■ = What's in the Boxes

■ = general Info

■ = examples.

SOCIOLOGY

CANADIAN EDITION

John J. Macionis
Kenyon College

Juanne Nancarrow Clarke
Wilfrid Laurier University

Linda M. Gerber
University of Guelph

PRENTICE HALL CANADA INC.
Scarborough, Ontario

To teachers of sociology…

Canadian Cataloguing in Publication Data

Macionis, John J
    Sociology

1st Canadian ed.
ISBN 0-13-102088-9

1. Sociology. I. Clarke, Juanne N. (Juanne
Nancarrow), 1944–   . II. Gerber, Linda Marie,
1944–   . III. Title.

HM51.M33 1994   301   C93-095154-9

Prentice-Hall, Inc., Englewood Cliffs, New Jersey
Prentice-Hall International (UK) Limited, London
Prentice-Hall of Australia, Pty. Limited, Sydney
Prentice-Hall Hispanoamericana, S.A., Mexico City
Prentice-Hall of India Private Limited, New Delhi
Prentice-Hall of Japan, Inc., Tokyo
Simon & Schuster Asia Private Limited, Singapore
Editora Prentice-Hall do Brasil, Ltda., Rio de Janeiro

ISBN 0-13-102088-9

Acquisitions Editor Mike Bickerstaff
Developmental Editor Ed O'Connor
Copy Editor Chelsea Donaldson
Production Editor Dawn du Quesnay
Production Coordinator Sharon Houston
Permissions/Photo Research Robyn Craig
Cover Design Alex Li
Cover Image Rocco Baviera
Page Layout Steve Lewis

    3 4 5   AG   98 97 96 95

Printed and bound in the U.S.A.

Original U.S. edition published by Prentice-Hall, Inc.
Englewood Cliffs, New Jersey 07632.
Copyright © 1993, 1991, 1989, 1987 Prentice-Hall, Inc.

All Statistics Canada material is reproduced with the permission
of the Minister responsible for Statistics Canada, 1993.

BRIEF CONTENTS

P A R T   I
The Foundations of Sociology

1 The Sociological Perspective   1
2 Sociological Investigation   33

P A R T   II
The Foundations of Society

3 Culture   65
4 Society   99
5 Socialization   129
6 Social Interaction in
   Everyday Life   157
7 Groups and Organizations   181
8 Deviance   209

P A R T   III
Social Inequality

9 Social Stratification   243
10 Social Class in Canada   267
11 Global Inequality   293
12 Race and Ethnicity   321
13 Sex and Gender   349
14 Aging and the Elderly   383

P A R T   IV
Social Institutions

15 Family   407
16 Education   439
17 Religion   461
18 Politics and Government   491
19 The Economy and Work   525
20 Health and Medicine   555

P A R T   V
Social Change

21 Population and
    Urbanization   587
22 Collective Behavior and Social
    Movements   619
23 Social Change and
    Modernity   641

CONTENTS

Preface   xiv

P A R T   I
The Foundations of Sociology

CHAPTER 1
The Sociological Perspective   *1*

THE SOCIOLOGICAL PERSPECTIVE   2
Seeing the General in the Particular   3
Seeing the Strange in the Familiar   3
Putting People in Social Context   5
The Importance of Global Perspective   7

THE SOCIOLOGICAL PERSPECTIVE IN
    EVERYDAY LIFE   9
Sociology and Social Diversity   9
Sociology and Social Marginality: Race, Gender,
    and Age   9
Sociology and Social Crisis   9
Benefits of the Sociological Perspective   10

THE ORIGINS OF SOCIOLOGY   12
Science and Sociology   12
Social Change and Sociology   14

SOCIOLOGICAL THEORY   17
The Structural-Functional Paradigm   18
The Social-Conflict Paradigm   20
The Symbolic-Interaction Paradigm   22
Emerging Paradigms   23
Sports: Three Theoretical Paradigms in Action   25

Summary   29   Key Concepts   29
Suggested Readings   30

CHAPTER 2
Sociological Investigation   *33*

THE BASICS OF SOCIOLOGICAL
    INVESTIGATION   34
Ways of Knowing: Science and "Truth"   34
Common Sense versus Scientific Evidence   35

THE ELEMENTS OF POSITIVIST SOCIAL
    SCIENCE   36
Concepts, Variables, and Measurement   36
The Ideal of Objectivity   40
Some Limitations of Scientific Sociology   40
The Importance of Subjective Interpretation   42
Politics and Research   42
Gender and Research   43
Research Ethics   45

THE METHODS OF DATA COLLECTION   45
Experiments   43
Survey Research   47
Participant Observation   50
Secondary Analysis   53

METHODS OF INTERPRETING SOCIOLOGICAL
    DATA   55
Social-Conflict/Feminist Methods   55
Interpretive Research   56
The Interplay of Theory and Method   57

PUTTING IT ALL TOGETHER: TEN STEPS IN
    SOCIOLOGICAL INVESTIGATION   57

Summary   59   Key Concepts   60
Suggested Readings   61

P A R T   II
The Foundations of Society

CHAPTER 3
Culture   *65*

WHAT IS CULTURE?   66
Culture and Human Intelligence   68

THE COMPONENTS OF CULTURE   69
Symbols   69
Language   70
Values   75
Norms   77

"Ideal" and "Real" Culture 78
Material Culture and Technology 78

CULTURAL DIVERSITY: MANY WAYS OF LIFE IN
    ONE WORLD 80
Subcultures 80
Multiculturalism 80
Countercultures 82
Cultural Change 83
Ethnocentrism and Cultural Relativity 83

THEORETICAL ANALYSIS OF CULTURE 86
Structural-Functional Analysis 86
Social-Conflict Analysis 87
Symbolic Interaction Analysis 88
Cultural Materialism 89
Sociobiology 90

CULTURE AND HUMAN FREEDOM 93
Culture as Constraint 93
Culture as Freedom 93

Summary 94   Key Concepts 95
Suggested Readings 95

CHAPTER 4
Society 99

GERHARD AND JEAN LENSKI: SOCIETY AND
    TECHNOLOGY 100
Hunting and Gathering Societies 101
Horticultural and Pastoral Societies 102
Agrarian Societies 104
Industrial Societies 105
The Limits of Technology 107

KARL MARX: SOCIETY AND CONFLICT 108
Society and Production 110
Conflict in History 111
Capitalism and Class Conflict 112
Capitalism and Alienation 113
Revolution 114

MAX WEBER: THE RATIONALIZATION OF
    SOCIETY 114
Rationality and Industrial Capitalism 116
The Roots of Rationality 116
Rationality and Modern Society 117

EMILE DURKHEIM: SOCIETY AND
    FUNCTION 120
Social Fact: Society Beyond Ourselves 120
Function: Society in Action 121
The Individual: Society in Ourselves 121
Evolving Societies: The Division of Labor 122

CRITICAL EVALUATION: FOUR VISIONS
    OF SOCIETY 123

Summary 124   Key Concepts 125
Suggested Readings 126

CHAPTER 5
Socialization 129

THE IMPORTANCE OF SOCIAL
    EXPERIENCE 129
Human Development: Nature and Nurture 131
Social Isolation 132

UNDERSTANDING THE SOCIALIZATION
    PROCESS 134
Sigmund Freud: The Elements of Personality 134
Jean Piaget: Cognitive Development 135
George Herbert Mead: The Social Self 137

AGENTS OF SOCIALIZATION 140
The Family 140
Schooling 141
Peer Groups 142
The Mass Media 143
Public Opinion 145

SOCIALIZATION AND THE LIFE COURSE 145
Childhood 145
Adolescence 147
Adulthood 147
Old Age and Dying 149

RESOCIALIZATION: TOTAL INSTITUTIONS 151

SOCIALIZATION AND HUMAN FREEDOM 152

Summary 153   Key Concepts 154
Suggested Readings 155

CHAPTER 6
Social Interaction in Everyday Life 157

SOCIAL STRUCTURE: A GUIDE TO EVERYDAY
    LIVING 157

STATUS 158
Ascribed and Achieved Status 158
Master Status 159

ROLE 160
Role Conflict and Role Strain 161
Role Exit 162

THE SOCIAL CONSTRUCTION OF REALITY   162
The Thomas Theorem   163
Reality-Building in Global Perspective   163
Ethnomethodology   164

**DRAMATURGICAL ANALYSIS: "THE
    PRESENTATION OF SELF"**   165
Performances   165
Nonverbal Communication   166
Gender and Personal Performances   168
Idealization   169
Embarrassment and Tact   170

**INTERACTION IN EVERYDAY LIFE: TWO
    ILLUSTRATIONS**   172
Language: The Gender Issue   172
Humor: Playing with Reality   173

Summary   177   *Key Concepts*   178
Suggested Readings   178

CHAPTER 7
Groups and Organizations   181

SOCIAL GROUPS   182
Groups, Aggregates, and Categories   182
Primary and Secondary Groups   182
Group Leadership   184
Group Conformity   185
Reference Groups   187
Ingroups and Outgroups   187
Group Size   188
Social Diversity   190
Networks   190

FORMAL ORGANIZATIONS   191
Types of Formal Organizations   191
Origins of Bureaucracy   192
Characteristics of Bureaucracy   192
Bureaucracy versus Small Groups   194
The Informal Side of Bureaucracy   195
Limitations of Bureaucracy   195
Oligarchy   199
Gender and Race in Organizations   199
Humanizing Bureaucracy   200
Organizational Environment   201
Formal Organizations in Japan   202

**GROUPS AND ORGANIZATIONS IN GLOBAL
    PERSPECTIVE**   204

Summary   205   *Key Concepts*   205
Suggested Readings   206

CHAPTER 8
Deviance   209

WHAT IS DEVIANCE?   210
Social Control   210
The Biological Context   211
Personality Factors   212
The Social Foundations of Deviance   213

STRUCTURAL-FUNCTIONAL ANALYSIS   214
Emile Durkheim: The Functions of Deviance   214
Merton's Strain Theory   215
Deviant Subcultures   216
Hirschi's Control Theory   217

SYMBOLIC-INTERACTION ANALYSIS   219
Labeling Theory   219
The Medicalization of Deviance   221
Sutherland's Differential Association Theory   222

SOCIAL-CONFLICT ANALYSIS   222
Deviance and Capitalism   223
White-Collar Crime   224

DEVIANCE AND GENDER   225

CRIME   226
Types of Crime   227
Criminal Statistics   227
The "Street" Criminal: A Profile   229
Crime in Global Perspective   232

THE CRIMINAL JUSTICE SYSTEM   234
Police   234
Courts   235
Punishment   235

Summary   239   *Key Concepts*   240
Suggested Readings   241

PART III
Social Inequality

CHAPTER 9
Social Stratification   243

WHAT IS SOCIAL STRATIFICATION?   244

CASTE AND CLASS SYSTEMS   245
The Caste System   245
The Class System   247
Caste and Class Together: Great Britain   248
Another Example: Japan   249
The Former Soviet Union   250
Ideology   252

THE FUNCTIONS OF SOCIAL
    STRATIFICATION   253
The Davis-Moore Thesis   253

STRATIFICATION AND CONFLICT   255
Marx's View of Social Class   255
Why No Marxist Revolution?   258
Max Weber: Class, Status, and Power   259

STRATIFICATION AND TECHNOLOGY IN
    GLOBAL PERSPECTIVE   261

SOCIAL STRATIFICATION: FACTS
    AND VALUES   263

Summary   263   *Key Concepts*   264
Suggested Readings   265

CHAPTER 10
Social Class in Canada   267

DIMENSIONS OF SOCIAL INEQUALITY   268
Income and Wealth   268
Power   269
Occupational Status for Males and Females   269
Schooling   271

ASCRIPTION AND SOCIAL
    STRATIFICATION   272
Ancestry   272
Race and Ethnicity   272
Gender   273

SOCIAL CLASSES IN CANADA   274
The Upper Class   276
The Middle Class   277
The Working Class   277
The Lower Class   278

SOCIAL MOBILITY   280
Social Mobility: Myth and Reality   280

POVERTY IN CANADA   282
The Extent of Canada Poverty   282
Who Are the Poor?   282
Explaining Poverty   283
Homelessness   285
Class and Welfare, Politics and Values   288

Summary   289   *Key Concepts*   289
Suggested Readings   290

CHAPTER 11
Global Inequality   301

THE IMPORTANCE OF GLOBAL
    PERSPECTIVE   292

THE THREE WORLDS   302
The First World   302
The Second World   304
The Third World   305

THIRD-WORLD POVERTY   306
The Severity of Poverty   306
The Extent of Poverty   308
Third-World Women: Work and Poverty   310
Correlates of Third-World Poverty   310

GLOBAL INEQUALITY: THEORETICAL
    ANALYSIS   313
Modernization Theory   313
Dependency Theory   317
Canada and the Third World   323

THE FUTURE OF GLOBAL INEQUALITY   323

Summary   325   *Key Concepts*   326
Suggested Readings   327

CHAPTER 12
Race and Ethnicity   321

THE SOCIAL SIGNIFICANCE OF RACE AND
    ETHNICITY   322
Race   322
Ethnicity   323
Minorities   324

PREJUDICE   324
Stereotypes   325
Racism   325
Theories of Prejudice   326

DISCRIMINATION   328
Institutional Discrimination   328
Prejudice and Discrimination:
    The Vicious Cycle   328

MAJORITY AND MINORITY: PATTERNS OF
    INTERACTION   329
Pluralism   329
Assimilation   331
Segregation   332
Genocide   332

RACE AND ETHNICITY IN CANADA   333
Social Standing   336
Special Status Societies   338
Native Peoples (First Nations)   338
The Québécois   340

IMMIGRATION TO CANADA: A HUNDRED-YEAR
    PERSPECTIVE   341

RACE AND ETHNICITY: PAST AND FUTURE   345

Summary   345   Key Concepts   346
Suggested Readings   347

CHAPTER 13
Sex and Gender   349

SEX AND GENDER   350
Sex: A Biological Distinction   350
Sexual Orientation   351
Gender: A Cultural Distinction   352
Patriarchy and Sexism   354

GENDER AND SOCIALIZATION   357
Gender and the Family   357
Gender and the Peer Group   358
Gender and Schooling   359
Gender and the Mass Media   360
Gender and Adult Socialization   361

GENDER AND SOCIAL STRATIFICATION   362
Working Men and Women   362
Housework: Women's "Second Shift"   364
Gender, Income, and Wealth   364
Gender and Education   365
Gender and Politics   367
Minority Women   368
Are Women a Minority?   368
Violence against Women   369

THEORETICAL ANALYSIS OF GENDER   371
Structural-Functional Analysis   371
Social-Conflict Analysis   372

FEMINISM   374
Basic Feminist Ideas   374
Variations within Feminism   375
Resistance to Feminism   376

GENDER IN THE TWENTY-FIRST CENTURY   377

Summary   377   Key Concepts   378
Suggested Readings   379

CHAPTER 14
Aging and the Elderly   381

THE GRAYING OF CANADA   382

GROWING OLD: BIOLOGY AND CULTURE   385
Biological Changes   385
Psychological Changes   388
Aging and Culture   388
Aging and Social Stratification   391

TRANSITIONS AND ISSUES OF AGING   392
Social Isolation   393
Retirement   393
Aging and Income   394
Abuse of the Elderly   394

THEORETICAL ANALYSIS OF AGING   395
Structural-Functional Analysis: Aging and
    Disengagement   396
Symbolic-Interaction Analysis: Aging
    and Activity   396
Social-Conflict Analysis: Aging and Inequality   397

AGEISM   397
The Elderly: A Minority?   398

DEATH AND DYING   398
Historical Patterns of Death   399
The Modern Separation of Life and Death   400
Bereavement   400

Summary   401   Key Concepts   402
Suggested Readings   402

PART IV
Social Institutions

CHAPTER 15
Family   405

THE FAMILY: BASIC CONCEPTS   405

THE FAMILY IN CROSS-CULTURAL
    PERSPECTIVE   406
Marriage Patterns   407
Residential Patterns   411
Patterns of Descent   411
Patterns of Authority   411

THEORETICAL ANALYSIS OF THE FAMILY   411
Functions of the Family   411
Social Inequality and the Family   413
Other Theoretical Analyses   414

STAGES OF FAMILY LIFE   414
Courtship   414
Settling in: Ideal and Real Marriage   416
Child Rearing   417
The Family in Later Life   419

VARIETIES OF FAMILY LIFE   420
Social Class   420
Ethnicity and Race   421
Gender   422

TRANSITION AND PROBLEMS IN
      FAMILY LIFE   424
Divorce   424
Remarriage   426
Family Violence   427

ALTERNATIVE FAMILY FORMS   429
One-Parent Families   429
Cohabitation   430
Gay and Lesbian Couples   430
Singlehood   431

NEW REPRODUCTIVE TECHNOLOGY AND THE
      FAMILY   431
In Vitro Fertilization   432
Ethical Issues   432

THE FAMILY IN THE TWENTY-FIRST
      CENTURY   432

Summary   434   Key Concepts   435
Suggested Readings   436

CHAPTER 16
Education   439

EDUCATION: A GLOBAL SURVEY   439
Schooling in Japan   442
Schooling in Great Britain   442
Schooling in the Commonwealth of Independent
      States   443
Schooling in Canada   444

THE FUNCTIONS OF SCHOOLING   444
Socialization   446
Cultural Innovation   446
Social Integration   446
Social Placement   447
Latent Functions of Schooling   448

SCHOOLING AND SOCIAL INEQUALITY   449
Social Control   449
Streaming and Social Inequality   448
Testing and Social Inequality   449

Unequal Access to Higher Education   451
Credentialism   453
Privilege and Personal Merit   454

PROBLEMS IN THE SCHOOLS   454
School Discipline   454
Bureaucracy and Student Passivity   455
Dropping Out   455
Education and the World of Work   456

EDUCATION FOR TOMORROW   458

Summary   458   Key Concepts   459
Suggested Readings   459

CHAPTER 17
Religion   461

RELIGION: BASIC CONCEPTS   461
Religion and Sociology   461

THEORETICAL ANALYSIS OF RELIGION   464
The Functions of Religion   464
The Social Construction of the Sacred   466
Religion and Social Inequality   466
Liberation Theology   467

TYPES OF RELIGIOUS ORGANIZATIONS   468
Church and Sect   468
Cult   470

RELIGION IN HISTORY   471
Religion in Preindustrial Societies   471
Religion in Industrial Societies   471

WORLD RELIGIONS   472
Christianity   472
Islam   473
Hinduism   474
Buddhism   475
Confucianism   477
Judaism   477

RELIGION IN CANADA   478
Religious Affiliation   478
Religiosity   479
Correlates of Religious Affiliation   481

RELIGION IN A CHANGING SOCIETY   482
Secularization   482
Religious Revival   484
The Future of Religion   486

Summary   486   Key Concepts   487
Suggested Readings   488

CHAPTER 18
Politics and Government *491*

POWER AND AUTHORITY *491*
Traditional Authority *492*
Rational-Legal Authority *493*
Charismatic Authority *493*

POLITICS IN GLOBAL PERSPECTIVE *494*
Politics in History *494*
Contemporary Political Systems *495*

POLITICS IN CANADA *500*
Culture, Economics, and Politics *501*
Political Parties *502*
Politics and the Individual *508*

THEORETICAL ANALYSIS OF POWER IN
    SOCIETY *512*
The Pluralist Model *512*
The Power-Elite Model *512*

POWER BEYOND THE RULES *514*
Revolution *514*
Terrorism *515*

WAR AND PEACE *516*
The Causes of War *517*
Militarism and the Arms Race *517*
Nuclear Weapons and War *518*
The Pursuit of Peace *519*

Summary 520   Key Concepts 521
Suggested Readings 522

Chapter 19
The Economy and Work *525*

THE ECONOMY: HISTORICAL OVERVIEW *525*
The Agricultural Revolution *526*
The Industrial Revolution *526*
The Postindustrial Society *528*
Sectors of the Modern Economy *528*

COMPARATIVE ECONOMIC SYSTEMS *529*
Capitalism *529*
Socialism *530*
Socialism and Communism *531*
Democratic Socialism in Europe *531*
Relative Advantages of Capitalism and Socialism *531*
Changes in Socialist Countries *533*

WORK IN THE POSTINDUSTRIAL
    ECONOMY *534*
The Decline of Agricultural Work *535*
From Factory Work to Service Work *535*
The Dual Labor Market *535*
Labor Unions *536*
Professions *538*
Self-Employment *539*
Unemployment *540*
The Underground Economy *542*
Technology and Work *543*

CORPORATIONS *543*
Economic Concentration *545*
Foreign Ownership *545*
Conglomerates and Corporate Linkages *546*
Corporations and Competition *547*
Corporations and the Global Economy *548*

THE ECONOMY OF THE TWENTY-FIRST
    CENTURY *549*

Summary 550   Key Concepts 551
Suggested Readings 552

CHAPTER 20
Health and Medicine *555*

WHAT IS HEALTH? *556*
Health and Society *556*
Historical Patterns of Health *556*
Global Patterns of Health *558*

HEALTH IN CANADA *559*
Social Epidemiology: The Distribution of Health *559*
Environmental Pollution *562*
Cigarette Smoking *564*
Sexually Transmitted Diseases *566*
Ethical Issues: Confronting Death *570*

MEDICINE *571*
The Rise of Scientific Medicine *572*
Holistic Medicine *573*
Medicine and Economics in Global Perspective *574*

THEORETICAL ANALYSIS OF HEALTH AND
    MEDICINE *577*
Structural-Functional Analysis *577*
Symbolic-Interaction Analysis *578*
Social-Conflict Analysis *579*

Summary 581   Key Concepts 583
Suggested Readings 583

P A R T   V
Social Change

CHAPTER 21
Population and Urbanization   *587*

DEMOGRAPHY: THE STUDY OF
        POPULATION   *587*
Fertility   *588*
Mortality   *588*
Migration   *589*
Population Growth   *590*
Population Composition   *590*

HISTORY AND THEORY OF POPULATION
        GROWTH   *593*
Malthusian Theory   *593*
Demographic Transition Theory   *595*
World Population Today   *595*
The Importance of Demography   *597*

URBANIZATION: THE GROWTH OF CITIES   *598*
The Evolution of Cities   *598*
The Growth of North American Cities   *601*
Suburbs and Central Cities   *605*
Inter-Regional Population Movement   *606*

UNDERSTANDING CITIES: THEORY AND
        METHOD   *607*
European Theory: Urban Life versus Rural Life   *607*
Observing the City   *608*
Urban Ecology   *610*
Third-World Urbanization   *611*
The Historical Importance of Cities   *614*

Summary   614   Key Concepts   615
Suggested Readings   616

CHAPTER 22
Collective Behavior and Social
Movements   *619*

COLLECTIVE BEHAVIOR   *619*
Studying Collective Behavior   *620*
Crowds   *621*
Mobs and Riots   *622*
Contagion Theory   *623*
Convergence Theory   *623*
Emergent-Norm Theory   *623*
Crowds, Politics, and Social Change   *624*
Rumor and Gossip   *624*
Public Opinion   *625*

Panic and Mass Hysteria   *625*
Fashions and Fads   *626*

SOCIAL MOVEMENTS   *628*
Types of Social Movements   *629*
Deprivation Theory   *629*
Mass-Society Theory   *631*
Structural-Strain Theory   *631*
Resource-Mobilization Theory   *632*
"New Social Movements" Theory   *633*
Stages in Social Movements   *634*
Social Movements and Social Change   *636*

Summary   637   Key Concepts   638
Suggested Readings   638

CHAPTER 23
Social Change and Modernity   *641*

WHAT IS SOCIAL CHANGE?   *642*

CAUSES OF SOCIAL CHANGE   *643*
Culture and Change   *643*
Social Structure and Change   *644*
Ideas and Change   *644*
The Natural Environment and Change   *644*
Demography and Change   *646*

MODERNITY   *646*
Ferdinand Toennies: The Loss of Community   *648*
Emile Durkheim: The Division of Labor   *650*
Max Weber: Rationalization   *651*
Karl Marx: Capitalism   *652*
Understanding Modernity:
        The Theory of Mass Society   *652*
Understanding Modernity:
        The Theory of Class Society   *655*
Modernity and the Individual   *656*
Modernity and Progress   *658*

MODERNIZATION IN GLOBAL
        PERSPECTIVE   *659*

Summary   661   Key Concepts   662
Suggested Readings   662

Glossary   *664*

References   *670*

Photo Credits   *702*

Index   *704*

About the Authors   *713*

BOXES

Critical Thinking

The Montreal Massacre: Are Sociologists Bleeding
    Hearts? 7
A Brief History of Canadian Sociology 14
Patriarchy: A Feminist Perspective 24
The Samsa Controversy: The Interplay of Science and
    Politics 42
"The Traveler's Dilemma": In the Night Market of
    Taipei 88
Bureaucracy and the Information Revolution:
    A Threat to Privacy? 197
Date Rape: Exposing Dangerous Myths 228
Ideology: When Is Inequality Unjust? 254
Salaries: Are the Rich Worth What They Earn? 256
Why Poverty is a Women's Issue 286
Modernization and Women: What Are the
    Drawbacks? 307
Black Citizens of Canada: A History Ignored 334
Corporate Women: The "Mommy–Track"
    Controversy 366
The Sandwich Generation: Who Should Care for
    Aging Parents? 389
Are New Reproductive Technologies Immoral? The
    Catholic Church's View 433
Functional Illiteracy: Must We Rethink
    Education? 457
Regional Economic Disparities 544
The Irving Empire 547
Medicine and Women: Science or Sexism? 581
The Witches of Salem: Can Whole Towns
    Go Crazy? 627
Modern Society: What Do We Owe Others? 651

Cross–Cultural Comparison

Canadian and American Values: What Makes Us
    Different? 72
Sex among Children? The Social Construction of
    Childhood 144
The Foster Home as Total Institution 152
Human Emotions in Global Perspective 166
South Africa: Race as Caste 246
India: A Different Kind of Poverty 304
Growing (Very) Old in Abkhasia 392
Civil Religion in the United States 483
Poverty: The Leading Cause of Death in the Third
    World 560
Birth Control in China 598

Profile

C. Wright Mills 11
Auguste Comte 13
Herbert Spencer 19
W. E. B. DuBois 21
Gerhard Lenski and Jean Lenski 97?
Karl Marx 109
Max Weber 115
Emile Durkheim 121
George Herbert Mead 138
Charles Horton Cooley 183
Rosabeth Moss Kanter 200
Jessie Bernard 358
Dorothy Smith 359
Robert Ezra Park 609
Ferdinand Toennies 649

Social Diversity

What's in a Name? How Social Forces Affect Personal
    Choice 6
Technology and the Changing Status of Women 104
The Dionne Quintuplets 130
Physical Disability as Master Status 160
Crime and Social Marginality: Rocco Perri 213
"Fore Word" from Don Harron's *The Canadian
    Establishment* 274
Why Poverty Is a Women's Issue 286
When Worlds Collide: The Christopher Columbus
    Controversy 311
The Other-Worldly and the Ordinary: W.O. Mitchell's
    Who Has Seen the Wind? 462
Native Self -Government 506
The French-Canadians of Manchester, New
    Hampshire 527

A Decade of Change

The Elderly: A Financial Windfall 397
Trends in College Diplomas and
    Bachelor's Degrees 446
The 1980s: A Decade of Democracy 498

Sociology of Everyday Life

Three Useful (and Simple) Statistical Measures 37
Understanding Culture: Yekoh Ritual Among the
    Snaidanac? 70
Alienation and Industrial Capitalism 113

Telling Lies: Clues to Deceit   *170*
Rock and Roll: From Deviance to Big Business   *215*
Middle-Class Stampede?   *278*
Masculinity as Contest   *360*

The Stone Angel   *384*
In the Bathrooms of the Nation?   *503*
My Financial Career   *536*
Traditional Honor and Modern Dignity   *660*

Global Maps

1-1 Per capita Income in Global Perspective   *8*
3-1 Language in Global Perspective   *72*
3-2 Ethnocentric Images of the World   *81*
4-1 Spending on Science in Global Perspective   *114*
5-1 Television Ownership in Global Perspective   *140*
5-2 Child Labor in Global Perspective   *142*
7-1 Data Transmission in Global Perspective   *193*
8-1 Prostitution in Global Perspective   *234*
9-1 Income Disparity in Global Perspective   *262*
11-1 The Three Worlds   *296*
11-2 Nutrition in Global Perspective   *301*
13-1 Housework in Global Perspective   *356*
14-1 Life Expectancy in Global Perspective   *391*
15-1 Marital Form in Global Perspective   *410*
16-1 Illiteracy in Global Perspective   *441*
17-1 Christianity in Global Perspective   *474*
17-2 Islam in Global Perspective   *474*
17-3 Hinduism in Global Perspective   *476*
17-4 Buddhism in Global Perspective   *476*
18-1 Political Freedom in Global Perspective   *497*
19-1 Agricultural Employment in Global Perspective   *529*
19-2 Industrial Employment in Global Perspective   *529*
20-1 Medical Care in Global Perspective   *561*
20-2 HIV Infection of Adults in Global Perspective   *568*
21-1 Population Growth in Global Perspective   *591*
21-2 Urbanization in Global Perspective   *612*
23-1 Energy Consumption in Global Perspective   *646*

Canada Maps

8-1 Violent Crime Rates (per 100,000 population, 1991)   *236*
10-1 Median Incomes (by province and territory, 1990)   *270*
12-1 Percentage of Population Foreign-Born (by province and territory, 1991)   *344*
14-1 Percentage of the Population Aged 65 and Over (by province and territory, 1991)   *386*
15-1 Divorce Rates (per 100,000 population, by province and territory, 1991)   *426*
16-1 French Immersion Enrolment (percent by province and territory, 1989–90)   *448*
16-2 Participation Rate of the 1824 Age Group in Full-Time Post-Secondary Education (by province and territory, 1989)   *450*
17-1 Population Claiming "No Religion" (by province and territory, 1991)   *480*
18-1 Support for the Charlottetown Accord: Referendum 1992 (percent voting "yes" by province and territory)
19-1 Unemployment Rates (percent of labor force by province, 1991)   *541*
20-1 Deaths from Cancers of the Respiratory System (per 10,000 population by province and territory, 1991)   *565*
21-1 Birth Rates (by province and territory, 1991)   *589*

PREFACE

The text you are now reading had a history of its own, a full life, you might say, even before we made this Canadian Edition. *Sociology* by John J. Macionis was first published in the United States in 1987. It enjoyed such success there that four editions appeared within six years. There are good reasons for this success; for one thing, the writing is beguiling. Macionis weaves theory, research, factual stories, and history into a complex of ideas that invites the student to embark on an enlightening voyage of discovery. Also, the artwork contained in the book, the theme boxes, and the complementary teaching and learning aids are all exemplary.

A good part of the appeal of *Sociology* has always turned on the care Macionis has taken to guide his students in their voyage of discovery beyond the borders of the United States. The text has been applauded for its *international coverage* and its *global perspective*. Perhaps this emphasis is most explicit in the twenty-seven global maps that provide students with visual summaries of worldwide patterns of (among others) income, language, religion, and population growth.

We have tried in this first Canadian Edition of *Sociology* to build on the strengths of John Macionis's book while adding a distinctly Canadian perspective. We have done this in a variety of ways. On the most basic level, we have replaced American demographic data and research findings with the results of similar Canadian studies. At the same time, we have found it necessary to go far beyond the basics in our revisions. We recognize that Canadian sociology is not just American sociology transplanted to a different country. Canadian sociology has different areas of interest and, consequently, different theoretical emphases. We have our own history, tradition, journals, and problems. Canadian sociologists have made a number of important contributions to the international development of this science, and in a Canadian text these contributions must be acknowledged. Wherever necessary, we have, therefore, shifted emphasis in the text in order to highlight Canadian contributions and debates. In dealing with institutions or establishments such as education,

politics, and medicine, we have brought the full weight of Canadian sociological literature to bear. In addition, we have incorporated selections from Canadian artists, photographers, and writers to further enhance the identity of the text.

In short, we have worked as hard as possible to make this book both visually appealing and pedagogically sound. In this we have followed two rationales. First, we agree with the old maxim which states that learning is easiest when it is accompanied by delight. Second, we have felt compelled to emulate John Macionis's goal of providing our students with an introductory textbook without equal. We invite you to enjoy this book and through it to share your enthusiasm for Canadian society with your students.

The Organization of This Text

Part I introduces the foundations of sociology. Underlying the discipline is the *sociological perspective*—the focus of Chapter 1, which explains how this invigorating point of view illuminates the world in a new and instructive way. Chapter 2 spotlights *sociological investigation*, or the "doing of sociology," and explains how to apply the logic of science to the study of human society. We bring major research strategies to life using extended examples of well-known sociological work. By learning how sociologists see the world and carry out research, passive readers are transformed into active, critical participants in the issues, debates, and controversies that frame subsequent chapters.

Part II targets the foundations of social life. Chapter 3 presents the central concept of *culture*, emphasizing the cultural diversity that makes up our society and our world. Chapter 4 links culture to the concept of *society*, and presents four enduring models for understanding the structure and dynamics of human social organization. Assigned in sequence, this unique chapter provides students with the background necessary to fully comprehend the ideas of important thinkers—

including Karl Marx, Max Weber, and Emile Durkheim—that appear in subsequent chapters. Alternatively, instructors may assign each of the chapter's four parts at later points in the course. Chapter 5 focuses on *socialization*, explaining how we gain our humanity as we learn to participate in society. Chapter 6 provides a micro-level look at the patterns of *social interaction* that make up our everyday lives. Chapter 7 offers full-chapter coverage of *groups and organizations*, both of which are vital elements of social structure. Chapter 8 completes the unit by investigating how the operation of society promotes both *deviance* and *conformity*.

Part III provides a detailed analysis of various dimensions of social inequality. Because of its importance to human life, three chapters are devoted to *social stratification*. Chapter 9 introduces major concepts and presents a fundamental theoretical analysis of social inequality. This chapter is rich with illustrations of how stratification has changed historically, and how it varies around the world today. Chapter 10 surveys *social class in Canada*, presenting common perceptions of inequality and seeing how well they square with the facts. Chapter 11 extends the analysis with *a global view of social stratification*, investigating the extent of differences in wealth and power between rich and poor societies. Both Chapters 10 and 11 explain how social stratification in Canada is linked to trends in the rest of the world, just as they explore our society's role in global stratification. *Race and ethnicity*, important dimensions of social inequality both in North America and the rest of the world, are detailed in Chapter 12. The focus of Chapter 13 is *sex and gender*. Here we explain the biological foundation of sex and sexuality, and how societies transform the distinction of sex into systems of gender stratification. *Aging and the elderly*, topics of increasing concern to members of aging societies such as ours, are addressed in Chapter 14.

Part IV includes a full chapter on each social institution. Chapter 15, *the family*, underscores the diversity of family life both in Canada and in the world as a whole. Chapter 16, *education*, traces the expansion of schooling in industrial societies. Here again, educational patterns in Canada are made more meaningful through contrasts with those in many other societies. Chapter 17 discusses *religion*, revealing how the timeless human search for ultimate meaning affects social life in countless ways. Chapter 18, *politics and government*, includes discussions of the Canadian political system and political parties, as well as the larger issues of war and Peace. Chapter 19 focuses on *the economy and work*, highlighting industrialization, postindustrial-

ization, the emergence of a global economy, and what these transformations mean for the Canadian labor force. Chapter 20, *health and medicine*, shows that health is a social issue just as much as it is a matter of biological processes. Paralleling the discussions of the other institutions, this chapter explains the historical emergence of medicine, analyzes current medical issues from different points of view, and compares Canadian patterns to those found in other societies.

Part V examines important dimensions of social change. Chapter 21 focuses on the powerful impact of *population growth and urbanization* in Canada and throughout the world. Chapter 22 explains how people seek or resist social change through various forms of *collective behavior and social movements*. Chapter 23 concludes the text with an overview of *social change and modernity*, explaining how and why world societies change, and critically analyzing the benefits and liabilities of traditional and modern ways of life.

Features of *Sociology, Canadian Edition*

Although introductory sociology texts have much in common, they are not all the same. *Sociology* has a combination of many distinctive features.

Unsurpassed writing style. Most important, this text offers a writing style strongly praised as elegant and engaging. *Sociology* is an inviting text that encourages students to read—even beyond their assignments.

Intriguing chapter introductions. One of the most popular features of the U.S. editions was the engaging vignettes that begin each chapter. These openings in the Canadian Edition—which range from a look at the life of Paul Desmarais and Canada's economic elite to the controversy surrounding the Montreal Massacre—will spark the interest of the reader as they introduce important themes.

A celebration of Canadian cultural and social diversity. *Sociology* invites students from all social backgrounds to discover a fresh and exciting way to see their world and themselves. Readers will hear in this text the diverse voices of our society—people of Native, black, Asian, European, and Latino ancestry, as well as women and men of various class positions and at all points in the life course. Just as important, without flinching from the problems that marginalized people confront, this text does not treat these individuals simply as "social problems" but notes their achievements and contributions to Canadian society as well.

In addition, the text incorporates Canadian data, analyses, and examples wherever possible, and uses excerpts from Canadian literature (including Constance Beresford-Howe, Stephen Leacock, and W.O. Mitchell) to illustrate sociological concepts.

Finally, the Canadian Edition includes twelve *Canada maps*. These sociological maps explore the demographic, social, and political differences that exist within Canada's provinces and territories, through topics ranging from birth rates, to rates of violent crime, to support for the Charlottetown Accord. In light of the strong divisions that have emerged within this country over the last decade, it is more important than ever that students look beyond their own region to discover the diversity that is perhaps our greatest strength as a nation. A list of all twelve Canada maps follows the table of contents.

A global perspective. Sociology has long revealed how individual lives are shaped by placement in their own society. As we approach the new century, sociology is extending its reach by showing how Canada is itself affected by our country's position in the world as a whole. The Canadian Edition of *Sociology* enhances the global sophistication of students in a number of ways.

First, each chapter contains comparative material that focuses on the social diversity of our world. Just as importantly, the text explains that social trends in Canada—whether they be musical tastes, the price of wheat, or growing income disparity—are influenced by what happens elsewhere. More than ever before, understanding our society demands comprehending Canada's place in global context.

Second, this edition ties life in Canada to processes and trends in the larger world. Various chapters explain, for example, how growing economic inequality in this country is linked to the globalization of the economy, and how the wealth of Canada is linked to our relations abroad. This global emphasis in no way lessens the text's focus on Canada; on the contrary, it enhances conventional scholarship and provides greater accuracy.

Third and most significantly, the text includes twenty-seven *global maps*, typically one or two in every chapter. *Windows on the World* reveal global patterns such as income disparity, favored languages and religions, the power of television, the extent of prostitution, permitted marriage forms, the degree of political free-

dom, the incidence of HIV infection, and a host of other issues. Twenty-seven *Windows on the World* are listed along with the Canada maps after the table of contents.

We make a major commitment to world maps, first, because global sophistication begins by understanding basic geography. Students need to know in what *region* of the globe to find Somalia or Bosnia to understand the human drama that is unfolding in such places. Second, students need to see ways in which rich and poor nations differ. Understanding the effects of industrialization, for example, depends upon spotlighting global wealth and poverty, birth rates, the extent of child labor, and what proportion of women are in the labor force. *Windows on the World* graphically display all these factors and more.

All maps distort reality, since they portray a three-dimensional world in two dimensions. However, some biases are better than others. Most of us are familiar with the Mercator projection (devised by the Flemish mapmaker Gerhardus Mercator, 1512-1594; see top map). Mercator sought to accurately present the shape of countries (a vital concern to early sea-faring navigators) but, in doing so, he distorted their size. Thus greater distance from the equator inflates a land mass, so that Europe and North America have exaggerated dimensions (and, by implication, importance). By the same token, the Mercator map renders most Third-World countries smaller than they are. *Windows on the World* are drawn in a new, non-Eurocentric projection devised by cartographer Arno Peters (*Peters' Atlas of the World*; see bottom map). The Peters projection distorts the shape of some countries in service to the more important goal of displaying their correct relative size.

Inclusive focus on women and men. Beyond devoting a full chapter to the important concepts of sex and gender, *Sociology* considers gender in every chapter, showing how the topic at hand affects women and men differently, and that gender affects not only our answers about how society works but also the way we frame questions in the first place.

Rich and varied examples. Sociologist George Herbert Mead once described the ideal teacher as a person able to transform simple information into real knowledge. Mead's insight applies as much to books as to teachers; on virtually every page of *Sociology*, therefore, rich and illuminating illustrations show students the power of applying sociology to their everyday lives.

Theoretically clear and balanced. *Sociology* makes theory easy. The discipline's major theoretical approaches are introduced in Chapter 1 and are systematically

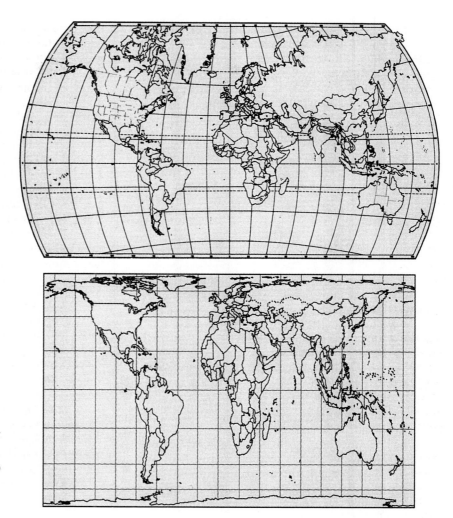

The Mercator projection (top) which correctly displays the shape of land masses, was vital to early sea-faring navigators. But it Eurocentrically inflates the dimensions of countries (like England) that are far from the equator. The Peters projection (bottom) is used in this text because it accurately presents the size (and, by implication, importance) of all nations.

reapplied in later chapters. In addition to the social-conflict, structural-functional, and symbolic-interaction paradigms, various chapters incorporate social-exchange analysis, ethnomethodology, cultural materialism and sociobiology. Chapter 4 provides an easy-to-understand introduction to important social theorists *before* their work is discussed in later chapters. The ideas of Gerhard and Jean Lenski, Max Weber, Karl Marx, and Emile Durkheim appear in distinct sections that may be assigned together or separately at different points in the course.

Emphasis on critical thinking. Critical thinking skills include the ability to challenge common assumptions, formulate questions, identify and weigh appropriate evidence, and reach reasoned conclusions. This text encourages students to discover as well as to learn, to seek out contradictions as well as to formulate consistent arguments, and to make connections among the various dimensions of social life.

Recent sociological research. *Sociology* blends classical sociological statements with the latest research, as reported in the leading publications in the field. On average, almost three-fourths of each chapter's citations are of articles and books published since 1980. The text also includes recent current events.

Learning aids. This text has specific features to help students learn. In each chapter, **key concepts**, identified by boldfaced type, are followed by a *precise, italicized definition*. An alphabetical listing of key concepts and definitions appears at the end of each chapter, and a complete **Glossary** appears at the end of the book.

Each chapter also contains a numbered **Summary** to assist students in reviewing material and assessing their understanding. Chapters end with lists of **Suggested Readings**, identifying books of lasting importance by Canadian and international sociologists and spotlighting noteworthy recent publications.

Outstanding images: photography and fine art. The authors and the publisher have developed a program of photography and artwork that plays a central role in this text. Not only are images of extraordinary quality, but they are the creations of artists of various social backgrounds and historical periods. In addition to widely celebrated art by Vincent Van Gogh and George Tooker, for example, this edition has paintings by Canadian artists William Kurelek, Carl Beam, Alex Colville, and Jane Ash Poitras.

Thought-provoking theme boxes. Although boxes are common to introductory texts, *Sociology* provides a wealth of uncommonly good ones. Each chapter typically contains several boxes, which fall into six types that strengthen central themes of the text. *Social Diversity* boxes focus on multicultural issues and enhance the voices of women and people of color. *A Decade of Change* boxes highlight important changes during the 1980s or project trends for the 1990s. *Critical Thinking* boxes teach students to ask sociological questions about their surroundings and help them to evaluate important, controversial issues. *Cross-Cultural Comparison* boxes provoke readers to think about their own way of life by examining the fascinating cultural diversity found in our world. *Sociology of Everyday Life* boxes show that, far from being detached from daily routines, many of sociology's most important insights involve familiar, everyday experiences. Finally, *Profile* boxes introduce many of the men and women who have shaped the discipline of sociology, from Emile Durkheim to Dorothy Smith.

Supplements

Sociology, Canadian Edition, is the heart of an unparalleled learning package that includes a wide range of proven instructional aids as well as several new ones. As the authors of the text, we maintain a keen interest in all the supplements to ensure their quality and compatibility with the text.

Instructor's Manual   This manual is of interest even to those who have shunned them in the past. The Instructor's Manual provides far more than chapter outlines and discussion questions; it contains statistical profiles, summaries of important developments and significant research, and supplemental lecture material for every chapter of the text. This supplement has been prepared by Canadian authors Juanne Nancarrow Clarke and Linda M. Gerber.

Test Item File.   A test item file is available in both printed and computerized forms. The file contains 2,300 items, incuding multiple-choice, true-false, and essay questions. Questions are divided into more simple "recall" items and more complex "inferential" items; answers to all questions are page-referenced to the text. Prentice Hall Test Manager is a test generator and classroom management system designed to provide maximum flexibility in producing tests and quizzes.

ABC News/Prentice Hall Video Library for Sociology Series I, II, & IV (Issues in Sociology).   Video is the most dynamic supplement you can use to enhance a class. But the quality of the video material and how well it relates to your course still makes all the difference. Prentice Hall and ABC News are working together to bring you the best and most comprehensive video ancillaries available in the post-secondary market.

Through its wide variety of award-winnng programs—*Nightline, Business World, On Business, This Week with David Brinkley, World News Tonight,* and *The Health Show*—ABC offers a resource for feature and documentary-style videos related to the chapters in *Sociology.* The programs have extremely high production quality, present substantial content, and are hosted by well-versed, well-known anchors.

Prentice Hall and its authors and editors provide the benefit of having selected videos and topics that will work well with this course and text and include notes on how to use them in the classroom. An excellent video guide in the Instructors Manual carefully and completely integrates the videos into your lecture. The guide has a synopsis of each video showing its relation to the chapter and discussion questions to help students focus on how concepts and theories apply to real-life situations.

These videos are also available on the *Sociology Laserdisk.*

Study Guide.   This workbook provides students with the opportunity to review the key ideas in each chapter of the text. A wide range of exercises and self-tests allows the student to assess personal learning as the course proceeds.

Other supplements available to aid in classroom teaching are

Prentice Hall Color Transparencies:
  Sociology Series
Film/Video Guide: Prentice Hall Introductory
  Sociology.
Sociology Laserdisk

Acknowledgments

Many people have helped us in preparing the Canadian Edition of *Sociology*. Among them are Laura Gerber, Elsie Kojola, Jackie Faubert, Gary Martin, Janette Moritz, Candice Shrigley, and Heather Barber. Their research assitance was much appreciated. Our thanks also go to our departmental colleagues, whose stimulating excitement about the field of sociology and whose expertise in particular areas was a great help, and to the staff of the Wilfrid Laurier and University of Guelph libraries, especially of the government document and periodical sections. We are particularly grateful to our students in Introductory Sociology.

Several instructors from across Canada reviewed parts of the manuscript in progress and offered many useful observations and suggestions:

William A. Adcock, Sheridan College
Jeanette A. Auger, Acadia University
Donna Jansen, Georgian College
Chris McCormick, Saint Mary's University
George Pollard, Carleton University
Peter Poole, Okanagan University College
Kathryn Schellenberg, University of Guelph
Craig Seaton, Trinity Western University
William L. Zwerman, University of Calgary

At Prentice Hall Canada we would like to thank the helpful editorial and production staff, including Mike Bickerstaff, Ed O'Connor, Dawn du Quesnay, Robyn Craig, Alex Li, Sharon Houston, Steve Lewis, and copy-editor Chelsea Donaldson.

Finally, we want to say thanks to family and friends who tolerated our preoccupation over many months.

Juanne Nancarrow Clarke
Linda M. Gerber

CHAPTER 1

THE SOCIOLOGICAL PERSPECTIVE

On December 6, 1989, fourteen women engineering students at Montreal's L'Ecole Polytechnique died at the hands of a young man named Marc Lepine. He was furious at feminists. He had tried to gain entrance to engineering at L'Ecole Polytechnique unsuccessfully and was enraged at the women who had been successful. Known as the Montreal Massacre, the end of Lepine's slaughter saw fourteen women dead, and thirteen injured. Lepine then killed himself.

Lepine's suicide note is instructive: (translated from French) "Would you note that I commit suicide today, 89,12,06, it's not for economic reasons ... but rather for political reasons. Because I have decided to send feminists, who have always ruined my life, back to their maker" (*Vancouver Sun*, Nov. 24, 1990).

Many people reacted to this incident with disbelief. This was partly because of the brutality and the numbers who were murdered, and partly because they were all young women engineering students chosen simply because the murderer considered them to be feminists. Thus this terrible event provoked people everywhere to confront a basic question: *What makes people do the things they do?*

There are, of course, many ways to look at human events. The *perspective*—or point of view—that people use determines which facts become important and sug-

gests how those facts can be woven together into coherent patterns of meaning. The police officers investigating the Montreal Massacre case used one perspective. They focused on piecing together what happened and on identifying the perpetrator. This point of view is concerned primarily with describing an event and establishing a course of action to be undertaken in accordance with the law.

A psychiatrist offers another perspective that might be applied to Marc Lepine's behavior. From a psychiatrist's point of view, the important issue is the state of mind that leads an individual to an act of such wanton violence. In this case, the psychiatric perspective would isolate a different set of facts and prescribe a response based on appropriate medical principles.

A sociologist brings yet another perspective to understanding human behavior. A sociologist attempting to make sense of this incident might note that the offender was male, and that the victims were females who were breaking new ground as women in engineering. The sociologist would observe that the murderer was an economically unsuccessful male who considered himself to be taking political action against feminists who were preventing his success. Notice that the facts noted by the sociological perspective differ in a crucial way from those noted by law enforcement officials or psychiatrists. Police are concerned with facts that pertain to this one specific situation. Knowing that an offender was male is useful only insofar as it leads to identifying *which* male was involved. Likewise, psychiatrists seek out the personal traumas that may have contributed to an explosive outburst by a particular person. Both police and psychiatrists share the assumption that, in important respects at least, every crime and every person are unique. In contrast, a sociologist looks beyond any *particular* event or person to understand how and why one *category* of people behaves differently from another.

These brief comparisons illustrate the important idea that, to a large degree, reality depends on the perspective we use. This chapter introduces the sociological perspective, which helps us to see how social forces affect our everyday lives.

The Sociological Perspective

A distinctive perspective is central to the discipline of **sociology**, which may be defined as *the scientific study of human society*. There are perhaps 2,500 sociologists in Canada, many of whom conduct research aimed at learning more about human behavior. In Chapter 2 ("Sociological Investigation"), we delve into how this research is carried out. As explained later in this chapter, sociologists also use various theoretical models to guide their research and teaching. But all sociologists

We can easily grasp the power of society over the individual simply by imagining how different our lives would be had we been born in place of any of these children from around the globe.

draw on one basic point of view in their quest to understand the social world.

Seeing the General in the Particular

Peter Berger (1963) describes the sociological perspective as *seeing the general in the particular*. This means that sociologists discern general social patterns in the behavior of particular individuals. Of course, each individual is in some ways unique, but people who fall in the same social categories—based, for instance, on sex, age, and social standing—behave in similar ways. In the Marc Lepine case just described, we might wonder if, as mentioned, violent crime is more common among males, the young, and the disadvantaged, for example, than among females, older people, and the more privileged. Sociological research confirms that this is indeed the case. Lepine's attack was very deliberately aimed at women. This might lead us to ask how frequently women are the victims of violence in our society. From this perspective, Lepine's attack stands out only for the method of violence he chose. While it is difficult to estimate the actual incidence of violence against women (because there is evidence that such crimes are significantly under-reported), a nation-wide survey from the mid-eighties estimated that there were 17,300 sexual assault incidents in Canada in 1981. Ninety percent involved female victims.

Although Marc Lepine did not know any of the students he killed, sociological research shows that women are thirteen times more likely to be assaulted by partners than by strangers. Wife abuse is a special case of violence against women. Linda Macleod (1980, 1987) estimated that almost 1 million wives are assaulted in this country each year. At least one in ten women is physically and/or sexually abused by a partner. Even then, on average, women are assaulted approximately thirty times before they call the police. In Ontario alone, there were seventy-eight shelters for women who had left violent and abusive husbands. These seventy-eight shelters provided housing for 9,838 women and over 11,000 children in 1989. No more than 5 percent of the victims of battering are male. Figure 1-1 shows the breakdown of sexual assault, spousal assault, and homicide victims by gender.

From a sociological point of view, the roots of violence against women lie in the pervasive social, economic, and political inequities faced by women on a daily basis. Furthermore, the pervasive fear of violence limits women's ability to achieve equity (Begin, 1991; De Keseredy and Hinch, 1991).

Seeing the Strange in the Familiar

The sociological perspective can also be described as *seeing the strange in the familiar*. This does not mean that sociologists focus on the bizarre elements of society. Rather, to make sociological observations requires

More and more women and people of color are found in universities and community colleges in Canada. The growing percentage of previously under-represented groups shows signs of changing even the disciplines taught within these schools. Native Studies and Women's Studies are two examples of new knowledge bases developed in recent decades in Canadian institutions of higher learning.

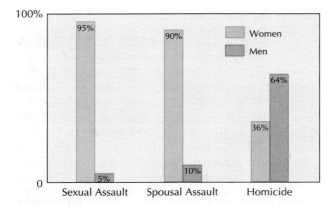

FIGURE 1-1   SEXUAL ASSAULT, SPOUSAL ASSAULT, AND HOMICIDE VICTIMS BY GENDER
SOURCE: Begin, 1991.

giving up the familiar idea that human behavior is simply a matter of what people *decide* to do, in favor of the initially strange notion that society influences our lives in key ways. Using the sociological perspective, we are likely to conclude that, in the words of Peter Berger (1963:23), "things are not what they seem."

We Canadians tend to overlook how society affects our thoughts, feelings, and actions. Using the sociological perspective, therefore, takes a bit of practice. The effort is worthwhile, however, because it provides a new level of understanding far richer than simple "common sense." Take the question of how you came to be a student at your particular university. For most people, specific reasons underlie the choice to attend one school or another:

I wanted to stay close to home.

This college has the best women's basketball team.

A journalism degree from this university ensures a good job.

My girlfriend goes to school here.

I wasn't accepted at the school I really wanted to attend.

Such responses are partly true, and they are certainly real to the people expressing them. But do they tell the full story? The sociological perspective provides additional insights that may not be readily apparent.

To approach the issue of university attendance sociologically, first step back from personal reasons that tell us only about *particular* choices, and think about more *general* patterns. What do students as a *category* of people have in common? A look around a university classroom suggests one answer. Although people of all ages attend university, most students are relatively young—generally between eighteen and twenty-four years of age. This is because our way of life traditionally has linked university attendance to this period of life. More than age is involved, however, because most university-age people in Canada are actually *not* enrolled in university (Colombo, 1992:74).

What else do young people who go to university have in common? Consider social background, which also shapes a person's range of opportunities. Traditionally, students who attend university come from families with annual incomes that are higher than average for Canada.

Of course, just as students fall into various categories, so do schools. Some are much more expensive than others, and going away to school costs more than attending classes while living at home.

There were an estimated 336,480 students enrolled in 204 community colleges in Canada in 1991–92 (*Corpus Almanac & Canadian Sourcebook*, 1993). At the same time, there were 554,021 students enrolled (as undergraduates and graduates) in sixty-nine universities in Canada (*Community Colleges and Related Institutions: Postsecondary Enrolment and Graduates*, 1993). Community colleges train students for particular jobs, and tend to be directed towards the needs of the labor market. Graduates are not expected to go on to further education, but rather to go on to paid employment. The training is usually for two or three years and the tuition is somewhat less than university tuition, in general. Universities, on the other hand, are designed to educate generalists in the arts and sciences who will then go on to further education in graduate schools or employment of one sort or another. With the exception of a few undergraduate "professional" programs such as Business and Economics, Medicine, and Law, universities do not train people for specific occupations. Typically the tenure for a general B.A. or B.Sc., the minimum degree, is three years. Graduate degrees can take up to ten years or more on average. The tuition for general arts at university ranges from about $1,300 to $3,500 per year (*Tuition and Living Accommodation Costs at Canadian Universities*, 1993). Because there are more community colleges, they are likely to be closer to home for more students. Living and travel expenses can then be expected to be less than similar expenses for university students who must travel farther or live away from home.

Furthermore, while it's not necessarily the case,

university students can expect to begin employment at and continue at a higher wage level than community college students. Since most college and university expenses are paid for by the students and their families, students with modest means are more likely to choose community colleges over universities. People from upper-middle and higher class backgrounds tend to be over-represented at universities (Levin, 1993). Older students with job and family responsibilities also favor community colleges, taking advantage not only of lower costs but of part-time and evening programs. Universities are typically the choice of younger, more affluent students who are able to study full time. Although it may initially seem strange to explain personal choices in terms of social forces, the sociological perspective empowers us as we come to understand how our own experiences—including the opportunities and barriers we face—are linked to where we are placed in the vast society around us. The box on page 6 illustrates further how social forces affect a seemingly personal matter: our choice of name.

Putting People in Social Context

Our society teaches us to view our lives in very personal terms, emphasizing personal choice. Thus everyday awareness carries a heavy load of personal responsibility, so that we pat ourselves on the back when we enjoy success and kick ourselves when things go wrong. Proud of our individuality, even in painful times, we resist the idea that we act in socially patterned ways. Indeed, when life goes awry we are often intent on attaching personal blame to people who may not be entirely responsible for their actions.

For this reason, a tragic event such as the attack described at the beginning of this chapter often provokes controversy about how much responsibility should be attached to the offenders. The box on page 7 looks critically at the spirited debate that appeared in the press after this crime.

Suicide: The Most Individual Act

There is perhaps no more compelling demonstration of how social forces affect human behavior than the study of suicide. What, after all, could be more personal than the act of taking one's own life? Perhaps this is why Emile Durkheim (1858–1917), a pioneer of sociology, writing a century ago, chose this as a topic of study. Durkheim was able to show that social forces are at work even in the apparent isolation of a self-destructive act.

Durkheim, who lived in France, examined records of suicide in various regions of Central Europe.[1] These documents revealed that some categories of people were much more likely than others to choose to commit suicide. Specifically, Durkheim found that men, Protestants, wealthy people, and the unmarried all had significantly higher suicide rates than did women, Catholics and Jews, the poor, and married people. What factor underlies these findings? Durkheim realized that the degree of *social integration* typical of particular categories of people significantly influences the propensity to commit suicide. That is, he found that high suicide rates corresponded with categories of people who were autonomous and individualistic. By contrast, he noted, suicide was less likely among those people who commonly have stronger social bonds.

Within the male-dominated societies of nineteenth-century Europe, men certainly had more autonomy than women. Whatever advantages this freedom afforded, reasoned Durkheim, it also meant that men killed themselves with greater frequency. Likewise, Catholic and Jewish ritual fosters stronger social ties and greater conformity than do individualistic Protestant doctrines. The result, he found, was that Protestants had a higher suicide rate than Catholics or Jews. The wealthy clearly have much more freedom than do the poor, but with the predictable result in terms of suicide rates. Finally, single people are less attached to others than married people are, which, consistent with Durkheim's theory, explained their greater likelihood of suicide.

A century later, statistical evidence continues to support Durkheim's analysis (Pescosolido & Georgianna, 1989; U.S. Bureau of the Census, 1991). Figure 1-2 shows the suicide rates for males and females; Figure 1-3 shows the suicide rate for males of different ages. Clearly, the suicide rate is higher for men than for women, and higher for elderly men who are more likely to be retired from the labor force and/or widowed, and for young men who may not yet have their own family established and may not yet have found employment. Following Durkheim's argument, we conclude that the higher suicide rate among men is due to their greater affluence and autonomy in Canadian society.

---

[1] This discussion is a much-abbreviated account of Durkheim's (1966; orig. 1897) considerably more complex analysis of suicide.

In contrast, poorer people and those with limited social choices are more socially rooted and have correspondingly lower rates of suicide.

In this way, we see general social patterns in even the most personal actions of individuals. Social forces are complex, of course, as a comparison of Figures 1-1 and 1-2 shows. We can see that social forces linked to gender produce similar patterns with regard to death from homicide and suicide. Gender operates consistently: men are more prone to both homicide and sui-

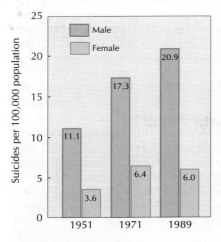

**FIGURE 1-2   SUICIDE RATES BY SEX,
1951, 1971, 1989**
SOURCE: Statistics Canada; Colombo, 1992:61.

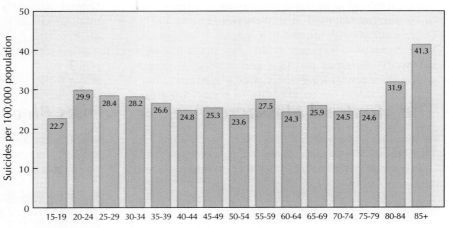

FIGURE 1-3   SUICIDE RATE FOR MEN BY AGE, 1989
SOURCE: Statistics Canada; Colombo, 1992:61.

SOCIAL DIVERSITY

What's in a Name? How Social Forces Affect Personal Choice

On the fourth of July in 1918, twins were born to Abe and Becky Friedman in Sioux City, Iowa. The first to arrive was called Esther Pauline Friedman; her sister was named Pauline Esther Friedman. Today, these women are known to almost everyone in North America, but by new names they later adopted: Ann Landers and Abigail ("Dear Abby") Van Buren.

These two women are among the thousands of people who changed their names to further their careers. This practice has been especially common among celebrities. At first glance, changing one's name may seem to be little more than a matter of particular preferences. But take a closer look at the following list from a sociological point of view. Historically, women and men of various national backgrounds have tended to adopt *English-sounding* names. Why? Because Canada and the United States have long accorded high social prestige to those of Anglo-Saxon background. How many of these well-known people can you identify from their original names?

1. Michael James Vijencio Gubitosi
2. Cherilyn Sarkisian
3. Cheryl Stoppelmoor
4. Robert Allen Zimmerman
5. Patsy McClenny
6. Nathan Birnbaum
7. Frederick Austerlitz
8. George Kyriakou Panayiotou
9. Aṇa Mae Bullock
10. Issur Danielovitch Demsky
11. Mladen Sekulovich

12. Gerald Silberman
13. Bernadette Lazzarra
14. Karen Ziegler
15. Ramon Estevez
16. Henry John Deutschendorf, Jr.
17. Allan Stewart Konigsberg
18. Judy Cohen
19. Eugene Maurice Orowitz
20. William Claude Dukenfield

1. Robert Blake; 2. Cher; 3. Cheryl Ladd; 4. Bob Dylan; 5. Morgan Fairchild; 6. George Burns; 7. Fred Astaire; 8. George Michael; 9. Tina Turner; 10. Kirk Douglas; 11. Karl Malden; 12. Gene Wilder; 13. Bernadette Peters; 14. Karen Black; 15. Martin Sheen; 16. John Denver; 17. Woody Allen; 18. Juice Newton; 19. Michael Landon; 20. W.C. Fields

cide than are women. The precise patterns may change, but in all such cases we are able to see how society is at work in our lives.

The Importance of Global Perspective

The sociological perspective reveals that our placement in the surrounding society has profound effects on our individual experiences. In recent years, many sociologists have extended this vision a step further by investigating how the position that Canada occupies in the larger world order affects us.

In global perspective, the United States and Canada are among the world's richest societies, as Global Map 1-1 shows. The mean average family income in Canada stands at more than $50,000 per

CRITICAL THINKING

The Montreal Massacre: Are Sociologists Bleeding Hearts?

In the weeks and months following the Montreal Massacre the press and the Canadian public in general debated its meaning and causes. Some focused on the psychopathology of Marc Lepine, some on Lepine's abuse as a child, some on the absence of adequate gun control legislation, and some on an anti-feminist backlash.

On one side of the controversy, a number of sociologists, social workers, and various other professionals pointed out that a wide range of social factors had to be considered in assessing responsibility for the tragedy. But others strongly objected to this position. Indeed, several nationally known commentators took the opportunity to belittle the sociological and feminist perspectives by arguing that such disciplines' concern for social forces merely obscured the basic issue: Marc Lepine was a *bad* person who had committed a morally repulsive act, for which he alone was responsible. Never mind, they added, what the "bleeding hearts" say.

Some denounced "psycho-socio babble" that blamed society, rather than Lepine, for the attack. Sociologists, they said, confused the issue by pointing to the way that Lepine's action results from patriarchy, sexism, and anti-feminist backlash. From this point of view, the issue is simpler: Lepine was crazy, and he acted in isolation. He could just as easily have decided to vent his rage on men, or minorities. Of course, these critics have a point. Lepine was certainly "crazy" in some sense. But is this the whole picture?

Sociologists would have to say no, and they also have a point. To begin, we must state clearly that sociological analysis is *not* a plea to turn loose people who commit violent crimes. But we must be prepared to face the truth that no human behavior is the product solely of what philosophers call "free will" or "simple choice." On the contrary, although human behavior involves choices, these choices are made within a constellation of influential social forces (not to mention whatever biological and psychological forces may also be at work). "Simple" is one thing human beings are not.

Consider one's sex: would anyone imagine a woman to be as likely as a man to commit this kind of crime? The fact is that males in Canada engage in many times more violent crimes than females do, as Chapter 8 ("Deviance") explains. And what about age? Are middle-aged men as likely as young men to "choose" such a murder spree? Hardly, as evidenced by the fact that people between the ages of fifteen and twenty-four represent only a fraction of the population of Canada but account for almost half of all violent crimes. Likewise, we know that categories of people who are poor are involved in more violence, both as victims and offenders, than are more affluent people. Finally, as we have already seen, crimes such as the Montreal Massacre are just the extreme end of a continuum in which women experience, in smaller and larger ways, daily violence and intimidation in their relationships with men. In our society, sexuality is all too often linked to rape and other brutal forms of violence.

No society can exist without demanding that people take some personal responsibility for their actions. For this reason, Canadians typically respond to morally outrageous behavior by seeking to attach blame to specific people. Many will argue that to blame "society" for a crime is to blame everyone and no one. But in this cultural climate of individualism, sociology injects a needed sense of balance. Embedded in society from the moment of birth, we learn to think, feel, and act as products of a larger social world. To think sociologically is not, therefore, to become a "bleeding heart." It is to understand ourselves and the world around us more fully and accurately. If our desire is to stop violence against women, we must not only punish individuals but address the societal attitudes that encourage people to see women as appropriate targets.

SOURCES: Macionis (1993); Maclean's, "Massacre in Montreal" Dec. 18, 1989: 14–18

year (Colombo, 1992:85). This affluence creates a range of personal choices for people in Canada—in terms of housing, health care, education, and opportunities for personal recreation—that are extraordinary. By contrast, as the map suggests, billions of the world's people contend with limited choices because they live in poor, strongly traditional communities. Chapter 11 ("Global Inequality") explores the causes and consequences of wealth and poverty on a global scale. For the present, merely keep in mind that the opportunities we face and the choices we make stem from both our placement in society and our country's standing in the world of nations.

A global awareness also helps us to learn about life closer to home. Social scientists have long recognized that studying others invariably provokes insights about ourselves. We could hardly consider the life of a young woman growing up in Saudi Arabia or a man coming of age in the African nation of Botswana without thinking about what it means to live in Canada.

WINDOW ON THE WORLD

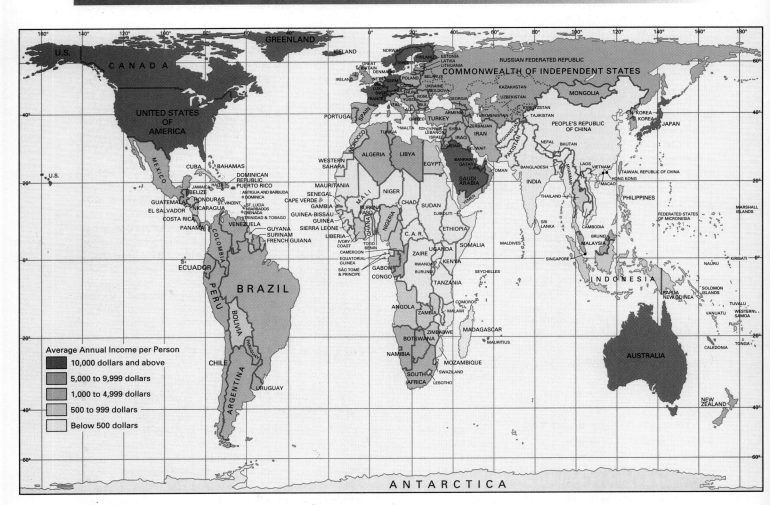

GLOBAL MAP 1-1   PER CAPITA INCOME IN GLOBAL PERSPECTIVE
Comprehending the range of opportunities and obstacles that confront us depends not only on understanding our place in a single society, but also on seeing our society's position in the world as a whole. Average people in Canada and the United States, where income is far higher than in most of the world, live longer and more comfortably than people who inhabit poor societies of Latin America, Africa, and Asia.

Thus almost every chapter of this text incorporates a global perspective into the discussion at hand.

As we approach the twenty-first century, learning about our own society demands familiarity with the rest of the world. And there is a very practical reason for this: the global restructuring of the economy and "freer" trade in and outside of Canada.

The Sociological Perspective in Everyday Life

As we have seen, members of our society often overlook the power of social forces. Yet some kinds of situations do prompt us to view the world sociologically even before we take our first course in sociology.

Sociology and Social Diversity

A Chinese student who has just arrived on an Alberta university campus is likely to notice social patterns that people in Canada take for granted. The strangeness of the surroundings alerts a foreigner that people's behavior reflects not only individual choice but also patterns of the larger society. In the same way, a Canadian encountering the social diversity of the world gains a heightened awareness of social forces. Our perspective widens as well when we confront unfamiliar social environments here at home—visiting strange neighborhoods, for example, or meeting people whose beliefs and patterns of behavior are quite different from our own.

Sociology and Social Marginality: Race, Gender, and Age

Sociologists use the term **social marginality** to refer to *the state of being excluded from social activity as an "outsider."* All people experience social marginality from time to time; for some categories of Canadians, however, being an outsider is commonplace. The more intense their social marginality, the more likely they are to make use of the sociological perspective.

No Canadian native person, for example, can live very long in Canada without being aware of how much race affects personal experiences. But because whites constitute the dominant majority in Canada, whites think about race only occasionally and tend to view race as an issue that applies only to people of

African, Asian, or native descent rather than to themselves as well.

Similarly, women of all races are more likely to see the world sociologically than are men. For several decades, women who have personally experienced the limitations that our society imposes on females have been comparing notes. The result has been a growing awareness by women that any person's particular choices, achievements, or failings reflect general social forces. Men, because of their dominant social position, generally fail to see patterns of sexual inequality as clearly and sometimes accuse women of exaggerating the problem. In the 1970s, Canadian women described the recognition of sexual inequality as "consciousness raising." It was also one way of gaining a sociological perspective.

The elderly often perceive social patterns more acutely than do young people. While this may be partly due to wisdom gained over a lifetime, another important factor is that the elderly often experience considerable social marginality. As Chapter 14 ("Aging and the Elderly") explains, the members of our society tend to define growing old as the loss of the capacity to engage in many important human endeavors, including physical recreation, work, and even sex. Since most elderly people are indeed physically and mentally capable of all these activities, they understand more clearly than the young the degree to which society defines what individuals are and how they should think and act.

In short, people who are placed on the outside of social life—due to their race, sex, age, or a host of other factors—are usually more aware of social patterns that others take for granted. They have stepped back from society (perhaps, more accurately, society has stepped back from them) and therefore take a more sociological view of the world.

Sociology and Social Crisis

American sociologist C. Wright Mills (1959) suggested that times of social disruption foster widespread sociological thinking. In Mills's life, the 1930s stood out as a decade of heightened sociological awareness. The Great Depression followed the stock market crash of 1929, throwing one-fourth of the labor force out of work. Under such circumstances, most unemployed people could not help but see general social forces at work in their particular lives. Rather than claiming, "Something is wrong with me; I can't find a job," they were likely to say, "There are no jobs to be found because the economy has collapsed!"

Because our way of life places such a high value on individualism and personal autonomy, we learn to think of advantaged people as especially capable and disadvantaged people as personally undeserving. The sociological perspective challenges this conclusion by showing that our life experiences also reflect larger forces, such as dramatic shifts in the economy, which may be completely beyond our control.

People very quickly develop a sociological perspective when the established patterns of society begin to shake and crumble. More recently, the decade of the 1960s also enhanced sociological awareness in North America. The civil rights, women's liberation, antiwar, and hippie movements all challenged accepted social patterns in a highly visible way. This social climate called attention to the ways in which personal experiences are shaped by forces beyond the people themselves—the political, economic, military, and technological elements of "the system." There is no doubt that, by pointing to social forces that affect the lives of all women and men, each of these movements has incorporated an element of the sociological perspective.

Worth noting, too, is that the converse is often true: sociological thinking sometimes fosters social disruption. In other words, gaining a sociological understanding of how "the system" works may well provoke attempts to change it. For example, as more and more women and men confront the power of gender, many are actively trying to reduce the traditional separation of men's and women's lives.

As these everyday examples suggest, an introduction to sociology is an invitation to discover a new way of looking at familiar patterns of social life. At this point, we might well consider whether this invitation is worth accepting. In other words, what are the benefits of learning to use the sociological perspective?

Benefits of the Sociological Perspective

The knowledge amassed by sociologists can be readily applied to our lives in countless ways. There are, however, four general benefits of exploring the sociological perspective. First, we start to realize that certain ideas we have come to accept as "true" have no basis in fact. *The sociological perspective challenges familiar understandings about ourselves and others, so that we can critically assess the truth of commonly held assumptions.*

As we have already seen, a good example of a widespread but misleading "truth" is that women and men in Canada are "autonomous individuals" who are responsible for their lives. By thinking this way, we are sometimes too quick to praise particularly successful people as being personally superior to those who have not fared as well. On the other side of the coin, people who do not measure up may be unfairly condemned as personally deficient. A sociological approach encourages us to ask whether these beliefs are actually true and, to the extent that they are not, why they are so widely held.

Second, the sociological perspective helps us see that, for better or worse, our own society operates in a particular and deliberate way. This is important because no one is able to live with complete disregard for society's rules. In the game of life, we may decide how to play our cards, but it is society that deals us the hand. The more we understand about how the game works, the more effective a player we will be. Put another way, *the sociological perspective allows us to recognize both the opportunities we have and the constraints that circumscribe our lives.* Knowledge of this kind is power. Through it, we come to understand what we are likely and unlikely to accomplish for ourselves, and how the goals we adopt can be realized more effectively.

Third, sociological thinking encourages a more active life. Without an awareness of how society operates, we are likely to passively accept the status quo. However, the greater our understanding of the operation of society, the more we can take an active part in shaping social life. *The sociological perspective, therefore, empowers us as active members of our world.* For some, this may mean embracing society as it is; other people, however, may attempt nothing less than changing the

entire world in some way. The discipline of sociology advocates no one particular political orientation, and sociologists themselves weigh in at points all across the political spectrum. But evaluating any aspect of social life—whatever one's eventual goal—depends on the ability to identify social forces and to assess their consequences.

Some thirty years ago, C. Wright Mills (1959) pointed out the importance of what he called the "sociological imagination" in helping people to actively engage the world around them. This pioneering sociologist is highlighted in the profile box. Others will be featured in boxes throughout this book.

A fourth and final benefit of sociological thinking is learning that our world contains a remarkable variety of human social patterns. North Americans represent a

PROFILE

C. Wright Mills (1916–1962)

Charles Wright Mills managed to cause a stir with most everything he did. Even arriving for a class at New York's Columbia University—astride his motorcycle and clad in a sweatshirt and boots—he was likely to turn some heads. During the conservative 1950s, Mills not only dressed a bit out of the mainstream; he produced a number of books that critically challenged most of the beliefs Americans took for granted. In the process, he won both followers and adversaries.

Mills's most enduring contribution was his insistence that people actively use what he described as the "sociological imagination" in their daily lives. Mills rejected sociology as a dry enterprise detached from life in favor of a vital process by which people became engaged in their social world. His hopeful vision was for a sociologically aware society forging a more gentle and just way of life.

The following excerpt spells out the first step in Mills's vision.* Here he suggests that we must learn to understand our individual lives in terms of the social forces that have shaped them.

When a society becomes industrialized, a peasant becomes a worker; a feudal lord is liquidated or becomes a businessman. When classes rise or fall, a man is employed or unemployed; when the rate of investment goes up or down,

*In this excerpt, Mills uses male pronouns which appear as he wrote them. Of course, his point applies to all people. It is interesting, and even ironic, that Mills, an outspoken critic of society, reflected in his writing the conventional practices of his time with respect to gender.

a man takes new heart or goes broke. When wars happen, an insurance salesman becomes a rocket launcher; a store clerk, a radar man; a wife lives alone; a child grows up without a father. Neither the life of an individual nor the history of a society can be understood without understanding both.

Yet men do not usually define the troubles they endure in terms of historical change. ... The well-being they enjoy, they do not usually impute to the big ups and downs of the society in which they live. Seldom aware of the intricate connection between the patterns of their own lives and the course of world history, ordinary men do not usually know what this connection means for the kind of men they are becoming and for the kinds of history-making in which they might take part. They do not possess the quality of mind essential to grasp the interplay of men and society, of biography and history, of self and world. ...

What they need ... is a quality of mind that will help them to [see] ... what is going on in the world and ... what may be happening within themselves. It is this quality ... that ... may be called the sociological imagination.

SOURCE: Mills, 1959:3–5.

scant 5 percent of the world's population and, as the remaining chapters of this book reveal, the rest of humanity lives in ways that often differ dramatically from our own. Like people elsewhere, we tend to define our own way of life as proper and "natural." But the cultural diversity of today's world presents us with countless competing versions of correct behavior. *The sociological perspective helps us to recognize human diversity and to begin to understand the challenges of living in a diverse world.*

The Origins of Sociology

Like the "choices" made by individuals, major historical events rarely "just happen." They are typically products of powerful social forces that are always complex and only partly predictable. So it was with the emergence of sociology itself. Having described the discipline's distinctive perspective and its benefits, we now consider how and why this discipline emerged in the first place.

Although human beings have mused about society since the beginning of our history, sociology is of relatively recent origin. It is one of the youngest academic disciplines—far younger than history, physics, or economics, for example. Only in 1838 did the French social thinker Auguste Comte, introduced in the box, coin the term *sociology* to describe a new way of looking at the world.

Science and Sociology

The nature of human society held the attention of the writings of virtually all the brilliant thinkers of the ancient world, including the Chinese philosopher K'ung Fu-tzu or Confucius (551–479 B.C.E.), and the Greek philosophers Plato (427–347 B.C.E.) and Aristotle (384–322 B.C.E.).[2]

Similarly, the Roman emperor Marcus Aurelius (121–180), the medieval theologian St. Thomas Aquinas (c. 1225–1274), the English playwright William Shake-

---

[2] Throughout this text, the abbreviation B.C.E. designates "before the common era." This terminology is used in place of the traditional B.C. ("before Christ") in recognition of the religious plurality of Canada. Similarly, in place of the traditional A.D. (anno Domini, or "in the year of our Lord"), the abbreviation C.E. ("common era") is employed.

speare (1564–1616), and a host of others reflected on the social world in their writings. Yet, as Emile Durkheim noted almost a century ago, none of these social thinkers approached society from a sociological point of view.

> *Looking back in history ... we find that no philosophers ever viewed matters [with a sociological perspective] until quite recently. ... It seemed to them sufficient to ascertain what the human will should strive for and what it should avoid in established societies. ... Their aim was not to offer us as valid a description of nature as possible, but to present us with the idea of a perfect society, a model to be imitated.* (1972:57; orig. 1918)

What made sociology different from what came before? Prior to the birth of sociology, philosophers and theologians were mostly concerned with imagining the "ideal" society, that is, life as it ought to be. None attempted an analysis of "real" society, as it actually was. Pioneers of the discipline such as Auguste Comte and Emile Durkheim reversed these priorities. Although they were certainly concerned with how human society could be improved, their major goal was to understand how society actually operates.

The key to achieving this goal, according to Comte, was the development of a scientific approach to studying society. Looking back over history, Comte sorted out efforts to understand society into three distinct stages (1975; orig. 1851–1854). The earliest era, extending through the medieval period in Europe, he termed the *theological stage*. At this point, thoughts about the world were guided by religion. More specifically, society was regarded as an expression of God's will—at least insofar as people and their religious leaders were capable of fulfilling a divine plan.

With the Renaissance, the theological approach to society gave way to what Comte called the *metaphysical stage*. During this period, people started to view society as a natural, rather than a supernatural, phenomenon. Human nature figured heavily in metaphysical visions of society; the English philosopher Thomas Hobbes (1588–1679), for example, suggested that society reflected not the perfection of God so much as the failings of selfish human nature.

What Comte heralded as the final, *scientific stage* in the long quest to understand society was prompted by scientists such as the Polish astronomer Copernicus (1473–1543), the Italian astronomer and physicist Galileo (1564–1642), and the English physicist and mathematician Isaac Newton (1642–1727). Comte's

This medieval drawing conveys the mix of apprehension and excitement with which early scientists began to question conventional understandings of the universe. Pioneering sociologists, too, challenged many ideas that had been long taken for granted, generating new and often controversial ideas.

contribution came in applying this scientific approach—first used to study the physical world—to the study of society.

Comte was thus a proponent of **positivism**, defined as *a means to understand the world based on science.* As a positivist, Comte believed that society conforms to invariable laws, much as the physical world operates according to gravity and other laws of nature.

Sociology emerged as an academic discipline in Canada and the United States at the beginning of this century, with early sociologists such as Lester Ward (1841–1913) pursuing Comte's vision of a scientific sociology. Even today, most sociologists continue to view science as a crucial element of sociology, but we

PROFILE

Auguste Comte (1798–1857)

What sort of person would invent *sociology*? Someone living in times of momentous change, no doubt. Comte grew up in the shadow of the French Revolution, which brought a sweeping transformation to his country. And if that wasn't sufficient, another revolution was going on at the same time: factories were sprouting up across Europe, recasting the lives of the entire population. Just as people enduring a storm cannot help but think of the weather, so those living during Comte's turbulent era became keenly aware of the state of society.

Drawn from a small town to the bustle and energy of Paris, Comte was soon deeply involved in the exciting events of his time. More than anything else, he wanted to understand the human drama that was unfolding all around him. Once equipped with the knowledge of how society operates, Comte believed people would be able to build a better future for themselves. He divided his new discipline into two parts: how society is held together (which he called *social statics*), and how society changes (*social dynamics*). From the Greek and Latin words meaning "the study of society," Comte came to describe his work as *sociology*.

have learned that scientific techniques cannot be applied to the social world in the same way they are applied to the physical world. As we shall explain in Chapter 2 ("Sociological Investigation"), the causes of human behavior are often far more complex than the causes of events in the natural world. Put another way, human beings, unlike mere physical objects, do not always act in predictable ways. We are creatures with considerable imagination and spontaneity; thus, our behavior can never be fully explained by any rigid "laws of society."

Social Change and Sociology

We have already suggested that the discipline of sociology sprang from revolutionary changes in society itself. European societies were buffeted by a number of great transformations during the seventeenth and eighteenth

---

CRITICAL THINKING

A Brief History of Canadian Sociology

John Porter is often considered Canada's foremost sociologist. His book, The Vertical Mosaic (1965) laid the groundwork for the Canadian sociologists' focus on Canadian society in the context of development and underdevelopment (particularly as compared to the United States), inequality and inequity, elites, French-English relations, and bureaucratic structures. Having graduated from the London School of Economics, Porter spent most of his career in Ottawa, at Carleton University where he held various posts ranging from faculty member, to department Chair, Dean, and Vice-President (Vallee, Canadian Encyclopedia, 1988).

S.D. Clark was a member of the faculty at the University of Toronto from 1938. While he is known as a sociologist, he was educated in history and sociology at the University of Saskatchewan, McGill, University of Toronto, and the London School of Economics before he joined U. of T. as a lecturer in the department of political economy. He directed the publication of a series of ten volumes on the Social Credit Movement. In the 1960s his interests turned to the economic consequences of social change. (Giffen, Canadian Encyclopedia, 1988).

Harold A. Innis was best known as a political economist. Nevertheless, his early political economic history of Canadian development has become a bedrock of sociological analysis. His first major work, The Fur Trade in Canada, 1930, argued the staple thesis of development, which became of critical importance. Even today, scholars interested in Canada's economic development take Innis's perspective into account. See for instance Gordon Laxer's Open for Business, discussed in Chapter 2, for a current analysis of Canadian economic development that addresses Innis's hypotheses.

centuries. As the social ground trembled under their feet, people were understandably drawn to the study of society.

Three key factors fueled the great reshaping of society during this period. First, rapid technological innovation in eighteenth-century Europe gave rise to factories and a new industrial economy. Second, these factories drew millions of people from the countryside, causing an explosive growth of cities. Third, people in these expanding industrial cities soon began to entertain new political ideas about democracy and individual rights. We shall briefly describe each of these three interrelated changes in turn.

A New Industrial Economy

During the Middle Ages, most people in Europe tilled fields near their homes while others engaged in

Canadian sociology arose from different traditions and continues to be, in many ways, distinct from American sociology. In fact, it is a discipline that reflects the country that has two major cultures and linguistic communities.

Sociology began in Canada, as in the United States, in the early part of this century. By 1920, sociology courses were being offered in a number of disciplines and sociology was included in the theology curricula. During this period the Canadian Political Science Association, formed in 1913, accepted sociologists as members. Sociology was taught and sociological research undertaken earlier in Quebec, at Laval, the University of Montreal, and later at the University of Quebec, than the rest of the country. This early French sociology was influenced by developments in Europe and tended towards investigations and discussion of economic and political trends and comparisons. English Canadian sociology began at McGill, following the American tradition on the one hand, and at the University of Toronto, following the British tradition, on the other hand.

Sociology as a distinct department did not begin at the University of Toronto until the 1960s. Before that time, social thinkers of sociological cast worked out of the department of Political Economy. Sociology at University of Toronto differed from the American influenced social issues and community study approach which characterized McGill. Modeled on British sociology, it tackled questions of political and economic history. The most influential sociologist in the early years was Harold A. Innis, whose emphasis on the way that the development of the Canadian economy depended on resource extraction and exportation (known as the staple approach) formed the backdrop for the development of the sociological perspective in Canada. This perspective focused on economic developments in this country, particularly the branch-plant nature of the Canadian state. Later, John Porter's The Vertical Mosaic, describing the internal inequities in Canadian society, became a landmark of Canadian sociology. More recently, Patricia Marchak (1975) in

Ideological Perspectives on Canadian Society, has described and compared the dominant and the counter-ideologies prevalent in different class groupings in Canadian society.

Sociology has played an important role in the development of Canadian social policy. For example, the medicare system arose out of the Royal Commission on Health Services (1964–65), which was strongly influenced by sociological research. Other royal commissions, including the Royal Commission on Bilingualism and Biculturalism (1963–69), and the Royal Commission on the Status of Women in Canada (1967–70), were also based, in part, on the findings of sociologists. In Quebec, La Commission d'enquête sur l'enseignement au Québec (1963–66) drastically altered the educational system in that province.

SOURCES: Adapted from Bruce & Fox (1987); Whyte & Vallee (1988); Spencer, 1981; and Helmes-Hayes (1988).

small-scale *manufacturing* (a word derived from Latin words meaning "to make by hand"). Many people worked where they lived; homes were centers of commercial endeavors such as baking, furniture making, and sewing of garments.

Early in the eighteenth century, new sources of energy, especially steam power, were harnessed to large machines. Factories began to spring up. Now, instead of laboring at home, or on land that families had worked for generations, workers became part of a vast and anonymous industrial work force, toiling away from home for strangers who owned the factories. More than just a new way to produce goods, factories set loose an expanding industrial economy that soon shook medieval society to its foundations. Traditional ways of life fell victim to the sweeping changes, and countless small, closely knit communities were swallowed up by the expanding scale of life. Steadily, factories drew people from the countryside to produce gargantuan cities.

The Growth of Cities

Factories sprouting across England and elsewhere in Western Europe became magnets attracting people in need of work. This "pull" was made all the more powerful by an additional "push" from the villages. As the English textile industry expanded, new industrialists fenced off more and more farmland to raise sheep—the source of wool. This "enclosure movement" pushed countless people from the countryside into the cities in search of jobs, which they could find in factories.

Not surprisingly, these new industrial cities soon reached unprecedented size. During the Middle Ages, towns had been small, self-contained worlds within defensive walls. As late as 1700—the dawning of the industrial era—London was the largest city in Europe with only 500,000 people. Within two centuries, that city's population had increased by *thirteen times* to 6.5 million (Chandler & Fox, 1974).

Urban growth on this scale took place across the European continent, dramatically changing people's lives. Not only were cities full of strangers, but the tremendous influx of people simply overwhelmed the cities' capacity to absorb them. Widespread social problems—including pollution, crime, and inadequate housing—were the order of the day. These social crises stimulated the development of the sociological perspective.

Political Change

During the Middle Ages, as Comte noted, most people thought of society as an expression of divine will. The feudal nobility claimed to rule by "divine right," as if the entire social order were simply God's plan for

The birth of sociology came at a time of rapid social change. The discipline developed in those regions of Europe where the Industrial Revolution most disrupted traditional ways of life, drawing people from isolated villages to rapidly growing industrial cities.

humanity. This belief is evident in lines from the old Anglican hymn "All Things Bright and Beautiful":

> *The rich man in his castle,*
> *The poor man at his gate,*
> *He made them high and lowly*
> *And ordered their estate.*

Considering, in hindsight, the new emerging economy and the rapid growth of cities, changes in political thought seem to have been inevitable. By the sixteenth century, the political conservatism that had characterized the medieval era was crumbling under a spirited attack on tradition, especially the notion that society reflected God's will. In the writings of Thomas Hobbes, John Locke (1632–1704), and Adam Smith (1723–1790), we find less concern with the moral obligations of people to society and more support for the idea that society is the product of self-interest. The key phrases in the new political climate, therefore, heralded the individual: *individual liberty* and *individual rights*. The American Declaration of Independence, which celebrated the separation of the American colonies from England, is a clear statement of these new political ideas. Here we read that each individual has "certain unalienable rights," including "life, liberty, and the pursuit of happiness." The political revolution in France that began soon afterward in 1789 was an even more dramatic effort to break with political and social traditions.

As he surveyed his society after the French Revolution, the French social analyst Alexis de Tocqueville exaggerated only slightly when he exclaimed that the changes we have described amounted to "nothing short of the regeneration of the whole human race" (1955:13; orig. 1856). In this context, it is easy to see why Auguste Comte and other pioneers forged the new discipline of sociology. Sociology flowered in precisely those societies that had experienced the most pronounced social changes. France, Germany, and England underwent a truly revolutionary social transformation, and in all three sociology had emerged by the end of the nineteenth century. In contrast, in societies touched less by these momentous events—including Portugal, Spain, Italy, and Eastern Europe—there was little development of the sociological perspective.

Individual sociologists reacted differently to the new social order, then, just as they respond differently to society today. Some found the emerging modern world deeply disturbing. Auguste Comte, for example, feared that people would be overpowered by change and uprooted from long-established local communities. Embracing social conservatism, he sought a rebirth of traditional family, community, and morality.

A different view of these massive changes characterized the thinking of German social critic Karl Marx (1818–1883), whose ideas are presented at length in Chapter 4 ("Society"). Marx worried little about the loss of traditional social patterns, which he detested. But neither could he condone the concentration of the great wealth produced by industrial technology in the hands of a small elite, while the masses faced only hunger and misery.

Clearly, Comte and Marx advanced radically different views on the problems of modernity. Yet they shared the conviction that society cannot be understood simply in terms of individual choice. The sociological perspective animates the work of each, revealing that people's individual lives are framed by the broader society in which they live. This lesson, of course, is as true today as it was in the nineteenth century. The major issues that concern sociologists are highlighted in subsequent chapters of this book. These important social forces include culture, social class, race, ethnicity, gender, the family, and the economy. They all involve ways in which individuals are guided, united, and divided in the larger arena of society.

Sociological Theory

Sociology involves more than adopting a distinctive point of view. Linking specific observations in a meaningful way focuses on another element of the discipline: theory. In the simplest terms, a **theory** is *the process of linking facts together in order to explain something*. To illustrate the use of theory in sociology, recall Emile Durkheim's investigation of suicide. Durkheim attempted to explain the fact that some categories of people (men, Protestants, the wealthy, and the unmarried) have higher suicide rates than others (women, Catholics, Jews, the poor, and the married). He did this by linking suicide rates to another fact—the degree of social integration typical of various categories of people. Through systematic comparisons, Durkheim refined his theory of suicide, learning that people with low social integration are more prone to take their own lives.

To illustrate further, how do we explain the fact that more men than women enroll in college science courses? Using the sociological perspective, we suspect that more than random individual choices are involved. One possible theory is that the sciences are more attractive to men than to women; perhaps men have a greater innate interest in science. A second premise is that the educational system has some formal or informal policy that limits the enrollment of women in science courses. Still another possibility is that our society encourages men to develop an interest in science while simultaneously discouraging this interest in women.

As this example shows, facts can be linked in different ways to generate a range of theoretical explanations. Merely linking facts together, therefore, hardly ensures that a theory is correct. To evaluate a theory, sociologists use methods of scientific research, described in the next chapter, to gather more information. This enables them to confirm some theories while rejecting or modifying others. Early in this century, for example, sociologists studying the rapid growth of cities theorized that urban living promoted impersonality and even mental illness. As we shall explain in Chapter 21 ("Population and Urbanization"), however, research has subsequently shown that living in a large city does not necessarily mean that people become socially isolated, nor does it diminish their mental health. Theory, then, is never static; sociologists continually refine theory through research, just as other types of scientists do.

In attempting to develop theories about human society, sociologists face a wide range of choices. What issues should they study? How should facts be linked together to form theories? Such questions are not answered haphazardly. Rather, theory building is guided by a general framework called a theoretical paradigm (Kuhn, 1970). Applied to sociology, a **theoretical paradigm** is defined as *a set of fundamental assumptions about society that guides sociological thinking and research*.

We suggested earlier that two of sociology's founders—Auguste Comte and Karl Marx—made sense of the emerging modern world in different ways. Such differences persist among sociologists today. Some are more concerned with ways societies stay the same; others focus on how societies change. Similarly, some direct attention to what joins people together, while others investigate how society divides people according to sex, race, or social class. Some sociologists seek to understand the operation of society as it is, while others see their work as encouraging what they consider to be desirable social change.

In short, sociologists often disagree about what the most interesting questions are; even when they agree about the questions, they may still differ over the answers. Nonetheless, sociological theory is far from chaotic, because sociologists share three major theoretical paradigms that allow them to analyze effectively virtually any dimension of society.

The Structural-Functional Paradigm

The **structural-functional paradigm** is a framework for building theory guided by the assumption that society is a complex system whose parts work together to promote stability. As its name suggests, the structural-functional paradigm has two components. First, society is composed of numerous kinds of **social structure**, defined as relatively stable patterns of social behavior. Social structures range from broad patterns such as family life and economic systems to situational behaviors such as greetings and other forms of face-to-face contact. Second, this paradigm links structures together in terms of their **social functions**, which refer to consequences for the operation of society as a whole. Thus all the elements of society—from families to a simple handshake—have important functions that help perpetuate society, at least in its present form.

The structural-functional paradigm owes much to the ideas of Auguste Comte, who tried to imagine how his own society could remain unified while undergoing massive change. Another who advanced this theoretical approach was the English sociologist Herbert Spencer (1820–1903), introduced in the box on page 19. One of the most influential thinkers of his time, Spencer studied both the human body and society. He came to believe that the two have much in common. The structural parts of the human body include the skeleton, muscles, and various internal organs. All these elements are interdependent, each having a function that contributes to the survival of the entire human organism. Likewise, reasoned Spencer, the elements of social life are interdependent, working to keep society operating with minimal disruption. The structural-functional approach, then, leads sociologists to identify the various parts of society, investigating the contribution of each.

Several decades after the death of Auguste Comte, Emile Durkheim expanded on the structural-functional paradigm in France. Like Spencer, his English counterpart, Durkheim investigated ways in which modern societies remain integrated. Because of the importance of his ideas to later chapters, Durkheim's analysis of social structures and their functions will be detailed in Chapter 4 ("Society"). As sociology developed, the approach of Herbert Spencer and Emile Durkheim was carried forward by Talcott Parsons (1902–1979) in the United States. The chief proponent

Herbert Spencer (1820–1903)

Herbert Spencer's most memorable idea was his assertion that the future would be characterized by "the survival of the fittest." Many people link this immortal phrase to the theory of species evolution developed by the natural scientist Charles Darwin (1809–1882). Spencer's concept of survival of the fittest, however, actually referred to society, not to living creatures. But this confusion over Spencer's remark suggests how deeply early sociological thought was influenced by comparisons between the social and natural worlds.

Spencer's view of society, which came to be known as *social Darwinism*, was built on the following principle: success would come to the most intelligent, ambitious, and productive people, who quite properly advanced their interests at the expense of the less able. Spencer endorsed the notion of the survival of the fittest, believing that this process would steadily improve society.

The key to successful social evolution, from Spencer's point of view, was simply not to meddle with society, especially its free-market economy. For this opinion, Spencer was widely applauded by early industrialists who sought to keep big business free of government regulation or social conscience. Indeed, John D. Rockefeller, who gobbled up companies to gain control of much of the American oil industry early in this century, often recited Spencer's words to young children in Sunday school, teaching them to think of the growth of giant businesses as merely the "survival of the fittest." But others objected to the idea that society was nothing more than a jungle where people selfishly used whatever resources they could muster to their own advantage. Critics found a pressing need for social welfare programs that would assist the poor. From Spencer's point of view, however, welfare damaged society by squandering social resources on its least worthy members.

Gradually, Spencer's doctrine of social Darwinism fell out of favor among social scientists, although it remains influential. Social Darwinism was actually discredited by facts that have since come to light: we now know that an individual's ability only partially accounts for personal success, and favoring the rich and powerful is not necessarily in the interest of society as a whole. In addition, from the standpoint of values, Spencer's ideas have been widely dismissed as a remarkably heartless view of society with little room for human compassion.

---

of the structural-functional paradigm in American sociology, Parsons sought to identify the major functions any and all societies had to perform in order to survive, and how they accomplished them.

Another contemporary sociologist whose work follows the structural-functional approach, Robert K. Merton (1968), has shown that social patterns can have many functions. For the same pattern, however, these functions differ depending on the point of view of specific categories of people. For example, traditional courtship behavior may benefit society by encouraging the formation of new families, but these practices may also confer advantages on men (by giving them disproportionate access to wealth and power) while limiting the opportunities of women (who may forgo professional advancement in favor of raising a family). Further,

Merton points out that some of the functions of any social pattern may be more obvious than others. The **manifest functions** of any social structure are *consequences that are recognized and intended by people in the society*. By contrast, **latent functions** are *consequences that go largely unrecognized and are unintended*. To illustrate, consider the rapid increase in automobile travel during this century. One manifest consequence of this technological innovation is that people and goods are easily transported from one place to another. Cars also serve a manifest function as *status symbols*, since we sometimes judge people's social standing by the things they own. But the rise in automobile transportation also has significant latent functions. Because they allow people to travel about in relative isolation, cars reinforce our cultural emphasis on personal autonomy.

Merton makes a further point: it is unlikely that *all* the effects of a single social structure will be useful. Merton used the term **social dysfunctions** to designate *undesirable effects of a social pattern on the operation of society.* One of the dysfunctions of our national reliance on private automobiles is that, with millions of them on the road, air quality has suffered, especially in large cities. No doubt, too, the easy travel made possible by cars has contributed to a decline in the strength of traditional families and local neighborhoods, changes lamented by many people in Canada.

Critical evaluation.   The positivist roots of the structural-functional paradigm are evident in this approach's tendency to see the social world as orderly and relatively fixed. The job of sociologists, from this point of view, is to employ scientific research to learn how society works. Despite its strong influence on the discipline of sociology, however, recent decades have revealed limitations of the structural-functional paradigm.

By assuming that society operates more or less "naturally," critics point out, structural-functionalism tends to overlook ways in which social arrangements are constructed. Social patterns vary widely from place to place, and they change over time; thus, the notion that any particular arrangements are natural seems hazardous at best. Further, by emphasizing social integration, structural-functionalism tends to pay less attention to divisions based on power conflict, social class, race, ethnicity, and gender, and downplays how such divisions generate tension and conflict. This focus on social stability at the expense of the important processes of conflict and social change gives the structural-functional paradigm a conservative character. As a critical response to this approach, sociologists have developed another theoretical orientation: the social-conflict paradigm.

The Social-Conflict Paradigm

The **social-conflict (or political economy) paradigm** is a framework for building theory based on the assumption that society is a complex system characterized by inequality and conflict that generate social change. This approach complements the structural-functional paradigm by highlighting not integration but division based on social inequality. Guided by this paradigm, sociologists investigate how factors such as social class, race, ethnicity, gender, and age are linked

to unequal distribution of valuable resources, including money, power, education, and social prestige. Therefore, rather than identifying how social patterns can be functional for society as a whole, this approach investigates how they are useful to some people and harmful to others. One sociologist who made his mark dealing with issues related to social inequality is introduced in the box.

The social-conflict paradigm leads sociologists to view society as an arena in which conflict emerges from the incompatible interests of categories of people who occupy different positions in society. Not surprisingly, dominant categories—the rich in relation to the poor, whites in relation to people of color, and men in relation to women—typically try to protect their privileges by supporting the status quo. Those with fewer privileges commonly counter these efforts by attempting to bring about a more equitable distribution of social resources.

To illustrate, Chapter 16 ("Education") explores how secondary schools in Canada prepare some students for university and emphasize vocational training for others. Thinking in terms of the structural-functional paradigm, we might wonder if society as a whole benefits from such "streaming" to the extent that students receive education according to their academic abilities. The social-conflict paradigm provides a contrasting insight: streaming confers privileges on some that it denies to others, perpetuating social inequality and promoting conflict between favored and disadvantaged categories of people.

Research guided by the social-conflict paradigm has shown that schools place students in university-preparatory streams not so much because of their superior intelligence but because of their privileged background. Virtually ensured of becoming part of the educational elite with a university degree, most of these men and women are likely to enter occupations that will provide both prestige and a high income. In the process, of course, the privileges of one generation are passed down to another. And what of the less privileged students? Schools commonly place them in vocational streams, sometimes with little regard for their actual abilities. There they receive no preparation for university so that, like their parents before them, they will enter occupations that confer little prestige and low income. From this point of view, "streaming" amounts to using the concept of ability to justify a practice that merely perpetuates privilege (Bowles & Gintis, 1976; Oakes, 1982, 1985).

Other important social conflicts in Canada are

PROFILE

W.E.B. DuBois (1868–1963)

The discipline of sociology is built on the work of many pioneers, not all of whom have received the attention they deserve. A case in point is William Edward Burghardt DuBois, whose work both as a scientist and social critic has gained attention only in recent decades.

Born to a poor family in a small Massachusetts town, DuBois showed extraordinary aptitude as a student. After graduating from high school, he went on to university, one of only a handful of young people from his town (and the only person of African descent) to do so. After graduating from Fisk University in Nashville, Tennessee, DuBois realized a childhood ambition and enrolled at Harvard, repeating his junior and senior years

and then beginning graduate study. He earned the first doctorate awarded by Harvard to a person of color.

DuBois believed that social research should be linked to contemporary problems, and for him, the vexing issue of race was a paramount concern. Although he was accepted in the intellectual circles of his day, DuBois believed that blacks and whites lived in two distinct social worlds that often erupted in conflict when they came in contact with one another. DuBois maintained that research—although scientifically rigorous and fair-minded—should be directed at answering questions that would improve society. Later in his life, DuBois reflected (1940:51):

> I was determined to put science into sociology through a study of the condition of my own group. I was going to study the facts, any and all facts, concerning the American Negro and his plight. ...

After taking a position at the University of Pennsylvania in Philadelphia, he set out to conduct the research that produced a sociological classic, *The Philadelphia Negro: A Social Study* (1899). In this systematic investigation of Philadelphia's African-American community at the turn of the century, DuBois chronicled both the strengths and weaknesses of people wrestling with overwhelming social problems. Running against the intellectual cur-

rent of the times (and especially social Darwinism), DuBois rejected the widespread notion of black inferiority, explaining the problems of African Americans largely in terms of white prejudice. He was critical not only of whites, but also of successful members of the black community whom he scolded for being so eager to win white acceptance that they abandoned all ties with those still in need. "The first impulse of the best, the wisest and the richest," he lamented, "is to segregate themselves from the mass. ..." (1899:317).

At the time *The Philadelphia Negro* was published, DuBois was optimistic about the chances of resolving the racial problems of the United States. By the end of his life, however, he had grown bitter, thinking that little had been done to advance social equality. At the age of 93, DuBois emigrated to Africa, and he died in Ghana two years later.

Although his research was not widely recognized at the time of his death, today DuBois's books are receiving the attention of a new generation of scholars. A model of sound sociology, his work also addresses many of the problems that continue to beset our society.

SOURCES: Based, in part, on Baltzell (1967) and DuBois (1967; orig. 1899).

Quebec nationalism, native self-government, labor strikes, and the drive for social equality for women. Overall, then, rather than viewing society as relatively stable, the social-conflict paradigm points out how social structure fosters continual conflict within a society, leading to change.

Finally, many sociologists who make use of the social-conflict paradigm attempt not only to understand society as it is but also to reduce social inequality.

This was the goal of Karl Marx, the social thinker who has had a singularly important influence on the development of the social-conflict paradigm. Marx had little patience with those who sought to use science only to understand how society works. In a well-known declaration (inscribed on his monument in London's Highgate Cemetery), Marx maintained: "The philosophers have only interpreted the world, in various ways; the point, however, is to change it."

Critical evaluation.   The social-conflict paradigm has developed rapidly in recent decades and is now a major part of sociology in Canada and elsewhere. As the paradigm itself would lead us to expect, more traditional sociological thinkers have voiced criticisms. One general concern is that this approach highlights power struggles as the dominant trait of societies, giving little attention to social unity based on functional interdependence and shared values. In addition, the social-conflict approach is often criticized for explicitly advocating change, thereby giving up at least some claim to scientific objectivity. As Chapter 2 ("Sociological Investigation") explains in detail, advocates of this approach respond that *all* social approaches have political consequences, albeit different ones.

An additional criticism, which applies equally to both the structural-functional and social-conflict paradigms, is that they envision society in terms of broad abstractions. A third theoretical paradigm views society more in terms of everyday, face-to-face interaction.

The Symbolic-Interaction Paradigm

Both the structural-functional and social-conflict paradigms share a **macro-level orientation**, meaning *a focus on broad social structures that characterize society as a system*. A macro-level approach to society is rather like investigating a city from high above in a helicopter—noting, for example, that highways facilitate traffic flow from one place to another, or that there are striking contrasts between the neighborhoods of the rich and the poor. The symbolic-interaction paradigm, by contrast, uses a **micro-level orientation**, meaning *a focus on situational patterns of social interaction*. Exploring urban life in this way means being at street level, observing, for example, face-to-face interaction in public parks or how people respond to a homeless person they pass on the street. The **symbolic-interaction paradigm**, then, is *a theoretical framework based on the assumption that society is continuously recreated as human beings construct reality through interaction*.

How are millions of distinct lives intertwined into the drama of society? One answer, discussed in detail in Chapter 6 ("Social Interaction in Everyday Life"), is that we become linked to one another as we build reality in countless social situations. Humans rarely respond to things or other people in direct, physical terms, as when someone ducks to avoid a punch. Mostly, we respond based on the meanings we attach to the surrounding world. Through this process of creating meaning, we define our identities, rights, and obligations toward one another. Notice, too, that the process of reality construction is highly variable. For example, one person may define a homeless man on a city street as "just a bum looking for a handout" and ignore him. Another, however, might define him as a "fellow human being in need" and offer some assistance. In the same way, one pedestrian may respond to a police officer walking nearby with a sense of security, while another may be overcome with a feeling of nervous anxiety. Sociologists guided by the symbolic-interaction approach view society as a mosaic of subjective meanings and responses.

The symbolic-interaction paradigm draws on the thinking of Max Weber (1864–1920), a German sociologist who emphasized that society is largely a matter of people's subjective perceptions. Weber's approach is considered at length in Chapter 4 ("Society").

From this general foundation, others have analyzed specific dimensions of social life. Chapter 5 ("Socialization") examines the thinking of sociologist George Herbert Mead (1863–1931), who explored how the human personality gradually emerges as a result of social experience. Chapter 6 ("Social Interaction in Everyday Life") presents the work of another sociologist, Erving Goffman (1922–1982). Goffman's contribution is described as *dramaturgical analysis* because it emphasizes the parallels between human beings and actors on a stage as we deliberately foster certain impressions in the minds of others. Some contemporary sociologists, including George Homans and Peter Blau, have created *social-exchange analysis*, which reveals how social interaction is often guided by what each person stands to gain and lose from others. Chapter 15 ("Family") applies this approach to the process of courtship, noting that individuals typically seek mates who offer at least as much—in terms of physical attractiveness, intelligence, and social background—as they provide in return.

Critical evaluation.   Perhaps the greatest strength of the social-interaction paradigm is that it reminds us that we shape our social world just as the world, in turn, shapes us. No sociological analysis can afford to ignore the spontaneity of individuals. Put differently, the symbolic-interaction paradigm overcomes a limitation of all macro-level approaches: while broad patterns like "the family" and "social inequality" certainly exist, such abstract concepts can mask the fact that society is fundamentally *people* interacting with one another. This

Nellie McClung (née Mooney) is one of Canada's most famous suffragists. McClung was born and raised in Manitoba, where she became a teacher at sixteen. She married a druggist, R.W. McClung, and moved to Manitou where she became active in the Woman's Christian Temperance Union. In 1908 McClung published her first novel, Sowing Seeds in Danny. The book became a national bestseller and was followed by numerous other books and articles. The McClungs moved to Winnipeg in 1911, where the Winnipeg Women's Rights and Reform movement welcomed Nellie as an effective and humorous speaker. She fought for suffrage for women, prohibition, factory safety legislation, dower rights for women, and many other reforms. McClung led the campaign for votes for Canadian women, and, she herself became one of the first women elected to the legislature in Alberta. She was one of the chief activists in the "Persons Case," which involved a court battle to have Canadian women legally declared "persons." Because of her efforts, and those of others like her, women were given the vote in 1918, allowed to sit in the House of Commons in 1919 and to be appointed to the Senate in 1929 (Hallett, 1988).

Many women contributed to the emergence of sociology, although their achievements have long been unrecognized. Harriet Martineau (1802–1876), born to a rich English family, translated the writings of Auguste Comte from French in 1853. Soon afterward, she established her own reputation as a sociologist with studies of slavery, factory laws, and women's rights.

Agnes McPhail was the only woman elected to the House of Commons in 1921, the first election in which women had the vote. She served the country in the legislature until 1940. McPhail began her career as a country school teacher and was involved in the Ontario agricultural co-operative movement and the United Farmers of Ontario. In fact, she entered parliament to represent the farmers of her region, but soon developed broader interests. During her active career, she became known for her support of "feminist causes," founded the Elizabeth Fry Society of Canada, and helped establish the Archambault Commission in 1935 to investigate Canada's prisons. She was also largely responsible for Ontario's first pay equity legislation, in 1951 (Black, 1988).

micro-level approach focuses more on how we as individuals actually experience society.

For just this reason, however, the symbolic-interaction paradigm sometimes leads to the error of ignoring larger social structures. Highlighting what is unique in each social scene risks overlooking the widespread effects of our culture, as well as factors like class, sex, and race.

Emerging Paradigms

Feminism

Feminist sociology encompasses both the micro and the macro perspectives of analysis. Both levels focus on women's lives. The micro level examines the reproduction of gender through such things as talk, body language, and emotion management. The macro level examines the myriad of constraints and forms of resistance in women's lives in such institutional realms as politics, economics, schooling, religion, and the family. The macro level of analysis has documented the patriarchal nature of the structure of societies, which characterizes virtually all realms of life.

In the past several decades, feminists have revolutionized the discipline of sociology. Feminist sociology continues to challenge the male-dominated discipline with critiques of methodology, theory, and all the substantive areas of the field. Feminist sociology, along with feminist analysis in other fields in the academy, has established a new field of work called Women's Studies. There are now departments of women's studies in virtually every university in Canada. Parallel to such developments has been a growing critique of the position and experience of women at all levels, from undergraduate to full professor, in the universities.

Mary O'Brien's work is an important example of the kind of revisioning of sociology undertaken by feminist scholars. See the Critical Thinking box, "Patriarchy: A Feminist Perspective".

Ethnomethodology

Ethnomethodology is a micro-level analysis of the ways that people, as members of society, make sense of their social lives in order to carry out activities. Garfinkel,

the founder of this perspective, showed how background understanding or assumptions are fundamental to the practice of social life. Further research has shown this to be true in a variety of settings. A common focus of ethnomethodology is conversation analysis. An example of a conversation analysis may be the best way to illustrate ethnomethodology in this brief space. Imagine a conversation in which you say "Hello, how are you?" to an acquaintance. Imagine that the acquaintance responds by saying, "Why?" The ongoing assumed social interaction has been disrupted. You expected your acquaintance to say, "Fine, and you?" The unexpected response has thrown the interaction into confusion. This is a small example of the myriad of complex assumptions that underlie the simplest of human social interactions. It is these common assumptions that are the subject matter of ethnomethodology. Further information about ethnomethodology may be found in Chapter 6 ("Social Interaction in Everyday Life").

The important characteristics of the structural-functional paradigm, the social-conflict paradigm, and the symbolic-interaction paradigm are summarized in Table 1-1. As we have explained, certain kinds of questions suggest the use of a particular theoretical paradigm. In many cases, however, the greatest benefits come from linking the sociological perspective to all three, as we shall now illustrate with an analysis of sports in North America.

CRITICAL THINKING

Patriarchy: A Feminist Perspective

Mary O'Brien's book, *The Politics of Reproduction*, is a good example of how feminist sociologists working within the social-conflict tradition are challenging many of the assumption of traditional, male sociology. O'Brien focuses on the Marxist view of patriarchy, originally put forward by Friedrich Engels, a colleague of Karl Marx, in 1848. Engels argued that in a capitalist world, men needed to control women in order that their property would be inherited by their biological children. Monogamy, Engels asserted,

was the family form best suited to ensuring patrilineal (father to son) succession. (For a more complete description of Engel's arguments, see Chapter 13, "Sex and Gender".)

O'Brien reversed Engels' argument. She suggests that the material base from which patriarchy arises is not the need to control property; rather, men seek to control property *in order to constrain and limit women's sexuality and reproduction*. Since men have no necessary assurance that babies born of women are their own,

they are alienated from reproduction. To gain control over this alienation, they have had to gain ownership of and control over women. They express this ownership in a myriad of ways, all of which tend to limit women's sexuality, change the ideology or practice of monogamy, and entrench the fundamental economic dependence of women on men.

SOURCE: O'Brien (1981)

TABLE 1-1   THE MAJOR THEORETICAL PARADIGMS: A SUMMARY

Theoretical Paradigm	Orientation	Image of Society	Illustrative Questions
Structural-functional	Macro-level	A system of interrelated parts that is relatively stable based on wide-spread consensus as to what is morally desirable; each part has functional consequences for the operation of society as a whole	How is society integrated? What are the major parts of society? How are these parts interrelated? What are the consequences of each for the operation of society?
Social-conflict	Macro-level	A system characterized by social inequality; any part of society benefits some categories of people more than others; conflict-based social inequality promotes social change	How is society divided? What are major patterns of social inequality? How do some categories of people attempt to protect their privileges? How do other categories of people challenge the status quo?
Feminist	Micro/macro	A gender-based hierarchy where men dominate women in all realms of social life including knowledge, the polity, the economy, education, etc.	Why is there a gendered hierarchy? What have been the effects of male dominance on men and women? How can such a structure be overturned?
Symbolic-interaction	Micro-level	An ongoing process of social interaction in specific settings based on symbolic communications; individual perceptions of reality are variable and changing	How is society experienced? How do human beings interact to create, sustain, and change social patterns? How do individuals attempt to shape the reality perceived by others? How does individual behavior change from one situation to another?
Ethnomethodology	Micro-level	Tenuous construction of reality based on assumptions of meanings observable best through the sense-making activities of individuals in communication with other individuals	How do I know what to do or to say in any situation? How do I know what you will do or say?

Sports: Three Theoretical Paradigms in Action

To people in Canada, sports seem indispensable. Almost everyone has engaged in some type of sport, from gym classes throughout the school years to recreational sports by young adults to fitness programs for elderly people. The sale of sporting goods is a multimillion-dollar industry, and most men and women observe and discuss sporting events each year. Television brings sports to millions of living rooms, not only as part of newscasts, but as regular programming averaging more than three hours a day (Coakley, 1990).

What new insights can the sociological perspective provide about this familiar element of our way of life? Each of the three major theoretical paradigms in sociology contributes part of the answer.

The Functions of Sports

A structural-functional approach directs attention to ways in which sports help society to operate. The manifest functions of sports include providing both recreation and a relatively harmless way to "let off steam," and contributing to the physical fitness of the population. Sports have important latent functions as well, from fostering social relationships to generating tens of thousands of jobs. Perhaps the most important latent function of sports is encouraging specific attitudes and patterns of behavior that are central to our way of life.

For example, the personal effort and discipline essential to success in sports make people successful in other areas as well. Additional social skills, too, such as learning to be a team player and to play by the rules, are developed through participating or watching sporting events. And sports generate the sense of personal competition that North Americans value so much in celebrating a "winner" (Spates, 1976a; Coakley, 1990). When he said, "Winning is not everything, but making the effort to win is," Vince Lombardi was speaking not only as a football coach; he was also speaking as a typical American.

Sports also have dysfunctional consequences, of course. For example, the obsession with winning can lead to excessive risk-taking and deleterious health consequences. In the case of Ben Johnson, it also led to national and even international humiliation. Johnson was caught with steroids in his system at the Seoul Olympics in 1988 and stripped of the gold medal he had just won. This crisis led critics of federal sports policies to say that policies that linked funding to performance outcomes had generated an ethic of victory at any cost.

In sum, the structural-functional paradigm suggests that sports contribute in a variety of ways to the operation of North American society. Perhaps the most important of these is teaching and reinforcing notions of competition and personal success, which are central to our way of life.

Sports and Conflict

A social-conflict analysis of sports begins by pointing out that sports are closely related to patterns of social inequality. Some sports—tennis, swimming, golf, and skiing, to name a few—are expensive, so participation is largely limited to well-to-do people. By contrast, the sports with mass appeal—football, baseball, and basketball—are those accessible to people at all income levels. In short, the games people play are not simply a matter of choice; they reflect patterns of economic inequality.

In Canada, sports are also oriented toward males (Lenskyj, 1986). Sexual discrimination has traditionally limited the opportunities of females in most sports,

The painting Father Image II by Native artist Jim Logan reminds us of the place of honor that Hockey Night in Canada holds in Canadian culture.

even when they have the talent, interest, and economic means to participate. The first modern Olympic Games held in 1896, for example, excluded women from competition entirely (Mangan & Park, 1987). Until quite recently, Little League teams also barred girls in most parts of the country. This exclusion has been defended by ungrounded sexual stereotypes that claim that girls either lack the ability to engage in sports or risk losing their femininity if they do so.

The role of women in sport today is founded in the view of women held in the nineteenth century. Then, any athletic involvement of girls or women was questioned because it might, it was believed, hinder their roles as childbearers. An article published in 1935 outlined the dangers of basketball for girls as follows. "In some cases, basketball can make too heavy a demand on the organic vitality of a growing girl ... a great deal of the excess energy is needed for the physical changes that are naturally taking place" (Lenskyj, 1986:19).

Thus, our society has encouraged males to be athletes while females are expected to be attentive observers and cheerleaders. Even when they both engage in sports, female performers are less likely to have audiences. A study of *Sports Illustrated*, for example, found there was very little coverage (6.8 percent) of female athletics (Kane, 1989). And when women athletes *are* the subject of reports they tend to be described in stereotypically feminine ways (Hillard, 1984). To illustrate: one of the most widely televised of "female" athletic activities is aerobic exercise. Here, seductive camera angles and skimpy costumes reinforce the idea that women are sex objects. But the fitness movement and political efforts by women are reducing this inequity. The number of high-school women in sports programs has increased. In addition, more women than ever before now play sports professionally, and women's sports enjoy growing spectator interest. Still, women continue to take a back seat to men in professional sports—particularly in those that provide the most earnings and social prestige.

Although our society traditionally excluded people of color as well from professional sports, the opportunity to earn a high income in athletics has expanded greatly in recent decades. The Toronto Blue Jays team that won the World Series in 1992, for example, included many visible minorities.

The increasing proportion of people of color in professional sports is largely due to the fact that individual athletic performances can be measured precisely. For this reason, white prejudice cannot easily diminish the achievement of nonwhite athletes. It is no doubt also true that many people of color make a particular effort to excel in athletics, where they recognize that greater opportunity can be found (Steele, 1990). In recent years, in fact, black baseball players have earned higher salaries, on the average, than white players.

Nonetheless, racial discrimination continues to shape professional sports. For example, while people of color are now common as players, almost all managers, head coaches, and owners of sports teams are still white (Jones, 1987). In 1987, Al Campanis, a vice-president of the Los Angeles Dodgers baseball team, conceded on national television that African Americans are good athletes, but he wondered aloud if they lacked the "necessities" to become team managers and executives. The furor that followed this racist remark revealed the extent of racial prejudice in American athletics, forty years after Jackie Robinson's breakthrough into the major leagues.

Furthermore, teams tend to position people of color in secondary positions, while whites take the starring roles. For example, about 70 percent of African-American players in the major leagues play the outfield (Staples, 1987; Center for the Study of Sport in Society, 1991). Figure 1-4 on page 28 shows the proportion of white and black players at the various positions in professional football and basketball, and includes Hispanic players in the case of baseball. The pattern is clear: in all three sports, the central positions have the highest proportion of white players.

Taking a wider view, one might also wonder who benefits most from professional sports. Although millions of fans follow their teams, the vast earnings they generate are controlled by the small number of people (again, predominantly white men) for whom teams are income-generating property. Team owners, highly competitive among themselves, together form a huge business that controls a vast national audience (Leifer, 1990). In the last decade or so, professional athletes have gained a larger share of what their teams earn. By 1990, for example, the average annual salary of major-league baseball players had risen to almost $900,000, which is thirty times the average in 1970 and far higher than the salaries of baseball's legendary greats in the past. Even so, in all professional sports, the lion's share of both power and profits remains in the hands of the few owners.

In sum, the social-conflict paradigm views professional sports in terms of patterns of social inequality. As noted earlier, sports may reflect the importance of competition and achievement to all of society, but they are also bound up with extensive inequalities based on sex, race, and economic power.

Sports as Interaction

At the macro-level, a sporting event can be understood as a formal system; at the micro-level, however, it is a complex drama of face-to-face interaction. In part, participants' behavior reflects their assigned positions and, of course, the rules of the game. Players also act spontaneously, however, so that the precise outcome of a game can never be predicted. According to the symbolic-interaction paradigm, sports are less a system than an ongoing process.

The symbolic-interaction paradigm also suggests that each player will look at the game at least somewhat differently. Some players, for example, thrive in a setting of stiff competition, playing the game simply for the thrill of winning. For others, however, love of the game may be greater than the need for victory; these people may actually perform worse under pressure. Still others use sports as a means to build personal friendships; they may avoid competition for fear that it will alienate people from one another (Coakley, 1986).

Beyond different attitudes toward competition, team members will also shape their particular realities according to the various prejudices, jealousies, and ambitions they bring to the field of play. Then, too, the behavior of any single player is likely to change over time. A rookie in professional baseball often feels self-conscious during the first few games in the big leagues. Eventually, however, a comfortable sense of fitting in with the team usually emerges. Coming to feel at home on the field was slow and painful for Jackie Robinson, who was initially only too aware that many white players, and millions of white baseball fans, resented his presence (Tygiel, 1983). In time, however, his outstanding performance and his confident and refined manner off the field won him the respect of the entire nation.

In spite of varied motives and perceptions, each player is expected to display team spirit and other elements of good sportsmanship. The dramaturgical approach of Erving Goffman (1959) suggests that athletes typically symbolize the ideals of honesty, hard work, and, above all, the will to win. In reality, of course, many fall far short of these ideals. For instance, frequent news accounts since the mid-1980s have documented the involvement of both amateur and professional athletes with illegal drugs, which has prompted controversial calls for mandatory drug testing.

The three theoretical paradigms certainly offer different insights, but none is more correct than the others. Applied to various social issues, each paradigm generates its own interpretations so that, to fully appreciate the sociological perspective, you should become familiar with all three. Together, they spark fascinating debates and controversies, many of which are covered in the chapters that follow.

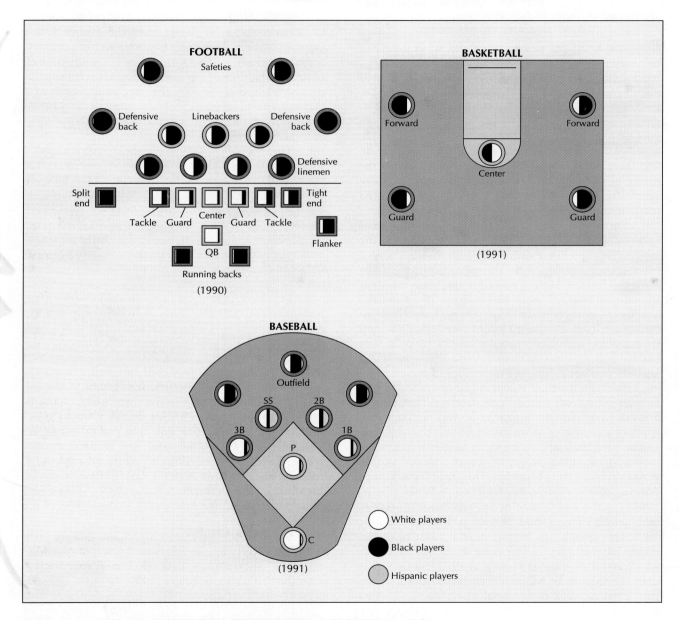

FIGURE 1-4   RACE AND PROFESSIONAL SPORTS: PATTERNS OF DISCRIMINATION
Professional athletics provide far greater opportunities for minorities than most other highly paid careers in North America. Even so, a pattern of "stacking" that places white athletes in central positions (outlined in blue) is evident in professional sports. These diagrams show the proportion of black and white players at each position in professional football and basketball, and the proportion of black, Hispanic, and white players for each position in professional baseball. Professional teams apparently consider whites more suitable for the central positions—generally deemed the "thinking" roles of the games.
(Center for the Study of Sport in Society, Northeastern University, 1991)

Summary

1.   Using the sociological perspective we recognize that individual lives are shaped by society. This point of view may be described as "seeing the general in the particular."

2.   Because people in Canada see events in terms of individual choice, the impact of society on our lives often goes unrecognized. Therefore, the sociological perspective may also be described as "seeing the strange in the familiar."

3.   By discovering that suicide rates are higher among some categories of people than others, Emile Durkheim was able to show how social forces affect even the most personal of our actions.

4.   The sociological perspective prompts us to recognize how our lives reflect both our position in society and our nation's standing in the larger world.

5.   The sociological perspective sometimes arises naturally, as when we enter an unfamiliar setting. Similarly, socially marginal people tend to perceive the effects of society more readily than others. During periods of social crisis, everyone is more likely to view the world sociologically.

6.   There are four general benefits to using the sociological perspective. First, it challenges our familiar understandings of the world, helping us to separate fact from fiction; second, it helps us to appreciate the opportunities and constraints that frame our lives; third, it encourages more active participation in society; fourth, it makes us aware of the diversity of social behavior in Canada and in the world as a whole.

7.   Auguste Comte gave sociology its name in 1838. Whereas previous social thought focused on what society ought to be, Comte's new discipline of sociology was based on the use of scientific methods to understand society as it is.

8.   Sociology emerged as a reaction to the rapid transformation of European society during the eighteenth and nineteenth centuries. The rise of an industrial economy, the explosive growth of cities, and the emergence of new political ideas were three dimensions of change that directed attention to the operation of society.

9.   Theory involves linking sociological insights in meaningful ways to explain social life. Theory building is guided by one or more theoretical paradigms.

10.   The structural-functional paradigm is a framework for exploring how social structures promote the stability and integration of society. This approach tends to minimize the importance of social inequality, conflict, and change.

11.   The social-conflict paradigm highlights social inequality, which often generates conflict resulting in change. At the same time, this approach tends to minimize the extent of social integration and social stability.

12.   In contrast to these two macro-level approaches, the symbolic-interaction paradigm is a micro-level framework for studying face-to-face interaction in specific settings. At this situational level of analysis, society is viewed as people acting in variable and somewhat unpredictable ways.

13.   Each of the three major theoretical paradigms provides important insights about the character of sports. The structural-functional paradigm emphasizes that sports reinforces the individualism and competition central to our way of life. The social-conflict paradigm links sports to patterns of social inequality. The symbolic-interaction paradigm portrays sports as the interplay of individuals who generate meaning as they engage one another on the field of play.

14.   Because each paradigm highlights different dimensions of any social issue, the richest sociological understanding is derived from applying all three.

Key Concepts

latent functions   the unrecognized and unintended consequences of any social pattern

macro-level orientation   a focus on broad social structures that characterize society as a system

manifest functions the recognized and intended consequences of any social pattern

micro-level orientation a focus on situational patterns of social interaction

positivism a means to understand the world based on science

social-conflict paradigm a framework for building theory based on the assumption that society is a complex system characterized by inequality and conflict that generate social change

social dysfunction the undesirable consequence of any social pattern for the operation of society

social function the consequence of any social pattern for the operation of society

social marginality the state of being excluded from social activity as an "outsider"

social structure a relatively stable pattern of social behavior

sociology the scientific study of human society

structural-functional paradigm a framework for building theory based on the assumption that society is a complex system whose parts work together to promote stability

symbolic-interaction paradigm a theoretical framework based on the assumption that society is continuously recreated as human beings construct reality through interaction

theoretical paradigm a set of fundamental assumptions that guides thinking and research

theory the process of linking facts together in order to explain something

Suggested Readings

These two paperbacks are readable classics that describe the sociological perspective and the benefits of learning to think sociologically.

C. Wright Mills. *The Sociological Imagination.* New York: Oxford University Press, 1959.

Peter Berger. *An Invitation to Sociology.* Garden City, NY: Anchor Books, 1963.

This paperback provides sixty-six supplementary readings that follow the chapter flow of the book you're now reading. For each topic, classic essays by sociology's "greats" are accompanied by articles highlighting contemporary and cross-cultural issues.

John J. Macionis and Nijole V. Benokraitis, eds. *Seeing Ourselves: Classic, Contemporary, and Cross-Cultural Readings in Sociology.* 2nd ed. Englewood Cliffs, NJ: Prentice Hall, 1992.

This collection of essays examines the potential contribution of sociology to various areas of social life and points to factors that have limited the discipline's significance in the past.

Edgar F. Borgatta and Karen S. Cook. *The Future of Sociology.* Newbury Park, CA: Sage Publications, 1988.

This recent sociological analysis of suicide in modern Japan supports Durkheim's contention that social forces are at work in even the most personal of actions.

Mamoru Iga. *The Thorn in the Chrysanthemum: Suicide and Economic Success in Modern Japan.* Berkeley: University of California Press, 1986.

This book contains autobiographical sketches by twenty contemporary sociologists that together suggest the achievements and shortcomings of the discipline.

Bennett M. Berger. *Authors of Their Own Lives: Intellectual Autobiographies by Twenty American Sociologists.* Berkeley: University of California Press, 1990.

The following books describe the history of sociology. The first, a general intellectual history of the discipline, delves into sociology's European roots. The second details the development of U.S. sociology at the University of Chicago in the years after World War I. The third introduces four women social scientists and explores historical barriers to the acceptance of women in sociology. The fourth, fifth, and sixth examine the history of sociology in Canada.

Randall Collins and Michael Makowsky. *The Discovery of Society.* New York: Random House, 1984.

Martin Bulmer. *The Chicago School of Sociology: Institutionalization, Diversity, and the Rise of Sociological Research.* Chicago: University of Chicago Press, 1984.

Ellen Fitzpatrick. *Endless Crusade: Women Social Scientists and Progressive Reform.* New York: Oxford University Press, 1990.

Marlene Shore. *The Science of Social Redemption: McGill, the Chicago School, and the Origins of Social Research in Canada.* Toronto: University of Toronto Press, 1987.

Robert J. Brym and Bonnie J. Fox. *From Culture to Power: The Sociology of English Canada.* Don Mills, ON: Oxford University Press, 1989.

Harry H. Hiller. *Society and Change: S.D. Clarke and the Development of Canadian Sociology.* Toronto: University of Toronto Press, 1987.

This useful paperback book for the beginning student includes a discussion of theoretical paradigms in sociology as well as information about how to gather data for writing papers.

Pauline Bart and Linda Frankel. *The Student Sociologist's Handbook*. 4th ed. New York: Random House, 1986.

A comprehensive sociological analysis of sports is found in the following:

Ann Hall, et al. *Sport in Canadian Society*. Toronto: McClelland & Stewart Inc., 1991.

Helen Lenskyj. *Out of Bounds: Women, Sport, and Sexuality*. Toronto: Women's Press, 1986.

Barry D. McPherson, et. al. *The Social Significance of Sport: An Introduction to the Sociology of Sport*. Illinois: Human Kinetics Books, 1989.

These books examine aspects of Canadian society from a structural-functional perspective.

Everett Hughes. *French Canada in Transition*. Chicago: University of Chicago Press, 1943.

S.D. Clark. *The Suburban Society*. Toronto: University of Toronto Press, 1966.

This classic book looks at Canada from a social-conflict, or political economy perspective.

John Porter. *The Vertical Mosaic: An Analysis of Class and Power in Canada*. Toronto: University of Toronto Press, 1968.

The following books are written by three Canadian feminist sociologists.

Mary O'Brien. *The Politics of Reproduction*. London: Routledge, Kegan, Paul, 1981.

Meg Luxton. *More than a Labour of Love*. Toronto: Women's Press, 1981.

Dorothy Smith. *The Everyday World as Problematic*. Toronto: University of Toronto Press, 1987.

Here are some examples of sociology done from a symbolic-interaction perspective.

Rex Lucas. *Minetown, Milltown, Railtown: Life in Canadian Communities of Single Industry*. Toronto: University of Toronto Press, 1971.

W. Shaffir. *Life in a Religious Community: The Lubavitcher Chassidim in Montreal*. Toronto: Holt, Rhinehart and Winston, 1974.

The following is a good introduction to ethnomethodology.

Roy Turner, ed. *Ethnomethodology: Selected Readings*. Harmondsworth: Penguin, 1974.

The following is an analysis of multiple murderers.

Elliott Leyton. *Hunting Humans: The Rise of the Modern Multiple Murderer*. Toronto: McClelland & Stewart, 1986.

SOCIOLOGICAL INVESTIGATION

Linda Davis enrolled in university in 1979, full of energy and drive. She was determined to earn good grades, graduate, and begin, as she put it, "a professional career that I will use the rest of my life." She made little effort to contain her excitement when she spoke of her plans to become a physical therapist.

Davis studied hard, but soon realized that her grades were falling short of the high marks she had taken for granted in high school. As the first year came to a close, her aspirations had diminished, and she doubted her ability to gain admission to the specialized therapy program she had set her sights on for so long.

By the middle of her second year, Davis no longer expressed interest in becoming a physical therapist; instead, she successfully applied to a less rigorous nursing program. She was still pleased with her accomplishments, but more than a little relieved that the pressure to achieve was now less intense than it had been. Davis began spending more and more time with her new boyfriend, Stan, and she often spoke of their future together. Those around her could see her career ambitions slowly fading.

Dorothy Holland and Margaret Eisenhart, teachers and researchers at two different universities, had followed the university career of Linda Davis, and they suspected that her experiences were not unique. Hol-

land and Eisenhart had long wondered why so few women pursue study and occupations in the sciences. They set out to answer this question by monitoring the changes in two dozen women by interviewing them at several points during their early university years. Using the skills of sociological investigation, the two researchers sketched the course of these women's lives in university during the 1980s, and found that their experiences were remarkably similar to those of Linda Davis. Holland and Eisenhart (1991) soon concluded that they had documented a more general pattern: the achievements and career choices of women in college—both in and out of the sciences—often fall short of their early expectations. Intrigued by this finding, Holland and Eisenhart extended their research, continuing to interview subjects in their final years of university and for five years following graduation. The general pattern of declining performance continued. Linda Davis's subsequent life exemplifies this trend.

By the time of graduation, Davis's view of herself and her future had clearly changed. The urge for career success had now taken a back seat to settling down with a husband and children. Asked how she might pursue a nursing career and care for a family, Davis responded simply, "If I had to make a decision between family and career, then there's no question—my family."

The years that followed confirmed these priorities. After graduation, Davis married Stan and found a full-time job at a local hospital. But the marriage lasted only a few years. Speaking to Holland and Eisenhart after her divorce, however, Davis explained that she was engaged to be married again. And what of her plans to work? Confident that her second marriage would be more successful, Davis looked forward to working only half time; before long she hoped to stop working entirely long enough to have at least two children.

From the life histories of Linda Davis and others, Holland and Eisenhart formulated the thesis that the university years—crucial in launching the careers of men—often are a time of compromise for women. Their research is a fascinating look at the campus scene, including insights about how women interact with faculty, the value they place on romantic attachments with men, and how university culture affects their relationships with other women.

Information of this kind stands as evidence of the power of the sociological perspective to uncover patterns (and also to identify problems) that other points of view overlook. But most important for our purposes, this research demonstrates the *doing* of sociology, the process of *sociological investigation*. We all are struck by curious social patterns, questions that all-too-often slip away unanswered. The discipline of sociology can impart a host of skills and procedures that makes us more able to find answers or, even if we never choose to conduct research ourselves, better equipped to evaluate the answers provided by others.

Many people think that scientists work only in laboratories, carefully taking measurements using complex equipment. But as Holland's and Eisenhart's study illustrates, sociologists also conduct scientific research on the campus, in neighborhoods, at workplaces, and even in prisons—in short, wherever people are living their lives.

This chapter introduces the most common methods that sociologists use to conduct research. Along the way, we shall encounter problems that test the talents of even the most seasoned women and men in this field of study. Some of these problems involve gathering information about complex and sometimes personal topics; others introduce debates about the role of personal politics and values in sociological research. The question of how facts and politics relate to one another is raised by the research by Holland and Eisenhart: should their goal be simply to *learn* about the lives of women on university campuses or, alternatively, to offer a prescription for *change* according to

the researchers' own values? We shall begin the various tasks of this chapter with the basics of positivist social research.

The Basics of Positivist Sociological Investigation

Sociological investigation begins with two simple requirements. The first was suggested in Chapter 1: *Look at the world using the sociological perspective.* Suddenly, from this point of view, our surroundings appear full of curious patterns of behavior that call out for further study.

Holland and Eisenhart did exactly this when they began to explore why so few women opted for careers in the sciences. But a sociological imagination prompted them to delve further into how women are influenced in their life choices by the surrounding campus culture.

This brings us to the second requirement for a sociological investigator: *Be curious and ask questions.* What patterns are evident among people living on a campus or in any other setting? Why do they live as they do? How do they understand their own lives? What factors unite and divide the community?

These two requirements—seeing the world sociologically and asking questions—are fundamental to sociological investigation. Yet they are only the beginning. They can draw us into the social world, stimulating our curiosity. But then there is the more difficult matter of finding answers to our questions. To understand the kind of answers sociology offers, consider various ways to recognize any piece of information as "true."

Ways of Knowing: Positivist Science and "Truth"

Saying we "know" something can mean any number of things. Many people, for instance, claim to believe in the existence of God. Few would assert that they had had direct contact with God, but they are believers all the same. This kind of knowing is often called "faith." A second kind of truth lies in the pronouncement of some recognized expert. When we want to know how to spell a word correctly, for example, we turn to a dictionary, acknowledging the book's editors as language experts. In still other cases, ordinary people define truth through

There are many kinds of truth. The Emergence of Clowns *by U.S. artist Roxanne Swentzell presents the story of creation according to the Santa Clara Pueblo. Life began, they believe, when four clowns emerged onto the earth's surface, each facing in a different direction. All of the world's people have creation beliefs of this kind (including the biblical accounts in Genesis). As members of a scientific society, we may too easily dismiss such stories as "myth." Whether or not they are entirely factual, they do convey basic truths about the way in which each society searches for human origins and struggles to find meaning in the universe. It is science, not "myth," that is powerless to address such questions.*

Heard Museum, Phoenix, AZ

simple agreement. This way of knowing is called "consensus." We simply "know" that sexual intercourse among young children is wrong, for instance, because virtually everyone says so. Of course, people in other times and places may recognize some different "truth." The Trobriand Islanders of New Guinea, for instance, shrug off sexual intercourse among children too young to reproduce as harmless.

As a final illustration of the variability of truth, imagine being a CUSO volunteer who has just arrived in a small, traditional society. With the goal of helping the local people to grow more food, you soon take to the fields, where you observe farmers carefully placing a dead fish directly on top of the ground where they have planted a seed. Curious, you ask about this practice, and they reply that the fish is a gift to the god of the harvest. A local elder adds sternly that the harvest was poor one year when no fish were offered as gifts.

From the local people's point of view, using fish as gifts to the harvest god makes sense. They believe in it, their experts endorse it, and everyone seems to agree that the system works. But, with scientific training in agriculture, you have to shake your head and wonder. The scientific "truth" in this situation is something entirely different: the decomposing fish fertilize the ground, producing a better crop.

As yet another way of knowing, **science** is defined as *a logical system that bases knowledge on direct, systematic observation.* Sometimes at odds with faith, the wisdom of "experts," and general agreement, scientific knowledge is based on **empirical evidence,** meaning *information we are able to verify with our senses.*

Our CUSO example does not mean, of course, that people in traditional societies ignore what their senses tell them, nor that members of technologically advanced societies reject all ways of knowing except science. A medical researcher seeking an effective treatment for cancer, for example, may still practice her religion as a matter of faith; she may turn to experts when making financial decisions; and she may derive political opinions from people around her. Yet none of these approaches affects her work as a scientist.

Common Sense Versus Positivist Scientific Evidence

Here are six statements that many Canadians consider "true" based on their common sense, although each is at least partly contradicted by scientific evidence.

1. **Poor people are far more likely to break the law than rich people.** Chapter 8 ("Deviance") explains that official arrest statistics would seem to bear this out. But research also reveals that, while people of all social backgrounds break the law, the criminal

justice system is more likely to prosecute wrong-doing by poor people while treating offenses by the well-to-do more leniently.

2. **Canada is a middle-class society in which most people are more or less equal.** However, in 1990, approximately 3,821,000 Canadians had incomes below the poverty line, including some 1,013,000 children. Moreover, there were 400 food banks across the nation in 1990 (Colombo, 1993:88). If people are equal, then, some are much "more equal" than others.

3. **Most poor people ignore opportunities to work.** Chapter 10 ("Social Class in Canada") suggests that this is true of some but not most poor people. The greatest proportion of poor people are from three groups. Sixty-six percent of all unattached women over sixty-five are poor; 60 percent of single-parent mothers under sixty-five with children under eighteen are poor; and 57 percent of unattached men over sixty-five are poor (Colombo, 1992). Clearly, these categories of people have serious constraints upon their ability to be active in the labor force.

4. **Differences in the social behavior of males and females are "human nature."** Much of what we call "human nature" is created by the society in which we are raised, as Chapter 3 ("Culture") details. Further, as Chapter 13 ("Sex and Gender") argues, some societies define "masculine" and "feminine" very differently than we do.

5. **People change as they grow old, losing many former interests while becoming focused on their health.** Chapter 14 ("Aging and the Elderly") reports that researchers have learned that aging actually changes our personality very little. Problems of health do increase in old age but, on balance, elderly people retain their distinctive personalities.

6. **Most people marry because they are in love.** To members of our society, few statements are so self-evident. But as surprising as it may seem, cross-cultural research shows that, in most societies, marriage has little to do with love. Chapter 15 ("Family") explains why this is the case.

These examples confirm the old saying that "It's not the things we don't know that get us into trouble as much as the things we *do* know that just aren't so." We have all been brought up believing conventional truths,

being bombarded by expert advice, and being pressured to accept the opinions of friends. As adults, we must learn to evaluate critically what we see, read, and hear to separate what is true from what is not. As a scientific discipline, sociology can help us to do that. Like any way of knowing, science has limitations, as we shall see. But scientific sociology is a useful way to assess accurately many kinds of information.

The Elements of Positivist Social Science

Positivist social science *seeks to model itself on the physical sciences through criteria such as objectivity, replicability, causality, experimentation, quantification, and generalization.* Positivist sociologists apply science to the study of society in much the same way that natural scientists investigate the physical world.

The work of social scientists lies in identifying ways in which various dimensions of social life are interrelated. Thus a sociologist might ask questions such as:

> *What segments of the population are least likely to vote in national elections? Why?*
>
> *Are abused children at risk of becoming child abusers themselves?*
>
> *Are city dwellers less neighborly than people living in rural areas?*

To answer these questions, positivist sociologists use the elements of science to gather empirical evidence. The following sections of this chapter introduce many important components of scientific investigation.

Concepts, Variables, and Measurement

A crucial element of science is the **concept**, *a mental construct that represents some part of the world, inevitably in a somewhat simplified form.* "Society" is itself a concept, as are the structural parts of societies, including "religion" and "the economy." Sociologists also use concepts to describe individuals, as when we speak of their "sex," "race," or "social class."

A **variable** is *a concept whose value changes from case to case.* The familiar variable "price," for example, refers to the value of items in a supermarket. Similarly, people use the sociological concept "social class"

SOCIOLOGY OF EVERYDAY LIFE

Three Useful (and Simple) Statistical Measures

Everyone talks about "averages": the average age of the Canadian population, the average price of a litre of gasoline, or the average winnings from provincial lotteries. In sociological research, three different statistical measures are used to describe what is average or typical.

Assume that we wish to describe the salaries paid to seven members of the local city council:

$14,250	$64,000	$21,750
$23,000	$23,000	$14,000
$18,500		

The simplest statistical measure is the **mode**, defined as *the value that occurs most often in a series of numbers*. In this example, the mode is $23,000, since that value occurs twice, while each of the others occurs only once. If all the values were to occur only once, there would be no mode; if two values occurred twice, there would be two modes. Although easy to identify, the mode is rarely used in sociological research because it provides information about only some, rather than all, of the values.

A more common statistical measure, the **mean**, refers to *the arithmetic average of a series of numbers*, and is calculated by adding all the values together and dividing by the number of cases. The sum of the seven incomes is $178,500; dividing by 7 yields a mean income of $25,500. Notice that the mean income is actually higher than the income of six of the seven council members. Because the mean shows the effects of any especially high or low value (in this case, the $64,000 income), it has the drawback of giving a distorted picture of any distribution with extreme scores.

The **median** is *the value that occurs midway in a series of numbers arranged in order of magnitude or, simply, the middle case*. Here the median income for the seven people is $21,750, since three incomes are higher and three are lower. (With an even number of cases, the median is halfway between the two middle cases.) In case of one extreme score (or more), the median gives a better picture of what is "average" than the mean does.

In conducting research, how we define a variable affects its value; therefore, researchers must specify definitions carefully. **Operationalizing a variable** means *specifying exactly what is to be measured in assigning a value to a variable*. If we were measuring the social class of particular individuals, for example, we would have to decide exactly what elements to measure. After choosing to examine several measures (such as income, occupational prestige, and education), we would then devise a way to combine them into a composite measure of "social class." When reporting the results of positivist research, sociologists should explain how all variables are operationalized, so that readers understand the conclusions.

---

to describe (and often to evaluate) people as "upper class," "middle class," "working class," or "lower class." The use of variables depends on **measurement**, *determining the value of a variable in a specific case*. Some variables are easy to measure; we can determine our weight simply by stepping on a scale. Measuring sociological variables, however, is often more difficult than taking physical measurements.

For example, how would you measure a person's "social class"? You might do this crudely by looking at how the person dresses, listening to patterns of speech, or by noting a home address. More precisely, you might investigate the individual's income, occupation, and education. But in sociological investigation, researchers must recognize that a variable can be measured in more than one way. A person with very high income may seem to be "upper class." But what if the income comes from selling automobiles, an occupation most people think of as "middle class"? And if the individual has only an eighth-grade education, you might think of the person as "lower class." To resolve this dilemma, sociologists may sensibly (if somewhat arbitrarily) combine these three measures—income, occupation, and education—into a single composite assessment of social class described in Chapter 9 ("Social Stratification") and Chapter 10 ("Social Class in Canada").

Another problem arises when sociologists seek to describe a number of people with respect to a variable like income. Reporting a stream of numbers does not easily convey information about the people as a whole, so sociologists use various *statistical measures* to describe people collectively. The box explains the calculation and the meaning of some of the simplest summary statistics—averages.

Reliability and Validity of Measurement

Useful measurement involves two further considerations. **Reliability** is *the quality of a measurement that is* *both internally consistent and consistent over time.* A measure is reliable if repeated measurements produce the same result. An unreliable technique for measuring social class is of little use to sociologists just as a scale giving inconsistent readings of weight would be useless to a physicist, or an elastic ruler would be useless to a draftsperson.

Even consistency is no guarantee of validity, however. **Validity** means *the quality of measuring precisely what one intends to measure.* Say you want to investigate how religious people are, and you decide to do so by asking how often they attend religious services. Notice that, in trying to gauge *religiosity,* what you are actually measuring is *attendance at services,* which may or may not amount to the same thing. Generally, religious people do attend services more frequently, but people may participate in religious rituals for social reasons, out of habit, or because of a sense of duty to someone else. Moreover, many devout believers avoid organized religion altogether. Thus, even when it yields consistent results (reliability), any measurement can still miss the real, intended target (and lack validity). In sum, sociological research is no better than the quality of measurement that it employs.

Relationships Among Variables

The real payoff in positivist sociological investigation comes from determining the relationships among variables. Ideally, scientists relate variables in terms of **cause and effect,** *a relationship in which change in one variable is caused by change in another.* A familiar cause-and-effect relationship occurs when a girl teases her brother until he becomes angry. *The variable that causes the change* (in this case, the teasing) is called the **independent variable.** *The variable that changes* (the behavior of the brother) is called the **dependent variable.** The value of one variable, in other words, is dependent on the value of another. Linking variables in terms of cause and effect allows researchers to *predict,* that is, to use what they do know to speculate about what they don't know.

Because science puts a premium on prediction, people may incorrectly infer cause and effect just because two variables seem to be related. But often, variables change together even though there is no causal link between them. For example, people probably steal more cars in Canada when the temperature goes up, but this does not mean that heat turns people into car thieves. More likely, warm weather encourages people to spend time outdoors and also prompts drivers to leave car windows open. Thus, cause and effect may be hidden within a complex web of factors, not always readily apparent.

To illustrate further, we might puzzle over the fact that juvenile delinquency is more common among young people who live in crowded housing. We could operationalize the variable "juvenile delinquency" in terms of the number of arrests of a person under the age of eighteen, and operationalize the variable "crowded housing" to mean the amount of square feet of living space per person. Because delinquency rates are high in areas that are densely populated, we would be tempted to conclude that crowding in the home (the independent variable) causes delinquency (the dependent variable). But does the fact that the two vary together indicate a causal connection?

Not necessarily. *When two (or more) variables are related in some way,* they demonstrate **correlation.** We know there is some relationship between these two variables because they change together, as shown in Part (a) of Figure 2-1 on page 39. This *may* mean that crowding causes delinquency, but there are other possibilities as well. Think for a minute about who lives in

Men who drink coffee are more likely than tea drinkers to die from a heart attack. Does this mean that coffee causes heart disease? No—the link between those two variables is spurious. Both coffee drinking and heart disease are caused by a third variable, high levels of stress.

crowded housing and whose mischief is likely to attract the attention of police. The answer: people with less power and choice—the poor. Crowded housing and juvenile delinquency may be found together because *both* are caused by a third factor—poverty—as shown in Part (b) of Figure 2-1. In other words, the apparent relationship between crowding and delinquency is "explained away" by a third variable—low income—that causes them both to change. The term **spurious correlation** means *an apparent, although false, association between two (or more) variables caused by some other variable.*

Unmasking a correlation as spurious is often tricky, but it can be done using scientific **control**, meaning *the ability to neutralize the effect of one variable in order to assess the relationships among other variables.* In the example above, we can determine whether the relationship between housing density and delinquency persists if income is held the same. To do this, we measure the two variables only among persons of the same income. If the relationship between density and delinquency still exists (that is, if young people living in more crowded housing have higher rates of delinquency), we gain confidence that crowding does in fact cause delinquency. But if the relationship disappears, as shown in Part (c) of the figure, we know we have been dealing with a spurious correlation. Research has, in fact, shown that the apparent correlation between crowding and delinquency virtually disappears if the effects of income are controlled (Fischer, 1984). So we have now sorted out the relationship among the three variables, as illustrated in Part (d) of the figure. Housing density and juvenile delinquency have a spurious correlation, because our evidence suggests that both variables rise or fall according to people's income.

To sum up, correlation means only that two (or more) variables change together. Cause and effect implies not only correlation but also that change in one variable actually causes change in another. A researcher can conclude that two variables are linked by cause and effect only after demonstrating (1) the two variables are correlated; (2) the independent (or causal) variable precedes the dependent variable in time; and (3) there is no evidence that a third variable is responsible for a spurious correlation between the two.

Identifying cause-and-effect relationships enables researchers to make predictions. The natural sciences can predict with much greater accuracy than the social sciences, however, since laboratory conditions used to study the physical world allow scientists to control a number of variables. The sociologist faces a

considerably more difficult task. In a world of countless social forces, to which each of us reacts at least somewhat differently, relationships of simple cause

FIGURE 2-1 CORRELATION AND CAUSE: AN EXAMPLE

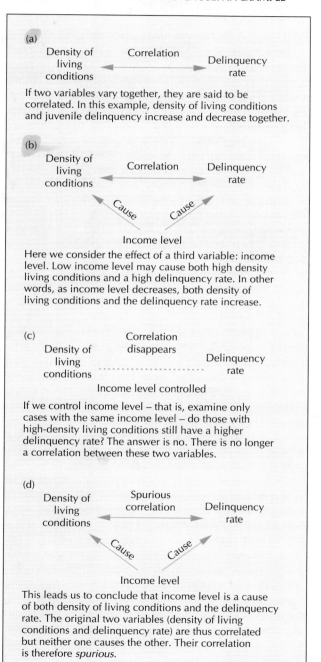

(a)

Density of living conditions ←— Correlation —→ Delinquency rate

If two variables vary together, they are said to be correlated. In this example, density of living conditions and juvenile delinquency increase and decrease together.

(b)

Density of living conditions ←— Correlation —→ Delinquency rate

Cause   Cause

Income level

Here we consider the effect of a third variable: income level. Low income level may cause both high density living conditions and a high delinquency rate. In other words, as income level decreases, both density of living conditions and the delinquency rate increase.

(c)

Density of living conditions — Correlation disappears — Delinquency rate

Income level controlled

If we control income level – that is, examine only cases with the same income level – do those with high-density living conditions still have a higher delinquency rate? The answer is no. There is no longer a correlation between these two variables.

(d)

Density of living conditions ←— Spurious correlation —→ Delinquency rate

Cause   Cause

Income level

This leads us to conclude that income level is a cause of both density of living conditions and the delinquency rate. The original two variables (density of living conditions and delinquency rate) are thus correlated but neither one causes the other. Their correlation is therefore *spurious*.

and effect are rare. Often sociologists must be satisfied with demonstrating only correlation. When relationships of cause and effect can be shown, they are usually complex, involving a large number of variables.

The Ideal of Objectivity

Assume that ten people who work for a magazine in Halifax, Nova Scotia, are putting together a story about that area's best restaurants. With their employer paying all the expenses, they set out for a week of fine dining. Later, when they get together to compare notes, will one restaurant be everyone's clear favorite? Perhaps, but that hardly seems likely.

In scientific terms, each of the ten would probably operationalize the concept "best restaurant" differently. For one, it might be a place that serves delicious seafood at reasonable prices; for another, the choice might turn on a rooftop view of the coastline; for yet another, stunning decor and attentive service might be the deciding factor. Like so many other things in our lives, the best restaurant may well be mostly a matter of individual taste.

Personal values are fine when it comes to restaurants, but they pose a challenge to scientific research. On the one hand, sociologists and other scientists have personal opinions about whatever they study; on the other, science strives for **objectivity**, *a state of personal neutrality in conducting research.* Scientific objectivity is an ideal rather than a reality, of course, since complete impartiality is virtually impossible for any researcher to achieve. But following scientific methods promotes objectivity so that even unconscious biases will not seriously distort a researcher's work. As an additional safeguard, researchers who identify their personal leanings along with their formal findings help readers evaluate conclusions in the appropriate context.

The influential German sociologist Max Weber wrestled with the problem of personal values distorting scientific study. Weber knew the personal values of a sociologist would play a part in the selection of topics to be studied. Why, after all, would one person study world hunger, another investigate the career aspirations of university women, and still another examine religious cults? While conceding that research would be *value-relevant*, Weber admonished researchers to be *value-free* in their pursuit of objective evidence. Research, he claimed, must be carried out dispassionately in order to study the world *as it is* rather than as we think *it should be.* This detachment, for Weber, set science apart from the world of politics. While politicians are committed to some particular outcome, scientists must cultivate an open-minded readiness to accept the results of their investigations, whatever they may be.

Most sociologists accept Weber's argument, even if few are confident that we can ever be entirely aware of our own biases. Social identity makes everyone—researchers included—think and see the world in particular ways. Moreover, sociologists are not "average" people: most are white men who are highly educated and live in cities. In addition, although the opinions of sociologists cover a broad political spectrum, they are more liberal than the population as a whole, and even more liberal than members of many other academic disciplines (Wilson, 1979). Turning the sociological perspective on the discipline itself, you should be aware that social background can and does affect sociological research, just as your own background and personal history will affect how you interpret this work.

One way to limit distortion caused by personal values is through **replication**, *repetition of research by others in order to assess its accuracy.* If other researchers repeat a study using the same procedures and obtain the same results, they can conclude that the original research (as well as their own) was conducted objectively. The need for replication in scientific investigation is probably the reason that the search for knowledge is called *re*search in the first place. Although only a small proportion of social science research is subjected to replication (far less than in the natural sciences), this process sometimes sparks conflict. The box on pages 42–43 describes a recent controversy arising from replication of well-known research.

Some Limitations of Positivist Scientific Sociology

Science first revealed the operation of the natural world. People also utilize science to study the social world, but doing so requires recognizing several important limitations.

1. **Because human society is so complex, and human behavior, attitudes, feelings, and bodies etc. are so varied, sociologists cannot predict individual behavior with precision.** Astronomers can calculate the movement of planets with remarkable precision, and they announce years in advance when a comet will next be visible from the earth. Humans, however, are more than physical beings; creative

minds ensure that no two people react in exactly the same way to any event. Therefore, sociologists speak of "probabilities" that categories of people will act in some way, while rarely expressing certainty, especially about the behavior of a specific individual.

2. **Because humans respond to their surroundings, the mere presence of a researcher may affect the behavior being studied.** An astronomer gazing at the moon has no effect whatever on the celestial body, but people often react to being observed. Some may become anxious or defensive; others may try to "help" the researcher by providing the answers or actions they think are expected of them.

3. **Social patterns change constantly; what is true in one time or place may not hold in another.** Atoms and molecules do not consciously shape their environment, but human beings do, in remarkably variable ways. The study of society, therefore, must take account of diversity and the human capacity for change.

4. **Because sociologists are part of the social world they study, objectivity in social research is especially difficult.** Chemists are not often personally affected by what goes on in test tubes. But sociologists live in the society they study. Therefore, sociologists often have difficulty in controlling—or even recognizing—personal values that may distort their work.

5. **Isolating concepts and variables from their social context and process may strip them of their meaning.** Durkheim considered that the successful result of the intention to end one's life constituted suicide. Jack Douglas (1967) studied suicide notes and discovered that the meaning of suicide varies considerably from person to person. Some people, for example, committed suicide not out of the intention to end their life but for other reasons, such as to seek revenge against someone.

6. **The search for causality may be premature.** This is not only because of the complexity of the social world, but also because of the frequent gap between what people understand to be the causes of their behavior and what sociologists may think to be the cause. Linda Davis in the introductory essay to this chapter felt that she changed her emphasis from career to family because she learned to value family more. Whereas the researchers saw her change as a compromise resulting from the culture of university life. Which notion of cause is correct?

A basic lesson of social research is that being observed affects how people behave. Researchers can never be certain precisely how this will occur, however: some people become shy as the subject of attention, while others become highly animated. In neither case does the researcher witness natural behavior.

The Importance of Subjective Interpretation

The logic of science cannot eliminate subjectivity from research. Nor would that be desirable, since creative thinking is vital to sociological investigation in three key ways.

First, science is basically a series of steps that guide research, rather like a recipe used in cooking. Just as more than a recipe is required to make a great chef, so scientific procedure will never, by itself, produce a great sociologist. Also needed is an inspired human imagination. Robert Nisbet (1970) points out that insight comes not from science itself but from the lively thinking of creative human beings. The genius of physicist Albert Einstein, anthropologist Margaret Mead, or sociologist Max Weber resulted not only from their use of the scientific method but also from their curiosity and imagination.

Second, science cannot embrace the vast and complex range of human motivations and feelings, including greed, love, pride, and despair. Science helps us gather facts about how people act, but it can never fully explain how people make sense of what they do (Berger & Kellner, 1981).

Third, data cannot speak for themselves. Sociologists and other scientists must always face the ultimate task of *interpretation*: creating meaning from a collection of observations. For this reason, sociology (like other disciplines) is an art as well as a science.

Politics and Research

As Max Weber observed long ago, a narrow line separates politics from science. Most sociologists endorse Weber's goal of value-free research. But a growing number of researchers are challenging the notion that politics and science can—or should—be distinct.

Alvin Gouldner (1970a, 1970b) was among the first to claim that "value-free" research paints a "storybook picture" of sociology. All aspects of social life, he

CRITICAL THINKING

The Samoa Controversy: The Interplay of Science and Politics

Margaret Mead was a pioneer of social research whose work in other societies helped us to think more critically about our own. Her career also alerts us to the fact that research—especially about controversial issues—is not easy to separate from our personal values.

Margaret Mead (1901–1978) remains the most prominent anthropologist* in American history. Several years after her death, however, replication of one of her most well-known studies raised questions about her objectivity and, more generally, about the interplay of science and politics.

Early in her career Mead investigated how children grew up in Samoa, an island in the South Pacific. She concluded that, far from a simple biological process, the experience of growing up varies significantly from one society to another. Her results immediately became part of a raging debate as to whether biology or environment ("nature" or "nurture") has a

---

* Closely related to sociology, anthropology studies human culture, often with a focus on preindustrial rather than industrial societies.

greater influence on human behavior.

The dominant position early in this century was that biology was more influential, not just in shaping adolescence but in guiding all human behavior and making some people different from others. When Mead's work was published, the United States was struggling with cultural diversity resulting from decades of immigration. Some individuals, opposed to admitting "foreigners" on the ground that they were biologically inferior, had successfully pressured Congress to restrict immigration. Other Americans thought people everywhere were essentially alike, differing only in their ways of life.

A leading figure on the environmental side of the debate was Margaret Mead's graduate school mentor, Franz Boas. Adopting his views, Mead espoused the belief that people differ only according to their environment.

argues, have political implications since any social arrangements are likely to benefit some people more than others. In short, Gouldner concludes, what is *social* is inevitably *political*. This also holds true for research, which reflects people's political values and has political consequences.

If sociologists have no choice about their work being political, Gouldner continues, they do have a choice about *which* positions are worthy of support. Moreover, sociologists have an obligation to endorse such political objectives. Although this viewpoint is not limited to sociologists of any one political orientation, it is especially strong among those influenced by the ideas of Karl Marx. As noted in Chapter 1 ("The Sociological Perspective"), Marx asserted that while it is important to understand the world, the crucial task is to change it (1972:109; orig. 1845).

In recent years, many colleges and universities have become embroiled in what has become known as the *political correctness debate*. In simple terms, this controversy pits the Weberian defense of value-free teaching and research against the Marxist view that knowledge is related to power and that it should be used for needed social and political change.

Gender and Research

One political dimension of research involves gender—the relative social standing of females and males. Sociologists are becoming increasingly aware that gender-related issues can play a major part in their work. Margrit Eichler (1988) identifies five dangers to sound research that relate to gender.

1. **Androcentricity.** Androcentricity (*andro* is the Greek word for "male"; *centricity* means "being centered on") refers to approaching an issue from a male perspective. Sometimes researchers approach a setting as if only the activities of men are important while ignoring what women do. For years, research in the area of occupations focused on the paid work of men while overlooking the

Not surprisingly, both Boas and Mead opposed what they viewed as false biological doctrine being used to justify the exclusion and unfair treatment of some people.

Mead's first book, *Coming of Age in Samoa* (1928), was powerful ammunition for the environmental side of what Chapter 5 ("Socialization") presents as the "nature-nurture debate." If growing up in Samoa revealed little of the turbulence typical of adolescence in North America, Mead concluded, environment must far outweigh biology in shaping humanity. Therefore, no category of people is inherently different—and certainly not better—than another.

Mead's research went a long way toward discrediting biological views of human behavior. Yet shortly after her death, Derek Freeman, who had also conducted research in Samoa, challenged Mead's conclusions about the importance of biology to human behavior. In Freeman's view, Mead had selectively represented Samoan society according to her personal politics. For his part, Freeman argued that biology plays a greater role in human behavior than Mead was willing to recognize.

Scholars still debate this issue. To those who side with Freeman, Mead was a young (twenty-four years old when she arrived in Samoa in 1925) and unseasoned researcher, prompted by her teacher to produce evidence supporting an environmental doctrine of human behavior. Her conclusions are too "neat," critics claim, suggesting that she saw only what she was looking for. In short, they assert, Mead's work is more "politically correct" than it is scientifically factual.

To others, however, Freeman stands as the villain in the controversy. Mead's defenders argue that, especially given the limited development of research skills at that time, her conclusions are basically sound. It is Freeman, they charge, who is playing politics by rigidly advocating a view of human behavior largely determined by biology. Those in Mead's camp conclude that Freeman has gained fame and fortune by unjustly attacking the work of a great scientist.

No doubt, some truth can be found on both sides of this recent controversy. One point, however, seems clear: human beings are passionate and political creatures who often fall short of the scientific goal of complete objectivity in research.

SOURCES: Based on Mead (1961; orig. 1928), Freeman (1983), Holmes (1983), and Weiner (1983).

Margrit Eichler is one of Canada's foremost feminist scholars. She has written extensively about feminist insight into policy and has provided thoughtful and critical analyses of such topics as new reproductive technologies, the family, and methodology.

housework traditionally performed by women (Counts, 1925; Hodge, Treiman, & Rossi, 1966). Similarly, until recently studies of status attainment were based on fathers and sons (Blau & Duncan, 1967; Sewell, Haller, & Ohlendorf, 1970). Clearly, research that seeks to understand human behavior cannot ignore half of humanity.

Eichler notes that the parallel situation of *gynocentricity*—seeing the world from a female perspective—is equally limiting to sociological investigation. However, in patriarchal Canada, this problem arises much less frequently.

2. **Overgeneralizing**. This occurs when research that focuses on members of one sex is used to support conclusions about both sexes. Historically, sociologists have studied men and then made sweeping claims about "society." This approach ignores the experiences of half the population. Gathering information about a community from public officials or other prominent persons (who are likely to be men), and then drawing conclusions about the community as a whole, would constitute overgeneralizing.

Sylvia Hale (1987) discovered that the general theory that women were poor managers within the Indian Civil Service was borne out by the lack of productivity and lack of respect of those who were working under them. But, when the reasons for women's underachievement as managers were ex-

amined in depth, it became clear that they had all of the qualities of good managers, including a good work ethic, commitment, knowledge, education, and dedication. The problem was that their male bosses constantly undermined their work, failed to support their decisions, and allied themselves against the managers with the workers whom the women managers were attempting to direct. The theory that women made poor managers was thus an overgeneralization because it ignored the whole context of their work.

Here, again, the problem can occur in reverse. For example, in an investigation of child-rearing practices, collecting data only from women would allow researchers to draw conclusions about "motherhood" but not about the more general issue of "parenthood."

3. **Gender insensitivity**. This refers to the failure of a researcher to consider the variable of gender at all. As is evident throughout this book, social forces often affect men and women quite differently. For example, failing to consider the importance of gender in a study of growing old in Canada would ignore important information such as the fact that most elderly men live with spouses while elderly women typically live alone.

4. **Double standards**. Researchers must be careful not to distort what they study by evaluating women and men using different standards. This might happen as a researcher investigating families describes a couple as "man and wife." This inconsistency involves more than words if the researcher defines the man as the "head of household" and treats him accordingly, while assuming that the woman simply engages in family "support work."

5. **Interference**. Beyond affecting researchers, gender often shapes the attitudes of subjects, which can also distort a study. The problem of "interference" occurs if a subject reacts to the sex of the researcher rather than to the research itself. For instance, while studying a small community in Sicily, Maureen Giovannini (1992) reported that many men responded to her as a woman to the point that she was unable to work effectively as a researcher. Gender dynamics prevented activities like private conversations with men that were deemed inappropriate for single women. In addition, local residents denied Giovannini access to places considered "off-limits" to members of her sex.

Of course, researchers can choose to focus their work on one sex or the other. Indeed, pervasive attention to men at the expense of women in the past encouraged some researchers—including Dorothy Holland and Margaret Eisenhart, whose study of the university campus is presented at the beginning of this chapter—to make special efforts to investigate the lives of women. But sociologists, as well as others who read their work, should think critically about how gender affects the process of sociological investigation.

Research Ethics

Like all investigators, sociologists must be mindful that research can be harmful as well as helpful to subjects or communities. For this reason, the American Sociological Association—the major professional association of sociologists in North America—has established formal guidelines for the conduct of research (1984).

The primary ethical guideline is that sociologists strive for technical competence and objectivity in conducting their research. Sociologists must disclose research findings in full, without omitting significant data. Further, they must include all possible interpretations of data, and they are ethically bound to make their results available to other qualified sociologists, some of whom may wish to replicate the work.

Researchers must strive to protect the rights, privacy, and safety of anyone involved in a research project. Sociologists are obligated to terminate any research, however promising it may seem, if they become aware of any potential danger to participants. Even if research is likely to cause subjects discomfort or inconvenience, sociologists must ensure in advance that all participants understand and accept any risks.

Subjects who agree to take part in research are entitled to full anonymity, even if sociologists come under legal pressure to release confidential information. Researchers should never promise such consideration, therefore, unless they are willing and able to carry through on their commitment.

Sociologists are ethically bound to present accurately the purpose of their work. They must inform subjects, in advance, of any political organization or business that they represent, and this information must also be furnished in reports of research findings. Since private or public agencies sometimes try to constrain the research process, a sociologist must never accept funding from an agency if doing so will require violating any of the ethical guidelines mentioned here. All sources of research funding must be disclosed in the publication of findings.

Finally, there is a global dimension to research ethics. Sociologists have been called on to collect data for government agencies. Professional ethics, however, demand that sociologists never use their professional role as a "cover" while gathering intelligence information for any government. In addition, when researchers do work abroad, they must understand what people in *that* setting are likely to perceive as a violation of privacy or a source of personal danger. In short, sociologists must gain familiarity with a cultural setting before they conduct research there.

Methods of Data Collection

A **research method** is *a strategy for systematically conducting research.* Four commonly used methods of sociological investigation are introduced here. None is inherently better or worse than any other; but in the same way that a carpenter selects a particular tool for a particular task, distinctive strengths and weaknesses make each method suitable for certain kinds of research.

Experiments

The logic of positivist science is most clearly expressed in the **experiment**, *a research method for investigating cause and effect under highly controlled conditions.* Experimental research is *explanatory*, meaning that it investigates not just what happens but why. Typically, researchers devise an experiment to test a specific **hypothesis**, *an unverified statement of a relationship between variables.*

Ideally, experimental research is conducted in three steps that provide the empirical evidence needed for a researcher to accept or reject the hypothesis. First, the experimenter measures the dependent variable; second, the investigator exposes the dependent variable to the effects of the independent variable (sometimes called the "treatment"); and third, the researcher measures the dependent variable again to see if the predicted change has taken place. If the expected change has occurred, the experiment lends support to the hypothesis; if not, the hypothesis is discounted.

Successful experiments require that researchers carefully control all factors that might affect what is being measured. This is most easily accomplished in a

Social calamities—whether caused by nature or by people themselves—provide opportunities for field research that could never be created in a laboratory. Such studies show that disasters not only destroy property but also shred the fabric of social life, causing human suffering that may continue long after physical structures have been repaired.

laboratory, an artificial setting specially constructed for this purpose. Oftentimes, scientific investigators enhance experimental control by dividing subjects into an *experimental group* and a *control group*. At the outset, the dependent variable is measured for members of both groups, but only the experimental group is subjected to the independent variable or treatment. Then both groups are measured again. A host of factors (such as some news event) occurring during the research might cause change in the experimental group, but such factors would affect the control group as well. By comparing the before and after measurements of the two groups, the researcher is able to assess how much of the observed change is actually due to the independent variable.

Not all experimental research takes place in a laboratory. Sociologists can conduct experiments in any number of everyday locations. Such "field experiments" have the advantage of allowing researchers to observe subjects in their natural habitats. In addition, field experiments study phenomena that could never be artifically created in a laboratory. For example, sociologist Kai Erikson (1976) investigated the aftermath of a deadly flood in Buffalo Creek, West Virginia, in 1972. Erikson found that the social damage caused by disruption of community ties was just as serious—and lasted much longer—than physical damage to property. However, the inability to control the field environment means researchers can test only hypotheses that are more general than they might be in a laboratory setting. Moreover, sociologists cannot replicate certain field experiments because precisely the same conditions (such as the Buffalo Creek flood) do not occur again.

In the field or the laboratory, subjects may change their behavior simply in response to a researcher's attention, as one classic experiment discovered. In the late 1930s, the Western Electric Company investigated productivity at its Hawthorne factory near Chicago (Roethlisberger & Dickson, 1939). One experiment tested the hypothesis that increasing the available lighting would raise worker output. First, productivity (the dependent variable) was measured; then lighting (the independent variable) was changed; finally, productivity was measured again. Productivity increased, supporting the hypothesis. But when the research team subsequently *reduced* the lighting, productivity again increased, contradicting the initial hypothesis. In time, the researchers realized that the workers were working harder simply because people were paying attention to them. Since then, social scientists have used the term **Hawthorne effect** to refer to *a change in a subject's behavior caused by the awareness of being studied.*

A Laboratory Experiment: The Stanford County Prison

The social dynamics of prisons comprises an important topic of study, although social scientists are rarely able to perform this kind of research "in the field." Philip Zimbardo nonetheless sought to investigate prison violence in an artificial "laboratory" (Zimbardo, 1972; Haney, Banks, & Zimbardo, 1973).

Zimbardo was skeptical of the common-sense idea that prison violence is caused by the characteristics of individual prisoners who are in jail precisely because of antisocial or violent behavior. Also he doubted that prison guards are simply the kind of people who enjoy pushing other people around. Rather,

Zimbardo suspected that, once inside a prison, even the healthiest and most emotionally stable person would be prone to violent behavior. This led to the hypothesis that *the character of prison itself, and not the personalities of prisoners and guards, causes prison violence.* Thus, the prison setting was treated as the independent variable capable of causing change in the dependent variable, people's behavior.

To test this hypothesis, Zimbardo's research team placed an ad in a local newspaper in Palo Alto, California, offering young men $15 a day to help with a two-week research project. Each of the seventy who responded was given a series of physical and psychological tests. The researchers selected the twenty-four deemed the healthiest, both physically and mentally. Then the men were randomly assigned to two groups; half were designated "prisoners" and half became "guards." The guards and prisoners were to spend the next two weeks in the "Stanford County Prison," a mock prison specially constructed in the basement of the psychology building on the Stanford University campus.

The "prisoners" were surprised when the Palo Alto police "arrested" them at their homes soon afterward. After being searched and handcuffed, they were taken to the local police station to be fingerprinted. Then they were transported to the "prison" on the Stanford campus. There each met other "prisoners," as well as the "guards," who had been instructed to keep the prison secure at all times. Zimbardo and his associates sat back with a video camera to see what would happen next.

The experiment soon became more than anyone had bargained for. The researchers observed both guards and prisoners acting in stereotypical fashion, quickly losing their sense of basic human decency. Guards insulted the prisoners, forcing them to engage in humiliating tasks such as cleaning out toilets with their bare hands. The prisoners reacted with bitterness and hostility. Within four days, five prisoners had to be removed from the study "because of extreme emotional depression, crying, rage and acute anxiety" (1973:81). Before the end of the first week, the situation had deteriorated so badly that the researchers canceled the experiment. Zimbardo explains (1972:4): "The ugliest, most base, pathological side of human nature surfaced. We were horrified because we saw some boys (guards) treat others as if they were despicable animals, taking pleasure in cruelty, while other boys (prisoners) became servile, dehumanized robots who thought only

of escape, of their own individual survival and of their mounting hatred for the guards."

What unfolded in the "Stanford County Prison" supported Zimbardo's hypothesis that prison violence is rooted in the social character of prisons themselves, rather than the personalities of guards and prisoners. His findings also raise questions about the way our society operates prisons, suggesting the need for basic prison reform. Just as important, the experiment reveals how research itself can threaten the physical and mental well-being of subjects. Such dangers are not always as immediately apparent as they were in this case. Therefore, researchers must consider carefully potential harm to subjects at all stages of their work and end any study, as Zimbardo responsibly did, if subjects appear to be threatened.

Survey Research

A **survey** is *a research method in which subjects respond to a series of items in a questionnaire or an interview.* Perhaps the most widely used of all research methods, surveys are particularly well suited to studying what investigators cannot observe directly, such as political attitudes, religious beliefs, or the private lives of couples. Although surveys can be used to study the relationship among variables, they are most useful for *descriptive* research, in which the responses of subjects help a sociologist to understand and describe a social setting, such as an urban neighborhood or a gambling casino.

Population and Sample

In survey research, a **population** refers to *the people who are the focus of research.* We might wish, for example, to learn how much schooling is typical of adults living in a particular city. In this case, all the adults in the city would be the survey population. Sometimes every adult in the country is the survey population, as in the familiar polls that are taken during political campaigns. However, contacting such a vast number of people would be virtually impossible as well as extremely expensive and time-consuming. Researchers skirt this problem by using a **sample**, meaning *a part of a population selected to represent the whole.* The precise size of a sample varies. We use the logic of sampling all the time. If you look around the classroom and notice five or six students nodding off, you might conclude that class finds the teacher to be dull. Such a conclusion involves making an inference about *all* the people (the "population") after observing *some* of the people (the "sample"). But how can we know if a sample actually represents the entire population?

The most common assurance is *random sampling,* ensuring that each element in the population has the same chance of being included in the sample. If this is the case, mathematical laws of probability make a representative sample likely within known limits. Seasoned researchers use computers to generate random samples. Novice researchers, however, sometimes assume that "randomly" walking up to people on the street produces a random sample. Unfortunately, this is unlikely for two reasons. First, any part of a city—whether a rich neighborhood or a university town—is likely to contain more of some kinds of people than others. Second, any researcher is apt to find some people more approachable, again introducing a bias.

Although good sampling is not simple, it offers a considerable savings in time and expense. We are spared the tedious task of contacting everyone in a population, while obtaining essentially the same results.

Questionnaires and Interviews

Selecting subjects is only the first step in carrying out a survey. Also needed is a plan for asking questions and recording answers. Surveys employ two general techniques: questionnaires and interviews.

A **questionnaire** is *a series of questions presented to subjects.* In most cases, subjects select a response from several provided by the researcher (similar to multiple-choice examination questions). Limiting responses with what is called a *closed-ended format* makes analyzing results relatively easy. In some cases, however, a researcher may want subjects to respond freely. An *open-ended format* allows subjects to express various shades of opinion. Of course, the researcher later has to make sense out of what can be a bewildering array of answers.

Deciding how to present questions to subjects forms another part of the research strategy. Most often, a questionnaire is mailed and respondents are asked to complete the form and then to mail it back. This technique is called a *self-administered survey.* Since no researcher is present when subjects read the questionnaire, it must be both inviting and clearly written. A self-administered questionnaire should always be *pretested* with a small number of people before sending it to all the subjects. This small investment of time and money may avoid the costly problem of finding

out—too late—that instructions or questions were confusing.

Using the mail has the advantage of including a large number of people over a wide geographical area in the study at relatively small expense. At the same time, people may treat such questionnaires as "junk mail," so that typically fewer than half are completed and returned. Researchers often employ follow-up mailings to coax reluctant subjects.

Worth remembering, too, is that many people are not capable of completing a questionnaire on their own. Young children obviously cannot, nor can many hospital patients, and as many as one-third of adults simply have too much difficulty with reading and writing to wade through a comprehensive questionnaire (Kozol, 1985a).

An **interview** is *a series of questions administered personally by a researcher to respondents.* Generally, open-ended interviews are most useful because they allow the researcher to ask follow-up questions that probe and clarify the subject's responses. In the ensuing conversation, however, the researcher must avoid influencing the subject, which can be done by making as small a gesture as raising an eyebrow when a person begins to answer. In comparing the interview with the questionnaire, investigators have found that a subject is more likely to complete a survey if contacted personally by the researcher. However, a disadvantage of interviews is that tracking people down and personally interrogating them is costly and time-consuming, especially if all subjects do not live in the same area.

In both questionnaires and interviews, the wording of questions has a significant effect on answers (Fowler, Jr., & Mangione, 1989). Language with an emotional charge generally sways subjects. For example, a person might endorse the statement "I approve of my child having teachers representing all political opinions" and yet reject the same statement if the words "including radicals" are added at the end. Similarly, using the term "welfare mothers" for "women who receive public assistance" injects an emotional element into a survey. In other cases, the wording of questions may suggest what other people think, thereby subtly guiding the respondent. People would be more likely to respond positively to the question "Do you *agree* that the police force is doing a good job?" than they would to the question "Do you *think* that the police force is doing a good job?" simply because the phrase "do you agree" suggests that others endorse the statement. In short, researchers must strive to use language that suggests no correct response.

Researchers should also avoid double-questions like "Do you think that the government should spend less money for military defense and more for domestic social programs?" The problem here is that a subject could very well agree with one part of the question but dispute the other, so that saying yes or no distorts the actual opinion the researcher is seeking.

Surveys at Work: The Case of Anti-Semitism in Quebec

On September 17, 1991, Mordecai Richler, a prominent Canadian novelist with an international reputation (and a Jew), wrote an article on French-Canadian nationalism in the *New Yorker* in which he alleged that French Canadians were anti-Semitic. His statements were the beginning of passionately felt and argued controversy. Are French-Canadians anti-Semitic? If so, are they more anti-Semitic than English Canadians? If they are more anti-Semitic, what is the explanation? A team of sociologists headed by Paul Sniderman attempted to answer these two questions.

Sniderman used the data from an existing survey entitled the *Charter of Rights Study Survey* (1993). The study used random digit dialing (RDD) of a random sample (2,084 people) of the 97 percent of the Canadian households that have telephones. The Quebec sam-

pling strategy was specifically designed to yield a representative sample of the province. Care was taken that the Quebec response rate was equal to that in the rest of the country, and that those who responded filled the same demographic categories as those in the rest of Canada. In other words, the survey was designed to include the right proportions of male and female, older and younger, urban-dwellers and rural-dwellers, etc., in order to reflect the total population of the country, and of Quebec. The accuracy of this method is demonstrated by the similarities between the sample and the population of Canada, as portrayed in Table 2-1. Notice, for example, that the average age of Canadians, according to the 1986 Census, was 42 years; while the average age of the Charter sample was 43 years.

The next problem for the researchers was the wording of the questions. A review of the literature on explanations for prejudice identified several common bases for prejudicial attitudes. These included:

1. **Personality type** of the individual: apparently people with authoritative personalities are more likely to express prejudice.

2. **Normative prejudice**, such as is found in South Africa, where prejudice has been normative and even legislated into prevailing policy.

TABLE 2-1   SAMPLE AND POPULATION CHARACTERISTICS: A COMPARISON

Variable	1986 Census of Canada*	Charter	1986 Census Quebec Only	Charter Sample Quebec Only
Mean age of respondents	42	43	42	41
Highest level of schooling				
High school graduation or less	55%	56%	58%	59%
College, Technical School, some University, etc.	35%	28%	31%	30%
University Degree(s)	10%	15%	9%	11%
Sex				
Female	51%	51%	52%	52%
Male	49%	49%	48%	48%
Marital Status				
Married (Living with partner)	65%	66%	64%	66%
Never been married	22%	23%	24%	22%
Separated, Divorced, Widowed	13%	11%	12%	12%
Employment Status				
Employed	62%	63%	57%	55%
Not in labor force	31%	29%	35%	37%
Unemployed	7%	8%	8%	8%

*Statistics Canada Public Use Sample Tapes

3. **Normative conformity**, in which conformity itself is seen as an important norm.

4. **Nationalism.** With respect to Quebec, it has been suggested that one of the consequences of French nationalism may be a derogation of other groups. These four competing hypotheses were operationalized through a series of questions and found reliable.

The questionnaire was designed to identify not only whether French-speaking Quebeckers held more anti-Semitic views than English-speaking Canadians (the dependent variable), but also to examine which of these factors was the underlying cause of those views (the independent variables). The five questions used were as follows (1993:247):

We realize no statement is true of all people in a group, but generally speaking, please tell me whether you agree or disagree with the following statements. Would you say you agree strongly, agree somewhat, disagree somewhat or disagree with this statement?

Most Jews don't care what happens to people who aren't Jewish.

Most Jews are pushy.

Jews have made an important contribution to the cultural life of Canada.

Jews are more willing than others to use shady practices to get ahead.

Most Jews are warm and friendly people.

Note the carefully worded introduction, which was designed to make respondents feel comfortable expressing their views candidly by qualifying the responses. Given the sensitive nature of the topic, this was deemed necessary in order to combat what sociologists refer to as the *social desirability effect*, whereby respondents are unwilling to commit themselves to an opinion which might place them outside the "normal" range of opinion. By acknowledging that the statements could not be applied to all Jews, the researchers allowed respondents freer reign in expressing their attitudes. Even if respondents agreed strongly with one of the negative statements, they could rest assured that they fell within "acceptable norms," since the response was not going to be taken as a blanket condemnation of all Jews.

Findings. The researchers found that French-speaking Quebeckers were, in fact, more anti-Semitic than English-speaking Canadians. While the personality basis for anti-Semitism was conspicuously weak, the cultural basis for anti-Semitism was strong and related more to the high value placed on conformity in Quebec (normative conformity) than on nationalist sentiment, as had been suggested by some commentators. French-speaking Quebeckers were significantly more likely than English-speaking Canadians to express support for conformity as a value. "They place a greater priority on people learning to fit in and get along with others" and on the larger society being "a unified body pursuing a common goal" (1993:264). They are therefore more likely to distrust and dislike those who try to be different.

Conclusions The authors make the point that while Francophone Quebecois are overall more anti-Semitic than other Canadians, most are not anti-Semitic at all. Moreover, on every test but one, a majority expressed positive sentiments regarding Jews. "Quebeckers differ from other Canadians not so much in their readiness to submit to the full syndrome of anti-Semitic ideas but rather in their willingness to accept one or two negative characterizations of Jews" (265). Quebecois were as tolerant as English-speaking Canadians and were as willing as Anglophones to support such things as the rights of groups with unpopular points of view to hold public rallies; and the need for restrictions on the rights of Canada's security service to wiretap. Finally, the researchers warned that to say that anti-Semitism is more of a problem in Quebec is not to say that it does not exist elsewhere in Canada.

Participant Observation

Participant observation is *a method in which researchers systematically observe people while joining in their routine activities.* This method allows researchers to gain an inside look at social life in settings ranging from night clubs to religious seminaries. Participant observation is commonly employed by cultural anthropologists to study other societies. Cultural anthropologists refer to participant observation as *fieldwork*; their description of an unfamiliar culture is termed an *ethnography*. Sociologists usually call the account of people in a particular setting a *case study*.

Sociologists beginning a case study may have

Sociologists who conduct research in other countries should be aware that what they may think are "innocent questions" may cause discomfort or even offense to others. Canada's growing social diversity raises the importance of this kind of sensitivity for research carried out at home as well.

only a vague understanding of the social patterns they wish to investigate. Thus, participant observation is *descriptive* and often *exploratory.* Researchers usually begin with few, if any, specific hypotheses to test, since they may not know initially what the important questions will turn out to be. Compared to experiments and survey research, then, participant observation has fewer hard and fast rules. A research plan must be flexible enough to adapt to unexpected circumstances. Initially, a researcher is likely to be concerned with gaining entry into what may be an unfamiliar social setting. In time, observations provoke many specific questions, and answers are organized into a detailed description of a way of life.

As its name suggests, participant observation has two sides. On the one hand, gaining an "insider's" look depends on becoming a participant in the setting— "hanging out" with others, attempting to act, think, and even feel the way they do. Unlike other research methods, participant observation requires a researcher to become immersed in a social setting, not for a week or two, but usually for a period of years. On the other hand, for the duration of the study, the researcher must also maintain the role of "observer," standing back from the action and applying the sociological perspective to social patterns that others take for granted. The twin roles of "insider" participant and "outsider" often come down to a series of careful compromises. Such

tensions appear as a regular feature in the *field notes,* a daily record of how the research proceeds. These notes form the basis for the final research report, and should convey not only a researcher's conclusions but something of the research experience itself.

Sociologists often work alone in this kind of study, so they must remain mindful that results depend on the interpretations of a single scientist. Participant observation is typically **qualitative research**, meaning *inquiry based on subjective impressions.* Unlike surveys, participant observation usually involves little **quantitative research**, *investigation based on the analysis of numerical data.* Because personal impressions play a central role in participant observation, some scientists disparage this method as lacking in scientific rigor. Yet its personal approach can be a strength; while a highly visible team of sociologists attempting to administer formal surveys would disrupt many social settings, a sensitive participant-observer can often gain considerable insight into people's natural behavior.

A Case Study: Street Corner Society

A classic illustration of participant observation was carried out in the late 1930s by William Foote Whyte. A graduate student at Harvard University, Whyte was fascinated by the lively street life of a nearby, rather run-down section of Boston. He embarked on a four-year study of this neighborhood, which he called "Cornerville" to protect the privacy of its inhabitants.

Cornerville was home to first- and second-generation Italian immigrants. Many were poor and lived quite unlike the more affluent Bostonians familiar to Whyte. To many, Cornerville was a place to avoid: a poor, chaotic slum that was home to racketeers. Unwilling to accept easy stereotypes, Whyte set out to discover for himself exactly what kind of life went on inside this community. His celebrated book, *Street Corner Society* (1981; orig. 1943), describes Cornerville as a highly organized community with its own code of values, complex social patterns, and distinctive social conflicts.

Whyte's research points up the advantages of participant-observation as well as some of its pitfalls. He could have taken his clipboard and questionnaire to one of Cornerville's community centers and asked local people to talk about their lives. Or he could have asked members of the community to come to his office at Harvard for interviews. In either case, the information he gathered would certainly have been misleading, since as we have already seen, the awareness of being observed often alters the behavior of subjects. Many Cornerville residents would probably have refused to

What is different often excites the sociological imagination. Participant observation is well suited for exploring an unfamiliar setting like this urban community in India. But research of this kind demands extensive preparation. To begin, investigators must acquire necessary language skills, and they need to gain at least a basic understanding of the new culture. To minimize these difficulties, researchers often study communities with which they have at least some previous experience.

talk to him at all under those circumstances. Whyte realized that he had to downplay the role of observer if people were to be comfortable in his presence. Therefore, he tried to become part of Cornerville's everyday social patterns.

One night early in his study, Whyte joined a group of people in Cornerville who frequented a gambling establishment. After listening to a story about how gambling was organized, Whyte asked naively, "I suppose the cops were all paid off?" The man's reaction taught Whyte something about the tension between being a participant and being an observer:

> *The gambler's jaw dropped. He glared at me. Then he denied vehemently that any policeman had been paid off and immediately switched the conversation to another subject. For the rest of that evening I felt very uncomfortable.*

The next day [a local acquaintance] explained the lesson of the previous evening. "Go easy on that 'who,' 'what,' 'why,' 'when,' 'where' stuff, Bill. You ask those questions and people will clam up on you. If people accept you, you can just hang around, and you'll learn the answers in the long run without even having to ask the questions" (1981:303).

Gaining insider status—becoming a participant—was the crucial first step in Whyte's research. But how could an upper-middle-class Anglo-Saxon graduate student from Harvard become part of the life of a poor Italian immigrant community like Cornerville?

Gaining entry or "breaking in" to a strange social environment is difficult, often embarrassing, and sometimes even dangerous, as Whyte soon found out. On another evening, Whyte dropped in at a local bar, hoping to buy a woman a drink, and encourage her to talk about Cornerville. He looked around the room, but could find no woman alone. Presently, he noticed a fellow talking with two women, which he took to be an opportunity:

> *I approached the group and opened with something like this:*
>
> *"Pardon me. Would you mind if I joined you?"*
> *There was a moment of silence while the man stared at me. Then he offered to throw me down the stairs. I assured him that this would not be necessary, and demonstrated as much by walking right out of there without any assistance.* (1981:289)

This experience taught Whyte another important lesson: imposing on people is not only impolite, it can be hazardous to the researcher. Fortunately, however, his luck soon took a turn for the better when he met a young man named "Doc" in the local community agency. Doc listened sympathetically to the problem and took Whyte under his wing, introducing his new friend to others in the neighborhood. This was the real start of Whyte's research because, with Doc's help, he soon became a regular among the people of Cornerville.

Whyte's friendship with Doc illustrates the importance of a *key informant* in field research. Key informants introduce a researcher to a community, and often can suggest how to find out specific information. But using a key informant has its dangers too. Because any key informant is familiar with only part of a community, such help may introduce bias into research. Moreover, once identified with a key informant, a researcher may be labeled in some way by others. In sum, while a key informant is invaluable at the outset, the participant-observer should soon seek a broader range of contacts.

Over several years of research, Whyte gradually settled in as a comfortable resident of Cornerville. He learned that it was hardly the disorganized slum some thought it to be. Many immigrants were working hard to become "established," and many were proud to have sent children to university. Whyte discovered social divisions in Cornerville, and he even found a few criminals. Yet he was able to see that this distinctive Boston neighborhood was composed mostly of people who, though poor, were working hard to build a future for themselves.

In sum, participant observation creates tensions and spotlights important contrasts. Its flexibility lets a researcher respond to an unfamiliar setting, but makes replication quite difficult. Sympathetic understanding requires involvement, while scientific observation demands detachment. Often a researcher works alone with little funding, but the time required to become familiar with a community makes this a costly type of research. Perhaps for all these reasons, participant-observation research is used less often than other methods described in this chapter. Yet the depth of understanding gained through research of this kind has greatly enriched our knowledge of many types of human communities.

Secondary Analysis

Not all research requires investigators personally to collect their own data. In many cases, sociologists engage in **secondary analysis**, *a research method in which researchers utilize data collected by others.*

The most widely used data are statistics gathered by government agencies. Statistics Canada, a branch of the Canadian government, systematically and regularly gathers information about the Canadian population which is used for both research and policy-making. The Bureau of the Census in the United States performs a similar function. Global analysis can benefit from various publications of the United Nations and the World Bank. A wide range of data is as close as the library.

Secondary analysis may also mean using data collected by other individual researchers. The obvious advantage of using available data—whether government statistics or the results of research studies—is a savings in time and money. This strategy enables sociologists with low budgets to undertake research that might otherwise be impossible. Just as important, the quality of government data is generally better than

Most census data are obtained from questionnaires that officials send and receive back through the mail or deliver and pick up by hand. This strategy, although generally quite efficient, is likely to undercount the homeless or others who lack a customary street address. This is a picture of Olaf Solheim, a man evicted from a roominghouse in Vancouver's West End to make room for tourist housing for Expo '86. Less than six weeks later, Solheim was dead. Modern sociologists are committed to doing the kind of research that does not rely solely on government statistics, but that also allows voices like Solheim's to be heard.

what even well-funded researchers could hope to obtain on their own.

Secondary analysis has inherent problems. For one thing, some researchers may not evaluate the accuracy of their data with a critical eye. Was information gathered in a systematic and unbiased way? Using second-hand data sometimes is a bit like buying a used car. While bargains can be found, there is potential for a poor choice.

Emile Durkheim's nineteenth-century study of suicide, described in Chapter 1 ("The Sociological Perspective"), is one of the best-known sociological investigations making use of existing records. But Durkheim's research also illustrates some of the dangers of this approach. He relied on official death records to investigate suicide rates among various types of people. But he had no way to check how many accidents were incorrectly classified as suicides, or what number of suicides were recorded as accidents or deaths due to some other cause. Sociologists who utilize others' data, then, must guard against distortions.

A second problem is that available data may have been collected for purposes different from those of a subsequent researcher. The way in which others phrased questions or selected respondents may not precisely fit the needs of a subsequent researcher. We are dealing with a trade-off here: any shortcomings in the data must be balanced against the ease by which they are obtained.

Content Analysis

Another type of secondary analysis is called **content analysis**. This entails *the counting or coding of the content of written, aural, or visual materials*, such as television and radio programming, novels, magazines, advertisements. Content analysis has a long tradition in sociology. One of the best known early content analyses of this century in America is *The Polish Peasant in Europe and America* by Thomas and Znaneicki (1919–1971), which used diaries and letters written to and from Polish immigrants to America to describe the adjustment processes of new American immigrants. A 1977 study by the Montreal YWCA Women's Center of gender roles in thirty-eight Grade One readers used in Montreal Anglophone schools is another example of the use of content research. The study found that gender stereotypes were mirrored in the books. The males were portrayed as central characters and as active, competitive problem-solvers. Females were less often included and when they were tended to be portrayed in passive, domestic roles and occupations. The males were shown in seventy-eight different occupations; most females were housewives, and those who weren't were described as nurses, librarians, teachers, or cooks (Mackie, 1983). Recent research by Nancarrow Clarke (1991) on the "treatment" of cancer, heart disease, and AIDS in the media, described in Chapter 3 ("Culture") provides another example of content analysis.

Historical Research: *Open For Business*

Since we are all trapped in the present, secondary analysis provides a key to investigating the past. Gordon Laxer's book, *Open for Business: The Roots of Foreign Ownership in Canada* (1989), is an important contribution to the age-old Canadian debate about the reasons for the Canadian economy's high level of dependence on the United States and other foreign owners. Laxer rejected what have become the conventional explanations: geographical closeness to a powerful and expanding economy, our relative lack of technological development, merchant and banking elite influences, and a reliance on the export of raw materials. Focusing on forces beyond our control, he pointed out, tends to make Canadian failure to develop independently seem inevitable. Instead, Laxer chose to examine the internal social and political forces that

have shaped Canada's development policies, by comparing Canada with other "late-followers" such as Germany, Japan, Sweden, and Russia (countries that were somewhat behind the U.S.A. and Great Britain in their economic development).

Laxer points out that at the turn of the century, Canada was the eighth largest manufacturing country in the world, a fact that was particulary surprising given its relatively small population. Early economic development was not due to American investment; rather, it was Canada's already developed industry, the nature of its labor force and its standard of living that attracted American companies. Before Canada became a "branch-plant" economy, Canadians were exporting sophisticated industrial goods, developed and made by Canadian-owned businesses, to such markets as Britain, France, and Germany.

An important cause of the demise of Canadian economic independence, Laxer found, was the weakness of the organized farmers' movements from before Confederation to World War I. (Agrarian movements, because of their attachment to the land, were important elsewhere in protecting countries against economic penetration and the exploitation of the land and natural resources by foreign capitalists.) The weakness of the Agrarian movements resulted partly from a loyalty to Britain and partly from internal divisions (e.g., French, English; Protestant, Catholic; and class divisions). As a result, banks did not encourage Canadians to invest in their own country. Moreover because of weak agrarian policies, the development of the West was delayed about twenty years, which in turn slowed the pace and scale of Canadian industrial development in the period immediately preceding the first major invasion of American branch-plants. Finally, the weakness of agrarian and populist nationalism allowed open-door policies with regard to foreign investment.

Laxer concludes his book with a warning to Canadians. He states that internal problems resulting from Anglophone/Francophone tensions, regionalism, ethnic, religious, and other divisions, must be solved on an equitable basis of mutual respect so that Canadians form a united front for strong economic development policies. Looking at history, Laxer suggests, provides us with clues to the future development of the Canadian economy.

We have introduced four major methods of gathering sociological data, which are summarized in Table 2-2. We now turn to consider the various ways in which these data may be used.

TABLE 2-2   FOUR RESEARCH METHODS: A SUMMARY

Method	Application	Advantages	Limitations
Experiment	For explanatory research that specifies relationships among variables; generates quantitative data	Provides greatest ability to specify cause-and-effect relationships; replication of research is relatively easy	Laboratory settings have artificial quality; unless research environment is carefully controlled, result may be biased
Survey	For gathering information about issues that cannot be directly observed, such as attitudes and values; useful for descriptive and explanatory research; generates quantitative or qualitative research	Sampling allows surveys of large populations using questionnaires; interviews provide in-depth responses	Questionnaires must be carefully prepared and may produce low return rate; interviews are expensive and time-consuming
Participant observation	For exploratory and descriptive study of people in a "natural" setting; generates qualitative data	Allows study of "natural" behaviour; usually inexpensive	Time-consuming; replication of research is difficult; researcher must balance roles of participant and observer
Secondary analysis	For exploratory, descriptive, or explanatory research whenever suitable data are available	Saves time and expense of data collection; makes historical research possible	Researcher has no control over possible bias in data; data may not be suitable for current research needs

Methods of Interpreting Sociological Data

Collecting data is one important aspect of sociological research. We have described several methods, each of which may be appropriate for various types of work, and for various paradigms. But once the data has been collected, how does one go about interpreting the results? Even in the case of a straightforward lab experiment, aimed at answering a straighforward quantitative question, interpretation can be tricky. Positivist approaches aim to take as much of the guesswork out of interpretation as possible, by striving for scientific rigor in their research methods. However, as we have seen, sociology is an inexact science, since it deals with human beings, not abstractions. For this reason, several branches of sociology have emerged that, to varying degrees, reject the very notion of applying the positivist values of reliability and objectivity to sociology.

Social-Conflict/Feminist Methods

The aim of research in the social-conflict tradition is not simply to describe the world in objective terms, but to work to change the inequities that exist in society. For this reason, the social-conflict approach to sociological interpretation is central to feminist sociological research in Canada. Many of the assumptions and goals described as aspects of positivist sociology are irrelevant to or contradicted by work in this tradition. Thus, a social-conflict researcher, given the same data as a positivist researcher, would likely arrive at a very different interpretation of the results, based on the assumptions with which they began their study.

Researchers in this tradition do not strive to be "objective." Indeed, objectivity is considered both undesirable and unattainable. Rather, they *begin* with the assumption, developed from close readings of Marx and neo-Marxists as well as feminist scholars, that the economic world of capitalism and patriarchy underlies all social action and social institutions. Data, in whatever form they are obtained, are analyzed to uncover the evidence of this economic basis. Since straight, quantitative analysis is meant to describe without imposing value judgments, many feminist scholars consider this methodology unsuited to feminist research. Others claim that feminist sociology can and should benefit from the full range of research "tools" available.

Feminist Research: Two Examples

How are women's lives affected by a capitalist and patriarchal social order? Dorothy Smith and Meg Luxton, two Canadian sociologists, have both done sociological research based on the decription and analysis of this question.

In a series of essays (1977, 1979, 1983), Dorothy Smith notes the ways in which relations between men and women depend on economic conditions. Her argument begins with the idea that in the early homesteading period, the division of labor between the sexes was fairly evenly split. Men and women depended on one another for housebuilding, clearing land, growing and harvesting gardens, caring for livestock, and preserving foodstuffs for winter. This situation of approximate equality changed as the economic unit moved to cash production. As land speculation led to increased prices and expensive mortgages on houses and machinery, families had to produce more than they themselves needed for their own subsistence. They needed profits to pay off bank loans and to buy equipment and other goods. But legally, only men could own property and borrow money at the bank. In this situation wives earned nothing and all of the results of their labor benefited their husbands/owners. The result was drudgery and a loss of power for the women. As late as 1973, the powerlessness of the farm wife was underscored in the Supreme Court decision regarding Irene Murdoch. Murdoch had worked on the family farm for twenty-five years. When she and her husband divorced, the Court decided that she had no right to any of the farm property. Women's organizations in Canada rallied in opposition to this injustice, Murdoch took her case to the Supreme Court and lost. Her case, however, was important. During the 1970s, province after province began to define marriage as a partnership of equals whose assets should be divided equally upon divorce (Anderson, 1991). By the late 1980s, Rosa Becker had won her right to the financial assets of a 25-year common law partnership.

Women's work is still undervalued and women continue to play a subservient role to their husbands in the home and in corporations. Their services are used to reproduce the labor power of their husbands and children. Meg Luxton's book *More Than A Labour of Love* (1980), describes the process whereby women work to reproduce labor power for a corporation in a single-industry mining town in Flin Flon, Manitoba. She describes the way in which the lives of the women are constrained by the requirements of the corporations. The rhythms of women's lives and the lives of their children revolve around the need of the husband for sleep, food, rest, and relaxation, all in the interest of maintaining his employment. Luxton also documents the ways in which his frustrations at work are carried home to be vented on the wife. In extreme cases, wives contend not only with surplus anger and frustration but become the victims of violence, as their husbands act out their frustrations with the corporation.

Neither Dorothy Smith nor Meg Luxton is concerned with the explication and operationalization of concepts into quantitative variables. Causality is not determined mathematically on the basis of numerical measurements of variables, but from a subjective analysis of the situation. In their world view, exploitation and injustice in power, gender, class, and race characterize social relations, and the relations among these conditions over time and place need explaining. Change towards justice is ultimately the goal. Sociology, in this tradition, is done very differently from positivist sociology.

Interpretive Research

Interpretive research differs from both political economy and positivist science. Its goal is to understand meanings and the way people construct meanings as they create their social worlds in interaction with others. Following Weber, the method used in this research endeavor is **verstehen**, a methodological approach based on the empathetic understanding of the perspectives and the world view of the other. Anne Martin Mathews' (1977) paper, The Newfoundland Migrant Wife, provides an illustration of this method. Martin Mathews noted that the experience of women in migration had been for the most part ignored. While there were studies of sex differentials in migration distance, age at migration, destination type, and the like, such studies merely compared the numbers of males and females to fall into the relevant categories. More detailed studies of adjustment to migration tended to examine the family as a unit, based on the assumption that what is good for the husband is good for the entire family.

Prior to the women's movement, only superficial reference was made to the fact that women's experience might differ from that of men. From the early seventies, some researchers began to pay attention to the differences between the expressed experiences of men and women in migration. Their findings underlined the fact that their experiences were often quite different. Martin Mathews extended this research and found that women generally felt they had very little say in the decision to migrate, while the men tended to feel that they had the absolute power to make such a decision.

The concerns of positivist sociology are not the concerns of interpretive work. Research in this tradition is not objective. Rather, the subjective descriptions of actual people involved in the routines of their lives are the focus. The richness of the data in the Martin Mathews study illustrates a part of the value of interpretive work.

One wife said:

> If I had my time over, I could have stayed in Newfoundland. I hate it up here. There's nothing here for me. People don't know how to be friendly. They don't have any respect for people here like in my hometown. I will never stay in this God-forsaken blood-hole.

> Well, Fred was up here and I was alone down there ... but I get so homesick. Hamilton will never be home to me. I know I should have stayed home where I would have been happy.

A husband said:

> My wife didn't want to leave really, but she eventually goes along with my ideas.

The research activity itself is not thought to be objective in interpretive work. Rather the collection of data (and in fact, all of the stages of research) are recognized as social events. The researcher both influences and is, in turn, influenced by the person whose life experiences he or she is portraying. Validity inheres in the depth, richness, and thickness of the description of the behavior being investigated. Nor is reliability tested by such statistical reliability measures as "coefficient alpha." The notion of reliability, so important in positivist research, is not possible in interpretive work, since any one researcher or group of researchers sees, hears, records, and interprets out of his/her/their social context. Each replication of a "similar situation" will, then, to an extent, always reflect the social characteristics of the researcher. Interpretive researchers are not interested in generalizations, but in the depth and detail of meaning in social contexts.

Ethnomethodology, which is described in Chapter 6 ("Sociology of Everyday Life") is another method which falls within the interpretive tradition. The focus in Ethnomethodology is on how and through what processes members (persons in interaction in society) make sense of their ongoing-taken-for-granted worlds.

The Interplay of Theory and Method

Methods of sociological investigation guide the discovery of facts about our social world. Facts, however, are not usually the final goal of research. As suggested in Chapter 1 ("The Sociological Perspective"), what sociologists really strive for is the development of theory—combining facts into cogent patterns of meaning.

In sociological investigation, researchers link facts and theory in two ways. **Deductive logical thought** is *reasoning that transforms general ideas into specific hypotheses suitable for scientific testing.* From a general understanding of some issue, in other words, the researcher *deduces* a hypothesis and selects a method by which to test it. Of course, the data collected may or may not support the hypothesis. Data supporting the hypothesis suggest that the general theory is on the right track. Faced with data refuting the hypothesis, a researcher infers that the theory should be revised or perhaps rejected entirely. The deductive logical model, then, proceeds from the general (theory) to the specific (facts used for evaluation).

Philip Zimbardo's Stanford County Prison experiment illustrates how this model operates. Zimbardo began with the general idea that prisons themselves alter human behavior. He then fashioned a specific hypothesis: placed in a prison setting, even emotionally well-balanced young men would exhibit violent behavior. Zimbardo confirmed this hypothesis when violence erupted soon after the experiment began. Had his experiment produced amicable behavior between "prisoners" and "guards," his original theory would clearly have required reformulation.

A second type of logical thought works in the other direction. Through **inductive logical thought**, or *reasoning that builds specific observations into general theory*, a researcher uses inductive reasoning to organize specific observations into a more general theory about human behavior.

In most cases, researchers make use of *both* types of logical thought, as represented in Figure 2-2. Sociological investigation often begins with general ideas that lead (deductively) to hypotheses, which in turn are evaluated on the basis of specific observations. These observations then (inductively) guide the modification of the original theory.

Putting It All Together: Ten Steps in Sociological Investigation

Any research project in sociology should include each of the following ten steps.

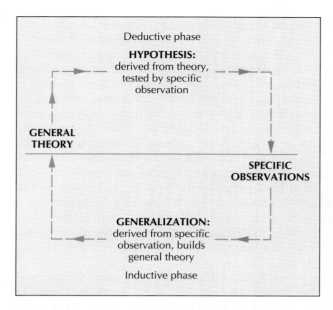

Deductive phase

HYPOTHESIS:
derived from theory,
tested by specific
observation

**GENERAL
THEORY**

**SPECIFIC
OBSERVATIONS**

GENERALIZATION:
derived from specific
observation, builds
general theory

Inductive phase

**FIGURE 2-2   DEDUCTIVE AND INDUCTIVE LOGICAL
THOUGHT**

1. **Define the topic of investigation.** The ideas for social research come from all over; just remain curious and observe the world using the sociological perspective. As Max Weber suggested, the issue you choose for study is likely to have some personal significance.

2. **Find out what has already been learned about the topic.** You are probably not the first person to develop an interest in a particular issue. Spend time in the library to learn what theories and methods of sociological investigation have been applied to your topic. Theory guides the kinds of questions you ask, and research methods indicate strategies for discovering answers. In reviewing the research that has already been done, note problems that may have come up before.

3. **Assess the requirements for carrying out research on the topic.** What resources are necessary to support your research? How much time will you need? Can you do the work yourself? If not, how much help is required? What expenses will you have along the way? What sources of funding might be available to support your research? You must answer all these questions before you actually begin to design the research project.

4. **Specify the questions you are going to ask.** Are you seeking to explore an unfamiliar social setting? To describe some category of people? Or to investigate cause and effect among variables? If your study is exploratory, identify general questions that will guide the work. If it is descriptive, specify the population and the characteristics of interest. If explanatory, state the hypothesis to be tested and carefully operationalize each variable.

5. **Consider the ethical issues involved in the research.** Not all research raises serious ethical issues, but you should be sensitive to this matter throughout your investigation. Will you promise anonymity to the subjects? If so, how will you ensure that anonymity will be maintained? Can the research harm anyone? How might you design the study to minimize the chances for injury?

What we "see" in our surroundings, or in the research data we derive from them, depends on us as well as on what we study. To illustrate, examine this painting by Alex Colville called The Traveller. *We "know" that this is a painting of a person in a car on a snowy road about to drive over a bridge. We "see" that the driver is being directed by the figure on the right of the car. Why does the "meaning" of the painting, then, remain obscure? Often, the challenge of making sense out of data in sociological research is akin to trying to interpret an image like this.*

6. **Devise a research strategy.** Consider all major research strategies—as well as innovative combinations of approaches—before deciding how to proceed. Keep in mind that the appropriate method depends on the kind of questions you are asking as well as the resources available to support your research.

7. **Use the method to gather data.** The collection of data is carried out according to the research method you have chosen. Be sure to accurately record all information in a way that will make sense later (it may be some time before you actually write up the results of your work). Remain vigilant for sources of bias that may creep in and distort the research.

8. **Interpret the findings.** Scrutinize the data in terms of the initial questions and decide what answers the data suggest. If your study involved a specific hypothesis, you should be able to confirm, reject, or modify the hypothesis based on the data. Keep in mind that there may be several ways to interpret the results of your study, consistent with different theoretical paradigms, and you should consider them all. Ask other people to review your work and suggest alternative interpretations. Be on guard against the ever-present danger that personal values or expectations will affect how you make sense out of the data you have collected.

9. **Based on the findings, state your conclusions.** Prepare a final report indicating what you have learned from the research. Consider the contributions of your work both to sociological theory and to improving sociological methods of research. What is the value of your research to other people in general? Finally, evaluate your own work. What problems arose during the research process? What questions are left unanswered? Note ways in which your own biases may have affected your conclusions.

10. **Publish your research!** There are many ways to present your work including public presentations on campus and at professional meetings. The important point is to share what you have learned with others, and to let others respond to your work. Doing this, you gain a place among countless men and women who have expanded our understanding of human behavior.

Summary

1. Positivist sociological investigation uses the logic of science to learn about the social world.

2. Science is a fundamental part of all positivist sociological research and, more broadly, helps us to critically evaluate information we encounter every day.

3. Two basic requirements for sociological investigation are (1) using the sociological perspective to view the surrounding world and (2) being curious and asking questions about society.

4. Science is a particular way of understanding the world based on empirical evidence. As such, science often contradicts our common sense.

5. Measurement, in positivist research, is the process of determining the value of a variable in any specific case. Sound measurement has both reliability and validity.

6. Positivist science seeks to specify the relationship among variables. Ideally, researchers seek relationships of cause and effect in which an independent variable can be used to predict change in a dependent variable. Often, however, research involves only correlation.

7. The positivist scientific ideal is objectivity. Although the issues studied typically reflect personal interests, value-free research depends on suspending personal values and biases to the greatest extent possible.

8. Issues involving gender often generate bias in research. Investigators should avoid examining issues from the point of view of only one sex, or basing generalizations about humanity on data collected from only men or women.

9. The logic of positivist science developed primarily through study of the natural world. However, we now recognize that application of science to the study of human behavior has inherent limitations.

10. Curiosity and imagination, which spring from the human mind and not from science, are vital to research. Since human reality revolves around meanings, the process of interpretation stands at the core of all sociological investigation.

11. Many sociologists argue that research inevitably involves political values, and some assert that sociological research, therefore, should promote desirable social change.

12. Because sociological research has the potential to harm subjects, sociological investigators are bound by ethical guidelines.

13. Experiments attempt to specify the relationship between two (or more) variables; they are best performed under controlled conditions.

14. Surveys gather people's responses to statements or questions. Surveys utilize both questionnaires and interviews.

15. Participant observation involves directly observing a social setting for an extended period of time. In this research method, the investigator functions both as a participant in the setting and as a careful observer of it.

16. Secondary analysis, or making use of available data, is often preferable to collecting one's own data; it also allows study of historical issues.

17. Some sociological methods, unlike positivist sociology, choose to focus more on methods of interpreting data than on the ways in which the data is collected.

18. Social-conflict and feminist research begin with quite different assumptions from positivist sociology. They reject the ideal of objectivity and attempt to uncover the effects of capitalism and patriarchy in the everyday lives of men and women.

19 Interpretive research is nether objective nor replicable; it seeks rich, thick description rather than quantitative analysis of relationships.

20. Theory and research are closely linked. Deductive thought transforms general ideas into specific hypotheses suitable for testing. Inductive thought organizes specific observations into general ideas. Most sociological investigation makes use of both types of logical thought.

Key Concepts

cause and effect a relationship between two variables in which change in one (the independent variable) causes change in another (the dependent variable)

concept a mental construct that represents some part of the world, inevitably in a somewhat simplified form

content analysis a methodology that involves the counting or coding of the content of written, aural, or visual materials

control the ability to neutralize the effect of one variable in order to assess the relationships among other variables

correlation a relationship between two (or more) variables

deductive logical thought reasoning that transforms general ideas into specific hypotheses suitable for scientific testing

dependent variable a variable that is changed by another (independent) variable

empirical evidence information we are able to verify with our senses

experiment a research method for investigating cause and effect under highly controlled conditions

Hawthorne effect a change in a subject's behavior caused by the awareness of being studied

hypothesis an unverified statement of a relationship between variables

independent variable a variable that causes change in another (dependent) variable

inductive logical thought reasoning that builds specific observations into general theory

interpretive research an interpretive method whose goal is to understand meanings and the way people construct meanings as they create their social worlds

interview a series of questions administered personally by a researcher to respondents

mean the arithmetic average of a series of numbers

measurement the process of determining the value of a variable in a specific case

median the value that occurs midway in a series of numbers arranged in order of magnitude or, simply, the middle case

mode the value that occurs most often in a series of numbers

objectivity the state of personal neutrality in conducting research

operationalizing a variable specifying exactly what is to be measured in assigning a value to a variable

participant observation a method in which researchers systematically observe people while joining in their routine activities

population the people who are the focus of research

positivist social science an approach that seeks to model itself on the physical sciences through criteria such as objectivity, replicability, causality, experimentation, quantification, and generalization

qualitative research inquiry based on subjective impressions

quantitative research inquiry based on the analysis of numerical data

questionnaire a series of questions presented to subjects

reliability the quality of consistent measurement

replication repetition of research by others in order to assess its accuracy

research method a strategy for systematically conducting research

sample a part of a population selected to represent the whole sciencea logical system that bases knowledge on direct, systematic observation

secondary analysis a research method in which a researcher utilizes data collected by others

spurious correlation an apparent, although false, relationship between two (or more) variables caused by some other variable

survey a research method in which subjects respond to a series of questions in a questionnaire or interview

validity the quality of measuring precisely what one intends to measure

variable concept whose value changes from case to case

Suggested Readings

The following books introduce the process of sociological investigation in terms that are easy for beginning students to understand.

Chava Frankfort-Nachmias and David Nachmias. *Research Methods in the Social Sciences*. 4th ed. New York: St. Martin's Press, 1992.

Morton M. Hunt. *Profiles of Social Research: The Scientific Study of Human Interactions*. New York: Russell Sage Foundation/Basic Books, 1986.

The first of these books is a new edition of a classic account of interviewing. The second, described at the beginning of this chapter, applies these methods to the study of women's lives on the university campus.

Robert K. Merton, Marjorie Fiske, and Patricia Kendall. *The Focused Interview: A Manual of Problems and Procedures*. 2nd ed. The Free Press, 1990.

Dorothy Holland and Margaret Eisenhart. *Educated in Romance*. Chicago: University of Chicago Press, 1990.

The first of these books analyzes a basic research strategy; the second illustrates its use in the study of an African-American community in Philadelphia.

Danny L. Jorgensen. *Participant Observation: A Methodology for Human Studies*. Newbury Park, CA: Sage, 1989.

Elijah Anderson. *Street Wise*. Chicago: University of Chicago Press, 1990.

These books explore the neglected issue of how gender and sexism can affect the research process.

Tony Larry Whitehead and Mary Ellen Conaway, eds. *Self, Sex, and Gender in Cross-Cultural Fieldwork*. Urbana, IL: University of Illinois Press, 1986.

Margrit Eichler. *Nonsexist Research Methods: A Practical Guide*. Winchester, MA: Unwin Hyman, 1988.

"Focus groups"—small groups that interact intensively in an attempt to answer some basic questions—are widely used in industry. This book details the operation of focus groups, including how to recruit members, how to conduct group discussions, and how to analyze data.

Davis W. Stewart and Prem N. Shamdasani. *Focus Groups: Theory and Practice*. Newbury Park, CA: Sage, 1990.

All researchers need to develop skills to communicate their findings to others in a comprehensive and interesting way.

These two books (the second aimed at more advanced writers) can help you to do just that.

> The Sociology Writing Group. *A Guide to Writing Sociology Papers.* New York: St. Martin's Press, 1986.
>
> Howard S. Becker, with a chapter by Pamela Richards. *Writing for Social Scientists: How to Start and Finish Your Thesis, Book, or Article.* Chicago: University of Chicago Press, 1986.

Written by a former Gallup organization official, this short book explores the role of polls in American politics.

> Irving Crespi. *Public Opinion, Polls, and Democracy.* Boulder, CO: Westview Press, 1989.

Sociologists continue to debate the links among research, politics, and personal values. The first book listed below is one of the best efforts to explore this controversy-filled area. The second is a recent history of the discipline suggesting that particular social values and priorities deeply influenced the work of pioneering sociologists.

> Alvin W. Gouldner. *The Coming Crisis of Western Sociology.* New York: Avon Books, 1970.
>
> Arthur J. Vidich and Stanford M. Lyman. *American Sociology: Worldly Rejections of Religion and Their Directions.* New Haven, CT: Yale University Press, 1985.

For a discussion of historical methods in sociology see the following.

> P. Abrams. *Historical Sociology.* Shepton Mallet, Somerset: Open Book Publishers, 1982.

For an eclectic, fun overview of perspectives and their methods see the following.

> Howard Boughey. *Insights of Sociology: An Introduction.* Boston: Allyn and Bacon, 1978.

The following books and articles either discuss or illustrate alternative methods of sociological research.

> Harold Garfinkel. *Studies in Ethnomethodology.* Englewood Cliffs, NJ: Prentice-Hall, 1967.
>
> Erving Goffman. *The Presentation of Self in Everyday Life.* Garden City, NJ: Doubleday, 1959.
>
> A Hochschild. *The Managed Heart.* California: University of California Press, 1983.
>
> Elliott Leyton. *Hunting Humans: The Rise of the Modern Multiple Murder.* Toronto: McClelland & Stewart, 1986.
>
> Dorothy Smith. "The Social Construction of Documentary Reality." *Sociological Inquiry,* 44.4:257–68, 1974.
>
> Dorothy Smith. *The Everyday World as Problematic: A Feminist Sociology.* Toronto: University of Toronto Press, 1987.

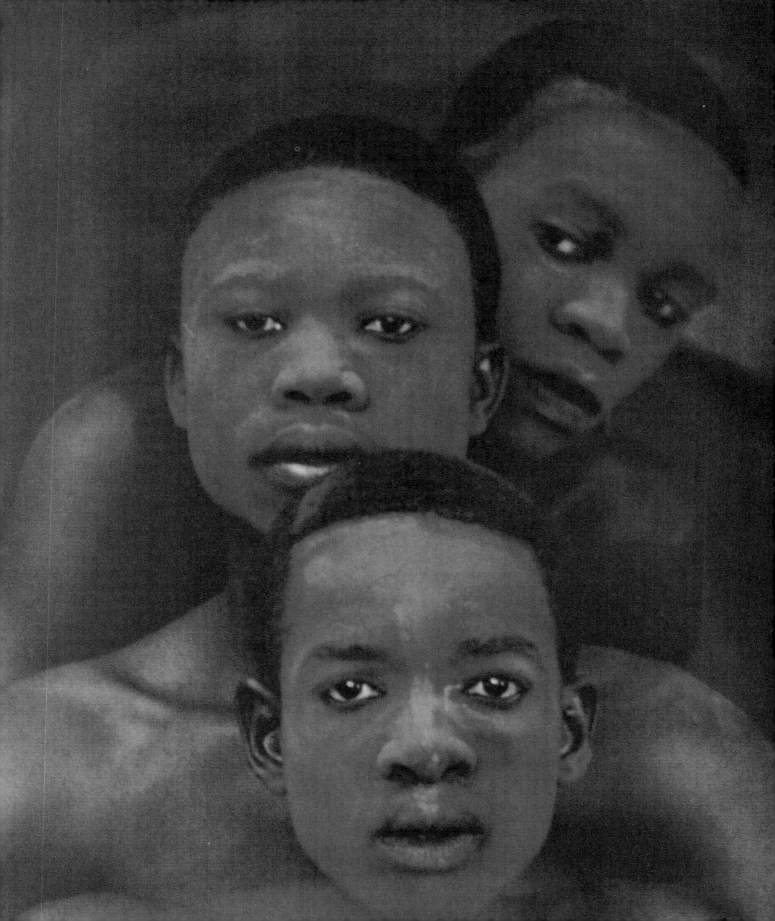

CHAPTER 3

CULTURE

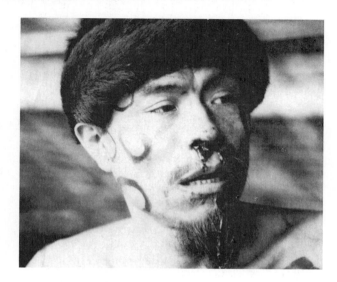

A small aluminum motorboat chugged steadily along the muddy Orinoco River, deep within South America's vast tropical rainforest. Anthropologist Napoleon Chagnon was nearing the end of a three-day journey to the home territory of the Yąnomamö, one of the most technologically primitive societies remaining on earth.

Some twelve thousand Yąnomamö live in villages scattered along the border of Venezuela and Brazil. Their way of life could hardly be more different from our own. The Yąnomamö wear little clothing, and live without electricity, automobiles, or other conveniences people in Canada take for granted. Their traditional weapons, used for hunting and warfare, are the bow and arrow. They have had little contact with the outside world. Thus Chagnon would be as strange to them as they would be to him.

By two o'clock in the afternoon, Chagnon had almost reached his destination. The hot sun made the humid air almost unbearable. The anthropologist's clothes were soaked with perspiration; his face and hands were swollen from the bites of innumerable gnats that swarmed around him. But he hardly noticed, so preoccupied was he with the fact that in just a few moments he would be face to face with people unlike any he had ever known.

Chagnon's heart pounded as the boat slid onto the riverbank near a Yąnomamö village. Sounds of activity came from nearby. Chagnon and his guide climbed from the boat and walked toward the village, stooping as they pushed their way through the dense undergrowth. Chagnon describes what happened next:

I looked up and gasped when I saw a dozen burly, naked, sweaty, hideous men staring at us down the shafts of their drawn arrows! Immense wads of green tobacco were stuck between their lower teeth and lips making them look even more hideous, and strands of dark green slime dripped or hung from their nostrils—strands so long that they clung to their [chests] or drizzled down their chins.

My next discovery was that there were a dozen or so vicious, underfed dogs snapping at my legs, circling me as if I were to be their next meal. I just stood there holding my notebook, helpless and pathetic. Then the stench of the decaying vegetation and filth hit me and I almost got sick. I was horrified. What kind of welcome was this for the person who came here to live with you and learn your way of life, to become friends with you? (1983:10)

Fortunately for Chagnon, the Yąnomamö villagers recognized his guide and lowered their weapons.

Reassured that he would at least survive the afternoon, Chagnon was still shaken by his inability to make any sense of the people surrounding him. And this was to be his home for a year and a half! He wondered why he had forsaken physics to study human culture in the first place.

The 5 billion people living on the earth are members of but one biological species: *Homo sapiens*. Even so, any of us can be overwhelmed by how dissimilar we are from one another, differences not of biology but of culture. Entering the world of the Yanomamö, Chagnon experienced a severe case of **culture shock**: *personal disorientation that accompanies exposure to an unfamiliar way of life*. Like most of us, Chagnon had been raised to keep his clothes on, even in hot weather, and to use a handkerchief when his nose was running—especially in front of others. The Yanomamö clearly had other ideas about how to live. The nudity that embarrassed Chagnon was customary to them. The green slime hanging from their nostrils was caused by inhaling a hallucinogenic drug, a practice common among friends. The "stench" that made Chagnon recoil in disgust no doubt smelled like "Home Sweet Home" to the inhabitants of that Yanomamö village.

Human beings the world over have very different ideas about what is pleasant and repulsive, polite and rude, true and false, right and wrong. This capacity for startling difference is a wonder of our species: the expression of human culture.

What Is Culture?

Culture is defined as *the beliefs, values, behavior, and material objects shared by a particular people*. But culture involves more than simply adding up all the ways people act and think, and assessing the sum of their possessions (Soyinka, 1991). Culture melds past and present, synthesizing achievement and aspiration. In short, culture comprises a complete social heritage.

To begin, however, we must divide culture into its components. Sociologists distinguish between **nonmaterial culture**, *the intangible creations of human society* (ideas ranging from altruism to zen), and **material culture**, *the tangible products of human society* (objects ranging from armaments to zippers). The terms *culture* and *society* are sometimes used interchangeably, but their precise meanings are different. Culture refers to a shared way of life. Society, the topic of the next chapter, is the organized interaction among people within a geographical or political boundary, which is guided by culture. Neither society nor culture could exist without the other.

In everyday life the way we dress, when and what we eat, where we work, and how we spend our free time are all grounded in culture. Our culture leads us to sleep in houses of wood and brick, while people of other cultures live in huts fashioned from brush, igloos of ice, or tepees made of animal skins. In addition, culture frames the meanings we attach to our lives, indicating standards of success, beauty, and goodness, as well as reverence for a divine power, the forces of nature, or long-dead ancestors. Culture also shapes our personalities—what we commonly (yet inaccurately) describe as "human nature." The Yanomamö, who are fierce and warlike, strive to develop these "natural" qualities in their children. The Tasaday of the Philippines, by contrast, are so peace-loving that there is no word in their language for violence. The cultures of North America and Japan stress achievement and hard work; but Americans value competition and individualism, while the Japanese emphasize cooperation and self-denying obedience to authority. In short, culture is a blueprint for virtually every dimension of our lives, from the might of enormous corporations to the meaning of a shy smile.

Sociologists, then, use the concept of culture more broadly than others do. In everyday conversation, "culture" usually refers to sophisticated art forms such as classical literature, music, dance, and painting. As used here, however, the term refers to *everything* that is part of a people's way of life—from Motown to Mozart, fish sticks to fine cuisine, ping pong to polo.

No cultural element is inherently "natural" to humanity, although most people around the world view their particular way of life that way. What sets humans apart from other species is the capacity to create culture, which we learn as members of a society. And although culture is transmitted from generation to generation, specific elements of culture are all subject to change.

Every other living species—from ants to antelopes—behaves in uniform ways. To a world traveler, the enormous diversity of human life stands out in contrast to the behavior of, say, cats, which is the same everywhere. Most living creatures respond to biological forces we call *instincts*, strategies for their survival that change only over long periods of time. A few animals—notably chimpanzees and related primates—have the capacity for basic elements of culture, as researchers have noted by observing them use tools and teach simple skills to their offspring. But the creative power of humans far exceeds that of any other form of life, so that *only people rely on culture rather* *than instinct to ensure the survival of their kind* (Harris, 1987).

To understand how this came to be, we must briefly review the history of our species on the earth.

A global perspective reveals that human beings create remarkably diverse ways of life. Such differences begin with outward appearance: contrast the women shown here from Iran, Kenya, New Guinea, and Egypt, and the men from Taiwan (Republic of China), Peru, India, and New Guinea. Less obvious, but of even greater importance, are internal differences, since culture also shapes our goals in life, our sense of justice, and even our inner-most personal feelings.

Culture and Human Intelligence

In a universe perhaps 15 billion years old, our planet is a relatively young 4.5 billion years of age, and the human species is a wide-eyed infant of only 40,000. Not for a billion years after the earth was formed did the first life forms appear. Far later on—some 65 million years ago—our history took a crucial turn with the appearance of the mammals we call primates.

Primates evolved into highly intelligent life forms, with the largest brains relative to body size of all living creatures. Further change occurred as the human line diverged from that of our closest relatives, the great apes, about 12 million years ago. Our common lineage shows through, however, in traits that the human species shares with today's chimpanzees, gorillas, and orangutans: great sociability, affectionate and long-lasting bonds for child rearing and mutual protection, the ability to walk upright (normal in humans, less common among other primates), and hands that manipulate objects with great precision.

Studying fossil records, scientists conclude that the first creatures with clearly human characteristics lived about 2 million years ago. These distant ancestors, with their limited mental capacity, still grasped such cultural fundamentals as the use of fire, tools, and weapons, and the creation of simple shelters. Although these "stone age" achievements seem modest, they mark the point at which our ancestors embarked on a distinct evolutionary course, making culture the primary strategy for human survival.

Consider for a moment what newcomers to the earth humans are. To make the time frame of human evolution clearer, Carl Sagan (1977) suggests superimposing the 15-billion-year history of our universe on a single calendar year. The life-giving atmosphere of our planet did not develop until the autumn, and the earliest human-like beings did not appear until December 31—the last day of the year—at 10:30 at night! Yet not until 250,000 years ago, which is mere minutes before the end of Sagan's "year," did our own species finally emerge. These *Homo sapiens* (derived from Latin meaning "thinking person") have continued to evolve so that, about 40,000 years ago, humans who looked very much like ourselves lived on the earth. With larger brains, these "modern" *Homo sapiens* produced culture at a rapid pace, as the wide range of tools and cave art from this period suggests. Still, what we call "civilization," based on permanent settlements and specialized occupations, began in the Middle East only about 12,000 years ago (Hamblin, 1973; Wenke, 1980). In terms of Sagan's "year," this cultural flowering occurred during the final *seconds* before midnight on New Year's Eve. And what of our modern, industrial way of life? Begun only 300 years ago, in Sagan's scheme, it amounts to a mere millisecond flash.

Human culture, then, is an evolutionary strategy for survival. Culture first evolved as our ancestors descended from the trees into the tall grasses of central Africa, where walking upright and hunting in organized groups had clear advantages. The human capacity to create a way of life—as opposed to simply acting

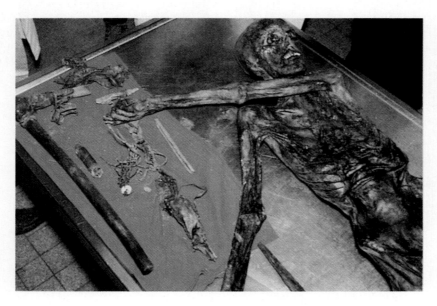

A man frozen inside a glacier for some 5,300 years was recently discovered high in the European Alps. Remarkably preserved, he provides us with evidence of the development of culture among our distant ancestors. The man was about thirty years of age—old for his time—and stood just five feet, three inches tall, reflecting a lower standard of living than we have today. This reliance on animal skins is evident in his leather jacket stitched with thongs and his leather boots, which he filled with hay to insulate his feet from the cold. The man's tools included a bow and feathered arrows, a bronze-headed ax, a knife with a stone blade, and a leather pouch which held a piece of flint to spark a fire. His concern with his appearance is suggested by a stone necklace and numerous tattoos on his body.

out biological imperatives—emerged over millions of years as the size of the human brain increased. Gradually, the biological forces we commonly call instincts were replaced by a more efficient survival scheme: humans gained the mental power *to actively fashion the natural environment for ourselves*. At this point, human nature no longer turned on instinct but on culture (Barash, 1981). Ever since, people have made and remade their worlds in countless ways, which explains today's fascinating (and, as Napoleon Chagnon's experiences show, sometimes disturbing) cultural diversity.

The Components of Culture

Although people the world over express their humanity differently, all cultures have five common components: symbols, language, values, norms, and material culture. We begin with the one that underlies the rest: symbols.

Symbols

The human world is grounded not in objects and action, but in *meaning*. In short, the surrounding environment is *symbolic*. A **symbol** is *anything that carries a particular meaning recognized by members of a culture*. A whistle, a wall of graffiti, a flashing red light, and a fist raised in the air all serve as symbols. We can see the human capacity to create and manipulate symbols in the simple act of winking the eye. In some settings this action conveys interest; in others, understanding; in still others, insult.

Symbols are the basis of culture, and the foundation of everyday reality. Generally, we become so fluent in the language of our culture's symbols that we take them for granted. Often, however, we sense their importance when symbols are used in an unconventional way. During the Meech Lake controversy, many Canadians were shocked by reports of the Quebec flag being desecrated in Brockville, Ontario, and the Canadian flag being burned in Quebec. We also recognize the power of symbols when we enter a society with an unfamiliar culture. Culture shock stems from an inability to attach meaning to our surroundings. Like Napoleon Chagnon confronting the Yanomamö, we feel lost, unsure of how to act, and sometimes frightened—a consequence of being outside the symbolic web of culture that joins individuals in meaningful social life.

Cultural variation means that an action or object with a specific meaning in one culture may have a very different significance in another. To people in North America, a baseball bat symbolizes sport and relaxation; but the Yanomamö would probably view this well-carved club with thoughts of hunting or war. A dog is a beloved household pet to millions of Canadians, but a regular meal to millions of Chinese. Likewise, the cows that are sacred to millions of Hindus in India are routinely consumed as "quarter-pounders" by hungry Canadians. Thus symbols not only bind people together but also separate people who live in the various societies of the world.

Hockey is an important ritual with symbolic significance for Canadians. For instance, the 1972 Canada/U.S.S.R hockey series galvanized the nation partly because the Soviets were seen as much more than rival sportsmen. They were also cultural interlopers, threatening the country's image of itself as the inventor and most perfect practitioner of this particular sport. The following box describes the game as it might appear to a sociologist who was completely unfamiliar with Canadian culture.

In practice, behavior that seems quite normal to us may spark offense among people of other societies. Women serving in the Gulf War recently discovered that simply wearing shorts in an Islamic society like Saudi Arabia was widely condemned as inappropriate. Countless gestures are imbued with different meanings in various cultures. Placing the thumb between the first and second fingers means good luck in Portugal or Brazil, yet it is an invitation to sex among the Germans. In Canada, we use the "A-OK" gesture made with thumb and forefinger to express approval and pleasure; in France and Belgium, however, the same symbol conveys the insulting meaning "You're worth zero" (Ekman et al., 1984). The lesson for travelers is obvious: understanding something about your cultural surroundings can save you from embarrassment—or worse.

To some degree, of course, symbolic meanings vary even within a single society. A fur coat, prized as a symbol of success by one person may represent the inhumane treatment of animals to another. Similarly, a flag that represents regional pride to one individual may symbolize centuries of oppression to someone else.

Cultural symbols also change over time. Blue jeans were introduced as sturdy and inexpensive clothing worn by people engaged in physical labor. In the liberal political climate of the 1960s, this working-class

Understanding Culture: Yekcoh Ritual Among the Snaidanac

Just when field workers think they have visited all tribal peoples and been exposed to all types of cultures, new discoveries are made of poorly understood or previously unexplored cultures. This report represents a first attempt by our research team to provide a summary of some of our initial observations about the Snaidanac culture.

What first drew the attention of our research team to this culture was the discovery of a ritualistic practice relatively unknown in other cultures. The practice primarily occurs at a particular time of the year when the ecosystem undergoes a fundamental metamorphosis which our field team has labelled "froide" conditions. For conceptual clarification, we refer to the contrasting conditions in the annual cycle as "chaude." When chaude prevails, this practice seldom occurs. However, when froide prevails, the practice reaches unusual intensity. As froide begins to encroach on chaude (a type of overlap period), the practice sometimes produces severe eruptions of boisterous behavior which are still to be fully understood. At that point, the ritual ends until a new cycle begins.

The ritualistic practice appears to have its earliest symptoms in the behavior of the young. Children are all issued a type of color-coded leather foot covering (females wear white, males wear black) which acquaints them with elementary forms of the ritual that, in contrast, primarily involves adolescents and adults. The prepubescent phase involves attaining a euphoric consciousness by propelling oneself around translucent surfaces which are diligently maintained in every village. As far as we can tell, these rectangular surfaces and their enclosed structures are a type of temple which include small cubicles for secret meetings and places for the preparation of the body (such as water purification and the administration of magical lotions). No one lives at these temples, but the devout make pilgrimages to the temple several times a week.

At an early age, the young are given an elongated wooden hammer (actually their shape is difficult to describe), and, almost as preparation for warfare, they are issued head ballasts. It at first appeared to our field personnel that the tribal group was expecting an imminent battle, but rather than use these armaments as a defense against invasion (such as warriors encountered in other cultures), much to our surprise, they use this battle gear in combat against each other.

As the young males mature (females appear to be excluded from the ritual), those who are most successful at this ritualistic type of combat become cultural heroes and are known not just in one village but in all villages. We confirm that their bravery and heroism is incredible,

aura made jeans popular among affluent students—many of whom wore them to identify with working people. A decade later, "designer jeans" emerged as fashionable "status symbols," signifying big clothing budgets, the opposite of their working-class roots. In recent years, jeans appear to be gaining favor once again, this time simply as comfortable apparel.

In sum, symbols allow people to make sense of their lives. In a world of cultural diversity, the use of symbols may cause embarrassment and even conflict, but without symbols human existence would be meaningless.

Language

Helen Keller (1880–1968) was blind and deaf from birth. Cut off from the symbolic world around her, she literally lived apart from society. Only when her teacher, Anne Mansfield Sullivan, broke through her isolation with the concept of language did Helen Keller begin to realize her human potential. This remarkable woman, who later became a renowned educator herself, recalls the moment she acquired language:

> We walked down the path to the well-house, attracted by the smell of honeysuckle with which it was covered. Someone was drawing water, and my teacher placed my hand under the spout. As the cool stream gushed over one hand, she spelled into the other the word water, first slowly, then rapidly. I stood still, my whole attention fixed upon the motions of her fingers. Suddenly I felt a misty consciousness as of something forgotten—a thrill of returning thought; and somehow the mystery of language was revealed to me. I knew then that "w-a-t-e-r" meant the wonderful cool something that was flowing over my hand. That living word awakened my soul; gave it light, hope, joy, set it free! (1903:21–24)

and many lose teeth, break their bones, or have exposed cuts on their skin as a consequence of the intensity of their flagellation against other bodies on the translucent altar. The most successful ritualist combatants are given sainthood through a lottery system that determines the combatant group to which the promising combatant will belong. These combatant groups are often given names from the naturalistic world such as part of a tree, underground liquids, bush fires or the names of animals found in their ecosystem.

The most important forms of the ritual take place in enormous temples where many people are present. Generally speaking, the rich and the privileged attend, but physical presence during the ritual is not necessarily important and others participate vicariously. In fact, rumor and gossip seems to carry the ritual to all corners of the society. At the beginning of the ritual, the unity of the culture is celebrated through a song which reaffirms the determination of its members to guard the society from external attack. The combatant-priests (or warriors) themselves seldom sing but wait for a respected deity to blow a mouth-piece signalling the commencement of the ritual in earnest. The significant part about this ritual is that it involves not only the priests of the ritual itself (as in all cultures), but also those observing the ritual. Behavioral responses vary from clapping hands or whistling to glum dejection, or even throwing objects at the combatant-priests. As in all rituals, the locals seem to leave the ritual site feeling much better. Oblations are usually available throughout the ritual for ingestion to enhance the sense of well-being.

The ritual has a rather uniform duration and occurs several times a week. However, Saturday night is the traditional ritual night, particularly for those away from the ritual center. The ritual is projected via electronic impulses (a technology which they have perfected) to boxes in dwellings and village centers where adults only are allowed. Here adults sip a brown intoxicating liquid and respond in various ways as the ritual unfolds. As the result of their dedication to this ritual, members of the society willingly give significant portions of their currency so that the ritualist performers can sustain their role as warriors and live a life of ease when away from the ritual field.

The ritual is known to exist elsewhere, but clearly is of much less importance in other societies. A careful linguistic analysis of the phonetic sounds used to describe the ritual has led us to refer to it as the Yekcoh ritual. Further comparisons of this and other rituals need to be made with other societies.

SOURCE: Adapted from Hiller, 1989: 281–282.

Language, the key to entering the world of culture, is *a system of symbols that allows members of a society to communicate with one another.* All cultures have a spoken language, although some, including the Yąnomamö, have no system of writing. Written symbols themselves are culturally variable, with societies in the Western world writing left to right, those in North Africa and Western Asia writing right to left, and people in Eastern Asia writing from top to bottom.

Global Map 3-1 shows the distribution of the world's three most widely spoken languages. Chinese is spoken by 21 percent (roughly 1 billion) of the world's people. More precisely, although all Chinese people who read and write use the same characters, they speak any of several dozen Chinese dialects, each of which is marked by distinctive pronunciation. The "official" dialect, taught in schools throughout the People's Republic of China and the Republic of Taiwan, is Mandarin (the dialect of Beijing, China's historic capital city). Cantonese (the language of Canton, which differs in sound from Mandarin roughly the way French does from Spanish) is the second most common Chinese dialect. English is the mother tongue of about 10 percent (500 million) of the world's people, and Spanish is the official language of 6 percent (300 million) of people worldwide. Notice, too, that, because of the dominance of the United States presently (and the U.K. earlier in the century) in the world order, English is steadily becoming a global language, since it is given preference as a second language in most of the world's societies.

For people throughout the world, cultural heritage is rooted in language. Thus language is the most important means of cultural transmission, the process by which one generation passes culture to the next. Just as our bodies contain the genes of our ancestors, so our everyday lives are grounded in the symbolic system of those who came before us. Through the unique power of language, we gain access to centuries of accumulated wisdom.

GLOBAL MAP 3-1   LANGUAGE IN GLOBAL PERSPECTIVE

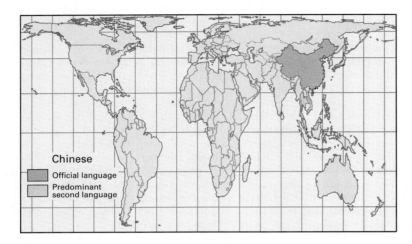

Chinese (including Mandarin, Cantonese, and dozens of other dialects) is spoken by one-fifth of the world's people, almost all of whom live in Asia.

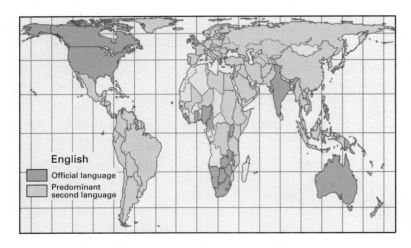

English is the mother tongue or official language in several world regions, and has become the preferred second language in most of the world.

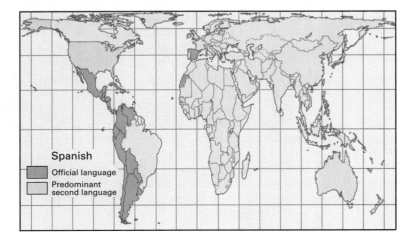

The largest concentration of Spanish speakers is in Latin America, and Spanish is the preferred second language of the United States.

Canadians are very familiar with the importance of language to culture. Although Canada is officially bilingual, in practice it is geographically unilingual, with a French-speaking majority in Quebec and northern New Brunswick, and English predominant everywhere else. The controversial Bill 101, which regulates the use of English in Quebec, and made French the only official language of the province, was an attempt to preserve the distinctive Quebecois culture. To many French-speaking Quebeckers, Bill 101 is essential to their survival as a nation; to some English-speaking Canadians, the law seems like an infringement on the rights of the minority English-speaking Quebeckers. The heated debates over language that characterize Canadian (and especially Quebec) politics are evidence of how strongly people feel about their language.

For most of human history, people have transmitted culture through speech, which is often termed the *oral cultural tradition*. Not until five thousand years ago did humanity devise writing, and even then only a few people learned to read and write. Even today, a substantial minority of Canadians are illiterate. According to a 1987 Southam survey, approximately 4.5 million Canadians cannot read or write. (Mackenzie, 1989:5). This is an almost insurmountable barrier to opportunity in a society that increasingly demands symbolic skills. Among the poorest societies of the world, four out of five people cannot use written language.

Language skills not only put us in touch with the past, they also free the human imagination. Connecting symbols in new ways, we can conceive of life other than as it is. Language—both spoken and written—distinguishes human beings as creatures aware of our limitations and ultimate mortality, yet able to dream and hope for a future better than the present.

Is Language Uniquely Human?

Of all the species of our world, are humans alone capable of speech and writing? Creatures great and small direct sounds and other physical cues to one another, and these are certainly forms of communication. But such signals are largely instinctual, so that humans stand alone with the mental capacity to create complex systems of symbols.

Still, research has shown that some animals have at least a rudimentary ability to use symbols in the process of communicating with one another and with humans. Allen and Beatrice Gardner taught a chimp named Washoe to use 160 different words of the American Sign Language. Washoe was able not only to attach words to objects but also to combine words to create new meanings. For example, when a researcher known to Washoe as Susan accidently stepped on Washoe's doll, the chimp urgently responded: "Up Susan; mine, please up; gimme baby; shoe up; please move up." Other studies have confirmed the ability of chimps to understand complex instructions (Gardner & Gardner, 1969; Premack, 1976; Harris, 1987).

Even more remarkably, under the direction of E. Sue Savage-Rumbaugh, a four-year-old pygmy chimpanzee named Kanzi not only has spontaneously created simple sentences, but has learned to react to spoken English she has not heard before. For example, Kanzi has correctly responded to requests like "Will you get a diaper for your sister?" which is a feat until now undocumented among nonhuman primates (Eckholm, 1985).

Chimpanzees lack the physical ability to form the consonant sounds made by humans. Nor have these specially trained animals been able to teach their language skills to others of their kind. But these recent achievements suggest that we should not chauvinistically assume that humans alone can lay claim to culture. With a limited symbolic capacity, some other species share, at least partly, in a world of culture.

Does Language Shape Reality?

If the Tasaday of the Philippines have no word for violence in their language, can they imagine deliberately hurting another person? Perhaps, but they cannot do so as readily as the Yąnomamö, whose language is rich with terms for fighting. Since language provides the building-blocks of reality, linguistic differences often mean that members of one culture experience the world differently from people who inhabit another symbolic world.

The names that we give to people affect our relationship to them. In an article about learning in Iqaluit at Arctic College, Jane Gyorgy (*Globe and Mail*, May 25, 1993:A22) explains something of the traditional naming practices of the Inuit.

An instructor spends a lot of time trying to explain to us the complex family relationships that bind her world. She says that each Inuit bears the name of a dead relative and actually becomes that dead person, inheriting his or her relationships as well. "I would like my mother to live in Igloolik," an Inuit uncle might say to a new mother, giving her new baby his late parent's name. So, if your daughter has your great-aunt's name, you may end up calling her

All animals are expressive. Only humans, however, confer symbolic meaning on facial gestures.

*Mother, especially if that aunt was like a mother to
you.*

*The Qallunaat—or white men—imposed a new sys-
tem on this uniquely Inuit family structure. First, it
was new first names from the church, followed by
new surnames from the government during the
1970s. Today, it's not unusual that children have
four or more names, their Inuit and Qallunaat
names. Likewise, because family names were
assigned almost at random, closely related families
may bear completely different names today. That
confuses what was, at least to Inuit, an entirely
understandable system.*

*"Do these relationships make it hard," a teacher-
classmate asks, mulling over problems in his community, "for a mother to discipline someone who is
her grandfather?" Is there somewhere in this language a better understanding of the cause and solution to the immense social problems in today's
North? Are they caused by Inuit being thrust out of
an environment in which everything was interrelated and explained, into our chaotic and vague culture
from the South? And, if we ever understand this language, will we see the North more clearly?*

Two anthropologists who specialized in linguistic
studies, Edward Sapir and Benjamin Whorf, argued
that language, rather than merely a series of labels,
stands between us and the world; words, that is, actually shape the reality we experience (Sapir, 1929, 1949;
Whorf, 1956). Sapir and Whorf challenge the common
assumption that the many human languages describe a
single reality. They remind us that every language has
words or expressions that have no precise counterpart
in other tongues. In addition, each language fuses symbols with particular emotions. Thus, as multilingual
people can attest, a single idea "feels" different if spoken in Spanish rather than in English or Chinese (Falk,
1987).

Formally, then, what is now called the
Sapir-Whorf hypothesis states that *people know the
world only in terms of their language*. Using different
symbolic systems, a Turk, a Brazilian, and a Filipino
actually experience "distinct worlds, not merely the
same world with different labels attached" (Sapir,
1949:162).

An example of how the Sapir-Whorf hypothesis
can be extended and applied to our everyday understanding of the world is found in the work of American
social critic Noam Chomsky. Chomsky demonstrates
the power of language (especially in the mass media) to
determine what people believe. For instance, he argues
that privately owned mass media reinforce and perpetuate social and economic inequities by presenting
"facts," images, and interpretations that either ignore or
rationalize such inequities (Chomsky & Herman,
1988).

The Sapir-Whorf hypothesis does not claim that
language rigidly limits human understanding. Various

senses and enormous mental capacity provide us with vast perceptive power, and human creativity further enables us to generate new symbols and to use familiar ones in new ways. Thus human inventions bring with them new symbols: the development of computers, for example, has added words and phrases like *bytes, interface,* and *E-mail* to our language. In addition, people sometimes intentionally change language. The desire for social equality in a predominantly white society led African Americans to replace the word *Negro* with the term *black* or *person of color.* A generation later, such symbolic changes have helped improve white people's perceptions of African Americans. Similarly, although adult males in English-speaking societies have long been called *men,* adult females often have been condescendingly referred to as *girls.* The recent emphasis on calling women *women* is both cause and effect of growing sexual equality. In short, a system of language generates strong *tendencies* to understand the world in a particular way, but does not *determine* how we do so.

Values

What accounts for the popularity of film characters like James Bond, Dirty Harry, Rambo, and Thelma and Louise? Each is ruggedly individualistic, suspicious of "the system," and relies primarily on personal skill and effort. Together, they suggest that North Americans celebrate an ideal of sturdy individualism, especially for men. Sociologists call such patterns **values,** *standards by which members of a culture distinguish the desirable from the undesirable, what is good from what is bad, the beautiful from the ugly* (Williams, 1970:27). Values are judgments, from the standpoint of the culture, of what ought to be. People express these broad principles in most aspects of their way of life.

Cultural values shape our personalities. We learn from families, schools, and religious organizations how to think and act according to approved principles, what personal goals are worthy, and how to properly relate to our fellow human beings.

In a society as large and diverse as Canada, of course, few cultural values are shared by everyone. Over time, people from throughout the world have entered Canada, producing a mosaic of cultural values. This contrasts with the greater cultural homogeneity of historically isolated societies such as Japan. Even so, the Canadian way of life is guided by a number of values that most people recognize and that tend to persist over time.

Australian artist Sally Swain alters a famous artist's painting to make fun of our culture's tendency to ignore the everyday lives of women. This spoof is entitled Mrs. Renoir Cleans the Oven.

Values: Inconsistency and Conflict

Cultural values are sometimes inconsistent or even outright contradictory (Lynd, 1967; Bellah et al., 1986). For example, the value that Americans place on equality of opportunity has long conflicted with the tendency to promote or degrade others because of their race, sex, or social background.

Then, too, values also change with time (or as a result of conflict), sometimes as temporary trends, sometimes as new cultural orientations. For example, some would claim that in Canada, the traditional value placed on the role of the state in caring for the less fortunate is being eroded by a new emphasis on individual responsibility.

In short, value inconsistencies and conflicts lead to strained and awkward balancing acts in how we view the world. Sometimes we try to ignore such contradictions.

CROSS-CULTURAL COMPARISON

Canadian and American Values: What Makes Us Different?

While there is no definitive list of values for any country, Sociologist Robin Williams suggests the following ten values are among the most central to the United States.

1. Equal opportunity
2. Achievement and success
3. Activity and work
4. Material comfort
5. Practicality and efficiency
6. Progress
7. Science
8. Democracy and free enterprise
9. Freedom
10. Racism and group superiority

What do you think the most important values held by Canadians are? How different would a Canadian "top ten" be from Williams' list?

What distinguishes us from our American neighbors?

Seymour Martin Lipset argues that the differences between Canadian and American values are rooted in the past. A central feature of the history of the U.S.A. was the war of independence from Great Britain. In a sense, Canada separated formally from Britain only in the 1980s with the repatriation of the Constitution. This difference is pivotal, Lipset argues, for cultural distinctions between the United States and Canada.

Canada, in his view, sits somewhere between the U.S.A. and Great Britain with respect to values. Lipset agrees with Williams that Americans place great value on freedom and individual initiative. He argues that

Canadians, on the other hand, stress conformity and obedience to the law. In the American West, outlaws such as Jesse James and Billy the Kid are lionized as heroes; in Canada it is the image of the Mountie—the policeman—that is admired.

Practically speaking, the Canadian tendency to emphasize the good of the collectivity over the good of the individual has resulted in social programs such as universal medical care. Until now, Americans have cherished the individual right to choose (and pay for) medical care as desired—with various sorts and levels of medical coverage for people with varying abilities to pay.

SOURCES: Williams (1970) and Lipset (1985).

Thus, in spite of a clearly stratified country, most Canadians believe that our society treats all people equally (Apostle, 1977). At other times, we decide to pursue one value at the expense of another, perhaps giving up an enjoyable area of university study for one that simply promises financial gains.

Values in Action: The Games People Play

Although we rarely think about cultural values, they affect every aspect of our lives. For example, children's games may seem like spontaneous fun, but they often provide important insights into what a culture defines as important.

Using the sociological perspective, James Spates (1976a) sees the familiar game King of the Mountain (also known as King of the Castle) as an expression of North American cultural values of achievement and success:[1]

---

[1] The excerpt presented here has been slightly modified on the basis of unpublished versions of the study, with the permission of the author.

In this game, the King (winner) is the one who scrambles to the top of some designated area and holds it against all challengers (losers). This is a very gratifying game from the winner's point of view, for one learns what it is like (however brief is the tenure at the top before being thrown off) to be an unequivocal success, to be unquestionably better than the entire competition. (1976a:286)

Each player endeavors to become number one at the expense of all other players. But success has its price, and King of the Mountain teaches that as well.

The King can never relax in such a pressurized position and constant vigilance is very difficult to endure, psychologically, for long. Additionally, the sole victor is likely to feel a certain alienation from others: whom can he trust? Truly, "it is lonely at the top."

Just as King of the Mountain exemplifies our cultural emphasis on winning, Tag, Keep Away, and Monkey in the Middle teach the lessons of being a loser. Spates observes that the loser in Tag, designated as "It," is singled out as unworthy of joining the group. This experience of being excluded is so difficult to bear that other players often allow themselves to be tagged just to end "It's" ordeal. All players thus learn the importance of competing successfully, as well as the dangers of not fitting in. Drawing on these sociological observations, we can better appreciate the prominence of competitive team sports in North American culture and why star athletes are often celebrated as cultural heroes.

Norms

Until recently, most women and men in Canada viewed sex as appropriate within marriage and largely for the purpose of having children. In the 1960s, however, the rules of sexual behavior changed so that sexual activity became widely redefined as a form of recreation, sometimes involving people who hardly knew each other. By the mid-1980s, the rules changed again. Amid growing fears of sexually transmitted diseases, especially the deadly acquired immune deficiency syndrome (AIDS), the "sexual revolution" came to an end, with more men and women limiting their sexual activity to one partner (McKusick et al., 1985; Smilgas, 1987).

Such patterns illustrate what sociologists call **norms**, *rules that guide behavior.* Many norms are *proscriptive,* mandating what we should *not* do. For example, health officials now warn us to avoid casual sex. *Prescriptive* norms, on the other hand, state what we *should* do. Following practices of "safe sex," for example, has become such a norm in recent years.

Norms also apply to various settings. Some rules have broad application; for example, parents expect children to obey them regardless of the setting. Other norms, however, are situation-specific. Applauding at the completion of a musical performance is expected; applauding at the end of a classroom lecture is acceptable, but rare; applauding at the completion of a sermon by a priest or rabbi would be considered rude.

Mores and Folkways

Norms vary in importance. William Graham Sumner (1959; orig. 1906), an early American sociologist, used the term **mores** (pronounced MORE-ays; the rarely used singular form is *mos*) to refer to *norms that have great moral significance.* Proscriptive mores, often called taboos, include our society's prohibition against adults having sexual relations with children. Examples of prescriptive mores are the requirements that people in

public places—from beaches to workplaces—wear sufficient clothing to conform to "standards of decency."

Because they are deemed vital to social life, mores usually apply to everyone, everywhere, all the time. For the same reason, violation of mores typically brings a swift and strong reaction from others. From early childhood, for example, Canadians learn that stealing, considered a serious wrong, will provoke a powerful response from the legal system.

Sumner used the term **folkways** to designate *norms of little moral significance.* Examples of folkways include norms guiding dress and polite behavior. Since they are viewed as less important than mores, folkways involve matters about which we allow people considerable personal discretion. Similarly, violations of folkways typically result in only mild penalties. For example, a man who does not wear a tie to a formal dinner party is violating one of the folkways we call "etiquette"; although the subject of some derisive comment, he is likely to be tolerated. However, if the man were to arrive at the dinner party wearing *only* a tie, he would be violating cultural mores and inviting far more serious sanctions.

Cultural norms, then, steer behavior by defining what is right and wrong, proper and improper. Although we sometimes bristle when others pressure us to conform, people generally embrace norms as part of the symbolic road map of culture that makes possible predictable and trustworthy interaction.

Social Control

Generally, students expect to remain quiet in class, listening attentively to the teacher and taking notes as necessary. The enthusiastic student who looks for every chance to speak is therefore courting criticism as a "nerd."

Punishments and rewards from others—termed *sanctions*—promote conformity to cultural norms. Sanctions are sometimes informal, illustrated by groans in the classroom when a student talks too much, and at times formal, ranging from grades in school to prosecution by the criminal justice system. Sanctions lie at the heart of a culture's system of **social control**: *various means by which members of society encourage conformity to cultural norms.*

After learning a wide range of cultural norms, we develop the capacity to respond critically to our own behavior. For most people, simply being aware of an act of theft gives rise to *guilt,* the discomfort that follows from a negative judgment we make of ourselves.

Both guilt and *shame*—the painful acknowledgment of the disapproval of others—stem from internalizing cultural norms, that is, building them into our own personalities. Internalizing norms was what the writer Mark Twain had in mind when he quipped that human beings "are the only animals that blush...or need to."

"Ideal and "Real" Culture

Values and norms do not describe actual behavior as much as they state how we *should* behave. Sociologists therefore distinguish between **ideal culture**, *social patterns mandated by cultural values and norms*, and **real culture**, *social patterns that actually occur*. This distinction comes to mind when we consider, for example, that most women and men acknowledge the importance of sexual fidelity in marriage although at least one-third of married people are sexually unfaithful to their spouses at some point in the marriage. Such discrepancies, common to all cultural systems, call to mind the old saying "Do as I say, not as I do."

Like all other elements of culture, norms vary over time and among different segments of the population. The cultural values and norms brought to North America by English and French settlers centuries ago continue to shape our way of life, but many current interpretations of those original norms and values would strike Sir Walter Raleigh or Madeleine de Vercheres as strange indeed. In addition, immigrants from societies throughout the world have introduced myriad cultural variations into our society, modifying our culture in ways that could never have been foreseen centuries ago.

Material Culture and Technology

In addition to intangible elements such as values and norms, every culture encompasses a wide range of tangible (from Latin meaning "touchable") human creations that sociologists term *artifacts*. The Yąnomamö gather forest materials to build huts and make hammocks. They craft bows and arrows to hunt and defend themselves, fashion tools for raising crops, and decorate their bodies with colored paints. Such examples of material culture among the Yąnomamö seem as strange to us as their language, values, and norms.

Material and nonmaterial elements of culture are closely related. The objects fashioned and used by a particular society typically express their cultural values. Because warfare is a central element of the Yąnomamö culture, they value militaristic skills and devote great care to making weapons. Poison-tipped arrows, for example, are among the Yąnomamö's most prized possessions.

In the same way, material elements of our own culture reflect the values we consider important. The cherished cultural values of privacy and autonomy come through in our society's high regard for single-family dwellings. Most Canadians aspire to owning a house for their immediate nuclear family, although fewer

Cultural patterns vary to some degree according to class position. Elites delight in the sounds of the violin, while ordinary people enjoy playing the fiddle. The two instruments are one and the same, of course, but one performance is defined as "high culture," while the other is termed "low culture," according to the social standing of the performers and the audience.

are willing to share that dwelling with aunts, uncles, cousins, or even aging parents. To other cultures, such practices would seem unnatural, even selfish.

Material culture reflects not only a society's values but also its **technology**, *the application of cultural knowledge to the task of living in a physical environment.* Technology links the world of nature and the world of culture. The Yąnomamö, with their relatively simple level of technology, intrude little on the natural environment. Keenly aware of the cycles of rainfall and the movement of animals they hunt for food, the Yąnomamö are guided by their environment. By contrast, technologically complex societies (such as those of North America) bring to bear far greater power in contending with the forces of nature, even reshaping the environment, at times, according to their own cultural values.

Because we place a high value on science and the sophisticated technology it has produced, people in Canada tend to judge cultures with simpler technology as less advanced. Some facts would support such an assessment. Life expectancy is one good measure of a society's level of well-being. Canadian females born in 1990 can expect to live almost to the age of eighty, males to about seventy-two. Napoleon Chagnon estimated the life expectancy of the Yąnomamö at only about forty years.

We must take care, however, to avoid self-serving judgments about the quality of life of people whose cultures differ from our own. Although the Yąnomamö are eager to gain modern technology (such as steel tools and shotguns), it may surprise you to learn that they are generally well fed by world standards, and are quite satisfied with their lives (Chagnon, 1983). Like other technologically simple societies, they adapt to the natural world rather than remaking it. By contrast, our culture drives a sophisticated technology with enormous impact on the environment—for better or worse. Thus, while our advanced technology has produced work-reducing devices and seemingly miraculous forms of medical treatment, it has also contributed to unhealthy levels of stress, opened threatening holes in the planet's ozone layer, and created weapons capable of destroying in a flash everything that humankind has managed to achieve throughout history.

Finally, technology is another cultural element that varies substantially within Canada. Although many of us cannot imagine life without stereos, televisions, and microwave ovens, some members of our society cannot afford such items, and others reject them on principle. The Old Order Mennonites, for example, who live in small farming communities across Waterloo County, Ontario, shun most modern conveniences. These religious beliefs may seem like a curious relic of

Standards of beauty—including how color should be used in everyday surroundings—vary significantly from one culture to another. Members of the Ndebele in South Africa lavishly paint their homes. Members of the societies of Europe and North America, by contrast, make far less use of color so that their surroundings seem subdued by comparison.

the past, yet the Mennonite communities thrive, grounded in strong families and individuals who enjoy a sense of identity and purpose.

Cultural Diversity: Many Ways of Life in One World

Between 1852 (when the government began keeping track of immigration) and 1990, more than 13 million people came to Canada from other countries (Immigrations Statistics, 1992). Early in this century, most hailed from Europe; in the 1990s, the majority will come from Asia and Latin America. This massive immigration has made Canada—far more than most nations of the world—a land of cultural diversity.

Cultural variety appears in some of the distinctive ways of life of various geographical regions of Canada: the Maritimes, Quebec, Ontario, the Prairies, the West Coast, and the North; in the rich diversity of religious life among Canadians; in a host of ethnic traditions; and among countless people who fashion their own individual lifestyles. Although sociologists sometimes speak of the "cloth of culture," we might more accurately characterize our society as a "patchwork quilt" or "mosaic." To understand our country's social patterns, then, we must move beyond dominant cultural patterns to consider cultural diversity.

Subcultures

Sociologists use the term **subculture** to refer to *cultural patterns that distinguish some segment of a society's population.* Teenagers, Native Canadians living on reserves, homeless people, and Northerners all display subcultural patterns. Occupations also foster distinctive subcultures, involving specialized ways of acting, speaking, and dressing, as anyone who has ever spent time with race-car drivers, jazz musicians, or even sociologists can attest. Rural people sometimes mock the ways of "city slickers," who in turn deride their "country cousins." Sexual orientation generates yet another subculture in our society, especially in cities like Toronto, Vancouver, Montreal, and Halifax, where relatively large numbers of gay men and women live.

Most societies encompass many ethnically based subcultures. Consider the former Yugoslavia, a small nation in southeastern Europe. The conflict that erupt-

ed in this nation at the end of the cold war was fueled by its astounding cultural diversity. This *one* small country (about the size of the Maritime provinces and with a population almost as large as Canada's) historically has made use of *two* alphabets, *three* major religions, and *four* major languages; it contained *five* major nationalities, has been divided into *six* separate republics, and absorbed cultural influences from *seven* other nations with which it shared borders. The cultural conflict that threw this nation into civil war reveals that subcultures are not only a source of pleasing variety but also of tensions and outright violence.

Multiculturalism

As well as being bilingual, Canadian society is officially **multicultural**, *a society that encourages ethnic or cultural heterogeneity.* Historically, our society downplayed cultural diversity, defining our way of life primarily in terms familiar to the English (and to a lesser degree French) immigrants who have socially dominated Canada. The legacy of this practice is a spirited debate over whether we should continue to stress French and English cultural contributions to the exclusion of those made by, for instance, the Chinese, Italian, Caribbean, Ukrainian, and East Indian peoples to this country.

For more than a century, historians have highlighted the role of descendants of the English and French, described events from their point of view, and pushed to the side the perspectives and accomplishments of other immigrants and of Native peoples. The European way of life was set up as an ideal to which all should aspire and by which all should be judged. Multiculturalists describe this singular pattern in Canada as **Eurocentrism**, *the dominance of European (particulary English) cultural patterns.* Molefi Kete Asante, a leading advocate of multiculturalism, suggests that like "the fifteenth-century Europeans who could not cease believing that the earth was the center of the universe, many today find it difficult to cease viewing European culture as the center of the social universe" (1988:7). An interesting example of the continued presence of Eurocentric ideas in Canada today was the recent widespread opposition to the decision to allow a Sikh, Baltej Singh Dhillon, to wear a Sikh turban rather than the famous traditional RCMP hat (*Calgary Herald*, 1992).

Although few deny that our culture has wide-ranging roots, multiculturalism has generated controversy because it requires us to rethink the norms and values at the core of our society. Not surprisingly, battles over how to describe our culture are now raging on many fronts.

One area of debate involves language. While Canada is officially bilingual, the Canadian population is actually composed of people with many different mother tongues. Table 3-1 gives a partial list of the mother tongues spoken in Canada. Despite the significant number of languages spoken here, minority languages are not officially recognized. This has led some critics to claim that the reality of multiculturalism is mostly symbolic. It "allows" minorities to maintain part of their cultures, perhaps during a transition phase to the dominant culture, while speaking one of the two official languages. Others point to the small minority of the population represented by each language, and claim that to accommodate all these groups would lead to an overly fractured Canadian society. To what extent should Canada encourage those who speak languages other than French or English to maintain their mother tongues? Should Canadian taxpayers support heritage language schools and courses?

An additional issue is how our schools—from the early grades through university—should teach about culture. It is among educators that the clash over multiculturalism has been most intense. Two basic positions have emerged from this discussion.

Proponents defend multiculturalism, first, as a way to capture a more accurate picture of our *past*. Proposed educational reforms seek, for example, to temper the simplistic praise directed at European explorers by realistically assessing the tragic impact of the European conquest on the Native peoples of this hemisphere. As detailed in Chapter 12 ("Race and Ethnicity"), from the point of view of the Native peoples of North America, contact with Europeans unleashed centuries of domination and death from war and disease. In addition, a multicultural approach would recognize the achievements of many women and men whose cultural backgrounds up to now have kept them on the sidelines of history. Second, proponents claim, multiculturalism is a means to come to terms with our country's even more diverse *present*. Children born in the 1990s can expect that, during their lifetimes, immigration from African, Asian, and Hispanic countries will increase significantly. Third, proponents assert that multiculturalism is a way to strengthen the academic achievement of immigrant and visible minority children and others who, from this point of view, find little personal relevance in traditional educational programs. In the U.S.A. to counter pervasive Eurocentrism, some multiculturalists are calling for **Afrocentrism**, *the dominance of African cultural patterns*, which they see as a corrective for centuries of minimizing or altogether ignoring the cultural achievements of African societies. Fourth and finally, proponents see multiculturalism as worthwhile preparation for all people in Canada to live in a world that is increasingly interdependent. As various chapters of this book explain, social patterns in this country are becoming more closely linked to issues and events elsewhere in the world. Multiculturalism undermines nationalistic prejudices by pointing out global connectedness.

Although multiculturalism has found widespread favor in the last several years, it has provoked its share of criticism as well. The argument most commonly voiced by opponents of multiculturalism is that any society remains cohesive only to the extent that its cultural patterns are widely shared. Multiculturalism, say critics, fuels the "politics of difference," encouraging divisiveness as individuals identify with only their own category rather than with the nation as a whole. Opponents also charge that multiculturalism erodes the claim to common truth by maintaining that ideas should be evaluated according to the race (and sex) of

TABLE 3-1   LANGUAGES SPOKEN IN CANADA

Mother Tongue	Percent of Population
English	63.1
French	24.3
Italian	1.8
German	1.7
Chinese	1.0
Ukrainian	0.8
Portuguese	0.6
Dutch	0.5
Polish	0.5
Greek	0.4
Spanish	0.3
Indo-Pakistani	n.a.
Yugoslav	n.a.
Native Indian	0.3
Hungarian	0.3
Vietnamese	0.2
Arabic	0.2
Finnish	0.1
Russian	0.1
Yiddish	0.1
Czech	0.1
Danish	0.1
Inuktituk	0.1
Japanese	0.1
Armenian	0.1
Norwegian	0.1
Swedish	n.a.

SOURCE: J.R.Colombo, The Canadian Global Almanac: A Book of Facts. *Toronto: MacMillan Canada, 1992, p. 72.*

those who present them. Are we to conclude that there is no common humanity, in other words, but only an "African experience," a "European experience," and so on? Second, critics are skeptical that multiculturalism actually benefits minorities as proponents say it does. First, the critics argue, multiculturalism seems to demand precisely the kind of racial segregation that we claim to deplore. Furthermore, a heritage-centered curriculum may well deny children a wide range of important knowledge and skills by forcing them to study from a single point of view.

Is there any common ground in this debate? Although sharp disagreements exist, the answer is yes. Virtually everyone agrees that all people in Canada need to gain greater appreciation of the extent of our cultural diversity. Further, because people of color are an increasingly large minority of the population, efforts in this direction are needed now. But precisely where the balance is to be struck is likely to remain a divisive issue for some time to come.

Countercultures

Cultural diversity in a society sometimes takes the form of active opposition to at least some widely shared cultural elements. **Counterculture** refers to *social patterns that strongly oppose popular culture.*

People who embrace a counterculture typically challenge the morality of the majority; when the defiance gains public attention, the majority may respond swiftly and strongly to repress what is perceived as a threat.

In many societies, youths form countercultures (Spates, 1976b, 1982, 1983). Most of us are familiar with the youth-oriented countercultures of the 1960s that attracted considerable media coverage. The hippies criticized the cultural mainstream as overly competitive, self-centered, and materialistic. Instead, they favored a cooperative lifestyle in which "being" took precedence over "doing," and the capacity for personal growth—or "expanded consciousness"—was prized over material possessions like homes and cars. Such differences led many hippies to "drop out" of the larger society, establishing new cultural centers like the Haight-Ashbury district of San Francisco, perhaps the best-known hippie community in the world.

During the same period, an array of political countercultures took root in opposition to the so-called "military-industrial complex" and particularly American involvement in the war in Vietnam. Political organizations such as Students for a Democratic Society (SDS) organized protest marches, while more radical groups carried out sporadic acts of violence against targets that to them exemplified the unjust and militaristic way of life in the United States. Thousands of draft

Conventional history has portrayed European expeditions to the so-called "New World" as sober efforts to bring religion and civilization to the child-like inhabitants of these societies. This message has long been a theme in European art, suggested here by a painting of the landfall of Columbus. More recently, historians have presented a more accurate view of events, explaining that the "explorers" were actually conquerors often intent on destroying existing civilizations in pursuit of wealth. The painting on the right suggests that the "discovery" of the Americas was more a pitched battle, illustrated by the assault on Tenochtitlán (today's Mexico City) by Hernando Cortes and his conquistadores.

resisters, protesting the war, escaped the U.S. military and emigrated from the U.S. to Canada. Countercultures develop not only their own values and political principles, but distinctive folkways, including dress, forms of greeting, and music. To many members of 1960s countercultures, for instance, blue jeans and "ethnic" clothing symbolized their identification with the "common people" of our society. Rock and roll music flourished as a countercultural anthem with far less of the middle-class respectability it enjoys today.

Although they have diminished in prominence since the 1960s, countercultures still exist. For example, various white supremacist groups with anti-Semitic, anti-Native and/or anti-non-whites views have emerged in Canada and elsewhere under names such as the Heritage Front, the Exalted Cyclops, the Church of Jesus and Christian-Aryan Nations (The *Halifax Chronicle Herald*, Sat. Feb. 29, 1992).

Cultural Change

The Greek philosopher Aristotle asserted that "There is nothing permanent except change." Caught up in day-to-day concerns, we may not notice changes because we are busy living our lives, not observing them. But cultural change happens continuously, even though it may only be evident over a period of years. Consider, for example, some recent changes in family life. As more and more women have joined the labor force, many are delaying marriage and children, or remaining single and having children all the same. The divorce rate in 1940 was 0.21 per 1,000 population; it now stands at 2.94 per 1,000 population—a considerable increase. And over the last generation, the number of single-parent households has increased rapidly. Many children now live with only one parent before they reach the age of eighteen.

Change in one part of a society's culture usually sparks other transformations as well. As noted earlier, for instance, women's rising participation in the labor force is linked to changing patterns of marriage. Such connections illustrate the principle of **cultural integration**, *the assertion that various parts of a cultural system are linked together.* Some parts of a cultural system, however, typically change more quickly than others. William Ogburn (1964) observed that technology moves quickly, generating new elements of material culture (like "test-tube babies") and outpacing nonmaterial culture (such as ideas about parenthood). Ogburn called this inconsistency **cultural lag**, *disrup-*

tion in a cultural system resulting from the unequal rates at which different cultural elements change. In a culture with the technical ability to allow one woman to give birth to a child by using another woman's egg, which has been fertilized in a laboratory with the sperm of a total stranger, how are we to apply the traditional terms motherhood and fatherhood?

There are three ways that such cultural changes are set in motion. The first is *invention*, the process of creating new cultural elements like video games, political parties, or polio vaccines. Consider the telephone (1876), the airplane (1903), and the aerosol spray can (1941)—all inventions that have had a tremendous impact on our culture. The process of invention goes on constantly, as indicated by the numerous applications received by the Canadian Patent Office each year.

Discovery, a second cause of cultural change, involves recognizing and understanding something already in existence—from a distant star, to the foods of another culture, to the muscle power of women. Discovery often results from scientific research; many medical breakthroughs occur this way. Yet discovery can also happen quite by accident, as when Marie Curie unintentionally left a rock on a piece of photographic paper in 1898 and thus discovered radium.

The third cause of cultural change is *diffusion*, the spread of cultural traits from one society to another. Missionaries and anthropologists like Napoleon Chagnon have introduced many cultural elements to the Yanomamö. Cultural elements from North America have likewise spread throughout the world: jazz music, with its roots deep in the culture of African Americans; computers, first built in the mid-1940s in a Philadelphia laboratory; insulin, discovered by Banting and Best in the 1920s at the University of Toronto; and the telephone, conceived by Alexander Graham Bell in Brantford, Ontario, in 1874.

Diffusion works the other way as well, so that much of what we assume is inherently "Canadian" actually comes from other cultures. As the technology of travel and communication makes the world smaller, the rate of cultural diffusion increases as well.

Ethnocentrism and Cultural Relativity

What is your favorite beverage? Milk? Soft drinks? Coffee? All of the beverages mentioned are favored by members of our culture. If you were to ask the same question of the Masai of eastern Africa, however, their answer might well be "Blood!". To us, of course, the idea of drinking blood is revolting, if not downright unnatural. But we should keep in mind that milk (which we all know is more healthful than soft drinks or coffee) is actually detested by billions of people in the world, including the Chinese (Harris, 1985).

As Global Map 3-2 suggests, people everywhere place their society at the center of the world. Since we all favor our own way of life, how do we respond to other people's social patterns when they offend our own ideas of what is proper? Even Napoleon Chagnon, trained as an anthropologist to have an open mind, recoiled with disgust at the "naked, sweaty, and hideous" Yanomamö. Later, Chagnon encountered several cultural practices that, from his point of view, seemed outrageous. For example, Yanomamö men share their wives sexually with younger brothers or friends. From the point of view of Yanomamö men, this practice symbolizes friendship and generosity. By our cultural standards, however, this behavior smacks of moral perversity and gross unfairness to women.

Common to people throughout the world is **ethnocentrism**, *the practice of judging another culture using the standards of one's own culture.* Inevitably, ethnocentrism creeps into our perceptions of other cultures because our understanding of the world is so closely tied to our own particular way of life. Why, for example, have Canadians traditionally referred to the area of the world dominated by China as the "Far East"? Such a term would have little meaning to the Chinese; "Far East" is an ethnocentric expression for an area that is far east of *Europe.* For their part, the Chinese use a character to designate their nation that is translated as "the middle kingdom," suggesting that they, too, see their society as the center of the world.

Societies promote some measure of ethnocentrism to enhance morale and solidarity among their members. But judging the cultural practices of others without understanding their cultural context yields not only a self-serving but a distorted view of other ways of life. The casual observer who puzzles at an Old Order Mennonite farmer tilling hundreds of acres with a team of horses rather than a tractor needs to understand the central role of hard work in the Mennonite way of life. Using tractors would violate their basic religious beliefs about living simply and, thus, even negate their very reasons for choosing farming as a way of life. From their point of view, in short, tractors would be their undoing.

An alternative to ethnocentrism is **cultural relativism**, *the practice of judging a culture by its own standards.* Cultural relativism is difficult because it requires not only understanding the values and norms of another society, but also suspending cultural standards we have known all our lives. Still, the effort is worth making for reasons of goodwill or self-interest. As the people of the world come into increasing contact with one another, the need to fully understand other cultures grows as well.

In the ever-expanding global economy, for example, international business is learning that success depends on cultural sophistication. When Coors first translated its slogan "get loose with Coors" into Spanish, would-be customers were startled to read "get the runs with Coors." Similarly, Kentucky Fried Chicken discovered that the Chinese thought that "licking one's fingers" made food seem anything but appealing. And Coca-Cola's early attempts to entice the Japanese to buy their soft drink involved a translation of "Coke adds life" that was read as "Coke brings your ancestors back from the dead," with results that are easy to imagine (Westerman, 1989:32).

Cultural sophistication underlies successful business ventures as well as a peaceful world order. But cultural relativity can also raise problems. Virtually every kind of behavior is found somewhere in a culturally diverse world, yet does that mean that anything and everything has equal claim to being morally right? What about Yanomamö men who routinely offer their wives to others, and react violently to women who allegedly commit some social impropriety? Sometimes, Chagnon reports, this goes as far as men shooting women with arrows or otherwise mutilating them. Even in the unlikely event that Yanomamö women accept this sort of treatment, should we adopt the culturally relative view that such practices are morally right simply because the Yanomamö themselves accept them?

As members of one human species, we might assume there would be some universal standards of proper conduct for people everywhere. But what are they? How can we avoid applying our own standards of fair play to everyone else? Sociologists have reached no consensus on this question, yet in a world in which societies confront each other amid ever-present problems such as hunger and war, this issue deserves careful thought.

The tension between ethnocentrism and cultural relativism often poses difficult problems for those who venture abroad. The box on pages 88–89 looks more closely at "the traveler's dilemma."

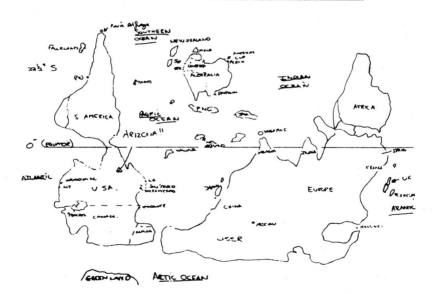

GLOBAL MAP 3-2 ETHNOCENTRIC IMAGES OF THE WORLD

One element of culture is how a person conceives of the world. The Eurocentric map, which places Europe in the center, is common in many parts of the world, reflecting Great Britain's historical dominance of the seas. Traditionally, European sea-farers measured their east-west location using as a standard the zero meridian of longitude, which runs north and south through Greenwich (near London). The first of the maps above, drawn by a young student in India, is Eurocentric. The second map, typical of students in Australia, presents a contrasting case. Here what we in North America might call "the Far East" is placed in the center of the map; moreover, the world is drawn from the point of view of being "down under."

In outdoor markets throughout the southern region of the People's Republic of China, dogs are a prized food. To a North American observer, selecting a puppy for dinner may seem cruel and unnatural. From the Chinese point of view, however, our common practice of drinking milk provokes disgust.

Theoretical Analysis of Culture

Culture allows us to understand ourselves and the world around us. Sociologists and anthropologists, however, have the special task of understanding culture. To understand something this complex requires several theoretical approaches.

Structural-Functional Analysis

Recall from Chapter 1 ("The Sociological Perspective") that structural-functional analysis sees society as a relatively stable system of integrated parts devised to meet human needs. Thus various cultural traits each help to maintain the overall operation of society.

The stability of cultural systems is rooted in core values (Parsons, 1964; Williams, 1970). In this way, structural-functionalism draws on the philosophical doctrine of *idealism*, the assertion that ideas (rather than, say, patterns of material production) are the basis of human reality. Expressed in a wide range of everyday activities, core values serve to bind all members of a society together.

Using a structural-functional approach, let us reconsider the Old Order Mennonite farmer plowing hundreds of acres with a team of horses. Within the Old Order Mennonite cultural system, rejecting tractors, automobiles, and electricity makes sense because it ensures that there is plenty of hard work. Continuous labor—usually outside the home for men and inside for women—functions to maintain the Old Order Mennonite value of discipline, which shapes their way of life. Long days of work, along with meals and recreation at home, define Old Order Mennonite culture and bind family members together. Their rejection of modern technology also has the function of making them self-sufficient (Fretz, 1989).

Of course, cultural traits have both functional and dysfunctional consequences. The Old Order Mennonite trait of "shunning," by which people cease social contact with anyone judged to have violated Mennonite mores, generates conformity but also provokes tension and, at the extreme, can cause a serious rift in the community.

Because cultures are strategies to meet human needs, we would expect that cultures the world over would have some elements in common since they were all devised by members of the same species. The term **cultural universals** refers to *traits found in every culture of the world.* Comparing hundreds of cultures, George Murdock (1945) found dozens of traits common to them all. One cultural universal is the family, which functions everywhere to control sexual reproduction and to oversee the care and upbringing of children. Another cultural universal, funeral rites, serves as a tellingly human response to the reality of death. Jokes, too, are found in all cultures, acting as a relatively safe means of releasing social tensions.

Critical evaluation. To its credit, the structural-functional paradigm explains culture as an organized system for meeting human needs. This approach allows researchers to grasp both cultural universals and cultural diversity. One limitation of the structural-functional paradigm, however, is its tendency to see cultural values as bridging social divisions. Often the cultural patterns favored by powerful people dominate a society, while shunting others to the margins. There is typically far more culture-based conflict in a society than structural-functional analysis suggests. Similarly, this paradigm emphasizes cultural stability, downplaying the extent of change.

Social-Conflict Analysis

The social-conflict paradigm views culture in a very different light. To social-conflict theorists, culture forms a dynamic arena of conflict generated by social inequality. This paradigm draws attention to the ways in which cultural traits serve the needs of some members of society at the expense of others.

Social-conflict analysis critically questions why certain values dominate in a society. What forces generate one set of values rather than another? Who benefits from these social arrangements? Many using this paradigm, especially sociologists influenced by Karl Marx, argue that values are shaped by a society's system of economic production. "It is not the consciousness of men that determines their existence," Marx asserted, "it is their social existence that determines their consciousness" (1977:4; orig. 1859). This shows the social-conflict paradigm's link to the philosophical doctrine of *materialism*, the assertion that how people fashion their material world (for example, a capitalist economy has a powerful effect on other dimensions of their culture. Such a materialist approach contrasts with the idealist leanings of structural-functionalism.

Social-conflict analysis, then, would suggest that the competitive and individualistic values of capitalist societies reflect their economy, and thus serve the interests of those who own factories and other productive enterprises. The culture of capitalism further teaches us to believe that the rich and powerful have more talent and discipline than others and therefore deserve

their wealth and privileges. Viewing capitalism as somehow "natural," then, leads some people to distrust efforts to lessen the economic disparity.

From a social-conflict point of view, however, strains fostered by social inequality exert continuous pressure toward change. The Native rights movement and the women's movement exemplify the drive for change supported by disadvantaged segments of the Canadian population. Both, too, have encountered opposition from defenders of the status quo.

Critical evaluation. The strength of the social-conflict paradigm lies in showing that, if cultural systems address human needs, they do so unequally. Put otherwise, this orientation holds that cultural elements "function" to maintain the dominance of some people over others. This inequity, in turn, promotes change. Because the social-conflict paradigm stresses the divisiveness of culture, however, this approach understates the ways in which cultural patterns integrate all

Funerals are often defined as a form of respect for the deceased. The social function of funerals, however, has much more to do with the living. For survivors, funerals reaffirm their sense of unity and continuity in the face of separation and disruption.

CRITICAL THINKING

"The Traveler's Dilemma": In the Night Market of Taipei

Avoiding ethno-centrism requires resisting the temptation to judge another way of life by our own standards. But this is usually easier said than done, as travelers often discover in disparate parts of the world.

Imagine, for instance, strolling through downtown Taipei, the capital city of Taiwan, the Republic of China. This island nation lies 150 miles off the shore of the Chinese mainland. Although it is a rapidly developing nation, its way of life is shaped by distinctive cultural traditions and a history of widespread poverty.

Taipei is a city frantic with activity. Streets are choked with people and motor scooters. From a Canadian point of view, drivers show little concern for pedestrians, making what seem to be intentional efforts to run

people down. The city reaches a frenzied pace after dark, when tens of thousands of people flood into the vast "night market." In thousands of outdoor stalls, just about everything is for sale. Vendors hawk familiar items such as clothing, fruits, and jewelry to the passing crowd, but also sell "snacks" like chicken feet, and, worse still, cook dogs that people in Canada think of as pets. Children with withered limbs lie on the ground, begging from the people who swarm around them.

Wandering into the night market's infamous "Snake Alley," visitors have their sensibilities pushed to the limit. For here—from the outsider's point of view, at least—cruelty and violence are elevated to the level of a sport. People are drawn to a stall by a man beckoning over a loudspeaker. At the back of the stall, several televisions "warm up" the crowd, displaying dog fights in which one animal tears another to pieces. The real show, however, begins as the master of cere-

monies displays dozens of huge, live snakes. "Who will drink the venom?" he taunts in Chinese, again in Japanese, and then in English. One or two young men—eager to display courage to their comrades—push forward. One of the snakes, raised overhead to

---

members of society. Thus we should consider both social-conflict and structural-functional insights to gain a fuller understanding of culture.

Symbolic Interaction Analysis

The symbolic interaction perspective also offers an important means of describing culture by looking at the meanings of aspects of culture (in their context and as they may be created and interpreted out of interaction). One aspect of cultural meaning that is amenable to description within this paradigm is that of illness. Nancarrow Clarke (1992) has studied the comparative "meanings" of cancer, heart disease, and AIDS in select print-based mass media. In particular she studied the disease imagery in *Time*, *Newsweek*, *Maclean's*, *Ladies Home Journal*, *Good Housekeeping*, and *Reader's Digest* (Jan. 1961–1965 and 1980–1985). Table 3-2 summarizes the results of this analysis.

The "media meanings" of these diseases may affect the experiences of people suffering from them. Although we do not have direct evidence of this, indirect evidence—the fact that people with cancer and AIDS feel stigmatized as persons, whereas those with heart disease tend not to—supports the hypothesis that there is a relationship between disease images and patients' experiences.

Critical evaluation. The strength of the symbolic interaction paradigm is its rich, detailed, and qualitative description of aspects of culture in context. However, working with this level of detail means it is impossible to generalize within this paradigm. The "meanings" found by Nancarrow Clarke, for example, may be more or less idiosyncratic to her coding and interpretations. Others may interpret the data somewhat differently, or develop different categorizations. Thus, the *reliability* of research in this

capture everyone's attention, is poked and taunted to provoke its full viciousness. Suddenly, the snake's head is punctured by a hook suspended from the ceiling and—as it continues to flash back and forth in anguish—the man tears the skin from the snake's body, handing it to members of the audience. Then, using skills learned from hundreds of such displays, the master of ceremonies squeezes venom from the body of the snake into a small glass. Paying for the prize, a spectator promptly chugs the fluid like so much whiskey as the crowd cheers. The process is repeated.

Looking away from this display, the traveler's eyes settle on a small monkey caged at the back of the stall. The observer soon stiffens as the monkey is snatched from the cage and thrust into the center of attention. "Pay to see him die!" the man shrieks. "See *real* blood now!" More cash is passed forward. One's mind whirls in disbelief. Can he mean it?

Would he really kill the monkey? Before the observer can regain wits enough to respond, the monkey is struck dead. Although a few turn and deliberately walk off, others continue to shout their approval, encouraging more of the same.

Snake Alley, an arena where cultural values collide, illustrates what might be called "the traveler's dilemma." On the one hand, ethnocentrism closes off insight and understanding by leading us to judge others quickly, simplistically, and thus unfairly. On the other hand, cultural relativism suggests that right and wrong are just a simple matter of convention so that, in the end, morality fades into the realm of arbitrary and meaningless posturing.

Is there a way to resolve "the traveler's dilemma?" Here are some guidelines. First, try to resist making judgments so that you can confront the unfamiliar with an open mind. We learn by being receptive to oth-

ers' ways of living. Second, try to imagine events from the standpoint of *them* rather than *us*. Witnessing the events of the night market, for instance, one might wonder if animals have a different significance in a society in which human poverty, hunger, and suffering are commonplace. Third, after a period of careful and critical thinking, we can and should try to make some judgment of the cultural practice. After all, a world in which everyone passively accepted their surroundings would be frightening. But, in making an evaluation, bear in mind that we can never experience the world as others do. Fourth, and finally, try to evaluate realistically our own way of life in light of others' cultural practices. Would an experience in the night market of Taipei change your view of fox hunts or boxing in Canada?

SOURCE: Based on the personal experiences of John Macionis in Taipei.

---

tradition suffers, to allow for what some would claim is greater *validity*.

Cultural Materialism

A fourth theoretical paradigm is derived from ecology, the natural science that delves into the relationship between a living organism and its environment. **Cultural materialism** (or cultural ecology), then, amounts to *a theoretical paradigm that explores the relationship of human culture to the physical environment*. This paradigm investigates how climate and the availability of food, water, and other natural resources shape cultural patterns.

Consider the case of India. This nation contends with widespread hunger and malnutrition, yet has cultural norms that prohibit the killing of cows. According to Hindu belief, cows are defined as sacred animals. To

North Americans who enjoy so much beef, this is puzzling. Why should Indians not consume beef to supplement their diet?

Investigating India's ecology, Marvin Harris (1975) concluded that the importance of cows greatly exceeds their value as a food source. Harris points out that cows cost little to raise, since they consume grasses of no interest to humans. And cows produce two valuable resources: oxen (the neutered offspring of cows) and manure. Unable to afford expensive farm machinery, Indian farmers rely on oxen to power their plows. For Indians, killing cows would be as clever as farmers in Canada destroying factories that build tractors. Furthermore, each year millions of tons of cow manure are processed into building material and burned as fuel (India has little oil, coal, or wood). To kill cows, then, would deprive Indians of homes and a source of heat. In short, there are sound ecological reasons to culturally protect the cow.

Critical evaluation.   Cultural materialism expands our understanding of culture by highlighting its interplay with the environment. This approach reveals how cultural patterns arise among human beings in response to particular natural conditions. However, this paradigm has several limitations. First, we can only rarely draw simple or direct connections between the environment and culture because cultural and physical forces interact in subtle and complex ways. Further, this approach has less application to technologically sophisticated societies that extensively manipulate the natural world.

Sociobiology

Since its origin in the nineteenth century, sociology has had a rather uneasy relationship with biology. In part, there is rivalry because the two disciplines both study human life. In addition, however, sociology played a role in challenging early biological notions about society—for example, that some categories of people were inherently "better" than others—as expressions of racism and ethnocentrism rather than legitimate science.

By the middle of this century, sociologists and anthropologists had convincingly demonstrated that culture rather than biology is the major force shaping human lives. But does this mean that biology has *nothing* to do with how we live? Providing an answer to this question is the focus of **sociobiology**, *a theoretical paradigm that studies ways in which biological forces affect human culture.* Some sociologists are skeptical about this new paradigm, but others think that it may offer useful insights into human culture.

Sociobiology and Human Evolution

The scientific view of how life developed on earth is based on the theory of evolution. In his book, *The Origin of Species*, Charles Darwin (1859) asserted that living organisms change over long periods of time as a result of the process of *natural selection*, a matter of four simple principles. First, all living things live and reproduce within a natural environment. Second, each species displays some random variability in genes, basic units of life that carry traits from one generation to the next. Darwin considered this variation as the way a species "tries out" new life patterns in a particular environment. Third, based on this variation, some organisms endure better than others. Survivors pass on their advantageous genetic variation to offspring. Fourth and

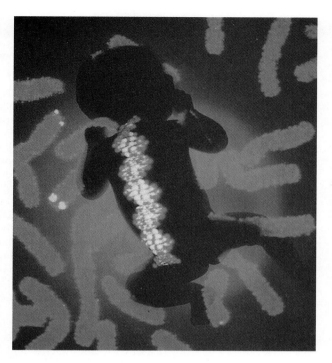

Debate continues about the role of biology in shaping human behavior. The truth is that scientists are only beginning to "map" genetic factors that guide physical development. Present evidence suggests that our biology does have some subtle influence on how individuals think and act. But in the bigger picture, our human nature demands that we create culture, and we learn this way of life through social experience.

finally, over thousands of generations the traits that promote survival and reproduction in a species grow dominant while traits that decrease the propensity for survival disappear. Naturally selected traits form the "nature" of a species, and they become pronounced as the species adapts to its environment.

Sociobiology and Human Culture

Darwin's insights revolutionized the study of biology. But in applying his ideas to human behavior a number of problems arise. Simply put, nonhuman behavior is largely regulated by encoded genetic programs so that all ants or bees, for example, behave much the same. These insects interact in complex ways and thus form "societies." But they are unable to creatively fashion their lives as humans can, making them prisoners of their own biology (Berger, 1967). Freed from biological instinct, humans thrive in diverse and changing cultures.

TABLE 3-2   SUMMARY OF MEDIA IMAGES

	Cancer	Heart Disease	AIDS
Moral Worth	Cancer is described as an evil, immoral predator.	Heart disease is described as a strong, active, painful attack.	Little is said about the nature of the disease other than it debilitates the immune system. Much is said about the moral worth of the victim of the disease.
Euphemisms	Euphemisms such as the "Big C" are used rather than the word *cancer*.	Heart disease, stroke, coronary/arterial occlusion, and all the various circulatory system diseases are usually called the *heart attack*.	Acquired immune deficiency syndrome is called AIDS. The opportunistic diseases that attack the weakened immune system often are not mentioned.
Societal View	Cancer is viewed as an enemy. Military imagery and tactics are associated.	The heart attack is described as a mechanical failure, treatable with available new technology and preventable with diet and other lifestyle changes.	AIDS is viewed as an overpowering enemy, an epidemic, a scourge.
Location of Disease	The whole self, particularly the emotional style of the person and the disease, is subject to discussion. Because the disease spreads and because the spread often is unnoticed through symptoms or medical perusal, the body itself becomes potentially suspect.	It occurs in a particular part that is indeed interchangeable with other parts located in a specific area.	Is described as affecting the immune system and resulting from mostly immoral behavior—connotes "shameful" sexual acts and drug abuse.
Optimism/Pessimism	Cancer is associated with hopelessness, fear, and death.	There is a degree of optimism about the preventability and the treatability of the disease.	Is associated with fear, panic, and hysteria because it is contagious through body fluids, primarily blood and semen.
Preventability	Prevention through early medical testing is advised.	The heart attack is described as very preventable. Recurrent specific listings of necessary lifestyle changes are often given.	Prevention through monogamous sexual behavior (or abstinence) and avoidance of unsterilized needles and drug abuse.
Causes (Specificity)	There are innumerable potential causes listed. They range from sperm to foodstuffs to the sun.	There is a specific and limited list of putative causes offered again and again.	Initially, the causes for AIDS were very general. Being homosexual, a drug user, or a Haitian was considered risky.
Causes (Sociopolitical)	There is little consideration of the sociopolitical, environmental causes.	There is little mention of sociopolitical causes.	There is little mention of sociopolitical causes.
Causes (Uncertainty)	There is uncertainty about cause.	There is uncertainty about cause.	There is uncertainty about cause.

SOURCE: Juanne Nancarrow Clarke, "Cancer, Heart Disease, and AIDS: What Do the Media Tell us About These Diseases?" Health Communication, 4(2), pp. 105–120.

But sociobiologists correctly note that the world's cultures are not nearly as different as they *could be*, as evidenced by cultural universals. In other words, because human beings all belong to a single species, people everywhere develop many of the same cultural patterns. Perhaps our common evolutionary history is somehow imprinted on the cultures we create.

Humans consume foods containing sucrose with delight, calling them "sweet." By contrast, people avoid foods that are "sour." Why? According to sociobiologist David Barash, the riddle of "sweetness" is rooted in human evolution:

> *Just as beauty is in the eye of the beholder, sweetness is in the mouth of the taster. To anteaters, ants are "sweet"; anteaters may even find sugar bitter—certainly they don't like it as much as we do. The reason is clear enough: we are primates, and some of our ancestors spent a great deal of time in trees, where they ate a great deal of fruit. Ripe fruit is more nutritious than unripe, and one thing about ripe fruit is that it contains sugars. It doesn't take much imagination to reconstruct the evolutionary sequence that selected for a strong preference among our distant ancestors for the taste that characterized ripe fruit. Genes that influenced their carriers to eat ripe fruit and reject the unripe ultimately made more copies of themselves than did those that were less discriminating.* (1981:39)

Sociobiologists extend this argument to other human behavior. Sex, for example, is certainly "sweet" to human beings, as it is to all forms of life. From a sociobiological standpoint, sex feels good because it is vital to reproducing our genes in the next generation. Further, we are all aware of what has long been called the "double standard" by which males engage in sexual activity more freely than females do. As sex researcher Alfred Kinsey put it, "Among all people everywhere in the world, the male is more likely than the female to desire sex with a variety of partners" (cited in Barash, 1981:49).

Speaking sociobiologically, nature has assigned the sexes very different roles in the reproductive process. We all know that children are the product of joining a woman's egg with a man's sperm. But these resources have a very different reproductive value. For a healthy man, sperm is a "renewable resource" produced by the testes through most of his life. A man releases hundreds of millions of sperm in a single ejaculation—technically speaking, enough "to fertilize every woman in North America" (Barash, 1981:47). A woman, however, carries from birth in her ovaries a limited allotment of follicles or immature eggs. She generally releases just one mature egg cell each month. Thus men are biologically capable of fathering thousands of offspring, while women can bear a relatively small number of children.

From a strictly biological point of view, men reproduce their genes most efficiently through a strategy of sexual promiscuity. But this strategy violates the reproductive interests of women. Each of a woman's relatively few pregnancies demands that she carry the child for the duration of the pregnancy, give birth, and perhaps nurse the child afterward. Thus, her most efficient reproductive strategy is selectively to seek a man whose own qualities (including the willingness to remain by her side after conception) will contribute to her child's survival and successful reproduction (Remoff, 1984). No one doubts that the double standard also reflects the historical domination of women by men (Barry, 1983). But sociobiology suggests that this cultural pattern, like many others, has an underlying bio-logic. Simply put, the double standard emerged worldwide because men and women benefit from different reproductive strategies.

Critical evaluation. A relative newcomer on the sociological scene, sociobiology has not yet established itself as a significant force in the field. Potentially, sociobiology offers insights about the biological roots of some cultural patterns—especially cultural universals. At present, however, it remains controversial for several reasons.

First, because so-called biological facts have historically been used (or more precisely, *mis*used) to justify oppression of one race or sex, some people suspect sociobiology of having the same agenda. Defenders respond, however, that sociobiology has no connection to the past pseudo-science of racial superiority. Quite the contrary, sociobiology stresses that humans of all cultures share but one evolutionary history, and thus have much in common.

The assertion that men are inherently superior to women also has no part in sociobiological thinking. Sociobiology does maintain that, from a biological standpoint, men and women differ in ways that no culture will ever completely eliminate—if, in fact, any culture intended to. As Barash points out, rather than asserting that males are somehow more worthy than females, this approach emphasizes that both sexes are equally vital to reproducing the human species.

A second issue raised by sociobiology's critics focuses on the lack of scientific proof for its claims. Edward O. Wilson (1975, 1978), generally considered to be the founder of this field of study, maintains that through future research sociobiologists will find clear evidence of the biological roots of human culture. Yet a generation of work by sociobiologists has yet to realize this ambitious goal. Further, it is highly doubtful that biological forces will ever be shown to *determine* human behavior in any direct sense. More likely, the value of sociobiology will lie in showing that biological forces make some cultural patterns more widely adopted than others. But even so, the biological forces Barash calls "whisperings within" definitely respond to cultural influences. The development of birth control techniques, for example, has allowed people in many cultures to separate sexual intercourse from reproduction and therefore to develop sexual attitudes very different from those that prevailed in the past.

The final value of both cultural materialism and sociobiology lies in reminding us that humans are physical creatures who create their culture in a physical environment. In this view, the forces of nature and the forces of culture are more intertwined than in opposition. Sociological and naturalist interpretations of human culture are not irreconcilable, nor inconsistent. Each provides a partial analysis of our symbolic world, and we increase our understanding by drawing on them both.

Culture and Human Freedom

We have introduced the elements of human culture, considered culture's complexity, and examined several approaches to cultural analysis. Now we turn to how culture affects the individual. Does culture enhance or inhibit our capacity to think critically and to make choices?

Culture as Constraint

Over the long course of human evolution, culture became our strategy for survival. But though we can hardly live without it, culture does have some negative consequences. By experiencing the world through sym-

Although culture is the key to realizing our human potential, we sometimes experience our way of life as threatening and overwhelming. In this pencil sketch from World War II, Alex Colville portrays the despair and exhaustion of a German prisoner of war.

bols and meaning, we become detached, susceptible to the experience of alienation unknown to other life forms. Further, established cultural systems sometimes impose a form of social inertia on our lives, driving us to relive troubling patterns from the past. Extensive social inequality is supported by Canadian culture, for example, by which some enjoy great privilege while others struggle simply to get by. Women of all social classes have often felt powerless in the face of cultural patterns that reflect the dominance of men.

Similarly, our cultural insistence on competitive achievement encourages us to strive for excellence, yet cultural patterns also isolate us from one another. Material comforts improve our lives in many ways, yet foster a preoccupation with objects that diverts us from the security and satisfaction of close relationships or strong religious faith. Our emphasis on personal freedom affords us privacy and autonomy, yet our culture often denies us the support of a human community in which to share the problems of life (Slater, 1976; Bellah et al., 1986). Thus while culture is as vital to humans as biological instinct is to other forms of life, it poses special problems for us.

Culture as Freedom

Human beings may appear to be prisoners of culture, just as other animals are prisoners of biology.

But careful thought about the ideas presented in this chapter suggests a crucial difference. Over millions of years of human evolution, the unfolding of culture gradually took our species from a world shaped largely by biology to a world we shape for ourselves.

Therefore, although culture seems at times to circumscribe our lives, it embodies the human capacity for hope and creative choice. The evidence that supports this conclusion lies all around us. Fascinating cultural diversity exists in our own society, and even greater variety is found around the world. Furthermore, far from being static, culture is ever-changing. And although it sometimes functions as a constraint, culture also presents a continuous source of human opportunity. The more we discover about the operation of our culture, the greater our ability to use the freedom it offers us.

Summary

1. Culture refers to patterned ways of human life. Although several species have simple forms of culture, only human beings rely on culture for survival.

2. Culture emerged over the long course of human evolution as the brain gradually enlarged. Basic elements of culture appeared some 2 million years ago; the complex culture that we call civilization emerged during the last 12,000 years.

3. Through symbols, which are the basis of culture, we attach meaning to objects and action. Language is the symbolic means with which we transmit culture from generation to generation.

4. Values are cultural elements that shape our orientation to the world around us.

5. Cultural norms guide human behavior. Mores consist of norms of great moral significance; folkways are norms of lesser moral significance in which greater individual discretion is allowed.

6. Values and norms are expressions of ideal culture; in practice, real culture varies considerably from these standards.

7. Material creations reflect cultural values as well as a society's technology.

8. Culture involves not only common patterns but social diversity. Subcultures are distinctive cultural forms that characterize a segment of society; countercultures are strongly at odds with widely accepted cultural patterns. Multiculturalism refers to efforts to enhance awareness and appreciation of cultural diversity.

9. Culture is never static: invention, discovery, and diffusion all generate cultural change. Not all parts of a cultural system change at the same rate, however; this produces cultural lag.

10. Having learned the standards of one culture, we often evaluate other cultures ethnocentrically. The alternative to ethnocentrism, called cultural relativism, means judging different cultures according to their own standards.

11. The structural-functional paradigm views culture as a relatively stable system built on core values. Specific cultural traits are understood in terms of their function in maintaining the entire cultural system.

12. The social-conflict paradigm envisions cultural systems as dynamic arenas of social inequality and conflict. Cultural patterns typically benefit some categories of people more than others.

13. The symbolic-interaction paradigm examines culture in terms of how we create meaning through interaction in a particular cultural context.

14. The cultural-ecology paradigm explores ways in which human culture is shaped by the natural environment.

15. Sociobiology studies the influence of humanity's evolutionary past on present patterns of culture.

16. Culture can constrain human needs and ambitions; yet as cultural creatures we have the capacity to shape and reshape the world to meet our needs and pursue our dreams.

Key Concepts

Afrocentrism   highlighting the viewpoint of people of African descent

counterculture   social patterns that strongly oppose popular culture

cultural integration   the close relationship among various parts of a cultural system

cultural lag   disruption in a cultural system resulting from the unequal rates at which different cultural elements change

cultural materialism   a theoretical paradigm that explores the relationship of human culture and the physical environment

cultural relativism   the practice of judging a culture by its own standards

cultural universals   traits found in every culture

culture   the beliefs, values, behavior, and material objects shared by a particular people

culture shock   personal disorientation that accompanies exposure to an unfamiliar way of life

ethnocentrism   the practice of judging another culture by the standards of one's own culture

Eurocentrism   the dominance of European (especially English) culture

folkways   norms that have little moral significance

ideal culture   social patterns consistent with cultural values and norms

language   a system of symbols that allows members of a society to communicate with one another

material culture   tangible elements of culture such as clothing and cities

mores   norms that have great moral significance

multiculturalism   a policy of encouraging ethnic or cultural heterogeneity

nonmaterial culture   intangible elements of culture such as values and norms

norms   rules and expectations by which a society guides the behavior of its members

real culture   actual social patterns that typically only approximate cultural values and norms

Sapir-Whorf hypothesis   the assertion that people perceive the world only in terms of the symbols provided by their language

social control   the process by which members of a society encourage conformity to cultural norms

sociobiology   a theoretical paradigm that studies ways in which biological forces affect human culture

subculture   cultural patterns that distinguish some segment of a society's population

symbol   anything that carries a particular meaning recognized by members of a culture

technology   the application of cultural knowledge to the task of living in a physical environment

values   culturally defined standards of desirability, goodness, and beauty that serve as broad guidelines for social life

Suggested Readings

Napoleon Chagnon's account of the Yąnomamö offers fascinating insights into a culture very different from our own. It is also a compelling tale of carrying out fieldwork in an unfamiliar world.

Napoleon A. Chagnon. *Yąnomamö: The Fierce People.* 3rd ed. New York: Holt, Rinehart and Winston, 1983.

Cannibalism is a practice almost impossible for Westerners to comprehend. Yet, as this book explains, this consuming passion is quite acceptable to some cultures.

Peggy Reeves Sanday. *Divine Hunger: Cannibalism as a Cultural System.* Cambridge, UK: Cambridge University Press, 1986.

This book compares the cultures of the two largest societies in North America.

Seymour Martin Lipset. *Continental Divide: The Values and Institutions of the United States and Canada.* New York: Routledge, 1990.

This book traces the development of English, and explains why it is becoming the global language.

Bill Bryson. *The Mother Tongue.* New York: William Morrow, 1990.

Marvin Harris uses the cultural-ecology paradigm to explain many puzzling cultural practices.

Marvin Harris. *Good to Eat: Riddles of Food and Culture.* New York: Simon and Schuster, 1985.

Shkilnyk's book offers a telling and touching description of the devastating effect of the state on the Grassy Narrows band in Northern Ontario. The band was forced to relocate from its reserve to a narrow strip of land, in order to facilitate the provision of some modern amenities, such as a school, electricity, improved housing, and social services.

Anastasia M. Shkilnyk. *A Poison Stronger Than Love: The Destruction of an Ojibwa Community.* New Haven, CT: Yale University Press.

The following books describe cultural, class, regional, and racial divisions within Canadian society.

S. Crean and M. Rioux. *Two Nations.* Toronto: James Lorimer, 1983.

S. Ramcharan. *Racism: Non-Whites in Canada.* Toronto: Butterworths, 1982.

P.S. Li and B.S. Bolaria., eds. *Racial Minorities in Multicultural Canada.* Toronto: Garamond Press, 1984.

Mel Watkins. *Dene Nation: The Colony Within.* Toronto: University of Toronto Press, 1977.

Pierre Vallières. *White Niggers of America.* Toronto: McClelland and Stewart, 1971.

W. Clement. *The Canadian Corporate Elite: An Analysis of Economic Power.* Toronto: McClelland and Stewart, 1975.

S.M. Crean. *Who's Afraid of Canadian Culture?* Don Mills, ON: General Publishers, 1976.

R. Mathews. *The Creation of Regional Dependancy.* Toronto: University of Toronto Press, 1983.

For a description of Canadian ideology, culture, and values, see the following.

M. Patricia Marchak. *Ideological Perspectives on Canada.* Toronto: McGraw-Hill Ryerson, 1975.

R. Breton, J.G. Reitz, and V.F. Valentine. *Cultural Boundaries and the Cohesion of Canada.* Montreal: Institute for Research in Public Policy, 1980.

G. Caldwell and E. Waddell. *The English of Quebec: From Majority to Minority Status.* Quebec: Institut québecois de recherche sur la culture, 1982.

R.J. Bryan and R.J. Sacouman. *Underdevelopment and Social Movements in Atlantic Canada.* Toronto: Hogtown Press, 1979.

For a classic Canadian community study, see the following.

D.H. Clairmont and D.W. Magill. *Africville: The Life and Death of a Black Community.* Toronto: University of Toronto Press, 1974.

SOCIETY

Space technology, while still in its infancy, has already sent astronauts to the moon, probed the clouds of Venus, mapped the craters of Mars, and carried video cameras hundreds of millions of miles to the edge of the solar system. The achievements that many people now take for granted, our ancestors surely would have found almost incomprehensible. Through most of the millennia of human history, the greatest distance people could put between themselves and the earth was the reach of a tall tree. And, until the proliferation of steam locomotives in the nineteenth century, human beings could travel no faster than about forty kilometers per hour—the speed of a swift horse. Many subsequent train travelers were terrified as locomotives reached seventy kilometers per hour, fearing that, at such speeds, the breath would be sucked from their bodies. Today, by contrast, space shuttle passengers confidently rocket from earth at speeds of 25,000 kilometers per hour and settle into an orbit almost 420 kilometers above our planet's surface.

The National Aeronautics and Space Administration (NASA), at the forefront of space exploration in the United States, recently has turned its attention from probing the universe to healing environmental damage to the earth. During the 1990s, the agency intends to launch a program called Mission to Planet Earth, in which a number of satellites will be used to investigate global warming, the loss of the earth's forests, and the spread of our planet's deserts. This effort reveals an important truth about humankind: as our species has gained technological power, we have both improved our lives and simultaneously threatened our very existence.

To understand how we have come to this point, we need to explore the changes to the nature of society wrought by technological advances. This chapter begins with an historical survey of the development of technology and its effects on societies—expanding our capabilities, changing the ways in which we organize our lives, and forcing us to confront new and unexpected problems. The chapter continues by exploring other dimensions of society—social conflict, changing patterns of human ideas, and social integration—that are both cause and effect of technological development.

The concept **society** refers to *people who interact within a limited territory and who share a culture.* This deceptively simple term will be explored from four vantage points, each of which has broadened the scope of sociology and will be used in later chapters.

Gerhard and Jean Lenski describe the changing character of human society over the last ten thousand years. Focusing on how *technology* shapes social life, their analysis shows that a technological breakthrough often has revolutionary consequences for society as a whole. The remainder of the chapter presents classic visions of society developed by three of sociology's founders. Like the Lenskis, **Karl Marx** also understood human history as a long and complex process of social change. For Marx, however, the story of society spins around *social conflict*, which results from inequality rooted in how people produce material goods. **Max Weber** recognized the importance of productive forces as well, but he sought to demonstrate the power of *human ideas* to shape society. Weber believed that modern society turns on human rationality, a world view that encourages change. Finally, **Emile Durkheim** investigated patterns of *social integration*, that is, how societies are held together. Identifying various sources of solidarity, Durkheim explored what makes modern societies distinctive.

All four visions of society address important questions: How do societies of the past and present differ from one another? How and why do societies change? What forces divide a society? What forces hold a society together? Are societies improving the human condition or making it worse? The theorists included in this chapter all investigated these questions, although they disagree on the answers. Thus, similarities and differences will be highlighted as we proceed.

Gerhard and Jean Lenski: Society and Technology

For hundreds of years, a small society called the Ona lived at the southernmost tip of South America. As they gathered vegetation and hunted game, the Ona may well have observed the Portuguese explorer Ferdinand Magellan sail in 1520 through the straits that now bear his name. Although the Ona endured for centuries with little change, the encroachment of people with more complex technology gradually reduced their land holdings. Many Ona fell victim to foreign diseases; others simply gave up the old ways. The death of the last full-blooded member of the Ona was recorded in 1975 (Lenski and Lenski, 1987:127–29).

As members of the industrialized world, accustomed to rapid transportation and global communication, we might regard the Ona merely as a curious vestige of the past. But the story of the Ona tells us much about our own past, and helps us to better understand how we live today. Gerhard and Jean Lenski, introduced in the box, have chronicled the great differences among societies that have flourished and declined throughout human history. They explain how technologically simple people like the Ona—the only type of human society until about ten thousand years ago—have now all but disappeared as the world evolves, driven by powerful industrial technology.

The Lenskis call the focus of their research **sociocultural evolution**, *the process of social change that results from gaining new cultural information, particularly technology* (Lenski, Lenski, and Nolan 1991:65). This approach draws on the biological concept of evolution to explore how societies, like living organisms, change over time as they gain greater ability to manipulate their physical environments. The Lenskis see technology as vital to defining other cultural patterns. Societies with rudimentary technology can support only a small number of people who adopt a simple way of life. Technologically complex societies—while not necessarily "better" in many respects—develop large populations engaged in highly diverse activities.

The Lenskis also explain that the amount of technological information a society has in its grasp affects the rate at which it changes. Because of their simple technology, societies like the Ona evolve very slowly. In striking contrast, highly industrialized societies, with access to much more technological information, change so quickly that people witness dramatic transformations during their lifetimes. Consider some familiar elements of North American culture that would probably puzzle, or even alarm, people who lived just a few generations ago: laser surgery, test-tube babies, genetic engineering, the threat of nuclear holocaust, computers, smart bombs, electronic surveillance, transsexualism, space shuttles, and artificial hearts (Lenski and Lenski, 1982:3).

As a society extends its technological reach, the effects ripple through the cultural system causing many more changes. A single innovation (say, harnessing the power of the wind) can be applied to many existing cultural elements (to produce windmills, kites, sailing ships, and eventually airplanes). Consider, as more recent examples, the many ways modern life has been changed by the computer or unleashing the power of the atom.

Drawing on the Lenskis' work, we will describe four general types of societies distinguished by their level of technology: hunting and gathering societies,

Gerhard Lenski and Jean Lenski

Gerhard Lenski is a contemporary American sociologist known for his research on religion, social inequality, and history. Jean Lenski, a writer

and poet, has collaborated with her husband on sociological research projects. Together, they have brought to the attention of their colleagues in the field of sociology a wide range of research on the role of technology in human societies.

The Lenskis' approach to understanding society has much in common with that of Marvin Harris, the cultural ecologist described in Chapter 3 ("Culture"). Recall that cultural ecology focuses on how specific practices help a society to survive in a particular natural environment. The Lenskis highlight the role of technology in channeling the power of a society to produce and process material resources from their surroundings.

Cultural ecology and sociocultural evolution differ, however, in one

important respect. While both emphasize that the natural environment shapes cultural patterns, the Lenskis' analysis explains why this is true of some societies more than others. With little ability to manipulate nature, technologically simple societies are influenced the most by their surroundings. Technologically sophisticated societies, by contrast, bring greater technological resources to their interaction with the physical world, even recasting nature according to their own designs. Therefore, technologically simple societies tend to resemble one another, with minor variations that reflect different natural environments. More technologically complex societies, on the other hand, reveal the striking cultural diversity described in Chapter 3.

---

horticultural and pastoral societies, agrarian societies, and industrial societies.[1]

Hunting and Gathering Societies

Hunting and gathering refers to *simple technology to hunt animals and gather vegetation.* From the emergence of our species until about ten thousand years ago, all humans were hunters and gatherers. Although hunting and gathering societies were common several centuries ago, only a few persist today including the Pygmies of central Africa, the Bushmen of southwestern Africa, the Aborigines of Australia, the Kaska Indians of the southern Yukon and northwest British Columbia, and the Tasaday of the Philippines.

Food production is inefficient at this early stage of sociocultural evolution so that the people's primary task involves searching for game and edible plants. In

harsh environments, this work goes on continually; in areas where food is plentiful, however, hunters and gatherers may enjoy considerable leisure. In any case, food production requires a large amount of land, so hunting and gathering societies are scattered at some distance from one another and are limited to several dozen people. They are also typically nomadic, moving on as they deplete vegetation in one area, or in pursuit of migratory animals. Although periodically returning to earlier sites, they rarely form permanent settlements.

Hunting and gathering societies are organized as family groups. The family obtains and distributes food, teaches necessary skills to children, and protects its members. While most activities are shared by everyone and center on seeking their next meal, some specialization occurs by age and sex. The very young and the very old are expected to contribute only what they can, while healthy adults secure most of the food. The gathering of vegetation—the more reliable food source—is typically the work of women, while men do the less certain work of hunting. Therefore, although the two sexes have somewhat different responsibilities, most hunters and gatherers probably viewed men and

---

[1] This account examines only the major types of societies described by the Lenskis.

In technologically simple societies, successful hunting wins men great praise. However, the gathering of vegetation by women is a more abundant and dependable source of nutrition.

women as having comparable social importance (Leacock, 1978).

Hunting and gathering societies have few formal leaders. Most recognize a *shaman*, or spiritual leader, who enjoys high prestige but no greater material rewards. Because of the society's limited technology, even the shaman must help procure food. Men who hunt with exceptional skills are admired, as are women who are unusually productive in gathering vegetation. But, overall, the social organization of hunters and gatherers is relatively simple and egalitarian.

Hunting and gathering societies rarely use their handcrafted weapons—the spear, the bow and arrow, and the stone knife—to wage war. Although peaceful toward each other, they are often ravaged by the forces of nature. Storms and droughts can easily destroy their food supply, and their simple skills leave them vulnerable to accident and disease. Continual risks encourage cooperative activities and sharing of food, strategies that increase everyone's odds of survival. Nonetheless, many die in childhood, and perhaps half perish before the age of twenty (Lenski, Lenski, and Nolan 1991:91).

During this century, technologically complex societies have slowly closed in on the remaining hunters and gatherers, so that these simple societies face depletion of game and vegetation. The Lenskis predict that the 1990s may well see the end of hunting and gathering societies on earth. Their plight is tragic. Fortunately, study of this way of life has already produced valuable information about human history and our fundamental ties to the natural world.

Horticultural and Pastoral Societies

Ten to twelve thousand years ago, a new technology began to change many hunting and gathering societies. **Horticulture** is a *technology based on using hand tools to cultivate plants.* The most important tools of horticulturalists are the hoe to work the soil and the digging stick to punch holes in the ground for seeds. These tools were first developed in fertile regions of the Middle East and Southeast Asia and were carried by cultural diffusion as far as Western Europe and China by about six thousand years ago. In Central and South America, the cultivation of plants emerged independently about nine thousand years ago, although horticulture was less efficient there because of the rocky soil and mountainous terrain.

Not all societies were quick to abandon hunting and gathering in favor of horticulture. Hunters and gatherers living amid plentiful vegetation and game probably had little reason to embrace the new technology (Fisher, 1979). The Yanomamö, described in Chapter 3 ("Culture"), illustrate the common practice of combining horticulture with more traditional hunting and gathering (Chagnon, 1983). Then, too, in particularly arid regions, horticulture was of relatively little value. People in such regions developed **pastoralism**, *technology that supports the domestication of animals.* Some societies combined horticulture and pastoralism to produce more varied foods. Today, many horticultural-pastoral societies are found in South America, Africa, the Middle East, and Asia.

The domestication of plants and animals transformed societies in various ways. First, producing more food enabled societies to grow, and populations climbed into the hundreds. Societies that emphasized pastoralism remained nomadic, leading their herds to fresh grazing lands. Those that adopted horticulture as their primary technology formed settlements of several hundred people, relocating only when they depleted the soil. As such settlements were joined by trade, they formed multicentered societies with overall populations often exceeding five thousand.

Domesticating plants and animals increased efficiency to the point of generating a *material surplus,* more resources than necessary to sustain day-to-day living. At this point, not everyone had to produce food, so some people could fashion crafts, engage in trade, or serve as full-time priests. In comparison to hunting and gathering societies, horticultural and pastoral societies display far more specialized and complex social arrangements.

The religious beliefs of hunters and gatherers recognize numerous spirits inhabiting the world. Horticulture, however, encourages the emergence of ancestor worship and a conception of God as Creator. Pastoral societies carry this belief further, perceiving God as directly involved in the well-being of the entire world. Both Christianity and Judaism were originally pastoral religions.

Expanding productive technology also intensifies social inequality. As some families produce more food than others, they assume positions of relative privilege and power and form alliances with other privileged

Pastoralism has historically been common in arid regions of the world where little can be grown. Pastoral people still flourish today in Northern Africa, living much as they did a thousand years ago.

families, so that social advantages persist over many generations. From the power of such elites, rudimentary government emerges. However, technology also limits this power. Without the ability to communicate or travel quickly, a ruler can control only a small number of people. Furthermore, the exercise of power often breeds opposition, and there is evidence of frequent revolts and other forms of political conflict in these societies.

The domestication of plants and animals enabled societies to become much more productive than was possible relying on hunting and gathering. But advancing technology is never entirely beneficial. The Lenskis suggest that technological progress is sometimes accompanied by ethical regression. Throughout history, greater production has paralleled a rise in social inequality, with privileged members of society less willing to share their resources. Horticulturalists and pastoralists also stand out as more warlike, just as they may engage in slavery and, in some cases, cannibalism.

Agrarian Societies

About five thousand years ago, another technological revolution surrounded **agriculture**, *the technology of large-scale farming using plows powered by animals or advanced energy*. Agrarian technology first appeared in the Middle East, and gradually diffused throughout the world. The Lenskis assert that the profound social significance of the animal-drawn plow, along with other technological innovations of the period—including irrigation, the wheel, writing, numbers, and the expanding use of metals—clearly qualifies this era as "the dawn of civilization" (1991:160).

Animal-drawn plows cultivated vast fields in contrast to the garden-sized plots worked by horticulturalists. Plows have the additional advantage of turning, and thereby aerating, the soil to increase fertility. Agrarian people can thus farm the same land for decades, encouraging permanent settlements. Large food surpluses, transported on animal-powered wagons, allowed agrarian societies to expand to unprecedented size both in terms of population and land area. As an extreme case, the Roman Empire at its height (about 100 C.E.) boasted a population of 70 million spread over some 2.8 million square kilometers (Stavrianos, 1983; Lenski, Lenski, and Nolan, 1991).

As always, greater surplus means more specialization. Tasks once performed by everyone, such as clearing land, building, and processing food, became distinct occupations. Money emerged around this time as a universal standard of value which, unlike the older barter system, could forge countless specialized activities into an expanding economy. Trade further sparked the growth of cities. Ancient Rome reached 1 million

---

S O C I A L   D I V E R S I T Y

Technology and the Changing Status of Women

In technologically simple societies of the past, women produced more food than men did. Hunters and gatherers valued meat highly, but men's hunting was not a dependable source of nourishment. Thus vegetation gathered by women was the primary means of ensuring survival. Similarly, tools and seeds used in horticulture developed under the control of women, who already had primary responsibility for providing and preparing food. With women handling the cultivation of plants for food, men typically engaged in trade and tended herds of animals. Only at harvest time did everyone pitch in and work together.

About five thousand years ago, societies discovered how to mold metals. Metal tools spread by cultural diffusion, primarily along trade networks made up of men. Thus men invented the metal plow and, since they already managed animals, soon devised the notion of hitching the device to cattle. This initiated the transition from horticulture to agriculture and thrust men for the first time into a dominant position in the production of food. Elise Boulding explains how this technological breakthrough undermined the social position of women:

The shift of the status of the woman farmer may have happened quite rapidly, once there were two male specializations relating to agriculture: plowing and the care of cattle. This situation left women with all the subsidiary tasks, including weeding and carrying water to the fields. The new fields were larger, so women had to work just as many hours as they did before, but now they worked at more secondary tasks. ... This would contribute further to the erosion of the status of women.

SOURCES: Based on Boulding (1976) and Fisher (1979).

people, and cities in modern agrarian societies such as India and Egypt are now many times that size. As population increased, social life became steadily more individualistic and impersonal.

Agrarian societies exhibit dramatic social inequality. In many cases a whole segment of the population is relegated to slavery or serfdom. Freed from the need to work, elites engage in the study of philosophy, art, and literature. This explains the historical link between "high culture" and social privilege.

In horticultural societies, women gain prestige because they produce much of the food. Agricultural technology, however, seems to have propelled men into a position of clear social dominance (Boulding, 1976; Fisher, 1979). The box looks more closely at the declining position of women at this point in the course of sociocultural evolution.

Religion plays an important role in reinforcing the power of agricultural elites. Religious doctrine typically propounds the idea that people are morally obligated to perform their tasks according to their place in the social order. Chinese emperors could mobilize their people to build the Great Wall (still the only human creation visible from space), the Forbidden City, and other massive public works only because they were defined as gods with virtually absolute power.

In agrarian societies, then, the elites gain unparalleled power. To maintain control of large empires, leaders require the services of a wide range of administrators. Along with the growing economy, then, the political system becomes established as a distinct part of society.

In relation to societies described so far, the Lenskis conclude that agrarian societies have greater internal diversity and social inequality. And unlike horticultural and pastoral societies, agrarian societies exhibit distinct characteristics from one another because advancing technology gives them increasing control over the natural world.

Industrial Societies

Industrialism, as found in Canada and much of the northern hemisphere, is *the technology that powers sophisticated machinery with advanced fuels.* Before the industrial era, the major source of energy was the muscle power of humans and other animals. At the dawning of the Industrial Revolution, about 1750, flowing water and then steam were used to power ever-larger and more efficient machinery.

Once industrial technology appeared, change increased exponentially, as shown in Figure 4-1. Industrial societies transformed themselves more in a century than they had in thousands of years before. As explained in Chapter 1 ("The Sociological Perspective"), this stunning change stimulated the birth of sociology itself. During the nineteenth century, railroads and steamships revolutionized transportation, and steel-framed skyscrapers recast the urban landscape, dwarfing the cathedrals that symbolized an age gone by.

Early in the twentieth century, automobiles further reshaped Western societies, and electricity was fast becoming a part of everyday life. Electronic communication, including the telephone, radio, and television, were gradually making a large world seem smaller and smaller. More recently, transportation technology has given humanity the capacity to fly faster than sound and even to break entirely the bonds of earth. Nuclear power, used for destruction ten years before it generated electricity, has also forever changed the world. During the last generation, computers have ushered in an "information revolution," dramatically increasing humanity's capacity to process information.

In agrarian societies, most men and women work in the home. Industrial machinery, however, led to the creation of factories, a far less personal setting for work. Lost in the process were not just close ties but

FIGURE 4-1   THE INCREASING RATE OF TECHNOLOGICAL INNOVATION
This figure illustrates the increasing rate of technological innovation in Western Europe after the beginning of the Industrial Revolution in the mid-1700s. The rate accelerates because each innovation combines with existing cultural elements to produce many further innovations.
SOURCE: Lenski, Lenski & Nolan, 1991:57

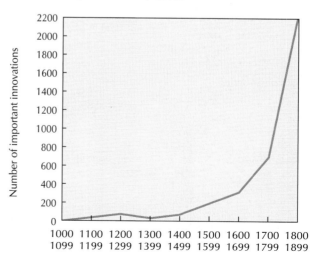

many of the traditional values, beliefs, and customs that had guided agrarian life for centuries.

Industrialism engendered societies of unparalleled prosperity. Although health in industrial cities was initially poor, a rising standard of living and advancing health-related technology gradually controlled diseases that had for centuries killed both children and adults. Consequently, life expectancy increased, fueling rapid population growth. Industrialization also concentrated the increasing population. Agrarian people were dispersed over the land, with perhaps one in ten living in cities. In industrial societies, however, a majority of the population clusters in cities.

Occupational specialization, which expanded over the long course of sociocultural evolution, has become more pronounced than ever. Industrial people often identify one another in terms of their jobs, rather than according to their family background (the common practice in technologically simple societies, where kinship is paramount). Rapid change and movement from place to place also prompt cultural diversity, leading to the emergence of numerous subcultures and countercultures, as described in Chapter 3 ("Culture").

The family, too, has been reshaped by industrial technology, with far less of its traditional significance as the center of social life. No longer does the family serve as the primary setting for economic production, learning, and religious worship. And so-called "traditional" families have given way to increasing numbers of single people, divorced people, single-parent families, and stepfamilies. These new family variations also reflect technological advance, as Chapter 15 ("Family") describes in detail.

The Lenskis suggest that early industrialization concentrated the benefits of advancing technology on only a small segment of the population, with the majority living in poverty. In time, however, the material products of industrial progress have been extended to more of the population. Poverty remains a very serious problem in industrial societies, but compared to the situation a century ago, the standard of living has risen, and economic, social, and political inequality has diminished. Some social leveling, detailed in Chapter 9 ("Social Stratification"), occurs because industrial societies require a literate and skilled labor force. In contrast to the dramatic social inequality common to

---

TABLE 4-1   SOCIOCULTURAL EVOLUTION: A SUMMARY

Type of Society	Historical Period	Productive Technology	Population Size
Hunting and Gathering Societies	Only type of society until about 10,000 years ago; still common several centuries ago; the few examples remaining today are threatened by extinction	Primitive weapons	25–40 people
Horticultural and Pastoral Societies	From about 10,000 years ago, with decreasing numbers after about 3000 B.C.E.	Horticultural societies use hand tools for cultivating plants; pastoral societies are based on the domestication of animals	Settlements of several hundred people, interconnected to form societies of several thousand people
Agrarian Societies	From about 5,000 years ago, with large but decreasing numbers today	Animal-drawn plow	Millions of people
Industrial Societies	From about 1750 to the present	Advanced sources of energy; mechanized production	Millions of people

agrarian societies, industrial societies gradually provided some schooling and extended political rights to almost everyone. In global perspective, industrialization has also intensified demands for political participation among the people of South Korea, Taiwan, the People's Republic of China, the former Soviet Union, and the societies of Eastern Europe.

However, even today women are a neglected majority, according to the conclusions reached in the 1993 United Nations Human Development Report. Thirty-three countries presently keep gender-based statistics. According to the data in these statistics, "no country treats its women as well as it treats its men." In spite of the growing struggle among women as well as changes in national laws, women's quality of life is still inferior to that of men. The discrimination against women in industrial countries is mainly in salary and employment opportunities. In developing countries the disparities also occur in health care, nutrition, and education. The report also notes that if women's unpaid housework were considered as productive, global output would increase by 20 to 30 percent (*Globe & Mail*, May 25, 1993).

A summary of how technology shapes societies is presented in Table 4-1 on pages 106–107. Sociocultural evolution continues apace. We will explore the emerging *postindustrial* society in later chapters.

The Limits of Technology

The technological might of industrial societies is unparalleled in human history. However, technology offers no "quick fix" for many social problems. Poverty remains the plight of millions of women and men in this country (detailed in Chapter 10, "Social Class in Canada") and of 1 billion people worldwide (Chapter 11, "Global Inequality"). Moreover, the capacity to reshape the world has created new problems that our ancestors could hardly have imagined. Industrial societies confer greater personal freedom, yet this often comes at the expense of the sense of community that characterized agrarian life. Furthermore, our ability to manipulate nature, coupled with our failure to restrain human greed, has wrought a staggering problem of global pollution. Perhaps most important, although

Type of Society	Settlement Pattern	Social Organization	Examples
Hunting and Gathering Societies	Nomadic	Family-centered; specialization limited to age and sex; little social inequality	Pygmies of central Africa Bushmen of southwest Africa Aborigines of Australia Tasaday of the Philippines Kaska Indians of Canada
Horticultural and Pastoral Societies	Horticulturalists form relatively small permanent settlements; pastoralists are nomadic	Family-centered; religious system begins to develop; moderate specialization; increased social inequality	Middle Eastern societies about 5000 B.C.E. Various societies today in New Guinea and other Pacific islands Yąnomamö today in South America
Agrarian Societies	Cities become common, though they generally contain only a small proportion of the population	Family loses significance as distinctive religious, political, and economic systems emerge; extensive specialization; increased social inequality	Egypt during construction of the Great Pyramids Medieval Europe Numerous nonindustrial societies of the world today
Industrial Societies	Cities now contain most of the population	Distinct religious, political, economic, educational, and family systems; highly specialized; marked social inequality persists, diminishing somewhat over time	Most societies today in Europe and North America Japan

Technology can threaten as well as serve humanity, a lesson symbolized by the utter destruction of Hiroshima by the armed forces of the United States at the end of World War II using a single, "primitive" atomic bomb. Weeks after the blast, heavily radiated people walked about the city—many aimlessly—due to their illness and the disorientation caused by losing their homes, families, and social routines.

industrial societies engage in warfare far less frequently than their technologically simpler counterparts, war now poses unimaginable horrors. Should nations ever unleash the present generation of nuclear weapons, human society would almost certainly regress to a technologically primitive state if, indeed, we survived at all. In some respects, technological advances have brought the world's people closer, creating a "global village." Yet in the wake of technological progress lie daunting problems of establishing peace and justice—problems that technology alone can never solve.

Karl Marx: Society and Conflict

The first of our classical visions of society comes from Karl Marx. Few observed the industrial transformation of Europe as keenly as he did. Marx spent most of his adult life in London, then the capital of the vast British Empire, and a city that symbolized the wealth and power of the new social order. He was awed by the productive power of industry; not only were European societies producing more goods than ever before, but resources from around the world were being funneled through their factories at a dizzying rate.

Beyond the new technology, Marx was also keenly aware of the concentration of industry's riches in the hands of a few. A walk almost anywhere in London revealed dramatic extremes of affluence and squalor. A handful of aristocrats and industrialists lived in massive mansions well staffed by servants, where they enjoyed luxury and privileges barely imaginable to most of their fellow Londoners. The majority, however, labored long hours for low wages, living in slums or even in the streets, where many eventually succumbed to poor nutrition and disease.

Marx was both saddened and angered by the social inequities he saw around him. The technological miracles of industrialization had finally made possible human society without want. Instead, however, indus-

PROFILE

Karl Marx (1818–1883)

Few names evoke a response as strong as Karl Marx. Some consider him a genius and a prophet, others see only evil in his ideas. Everyone agrees that Marx stands among the social thinkers who have had the greatest impact on the world's people. Today, more than one-fifth of all humanity live in societies that consider themselves Marxist.

Controversy surrounded Marx even during his own lifetime. Born in the German city of Trier, he earned a doctorate in 1841 and began working as a newspaper editor. But because of his relentless social criticism, he clashed with government authorities and was driven out of Germany to Paris. Soon he was forced from France as well and he spent the rest of his life in London.

Along with Max Weber and Emile Durkheim, Marx was a major figure in the development of sociology, as we saw in Chapter 1 ("The Sociological Perspective"). However, his ideas received relatively little attention in North America until the 1960s.

Why? The answer lies in Marx's explicit criticism of industrial-capitalist society. Early American sociologists dismissed his ideas as mere "politics" rather than serious scholarship. For Marx, though, scholarship was politics. While most sociologists heeded Max Weber's call for value-free research by attempting to minimize or conceal their own values (see Chapter 2, "Sociological Investigation"), Marx's work was explicitly value-laden. Marx did not merely observe society; he offered a rousing prescription for profound social change. As we in North America have come to recognize the extent to which values shape all ideas, Marx's social analysis has finally gained the attention it deserves as an important part of sociology.

SOURCE: Based, in part, on Ritzer (1983).

All societies use art to convey political ideas. This fact is most evident in socialist countries where, following Marx's thinking, people are expected to apply the lessons of economic revolution to all dimensions of social life. Stephan Carpov's hopeful painting Friendship of the People *(1924) represents the vision of a new human race that shined brightly at the dawning of socialism.*

try had done little to improve the lives of most people. To Marx, this represented a fundamental contradiction: in a society so rich, how could so many be so poor? Just as important, Marx asked, how can this situation be changed? Many people, no doubt, think of Karl Marx as a man determined to tear societies apart. But he was motivated by compassion for humanity and sought to help a society already badly divided to forge a new and just social order.

The key to Marx's thinking lies in the concept of **social conflict**, *struggle between segments of society over valued resources.* Social conflict can, of course, take many forms: individuals may quarrel, some sports teams have long-standing rivalries, and nations sometimes go to war. For Marx, however, the most significant form of social conflict arises from the way a society produces material goods.

Society and Production

The nineteenth-century societies Marx observed had industrial-capitalist economies, similar to those found today in North America, Western Europe, and elsewhere. Analyzing capitalist society, Marx designated a small part of the population as **capitalists**, *people who own factories and other productive enterprises.* A capitalist's goal is profit, which is made by marketing a product for more than it costs to produce. The vast majority of the population fell into the category of industrial workers that Marx termed the **proletariat**, *people who provide labor necessary to operate factories and other productive enterprises.* Workers sell their labor for the wages needed to live. To Marx, an inevitable conflict between capitalists and workers stems from the productive process itself. To maximize profits, capitalists try to minimize wages, generally their single greatest expense. Workers, however, want wages to be as high as possible. Since profits and wages come from the same pool of funds, ongoing conflict occurs. Marx argued that this conflict could be resolved only by fundamentally changing the capitalist system. This revolutionary economic upheaval, he believed, would eventually come to pass.

Marx's analysis of society draws on the philosophical approach called *materialism,* which asserts that the production of material goods shapes all aspects of society. Marx did not think that, once established, an economic system neatly or simplistically determines cultural values, politics, and family patterns. But just as the Lenskis argue the fundamental importance of tech-

nology, so Marx contended that the economic system exerts a key influence in every society:

> [T]he economic structure of society [is] the real foundation ... The mode of production in material life determines the general character of the social, political, and spiritual processes of life. (1959:43; orig. 1859)

Marx therefore viewed the economic system as the social *infrastructure* ("infra" is Latin meaning "below"). Other social institutions, including the family, the political system, and religion, are built on this foundation, becoming society's *superstructure*. These institutions extend economic principles and patterns into other areas of life, as illustrated in Figure 4-2. In practical terms, social institutions reinforce the domination of the capitalists, by legally protecting their wealth, for example, and transmitting property from one generation to the next through the family.

FIGURE 4-2   KARL MARX'S MODEL OF SOCIETY
This diagram illustrates Karl Marx's materialistic approach: that the process of economic production shapes the entire society. Economic production involves both technology (industry, in the case of capitalism) and social relationships (for capitalism, the relationship between the capitalists, who control the process, and the workers, who are simply a source of labor). Upon this infrastructure, or economic foundation, are built the major social institutions, as well as core cultural values and ideas. Taken together, these additional social elements represent the society's superstructure. Marx maintained that all the other parts of the society are likely to operate in a manner consistent with the economic system.

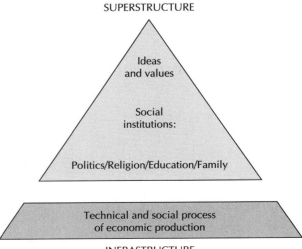

Generally speaking, most members of industrial-capitalist societies do not view their legal or family systems as hotbeds of social conflict. On the contrary, individual rights to private property come to be defined as "natural." To illustrate, we tend to believe that individuals live in poor-quality housing because they cannot afford something better. And no one expects a business to provide better housing unless doing so would be profitable. Similarly, we find it easy to characterize people who are out of work as lacking the skills or motivation to become employed. Marx challenged this kind of reasoning, asserting that it stemmed from a social system—preoccupied with the "bottom line"— that treats human well-being as a market commodity. Poor housing and unemployment are not inevitable; nor is it true that some people "simply don't deserve more." Substandard housing and chronic unemployment merely constitute one set of human possibilities generated by capitalism (Cuff and Payne, 1979).

This realization led Marx to claim that capitalism promotes **false consciousness**, *any belief suggesting that the shortcomings of individuals, rather than society, are responsible for widespread social problems.* Marx was saying, in effect, that industrial capitalism itself was responsible for many of the social problems he saw all around him. False consciousness, he maintained, not only victimizes people, it obscures the real cause of their problems.

Conflict in History

Marx believed that the power of ideas lies in action. He studied how societies have historically changed, noting that often a shift occurred gradually, following an evolutionary pattern; yet sometimes it happened rapidly, in revolutionary fashion. Marx observed (as do the Lenskis) that change is partly prompted by technological advance. But he steadfastly held that conflict underlies all transformations in society. In Marx's terms, the earliest hunters and gatherers formed primitive communist societies. The word *communism* means, simply, that the production of food and other material goods involves a common effort shared more or less equally by all members of society. Because the resources of nature were available to all hunters and gatherers (rather than privately owned), and because everyone performed similar tasks (rather than dividing the labor into specialized pursuits), there was little possibility for social conflict.

Marx noted that horticulture introduced significant social inequality. Among horticultural, pastoral, and early agrarian societies—which Marx lumped together as the "ancient world"—frequent warfare produced military captives who typically became slaves. A small elite (the "masters") used the labor of slaves to generate riches for themselves. From earliest civilizations, then, masters and slaves were locked into an irreconcilable pattern of social conflict (Zeitlin, 1981).

Agriculture brought still more wealth to members of the elite, fueling further social conflict. Agrarian serfs, occupying the lowest reaches of European feudalism from about the twelfth to the eighteenth centuries, were only slightly better off than slaves. In Marx's view, the power of both church and state defended and legitimized agrarian inequality by declaring that the existing social order embodied God's will. Thus, Marx viewed feudalism as little more than "exploitation, veiled by religious and political illusions" (Marx and Engels, 1972:337; orig. 1848).

Gradually, new productive forces undermined the feudal order. Commerce grew steadily throughout the Middle Ages, mostly carried out by peasants who had settled in the cities to escape feudal obligations to the nobility. Such people formed a new social category, the *bourgeoisie* (a French word meaning "of the town"). Profits earned in the expanding market brought the bourgeoisie increasing wealth. After the mid-eighteenth century, with factories at their command, the bourgeoisie became true capitalists with power rivaling that of the landed nobility. While the nobility regarded this upstart class of men and women "of commerce" with disdain, the capitalists firmly took control of the emerging industrial-capitalist societies of Europe. Following Marx's analysis, then, technological change powered only part of the Industrial Revolution. More important, the agrarian economy, with its elite class of nobles, was overthrown from below by capitalists who presided over the emerging industrial economy.

Industrialization also fostered the development of the proletariat. English capitalists converted fields once tilled by serfs into grazing land for sheep, because these animals provided wool for the prospering textile industry. As serfs migrated to the cities to work in factories, they took their place among the burgeoning industrial proletariat. Marx believed that these workers would one day join together to form a unified class, setting the stage for historic confrontation, this time between capitalists and the exploited workers.

Much of Marx's analysis centers on the destructive aspects of industrial capitalism—especially how it

Fildes's painting Awaiting Admission to the Casual Ward *shows the numbing poverty commonplace among immigrants to cities that grew rapidly soon after the Industrial Revolution began. Marx saw in such suffering a fundamental contradiction of modern society: industrial technology promised material plenty for all, yet capitalism concentrated wealth in the hands of a few.*

promotes class conflict and alienation. In examining his views on each of these topics, we come to understand why he advocated the overthrow of this type of society.

Capitalism and Class Conflict

"The history of all hitherto existing society is the history of class struggles." With this observation, Marx and his collaborator Friedrich Engels began their best-known work, the "Manifesto of the Communist Party" (1972:335; orig. 1848). The idea of social class lies at the heart of Marx's critique of capitalist society. Industrial capitalism, like earlier types of society, encompasses two major social classes, reflecting positions people hold in the productive system. Capitalists and proletarians are the historical descendants of dominant and oppressed classes in earlier societies: masters and slaves in the ancient world, nobility and serfs in feudal systems. In each case, one class controls the other, as productive property. Marx used the term **class conflict** (and sometimes *class struggle*) to refer to *the struggle between social classes over the distribution of wealth and power in society.*

Class conflict, then, dates back to civilizations long dead. What distinguishes the conflict in capitalism, however, is oppression that is obvious to all. In feudal societies, tradition and mutual obligations bound serfs and nobles together. Industrial capitalism dissolved those ties, so that people confronted each other merely in terms of "naked self-interest" and "callous cash payment." With no personal ties to their oppressors, Marx concluded, the proletariat had little reason to tolerate their suffering.

Even though industrial capitalism had brought class conflict out in the open, Marx realized that fundamental social change would require several key steps. First, he claimed, workers must become aware of their shared oppression and its true cause (industrial capitalism). Second, they must *organize* and *act* to address their problems. In other words, they must recognize that they suffer not from personal failings (as capitalist beliefs suggest), nor because other workers compete for their jobs. Rather, their suffering arises from the structure and workings of capitalism itself. In short, workers must adopt a Marxist version of the sociological perspective to replace false consciousness with **class consciousness**, *the recognition by workers of their unity as a class in opposition to capitalists and, ultimately, to capitalism itself.* Because the inhumanity of early capitalism seemed so obvious to Marx, he firmly believed that industrial workers would inevitably rise up en masse to destroy industrial capitalism. In doing so, they would cease to be merely a social class *in* themselves and become a social class acting *for* themselves.

And what of their adversaries, the capitalists? The formidable wealth and power of capitalists, protected by the institutions of society, might seem invulnerable. But Marx saw a weakness in the capitalist armor. Motivated by a desire for personal gain, capitalists fear the competition of other capitalists. Thus Marx thought that capitalists would be reluctant to band together, even though they, too, share common interests. Furthermore, he reasoned, by competing with one another, capitalists keep wages low; this strategy further bolsters the resolve of workers to forge an alliance against them. In the long run, Marx claimed, capitalists could only contribute to their own undoing.

Capitalism and Alienation

Marx also condemned capitalism for producing widespread **alienation**, *the experience of separation resulting from powerlessness.* Dominated by capitalists and dehumanized by their jobs (especially monotonous and repetitive factory work), workers find little satisfaction and feel individually powerless to improve their situation. Capitalist society itself gives rise to a major contradiction, observed Marx: as human beings have acquired and used technology to gain power over the world, the productive process itself has increasingly exerted power over human beings.

The basic problem here is that workers find industrial-capitalist work unsatisfying. They view themselves merely as a commodity, a source of labor, bought by capitalists and discarded when they are no longer needed. Marx cited four ways in which industrial capitalism alienates workers.

1. **Alienation from the act of working.** Ideally, people work both to meet their immediate needs and to develop their long-range potential. Capitalism, however, denies workers a voice in the fruits of

SOCIOLOGY OF EVERYDAY LIFE

Alienation and Industrial Capitalism

When we think of work that might produce experiences of social alienation, we probably think first about assembly line manufacturing jobs and other so-called "blue collar" work. However, alienation can occur in other guises as well. Martin Shapiro is a physician who went through medical school at McGill University beginning in 1969. During his time there, he was confronted with "many disturbing aspects of social interventions, in hospitals as well as in medical schools." He published *Getting Doctored* as a critical memoir of his experiences at McGill and later as a resident doctor in Los Angeles. Building on Marx, the three components of alienation that he noted were first, alienation of labor or productive activity, which he says results in fragmented productive activity. He notes that, with the emphasis on specialization in our medical system, doctors may feel that they work on an assembly line, and consequently lose their commitment to the whole person or the whole process of health. Second, Shapiro points to doctors' alienation from the product of their labor. Because the work of physicians is so specialized, they rarely have an opportunity to actively work towards the promotion of health. Rather they are faced almost continually with piece work—repairing a broken part of the body. Third, Shapiro notes alienation of people from one another in medicine. For example, in the hospital hierarchy people at different levels relate in stereotypical and predictable ways towards those at other levels of the hierarchy. Patients, too, come to be treated, says Shapiro, as commodities whose value is seen in the "differentness" of their symptoms. The following excerpt shows how physicians may separate themselves morally from their patients:

> ... at least some of the information physicians collect in their interviews with patients and usually accept on faith, is inaccurate. Ironically, it is only for particular parts of a medical history that many physicians reserve their scepticism, and written medical records reflect this bias: "This patient denies sexual contact"; "the patient claims he drinks two or three beers a day." *(Shapiro, 1978:69.)*

production or the productive process itself. Further, work is often tedious, involving countless repetitions of routine tasks. The modern-day replacement of human labor by machines would hardly have surprised Marx; as far as he was concerned, capitalism had turned human beings into machines long ago.

2. **Alienation from the products of work.** The product of work belongs not to workers but to capitalists, who dispose of it in exchange for profits. Thus, Marx reasoned, the more workers invest of themselves in the products of their labor, the more they lose.

3. **Alienation from other workers.** Marx celebrated work as the productive affirmation of human community. Industrial capitalism, however, makes work competitive rather than cooperative. As the box illustrates, work often provides little chance even for human companionship.

4. **Alienation from humanity.** Industrial capitalism alienates workers from their own human potential. Marx argued that a worker "does not fulfill himself in his work but denies himself, has a feeling of misery rather than well-being, does not freely develop his physical and mental energies, but is physically exhausted and mentally debased. The

Marxism, one of the world's most influential social movements, has shaped the economic and political life of one-fifth of the world's people. For years, the conventional wisdom in the United States was that, once established, socialism stifled its opposition, making its overthrow impossible. But that notion collapsed along with the governments of Eastern Europe and the former Soviet Union. The political transformation of this world region is symbolized by the removal of statues of Vladimir Lenin (1870-1924), architect of Soviet Marxism, in city after city during the last few years.

worker, therefore, feels himself to be at home only during his leisure time, whereas at work he feels homeless" (1964a:124–25; orig. 1844). In short, industrial capitalism distorts an activity that should bring out the best qualities in human beings into a dull and dehumanizing experience.

Marx viewed alienation, in its various forms, as a barrier to social change. But he hoped that industrial workers eventually would overcome their alienation as they united into a true social class, aware of the cause of their problems, and galvanized to transform society.

Revolution

The only way out of the trap of capitalism, contended Marx, was to refashion society. He envisioned a more humane and egalitarian productive system, which he termed *socialism*. Marx knew well the obstacles to a socialist revolution; even so, he was disappointed that workers in England did not overthrow industrial capitalism during his lifetime. Still, convinced of the basic immorality of capitalist society, he was sure that, in time, the working majority would realize they held the key to a better future in their own hands. This transformation would certainly be revolutionary, and perhaps even violent. The end product, however, would be a cooperative socialist society that would meet the needs of all.

The discussion of social inequality in Chapter 9 ("Social Stratification") reveals more about changes in industrial-capitalist societies since Marx's time, and why the revolution he longed for has not taken place. Later chapters also suggest why people in the societies of Eastern Europe and the former Soviet Union recently revolted against established socialist governments. Marx, however, looked toward the future with hope (1972:362; orig. 1848): "The proletarians have nothing to lose but their chains. They have a world to win."

Max Weber:
The Rationalization of Society

With a broad understanding of law, economics, religion, and history, Max Weber produced what many regard as the greatest individual contribution to sociology. Weber's ideas span such a wide range that they are difficult to summarize. The present discussion focuses on Weber's vision of modern society and how our world differs from earlier societies.

Weber's analysis of society reflects the philosophical approach called *idealism*, which emphasizes how human ideas shape society. Weber understood the power of technology, and he shared many of Marx's ideas about social conflict. But he departed from Marx's materialist views, arguing that societies differ from one another primarily in terms of how human beings think about the world. For Weber, human consciousness—ideas, beliefs, and values—was a transforming force. Thus he saw modern society as the result of not just new technology and new means of production but new ways of thinking as well. An emphasis on ideas, in contrast to Marx's focus on material production, has led scholars to characterize Weber's work as "a debate with the ghost of Karl Marx" (Cuff and Payne, 1979:73–74).

Weber conducted his research comparatively, contrasting social patterns in different times and places. To facilitate comparisons, he used the **ideal type**, *an abstract statement of the essential characteristics of any social phenomenon.* He explored religion through constructing ideal types of "Protestants," "Jews," "Hindus," and "Buddhists," even though no individual may precisely conform to the models. Similarly, we have already described entire societies in ideal terms, comparing "hunters and gatherers" to "industrial people." An ideal type has much in common with the more familiar idea of stereotype, in that both are abstract conceptualizations. Unlike a stereotype, however, an ideal type is essentially factual and emotionally neutral rather than being infused with unfair positive or negative connotations (Theodorson and Theodorson, 1969). Finally, Weber's use of the word *ideal* does not imply that something is "good" or "the best"; "criminals" as well as "priests" can be analyzed as ideal types.

PROFILE

Max Weber (1864–1920)

To be called merely a "sociologist" would probably have offended Max Weber. Not that he was indifferent to the study of society; in fact, he spent most of his life exploring the intricacies of our social arrangements. But Weber's contribution to understanding humanity is so broad and rich that no single discipline can properly claim him.

The product of a prosperous German family, Weber completed law school and set off on a legal career. But he soon felt confined by the constraints of legal practice. Continuing his studies, he became a university professor. His curiosity racing across the entire human condition, he integrated many approaches into his rich scholarship.

Throughout his life, Weber's family ties continued to influence his work. His mother's devout Calvinism no doubt prompted Weber's study of world religions and the link between Calvinism and the rise of industrial capitalism. From his father, a notable politician, Weber clearly gained insights into the workings of bureaucracy and political life.

Weber flirted with politics, and his wife Marianne was a leading feminist of her time. But Weber found politics to be incompatible with his work as a scholar. Politics, he claimed, demands action and strong personal conviction, while scholarship requires impartiality and patient reflection. Late in his life, Weber began urging his colleagues to become involved in politics as citizens outside the classroom, while striving for scientific neutrality in their professional work.

For many reasons, Weber's life was far from happy. He did not get along well with his father, and soon after his father's death Weber began to suffer from psychological problems. Illness sharply limited his ability to work during the remainder of his life. Even so, the exceptional number of major studies he conducted has led many to call him the most brilliant sociologist in history.

Rationality and Industrial Capitalism

Rather than categorizing societies in terms of technology or productive systems, Max Weber highlighted differences in the ways people view the world. In simple terms, Weber concluded that members of preindustrial societies embrace tradition, while industrial capitalism fosters *rationality*.

By **tradition**, Weber meant *sentiments and beliefs passed from generation to generation*. Thus social patterns in traditional societies are guided by the past. People evaluate particular actions as right and proper precisely because they have been accepted for so long.

Modern society takes a different approach, according to Weber, encouraging **rationality**, *deliberate, matter-of-fact calculation of the most efficient means to accomplish any particular goal*. Sentiment has no place in a rational world view, which is largely indifferent to the past. Ideally speaking, Weber continued, modern people treat tradition simply as a form of information with no special claim on them. We choose to think and act on the basis of present and future consequences, evaluating jobs, schooling, and even relationships in terms of what we contribute to them and what we expect to receive in return.

Weber viewed both the Industrial Revolution and the rise of capitalism as evidence of a historical surge in rationality. He used the phrase **rationalization of society** to denote *the historical change from tradition to rationality as the dominant mode of human thought*. Modern society, therefore, has been "disenchanted" as scientific thinking and technology have swept away sentimental ties to the past.

To conceptualize the impact of rationalization on the modern world, Global Map 4-1 on page 118 shows expenditures on the sciences for the world's nations. The Commonwealth of Independent States and the United States spend a great deal on scientific projects. Many of the more traditional societies in Latin America, Africa, and Asia devote far less of their resources to scientific pursuits.

Weber's comparative perspective—and the data found in the map—suggest that societies value technological achievements differently. What one society might herald as a technological breakthrough, another might deem unimportant, and a third might strongly oppose as a threat to an established way of life. Elites in ancient Greece, for instance, devised many surprisingly elaborate mechanical devices to perform household tasks. Well served by slaves, however, they viewed their inventions as merely entertaining. In Canada today, the Old Order Mennonites are guided by their traditions to staunchly oppose modern technology.

In Weber's view, then, technological innovation is encouraged or hindered by the way people understand their world. He concluded that many societies in history held the technological keys to industry, but only in the supportive cultural climate of Western Europe did the Industrial Revolution actually take root (1958; orig. 1904–5).

Here we note another crucial difference between two great sociologists. Weber considered industrial capitalism as the essence of rationality, since capitalists pursue profit in eminently rational ways. Marx dismissed capitalism as the antithesis of rationality, claiming that this economic system failed to meet the basic needs of most of the people (Gerth and Mills, 1946:49).

The Roots of Rationality

Weber elaborated on his analysis of modern rationality by noting that industrial capitalism actually developed in the wake of Calvinism—a Christian religious movement spawned by the Protestant Reformation. Weber knew that Calvinists, as an ideal type, approached life in a highly disciplined and rational way. But how did a religion spark the development of a new economy?

Central to the doctrine of John Calvin (1509–1564) is *predestination*, the idea that an all-powerful God has selected some people for salvation and others for eternal damnation. With everyone's fate predestined before birth, Calvinists were taught that people could do nothing to alter their destiny. Nor could they even know what their fate was. The only certainty was what hung in the balance: heavenly glory or hellfire for all of eternity.

The lives of Calvinists, then, were framed by visions of salvation or damnation. For such people, the anxiety of not knowing one's fate can only be imagined. Calvinists gradually came to a resolution of sorts: those chosen for glory in the next world, they concluded, should see signs of divine favor in *this* world as well. This conclusion prompted Calvinists to interpret worldly prosperity as a sign of God's grace. Anxious to acquire this reassurance, Calvinists threw themselves into a quest for success, applying rationality, discipline, and hard work to their tasks. This pursuit of riches was not for its own sake, however, since self-indulgently spending money was clearly sinful. Calvinists also were little moved to share their wealth with the poor because poverty was seen as a sign of God's rejection. Their ever-present purpose was to carry out what they held to be their personal *calling* from God as effectively as possible.

All the same, Calvinists built the foundation of capitalism as they reinvested their profits for greater success. Their deliberate and pious plan was to use wealth to generate more wealth, to practice personal thrift, and to eagerly embrace the technological advances that accompanied the Industrial Revolution.

These traits, Weber explained, distinguished Calvinism from other world religions. Catholicism, the traditional religion in most of Europe, encouraged an "otherworldly" acceptance of life as it was in hopes of greater rewards in the life to come. For Catholics, material wealth had none of the spiritual significance that so motivated the Calvinists. And so it was, Weber concluded, that industrial capitalism became established primarily in areas of Europe where Calvinism held sway.

Weber's study of Calvinism provides striking evidence of the power of ideas (which Marx considered merely a reflection of the productive process) to shape all of society. Weber's analysis does not imply, however, that something as complex as industrial capitalism sprang full blown from a single source. On the contrary, such simplicity would have offended Weber, whose work was partly in response to what he saw as Marx's narrow explanation of modern society in terms of economics. Later in his career, in fact, Weber (1961; orig. 1920) stressed that the development of industrial capitalism stemmed from a complex web of factors, including both economic and legal considerations as well as a distinctive world view (Collins, 1986).

But Weber never wavered in his contention that the defining characteristic of the modern world was rationality. As religious fervor diminished among later generations of Calvinists, he noted, success-seeking personal discipline remained. A *religious* ethic became simply a "*work* ethic," in pursuit of profit rather than the glory of God. From this point of view, industrial capitalism appears as "disenchanted" religion, with wealth now valued for its own sake. It is revealing that *accounting,* by which early Calvinists meant a daily record of moral deeds, now refers simply to money.

Rationality and Modern Society

Weber contended that rationality, which had spawned the Industrial Revolution and the development of capitalism, had defined the character of modern society.

Rationality influences modern social life in various ways.

1. **Distinctive social institutions.** Rationality promotes the emergence of distinctive **social institutions**, defined as *the major spheres of social life organized to meet basic human needs.* Among hunters and gatherers, the family was the center of virtually all activities. Gradually, however, other social institutions, including religious, political, and economic systems, emerged separate from the family. In modern societies, institutions of formal education and health care have also appeared. These social institutions—each detailed in a later chapter—are rational strategies for more efficiently addressing human needs.

2. **Specialization.** Distinctive social institutions encourage the pursuit of specialized activities. In traditional societies, everyone shares in carrying out many of the same tasks. Modern rationality, however, guides people into narrow pursuits like biological research, welding, or driving a taxi.

3. **Personal discipline.** Modern society puts a premium on adopting a disciplined approach to achieving life goals. For early Calvinists, of course, discipline was rooted in religious belief. Although now distanced from its religious origin, discipline is still encouraged by cultural values such as achievement, success, and efficiency.

4. **Awareness of time.** Central to a rational world view is a keen awareness of time. In modern societies, the traditional rhythm of sun and seasons gives way to scheduling according to the precise hour and minute. In addition, rationality turns people's attention from the past to the present and to the future, as they seek to improve their lives.

5. **Technical competence.** Members of traditional societies evaluate one another largely on the basis of *who* they are—how they are connected to others in the web of kinship. Modern rationality, in contrast, encourages us to judge people according to *what* they are—that is, their technical skills and personal abilities.

6. **Impersonality.** Because technical competence takes priority over personal relationships in a rational society, the world becomes more and more anonymous. Modern society increasingly turns on the interplay of specialists concerned with particular tasks, rather than the interaction of people sensitive

to human feelings. Weber explained that we tend to devalue personal feelings and emotions as "irrational" because they sometimes run counter to rational principles.

7. **Large-scale organizations**. Finally, modern rationality is exemplified in the expansion of large-scale organizations. As early as the horticultural era, organizations deliberately administered activities like religious celebrations, public works, and warfare. As societies became larger and more com-

plex, so did their organizations. In medieval Europe, the Catholic Church had become an enormous organization with thousands of officials; today's federal government has hundreds of thousands of employees.

Rational Organization: Bureaucracy

Weber argued that rationality did not fully characterize the medieval church because its purpose was largely to preserve tradition. Truly rational organizations,

WINDOW ON THE WORLD

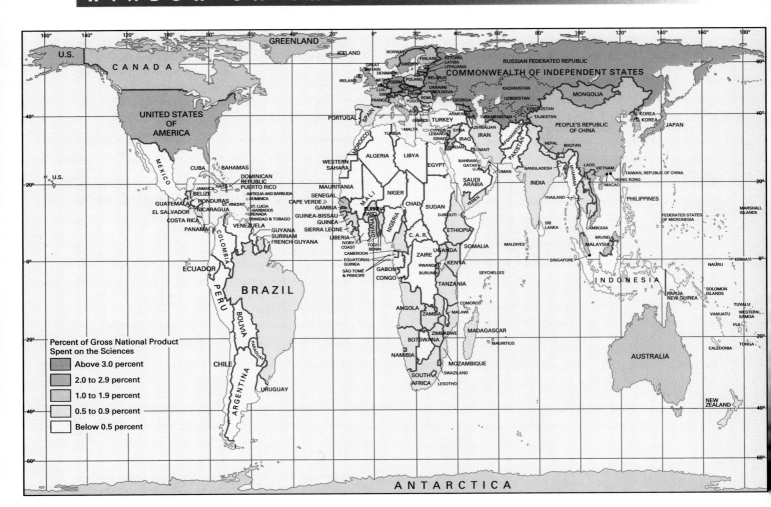

GLOBAL MAP 4-1   SPENDING ON SCIENCE IN GLOBAL PERSPECTIVE
In general, industrial societies spend relatively more of their gross national product (the value of all goods and services produced annually) on scientific pursuits than less industrialized societies do. From Weber's point of view, such expenditures are an indicator of a society's world view: less industrialized societies embrace tradition while more industrialized nations espouse rationality as a source of meaning.

in which tradition has been subsumed by efficiency, emerged only in the last few centuries in Western societies. The organizational type Weber termed *bureaucracy* accompanied capitalism as an expression of rationality.

Bureaucracy, the organizing principle of modern businesses, government agencies, labor unions, and universities, is explored in depth in Chapter 7 ("Groups and Organizations"). For now, it is important to recognize that Weber viewed bureaucracy as the clearest expression of a rational world view because its organizational elements—offices, duties, and policies— all are designed to achieve specific goals as efficiently as possible. In addition, any part of the organization is subject to modification to increase organizational efficiency. By contrast, traditional social organization places little emphasis on efficiency and is typically hostile to change. Weber asserted that bureaucracy had done for society as a whole what industrialization had done for the production of material goods:

> *The decisive reason for the advance of bureaucratic organization has always been its purely technical superiority over any other form of organization. The fully developed bureaucratic apparatus compares with other organizations exactly as does the machine with the nonmechanical modes of production.* (1978:973; orig. 1921)

Rational bureaucracy, Weber explained, also has a natural affinity to capitalism:

> *Today, it is primarily the capitalist market economy which demands that the official business of public administration be discharged precisely, unambiguously, continuously, and with as much speed as possible. Normally, the very large capitalist enterprises are themselves unequaled models of strict bureaucratic organization.* (1978:974; orig. 1921)

Rationality and Alienation

So far, we have emphasized the unparalleled efficiency of modern society. Worth remembering, however, is that Karl Marx reached much the same conclusion, at least as far as the productive efficiency of capitalism was concerned. But Marx ultimately rejected this type of society because of widespread alienation and other destructive consequences of economic inequality inherent in industrial-capitalist systems.

Weber, too, criticized modern society, but for different reasons. For him, the primary problem was not the economic inequality that so troubled Marx. Rather, the price of rational efficiency appeared to be alienation and dehumanization—people stifled by bureaucratic impersonality and regulation.

Large-scale organizations, Weber observed, tend to treat people as cases rather than as individuals. In

Max Weber agreed with Karl Marx that modern society is alienating, but the two thinkers saw different causes for this estrangement. For Marx, economic inequality is the culprit; for Weber, the issue is pervasive and dehumanizing bureaucracy. George Tooker's painting Landscape *echoes Weber's sentiments.*

addition, much of modern society's highly specialized work involves tedious repetition. Perhaps most important, Weber feared that the human spirit was being extinguished by rational formality. In the end, Weber envisioned modern society as a vast and growing system of rules and regulations that sought to direct virtually every human endeavor. In this way, he observed, human beings were becoming alienated from their own spontaneity and creativity.

An irony found in the work of Marx appears once again in Weber's analysis: rather than serving humanity, modern society turns on its creators and enslaves them. In language reminiscent of Marx's description of the human toll of industrial capitalism, Weber portrayed the modern individual as "only a small cog in a ceaselessly moving mechanism which prescribes to him an endlessly fixed routine of march" (1978:988; orig. 1921).

An example of the casualties of modern bureaucracy is found in the research of Canadian sociologist Elliot Leyton. Leyton examined the impact of the bureaucratic Worker's Compensation Board on the citizens of a small mining community in Newfoundland called St. Lawrence. Here the main source of income is the florspan mining, which has been found to lead to lung cancer and other diseases of the respiratory system. Whenever the company doctor declared a man unable to work, he became eligible for a disability pension and his "case" was referred to the Compensation Board. However, the amount of pension benefits meted out by the Board varied greatly from worker to worker. Some received their full benefits, some half, and some were given no pension at all. To receive his benefits, the miner had to submit evidence showing a causal link between his work in the mines and the disease he had contracted. Although the Board accepted in principle that such a link existed, it often disputed the evidence in individual cases. Therefore, it was the miners who submitted the most convincing paperwork who received the greatest benefits. To the miners whose claims were rejected, the process seemed grossly unfair and arbitrary. But those who administered the fund continued to insist that the judgment in each case was made on sound scientific principles. As a consequence, in an effort to act rationally and on the basis of scientific and objective proof, the miners and their families were often treated cruelly and without any regard for their suffering (Handleman and Leyton, 1978).

Despite obvious advantages of modern society over earlier types of societies, Weber ended his life deeply pessimistic. More and more, the modern world was coming to resemble a vast "machine," which, he worried, "chained" people to their work despite their efforts to "squirm free." Weber wondered if the logical conclusion of the rationalization of society would be to reduce people to mere robots.

Emile Durkheim: Society and Function

"To love society is to love something beyond us and something in ourselves." These are the words of Emile Durkheim, another architect of sociology, introduced in the box. In this curious phrase[2] we find one more influential vision of human society.

Social Fact: Society Beyond Ourselves

The starting point for understanding the work of Emile Durkheim is the concept of **social fact**, *any social pattern that people confront as an objective reality beyond themselves.* Familiar examples of social facts include cultural norms and values, described in the last chapter ("Culture"), or the degree of social integration that Durkheim found to influence suicide rates, as explained in Chapter 1 ("The Sociological Perspective").

Durkheim's concept of social fact becomes clearer with three additional observations. First, society has *structure* because social patterns exist in orderly relation to one another. Second, because the social world surrounds us, such patterns shape our thoughts and actions. Third, social patterns constitute "facts" because they have an objective existence apart from any individual's subjective experience of them.

For Durkheim, then, society is more than the sum of its parts. He envisioned society as an elaborate, collective organism, with a certain life and momentum of its own. Society confronts its creators, demanding a measure of obedience, and we experience society as we feel the urge of morality. A first-grade classroom, a family having dinner, and a country auction are commonplace situations that have an existence apart from any particular individual who has ever participated in them. These patterns not only shape behavior, but affect our thoughts and feelings as well. In Durkheim's view, soci-

---

[2] *Sociology and Philosophy,* 1974:55; orig. 1924.

Emile Durkheim (1858–1917)

Why would wanting to be a sociology professor be controversial? Because there *weren't* any, at least not in

France, until Emile Durkheim became the first in 1887. Up to this time, researchers studied human behavior almost exclusively in terms of biology and psychology. But Durkheim argued that one cannot comprehend humanity by looking at the individual. Instead, he maintained, understanding individuals demands examining their society.

In Chapter 1 ("The Sociological Perspective"), we encountered persuasive evidence of society's power to shape people's lives. By studying suicide, among the most personal and individualistic of actions, Durkheim showed that where people are embedded in society—as women or

men, rich or poor, and as followers of various religions—affects their suicide rates.

Durkheim is introduced here because his work, like that of Marx and Weber, is referred to extensively in later chapters. Durkheim's contributions to the understanding of crime are especially significant and figure prominently in Chapter 8 ("Deviance"). He also spent much of his life investigating religion, and we include his ideas on this subject in Chapter 17 ("Religion"). Just as important, Durkheim is one of the major architects of the structural-functional paradigm, which is used in almost every chapter that follows.

---

ety precedes us, makes claims on us while we are here, and continues after we are gone.

Function: Society in Action

The next step in understanding Durkheim's vision of society involves the concept of *function*. Along with Herbert Spencer, introduced in Chapter 1, Durkheim helped to formulate what we now call the "structural-functional paradigm" in sociology. Durkheim argued that we discern the function of social facts not in the experience of individuals, but in their contribution to the general life of society itself.

Without sociological insight, Durkheim reasoned, common sense leads us to misunderstand events solely in terms of ourselves or other individuals. Crime, for example, brings to mind harm that offenders inflict on their victims. For Durkheim, though, the function of crime has little to do with particular people but involves society as a system. As Chapter 8 ("Deviance") explains, the way people identify and respond to particular acts as criminal vitalizes society as a moral system. Thus most people never recognize the social function of crime: to sustain the moral power of society. For this reason, Durkheim rejected the common view of crime

as "pathological." On the contrary, he concluded, crime is quite "normal" for the most basic of reasons: no society could exist without it (1964a, orig. 1895; 1964b, orig. 1893).

The Individual: Society in Ourselves

Durkheim contended that, while society is "beyond us," it is simultaneously "something in ourselves." Individuals, in other words, build personality by internalizing social facts. Through society and the social restraints we learn growing up, we nurture our humanity. That is, the moral education of society—through norms and values—regulates the natural insatiability of human beings. We are in danger of being overpowered by desire, Durkheim observed, because "the more one has, the more one wants, since satisfactions received only stimulate instead of filling needs" (1966; orig. 1897). Society, then, must necessarily instill restraints in each of us.

The need for societal regulation is illustrated by Durkheim's study of suicide (1966; orig. 1897), detailed in Chapter 1. In nineteenth-century France, as well as in Canada today, it is precisely the *least* regulated categories of people that suffer the *highest* rates of suicide. The greater autonomy afforded to men, for example, yields a suicide rate three times higher than that among women (Colombo, 1992).

Modern societies, however, have less of a hold on us. While Durkheim found some reasons to praise individualism, he warned of a rise in **anomie**, *a condition in which society provides individuals with little moral guidance.* The familiar—if uncommon—image of people leaping from office buildings during a stock-market crash exemplifies the extreme case of anomic suicide. Here, a radical collapse of the social environment disrupts society's support and regulation of the individual, sometimes with fatal results. Interestingly, sudden affluence does much the same thing, tearing individuals out of established social patterns and overwhelming them with unregulated free choice. The record of reckless behavior leading to accidental death among rock performers of recent decades who experienced sudden stardom clearly reveals the danger of self-destructiveness in extreme individualism.

Although he was an outspoken defender of individual rights, Durkheim never doubted that the needs of the individual must be balanced by the claims and guidance of society. Nowhere has this balance become more precarious than in the modern world.

Evolving Societies: The Division of Labor

Like Marx and Weber, Durkheim experienced first-hand the rapid social changes that were transforming European societies during the nineteenth century. Durkheim saw in these changes new forms of social organization.

Historical study led Durkheim to conclude that societies with simple technology have strong traditions, and operate as powerful moral systems demanding unbending conformity. The *collective conscience* of traditional societies is so strong that the community moves quickly to punish any person who dares to differ very much from accepted ways of life. Durkheim called this intense moral consensus **mechanical solidarity**, meaning *social bonds, common to preindustrial societies, based on shared moral sentiments.* In horticultural and agrarian societies, for example, social solidarity is *based on likeness*, or shared experiences, since everyone acts and thinks mostly the same. Durkheim called such solidarity "mechanical" because people feel a more or less automatic sense of belonging.

The decline of mechanical solidarity marked the emergence of modern society. But, continued Durkheim, a new type of solidarity emerged to fill some of

Historically, most members of human societies have engaged in the same basic activities: building shelters and obtaining food. Modern societies, claimed Durkheim, have a rapidly expanding division of labor. Increasing specialization is evident on the streets of societies beginning to industrialize: providing people with their weight is the livelihood of this man in Istanbul, Turkey; on a Bombay street in India, another earns a small fee for cleaning ears.

the void left by vanished traditions. This new social integration Durkheim dubbed **organic solidarity**, defined as *social bonds, common to industrial societies, based on specialization*. Social solidarity, *based on difference*, arises among people who, although conforming less in moral terms, find that specialization makes them need one another. Therefore, Durkheim summed up this entire historical process as a growing **division of labor**, or *specialized economic activity*. As we have already seen in Max Weber's analysis, modern societies rationally promote efficiency through specialization. From Durkheim's point of view, the result is a complex web of functional interdependence by which each person relies on tens of thousands of others—most complete strangers—who help produce the products and provide the services we use every day.

Modern organic solidarity, then, shares with traditional mechanical solidarity the function of maintaining the unified operation of society. But while the former system is grounded in morality, the latter owes its force to practicality. Thus members of modern societies depend more and more on people we trust less and less. Why, after all, should we trust people we hardly know? And people whose beliefs probably differ from our own? Durkheim's answer: "because we can't live without them." But he knew that trust comes hard in a world that has lost much of its moral foundation. This prompts what we might call "Durkheim's Dilemma": that the positive benefits of modern society, including technological advance and greater personal freedom, are achieved at the cost of undermining morality and unleashing the ever-present danger of anomie.

Durkheim certainly found much to celebrate in modern society, especially individualism, privacy, and freedom of choice. Like Marx and Weber, though, he had misgivings about the direction society was taking. Still, of the three, Durkheim was the most optimistic. Confidence in the future sprang from his hope that we could enjoy greater freedom while creating for ourselves the moral regulation that had once been forced on us by tradition.

Critical Evaluation: Four Visions of Society

This chapter opened with several important questions about human societies. We will conclude by probing how these questions are answered in light of the four visions of society we have examined.

How Have Societies Changed?

According to the model of sociocultural evolution spelled out by the Lenskis, societies throughout history differ primarily in terms of their *technology*. Modern society is distinctive essentially because of its large-scale industrial productivity. Karl Marx, who also stressed historical differences in the productive system, was more concerned with demonstrating that material production in all historical societies (except perhaps for simple hunters and gatherers) generates social conflict. For Marx, modern society stands out only in that social conflict has become more obvious. In contrast to Marx, Max Weber distinguished societies in terms of characteristic modes of human thought. Preindustrial societies, he claimed, were traditional, while modern societies embrace a rational view of the world. Finally, for Emile Durkheim, societies differ in how they are bound together. Preindustrial mechanical solidarity is based on likeness; this gives way in industrial societies to organic solidarity based on difference.

Why Do Societies Change?

Here again, the visions we have considered bring to bear different insights. The Lenskis see social change primarily as a matter of technological innovation that, over time, can transform an entire society. Marx pointed to the struggle between classes as the "engine of history," pushing societies toward revolutionary reorganization. Weber's idealist approach complemented Marx's materialism, showing that particular modes of thought also contribute to social change. He demonstrated how the rational underpinnings of Calvinism bolstered the Industrial Revolution, which, in turn, reshaped much of modern society. Finally, Durkheim believed that an expanding division of labor was propelling the increasing complexity of human societies.

How Are Societies United and Divided?

The Lenskis hold that all societies are united by cultural patterns, although these patterns change according to a society's level of technological development. They note, too, that inequality tends to intensify as technology becomes more complex, although diminishing somewhat with the onset of industrialization. Marx argued that material production has drawn classes into conflict with one another throughout history.

From his point of view, a unified and just social order could only emerge if production became a truly cooperative enterprise. Without denying the importance of economic rifts, Weber claimed that members of a society share a distinctive world view. Just as tradition has fused people together in the past, so rational, large-scale organizations now link the lives of modern individuals. Guided by the structural-functional paradigm, Durkheim focused on social integration. He contrasted the mechanical solidarity of preindustrial societies with modern society's organic solidarity, a change he explained in terms of an increasing division of labor. Durkheim's analysis also helps to clarify the modern tolerance (and sometimes encouragement) of individuals cultivating a distinctive personality.

Are Societies Improving?

The visions presented in this chapter differ on the question of human progress. From their survey of history, the Lenskis conclude that industrial societies provide important advantages, such as a higher standard of living and a longer life span. But the potential threat to our planet posed by advancing technology—through war or environmental pollution—makes it problematic to equate technological advance with improved quality of life. Without passing judgment on all the consequences of technological advances, the Lenskis predict that change will continue to be rapid, and perhaps more dramatic than ever.

Marx applauded the power of advancing technology, but he concluded that only the few would enjoy its benefits until society underwent a radical restructuring. He looked to the future for a final resolution of historical class conflict as socialism placed the productive system under the control of all the people.

Weber found little comfort in Marx's vision, fearing that socialist revolution would only intensify the power of large-scale organizations to dominate the lives of individuals. As explained in Chapter 19 ("The Economy and Work"), Weber's forecast that state control of everyday life would expand—especially under socialism—helps to explain the recent overthrow of governments in Eastern Europe and the former Soviet Union. Despite the successes of these systems in promoting economic equality, in other words, they sharply limited political participation. Recognizing that the expansion of organizations would take on global proportions made Weber's view of the course of human society the most pessimistic of all.

Durkheim, by contrast, holds the most optimistic view. He saw in the twilight of tradition the possibility for greater freedom than individuals had ever known. Individualism has its dangers, however, as Durkheim's concern with anomie suggests. Despite this reservation, Durkheim comes closest to applauding the history of human societies as a march of genuine "progress."

The significant differences among these four approaches do not mean that any one of them is, in an absolute sense, right or wrong. Society is exceedingly complex, and we shall return to each of these visions in later chapters.

Summary

Gerhard and Jean Lenski

1. The Lenskis' model of sociocultural evolution explores the societal consequences of technological advance.

2. The earliest and simplest societies, based on hunting and gathering, are composed of a small number of family-centered nomads. These societies are rapidly vanishing from the world.

3. Horticulture emerged about ten thousand years ago, with the invention of hand tools for cultivation. Pastoral societies are nomadic, domesticating animals and engaging in extensive trade.

4. Agriculture, which appeared some five thousand years ago, involves large-scale cultivation using animal-drawn plows. This technology allows societies to grow into vast empires with more productivity, specialization, and inequality.

5. Industrialization began only 250 years ago in Europe, as sophisticated machinery was powered with advanced sources of energy. In industrial societies, change typically happens quickly. Most people live in cities, and highly specialized activities take place separate from the family.

Karl Marx

6. Marx pointed out the conflict between social classes. Classes are production-based, making Marx's analysis a materialist one.

7. Social conflict has characterized human history. Conflict in "ancient" societies involved masters and slaves; in agrarian societies, nobility and serfs; in industrial-capitalist societies, the bourgeoisie and the proletariat.

8. Industrial capitalism alienates workers in four ways: from the act of working, from the products of their labor, from other workers, and from human potential.

9. Marx believed that workers could overcome elites and their own false consciousness to overthrow the industrial-capitalist system.

Max Weber

10. The idealist approach of Max Weber reveals that ways of thinking have a powerful effect on society.

11. The rationality of modern s̶ the tradition that directed ' described the historical pr modern-day life as the rat.

12. Weber feared that rationality, anonymous organizations, would still creativity.

Emile Durkheim

13. Durkheim characterized the way society confronts individuals as external, objective facts.

14. His approach relates social elements to the larger society through their functions.

15. Societies require solidarity; mechanical solidarity is based on traditional likeness, while organic solidarity is based on the division of labor, or productive specialization.

Key Concepts

agriculture the technology of large-scale farming using plows powered by animals or advanced energy

alienation the experience of separation resulting from powerlessness

anomie Durkheim's designation of a condition in which society provides individuals with little moral guidance

capitalists people who own factories and other productive enterprises

class conflict Marx's term for the struggle between social classes over the distribution of wealth and power in society

class consciousness Marx's term for the recognition by workers of their unity as a social class in opposition to capitalists and to capitalism itself

division of labor specialized economic activity

false consciousness Marx's description of any belief suggesting that the shortcomings of individuals, rather than society, are responsible for widespread social problems

horticulture technology based on using hand tools to cultivate plants

hunting and gathering simple technology to hunt animals and gather vegetation

ideal type an abstract statement of the essential characteristics of any social phenomenon

industrialism technology that powers sophisticated machinery with advanced fuels

mechanical solidarity Durkheim's term for social bonds, common to preindustrial societies, based on shared moral sentiments

organic solidarity Durkheim's designation of social bonds, common to industrial societies, based on specialization

pastoralism technology that supports the domestication of animals

proletariat people who provide labor necessary for the operation of factories and other productive enterprises

rationality deliberate, matter-of-fact calculation of the most efficient means to accomplish any particular goal

rationalization of society Weber's characterization of the historical change from tradition to rationality as the dominant mode of human thought

social conflict struggle between segments of society over valued resources

social fact Durkheim's term for any social pattern that people confront as an objective reality beyond themselves

social institution a major sphere of social life organized to meet a basic human need

society people who interact in a limited territory and share a culture

sociocultural evolution the Lenskis' term for the process of social change that results from gaining new cultural information, particularly technology

tradition sentiments and beliefs passed from generation to generation

Suggested Readings

A comprehensive account of Gerhard and Jean Lenski's analysis of human societies is found in the following textbook.

Gerhard Lenski, Jean Lenski, and Patrick Nolan. *Human Society: An Introduction to Macrosociology.* 6th ed. New York: McGraw-Hill, 1991.

These essays, in two volumes, point out various misconceptions about our human ancestors.

Tim Ingold, David Riches, and James Woodburn, eds. *Hunters and Gatherers 1: History, Evolution and Social Change,* and *Hunters and Gatherers 2: Property, Power and Ideology.* New York: Berg, 1988.

This book highlights the distinctive ways in which women are defined, with particular attention to virginity, motherhood, and other expressions of sexuality.

Shirley Ardener, ed. *Defining Females: The Nature of Women in Society.* New York: Berg, 1991.

Using the thinkers included in this chapter, as well as literary figures, this book examines the emergence of sociology amid the changes of the nineteenth century.

Bruce Mazlish. *A New Science: The Breakdown of Connections and the Birth of Sociology.* New York: Oxford University Press, 1989.

This is one of the best sources of essays by Karl Marx and Friedrich Engels.

Robert C. Tucker, ed. *The Marx-Engels Reader.* 2nd ed. New York: W.W. Norton, 1978.

Perhaps Max Weber's best-known study is his analysis of Protestantism and capitalism.

Max Weber. *The Protestant Ethic and the Spirit of Capital-*

ism. New York: Charles Scribner's Sons, 1958 (orig. 1904–5).

This collection of essays demonstrates the multifaceted ways in which Max Weber incorporated history, politics, and social criticism into his work.

Wolfgang J. Mommsen. *The Political and Social Theory of Max Weber: Collected Essays.* Chicago: University of Chicago Press, 1989.

This is one of the most thorough studies of Emile Durkheim and his pioneering work in sociology.

Steven Lukes. *Emile Durkheim, His Life and Work: A Historical and Critical Study.* New York: Harper and Row, 1972.

Sociological theory has yet to respond adequately to the large number of women who entered sociology in recent decades. This book takes a step in that direction.

Ruth A. Wallace, ed. *Feminism and Sociological Theory.* Newbury Park, CA: Sage Publications, 1989.

The following is a brief sampling of some classics in Canadian sociology focused on the structure and development of Canadian society.

S.D. Clark. *The Social Development of Canada.* Toronto: University of Toronto Press, 1942.

Wallace Clement. *The Canadian Corporate Elite: An Analysis of Economic Power.* Toronto: McClelland and Stewart, 1974.

Dennis Forcese. *The Canadian Class Structure.* 2nd Edition. Toronto: McGraw Hill, 1980.

John Porter. *The Vertical Mosaic.* Toronto: University of Toronto Press, 1965.

C H A P T E R

5

SOCIALIZATION

On a cold winter day in 1938, a social worker walked anxiously to the door of a farmhouse in rural Pennsylvania. Investigating possible child abuse, the social worker soon discovered a five-year-old girl hidden in a second-floor storage room. The child, whose name was Anna, was wedged into an old chair with her arms tied above her head so that she could not move. She was dressed in a few filthy garments, and her arms and legs were like matchsticks—so thin and frail that she could not use them (Davis, 1940:554).

Anna's situation was both moving and tragic. She was born in 1932 to an unmarried and mentally impaired woman of twenty-six who lived with her father. Enraged by his daughter's "illegitimate" motherhood, the grandfather initially refused to even allow the child in his house. Anna therefore spent the first six months of her life in various institutions. Finally, because her mother was unable to pay for such care, Anna was forced to live with her mother and grandfather.

At this point, her ordeal intensified. To avoid the grandfather's hostility, Anna's mother moved her to a room that resembled an attic, where she received little attention and just enough milk to keep her alive. There she stayed, with essentially no human contact, for five years.

Upon learning of the discovery of Anna, sociologist Kingsley Davis travelled immediately to see the child, who had been transported by local authorities to a county home for children. He was appalled by her condition. Anna was emaciated, devoid of strength, and she displayed virtually no human qualities. She could not laugh, smile, speak, or even show anger. She was completely unresponsive, as if the world around her did not even exist. Not surprisingly, people initially thought she was deaf and blind (Davis, 1940).

The Importance of Social Experience

Anna is a deplorable but instructive case of a human being deprived of virtually all social contact. Although Anna was physically alive, she had none of the capacities associated with full humanity. Her plight revealed that, without social experience, an individual develops little or no capacity for thought, emotion, and meaningful behavior. In short, an individual who has no social interaction is likely to remain an *object* rather than to become a *person*.

This chapter explores what Anna was deprived

of—the means by which we become fully human. We call this process **socialization**, *lifelong social experience by which individuals develop human potential and learn* *the patterns of their culture*. Unlike other living species for which behavior is determined biologically, human beings rely on social experience to learn the intricacies

The Dionne Quintuplets

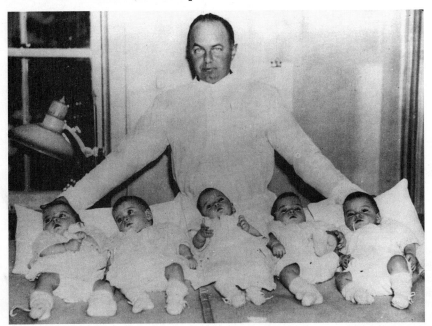

In May of 1934, the world's attention was drawn to a small Northern Ontario town by the birth of identical quintuplets. The chance of this multiple birth was one in 54 million. Until this time, there was no record of quintuplets living more than a few days, but Annette, Yvonne, Emilie, Cecile, and Marie Dionne all lived to be at least young adults.

From the start, their lives were unlike those of most children. They were separated from their parents from birth until they were nine years of age, and raised by a doctor and nurses in uniform, where they were on constant display to strangers. They were a media sensation and an enormously successful cottage industry for the doctor, their parents, and other citizens of their home town of Callan-dar, which became known as Quint-land. At the height of their fame, they were a 500-million-dollar asset for the townspeople. Several cities wanted to house them and three world fairs wanted to exhibit them. By the end of 1936, they were, according to *Time* magazine, the world's greatest news picture story— to many people Canada became known as the home of the "Quints."

In 1963, James Brough wrote a book based on interviews with Cecile, Marie, and Annette. Yvonne did not take part and Emilie had died in a convent when she was 20 years old of an epileptic seizure. Brough told a story of bitter, angry women who had felt like prisoners all their young lives; who resented the facts that they could never be alone, that

their father opened their mail, and that they were not allowed any friends outside of the family. They were treated as a single entity, obligated to dress alike and never to their own taste. The Quints were raised in French, their siblings in English. When they returned home after they were nine, they felt they were treated as slaves and yet, because they had some money of their own, had to pay for the whole family to do certain things such as attend shows.

At 21 years of age, the four surviving sisters moved to Montreal, where they clung together for emotional support. They did not know how to handle money, how to enter a store, shop, or choose clothing. On their own, they began lives marred by continual difficulties including mental and physical illnesses, excessive alcohol consumption, and divorce (Berton, 1977).

The experience of the Dionne sisters was in some ways the opposite of Anna's. They too were separated from their parents for the crucial young years of their lives. Rather than isolation, however, they were constantly in contact with one another. Each was always with her four sisters and together they were the object of the gaze and comment of millions of people over their lifetimes. Yet this highly public form of socialization was just as confusing, contradictory, and inadequate as the private neglect experienced by Anna and others like her. The Dionne story reminds us that successful socialization requires more than just contact with society, and that in the presence of contradictory and deviant social experiences, "personality" may not develop fully.

of their culture in order to survive. Social experience is also the foundation of **personality**, which refers to *a person's fairly consistent pattern of thinking, feeling, and acting*. Personality is constructed from our social surroundings and how we learn to respond to them. As personality develops, we simultaneously become distinctive individuals and share a culture. In the absence of social experience, as the case of Anna shows, personality simply does not develop.

Social experience is obviously as vital for society as it is for individuals. A society extends both forward and backward in time, far beyond the life span of any person. As explained in Chapters 3 ("Culture") and 4 ("Society"), every society teaches something of its past way of life to its new members. The complex and life-long process of socialization is the way in which society transmits culture from one generation to another (Elkin & Handel, 1984).

Human Development: Nature and Nurture

Virtually helpless at birth, the human infant needs others to provide for its care and nourishment. A child also relies on others to teach patterns of culture. Although Anna's experience makes these facts very clear, a century ago most people mistakenly believed that human behavior was the product of biology.

Chapter 3 ("Culture") described Charles Darwin's ground-breaking work in the mid-nineteenth century. In brief, Darwin's theory of evolution held that a species gradually changes over thousands of generations as genetic variations promote more successful survival and reproduction. As Darwin's influence grew, others applied his ideas to the understanding of human behavior. By the end of the nineteenth century, most people spoke of human behavior as if it were instinctive, part of the "nature" of the human species.

Such notions are still with us. People sometimes claim, for example, that our economic system reflects "instinctive human competitiveness," that some people are "born criminals," or that women are more emotional while men are more rational (Witkin-Lanoil, 1984). The term *human nature* is often used to mean personality traits that people are supposedly born with, just as we are born with five senses. More accurately, however, human nature involves the creation and learning of cultural traits, as we shall see.

Darwin's thinking was also misconstrued by people trying to explain how societies varied from one another. Centuries of world exploration and empire

Human infants display various reflexes, biologically based behavioral patterns that enhance survival. The sucking reflex, which actually begins before birth, enables the infant to obtain nourishment. The grasping reflex, triggered by placing a finger on the infant's palm, causes the hand to close. This response helps the infant to maintain contact with a parent and, later on, to grasp objects. The Moro reflex, which occurs when an infant is startled, causes the infant to swing both arms outward and then bring them together on the chest. This action, which disappears during the first months of life, probably developed among our evolutionary ancestors so that a falling baby could grasp the body hair of a parent.

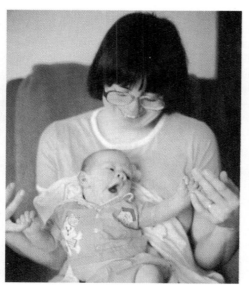
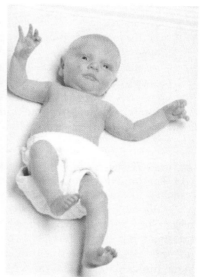

building brought Western Europeans into contact with people whose behavior was quite different from their own. They attributed such contrasts to biological differences rather than to cultural diversity. Thus Europeans and North Americans viewed the members of technologically simple societies as biologically less evolved, and, therefore, less human. This self-serving and ethnocentric view helped them justify their colonial practices. It is easy to enter another society, exploit its resources, and perhaps enslave its people if you believe they are not truly human.

The research on the relationship between "race" and intelligence by Professor Philip Rushton of the University of Western Ontario is an example of modern "Social Darwinism." Rushton claimed to have demonstrated scientifically that orientals were "smarter" than whites or blacks, and that blacks were the least "intelligent" of the three races. The widespread outrage that resulted from the presentation and publication of this work indicates the dramatic decline in the social acceptability of Social Darwinist theories today. Even the conceptualization of the hypothesis that there is a relationship between race and behavior is seen today as a piece of racist behavior.

In the first half of the twentieth century, psychologist John B. Watson (1878–1958) devised an approach called *behaviorism*, which held that specific patterns of behavior are not instinctive but learned. Arguing that all of the world's cultures have the same biological foundation, Watson rejected the idea that cultural variations reflect any evolutionary distinctions. To Watson, human behavior was malleable, open to the influence of any imaginable environment:

> Give me a dozen healthy infants … and my own specified world to bring them up in, and I will guarantee to take any one at random and train him to become any type of specialist that I might select—doctor, lawyer, artist, merchant-chief, and yes, even beggar-man and thief—regardless of his talents, penchants, tendencies, abilities, vocations, and race of his ancestors. (1930:104)

Watson was aware that he was overstating his case, but he was convinced that linking human behavior to biology was fundamentally wrong and that nurture—or learning—was far more influential than "nature."

Watson's assertions were supported by the research of anthropologists that showed variable cultural patterns, even among societies with similar technology. An outspoken proponent of the "nurture" view, anthropologist Margaret Mead summed up the evidence: "The differences between individuals who are members of different cultures, like the differences between individuals within a culture, are almost entirely to be laid to differences in conditioning, especially during early childhood, and this conditioning is culturally determined" (1963:280; orig. 1935).

Today, social scientists are cautious about describing any type of behavior as instinctive. Even sociobiology, discussed in Chapter 3, does not challenge the assertion that human behavior is primarily guided by the surrounding culture. This does not mean that biology plays *no* part in human behavior. Human life, after all, depends on the functioning of the human body. We also know that children share some biological traits with their parents, especially physical characteristics such as height, weight, hair and eye color, and facial features. Intelligence and personality characteristics (for example, how one reacts to stimulation) have some genetic component, as does the potential to excel in such activities as art and music (Herrnstein, 1973). But whether or not a person develops any inherited potential depends on the opportunities associated with social position (Plomin & Foch, 1980; Goldsmith, 1983). Overall, clear evidence supports the conclusion that nurture is far more important than nature in shaping human behavior. Finally, bear in mind, as suggested in Chapter 3, that what we call human nature is the creation, learning, and modification of culture. Thus, nature and nurture stand not so much in opposition as intertwined.

Social Isolation

For obvious ethical reasons, researchers cannot subject human beings to experimental isolation. Consequently, much of what we know about this issue comes from rare cases of children subjected to abuse, like Anna. Even then, researchers typically enter the picture at the end of an ordeal and have to piece together what happened over a period of years. Researchers have, however, studied the effects of social isolation on animals.

Effects of Social Isolation on Nonhuman Primates

A classic investigation of the effects of social isolation on nonhuman primates was conducted by psychologists Harry and Margaret Harlow (1962). The Harlows placed rhesus monkeys—whose behavior is in some ways surprisingly similar to that of humans—in various conditions of isolation to observe the consequences. They found that complete social isolation for a period of even six months (with adequate nutrition) seriously disturbed the monkeys' development. When isolated monkeys subsequently encountered others of their kind, they were fearful and unable to defend themselves against aggression.

The Harlows modified their experiment, isolating infant rhesus monkeys in cages but with an artificial "mother" of wire mesh with a wooden head and the nipple of a feeding tube where the breast would be. These monkeys survived physically, but they, too, were subsequently unable to interact with other monkeys. A further variation of the research, however, showed that when the artificial mother was covered with soft terry cloth, the infant monkeys clung to it and apparently derived emotional benefit from the closeness. These monkeys later displayed less emotional distress. The Harlows thus concluded that normal emotional development requires affectionate cradling as part of mother–infant interaction.

The Harlows also made two other discoveries. First, as long as they were surrounded by other infants, monkeys were not adversely affected by the absence of a mother. This suggests that deprivation of social experience, rather than the specific absence of maternal contact, has devastating effects. Second, the Harlows found that, when socially isolated for shorter periods of time (about three months), infant monkeys eventually regained normal emotional patterns after rejoining others. The damage of short-term isolation, then, can be overcome; longer-term isolation, however, appears to inflict on monkeys irreversible emotional and behavioral damage.

Effects of Social Isolation on Children

The case of Anna, described at the beginning of this chapter, is the best-known instance of the long-term social isolation of a human infant. After her discovery, however, Anna benefited from extensive social contact and she soon showed some improvement. When Kingsley Davis (1940) visited her in the county home after ten days, he noted that she was more alert and showed some human expression, even smiling with obvious pleasure. During the next year, Anna made slow but steady progress, as she experienced the humanizing effects of socialization, showing greater interest in other people and gradually learning to walk. After a year and a half, she could feed herself, walk alone for short distances, and play with toys.

Consistent with the observations of the Harlows, however, it was becoming apparent that Anna's five years of social isolation had left her permanently damaged. At the age of eight her mental and social development was still less than that of a two-year-old. Not until she was almost ten did she show the first signs of using language. Complicating the problem is the fact that

The personalities we develop depend largely on the environment in which we live. As William Kurelek shows in this painting, Prairie Childhood, *based on his childhood in the Alberta prairies, a young person's life on a farm is often characterized by periods of social isolation and backbreaking work. How would such a boy's personality be likely to differ from that of his wealthy cousin raised in Montreal?*

Anna's mother was mentally retarded, so that Anna may have been similarly disadvantaged. The puzzle was never untangled, because Anna died at age ten from a blood disorder, possibly related to her long years of abuse (Davis, 1940).

A second, quite similar case reveals more about the long-range effects of social isolation. At about the same time that Anna was discovered, another girl of about the same age was found under strikingly similar circumstances. After more than six years of virtual isolation, this girl—known as Isabelle—showed the same lack of human responsiveness as Anna (Davis, 1947). Unlike Anna, though, Isabelle benefited from an intensive program by psychologists to aid her development. Within a week, Isabelle was attempting to speak, and a year and a half later, her vocabulary was nearly two thousand words. The psychologists concluded that Isabelle had progressed through what is normally about six years of development with two years of intensive effort. By the time she was fourteen, Isabelle was attending Grade six classes in school, apparently well on her way to at least an approximately normal life.

A final case of childhood isolation involves a thirteen-year-old girl in California isolated in a small room from the age of about two. For years Genie had been victimized by her parents in a host of ways, including being deprived of social contact. Upon discovery, her condition was similar to that of the two other children we have described. Genie was emaciated (weighing only about 26 kilograms) and had the mental development of a one-year-old. She was given intensive treatment by specialists and is alive today. Yet even after years of care, her ability to use language is little better than that of a young child (Curtiss, 1977; Pines, 1981). All the evidence points to the crucial role of social experience in personality development. Human beings are resilient creatures, sometimes able to recover from even the crushing experience of prolonged isolation. But there is a point—precisely when is unclear from the limited number of cases—at which social isolation in infancy results in irreparable developmental damage.

Understanding the Socialization Process

Socialization is a highly complex process, and no one researcher to date has fully explained how we gain our humanity. The following sections introduce several thinkers who have made important contributions to our understanding of social development.

Sigmund Freud stands among the pioneers who charted the human personality. His daughter Anna Freud, also shown here in a 1913 family photograph, further developed her father's theory of psychoanalysis.

Sigmund Freud: The Elements of Personality   Oct 12/95

Sigmund Freud (1856–1939) lived in Vienna at a time when most Europeans linked human behavior to biological forces. Freud himself was trained in the natural sciences and began his career as a physician. His importance today, however, is based on his ground-breaking analysis of personality from which he developed his theory of psychoanalysis. Many aspects of this work have direct bearing on understanding socialization.

Basic Human Needs

Freud contended that biology plays an important part in personality development, although he never reduced human behavior to simple biological instinct. For Freud, instinct meant general human needs or drives. Freud ultimately decided that two human drives underlie all others. First, he claimed, humans have a basic need for bonding, which he described as the life instinct, or *eros* (from the Greek god of love). In Freud's view, this life instinct manifests itself in the pursuit of sensory pleasure, including sex. Second, he asserted that people also have an aggressive drive, which he called the death instinct, or *thanatos* (from Greek meaning "death"). Freud postulated that these opposing forces generate tension in the personality, even though we are not necessarily conscious of this interplay of forces. Together, he maintained, these drives form the foundation of the human drama.

Freud's Model of Personality

Freud incorporated both basic drives and the influence of society into a broader model of personality with three parts: id, ego, and superego. The **id** represents *the human being's basic drives*, which are unconscious and demand immediate gratification. (The word *id* is simply Latin for "it," suggesting the tentative way in which Freud explored the unconscious mind.) Rooted in our biology, the id is present at birth so that, from a Freudian point of view, a newborn is basically a bundle of needs that demands attention, touching, and food. Since society opposes such a self-centered orientation, the id's desires inevitably encounter resistance. To avoid frustration, the child learns to approach the world realistically. This is accomplished through the ego, the second component of the personality, which gradually emerges from the id. The **ego** (Latin for "I") represents *a person's conscious efforts to balance innate pleasure-seeking drives with the demands of society*. The ego arises as we gain awareness of our distinct existence; it develops as we face up to the fact that we cannot have everything we want. Finally, the human personality develops the **superego** (Latin meaning "above" or "beyond" the ego), which is *the presence of culture within the individual*. In this intriguing overlay of personality, we see *why* we cannot have everything we want. The superego consists of the internalized values and norms of our culture, and takes the form of conscience. First expressed as the recognition of parental control, the superego eventually matures as the child learns that parental control is itself a reflection of the moral demands of the larger culture.

From a child's point of view, the world first appears as a bewildering array of physical sensations and need satisfactions. With the gradual development of the superego, however, the child's comprehension extends beyond pleasure and pain to the moral concepts of right and wrong. In other words, initially a child can feel good only in the physical sense. Later, though, a child feels good for behaving in culturally appropriate ways and feels bad (the experience of guilt) for failing to do so.

In a well-adjusted personality, the ego successful-ly manages the opposing forces of the id and the superego. If conflicts are not successfully resolved, personality disorders result. Freud viewed childhood as the critical period in the formation of an individual's basic personality, and he regarded conflicts experienced during this stage of life as an unconscious source of personality problems later on.

Freud called society's efforts to control human drives *repression*. In his view, some repression is inevitable, since people must be coerced into looking beyond themselves. Often, the competing demands are resolved through compromise, so that basic needs are redirected into socially approved forms. This process, which Freud named *sublimation*, transforms fundamentally selfish drives into socially acceptable activities. For example, sexual urges may lead to marriage, and aggression can be expressed in a sports stadium.

Critical evaluation. Freud's work sparked controversy in his own lifetime and some of that controversy still smolders today. The world he knew vigorously repressed human sexuality, and few of his contemporaries were inclined to concede that sex was a basic human need. Recently, Freud has drawn fire for his depictions of humanity in allegedly male terms, thereby distorting the lives of women (Donovan & Littenberg, 1982). But Freud provided a foundation that influenced virtually everyone who later studied the human personality. Of special importance to sociology is his notion that we internalize social norms, and that childhood experiences have lasting importance to socialization.

Jean Piaget: Cognitive Development

Oct 10/95

Jean Piaget (1896–1980) also stands among the foremost psychologists of the century. Much of his work centered on human *cognition*—how people think and understand. Early in his career, Piaget was fascinated by the behavior of his three children, wondering not only what they knew, but *how* they understood the world. Systematic observations led him to conclude that children's conceptions of the world vary with age. Piaget identified four stages of cognitive development, each a product of biological maturation and increasing social experience.

The Sensorimotor Stage

The first step in human development, according to Piaget, is the **sensorimotor stage**, *the level of human* *development in which people experience the world only through sensory contact.* In this stage, which corresponds roughly to the first two years of life, the infant explores the world by touching, looking, sucking, and listening. By about four months of age, children learn to distinguish their own bodies from their surroundings. Nearing the end of this stage, children comprehend what Piaget called *object permanence,* realizing that objects continue to exist even if the youngster cannot sense them directly. Young infants, for example, may think that an adult leaving the room actually has ceased to exist (and respond accordingly).

Children gain skill at imitating the actions or sounds of others during the sensorimotor stage, but they have no comprehension of symbols. Thus, very young children do not think; they know the world only in terms of direct physical experience.

The Preoperational Stage

The second level in Piaget's account of development is the **preoperational stage,** *the level of human development in which individuals first use language and other symbols.* Typically, this stage extends from age two to seven. Using symbols, children can now engage the world mentally—that is, they are able to think about things they cannot sense directly. As they begin to attach meaning to the world, they learn to distinguish between ideas and objective reality. At this age, children realize that their dreams are not real, and they appreciate the element of fantasy in fairy tales (Kohlberg & Gilligan, 1971; Skolnick, 1986). Unlike adults, however, they identify the names and meanings only of specific things. A child at this stage who takes pleasure in describing a favorite toy, for example, will be unable to describe the qualities of toys in general.

Without a grasp of general concepts, a child cannot abstractly conceive of size, weight, and volume. In one of his best-known experiments, focusing on a principle Piaget called *conservation of matter,* the researcher placed two identical glasses, containing equal volumes of water, on a table. He then asked several children aged five and six if the amount in each glass was the same. They nodded that it was. The children then watched Piaget take one of the glasses and pour its contents into a taller, narrower glass, raising the level of the water. He asked again if each glass held the same amount. The typical five- and six-year-old now insisted that the taller glass held more water. But children over the age of seven, who are able to think more abstractly, could usually comprehend that the amount of water remained the same.

During the preoperational stage, children still have a very egocentric view of the world (Damon, 1983). For example, we have all seen young children place their hands in front of their faces and exclaim, "You can't see me!". They assume that if they cannot see you, then you are unable to see them. This illustrates that they perceive the world only from their own vantage point and have yet to learn that a situation may appear different to another person.

The Concrete Operational Stage

Next, in Piaget's model, comes the **concrete operational stage,** *the level of development at which individuals first use logic to understand their surroundings.* At this point, typically between seven and eleven, children make significant strides in comprehending and manipulating their environment. Having gained the capacity for logical thought, they now connect what they experience in terms of cause and effect. In addition, girls and boys can attach more than one symbol to a particular event or object. For instance, if you say to a girl of six, "Today is Wednesday," she might respond, "No, it's my birthday!" belying the limitation of being able to use but one symbol at a time. Within a few years, however, she would be able to respond, "Yes, this Wednesday is my birthday!". However, during the concrete operational stage, the thinking of children remains focused on concrete objects and events. They may understand that hitting brothers without provocation will bring punishment, but children still cannot conceive of situa-

In a well-known experiment, Jean Piaget demonstrated that children over the age of seven entered the concrete operational stage of development as they came to recognize that the quantity of liquid remained the same when poured from a wide beaker into a tall one.

oct 12/95

tions in which hitting a brother would be fair or why parents punish. In a final development during the concrete operational stage, children transcend their earlier egocentrism, imagining themselves in the position of another person. As we shall explain shortly, perceiving a situation from another's point of view is the foundation of complex social activities, such as games.

The Formal Operational Stage

The fourth level in Piaget's model, the **formal operational stage**, refers to *the level of human development at which people use highly abstract thought and are able to imagine alternatives to reality*. By about the age of twelve, children begin to reason using abstract qualities rather than thinking only of concrete situations. If, for example, you were to ask a child of seven or eight, "What would you like to be when you grow up?" you might prompt a concrete response, such as "A teacher." Once the final stage of cognitive development is attained, however, the child is capable of responding abstractly, "I would like a job that is exciting." At this point, the child has acquired the marvelous human quality of imagination, which frees us from the immediate bounds of our lives. Children capable of formal operations often display a keen interest in imaginative literature like science fiction (Skolnick, 1986). They also are able to comprehend metaphors. Hearing the phrase "A penny for your thoughts" might lead a younger child to think of money, but the older child will recognize a gentle invitation to intimacy.

Critical evaluation. If Freud envisioned humanity torn by the opposing forces of biology and society, Piaget believed the human mind to be active and creative, so that children soon learn to shape their own social world, an achievement that is well documented by other research (Corsaro & Rizzo, 1988). His contribution to understanding socialization lies in showing that this capacity unfolds gradually as the result of biological maturation and growing social experience.

In global perspective, there is some question as to whether people in every culture progress through Piaget's stages, and do so in the same time frame. For instance, living in a society that changes very slowly is likely to inhibit the ability to imagine the world being very different. In addition, Carol Gilligan (1982) has suggested that we have yet to examine adequately how gender affects the process of social development. Her studies show that boys and girls take a somewhat dif-

ferent approach to moral reasoning, with boys embracing abstract standards of right and wrong while girls morally evaluate events according to how they affect others. Finally, among both women and men, as many as 30 percent of thirty-year-olds appear not to reach the formal operational stage at all (Kohlberg & Gilligan, 1971). This finding again underscores the importance of social experience in the development of personality. Regardless of biological maturity, people who are not exposed to highly creative and imaginative thinking are less likely to develop this capacity in themselves.

George Herbert Mead: The Social Self[1]

What exactly is social experience? How does it enhance our humanity? These fundamental questions guided the work of George Herbert Mead, who is introduced in the box. Among sociologists, Mead is widely regarded as having made the greatest contribution to explaining the process of socialization.

Mead's approach (1962; orig. 1934) has often been described as *social behaviorism*, suggesting a connection to the thinking of psychologist John B. Watson, described earlier. Mead agreed with Watson that environment influences human behavior, but he saw a basic error in Watson's approach. By focusing on behavior itself, Mead reasoned, Watson ignored mental processes—the key to our humanity—and treated the behavior of humans and other animals as essentially the same. Mead conceded to Watson the difficulty of studying the human mind, but he pressed ahead, certain that the key to social experience lay not in how humans act but in how we think.

The Self

Mead's central concept is the **self**, *a dimension of personality composed of an individual's self-conception*. Mead's genius lay in seeing that the self is inseparable from society, a connection explained in a series of steps.

First, Mead asserted, *the self emerges from social experience*. The self is not biological, it is not the same as any part of the body, and it does not exist at birth. Mead rejected the notion that personality is guided by biological drives (as asserted by Freud) or biological maturation (as Piaget claimed). For Mead, the self simply develops through social experience and *only*

---

[1] This section reflects suggestions by Howard Sacks of Kenyon College.

George Herbert Mead (1863–1931)

Few people were surprised that George Herbert Mead became a college professor. He was born to a Massachusetts family with a strong intellectual tradition, and both his parents were academics. His mother served for ten years as president of Mount Holyoke College, and his father was both a preacher and teacher at a number of colleges.

But Mead also had a hand in shaping his own life, and in some unexpected ways. Early on, he rebelled against the strongly religious atmosphere of his home and community. After completing college, he travelled around the Pacific Northwest, surveying for the railroad and reading as much as he could. Restless about his future, he gradually settled on the idea of studying philosophy, which he did at Harvard and abroad.

Mead took a teaching position at the new University of Chicago. But his outlook still veered far from the conventional. For one thing, he rarely published, an activity expected of many academics. Mead's fame spread after his death when colleagues and former students published a collection of his lecture notes. For another, Mead drew together ideas from a wide range of disciplines to generate new and fascinating insights that helped launch the new field of social psychology. Finally, never content with life as it was, Mead was an active reformer, often championing controversial causes. His firm belief in the human capacity for change gave him confidence that society could overcome its problems. In addition to teaching, then, Mead labored to improve the lives of the city's disadvantaged.

George Herbert Mead envisioned both an individual life and the course of an entire society as unpredictable and ongoing. His own life exemplifies the themes of his work: the power of society to shape individuals and the power of people to shape society.

SOURCES: Based, in part, on Coser (1977) and Schellenberg (1978).

---

through social experience. In the absence of social interaction, as we see from the cases of isolated children, the body may grow but no self will emerge.

Second, Mead explained, *social experience is based on the exchange of symbols.* By using symbols, people create meaning in their interaction. People use words, a wave of the hand, and a smile symbolically. Thus, while Mead agreed with Watson that human behavior can be shaped by manipulating rewards and punishments, he maintained that this ignores distinctively human characteristics in our behavior. We can train a dog, after all, to respond to a command, but the dog attaches no meaning to its action. Human beings, by contrast, search for meanings as we infer intention as well as observe action. In short, a dog responds to *what you do*; a human responds to *what you have in mind* as you do it.

Return to our friendly dog for a moment. Using reward and punishment, you can train a dog to walk to the porch and return with an umbrella. But the dog grasps no meaning in the act, no intention behind the command. Thus, if the dog cannot find the umbrella, it is incapable of the *human* response: to look for a raincoat instead. Human beings do this because we understand actions in terms of meanings.

The third step in Mead's analysis is the assertion that *understanding someone's intentions requires imagining the situation from that person's point of view.* Our symbolic capacity empowers us to imaginatively place ourselves in another person's shoes, and to see ourselves as that person does. Intentional social action depends on being able to envision how others will respond to us even before we act. Even the simplest act of tossing a ball requires stepping outside of ourselves to imagine how another will respond to our throw. Social interaction, then, involves seeing ourselves as others see us—a process that Mead termed *"taking the role of the other."*

The Looking-Glass Self

How we think about ourselves is inseparable from how others think of us. Charles Horton Cooley (1864–1929), one of Mead's colleagues, suggested that others represent a mirror or looking glass in which we perceive ourselves as they see us. Cooley (1964; orig. 1902) used the phrase **looking-glass self** to capture *the idea that the self is based on how others respond to us.* Whether we think of ourselves as clever or clumsy, worthy or worthless, handsome or homely, depends in large measure on what we think others think of us.

The I and the Me

The notion that "the self thinks about itself" suggests an important dualism. First, *the self is subject*, a point brought home as humans initiate social action. Mead claimed humans are innately active and spontaneous. For simplicity, he dubbed this subjective element of the self the *I* (the subjective form of the first-person pronoun). Second, *the self is object*, that is, how we imagine ourselves from the perspective of someone else. Mead called this objective element of the self the *me* (the objective form of the first-person pronoun). Social experience begins as a person initiates action (the I-phase of the self) and then guides the action (the me-phase of the self) by reflectively taking the role of the other. All social experience involves a continuous interplay of the I and the me: our actions are spontaneous yet guided by how others respond to us.

Mead stressed that thinking, too, has a social dimension. Our thoughts are partly creative (representing the I), but in thought we also become objects to ourselves (representing the me), as we imagine how others would respond to our ideas.

Development of the Self

According to Mead, the self develops by gaining sophistication in taking the role of the other. Like Freud and Piaget, Mead regarded early childhood as crucial to this process. However, he did not think the development of the self was rigidly linked to age. Both Freud and Piaget emphasized the role of biology in personality development, but Mead consistently minimized the importance of biological forces. Thus Mead thought that the self emerged over time due simply to more and more social experience.

Mead declared that infants with limited social experience respond to others only in terms of *imitation*. They mimic behavior but do not understand underlying intentions. Without symbolic interaction, Mead concluded, no self exists.

As children learn to use language and other symbols, the self becomes evident in the form of *play*. Children begin to experience the complex behavior they observe around them by role playing. At first, they model themselves on significant people—such as parents—sometimes called *significant others*. Playing "Mommy and Daddy," for example, helps children imagine the world from their parents' point of view.

Gradually, children learn to take the roles of several others simultaneously. In other words, the developing self is able to initiate distinctive actions in response to various others. This is the key to moving from simple play involving one role to more complex *games* involving many roles at once. Doing so, a person's self becomes more complex, based now on numerous "looking-glasses." The box on the opposite page profiles Mead.

At times people develop multiple selves. This process may be related to the experience of extreme abuse in children. Sylvia Fraser, a Canadian novelist, describes her own experience of sexual abuse and the development of another personality in the following.

> *When the conflict caused by my sexual relationship with my father became too acute to bear, I created a secret accomplice for my daddy by splitting my personality in two. Thus, somewhere around the age of seven, I acquired another self with memories and experiences separate from mine, whose existence was unknown to me. My loss of memory was retroactive. I did not remember my daddy ever having touched me sexually. I did not remember ever seeing my daddy naked. I did not remember my daddy ever seeing me naked. In future, whenever my daddy approached me sexually I turned into my other self, and afterwards I did not remember anything that had happened. (Fraser, 1987)*

A final step in the development of the self involves acquiring the ability to see ourselves as society in general does. Figure 5-1 on page 140 shows how this constitutes an extension of play and games. Even in a game, the others involved are limited. Going a step further, we eventually learn to take the role of virtually anyone in any situation. This depends on recognizing that people throughout society share cultural norms and values. As they incorporate general cultural patterns into the self, children begin to respond to themselves as they imagine anyone might. Mead used the term **generalized other** to refer to *widespread cultural norms and values we use as a reference in evaluating ourselves.*

Finally, the socialization process does not end with the emergence of the self. Quite the contrary: Mead claimed that socialization continues as long as we have social experience. Furthermore, changing social circum-

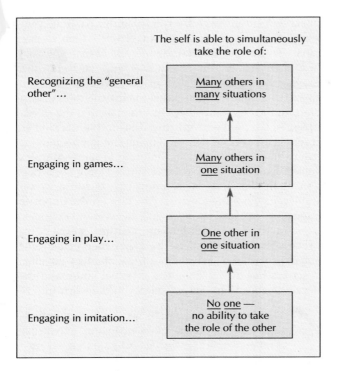

The self is able to simultaneously take the role of:

Recognizing the "general other"...

Many others in many situations

Engaging in games...

Many others in one situation

Engaging in play...

One other in one situation

Engaging in imitation...

No one — no ability to take the role of the other

FIGURE 5-1   BUILDING ON SOCIAL EXPERIENCE
George Herbert Mead described the development of self as the process of gaining social experience. This is largely a matter of taking the role of the other with increasing sophistication.

stances can reshape who we are. The self may change, for example, if someone becomes rich, divorced, or disabled. But we are not pawns, simply moved by others. Mead steadfastly maintained that social experience is based on interaction, so that society shapes us, but we also act back on society. In short, as active and creative beings, we play a large part in our own socialization.

Critical evaluation.   George Herbert Mead's contribution to the understanding of socialization lies in exploring social experience itself. He succeeded in showing how symbolic interaction underlies the self as well as society.

Mead's view is sometimes criticized for being radically social—meaning that it recognizes no biological element in the emergence of the self. In this, he stands apart from Freud (who identified general drives within the human organism) and Piaget (whose stages of development are tied to biological maturation).

Mead's concepts of the I and the me are often confused with Freud's concepts of the id and the superego. One difference is that Freud rooted the id in the biological organism, while Mead rejected any link

between the self and biology (although he never specified the origin of the I). Freud's concept of the superego and Mead's concept of the me both reflect the power of society to shape personality. But for Freud, superego and id are locked in continual combat. Mead, however, understood the I and the me as working closely and cooperatively together (Meltzer, 1978).

Agents of Socialization

We are affected in at least some small way by every social experience we have. In modern industrial societies, however, several agents of socialization have pronounced importance.

The Family

The family is usually the most important agent of socialization. As we have seen, infants are dependent on others to meet their needs, and this responsibility almost always falls on parents and other family members. Typically, the family stands as a child's entire social world, at least until the onset of schooling, and it remains central to social experiences throughout the life course (Riley, Foner, & Waring, 1988). The family also plays a crucial part in transmitting culture from one generation to the next. Through countless family activities, children are taught to reproduce social patterns familiar to adults.

Family-based socialization is not all intentional. Children learn continuously from the kind of environment that adults create. Whether children learn to think of themselves as strong or weak, smart or stupid, loved or simply tolerated, and whether they believe the world to be trustworthy or dangerous, largely stem from this early environment.

Although parents do not solely determine the course of their children's development, many attitudes, interests, goals, beliefs, and prejudices are acquired in the family. Also, from infancy boys and girls receive both conscious and unconscious guidance from family members in how to be "masculine" and "feminine" (Tavris & Wade, 1984; Witkin-Lanoil, 1984). In sum, much of what we consider to be innate in ourselves actually comes from patterns of socialization learned in the family.

Parenting styles vary from home to home, but research points to the importance of *attention*, paid by parents to children, in the social development of children. Physical contact, verbal stimulation, and responsiveness from parents have all been shown to foster intellectual growth (Belsky, Lerner, & Spanier, 1984).

Another crucial function of the family is providing children with a social position. In other words, parents not only bring children into the physical world, they also place them in society in terms of social class, religion, race, and ethnicity. In time, all these elements of social identity become part of a child's self-concept. Of course, this social placement may change in at least some respects, but it affects us throughout our lives.

Investigating the importance of social class to socialization, Melvin Kohn (1977) interviewed working-class and middle-class parents in the United States. He found that working-class parents tend to stress behavioral conformity in rearing their children. Middle-class parents, however, typically tolerate a wider range of behavior and show greater concern for the intentions and motivations that underlie their children's actions. Kohn explained this difference in terms of the education and occupations common to parents in each category. Working-class parents usually lack higher education and often have jobs in which they are closely supervised and expected to do as they are told. This leads them to foster similar obedience and conformity in their children. By contrast, with more schooling, middle-class parents typically have jobs that provide greater autonomy and encourage the use of imagination. These parents are therefore likely to inspire the same qualities in their children. Such differences in socialization have long-term effects on children's ambitions, partly explaining why middle-class children are more likely than working-class children to go to university themselves and are generally more confident of success in university and in later careers (Wilson, 1959; Ballantine, 1989). In many ways, then, parents teach children to follow in their footsteps, and to adapt to the constraints or privileges of their inherited social positions.

Interestingly, children are aware from a very early age of the accessories of class. Bernd Baldus and Verna Tribe (1978) presented children in grades one, three, and six with sets of pictures of two men, one who was "well" dressed and one who was casually dressed, two houses (one from a high income area of the city), two dining rooms, and two cars, again reflecting expensive taste on the one hand, and less expensive taste on the other. Children's ability to match person and appropriate taste level did increase with the grade level, but it was not affected by gender, the school environment, or their own social class origin. Interestingly, the children

were able to give "character" descriptions of the two men. The well dressed man was described as cheerful, nice, smart, and likeable, while the casually dressed man was described as tough, lazy, and likely to swear, steal, drink, or be uncaring regarding his family. Clearly, when children learn about class, they are actually learning to assign different values to different people. This, in return, can have an effect on how they value themselves—in short, their self-esteem.

Schooling

Schooling introduces children to new people and experiences. In school, children learn to interact with others who are initially strangers and who may have social backgrounds that differ from their own. As children consider social diversity, they are also likely to become self-conscious of their own social identities and respond to others accordingly. For example, one study of kindergarten children in the United States documented the tendency for blacks and whites to form same-race play groups (Finkelstein & Haskins, 1983). Similarly, boys and girls tend to form distinct play groups, grasping more of the importance that our culture attaches to sex (Lever, 1978).

Formally, schooling teaches children a wide range of knowledge and skills. The early grades are devoted to basic abilities like reading, writing, and arithmetic. Secondary schools and universities subsequently convey more specialized material needed to perform various occupational roles. But what children learn in school goes far beyond the official curriculum. What is often called the *hidden curriculum* teaches them important cultural values. Activities such as spelling bees and sports encourage children to be competitive and to value success. Children also receive countless subtle messages that their society's way of life is morally good.

Children's value in the family is based on personal relationships: they are loved because of *who they are*. Thus school presents a new experience for children, with evaluations of skills like reading based on impersonal, standardized tests. Here, the emphasis shifts from who they are to *how they perform*. As such evaluations define personal abilities, they greatly affect how children come to view themselves. At the same time, the confidence or anxiety that children develop at home can have a significant effect on how well they perform in school (Belsky, Lerner, & Spanier, 1984). Finally, the school gives most children their first experience with rigid formality. The school day is organized according to a strict time schedule, subjecting children to impersonal regimentation and fostering traits such as punctuality that will be expected by many large organizations later in life.

Finally, schools further socialize children into culturally approved sex roles. As Raphaela Best (1983) points out, instructional activities for boys and girls often differ, so that boys engage in more physical activities and spend more time outdoors, while girls tend to be more sedentary, sometimes even helping the teacher with various housekeeping chores. Such gender distinctions continue through the university years. University women encounter pressure to select majors in the arts, humanities, or social sciences, while men are steered toward the physical sciences. Further, the informal campus culture provides more support for the academic achievement of men, while making romantic life a central concern of women (Holland & Eisenhart, 1990).

Overall, schooling plays a vital part in guiding child development. Schools help children adjust to living in a large, impersonal world and also teach them the knowledge and skills necessary to successfully perform adult roles. All this is done without disturbing larger patterns of social inequality. As Chapter 16 ("Education") explains, schooling perpetuates social inequality by linking the extent and type of education that children receive to gender and social class.

Peer Groups

By the start of school, children have discovered another new setting for social activity in the **peer group**, *a social group whose members have interests, social position, and age in common.* A young child's peer group generally consists of neighborhood playmates; later, peer groups are composed of friends from school or other activities.

The peer group differs from the family and the school because it affords an escape from the direct supervision of adults. Of course, this constitutes much of the attraction of peer groups in the first place. With considerable independence, peer groups offer individuals valuable experience in forging social relationships on their own and developing a sense of themselves apart from their families. Peer groups also provide the opportunity to discuss interests that may not be shared by adults (such as styles of dress and popular music) as well as topics young people may wish to avoid in the presence of parents and teachers (such as drugs and sex).

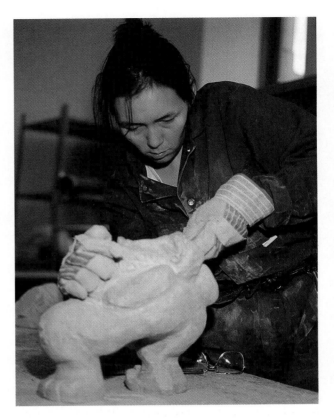

This photo of an Inuit artist from Rankin Inlet, Theresa Sivanertok, illustrates one of the ways in which aboriginal Canadians have become recognized and admired by non-Native Canadians. Being a "successful" artist not only can have a positive effect on a young person's self image, it can also help to open doors that had been previously shut because of pervasive prejudice in the society as a whole.

The ever-present possibility of activity not condoned by adults is, no doubt, the reason parents have long expressed concern about who their children's friends are. Especially in a society that is changing rapidly, peer groups often rival parents in influence. This is simply because the interests and attitudes of parents and children may differ considerably—as suggested by the familiar phrase "the generation gap." The importance of peer groups typically peaks during adolescence, when young people begin to break away from their families and think of themselves as responsible adults. It is during this stage of life that individuals typically draw the greatest identity from peer groups, and they are often anxious in their efforts to conform. The reward of belonging to a peer group eases some of the uneasiness provoked by breaking away from the family.

The conflict between parents and peers may be more apparent than real, however, for even during adolescence children remain strongly influenced by their families. While the peer group may guide such short-term concerns as style of dress and musical taste, parents retain more sway over the long-term aspirations of their children. For example, one study found that parents had more influence than even best friends on young people's educational aspirations (Davies & Kandel, 1981).

Finally, a neighborhood or school forms a social mosaic of many peer groups. As we will see in Chapter 7 ("Groups and Organizations"), members tend to perceive their own peer group in positive terms while discrediting others. Therefore, *many* peer groups are important to the socialization process as individuals conform to their own groups while forming an identity in opposition to others. In some cases, too, people are strongly influenced by peer groups they would like to join. For example, upon entering a new school, a young man with a desire to excel at basketball may wish to become part of the basketball players' social crowd. He is likely to adopt what he sees as the social patterns of this group in the hope of eventual acceptance. This represents what sociologists call **anticipatory socialization**, *the process of social learning directed toward gaining a desired position.* Later in life, jobs are likely to prompt further anticipatory socialization. For instance, a young lawyer who hopes to eventually become a partner in her law firm may conform to the attitudes and behavior of other partners to encourage her inclusion into this rarefied group.

The Mass Media

The **mass media** are *impersonal communications directed to a vast audience.* The term "media" is derived from Latin meaning "middle," so that media function to connect people. In large industrial societies, media take on a mass scale so that television, radio, newspapers, and magazines link tens of millions of people. In Canada, the mass media have an enormous impact on our attitudes and behavior. For this reason, we need to critically consider the content of the media. Often media sources claim to present world events in a factual manner. Some sociologists, however, argue that the media tend to support the *status quo*, while portraying people who challenge the system in negative terms (Gans, 1980; Parenti, 1986).

Introduced in 1939, television rapidly became part of the Canadian scene after 1950. At that time,

fewer than 9 percent of all households had one or more television sets. By 1990, this proportion had soared to 99 percent (while only 16.3 percent had home computers). Video cassette recorders (VCRs), the fastest-growing appliance in history, are already found in 66.3 percent of homes, up from 6.4 percent in 1983. Of all households, 71.4 percent have cable television coverage (Colombo, 1992:87). Clearly, "the tube" now has profound significance for socialization.

The latest statistics show that the average household in Canada has a television turned on for three hours a day (Colombo, 1992:566). Before most children learn to read, watching television has become a regular routine, and young girls and boys in the United States actually spend more hours in front of a television than they do in school (Anderson & Lorch, 1983; Singer, 1983). Canadian children are not far behind in their viewing habits. Indeed, television may very well consume more of children's time than interacting with parents. Overall, television is now the most powerful mass medium (Singer & Singer, 1983).

There is almost one television set for every person in Canada, but television is far from common in many other countries. Global Map 5-1 on page 144 provides a look at where in the world this medium is found.

Joe Camel, the debonair dromedary, has sent the sales of Camel cigarettes soaring. Since this ad campaign began, the proportion of Camels sold to minors, in violation of the law, has risen to one-fourth. The increase attests to the marketing power of the mass media, but also raises ethical questions about how the public should regulate this power.

Television does more than provide entertainment; it programs many of our attitudes and beliefs. For example, television has traditionally portrayed men and women according to cultural stereotypes, showing, for instance, men in positions of power and women as mothers or subordinates (Cantor & Pingree, 1983; Ang, 1985; Holmes & Taras, 1992). As Chapter 13 ("Sex and Gender") describes in detail, advertising in the mass media contributes to gender stereotyping (Courtney & Whipple, 1983). Similarly, television shows have long presented affluent people in favorable

terms, while suggesting that less affluent people (Archie Bunker is the classic example) are ignorant and wrongheaded (Gans, 1980). In addition, although racial and ethnic minorities tend to watch more television than others, they have until recently been all but absent from programming. The successful 1950s comedy *I Love Lucy*, for example, was initially shunned by major television producers because it featured Desi Arnaz—a Hispanic—in a starring role. Even today, television often portrays minorities in ways that are attractive and non-threatening to white middle-class

WINDOW ON THE WORLD

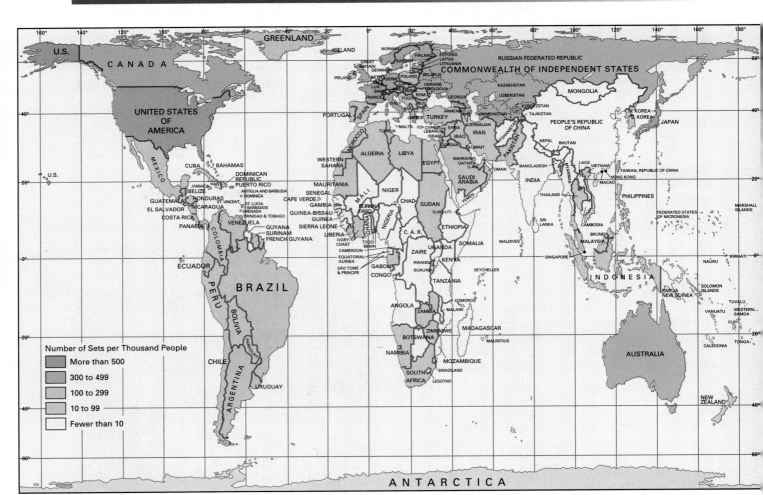

GLOBAL MAP 5-1   TELEVISION OWNERSHIP IN GLOBAL PERSPECTIVE
The mass media have the greatest influence in industrialized societies like the United States and Canada. In less technologically complex societies, people are more likely to communicate in the traditional manner, through face-to-face talk. This pattern is evident in the number of television sets per thousand people: in the United States there is roughly one set for every woman, man, and child in the country.

people (as in the affluent African-American family on *The Cosby Show*). The number of visible minorities making appearances in all the mass media has increased mainly because advertisers recognize the marketing advantages of appealing to these large segments of North American society (Wilson & Gutierrez, 1985).

One dimension of television in which significant change has taken place is news reporting. Recognition of social diversity today is now greater than it was even a decade ago. In large measure, this stems from deliberate personnel policies. Still, over 90 percent of the experts we see on television are men, as are 77 percent of the newsreporters and 70 percent of the voiceovers. Women hold 28 percent of the CBC management positions, yet they are still over-represented in the bottom two of nine levels. Available evidence, then, suggests that Canadians continue to value the male voice and presence over that of the female (Holmes & Taras, 1992). Minorities face similar invisible barriers to those faced by women.

Television continues to influence us through what it ignores, such as the lives of the poor, of homosexuals, and of aboriginal and other racial minorities. In this way, television sends the message that these categories of people do not matter or—even more incorrectly—that they do not exist at all. Television has unquestionably enriched our lives in many respects, bringing into our homes a wide range of entertaining and educational programming. Furthermore, this "window on the world" has increased our awareness of diverse cultures and provided a means of addressing current public issues. At the same time, the power of television has made it a controversial medium, and especially to the extent that it supports traditional stereotypes.

Public Opinion

Public opinion is defined as *the attitudes of people throughout a society about one or more controversial issues*. Although family and peer groups have the greatest impact on socialization, our attitudes and behavior are also influenced by what we perceive to be the opinions of other members of our society. As discussed in Chapter 6 ("Social Interaction in Everyday Life"), people often conform to the attitudes of others—even complete strangers—to avoid being singled out as different. The mass media track the latest trends, and there is little doubt that both adults and children mimic

these patterns. For example, the clothing industry's success in marketing new fashions several times a year illustrates people's tendency to adopt, within their budgets, what the trend makers define as desirable.

Public opinion sometimes exaggerates the degree of conformity in Canada. We have all heard people say that homosexuals are "weird," that noncompetitive men "lack character," and that women who are assertive are "pushy." But it is worth remembering that our culture is highly diverse, and no one ever conforms completely to so-called dominant values and norms. Even people who publicly conform to these notions are apt to experience private anxiety about their failure to live up to unrealistic cultural expectations.

Beyond the agents of socialization we have described, other spheres of life play a part in social learning as well. These include religious organizations, the workplace, the military, and social clubs. As a result, socialization inevitably involves inconsistencies as we learn different information from various kinds of social experiences. In the end, socialization is not a simple learning process; it is a complex balancing act in which we encounter a wide range of ideas as we try to forge our own distinctive personalities and world views.

Socialization and the Life Course

Although discussions of socialization focus on childhood, the process continues throughout our lives. Members of all societies organize social experience according to age to produce distinctive stages of the life course; in industrial nations, these are commonly understood to include childhood, adolescence, adulthood, and, as a final phase of adulthood, old age. Socialization has characteristic traits during each stage.

Childhood

Charles Dickens's classic novel *Oliver Twist* is set in London early in the nineteenth century, when the Industrial Revolution was bringing sweeping changes to English society. Oliver's mother died in childbirth and, barely surviving himself, he began life as an indigent orphan, "buffeted through the world—despised by all, and pitied by none" (Dickens, 1886:36; orig. 1837–1839). Knowing little pleasure in his early years, Oliver Twist began a life of toil and drudgery in a workhouse, laboring long hours to pay for filthy shelter and meager food.

In our present culture, *childhood*—roughly the first twelve years of life—is a time of freedom from the burdens of the adult world. But during the Middle Ages in Europe—and, as Oliver Twist testifies, long afterward—children's lives mirrored those of adults. Historian Philippe Ariès (1965) explains that medieval Europeans did not share our conception of childhood; as soon as children were able to survive without con-stant care, they took their place in the world as adults. This meant that poor children worked long hours, just as most adults did. Although "child labor" is now illegal in Canada, this pattern persists in preindustrial societies throughout Latin America, Africa, and Asia. Global Map 5-2 shows that work is commonplace for children in poor societies of the world.

The notion of young children working long hours may be startling because our common sense suggests that youngsters are very different from adults—inexpe-

WINDOW ON THE WORLD

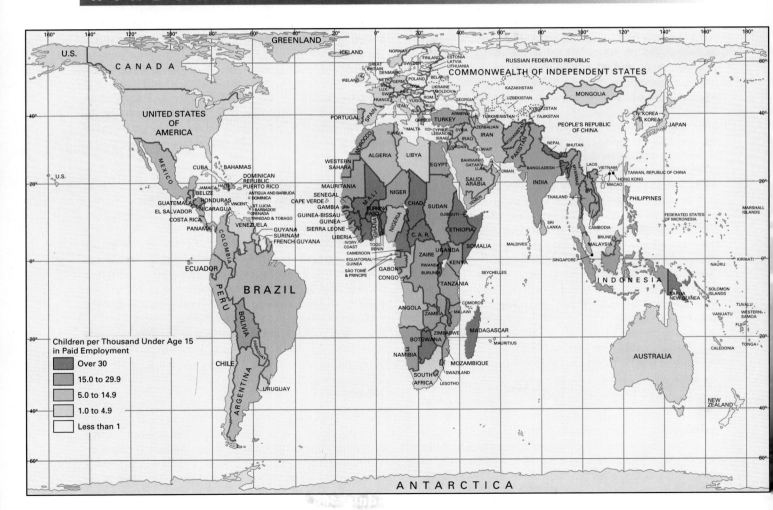

GLOBAL MAP 5-2   CHILD LABOR IN GLOBAL PERSPECTIVE
Industrialization has the effect of prolonging childhood and discouraging children from engaging in work and other activities deemed suit-able only for adults. Thus child labor is relatively uncommon in the United States and other industrial societies. In less industrialized nations of the world, however, children form a vital economic asset and they typically begin working as soon as they are able.

rienced in the ways of the world and biologically immature. But much of this difference is rooted in society and
culture. Because technologically complex societies are
more affluent, everyone does not need to work. In addition, such societies extend childhood to allow time for
learning many complex skills required for adult activities. These facts encourage us to define children and
adults in contrasting ways, with "irresponsible" children
looked after by "responsible" adults (Benedict, 1938). In
global perspective, however, this pattern is far from an
inevitable consequence of biological maturation. Many
characteristics of childhood—and even whether it exists
at all—are highly variable among the world's cultures.
The box on page 148 provides an example.

Recently, sociologists and psychologists have
found evidence that childhood is changing yet again,
this time becoming shorter. Especially among affluent
families, children are subjected to mounting pressures
to dress, speak, and act like adults (Elkind, 1981; Winn,
1983). Evidence of what is called the "hurried child"
pattern includes ten-year-old boys in designer jeans, and
girls of the same age adorned with jewelry, makeup, and
perfume. The mass media now interject into a child's
world sexuality, violence, and a host of other issues that
were considered only a generation ago to be strictly
adult topics. Young children may routinely watch films
that graphically depict violence and listen to rock music
that contains sexually explicit lyrics. Pressure to grow
up quickly is also exerted in the home because greater
numbers of mothers work, requiring children to fend
more for themselves. Furthermore, today's parents are
often delighted if their children can read, spell, or discuss world events before their peers can, believing that
this indicates greater intelligence. Schools also encourage rapid maturation by emphasizing achievement,
which reflects positively on both parents and teachers.
In the view of child psychologist David Elkind (1981),
the "hurried child" pattern is a detrimental change in
our society's conception of childhood because children
are confronting issues that they lack the experience to
understand, let alone successfully resolve.

Adolescence

As childhood emerged as a distinct stage of life in
industrial societies, adolescence came into focus as a
buffer stage between childhood and adulthood, corresponding roughly to the teenage years. This stage of life
offers time to learn various specialized skills required
for adult life.

We generally associate adolescence with emotional and social turmoil; young people experience conflict
with their parents and struggle to develop their own,
separate identities. Since adolescence generally occurs at
the same time as the onset of puberty, we often attribute
much of the social and emotional turmoil of this stage
of life to physiological changes. However, thinking sociologically, the instability of adolescence also reflects
inconsistencies in socialization. For example, adults
expect adolescents to be increasingly self-reliant and
responsible for themselves, yet adults view teenagers as
unequipped for the occupations that would give them
financial independence. The adult world also gives adolescents mixed messages about sexuality; sexual activity
is often encouraged by the mass media, while parents
urge restraint. Consider, too, that an eighteen-year-old
male may face the adult responsibility of going to war,
while simultaneously being denied the right to drink
alcohol.

Definitions of adolescence are somewhat contradictory. For instance, the ages at which Canadian
teenagers can drive a car, vote, and drink alcoholic beverages are frequently different. Without minimizing the
role of biological forces in adolescence, this is a time of
social contradictions when people are no longer children but not yet adults. As is true of all stages of life,
the experience of adolescence varies according to social
background. Young people from working-class families
often move directly into the adult world of work and
parenthood after completing high school. Those from
wealthier families, however, have the resources to
attend university and perhaps graduate school, which
may extend adolescence into the later twenties and
even the thirties (Skolnick, 1992). Poverty, too, can
extend adolescence. Especially in the inner cities, many
young people cannot attain full adult standing because
jobs are not available or accessible.

Cross-cultural research offers further evidence
that adolescence is not simply a matter of biological
maturation. When anthropologist Margaret Mead studied the culture of the Samoan Islands in the 1920s, she
found that boys and girls were simply defined as adults
when they reached their mid-teens. In the Samoan culture, unlike our own, childhood and adulthood did not
differ radically from each other, so the transition
between the two stages of life was not dramatic (M.
Mead, 1961; orig. 1928).

Adulthood

There are two major characteristics of the stage of life
we call *adulthood*, which our culture defines as begin-

CROSS-CULTURAL COMPARISON

Sex among Children? The Social Construction of Childhood

Should children be sexual? Most people in Canadian society find sexual activity among children to be disturbing and unnatural. Anthropologist Ruth Benedict explains that the Zuni—a Native American society of New Mexico—also discourage childhood sexuality, but not for the same reason. According to Zuni culture, sex is simply a means of reproduction, so the activity has little significance before reaching puberty, when reproduction is possible. Among the Melanesian cultures of Southeast New Guinea, Benedict found easy acceptance of sexual activity among children. Rather than reacting with alarm as we commonly would, adults in this society typically laugh it off, believing that no harm can result.

Certainly, the reproductive immaturity of children is a biological reality (although puberty now occurs earlier in life due to social changes). But the significance of being young extends far beyond biology to culture.

How do comparisons of this kind help us to better understand our own way of life? Ruth Benedict suggests that, unlike many other cultures, our culture defines childhood and adulthood *in opposition*. Thus socialization cannot be a simple matter of accumulating information as we grow.

On the contrary, to learn to be adults in North America, we must *unlearn* many of the proscriptions imposed in childhood. Perhaps, observed Benedict, this may offer some insight into the widespread sexual anxieties among adults in our culture:

> The adult in our culture has often failed to unlearn the wickedness or the dangerousness of sex, a lesson that was impressed upon [the child] strongly during [the] most formative years. (1938:165)

SOURCE: Benedict (1938).

ning in the twenties. First, adulthood is the period during which most of life's accomplishments typically occur. In other words, having been socialized into society's conception of adulthood, people embark on careers and raise families of their own. Second, especially in later adulthood, people reflect on what they have accomplished, feeling great satisfaction or perhaps coming to the sobering realization that many of the idealistic dreams of their youth will never come true.

Early Adulthood

Personalities are largely formed by the start of adulthood. Even so, a marked shift in an individual's life situation—brought on by dislocations such as unemployment, divorce, or serious illness—may result in significant change to the self (Dannefer, 1984). Early adulthood—until about the age of forty—is generally a time of working toward many goals set earlier in life.

Young adults learn to manage for themselves a host of day-to-day responsibilities that had been handled by parents or others. Beginning a family, people draw on the experience of having lived in the family of their parents, although as children they may have perceived little of adult life. In addition, young adults typically try to master patterns of intimate living with another person who may have just as much to learn. Early adulthood also involves juggling conflicting priorities: parents, spouse, children, and work (Levinson

et al., 1978). Women, especially, face up to the difficulty of "doing it all," since our culture confers on them primary responsibility for child rearing and household chores, even if they have demanding occupations outside the home (Hochschild, 1989). There has been a dramatic increase in the labor force participation of women since not long after World War II. Presently, married women with pre-school children have a 64.6 percent employment rate, and those whose children are between 6 and 15 years of age have a 76.8 percent participation rate (*Women in the Labour Force*, 1990–1991:990).

In short, women today are often caught between traditional femin*ine* ideals learned as children and the more contemporary femin*ist* ideals learned as adults (Sexton, 1980; cited in Giele, 1982:121).

Middle Adulthood

Young adults usually cope optimistically with such tensions. But in middle adulthood—roughly the years between the ages of forty and sixty—people begin to sense that marked improvements in life circumstances are less likely. Greater reflection characterizes middle adulthood, as people assess their achievements in light of earlier expectations. They become more aware of the fragility of health, which is typically taken for granted by the young. Women who have already spent many years raising a family can find middle adulthood especially trying. Children grow up and require less attention, husbands become absorbed in their careers, leaving some women with spaces in their lives that are difficult to fill. Women who divorce during middle adulthood may experience serious financial problems (Weitzman, 1985). For all these reasons, many women mark middle adulthood by returning to school and beginning new careers. Neither education nor a career is easy after several decades of working primarily in the home.

The traditional conception of femininity also stresses the importance of physical attractiveness. Both older men and older women face the reality of physical decline, but our society's traditional socialization of women has made good looks crucial, so that wrinkles, weight gain, and loss of hair are more traumatic for women than for men. Naomi Wolfe argues that as women's participation in the labor force has increased, so too have the demands and strictures of what Wolfe terms the "Beauty Myth" (Wolfe, 1990). She claims that the focus on women's appearance handicaps their free and equal participation in the work force. Not only do women have to sell their skills, but they also have to look appropriate. This costs both time and money that might otherwise be spent on job development. Men, of course, experience their own particular difficulties. Some confront limited achievement, knowing that their careers are unlikely to change for the better. Others, realizing that the price of career success has been neglect of family or personal health, harbor deep uncertainties about their self-worth even as they bask in the praise of others (Farrell & Rosenberg, 1981). Women, too, who devote themselves singlemindedly to careers in early adulthood, may experience regrets about what they have given up in pursuit of occupational success.

Constance Beresford-Howe, a Canadian novelist, often writes about people who make immense changes during adulthood. Her novel, *A Serious Widow*, begins with the funeral of Rowena Hill's husband of thirty years and her discovery that he was a bigamist. Over the course of the novel, as Rowena re-edits her biography and the history of the marriage, she makes a number of surprising changes in her lifestyle and relationships. In the following scene, she reviews her wardrobe, finds it inadequate, and sews herself a new outfit:

Refreshed by this encounter, I wrap myself in a towel and cross the bedroom to get dressed. But a survey of the cupboard (half empty, now, with most of Edwin's things packed away) does nothing to encourage the idea of rebirth. My clothes are all depressing reminders of many things, in particular my dressmaking inadequacies. The brown checked skirt that never did hang quite straight. The grey dress I made three years ago that looks even more boring whenever I try to brighten it up with a new scarf or belt. The beige skirt, baggy at the seat with age. Fretfully I push these dreary articles about on their hangers. Catching my eye in the mirror, it occurs to me that I look better in the bath towel pegged under my arms than in any of my clothes. The ruby colour and the soft pile are both pleasing. Turning first one way and then another, I look at my reflection thoughtfully. ... Certainly it would take a bolder spirit than mine to wear such a rich red any place where other people could see it. But just to lounge around in at home ... The longer I look at myself the better I like the way the ruby colour makes my hair look darker and my shoulders whiter. After a minute, I pull the matching towels out of the linen cupboard. There is enough material for a wraparound skirt and a sort of tabard top. Half furtively I uncover the sewing machine and sit down. A few hours with scissors and thread ... Why not? It's not exactly fishing, Ethel, but maybe it's not far off. (Beresford-Howe, 1991).

Rowena Hill's midlife crisis may well have involved some of the personal transitions we have described. But her story also illustrates that the greatest productivity and personal satisfaction may occur after the middle of life. Socialization in our youth-oriented culture has convinced many people that life ends at forty. As average life expectancy in Canada has increased, however, such limiting notions about growing older have begun to change. Major transformations may become less likely, but the potential for learning and new beginnings continues all the same.

Old Age and Dying

Old age comprises the later years of adulthood and the final stage of life itself, beginning about the mid-sixties. Here again, societies attach different meanings to a particular time of life. Among preindustrial people, advancing age typically affords great influence and respect. As noted in Chapter 14 ("Aging and the Elderly"), this stems from two main sources: in traditional societies, the elderly usually control land and other wealth, and in societies that change slowly, elders amass a lifetime of wisdom (Sheehan, 1976; Hareven, 1982).

In industrial societies, however, younger people

The sociological perspective suggests that, far from being simple expressions of our biology, stages of the life course are shaped by society. In industrial societies, elderly people are deemed ready for "retirement," which often means finishing their lives with little meaningful activity. In preindustrial societies, including the People's Republic of China, older people are a vital resource. Thus their productive work continues as long as they are able.

typically work apart from the family, lessening the influence of the elderly. Also, rapid change promotes a definition of what is older as marginal or even obsolete. To younger people, the elderly are unaware of new trends and fashions, and their knowledge and experience often seem irrelevant. As we have already observed, the youth orientation in North America tends to rate everyone by the standards of physical beauty, activities, and attitudes of the young.

No doubt, however, this youth orientation will diminish as the proportion of older people steadily increases. The percentage of those in North America over the age of sixty-five has grown substantially since the beginning of this century, so that today more men and women are elderly than in their teens. Moreover, life expectancy is still increasing, so more and more individuals will live well past the age of sixty-five. Looking to the next century, *A Portrait of Seniors in Canada* (1990) predicts that the fastest-growing segment of our population will be those over eighty-five. It is projected that there will be almost six times as many people over that age a century from now as there are today.

At present, the final phase of socialization differs in an important way from learning earlier in life. For the young, advancing age typically means entering new roles and assuming new responsibilities. Old age, however, involves the opposite process: leaving roles that have long infused life with social identity and meaningful activity. Retirement is one clear example. Although retirement sometimes fits the common image of being a period of restful activity, it often means the loss of familiar routines, and sometimes outright boredom. Like any life transition, retirement demands that a person learn new and different ways of living while simultaneously *unlearning* patterns and routines that guided earlier stages in life. A comparable transition is required of the nonworking wife or husband who must change routines to accommodate a spouse now spending more time at home.

Today most people assume that death occurs in old age. Historically, however, death was caused by disease or accident during any stage of life, because living standards were lower and medical technology was primitive. By contrast, in industrial societies, although death can still occur at any time (especially among the poor), more and more people reach old age. In 1971, people aged sixty-five and over were 8.2 percent of the population. By 1986, this figure had risen to 10.7 percent and by 2001 it is expected to reach 14 percent (Colombo, 1992:57). More and more men and women reaching old age can look forward to decades of life, but patterns of socialization in this stage of the life course cannot be separated from the realization of impending death.

After observing many dying people, Elisabeth Kübler-Ross (1969) described death as an orderly transition involving five distinct stages. Because our culture tends to ignore the reality of death, a person's first reaction to the prospect of dying is usually *denial* and avoiding contact with anything that might suggest the inevitability of death. The second stage is *anger*: here the person has begun to accept the idea of dying but views it as a gross injustice. In the third stage, anger gives way to *negotiation*, the attitude that death may not be inevitable and that a bargain might be struck with God to allow life to continue. The fourth stage, *resignation*, is often accompanied by psychological depression. Finally, adjustment to death is completed in the fifth stage, *acceptance*. At this point, rather than being paralyzed by fear and anxiety, the person sets out to use constructively whatever time remains.

As the proportion of women and men in old age increases, we can expect our culture to become more comfortable with the idea of death. Today, for example, death is more widely discussed than it was earlier in this century, and many people view death as preferable to months or even years of suffering and social isolation in hospitals and rest homes. In addition, married couples are more likely to anticipate their own deaths in discussions and estate planning. This may ease somewhat the disorientation that usually accompanies the death of a spouse—a greater problem for women, who usually outlive their husbands.

This brief examination of the life course leads to two general conclusions. First and most important, although linked to the biological process of aging, the essential characteristics of each stage of life are socially constructed. For this reason, a stage of life may be experienced differently by people in other cultures. Second, each period of the life course presents characteristic problems and transitions that involve learning something new and, in many cases, unlearning what has become familiar.

Two additional points are worth noting. Just because social experience is organized according to age in every society, this in no way negates the effects of other social forces, such as social background, race, ethnicity, and gender. Thus, the general patterns we have described are all subject to further modification as they apply to various categories of people. Finally, people's typical life experiences vary depending on when, in the history of the society, they were born. A **cohort** is *a category of people with a common characteristic, usually their age.* Age-cohorts are likely to have similar reactions to particular issues to the extent that they were influenced by the same major events (Riley, Foner, & Waring, 1988). Women and men born early in this century, for example, were influenced by two world wars and an economic depression unknown to many of their children. In this sense, too, general patterns pertaining to the life course will vary.

Resocialization: Total Institutions

This chapter has focused on socialization as experienced by the vast majority of individuals in countless familiar settings. Some people, however, experience a different type of socialization—often against their will—in prisons or mental hospitals where they are confined. This is the special world of a **total institution**, *a setting in which people are isolated from the rest of society and manipulated by an administrative staff.*

According to Erving Goffman (1961), total institutions have three distinctive characteristics. First, staff members supervise all spheres of daily life, including where residents (often called "inmates") eat, sleep, and work. Second, a rigid routine subjects inmates to standardized food, sleeping quarters, and activities. Third, formal rules govern how inmates behave in every setting, from how they dress to when and where they may smoke.

Total institutions impose such regimented routines with the goal of **resocialization**, *deliberate control of an environment to radically alter an inmate's personality.* The power of a total institution to do this lies in depriving people of any other source of social experience. An inmate's isolation is achieved through physical barriers such as walls and fences (usually with barbed wire and guard towers), barred windows, and locked doors. Cut off in this way, the inmate's entire world can be manipulated by the administrative staff to produce lasting change—or at least immediate compliance—in the inmate.

Resocialization is a two-part process. First, the staff attempts to erode the new inmate's established identity. This involves a series of experiences that Goffman describes as "abasements, degradations, humiliations, and profanations of self" (1961:14). For example, inmates are required to surrender personal possessions, including clothing and grooming articles normally used to maintain a person's distinctive appearance. In their place, inmates receive standard-issue items that make everyone alike. In addition, inmates are given standard haircuts, so that, once again, what was personalized becomes uniform. The staff also processes new inmates by searching, weighing, fingerprinting, and photographing them, and by issuing them a serial number. Once inside the walls, individuals surrender the right to privacy: guards often demand that inmates undress publicly as part of the admission procedure, and guards routinely conduct surveillance and searches of inmates' living quarters. These "mortifications of self" undermine the identity and autonomy that inmates bring to the total institution from the outside world.

The second part of the resocialization process turns on efforts to systematically build a different self. The staff manipulates inmate behavior through a system of rewards and punishments. The privilege of keeping a book or receiving extra cigarettes may seem trivial from the vantage point of outsiders, but, in the rigid environment of the total institution, they can be powerful motivations toward conformity. Noncompliance carries the threat that privileges will be withdrawn or, in more serious cases, that the inmate will suffer physical pain or isolation, even from other inmates. The duration of confinement in a prison or mental hospital also has to do with policy, which is related to the degree of cooperation with the staff an inmate displays. Goffman emphasized that conformity in a total institution must reflect both inward motivation as well as outward behavior. Even a person who does not outwardly violate the rules, in other words, may still be punished for having "an attitude problem."

Socialization and Human Freedom

Through socialization, society shapes how we think, feel, and act. If society has this power over us, in what sense are we free? This chapter ends with a closer look at this important question.

Children and adults throughout North America delight in watching the Muppets, stars of television and film. Observing the expressive antics of Kermit the Frog, Miss Piggy, and the rest of the troupe, one almost believes that these puppets are real rather than mere objects animated by movement that originates backstage. The sociological perspective suggests that human beings are like puppets in that we, too, respond to the backstage guidance of society. Indeed, more so, in that society affects not just our outward behavior but our innermost thoughts and feelings.

But our analysis of socialization also reveals where the puppet analogy ultimately breaks down. Viewing human beings as the puppets of society leads

CROSS-CULTURAL COMPARISON

The Foster Home as Total Institution

Resocialization in a total institution can considerably change a human being. The rebuilding of the self is extremely difficult, however, and no two people are likely to respond to any such program in precisely the same way (Irwin, 1980). Some inmates may experience "rehabilitation" or "recovery" (meaning change that is officially approved), while others may gradually sink into an embittered state because of the perceived injustice of their incarceration. Furthermore, over a considerable period of time, the rigidly controlled environment of a total institution may render people completely *institutionalized*, incapable of the independence required for living in the outside world.

Resocialization sometimes occurs in foster homes, as the following excerpt illustrates. April Raintree, a Métis foster child, is separated from her sister and sent to a new foster home. This is the first welcome she receives from her new foster "mom". Notice the racial stereotyping.

… I was taken to a small farming community further south of Winnipeg on the outskirts of Aubigny, to the DeRosier farm. It was a Friday afternoon when we arrived. While Mrs. Semple talked with Mrs. DeRosier, I studied my new foster mother with great disappointment. She was a tall woman with lots of make-up and badly dyed hair. If she had been a beauty once, the only thing left of it now was vanity. Her voice was harsh and grating. The more I watched her, the more positive I became that she was putting on an act for Mrs. Semple's benefit. I wondered why Mrs. Semple couldn't figure that out but then I thought it was okay as long as Mrs. DeRosier gave me a good home. After my social worker's departure, Mrs. DeRosier turned to me. I looked up at her with curiosity. She went to the kitchen drawer, took out a strap and laid it on the table near me. She told me the routine I would be following but in such a way that it made me think she had made this speech many times before.

"The school bus comes at eight. You will be up at six, go to the hen house and bring back the eggs. While I prepare breakfast, you will wash the eggs. After breakfast you will do the dishes. After school, you'll have more chores to do, then you will help me prepare supper. After you do the supper dishes, you will go to your room and stay there. You'll also keep yourself and your room clean. I know you half-breeds, you love to wallow in filth. You step out of line once, only once, and that strap will do the rest of the talking. You don't get any second chances. And if you don't believe that I'll use it, ask Raymond and Gilbert. And on that subject, you will only talk to them in front of us. I won't stand for any hanky-panky going on behind our backs. Is that clear? Also you are not permitted the use of the phone. If you want letters mailed, I'll see to it. You do any complaining to worker, watch out. Now, I'll show you where your room is." (Culleton, 1983)

SOURCE: Culleton (1983).

into the trap that Dennis Wrong (1961) has called an "oversocialized" conception of the human being. In part, Wrong wishes to remind us that we are biological as well as social creatures, a point emphasized by Sigmund Freud, who identified general human drives. To the extent that any biological force affects our being, we can never be entirely shaped by society.

The fact that human beings may be subject to *both* biological and social influences, however, hardly advances the banner of human freedom. Here is where the ideas of George Herbert Mead are of crucial importance. Mead recognized the power of society to act on human beings, but he argued that human spontaneity and creativity (conceptualized in the I) empower us to continually *act back* on society. Thus the process of socialization affirms the human capacity for choice as we reflect, evaluate, and act. Therefore, although the process of socialization may initially suggest that we respond like puppets to forces beyond our control, Peter Berger points out that "unlike the puppets, we have the possibility of stopping in our movements, looking up and perceiving the machinery by which we have been moved" (1963:176). Doing this, we can act to change society by, so to speak, pulling back on the strings. And, Berger adds, the more we utilize the sociological perspective to study how the machinery of our society works, the freer we are.

Summary

1. Socialization is a process through which social experience confers on the individual the qualities we associate with being fully human. For society as a whole, socialization is the means of transmitting culture to each new generation.

2. A century ago, people thought most human behavior was grounded in biological instinct. Today, we understand human behavior to be mostly a product of nurture rather than nature. So-called "human nature," then, is the capacity to create variable cultural patterns.

3. The damaging effects of social isolation reveal the importance of social experience to human development.

4. Sigmund Freud envisioned the human personality as composed of three parts. The id represents general human drives (the life and death instincts), which Freud claimed were innate. The superego represents cultural values and norms internalized by individuals. Competition between the needs of the id and the restraints of the superego are mediated by the ego.

5. Jean Piaget believed that human development reflects both biological maturation and increasing social experience. He asserted that socialization involves four major stages of development: sensorimotor, preoperational, concrete operational, and formal operational.

6. To George Herbert Mead, socialization is based on the emergence of the self, which he viewed as partly autonomous (the I) and partly guided by society (the me).

7. Charles Horton Cooley used the term looking-glass self to underscore that the self is influenced by perceptions of how others respond to us.

8. Commonly the first setting of socialization, the family has the greatest influence in shaping a child's attitudes and behavior.

9. School exposes children to greater social diversity and introduces the experience of being evaluated according to impersonal, universal standards of performance. In addition to formal lessons, the hidden curriculum teaches cultural lessons about race and gender.

10. Members of youthful peer groups are subject to adult supervision less than in the family or in school. Peer groups take on increasing significance in adolescence.

11. The mass media, especially television, have a considerable impact on the socialization process. The average Canadian household has a television turned on for three hours a day.

12. Public opinion plays a key role in the socialization process because popular attitudes and widespread values influence how we think and act.

13. As is true of each phase of the life course, the characteristics of childhood are socially constructed. During the Middle Ages, European societies scarcely recognized childhood as a stage of life. In

industrial societies such as Canada, we define childhood as much different from adulthood.

14. Members of our society consider adolescence, the transition between childhood and adulthood, to be a difficult period. However, this is not the case in all societies.

15. During early adulthood, socialization involves settling into careers and raising families. Later adulthood is marked by considerable reflection about earlier goals in light of actual achievements.

16. In old age, people make many transitions, including retirement and establishing new patterns of social life. While the elderly typically enjoy high prestige in preindustrial societies, industrial societies are more youth-oriented.

17. Members of industrial societies typically fend off death until old age. Adjustment to the death of a spouse (an experience more common to women) and acceptance of the inevitability of one's own death are part of socialization for the elderly.

18. Total institutions such as prisons and mental hospitals have the goal of resocialization—radically changing the inmate's personality.

19. Socialization demonstrates the power of society to shape our thoughts, feelings, and actions. Yet, as George Herbert Mead pointed out, the relationship between the self and society is a two-way process: each shapes the other through social interaction.

Key Concepts

anticipatory socialization the process of social learning directed toward gaining a desired position

cohort a category of people with a common characteristic, usually their age

concrete operational stage Piaget's term for the level of development at which people first use logic to understand their surroundings

ego Freud's designation of a person's conscious attempt to balance pleasure-seeking drives with the demands of society

formal operational stage Piaget's term for the level of human development at which people use highly abstract thought and are able to imagine alternatives to reality

generalized other George Herbert Mead's term for widespread cultural norms and values we use as a reference in evaluating ourselves

id Freud's designation of the human being's basic drives

looking-glass self Cooley's assertion that the self is based on how others respond to us

mass media impersonal communications directed toward a vast audience

peer group people who interact regularly, usually with common interests, social position, and age

personality a person's fairly consistent pattern of thinking, feeling, and acting

preoperational stage Piaget's term for the level of human development in which the individual first uses language and other symbols

public opinion the attitudes of people throughout a society about one or more controversial issues

resocialization deliberate control of an environment intended to radically alter an inmate's personality

self George Herbert Mead's term for a dimension of personality encompassing an individual's self-conception

sensorimotor stage Piaget's term for the level of human development in which people experience the world only through sensory contact

socialization lifelong social experience by which individuals develop human potential and learn patterns of their culture

superego Freud's designation of the presence of culture within the individual in the form of internalized values and norms

total institution a setting in which people are isolated from the rest of society and manipulated by an administrative staff

Suggested Readings

Many dimensions of socialization are covered in these three books. The first focuses on infancy, the second encompasses the entire life course. The third offers a Canadian perspective on the topic.

> Judith Rich Harris and Robert Liebert. *Infancy and the Child.* Englewood Cliffs, NJ: Prentice Hall, 1992.
> Grace Craig. *Human Development.* 6th ed. Englewood Cliffs, NJ: Prentice Hall, 1992.
> Frederick Elkin and Gerald Handel. *The Child and Society: The Process of Socialization.* 2nd ed. New York: Random House, 1973.

This analysis of Freud's theories and research examines the implications of his work for a broad range of social issues.

> Paul Roazen. *Encountering Freud: The Politics and Histories of Psychoanalysis.* New Brunswick, NJ: Transaction Books, 1989.

George Herbert Mead's analysis of the development of the self is presented in this paperback, compiled after Mead's death by many of his students.

> George Herbert Mead. *Mind, Self, and Society from the Standpoint of a Social Behaviorist.* Charles W. Morris, ed. Chicago: The University of Chicago Press, 1962; orig. 1934.

The first of these two books is a classic study of the history of the family, exploring changing conceptions of childhood. The second book describes the recent development of the "hurried child" pattern in the United States.

> Philippe Ariès. *Centuries of Childhood: A Social History of Family Life.* New York: Vintage Books, 1965.
> David Elkind. *The Hurried Child: Growing Up Too Fast Too Soon.* Reading, MA: Addison-Wesley, 1981.

An overview of what is known about adolescent stress, these essays include evidence about which intervention programs have proved useful for practitioners.

> Mary Ellen Colton and Susan Gore, eds. *Adolescent Stress: Causes and Consequences.* Hawthorne, NY: Aldine de Gruyter, 1991.

This book, a compilation of fourteen essays on how people organize their lives by age in various societies, offers historical and cross-cultural material on the links between age, power, and retirement.

> David I. Kertzer and K. Warner Schaie, eds. *Age Structuring in Comparative Perspective.* Hillsdale, NJ: Lawrence Erlbaum, 1989.

This collection of fourteen essays explores the distinctive elements of socialization among African-American children.

> Harriette Pipes McAdoo and John Lewis McAdoo, eds. *Black Children: Social, Educational, and Parental Environments.* Beverly Hills, CA: Sage Publications, 1985.

Gay people are deprived of many of the social supports that heterosexuals take for granted. As a result, a gay folklore has emerged that is influential in the social development of millions of Americans. This book examines the growing folklife of the gay subculture.

> Joseph P. Goodwin. *More Man than You'll Ever Be: Gay Folklore and Acculturation in Middle America.* Bloomington, IN: Indiana University Press, 1989.

Reviewing decades of research about children and television, this researcher concludes that we still have much to learn.

> Carmen Luke. *Constructing the Child Viewer: A History of the American Discourse on Television and Children, 1950–1980.* New York: Greenwood, 1990.

How have the mass media shaped the way whites perceive minorities? This book spotlights images of African Americans, Hispanic Americans, Native Americans, and Asian Americans, as presented by the mass media.

> Clinty C. Wilson II and Felix Gutierrez. *Minorities and Media: Diversity and the End of Mass Communication.* Beverly Hills, CA: Sage, 1985.

The following two books examine the role of gender in socialization.

> Ray Raphael. *The Men from the Boys: Rites of Passage in Male America.* Lincoln: University of Nebraska Press, 1988.
> Dorothy C. Holland and Margaret A. Eisenhart. *Educated in Romance: Women, Achievement, and College Culture.* Chicago: The University of Chicago Press, 1990.

Personality is shaped to some extent by the particular times in which we live. How the 1960s influenced a generation of men and women is suggested by this historical look at a turbulent decade.

> Joan Morrison and Robert K. Morrison. *The Sixties Experience: Sights and Sounds of the Decade of Change in the Words of Those Who Lived It.* New York: Times Books, 1987.

A classic book on socialization amongst an elite community in Canada is as follows:

> John R. Seeley (et al.). *Crestwood Heights: A Study of the Culture of Suburban Life.* New York: Wiley, 1963.

For a detailed examination of the lives of three generations of women in Flin Flon, Manitoba, read the following:

> Meg Luxton. *More Than A Labour of Love.* Toronto: Women's Press, 1980.

The impact of Canadian public policy on family life is the focus of Eichler's book.

> Margrit Eichler. *Families in Canada Today: Recent Changes and their Policy Consequences.* 2nd Edition. Toronto: Gage, 1988.

SOCIAL INTERACTION IN EVERYDAY LIFE

If you stop to think about it, a cemetery has a hard time selling its product. Brochures—like the one that just arrived in the mail—announce "limited-time offers"; in this case, $395 will buy two burial spaces in the "Garden of the Praying Hands." But isn't there something wrong with trying to sell burial plots as if they were cars, even if many people (sooner or later) need them? For one thing, someone opening the morning mail still might be grieving over the death of a family member, and hardly needs to be reminded of the loss. More generally, social rules demand that we treat death with a special respect. People selling cemetery plots must be as dignified and low key as possible, acting quite differently from dealers who hawk automobiles. Consider, as examples, some of the following lines common to the car business that you will never read in cemetery advertising:[1]

1. *We're dealing.*
2. *How do we keep prices low? Volume.*
3. *Doing business at the same location for years.*
4. *Our customers never go anywhere else.*
5. *We're having a midnight madness sale.*

6. *The boss says everything must go.*
7. *Push it, pull it, tow it in.*

Such contrasts are among the fascinating patterns that compose everyday life, the topic of this chapter. The chapter begins by presenting many of the building blocks of our common experiences, continues by exploring the almost magical way in which face-to-face interaction generates reality, and concludes with a look at humor and what our jokes tell us about ourselves.

The key concept throughout is **social interaction**, *the process by which people act and react in relation to others*. Social interaction is the key to creating the reality we perceive. We interact, moreover, according to particular social guidelines.

Social Structure: A Guide to Everyday Living

Earlier chapters have described social life as an organized system. Chapter 3 ("Culture") examined the symbolic web that unites members of society into a culture, directing everyday interaction with norms and values. Chapter 4 ("Society") explained that the social

---

[1] This opening is adapted from a news feature by Mike Harden (1989).

world is shaped by its technological development, its economic system, and its particular world view and moral beliefs. Chapter 5 ("Socialization") showed how individuals gain humanity only as they engage others in society.

Although we have encountered ample evidence of the power of society, the notion that our behavior is socially patterned often provokes some initial resistance. Few of us will readily admit to being part of any kind of system. Instead, we prefer to highlight the unique elements of our personalities. But behaving in patterned ways does not threaten our individuality. Quite the contrary: social structure in everyday life actually serves to promote our individuality.

Social structure enhances our lives in two key ways. First, becoming fully human is possible only through social life, as Chapter 5 ("Socialization") explained. Human development occurs as we blend our unique qualities with the values and norms of the larger culture to produce distinct personalities. Second, in the absence of social structure, we would have no way of making sense out of any social situation. The social world can be disorienting, even frightening, when behavioral guidelines are unclear. Entering an unfamiliar setting generally inhibits us from freely expressing ourselves. Stepping onto a university campus for the first time, for example, we feel understandable anxiety at not knowing quite what to expect. Therefore, we look to others for clues about what sort of behavior is appropriate. Only after we understand the behavioral standards that apply to the situation are we likely to feel comfortable enough to "act like ourselves."

This is not to deny that social structure places some constraints on everyday life: established social patterns inevitably discourage the unconventional. Traditional values and norms in North America, for example, still reflect the expectation that males will be dominant and assertive in social situations and that females will adopt a subordinate and supportive stance. By pressuring each of us to fit neatly into "feminine" or "masculine" categories, social structure gives us identity but at the cost of limiting individual freedom to think and act according to personal preference.

Keep in mind, however, that social structure *constrains and guides* human behavior, rather than *rigidly determining* it. A saxophone is designed to make only certain kinds of sounds just as "fatherhood" encompasses specific patterns of behavior. Like musical instruments, however, any social arrangement can be "played" creatively in a wide range of ways.

Status

Among the most important components of social interaction is **status**, which refers to *a recognized social position that an individual occupies*. The sociological meaning of the term "status" differs markedly from its everyday meaning of "prestige." In common usage, a bank president has more "status" than a bank teller. Sociologically, however, both "bank president" and "bank teller" are statuses because they represent socially defined positions, even though one does confer more power and prestige than the other.

Every status involves various rights, duties, and expectations. The statuses people occupy therefore guide the way they act in any setting. In the university classroom, for example, professors and students have different and well-defined rights and duties. Similarly, family interaction turns on the interplay of mother, father, daughters, and sons (and sometimes members of extended families). In all these situations, statuses define people in terms of each other, thereby forging relationships among individuals. A status, then, also defines who and what we are in relation to specific others.

We all simultaneously hold many statuses. The term **status set** refers to *all the statuses a person holds at a given time*. A girl may be a *daughter* to her parents, a *sister* to her siblings, a *friend* to members of her social circle, and a *goalie* to others on her hockey team. Just as status sets branch out in different directions, they also change over the life course. A child grows into an adult, a student becomes a lawyer, and people marry to become husbands and wives, sometimes becoming single again as a result of divorce or death. Joining an organization or finding a job enlarges our status set; retirement or withdrawing from activities diminishes it. Individuals gain and lose dozens of statuses over a lifetime.

Status plays an important part in how we define ourselves. Occupational status, for example, forms a major part of most people's self-concept. Even after retirement, for instance, a man may still think of himself as a professor and be similarly defined by others.

Ascribed and Achieved Status

Sociologists use a helpful distinction to describe how people obtain various statuses. An **ascribed status** is *a social position that is received at birth or involuntarily* *assumed later in the life course.* Examples of ascribed statuses include being a daughter, a Native Canadian, a teenager, or a widower. Ascribed statuses are matters about which people have little or no choice.

By contrast, an **achieved status** refers to *a social position that is assumed voluntarily and that reflects a significant measure of personal ability and effort.* Among achieved statuses in Canada are being an honors student, an Olympic athlete, a wife, a computer programmer, or a thief. In each case, the individual has a definite choice in the matter.

Most statuses actually involve a combination of ascription and achievement. That is, people's ascribed statuses influence the statuses they are likely to achieve. Children cannot be lawyers until they become adults. Moreover, the adults who earn a law degree are likely to have another ascribed trait in common: being born into relatively privileged families. More generally, any person of a privileged gender, race, ethnicity, or age has far more opportunity to achieve desirable statuses than does someone without such advantages. By the same token, many less desirable statuses, such as criminal, welfare recipient, or drug addict, are more easily "achieved" by people disadvantaged by ascription.

Master Status

Among the many statuses a person holds at any time, one often overshadows all the others. A **master status** is *a status that has exceptional importance for social identity, often shaping a person's entire life.* In our society, a person's occupation—largely due to achievement—often ranks as a master status. This is because occupation conveys so much information, including some idea of a person's education, income, and family background. No doubt, this is why adults typically introduce themselves by stating their occupations along with their names. Other master statuses, however, are based on ascription. For an Eaton or a Vanier, family name stands out in the minds of others. Similarly, people of color know that race can sometimes undermine personal achievements.

Serious disease can also underlie a master status. Sometimes even lifelong friends avoid cancer patients. Orville Kelly gives an example of the stigmatic effect of a cancer diagnosis when he recounts the story of a woman who reported to him that she was so thankful that her husband hadn't suffered from cancer. Kelly then asked what he had suffered from. The woman

In any rigidly ranked setting, no interaction can proceed until people assess each other's social standing. In traditional Indian society, each individual wears a caste mark on the forehead, which serves as a master status guiding subsequent behavior.

answered "heart disease." When Kelly asked how he was doing, she said, "oh, he died of a heart attack" (Kelly, 1979:5). Even though her husband had died, the woman expressed relief that the death was as the result of heart disease and not cancer. For persons with acquired immune deficiency syndrome (AIDS), disease may result in social isolation.

Most societies of the world limit the opportunities of women, whatever their abilities, so that sex, too, can serve as a master status. Additionally, the physically disabled can be made to feel dehumanized by people who perceive them only in terms of their handicaps. In the box on page 160, several people with physical disabilities describe this problem.

Physical Disability as Master Status

Following are some comments from people with two very different diseases, both of which may have profound effects on the whole round-of-life including self-concept, primary relationships, acquaintance relationships, and work life.

First is a person with cancer. Amongst strangers, neighbors, and acquaintances, the term cancer is mentioned with particular care. One woman told of her trips to the hairdresser, to whom she had been going for many years, during her chemotherapy treatment. "My hairdresser says to me, 'Your hair is falling out', and I was too shocked and ashamed to give her the truth. So I just said, 'Oh, I don't know what it could be.'" She stopped going to the hairdresser. She couldn't face this stranger with her pain and shame. They had always had a good but distant professional relationship and she had had her hair done there for ten years. She had told her hairdresser the things of which she was proud. Her hairdresser knew that she had three children, knew their names and ages and the name of her husband. She didn't understand herself and was surprised by her reaction and said:

I don't know why it is. Maybe it is

something lacking in me. Maybe it's just my nature. I don't know. I'm not that open. I don't know what it is, but I can't go around telling everybody. I just can't do it. It's not really that I'm trying to keep it a secret. Or maybe I am. I don't know what it is.

Notice that the diagnosis of cancer is thought to be so overwhelming as to diminish the person with the disease. The irony, then, is that it is assumed to be a status of such proportions that its very naming is problematic. The same woman had been trying to sell her home. When people learned from the real estate agent that she had cancer, they lost interest.

We just had to change real estate companies and agents. And this time, we didn't tell. Soon several people looked at the house and then we finally sold it. (Nancarrow Clarke, 1985:30)

Second, listen to a person with chronic fatigue syndrome or myalgic encephalomyelitis (CFS or ME):

Well, when I first got diagnosed because there was such a stigma ... you know, like it's a psychological thing and I felt embarrassed. I didn't really tell anybody other than my immediate family and my very closest friends, whereas now when I'm talking I'll just say what I

have because how are people going to learn if they don't know what it is and how if affects us. So in the beginning, I felt embarrassed. I cried ... I mean I didn't cry when I had the growth as much as I cried when I got diagnosed with CFS because it was such a negative ... I felt ... you know, and I went to a support group and I said why do I feel like we're a group that has ... you know, where we should be shipped on an island all by ourself because ...

I mean I wouldn't even say half of my complaints because they were so weird ... like my fingers hurt, my joints hurt or I feel like I have arthritis but I'm too young to have arthritis. You know, half the time you didn't even tell them because you felt like you were a hypochondriac.

Notice here how the disease is seen as a threat to the very self of the sufferer. She experiences social isolation, embarrassment, and stigma. There is continuing debate about whether CFS is just an excuse for a break for hard-driving, ambitious young people (hence the early name, the "Yuppie flu"), a psychosomatic disorder, or a biologically-base, and therefore "real" disease. Those with the disease suffer from the current lack of clarity as to its cause and treatment.

Role

Besides status, a second major component of social interaction is **role**, *patterns of expected behavior attached to a particular status.* Ralph Linton (1937) described a role as the dynamic expression of a status. The various obligations and privileges attached to a status, in other words, call out a particular role. The student role, for example, involves responsibility to professors and other students, as well as the privilege of being able to devote much of one's time to personal enrichment through academic study. Thus, individuals *hold* a status, and *perform* a role. Cultural norms suggest how a person holding a particular status ought to act, which is often called a *role expectation*. As noted in Chapter 3 ("Cul-

ture"), however, real culture only approximates ideal culture, so that actual role performance varies according to an individual's unique personality. In addition, cultural diversity in a society ensures that people will perform comparable roles quite differently.

Like a status, a role is *relational*, organizing our behavior toward some other person. The parent's role, for example, centers on responsibilities toward a child. Correspondingly, the role of daughter or son consists largely of obligations toward a parent. Other examples of such role pairs include wives and husbands, baseball pitchers and catchers, physicians and patients, and performers and members of an audience.

Because individuals occupy many statuses simultaneously—a status set—they perform multiple roles.

The total number of roles usually exceeds the number of statuses because each status can require an individual to carry out several roles in relation to various other people. Robert Merton (1968) introduced the term **role set** to identify *a number of roles attached to a single status.* Figure 6-1 illustrates the status set and corresponding role sets of one individual. Four statuses are presented, each linked to a different role set. First, this student occupies the status of student with corresponding roles toward her professors and her colleagues in the classroom. Second, she occupies the status of family member wherein she has role relationships with her parents, her brothers and sisters as well as her wider, extended family members including (sometimes) grandparents, aunts and uncles, cousins, and others. Third, she occupies the status of a "part-time" employee and has a role in relationships with her boss as well as her fellow workers. Finally, she has a status in a friendship network which may include "primary" commitment to a best friend or a "romantic" partner as well as wider social roles with various other friends. Of course, Figure 6-1 lists only some of this person's status and role sets, since anyone generally occupies dozens of statuses at one time, each linked to a role set.

Role Conflict and Role Strain

The personal performances required by an array of role sets often make heavy demands on an individual's time and energy. This holds especially true for members of industrial societies in which people routinely assume many statuses and an even greater number of roles. As students working at the same time as studying can testify, carrying out the role of student as well as the role of employee taxes both their physical and emotional strength. Sociologists define such **role conflict** as *incompatibility among roles corresponding to two or more different statuses.*

We experience role conflict when we find ourselves pulled in various directions while trying to respond to the many statuses we hold. Politicians, for example, sometimes decide not to run for public office because the demands of such a campaign would impoverish their family life; in other cases, ambitious people sometimes defer having children or choose to remain childless in order to build their careers as quickly as possible.

Even the many roles linked to a single status may make competing demands on us. The concept of **role strain** refers to *incompatibility among roles corresponding to a single status.* A plant supervisor may wish to be a

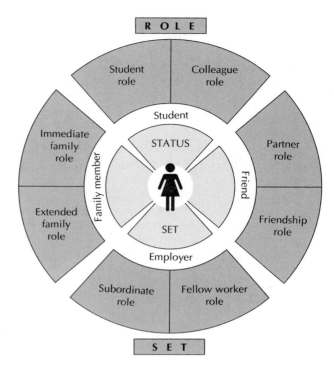

FIGURE 6–1   STATUS SET AND ROLE SET

good friend and confidant to other workers. At the same time, however, a supervisor's responsibility for everyone's performance may require maintaining some measure of personal distance. In short, performing the roles attached to even one status may involve a "balancing act" of trying to fulfill various duties and obligations.

Individuals handle problems associated with conflicting roles in a number of ways. One simple strategy for reducing role conflict is to define some roles as more important than others. A university student, for instance, might devote most of her efforts to studying and put her "romantic" life on hold, at least for the present. Resolving role conflict in this way, however, depends on being able to find satisfaction in studying—an option unavailable to many students.

Setting priorities also reduces the strain among roles linked to a single status. Adopting this approach, a person concentrates on one particular role (from among the many tied to a status), while downplaying another with which it conflicts. A promising rower, for example, may decide that maintaining a good rowing season is more important than getting good grades.

Another strategy for minimizing role conflict is "insulating" roles from one another (Merton, 1968). Instead of downplaying a particular role, people "compartmentalize" their lives so that they perform roles linked to one status in one place for part of the day, while roles corresponding to another status dominate activity elsewhere or at some other time. For example, a student may try to leave his studies behind him when he goes to work as a waiter in a restaurant.

Role Exit

Recent research has focused on *role exit*, the process by which people disengage from social roles that have been central to their lives. Helen Rose Fuchs Ebaugh (1988) began to study this issue as she herself left the life of Catholic nun to become a university sociologist. Studying a range of "exes," including ex-nuns, ex-doctors, ex-husbands, and ex-alcoholics, Ebaugh found many common elements to the process of "becoming an ex."

According to Ebaugh, people considering role exit typically begin by reflecting critically on their existing lives, raising doubts about their ability or willingness to carry out that role. As they focus on alternative roles, they may ultimately reach a turning point and decide to pursue a new life. In the subsequent "ex-role," they disengage from the previous situation, building a new sense of self, which emerges through changes in outward appearance and behavior (an ex-nun, for example, may begin to wear stylish clothing and make-up). "Exes" must also grapple with changing responses from those who may have known them in their earlier role, as well as those who do not realize how new and unfamiliar their present role may be. Forming new relationships is especially challenging for an "ex," since many new social skills must be learned. Ebaugh reports, for example, that nuns who begin dating after decades in the church are often startled to learn that sexual norms are now vastly different from those they knew as teenagers. In her study of women with cancer, Nancarrow Clarke found that, much as the experience of chemotherapy (including weight gain or loss, hair loss, funny tastes, nausea, and so on) was often very hard, the end of treatment had its own, and frequently more complicated, terrors. People seem to feel some safety or protection in being "under the care of a doctor." Thus, leaving the patient role, a type of role exit, raises new fears. As one woman said:

The funny thing is as much as I hated chemotherapy and vomiting and everything, as soon as I learned that I was near the end, I started to get scared. It's like any weaning process—I felt that my life depended on the recurrent poisoning of my system.

Right after it ended, I was full of new symptoms. For a while, I thought the cancer could reassert itself and I'd soon die. I was paranoid and afraid. (Nancarrow Clarke, 1985:21)

In modern society, fewer and fewer people expect to spend their entire lives in one job or one marriage or one state of health. The study of role exit, therefore, promises to attract greater attention.

The Social Construction of Reality

Over fifty years ago, the Italian playwright Luigi Pirandello skillfully applied the sociological perspective to social interaction. In *The Pleasure of Honesty*, Angelo Baldovino—a brilliant man with a rather checkered past—enters the fashionable home of the Renni family and introduces himself in a most peculiar way:

Inevitably we construct ourselves. Let me explain. I enter this house and immediately I become what I have to become, what I can become: I construct myself. That is, I present myself to you in a form suitable to the relationship I wish to achieve with you. And, of course, you do the same with me. ... (1962:157–158)

This curious statement suggests that, while social interaction is guided by status and role, each human being has considerable ability to shape what happens moment to moment. "Reality," then, is not as fixed as we may think. The social world does have an objective existence, of course; it existed long before we were born, affects us throughout our lives, and will continue long after we die. But, in everyday terms, society is nothing more than the behavior of countless people. If society affects individuals, then individuals creatively shape society (Berger & Luckmann, 1967).

The phrase **social construction of reality** refers to *the process by which individuals creatively shape reality through social interaction.* This idea stands at the foundation of the symbolic-interaction paradigm in sociology, as described in earlier chapters. In this context, Angelo Baldovino's remark suggests that, especially in an unfamiliar situation, quite a bit of "reality" remains unclear in everyone's mind. Pirandello's character will simply use his ability to "present himself" in terms that he thinks suit his purposes. As others do the same, a complex reality emerges, although few people are so "up front" about their deliberate efforts to foster an impression.

Social interaction, then, amounts to a process of negotiating reality. Usually, interaction results in at least some agreement about how to define a situation. But participants rarely share precisely the same perception of events. Subjective realities vary because social interaction brings together people with different purposes, interests, and hidden agendas, each of whom is seeking a somewhat different shaping of reality.

This short excerpt from Margaret Atwood's short story "True Trash" illustrates one way that names and clothing styles construct a certain type of person.

> *Eleven years later Donny is walking along Yorkville Avenue, in Toronto, in the summer heat. He's no longer Donny. At some point, which even he can't remember exactly, he has changed into Don. He's wearing sandals, and a white Indian-style shirt over his cut-off jeans. He has longish hair and a beard. The beard has come out yellow, whereas the hair is brown. He likes the effect: WASP Jesus or Hollywood Viking, depending on his mood. He has a string of wooden beads around his neck.*
>
> *This is how he dresses on Saturdays, to go to Yorkville; to go there and just hang around, with the crowds of others who are doing the same. Sometimes he gets high, on the pot that circulates as freely as cigarettes did once. He thinks he should be enjoying this experience more than he actually does.*
>
> *During the rest of the week he has a job in his father's law office. He can get away with the beard there, just barely, as long as he balances it with a suit. (But even the older guys are growing their sideburns and wearing colored shirts, and using words like "creative" more than they used to.) He doesn't tell the people he meets in Yorkville about this job, just as he doesn't tell the law office about his friends' acid trips. He's leading a double life. It feels precarious, and brave. (Wilderness Tips, 1990)*

The Thomas Theorem

W.I. Thomas (1966:301; orig. 1931) succinctly expressed an insight in what has come to be known as the **Thomas theorem**: *situations that are defined as real are real in their consequences.* Applied to social interaction, his observation means that although reality is initially "soft" or fluid, as it is fashioned, it can become "hard" in its effects.

Reality-Building in Global Perspective

Of course, people do not construct everyday experience "out of thin air." Rather, we creatively manipulate elements in the surrounding culture. For this reason, residents of subsidized housing build somewhat different realities than do people living in affluent communities, such as Westmount in Montreal. In global perspective, reality varies even more, so that social experiences common to, say, women in Saudi Arabia would seem unreal to many women in Canada. Similarly, social reality changes over time. People living in ancient Japan forged social worlds that were very different from those typical of the Japanese today.

George Littlechild's painting, Red Horse Boarding School, *is a poignant reminder of a sad chapter in Canadian history. In an effort to "Christianize" and "civilize" them, Native children were taken from their families and out of their reserve communities. Then they were sent to boarding schools where they learned new values, customs, norms, and language. From the perspective of the Canadian government, this practice was motivated by beneficence. However, the consequences for both the children and their communities have proven to be devastating.*

Because social reality is grounded in the surrounding culture, any object or action is subject to different interpretations, depending on the cultural context. The meanings people attach to the two sexes, to stages of the life course, or even to the days of the week vary from culture to culture. Supporting this conclusion, Wendy Griswold (1987) asked people from different societies—the West Indies, Great Britain, and the United States—to interpret several novels. She found that the messages her respondents drew from what they read differed and, furthermore, were consistent with the basic "blueprint" of their culture. What people see in a book—or anything else—is guided by their social world.

This variability of human experience leads to an interesting question: since people everywhere are members of a single species, don't we all share many of the same basic feelings? A number of researchers have conducted cross-cultural investigations of human emotions. The answer to the question is yes—and no—as the box on pages 166–67 explains.

Ethnomethodology

It is hardly surprising that human beings take for granted most of the reality they create. After all, what would social life be like if we questioned every situation we experienced? For some sociologists, however, challenging the patterns of conventional behavior yields rich insights into the organization of everyday life.

Ethnomethodology is a specialized approach within the symbolic-interaction paradigm. The term itself has two parts: the Greek *ethno* refers to understandings of cultural surroundings that people share, and "methodology" designates a system of methods or principles. Combining them makes **ethnomethodology**, *the study of the everyday, common-sense understandings that people have of the world*. Ethnomethodology was devised in the 1950s by Harold Garfinkel, a sociologist dissatisfied with the then-widespread view of society as a broad "system" with a life of its own (recall the approach of Emile Durkheim, described in Chapter 4, "Society"). Garfinkel wanted to explore how we create rules and expectations in countless familiar, everyday situations (Heritage, 1984). For example, people readily expect certain behavior when sitting down to dinner in a restaurant, when beginning to take a final examination, or when driving onto a freeway. As important as such conventional understandings may be, Garfinkel (1967) maintained that few of us ever think much about them.

In the rebellious social climate of the 1960s, Garfinkel developed a distinctive technique for exposing the unacknowledged patterns of everyday life: *break the rules*. In other words, a good way to tease out the conventional realities is to deliberately ignore them.

In a series of experiments, Garfinkel (1967) and

Cultures frame reality differently. This man lay on the street in Bombay, India, for several hours and then quietly died. In the United States, such an event would probably have provoked someone to call the rescue squad. In a poor society in which death on the streets is a fact of everyday life, however, many Indians responded not with alarm but with simple decency by stopping to place incense on his body before continuing on their way.

his students mapped everyday life by refusing to "play the game." Some entered stores and insisted on bargaining for standard-priced items, others recruited people into simple games (like tic-tac-toe) only to intentionally flout the rules, still others initiated conversations and slowly moved closer and closer until they were almost nose to nose with their quarry. At the very least, this rule violation was met with bewilderment; often "victims" responded with anger. One of Garfinkel's students reported, for example, the following exchange (1967:44):

> *Acquaintance: "How are you?"*
>
> *Student: "How am I in regard to what? My health, my finances, my school work, my peace of mind, my ..."*
>
> *Acquaintance (now red in the face and suddenly out of control): "Look! I was just trying to be polite. Frankly, I don't give a damn how you are."*

This deliberate lack of social cooperation allows the researcher to see more clearly the unspoken rules of everyday life. One measure of the importance of these rules is that people find their violation unpleasant, even threatening.

Because of its provocative character and its focus on commonplace experiences, ethnomethodology has gained a reputation as less-than-serious research. Even so, ethnomethodology has succeeded in heightening awareness of many unnoticed patterns of everyday life.

Dramaturgical Analysis: "The Presentation of Self"

Erving Goffman (1922–1982) shared with Garfinkel an interest in the patterned character of everyday life. Goffman argued that people socially constructing reality have much in common with actors performing on a stage. Calling to mind a director scrutinizing the action in a theater, Goffman termed his approach **dramaturgical analysis**, *the investigation of social interaction in terms of theatrical performance.*

Dramaturgical analysis offers a fresh look at two now-familiar concepts. In this theoretical scheme, a status mirrors a part in a play, and a role serves as a script, supplying dialogue and action for each of the characters. In any setting, then, each of us plays a role, like an actor, and also forms part of the audience. Goffman called the intricate interaction that makes up everyday

life the **presentation of self**, *ways in which individuals, in various settings, try to create specific impressions in the minds of others.* This process, sometimes termed *impression management,* contains several distinctive elements (Goffman, 1959, 1967).

Performances

As we present ourselves to others, we convey information—consciously and unconsciously—about how we wish to be understood. Goffman called these efforts, taken together, a *performance.* Dress (costume), the objects people carry with them (props), and our tone of voice and gestures (manner) are all part of a performance. In addition, everyone takes account of the setting in crafting a performance. People may joke loudly on a sidewalk, for instance, but assume a more reverent manner when they enter a church. Equally important, individuals often design settings, such as their home or office, to invoke desired reactions in others. A setting, then, is a stage that enhances a person's performance by providing numerous specific pieces of information.

Consider, for example, how a physician's office guides social interaction and conveys appropriate information to an audience of patients. Physicians enjoy considerable prestige and power in Canada, which is evident to patients immediately upon entering the doctor's office. First, the physician is nowhere to be seen. Instead, in what Goffman describes as the "front region" of the setting, the patient encounters a receptionist who functions as a gatekeeper, deciding if and when the patient can meet the physician. A simple survey of the doctor's waiting room, with patients (often impatiently) waiting to gain entry to the inner sanctum, leaves little doubt that the medical team controls events.

The physician's private office and examination room constitute the "back region" of the setting. Here the patient confronts a wide range of props, such as medical books and framed degrees, that reinforce the impression that the physician, and not the patient, has the specialized knowledge necessary to guide their interaction. In the office, the physician usually remains seated behind a desk—the larger, the greater the statement of power—while the patient is provided with only a chair.

The physician's appearance and manner convey still more information. The usual costume of white lab coat may have the practical function of keeping clothes from becoming soiled, but its primary function is to let others know at a glance the physician's status. A stethoscope around the neck or a black medical bag in hand

CROSS-CULTURAL COMPARISON

Human Emotions in Global Perspective

On a Vancouver sidewalk, a woman reacts angrily to the skateboarder who hurtles past her. Apart from a few choice words, her facial expression broadcasts a strong emotion that any Canadian can recognize. But would an observer from New Guinea be able to interpret her emotion? In other words, do people everywhere share similar emotions, and do they express them in the same way?

Paul Ekman (1980) and his colleagues have studied emotions around the world and even among members of a small society in New Guinea. Their conclusion is that people everywhere feel the same basic emotions—including anger, fear, happiness, disgust, surprise, and sadness. Moreover, people all over the globe recognize that these feelings are expressed by the same distinctive facial gestures. To Ekman, this commonality suggests that much of our emotional life is universal—rather than culturally specific—with the display of emotion biologically programmed in our facial features, muscles, and central nervous system.

But the reality of emotions is only partly rooted in our biology. Ekman and others have noted three ways in which emotional life differs significantly in global perspective. First, what *triggers* an emotional response is highly variable from one culture to another. Whether a particular situation is defined as an insult (causing anger), a loss (calling out sadness), or a mystical event (provoking surprise and awe) depends on the cultural surroundings of the individual. Second, people *display* emotions according to the norms of their culture. Every society has certain rules about when, where, and to whom people may exhibit certain emotions. People in Canada typically approve of emotional expression among family members, but consider such behavior out of place at work. Similarly, we expect children to express emotions to parents, although parents are taught to guard their emotions in front of children. Third, cultures differ in terms of how people *cope* with emotions. Some societies encourage the expression of feelings, while oth-

ers belittle emotions and demand that their members suppress them. Societies also display significant gender differences in this regard: in Canada, people tend to regard emotional expression as feminine, expected of women but a sign of weakness among men. In other societies, however, this sex-typing of emotions is less pronounced or even reversed. In sum, emotional life in cross-cultural perspective has both common and variable dimensions. People around the world experience many of the same human feelings. But what sparks a particular emotion, how a person expresses feelings, and what people think about emotions in general are variable products of social learning. In global perspective, therefore, everyday life differs not only in terms of how people think and act, but how they infuse their lives with feeling.

SOURCES: Ekman (1980a, 1980b), Lutz & White (1986), and Lutz (1988).

---

has the same purpose. A doctor's highly technical terminology—occasionally necessary, but frequently mystifying—also emphasizes the hierarchy in the situation. The use of the title "Doctor" by patients who, in turn, are frequently addressed only by their first names also underscores the physician's dominant position. The overall message of a doctor's performance is clear: "I can help you, but you must allow me to take charge."

Waitzkin (1989) has demonstrated how doctors control the talk in a patient–doctor encounter in order to reinforce a narrow, individualistic, medical definition of a situation. He makes the point that much illness and disease results from social inequities or environmental degradation, and that the most valuable techniques for health provision often include or require social and political action. But, because of various strategies of questioning and interrupting doctors are

able to keep the focus on the biomedical model of disease to the exclusion of the wider context (Waitzkin, 1989).

Nonverbal Communication

Novelist William Sansom describes a fictional Mr. Preedy, an English vacationer on a beach in Spain:

> He took care to avoid catching anyone's eye. First, he had to make it clear to those potential companions of his holiday that they were of no concern to him whatsoever. He stared through them, round them, over them—eyes lost in space. The beach might have been empty. If by chance a ball was thrown his way, he looked surprised; then let a smile of amusement light his face [Kindly Preedy],

Would people anywhere in the world see in these facial expressions anger, fear, happiness, disgust, surprise, and sadness? Research supports the conclusion that all human beings experience the same basic emotions and display them to others in ways characteristic of our species. Culture plays a central part, however, in setting the range of situations that triggers one or another emotion.

looked around dazed to see that there were people on the beach, tossed it back with a smile to himself and not a smile at the people. ...

... [He] then gathered together his beach-wrap and bag into a neat sand-resistant pile [Methodical and Sensible Preedy], rose slowly to stretch his huge frame [Big-Cat Preedy], and tossed aside his sandals [Carefree Preedy, after all]. (1956; cited in Goffman, 1959:4–5)

Through his conduct, Mr. Preedy offers a great deal of information about himself to anyone caring to observe him. Notice that he does so without uttering a single word. This illustrates the process of **nonverbal communication**, *communication using body movements, gestures, and facial expressions rather than speech.*

Through nonverbal communication, we use the body to convey information to others, as suggested by the more common phrase *body language*. Facial expressions form the most significant element of nonverbal communication. As noted earlier, smiling and other facial gestures constitute an almost universal language to express basic emotions like pleasure, surprise, and anger. Further, people express particular shades of meaning with their faces according to the demands of the situation. We distinguish, for example, between the casual, lighthearted smile of Kindly Preedy on the beach, a smile of embarrassment, and a full, unrestrained smile of self-satisfaction we often associate with the "cat who ate the canary."

Eye contact is another important element of nonverbal communication. Generally, we use eye contact to initiate social interaction. Someone across the room "catches our eye," for example, sparking a conversation. Avoiding the eyes of another, by contrast, discourages communication. Hands, too, speak for us. Common hand gestures in our culture convey, among other things, an insult, a request for a ride, an invitation for someone to join us, or a demand that others stop in their tracks. Gestures also supplement spoken words. Pointing in a menacing way at someone, for example, intensifies a word of warning, as shrugging the shoulders adds an air of indifference to the phrase "I don't know," and rapidly waving the arms lends urgency to the single word "Hurry!"

Most nonverbal communication is culture-specific. Hand gestures and body movements have different meanings from place to place, so that many gestures significant to North Americans mean nothing—or something very different—to members of other societies, as explained in Chapter 3 ("Culture"). For instance, what many of us call the "A-OK" gesture with thumb touching forefinger means "You're a zero" to the French, and conveys a crude word for "rectum" to many Italians (Ekman, Friesen, & Bear, 1984).

Individuals deliberately express many elements of nonverbal communication. Sometimes, however, the information we unintentionally give off contradicts our intended performance. Listening to her teenage son's explanation for returning home at a late hour, for example, a mother begins to doubt his words because he avoids her eyes. The guest on a television talk show claims that her recent divorce is "the best thing that ever happened to me," but the nervous swing of her leg suggests otherwise. Such nonverbal communication may provide clues to deception, in much the same way that a lie detector measures subtle physical changes in breathing, pulse rate, perspiration, and blood pressure that signal the stress of telling lies. Does this mean that careful observers can detect dishonesty in someone else's performance? Paul Ekman believes they can, as the box on pages 170–71 explains.

Gender and Personal Performances

Because women are socialized to be less assertive than men, they tend to be especially sensitive to nonverbal communication. In fact, *gender*—which involves distinct social expectations for females and males—is a central element in personal performances. In other words, because women and men are subject to different cultural norms and have unequal social power, the members of each sex typically behave differently in most settings. Based on the work of Nancy Henley, Mykol Hamilton, and Barrie Thorne (1992), we can extend the conventional analysis of personal performances to spotlight the importance of gender.

Demeanor

Goffman (1967) links *demeanor*—general conduct or deportment—to social power. Simply put, people in positions of power have far greater personal discretion in how they act; those subject to supervision act more formally and self-consciously. Office behavior such as swearing, removing shoes, or putting feet up on the desk may well be considered acceptable for the boss, but not for subordinates (Henley, Hamilton, & Thorne, 1992). Similarly, people in positions of dominance can interrupt the performances of others with impunity, while those subject to their power are expected to display deference by becoming silent (Smith-Lovin & Brody, 1989).

For women, who generally occupy positions of low power, demeanor is a matter of particular concern. As Chapter 13 ("Sex and Gender") explains, about half of all working women in Canada hold clerical or service jobs that place them under the control of supervisors, who are usually men. Women, then, must craft their personal performances more formally than men, and display a greater degree of deference in everyday interaction.

Use of Space

How much space does a personal performance require? Here again, power plays a key role, since using more space conveys a nonverbal message of personal importance. According to Henley, Hamilton, and Thorne (1992), men use significantly more space than women do. Typically, men command more space when they stand before a convention audience making a presentation or even when they lounge casually about the beach on vacation. Why? Because our society traditionally has measured femininity by how little space women occupy (the standard of "daintiness"), while men enhance their masculinity by controlling as much territory as possible (the standard of "turf").

Susan Brownmiller, in *Femininity*, poignantly describes her personal experience in developing feminine body utilization. As she says,

*My mother gave me curtsy lessons before I was five.
At the drop of a cue, "And this is our daughter,
Susan," I'd gather the ends of my short, pleated
skirt—elbows in, wrists down, fingers up—and fall
to the ground on one tender-skinned knee.
Grownups were enchanted. So was I, for Shirley*

Temple, Deanna Durbin and all the storybook princesses stood at my side. I had mastered my first serious training in feminine movement, and I found it was something at which I excelled. (Brownmiller, 1984:171)

The concept of **personal space** refers to *the surrounding area over which a person makes some claim to privacy.* In Canada, we typically remain at least several feet from others, maintaining somewhat greater personal space than people in more densely populated societies such as Japan. But this distance varies significantly by sex. In daily life, men readily intrude on the personal space of women. A woman's intrusion into a man's personal space, however, is likely to be construed as a sexual overture. Here again, women have less power to define a specific reality than men do.

Staring, Smiling, and Touching

Eye contact encourages interaction. Women more than men actively maintain interaction, generally sustaining eye contact longer. One exception is *staring*. Men in our society often make women the objects of stares, which reflects both the dominance of men in Canada and the tendency to define women as sexual objects.

Although frequently conveying pleasure, *smiling* can also project a wide range of meaning. In a male-dominated world, women often smile to indicate appeasement, or acceptance of submission. For this reason, Henley, Hamilton, and Thorne maintain, women smile more than men; in extreme cases, smiling may reach the level of nervous habit.

Finally, *touching* constitutes an intriguing social pattern. Mutual touching generally conveys intimacy and caring. Apart from close relationships, however, touching is generally something men do to women. A male physician touches the shoulder of his female nurse as they examine a report, a young man who has just begun dating touches the back of his woman friend as he guides her across the street, or a male skiing instructor excessively and unnecessarily touches his female students. In these examples—as well as many others—the touching may evoke little response, so common is it in everyday life. But it amounts to a subtle ritual by which men express their dominant position in an assumed hierarchy that subordinates women.

Idealization

Complex motives underlie all human behavior. Even so, Goffman suggests, performances tend to *idealize* our intentions. That is, we try to convince others that what we do reflects ideal cultural standards rather than less virtuous motives.

Idealization is easily illustrated by returning to the world of physicians and patients. In a hospital, physicians engage in a performance commonly described as "making rounds." Entering the room of a patient, the physician often stops at the foot of the bed and silently examines the patient's chart. Afterwards, physician and patient briefly converse. In ideal terms, this routine involves a physician making a personal visit to inquire about a patient's condition.

In reality, something less exemplary is usually going on. A physician who sees perhaps thirty-five patients a day may remember little about most of them. Reading the chart gives the physician the opportunity to rediscover the patient's identity and medical problems. Openly revealing the actual impersonality of much medical care would undermine the culturally ideal perception of the physician as deeply concerned about the welfare of others. Idealizing the behavior of physicians also encourages patients to "follow doctor's orders," which, they assume, are in their own best interest. No doubt this is often the case. But, as Chapter 20 ("Health and Medicine") explains, physicians often prescribe drugs, order tests, admit patients to hospitals, and perform surgery with a keen awareness of what's in it for themselves (Kaplan et al., 1985).

Idealization is woven into the fabric of everyday life in countless ways. Physicians and other profession-

Women and men use space in different ways. Because controlling space is a measure of power, men typically take up as much space as they can—even while relaxing—while women try to use as little as possible.

SOCIOLOGY OF EVERYDAY LIFE

Telling Lies: Clues to Deceit

On September 15, 1938, Germany's chancellor Adolf Hitler and Britain's prime minister Neville Chamberlain met for the first time, as the world looked on in hopes of avoiding war. Although his plans for war were already well under way, Hitler assured Chamberlain that peace could be preserved. Chamberlain believed what he heard, writing soon afterward, "In spite of the hardness and ruthlessness I thought I saw in his face, I got the impression that here was a man who could be relied upon when he had given his word" (Ekman, 1985:15–16). In retrospect, we can see that Chamberlain should have paid less attention to the message Hitler *gave* and more to the contradictory nonverbal signals he *gave off*.

Detecting lies is a difficult task, because no bodily gesture directly indicates deceit as, for example, a smile indicates pleasure. Even so, because each performance involves so many expressions, few people can confidently lie without allowing some piece of contradictory information to arouse the suspicions of a careful observer. The key, therefore, to identifying deceit is to scan a complete

Telling lies is no easy task because most people lack the ability to manipulate correctly their facial muscles. Looking at the three faces below, the expression of grief in Figure A is probably genuine, since few people can deliberately lift the upper eyelids and inner corners of the eyebrows in this way. Likewise, the apprehension shown in Figure B also appears authentic, since intentionally raising the eyebrows and pulling them together is nearly impossible. People who fake emotions usually do a poor job of it, illustrated by the phony expression of pleasure shown in Figure C. Genuine delight, for most people, would produce a balanced smile.

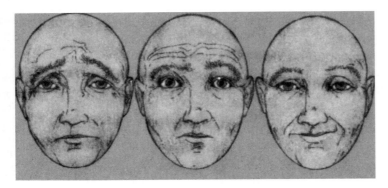

FIGURE A   FIGURE B   FIGURE C

als typically idealize their motives for entering their chosen careers. They describe their work as "making a contribution to science," perhaps "answering a calling from God," or "serving the community." Rarely do such people concede the less honorable, although common, motives of seeking the high income, power, and prestige these occupations confer. More generally, we all smile and make polite remarks to people we do not like. Such small hypocrisies ease our way through social interactions. Even when we suspect that others are putting on an act, we are unlikely to openly challenge their performance, for reasons that we shall explain next.

Embarrassment and Tact

The presidential candidate enters the room and stumbles over the rug; the eminent professor consistently mispronounces a simple word; the visiting dignitary rises from the table to speak, unaware of the napkin that still clings to her dress. As carefully as individuals may craft their performances, slipups of this kind frequently occur. The result is *embarrassment*, which in a dramaturgical analysis means the discomfort that follows a spoiled performance. Goffman describes embarrassment simply as "losing face."

Embarrassment looms as an ever-present danger because, first, idealized performances typically contain some deception. Second, most performances involve a complex array of elements, any one of which if badly done can shatter the intended impression.

Curiously, an audience often overlooks flaws in a performance, thereby allowing the individual to avoid embarrassment. We discreetly inform a man that his zipper is open (creating limited embarrassment) only to help him avoid an even greater loss of face. In Hans Christian Andersen's classic fable "The Emperor's New Clothes," the child who blurts out that the emperor is naked tells the truth, but is scolded for being rude.

performance with an eye for any discrepancies in the information that is conveyed.

Specifically, Ekman suggests scrutinizing four types of information provided by a performer—words, voice, body language, and facial expression. *Language* serves as the major channel of communication in social interaction. But a liar can manipulate words with relative ease by mentally rehearsing what will be said. One clue to deceit, however, is a simple slip of the tongue—something the performer did not mean to say in quite that way. For example, a young man who is deceiving his parents by claiming that his roommate is a male friend rather than a female lover might inadvertently use the word *she* rather than *he* in a conversation about his living arrangements. The more complicated the deception, the more likely a performer is to make a revealing mistake.

Voice, meaning the qualities of speech other than words, also contains clues to deception. Tone and patterns of speech are especially important because they are hard to control. A person trying to hide a powerful emotion, for example, cannot easily prevent the voice from trembling or breaking. Similarly, the individual may speak quickly (suggesting anger) or slowly (indicating sadness). Nervous laughter, inappropriate pauses between words, or nonwords, such as *ah* and *ummm*, also hint at discomfort.

A "leak" of *body language* that a performer is unable to conceal may tip off an observer to deception as well. Subtle body movements, for example, give the impression of nervousness, as do sudden swallowing or rapid breathing. These are especially good clues to deception because few people can control them. Sometimes, *not* using the body in the expected way to enhance words—as when a person tries to fake excitement—also suggests deception.

Uncontrollable *facial expressions* may give away a phony performance. A sad person feigning happiness, for example, generally "flashes" momentary frowns through a crooked smile. In this case, the concealed emotion "leaks" through the deliberate facade. A signal of fear or worry is raising and drawing together the eyebrows, a movement virtually impossible for most people to make voluntarily. Crossing the face of a person who is supposedly at ease, this expression sounds the alarm of deception.

In sum, lies are detectable, but the ability to notice relevant clues usually requires training. Knowing the other person well makes detecting deception much easier; parents, for example, can usually spot deception in their children. Clues to deception are also more evident if a person is trying to contain strong emotions. Even so, some have (or develop) the ability to carefully manage their verbal and nonverbal performances. There are, in short, both good and bad liars.

SOURCE: Ekman (1985).

Members of an audience not only ignore flaws in a performance, Goffman explains, they often help the performer recover from them. *Tact* is an effort to help another person "save face." After hearing an educated person make an embarrassingly crude remark, for example, people may handle the situation in a variety of tactful ways. No response at all may signal the pretense that the statement was never made. Mild laughter may indicate they wish to dismiss what they have heard as a joke. Or a listener may simply respond, "I'm sure you didn't mean that," suggesting that the statement will not be allowed to destroy the actor's overall performance.

Why is tact such a common response? Simply because embarrassment provokes discomfort not only for one person but for *everyone*. Just as members of a theater audience feel uneasy when an actor forgets a line, people who observe a poor performance are reminded of how fragile their own performances often are. Socially constructed reality thus functions like a dam holding back a sea of chaotic possibility. Should one person's performance spring a leak, others tactfully assist in making repairs. Everyone, after all, is engaged in jointly building reality, and no one wants it to be suddenly swept away.

Goffman's research shows that although individuals interact with a considerable degree of individuality and spontaneity, everyone's social interactions are constructed out of similar, patterned elements. Almost four hundred years ago, Shakespeare wrote:

All the world's a stage,
And all the men and women merely players.
They have their exits and their entrances,
And one man in his time plays many parts.

(As You Like It, II. vii.)

Of course, human behavior is never as rigidly scripted as a stage performance. In a lifetime, though, each individual does assume many roles in ways that combine social structure with expressions of a unique personality. But although human behavior does not simply consist of stage and script, Shakespeare's observation still contains a good measure of truth.

Interaction in Everyday Life: Two Illustrations

We have now examined a number of dimensions of social interaction. The final sections of this chapter illustrate these lessons by focusing on two important, yet quite different, elements of everyday life.

Language: The Gender Issue

As explained in Chapter 3 ("Culture"), language is the thread with which members of a society weave the symbolic web we call culture. In everyday life, language conveys meaning on more than one level. Besides the *manifest* content, or what is explicitly stated, the *latent* content conveys various additional assumptions about reality. One latent message involves gender. Language defines men and women differently in at least three ways (Henley, Hamilton, & Thorne, 1992).[2]

The Control Function of Language

A young man drives into the gas station, eager to display his new motorcycle, and proudly says, "Isn't she a

---

[2] The following sections draw primarily on Henley, Hamilton, & Thorne, 1992. Additional material comes from Thorne, Kramarae, & Henley, 1983; MacKay, 1983; and others as noted.

beauty?" On the surface, the question has little to do with females and males. Yet, curiously, a common linguistic pattern confers the female "she," rather than male "he," on the man's prized possession.

Men often use language to establish control over their surroundings. That is, a man attaches a female pronoun to a motorcycle, car, yacht, or other object because it reflects *ownership*. Conversely, for a man or a woman to use a male pronoun in such cases sounds awkward.

A more obvious control function of language relates to people's names. Traditionally in Canada, and in many other parts of the world, a woman takes the family name of the man she marries. While few today consider this an explicit statement of a man's ownership of a woman, it certainly reflects historical male dominance. For this reason, an increasing proportion of women have retained their own name (more precisely, the family name obtained from their father) or merged two family names.

The Value Function of Language

Language usually attaches greater value, force, or significance to what is defined as masculine. This pattern is deeply rooted in the English language, in ways that probably few men or women realize. For instance, the laudatory adjective "virtuous," meaning "morally worthy" or "excellent," is derived from the Latin word *vir* meaning "man." By contrast, the pejorative adjective "hysterical" is derived from the Greek word *hyster*, meaning "uterus."

In numerous, more familiar ways, language also confers different value on the two sexes. Traditional masculine terms such as "king" or "lord" have retained their positive meaning, while comparable terms, such as "queen," "madam," or "dame" have acquired nega-

Hand gestures vary widely from one culture to another. Yet a chuckle, grin, or smirk in response to someone's performance is universally defined as not taking the person seriously. Therefore, the world over, people who cannot restrain their mirth tactfully cover their faces.

tive connotations in contemporary usage. Language thus both mirrors social attitudes and helps to perpetuate them.

Similarly, use of the suffixes "ette" and "ess" to denote femininity generally devalues the words to which they are added. For example, a *major* has higher standing than a *majorette*, as does a *host* in relation to a *hostess*.

The Attention Function of Language

Language also shapes reality by directing greater attention to masculine endeavors. The most obvious example is our use of personal pronouns. In the English language, the plural pronoun "they" is neutral in referring to both sexes. But the corresponding singular pronouns "he" and "she" are sex linked. According to traditional grammatical practice, "he" along with the possessive "his" and objective "him" are used to refer to *all people*. Thus, we assume that the masculine pronoun in the bit of wisdom "He who hesitates is lost" refers to women as well as to men. But this practice also reflects the traditional cultural pattern of ignoring the lives of women. Some research suggests that people continue to respond to allegedly inclusive or generic male pronouns as if only males were involved (Martyna, 1978, 1980; MacKay 1983). To many women, especially those who embrace feminism, encountering male pronouns sends a disconcerting message that women are of peripheral importance (MacKay, 1983).

For a century, advocates of gender equality have urged creation of a gender-neutral, third-person singular personal pronoun. In 1884, one language critic offered the new word "thon" (from "that" + "one") to solve the pronoun problem, as in "the successful person is thon who is well-prepared" (Converse, 1884; cited in Kramarae, Thorne, & Henley, 1983:175). The awkward sound of this phrasing suggests how firmly established traditional patterns are in our everyday lives. More recently, the plural pronoun "they" has gained currency as a singular pronoun ("*Everyone* should do as *they* please"). This usage remains controversial because it violates grammatical rules.

Recently, the Ontario Women's Directorate published a booklet entitled *Words that Count Women In* (1992). On the first page, the authors make the point that sexist language is so very prevalent that it can even be found in the one piece of music that all Canadians are exposed to and most sing thousands of times over their lifetimes. The national anthem begins with the famous words,

O Canada! Our Home and Native Land!
True patriot love in all thy sons command.

The editors go on to question where such wording leaves all Canadian women and girls. Can only men love their country? "O Canada," the symbol of our democratic spirit, excludes half the population. The Directorate's publication examines some of the most common assumptions and barriers that have made transition to gender-inclusive language somewhat troublesome. Some of their suggestions for bias-free wordings are included in Table 6-1.

Humor: Playing with Reality

It has been suggested that comedy is Canada's greatest cultural export (Johnson, 1993:32). Certainly, humor plays a vital part in our everyday lives. Comedians are among our favorite entertainers, most newspapers contain cartoon pages, and even professors and the clergy incorporate humor in their performances. Like many aspects of everyday life, humor is largely taken for granted. While everyone laughs at a joke, few people think about what makes something funny or why humor is found among humans everywhere in the world. Many of the ideas developed in this chapter provide insights into the character of humor, as we shall now see.[3]

The Foundation of Humor

Humor stems from the contrast between two incongruous realities. Generally, one socially constructed reality can be termed *conventional* because it describes what people expect in a specific setting. The other reality, dubbed *unconventional*, represents a significant violation of cultural patterns. Humor, therefore, arises from contradiction, ambiguity, and "double meanings" generated by two differing definitions of the same situation. Note how this principle works in these simple pieces of humor:

Steve Martin muses: "I like a woman with a head on her shoulders. I hate necks!"

A car pulls alongside the steaming wreck and the driver calls out: "Have an accident?"

"No thanks," comes the reply. "Just had one!"

---

[3] The ideas contained in this discussion are those of John J. Macionis (1987), except as otherwise noted. The general approach draws on work presented earlier in this chapter, especially on the ideas of Erving Goffman.

TABLE 6-1   EXAMPLES OF BIASED AND BIAS-FREE WORDS

Biased	Bias-free	Biased	Bias-free
The Work World		**Stereotypes**	
alderman	municipal councillor	femme fatale	seducer
anchorman	anchor	kingmaker	power behind the throne, eminence grise
career girl, career woman	professional, manager, executive	lady luck	luck
cleaning lady	cleaner	maiden voyage	first voyage
engineman	engine operator	man of letters	scholar, writer, literary figure
foreman	supervisor	one-up-manship	upstaging, competitiveness
longshoreman	dockhand, shorehand	workmanship	quality construction, expertise
newsman	journalist, reporter, newshound	**Turns of Phrase**	
World of Play		All men are created equal.	We are all created equal.
		Boys will be boys.	Kids will be kids.
horseman, horsewoman	rider	A fool and his money are soon parted.	Fools and their money are soon parted.
sportsman	sports buff, sports enthusiast, athlete	Man does not live by bread alone.	We don't live by bread alone.
Roles People Play		A man's home is his castle.	Your home is your castle.
alumni	graduates	no-man's land	limbo, dead zone, unclaimed territory
boys in blue	armed forces	to a man	to a one, to a person, without exception
corporate wife	corporate spouse	**Put-downs**	
layman	layperson, uninitiated, nonprofessional	fall guy	chump, dupe, scapegoat
The Human Family		manhandle	abuse, mistreat
brotherhood	kinship, community	nervous Nellie	worrywart, worrier
common man	common person, average person	prodigal son	spendthrift, returned prodigal
fatherland	native land	tomboy	rough and tumble child
fellowship	camaraderie		
sons of God	children of God		

SOURCE: *Adapted from* Words that Count Women Out *In, Toronto: Ontario Women's Directorate, 1992.*

In each of these examples, the first sentence represents a conventional reality. A man seeks a woman who is sensible and intelligent. One driver offers help to another. There is nothing startling here. The second sentence in each example, however, provides an unconventional meaning that collides with what we take for granted. In the Steve Martin joke, the assertion "I hate necks!" suddenly transforms the entire statement into an unexpectedly grotesque image. Similarly, the motorist who replies, "Just had one," absurdly transforms an offer of help into an invitation to further injury. All humor is grounded in such contrasting realities.

The same simple pattern characterizes the humor of other well-known comedians:

Groucho Marx, trying to sound manly: "This morning, I shot a lion in my pajamas." He then turns to the camera and adds, "What the lion was doing in my pajamas I'll never know …"

On the television show "M*A*S*H", Hawkeye Pierce observes Colonel Henry Blake gallivanting around with a young woman half his age and dryly responds, "There's an age problem there; she's twenty-two and his wife's forty-eight."

Like the other two examples, each of these jokes contains two major elements, a conventional assertion followed by an unconventional one. The greater the opposition, or incongruity, between the two definitions of reality, the greater the potential for humor. The humor that opens this chapter flows from contrasting the hucksterism of car dealers with the formality and dignity expected of those who provide funeral services.

When telling jokes, people can strengthen this opposition in various ways. One technique, often used by Groucho Marx, George Burns, Gracie Allen, and other comedians of the screen, is to present the first, or conventional, remark in conversation with another actor, then to turn toward the audience (or the camera) when delivering the second, or unconventional, line. This "shift of channel" underscores the incongruity of the two parts. To fashion the strongest contrast, comedians must pay careful attention to their performances—the precise words they use, as well as the timing of each part of the delivery. A joke is "well told" if the comic creates the sharpest possible opposition between the realities, just as humor falls flat in a careless performance. Since the key to humor lies in the opposition of realities, it is not surprising that the climax of a joke is called the *punch line*.

The Dynamics of Humor: "Getting It"

Someone who does not understand both the conventional and unconventional realities embedded in a joke offers the typical complaint: "I don't get it." To "get" humor, members of an audience must understand the two realities involved well enough to perceive their incongruity.

But there is something more to getting a joke, because some of the information listeners must grasp is usually left unstated. The audience, therefore, must pay attention to the stated elements of the joke and then inferentially complete the joke in their own minds. Consider the following exchange, from the well-known television show "Cheers":

> Sam: "Diane, you're drunk."
>
> Diane: "Yes, Sam, and you're stupid, but I'll be sober in the morning."

In this case, "getting" the joke depends on following the logic well enough to mentally complete Diane's line with the words "... and you'll *still* be stupid."

A more complex joke was written on the wall of a college restroom:

> Dyslexics of the World, Untie!

This joke demands much more of the audience. One must know, first, that dyslexia is a condition in which people routinely reverse letters; second, one must identify the line as an adaptation of Karl Marx's call to the world's workers to unite; third and finally, one must recognize "untie" as an anagram of "unite," as one might imagine a disgruntled dyslexic person would write it.

Why would an audience be required to make this sort of effort in order to understand a joke? Simply because our reaction to a joke is heightened by the pleasure of having completed the puzzle necessary to "get it". This pleasure partly derives from satisfaction at our mental abilities. Additionally, "getting" the joke

Humor is often based on incongruous definitions of reality or on jarring juxtapositions. In the world of Bob and Doug McKenzie, Canada, the Great White North, turned out not to be a land "flowing with milk and honey" so much as one that was clogged with junk food and beer.

confers a favored status as an "insider" in the larger audience. These insights also explain the frustration that accompanies not getting a joke: the fear of mental inadequacy coupled with a sense of being socially excluded from a pleasure shared by others. Not surprisingly, "outsiders" in such a situation may fake "getting" the joke; others may tactfully explain a joke to them to end their sense of being left out.

But, as the old saying goes, if a joke has to be explained, it couldn't be very funny. Besides taking the edge off the language and timing on which the *punch* depends, an explanation completely relieves the audience of any mental involvement, substantially reducing their pleasure.

The Topics of Humor

People throughout the world smile and laugh, providing ample evidence that humor is a universal human trait. But because people live in diverse cultures, they differ in what they find funny. Musicians frequently travel to perform for receptive audiences around the world, suggesting that music may be the "common language" of humanity. Comedians rarely do this, demonstrating that humor does not travel well.

What is humorous to the Chinese, then, may be lost on people in North America. To some degree, too, the social diversity of our society means that people will find humor in different situations. Newfoundlanders, southerners, and westerners have their own brands of humor, as do Native people and Anglos, fifteen- and forty-year-olds, bankers and construction workers.

For everyone, however, humor deals with topics that lend themselves to double meanings or *controversy*. For example, the first jokes many of us learned as children concerned what our culture defines as a childhood taboo: sex. The mere mention of "unmentionable acts" or even certain parts of the body can dissolve young faces in laughter.

The controversy inherent in humor often walks a fine line between what is funny and what is considered "sick." During the Middle Ages, the word *humors* (derived from the Latin *humidus*, meaning "moist") referred to a balance of bodily fluids that determined a person's degree of health. Most cultures value the ability to take conventional definitions of reality lightly (in other words, having a "sense of humor"). In fact, empirical evidence supports the old saying "Laughter is the best medicine": maintaining a sense of humor does contribute to a person's physical health partly by decreasing stress (Robinson, 1983; Haig, 1988). At the extreme, however, people who always take conventional reality lightly risk being defined as deviant or even mentally ill (mental hospitals have long been dubbed "funny farms").

Every social group considers some topics too sensitive for humorous treatment. A violation may result in the comedian being admonished for telling a "sick" joke, one that pokes fun at a situation that is expected to be handled with reverence. Some topics, in other words, are "off limits," because people expect them to be understood in only one way. People's religious beliefs, tragic accidents, or appalling crimes are the stuff of "sick" jokes.

The Functions of Humor

As a widespread means of communication, humor has survival value for any society and for the entire human species. A structural-functional analysis suggests that humor has a valuable function as a social "safety valve," allowing people to release potentially disruptive sentiments with little consequence. Put another way, jokes express ideas that might be dangerous if taken seriously, as in the case of racial and ethnic jokes. Called to account for a remark that could be defined as offensive, a person may defuse the situation by simply stating, "I didn't mean anything by what I said—it was just a joke!" Likewise, rather than taking offense at another's behavior, a person might use humor as a form of tact, smiling, as if to say, "I could be angry at this, but I'll assume you were only kidding."

In Canada, we often use humor to express our common identity. By laughing at ourselves and putting ourselves down, we reinforce a sense of our common bond. In the following joke, we are all being made fun of:

> *After all, [Canada's] idea of a joke is spending a year debating a constitutional accord as if it were a matter of life and death, then changing the subject. Canada is a nation without a punch line.* (Johnson, 1993:32)

In the midst of the deep divisions caused by the constitutional discussions, the joke reminds us that we have a common national identity. We are "insiders" to the joke, not only because we are familiar with the events being referred to, but also because we recognize in the situation as it is described a pattern that in some way characterizes us as a nation. Would the joke seem as funny if the writer were an American?

Humor is a natural response of the outsider—the drifter or social misfit—to mainstream society. We love to hear the patient say to the psychiatrist, "You're sicker than I am!" Much of the humor in Bruce McDonald's film, Highway 61, turns on the discovery made by Pokey and Jackie that the "straight" people they meet in their wanderings are actually weirder and more maladjusted than they are. Here, a shotgun-toting Mr. Watson punishes Pokey (left) and Jackie (right) for stealing his wife's dress by forcing them to endure an excruciatingly off-key singing performance by his daughters.

Like theatre and art, humor also allows a society to challenge orthodox ideas and to explore alternatives to the status quo. Sometimes, in fact, humor may actually promote social change by loosening the hold of convention.

Humor and Conflict

If humor holds the potential to liberate, it can also be used for subjugation. Men who tell jokes about feminists, for example, typically are voicing some measure of hostility to the interests of women (Benokraitis & Feagin, 1986; Powell & Paton, 1988). Similarly, jokes at the expense of homosexuals reveal the tensions surrounding sexual orientation in North America.

"Put-down" jokes, which make one category of people feel good at the expense of another, are common around the globe. After collecting and analyzing jokes from many societies, Christie Davies (1990) concluded that conflict among ethnic groups is a driving force behind humor virtually everywhere. Typically, jokes label some disadvantaged category of people as stupid or ridiculous, thereby imputing greater wisdom and skills to those who share the humor. In Canada, Newfoundlanders have long been the "butt" of jokes, as have Poles in the United States, the Irish in Scotland,

the Sikhs in India, the Hausas in Nigeria, the Tasmanians in Australia, and the Kurds in Iraq.

Disadvantaged people, of course, also make fun of the powerful. Women in Canada have long joked about men, just as African Americans portray whites in humorous ways, and poor people poke fun at the rich. Throughout the world, people target their leaders with humor, and officials in some countries take such jokes seriously enough to vigorously repress them.

The significance of humor is therefore much greater than first impressions suggest. Michael Flaherty (1984, 1990) points out that socially constructing reality is constant and demanding work. Furthermore, the reality that emerges may suffer by comparison to what we are able to imagine. As long as we maintain a sense of humor, however, we are never prisoners of the present. Rather, in laughter we assert our freedom. And, in doing so, we change the world and ourselves just a little. Although quite different, the impact of gender in our language and the way humor plays with reality are both important dimensions of everyday life. Each demonstrates our power to socially construct a world of meaning and then to react to what we have made. Each also demonstrates the value of the sociological perspective for understanding—and more actively participating in—this process.

Summary

1. Social life is patterned in various ways. By guiding behavior within culturally approved bounds, social structure helps to make situations more understandable and predictable.

2. A major component of social structure is status. Within an entire status set, a master status has particular significance.

3. Ascribed statuses are essentially involuntary, while achieved statuses are largely earned. In practice, however, many statuses incorporate elements of both ascription and achievement.

4. Role is the dynamic expression of a status. Like statuses, roles are relational, guiding people as they interact.

5. When roles corresponding to two or more statuses are incompatible, role conflict results. Likewise, incompatibility among various roles linked to a single status (the role set) can generate role strain.

6. The phrase "social construction of reality" conveys the important idea that people build the social world as they interact.

7. The Thomas theorem states, "situations defined as real are real in their consequences."

8. People build social reality using elements of their culture and according to their available social resources.

9. Ethnomethodology refers to a means of exploring the structure of everyday social situations by violating patterns of expected behavior.

10. Dramaturgical analysis explores how people construct personal performances. This approach views everyday life in terms of theatrical performances.

11. People speak, use body language, and fashion physical settings to assist their performances.

Often these performances attempt to idealize underlying intentions.

12. Women and men craft their situational behavior differently based on their different relative social power.

13. Social behavior carries the ever-present danger of embarrassment. Tact is a common response to a "loss of face" by others.

14. Language constitutes a major element in forming social reality. In various ways, language defines females and males differently, generally to the advantage of males.

15. Humor stems from the contrast between conventional and unconventional social realities. Because comedy is framed by the specific culture, people throughout the world find humor in very different situations.

Key Concepts

achieved status   a social position that is assumed voluntarily and that reflects a significant measure of personal ability and effort

ascribed status   a social position that is received at birth or involuntarily assumed later in the life course

dramaturgical analysis   the investigation of social interaction in terms of theatrical performance

ethnomethodology   the study of the everyday, common-sense understandings that people have of the world

master status   a status that has exceptional importance for social identity, often shaping a person's entire life

nonverbal communication   communication using body movements, gestures, and facial expressions rather than speech

personal space   the surrounding area over which a person makes some claim to privacy

presentation of self   the ways in which individuals, in various settings, try to create specific impressions in the minds of others

role   patterns of expected behavior attached to a particular status

role conflict   incompatibility among the roles corresponding to two or more different statuses

role set   a number of roles attached to a single status

role strain   incompatibility among roles corresponding to a single status

social construction of reality   the process by which individuals creatively shape reality through social interaction

social interaction   the process by which people act and react in relation to others

status   a recognized social position that an individual occupies

status set   all the statuses a person holds at a given time

Thomas theorem   the assertion that situations that are defined as real are real in their consequences

Suggested Readings

Drawing on the sociological perspective, this paperback provides many rich insights into everyday life.
David A. Karp and William C. Yoels. *Sociology and Everyday Life.* Itasca, IL: Peacock, 1986.

These two readable classics in sociology are readily available in paperback.
Erving Goffman. *The Presentation of Self in Everyday Life.* Garden City, NY: Doubleday Anchor Books, 1959.

Peter L. Berger and Thomas Luckmann. *The Social Construction of Reality: A Treatise in the Sociology of Knowledge.* Garden City, NY: Doubleday Anchor Books, 1967.

Fiske offers an intriguing, multidisciplinary thesis that all interaction can be reduced to basic social forms.
Alan Paige Fiske. *Structures of Social Life: The Four Elementary Forms of Human Relations.* New York: The Free Press, 1991.

Television is central to everyday lives in North America. This book brings together thirteen essays that explore television and women from a feminist perspective.

Mary Ellen Brown, ed. *Television and Women's Culture: The Politics of the Popular*. Newbury Park, CA: Sage, 1990.

A fascinating study of role conflict, this account delves into the lives of gay men who became Roman Catholic priests.

James G. Wolf. *Gay Priests*. San Francisco: Harper & Row, 1989.

The everyday lives of women—especially women of color—in North American society have long been overlooked. This paperback offers an oral history of one African-American woman's life as told to her sociologist granddaughter.

Mamie Garvin Fields with Karen Fields. *Lemon Swamp and Other Places*. New York: The Free Press, 1985.

A crucial aspect of personal performances is their believability. This book explores persuasiveness in face-to-face interaction, in the mass media, and in large organizations.

Kathleen Kelley Readron. *Persuasion in Practice*. Newbury Park, CA: Sage, 1991.

Here is a recent book by an analyst of deceit whose ideas were noted in this chapter.

Paul Ekman. *Why Kids Lie: How to Encourage Truthfulness*. New York: Charles Scribner's Sons, 1989.

This sociological study explores the process of *leaving* roles.

Helen Rose Fuchs Ebaugh. *Becoming an EX: The Process of Role Exit*. Chicago: University of Chicago Press, 1988.

An excellent collection of articles on ethnomethodology can be found in the following book:

Roy Turner, ed. *Ethnomethodology: Selected Readings*. Harmondsworth: Penguin, 1974.

Haas and Shaffir studied medical students at McMaster University in Hamilton. The following article describes some processes through which they become "professional."

Jack Haas and William Shaffir. "The Professionalization of Medical Students: Developing Competence and a Cloak of Competence." *Symbolic Interaction*, 71–88, 1977.

The authors observed and participated in hustling in order to write this rich and detailed description of the life of professional hustlers.

Robert Prus and C.R.D. Sharper. *Road Hustler: Career Contingencies of Professional Card and Dice Hustlers*. Lexington, Mass.: Lexington Books, 1977.

The following book examines the political economy in social psychology interactions.

Peter W. Archibald. *Social Psychology as Political Economy*. Toronto: McGraw-Hill Ryerson, 1978.

This book is a fascinating inside account of the multiple murderer.

Elliott Leyton. *Hunting Humans: The Rise of the Modern Multiple Murderer*. Toronto: McClelland & Stewart, 1986.

Physical attractiveness is a topic of growing interest in social science. This book offers a good introduction to the issue.

Elaine Hatfield and Susan Sprecher. *Mirror, Mirror ... The Importance of Looks in Everyday Life*. Albany, NY: SUNY Press, 1986.

The centrality of gender to language and everyday reality is explored in this collection of essays; the editors also provide a comprehensive and annotated bibliography.

Barrie Thorne, Cheris Kramarae, and Nancy Henley. *Language, Gender and Society*. Cambridge: Newbury House, 1983.

As the negative tone of the phrase "woman driver" suggests, North American culture has traditionally denied women the mobility it afforded to men. In this book, Virginia Scharff examines the gradual process by which women entered the automobile age.

Virginia Scharff. *Taking the Wheel: Women and the Coming of the Motor Age*. New York: The Free Press, 1991.

This report of research on a Pacific island suggests ways in which emotions, and how people think about them, are culturally variable.

Catherine A. Lutz. *Unnatural Emotions: Everyday Sentiments on a Micronesian Atoll and Their Challenge to Western Theory*. Chicago: University of Chicago Press, 1988.

Relatively little attention has been paid to the sociological analysis of humor. The following two books introduce various approaches.

Marvin R. Koller. *Humor and Society: Explorations in the Sociology of Humor*. Houston: Cap and Gown Press, 1988.
Christie Davies. *Ethnic Humor Around the World: A Comparative Analysis*. Bloomington: Indiana University Press, 1990.

GROUPS AND ORGANIZATIONS

Nine-year-old Alicia Martin was playing in front of her New Hampshire home when her ball rolled into the next yard. Annoyed at the child's carelessness, her eighty-eight-year-old neighbor refused to return the ball. Alicia's parents then did the properly American thing: they *sued* their neighbor, winning a court judgment for $30.20.

Although far from typical, this story of neighborhood relations points to an emerging trend in the United States: the increasing use of lawyers and the courts to settle issues that once were resolved with some hasty apologies and a handshake. The number of lawyers in the United States is fast approaching 1 million; already there is one lawyer for every 300 people in the country.

With some 18 million lawsuits filed yearly in the U.S. (roughly one for every ten adults), some observers are asking whether the United States has too many lawyers. Former vice-president Dan Quayle (an attorney married to an attorney) pointedly asked the American Bar Association if the United States really needs 70 percent of the world's lawyers. Most countries have few if any lawyers, but even among industrial nations, the United States has a lawyer/population ratio almost twice that of Canada, more than three times that of Germany and twenty-five times that of Japan (Cohn, 1991; Johnson, 1991).

American reliance on formal litigation, of course, has a number of causes beyond the large number of attorneys. The U.S. embrace of the notion of individual rights makes people quick to perceive infringements on their rights and interests. More broadly, the United States has become a vast, complex, and impersonal society, in which many traditional social clusters like neighborhoods (and perhaps even families) play smaller roles than in the past. Across the country, individuals recognize fewer obligations to their neighbors and, in many cases, do not even want to know them.

Canada, which former prime minister Joe Clark has called a "community of communities," is not as individualistic as the United States. It may be a long time before we catch up to the Americans, but since the Charter of Rights and Freedoms was added to our Constitution Act in 1982, Canadians have become more litigious—that is, more inclined to file lawsuits. As in the U.S., the proliferation of secondary relationships and the emphasis upon individual rights make lawsuits more likely.

This chapter examines the importance of *social groups*, the clusters of people with whom we interact during our daily lives. As we shall explain, the scope of group life has expanded during this century, from the small and personal families and neighborhoods of the past to the vast and anonymous bureaucracies and businesses that sociologists describe as *formal organizations*. We now turn to explaining how groups and organizations operate, and assessing the impact they have on our lives.

Social Groups

Virtually everyone moves through life with a sense of belonging; that is the experience of group life. A **social group** is defined as *two or more people who identify with one another and have a distinctive pattern of interaction*. As human beings, we continually come together to form couples, families, circles of friends, neighborhoods, churches, businesses, clubs, and numerous large organizations. Whatever the form, groups encompass people with shared experiences, loyalties, and interests. In short, while maintaining their individuality, the members of social groups also think of themselves as a special "we."

Groups, Aggregates, and Categories

Not every collection of people constitutes a social group. The term *aggregate* refers to people who are in the same place at the same time but who interact little, if at all, and have no sense of belonging together. People riding together on a subway, for example, form an aggregate, not a social group.

People who have some status in common, such as "mother," "sergeant," "homeowner," or "Roman Catholic" are considered a *category*. They do not constitute a social group because, while they may be aware of others like themselves, most are strangers who never socially interact.

People in some aggregates and categories *could* fuse into a social group, if the right circumstances gave them a shared identity and produced interaction over a period of time. In the event of crises or disasters like mine explosions, floods, earthquakes or train accidents, people who face a common plight are likely to develop a sense of group awareness and to help each other. Similarly, a house fire or other tragic event often renews a neighborhood's community spirit as people pitch in to assist the family in need.

Primary and Secondary Groups

People frequently greet one another with a smile and the simple phrase, "Hi! How are you?" The response is usually a well-scripted, "Just fine, thanks. How about you?" or the typically Canadian, "Not too bad!". These answers, of course, may be far from truthful, but in most cases, providing a detailed account of how you *really* are doing would prompt the other person to beat a hasty retreat.

Social groups fall into two types according to the degree of personal concern members display toward each other. According to Charles Horton Cooley, who is introduced in the box on page 183, a **primary group** refers to *a small social group in which relationships are both personal and enduring*. Bound together by strong and lasting loyalties that Cooley termed *primary relationships*, people in primary groups share many activities, spend a great deal of time together, and feel they know one another well. As a result, they typically display genuine concern for each other's welfare. The family is the most important primary group in any society.

Cooley called personal and tightly integrated groups *primary* because they are among the first groups we experience in life. In addition, the family and peer groups hold primary importance in the socialization process, shaping personal attitudes and behavior. We look to members of our primary groups for clues to our

Around the world, families are the most significant primary group. Weddings are one example of various rituals that reaffirm the primary bonds of family life, linking the generations with ties of identification and duty. Here members of a wedding party in Monrovia, Liberia, commemorate their celebration through a family photograph.

PROFILE

Charles Horton Cooley (1864–1929)

Many men and women fear that the world is becoming so fast paced and impersonal that people are losing touch with one another. This is nothing new: Charles Horton Cooley shared this concern a century ago as he grew up in a small town and witnessed rapid change.

Cooley's home was in Ann Arbor, Michigan, where he spent his childhood and returned to teach, serving on the faculty of the University of Michigan from 1892 until his death. His major contribution to sociology was exploring the character of the primary group. Cooley noted a disturbing trend: with the growth of cities and factories, people seemed to become ever more individualistic and competitive, displaying less concern for the traditional family and local neighborhood. This transformation made Cooley uneasy because he was convinced of the crucial importance of small, cooperative social groups to human life. Without them, he wondered, how could people experience a feeling of belonging and develop a sense of fairness and compassion?

Cooley hoped that calling attention to the importance of primary groups would encourage the preservation of traditional values and a socially cohesive way of life. Certainly, society has continued to change since Cooley's lifetime, and not entirely in ways he would have wished. But, as a testament to the value of his insights, many of Cooley's social concerns are with us still.

SOURCES: Rieff (1962) and Coser (1977).

social identity as well, which is why members of any primary group almost always think of themselves in the first-person plural, as "we."

The strength of primary relationships gives many individuals considerable comfort and security. In the familiar social circles of family or friends, people feel they can "be themselves" without constantly worrying about the impressions they are making.

Members of primary groups generally provide one another with personal, financial, and emotional support. Even so, people generally think of a primary group as an end in itself rather than as a means to other ends. For example, we readily call on family members or close friends to help us move into a new apartment, without expecting to pay for their services. And we would do the same for them. For this reason, a friend who never returns a favor leaves us feeling "used" and questioning the depth of the friendship.

Members of a primary group look at fellow members as unique individuals rather than interchangeable, faceless functionaries. We usually do not care who cashes our cheques at the bank or pumps fuel for our cars at the corner service station. Yet in primary groups—especially the family—we are bound to others by deep ties of emotion and loyalty. Although brothers and sisters experience periodic conflict, they always remain siblings.

In contrast to the primary group, the **secondary group** is *a large and impersonal social group based on a specific interest or activity.* Secondary groups are typically larger than primary groups. For example, people who work together in an office, enroll in the same course, live in the same city neighborhood, or belong to a particular political organization form secondary groups.

In most respects, secondary groups have precisely the opposite characteristics of primary groups. *Secondary relationships* usually involve little personal knowledge of one another and weak emotional ties. Groups built on such ties vary in duration, but they are frequently of short term, beginning and ending without particular significance. Students in a university course, for instance, who may not see one another after the semester ends, exemplify the secondary group. Because secondary groups focus on a particular interest or activity, members have little chance to develop a deep concern for one another's overall welfare. In some cases, as among co-workers who share an office, relationships are transformed from secondary to primary with the passing of time. People in a secondary group sometimes think of themselves as "we," but the boundary that distinguishes members from nonmembers is usually far less clear than in primary groups.

While secondary relationships are not particularly intense, people depend on them to achieve specific ends. Primary relationships have a *personal orientation*, then, while secondary relationships have a *goal orientation*. This does not mean that secondary ties need be formal and unemotional. On the contrary, social interactions among students, co-workers, and business associates can be enjoyable even if they are rather impersonal.

In primary groups, members define each other according to *who* they are; members of secondary groups look to one another for *what* they are, that is, what they can do. In secondary groups, in other words, we are always mindful of what we offer others and what we receive in return. This "scorekeeping" comes through most clearly in business relationships. Likewise, neighbors typically expect that a neighborly favor will be reciprocated.

The goal orientation of secondary groups encourages members to carefully craft their behavior. In these roles, then, we remain characteristically impersonal and polite. The secondary relationship, therefore, is one in which the question "How are you?" may be asked without really wanting a truthful or informative answer.

The characteristics of primary and secondary groups are summarized in Table 7-1. As the figure suggests, we have described these two types of social groups in ideal terms; neither one precisely describes actual groups in our lives. But placing these concepts at

opposite ends of a continuum provides a helpful shorthand for describing and analyzing group life.

By spotlighting primary and secondary ties, we can track changes in society itself. In general, primary relationships dominate in preindustrial societies, as people live and work within families and local villages. Strangers stand out in the social landscape. By contrast, secondary ties take precedence in modern, industrial societies, where people assume highly specialized social roles. In today's world, we all routinely engage in impersonal, secondary contacts with virtual strangers— people about whom we know very little and whom we may never meet again (Wirth, 1938).

Group Leadership

Social groups vary in the extent to which members recognize leaders—people charged with the responsibility for directing the group's activities. Some friendship groups grant someone the clear status of leader; others do not. Within families, parents have leadership roles, although husband and wife may disagree about who is really in charge. In secondary groups like corporations, leadership is likely to involve a formal chain of command with clearly defined duties.

Leaders are generally thought to possess extraordinary personal abilities, but decades of research have failed to produce convincing evidence of so-called "natural leaders." No particular individual traits seem to qualify a person as a leader; rather, the needs of the group itself dictate the type of leader who will be most effective (Ridgeway, 1983; Ridgeway & Diekema, 1989).

Two different leadership roles commonly emerge in groups (Bales, 1953; Bales & Slater, 1955). **Instrumental leadership** refers to *group leadership that emphasizes the completion of tasks*. Members look to instrumental leaders to "get things done." **Expressive leadership**, by contrast, *emphasizes collective well-being*. Expressive leaders take less of an interest in the performance goals of a group than in providing emotional support to group members and minimizing tension and conflict among them.

Because they concentrate on performance, instrumental leaders usually forge secondary relationships with other group members. Instrumental leaders give orders or punish people according to their contribution to the group's efforts. Expressive leaders, however, cultivate more primary relationships. They offer sympathy to a member having a tough time, work to keep the group united, and lighten serious moments with

TABLE 7-1	PRIMARY GROUPS AND SECONDARY GROUPS: A SUMMARY	
	Primary Group	**Secondary Group**
Quality of relationships	Personal orientation	Goal orientation
Duration of relationships	Usually long term	Variable; often short term
Breadth of relationships	Broad; usually involving many activities	Narrow; usually involving few activities
Subjective perception of relationships	As an end in itself	As a means to an end
Typical examples	Families; close friendships	Co-workers; political organizations

humor. While successful instrumental leaders gain a more distant *respect* from group members, expressive leaders generally enjoy more personal *affection*.

In the past, this differentiation of leadership has been linked to gender. In the traditional North American family, cultural norms bestow instrumental leadership on men. As fathers and husbands, they assume primary responsibility for providing family income, making major family decisions, and disciplining children. By contrast, expressive leadership has traditionally been the purview of women. Mothers and wives historically have been expected to lend emotional support and to maintain peaceful relationships among all family members (Parsons & Bales, 1955). This division of labor partly explains why many children have greater respect for their fathers, but closer personal ties with their mothers (Macionis, 1978). Changes in family gender roles have blurred the gender-linked distinction between instrumental and expressive leadership. In other group settings, women and men are both assuming leadership roles.

Decision-making styles also distinguish types of leaders. *Authoritarian leaders* focus on instrumental concerns, make decisions on their own, and demand strict compliance from subordinates. Although this leadership style wins little affection from group members, they may praise an authoritarian leader in a crisis situation requiring immediate decisions and strong group discipline. *Democratic leaders* are more expressive, and try to include everyone in the decision-making process. Although less successful during crises, when there is little time for discussion, democratic leaders can otherwise draw on the ideas of all members to forge reflective and imaginative responses to the tasks at hand. *Laissez-faire leaders* (from the French phrase meaning roughly "to leave alone") downplay their position and power, allowing the group to function more or less on its own. Laissez-faire leaders generally are least effective in promoting group goals. Leadership style in a particular case depends, in large part, on the traits and needs of the group itself (White & Lippitt, 1953; Ridgeway, 1983).

Group Conformity

Groups influence the behavior of their members, often promoting conformity. Some amount of group conformity provides a secure feeling of belonging; group pressure, however, can be considerable and unpleasant. Even interaction with strangers can promote confor-

mity, as a classic experiment by Solomon Asch (1952) showed.

Asch's Research

Asch formed groups of six to eight people, allegedly to study visual perception. He arranged with all but one member of the group to create a situation in which the remaining subject would be pressured to accept conclusions that were quite unreasonable. Sitting around a table, group members were asked one at a time to match a "standard" line, as shown in Figure 7-1 on "Card 1," to one of three lines on "Card 2." Anyone with normal vision could easily see that the line marked "A" on the right card would be the correct choice. Initially, everyone gave correct answers. Then Asch's secret accomplices began answering incorrectly, causing the naive subject to become bewildered and uncomfortable. Asch found that more than one-third of all subjects placed in such an awkward situation chose to conform to the others by answering incorrectly. Many of us are apparently willing to compromise our own judgment to avoid the discomfort of being different from others, even from people we do not know.

Milgram's Research

In the early 1960s, Stanley Milgram—a one-time student of Solomon Asch—conducted a controversial conformity experiment of his own. In Milgram's initial study (1963, 1965; Miller, 1986), a researcher explained to pairs of participants that they were about to engage in a study of memory. One took the role of

FIGURE 7-1   THE CARDS USED IN ASCH'S EXPERIMENT IN GROUP CONFORMITY
SOURCE: Asch, 1952:452–53.

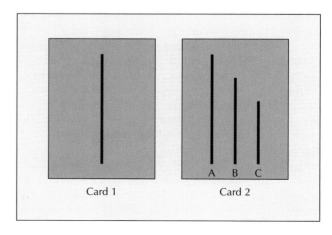

"teacher" and the other—who was an insider to the study—became the "learner."

The learner sat in a forbidding contraption resembling an electric chair with electrodes attached to one arm. The researcher then instructed the teacher to read aloud pairs of words. In subsequent trials, the teacher repeated the first word of each pair and asked the learner to recall the corresponding second word. As mistakes occurred, the researcher instructed the teacher to administer a shock to the learner using a "shock generator," marked to regulate electric current ranging from 15 volts (labeled "mild shock") to 300 volts (marked "intense shock") to 450 volts (marked "Danger: Severe Shock" and "XXX"). Beginning at the lowest level, the researcher instructed teachers to increase the shock by 15 volts every time the learner made a mistake. The experimenter explained to the teacher that the shocks would become "extremely painful" but cause "no permanent tissue damage."

The results provided striking evidence of the ability of leaders to obtain compliance. None of forty subjects assigned in the role of teacher during the initial research even questioned the procedure before 300 volts had been applied, and twenty-six of the subjects—almost two-thirds—went all the way to 450 volts (even though no real shocks would be administered).

In later research, although the proportion of subjects who applied the maximum shock varied, Milgram's subjects administered shocks to people who verbally objected, people who protested that they had heart conditions, and many even turned up the voltage as individuals screamed and then feigned unconsciousness. Understandably, many subjects found the experiment extremely stressful, the source of controversy ever since. No less disturbing is the implication of Milgram's research that people who commit atrocities against fellow human beings—as did hundreds of German soldiers during the Nazi regime—are more or less ordinary people who are "just following orders."

Milgram (1964) then modified his research to see if Solomon Asch had found a high degree of group conformity only because the task of matching lines seemed trivial. What if groups pressured people to administer electrical shocks? To investigate, he varied the experiment so that a group of three "teachers," two of whom were his accomplices, made decisions jointly. Milgram's rule was that each of the three teachers would suggest a shock level when the learner made an error, and the shock actually given would be the *lowest* of the three suggestions. This gave the naive subject the power to lessen the shock level regardless of what the

Social organization depends on some measure of obedience and conformity. But who we recognize as legitimate leaders and the extent to which we respect them depend on a host of political factors that vary from situation to situation.

other two "teachers" suggested. The accomplices recommended increasing the shock level with each error, placing group pressure on the third member to do the same. Responding to this pressure, subjects applied voltages three to four times higher than in experiments when they were acting alone. Thus Milgram's research suggests that people are surprisingly likely to follow not only the directions of "legitimate authority figures," but also groups of "ordinary individuals."

Janis's Research

Even the experts succumb to pressure for group conformity, according to Irving L. Janis (1972, 1989). Janis contends that a number of foreign policy errors made by the United States, including the failure to foresee the Japanese attack on Pearl Harbor in World War II, the disastrous U.S. invasion of Cuba's Bay of Pigs in 1961, and the ill-fated involvement in the Vietnam War, may have been the result of group conformity among the highest-ranking political leaders.

We often think that a group's "brainstorming" will improve decision making. However, Janis argues that group decision making sometimes backfires. First, rather than examining a problem from many points of view, groups often seek consensus, thereby narrowing the range of options. Second, groups may develop a distinctive language, adopting terms that favor a single interpretation of events. Third, having settled on a position, members of the group may come to see anyone with another view as the "opposition." Janis called this process "**groupthink**," *a limited understanding of some issue due to group conformity.*

The effect of groupthink was apparent when federal and provincial party leaders came together on the "yes" side during the constitutional referendum battle of October 1992 and assumed that Canadians would obediently follow suit: they failed to explain why the Charlottetown accord would be good for Canada, opting instead for a slick advertising campaign. Anyone who pointed out that the hard-sell approach of our leaders might backfire was dismissed as talking nonsense. The use of the term "enemies of Canada" to describe the opponents of the accord who carefully explained their objections and fears, is also consistent with groupthink.

Of course, Canadian and U.S. leaders are not the only ones who can be blinded by group consensus. In 1991, a group of eight top government officials carried out a short-lived seizure of power in the Soviet Union. From their point of view, their actions did not constitute an illegal "coup" but a necessary and patriotic act to save their country from reform that had slipped out of control. Despite access to vast amounts of information through government agencies, however, these leaders failed to accurately anticipate the reaction of their opponents, foreign governments, and even their own people to their power grab.

Reference Groups

How do we know if a particular decision is a good one? Frequently, we evaluate our views in relation to those of others, often using some **reference group**, *a social group that serves as a point of reference for people making evaluations or decisions.*

A young man who imagines his family's response to a woman he is dating is using his family as a reference group. Similarly, a banker who assesses her colleagues' reactions to a new loan policy is using her co-workers as a standard of reference. As these examples suggest, reference groups can be primary or secondary. And because we are often strongly motivated to conform to a group, the attitudes of group members can greatly affect personal evaluations.

Groups of which we are *not* members also can be used for reference. People preparing for job interviews typically anticipate how those in the company dress and act, and they adjust their personal performances accordingly. The use of groups by nonmembers illustrates the process of *anticipatory socialization,* described in Chapter 5 ("Socialization"). By conforming, individuals hope to win acceptance to the group.

Stouffer's Research

Samuel A. Stouffer (1949) and his associates conducted a classic study of reference group dynamics during World War II. In a survey, researchers asked soldiers to evaluate the chances of promotion for a competent soldier in their branch of the service. Common sense suggests that soldiers serving in outfits with a relatively high promotion rate would be optimistic about their future advancement. Yet survey results revealed just the opposite: soldiers in branches of the service with low promotion rates were actually more optimistic about their own chances for advancement.

The key to this paradox lies in recognizing the groups against which the soldiers measured their progress. Those in branches with lower promotion rates compared their advancement with people like themselves; typically, they had not been promoted, but neither had many others, so they did not feel deprived and expressed favorable attitudes about their chances for promotion. Soldiers in a service branch with a higher promotion rate, however, could easily think of people who had been promoted sooner or more often than they had. Using these people as a reference group, even soldiers who had been promoted were likely to feel they had come up short. These were the soldiers who voiced more negative attitudes in their evaluations.

Stouffer's research demonstrates that we do not make judgments about ourselves in isolation, nor do we compare ourselves with just anyone. Instead, we use specific social groups as standards in developing individual attitudes. Regardless of our situation in *absolute* terms, then, we perceive well-being subjectively, *relative* to some specific reference group (Merton, 1968; Mirowsky, 1987).

Ingroups and Outgroups

Differences among groups in political outlook, social prestige, or even manner of dress, may lead us to embrace one while avoiding others. Across North America, for example, students wear high-school jackets and place school decals on car windows to indicate that, to them, school serves as an important social group. Students attending another school may become the targets of derision simply because they belong to a rival group.

This illustrates an important process of group dynamics: the opposition of ingroups and outgroups. An **ingroup** is *a social group commanding a member's esteem and loyalty.* An ingroup exists in relation to an **outgroup**, *a social group toward which one feels competition or opposition.* Many social groups follow this pattern. A sports team, the Montreal Canadiens for example, is both an ingroup to its members and an outgroup for members of opposing teams like the Toronto Maple Leafs. A town's active New Democrats are likely to think of themselves as an ingroup in relation to the local Tories. All ingroups and outgroups work on the principle that "we" have valued characteristics that "they" lack.

Tensions among groups often help to sharpen their boundaries and to give people a clearer social identity. However, distinguishing groups in this way promotes self-serving distortions of reality. Research has shown that the members of ingroups hold overly positive views of themselves and unfairly negative views of various outgroups (Tajfel, 1982). Ethnocentrism, for example, grows out of the tendency to overvalue one's own "group," while undervaluing other cultures as outgroups.

When an ingroup has greater social power than an outgroup it opposes, serious personal and social problems may result. For example, whites have historically viewed people of color in negative terms and subjected them to certain social, political, and economic disadvantages. Internalizing these negative attitudes, people of African, Asian, and Native-American descent often struggle to overcome negative self-images based on stereotypes held by the larger society. The operation of particular ingroups and outgroups often mirrors patterns of social inequality in the larger society. Clarifying group boundaries, then, may foster both loyalty (to the ingroup) and social tension and conflict (with the outgroup).

Group Size

If you are the first person to arrive at a party, you can observe a fascinating process in group dynamics. Until about six people enter the room, everyone generally shares a single conversation. But as more people arrive, the group soon divides into two or more smaller clusters. It is apparent that size plays a crucial role in how group members interact.

To understand why, consider the mathematical connection between the number of people in a social group and the number of relationships among them, as shown in Figure 7-2. Two people form a single relationship; adding a third person generates three relationships; a fourth person yields six. Adding people one at a time—a process mathematicians describe as an *arithmetic progression*—rapidly increases the number of relationships in a *geometric progression.* By the time six people join one conversation, fifteen different relationships connect them, so the group usually divides at this point.

German sociologist Georg Simmel (1858–1918) explored the social dynamics in the smallest social

Ingroups and outgroups are often based on dimensions of inequality. In 1961 black residents of Africville, then a district in Halifax, were powerless to prevent the demolition of their 120-year-old community. Here the home of Deacon Ralph Jones is boarded up during relocation. Many white Haligonians felt Africville was a "blot on the face of Halifax". The reality of race in Canada is that people of color have often, and still do, find themselves cast in the role of an outgroup.

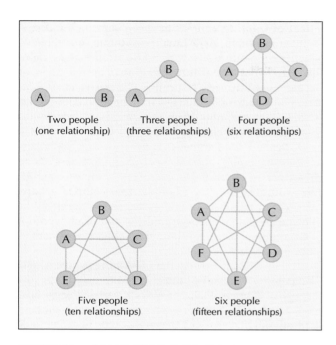

FIGURE 7-2   GROUP SIZE AND RELATIONSHIPS

groups. Simmel (1950; orig. 1902) used the term **dyad** to designate *a social group with two members*. Love affairs, marriages, and the closest friendships are dyadic. Simmel identified two special qualities of the dyad. First, they are typically less stable than groups with many members. Both members of a dyad must actively participate in the relationship; if either withdraws, the group collapses. Because the stability of marriages is important to society, this dyad is supported with legal and often religious ties. In contrast, a large group is inherently more stable. The federal Liberal riding association of Restigouche, New Brunswick does not dissolve if a few members drop out or, for that matter, if half of its executive resigns.

Second, social interaction in a dyad is typically more intense than in other groups. In such a one-to-one relationship, neither member shares the other's attention with anyone else. For this reason, dyads also have the potential to be the most meaningful social bonds we ever experience. Because marriage in our culture is dyadic, powerful emotional ties generally unite husbands and wives. As we shall see in Chapter 15 ("Family"), however, marriage in other societies can involve more than two people. In that case, the marriage is more stable although the many marital relationships, viewed individually, are typically less strong.

Simmel also probed the **triad**, *a social group with three members*. A triad encompasses three relationships, each uniting two of the three people. Two can form a coalition to press their views on the third, or two may intensify their relationship, leaving the other feeling like a "third wheel." For example, the members of a triad, two of whom develop a romantic interest in each other, are likely to understand the old saying "Two's company, three's a crowd."

Despite characteristic problems, a triad is more stable than a dyad. If the relationship between any two of the group's members becomes strained, the third can act as a mediator to restore the group's vitality. Similarly, members of a dyad (say, a married couple) often seek out a third person (a trusted friend or counselor) to air tensions between them.

As groups grow beyond three members, they become progressively more stable because the loss of even several members does not threaten the group's existence. At the same time, increases in group size typically reduce the intense personal interaction possible only in the smallest groups. So larger groups are based less on personal attachments than their smaller counterparts and are more dependent on formal rules and regulations. Such formality helps a large group persist over time, but that does not mean that a large group is immune to change. After all, numerous members give large groups considerable contact with the outside world, which opens the door to new attitudes and behavior (Carley, 1991).

Does a social group have an ideal size? The answer depends on the group's purpose. A dyad offers unsurpassed emotional intensity, while a group of several

A distinctive characteristic of a triad is that the social bond that joins two members can intensify, to the exclusion of the third.

dozen people is likely to be more stable, capable of accomplishing larger, more complex tasks, and better able to assimilate new members or ideas. People typically find more personal *pleasure* in smaller groups, while deriving greater *satisfaction* from accomplishing tasks in larger organizations (Slater, 1958; Ridgeway, 1983; Carley, 1991).

Social Diversity

Social diversity also affects the behavior of group members, especially the likelihood that they will interact with someone of another group. Peter Blau (1977, 1982; South & Messner, 1986) points out four ways in which the structure of social groups regulates intergroup association.

First, extending Simmel's analysis, Blau identifies a further consequence of group size. The larger a group, he claims, the more likely any individual member is to maintain relationships exclusively within the group; the smaller the group, by contrast, the greater the odds that members will reach beyond their immediate social circle. To illustrate, increasing the number of international students on a campus may well have the effect of enabling these students to maintain their own distinctive social group. Thus intentional efforts to promote social diversity may well have the unintended

Today's university campuses value social diversity. One of the challenges of multiculturalism is ensuring that all categories of students are integrated into campus life. But as the number of minority students increases, according to Blau's theory of group dynamics, these individuals are able to form a group unto themselves, perhaps interacting less with others.

effect of limiting contact between international students and others. As a broader example, members of smaller communities (say, based on ethnicity) are more likely to marry out of their group than are members of larger communities (Gurak & Fitzpatrick, 1982). French-Canadians in a small francophone community in Manitoba are more likely to marry non-francophones than are their counterparts in Quebec.

Second, Blau argues that the more internally heterogeneous groups are, the more likely members of one group are to interact with members of another group. We would expect, for example, that campus groups that recruit members of both sexes and of various ethnic and geographic backgrounds, would promote more intergroup contact than those who choose members of one social type.

Third, Blau asserts that the greater the overall social parity within a setting, the more likely it is that people of diverse backgrounds will mingle and form social ties. In socially diverse settings, then, members typically forge social ties that transcend their own cultural, ethnic, or racial categories.

Fourth, Blau contends that physical space affects the chances of contacts among groups. To the extent that a social group is physically segregated from others (by having its own dorm or dining area, for example), its members are less apt to engage other people.

Networks

Not all social interaction takes place within well-defined groups. A **network** is *a web of social ties that links people who may have little common identity and interaction.* A network resembles a social group in that it joins people in relationships. But unlike people in groups, network members typically feel little sense of membership and rarely have direct contact with one another. The boundaries of networks are thus less clear cut than those of groups. If we think of a group as a "circle of friends," we might describe a network as a "social web" expanding outward, with most members connected indirectly through others.

Network ties may be close, as among college friends who years later keep in touch by mail and telephone. More commonly, however, a network includes people we *know of*—or who *know of us*—but with whom we interact infrequently, if at all. For this reason, social networks have been described as "clusters of weak ties" (Granovetter, 1973).

Network ties may be weak, but they can serve as a significant resource. For example, many people rely on their networks to find jobs. Even the scientific genius Albert Einstein needed a hand in landing his first job. After a year of unsuccessful interviewing, he obtained employment only when the father of one of his classmates put him in touch with an office manager who hired him (Clark, 1971; cited in Fischer, 1977:19). As the saying goes, *who you know* is often just as important as *what you know.*

A survey by Nan Lin (1981) determined that almost 60 percent of 399 men in one city in the United States had found a job through networks. Lin concluded that networks were the greatest single occupational resource, but he also found that networks do not provide equal advantages to everyone. The sons of men with important occupational positions gained the greatest advantages from networks. This finding supports the notion that networks link people of similar social background, thereby perpetuating social privilege.

Peter Marsden (1987) discovered that the most extensive social networks are maintained by people who are young, well educated, and living in urban areas. The networks of men and women tend to be the same size, although women include more relatives in their networks while those of men encompass more co-workers (Moore, 1990). Women's networks, therefore, may not carry the clout that the "old-boy" networks do. In response, many women have begun to pay more attention to building networks in the world of work. Women's networks provide the support, mentors, camaraderie, and business contacts that women might otherwise lack (Speizer, 1983; Coppock, 1987). The National Action Committee on the Status of Women (NAC), as an umbrella group representing over 500 women's groups with a wide variety of goals, is undoubtedly the organizational framework for a vast network of women stretching across Canada.

In a study of "intimate networks" in East York (a Toronto borough), Wellman (1979) found that almost everyone could name one to six intimates outside the home, only half of whom were kin. While most of their intimate contacts lived within Metro Toronto, only 13 percent were in the neighborhood. In other words, Wellman's respondents felt close to people who were widely dispersed. Neither weak-tie networks nor the intimate variety are geographically bound.

Formal Organizations

A century ago, social life was centered in small groups—the family, friendship, and working groups, and the local neighborhood. Today, our lives revolve far more around **formal organizations,** *large, secondary groups that are organized to facilitate achieving their goals efficiently.* Formal organizations, such as corporations or branches of government, differ from small family or friendship groups in more than simply the size of their membership. Their greater size renders social relationships less personal, and also fosters a planned or formal atmosphere. People design formal organizations to accomplish specific tasks, rather than to meet personal needs.

With a population exceeding 27 million, Canada performs countless, complicated tasks ranging from educating expectant parents to delivering the mail. Most of these responsibilities are carried out by large, formal organizations. Canada's federal government, the nation's largest formal organization, is itself a major employer with multiple divisions encompassing an array of more specialized organizations with specific goals. These large groups develop lives and cultures of their own so that, as members come and go, the statuses they fill and the roles they perform remain unchanged over the years.

Types of Formal Organizations

Amitai Etzioni (1975) has identified three types of formal organizations, distinguished by the type of member affiliation—normative organizations, coercive organizations, and utilitarian organizations.

Normative Organizations

People join *normative organizations* to pursue goals they consider morally worthwhile, and derive personal satisfaction, perhaps social prestige, but no monetary reward for their efforts. Sometimes called *voluntary associations,* these include community service groups (such as the Lions Club, Kiwanis, or the Red Cross) political parties, religious organizations, and numerous other confederations concerned with specific social issues. Because women have historically been excluded from much of the paid labor force, they have played a greater part than men in civic and charitable organizations.

Coercive Organizations

In Etzioni's typology, *coercive organizations* are distinguished by involuntary membership. That is, people are forced to join the organization as a form of punishment (prisons) or treatment (psychiatric hospitals). Coercive organizations have extraordinary physical features, such as locked doors, barred windows, and security personnel (Goffman, 1961). They are designed to segregate people as "inmates" or "patients" for a period of time, and sometimes radically alter people's attitudes and behavior. Recall from Chapter 5 ("Socialization") the power of coercive total institutions to transform a human being's overall sense of self.

Utilitarian Organizations

According to Etzioni, people join *utilitarian organizations* in pursuit of material rewards. Large business enterprises, for example, generate profits for their owners and income in the form of salaries and wages for their employees. Joining utilitarian organizations is usually a matter of individual choice (assuming one is hired by the firm of one's choosing), although, obviously, most people must join one utilitarian organization or another to make a living. While utilitarian organizations certainly offer greater individual freedom than coercive organizations, they provide less autonomy than normative organizations. This is because most people have little choice but to spend something approaching half of their waking hours at work, and because most workers have only limited control over their jobs.

From differing vantage points, any particular organization may fall into *all* of these categories. A psychiatric hospital, for example, serves as a coercive organization for a patient, a utilitarian organization for a psychiatrist, and a normative organization to a part-time hospital volunteer.

Origins of Bureaucracy

Formal organizations date back thousands of years. Religious and political administrations extended the power of elites over millions of people living in vast areas. Formal organization also allowed rulers to collect taxes, undertake military campaigns, and construct monumental structures such as the Great Wall of China.

The effectiveness of these early organizations was limited, however. This was not because the elites lacked grandiose ambition; rather it was due to the traditional character of preindustrial societies. Long-established cultural patterns placed greater importance on "God's will" than on organizational efficiency. Only in the last few centuries did there emerge what Max Weber called a "rational world view," as described in Chapter 4 ("Society"). In the wake of the Industrial Revolution, the organizational structure called *bureaucracy* became commonplace in Europe and North America.

Bureaucracy is *an organizational model rationally designed to perform complex tasks efficiently*. Through bureaucratic organization, officials deliberately enact and revise policy to make the organization as efficient as possible. To appreciate the power and scope of bureaucratic organization, consider the telephone system in North America. Each of about 180 million telephones can be used to reach any other telephone in homes, businesses, and automobiles within seconds. This major organizational feat reaches far beyond the imagination of the ancient world. Of course, the telephone system depends on technological developments such as electricity. But neither could the system exist without the organizational capacity to keep track of every telephone call—noting which phone was used to call which other phone, when, and for how long—and presenting all this information to millions of telephone users in the form of monthly bills.

In global context, the availability of telephones and other forms of electronic communication is one indicator of the extent of bureaucratic organization. As shown in Global Map 7-1 on page 193, facsimile (fax) machines and other devices for data transmission are most common in the United States and Canada, Western Europe, Japan, and Australia and New Zealand. In most nations of the world, however, such devices are limited to government officials, large businesses, and urban elites. Thus the proliferation of bureaucracy is closely tied to economic development.

Characteristics of Bureaucracy

What are the characteristics of an efficient organization? Max Weber (1978; orig. 1921) argued that six key elements define the ideal bureaucratic organization.

1. **Specialization.** Through most of human history, all people's lives centered on securing food and shelter. Bureaucracy embodies a whole different set of imperatives by assigning people highly specialized tasks that correspond to organizational offices.

2. **Hierarchy of offices.** Bureaucracies arrange offices vertically to form a hierarchy, according to each official's responsibilities. Each employee is thus supervised by "higher-ups" in the organization while, in turn, supervising others in lower positions.

3. **Rules and regulations.** Tradition holds scant sway in bureaucracy. Instead, operations are guided by

rationally enacted rules and regulations. These rules guide not only the organization's own functioning but, as much as possible, its larger environment. Ideally, a bureaucracy seeks to operate in a completely predictable fashion.

4. **Technical competence.** Bureaucratic officials are expected to have the technical competence to carry out the duties of their offices. Bureaucracies typically evaluate new staff members according to specified criteria and subsequently monitor their

performance. This practice of impersonal evaluation based on performance contrasts sharply with the custom, followed through most of human history, of favoring relatives—whatever their talents—over strangers.

5. **Impersonality.** In bureaucratic organizations, rules take precedence over personal feelings. Ideally, this ensures uniform treatment for each client, supervisor, or subordinate. From this detached approach stems the notion of the "faceless bureaucrat."

WINDOW ON THE WORLD

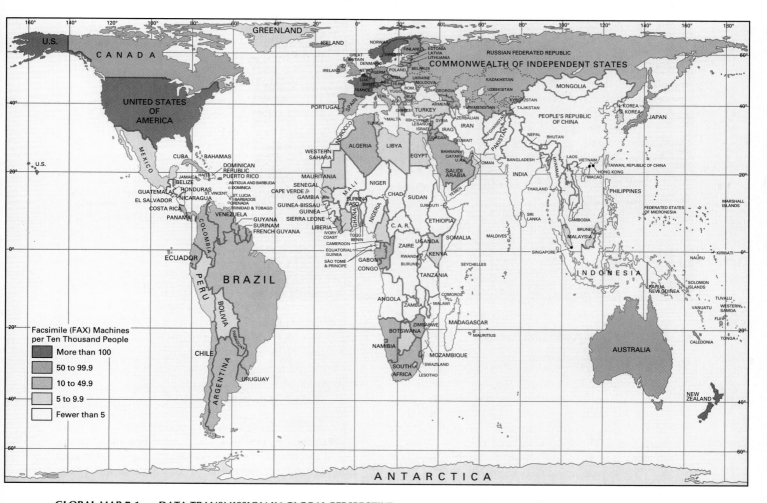

GLOBAL MAP 7-1   DATA TRANSMISSION IN GLOBAL PERSPECTIVE

The expansion of formal organization depends partly on available technology. Facsimile (fax) machines and other devices for transmitting data are most widespread in economically developed regions of the world, including the United States, Canada, Western Europe, Japan, and Australia. In poor societies, such devices are all but unknown. Note, too, that the wealthy elite in small nations like Kuwait make use of advanced technology to support their global business operations.

Although formal organization is vital to modern, industrial societies, it is far from new. Twenty-five centuries ago, the Chinese philosopher and teacher K'ung Fu-Tzu (known to Westerners as Confucius) endorsed the idea that government offices should be filled by the most talented young men. This led to one of the world's first systems of civil service examinations. Here, would-be bureaucrats compose essays to demonstrate their knowledge of Confucian texts.

6. **Formal, written communications.** Certainly, some truth lies in the adage that the heart of bureaucracy is not people but paperwork. Rather than casual, verbal communication, bureaucracy demands formal, written letters, memos, and reports. Over time, this correspondence accumulates into vast *files*—more recently on computers rather than hard copy. These accumulated records or documents guide an organization in roughly the same way that personality guides the individual.

Bureaucracy versus Small Groups

In small groups, especially primary groups like the family, people are valued for who they *are*, that is, for the personal relationships they maintain. By contrast, the value of bureaucratic organizations lies in what they *do*. As a path to efficient performance, then, bureaucracy serves as a means to an end.

Bureaucratic organization promotes efficiency by carefully recruiting personnel and limiting the variable and unpredictable effects of personal tastes and opinions. In smaller, informal groups, members have considerable discretion in their behavior, they respond to each other personally, and consider one another more or less equal in rank. Weber believed, however, that such traits compromised organizational efficiency. He concluded that a rigid and impersonal organizational system maximizes performance, but does not necessarily enhance the personal satisfaction of members. Table 7-2 summa-

TABLE 7-2	SMALL GROUPS AND FORMAL ORGANIZATIONS: A COMPARISON	
	Small Groups	Formal Organizations
Activities	Members typically engage in many of the same activities	Members typically engage in various highly specialized activities
Hierarchy	Often informal or nonexistent	Clearly defined, corresponding to offices
Norms	Informal application of general norms	Clearly defined rules and regulations
Criteria for membership	Variable, often based on personal affection or kinship	Technical competence to carry out assigned tasks
Relationships	Variable; typically primary	Typically secondary, with selective primary ties
Communications	Typically casual and face to face	Typically formal and in writing
Focus	Person oriented	Task oriented

rizes the differences between small social groups and large formal organizations.

The Informal Side of Bureaucracy

In Weber's ideal bureaucracy, every activity is deliberately regulated. In actual organizations, however, human behavior often diverges from bureaucratic blueprints. Sometimes informality helps to meet a legitimate need overlooked by formal regulations. In other situations, such as cutting corners in one's job, informal behavior clearly violates official rules (Scott, 1981).

Personality, for example, greatly affects patterns of organizational leadership. Formally, power resides in offices, not with the people who occupy them, but studies of corporations reveal that the qualities and quirks of individuals—including their charisma or skill in interpersonal relations—have a tremendous impact on organizational outcomes (Halberstam, 1986). Mikhail Gorbachev played a central role in the restructuring of Soviet society and in setting in motion the massive changes that would eventually lead to the breakup of the Soviet Union. In Canada, the structure, operating style, and message of the Reform Party are a reflection of one man—it's founder, Preston Manning.

Authoritarian, democratic, and laissez-faire types of leadership—described earlier in this chapter—also reflect individual personality as much as any organizational plan. Then, too, decision making within an organization does not always conform to official regulations. The continuous saga of conflict-of-interest charges against politicians, real estate flips, insider trading on the stock market, computer-based theft, and many instances of fraud suggest that officials and their friends may personally benefit through abuse of organizational power. In the "real world" of organizational life, officials who attempt to operate strictly by the book may even find themselves denied the promotions and power that are based on informal alliances. In some organizations, too, people in leadership positions rely on the fact that much of their own work will be handled by subordinates. Many secretaries, for example, have more authority and responsibility than their official job titles and salaries suggest.

Communication offers another example of how informality creeps into large organizations. Formally, memos and other written communications disseminate information through the hierarchy. Typically, however, individuals cultivate informal networks or "grapevines" that spread information much faster, if not always as accurately. Grapevines are particularly significant to subordinates because executives often attempt to conceal important information from them.

Sometimes employees modify or ignore rigid bureaucratic structures to advance their own interests. A classic study of the Western Electric factory in Chicago revealed that few employees reported fellow workers who violated rules, as they were required to (Roethlisberger & Dickson, 1939). On the contrary, those who *did* were socially isolated, labeled by other workers as "squealers" who could not be trusted. Although the company formally set productivity standards, workers informally created their own definition of a fair day's work, criticizing those who exceeded it as "ratebusters" and others who fell short as "chiselers."

Such informal social structures suggest that people often resist the dehumanizing aspects of bureaucracy. Organizational informality also reveals that human beings have the creative capacity to personalize even rigidly defined social situations.

Limitations of Bureaucracy

Weber touted the ideal bureaucracy as a model of efficiency. Still, real-life formal organizations certainly have their limitations, even when it comes to the performance of specific tasks. Anyone who has ever tried to replace a lost driver's license, return defective merchandise to a discount chain store, or change an address on a magazine subscription knows that large organizations can be maddeningly unresponsive to individual needs.

Of course, no organizational system will ever eradicate human failings. Moreover, some problems occur because organizations are *not* truly bureaucratic. But, as Weber himself recognized, even the pure form of bureaucracy has inherent limitations. Perhaps the most serious limitation of bureaucracy is its potential to *dehumanize* those it purports to serve. To operate efficiently, each client must be treated impersonally as a standard "case." In other words, in striving for efficiency, organization members lose the ability to personally know their clients or customers and to provide individual attention.

Weber also feared that bureaucratic impersonality would *alienate* those who worked in large organizations. A human being in a formal organization, he claimed, was often reduced to "a small cog in a ceaselessly moving mechanism" (1978:988; orig. 1921). Although formal organizations are intended to serve humanity, Weber worried that humanity would eventually end up serving formal organizations.

The ambivalence of many people toward bureaucracy, then, is understandable. On the one hand, formal organizations advance many of our deeply held cultural values (see Chapter 3, "Culture"), including efficiency, practicality, and achievement. On the other hand, bureaucracies threaten the cherished ideals of democracy and individual freedom. In addition, the growth of formal organizations has prompted a decline in individual privacy (Long, 1967; Smith, 1979). The box on page 197 provides details.

Bureaucratic Waste and Incompetence

"Work expands to fill the time available for its completion." Enough truth underlies C. Northcote Parkinson's (1957) tongue-in-cheek assertion that it is known today as Parkinson's Law.

To illustrate, assume that a bureaucrat processes fifty applications in an average day. If one day this worker had only twenty-five applications to examine, how much time would the task require? The logical answer is half a day. But Parkinson's Law suggests that

According to Max Weber, bureaucracy is an organizational strategy that promotes efficiency. Impersonality, however, also fosters alienation among employees, who may become indifferent to the formal goals of the organization. The behavior of this municipal employee in Bombay, India, is understandable to members of formal organizations almost anywhere in the world.

if a full day is available to complete the work, a full day is how long it will take. Because organizational employees have little personal involvement in their work, few are likely to seek extra work to fill their spare time. Bureaucrats strive to *appear* busy,[1] however, prompting organizations to take on more employees. The added time and expense required to hire, train, supervise, and evaluate a larger staff makes everyone busier still, setting in motion a vicious cycle that results in *bureaucratic bloat*. Ironically, the larger organization may accomplish no more real work than it did in its leaner incarnation.

Laurence J. Peter (Peter & Hull, 1969) devised the Peter Principle, which states that *bureaucrats are promoted to their level of incompetence*. The logic here is simple: employees competent at any level of the organizational

---

[1] It is now possible for employees to look *very* busy at their computers when in fact they are sending personal messages or exchanging gossip through electronic mail.

CRITICAL THINKING

Bureaucracy and the Information Revolution: A Threat to Privacy?

A century ago, people who wanted personal privacy built a fence around their houses and hung "Beware of Dog" signs on the gates. Today, however, fences and dogs do little to protect people from some kinds of intrusions. More people now have access to detailed information about each one of us than ever before.

Why? Because of the growth of formal organizations. Without a doubt, bureaucracy is essential to a vast and complex society, but the cost is ever-larger banks of personal information. Automobile drivers must be licensed, but doing so requires gathering information about everyone who legally operates a vehicle. Similarly, Revenue Canada, Health and Welfare, and programs that benefit veterans, students, the poor, and unemployed people must each collect extensive information.

The explosive growth of credit in the country's economy has also fueled the drive for information. In the past, local merchants offered credit to customers with no more paperwork than an I.O.U. Today, people in North America carry more than 1 billion credit cards, enabling them to obtain credit from total strangers—at home and when traveling abroad.

This information revolution has spawned a new growth industry: maintaining files about people's place of residence, marital status, employment, income, debts, and history of paying their bills on time. Further eroding our privacy, computers now disseminate this information more widely and more rapidly than ever before. Because addresses are easily added to mailing lists, we are now deluged by so-called junk mail, which makes up a large component

The Information Revolution—the ability to process and store information efficiently—has transformed organizational life in Canada. At the center of this transformation is the computer. While improving our lives in various ways, computers also amass a vast amount of data about each of us, thus generating an unprecedented threat to personal privacy.

of all correspondence. Of greater concern is the fact that information circulates from organization to organization, generally without the knowledge or consent of the people in question.

In response, privacy legislation has been enacted in Canada by provinces as well as the federal government. The federal Privacy Act (1978; amended in 1982) gives citizens access to information contained about them in government files and allows for procedures to correct erroneous information. Canadians also have access to information (e.g., con-

sultants' reports) that contributes to the making of government decisions and policy.

Of particular concern to Canadians is the information stored in connection with our Social Insurance Numbers (SIN), which in some organizations have become employee identification numbers as well. The amount of personal information associated with one's SIN, the multiple uses of the number, and the possibility of merging massive files make SINs a particularly sensitive issue. Access by one government department or agency, such as Revenue Canada or the RCMP, to SIN-related data or Statistics Canada files would also be a worrisome invasion of privacy. It is possible, as well, for unauthorized users—from anywhere in the world in fact—to gain access to and to link the various files containing personal information about us.

One might conceive of a *single* all-purpose card for Canadians which we would use as identification, credit card, medical card, unemployment insurance, and so forth. This single card could have an up-dated photograph *and a fingerprint*, making it difficult, for example, to collect unemployment insurance and welfare at the same time (perhaps under different names). The technology is available to produce and administer such a supercard—and there might even be administrative advantages to doing so—but the potential for information abuse and the sacrifice of personal privacy make the supercard a chilling prospect.

SOURCES: Smith (1979); Rubin (1988); and Miller (1991).

hierarchy are likely to be promoted to higher positions. Eventually, however, when they reach a position where they are in over their heads and perform poorly, they are no longer eligible for promotion. They are thereby doomed to a future of inefficiency. Adding to the problem, by this time they have almost certainly acquired enough power to protect their interests, avoiding demotion or dismissal by hiding behind rules and regulations and taking credit for work actually performed by their more competent subordinates.

Bureaucratic Ritualism

For many of us, the concept *bureaucracy* conjures up images of *red tape* (derived from the red tape used by eighteenth-century English officials to wrap official parcels and records; Shipley, 1985). Red tape refers to a tedious concern with organizational procedures. In Robert Merton's view (1968), red tape amounts to a type of group conformity. He coined the term **bureaucratic ritualism** to signify *a preoccupation with rules and regulations as ends in themselves rather than as the means to organizational goals.*

Bureaucratic ritualism occurs when people become so intent on conforming to rules that they thwart the goals of the organization. Besides reducing individual and organizational performance, ritualism stifles creativity and imagination, robbing the organization of the talents, ideas, and innovations necessary to operate more efficiently as circumstances change (Whyte, 1957; Merton, 1968). In bureaucratic ritualism, we see one form of the alienation that Max Weber feared would arise from bureaucratic rigidity.

Bureaucratic Inertia

Weber noted that "once fully established, bureaucracy is among the social structures which are hardest to destroy" (1978:987; orig. 1921). Through **bureaucratic inertia**, *the tendency of bureaucratic organizations to persist over time*, formal organizations take on a life of their own and perpetuate themselves. Occasionally, a formal organization that meets its organizational goals will simply disband: more commonly, an organization redefines its goals so that it can continue to provide a livelihood for its members. In the United States, the National Association for Infantile Paralysis (sponsor of the well-known March of Dimes), was created to help find a cure for polio. It succeeded with the development of the Salk vaccine in the early 1950s. But the organization did not dissolve then; it simply redirected its efforts toward other medical problems such as birth defects (Sills, 1969). Similarly, as the need for service to veterans declined, Canadian War Amputations turned its attention to the needs of child amputees. Bureaucratic inertia usually leads formal organizations to devise new justifications for themselves after they have outlived their originally intended purpose.

George Tooker's painting Government Bureau *is a powerful statement about the human costs of bureaucracy. The artist depicts members of the public in monotonous similitude—reduced from human beings to mere "cases" to be disposed of as quickly as possible. Set apart from others by their positions, officials are "faceless bureaucrats" concerned more with numbers than with providing genuine assistance.*

Government Bureau, 1956. Egg tempera on gesso panel. 19⅝ x 29⅝ inches. The Metropolitan Museum of Art, George A. Hearn Fund, 1956. (56.78)

Oligarchy

Early in this century, Robert Michels (1876–1936) pointed out that one of the consequences of bureaucracy is **oligarchy**, *the rule of the many by the few* (1949; orig. 1911). The earliest human societies did not possess the organizational means for even the most power-hungry ruler to control everyone. The development of formal organizations, however, enhanced the opportunities for a small elite to dominate society. According to what Michels called "the iron law of oligarchy," the pyramid-like structure of bureaucracy places a few leaders in charge of vast and powerful government organizations.

Weber credited bureaucracy's strict hierarchy of responsibility for increasing organizational efficiency. Applying Weber's thesis to the organization of government, Michels added that this hierarchical structure discourages democracy. While government leaders are expected to subordinate personal interests to organizational goals, people who occupy powerful positions can—and often do—use their access to information and the media and numerous other advantages to promote their personal interests. Oligarchy, then, thrives in the hierarchical structure of bureaucracy, and undermines people's control over their elected leaders.

The Canadian political system puts power in the hands of party elites—particularly in those of the governing parties—by the requirement of party discipline. When all of the elected representatives of the Progressive Conservative Party vote *with* the party, they effectively support the policies of their own leaders instead of responding to the concerns of their constituencies or regions. In most parties, the elite has some influence on the choice of candidates to run for election at the riding level, but in 1993 the federal Liberals took an active role in promoting certain individuals and parachuting star candidates into selected ridings. Their goal was to muster an impressive Team Liberal with at least 25 percent female candidates for the federal election of that year—at the expense of grassroots involvement and participation.

Gender and Race in Organizations

Rosabeth Moss Kanter, introduced in the box, has analyzed how ascribed statuses such as gender and race figure in the power structure of bureaucratic hierarchies. To the extent that an organization has a dominant social composition, the gender- or race-based ingroup enjoys greater social acceptance, respect, credi-

The notion that organizations can muster vast resources to perpetuate themselves is called into question by the rapid and sweeping changes in Eastern Europe and the former Soviet Union. Oligarchies, it turns out, are more vulnerable to popular opposition than the thinking of Robert Michels suggests they are.

bility, and access to informal social networks. In North American society, the most powerful positions are generally held by well-to-do white men. By contrast, women, people of color, and those from economically disadvantaged backgrounds sometimes feel like members of socially isolated outgroups. Often uncomfortably visible, they are taken less seriously and have lower chances of promotion than others. Understandably, these people generally believe they must work twice as hard as those in dominant categories to maintain their present positions, let alone advance to higher positions (Kanter, 1977; Kanter & Stein, 1979:137). Bassett (1985) found a similar belief among Canadian career women and refers to this requirement as one of society's *double standards*.[2]

Kanter (1977) finds that providing more opportunities for some members of corporations and not others

---

[2] Charlotte Whitton, the late mayor of Ottawa, put it as follows: "A woman has to be twice as good as a man to get ahead—fortunately, it's not difficult." (Cited in Bassett, 1985:45.)

Rosabeth Moss Kanter

How did a woman who began her career studying communes and other utopian settlements end up shaping the real-world decisions of some of the most successful corporations in the United States? Timing had a lot to do with it; many ideas about organizations originally advanced in the 1960s have now found a receptive audience in the 1990s. Rosabeth Moss

Kanter, a professor of business administration at Harvard University, has shown businesses how their organizational patterns can influence productivity, performance, and profits. For her work, Kanter has been awarded numerous honorary doctoral degrees and has been the subject of feature stories in national publications. Her achievements rank her among the most influential women in American society.

Kanter's career is divided between academic duties and Goodmeasure, Inc., a corporate consulting firm she and her husband founded. She is the author of several widely read books that apply sociological insights to the task of making corporations more effective. What lessons does Kanter offer corporate executives that warrant fees as high as $15,000 for a single appearance? She challenges conventional organizational wisdom by demonstrating that *people*—not technology or machin-

ery—are a corporation's most important resource. In the long run, she maintains, an organizational environment that develops human potential will ensure success. Reflecting on her career, Kanter explains:

> I remember when participation was what was being talked about on college campuses by Vietnam war protesters or people looking for student power. Now it's a respectable concept in corporate America, and now very large companies are figuring out how to divide themselves into small units. Many ideas and values of the '60s have been translated into the workplace. Take, for example, the right of workers to free expression, the desirability of participation and teamwork, the idea that authority should not be obeyed unquestioningly, the idea that smaller can be better because it can create ownership and family feeling. All of these are mainstream ideas.

SOURCES: Murray (1984) and McHenry (1985).

---

has important consequences for everyone's on-the-job performance. Beyond the popular wisdom that being smart and "hustling" helps people get ahead, her research indicates that an organization's policies greatly influence employee performance. According to Kanter, organizations that offer everyone a chance for promotion typically motivate employees to become "fast-trackers," with higher aspirations, greater self-esteem, and a stronger commitment to the organization. By contrast, companies made up of "dead-end" jobs encourage a "just-get-by" attitude among workers, who have little aspiration, poor self-concept, and minimal loyalty to the organization.

Kanter adds that widely shared responsibility and opportunity also promote flexible leadership and heighten concern among officials for the morale of subordinates. Leaders in positions of little real power often jealously guard what privileges they do have, and rigidly supervise subordinates. Table 7-3 on page 201 summarizes Kanter's findings. In her view, organizations

must "humanize" their structure to bring out the best in their employees and improve the "bottom line."

Humanizing Bureaucracy

Humanizing bureaucracy means *fostering an organizational environment that develops human resources.* Research by Kanter (1977, 1983, 1989; Kanter & Stein, 1980) and others (cf. Peters & Waterman, Jr., 1982) shows that humanizing bureaucracy produces both happier employees and healthier profits. Based on the discussion so far, we can identify three paths to a more humane organizational structure.

1. **Social inclusiveness.** The social composition of the organization should, ideally, make no one feel "out of place" because of gender, race, or ethnicity. The performance of all employees will improve to the extent that no one is subject to social exclusion.

TABLE 7-3   KANTER'S RESEARCH: A SUMMARY

	Advantaged Employees	Disadvantaged Employees
Social composition	Being represented in high proportions helps employees to more easily fit in and to enjoy greater credibility; they experience less stress, and are usually candidates for promotion	Being represented in low proportions puts employees visibly "on display" and results in their not being taken seriously; they tend to fear making mistakes and losing ground rather than optimistically looking toward advancement
Power	In powerful positions, employees contribute to high morale and support subordinates; such employees tend to be more democratic leaders	In positions of low power, employees tend to foster low morale and restrict opportunities for subordinates to advance; they tend to be more authoritarian leaders
Opportunity	High opportunity encourages optimism and high aspirations, loyalty to organization, use of higher-ups as reference groups, and constructive responses to problems	Low opportunity encourages pessimism and low aspirations, weak attachment to the job, use of peers as reference groups, and ineffective griping in response to problems

SOURCE: Based on Rosabeth Moss Kanter, *Men and Women of the Corporation* (New York: Basic Books, 1977), pp. 246–49.

2. **Sharing of responsibilities.** Humanizing bureaucracy means reducing rigid, oligarchical structures by spreading power and responsibility more widely. Managers cannot benefit from the ideas of employees who have no channels for expressing their opinions. Knowing that superiors are open to suggestions encourages all employees to think creatively, increasing organizational effectiveness.

3. **Expanding opportunities for advancement.** Expanding opportunity reduces the number of employees stuck in routine, dead-end jobs with little motivation to perform well. Employees at all levels, therefore, should be encouraged to share ideas and to try new approaches, and no position should be ruled out as the start of an upward career path.

Critical evaluation.   Kanter's work takes a fresh look at the concept of bureaucracy and its application to business organizations. Perhaps rigid formality may have made sense in the past, when uneducated workers were hired primarily as a source of physical labor. But today, employees can contribute a wealth of ideas to bolster organizational efficiency if the organization encourages and rewards innovation.

Kanter's suggested changes may encounter resistance, however, since they mandate a redistribution of power. Interestingly, some research suggests women leaders are especially likely to embrace the kinds of changes Kanter advocates; if so, we might expect organizations to evolve as women gradually fill more executive positions traditionally held by men (Helgesen, 1990). But whether leaders are women or men, Kanter maintains, loosening up rigid organization is the key to improved performance. Comparing forty-seven companies with strictly bureaucratic structures to competitors of similar size but with more flexible approaches, Kanter (1983) found that flexibility increased profits. She argues, therefore, that bureaucratic structure limits an organization's success to the extent that it treats employees as a group to be controlled rather than as a resource to be developed. Thus, while the basic bureaucratic model may still promote efficiency, productivity is enhanced by flexible management styles, coupled with efforts to spread power and opportunity throughout the organization (Kanter, 1985).

It is worth noting that there are some similarities between Kanter's recommendations and those based upon the Japanese model described below.

Organizational Environment

How any organization operates depends on more than its internal structure. Recently, researchers have stressed the importance of the **organizational environment**, *a range of factors outside an organization that affect its operation.* Such factors include technology, politics, the economy, population patterns, and other organizations.

Technology is an especially important factor in an organizational environment. As we have already suggested, modern organizations could not exist without the technical capacity to communicate provided by telephone systems and facsimile (fax) machines, and the ability to process and store information afforded by copiers and computers. Technological changes currently under way are likely to have two somewhat contradictory consequences for organizational structure. On the one hand, the proliferation of personal computers and facsimile machines gives individuals throughout an organization access to more information than ever before; this may produce some leveling in the traditional hierarchy that concentrates information and decision making at the top of an organizational pyramid. On the other hand, however, computer technology also enables organizational leaders to monitor the activities of workers more than ever before in Big Brother-like fashion; this is likely to enhance the concentration of power in the executive suite (Markoff, 1991).

A second key dimension of the organizational environment is *politics*. Changes in law often have dramatic consequences for the operation of an organization, as many industries have learned in the face of new environmental standards. In global perspective, a dramatic change like the reorganization of the Soviet government in 1991 rippled throughout virtually every organization in that country.

Third, the state of the *economy* has obvious importance for an organization's well-being. Clearly, businesses may expand or contract along with economic cycles affecting the demand for their products or services: less obvious is the fact that contraction in size will have an impact on the level of bureaucratization within the firms themselves. Small companies that go through periodic boom–bust cycles must re-shape their bureaucratic structures repeatedly (Schellenberg, 1991). Needless to say, the ability to get a new organization off the ground depends on the availability of funds, which varies according to economic trends and banking policies (Pennings, 1982).

Fourth, *population patterns*—such as the size and composition of the surrounding populace—also affect organizations. The average age, typical education, and social diversity of a local community shapes both the available work force and the market for an organization's products or services.

Fifth, *other organizations* also form part of the organizational environment. The people who operate a hospital, for example, must be responsive to organizations of doctors, nurses' associations, and unions of other hospital workers. They must also interact with medical schools, ministries of health, political parties, research institutes, suppliers of medical equipment, and drug companies (brand-name and generic).

In short, no organization operates in a social vacuum. On the contrary, organizations are linked in many ways—in terms of structure as well as attitudes and values—to the surrounding society. This is especially evident when one looks at organizations cross-culturally.

Formal Organizations in Japan

Because of Japan's extraordinary success, Japanese corporations have captured the attention of people around the world and sparked many debates about organizational structure. Since the end of World War II, Japan's economy has surged ahead much faster than our own. Although geographically smaller than the Yukon, Japan's gross national product in 1990 was more than five times that of Canada.

Businesses in Japan have a distinctive organizational environment: a culture rooted in strong collective identity and solidarity. While most members of our society prize rugged individualism, the Japanese maintain traditions of cooperation. This cohesiveness results in relatively low levels of social problems—such as alcoholism, violence, and drug abuse—compared to more rootless and competitive societies like the United States (Ouchi, 1981). Japanese cities also lack the abject poverty and crime found in much of urban America. Even late at night, a person can walk safely through downtown Tokyo. Japanese solidarity also underlies the remarkably small number of lawyers in that society. Among the Japanese, obligations and disputes are typically settled according to traditional norms rather than by resorting to formal legal procedures.

Because of Japan's social cohesiveness, formal organizations in that country contradict the conventional wisdom of Western societies; they appear to be extremely large primary groups. In Canada and the United States, where many companies have experimented with Japanese organizational principles, even the humanized bureaucracies have many more secondary relationships. William Ouchi (1981) highlights five distinctions between formal organizations in Japan and their counterparts in industrial societies of the West. In each case, the Japanese organization reflects that society's more collective orientation.

1. **Hiring and advancement.** Organizations in the West hold out promotions and raises in salary as prizes won through individual competition. In Japanese organizations, however, companies hire new graduates together and all employees in a particular age cohort receive the same salary and responsibilities. As one employee moves ahead, so do they all. Only after several years is anyone likely

to be singled out for special advancement. This corporate approach generates a common identity among employees of the same age.

2. **Lifetime security.** Employees in North America rarely remain with one company for their entire careers; rather, we expect to move from one company to another in pursuit of personal goals. For their part, companies are quick to lay off employees (or even close plants) when economic setbacks strike. By contrast, Japanese companies typically hire employees for life, fostering strong, mutual loyalties among members of an organization. Japanese companies avoid layoffs by providing workers with other jobs in the organization, along with any necessary retraining.

3. **Holistic involvement.** For North American employees, work and private lives are usually distinct. Japanese organizations differ by playing a broad role in their employees' lives, to the point of being described as "welfare corporations" (Lincoln & Kalleberg, 1985). Companies often provide dormitory housing or mortgages for the purchase of homes, sponsor recreational activities, and schedule a wide range of social events in which every worker participates. Employee interaction outside the workplace strengthens collective identity, while offering the respectful Japanese worker an opportunity to more readily voice suggestions and criticisms in a neutral setting.

4. **Nonspecialized training.** Bureaucratic organization in North America is based on specialization; many people spend an entire career at a single task. From the outset, a Japanese organization trains employees in all phases of its operation, again with the idea that employees will remain with the organization for life. Ideally, nonspecialized training helps workers understand how each job relates to the organization's overall operation. As a result, Japanese workers generally have more technical knowledge than their Western counterparts (Sengoku, 1985). Broad training also enables the company to move employees from job to job more easily as circumstances dictate.

5. **Collective decision making.** In the West, most organizational decisions are made by a handful of executives. This cultural pattern is evident in the well-known sign on the desk of former U.S. president, Harry Truman: "The buck stops here." Although leaders of Japanese organizations also take responsibility for company performance, they involve workers in any decision that affects them. A closer working relationship is also encouraged by greater economic equality between management and workers: the salary differential between executives and the lower-ranking employees is smaller than that found in the West. Additionally, Japanese companies typically encompass many semi-autonomous working groups, called "quality circles." Instead of responding simply to the directives of superiors, all employees in Japan share managerial responsibilities.

Japan is a fascinating blend of the old and the new. Traditional loyalties and patterns of deference—of the young toward the old and women toward men—are still evident in modern, corporate life.

These characteristics give the Japanese a strong sense of organizational loyalty. The cultural emphasis on *individual* achievement in our society finds its parallel in Japanese *groupism*. By tying their personal interests to those of their company, workers realize their ambitions through the organization.

Finally, internal solidarity allows Japanese organizations to map long-term strategies. Akio Morita, a founder of the SONY corporation, quipped that Japanese businesses operate by looking ten years ahead, while U.S. corporations think ahead only about the next ten minutes. The kernel of truth in this exaggeration is that top-heavy management and pursuit of short-term profits have hurt the global competitiveness of North American businesses.

Groups and Organizations in Global Perspective

In recent years, the emphasis in the study of formal organizations has shifted from the organizations themselves to the environment in which they operate. In part, this change stems from a growing global focus on organizational research, which shows that the structure and performance of organizations reflect a host of broad societal factors.

Despite Weber's depiction of bureaucracy as a singular organizational form, formal organizations actually developed quite differently in various world regions. Several centuries ago, most businesses in Europe and North America were small family enterprises. But as Western societies were rocked by the Industrial Revolution, the rational world view, described by Max Weber, came to the fore. Primary relationships were defined as a barrier to organizational efficiency. Thus, Western organizational tradition scorns nepotism (favoritism shown to a family member) or other forms of personal bias. This helps to explain why Weber's model of bureaucracy—widely embraced by organizations in Europe and North America—maintains that the key to efficiency is impersonal, secondary relationships based on technical specialization and impartiality.

The development of formal organizations in Japan followed a different route. Historically, that society was even more socially cohesive, organized according to family-based loyalties. As Japan industrialized, people there did not see primary relationships as a threat to efficiency, as Westerners did. On the contrary, the Japanese modeled their large businesses on the family and, as that nation modernized, traditional family loyalties were transferred to corporations. From our point of view, then, the Japanese seem to be simultaneously modern and traditional as they promote organizational efficiency by cultivating personal ties. Perhaps Japanese workers are now becoming more individualistic; the startling economic success of the Japanese is prompting some to leave the big industrial corporations in search of higher salaries offered by newer financial organizations. Yet the Japanese model still demonstrates a basic truth: organizational life need not be impersonal. Economically challenged as never before, Canadian businesses are taking a closer look at organizational patterns elsewhere, especially in Japan. In fact, many efforts to humanize bureaucracy in this country are clear attempts to mimic the Japanese way of doing things.

Beyond the benefits for Canadian businesses there is another reason to study the Japanese approach carefully. Our society is less socially cohesive now than the more family-based society Weber knew. A rigidly bureaucratic form of organization only atomizes society further. Perhaps by following the lead of the Japanese, our own formal organizations can promote—rather than diminish—a sense of collective identity and responsibility.

Beyond Japan, organizations throughout the world are developing distinctive structures based on their distinctive environments. Businesses in Poland are gaining vitality as that country establishes a convertible currency and opens its markets to global trade. European nations are forging a new and promising multinational economic system. The Communist party in the People's Republic of China has clamped down on organizations throughout the country. In the former Soviet Union, associations of all kinds are coming out from under rigid political control for the first time in three-quarters of a century. Each of these developments will have an effect on organizational patterns in Canada. To seize the opportunities inherent in the changes sweeping the world, we must maintain a sense of openness and curiosity about the possibilities for reorganizing our future.

Summary

1. Social groups are important building blocks of societies, fostering common identities and distinctive patterns of interaction.

2. Primary groups tend to be small and person-oriented; secondary groups are typically large and goal-oriented.

3. Leadership often involves two distinctive roles: instrumental leaders are concerned with a group's goals; expressive leaders focus on the collective well-being of members.

4. The process of group conformity is well documented by researchers. Because members often seek consensus, groups do not necessarily generate a wider range of ideas than do individuals working alone.

5. Individuals use reference groups—both ingroups and outgroups—to make decisions and evaluations.

6. Georg Simmel argued that dyads have a distinctive intensity but lack stability because of the effort necessary to maintain them. A triad can easily dissolve into a dyad by excluding one member.

7. Peter Blau has shown that structural characteristics of groups—including size, internal homogeneity, relative social parity, and physical segregation—all affect the behavior of group members.

8. Social networks are grouplike relational webs that link people who typically have little common identity and uncertain interaction.

9. Formal organizations are large, secondary groups that seek to perform complex tasks efficiently. Depending on their members' reasons for joining, formal organizations can be classified as normative, coercive, or utilitarian.

10. Bureaucratic organization expands in modern societies and allows the efficient performance of many complex tasks. Bureaucracy is based on specialization, hierarchy, rules and regulations, technical competence, impersonal interaction, and formal, written communications.

11. Limitations of bureaucracy include the inability to deal efficiently with special cases, depersonalizing of the workplace, and the fostering of ritualism among some employees. Further, as Max Weber recognized, bureaucracy resists change.

12. Formal organizations are often oligarchies. Rosabeth Moss Kanter's research has shown that the concentration of power and opportunity in corporations can compromise organizational effectiveness.

13. Humanizing bureaucracy means recognizing that people are an organization's greatest resource. To develop human resources, organizations must not allow people of any one gender or race to dominate decision making; rather, responsibility and opportunity should be available to everyone at all levels.

14. Recently, researchers have shifted attention from organizations themselves to the organizational environment. Technology, politics, the economy, population patterns, and other organizations are among the external factors that influence organizations.

15. Formal organization in Japan differs from the Western, bureaucratic model because of the collective spirit of Japanese culture. Formal organizations in Japan are based on more personal ties than are their counterparts in Canada.

Key Concepts

bureaucracy an organizational model rationally designed to perform complex tasks efficiently

bureaucratic inertia the tendency of bureaucratic organizations to persist over time

bureaucratic ritualism   a preoccupation with organizational rules and regulations as ends in themselves rather than as the means to organizational goals

dyad   a social group with two members

expressive leadership   group leadership that emphasizes collective well-being

formal organization   a large secondary group that is formally organized to facilitate achieving its goals efficiently

groupthink   a limited understanding of some issue due to group conformity

humanizing bureaucracy   fostering an organizational environment that develops human resources

ingroup   a social group commanding a member's esteem and loyalty

instrumental leadership   group leadership that emphasizes the completion of tasks

network   a web of social ties that links people who may have little common identity and interaction

oligarchy   the rule of the many by the few

organizational environment   a range of factors outside an organization that affect its operation

outgroup   a social group toward which one feels competition or opposition

primary group   a small social group in which relationships are both personal and enduring

reference group   a social group that serves as a point of reference for people making evaluations or decisions

secondary group   a large and impersonal social group based on some special interest or activity

social group   two or more people who identify with one another and have a distinctive pattern of interaction

triad   a social group with three members

Suggested Readings

These two books delve into many of the issues addressed in this chapter.

> Richard H. Hall. *Organizations: Structures, Processes, and Outcomes.* Englewood Cliffs, NJ: Prentice Hall, 1991.
> Cecilia L. Ridgeway. *The Dynamics of Small Groups.* New York: St. Martin's Press, 1983.

This article deals with "intimate networks" in a Toronto borough, revealing that these close ties extend throughout the metropolitan area and beyond.

> Barry Wellman. "The Community Question: The Intimate Networks of East Yorkers." *American Journal of Sociology* 84(5): 1201–1231, 1979

Controversy has dogged the obedience experiments of Stanley Milgram for more than thirty years. This book reviews Milgram's work and related studies, and tackles broad ethical questions such research raises.

> Arthur G. Miller. *The Obedience Experiments: A Case Study of Controversy in Social Science.* New York: Praeger, 1986.

This book, by the originator of the term "groupthink," examines organizational leadership.

> Irving L. Janis. *Crucial Decisions: Leadership in Policy-making and Crisis Management.* New York: The Free Press, 1989.

This intriguing book argues that women typically adopt a more humanized leadership style in managerial positions that works to the advantage of corporations.

> Sally Helgesen. *The Female Advantage: Women's Ways of Leadership.* New York: Doubleday, 1990.

This analysis of factors affecting the careers of Canadian women is based on in-depth interviews and a Goldfarb poll commissioned by Bassett (a television journalist).

> Isabel Bassett. *The Bassett Report: Career Success and Canadian Women.* Toronto: Collins, 1985

Throughout the world, women have played a large part in voluntary associations. The first of these two books investigates the unpaid work of U.S. women outside the home. The second analyzes women's associations in the context of national politics in India.

> Arlene Kaplan Daniels. *Invisible Careers: Women Civic Leaders from the Volunteer World.* Chicago: University of Chicago Press, 1988.
> Patricia Caplan. *Class and Gender in India: Women and Their Organizations in a South Indian City.* New York: Tavistock, 1985.

This brief book spells out strategies for effectively organizing people into task groups.

> Carl E. Larson and Frank M.J. LaFasto. *Teamwork: What Must Go Right/What Can Go Wrong.* Newbury Park, CA: Sage, 1989.

The first of these books challenges the conventional belief that traditional social patterns run counter to bureaucracy, revealing how both are shaped by the same cultural forces. The second, by a renowned organizational researcher, brings together essays showing that government bureaucracies are far more varied than Weber's model suggests.

Michael Herzfeld. *The Social Production of Indifference: Exploring the Roots of Western Bureaucracy.* New York: Berg, 1991.

James Q. Wilson. *Bureaucracy: What Government Agencies Do and Why They Do It.* New York: Basic Books, 1989.

According to Diane Francis, corporate concentration is particularly alarming in Canada. Here she tells the story of the small number of families and corporations that effectively run our country.

Diane Francis. *Controlling Interest: Who Owns Canada?* Toronto: Macmillan, 1986.

These two books exemplify the growing trend of applying sociological analysis to problems of corporate management. The first, by one of the best-known sociologists in the field of formal organizations, examines the future of corporate organization. The second, by a noted futurist, argues that simply "doing more of the same" in a changing society will surely lead to declining business.

Rosabeth Moss Kanter. *When Giants Learn to Dance: Mastering the Challenges of Strategy, Management, and Careers in the 1990s.* New York: Simon and Schuster, 1989.

Alvin Toffler. *The Adaptive Corporation.* New York: McGraw-Hill, 1985.

This collection of articles dealing with Canadian industrial relations includes Canada-U.S.-Europe comparisons.

John Anderson and M. Gunderson. *Union Management Relations in Canada.* Don Mills, Ontario: Addison-Wesley, 1982.

This is one of the better books contrasting formal organizations in the United States with those in Japan.

Boye De Mente. *Japanese Etiquette and Ethics in Business.* 5th ed. Lincolnwood, IL: NTC Business Books, 1987.

Challenging the notion that formal organizations are based on cool-headed, rational behavior, some organizations deliberately foster emotional intensity among their members. This study highlights companies such as Mary Kay cosmetics and Amway products that have used emotional, motivational techniques successfully.

Nicole Woolsey Biggart. *Charismatic Capitalism: Direct Selling Organizations in America.* Chicago: The University of Chicago Press, 1989.

DEVIANCE

MAR. 3 1991

Sirens sliced through the night as police cruisers joined in angry pursuit of the 1988 Hyundai through a suburban neighborhood in Los Angeles. As the black-and-white cars closed in on their quarry, a helicopter chattered overhead, its powerful floodlight bathing the surreal scene in a shimmering brilliance.

Twenty-five-year-old Rodney Glen King, the lone occupant of the Hyundai, brought his car to a halt, opened his door, and stumbled into the street. In an instant, police swarmed around him, and a sergeant lunged forward, staggering King with the discharge of a 50,000-volt Taser stun gun. Unarmed and now helpless, King fell to the pavement. As a group of eleven police officers looked on, three officers took turns kicking King and striking him with their clubs as he tried in vain to protect himself. By the time the beating ended, King had sustained a crushed cheekbone, a broken ankle, damage to his skull, a burn on his chest, and internal injuries.

The capture and beating of an unemployed construction worker by police might have attracted little public notice except for one extraordinary coincidence: the resident of a nearby apartment building had observed the event through the eyepiece of his video-camera. In a matter of hours, the flagrant abuse of power was being replayed on television screens across the United States and beyond.

The King incident touched off a firestorm of public debate over the operation of police departments in Los Angeles and elsewhere. In Washington, DC, the attorney general ordered a national investigation of the extent of police misconduct. To some critics, the scene was all too familiar: a black man being brutalized by white police for little or no reason. Sociologist and law professor Jerome Skolnick explained the need for caution in asserting that the case was racially motivated. But, he concluded, "racist police are more likely to be brutal and brutal police are more likely to be racist." Other critics declared that the King episode was notable only because the Los Angeles police had been caught in the act: during the previous year, that city's police department had paid $10 million to compensate citizens who claimed they, too, had been victims of abuse.

The officers involved in the King incident soon stood charged with assault with a deadly weapon and use of excessive force. But many Americans wondered if the police are being asked to perform an almost impossible task: maintaining some semblance of order in cities seething with crime, drugs, and poverty. Typically for little pay, police routinely risk personal harm as they try to hold back the rising tide of violence, often feeling that they have little support from the courts and little understanding from the public.[1]

Canadians were not untouched by the events in Los Angeles, for they suspected that racism sometimes motivated the actions of their own police officers. Several incidents in Montreal and Toronto in which unarmed blacks were shot, met with rage in the black community, deep concern in the wider community, enquiries into police conduct and, in Ontario, the requirement that police file reports each time they unholster their guns.

Every society struggles to establish standards of justice, to reward people who play by the rules, and to punish those who do not conform. This chapter investigates questions of deviance, crime, and punishment in modern society. How do societies create a moral code in the first place? Is deviance inevitable, or can it be checked? Why are some people more likely than others to be charged with offenses? How has the scope of the crime problem changed in recent decades? And what are the legitimate purposes of the criminal justice system? We shall begin by defining several basic concepts.

What Is Deviance?

Deviance is *the recognized violation of cultural norms.* Norms guide virtually all human activities; the concept of deviance covers a correspondingly broad spectrum. One distinctive category of deviance is **crime**, *the violation of norms formally enacted into criminal law.* Even criminal deviance spans a wide range, from minor traffic violations to serious offenses such as rape and murder. A subcategory of crime, **juvenile delinquency**, refers to *the violation of legal standards by the young.*

Some instances of deviance barely raise eyebrows; other cases command greater attention, and some demand a swift and severe response. Canadians may pay little attention to mild nonconformity like left-handedness or boastfulness, but we take a dimmer view of a Mohawk hairstyle or a child flunking out of school. The vast majority define an act like violent rape as most serious, demanding a response by the police. Not all deviance involves action or even choice. For some categories of individuals, just *existing* may be sufficient to provoke condemnation from others. To some whites, who are in the majority, the mere presence of people of color may cause some discomfort. Similarly, many peo-

Each and every normative pattern creates the possibility for deviance. Many societies retain traditional norms that women should be soft and submissive; in this context, women who develop their physical strength—or those who are assertive—may be viewed as deviant.

ple of all races consider the poor disreputable, because they do not conform to conventional middle-class standards. Gay men and lesbians also confront derision and hostility from those who are intolerant of their sexual orientation.

Examples of nonconformity that come readily to mind—swimming in the nude, neglecting a pet, driving while intoxicated—involve overtly breaking some rule. But since we all have shortcomings, we sometimes define especially righteous people—those who *never* raise their voices or who are enthusiastic about paying their taxes—as deviant, even if we accord them a measure of respect (Huls, 1987). Deviant actions or attitudes, then, can be negative or positive. In either case, however, deviance stems from *difference* that causes us to react to another person as an "outsider" (Becker, 1966).

Social Control

Members of every society are subject to *social control,* attempts by society to regulate the behavior of individ-

---

[1] This account is based on Lacayo (1991) and Morrow (1991).

uals. Like norms, social control takes many forms. Socialization, discussed in Chapter 5, constitutes a complex process of social control in which family, peer groups, and the mass media influence people's attitudes and behavior. Through social control, people earn a positive response for conforming and a negative response for deviant attitudes or actions. Praise from parents, high grades in school, and positive recognition from people in the community encourage conformity to conventional patterns of thought and behavior.

Many instances of deviance provoke only informal responses, such as a scowl or a bit of friendly criticism. Charges of more serious deviance, however, may propel an individual into the **criminal justice system**, *a formal system that responds to alleged violations of law using police, courts, and punishment.*

Canadians reacted with horror to the killing of 14 women on December 6, 1989, in a classroom at L'Ecole Polytechnique in Montreal. In a suicide note discovered after the massacre, Marc Lepine claimed that "feminists" had frustrated his education and career plans. Here, one of Lepine's victims is rushed to an ambulance moments after the shooting.

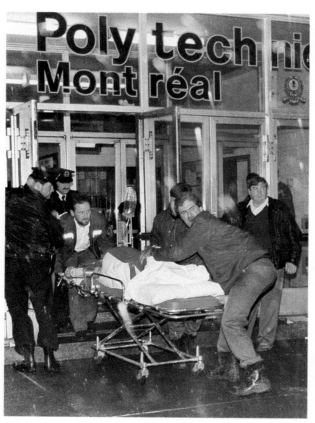

In sum, although we think of deviance simply in terms of individual choice or personal failings, society actually shapes the world of good and evil. How a society defines deviance, who is targeted as deviant, and what people decide to do about nonconformity are all issues of social organization. Only gradually, however, have people recognized this essential truth, as we shall now explain.

The Biological Context

Chapter 5 ("Socialization") noted that human behavior was understood—or, more correctly, misunderstood—during the nineteenth century as an expression of biological instincts. Understandably, then, early interest in criminality emphasized biological causes.

Early Research

In 1876 Caesare Lombroso (1835–1909), an Italian physician who worked in prisons, suggested that criminals had distinctive physical features—low foreheads, prominent jaws and cheekbones, protruding ears, hairiness, and unusually long arms that made them resemble human beings' apelike ancestors. In essence, Lombroso viewed criminals as evolutionary throwbacks to lower forms of life. Toward the end of his career he acknowledged the importance of social forces in criminality, but his early assertion that some people were literally "born criminals" gained currency among powerful people who dismissed the idea that failings in social arrangements might account, in part, for criminal deviance (Jones, 1986).

Although popular for a time, Lombroso's research was flawed. He failed to realize that the physical features he noted among prisoners appeared to the same degree in the population as a whole. Several decades later the British psychiatrist Charles Buckman Goring (1870–1919) probed the matter more carefully, comparing thousands of convicts and noncriminals. He found great physical variation within both categories, but no overall physical differences of the kind Lombroso used to distinguish criminals from noncriminals (1972; orig. 1913).

Delinquency and Body Structure

Although Lombroso's work had been discredited, others continued to search for alleged biological explanations of criminality. William Sheldon (1949) suggested that body structure was significant. He described three general types of body structure: *ectomorphs*, who are tall, thin, and fragile; *endomorphs*, who are short and fat; and *mesomorphs*, who are muscular and athletic. After analyzing the body structure and criminal history of hundreds of young men, Sheldon found criminality to be more common among men with the mesomorphic body type. Criminality, according to Sheldon, is linked to a muscular, athletic build.

Sheldon and Eleanor Glueck (1950) agreed with William Sheldon. However, the Gluecks cautioned that a powerful build is not necessarily a *cause* of criminality. Mesomorphic men, they suggested, were somewhat less likely to be raised with affection and understanding from family members; consequently, they showed less sensitivity toward others and tended to react aggressively to frustration. Young, muscular men also have the physical capacity to become the "bullies on the block" (Gibbons, 1981). Moreover, expecting muscular and athletic boys to be more physically aggressive than others, people may treat them accordingly, thereby provoking aggressive behavior in a self-fulfilling prophesy.

Recent Research

Since the 1960s, increasing knowledge of genetics has rekindled interest in the biological origins of criminality. Some investigators have focused on unusual genetic patterns that may engender criminality in some people (Vold & Bernard, 1986). The sex of human beings is determined by chromosomes: females have two X chromosomes and males have one X and one Y. Perhaps once in a thousand cases, a genetic mutation yields a male with an extra Y chromosome, an XYY pattern. Such men seem more likely than others to end up in prisons or mental institutions. Initially, researchers thought the XYY pattern triggered criminal violence, but it appears now that such men are only taller and perhaps less intelligent than average. Probably whatever greater criminality occurs among XYY men is the result of a tendency by others to define them as threatening and less capable, which is a social barrier to acceptance and a good job (Hook, 1973; Suzuki & Knudtson, 1989).

As of now, there is no convincing evidence that criminality stems from any specific genetic flaw. However, there is support for the notion that overall genetic composition, in combination with social influences, can account for some criminality. In other words, biological factors probably have a small but real effect on whether or not individuals engage in criminal activity (Rowe, 1983; Rowe & Osgood, 1984; Wilson & Herrnstein, 1985; Jencks, 1987). The new field of sociobiology is tackling a number of intriguing questions relating

to deviance, such as why men engage in violence more than women, and why parents are more likely to abuse disabled or foster children than healthy or biological children (Daly & Wilson, 1988).

Critical evaluation. Most biological theories have tried to explain crime in terms of people's physical traits. Early research focused on rare and abnormal cases, which, under any circumstances, could explain only a small proportion of all crimes. More recent sociobiological research suggests that specific biological traits may be related to criminality but, as yet, too little is understood about the links between genetics and human behavior to warrant assumptions of causation. In any case, an individualistic biological approach cannot address the issue of how some kinds of behaviors come to be defined as deviant in the first place. Therefore, although there is much to be learned about how human biology may affect behavior, research currently places far greater emphasis on social influences on human behavior (Gibbons & Krohn, 1986; Liska, 1991).

Personality Factors

Like biological theories, psychological explanations of deviance spotlight the individual, focusing on abnormalities in the individual personality. Though some abnormalities are hereditary, psychologists believe that most result from social experience. According to this view, deviance is thought to be the result of "unsuccessful" socialization.

The research of Walter Reckless and Simon Dinitz (1967) illustrates a psychological approach to explaining juvenile delinquency. They claimed that the odds of young boys engaging in delinquency are reduced to the extent that they develop strong moral values and a positive self-image. Reckless and Dinitz called their analysis containment theory.

They began their research by asking teachers to identify boys about age twelve who seemed likely to engage in delinquent acts and to pick out those who were not. Interviews with both categories of boys and their mothers provided information on each boy's self-concept—how he viewed himself and how he related to the world around him. The "good boys" displayed strong consciences (or superegos, in Sigmund Freud's terminology), coped well with frustration, and identified positively with cultural norms and values. The "bad boys" had weaker consciences, little tolerance for frustration, and identified less strongly with conventional culture. Over a four-year period, the researchers found that the "good boys" did indeed have fewer contacts with the police than the "bad boys." Since all the boys studied lived in areas where delinquency was widespread, the researchers concluded that boys who managed to stay out of trouble had strong consciences and positive self-concepts that, taken together, served as "an internal buffer which protects people against [violation] of the social and legal norms" (Reckless, 1970:401).

Critical evaluation. Psychological research has demonstrated that personality patterns have some relationship to delinquency and other types of deviance. Nevertheless, the vast majority of serious crimes are committed by people whose psychological profiles are normal. This finding limits the value of the psychological approach. Also, because this analysis focuses on individuals, it ignores how definitions of what is "normal" and "abnormal" vary from society to society. Finally, psychological research sheds little light on why, among people who behave in the same manner, some are defined as deviant while others are not.

Both biological and psychological approaches view deviance as an individual attribute without exploring how conceptions of right and wrong initially arise and without investigating the deviant person's place in the larger society. We now address these issues by delving into sociological explanations of deviance.

The Social Foundations of Deviance

Canadians have long viewed deviance in terms of the free choice or personal failings of individuals. But all behavior—deviance as well as conformity—is shaped by society. Three *social* foundations of deviance are identified below; they will be detailed in the following sections of the chapter.

1. **Deviance varies according to cultural norms.** No thought or action is inherently deviant; it becomes deviant only in relation to particular norms. The life patterns of rural Albertans, residents of Newfoundland fishing villages, Ontario suburbanites, and West Vancouverites differ in highly significant ways: as a result, their values and behavioural standards are different. Laws, too, differ from place to place. Quebeckers can drink at a younger age than Ontarians and are able to purchase wine and beer at corner stores, whereas Ontarians have only recently seen the arrival of beer with 0.5% alcohol

content in their grocery stores. Lotteries were illegal in Canada until 1969 but are now conducted in regionally diverse guises by the federal and provincial governments. Casinos are legal in Ontario, and may even be allowed on Indian reserves. They are also legal in Manitoba—but definitely *not* on Indian reserves.[2] Workers from Quebec can work in New Brunswick, but workers from New Brunswick cannot work legally in Quebec. And, while the Divorce Act establishes maintenance orders across Canada, the *enforcement* of support payments varies by province. In other words, what is deviant or even criminal is not uniform across the country.

   In global context, deviance is even more diverse. Albania outlaws any public display of religious faith, such as making the sign of the cross; Cubans can be prosecuted for "consorting with foreigners"; and U.S. citizens risk arrest by their own government if they travel to Libya or Iraq.

2. **People become deviant as others define them that way.** Even within a particular setting, people selectively apply cultural norms. Everyone violates norms from time to time, even to the extent of breaking the law. For example, most of us have at some point walked around talking to ourselves, "borrowed" supplies such as pens and paper from the workplace or driven faster than allowed by the law. Others may or may not take note of our actions; even if they do, they may or may not define what they see as mental illness, theft, or a traffic violation. In short, deviance is a product of the perceptions, definitions, and responses of others.

3. **Both rule-making and rule-breaking involve social power.** As explained later in this chapter, Karl Marx considered norms, and especially laws, as devices to protect the interests of powerful people. For example, the owners of an unprofitable factory have a legal right to close their business, even if doing so puts thousands of people out of work. If workers commit an act of vandalism that closes the same factory for a single day, however, they are likely to be defined as criminal. Also, poor people may be looked upon as deviant for exactly the same behavior that powerful people engage in with

---

[2] Several reserve-based Indian communities have attempted to establish casinos, in part as a test of their sovereignty. So far, Ontario has been more receptive than Manitoba to the possibility of allowing casinos on reserves. Otherwise provincial governments are eager to have a monopoly on casinos.

impunity. A homeless person who stands on a street corner denouncing the city government risks arrest for disturbing the peace; a mayoral candidate can do the same thing while receiving extensive police protection. In short, norms and their application are linked to social inequality.

Structural-Functional Analysis

Deviance is inherent in the operation of society. The structural-functional paradigm examines how deviance makes important contributions to a social system.

Emile Durkheim: The Functions of Deviance

A pioneering study of deviance was carried out by Emile Durkheim, whose vision of society is outlined in Chapter 4 ("Society"). In Durkheim's day, as now, most people thought that deviance meant destruction. Durkheim conceded that the costs of deviance are great, but he argued that the positive functions of deviance are even greater. In fact, he concluded, in the absence of deviance, society could not exist at all. Durkheim (1964a, orig. 1895; 1964b, orig. 1893) cited four major functions of deviance.

1. **Deviance affirms cultural values and norms.** Culture turns on moral choices: people must prefer some attitudes and behaviors to others. Conceptions of what is morally right exist only in antithesis to notions of what is wrong. For example, respect for law is strengthened as a society condemns those who violate legal standards. Deviance, therefore, is indispensable to the process of generating and sustaining cultural values.

2. **Responding to deviance clarifies moral boundaries.** In defining people as deviant, a society sets the boundary between right and wrong. For example, a university marks the line between academic honesty and dishonesty through disciplinary procedures that declare some behavior as intolerable plagiarism.

3. **Responding to deviance promotes social unity.** People typically react to serious deviance with collective outrage. In doing so, Durkheim explained, they reaffirm the moral ties that bind them. For example, the murder of fourteen female engineering students at Montreal's L'Ecole Polytechnique

on Dec. 6, 1989, was met with reactions of horror and profound grief by the larger community. Artists commemorated the incident with songs, poems, and artworks. Others participated in vigils and "Take Back the Night" walks. Men expressed their solidarity with women by wearing white ribbons on the third anniversary of the massacre, and stricter gun-control legislation was enacted.

4. **Deviance encourages social change.** People who push society's moral boundaries are able to suggest alternatives to the status quo, thereby provoking change. Today's deviance, Durkheim noted, may well become tomorrow's morality (1964a:71). For example, in the 1950s, the older generation of North Americans denounced rock and roll music as a threat to the morals of youth and an affront to traditional musical tastes. Since then, however, rock and roll has been swept up in the musical mainstream, as the box explains.

An Illustration: The Puritans of Massachusetts Bay

Durkheim's functional analysis of deviance is supported by Kai Erikson's (1966) historical research about the early Puritans of Massachusetts Bay. This highly religious "society of saints," Erikson discovered, created deviance in order to clarify moral boundaries. Durkheim could well have had the Puritans in mind when he asked us to

> *imagine a society of saints, a perfect cloister of exemplary individuals. Crimes, properly so called, will there be unknown; but faults which appear [insignificant] to the layman will create there the same scandal that the ordinary offense does in ordinary consciousness. ... For the same reason, the perfect and upright man judges his smallest failings with a severity that the majority reserve for acts more truly in the nature of an offense.*
> (1964a:68–69)

Deviance, in short, is inevitable in society, however righteous individuals may be.

The kind of deviance the Puritans created changed over time, depending on the moral questions they confronted. Whether or not they could continue their tradition of lively dissent, how they should respond to outsiders who joined them, and what their religious goals should be—all such questions were answered through celebrating some members while defining others as deviant.

Finally, Erikson discovered that although the definition of deviance changed, the proportion of Puritans declared to be deviant remained stable over time. To Erikson, this fact supported Durkheim's idea that deviants serve as moral markers, outlining the changing boundaries of conventional attitudes and behavior for a society. By constantly defining a small portion of their members as deviant, Puritan society ensured that the social functions of deviance were carried out.

Merton's Strain Theory

Robert Merton (1938, 1968) has amplified Durkheim's structural-functional analysis by linking deviance to certain societal imbalances. Merton's theory begins with the observation that financial success stands as a widespread *goal*. We expect people to pursue financial success according to certain approved *means*, such as schooling and hard work, and not through theft or other dishonest activities. Therefore, to the extent that people are willing and able to seek success according to such rules, *conformity* should result.

But not everyone who desires success has the opportunity to achieve it legitimately. Moreover, even successful people may be lured by the promise of further gain to violate cultural norms. Corporate executives, for example, may engage in dishonest business practices or embezzle company funds, and many

Rock and Roll: From Deviance to Big Business

Rock and roll exploded onto the national scene in the early 1950s, bursting with energy and inciting controversy. With roots in the rhythm and blues of African Americans, rock was initially taboo, a musical style that few white-owned record companies or radio stations were willing to promote. To make matters worse, rock and roll had long been synonymous with sex; the phrase originally referred to sexual intercourse. Little wonder that rock and roll soon became the anthem of rebellion among members of the emerging youth subculture, who delighted in flouting parental authority. By the 1960s, protest music and drug-based psychedelic rock urged listeners to challenge parents, police, and anyone else linked to "the system." In short, rock and roll seemed to oppose everything our culture valued, and to advocate attitudes and actions our way of life had long condemned.

Representing the conventional musical tastes of the 1950s, singers like Perry Como and Doris Day were upstaged by the gyrating Elvis Presley—the first superstar of rock and roll. Although dismissed by critics as vulgar and lacking talent, Pres-

ley started rock and roll on a ride that has accelerated ever since. But there was strong resistance to the new music. Church groups campaigned to suppress rock and roll, burning records and condemning the antics of singers as sexually suggestive and their lyrics (mild by today's standards) as obscene.

Gradually, however, our culture embraced rock and roll. Why? For one compelling reason: there was so much money to be made from it. By the early 1960s, the Beatles were not only selling millions of records but had discovered a vast market for side-line products, concert tours, and

successful films. Coca-Cola jumped on the bandwagon and for the first time used rock music in advertising.

Rock music is now bigger business than anyone two generations ago could have imagined. From 5 percent of record sales in 1955, rock is now a multibillion-dollar industry, accounting for more than 80 percent of sales of all recorded music. Promoter Dick Clark had it right when he quipped, "I don't make culture, I sell it" (cited in Chapple & Garofalo, 1977:305).

SOURCES: Chapple & Garofalo (1977) and Gillett (1983).

wealthy men and women misrepresent their income to Revenue Canada. Merton called this type of deviance *innovation*—attempting to achieve culturally approved goals using unconventional means. Table 8-1 shows that innovation involves accepting the goal of success while rejecting conventional means of attaining that goal.

According to Merton, innovation grows out of "strain" between the value of success and the limited opportunity to become successful in approved ways. The poor, especially, experience this strain as their aspirations are frustrated by a lack of educational and job opportunities. To alleviate this strain, people may resort to making their own rules, stealing, selling illegal drugs, or engaging in other kinds of street hustling and racketeering. The Social Diversity box "Crime and Social Marginality: Rocco Perri", which highlights the life of mobster Rocco Perri, explains why Merton's "innovation" has been historically attractive to people at the margins of our society.

The inability to become successful by normative means may also prompt what Merton calls *ritualism* (see Table 8-1). Ritualists resolve the strain of not having realized their goals by abandoning them in favor of compulsively conforming to cultural norms as a means of seeking respectability. Ritualism, Merton suggests, is common among people of modest social standing who have little opportunity to gain more in life but fear risking what they have through innovation. Consider the "bureaucratic ritualist," described in Chapter 7 ("Groups and Organizations"): the lower-level official, obsessed with rules, who loses sight of their overall purpose. In Merton's view, such deviance stems from

giving up the pursuit of success; however, ritualists may gain the reputation of being "good citizens" because they rigidly adhere to the rules.

A third response to the inability to succeed is *retreatism*—the rejection of both the goals and the norms of one's culture. Retreatists are society's dropouts. They include many of the alcoholics, drug addicts and street people we find on the streets of Vancouver, Toronto, or Montreal. The deviance of retreatists lies in their unconventional way of life and, perhaps more seriously, their acceptance of their situation.

The fourth response to failure is *rebellion*. Like retreatists, rebels reject both the cultural definition of success and the normative means of achieving it. Rebels, however, go further by advocating radical alternatives to the existing social order. They may promote unconventional values and norms through political revolution or zealous religious activity. Either way, rebels withdraw from established society, forming a counterculture.

Deviant Subcultures

Richard Cloward and Lloyd Ohlin (1966) extended Merton's theory in their investigation of delinquent youths. They maintain that criminal deviance results not simply from limited legitimate opportunity but also from accessible illegitimate opportunity. In short, some patterns of deviance and conformity can be explained in terms of the *relative opportunity structure* various categories of young people face in their lives.

The life of Rocco Perri, described in the box on page 218, illustrates the impact of alternative opportunity structures. As a poor immigrant, Perri was denied access to success through higher education. Yet his world did provide illegitimate opportunities for success as a bootlegger. Where relative opportunity favors what Merton might call "organized innovation," Cloward and Ohlin predict the development of *criminal subcultures*. These subcultures offer the knowledge, skills, and other resources people need to succeed in unconventional ways.

But in many poor and highly transient neighborhoods, organized innovation may be lacking. Here, delinquency is likely to surface in the form of *conflict subcultures* where violence explodes as an expression of frustration and a claim to territorial supremacy. Finally, among those who fail to achieve success even through criminal means, *retreatist subcultures* may arise. Consistent with Merton's analysis, such subcultures comprise dropouts who may use alcohol or other drugs.

TABLE 8-1	MERTON'S STRAIN THEORY OF DEVIANCE	
Individual Responses to Dominant Cultural Patterns	**Cultural Goals**	**Cultural Means**
Nondeviant response		
Conformity	Accept	Accept
Deviant responses		
Innovation	Accept	Reject
Ritualism	Reject	Accept
Retreatism	Reject	Reject
Rebellion	Reject current goals but promote new ones	Reject current means but promote new ones

SOURCE: Based on Robert K. Merton, *Social Theory and Social Structure* (New York: Free Press, 1968), pp. 230–46.

Albert Cohen (1971) suggests that delinquency is most pronounced among lower-class youths because society offers them little opportunity to achieve success in conventional ways. Because conventional definitions of success call for acquiring wealth and all its trappings, they find little basis for self-respect in their impoverished condition. In response, they may create a delinquent subculture that defines them in more favorable terms. These subcultures, Cohen says, "define as meritorious the characteristics [these youths] *do* possess, the kinds of conduct of which they *are* capable" (1971:66). For example, because the dominant culture values the calculated pursuit of wealth, a delinquent subculture may extol stealing "for the hell of it." In short, members of a delinquent subculture publicly flout conventional norms while carefully conforming to their own standards.

Walter Miller (1970) agrees that delinquent subcultures are most likely to develop in the lower classes where society provides the least legitimate opportunity. He describes six focal concerns of delinquent subcultures: (1) *trouble*, arising from frequent conflict with teachers and police; (2) *toughness*, the value placed on physical size, strength, and athletic skills, especially among males; (3) *smartness*, the ability to succeed on the streets, to outthink or "con" others, and to avoid being similarly taken advantage of; (4) *excitement*, the search for thrills, risk, or danger to gain needed release from a daily routine that is predictable and unsatisfying; (5) a concern with *fate*, derived from the lack of control these youths feel over their own lives; and (6) *autonomy*, a desire for freedom often expressed as resentment toward figures of authority.

Hirschi's Control Theory

A final argument that builds on Durkheim's analysis of deviance is Travis Hirschi's (1969) *control theory*. Hirschi assumes that everyone finds at least some deviance tempting. What requires explanation, then, is not deviance, but *conformity*. He suggests that conformity arises from four types of social controls.

1. **Attachment.** Strong social attachments to others encourage conformity; weak relationships in the family, peer group, and school leave people freer to engage in deviance.

2. **Commitment.** The higher one's commitment to legitimate opportunity, the greater the advantages of conformity. A young person bound for university, with good career prospects, has a high stake in conformity. In contrast, someone with little confidence in future success has a low investment in conformity and is more likely to follow a deviant path.

3. **Involvement.** Extensive involvement in legitimate activities, such as holding a job, going to school and completing homework, or pursuing hobbies, inhibits deviance. People with little legitimate involvement—who simply "hang out" waiting for something to happen—have time and energy for deviant activity.

4. **Belief.** Strong beliefs in conventional morality and respect for authority figures also restrain tendencies toward deviance; people with weak beliefs are more vulnerable to whatever temptation deviance presents.

Hirschi's analysis explains many kinds of deviant behavior, and it has gained support from subsequent research (Wiatrowski, Griswold, & Roberts, 1981; Sampson & Laub, 1990). Here, again, a person's social

No social class stands apart from others as being criminal or free from criminality. According to various sociologists, however, people with less stake in society and their own future typically exhibit less resistance to some kinds of deviance. Photographer Stephen Shames captured this scene in the Bronx, New York, in 1983.

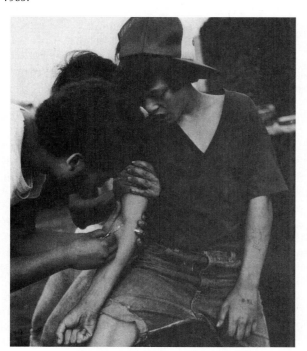

Crime and Social Marginality: Rocco Perri

Rocco Perri

Al Capone

During Prohibition (which outlawed the sale of liquor in Canada from about 1918 to 1924) a young Hamilton, Ontario grocer named Rocco Perri saw an opportunity to augment his income by selling bootleg liquor at the back of his store. He was remarkably successful. By the time American Prohibition (1920 to 1933) opened up vast markets in the U.S., "Perri had the organization and the experience to take quick advantage of the opportunity ... Before long Perri was a major supplier to gangsters like Al Capone" (Carrigan, 1991:174) and had become "King of the Bootleggers."

Rocco Perri's "formidable criminal organization" was one of many spawned by prohibition and linked to U.S. gangs through a wide range of activities including gambling, prosti-

tution, and extortion—the latter activities becoming more important as prohibition wound down. As these gangs manoeuvred for position, anticipating new post-war opportunities, Perri became an early victim of the competition, diasappearing in Hamilton in 1944.

Perri is one of Merton's "innovators"—one who pursues the culturally approved goal of success by unconventional means. His type of deviance is a product of ambition coupled with a lack of legitimate opportunity. Defined by background, language, and religion as second class citzens, immigrants confronted time and again the barriers of prejudice and discrimination. While the vast majority remained "conformists " (in Merton's terminology), some saw

in organized crime a means to achieve their most cherished goals.

However, even highly successful gangsters found that they were denied the prestige accorded to members of more "respectable" families. To overcome this marginality, some tried to distance themselves from their ethnic origins by changing their names, among other things. For example, American Mafia boss Al Capone's first employer (a reputed Mafia boss himself) was a fellow immigrant who adopted the name Mr. Frankie Yale and called his establishment on Coney Island the Harvard Inn. After Capone became a leader of the Chicago rackets, he insisted on being called Anthony Brown and avoided hiring men who displayed any of the ethnic traits he sought to leave behind. "The Big Fellow hires nothing but gentlemen" (Allsop, 1961).

Although the means he chose to achieve success were hardly commendable, Rocco Perri's ambitions were modeled on those of the surrounding culture. His deviance—which brings to mind that of thousands of young people dealing drugs in today's cities—was motivated by the hunger for success amid limited opportunity.

SOURCES: Allsop (1961); Carrigan (1991).

---

ranking is crucial in generating a stake in conformity or, conversely, in allowing everyday temptations to cross the line into actual deviance.

Critical evaluation. Durkheim's pioneering work in the functions of deviance remains central to sociological thinking. Even so, recent critics point out that a community does not always come together in reaction to crime; sometimes fear of crime has a chilling effect on interaction (Liska & Warner, 1991). When, in 1991–92, several teenage girls were murdered in Burlington and St. Catharines (in southern Ontario),

the communities pulled together in searches, concern for the families involved, and moves to demand stricter parole and gun-control legislation. But at the same time anxious parents expressed concern for the safety of their own daughters through earlier curfews, restrictions on movement, and closer parental surveillance, thereby changing the ways in which many teenage girls interacted with their peers.

Various structural-functional theories derived from Durkheim's analysis—especially Merton's strain theory—have also enjoyed widespread support. Merton's theory has much credibility, but it also has several limitations. First, no evidence shows precisely how deviance is caused by societal "strain." After all, most people who cannot realize their dreams keep playing by the rules all the same. Second, Merton offers only a few clues as to which categories of people would choose one response to strain over another. Third, Merton's approach explains some kinds of deviance (theft, for example) far better than others (such as crimes of passion, or white-collar crime). Fourth, we should recognize that not everyone seeks success in conventional terms of wealth, as strain theory implies. As explained in Chapter 3 ("Culture"), members of our society embrace many different cultural values and are motivated by various notions of personal success.

The general argument of Cloward and Ohlin, Cohen, Miller, and Hirschi—that deviance reflects the opportunity structure of society—has been confirmed by subsequent research (cf. Allan & Steffensmeier, 1989). However, these theories fall short in assuming that people use a single cultural standard for determining which attitudes and behavior are legitimate and illegitimate. Our society upholds various, sometimes competing, ideas of what is and is not deviant. A second problem lies in our defining deviance in terms that focus most attention on poor people. If crime is defined to include stock fraud as well as street theft, criminals are more likely to come from the ranks of well-integrated, affluent individuals. A third problem with this approach is that structural-functional theories imply that everyone who violates conventional cultural standards will be defined as deviant. Defining particular actions or attitudes as deviant, however, actually involves a highly complex process, as the next section explains.

Symbolic-Interaction Analysis

The symbolic-interaction paradigm directs attention to how people construct reality as they interact in countless everyday situations. In the early 1950s, sociologists began to apply this theoretical orientation to the study of deviance. Their work revealed that surprising flexibility underscores definitions of deviance and conformity.

Labeling Theory

The central contribution of symbolic-interaction analysis is **labeling theory**, *the assertion that deviance and conformity result from the response of others.* Labeling theory stresses the relativity of deviance, meaning the same behavior may be defined in any number of ways. Howard S. Becker therefore claims that deviance is nothing more than "behavior that people so label" (1966:9). Consider these situations: a woman takes an article of clothing from a roommate; a married man at a convention in a distant city has sex with a prostitute; a cabinet minister drives home intoxicated after a party. The reality of each of these situations depends on the response of others. The first could be defined as borrowing or as theft. The consequences of the second situation depend largely on whether news of the man's indiscretion follows him back home. In the third situation, the official might be defined as either an active socialite or a dangerous drunk. In the social construction of reality, then, a highly variable process of detection, definition, and response comes into play.

People sometimes contend with deviant labels for involvement in situations completely beyond their control. For example, victims of violent rape may be labeled as deviants because of the misguided assumption that they must have provoked the offender. Similarly, people with a serious disease may be viewed as deviant by others who cannot cope with the illness. Employers, friends, and even family members, for instance, sometimes shun people with Acquired Immune Deficiency Syndrome (AIDS).

Primary and Secondary Deviance

Edwin Lemert (1951, 1972) explains that being labeled as deviant can affect a person's subsequent behavior. Lemert calls activity that is initially defined as deviant *primary deviance.* What Lemert terms *secondary deviance* may follow if the deviant label becomes part of the person's self-concept and social identity. Initial labeling, then, can start someone down the road to fulfilling the expectations of others.

Stigma

The onset of secondary deviance marks the emergence of what Erving Goffman (1963) called a *deviant career.* Typically, this occurs as a consequence of acquiring a **stigma**, *a powerfully negative social label that radically changes a person's self-concept and social identity.* Stigma, then, operates as a master status (see Chapter 6, "Social Interaction in Everyday Life"), overpowering other dimensions of social identity so that an individual is "reduced in our minds from a whole and usual person to a tainted, discounted one" (1963:3). The person who is stigmatized may become socially isolated, allegedly because of personal failings.

Sometimes condemnation by an entire community is conveyed formally through what Harold Garfinkel (1956) calls a *degradation ceremony*. A criminal prosecution, for example, is much like a high-school graduation, except that people stand before others to be formally labeled in a negative rather than positive way.

More casually, adults socialize children to devalue stigmatized categories of people. Those stigmatized may include not only lawbreakers but also people of certain races and social classes, as well as those who are physically disabled or unconventional in a host of other respects. For some children, the most emotionally wrenching experience comes from realizing that a particular stigma applies to them personally. Confronted with bigotry, for example, a black child in Toronto may learn that, in the eyes of some people, being different means being ignored or even hated. Understandably, then, many people with physical limitations, gay people, and members of racial minorities have come together to counter stigma by recognizing and emphasizing their positive personal qualities.

Retrospective Labeling

Once stigmatized, a person may be subject to **retrospective labeling**, *the interpretation of someone's past consistent with present deviance* (Scheff, 1984). For example, after discovering that a man who has worked for years with the Boy Scouts has sexually molested a child, others rethink his past, perhaps musing, "He always did want to be around young children." Clearly, retrospective labeling involves a highly selective and prejudicial view of a person's past, guided more by the present stigma than by any attempt to be fair. But this process may nonetheless deepen a person's deviant identity.

Labeling and Mental Illness

Generally speaking, psychiatrists believe that mental disorders have a concrete reality that parallels diseases of the body. Factors such as heredity, diet, stress, and chemical imbalances in the body do account, in part, for some mental disturbances. However, much of what we label as "mental illness" is actually a matter of social definition (Thoits, 1985). Sometimes defining and treating the "mentally ill" boils down to an attempt to enforce conformity to conventional standards.

If a woman believes that Jesus accompanies her as she rides the bus to work each day, is she seriously deluded or merely expressing her religious faith in a graphic way? If a man refuses to bathe or observe common etiquette, much to the dismay of his family, is he insane or simply choosing a unconventional way of life? Is a homeless person loudly denouncing the city government while shivering on a street corner mentally ill or expressing justifiable anger?

According to psychiatrist Thomas Szasz, the label of insanity is widely applied to behavior that is merely "different." Therefore, Szasz concludes, the notion of mental illness should be abandoned (1961, 1970; Vatz & Weinberg, 1983). Illness, he asserts, afflicts only the body. Disease can ravage the brain; however, mental illness per se is a myth. Being different in thought or action may irritate others, but it does not justify labeling someone as sick. To do so, Szasz claims, simply enforces conformity to the standards of people powerful enough to get their way. Thus, for decades political dissidents in the Soviet Union reportedly were sent to mental hospitals for "rehabilitation"; similarly, homeless people in New York may be hospitalized for refusing an offer of a bed in a city shelter when outdoor temperatures fall below freezing.

Szasz's views are controversial; many of his colleagues reject the idea that all mental illness is a fiction. Others have hailed his work, however, for pointing to the danger of abusing medical practice in the interest of conformity.

Erving Goffman (1961) has also criticized the label of mental illness. He pointed out that commitment to a mental institution may reflect the desires of others as much as the needs of the patient. Forcible commitment, says Goffman, is often triggered by contingencies that have no direct bearing on the patient's mental condition:

> ... a psychotic man is tolerated by his wife until she finds herself a boyfriend, or by his adult children until they move from a house to an apartment; an alcoholic is sent to a mental hospital because the jail is full, and a drug addict because he declines to avail himself of psychiatric treatment on the outside; a rebellious adolescent daughter can no longer be managed at home because she now threatens to have an open affair with an unsuitable companion. ...
> One could say that mental patients distinctively suffer not from mental illness, but from contingencies. (1961:135)

The stigma of mental illness can transform a person's life, and should not be applied lightly. After all, most of us have experienced periods of extreme stress or other mental disability. Such episodes, although upsetting, are usually of passing importance. If, however, others use the occasion to attach a powerful label

In Winnipeg, a born-again Christian gives visible expression to his faith. When the city council warned that his signs violated civic by-laws, the man vowed to challenge any charges in court.

to us, they may initiate a self-fulfilling prophecy (Scheff, 1984).

The Medicalization of Deviance

Labeling theory, particularly the ideas of Szasz and Goffman, helps to explain an important shift in the way we understand deviance. Over the last fifty years, the growing influence of psychiatry and medicine in Canada and the United States has encouraged the **medicalization of deviance**, *the transformation of moral and legal issues into medical matters*. In essence, this amounts to a change in labels. Conventional moral judgment designates people or their behavior as "bad" or "good." However, the scientific objectivity of medicine passes no moral judgment; instead, science applies morally neutral diagnoses such as "sick" and "well."

Changing views on alcoholism illustrate this process. Until the middle of this century, alcoholics were generally considered morally deficient, easily tempted by the pleasure of drink. Gradually, however, specialists redefined alcoholism as a medical problem. Now most people view alcoholism as a disease, affecting people who are "sick" rather than "bad." Similarly, obesity, drug addiction, child abuse, and other behaviors that used to provoke cries of moral outrage are today widely defined as illnesses for which the people deserve help rather than punishment.

In some complex cases, moral and medical views alternate over time. For centuries, most North Americans considered homosexuality to be a moral issue, a straightforward example of being "bad" as measured against a heterosexual standard of "good." But the growing influence of psychiatry gradually led to the inclusion of homosexuality among medical conditions; in 1952, the American Psychiatric Association (APA) officially declared homosexuality as a "sociopathic personality disturbance." Such a pronouncement by medical authorities had a powerful influence on public opinion and, by 1970, some two-thirds of American adults agreed that homosexuality was a "sickness that could be cured."

More recently, however, yet another view has emerged: homosexual and bisexual people may be *different* without being *deviant*. Supporters of this view point to the lack of success in "curing" homosexuality and to the growing evidence that sexual orientation is not a matter of personal choice. In 1974, the APA switched again, redefining homosexuality as simply a "form of sexual behavior" (Conrad & Schneider, 1980:193–209).

In the wake of this shift to a more neutral view of homosexuality, many gay and straight people have countered traditional prejudices by labeling unwarranted hostility toward homosexuals as "homophobia." This strategy attempts to turn the tables on those who denounce gays by suggesting that deviance may lie in "conventional" people and not those they victimize.

Whether we define deviance as a moral or a medical issue has a number of profound consequences. First, consider *who responds* to deviance. An offense against common morality typically provokes a response by members of the community or police. Applying medical labels, however, places the situation under the control of clinical specialists, including counselors, psychiatrists, and physicians. A second difference is *how people respond* to a deviant. A moral approach defines the deviant as an "offender" subject to punishment; medically, however, "patients" cry out for treatment. Therefore, while punishment is designed to fit the crime, treatment programs are tailored to the patient and may involve virtually any therapy that might prevent future deviance (von Hirsh, 1986). Third, and most important, the two labels differ on the issue of *the personal competence of the deviant person*. Morally, people must take responsibility for their own behavior; they may do wrong, but they understand what they are doing and must face the consequences. Medically, sick people are not considered responsible for what they do. Defined as personally incompetent and unaware of what is in their own best interest, they become vulnerable to more intense, often involuntary, treatment. For this reason alone, attempts to define deviance in medical terms should be made only with extreme caution.

Sutherland's Differential Association Theory

Related to the issue of how we view others' behavior is how we learn to define our own. Edwin Sutherland (1940) suggested that social patterns, including deviance, are learned through association with others, especially in primary groups. Because of the complexity of socialization, people are exposed to forces encouraging criminality as well as those supporting conformity. The likelihood that a person will engage in criminal activity depends on the frequency of association with those who encourage norm violation compared with those who encourage conformity. This is Sutherland's theory of *differential association*.

Sutherland's theory is illustrated by a study of drug and alcohol use among young adults in the United States (Akers et al., 1979). Analyzing responses to a questionnaire completed by junior and senior high-school students, researchers found that the extent of alcohol and drug use among the respondents varied according to the degree to which peer groups encouraged such activity. The researchers concluded that young people adopt delinquent patterns if they receive praise and other rewards for doing so, defining deviance rather than conformity in positive terms. Nawaz (1978) found the same kinds of peer influences affecting the use of marijuana among Ontario high school students.

A learning approach to deviance also helps to explain the persistence of juvenile delinquency in specific neighborhoods (Shaw & McKay, 1972; orig. 1942). Once established in delinquent subcultures, older youths transmit skills and attitudes promoting deviance to younger boys and girls. The result of this cultural transmission is that delinquency takes on a life of its own, sometimes spanning decades.

Critical evaluation. Labeling theory links deviance not to *action* but to the *reaction* of others. Thus some people are defined as deviant while others who think or behave in the same way are not. The concepts of stigma, secondary deviance, and deviant career demonstrate how the label of deviance can be incorporated into a lasting self-concept.

Yet labeling theory has several limitations. First, because this theory takes a highly relative view of deviance, it glosses over how some kinds of behavior, such as murder, are almost universally condemned (Wellford, 1980). Labeling theory is thus most usefully applied to less serious deviance, such as certain kinds of sexual behavior and mental illness. Second, the consequences of deviant labeling remain unclear. Labeling sometimes promotes subsequent deviance, but it can also discourage people from engaging in further violations (Smith & Gartin, 1989). Thus questions remain as to when and how deviant labeling launches deviant careers. Third, labeling theory assumes that people resist the label of deviance. Probably most do, but some may seek to be defined as deviant (Vold & Bernard, 1986). For example, civil disobedience leading to arrest is a deliberate strategy for calling attention to social injustice. Fourth, we still have much to learn about how people respond to those who are labeled as deviant. One recent study found that the stigma of being a former mental patient resulted in social rejection only in cases when an individual was considered dangerous (Link et al., 1987).

Although Sutherland's differential association theory has exerted considerable influence in sociology, it overlooks instances of deviance that are impulsive rather than planned. Many deviant acts, such as shoplifting or cheating on an examination, may happen spontaneously, rather than signaling the onset of a deviant career. Put otherwise, young people sometimes drift into and out of deviant episodes, many of which are not serious (Matza, 1964; Elliot & Ageton, 1980). Furthermore, differential association theory offers little insight into why society's norms and laws define certain kinds of activities as deviant in the first place. This important question is addressed by social-conflict analysis, described in the next section.

Social-Conflict Analysis

The social-conflict paradigm links deviance to social inequality. This approach suggests that who or what is labeled as deviant depends on the relative power of categories of people.

Why, Alexander Liazos (1972) asks, does the term "deviance" bring to mind "nuts, sluts, and 'preverts'"? The answer, he suggests, is that such terms identify powerless people. In the power hierarchy, then, deviants inhabit the lowest levels. Bag ladies (not tax evaders) and unemployed men on street corners (not those who profit from wars) contend with the burden of deviance. Similarly, we tend to define the peer groups of poor youths as "street gangs," while those of affluent young people are simply called "cliques."

Social-conflict theory explains this pattern in three ways. First, the norms—including laws—of any society generally reflect the interests of the rich and powerful. People who threaten the wealthy, either by taking their property or by advocating a more egalitarian society, may be readily defined as "thieves" or "political radicals." As was noted in Chapter 4 ("Society"), Karl Marx argued that all social institutions tend to support the capitalist economic system and protect the interests of the rich, capitalist class. Richard Quinney makes the point succinctly: "Capitalist justice is by the capitalist class, for the capitalist class, and against the working class" (1977:3).

Second, even if their behavior is called into question, the powerful have the resources to resist deviant labels. Corporate executives who might order or condone the dumping of hazardous wastes are rarely held personally accountable for these acts. While such mischief poses dangers for all of society, it is not necessarily viewed as criminal.

Third, the widespread belief that norms and laws are natural and good obscures their political character. For this reason, we may condemn the unequal application of the law but give little thought to whether the *laws themselves* are inherently fair (Quinney, 1977).

Plains Cree artist George Littlechild explores the social and psychological aspects of Native-European relations. In Mountie and Indian Chief, *he brings the viewer "face to face with two very diverse cultures." Both figures are symbols of authority in their own right. Too often, though, in part as a result of the cultural divide, Native people have found themselves in conflict with Euro-Canadian law.*

Deviance and Capitalism

Steven Spitzer (1980) claims that the people who run the risk of being labeled as deviant are those who impede the operation of capitalism. First, capitalism is based on private control of property, so people who threaten the property of others—especially the poor who steal from the rich—are prime candidates for labeling as deviant. Conversely, the rich who exploit the poor are unlikely to be defined as deviant. Landlords, for example, who charge poor tenants unreasonably high rents, refuse to make repairs on their buildings, and evict those who cannot pay are not officially considered a threat to society: they are simply "doing business."

Second, because capitalism depends on productive labor, those who cannot or will not work risk deviant labeling. We commonly think of people who are out of work—even those unemployed through no fault of their own—as somehow personally inadequate.

Third, capitalism depends on respect for figures of authority, so those who resist society's leaders are likely to be labeled as deviant. Consider the deviant labels that attach to children who skip school or talk back to parents and teachers, adults who do not cooperate with employers or police, and anyone who opposes "the system."

Fourth, capitalism, like all economic systems, rests on the widespread acceptance of the status quo. Those who challenge or undermine the capitalist system, therefore, are subject to deviant labeling. In this category fall antiwar activists, environmentalists, labor organizers, and anyone who supports an alternative economic system.

By contrast, whatever enhances the operation of capitalism attracts positive labels. Athletes, for example, are praised because sports express the values of individual achievement and competition vital to capitalism. Additionally, Spitzer notes, we define the use of drugs for escape (marijuana, psychedelics, heroin, and crack) as deviant, while we endorse consuming drugs that promote adjustment to the status quo (such as caffeine).

Deviant individuals, Spitzer continues, fall into one of two general categories. The system defines people who are a "costly yet relatively harmless burden" to capitalism as *social junk* (1980:184). People devalued in this way do not support themselves by working, typically depending on others or the government for their well-being. Such nonproductive, but nonthreatening, members of society include Robert Merton's retreatists (for example, those addicted to alcohol or other drugs) and the elderly, physically disabled, mentally retarded, or mentally ill. Defined as moderately deviant, these people are typically subject to control by social welfare agencies.

People who threaten capitalism, meanwhile, are labeled as *social dynamite*. Those in this second category range from members of the inner-city "underclass," to alienated youths, radicals, and revolutionaries—in Merton's terms, society's innovators and rebels. To the extent that they become threatening, such people are subject to control by the criminal justice system and, in times of crisis, by military forces.

Following Marx's lead, Spitzer claims that capitalism itself produces both "social junk" and "social dynamite." The unemployment and poverty that overwhelm much of these populations stem from the workings of the capitalist system. Having created these categories of people, capitalism must also control them—through the social welfare system and the criminal justice system. In the process of doing so, both systems apply deviant labels that place responsibility for social problems on the people themselves. Those who receive welfare because they have no other source of income are considered unworthy; poor people who vent their rage at being deprived of a secure life are labeled as rioters; anyone who actively challenges the government is called a radical; and those who attempt to gain illegally what they cannot otherwise acquire are called common thieves.

White-Collar Crime

"Reputable" Canadians have long been known to circumvent the law when doing so is likely to be immensely profitable (Carrigan, 1991:113–165). For example, Prohibition in the U.S brought tremendous money-making opportunities for Canadians—not only for the Mafia but also for numerous legitimate businesses that earned a little extra on the side. During World War II, when consumer goods were being rationed in favor of the production of armaments, big and small businesses and helpful government officials were caught up in wartime racketeering, supplying illegal goods through the black market. More recently, Canada has had its share of stock and real estate fraud, bid-rigging, tax evasion, and the fencing of stolen goods. These activities have cost tax-payers and consumers many millions of dollars, but the perpetrators rarely find themselves in the criminal courts. Although "detection capabilities have vastly improved," since 1967 when the RCMP organized commercial fraud units in all provinces, "less progress has been made with prosecutions" (Carrigan, 1991:164).

Marijuana use is not illegal simply because it is harmful. In fact, smoking tobacco is far more dangerous since it contributes to more than 300,000 premature deaths each year. The legal standing of a drug depends on many factors, including whether it promotes social adjustment or encourages escape and what potential profit it represents for businesses.

These activities exemplify **white-collar crime**, defined by Edwin Sutherland in 1940 as *crimes committed by persons of high social position in the course of their occupations* (Sutherland & Cressey, 1978:44). White-collar crime rarely involves uniformed police converging on a scene with drawn guns. Thus it does not refer to crimes such as murder, assault, or rape that happen to be carried out by people of high social position. Instead, white-collar crimes are acts by powerful people making use of their occupational positions to enrich themselves or others illegally, often causing significant public harm in the process (Hagan & Parker, 1985; Vold & Bernard, 1986). In short, white-collar offenses that occur in government offices and corporate board rooms are commonly dubbed crime in the suites rather than crime in the streets.

The public harm wreaked by false advertising, marketing of unsafe products, embezzlement, and bribery of public officials extends far beyond what most people realize. Some researchers contend that white-collar crime causes greater public harm than the more visible "street crime" (Reiman, 1990). The marketing of unsafe products and the failure to implement workplace safety regulations have been responsible for many deaths in Canada. Immeasurable sums of money are stolen every year through fraud. Since much of it goes undetected, and the overburdened fraud units do not have the manpower to prosecute all known cases, it is difficult to estimate the dollar value of white-collar crime. Among the roughly 600 cases under investigation or prosecution by the Ontario Provincial Police in 1989, frauds in the $10 to $15 million dollar range were common. One Toronto developer alone defrauded investors and creditors of roughly $93 million in the late 1980s (Carrigan, 1991). Clearly, the losses from this kind of crime far exceed the economic losses through common theft.

Elite deviance rarely results in criminal labeling of powerful people. Even when their actions lead to extensive public harm, it is far from certain that officials will be prosecuted. And in the event that white-collar criminals do face the music, the odds are they will not go to jail. As well, Sutherland noted that the public voices less concern about white-collar crime than about street crime, partly because corporate crime victimizes everyone—and no one. White-collar criminals don't stick a gun in anyone's ribs, and the economic costs are usually spread throughout the population.

As the "backbone of capitalism," corporations have immense power, influencing both the mass media and the political process. High corporate officials are frequently graduates of prestigious universities and professional schools, belong to exclusive social clubs, and have well-developed networks linking them to other powerful people in all walks of life. Many government officials, drawn from the ranks of corporate executives, regulate the very corporate enterprises in which they have spent most of their working lives. Not surprisingly, then, serious episodes of white-collar crime only make headlines from time to time.

Critical evaluation. According to social-conflict theory, the inequality in wealth and power that pervades our way of life also guides the creation and application of laws and other norms. This approach suggests that the criminal justice and social welfare systems act as political agents, controlling categories of people who threaten the capitalist system.

Like other approaches to deviance, however, social-conflict theory has its critics. First, this approach assumes that laws and other cultural norms are created directly by the rich and powerful. This is certainly an oversimplification, since many segments of our society influence, and benefit from, the political process. For example, laws also protect workers, consumers, and the environment, sometimes in opposition to the interests of capitalists. A second criticism holds that while social-conflict theory points to the social injury caused by the powerful, the average individual remains far more concerned about street crime. Third, this approach implies that criminality springs up only to the extent that a society treats its members unequally. However, according to Durkheim, all societies generate deviance, and crime is well known in societies far more socially and economically egalitarian than our own.

We have presented various sociological explanations for crime and other types of deviance. Table 8-2 presents a summary of the contributions of each approach.

Deviance and Gender

Anne Campbell (1991) points out that no variable is related to deviance more than gender: her own research shows that the vast majority of gang members are men. Curiously, however, analysis of gang behavior and other types of deviance rarely takes gender into account. Let us now examine how gender figures in to some of the theories we have already discussed.

Robert Merton's strain theory, for example, defines cultural goals in terms of financial success.

TABLE 8-2	SOCIOLOGICAL EXPLANATIONS OF DEVIANCE: A SUMMARY
Theoretical Paradigm	**Major Contribution**
Structural-functional analysis	While what is deviant may vary, deviance itself is found in all societies; deviance and the social response it provokes serve to maintain the moral foundation of society; deviance can also direct social change
Symbolic-interaction analysis	Nothing is inherently deviant but may become defined as such through the response of others; the reactions of others are highly variable; the label of deviance can lead to the emergence of secondary deviance and deviant careers
Social-conflict analysis	Laws and other norms reflect the interests of powerful members of society; those who threaten the status quo are likely to be defined as deviant; social injury caused by powerful people is less likely to be defined as criminal than social injury caused by people who have little social power

Traditionally, however, this preoccupation with material things has dominated the thinking of men while women have been socialized to define success in terms of relationships, particularly marriage and motherhood (Leonard, 1982). Only recently have women and men come to recognize the "strain" caused by cultural ideals of equality clashing with the reality of gender-based inequality.

Labeling theory, the major approach to deviance in symbolic-interaction analysis, offers some insights into ways in which gender influences how we define deviance. Since the behavior of females and males is judged by different standards, the very process of labeling stems from sex-linked biases. Further, Edwin Schur (1983) explains that because society generally places men in positions of power over women, men often escape direct responsibility for actions that victimize women. Frequently, men who engage in sexual harassment or other assaults against women are tagged with only mildly deviant labels ("Boys will be boys, after all!"); sometimes, they suffer no adverse consequences and, in some quarters, they may even gain social approval for their actions. In their analysis of woman abuse, DeKeseredy and Hinch (1991:127) note progress in that sexual harassment is now considered "a

compensatable injury under the provisions of the Ontario Worker's Compensation Act."

As a general rule, women who are victimized may have to convince an unsympathetic audience that they are not to blame for what happened. Research confirms an important truth: whether people define a situation as deviance—and, if so, whose deviance it is—depends on the sex of both the audience and the actors (King & Clayson, 1988). The box on pages 228–29 takes a closer look at the issue of date rape, in which many women and men are standing up for an end to a double standard that has long threatened the well-being of women.

Finally, a notable irony is that social-conflict analysis—despite its focus on social inequality—has neglected the importance of gender. If, as this approach asserts, economic oppression is a primary cause of crime, why do women (whose economic position is much worse than that of men) commit far *fewer* crimes than men do? The next section, in which we examine crime rates, answers this question.

Crime

Speak of crime and people immediately conjure up images of unsavory characters ducking into alleyways, waiting to prey on unsuspecting victims. But crime covers a surprisingly wide range of behaviors, including activities that in one time or place provoke a swift response while in another barely merit a raised eyebrow. In centuries past, a commoner who simply looked at the Chinese emperor in public was accused of a serious crime. Today a citizen of the People's Republic of China who expressed support for the nation's historic monarchy would likely face criminal charges.

All societies have a formal means of dealing with perceived violations of law. Generally, then, crime amounts to a violation of the criminal law enacted by government. Because jurisdictions define legal standards differently, what is a crime in one time and place may or may not be so at another. Technically, however, all crimes are constructed of two distinct elements: the *act* itself (or, in some cases, the failure to do what the law requires) and *criminal intent* (in legal terminology, *mens rea*, or "guilty mind"). Intent is a matter of degree, ranging from a deliberate action to negligence in which a person acts (or fails to act) in a manner that may reasonably be expected to cause harm. Juries weigh the degree of intent in determining whether, for example, someone who kills another is guilty of first-degree murder, second-degree murder, or manslaughter.

Types of Crime

In Canada, information on criminal offenses is obtained from the Uniform Crime Reporting system and reported in a Statistics Canada publication called *Canadian Crime Statistics*. Violent crime and property crime are recorded separately. **Violent crimes**, *crimes against people that involve violence or the threat of violence*, include murder, manslaughter, infanticide, assault, sexual assault, abduction, and robbery. **Property crimes** encompass *crimes that involve theft of property belonging to others*, including breaking and entering, motor vehicle theft, theft over $1000, theft of $1000 and under, possession of stolen goods, and fraud. A third category of offenses includes **victimless crimes**, *violations of law in which there are no readily apparent victims*—such as prostitution and gambling. There is also a separate category of Narcotic Control Act Offences regarding the use of illegal drugs, including cannabis or marijuana.

However, "victimless crime" is often a misnomer. How victimless is a crime when a young runaway is lured into prostitution and then made to believe that is her only way to live? And how victimless is the crime when a gambler falls so deeply into debt that he cannot make the mortgage payments or afford food for his family? In truth, the people who commit such crime can themselves be both offenders and victims.

Criminal Statistics

Canada's crime statistics suggest steady increases in both violent and property crime rates from 1962 to 1991. The violent crime rate in Canada rose from 221 per 100,000 population in 1962 to 1,099 in 1991, while the property crime rate rose from 2,000 to 6,395 (increases of 397 and 220 percent respectively). Figure 8-1 illustrates the trends in violent and property crimes over the period in question.

Canadians often pride themselves on having a much less violent society than the U.S. And, indeed, as Figure 8-2 shows, in 1985 the American violent crime rate was more than five times that of Canada. However, changes over time indicate that the difference between the two countries' rates is declining. Indeed, the ratios in Table 8-3 suggest that the U.S. homicide rate dropped from 3.9 times the Canadian rate in 1964 to 3.3 in 1986.

Crime statistics should be read with caution, however, since they include only the officially recorded offenses—that is, only those known to the police. Police learn about almost all homicides, but assaults—especial-

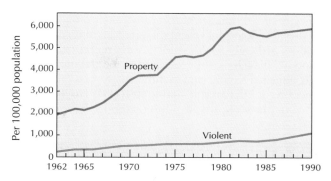

FIGURE 8-1   VIOLENT AND PROPERTY CRIME RATES IN CANADA, 1962–1990
SOURCE: Statistics Canada, Catalogue No. 85-205.

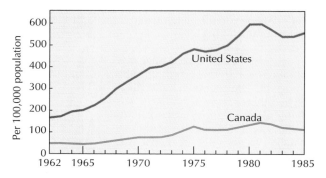

FIGURE 8-2   SERIOUS VIOLENT CRIME RATE,* CANADA AND THE U.S.A., 1962–1985
* The Canadian rate includes homicide, attempted murder, rape and aggravated sexual assault, wounding and aggravated assault, and robbery. The U.S. rate includes murder, forcible rape, robbery, and aggravated assault.
SOURCE: Statistics Canada, Catalogue No. 85-205; United States Department of Justice, Sourcebook.

TABLE 8-3	HOMICIDE RATES (PER 100,000 POPULATION): CANADA AND U.S.A., 1954–86		
	Canada	**U.S.**	**U.S./Canada Ratio**
1954–64	1.2	4.7	3.9
1965–75	2.1	7.8	3.7
1976–86	2.7	8.9	3.3

SOURCE: Adapted from Lenton (1989)

ly among acquaintances—are far less likely to be reported. Police records include even a smaller proportion of property crimes that are committed, especially those involving items of little value. Some victims may not realize that a crime has occurred, or they may assume they have little chance of recovering their property even if they notify the police and therefore fail to report.

As already noted, rape statistics reflect only a portion of all such assaults. Because of the traditional stigma attached to innocent victims, many women choose to remain silent after being attacked. However, in recent years improved public support for rape vic-

tims—including the establishment of rape crisis centers, increased sensitivity to rape-related trauma on the part of police and hospital personnel, and even the hiring of female police officers—has prompted more victims to come forward. In Canada, between 1987 and 1991 the sexual assault rate went from 87 per 100,000 population to 112. This probably reflects an increase in

CRITICAL THINKING

Date Rape: Exposing Dangerous Myths

Completing a day of work during a business trip to the courthouse in Tampa, Florida, thirty-two-year-old Sandra Abbott* pondered her return to her hotel. An attorney with whom she had been working—a pleasant enough man—made a kind offer of a lift. As his car threaded its way through the late afternoon traffic, their conversation was animated. "He was saying all the right things," Abbott recalled, "so I started to trust him." An invitation to join him for dinner was happily accepted. After lingering over an enjoyable meal, they walked together to the door of her hotel room. The new acquaintance angled for an invitation to come in, apparently eager to continue their conversation. Abbott hesitated. Sensing that he might have something more on his mind, she explained that she took an old-fashioned view of relationships. He could come in, she finally agreed, but only for a little while, and with the understanding that talking was *all* they would do.

Sitting on the couch in the room, soon Abbott was overcome with drowsiness. Feeling comfortable in the presence of her new friend, she let her head fall gently onto his shoulder and, before she knew it, she fell asleep. That's when the attack began. Abbott was startled back to consciousness as the man thrust himself sexual-

The 1992 rape conviction of heavyweight boxing champion Mike Tyson suggested that the problem of sexual violence against women is being taken more seriously.

ly upon her. She shouted "No!" but he paid no heed. Abbott describes what happened next:

> I didn't scream or run. All I could think of was my business contacts and what if they saw me run out of my room screaming rape. I thought it was my fault. I felt so filthy, I washed myself over and over in hot water. Did he rape me?, I kept asking myself. I didn't consent. But who's gonna believe me? I had a man in my hotel room after midnight. (Gibbs, 1991a:50)

Abbott knew that she had said "No!" and thus had been raped. She notified the police, who conducted an investi-

gation and turned their findings over to the state attorney's office. But the authorities backed away from Abbott. In the absence of evidence like bruises, a medical examination, and torn clothes, they responded, there was little point in prosecuting.

The case of Sandra Abbott is all too typical—not just in the U.S., but also in Canada. Even today, in most incidences of sexual attack, a victim files no police report, and no offender is arrested. So reluctant are the victims of such attacks to come forward that, in Canada, "somewhere between 60 and 90 percent of rapes go unreported" (DeKeseredy & Hinch, 1991:94). Where charges are not laid, the victim faces the bitter reality of simply trying as best she can to put a traumatic experience behind her.

The reason for such appalling inaction is that many people have a misguided understanding of rape. Three inaccurate notions about rape are so common that they might be called "rape myths." A first myth is that rape involves strangers. A sexual attack brings to mind young men who lurk in the shadows and suddenly spring on their unsuspecting victims. But this pattern is the exception rather than the rule: experts report that only one in five rapes involves strangers. For this reason, people have begun to speak more realistically about *acquaintance rape* or, more simply, *date rape*. A rape is typically committed by a man who is known to, and even trusted by, his victim: unfortu-

* A pseudonym; the facts of this case are from Gibbs (1991a).

both reporting and the willingness of the police to take the reports seriously.

One way to evaluate crime statistics is through a *victimization survey*, in which a representative sample of people is asked about being victimized. According to these surveys, actual criminality occurs at a rate about three times higher than indicated by official reports.

The "Street" Criminal: A Profile

Government statistics paint a broad-brush picture of people arrested for violent and property crimes. We now examine the breakdown of these arrest statistics by age, gender, social class, and race.

---

nately, being a "friend" (or even a husband) does not prevent a man from committing murder, assault, or rape.

A second myth about rape is that women provoke their attackers. Surely, many people think, a woman claiming to have been raped must have done *something* to encourage the man, to lead him on, to make him think that she really wanted to have sex. In the case described above, didn't Sandra Abbott agree to have dinner with the man? Didn't she willingly admit him to her room? Such thinking often paralyzes victims; women themselves often experience self-doubt about their actions after having been raped. But having dinner with a man—or even inviting him into her hotel room—is hardly a woman's statement of consent to have sex with him any more than it is an invitation to have him beat her with a club.

A third myth is the notion that rape is simply sex. If there is no knife held to a woman's throat, or if she is not bound and gagged, then how can sex be a crime? The answer is simply that *forcing a woman to have sex without her consent is rape*. To accept the idea that rape is sex we would also have to see no difference between brutal combat and playful wrestling. In the absence of consent, as Susan Brownmiller (1975) explains, rape is not sex but violence. "Having sex" implies intimacy, caring, and communication—none of which is present in cases of rape. Beyond the brutality of being physically violated,

date rape also undermines a victim's sense of trust.

The more people believe these myths about rape—that offenders are strangers, that victims provoke their attackers, and that rape is just spirited sex—the more women will become victims of sexual violence. The ancient Babylonians stoned married women who became victims of rape, claiming that the women had committed adultery. To a startling extent, ideas about rape have not changed over thousands of years, which helps explain why, even today, most rapes go unreported to police and, even when authorities are notified, prosecutions and convictions are rare.

When women *do* report sexual attacks, police judgment as to whether or not a criminal act had occurred depends upon the victim's reputation. When females referred to, by the Canadian police, as "women who can't be raped" or "open territory victims" filed complaints, 98 percent of them were dismissed as unfounded. "These women were prostitutes, known alcoholics, women who were drinking at the time of the offence, drug users, women on welfare, and unemployed women as well as women noted in police reports as 'idle'" (DeKeseredy and Hinch, 1991: 66–67). In his own research Hinch (1988) found this situation to exist as late as 1984.

Nowhere has the issue of date rape been more widely discussed than at colleges and universities. The cam-

pus is distinctive in several respects: students have easy access to one another, the collegiate setting encourages trust, and young people often have much to learn about relationships and about themselves. While this open environment encourages communication, it also allows for an alarming level of sexual violence. Studies in the U.S. estimate that one in six college women will be raped before she graduates. It is difficult to make estimates for Canada because of the limited amount of research on university date rape done in this country. What is known is that university men who abuse their dates do so, quite often, with the support of male friends who encourage and legitimate female victimization (DeKeseredy and Hinch, 1991:53–55)

To eliminate sexual violence we must begin by exposing the myths about rape. In addition, the campus must be transformed so that women and men interact with dignity and equality. Serious questions surround the role of alcohol in campus social life and the effect of traditional cultural patterns that define sex as a sport. To address the crisis of date rape, everyone needs to understand two simple truths: forcing sex without a woman's consent constitutes rape, and when a woman says "no," she means just that.

SOURCES: Gibbs (1991a, 1991b); DeKeseredy and Hinch (1991).

Age

Official crime rates rise sharply during adolescence and the early twenties, falling thereafter (Giffen, 1976; Hirschi & Gottfredson, 1983; Krisberg & Schwartz, 1983; Correctional Services Canada, 1991). Although people between the ages of twelve and twenty-four represent about 20 percent of the population, they account for about 60 percent of the people charged with property crimes and 35 percent of those charged with violent crimes. In contrast, those over 45 years of age make up about 32 percent of the population, but are responsible for only 5 percent of the property crime and 10 percent of violent crime. Crime rates are highest in the teen years and generally decline thereafter. Not suprisingly, 20- to 34-year-olds make up 25 percent of the Canadian population and 62 percent of the inmates in our prisons.

Gender

Official statistics suggest that the vast majority of crime is committed by males. Although each sex constitutes roughly half the population, males are much more likely than females to be arrested for serious crimes. In Canada, about 85 to 90 percent of arrests involve males and, once one gets behind prison walls, one finds that about 97 percent of the inmates are male. Although some research suggests that the criminal disparity between the sexes diminishes in the lower social classes, the overall pattern of female underrepresentation is striking (Hagan, Gillis, & Simpson, 1985). The proportion of females among those arrested is always low but varies considerably from one country to another: one study found Finland with a low of 6.7 percent, Canada at 9.8, the U.S. at 13.7 and New Zealand at 20.5 (Simon and Sharma, 1979).

Some of this gender difference stems from the reluctance of law enforcement officials to define women as criminals. Despite this, the arrest rate for women has been increasing in the United States, perhaps as a result of increasing sexual equality: between 1981 and 1990, it increased by 48.4 percent for women compared to 27.4 percent for men (U.S. Federal Bureau of Investigation, 1991). In addition, girls and boys display comparable patterns of delinquency in families where females and males are treated with relative equality (Hagan, Simpson, & Gillis, 1987).

Social Class

Although people commonly associate criminality with poverty, sociological research suggests that rich and

In Saudi Arabia, women cannot vote, drive a car, or appear in public without being veiled. Given this rigid regulation, crimes by women are rare. In Western societies, women have much more freedom over what they do and how they dress. This greater freedom is reflected in crime rates that are steadily moving closer to those of men. Even so, women have less power and remain subject to more extensive social control than men.

poor alike commit crimes, albeit somewhat different *kinds* of offenses. People arrested for violent and property crimes in North America and elsewhere disproportionately have low social standing (Wolfgang, Figlio, & Sellin, 1972; Clinard & Abbott, 1973; Elliott & Ageton, 1980; Braithwaite, 1981; Thornberry & Farnsworth, 1982; Wolfgang, Thornberry, & Figlio, 1987). Here the difference partly reflects the historical tendency to view poor people as less worthy or trustworthy than those whose wealth and power confers on them "respectability" (Tittle & Villemez, 1977; Tittle, Villemez, & Smith, 1978; Elias, 1986). Even the *strain* theory discussed above contributes to the expectation that more law-breakers will come from our less affluent neighborhoods. Police officers, then, are conditioned to focus their search for crime and its perpetrators in the poor sections of town rather than in the pristine office towers of business and government where embezzlement, insider trading, and bid-rigging occur.

The evidence also suggests that street crime disproportionately *victimizes* people of lower social position. Violent crime in particular is commonplace among the small number of chronically poor people living in inner-city neighborhoods—or in our isolated native communities. But only a small proportion of less advantaged people are ever convicted of crimes; most crimes are committed by relatively few hard-core offenders (Wolfgang, Figlio, & Sellin, 1972; Elliott & Ageton, 1980; Wolfgang, Thornberry, & Figlio, 1987; Harries, 1990). Additionally, as John Braithwaite notes, the connection between social standing and criminality "depends entirely on what form of crime one is talking about" (1981:47). If the definition of crime is expanded beyond street crime to include white-collar crime, the average "common criminal" has a much higher social position.

Race

Probing the relationship between race and criminality, we confront a raft of complex issues. Just as most people have long considered criminality the province of the poor, they have also associated crime with people of color. This despite clear evidence that most crimes are committed by whites.

In Canada, blacks and particularly Native people are arrested in disproportionate numbers. The effect of these arrest rates is apparent in the racial composition of our prison inmates; roughly 1 percent of Canada's population is black while this is true of 3.8 percent of federal inmates; aboriginals make up about 2 percent of

the population and 11.3 percent of the inmates (Correctional Service of Canada, 1991). This pattern is even more pronounced among female prisoners, where 8.8 percent are black and 15.4 percent are aboriginal. More disturbing yet is the observation that, in the prairie provinces, where natives make up about 6 percent of the population, 36 and 47 percent of male and female inmates in federal prisons are aboriginal. The overrepresentation of native people in provincial prisons is even more pronounced.

To the degree that prejudice related to color prompts police to arrest natives and blacks more readily than whites, and leads white citizens more readily to report members of these visible minorities to police as potential offenders, they are overly criminalized. The same prejudices may work in the courtroom. In the long run, even small biases by law enforcement officials and the public substantially distort the official link between race and crime (Liska & Tausig, 1979; Unnever, Frazier, & Henretta, 1980; Smith & Visher, 1981).

Second, race in Canada closely relates to social standing, which, as we have already shown, affects the likelihood of engaging in street crimes. Several researchers claim that membership in lower-class gangs promotes criminality. American sociologists Judith and Peter Blau (1982) take a different tack, suggesting that criminality—especially violent crime—is promoted by income disparity. That is, the Blaus argue that criminality is caused less by deviant subcultures than by the sting of poverty in the midst of affluence. Suffering the hardships of poverty in a rich society encourages people to perceive society as unjust and to disregard its laws. Because unemployment among African-American adults is two to three times higher than among whites, and because *almost half* of black children grow up in poverty (in contrast to about one in six white American children), we should expect proportionately higher crime rates for African Americans (Sampson, 1987). Research suggests that rigid systems of social inequality in other societies generate similar patterns of criminality (Messner, 1989). Since Canada's aboriginal population in particular is in economic circumstances very similar to those of American blacks (see Chapter 10, "Social Class in Canada"; Gerber, 1990), its higher crime rates are not surprising.

Crime statistics tend to be biased against reporting white-collar crimes. In the U.S., these are excluded from the official crime index. While the Canadian statistics do include fraud and "theft over $1000" (no "theft over $2 million" category) among property crimes, otherwise we, too, fail to identify typical white-collar crimes.

Clearly, this omission contributes to the view of the typical criminal as not simply poor but a person of color. If our definition of crime were broadened to include insider stock trading, toxic-waste dumping, embezzlement, bribery, and cheating on income tax returns, the proportion of white (and affluent) criminals would rise dramatically.

Crime in Global Perspective

By world standards, the United States stands out as having a lot of crime. Global comparisons fall short because nations define crimes differently and not every country collects data with care, but rough comparisons suggest that the homicide rate in the United States stands 3.3 times higher than in Canada and five times higher than that in Europe, and the rape rate 2.6 times higher (seven times Europe's). Figure 8-3 graphically illustrates global comparisons for rape and robbery. Although the patterns differ for each crime, we can conclude from these figures that Canada's rates, while lower than those in the U.S., are at the higher end of the range recorded for the other countries and that the United States contends with more crime than virtually any other country in the world (Kalish, 1988). New York City led all U.S. cities with 2,245 murders in 1990. Canada as a whole, with almost four times the population of New York City, had 656.

Why does the U.S. have such high crime rates? Elliot Currie (1985) suggests that the problem stems from its cultural emphasis on individual economic success, frequently at the expense of family and community cohesion. Currie also notes that, unlike European nations, the United States neither guarantees families a minimum income nor publicly funds childcare programs. Such public policy decisions, he claims, erode the fabric of society, fuel frustration among society's have-nots, and thus encourage criminal behavior. Furthermore, Currie asserts that the high level of unemployment and underemployment tolerated in the United States helps create a category of perpetually poor people whose opportunities to make money are often limited to criminal pursuits. The key to reducing crime, then, lies in *social change*, not in hiring more police and building more prisons. Canada falls between Europe and the United States in the provision of social services and income support, but in recent years our "safety nets" have become increasingly frayed. According to Currie's reasoning, we can expect rising crime rates.

Another contributing factor to the relatively high level of violence in the United States is widespread private ownership of guns. About 60 percent of the 20,000 murder victims each year in the United States are killed by guns. In recent years, the proliferation of high-powered, military-type weaponry has prompted police organizations and citizens' groups to press for gun control. The Brady Bill, passed in 1981, requires a seven-day waiting period for the purchase of handguns. No one thinks reining in the gun trade will end crime, for there are already as many guns in the hands of private individuals as there are people in the United States. Further, Elliot Currie argues that the causes of violence go far beyond the availability of guns. He notes that the number of Californians killed each year *by knives alone* exceeds the number of Canadians killed by weapons of all kinds. Most experts do think, however, that gun control would curb the level of violence.

Available evidence indicates that crime rates are skyrocketing in the largest cities of the world—cities like Sao Paulo, Brazil, where the population is soaring and most people are desperately poor. By and large, however, crime rates in less developed countries are lower than in Canada and the United States. Some

There are enough guns in the United States to arm every woman, man, and child; about half of all households contain one or more weapons of this kind. Guns are not the key to that country's high crime rate, since unarmed criminality in the United States is also high by world standards. But the ready availability of guns does contribute to accidental shootings—especially by children—and it also raises the risk that interpersonal violence will be deadly.

countries have high rates of violence (Columbia's recent drug war stands out), but the rates of property crime in North America dwarf those of most poor nations. Their lower crime rates reflect the traditional character of nonindustrial societies; there, strong families and cohesive residential neighborhoods informally control crime (Clinard & Abbott, 1973; *Der Spiegel*, 1989). By the same token, however, traditional social patterns promote a crime like prostitution by sharply limiting the opportunities available to women. Global Map 8-1 on page 234 shows the extent of prostitution in various world regions.

FIGURE 8-3   GLOBAL COMPARISONS: RATES FOR RAPE AND ROBBERY
SOURCE: Interpol data, as reported by Kalish, 1988.

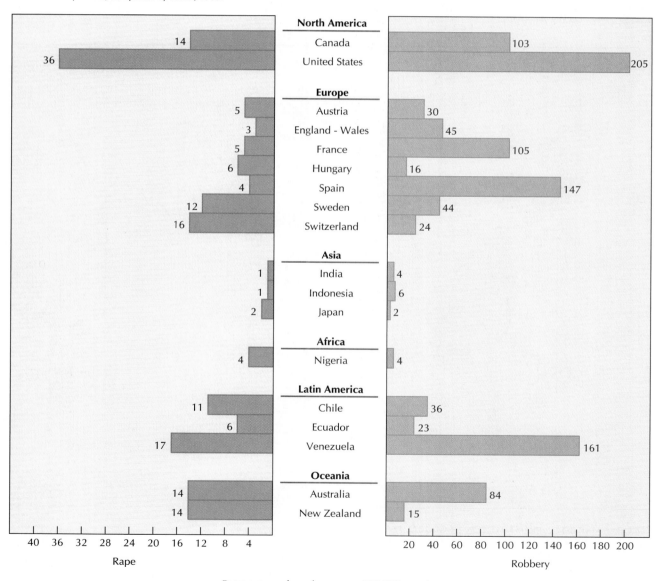

	Rape	Robbery
North America		
Canada	14	103
United States	36	205
Europe		
Austria	5	30
England - Wales	3	45
France	5	105
Hungary	6	16
Spain	4	147
Sweden	12	44
Switzerland	16	24
Asia		
India	1	4
Indonesia	1	6
Japan	2	2
Africa		
Nigeria	4	4
Latin America		
Chile	11	36
Ecuador	6	23
Venezuela	17	161
Oceania		
Australia	14	84
New Zealand	14	15

Rates are number of cases per 100,000 people

The Criminal Justice System

Through the criminal justice system, society formally responds to crime. We shall briefly introduce the key elements of this system: police, the courts, and the punishment of convicted offenders.

Police

The police generally serve as the point of contact between the public and the criminal justice system. In principle, the police maintain public order by uniformly enforcing the law. Since Canada's police officers

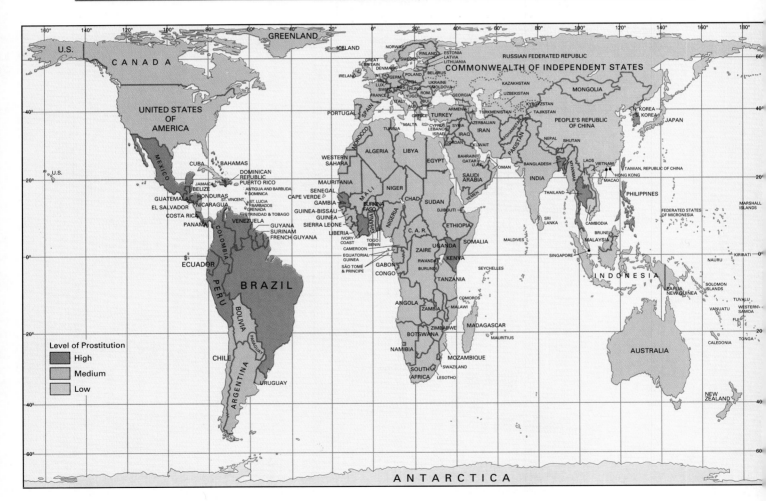

WINDOW ON THE WORLD

GLOBAL MAP 8-1   PROSTITUTION IN GLOBAL PERSPECTIVE
Roughly speaking, prostitution is widespread in societies of the world where women have low social standing in relation to men. Officially, at least, the now defunct socialist regimes in Eastern Europe and the Soviet Union, as well as the People's Republic of China, boasted of gender equality, including the elimination of "vice" such as prostitution. By contrast, in much of Latin America, a region of pronounced patriarchy, prostitution is commonplace. In many Islamic societies, where patriarchy is also strong, religious forces temper this practice. Western industrial societies also display a moderate amount of prostitution.

(1 per 475 people) cannot effectively monitor their entire populations, the police exercise considerable discretion about which situations warrant their attention and how to handle them.

Police discretion is a two-edged sword. On the one hand, police officers must have a good deal of latitude in decision making because of the magnitude of police responsibilities. On the other hand, however, the ability of police to pursue a situation as they see fit also fosters unequal treatment of some categories of people, as suggested by a number of incidents in Toronto and Montreal where black men (and sometimes youths) have been shot by police officers.

How, then, do police carry out their duties? In a study of police behavior in five U.S. cities, Douglas Smith and Christy Visher (1981; Smith, 1987) concluded that, because they must often act quickly, police rely on external cues to guide their actions. These researchers identified six factors that affect police when confronted with apparent crime. First, the more serious they perceive the situation to be, the more likely they are to make an arrest. Second, police assess the victim's preference as to how the matter should be handled. If a victim demands that police make an arrest, they are likely to do so. Third, police more often arrest suspects who appear uncooperative. Fourth, they are more likely to arrest suspects with whom they have had prior contact, presumably because this suggests guilt. Fifth, the presence of bystanders increases the likelihood of arrest. According to Smith and Visher, the presence of observers prompts police to act assertively because they want to appear in control of the situation, and also because an arrest moves the interaction from the street (the suspect's turf) to the police department (where law officers have the edge). Sixth, all else being equal, police are more likely to arrest people of color than whites. Smith and Visher concluded that this perception contributes to the disproportionately high arrest rates among these categories of people.

Finally, the greater numbers of police relative to population are found in cities with two key characteristics: high concentrations of minorities and large income disparities between rich and poor (Jacobs, 1979). This finding squares with Judith and Peter Blau's (1982) conclusion that striking inequality promotes criminal violence. Thus, the Northwest Territories and the Yukon have both the highest rates of violent crime (see Canada Map 8-1) and the largest numbers of police officers relative to their populations (one officer per 229 and 230 residents respectively in 1991). The higher crime rates in these areas may be partly alcohol-related and generated by underdevelopment or social disorganization: they may also reflect bias in police surveillance, arrests, and convictions as well as an emphasis upon crime control and law enforcement rather than crime prevention (LaPrairie, 1983; Depew, 1992). Thus police form an imposing presence where a volatile mix of social forces encourages social disruption.

Courts

After arrest, a suspect's guilt or innocence is determined by a court. In principle, our courts rely on an adversarial process involving attorneys—who represent the defendant on the one side and the Crown on the other—in the presence of a judge who monitors adherence to legal procedures. In practice, however, a large percentage of criminal cases are resolved prior to court appearance through **plea bargaining**, *a legal negotiation in which the prosecution reduces a defendant's charge in exchange for a guilty plea.* For example, a defendant charged with burglary may agree to plead guilty to the lesser charge of possession of burglary tools; another charged with selling cocaine may go along with pleading guilty to possession.

Plea bargaining has gained widespread acceptance because it spares the judicial system the time and expense of court trials. A trial is usually unnecessary if there is little disagreement as to the facts of the case. By selectively trying only a small proportion of the cases, the courts can also channel their resources into those deemed most important (Reid, 1991).

But in the process, defendants (who are presumed innocent) are pressured to plead guilty. A person can exercise the right to a trial, but only at the risk of receiving a more severe sentence if found guilty. In essence, then, plea bargaining undercuts the right of defendants as it circumvents the adversarial process. According to Abraham Blumberg (1970), defendants who have little understanding of the criminal justice system, as well as those unable to afford a good lawyer, are likely to suffer from this system of "bargain-counter justice."

Punishment

In 1831 the officials in an English town hanged a nine-year-old boy who was found guilty of the crime of setting fire to a house (Kittrie, 1971:103). The history of the United States records 281 youths executed for crimes committed as juveniles, and twenty-seven more are currently on death row, awaiting a Supreme Court decision on whether their ages should preclude their executions (Rosenbaum, 1989).

Canada, which had its last execution in 1962 and abolished the death penalty in 1976, has decided that young people under eighteen years of age have a *diminished capacity* for crime. Under our Young Offenders Act (operative since 1985), the minimum age for prosecution is twelve years: those twelve to seventeen years of age are tried according to criminal law, but in youth court. At no time is the identity of the young person to

be published, sentencing is normally limited to two years (three as a "life" sentence equivalent), incarceration is seen as the last resort, and the detention centers themselves are comfortable (Carrigan, 1991).

Clearly, approaches to punishment have changed over time and vary from country to country. Debate about the appropriateness of specific punishments as applied to adults and to juvenile offenders in particular raises the question of why societies punish in the first place. Four justifications of punishment are commonly advanced.

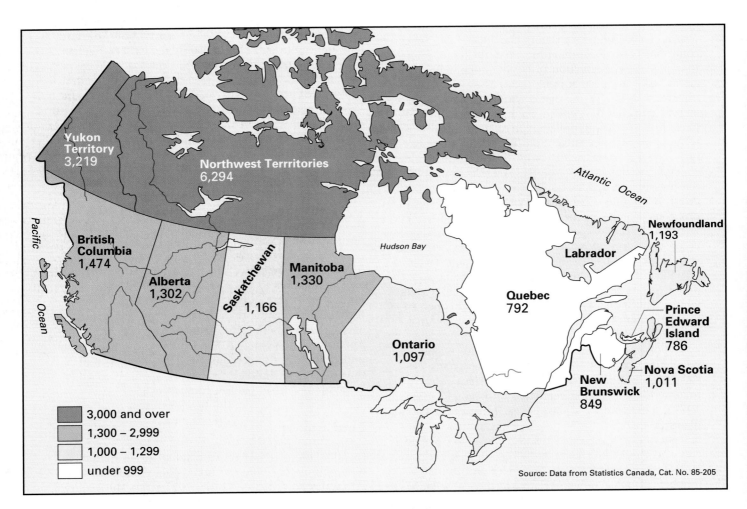

CANADA MAP 8-1   VIOLENT CRIME RATES (PER 100,000 POPULATION, 1991)

Retribution

The celebrated justice of the U.S. Supreme Court, Oliver Wendell Holmes, stated that "The first requirement of a sound body of law is that it should correspond with the actual feelings and demands of the community." Because people react to crime with a passion for revenge, Holmes continued, "the law has no choice but to satisfy [that] craving" (cited in Carlson, 1976).

From this point of view, punishment satisfies a society's need for **retribution**, *an act of moral vengeance by which society subjects an offender to suffering comparable to that caused by the offense.* Retribution is based on a view of society as a system of moral balance. When criminality upsets this balance, punishment exacted in comparable measure restores the moral order, as suggested in the biblical dictum "An eye for an eye."

Retribution stands as the oldest justification for punishment. During the Middle Ages, crime was widely viewed as sin—an offense against God as well as society—therefore warranting harsh punishment. Although sometimes criticized today because it overlooks the issue of reforming the offender, retribution remains a strong justification for punishment.

Deterrence

A second justification for punishment, **deterrence**, amounts to *the attempt to discourage criminality through punishment.* Punishment may deter in two ways. *Specific deterrence* demonstrates to an individual offender that crime does not pay. Through *general deterrence*, the punishment of one person serves as an example to others.

Deterrence is based on the Enlightenment notion that humans are calculating and rational creatures. From this point of view, people engage in deviance for personal gain, but if they think that the pain of punishment outweighs the pleasure of mischief, they will forgo temptation.

Initially, deterrence was instituted to reform a system of excessive punishments based on retribution. Why put someone to death for stealing, for example, if that crime could be discouraged with a prison sentence? As the concept of deterrence became better accepted, execution and physical mutilation of criminals were replaced by milder forms of punishment such as incarceration.

As shown in Figure 8-4, the use of imprisonment varies dramatically between countries. The U.S. has by far the highest level of incarceration at 426 per 100,000

Dutch painter Vincent Van Gogh (1853–1890) strongly identified with suffering people that he found around him. Perhaps this is why he included his own likeness in this portrait of the dungeon-like prisons of the nineteenth century. Since then, the stark isolation and numbing depersonalization of prison life has changed little. Prisons are still custodial institutions in which officials make few efforts at rehabilitation.

Vincent Van Gogh, 1853–1890. Prisoners' Round. Dutch, Pushkin State Museum, Moscow.

population; Canada with a much lower rate of 113 is still far ahead of most European countries.

Rehabilitation

The third justification for punishment, **rehabilitation**, involves *reforming the offender to preclude subsequent offenses.* Rehabilitation paralleled the development of the social sciences in the nineteenth century. According to early social analysts, crime and other deviance sprang from an unfavorable social environment, one pervaded by poverty or a lack of parental supervision, for example. Defenders of rehabilitation argued that, just as offenders learn to be deviant, they learn to obey the rules if placed in the right setting. *Reformatories* or

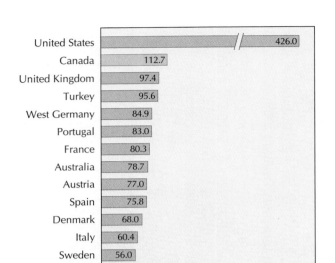

Country	Rate
United States	426.0
Canada	112.7
United Kingdom	97.4
Turkey	95.6
West Germany	84.9
Portugal	83.0
France	80.3
Australia	78.7
Austria	77.0
Spain	75.8
Denmark	68.0
Italy	60.4
Sweden	56.0
Norway	48.4
The Netherlands	40.0

Rate per 100,000 total population

FIGURE 8-4   RATES OF IMPRISONMENT IN SELECTED COUNTRIES: A COMPARISON
SOURCE: Correctional Service of Canada, Basic Facts About Corrections in Canada, 1991.

houses of correction, therefore, afforded offenders a controlled environment that might help them learn proper behavior (recall the description of total institutions in Chapter 5, "Socialization").

Rehabilitation resembles deterrence because it motivates the offender to conform to societal norms. But rehabilitation emphasizes constructive improvement while deterrence and retribution simply make the offender suffer. In addition, while retribution demands that the punishment fit the crime, rehabilitation focuses on the distinctive problems of each offender. Thus identical offenses might prompt similar acts of retribution, but different programs of rehabilitation. In Canada, rehabilitation is given high priority.

Social Protection

A final justification for punishment, **social protection**, refers to *rendering an offender incapable of further offenses either temporarily during a period of incarceration or permanently by execution.* One of the concerns expressed by the Canadian public is that dangerous offenders are given "life" sentences and then released on parole. After the murder of her daughter, Nina, in Burlington, Ontario, Priscilla DeVilliers has been

involved in a massive campaign to have parole and bail restricted for dangerous offenders. Her campaign has touched a responsive cord in an apprehensive public that does not feel adequately protected at present. When a dangerous man like Clifford Olson is granted early release and kills eleven young people, as he did in British Columbia in 1980–81, people question the level of social protection afforded them.[3]

Table 8-3 summarizes these four justifications of punishment.

Critical evaluation.   We have identified four aims of punishment. Assessing the actual consequences of punishment, however, is no simple task.

The value of retribution relates to Durkheim's ideas about the functions of deviance, presented earlier in this chapter. Recall that Durkheim believed that

TABLE 8-3	FOUR JUSTIFICATIONS OF PUNISHMENT: A SUMMARY
Retribution	The oldest justification of punishment that remains important today. Punishment is atonement for a moral wrong by an individual; in principle, punishment should be comparable in severity to the deviance itself.
Deterrence	An early modern approach, deviance is viewed as social disruption, which society acts to control. People are viewed as rational and self-interested, so that deterrence requires that the pains of punishment outweigh the pleasures of deviance.
Rehabilitation	A modern approach linked to the development of the social sciences, deviance is viewed as the product of social problems (such as poverty) or of personal problems (such as mental illness). Social conditions are improved and offenders subjected to intervention appropriate to their condition.
Social protection	A modern approach easier to effect than rehabilitation. If society is unable or unwilling to improve offenders or reform social conditions, protection from further deviance is afforded by incarceration or execution.

[3] At the time of Olson's release in 1980, he had not been serving a prison sentence for murder. He is now serving the maximum sentence of twenty-five years without the possibility of parole. He can expect to be released in the year 2007, when he is 67 years old. Peter Worthington has written about the 1980–81 murders of which Olson was convicted, as well as about many others he claims to have committed, in *Saturday Night* (July/August 1993).

responding to deviance increases people's awareness of shared morality. Punishing a person for a moral offense, moreover, draws together disparate members of society by reinforcing a shared sense of justice. For this reason punishment was traditionally carried out in public. Public executions occurred in England until 1868; the last public execution in the United States took place in Kentucky in 1936. Today the mass media ensure public awareness of executions carried out inside prison walls (Kittrie, 1971). Despite this publicity, it is difficult to prove scientifically that punishment upholds social morality.

To some degree, punishment serves as a specific deterrent. Yet our society also has a high rate of **criminal recidivism**, *subsequent offenses by people previously convicted of crimes.* Various studies of people released from prison showing that, substantial percentages have been rearrested and returned to prison within a few years raise questions about the extent to which punishment actually deters crime. In addition, only about one-third of all crimes are reported to police, and of these, only about one in five results in an arrest. The old adage that "crime doesn't pay" rings rather hollow when we consider that only a small proportion of offenses ever result in punishment.

General deterrence is even more difficult to investigate scientifically, since we have no way of knowing how people might act if they were unaware of punishments meted out to others. In the debate over capital punishment, critics of the practice point to the fact that the United States has a very high homicide rate despite the fact that it is the only Western industrial society that routinely executes serious offenders (Sellin, 1980; van den Haag & Conrad, 1983; Lester, 1987; Archer & Gartner, 1987; Bailey & Peterson, 1989; Bailey, 1990; Bohm, 1991). Furthermore, an examination of the Canadian homicide rates compiled by Lenton (1989) from 1954 to 1986 reveals no sudden increase in homicide rates either after 1962 when the last executions occurred or after 1976 when capital punishment was abolished: in fact, the rate went down for a few years after 1976.

Efforts at rehabilitation have sparked controversy as well. Prisons accomplish short-term social protection by keeping offenders off the streets, but they do very little to reshape attitudes or behavior in the long term. For this reason, penologists concede that prisons do not rehabilitate inmates (Carlson, 1976). Perhaps this is to be expected, since according to Sutherland's theory of differential association, placing a person among criminals for a long period of time should simply strengthen that person's criminal attitudes and skills. Prisons also tolerate a destructive level of physical and sexual violence. And because incarceration severs whatever social ties an inmate may have in the outside world, individuals may be prone to further crime upon their release, consistent with Hirschi's control theory. Finally, inmates returning to the surrounding world contend with the stigma of being ex-convicts, often an obstacle to successful integration in the larger society.

Ultimately, we should not assume that the criminal justice system can eliminate crime. The reason, echoed throughout this chapter, is simple: crime and deviance are more than simply the acts of "bad people": they are bound up inextricably in the operation of society itself.

Summary

1. Deviance refers to norm violations that span a wide range, from mild breaches of etiquette to serious violence.

2. Biological explanations of crime, from Lombroso's research in the nineteenth century to developing research in human genetics, has yet to produce much insight into the causes of crime.

3. Psychological explanations of deviance focus on abnormalities in the individual personality, which arise from either biological origins or the social environment. Psychological theories help to explain some kinds of deviance.

4. Social forces produce nonconformity because deviance (1) exists in relation to cultural norms, (2) involves a process of social definition, and (3) is shaped by the distribution of social power.

5. Sociology links deviance to the operation of society rather than the deficiencies of individuals. Using the structural-functional paradigm, Durkheim identified several functions of deviance for society as a whole.

6. The symbolic-interaction paradigm is the basis of labeling theory, which holds that deviance arises in the reaction of some audience to a person's

behavior. Labeling theory focuses on secondary deviance and deviant careers, which result from acquiring the stigma of deviance.

7. Social-conflict theory directs attention to the relationship between deviance and patterns of social inequality. Following the approach of Karl Marx, this paradigm holds that laws and other norms reflect the interests of the most powerful people in society. Social-conflict theory also spotlights white-collar crimes that cause extensive social harm, although the offenders are rarely defined as criminals.

8. Official statistics indicate that arrest rates peak in adolescence, then drop steadily with advancing age. Males are arrested more often than females for serious street crimes. Three-fourths of property crime arrests are of males, as are almost nine of ten arrests for violent crimes.

9. People of lower social position tend to commit more street crime than those with greater social privilege. When white-collar crimes are included among criminal offenses, however, the disparity in overall criminal activity diminishes.

10. The police exercise considerable discretion in their work. Research suggests that factors such as the seriousness of the offense, the presence of bystanders, and the race and sex of the suspect make arrest more likely.

11. Although ideally an adversarial system, our courts routinely resolve cases through plea bargaining. An efficient method of handling cases where the facts are not in dispute, plea bargaining nevertheless places less powerful people at a disadvantage.

12. Punishment has been justified in terms of retribution, deterrence, rehabilitation, and social protection. Because its consequences are difficult to evaluate scientifically, punishment—like deviance itself—sparks considerable controversy among sociologists and the public as a whole.

Key Concepts

crime the violation of norms formally enacted into criminal law

criminal justice system a formal system that responds to alleged violations of the law using police, courts, and punishment

criminal recidivism subsequent offenses by people previously convicted of crimes

deterrence the attempt to discourage criminality through punishment

deviance the recognized violation of cultural norms

juvenile delinquency the violation of legal standards by the young

labeling theory the assertion that deviance and conformity result from the response of others

medicalization of deviance the transformation of moral and legal issues into medical matters

plea bargaining a legal negotiation in which the prosecution reduces a defendant's charge in exchange for a guilty plea

property crimes crimes that involve theft of property belonging to others

rehabilitation reforming the offender to preclude subsequent offenses

retribution an act of moral vengeance by which society subjects an offender to suffering comparable to that caused by the offense

retrospective labeling the interpretation of someone's past consistent with present deviance

social protection rendering an offender incapable of further offenses either temporarily during a period of incarceration or permanently by execution

stigma a powerfully negative social label that radically changes a person's self-concept and social identity

victimless crimes violations of law in which there are no readily apparent victims

violent crimes crimes against people that involve violence or the threat of violence

white-collar crime crimes committed by people of high social position in the course of their occupations

Suggested Readings

These three books are valuable efforts to incorporate gender into the study of deviance. The first explains how women have virtually been ignored up to the present in studies of crime; the second applies labeling theory to gender issues: the third looks at women as victims.

Eileen B. Leonard. *Women, Crime and Society: A Critique of Theoretical Criminology*. New York: Longman, 1982.

Edwin M. Schur. *Labeling Women Deviant: Gender, Stigma, and Social Control*. Philadelphia: Temple University Press, 1983.

Walter S. DeKeseredy & Ronald Hinch. *Woman Abuse: Sociological Perspectives*. Toronto: Thompson Educational Publishing, 1991.

These two books present the history and many contemporary controversies surrounding crime and punishment in Canada and the United States.

Charles W. Thomas. *Corrections in America: Problems of the Past and the Present*. Newbury Park, CA: Sage, 1987.

D. Owen Carrigan. *Crime and Punishment in Canada: A History*. Toronto: McClelland and Stewart, 1991

This book offers eight essays dealing with the death penalty.

Robert M. Bohm. *The Death Penalty in America: Current Research*. Cincinnati, OH: Anderson Publishing, 1991.

This sociological account of mental illness delves into who in the United States is affected by such conditions and the social role of the mental patient.

Bernard J. Gallagher III. *The Sociology of Mental Illness*. 3rd ed. Englewood Cliffs, NJ: Prentice Hall, 1991.

Most research about youth gangs is by and about men. Anne Campbell provides a rare and insightful account of young women in New York street gangs.

Anne Campbell. *The Girls in the Gang*. 2nd ed. Cambridge, MA: Basil Blackwell, 1991.

A critical review of the case linking the XYY chromosome to crime is found in Chapter 6 of this study of the ethical consequences of human biology.

David Suzuki and Peter Knudtson. *Genethics: The Clash Between the New Genetics and Human Values*. Cambridge, MA: Harvard University Press, 1989.

This book shows the relativity of deviance, illustrating the extent to which the definition of deviant behavior varies with time and across cultures.

Robert B. Edgerton. *Deviance: A Cross-Cultural Perspective*. Menlo Park, California: Cummings, 1976.

CHAPTER 9

SOCIAL STRATIFICATION

On April 10, 1912, the ocean liner *Titanic* left the docks of Southampton, England, on its maiden voyage across the North Atlantic to New York.[1] A proud symbol of the new industrial age, the towering ship carried 2,300 passengers, some enjoying more luxury than most travelers today could imagine. Crowded into the lower decks, however, were poor immigrants, journeying to what they hoped would be a better life in North America.

On April 14, the crew received reports of icebergs in the area but paid little notice. Then, near midnight, as the ship steamed swiftly and silently westward, a lookout was stunned to see a massive shape rising out of the dark ocean directly ahead. Moments later, the ship collided with a huge iceberg, almost as tall as the *Titanic* itself, which opened the starboard side of the ship as if it were a giant tin can. Sea water exploded into the vessel's lower levels, and within twenty-five minutes people were crowding into the lifeboats. By 2 A.M. the bow of the *Titanic* was submerged and the stern reared high above the water. There on the deck,

silently observed by those in the lifeboats, stood hundreds of helpless passengers solemnly passing their final minutes before the ship disappeared into the frigid Atlantic (Lord, 1976).

The tragic loss of more than 1,600 lives shocked the world. Looking back dispassionately at this terrible incident with a sociological eye, however, we see that some categories of passengers had much better odds of survival than others. Of those holding first-class tickets, more than 60 percent were saved, primarily because they were on the upper decks, where warnings were sounded first and lifeboats were accessible. Only 36 percent of the second-class passengers survived, and of the third-class passengers on the lower decks, only 24 percent escaped drowning. On board the *Titanic*, class turned out to mean much more than the quality of accommodations: it was truly a matter of life or death.

The fate of the *Titanic* dramatically illustrates the consequences of social inequality for the ways people live—and sometimes whether they live at all. This chapter introduces a number of sociological ideas concerning social stratification. Chapter 10 continues the story by examining social inequality in Canada, and Chapter 11 explores where our society fits into a global system of wealth and poverty.

---

[1] This opening is adapted from a news feature by Mike Harden (1989).

What Is Social Stratification?

For tens of thousands of years, all of humanity was divided into small hunting and gathering societies. Although one person might enjoy praise from others for being swifter, stronger, or more skillful in collecting food, everyone had more or less the same social standing. As societies became more complex—a process detailed in Chapter 4 ("Society")—a monumental change came about. Entire categories of people came to enjoy more money, schooling, health, and power than others.

Such social inequality is not simply due to the varying abilities and efforts of people themselves. Rather, sociologists document that patterns of this kind reflect how societies produce and distribute valued resources. Sociologists use the concept **social stratification** to refer to *a system by which a society ranks categories of people in a hierarchy*. Social stratification is a matter of four fundamental principles.

1. *Social stratification is a characteristic of society, not simply a function of individual differences.* Social inequality stands as a basic dimension of how a society is organized. Sociologists try to identify ways people are unequal and to measure how unequal they are. Further, basic patterns of inequality—whether societies are divided into peasants and landlords, whether most people believe they share in a society's bounty, or whether the poor are few in number or legion—differ according to time and place. How people understand their social position also varies. In some societies, people attribute their standing simply to their birth; in others, individuals speak of social position as their "achievement," thought to reflect personal efforts and abilities. A focus on achievement characterizes industrial societies such as Canada and the United States, although people typically exaggerate its importance.

    Did a higher percentage of the first-class passengers on the *Titanic* survive because they were smarter or better swimmers than second- and third-class passengers? Hardly. They fared better because of their privileged position on the ship. Similarly, children born into wealthy families are more likely than those born into poverty to enjoy health, achieve academically, succeed in their life's work, and to live well into old age. Neither rich nor poor people are responsible for creating social stratification, yet this system shapes the lives of them all.

2. *Social stratification persists over generations.* To understand that stratification stems from society rather than growing out of individual differences, note how it persists over time. Social position is closely linked to the family, so that children assume the social positions of their parents. In agrarian societies, the vast majority of people spend their entire lives at one social level, as their children do after them. In industrial societies, too, social position is initially ascribed, although it sometimes changes over time as a result of personal efforts or, occasionally, by sheer chance.

    The concept of **social mobility** refers to *changes in people's positions in a system of social stratification*. Social mobility may be *upward* or *downward*. Our society celebrates the achievements of a Wayne Gretsky, a Michael J. Fox, a Lincoln Alexander or an Ed Mirvish, all of whom rose to prominence from more modest beginnings. People may also move downward socially as a result of business setbacks, unemployment, or illness. Nevertheless, as explained in Chapter 10 ("Social Class in Canada"), dramatic changes in social position are uncommon: for most people, social standing remains much the same over a lifetime. Somewhat more common is *horizontal* social mobility by which people move from one occupation to another that is comparable.

Human beings feel directly and personally the effects of triumph or failure. This idea is captured in this haunting photograph, a universal portrait of suffering, by Sebastiao Salgado. The essential sociological insight is that, however strongly individuals feel its effects, social standing is largely a consequence of the way in which a society (or a world of societies) structures opportunity and reward. In short, we are all the products of social stratification.

3. *Social stratification is universal but variable.* Social stratification is found everywhere. At the same time, its character and extent vary widely from one society to another. Among the members of technologically primitive societies, social differentiation is minimal and based mostly on age and sex. As societies develop sophisticated technology for growing food, they also forge complex and more rigid systems for distributing what they produce. Industrialization has the effect of increasing social mobility, and of reducing at least some kinds of social inequality.

4. *Social stratification involves not just inequality but beliefs.* Any system of inequality not only confers more resources on some people than on others, but it also defines these arrangements as fair. Just as *what* is unequal differs from society to society, then, so does the justification for inequality—the explanation of *why* people should be unequal. Virtually everywhere, however, people with the greatest social privileges express the strongest support for their society's system of social stratification, while those with fewer social resources are more likely to challenge the system.

Caste and Class Systems

In describing social stratification in particular societies, sociologists often use two opposing standards: "closed" systems that allow little change in social position, and "open" systems that permit considerable social mobility (Tumin, 1985).

The Caste System

A **caste system** amounts to *social stratification based on ascription.* A pure caste system, in other words, is closed, with no social mobility at all; birth alone determines one's destiny. People living in caste systems usually define their precise social standing simply by indicating the category to which they belong.

Illustrations: India and South Africa

A number of the world's societies approximate caste systems, including traditional village life in India and South Africa's system of racial apartheid. In the Indian caste system, a person is born into one of several thousand subcaste groups, which rank people in relation to others in countless local communities. Race is the key to social ranking in South Africa. Of a total population of some 40 million, roughly one South African in eight (about 5 million people) is of European ancestry. Yet this white minority commands an overwhelming share of wealth and power. Representing three-fourths of South Africans, 30 million blacks have far fewer rights and privileges. In a middle position are another 3 million South Africans, known as "coloreds," who are of mixed race, along with about 1 million Asians. The box on pages 246–47 explores the current state of South African apartheid.

In a caste system, birth determines the fundamental shape of people's lives in three crucial respects. First, traditional caste groups are linked to occupation so that families in each ranking perform one type of work from generation to generation. Although some occupations (such as farming) are open to all, castes are socially identified with the work their members do (priests, barbers, leather workers, and so on). In South Africa, whites hold almost all the desirable jobs, while the black majority is primarily consigned to manual labor and other work in service to whites.

Second, a rigid system of social stratification would break down quickly if people married outside their own castes. In such cases, what rank would their children hold? To keep the hierarchy clear, then, caste systems mandate that people marry others of the same social ranking. Sociologists call this pattern *endogamous* marriage (*endo* stems from the Greek, meaning "within"). Tradition in India directs parents to select their children's marriage partners, often when the children are quite young. Among such families, instances of cross-caste marriage are rare; when they do occur, a female typically marries a male of a higher position (Srinivas, 1971). In South Africa, sexual relationships and marriage between the races have been banned by law; although these regulations were eased in 1985, interracial marriage remains relatively rare since racial categories continue to live in separate areas.

Third, powerful cultural beliefs underlie caste systems. In India, Hindu traditions define acceptance of one's social position and fate as a moral duty; therefore, people must carry out their life's work, whatever it may be. Caste systems are typical of agrarian societies, because such beliefs foster the habits of diligence and discipline that agriculture demands. The same logic helps explain why caste systems break down as societies industrialize. Much of the intense pressure to end the racial caste system in South Africa stems from the

CROSS-CULTURAL COMPARISON

South Africa: Race as Caste

At the southern tip of the African continent lies South Africa, a territory about the size of Ontario or Quebec, with a population of almost 40 million. Long inhabited by people of African descent, the region was colonized by Dutch traders in the mid-seventeenth century. Early in the nineteenth century, the descendants of these settlers from the Netherlands were pushed inland by a new wave of British colonization. By the beginning of this century, the British had gained control of the country, calling it the Union of South Africa. In 1961 the Republic of South Africa formally severed ties with the United Kingdom and became politically independent.

But freedom was a reality only for the white minority. To ensure their political control, the whites developed the policy of *apartheid*, or separation of the races. A common practice for many years, apartheid was enshrined in law in 1948 so that whites could deny the black majority South African citizenship, ownership of land, and any formal voice in the government.

Under this policy, blacks became a subordinate caste, receiving only the education needed to perform the low-paying jobs deemed inappropriate for whites. In this racial caste system, even white housewives of limited means became accustomed to having a black household servant. Under such conditions, blacks were able to earn, on average, only one-fourth of what whites received. A final plank in the platform of apartheid was the forcible resettlement of millions of blacks to so-called homelands, dirt-poor districts set aside by whites to confine and control blacks. The overall effect was devastating on the black majority. In a land rich with natural resources, most blacks lived close to abject poverty.

The prosperous white minority has traditionally defended its privileges by viewing blacks as social inferiors. Increasingly, however, whites have been forced to rely on a system of brutal military repression to maintain their power. Without formal rights, blacks suspected of opposing white rule have been subject to arbitrary arrest and indefinite detention.

Despite its severity, this repression has not kept blacks—and a grow-

ing number of sympathetic whites—from challenging apartheid. Violent confrontations have been frequent, especially among younger blacks impatient for political and economic opportunity. During the 1980s, Canada imposed severe economic sanctions on South Africa—in part because our prime minister, Brian Mulroney, took a special interest in the issue. Corporations in Canada, the U.S., and a number of other countries severed direct economic ties with South Africa. This foreign divestment has staggered the South African economy, hurting both blacks and whites in the process. But it has accomplished its primary objective: to pressure the Pretoria regime to make significant reforms and begin dismantling apartheid.

In 1984, South Africans of mixed race and Asians were granted a limited voice in government. Blacks have also won the right to form labor unions, and are now permitted to enter a number of occupations once restricted to whites, resulting in economic gains for some workers. The government has also extended property rights to all people. Additionally, officials have abolished a host of "petty apartheid" regulations that segregated blacks and whites in

inconsistency of categorical ranking with a more talent-based industrial economy.

Members of various castes are also constrained in their social ties by traditional beliefs. Hindu thought defines higher caste groups in India as ritually "pure," while lower caste groups are deemed "polluted." The ingrained belief that a member of a higher caste is defiled by contact with a member of a lower caste forces the two to keep their distance in all routine activities. In the same way, many white South Africans support apartheid, claiming they are morally superior to the black majority and, thus, justly dominate them.

Since the Industrial Revolution, beliefs that rank entire categories of people as "better" or "worse" than others have gradually lost their force. In India, for example, the Hindu caste system now holds little significance for most people in large cities as people exercise greater choice about their marriage partners and their work (Bahl, 1991). As later chapters explain, such traditional attitudes, now cast as various "isms"—racism, sexism, ageism—are increasingly denounced as unjust. Sixty years ago, India outlawed its caste system, although it remains deeply embedded in village life even today. And in South Africa, the gradual erosion of apartheid is under way—albeit at a pace that many find excruciatingly slow—in the face of condemnation of that system by almost every other industrial society in the world.

South African performer John Clegg has blended familiar rock and roll with traditional African music and dancing. For his efforts, the apartheid government banned him on the grounds that his work brought the races together. In the currently more liberal climate, however, Clegg has enjoyed unprecedented popularity.

public places, including beaches and hospitals. In 1990, the release from prison of Nelson Mandela and the legalization of the anti-apartheid African National Congress opened the political system and raised the hope for more basic change. And, in 1992, a majority of white voters in a national referendum endorsed the principle of bringing apartheid to an end.

The reforms to date have enraged traditionalists who charge the government is selling out white interests. But despite many significant changes, the basic structure of apartheid remains intact. Winning the legal right to own property means little to millions of blacks who barely make enough money to survive; opening hospitals to South Africans of every race amounts to an empty gesture for nonwhites who cannot afford to pay for medical care; opening the ranks of the professions to blacks offers little real opportunity to men and women with minimal schooling. The harsh reality is that more than one-third of all black adults cannot find any work at all and, by the government's own estimate, half of all blacks live in desperate conditions.

The worst off are those called *ukuhleleleka* in the Xhosa language, which means the marginal people. Some 7 million blacks fall into this category, living on the edge of society and on the edge of life itself. In Soweto-by-the-Sea, an idyllic-sounding community, thousands of people live crammed into shacks built of discarded material like packing cases, corrugated metal, cardboard, sheet-rock, and pieces of pipe. There is no electricity for lights or refrigeration; without plumbing, people use buckets to haul sewage; women line up awaiting their turn at a single tap that provides water for more than a thousand people. Jobs are hard to come by, partly because Ford and General Motors have closed their factories in nearby Port Elizabeth, and partly because people keep migrating to the town from regions where life is even worse. Those who can find work are lucky to earn $200 a month.

South Africa has made some real progress toward breaking down apartheid, and expressed its determination to do more. Under discussion now are plans for eventual power sharing among all people. Yet to those who struggle simply to survive, the pace of change is agonizingly slow. Until traditional notions about race are finally dispelled, and until the underlying problem of intense and persistent poverty is addressed, South Africa will remain a society divided.

SOURCES: Fredrickson (1981), Wren (1991), Contreras (1992), and various news reports.

The Class System

A caste system bolsters stable, agrarian life; industrial societies, by contrast, depend on individual initiative and the development of specialized talents. Industrialization does not abolish social inequality, but it does change its character from a caste system to a **class system**, *social stratification based on individual achievement.*

Social "classes" are not as rigidly defined as castes. As people gain schooling and develop their individual talents, they are likely to experience at least some social mobility in relation to their parents and siblings, blurring class distinctions. Social categories also break down as people immigrate from abroad or move from rural areas to industrialized cities, lured by better jobs, greater opportunities for education, and the promise of a brighter future (Lipset & Bendix, 1967; Cutright, 1968; Grey, 1972; Treiman, 1970). Movement of this kind not only contributes to social diversity in industrial societies, but it also stimulates social mobility as newcomers take low-paying jobs, typically pushing others up the social ladder (Tyree, Semyonov, & Hodge, 1979). Furthermore, industrial societies generally extend political rights more broadly (Glass, 1954; Blau & Duncan, 1967). In other words, while castes each have distinctive privileges and duties, everyone in a class system—in principle, at least—stands equal before the law.

The success of entrepreneurs such as Toronto's "Honest Ed" Mirvish— whose drive transformed a young man of modest background into a multi-millionaire, philanthropist, and patron of the arts—encourages us to think that personal merit is the key to improving one's social standing.

Class systems stand on a relatively new conception of fairness: that talent and effort, rather than birth, should determine social position. People tend to think of their careers as matters of individual achievement and choice, rather than a duty passed from generation to generation as members of caste systems do. Greater individuality also translates into more freedom in marriage, with parents and cultural traditions playing a lesser role in children's selections of their mates.

Greater freedom and mobility confer on members of class systems characteristically lower **status consistency**, *consistent standing across various dimensions of social inequality*. Linking social ranking to birth (as in caste systems) generates high status consistency, meaning that an individual has the same relative standing with regard to wealth, prestige, power, ritual purity, or other dimensions of difference. Class systems, with their greater social mobility, offer less status consistency. In Canada, some people with prestigious occupations (such as priests) accumulate little wealth and wield only moderate social power. Such inconsistencies make class boundaries less clear than those separating castes.

Caste and Class Together: Great Britain

There are no pure caste or class systems; in every society, social stratification involves some combination of these two forms. The mix of caste and class is most pronounced in societies in which centuries of agriculture have recently given way to industrialization. A case in point is England, a nation that weaves together traditional caste distinctions and modern class differences.

The Estate System

In the Middle Ages, social stratification in England (which, together with Wales, Scotland, and Northern Ireland, comprise today's United Kingdom of Great Britain and Northern Ireland) took the form of a caste-like system of three *estates*. A hereditary nobility, or *first estate*, accounted for only 5 percent of the population. These nobles maintained wealth and power through the ownership of land (Laslett, 1984). Typically, they had no occupation at all, for to be "engaged in trade" or any other type of work for income was deemed "beneath" them. Well tended by servants, nobles used their extensive leisure time to cultivate refined tastes in art, music, and literature.

Vast landholdings were preserved from generation to generation by the practice of *primogeniture* (from Latin meaning "first born"). This law mandated that property be passed to only the eldest son rather than divided among all children. Under this system, however, younger sons fared less well; typically, they were forced to find other ways to support themselves. Thus many nobles entered the clergy—the *second estate*—where spiritual power was supplemented by the church's extensive landholdings. Others became military officers, lawyers, or took up work that has come down to us today as "honorable" callings for "gentlemen." In an age when few women could expect to earn a living on their own, a daughter of the nobility depended for her security on marrying well.

Below the nobility and the clergy, the vast majority of men and women formed the *third estate*, or commoners. With little property, most commoners or serfs worked parcels of land belonging to nobles. The phrase "one's *lot* in life" literally describes the daily plight of commoners during the Middle Ages. Unlike the nobility and the clergy, commoners had little access to schooling, so most remained illiterate.

As the Industrial Revolution gradually transformed England's economy in the nineteenth century, some commoners, especially those who made their way to cities, gained wealth and power that rivaled and sometimes surpassed that of the nobility. This economic expansion, along with the extension of education and legal rights to more people, soon blurred traditional social rankings as a class system emerged. In a pointed illustration of how far the pendulum has swung, a descendant of nobility, now making a living as a writer, was asked in a press interview if England's caste-like estates had finally broken down. Playfully she retorted, "Of course they have, or I wouldn't be here talking to someone like *you!*" (*New Haven Journal-Courier*, Nov. 27, 1986).

Great Britain Today

While individual achievement does have an impact on social stratification in Great Britain, today's class system retains the mark of a long, feudal past. The great wealth enjoyed by some people in contemporary Great Britain is achieved through their own efforts. Others, descendants of traditional nobility, still maintain inherited wealth, savor the highest prestige, attend expensive, elite universities, and wield considerable power to shape British society. A traditional monarch remains as Britain's head of state, and Parliament's House of Lords is composed of "peers," almost all of whom are of noble birth. Actual control of government, however, resides in the House of Commons, comprising commoners who are more likely to have achieved their positions through individual effort than through ascription.

Below the upper class, roughly one-fourth of the British population falls into the "middle class." Some are moderately wealthy, with high incomes from professions and business. These richer "commoners," along with members of the upper class, make up the 10 percent of Britons with significant financial holdings in the form of stocks and bonds (Sherrid, 1986). Most members of the British middle class, however, earn too little to accumulate substantial wealth.

Under the middle class, across a boundary that cannot be precisely defined, lie roughly half of all Britons, known as the "working class." As in Canada, members of the working class earn modest incomes, generally doing manual labor. Although the British economy expanded during the 1980s, traditional industries such as coal mining and steel production declined, subjecting many working-class families to unemployment. Some slipped into poverty, joining the remaining one-fourth of Britons who are socially and economically deprived. Lower-class people—or, more simply, "the poor"—are heavily concentrated in northern and western regions of the country plagued by economic decay.

Today Great Britain displays typical class-system traits: unequally distributed wealth, power, and prestige, but with some opportunity for significant movement up and down in the overall hierarchy. In one legacy of the estate system, however, movement between social classes occurs less frequently than in North America (Boyd et al., 1981; Kerckhoff, Campbell, & Winfield-Laird, 1985). Compared with people in Canada, therefore, Britons are more resigned to remaining in the social position to which they were born (Snowman, 1977). The greater rigidity of British stratification is exemplified in the importance attached to accent as a mark of social position. Distinctive patterns of speech develop in a society as categories of people are segregated from one another over long periods. In Great Britain, families of long-standing affluence and those living in chronic poverty speak so differently that they seem to be, as the saying goes, a single people divided by a common language.

Another Example: Japan

Social stratification in Japan also mixes the traditional and the contemporary. As in Great Britain, a modern emphasis on individual achievement has reshaped an ancient hierarchy of rank by birth.

Feudal Japan

For centuries, Japan was an agrarian society composed of nobles and commoners in one of the most rigidly stratified societies the world has ever known. This system dates back to the fifth century C.E., when an imperial family, claiming divine right to rule, formally presided over the country. More accurately, however, the imperial family maintained often uneasy alliances with a network of regional nobility. These nobles were men who excelled in military combat; such warlords—called *shoguns*—routinely fought among themselves, as did their counterparts in medieval England.

Below the nobility stood the *samurai*, or warrior caste. This second rank of Japanese society cultivated elaborate martial skills, often in highly ritualized form. Although not nobles themselves, the *samurai*'s role as defenders of the nobility placed them clearly above the common people. Like all Japanese of that time, the *samurai* dressed and behaved according to their rank, as demanded by traditional codes of honor.

As in England, the majority of people in Japan at this time in history were commoners, who labored for a lifetime to eke out only a bare subsistence for themselves and their families. Feudal society in Japan afforded commoners no political voice, just as European serfs had little political power. Unlike their European counterparts, however, Japanese commoners were not the lowest in rank. The *burakumin*, or "outcasts," stood further down on that country's hierarchy; such people were shunned as unworthy by even "common" Japanese. Much like the lowest caste groups in India, "outcasts" lived apart from others, engaged in the most distasteful occupations, and, like everyone else, had no opportunity to change their standing.

Japan Today

Important changes in nineteenth-century Japan—industrialization, the growth of cities, and the opening of Japanese society to outside influences —combined to weaken the traditional caste structure. In 1871 the Japanese legally banned the social category of "outcast," although even today people look down on women and men who trace their lineage to this rank. After Japan's defeat in World War II, the nobility too lost their legal standing, and since then fewer and fewer Japanese are willing to accept the notion that their emperor rules by divine right. Thus social stratification in contemporary Japan is a far cry from the rigid caste system in force centuries ago. Today, analysts identify a range of social gradations, including "upper," "upper-middle," "lower-middle," and "lower," but they disagree about what proportion of the population falls in each.

Although Japanese society now displays many of the traits of a class system, this nation's fascinating ability to combine the traditional with the modern still comes through in patterns of social inequality. Because many Japanese people revere past practices, family background is never far from the surface in assessing someone's social standing. Therefore, despite legal reforms that grant all people equal standing before the law, and a modern culture that stresses individual achievement, the Japanese continue to perceive each other through the centuries-old lens of caste.

This dynamic mix echoes from the campus to corporate boardrooms. The most prestigious universities—now gateways to success in the industrial world—admit students with outstanding scores on rigorous entrance examinations, a process detailed in Chapter 16 ("Education"). Still, the highest achievers and business leaders in Japan are products of privilege, with *samurai* or noble background. At the other extreme, "outcasts" continue to live in isolated communi-

Hereditary nobles, in principle at least, become enshrined in the traditions of their country. For this reason, Japan's Emperor Akihito enjoys the highest prestige and widespread popularity, especially among older people in his nation. Japan's transformation into the more egalitarian culture of an industrial society, however, has eroded the emperor's standing, shifting political power to a popularly elected prime minister.

nities cut off from opportunities to better themselves (Hiroshi, 1974; Norbeck, 1983).

Finally, traditional ideas about gender shape Japanese society to this day. Despite legal reforms that confer formal equality on the sexes, women are clearly subordinate to men in many important respects. More than twice the proportion of Japanese parents (73 percent) express the desire to send a son to college compared to a daughter (29 percent) and, predictably enough, women in Japan are far less likely than men to receive a university education (Brinton, 1988). As a consequence, women predominate in lower-level support positions in the corporate world, only rarely assuming leadership roles. In this sense, too, individual achievement in Japan's modern class system operates in the shadow of centuries of traditional privileges.

The Former Soviet Union

During the last decade, the new Commonwealth of Independent States—the former Union of Soviet Socialist Republics (USSR)—has experienced changes so dramatic that many observers have heralded a second Russian revolution. The history of this military superpower has been a grand experiment, first, to eliminate class differences and, more recently, to reintroduce some aspects of the Western market economy that will further transform social stratification in the world's largest country.

A Classless Society?

The current Soviet federation was born out of a revolution in 1917 that brought an abrupt end to a feudal estate system ruled by a hereditary nobility. The Russian Revolution transferred most farms, factories, and other productive property from private ownership to control by the state. This transformation was guided by the ideas of Karl Marx, who asserted that private ownership of productive property is the basis of social classes (see Chapter 4, "Society"). As the state gained control of the economy, the Soviet Union boasted of reaching a milestone in human history by becoming a classless society.

Analysts outside the Soviet Union were always skeptical of this claim, pointing out that Soviet society remained clearly stratified (Lane, 1984). The occupations of the Soviet people are clustered into four major categories, listed here in descending order of income, prestige, and power: (1) high government officials, also known as *apparatchiks*; (2) the intelligentsia, including lower government officials and professional workers—engineers, scientists, college professors, and physicians; (3) manual workers in state-controlled industries; and (4) the rural peasantry. This ranking of categories of people illustrates that the Soviet Union neither eliminated social classes nor eradicated social inequality. At the same time, however, a more modest claim can be advanced: because factories, farms, colleges, and hospitals were collectively owned and operated, the Soviet Union had less economic inequality than capitalist societies such as Canada or the United States.

The Second Soviet Revolution

Economic reforms were accelerated by Mikhail Gorbachev when he came to power in the Soviet Union in 1985. His economic program, popularly known as *perestroika*, meaning "restructuring," was put in place in response to a dire economic problem: while the Soviet system had succeeded in minimizing economic inequality, the overall standard of living lagged far behind that of other industrial nations. Gorbachev's program was designed to stimulate economic expansion by reducing inefficient centralized control of the economy.

Few Soviet people were satisfied with their living standards when Gorbachev began his campaign and, by most accounts, economic conditions today have plum-meted even further. Economic reform has been complicated by a host of factors, including the need to acquire advanced technology and to cut military spending. But perhaps most important is the popular reform movement that swept through many socialist societies. First in the countries of Eastern Europe and then in the Soviet Union itself, demands for wholesale change reached a fever pitch, spurred by shortages of consumer goods as well as a growing recognition that the ideal of a classless society was far from reality in socialist nations. Thus people blamed their plight and powerlessness on the small ruling classes of Communist party officials. After the Soviet Union was formed in 1917, the Communist party retained a monopoly of power, often brutally repressing any opposition. Until its hold over Soviet society was broken in 1991, some 18 million party members (about 6 percent of the Soviet people) not only made all the decisions about Soviet life, but also enjoyed privileges unknown to the vast majority of the population. These privileges included vacation homes, chauffeured automobiles, access to prized consumer goods, and elite educations for their children (Zaslavsky, 1982; Shipler, 1984; Theen, 1984). The second Soviet revolution, then, mirrors the first in one important respect: the goal is nothing less than the overthrow of the ruling class. By the winter of 1991, the Soviet Union had dissolved into a new federation of republics. Because the nation remains in flux, its future cannot be predicted. But it seems likely that the enormous political power held by a handful of party officials has come to an end.

The case of the Soviet Union demonstrates that social inequality involves more than simply economic resources. While Soviet society lacked the extremes of wealth and poverty found in Great Britain and the United States, elite standing in that nation was based on *power* rather than wealth. Thus, neither Mikhail Gorbachev nor Boris Yeltzin, despite their awesome power, ever earned more than an average worker in Canada or the United States, and neither man has anywhere near the personal wealth of Pierre Elliott Trudeau or George Bush.

And what about social mobility in the Soviet Union? Evidence suggests that during this century there has been more upward social mobility in the Soviet Union than in Great Britain, Japan, Canada, or even the United States. This is partly because Soviet society lacks the concentrations of wealth passed from generation to generation in other societies. Even more importantly, the Soviet Union's rapid industrialization and bureaucratization during this century pushed a large proportion of the working class and rural peasantry upward to occupations in industry and government. In the last few decades, however, Soviet society experienced decreasing social mobility. Most analysts contend that the country's earlier high rate of upward mobility stemmed from industrial development more than socialism (Dobson, 1977; Lane, 1984; Shipler, 1984).

The close link between societal transformation and personal changes in social standing exemplifies what sociologists call **structural social mobility**, *a shift in the social position of large numbers of people due more to changes in society itself than to individual efforts* (Tepperman, 1976). Half a century ago, industrialization created a vast number of new jobs that drew the Soviet people to cities from rural farming villages. Similarly, the growth of bureaucracy propelled countless Soviet citizens from the fields into the offices. Now, with the recent introduction of private property into the economy and new laws sanctioning individual ownership of business enterprises, further structural social mobility is likely, perhaps including greater economic inequality. But the hope is that everyone will enjoy a higher standard of living.

Ideology

Considering the extent of social inequality everywhere in the world, how do stratified societies persist without distributing their resources more equally? The caste systems of Great Britain and Japan lasted for centuries, placing most wealth and power in the hands of several hundred families. Even more striking, for two thousand years most people in India accepted the idea that their lives should be privileged or poor because of the accident of birth. One reason for the remarkable persistence of social hierarchies is that they are bolstered by **ideology**, *cultural beliefs that reflect and support the interests of certain categories of people.* Any cultural pattern—an idea or an action—is ideological to the extent that its consequences favor some people over others.

The ancient Greek philosopher Plato (427–347 B.C.E.) claimed that justice was primarily a matter of agreement about who should have what. To generate a high level of agreement about inequality, most people in a society are socialized to view their system as basically "fair." From Plato's point of view, then, cultural beliefs are necessary to legitimate any social hierarchy.

Karl Marx, too, understood this process, although he was far more skeptical about claims of fairness than Plato was. In Marx's view, the economy channels

wealth and power into the hands of a few, defining the process as simply "the laws of the marketplace." Further, the legal system defends the right to own private property as a basic human freedom, just as family members are merely "looking out for their own" when they funnel money and privileges from generation to generation. In short, Marx concluded, both resources and ideas come under the control of a society's elite, which helps to explain why social stratification is so difficult to change.

Though Plato looked more favorably on social hierarchy than Marx did, both thinkers recognized the essential role of ideology in maintaining social inequality. Ideology is rarely a simple matter of privileged people conspiring to generate self-serving ideas about social inequality. Typically, ideology takes the form of evolving cultural patterns that directly and indirectly justify according a disproportionate share of resources and privileges to certain categories of people. Through socialization, the primary means by which ideology is transmitted over time, most people learn to embrace their society's system of social hierarchy. As a result of learning certain conceptions of fairness, people who challenge the system generally question not the system itself but simply their own position in it.

The ideas that shore up social stratification change along with a society's economy and technology. Early agrarian societies depended on slaves to perform burdensome manual work. In ancient Greece, for example, the practice of slavery was justified by the widespread notion that people differed greatly in their intellectual capacities. Aristotle (384–322 B.C.E.) spoke for his times when he stated that some people deserve nothing more than slavery, which places them under the control of their natural "betters." Agrarian societies in Europe during the Middle Ages also required the routine labor of most people in the fields in order to support the small aristocracy. In this context, noble and serf alike were taught that occupation was rightfully determined by birth and each person's work was a matter of moral responsibility. In short, caste systems always rest on the assumption that social ranking is the product of a "natural" order.

With the rise of industrial capitalism, a new economic elite promoted the idea that valued resources come to those who display individual merit. Class systems celebrate individualism and achievement, defining wealth as virtually synonymous with intelligence and hard work. Poverty, the object of charity under feudalism, was transformed into a state of personal inadequacy. The box on page 254 takes a closer look at the transition from the medieval notion that social inequality is divinely sanctioned to the modern idea that stratification reflects personal effort and ability.

Throughout human history, social stratification has seemed unshakable to most people. However, challenges to the status quo do arise and sometimes succeed. Especially as traditions weaken, people begin to question cultural "truths" and unmask their political

In medieval Europe, people accepted rigid social differences, which divided them from birth until death, as part of a divine order for the world. This fifteenth-century painting by the Limbourg brothers—used to illustrate a book for the brother of the king—portrays life as orderly and cyclical. In this example, showing indoor life during January, the Duke of Berry is seated near the fireplace surrounded by a host of attendants that caters to his every whim. The firescreen behind him appears to give him a halo, surely intended by the artists to suggest a common notion of the time that nobles enjoyed their privileges by grace of God.

Limbourg Brothers, *"Le Duc de Berry à table"* Trés Riches Heures du Duc de Berry. January, fol 1v. Chantilly, Musée Condé.

foundations and consequences. For example, historic notions of a "woman's place" today seem far from natural and are losing their power to deprive women of opportunities. For the present, however, the contemporary class system still subjects women to caste-like expectations that they perform traditional tasks out of altruism and duty while men are financially rewarded for their efforts. To illustrate, far more power, prestige, and financial rewards are accorded to a chef (typically, a man) than to a family cook (usually a woman), although they perform much the same work. Yet, while these differences persist in Canada, there is little doubt that women and men are steadily becoming more equal in important respects. The continuing struggle for racial equality in South Africa also exemplifies widespread rejection of apartheid, which has shaped economic, political, and educational life. Apartheid has never been widely accepted by blacks, and it is losing support as a "natural" system among whites who reject ideological racism (Friedrich, 1987; Contreras, 1992).

[handwritten margin note: strict racial segregation as practiced in South Africa.]

The Functions of Social Stratification

Why are societies stratified at all? One answer, consistent with the structural-functional paradigm, is that social inequality has vital consequences for the operation of society. This argument was initially set forth half a century ago by Kingsley Davis and Wilbert Moore (1945).

The Davis–Moore Thesis

In 1945, Kingsley Davis and Wilbert Moore proposed a theory of social stratification that remains influential—and controversial—to this day. The *Davis–Moore thesis* begins with the observation that all societies are stratified to some degree. Therefore, the argument goes, social inequality must have some beneficial effects.

In their effort to identify these consequences, Davis and Moore note that society encompasses many occupational positions of varying importance. Some jobs are performed easily by virtually anyone, while the most important positions can be carried out only by people with rare talents who have received long and expensive education and training. Such functionally important positions usually subject individuals to substantial pressure and day-to-day responsibility as well.

CRITICAL THINKING

Ideology: When Is Inequality Unjust?

Inequality may or may not be unjust: Such judgments depend on cultural definitions of fairness. As a cultural issue, justifications for social stratification vary, displaying marked variety across history and from place to place.

A millennium ago, the feudal estate system was taking root in Europe. This rigidly stratified social order drew strength from the teachings of the church, which claimed social arrangements on earth reflected the will of God. As the expression of a divine plan, religious leaders asserted, God had assigned people on earth to distinctive stations. The majority of people endured a harsh life of serfdom, driving the feudal economy with their muscles. Most people born to such a life knew nothing else, but even imagining an alternative risked challenging not only the nobility but also the church and, ultimately, God. Although their lives were framed with far more comforts, the nobility fit into the same plan; their various duties of defending the realm and maintaining law and order were imbued with a sense of divine purpose. The religious justification that cloaked the entire medieval estate system, and which helped to sustain this form of inequality for centuries, is clearly expressed in the following lines from an old hymn sung by members of the official church of the realm, the Church of England:

The rich man in his castle,
The poor man at his gate,
He made them high and lowly
And ordered their estate.
All things bright and beautiful ...

During the Industrial Revolution, newly rich industrialists gradually toppled the feudal nobility, advancing a new ideology in the process. Capitalists scorned the notion that social hierarchy should rest on the accident of birth; a view that had been compelling to hundreds of generations living under feudalism soon became ludicrous once the economy had been reorganized. If there was a natural order to the world, the new thinking went, it was that society should be dominated by the most talented and hard-working individuals. Early industrialists like John D. Rockefeller (1839–1937), who made a vast fortune in oil, was fond of defending the wealth and power of his class as the product of personal effort and initiative, which, he asserted, was consistent with the laws of nature and the will of God. The poor, who in feudal societies had been the objects of charitable assistance (since, after all, being poor was not their own fault but part of a divine plan), were redefined as lacking ambition and ability and, consequently, scorned. The ideological shift from birth to individual achievement as the basis of social inequality was evident to the early nineteenth-century German writer Johann Wolfgang von Goethe, who quipped:

Really to own
What you inherit,
You first must earn it
With your merit.

Clearly, medieval and modern justifications of inequality differ dramatically—what an earlier era defined as just, a later one rejected as wrongheaded. Yet both cases illustrate the role of culture in defining a particular form of hierarchy as fair and beyond the power of society itself to change.

By conferring income, prestige, power, and leisure time on those who perform vital tasks, a society encourages the discovery and development of human resources. Further, a system of differential rewards motivates individuals to engage in the most significant activities possible. To illustrate, if a society values a Supreme Court justice more than a government clerk, it will accord greater benefits to the member of the high court. Similarly, if more skills and training are required to be a physician than to be a hospital orderly, a society bestows greater rewards on the physician. In all cases, effective performance of social roles demands unequal rewards, and a system of unequal rewards is, by definition, social stratification. According to the Davis–Moore thesis, a society could be egalitarian, but only to the extent that its members are prepared to have *any* person perform *any* job. Equality would also demand that someone who carries out a job poorly be rewarded just as much as another who performs well. Logic dictates that a system of equal rewards would not motivate people toward their best efforts and would thereby reduce a society's productive efficiency.

The Davis–Moore thesis is one explanation for why some form of stratification exists everywhere; it is not a defense of any *particular* system of inequality. Davis and Moore do not suggest precisely what reward should be attached to any occupational position. Rather, they merely point out that positions deemed crucial by a society must yield sufficient reward to draw talent away from less important positions.

Davis and Moore maintain that societies become more productive as they approach **meritocracy**, *a system of social stratification based entirely on personal merit*. Highly specialized industrial societies endeavor to develop the abilities and talents of each individual to the maximum. To become more meritocratic, a society must promote equality of opportunity for everyone; equality of condition, however, will not occur under this system given individual differences in ability and effort. Furthermore, as a society approaches a meritocracy, social mobility will blur social categories as people move up or down in the system depending on their performances.

Class systems are clearly more meritocratic than caste systems. In the latter, to the extent people speak of "merit" (from Latin, meaning "worthy of praise"), they mean the dutiful persistence in low-skill labor necessary to the operation of an agrarian society. Caste systems confer honor on those who remain "in their place."

Social organization based on caste inevitably wastes human potential. But then why do modern industrial societies retain many caste-like qualities? In no societies of the world, in fact, are rewards distributed solely on the basis of individual talent and achievement. This is because humans need to maintain the social fabric of kinship and community, both of which are eroded by unchecked personal ambition. For example, we favor members of our own families whether they are especially capable or not. In short, industrial class systems retain some elements of caste because of the need for social cohesion and stability.

Critical evaluation. Although the Davis–Moore thesis has made a lasting contribution to sociological analysis, Melvin Tumin (1953) argues that it is flawed in several respects. First, Tumin points to the difficulty of measuring the functional importance of any occupation. For example, the widely held notion that the work of physicians has great importance partly results from a policy of limiting the number of people entering the medical profession (through medical school admission practices) to ensure that physicians remain in great demand.

Further, actual rewards—especially income—may have little to do with an individual's functional importance to society. Wayne Gretzky's hockey contract *alone* (apart from income earned through endorsing products or other lucrative activities) gives him 21 times the income of the prime minister of Canada, who earned a salary of less than $140,000 in 1992. The box on page 256 takes a critical look at the link between pay and societal importance.

A second charge made by Tumin is that the Davis–Moore thesis exaggerates the consequences of social stratification when it comes to developing individual talents. Our society does reward individual achievement, but families also follow the caste-like practice of transferring wealth and power from generation to generation regardless of talent. Additionally, for women, people of color, aboriginal people and others with limited opportunities, the social hierarchy stands as a barrier to personal accomplishment. In practice, concludes Tumin, social stratification functions to develop some people's abilities to the fullest while guaranteeing that others will *never* reach their potential.

Third, by suggesting that social stratification benefits all of society, the Davis–Moore thesis ignores how social inequality promotes conflict and even outright revolution. This assertion leads us to the social-conflict paradigm, which provides a very different explanation for the persistence of social hierarchy.

Stratification and Conflict

Social-conflict analysis argues that, rather than benefiting society as a whole, social stratification ensures that some people gain advantages at the expense of others. This analysis draws heavily on the ideas of Karl Marx; additional contributions were made by Max Weber.

Marx's View of Social Class

Karl Marx, whose approach to understanding social inequality was detailed in Chapter 4 ("Society"), argued that the two major social classes correspond to the two basic relationships people have to the means of production: individuals can own productive property or they can labor for others. In medieval Europe, the nobility and clergy owned the productive land on which peasants toiled. Similarly, in industrial class systems, the *capitalists* (or the bourgeoisie) control factories, which utilize the labor of *workers* (the proletariat). So great are the disparities in wealth and power that arise from this productive system, Marx contended, that conflict between these two classes is inevitable. In time, he believed, oppression and misery would drive the working majority to organize and ultimately overthrow capitalism once and for all.

Marx's analysis was inspired by his observations

CRITICAL THINKING

Salaries: Are the Rich Worth What They Earn?

For an hour of work, a Canadian child-care worker earns about $6, a police officer about $27, a veterinarian about $32. The average worker —and even the prime minister and other high government officials—earn salaries that pale in comparison with popular athletes and entertainers.

In the U.S. John McEnroe garners about $400 an hour playing tournament tennis; singer and actress Dolly Parton is paid about $25,000 for every hour she performs in Las Vegas nightclubs. Bill Cosby commands about $100,000 an hour to take the stage, and boxer Mike Tyson earned about $1 million per minute throwing punches in heavyweight title bouts. Many Canadians—among them Raymond Burr, Michael J. Fox, Lorne Greene, Wayne Gretzky, and William Shatner—have gone to the U.S. in search of greater opportunity and remuneration. In September, 1993, Wayne Gretzky was rewarded for his move to the U.S. with a contract for $8 million annually, but even in Canada top athletes earn $3 and $4 million per year.

According to the Davis–Moore thesis, rewards reflect an occupation's value to society. But is Oprah Winfrey, who hosts American talk shows for some $25 million annually, worth twice as much to U.S. society as all one hundred of its senators (who, unlike Canada's, are elected and accountable to their constituencies)? Is Joe Carter of the Toronto Blue Jays worth as much as 35 or 40 of Canada's physicians or surgeons? In short, do earnings reflect the social importance of work?

Salaries in industrial-capitalist societies like Canada are a product of market forces. Defenders of the laws of supply and demand claim that the market impartially evaluates worth, rewarding each worker according to the supply of the talent in question and the public demand for it. According to this view, movie stars, top athletes, skilled professionals, and many business executives have rare talents that are much in demand; thus they may earn hundreds of times more than the typical worker. Only a handful of Canadian companies voluntarily reveal executive incomes, but in 1992, Steven Banner of Seagram Co. Ltd. earned $11 million. Are the highest earning half-of-one-percent in North America really worth the mega-million dollar incomes they earn each year?

Some critics claim that the market is not a good evaluator of occupational importance. First, critics maintain, the economy is dominated by a small proportion of people who manipulate the system for their own benefit. In Canada, thirty-two of our wealthiest families play "monopoly with the money of average Canadians" (Francis, 1986). Corporate executives pay themselves salaries and bonuses that have an uncertain connection to how well their companies perform. In 1990, for example, Steven J. Ross was the highest paid corporate leader in the United States, receiving $39 million in salary, bonuses, and one-time stock options, despite the fact that his company—Time Warner—actually fared below average for large corporations. In Canada, in 1992, Paul Stern of Northern Telecom Ltd. was to have earned $5 million, despite serious mismanagement. His departure, under a shadow, sent stock prices tumbling by almost 30 percent (Surtees, *Globe and Mail,* July 5, 1993).

In global perspective, Japanese executives earn far less than their counterparts in this country; this despite the fact that most Japanese corporations have handily outperformed their rivals in North America.

A second problem with the idea that the market measures the value of people to society is that many who make clear and significant contributions receive surprisingly little money. Tens of thousands of teachers, counselors, and health-care workers enhance the welfare of others every day for little salary, partly because many people do not think of income as the best measure of the value of their work. In 1987, the notorious "U.S. junk-bond king" Michael Milken earned $550 million dealing on Wall Street; in the process, he enriched a small number of investors other than himself while weakening the U.S. economy, according to Wall Street analysts. During the same year, Rachel Stuart counseled thirty-five poor women in rural Louisiana who were preparing to give birth. Her work helped them to deliver healthy babies. Since the cost of neonatal care for a single premature baby in the States runs as high as $200,000, Stuart probably saved the public millions; yet she is paid $4,000 a year for her work (Werman, 1989).

Using salary to measure social worth, then, only works to the extent that market forces actually gauge people's societal contribution. Some people view market forces as the most accurate measure of occupational worth. Others contend that lucrative activities may or may not be socially valuable. From this standpoint, the market system amounts to a closed game in which only a handful of people have the money to play.

John George Brown made a fortune a century ago as a painter who portrayed the world as most people wanted to see it. Others, including photographer Jacob Riis, found far less fame by capturing something closer to the truth. This is Riis's well-known image of "street arabs" who survived as best they could on the mean streets of the growing industrial cities.

of capitalism early in the nineteenth century, a time when society seemed irrevocably divided into contending classes. While the industrial revolution had yet to take hold in Canada, this was the era when wealthy American capitalists like Andrew Carnegie, J.P. Morgan, and John Jacob Astor (one of the few very rich passengers to perish on the *Titanic*) lived in fabulous mansions filled with priceless art and staffed by dozens of servants. Their fortunes were staggering: the wealth of John Jacob Astor is estimated at $25 million; Andrew Carnegie reportedly earned more than $20 million in a single year as the new century began (worth perhaps $80 million in today's dollars); all this at a time when the wages paid to the average U.S. worker totaled roughly $500 a year (Baltzell, 1964; Pessen, 1990).

Throughout the course of capitalist development, Marx claimed, the economy stands out as the social institution with the greatest influence on the rest of society. Other institutions serve, in general, to support the operation of the economy. This means, for example, that the family enables wealthy people to pass their accumulated savings and property from generation to generation, and the legal system defends this process through inheritance law. Similarly, exclusive schools bring children of the elite together, training them in the ways of their class, and encouraging the informal social ties that will benefit them throughout their lives. Overall, from Marx's point of view, the operation of capitalist society contributes to the *reproduction of the class structure*, meaning that class divisions are perpetuated over time.

Critical evaluation. By exploring how the capitalist economic system generates conflict between classes, Marx's analysis of social stratification has had an enormous influence on sociological thinking in recent decades. Because it is revolutionary—at least in a capitalist society—Marxism is also controversial.

One of the strongest criticisms of the Marxist approach is that it denies one of the central elements of the Davis-Moore thesis: that motivating people to perform various social roles requires some system of unequal rewards. Marx separated reward from performance, endorsing an egalitarian system based on the principle of "from each according to ability; to each according to need" (1972:388). Critics argue that severing rewards from performance goes a long way toward explaining the low productivity that has been characteristic of the former Soviet Union and other socialist economies around the world, and the recent efforts by these nations to reform their economies by introducing market elements. However, it is important to recognize that considerable evidence supports the view of humanity that underlies the Marxist position: that people are inherently social rather than unflinchingly selfish and individualistic (Clark, 1991; Fiske, 1991). Therefore, we should not assume that individual rewards (much less *monetary* compensation alone) constitute the only way to motivate people to perform their social roles.

Second, although capitalist society does perpetuate poverty and privilege from generation to generation, the revolutionary developments Marx considered inevitable have failed to materialize. Here lies a second major critique of his ideas. The next section explores why the socialist revolution Marx predicted and promoted has not occurred, at least in advanced capitalist societies.

Why No Marxist Revolution?

Despite Marx's prediction to the contrary, capitalism is still thriving. Even so, as we shall see, Western capitalism has evolved in some of the ways Marx anticipated.

Why have workers in modern industrialized countries not overthrown capitalism? Ralf Dahrendorf (1959) has suggested four overarching reasons.

First, in the century since Marx's death, the capitalist class has grown fragmented. Nineteenth-century companies were typically owned by *families*. Today, although some families continue to be important players in the corporate world, most major corporations are owned by numerous *stockholders*. Further, in industrialized countries like Canada, a large managerial class, whose members may or may not own a significant share of the companies they manage, has also emerged. The overall effect is that an increasing number of people have a direct stake in preserving the capitalist system.

Second, Marx's industrial proletariat has also been transformed by the so-called white-collar revolution. As Chapter 19 ("The Economy and Work") details, a century ago the vast majority of workers in North America filled the ranks of **blue-collar occupations**, *work involving mostly manual labor*, in factories or on farms. Today, most of the labor force holds **white-collar occupations**, *higher-prestige work involving mostly mental activity*. These jobs include positions in sales, management, and other service work, frequently in large, bureaucratic organizations. While these white-collar workers have much in common with the industrial working class described by Marx, evidence suggests that most do not think of themselves in those terms. For much of this century, then, the white-collar revolution has prompted many people to perceive their social positions as higher than those held by their parents and grandparents. Just as important, the overall standard of living of workers in North America has risen dramatically over the course of the century. As a result of this tide of upward social mobility, our society seems less sharply divided between the rich and poor than it did to people during Marx's lifetime.

Third, the plight of workers is not as desperate today as it was a century ago. Despite setbacks for many workers during the 1980s, the overall quality of life in Western societies has improved significantly since Marx's time. Moreover, workers have won the right to organize into labor unions that can make demands of management backed by threats of work slowdowns and strikes. Recently union membership has been declining in the U.S. while remaining stable in Canada. There is no doubt that well-established unions continue to enhance or protect the economic standing of the workers they represent. Further, labor and management now regularly engage in contract negotiations. If not always peaceful, worker-management disputes (including binding arbitration in some instances) are now institutionalized.

Fourth, legal protection has been widely extended during the last century. Laws now protect workers' rights and mandate safe working conditions, and workers have greater access to the courts for redressing grievances. Government programs such as unemployment insurance and welfare provide workers with substantially greater financial resources and safety nets than the capitalists of the last century were willing to grant them.

Taken together, these developments suggest that despite persistent and marked stratification, many of capitalism's rough edges have been smoothed out. Consequently, social conflict today is less intense than it was a century ago. Nonetheless, many sociologists continue to find value in Marx's analysis, often in modified form (Miliband 1969; Edwards, 1979; Giddens, 1982; Domhoff, 1983; Stephens, 1986; Clement & Williams, 1989; McAll, 1990; Satzewich & Wotherspoon, 1993; Teeple, 1993).

Advocates of social-conflict analysis respond with four key points of their own. First, wealth remains highly concentrated, just as Marx contended, in the hands of a capitalist class. Second, the jobs generated

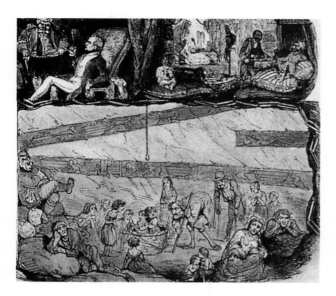

This cartoon, entitled "Capital and Labor," appeared in the English press in 1843, when the ideas of Karl Marx were first gaining attention. It links the plight of that country's coal miners to the privileges enjoyed by those who owned coal-fired factories.

by the white-collar revolution offer income and security no greater (and often less) than factory jobs did a century ago. In addition, much white-collar work is as monotonous and routine as factory work, especially the low-level clerical jobs commonly held by women. Third, they suggest, although labor organizations have certainly advanced the interests of workers over the last half century, regular negotiation between workers and management does not signal the end of social conflict. Many of the concessions workers have won came about precisely through the class conflict Marx described. Moreover, workers still struggle to gain concessions from capitalists and, in the 1990s, to hold on to the advances they have already made. Fourth, workers may have gained some legal protections, but the law has not changed the overall distribution of wealth in North American society, nor can "average" men and women use the legal system to the same advantage as the rich.

Therefore, social-conflict theorists conclude, the fact that no socialist revolution has taken place in Canada, the United States, or the other industrialized countries hardly invalidates Marx's analysis of capitalism. Our cultural values, emphasizing individualism and competition, may have curbed revolutionary aspirations in this country, but, as we shall see in Chapter 10 ("Social Class in Canada"), pronounced social inequality persists in our society, as does social

conflict—albeit less overtly and violently than in the nineteenth century.

Finally, some defenders of capitalist free-market economics contend that the collapse of communist regimes in Eastern Europe and the Soviet Union validates their long-standing arguments in favor of capitalism. To be fair, however, analysis of socialist and capitalist systems (detailed in Chapter 19, "The Economy and Work") are separate issues. Without denying the difficulties that have overwhelmed socialist societies in some parts of the world, many analysts claim that capitalism has yet to demonstrate its ability to address problems of poor public education and desperation among members of the urban underclass (Uchitelle, 1991). Table 9-1 summarizes the contributions of the two contrasting sociological approaches to these problems.

Max Weber: Class, Status, and Power

Max Weber, whose approach to social analysis is described in Chapter 4 ("Society"), agreed with Karl Marx that social stratification sparks social conflict, but he differed with Marx in several important respects.

Weber considered Marx's model of two social classes simplistic. Instead, he viewed social stratification as the interplay of three distinct dimensions. First is economic inequality—the issue so vital to Marx—which Weber termed *class* position. Weber's use of "class" refers not to crude categories, but to a continuum on which anyone can be ranked from high to low. Second is *status*, meaning level of social prestige. This, too, forms a continuum. Third, Weber noted the importance of *power*, yet another dimension of social hierarchy.

Marx believed that social prestige and power stemmed from the same factor: economic position. Thus, he saw no reason to treat them as distinct dimensions of social inequality. Weber disagreed, asserting that stratification in industrial societies has characteristically low status consistency, meaning that a person might have a high standing on one dimension of inequality while having a lower position on another. For example, bureaucratic officials might wield considerable power yet have little wealth or social prestige. So while Marx viewed social inequality in terms of two clearly defined classes, Weber saw something more subtle at work in the social stratification in industrial societies. Weber's key contribution in this area, then, lies in identifying rankings along a multidimensional

TABLE 9-1   TWO EXPLANATIONS OF SOCIAL STRATIFICATION: A SUMMARY

Structural-Functional Paradigm	Social-Conflict Paradigm
1. Social stratification keeps society operating. The linkage of greater rewards to more important social positions benefits society as a whole.	Social stratification is the result of social conflict. Differences in social resources serve the interests of some and harm the interests of others.
2. Social stratification encourages a matching of talents and abilities to appropriate positions.	Social stratification ensures that much talent and ability within the society will not be utilized at all.
3. Social stratification is both useful and inevitable.	Social stratification is useful to only some people; it is not inevitable.
4. The values and beliefs that legitimate social inequality are widely shared throughout society.	Values and beliefs tend to be ideological; they reflect the interests of the more powerful members of society.
5. Because systems of social stratification are useful to society and are supported by cultural values and beliefs, they are usually stable over time.	Because systems of social stratification reflect the interests of only part of the society, they are unlikely to remain stable over time.

SOURCE: Adapted in part from Arthur L. Stinchcombe, "Some Empirical Consequences of the Davis-Moore Theory of Stratification," *American Sociological Review*, Vol. 28, No. 5 (October 1963):808.

hierarchy. Sociologists often use the term **socioeconomic status** to refer to *a composite ranking based on various dimensions of social inequality.*

A population that varies widely in class, status, and power—Weber's three dimensions of inequality—creates a virtually infinite array of social groupings, all of which pursue their own interests. Thus, unlike Marx, who saw a clear conflict between two classes, Weber considered social conflict as a highly variable and complex process.

Weber also suggested that each of his three dimensions of social inequality stands out at different points in the history of human societies. Agrarian societies, he maintained, emphasize status or social prestige, typically in the form of honor or symbolic purity. Members of these societies gain such status by conforming to cultural norms corresponding to their rank. Industrialization and the development of capitalism level traditional rankings based on birth but generate striking financial disparities in the population; thus, Weber argued, the crucial difference among people lies in the economic dimension of class. Mature industrial societies, especially socialist societies, witness a surging growth of the bureaucratic state and accord tremendous power to high-ranking officials.

Finally, recall from Chapter 4 ("Society") Weber's disagreement with Marx about the future of industrial-capitalist societies. Marx, who focused almost exclusively on economics, believed that most social stratification could be eliminated by abolishing private ownership of productive property. Weber doubted that overthrowing capitalism would significantly diminish social stratification in modern societies because of the rising significance of power based on positions in formal organizations. In fact, Weber imagined that a socialist revolution might actually increase social inequality by expanding government and concentrating power in the hands of a political elite. Recent popular uprisings against entrenched bureaucracies in Eastern Europe and the Soviet Union lend support to Weber's position.

Critical evaluation.   Weber's multidimensional analysis of social stratification retains enormous influence among sociologists. Nevertheless, some analysts (particularly those influenced by Marx's ideas) argue that while social class boundaries have become less pronounced, striking patterns of social inequality persist in Canada as they do elsewhere in the industrial world.

As we shall see in Chapter 10 ("Social Class in Canada"), the enormous wealth of the most privileged Canadians contrasts sharply with the grinding poverty of those who are barely able to meet their day-to-day needs, such as those in households headed by single mothers or in many Inuit, Métis and Indian communities. The upward social mobility that historically blurred class lines in Canada ceased in the 1970s; during the 1980s, the extent of economic inequality in this country actually increased. Against this backdrop of economic polarization, the 1990s may well see a renewed emphasis on "classes" in conflict rather than on the subtle shadings of a "multidimensional hierarchy."

Stratification and Technology in Global Perspective

We can weave together a number of observations made in this chapter by considering the relationship between a society's technology and its type of social stratification. Gerhard and Jean Lenski's model of sociocultural evolution, examined in Chapter 4 ("Society"), puts social stratification in historical perspective, and also helps us to understand the varying degrees of inequality found around the world today (Lenski, 1966; Lenski, Lenski, & Nolan, 1991).

Simple technology limits the production of hunting and gathering societies to only what is necessary for day-to-day living. No doubt, some individuals are more successful hunters or gatherers than others, but the group's survival depends on everyone sharing what they have. With little or no surplus, therefore, no categories of people emerge as better off than others. Thus social stratification among hunters and gatherers (where it is based on age and sex) is less pronounced than among societies with more complex technologies.

Technological advances historically generate a productive surplus, while intensifying social inequality. In horticultural and pastoral societies, a small elite controls most of the surplus. Agrarian technology based on large-scale farming generates vastly greater abundance, which is unequally shared. In agrarian societies, then, various categories of people lead strikingly different lives. In one sense, agrarian societies seem egalitarian, since the vast majority of people are poor and work the land as peasants. However, the social distance between the favored strata—hereditary nobility—and the serfs looms as large as at any time in human history. In most cases, nobles wield godlike power over the masses.

In industrial societies, social inequality diminishes to some degree. The eclipse of tradition and the need to develop individual talents gradually erode caste rankings in favor of greater individual opportunity. The increasing productivity of industrial technology steadily raises the living standards of the historically poor majority. Specialized, technical work also encourages the expansion of schooling, sharply reducing illiteracy. A literate population, in turn, tends to press for a greater voice in political decision making, further diminishing social inequality. And, as already noted, additional technological advances transform much blue-collar labor into higher-prestige white-collar work. All these transformations help to explain why Marxist revolutions have occurred in agrarian societies— such as the Soviet Union (in 1917), Cuba (1959), and Nicaragua (1979)—where social inequality is most pronounced, rather than in industrial societies, as Marx predicted more than a century ago.

Finally, industrialization lessens the domination of women by men, which is generally strongest in agrarian societies. The movement toward social parity for the sexes derives from the industrial economy's need to cultivate individual talent as well as a growing belief in basic human equality. In short, reducing the intensity of social stratification is actually functional for industrial societies. This historical pattern, recognized by Nobel Prize-winning economist Simon Kuznets (1955, 1966), is illustrated by the "Kuznets Curve," shown in Figure 9-1.[2]

Current patterns of social inequality in global perspective generally accord with the Kuznets Curve. As shown in Global Map 9-1, industrialized societies of the world have somewhat less income inequality—one important measure of social stratification—than nations that remain predominantly agrarian. Specifically, mature industrial societies such as Canada or the United States and the nations of Western Europe exhibit less income inequality than many of the less industrialized societies of Latin America, Africa, and Asia. The

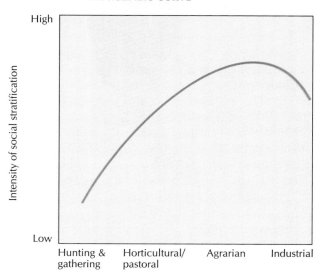

FIGURE 9-1   SOCIAL STRATIFICATION AND TECHNOLOGICAL DEVELOPMENT: THE KUZNETS CURVE

[2] The ideas of Simon Kuznets are discussed by Peter Berger (1986:43–46), whose interpretations are reflected in what appears here.

pattern, however, is far from perfectly consistent: income disparity reflects a host of factors beyond technology, especially political and economic priorities. Societies that have operated as socialist economic systems (including the People's Republic of China, the former Soviet Union, and the nations of Eastern Europe) display relatively little income inequality. Keep in mind, however, that an egalitarian society like the People's Republic of China has an average income level that is quite low by world standards; further, this society has pronounced social inequality on noneconomic dimensions such as political power.

Finally, even if the general global patterns suggested by Kuznets appear to hold, his analysis does not necessarily mean that industrial societies will gradually become less and less stratified. In the abstract, the principle of equal opportunity for all is widely endorsed; even so, this goal has not—and may never—become a

WINDOW ON THE WORLD

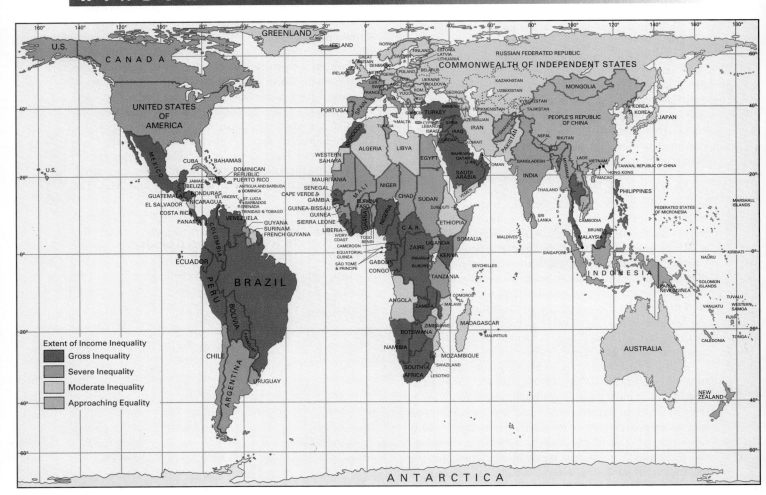

GLOBAL MAP 9-1   INCOME DISPARITY IN GLOBAL PERSPECTIVE
Societies of the world differ in the rigidity and intensity of social stratification as well as in their overall standard of living. This map highlights income inequality. Generally speaking, countries that have had centralized, socialist economies (including the People's Republic of China, the former Soviet Union, and Cuba) display the least income inequality, although their standard of living has been relatively low. Industrial societies with predominantly capitalist economies, including Canada, the United States, and most of Western Europe, have higher overall living standards, accompanied by severe income disparity. The less industrialized societies in Latin America and Africa (including Mexico, Brazil, and Zaire) exhibit the most pronounced inequality of income.

reality. The objective of social equality, like all concepts related to social stratification, is controversial, as the final section of this chapter explains.

Social Stratification: Facts and Values

The year was 2081 and everybody was finally equal. They weren't only equal before God and the law. They were equal every which way. Nobody was smarter than anybody else. Nobody was better looking than anybody else. Nobody was stronger or quicker than anybody else. All this equality was due to the 211th, 212th, and 213th Amendments to the Constitution and the unceasing vigilance of agents of the Handicapper General. ...

With these words, novelist Kurt Vonnegut, Jr. (1961) opens the story of "Harrison Bergeron," an imaginary account of a future in which social inequality has been totally abolished. Although the ideal of equality may be appealing in principle, Vonnegut is not celebrating this achievement in practice. Far from it: he describes a social nightmare in which every individual talent that makes one person different from another has been systematically neutralized by agents of the government. The most physically attractive people are required to wear masks that render them average-looking, intelligent people wear earphones that send distracting shrieks of noise every few seconds, and the legs of the best dancers are precisely fitted with weights to make their movements just as cumbersome as everyone else's.

In short, although we may imagine that social equality would liberate people to make the most of their talents, Vonnegut suggests that more likely everyone would be reduced to a lowest common denominator.

All accounts of hierarchy and equality involve such value judgments. The Davis-Moore thesis argues that social stratification is necessary to social life because some occupational roles have greater importance than others. Social inequality, from this point of view, reflects both variation in human abilities and the variable tasks of society. Just as importantly, how could absolute social equality be achieved in a world of human diversity? Vonnegut fears that it could only occur through the relentless efforts of officials like the agents of his fictitious "Handicapper General."

Social-conflict analysis, advocated by Karl Marx, also mixes facts and values. Marx rejected the argument that stratification serves human societies, condemning social hierarchy as a product of greed that favors the few at the expense of the many. Guided by egalitarian values, he opposed any social arrangements that prevented everyone from sharing equally in important resources. Rather than undermining the quality of life, Marx maintained that equality would enhance humanity, and could be realized if the corrupting effects of capitalism were eradicated.

The next chapter ("Social Class in Canada") takes a close look at inequality in our own society. But even people who agree on the basic facts often interpret them quite differently. The same holds true for Chapter 11 ("Global Inequality"); there, we shall examine not only how much inequality exists among societies of the world, but why this hierarchy of nations exists.

Summary

1. Social stratification involves ranking categories of people in a hierarchy. Such inequality is (1) a characteristic of society, not something that simply arises from individual differences; (2) universal, yet variable in form; (3) persistent over many generations; and (4) supported by cultural beliefs.

2. Caste systems, common in agrarian societies, are based on ascription and permit little or no social mobility. Caste hierarchy, which is supported by strong moral beliefs, shapes a person's entire life, including occupation and marriage.

3. Class systems, typical of industrial societies, reflect a greater measure of individual achievement. The emphasis on achievement allows for social mobility, so classes are less clearly defined than castes.

4. Socialist societies have historically claimed to be classless because of public ownership of productive property. Such societies, however, are unquestionably stratified, especially with regard to power.

5. Social stratification persists over time because of

support from various social institutions and the power of ideology to define inequality as just, natural, or the expression of divine will.

6. The Davis-Moore thesis states that social stratification is universal because it contributes to the operation of society. In class systems, unequal rewards motivate the most able people to perform the most important occupational positions.

7. Critics of the Davis-Moore thesis note that (1) it is difficult to determine objectively the functional importance of any occupational position; (2) stratification prevents many people from developing their abilities; and (3) social stratification often generates social conflict.

8. Karl Marx's social-conflict analysis has had an enormous influence on the sociological debate over social stratification. Marx recognized two major social classes in industrial societies: the capitalists, or *bourgeoisie*, who own the means of production and seek profits; and the *proletariat*, who provide labor in exchange for wages.

9. The socialist revolution that Marx predicted has not occurred in industrial societies like Canada. While some sociologists cite this fact as evidence that Marx's analysis was flawed, others point out that our society is still marked by pronounced social inequality and substantial class conflict.

10. Max Weber identified three distinct dimensions of social inequality: economic class, social status or prestige, and power. Taken together, these three dimensions form a complex hierarchy of socioeconomic standing.

11. Gerhard and Jean Lenski observe that, historically, technological advances have been associated with more pronounced social stratification. A limited reversal of this trend occurs in advanced industrial societies, as represented by the "Kuznets Curve."

12. Social stratification is a complex and controversial area of research because it deals not only with facts but with values that suggest how society should be organized.

Key Concepts

blue-collar occupations   work involving mostly manual labor

caste system   a system of social stratification based on ascription

class system   a system of social stratification based on individual achievement

ideology   cultural beliefs that reflect and support the interests of certain categories of people

meritocracy   a system of social stratification based entirely on personal merit

social mobility   changes in people's positions in a system of social stratification

social stratification   a system by which society ranks categories of people in a hierarchy

socioeconomic status   a composite ranking based on various dimensions of social inequality

status consistency   consistent standing across various dimensions of social inequality

structural social mobility   a shift in the social position of large numbers of people due more to changes in society itself than to individual efforts

white-collar occupations   higher-prestige work involving mostly mental activity

Suggested Readings

The first of these two books explores a number of issues raised in this chapter. The second, a historical account, traces how sociology has grappled with the study of social stratification.

Charles E. Hurst. *Social Inequality: Forms, Causes, and Consequences.* Needham Heights, MA: Allyn & Bacon, 1992.

Michael D. Grimes. *Class in Twentieth-Century American*

Sociology: An Analysis of Theories and Measurement Strategies. New York: Praeger, 1991.

This recent collection of essays brings together a number of influential points of view concerning social diversity and hierarchy.

David B. Grusky, ed. *Social Stratification: Class, Race, and*

Gender in Sociological Perspective. Boulder, CO: West-view, 1992.

This analysis of social stratification in Sweden points up the role of culture and national politics in the creation of this nation's extensive welfare system.

Sven E. Olsson. *Social Policy and Welfare State in Sweden.* Lund, Sweden: Arkiv, 1990.

This book compares social equality in three distinctive societies.

Sidney Verba with Steven Kelman, Gary R. Orren, Ichiro Miyake, Joji Watanuki, Ikuo Kabashima, and G. Donald Ferree, Jr. *Elites and the Idea of Equality: A Comparison of Japan, Sweden, and the United States.* Cambridge, MA: Harvard University Press, 1987.

Discussions about social hierarchy often revolve around the thorny question of whether, by nature, individuals are selfish or altruistic. This collection of a dozen essays presents comparative evidence of the existence of altruism in every culture.

Margaret S. Clark, ed. *Prosocial Behavior.* Newbury Park, CA: Sage, 1991.

This collection of reprinted articles appro equality from a number of perspectives.

James Curtis, Edward Grabb, Neil Gilbert (eds.). *Social Inequality in* Prentice Hall Canada, 1993.

John Porter and a number of colleagues set out to replicate and expand upon work by Blau and Duncan on American status attainment. This paper shows that Canada's social mobility rate is almost identical to that of the U.S.

Monica Boyd, John Goyder, Frank E. Jones, Hugh A. McRoberts, Peter Pineo and John Porter. "Status Attainment in Canada: Findings of the Canadian Mobility Study." *Canadian Review of Sociology and Anthropology* 18:657–673, 1981.

The rate of mobility in a society is largely a function of the shape or structure of its stratification system. Tepperman develops a model that deals with shifts in the shape of stratification systems, and in social mobility, with industrialization.

Lorne Tepperman. "A Simulation of Social Mobility in Industrial Societies." *Canadian Review of Sociology and Anthropology* 13:26–42, 1976.

SOCIAL CLASS IN CANADA

"It was hot and cold running politicians on New Year's Eve, 1983, at the spectacular villa of Paul Desmarais. Brian Mulroney, Pierre Trudeau, and Bill Davis tripped the light fantastic with tycoons and citizens of Tinsel Town at the Palm Beach mansion of this Montreal magnate" (Francis, 1986:48–51). Among the others invited that evening were Estée Lauder, Dinah Shore, Douglas Fairbanks, and several Liberal and Conservative senators. The setting was a "one-story cream stucco-and-stone mansion, with tall arched windows and yellow-and-white decor"—one of the finest homes in Palm Beach, Florida. The host, Paul Desmarais, is the chairman of a huge empire, Power Corporation of Canada, and the richest French-Canadian in the world. He is in the multibillion-dollar league.

Desmarais is unusual in that he established rather than inherited a dynasty. With his French political connections and business agressiveness, he managed to overcome the disadvantage of not being born into rich anglophone society. Born in Sudbury, Desmarais graduated from the University of Ottawa and plunged into business, taking over a nearly bankrupt bus company. "To save money, he did the maintenance himself on his fleet of nineteen buses and sometimes paid his drivers in bus tickets when there was not enough cash." He was helped in his move to bigger and better things by the demand for bilingual directors of major corporations, but he clearly had driving ambition, business smarts, timing, and the ability to cultivate appropriate contacts. One would not expect to learn that the man who built the Power Corp. empire is shy, stutters, and suffers serious asthma.

Paul and Jacqui Desmarais have one of Canada's best collections of works by Krieghoff and the Group of Seven—and beautiful homes in Montreal, the Laurentians, and Palm Beach. They also have a star-studded list of friends who often blend the political and the personal. When their son married the daughter of Jean Chrétien, the reception was held in the West Block of Parliament Hill. Economist and journalist Diane Francis refers to the marriage as "a match made in heaven, symbolizing more than any Desmarais deal an ability to match Power with power" (Francis, 1986).

The Desmarais family is one of about thirty-two families who control an inordinate amount of Canada's wealth. Canada's laws and tax structure allow or help them to maintain control of their business empires and other assets and to pass that control on to the next generation. The immense wealth of this handful of families places them in stark contrast to the hundreds of thousands of Canadian families struggling to keep their heads above water.

Dimensions of Social Inequality

We have long considered our society to be responsive to individual initiative. We have neither a feudal aristocracy nor, with the notable exception of our treatment of Natives, a caste system that rigidly ranks categories of people.

Even so, Canadian society is highly stratified. The rich not only control most of the money, but they also benefit from more schooling, they enjoy better health, and they consume a greater share of almost all goods and services than others do. On the other end of the socio-economic spectrum, poor families struggle from day to day simply to make ends meet. This chapter will explain that the popular perception of Canada as a society with a bulging middle class and a uniformly high quality of life does not square with many important facts.

We tend to underestimate the extent of stratification in our society. Our egalitarian values suggest that we experience equality of opportunity, widespread upward mobility and that, at the very least, we provide a broad social safety net that catches those who fall through the cracks. Generally, we fail to recognize that, in reality, birth confers on some people advantages and opportunities that others who are less fortunate could never imagine.

Social inequality in Canada is not easily recognized because our primary groups—including family, neighbors, and friends—typically have the same social standing as we do. At work, we tend to mix with others like ourselves. In effect, most of our daily interaction involves a narrow stratum of society, with only brief and impersonal encounters with people very different from ourselves. The mass media, even in their ads, project a largely middle-class picture of our social world, and recently governments have eagerly quoted statistics showing that Canadians, overall, have the highest standard of living in the world. The net effect of this bombardment with images of homogeneity is that the very rich and the very poor are largely invisible to the rest of us.

When people do acknowledge their differences, they often talk of inequality as if it were determined by a single factor such as money. More accurately, however, social class in Canada has several dimensions. *Socio-economic status* (SES), discussed in Chapter 9 ("Social Stratification"), amounts to a composite measure of social position that encompasses not only money but power, occupational prestige, and schooling.

Income

One important dimension of inequality involves **income**, *occupational wages or salaries and earnings from investments.* Statistics Canada reports that in 1991, the average family income in Canada was $53,131, marking a significant decline for two consecutive years. Those two years of decline eroded half of the gains made since the early 1980s (as measured in constant 1991 dollars). Figure 10-1 reveals the fluctuation in buying power of the average family from 1978 to 1991 and suggests that when the two end points are compared, there is actually very little improvement in the interval.

Table 10-1, which shows the distribution of income by quintile among all Canadian families from 1951 to 1991, suggests remarkable stability over time. Taking 1991 as the point of reference, the 20 percent of families with the highest earnings received 40 percent

FIGURE 10-1   AVERAGE FAMILY INCOME IN CONSTANT 1991 DOLLARS, 1978–1991
SOURCE: Statistics Canada, Catalogue No. 13-207.

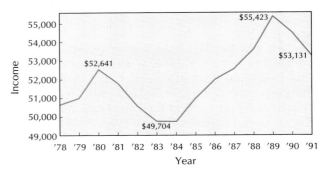

TABLE 10-1   DISTRIBUTION OF FAMILY INCOME BY QUINTILE* IN CANADA, 1951–1991, AND IN THE U.S., 1990

Quintile	Canada					U.S.
	1951	1961	1971	1981	1991	1990
Lowest	6.1	6.6	5.6	6.4	6.4	3.9
Second	12.9	13.5	12.6	12.9	12.2	9.6
Middle	17.4	18.3	18.0	18.3	17.6	15.9
Fourth	22.4	23.4	23.7	24.1	23.9	24.0
Highest	41.1	38.4	40.0	38.4	40.0	46.6
Total	100.0	100.0	100.0	100.0	100.0	100.0

* Quintiles divide those with income into five equal categories. The distribution refers to the percentage of total income going to each category.
SOURCES: Fréchette (1988); Statistics Canada, Catalogue No. 13-207; U.S. Bureau of the Census (1991).

of all income, while the bottom 20 percent made only 6.4 percent. In short, the bulk of the nation's income is earned by a small proportion of families, while the rest of the population makes do with far less.

A glance at the Canadian figures over a forty-year period suggests that little has changed in terms of the pattern of income distribution. The stability in the figures is quite surprising considering the fact that we experienced substantial economic growth during the period. In addition, our social welfare system, which is intended to redistribute income to those who are less well off, became firmly established during this interval. It would appear that increases in government transfer payments have been accompanied by decreases in primary income (Fréchette, 1988).

A comparison of the 1991 Canadian and 1990 American figures in Table 10-1 reveals a substantial difference between the two countries that is probably attributable to the more broadly based social welfare programs in our country which, however ineffectively, do indeed transfer income from the wealthy to the poor. Where our lowest quintile receives 6.4 percent of all income, in the U.S. the comparable figure is 3.9. In Canada, the highest quintile receives 40 percent of income where in the U.S. it receives 46.6 percent. Thus, the difference between rich and poor is more marked in the U.S. where income distribution is more clearly skewed towards the highest quintile. Furthermore, while the distribution of income within Canada has remained stable, within the U.S., income disparity actually increased during the 1980s, as a result of changes in the economy, new tax policies, and cuts in social programs that assist low-income people (Levy, 1987; Reich, 1989).

Canada Map 10-1 shows the median income for each province and territory within Canada, suggesting that 1990 incomes are lowest in Newfoundland, Prince Edward Island, and New Brunswick, and highest in the two territories and Ontario. Median incomes range from a low of $13,834 in Newfoundland to $23,405 in the Yukon.

Income is but one component of the broader economic factor of **wealth**, *the total amount of money and valuable goods that a person or family controls.* Wealth in the form of stocks, bonds, real estate, and other privately owned property is distributed even less equally than income. Paul Desmarais has to declare his "income" to Revenue Canada, but not the value of his mansions or business holdings. It is the control of these kinds of assets that really sets the wealthy apart from the aver-

age person or the poor in Canada. When the political left talks of establishing a wealth tax and an inheritance tax, it is this component of wealth that it seeks to redistribute.

Power

In Canadian society, as elsewhere, wealth stands as an important source of power. People who own substantial shares of corporations, for example, make decisions that create jobs for ordinary people or scale back operations, putting men and women out of work.

For this reason, the small proportion of families who own most of the property in Canada typically set the agenda in the Canadian political system (Clement, 1975; Francis, 1986), in part through the kinds of social and economic links illustrated in the Desmarais story at the beginning of this chapter. Chapter 18 ("Politics and Government") raises a question that has engaged sociologists for decades: Can a society maintain a political democracy if a small share of the population controls most of the wealth? Some analysts maintain that, while the rich may have some advantages, they do not dominate the political process. Others argue that, in general, the political system operates to serve the interests of the "super-rich."

Occupational Status for Males and Females

Occupation is a major determinant of income, wealth, and power. In addition, it is an important source of social prestige. So important is occupation to the nature of social interaction, that one of the first questions we want answered about a new acquaintance is, "What does she *do*?"—meaning *do for a living*. Once we learn that Bonnie Shnier Monik is the President of Gesco Industries, Inc., we can make numerous assumptions about her lifestyle, education, and income. We are likely to treat her with respect and listen more closely to her opinions. Knowledge of another person's occupation, or lack thereof, might lead to very different emotional and behavioral reactions from other people.

For more than half a century, sociologists have measured the relative social prestige of various occupations (Counts, 1925; Blishen, 1958; Hodge, Treiman, & Rossi, 1966; Blishen et al., 1987). Surveys requiring respondents to rank occupations in terms of prestige produce a ranking that reflects both income and education. Physicians, lawyers, and engineers (high on income and education) are ranked near the top on prestige while cashiers and janitors are ranked near the bottom. In global perspective, occupational prestige rankings tend to be roughly the same in all industrial societies (Ma, 1987).

Table 10-2 shows the ranking of various occupational categories in Canada in 1986, based on the Blishen scale, which uses income and education to assess socio-economic status and produces a ranking very similar to the survey-based prestige scales. When 514 census occupations are ranked, physicians and surgeons come out at the top with a score of 101.32, while

newspaper carriers and vendors have a score of 17.81. Collapsing occupations into broader categories automatically reduces the range of scores, but the data are still instructive. Among other things, one notes that in the middle range of occupations, the Blishen scores are lower for women than for men—particularly in the various white- and blue-collar categories. This, of course, is where the *pink ghetto* jobs are concentrated (i.e., the predominantly female jobs that are designated as having lower status and paid accordingly). Although males and females tend to have very similar educational levels, with the few differences usually resulting from *higher* educational attainment among females, one can see marked differences in male and female incomes. In

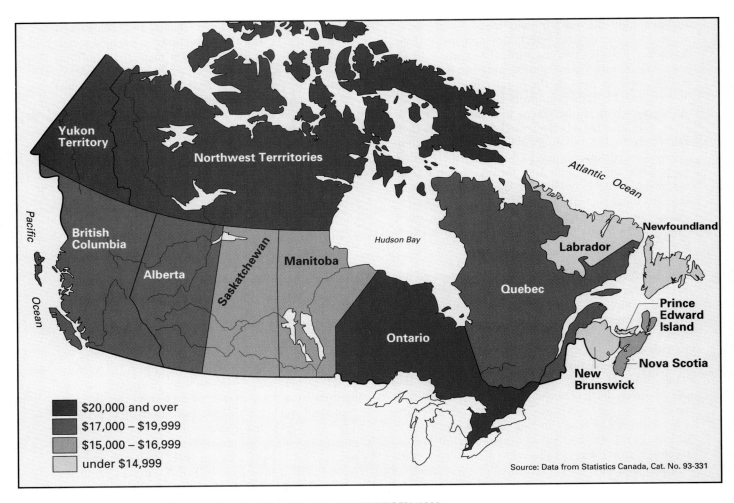

CANADA MAP 10-1   MEDIAN INCOMES BY PROVINCE AND TERRITORY, 1990

TABLE 10-2   OCCUPATIONAL CATEGORIES BY AVERAGE BLISHEN SCORES, YEARS OF SCHOOLING, INCOME, AND SEX, 1986

Occupation	Blishen Scores Male	Female	Years of Schooling Male	Female	Income ($) Male	Female
1. High-level management	69	67	14.0	14.0	62,555	36,637
2. Professional	65	65	15.0	15.0	38,226	27,672
3. Middle management	52	52	13.0	13.0	36,935	21,894
4. Semi-professional/technician	52	51	13.6	14.0	30,784	25,732
5. Upper (skilled) white collar	46	42	12.7	12.9	37,334	18,005
6. Upper (skilled) blue collar	44	37	11.0	11.6	28,572	18,476
7. Lower (unskilled) white collar	33	32	12.0	12.0	23,016	13,301
8. Lower (unskilled) blue collar	32	28	10.5	10.0	22,186	13,444
9. Farmers	28	28	10.0	14.0	26,528	–13,147*
10. Farm laborers	24	24	10.0	11.0	14,774	8,830

* The negative income reflects net losses for some farmers. Since there are relatively few female farmers, a large net loss for a small number of individuals can produce a negative average income for the category as a whole.
SOURCE: Creese, Guppy, & Meissner (1991:37), based on analysis of data collected for the 1986 General Social Survey.

most of the occupational categories, women earn about 60 percent of male income, but in the professional and semi-professional/technical categories, the figures are 72 and 84 percent respectively. (Women fare best in the *self-employed* segment of professionals, where they earn 88 percent of the income earned by their male counterparts.) In the upper white-collar category, which includes supervisors and skilled clerical, sales, and service occupation, women make less than 50 percent of male earnings.

Table 10-3 takes us ahead in time to 1991 and provides average income figures (based on the census) for males and females employed full time, all year in selected occupations. The occupations are ranked by male income. Physicians and surgeons have the highest incomes, although not as high as some of the negative publicity surrounding doctors would lead us to believe. Dentists are not too far behind physicians, but since their incomes do not come from public funds they are not as controversial (except in our incoherent private mutterings as we depart dentists' offices with frozen jaws and aching chequebooks). Elected members of legislative assemblies (also subject to loud public criticism) earn less than police officers and pharmacists. At the bottom of the income scale, one finds housekeepers and child care workers, with chefs, artists, musicians, and actors above them. Once again we see variation in the size of the gap between male and female incomes. In only *two* of the selected occupations (sociologists and radio and television announcers) do women actually make (slightly) more than men. Whatever the gender of the recipient, the range of average incomes for various occupations is substantial in Canada and implies vastly different lifestyles.

Schooling

Education, as an important determinant of labor force participation, occupation, and income, is highly valued in the world's major industrial countries. In 1988, Canada ranked third after the U.S. and Germany in the proportion of adults, twenty-five years of age and over, with at least a high school education—at 64.2 percent compared with 76.1 percent in the U.S. (Secretary of State, 1992:38). Although industrial societies generally define schooling as everyone's right, the opportunity for formal education is not always equal. In Canada, traditionally, women did not pursue formal education as far as their male counterparts; however, in recent years, more than half of the community college diplomas and undergraduate degrees have been earned by women (though they have not caught up with men in earning master's and doctoral degrees). Table 10-2 suggests that while educational differences between men and women employed in similar jobs are minimal, overall, women have completed slightly more years of schooling than their male colleagues. As Chapter 16 ("Education") points out, Canadians of Asian and black origin are slightly more likely than their British or French counterparts to have completed high school and university. It is the *Native* population that has much lower completion rates.

Schooling not only promotes personal development but also affects an individual's occupation and income. Most of the occupations in the top half of Table 10-3 require university degrees and, in some cases, advanced degrees. Individuals with higher levels of schooling are more likely to be in the labor force, to be employed rather than unemployed, and to earn higher incomes (Secretary of State, 1992).

TABLE 10-3 AVERAGE INCOME FOR SELECTED OCCUPATIONS FOR THOSE WORKING FULL TIME, ALL YEAR, 1990 (RANKED BY MALE INCOME)

Occupation	Male	Female
Physicians & surgeons	$111,261	$73,071
Dentists	99,280	67,997
Lawyers & notaries	86,108	50,012
Athletes	75,358	n.a.
General managers & other senior officials	74,425	40,633
Osteopaths & chiropractors	68,404	45,368
University teachers	65,671	49,000
Veterinarians	57,542	39,262
Architects	53,083	36,083
Economists	52,739	51,369
Civil engineers	50,389	38,137
Police officers & detectives	49,497	38,415
Pharmacists	48,949	35,100
Biologists & related scientists	47,725	35,597
Members of legislative bodies	47,539	37,360
Secondary school teacher	47,385	41,667
Elementary & kindergarten teachers	45,471	37,694
Real estate sales	43,544	35,093
Systems analysts, computer programmers	43,025	35,932
Writers & editors	41,552	33,007
Sociologists	41,549	41,830
Radio & television announcers	36,614	37,563
Nurses	35,964	33,317
Secretaries & stenographers	33,839	23,880
Actors/actresses	33,359	22,879
Photographers & camera operators	31,323	22,949
Tool & die makers	30,646	25,860
Carpenters	29,565	19,512
Painters, paperhangers	28,763	23,483
Musicians & singers	27,036	20,066
Orderlies	24,984	23,599
Painters, sculptors, & related artists	22,396	14,533
Cashiers & tellers	21,913	17,243
Chefs & cooks	21,079	16,294
Child care workers	20,987	13,252
Farmers	19,649	12,871
Housekeepers, servants	19,210	14,053

SOURCE: Statistics Canada 1991, Cat. No. 93–332

Ascription and Social Stratification

To a large extent, the class system in Canada rewards individual talent and effort. But, as explained in Chapter 9 ("Social Stratification"), class systems still rest on ascription: who we are at birth greatly influences what we become later in life.

Ancestry

Ancestry, or what we commonly call *social background*, determines our point of entry into the system of social inequality. Some families in Canada, including the Reichmans, Blacks, Bentleys, Irvings, and Desmarais, are known around the world. On a more modest scale, certain families in practically every Canadian community have wealth and power that have become well established over several generations.

Being born to privilege or poverty sets the stage for our future schooling, occupation, and income. Although there are numerous "rags to riches" stories in Canada, many of the richest individuals—those with hundreds of millions of dollars in wealth—derived their fortunes primarily from inheritance. By the same token, the "inheritance" of poverty and the lack of opportunity that goes with it just as surely shapes the future for those in need. Families are able to transmit their levels of property, power, aspiration, and possibilities from one generation to the next, but, as we shall see in the section on social mobility, they do this mainly through their impact upon the educational attainments of the younger generation.

Race and Ethnicity

Although we tend to think of our society as largely egalitarian, race and ethnicity remain important determinants of social position. In Chapter 16 ("Education") we saw that, in Canada, people of black and Asian origin have higher levels of educational attainment than those of British and French origin and that they also have high levels of labor force participation. The Native population, on the other hand, has not aquired the same levels of education or gained access to the labor force to the same extent. Table 10-4 suggests that race and ethnicity do have a bearing on income in Canada.

Observing income levels for males alone—because the female pattern is quite different—one notes that, for either average or median incomes, the categories are ranked in the same order: British, French, Asian, black, and Native. Average income is about $6,000 lower for blacks than for the British; the average income for Natives, in turn, is about $6,000 lower than for blacks. Median incomes reveal smaller gaps between the first four categories followed by a drop of $7,500 between blacks and Natives. Overall, male Native income is about half that of the British males.

TABLE 10-4 AVERAGE AND MEDIAN INCOMES* BY SEX, FOR SELECTED CATEGORIES, CANADA 1985**

Category	Average Income ($)		Median Income ($)	
	Male	Female	Male	Female
British	24,087	12,579	20,214	9,450
French	21,343	11,772	18,544	8,815
Asian	20,738	13,441	16,479	10,650
Black	18,285	13,049	16,057	10,891
Native	12,581	8,579	8,537	6,829

* For all those with income.
** Latest data available.
SOURCE: Statistics Canada, Profile of Ethnic Groups—Dimensions, *1989.*

Whether we are looking at average or median incomes for females, they are consistently lower than the comparable figures for males, but the ranking of categories is very different. While women, overall, seem to have difficulty translating their educational attainments into well-paid occupations, this appears to be less true of women of color, who have *higher* incomes (average or median) than their British and French counterparts. Native women, on either measure, have substantially lower incomes; they are clearly disadvantaged in terms of both gender and ethnicity (Gerber, 1990).

However, Figure 10-2 reveals that the income gap between Native people who are employed full time and other groups is substantially less, perhaps indicating that the barriers they face are in *finding* employment

more than in wage discrimination once employed. Within this select group of individuals employed full time, all year, male incomes can be ranked as before, but the differences between categories are much smaller. Women in all categories have lower incomes than men, but the differences among the women are diminished as well.

It is Figure 10-3 that most clearly reveals the extent to which each ethnic or racial category is firmly rooted in what one might call upper-middle-class comfort. Keeping in mind that $35,000 in 1985 was a fairly substantial income ($35,000 and over was the upper cut-off point in 1986 census tables) note that, of *all* British-origin males fifteen years of age and over, 20.6 percent had incomes of that magnitude or greater. The comparable figures for the other categories are substantially lower and in the same rank order as before. Once again, Natives fare the worst, with only 4.9 percent of males earning incomes above $35,000. In none of the categories does the equivalent female population have even 4 percent in the high income bracket. While it is true that income is only one component of social class, race and ethnicity are clearly associated with differential placement on our socio-economic hierarchy.

Gender

Societies also place men and women in different social positions. Of course, people of both sexes are born into

FIGURE 10-2 AVERAGE INCOME BY SEX FOR SELECTED CATEGORIES FOR FULL TIME, ALL YEAR WORKERS, 1985*

* Latest data available.
SOURCE: Adapted from Statistics Canada, Profile of Ethnic Groups—Dimensions, *1989.*

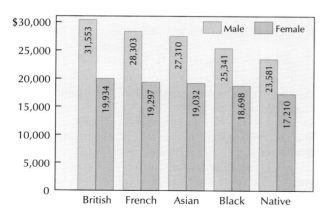

FIGURE 10-3 PERCENTAGE OF TOTAL POPULATION 15 YEARS OF AGE AND OVER EARNING $35,000 OR MORE, 1985*

* Latest data available.
SOURCE: Adapted from Statistics Canada, Profile of Ethnic Groups—Dimensions, *1989.*

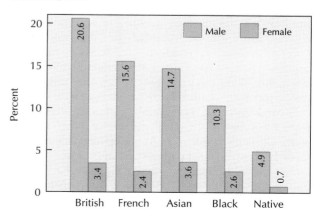

"Fore Word" from Don Harron's **The Canadian Establishment**

That's all they ast me to rite, them eddyters at Debunk's. Fore word about the relayshuns the wife and I has down to Tronto in the high mucky-muck area of town. So I rit down the fore word: "Them ritches is differnt." Wernt good enuff, the pubelisher sed. First off, sumbuddy name of Effscotch Fitsgeritol rit the same blame thing yeers ago. Second off, fore words in books is spose to run on fer a cuppla pages. Shows yuh the power of inflayshun.

To begin at our beginning, us Farquharsons immigrunted here from Ireland in yer forties—not yer 19 but yer 18 forties. We got kick out of Ballyhilly in yer County Antrum by the same bunch had boot us outta Scotland a cuppla sentrys earlier, them overlard Anglican Saxaphones. They didden want us pessants on their land; they wanted sheep, on accounta yuh kin skin them morn once. So we hung round Ireland fer a hunnert yeers tryna grow potaters, but the hole country got over-run with them same blame absentee Anglish landlards. This time they wanted to stop plantin potaters, and it look like they was aimin fer to plant Farquharsons insted. So that's why we lit out fer Uppity Canada, yer boat peeple of a sexysintenniel ago.

So Valry Rozedale and me cum from common incesters, and wen we started we wuz all in the same boat. Wen her fokes left Ireland ther wernt no lace curtins on ther shanty eether, and they kep the pig in the house jist like everybuddy elts. So how cum over here in Canada, where there's sposed to be no clash sistern and we're all cremated equal, that this Rozedale woman is close to yer tops while Charles Ewart Farquharson is scrapin bottoms?

[...]

Now I got no mind to be among caféteria sassiety downtown with my name in yer Socialist Register. But I jist wonder how our branch of our family tree ends up tryna scratch a livin wile our city cussin sits around eatin canopys offen a tray and drinkin cavvyar. I know we're sposed to be content with our lot in life, but sumtimes I wish mine wernt so darn far north. Mebby the trubble start wen us Farquharsons got off the boat and rushed off in all drekshuns. I dunno why my grate granfather hedded strait fer the lumbar regions, becuz that stuff run out after a few ginrations, and we bin outa our tree on our land fer quite sum time.

I gess Valry's bunch didden move too much wen they got offa the boat. They hung around Yorkvile, witch is what Tronto was call at the time. Not too much goin on down there in them daze, jist a few tooriests windershoppin as they stared at everybuddy's buteeks. The mane action

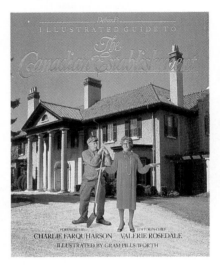

Canadian humorist Don Harron poses as both Charlie Farquarson and his rich city cousin, Valerie Rosedale.

seem to be over on Jarvis Street and that's wher Valry's fokes open a meet market speshulizing in tender loins. They don't menshun that parta ther famly history much, but Valry gits downrite boastfull wen she tells about her gramma bein one

families at every social level. Women born into families of high social standing, therefore, draw on many more social resources than men born into disadvantaged families. Yet, women earn less income, accumulate less wealth, enjoy less occupational prestige, and place lower in *some* aspects of educational achievement when compared to men (Bernard, 1981; Lengermann & Wallace, 1985; Creese et al., 1991). We have already seen that women are uniformly disadvantaged with respect to income and that, on several of the measures used, women (in each of the racial and ethnic categories) are worse off than Native men. Women, in effect are *very* severely disadvantaged with respect to income.

Later in the chapter, you will discover that women do not "inherit" the social position of their fathers to the extent that men do. You will also learn that households headed by women are many times more likely to be poor than are those headed by men. Chapter 13 ("Sex and Gender") further examines the link between gender and social stratification.

Social Classes in Canada

As Chapter 9 ("Social Stratification") explained, people living in rigid caste systems consider relative social rankings to be clear and obvious to everyone. Defining the social categories in a more fluid class system, however, poses a number of challenges.

Consider the joke about the fellow who orders a pizza, asking that it be cut into six slices because he isn't hungry enough to eat eight. While sociologists acknowledge extensive social inequality in Canada, they have

of the founderers of a place fer wayword girls call Hav-a-Gal Callitch. It musta bin kinda a haffway house, becuz as soon as Jarvis Street started gettin fulla rundown peeple they mooved uptown lickety-spit. The "Condemm" sine was put up in front of the old billding by yer Bored of Helth and in no time it was bot up by them Canajun Broadcastering Commontaters, hoo have bin tryna prop up the condemm place ever since.

Everybuddy elts move northa Bloor Street fer to git away frum it all. That's wen this place Rozedale start up I gess. Now, cussin Valry is one of them, even tho she was *knée* (pardon my French) a Farquharson. I dunno wether her husbin's peeple name the place Rozedale or name therselfs after the place, but I suspek that after bein with that Jarvis crowd, they change their name so's they cood git a fresh start movin into a hireclass naberhood. I mind last time we had a family reonion was jist afore World War One, and its the oney time I ever got to meet any kin of them Rozedales, and they turn out to be mostly old Coots and Ferries. Charles Rozedale (that's his name, witch makes me, I spose, the udder Charlie), his mother was one of yer old Ottawa Coots, and his father was an old Toronto Ferrie. Now yer Coots and yer Ferries is offshoots of yer

Farquharson klansmen, so that'd make Mr. and Miz Rozedale first cussins to themsels. No wonder they looks so much alike, give er take his wallrust mustash. They say breeding tells, and inter-marge sure shows on the faces of our family.

But the thing that reely sticks up my craw is that both them uses this made-up name of Rozedale fer to cover up their backgrounds. And yet whenever there's a Rabbi Burns nite or Sin Andrews Balls, the both of them is out there shakin a boot and wavin ther Farquharson kilt, him in a minny and hern a maxy. Resta the yeer she never menshuns that she is reely an old Farquharson. I bleeve she was also a Leitch on her mother's peeple's side.

[...]

And do you know wat reely gits my dandruff up? Mosta these urbane plutocraps becomes country gentilemen on weak ends, by buyin up good farmland and doin nothin with it but a little horsin around on the side and raisin a lotta Cane in ther leesure time. And wat's it all fur? So's that in November they kin show off their animal pets down to yer Royls Winterfare on Exhibitionist grounds at yer Hores Paliss nex to yer Colossalsemen. They puts on pink coats and plug hats and jumps over fensus in the big ring tryna git into their cups. If you ast me it's jist a bun-

cha horses showin ther arses to a buncha horses arses showin ther horses.

Fore word? Looks more like fore page! And I still haven't sed my fore word about my Uppity Canajan cussins. How 'bout "The ritch is indifferent"? The wife and former sweethart, Valeda, she thinks that's sour gripes, on accounta Valry Rozedale takes a cuppla dozen of our aigs regler every other weak, and pays me fer haulin her ashes, blowin her snow, and cleenin her sceptic tank at her summer place up yer Go Home Bay. But that's the differnts atween yer country mouse and yer town rat. We hasta hussle fer to make our ends meat, and them high mucky-mucks jist has to sit ther watchin their tickers tape and clippin ther coopons. As a aggravacultured worker I feel sumtimes like I'm yer vanishin Canajun. I aint exactly on the outs with the resta sassiety but I sure am a long ways frum beein in.

So if money is the root of all evil, then wat is the root of all money? Everybody wants to make the stuff, but the rich makes money with money, and if they has lotsa money then they makes lotsa money. Sure the ritch is differnt, but what's the differents? "The Rich Has Credit." That's my fore word. ...

SOURCE: Harron 1984:7–10.

long debated precisely how to divide up this social hierarchy. Some who follow Karl Marx's thinking about classes contend that there are two major categories; other sociologists suggest that our society breaks down into as many as six or seven classes (Warner & Lunt, 1941). Still others endorse Max Weber's contention that there are no clear classes at all; rather, Weber argued, people have different positions on various dimensions of social inequality. From this point of view, Canada does not contain clear classes but rather a complex status hierarchy.

The task of defining classes within the Canadian context would be far less difficult were it not for the relatively low level of status consistency. Especially toward the middle of the class system, an individual's social standing on one dimension often contradicts that person's position on another (Tepperman, 1979;

Gilbert & Kahl, 1987). A government official, for example, may control a multimillion-dollar budget yet earn a modest income. Similarly, members of the clergy typically enjoy ample prestige while possessing only moderate power and little property. Or consider a lucky professional gambler who accumulates considerable wealth yet has little power or prestige.

Finally, the social mobility typical of class systems—again, most pronounced near the middle—means that social position often changes over the life course. This further blurs the lines between social classes.

Despite these problems of definition, it is useful to think of four general social classes in Canada: the upper class, the middle class, the working class, and the lower class. As we shall explain, however, some categories are more clear-cut than others.

The Upper Class

The upper class, encompassing perhaps 3 to 5 percent of the population, derives much of its income from inherited wealth, in the form of stocks and bonds, real estate, and other investments. And this income may be substantial. In May 1989, the *Financial Post* magazine, "Moneywise" profiled fifty of the richest individuals and families in Canada, each of them with a minimum net worth of at least $125 million and seven worth at least $1 billion. The upper class is thus comprised of what Karl Marx termed "capitalists," those who own or control most of the nation's productive property. Despite this immense wealth, many members of the upper class work as top executives in large corporations—sometimes earning salaries of $500,000 or more—and as senior government officials, further enhancing their power to shape events in the nation and, increasingly, the entire world.

Members of the upper class also attain the highest levels of education, typically in the most expensive and highly regarded schools and colleges. Historically, though less so today, the upper class has been composed of people of British origin (Porter, 1975; Clement, 1975; Tepperman, 1979).

A useful distinction is sometimes made between the "upper-upper class" and the "lower-upper class." The *upper-upper class*, often described as "society" or "bluebloods," includes less than 1 percent of the Canadian population. Membership is usually the result of ascription or birth, as suggested by the old quip that the easiest way to become an "upper-upper" is to be born one. These families possess enormous wealth, primarily inherited rather than earned. For this reason, members of the upper-upper class are said to have *old money*.

Set apart by their wealth, members of the upper-upper class live in a world of exclusive affiliations. They inhabit elite neighborhoods, such as Forest Hill in Toronto or Westmount in Montreal. Schools extend this privileged environment. Their children typically attend private schools like Upper Canada College with others of similar background, completing their formal education at high-prestige universities like Cambridge, Oxford, or Harvard. In the historical pattern of European aristocrats, they study liberal arts rather than vocationally directed subjects. Women of the upper-upper class often maintain a full schedule of volunteer work for charitable organizations. For example, women from Toronto's upper-crust neighbourhoods are the backbone of the Toronto Symphony and the National Ballet: old-money families support these organizations, offering their time as well as funds. While helping the larger community, these activities are not entirely altruistic; volunteer work is a means by which women forge networks that identify them as members of the city's elite.

The remaining 2 to 4 percent of the population that make up the upper class falls into the *lower-upper class*. From the point of view of the average Canadian,

A popular distinction in North America and elsewhere sets off the "new rich" from people with "old money." Men and women who suddenly begin to earn high incomes tend toward public extravagance perhaps because they enjoy the new thrill of high-roller living and want others to know of their success. Those who grow up surrounded by wealth, by contrast, are more used to their privileges and more quiet about them. In short, the "conspicuous consumption" of the lower-upper class differs from the more private pursuits and characteristic understatement of the upper-upper class.

such people seem every bit as privileged as the upper-upper class. The major difference, however, is that "lower-uppers" depend on earnings rather than wealth as their primary source of income. Few people in this category inherit a vast fortune from their parents, although the majority do inherit some wealth. Especially in the eyes of members of "society," the lower-upper class constitutes the "new rich," people who can never savor the highest levels of prestige enjoyed by those with rich and famous grandparents. Thus, while the "new rich" typically live in expensive homes, they often find themselves excluded from the most prestigious clubs and associations maintained by "old-money" families. These clubs have long lists of would-be members, who undergo extensive "checks" into their suitability and require the sponsorship of several existing members.

Historically, the dream of great success has meant joining the ranks of the lower-upper class through exceptional accomplishment. The entrepreneurial individual who makes the right business moves with split-second timing, the athlete who accepts a million-dollar contract to play in the big leagues; the clever computer whiz who designs a new program that sets a standard for the industry—these are the lucky and talented achievers who reach the level of the lower-upper class. Their success stories fascinate most of us because this kind of upward social mobility has long stood as a goal which, however unlikely, is still within the realm of the possible. A dual-earner family in which both wife and husband are professionals *can* make it into this lower-upper stratum of the upper 5 percent of families (as measured by income). Members of the upper-upper class, in contrast, move in rarefied circles far from the everyday reality of the rest of us: we know so little about them that we cannot emulate them.

The Middle Class

The middle class includes about 40 to 50 percent of the Canadian population. Being so large, the middle class exerts tremendous influence on patterns of North American culture. Television and other mass media usually portray middle-class people, and most commercial advertising is directed at these "average" consumers. The middle class encompasses far more racial and ethnic diversity than the upper class. While many upper-class people (especially "upper-uppers") know each other personally, such exclusiveness and familiarity do not characterize the middle class.

The top half of this category is often termed the *upper*-middle class. Family income would be above $50,000, and potentially much higher if both wife and husband work. High income allows upper-middle-class families gradually to accumulate considerable property—a comfortable house in a fairly expensive area, several automobiles, and some investments. Virtually all upper-middle-class people receive university educations, and postgraduate degrees are common. Many work in white-collar fields such as medicine, engineering, and law, or as business executives. Lacking the power of the upper class to influence national or international events, the upper-middle class often plays an important role in local political affairs.

The rest of the middle class typically works in less prestigious white-collar occupations (as bank tellers, middle managers, and sales clerks) or in highly skilled blue-collar jobs (including electrical work and carpentry). Family income is sufficient to provide a secure, if modest, standard of living. Middle-class people generally accumulate a small amount of wealth over the course of their working lives, and most eventually own a house. Middle-class men and women are likely to be high-school graduates themselves. If they do send their children to university, it is more likely to be the one closest to home to save on accommodation.

The Working Class

Including about one-third of the population, the working class refers to people who have lower incomes than those in the middle class and virtually no accumulated wealth. In Marxist terms, the working class forms the core of the industrial proletariat. The blue-collar occupations of the working class generally yield a family income that is somewhat below the national average, although unionized blue-collar workers, especially if there are two in the family, can contribute to family incomes that are well above that level.

Besides generating less income than the occupations of the middle class, working-class jobs typically provide less personal satisfaction. Tasks tend to be routine, requiring discipline rather than imagination, and workers are usually subject to continual supervision by superiors. Working-class families, in response to this kind of work experience, tend to instill in their children the values of obedience, conformity to conventional beliefs and practices, and respect for authority. University is less likely to be part of the experience of children of working-class parents. The many working-class families who own their own homes are likely to own them in lower-cost neighborhoods.

Middle-Class Stampede?

Who participates in community festivals? Surely, the Calgary Stampede, for example, draws a cross-section of the community (and of Canadians from a wide geographic area) into a generalized tension-release ritual. Without a doubt. "Yahoos" and "yippees" will be part of the spontaneous vocabulary of people everywhere. Right?

Richard J. Ossenberg set out to show that, while homogeneous communities might give rise to generalized participation, complex urban centers like Calgary would elicit differentiated or selective participation. His research involved "a systematic pub-crawl on two evenings of the weeklong Stampede" held every July. He expected to find that members of the middle class, who are more "sensitive to legal and other restrictive norms," might be most likely to respond to the relaxation of social controls with "festival-related aggressive/expressive behaviour."

Ossenberg had already carried out extensive analysis of Calgary bar behavior as a way of discovering the social class structure in Calgary, so he knew which nine of the city's beer parlors and lounges would represent a "cross-section of social-class-related drinking establishments." Those chosen for the study were close to the Stampede Grounds; two were upper-class, three were middle-class and four were lower-class. The establishments are described as follows:

> The upper-class establishments are usually patronized by the elite oil and ranching group as well as the *nouveau riche* and the occasional white-collar couple celebrating an anniversary. The middle-class bars are patronized by clerical workers, small businessmen, and generally middle-range employees of the larger local firms, with the occasional laborers drifting in. The lower-class bars are the clearest in definition. They are patronized by service personnel, laborers, winos and deprived Indians as well as by members of newly-arrived immigrant groups.

During the two evenings of observation "only about one in ten of the tipplers at the lower-class establishments wore Western cowboy costume, and most of those who did were completely ignored by the other patrons." The noise level was lower than usual, fights broke out less frequently, prostitutes were more in evidence and patrons stuck to the normal men's parlor and "ladies and escorts" pattern, even though restrictions were lifted during the Stampede. And there were virtually no rodeo-related "yahoos" to be heard.

In the middle-class establishments—two cocktail lounges and one beer parlor in a posh hotel—90 percent or more of the patrons were in cowboy or Western costumes. In fact, the researchers were ridiculed for their lack of such attire. The noise levels were intolerable, "yippees' and "yahoos" filled the air, while back slapping and necking were the norm. Executives interacted freely with their secretaries and tourists or strangers were readily accepted and even invited out to house parties. Call girls, rather than streetwalkers, made their appearances.

The two upper-middle-class cocktail lounges in Calgary's plush, reputable hotels presented a very different picture. About 25 percent of patrons were costumed, but the noisy celebration was missing. Here, as in the working-class bars, it was "business as usual." The few costumed patrons who tried to liven up the scene soon left in disgust: "Let's blow this joint—it's like a graveyard."

Ossenberg concluded that Stampede week is "functional" for people who are inhibited in their daily lives and "look forward to the 'green light' of tolerated deviance during a community festival." Behavior during such festivals reflects the social structure of the city but does not reinforce solidarity across class lines. It is, in effect, a "middle-class 'binge'."

SOURCE: Adapted from Ossenberg, 1979.

As these facts suggest, working-class people lack the power to shape events, leading many to cultivate a sense of fatalism about their lives. Families live in modest neighborhoods because they cannot afford better housing. They may want their children to attend university but lack the money to send them. Many find little satisfaction in their jobs, and opportunities for upward mobility are scarce. Still, working-class families express a great deal of pride in the possessions they have and compare themselves favorably to those who are not working at all.

The Lower Class

The 20 percent of our population with the lowest family income makes up the lower class, whose lack of income renders life unstable and insecure. In 1990,

North American television programming has typically portrayed people in a relatively narrow range of the class structure, from middle class to lower-upper class. In the last decade or so, however, an increasing number of shows have featured working-class families—belated recognition of the fact that at least one-third of all families think of themselves in these terms. Roseanne Arnold, herself from a working-class family, is the star of one of the most popular shows on television.

Life expectancy is closely related to social-class position. Poor people—especially males—have a strikingly high rate of death and injury from illness, accident, and violence. To some extent, this reflects their dangerous environment; in addition, it may indicate that people caught up in poverty have little reason to think that the future will be brighter than the present.

close to 4 million people (roughly 14 percent of our population) were classified by the federal government as poor. While some of these people are supported entirely by social welfare payments, others are among the "working poor"—those whose incomes from working at full-time jobs fall short of what is required to cover necessities like food, shelter, and clothing.

The poor typically work in low-prestige jobs that provide minimal income and little intrinsic satisfaction. Some have managed to complete high school, but college diplomas and university degrees are relatively rare. In fact, many lower-class men and women are functionally illiterate.

Lower-class families find themselves segregated into specific, less desirable neighborhoods—some of which are ethnically or racially distinct. Although there are many poor people in small towns and rural areas—

where resource-based industries have collapsed or plants closed—physical segregation of the poor is most starkly apparent in cities where large numbers of poor people live in rental housing shunned by the other social classes.

Lower-class children learn early on the harsh reality that many people consider them only marginal members of society. Observing their parents and other lower-class adults, they may conclude that their own future holds little hope for breaking the cycle of poverty. Lower-class life, then, often generates self-defeating resignation, as these people are cut off from the resources of an affluent society: welfare dependency, as a lifestyle, can be passed from one generation to the next. Some of the poor simply give up, but others work sometimes at two or three jobs to make ends meet, going to all kinds of lengths to avoid going on welfare.

Social Mobility

Ours is a dynamic society marked by a significant measure of social mobility. As we noted in the last chapter, social mobility involves individuals moving upward or downward in the stratification system. Earning a university degree, securing a higher-paying job, or succeeding in a business endeavor contributes to *upward social mobility*, while dropping out of school, losing a job, or having a business enterprise fail may signal the onset of *downward social mobility*.

Social mobility is not just a matter of the changing fortune of individuals. Changes in society itself account for most social mobility, at least over long periods. During the first half of this century, for example, industrialization expanded the economy, dramatically raising living standards for the majority of Canadians. Even without being very good swimmers, so to speak, people were able to "ride a rising tide of prosperity." As explained presently, *structural social mobility* in a downward direction has more recently dealt many people economic setbacks.

In studying social mobility, sociologists distinguish between changes within a single generation and shifts between generations of a family. **Intragenerational social mobility** refers to *a change in social position occurring during a person's lifetime*. Sociologists pay even greater attention to **intergenerational social mobility**, *upward or downward social mobility of children in relation to their parents*. Social mobility across generations reflects changes in society that affect virtually everyone. Another way of looking at the question of social mobility is to ask about the extent of equality of opportunity in comparison with "inherited" social standing—or about how much social mobility, upward or downward, is driven by individual competition (Creese et al., 1991)

Social Mobility: Myth and Reality

Although "the American Dream" may be attributed to people south of the border, Canadians have traditionally shared the idea that those who apply themselves can "get ahead" and that each new generation will do better than the last.

But how much social mobility is there in Canada? Using data obtained from the 1986 General Social Survey, Creese, Guppy, and Meissner (1991) found that Canadians have been a little more likely to experience upward than downward mobility. Among women,

48 percent moved up, while 40 percent moved down: the comparable figures for men are 39 and 36 percent respectively. Only 12 percent of women and 26 percent of men experienced no mobility at all, meaning that they were in the same occupational category as their fathers. Francophones experienced less mobility than anglophones, and family background was more important for them.

Creese et al. also found that occupational inheritance occurs most commonly among men whose fathers are in the professional, white-collar, and farming categories. Women experience little occupational inheritance from their fathers, mainly because of the types of occupations available to daughters. Men also experience

On November 6, 1992, hundreds of people lined up for hours in hopes of landing one of the minimum-wage jobs being offered at a motel north of Toronto. Such sights are an increasingly common part of the postindustrial economy. Although the 1980s were a boom time for the wealthiest people in Canada, they brought no gains to most middle-income families and a slight drop in living standards for the poor.

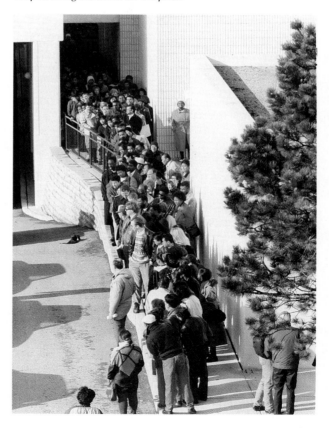

more upward intragenerational mobility than women as well as more long-range upward mobility during their careers (i.e., upward across several occupational categories). Among men, being foreign-born is associated with more upward mobility and less downward mobility than is the case for the Canadian-born.

There has been substantial upgrading of educational levels between generations. The higher the level of education and occupation of one's father, the more years of schooling one is likely to complete. Furthermore, according to Creese et al., a person's first job in the labor market is *principally* affected by his or her level of education. Parental education and occupation have an impact, not directly, but through their effects on the educational attainment of the younger generation. Once in the labor force, 56 percent of women and 49 percent of men stayed at the same job level throughout their careers.

Education, then, is the key to occupational mobility in Canada. If family background has an impact, it is through its effect on schooling. But, as we saw earlier, it seems that francophones, people of color, and, in particular, women have difficulty translating their educational accomplishments into higher-status, well-paid work.

Others have also noted the general lack of occupational inheritance in Canada. In a study of occupational mobility over four generations, Goyder and Curtis (1979) found that the occupations of great-grandfathers had no bearing whatsoever on those of their great-grandsons. Occupationally speaking, the descendants were all over the map. On the basis of their findings and those of others who have studied the extreme upper and lower ends of the spectrum, Goyder and Curtis conclude that the "two types of processes may well occur together: high over-all three-generation mobility in the general population along with low three-generation mobility in poverty and elite groups" (p. 229). In other words those at the very top and bottom of the socio-economic ladder may experience substantial occupational inheritance while those in the middle do not.

Historically, women have had less opportunity for upward mobility than men. As we shall see in Chapter 13 ("Sex and Gender"), the majority of working women hold clerical positions (such as secretaries) and low-paying service jobs (such as waitresses). These jobs offer little chance for advancement, creating barriers to upward social or economic movement. Divorce also commonly results in downward social mobility for women—but not men—as Chapter 15 ("Family") explains. Data reflecting income change during the 1980s

reveal a narrowing of the gap between the earnings of women and men, with the female to male income ratio increasing from about 60 to 70 percent over the decade.

For generations of immigrants as well as the Canadian-born, Canada has been a land of opportunity. In global perspective, however, the rates of social mobility in this country have been about the same as those of the United States and other industrial societies. As the economies of the world become more interrelated, we can expect that the structural shifts—both upward and downward—that occur in Europe and Japan will mirror those we experience here in North America.

In the last few years, Canada—in the company of much of the industrial world—has been going through economic restructuring and upheaval that will undoubtedly upset normal patterns of mobility. Much of the industrial production that provided highly-paid jobs for Canadians has been transferred to the United States (partly in response to the Free Trade Agreement) and to developing countries overseas. Throughout the negotiation of the North American Free Trade Agreement (NAFTA), companies were already moving to Mexico, from Canada and the U.S., in anticipation of more open borders. While industrial jobs migrate out of the country, a growing proportion of the new jobs being created in Canada are in the service sector, which often requires lower skill levels and pays poorly. In the meantime, a large number of highly specialized jobs remain unfilled because Canada has not produced a workforce with the required skills.

The process of deindustrialization has hurt the standard of living of Canadians and shaken our confidence. Industrial jobs are giving way to service jobs, full-time employment is disappearing and being replaced by part-time work, and real income declined between 1989 and 1990. Compared to a generation ago, far fewer now expect to improve their social position and a growing number of Canadians worry that their children will not be able to maintain the same standard of living as themselves. The standard of living in Canada has stopped rising, even though women and men are working harder than ever and more families have two or more people in the labor force.

The mixed performance of Canada's economy through the 1980s, which mirrors that of other industrialized countries, has generated intense controversy and debate—particularly with respect to the role of government in the economy, job creation, income maintenance, and the alleviation of poverty.

Poverty in Canada

Social stratification simultaneously creates "haves" and "have-nots." Poverty, therefore, inevitably exists within all systems of social inequality. The concept of poverty, however, is used in two different ways. **Relative poverty**, the universal societal trait, refers to *the deprivation of some people in relation to those who have more*. The richest and most egalitarian of societies have some members who live in relative poverty. Much more serious is **absolute poverty**, or *a deprivation of resources that is life threatening*. Defined in this way, poverty is a pressing, but solvable, human problem. As the next chapter ("Global Inequality") explains, the global dimensions of absolute poverty place the lives of perhaps 1 billion people—one in five of the earth's entire population—at risk. Even in affluent Canada, with its social welfare safety net the wrenching reality of poverty results in hunger, inadequate housing, and poor health for those at the lower end of our income scale.

The Extent of Canadian Poverty

Statistics Canada defines the "poverty line" as that below which people spend roughly 60 percent of pre-tax income on food, clothing, and shelter. In 1990, the income cut-offs for families of four were $19,117 in rural areas to $28,081 in a city of more than 500,000. Based upon this point of reference, there were close to 4 million Canadians in 1990 who had incomes below the poverty line (Colombo, 1992:88)—about 15 percent of the Canadian population. If one notes that families in the lowest quintile (Table 10-1) have incomes below $25,000, it would appear that most of them live below the poverty line and have severe difficulties making ends meet.

Our lack of progress in eliminating poverty prompted a United Nations committee to sharply criticize the Canadian government "for allowing poverty and homelessness to persist at disturbing levels in one of the world's richest countries" (York, 1993:A1). The report goes on to criticize Canada for the fact that, over the past decade, we have made "no measurable progress" in alleviating poverty. We have been criticized by the U.N. committee because of poverty among more than half of our single mothers, a million children who are poor, and dependence on voluntary food-banks to deal with hunger.

Poverty means hunger, and many of the people at lower income levels are forced to rely on food banks and soup kitchens, both of which, in Canada, are run by voluntary organizations. The demand for food banks has increased substantially over the past few years to a point where, in 1992, Canada's 372 food banks were serving, on a regular basis, 2 million people, 40 percent of whom were under sixteen years of age (Colombo, 1992:88). The fact that so many people feel the need to resort to food banks, which function only because some people volunteer to staff them while others donate food, is particularly distressing in a country where we *have* the resources to alleviate poverty, if only we had the political will.

Who Are the Poor?

Although no single description covers all poor people, poverty is pronounced among certain categories of our population. Children, women, certain visible minorities (specifically Natives) and those who live in rural areas are all at higher risk of being poor. Regional disparities, in economic development and income, are also in evidence in that poverty is a particularly acute problem in the Atlantic provinces, Quebec, and the North. Any combination of the above factors suggests that the problem of poverty is especially serious.

Age

The burden of poverty falls most heavily on children. In 1990, 17.4 percent of people under age eighteen (almost 1 million children) were officially classified as poor. From another perspective, slightly more than four in ten poor Canadians are children under the age of eighteen.

A generation ago, the elderly were at greatest risk for poverty. The poverty rate for women and men over the age of sixty-five was 19.3 percent in 1990 (yielding about 600,000 elderly poor). Although the situation of our elderly has improved over time with better pension support from the government and private employers, the growing numbers of elderly people suggest that this category will increasingly contribute to the numbers of poor people in Canada. The appearance of the baby boomers among the retired, following difficult economic times and cutbacks in government services, means that in the future we are likely to see an increase in the number of the elderly poor.

Education

Education is another factor that determines the likelihood of having an income below the poverty line. People who have higher levels of education are less likely to be unemployed and more likely to have higher incomes. Not surprisingly, the better educated are less likely to fall below the poverty line—as indicated in Figure 10-4 where the incidence of poverty drops with each added level of education. The figure also shows that unattached individuals at all levels of education have higher levels of poverty than their counterparts living in families.

Race and Ethnicity

The likelihood of experiencing poverty is related to race and ethnicity in Canada, but the ranking of various categories is not necessarily what one might expect. Those of British origin are not at the top of the income hierarchy: in fact, in a ranking of sixty ethnic and racial categories by average male income for those employed full time all year (Gerber, 1990:79), those of English origin rank twenty-fifth. The French, too, are near the middle. Canadians of Welsh and Scottish background appear in the top fifteen, along with those of Jewish and Japanese descent.

In the bottom fifteen categories one finds blacks, West Indians, Latin Americans, some of the Asian groups and the Métis, Inuit, and North American Indians. The only categories that rank below the North American Indians are groups that tend to be recent immigrants and possibly refugees—Chileans and "other" Latin Americans, Vietnamese, Haitians, Laotians, and Cambodians. While male income for those employed full time is only *one* indicator of economic well-being, the rank ordering by race or ethnicity is

FIGURE 10-4   POVERTY AMONG CANADIAN FAMILIES AND UNATTACHED INDIVIDUALS, 1990, BY EDUCATION OF HEAD (PERCENTAGES BELOW THE POVERTY LINE)
SOURCE: Adapted from Statistics Canada, Income Distribution by Size in Canada, 1991. *Cat. No. 13-207*

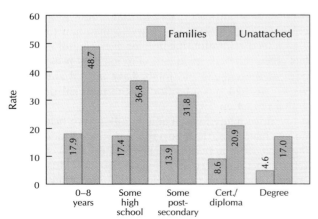

suggestive. One would expect to find that more of the people in the bottom fifteen categories have incomes below the poverty line.

Gender and Family Patterns

The disparity in male and female incomes and the fact that lone-parent families tend to be headed by females contribute to higher rates of poverty among women. In fact, women who head households bear the brunt of poverty. On their shoulders falls the financial burden of raising children, which makes working for income difficult. For those able to work, low-paying jobs are the norm. Of all poor families, 61 percent are headed by women with no husband present. In marked contrast, only 27 percent of poor families are headed by single men.

Because single-parent families are at higher risk of poverty, divorce typically threatens the economic security of children. Family income is likely to plummet in the wake of separation or divorce.

Sociologists investigating women's increased risk of poverty describe a process called the **feminization of poverty**, *the trend by which women represent an increasing proportion of the poor.* The box takes a closer look at this phenomenon.

Explaining Poverty

The presence of close to 4 million poor people in one of the world's most affluent societies raises serious social and moral concerns. It also sparks considerable controversy within Canada—and from abroad. Many Canadians concur with the U.N. committee mentioned earlier, arguing that our government should take a much more active role in eradicating poverty. Others feel that the poor must bear responsibility for themselves. It is also possible to argue, as some do, that *both* governments and the poor themselves need to contribute to the solution. We now turn to arguments underlying each of these two approaches to the problem of low income, which together frame a lively and pressing political debate.

Proponents of one side of the issue hold the following view: *The poor are primarily responsible for their own poverty.* In this land of immigration and once seemingly unlimited resources and opportunities, we have embraced the notion that people are largely responsible for their own social standing. This approach assumes that our society offers considerable opportunity for anyone able and willing to take advantage of it. The poor,

A widespread stereotype links poverty to minorities and people of color in the larger cities of Canada. Although minorities are more likely to be disadvantaged, most poor people in Canada are white. Furthermore, although inner cities have the greatest concentration of poverty, rural people are actually at higher risk of poverty than their urban counterparts. Here, a family of Nova Scotia farm laborers stand in their plywood trailer, which is equipped neither with running water nor plumbing.

then, are those with fewer skills, less schooling, lower motivation, or, perhaps, a debilitating drug addiction—in sum, people who are somehow undeserving.

Anthropologist Oscar Lewis (1961) illustrates this approach in his studies of Latin American poverty. Lewis claims that the poor become entrapped in a *culture of poverty* that fosters resignation to one's plight as a matter of fate. Socialized in this environment, children come to believe that there is little point to aspiring to a better life. The result is a self-perpetuating cycle of poverty, at least as long as people tolerate their condition.

Edward Banfield (1974) adds the contention that, where there are areas of intense poverty, there exists a distinctive lower-class subculture that denigrates and erodes personal achievement. One element of this sub-

culture, a present-time orientation, encourages living for the moment rather than looking toward the future by engaging in hard work, saving, and other behavior likely to promote upward social mobility. In Banfield's view, poor people who live largely for the moment perpetuate their own poverty; he defines this kind of behavior as basically irresponsible, and he concludes that the poor reap more or less what they deserve.

The other view of the issue follows this reasoning: *Society is primarily responsible for poverty.* This alternative position, argued by William Ryan (1976), holds that society—not the poor—is responsible for poverty because of the way it distributes resources. Looking at this problem in global context, societies that distribute wealth very unequally face a significant poverty problem; societies that strive for more equality (such as Sweden and Japan) lack such extremes in income. Poverty, Ryan insists, is not inevitable; this problem is simply a matter of low incomes, not personal deficiencies. Ryan interprets any lack of ambition on the part of poor people as a *consequence* rather than a *cause* of their lack of opportunity. He therefore dismisses Banfield's analysis as little more than "blaming the victims" for their own suffering. In Ryan's view, social policies that empower the poor would give them real economic opportunity, and this should yield greater equality.

Critical evaluation. Each of these explanations of poverty has won its share of public support, and each has advocates among government policy makers. Some, particularly on the right of the political spectrum, believe that society should strive to encourage equality of opportunity, but should otherwise adopt a laissez-faire attitude toward the poor. Others, on the left, hold that society should actively reduce poverty by redistributing income in a more equitable manner. This could be accomplished through programs like a comprehensive child-care package that would allow poor mothers to gain skills necessary to maintain jobs or a guaranteed minimum income for every family. Canada has given serious consideration to national programs in both of these areas and might have moved ahead had we not turned our attention to the national debt and deficit reduction.

Since many low-income families have heads who do not have jobs, their poverty is attributed to *not holding a job.* But the *reasons* that people do not work are a reflection on society as much as the individuals concerned. Most women who are poor claim they cannot work because they need to care for their children.

In Canada, few employers provide child-care pro-

In The Potato Eaters, *Vincent Van Gogh portrayed suppertime among the Dutch peasants of his day as a kind of sacramental sharing of the fruits of the earth. This affirmation of the dignity of the poor was considered a radical statement at the time. In nineteenth-century Holland, as often today, the poor were dismissed as morally unworthy and deserving of their bitter plight.*

grams for workers, and few low-paid workers can afford to obtain this service from the private sector. Where child-care subsidies are provided, parents may still find that, when all costs are taken into consideration, it is cheaper to stay at home and take care of one's own children. (In August of 1993, an Ontario woman became the center of controversy by giving up a job in social work paying over $40,000 per year on the grounds that, when all work-related expenses, including child care, were taken into consideration, she would be almost as well off on welfare, taking care of her own children.) Most poor men report that either there are no jobs to be found, illness or disability has sidelined them, or, in the case of the elderly, they have retired. Overall, poor adults are poor, not by choice, but because they feel they have few alternatives.

But not all poor people are jobless. At various points in this chapter, tables and figures refer to salaries of people who work full-time all year. Many of these salaries—for women, for certain occupations, and for specific ethnic and racial categories—are low relative to the official poverty line. If these people, working full time, have incomes that are below the poverty line for individuals, what happens if they are single parents with two or three children? The *working poor* are the men and women who labor for at least fifty weeks of the year and yet cannot escape poverty. Since full-time jobs have decreased in numbers and have been replaced with part-time jobs, many people who involuntarily work part-time are also included among the working poor. Such "working poverty" places the poor in a bind: their jobs provide low wages that barely

allow them to make ends meet, but consume the time and energy needed to obtain training or schooling that might open new doors. People in this situation are often reluctant or simply unable to risk the jobs they do have in hopes of finding something better. Even with minimum wages of $4.75 to $6.50, depending on the province (1992), a full-time worker could not support a family above the official poverty line.

Clearly, individual ability and initiative play a part in shaping everyone's social position. On balance, though, evidence points to society—not individual character traits—as the primary source of poverty. Some poor people do lack ambition. Overall, however, the poor are *categories* of people, who for reasons beyond their control, lack the opportunities that are available to others.

Homelessness

Many low-income people in Canada lack the resources to support even basic housing; as a society, we have failed to ensure an adequate supply of affordable housing. In light of the enormous wealth of our country and its commitment to providing opportunity and/or social safety nets for everyone, homelessness may be fairly described as a scar on our society that demands an effective response. It is a scar that is formed by thousands of people, across the country, living on the streets, in various (often temporary) shelters and even in our jails.

The familiar stereotypes of homeless people—men sleeping in doorways and women carrying everything

CRITICAL THINKING

WHY POVERTY IS A WOMEN'S ISSUE

Female income for those working full time all year has averaged about 66 percent of male income for several years, rising to almost 70 percent in 1991. The fact that among those fifteen to twenty-four years of age the female-to-male earnings ratio was 86.4 percent (Statistics Canada, *The Daily,* Jan. 14, 1993:3) suggests that we will see continued improvement as the younger generation matures to make up more of the labor force. Less encouraging is the observation that, for all those with income in 1990, female *median* income was $13,564 or 53 percent of male median income ($25,571). In other words, half of our women have incomes that are below the poverty line of $14,155 for one person living in a city of 500,000 or more (Colombo, 1992:88). If these women happen to be single mothers, these low incomes become even more inadequate to meet their needs. With an increase in the numbers of female lone-parent families one sees a clear example of the *feminization of poverty.*

Figure 10-5 reveals that among families with heads under 65 years of age, lone-parent families headed by females have an average income that is lower than that of lone-parent families headed by males. Two-parent families have substantially higher incomes. Figure 10-6 shows that, of all families with low income, 61 percent are headed by women. Clearly, women and children are over-represented among Canada's poor. In addition, elderly women (65 years of age and over) had a median income of about $11,000 in 1990, suggesting that a large majority lives below the poverty line. Since women outlive men by about seven years, it is not surprising to find that women predominate among the elderly poor (see Chapter 14, "Aging and the Elderly").

As with many other indicators of economic well-being, regional disparities are apparent in the distribution of female lone-parent families. Figure 10-7 shows that, in 1986, female lone-parent families were much more prevalent in some cities than others—ranging from about 8.5 percent of families in Oshawa, Ontario, to 14 percent in Saint John, New Brunswick. The percentages in each of these cities may have increased since 1986, but it is likely that the rank order would be very similar

FIGURE 10-5   AVERAGE FAMILY INCOME* BY FAMILY STATUS, 1990
* Includes families in which the head is under age 65, with children less than age 18 living at home.
SOURCE: Statistics Canada, Lone-Parent Families in Canada, 1992. *Cat. No. 89-522E, p. 35.*

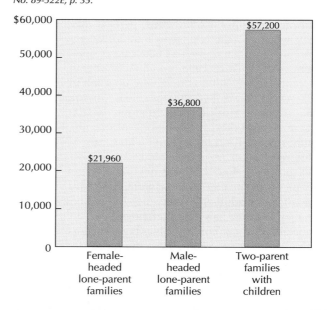

they own in a shopping bag—have recently been undermined by the reality of the "new homeless," those thrown out of work because of plant closings, people forced out of apartments by rising rents, condominium conversions, or "gentrification" (e.g., converting rooming houses back into expensive single-family homes), and others unable to meet mortgage or rent payments because they must work for low wages. Today, no stereotype of the homeless paints a complete picture because such people are now a highly varied segment of our society. But virtually all homeless people have one status in common: *poverty.* For that reason, the

today. Note that the urban areas of Quebec and the Atlantic provinces are all above the average for Canada as a whole: the four with the lowest percentages of female lone-parent families are in southern Ontario.

Although women in general as well as elderly women are at risk of poverty, it is the gradual increase in the proportion of female lone-parent fami-lies—from 9.3 percent of families in 1961 to 13 percent in 1986—that most clearly contributes to the feminization of poverty.

FIGURE 10-6   PERCENTAGE OF FAMILIES WITH LOW INCOME* BY FAMILY STATUS, 1990
* Includes families in which the head is under age 65, with children less than age 18 living at home.
SOURCE: Statistics Canada, Lone-Parent Families in Canada, 1992. Cat. No. 89-522E:35.

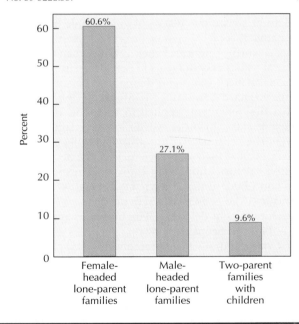

FIGURE 10-7   FEMALE LONE-PARENT FAMILIES AS A PERCENTAGE OF TOTAL FAMILIES IN PRIVATE HOUSEHOLDS
SOURCE: Statistics Canada, Metropolitan Atlas Series. Cat. No. 98-106, 1989.

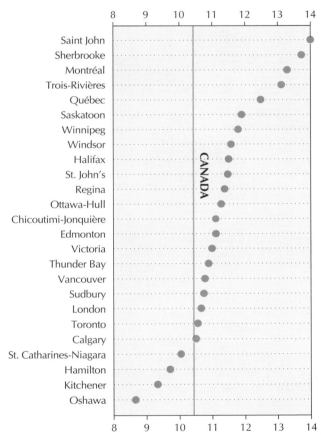

approaches already used in explaining poverty also apply to homelessness. One side of the debate places responsibility on *personal* traits of the homeless themselves. Perhaps one-third of homeless people are mentally ill; others are addicted to alcohol or other drugs. Some, for whatever reason, seem unable to cope in a complex and highly competitive society (Bassuk, 1984; Whitman, 1989). On the other side of the debate, advocates assert that homelessness results from *societal* factors, including a lack of low-income housing and the economic transition toward low-paying jobs described earlier (Kozol, 1988; Shutt, 1989). Advocates of this

The increase in homelessness during the 1980s intensified the controversy over poverty in Canada. Some homeless people have personal problems that render them unable to cope with a demanding world. But how much of this is cause and how much is effect remains a hotly contested issue. What is clear is that major causes of rising homelessness include economic stagnation, a declining stock of low-income housing, and cutbacks in social service programs.

position are quick to point out that fully one-third of all homeless people are now entire families, and children are the fastest growing category of the homeless. The closing of a plant, making it necessary for an individual to take a job at McDonald's—at $950 per month, or $11,500 per year—makes it virtually impossible to support a family.

No one disputes that a large proportion of homeless people have personal difficulties to some degree, although how much is cause and how much effect is difficult to untangle. But structural changes in the Canadian economy, and government policies that reduce support for lower-income people have all contributed to homelessness.

A comprehensive response to homelessness must consider both personal and societal dimensions of the problem. Increasing the supply of low-income housing (other than shelters) is one important step. Additionally, low-income people must have the opportunity to earn the income necessary to pay for housing. Home-

lessness, however, is not only a housing problem, it is also a *human* problem. People who endure months or years of insecure living come to need various types of social services.

Class and Welfare, Politics and Values

This chapter has presented a great many facts about social class in Canada. In the end, however, our understanding of what it means to be wealthy and privileged or poor and perhaps homeless also turns on politics and values. Understandably, support for the notion that social standing reflects personal merit, effort and responsibility is strongest among people who are well-off and support the Conservative and Reform parties politically. The idea that society should distribute wealth and other resources more equally finds greatest favor among those with relatively few advantages or those on the political left.

However much we may recognize the fact that structural constraints place insurmountable barriers in the paths of some categories of people, we still share a general North American belief in a meritocracy. These cultural values encourage us to see successful people as personally meritorious and the poor as personally deficient. Richard Sennett and Jonathan Cobb (1973) called this judgment, applied to the poor, the *hidden injury of class.* In other words, poverty significantly lowers the self-image of disadvantaged people, while others display their affluence as a personal "badge of ability." Values supporting individual responsibility also contribute to negative views of social welfare programs and the people who rely on them. While advocates for the poor defend welfare programs as necessary for millions of people lacking opportunities and advantages, our cultural values promote the view that social welfare programs undermine initiative. Accepting assistance of this kind thus becomes personally demeaning, which helps explain why many people who are eligible for assistance are reluctant to apply for it.

Finally, the drama of social stratification extends far beyond Canada's borders. The most striking social disparities are found not by looking inside one country but by comparing living standards in various parts of the world. In Chapter 11, we broaden our investigation of social stratification, focusing on global inequality.

Summary

1. Social inequality in Canada involves disparities in a host of variables, including income, wealth, and power.

2. White-collar occupations generally confer more prestige and higher incomes than blue-collar jobs. The pink-collar occupations typically held by women offer little social prestige or income.

3. Schooling is also a resource that is distributed unequally. About three-fourths of people over age twenty-five have completed high school, but only one-fifth are college graduates.

4. Ascription exerts a powerful effect on stratification in Canada; ancestry, race or ethnicity and gender are all related to social position.

5. The upper class, which is small (perhaps 4 or 5 percent of the population) includes the richest and most powerful families. Members of the upper-upper class, or the old rich, derive their wealth through inheritance over several generations; those in the lower-upper class, or the new rich, depend on earned income as their primary source of wealth.

6. The middle class encompasses 40 to 50 percent of the Canadian population. The upper-middle class may be distinguished on the basis of higher income, higher-prestige occupations, and more schooling.

7. The working class comprises about one-third of our population. With below-average income, working-class families have less financial security than those in the middle class. Few working-class people attain more than a high-school education, and they commonly work in blue-collar or lower white-collar jobs.

8. About one-fifth of the population belong to the lower class. Most live near or below the official poverty threshold.

9. Social class affects nearly all aspects of life, beginning with health and life expectancy, and encompassing a wide range of attitudes and patterns of family living.

10. Social mobility is common in Canada as it is in other industrial societies. For only 12 percent of women and 26 percent of men is there no intergenerational mobility; typically, however, only small changes (upward or downward) occur from one generation to the next.

11. Since the early 1970s, changes in the Canadian economy have reduced the standard of living for low- and moderate-income families. In one important trend, manufacturing industries have declined in Canada, paralleling growth in low-paying service-sector jobs.

12. Some 4 million people in Canada are officially classified as poor. About one million of the poor are children under the age of eighteen. A growing share of poor families are headed by women, but the elderly, Natives, and certain other racial and ethnic categories are over-represented among the poor.

13. Oscar Lewis and Edward Banfield advanced the "culture of poverty" thesis, suggesting that poverty can be perpetuated by the social patterns of the poor themselves. Opposing this view, William Ryan argues that poverty is caused by the unequal distribution of wealth in society. Although Banfield's view is consistent with our society's cultural pattern of personalizing social position, Ryan's view is supported by more evidence.

Key Concepts

absolute poverty a deprivation of resources that is life-threatening

feminization of poverty the trend by which women represent an increasing proportion of the poor

income   occupational wages or salaries and earnings from investments

intergenerational social mobility   upward or downward social mobility of children in relation to their parents

intragenerational social mobility   a change in social position occurring during a person's lifetime

relative poverty   the deprivation of some people in relation to those who have more

wealth   the total amount of money and valuable goods that any person or family controls

Suggested Readings

The first of these books explains how the lives of privileged women differ from those of privileged men; the second argues that elite class standing does not override the significance of race in the United States.

Susan A. Ostrander. *Women of the Upper Class.* Philadelphia: Temple University Press, 1984.

Lois Benjamin. The Black Elite: Facing the Color Line in the Twilight of the Twentieth Century. Chicago: Nelson-Hall, 1991.

This readable and insightful book probes middle America during a time of economic decline.

Barbara Ehrenreich. *Fear of Falling: The Inner Life of the Middle Class.* New York: Harper Collins, 1990.

This collection of readings deals with various dimensions of social inequality, its causes and consequences.

James Curtis, Edward Grabb, Neil Guppy, and Sid Gilbert. *Social Inequality in Canada.* Scarborough, Ont.: Prentice Hall, 1988.

This sociological classic is still cited regularly in studies on social stratification.

John Porter. *The Vertical Mosaic: An Analysis of Class and Power in Canada.* Toronto: University of Toronto Press, 1965.

This book deals with Canadian capitalism and the people who control the economy.

William K. Carroll. *Corporate Power and Canadian Capitalism.* Vancouver: University of British Columbia Press, 1986.

This study looks at various aspects of social class including its interaction with gender and ethnicity.

Alfred A. Hunter. *Class Tells On Social Inequality in Canada.* (2nd ed.) Toronto: Butterworths, 1986.

GLOBAL INEQUALITY

Half an hour from the center of Cairo, Egypt's capital city, the bus turned onto a dirt road and jerked to a stop. It was not quite dawn, and the Mo'edhdhins would soon climb the minarets of Cairo's many mosques to call the Islamic faithful to morning prayers. The driver turned, genuinely bewildered, to the busload of students and their instructor. "Why," he said, mixing English with some Arabic, "do you want to be *here*? And in the middle of the night?"

Why, indeed? No sooner had we left the bus than smoke and stench, the likes of which we had never before encountered, overcame us. Eyes squinting, hand-kerchiefs pressed against noses and mouths, we moved slowly uphill along the path ascending mountains of trash and garbage that extended for miles. We had reached the Cairo Dump, where the fifteen million people of one of the world's largest cities deposit their trash and garbage.[1]

We walked stiffly and with great care, since only a scattering of light came from small fires smoldering

around us. Suddenly, spectral shapes appeared out of the shadows. After a moment, we identified them as dogs peering curiously through the curtain of haze. As startled as we were, they quickly turned and vanished into the thick air. Ahead of us, we could see blazing piles of trash encircled by people seeking warmth and companionship.

Human beings actually inhabit this inhuman place, creating a surreal scene, like the aftermath of the next war. As we approached, the fires cast an eerie light on their faces. We stopped some distance from them, separated by a vast chasm of culture and circumstances. But smiles eased the tension, and soon we were sharing the comfort of their fire. At that moment, the melodious call to prayer sounded across the city.

The people of the Cairo Dump, called the Zebaleen, belong to a religious minority—Coptic Christians—in a predominantly Muslim society. Barred by religious discrimination from many jobs, the Zebaleen use donkey-carts and small trucks to pick up refuse throughout the city and bring it here. The night-long routine reaches a climax at dawn when the hundreds of Zebaleen gather at the dump, swarming over the new piles in search of anything of value. That morning, we watched men, women, and children accumulate bits of metal and ribbon, examine scraps of discarded food,

---

[1] This portrayal is based on a visit by John J. Macionis to the Cairo Dump in 1988 with more than 100 students. It also draws on the discussion found in Spates & Macionis, 1987, and conversations with James L. Spates, who has also traveled to the Cairo Dump.

and slowly fill their baskets with what would get them through another day. Every now and then, someone gleefully displayed a "precious" find that would bring the equivalent of a few dollars in the city. Watching in silence, we became keenly aware of our sturdy shoes and warm clothing, and self-conscious that our watches and cameras represented more money than most of the Zebaleen earn in a year.

Although unfamiliar to most North Americans, the Zebaleen of the Cairo Dump are hardly unique. Their counterparts live in almost every country of the world. In poor societies around the globe, as we shall see, poverty is not only more widespread than in North America, but also far more severe.

The Importance of Global Perspective

Why should we study unfamiliar parts of the world, especially in a course primarily concerned with North America? Earlier chapters have explained that our society shapes how we behave, what we think, and even molds our self-image. Taken one step further, the same logic applies to the relationship of Canada to other nations. To understand our own society, we must explore how our part of the world fits into the larger global order. Extending the sociological perspective in this way is particularly important today, as political changes sweep through Latin America, Eastern Europe, the former Soviet Union (now the Commonwealth of Independent States), the Middle East, and South Africa, and rapid economic development reshapes many countries in Eastern Asia. All these global realignments affect our country and the lives of each one of us.

This chapter highlights an important theme of the text: that our world has grown increasingly interdependent. St. Augustine, a scholar of the early Christian era, once described the world as a book, noting that those who concentrate only on their own society read just a single page. Beyond academic arguments, there is also a very practical reason to learn more about the larger world: success, for most workers of the twenty-first century, will depend on being "globally competent." No future investment banker in Toronto will be able to neglect what happens on the trading floor of the Tokyo stock exchange, just as no prairie farmer will dare to ignore wheat production in the Ukraine or Georgia. Canada's economic activity increasingly involves international trade and one can expect a large percentage of new jobs to have an international component. As is the case in the U.S. (Macionis, 1991), the Canadian economy depends on imbuing the workforce with a global vision. More broadly, making sound decisions about the future of our nation also depends on understanding the various roles Canada can play in the larger world order. For all these reasons—and with much of the contemporary world seized by political and economic change—looking beyond our own borders has never been more important than it is today.

The Three Worlds

Just as Chapter 3 ("Culture") emphasized the need to recognize cultural variation in the world, this chapter focuses on the character, causes, and consequences of global inequality. While pronounced social stratification divides members of our society, Canada stands among the richest nations in the world. Because the average Canadian family is very well off by world standards, even most people living below what we define as the poverty line enjoy a much higher standard of living than the majority of those in the poorest nations on earth. We begin our study of global inequality by dividing the world's societies into three broad categories or "worlds."

First, however, a word of caution. There are roughly 180 nations on earth (the precise number changes frequently in response to political events). To sort them all into only three sweeping categories ignores striking differences in their ways of life. The societies in each category have rich and varied histories, speak dozens of languages, and encompass diverse peoples whose cultural distinctiveness serves as a source of pride. However, the three broad categories that follow are widely used to group societies together based on (1) their level of technological development, and (2) their political and economic systems.

The First World

The term **First World** refers to *industrial societies that have predominantly capitalist economies*. They are not called "first" because they are "better" or "more important" than other countries, but rather because the Industrial Revolution came first to these nations, beginning two centuries ago. Chapter 4 ("Society") explained that industrialization increases a society's

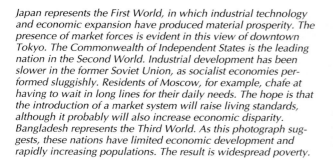

Japan represents the First World, in which industrial technology and economic expansion have produced material prosperity. The presence of market forces is evident in this view of downtown Tokyo. The Commonwealth of Independent States is the leading nation in the Second World. Industrial development has been slower in the former Soviet Union, as socialist economies performed sluggishly. Residents of Moscow, for example, chafe at having to wait in long lines for their daily needs. The hope is that the introduction of a market system will raise living standards, although it probably will also increase economic disparity. Bangladesh represents the Third World. As this photograph suggests, these nations have limited economic development and rapidly increasing populations. The result is widespread poverty.

productive capacity one hundred-fold, which greatly raises living standards. In historical context, the economic activity surrounding the care of household pets in the United States today exceeds the economic enterprise of all of Europe during the Middle Ages.

Global Map 11-1 on page 296 identifies nations of the First World. Shown in blue, this region includes the nations of Western Europe such as the United Kingdom (made up of England, Scotland, Wales, and Northern Ireland). It was in southeastern England that industrialization began about 1775. Also part of the First World are the United States and Canada, where the Industrial Revolution got under way around 1850. On the African continent, the advanced economic development of South Africa places this country (more precisely, its *white minority*) in the First World. Israel stands alone in the Middle East as a First-World nation. Also ranking in the First World is Japan, the most economically powerful nation in Asia. And, in the world region known as Oceania, Australia and New Zealand belong to the First World.

Collectively, the First World covers roughly 25 percent of the earth's land area, includes parts of five continents, and lies mostly in the northern hemisphere. In 1992, the population of the First World was approaching 800 million, just over 15 percent of the earth's people. By global standards, the First World is not densely populated.

Despite significant cultural differences, First-World nations now share an industrial capacity that generates, on average, a rich material life for their people. The world's income is concentrated among the minority of humanity living in the First World. The economies of these nations are predominantly capitalist, so that a market system (or "private enterprise"), rather than government, controls most production. Since World War I, the United States has been the dominant nation (often termed a "superpower") of the First World. Because the United States, Canada, and Western Europe are linked by political and economic alliances, the First World is sometimes referred to as "the West."

The Second World

The **Second World** is composed of *industrial societies that are currently transforming their socialist economies.* Industrialization took hold in much of this broad region of the world only in the twentieth century. This accounts, in part, for the lesser economic strength of the Second World in relation to the First World. Second-World nations have less powerful industrial capacities: proportionately more of their people live in rural areas and remain in agricultural production. (Chapter 19, "The Economy and Work," compares the performance of capitalist and socialist economies.)

In Global Map 11-1, the Second World appears in red. During this century, the dominant nation in the Second World was the Union of Soviet Socialist Republics (U.S.S.R.), which, in 1992, was recast as the Commonwealth of Independent States. The former Soviet Union's military strength rivaled that of the United States, giving it "superpower" status. After World War II, the Soviet Union took control of most of Eastern Europe, including the Baltic countries, Poland, the German Democratic Republic (East Germany), Czechoslovakia, Hungary, Romania, and Bulgaria. In 1989, most of Eastern Europe was transformed by the popular overthrow of established social-

WINDOW ON THE WORLD

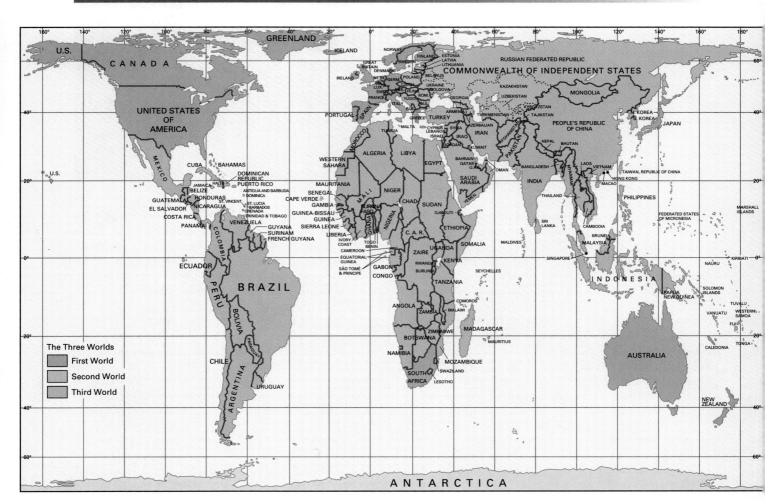

GLOBAL MAP 11-1   THE THREE WORLDS

ist governments, the opening of borders to the West, and the call for Western-style market systems. Within a year, the "two Germanys" were rejoined, so that the united Germany is shown on the map as part of the First World. In 1991, change accelerated in the Soviet Union as well, as leaders ended the historic monopoly on power enjoyed by that nation's Communist party. After the Baltic republics of Estonia, Latvia, and Lithuania won their independence, the remaining republics of the old Soviet Union formed the current new federation. Reform toward a market economy is currently underway throughout the new Commonwealth of Independent States. The future course of the Second World is unclear; perhaps the concept of a "second world" may soon be obsolete. For the present, the Soviet-led alliance that was long called the "Eastern bloc" appears to have disintegrated. In the future, no doubt, the political systems of these countries will continue to evolve.

The Second World spans roughly 15 percent of the earth's land area. Most of it lies in the Commonwealth of Independent States, which, stretching from Europe to Asia, is geographically the largest nation on earth. Roughly 500 million people or 10 percent of humanity live in the Second World. Like the First World, this region is not densely populated by global standards.

The Third World

The **Third World** encompasses *primarily agrarian societies, in which most people are poor*. In these countries, economic activity centers on farming; in fact, slightly more than half of the world's people are rural peasants. Many are staunchly traditional, following the folkways of their ancestors. Industrial technology plays a limited role in the lives of such people; its impact is evident mostly in Third-World cities. With more simple technology, Third-World societies are less productive by world standards. This pattern holds true even though some Third-World countries—notably the oil-rich nations of the Middle East—have an extremely high average standard of living due to the great wealth of *some* of their people. Global Map 11-1 indicates that the Third World, shown in green, spans most of the globe. In our hemisphere, Third-World countries range from the poor but industrializing nation of Mexico, on the southern border of the United States, to all the nations of Central America and South America. Moving across the Atlantic Ocean, the continent of Africa (except for South Africa) falls into the Third World. Included, too, is the Middle East except Israel, and all of Asia except Japan.

The Third World represents about 60 percent of our planet's land area including most of the countries near and below the equator. More significantly, 77 per-

In our hemisphere, the nations of central and south America are among the poorest. Here, unsafe housing, high rates of disease, and crushing foreign debt have propelled tens of thousands of Argentinos into the streets to demand change. The problem is stated simply on the banner, which reads, "Argentinos are hungry."

cent of the world's 5.5 billion people live in the Third World. Population density is very high throughout the Third World: in India, for instance, it is 100 times that of Canada or ten times that of the United States. Because of its large and rapidly increasing population, coupled with low economic productivity, the Third World faces poverty on a massive scale. Hunger, unsafe housing, and high rates of disease all plague Third-World nations.

Although they share poverty, less-developed societies have no single economic system in common. Some poor countries, such as the People's Republic of China (with 1.2 billion people, the world's most populous nation), maintain a predominantly socialist economy. Other nations, like India and Egypt, blend elements of government socialism and market capitalism. Still others, including Brazil and much of Latin America, have adopted a capitalist approach. We shall examine some of the consequences of the form of economic system a country embraces both in this chapter and in later chapters concerned with politics and economics. For now, we must recognize that all Third-World societies share a common plight: devastating poverty.

This identification of "three worlds" is the foundation for understanding the problem of global inequality. For people living in an affluent nation such as Canada, the scope of the problem is difficult to grasp. From time to time, televised scenes of famine in the poorest countries of the world, including Ethiopia and Bangladesh, give people in Canada a shocking glance at the absolute poverty that makes daily living a life-and-death struggle for so many. Behind these images lie cultural, historical, and economic forces that we shall explore in the remainder of this chapter.

Third-World Poverty

Poverty always means suffering. Third-World poverty, however, typically involves more severe hardship than poverty in this country (see Chapter 10, "Social Class in Canada"). This does not mean, of course, that deprivation among Canadians constitutes only a minor issue. Canada, as one of the world's richest countries, with a quality of life index at or near the top (depending upon the year) has been harshly criticized by a United Nations committee (June, 1993) for making no headway in alleviating avoidable poverty and homelessness within its boundaries. Yet, in global perspective, poverty in the Third World is *more severe* and *more extensive* than in Canada.

The Severity of Poverty

Poverty in the Third World is more severe than it is in rich societies such as Canada. The data in Table 11-1 suggest why. The first column of figures shows, for selected countries, the gross domestic product (GDP).[2] Income earned abroad by individuals or corporations is excluded from this measure, differentiating GDP from gross national product (GNP), which includes foreign earnings. For countries that invest heavily abroad (Kuwait, for example) GDP is considerably less than GNP; for countries in which other nations invest heavily (Hong Kong), GDP is considerably higher than GNP. For societies that both invest heavily abroad and have considerable foreign investment (including Canada), the two measures are roughly comparable. For the present purpose, simply notice the striking differences in the power of the various world economies. Industrial societies typically have a high economic output due mainly to their productive industrial technology. A large First-World nation like the United States had a 1990 GDP of more than $5 trillion (that of a much smaller Canada is $488 billion); the GDP of the former Soviet Union, the largest Second-World country, stood at about $2 trillion. The rest of the table shows that Third-World countries around the globe, with little industrial technology, had far lower GDPs.

The second column of figures in Table 11-1 indicates "per-person income" for these countries, calculated by dividing the country's economic output by the total population. The resulting figures for First-World nations are relatively high—about $19,000 for Canada, for example. Income levels in Second-World societies are significantly lower than those in the First World. But the most dramatic difference involves the Third World. In many poor societies, per-person income is below $1,000 a year. At roughly $180, per-capita income in Bangladesh amounts to less than 1 percent of that found in Canada. In simple terms, this means that the typical person in this poor Asian nation labors all year to make what the average worker in Canada earns in several days.[3]

---

[2] Gross domestic product refers to all the goods and services produced by a society's economy in a given year.

[3] The per-person income figures for the poorest of the world's societies are understated to the extent that they exclude products grown for home consumption or bartered with others. But even if the figures were doubled to neutralize this bias, per-capita income of Third-World societies remains well below that of rich nations.

TABLE 11-1 WEALTH AND WELL-BEING IN GLOBAL PERSPECTIVE, 1990

Country	Gross Domestic Product ($ billion)	Per-Person Income ($)	Quality of Life Index
First World			
Japan	2,818	23,810	.993
Canada	488	19,030	.983
Sweden	167	21,570	.982
United States	5,156	20,910	.976
United Kingdom	717	14,610	.967
Germany	1,189	20,440	.959
Second World			
Czechoslovakia	50	9,709	.920
Hungary	29	8,260	.911
Soviet Union	2,000	8,662	.908
Bulgaria	16	2,320	.899
Poland	68	6,879	.863
Third World			
Latin America			
Argentina	200	2,160	.854
Mexico	400	2,010	.838
Brazil	319	2,540	.759
Colombia	39	1,200	.757
Nicaragua	3	850	.612
El Salvador	6	1,070	.524
Bolivia	5	620	.416
Africa/Middle East			
Saudi Arabia	80	6,020	.697
Lebanon	3	1,150	.592
Iran	150	3,200	.577
Egypt	32	640	.394
Cameroon	11	1,000	.328
Zaire	10	260	.299
Nigeria	29	250	.242
Burkina Faso	2	350	.081
Sierra Leone	220	890	.048
Asia			
Hong Kong	53	10,300	.934
South Korea	211	4,400	.884
Thailand	69	1,220	.713
P. R. of China	417	350	.614
Pakistan	36	370	.311
India	235	340	.308
Bangladesh	20	180	.186

SOURCES: United Nations Development Programme, Human Development Report 1991, New York: Oxford University Press, 1991; The World Bank, World Development Report 1991: The Challenge of Development, New York: Oxford University Press, 1991.

The third column of Table 11-1 provides a measure of the quality of life in the various nations. Income is obviously one important component of well-being, although certainly not the only one. The index used here, calculated by the United Nations, reflects not only income but education (adult literacy and average years of schooling) and longevity (how long people typically live). Index values are decimals that fall between hypothetical extremes of 1 (highest) and zero (lowest). Japan has the highest rating of world societies (.993), and the African nation of Sierra Leone has the lowest (.048). Canada has a quality of life index of .983, placing us second in the world in 1990 (United Nations Development Programme, 1991). In 1992, Canada was ranked first, ahead of Japan.

One key reason that quality of life differs so dramatically among the societies of the world is that economic productivity is lowest in precisely the regions of the globe where population is highest. Figure 11-1 shows the division of global income and population for each of the "three worlds." The First World is by far the most advantaged: here two-thirds of the world's income is spread among only 15 percent of the world's people. The people of the Second World are less well off, but they, too, claim a disproportionately large share of global income. In the Third World, 20 percent of

FIGURE 11-1 THE RELATIVE SHAPE OF GLOBAL INCOME BY WORLD REGION

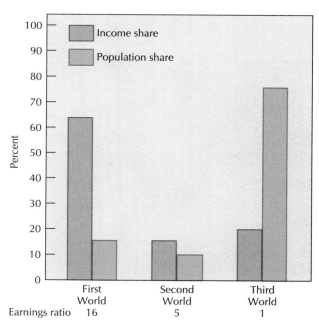

global income supports a full 75 percent of humanity. Factoring together income and population, for every dollar received by a Third-World worker, a person in the Second World takes home five dollars and a worker in the First World earns sixteen dollars.

Bear in mind that, beyond overarching global patterns, each society is *internally* stratified. As a result, affluent Canadians live worlds apart from the most disadvantaged people on our planet, such as Cairo's Zebaleen, described in the chapter opening.

Relative Versus Absolute Poverty

A distinction made in the last chapter has an important application to global inequality. The members of rich societies typically focus on the *relative poverty* of some of their members, highlighting how some people lack resources that are taken for granted by others. Relative poverty, by definition, exists in every society, even in the First World. But especially important in a global context is the concept of *absolute poverty*, a lack of resources that is life threatening. Commonly, human beings living in absolute poverty lack the nutrition necessary for health and long-term survival.

In a rich society like Canada, most people described as poor are deprived in the relative sense. That is, women, men, and children fall short of the standard of living that we like to think is the birthright of everyone in our society. But absolute poverty, too, exists in Canada. Inadequate nutrition that leaves children, elderly people, or Native people on reservations vulnerable to illness and even outright starvation is a stark and tragic reality. By global standards, however, immediately life-threatening poverty in Canada strikes a relatively small proportion of the population. Third-World societies face a severe problem of absolute poverty, involving one-fifth of the population—1 billion people—who lack nutrition adequate for a safe and productive life.

The Extent of Poverty

Poverty in the Third World is more extensive than it is in Canada. Chapter 10 ("Social Class in Canada") indicates that about 14 percent of the Canadian population is officially classified as poor. In the societies of the Third World, however, *most* people live no better than the poor in our country, and at any given time, about 20 percent of Third-World people are near absolute poverty. In some parts of the world (such as East Asia), the extent of absolute poverty is not so great; in other regions (rural areas in Central America and Africa, for example), half the population is malnourished. In the world as a whole, 100 million people have no shelter and approximately 1 billion people do not eat enough to allow them to work regularly. Of these, at least 800 million are at risk for their lives (Sivard, 1988;

Canada enjoys a large share of the world's wealth. Even so, the standard of living among the poorest of our people is little better than that of the poor throughout the Third World. The plight of some children growing up on certain reserves in Northern Ontario (left) is remarkably similar to that of many children in Nicaragua.

Helmuth, 1989; United Nations Development Programme, 1991).

Global Map 11-2 illustrates nutritional resources in various world regions. If anything the problem in the First World is too much nutrition: on average, a person living in the First World consumes more than 3,500 calories daily, which contributes to obesity and related health problems. People in much of the Third World, by contrast, do not have adequate nutrition. Especially in parts of central Africa, the problem of hunger regularly reaches crisis proportions.

Simply stated, in many parts of the world, people die every minute of every day from lack of basic nutrition. In the ten minutes it takes to read through this section of the chapter, about three hundred people in the world will die of starvation. This amounts to more than 40,000 people a day, or 15 million people each year. Even more than in Canada, the burden of poverty

WINDOW ON THE WORLD

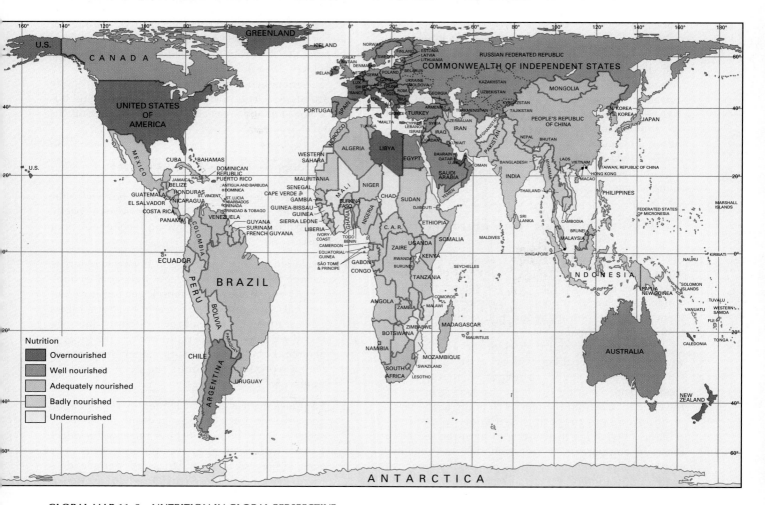

GLOBAL MAP 11–2 NUTRITION IN GLOBAL PERSPECTIVE
To remain healthy, an average, active adult requires 2,500 to 3,000 calories a day in food energy. Women and men in many poor societies are not well nourished: hundreds of millions of people survive on fewer than 2,000 calories daily despite engaging in extensive physical labor. By contrast, members of rich societies are typically overnourished—consuming in excess of 3,500 calories each day—just as they are less active physically. Although not as immediately life threatening as undernourishment, overconsumption contributes to obesity and a host of longer-term health problems.

in the Third World falls on children. Across the Third World, about one child in four dies before reaching the age of five.

To remain healthy, an average, active adult requires 2,500 to 3,000 calories a day in food energy. Women and men in many poor societies are not well nourished: hundreds of millions of people survive on fewer than 2,000 calories daily despite engaging in extensive physical labor. By contrast, members of rich societies are typically overnourished—consuming in excess of 3,500 calories each day—just as they are less active physically. Although not as immediately life threatening as undernourishment, overconsumption contributes to obesity and a host of longer-term health problems.

Two further comparisons suggest the human toll of global poverty. First, at the end of World War II, the United States obliterated the Japanese city of Hiroshima with an atomic bomb. The worldwide loss of life from starvation reaches the Hiroshima death toll *every three days*. Second, the death toll from hunger in just the last five years equals the number of deaths from war, revolution, and murder during the last 150 years (Burch, 1983). Given the magnitude of this problem, easing world hunger is one of the most serious responsibilities facing humanity today.

Third-World Women: Work and Poverty

Even more than in rich societies, in the Third World women are disproportionately the poorest of the poor. In societies poor to begin with, the opportunities for women are sharply limited by traditions that accord them primary responsibility for child rearing and maintaining the household.

Especially in rural regions of the Third World, women face "an appalling workday of 16 to 18 hours" (Plewes & Stuart, 1991). Much of women's work—cleaning and repairing the home, gathering firewood, traveling to and from the market, tending to the needs of children, and preparing meals for the family—remains "invisible" to those who monitor the labor force. In comparison to rich societies, in the Third World more of women's work is not paid, making the economic position of women correspondingly weaker.

Even Third-World women who work for pay are at a greater disadvantage than their counterparts in rich societies. As Chapter 13 ("Sex and Gender") details, in Canada and the rest of the industrialized world, women receive less income for their efforts than men do. In the largely agrarian societies of the Third World, traditional subordination of women to men is more pronounced, making the gender differences in salary even greater. Third-World women have less access to education than men have, a pattern that has diminished in industrial societies (United Nations, 1988). Lacking education, Third-World women have far fewer choices about their lives.

Finally, the United Nations estimates that roughly 90 percent of land in the Third World is formally owned by men (in rich societies, men control a lesser proportion of wealth). In reality, wives and mothers exert considerable control over property that formally belongs to husbands and sons. Nevertheless, strong traditions reinforced by law give men ultimate control of the land, the chief source of wealth in agrarian societies (Cebotarev, 1988).

Overall, then, Third-World poverty is both severe and extensive. The burden of poverty is heavy, and it is not shared equally; women are generally among the most disadvantaged.

Correlates of Third-World Poverty

What accounts for severe and extensive poverty in the Third World? The rest of this chapter weaves together explanations from the following facts about poor societies.

1. **Technology.** The Third World is largely agrarian, lacking the productive power of industrial technology. Energy from human muscles or beasts of burden falls far short of the force from steam, oil, or nuclear fuels; this technological disparity limits the use of complex machinery. Moreover, the focus in agrarian societies on farming, rather than on specialized production, limits the need to develop human skills and abilities.

2. **Population growth.** As Chapter 21 ("Population and Urbanization") explains in detail, Third-World societies have the highest birth rates in the world. Despite high death rates from poverty, the populations of poor societies in Africa, for example, double every twenty-five years. In such countries, more than half the people are not yet through their teens, so that they are just entering their childbearing years. Future population growth, therefore, looms large. Even a developing economy would

not be able to support the inevitable surges in population. Typically, then, economic growth is overwhelmed by population growth, resulting in little or no real increase in people's standard of living.

3. **Cultural patterns.** Societies yet to industrialize usually embrace tradition. Families and community groups pass down folkways and mores from generation to generation. Adhering to long-established ways of life, such people resist innovations —even those that promise a richer material life.

    The members of poor societies often accept their fate, although it may be bleak, in order to maintain a sense of family vitality and cultural heritage. Although such attitudes discourage development, they bolster strong social bonds. The Cross-Cultural Comparison box "India: A Different Kind of Poverty" explains why traditional people in India respond to their poverty differently than poor people in the West generally do.

4. **Social stratification.** The modest wealth of Third-World societies is distributed very unequally among their people. Chapter 9 ("Social Stratification") explained that social inequality is more pronounced in agrarian societies, where land is a vital resource, than in industrial societies. In the farming regions of Bangladesh in Central Asia, for example, 10 percent of all landowners own more than half the land, while almost half of farming families possess little or no land of their own (Hartmann & Boyce, 1982). According to another estimate, the richest 10 percent of landowners in Central America control more than three-fourths of the region's land (Barry, 1983). Such concentrations of land and wealth have prompted widespread demands for land reform in many agrarian societies.

5. **Global power relationships.** A final cause of global poverty lies in the relationships among the nations of the world. Much of the wealth of the Third World has enriched the First World. Historically, this stems from **colonialism**, *the process by which some nations enrich themselves through political and economic control of other countries.* The societies of Western Europe colonized and maintained control over much of Latin America for more than 300 years; much of Africa endured a century of colonization; parts of Asia were also under domination by colonial powers for long periods. Some analysts claim that this global exploitation spurred certain nations to *develop* economically at the expense of others that were systematically *underdeveloped.*

During the twentieth century, about 130 former colonies gained their independence, leaving only a small number of countries as formal colonies today (Strang, 1990). As we shall see, however, a continuing pattern

Life for both women and men throughout the Third World is more often than not a matter of continual labor to meet basic needs. But because social inequality between the sexes is pronounced in agrarian societies, the relative disadvantages endured by women are greater than for women living in industrial societies.

CROSS-CULTURAL COMPARISON

India: A Different Kind of Poverty

Most North Americans know that India is one of the poorest societies on earth: typical personal income in this Asian nation stands at only $340 a year (see Table 11-1). Hunger pervades this vast society, where one-third of the world's starving people can be found. But few members of our society fully comprehend the reality of poverty in India. Most of the country's 750 million people live in conditions far worse than those of us who are labeled as "poor." A traveler's first experience of Indian life is sobering and sometimes shocking; in time, however, the outsider learns that, in India, people understand poverty differently from us. Arriving in Madras, one of India's largest cities, a visitor immediately recoils from the smell of human sewage, which hangs over the city like a malodorous cloud. Untreated sewage also renders much of the region's water unsafe to drink. The sights and sounds of Madras are strange and intense—streets are choked by motorbikes, trucks, carts pulled by oxen, and waves of people. Along the roads, vendors sitting on burlap cloth hawk fruits, vegetables, and prepared foods. Seemingly oblivious to the urban chaos all around them, people work, talk, bathe, and sleep in the streets. Tens of millions of homeless people fill the cities of India.

Madras is also dotted by more than a thousand shanty settlements,

Third-World societies may be poor, but strong traditions and vital families place everyone in a network of social support. Thus people endure poverty with the help of their kin, which contrasts to the often isolating poverty in the United States.

home to roughly half-a-million people, many of whom converge on the city from traditional rural villages in search of a better life. Shantytowns are clusters of huts constructed of branches, leaves, and discarded material. These dwellings offer little privacy and no refrigeration, running water, or bathrooms. The visitor from North America understandably feels uneasy entering such a community, since the poorest sections of its inner cities abound with frustration and,

oftentimes, outright violence. But here, too, India offers a sharp contrast. No angry young people hang out at the corner, no drugs pervade the area, and there is surprisingly little danger. Instead, the social units of shantytowns are strong families —children, parents, and sometimes elderly grandparents—who extend a smile and a welcome. In traditional societies like India, ways of life change little, even over many generations. Moreover, the lives of traditional Indians are shaped by *dharma* —the Hindu concept of duty and destiny—that presses people to accept their fate, whatever it may be. Mother Teresa, who has won praise for her work among the poorest of India's people, goes to the heart of the cultural differences: "Americans have angry poverty," she explains. "In India, there is worse poverty, but it is a happy poverty."

No one who lives on the edge of survival can be called truly "happy." The deadly horror of poverty in India, however, is eased by the strength of families and traditional communities, a sense of purpose to life, and a world view that encourages each person to accept whatever society offers. As a result, the visitor comes away from the first encounter with Indian poverty in confusion: "How can people be so poor, and yet apparently content, vibrant, and so *alive?*"

SOURCE: Based on research by John J. Macionis in Madras, India, November, 1988.

of domination has emerged. **Neocolonialism** (*neo* comes from Greek, meaning "new") amounts to *a new form of international, economic exploitation that involves not direct political control but the operation of multinational corporations.* **Multinational corporations**, in turn, are simply *large corporations that operate in many different countries.* As Chapter 19 ("The Economy and Work") explains, multinational corporations historically developed through rapid corporate growth and mergers. These corporations now wield such vast economic power that corporate decision makers can—and often do—manipulate the political systems in countries where they do business.

Global Inequality: Theoretical Analysis

There are two major explanations for the unequal distribution of the world's wealth and power—*modernization theory* and *dependency theory*. Each suggests not only why so many of the world's people are poor, but why we as North Americans enjoy such comparative advantages.

The two explanations overlap to some extent. Both acknowledge enormous inequality on our planet, and they agree that changes are needed to guarantee the future security of humanity, rich and poor alike. Yet, emphasizing different factors, each reaches a different conclusion about where responsibility lies for global poverty.

Modernization Theory

Modernization theory is a model of economic and social change that explains global inequality in terms of differing levels of technological development among societies. Modernization theory developed in the 1950s, a period of fascination with technology in the United States and a time of hostility to U.S. interests in much of the Third World. Socialist nations of the Second World were gaining influence in the Third World by asserting that Third-World countries simply could not make economic progress under the sway of the capitalist First World. In response, U.S. policy makers framed a broad defense of the First World and its free-market economy that has shaped official foreign policy toward poor nations ever since.[4] Canada's approach to Third World issues is largely consistent with that of its powerful neighbor to the south.

Historical Perspective

According to modernization theorists, the *entire world* was poor as recently as several centuries ago. Because poverty has been the norm throughout human history, *affluence*—not deprivation—demands an explanation.

---

[4] The following discussion of modernization theory draws primarily on Rostow (1960, 1978), Bauer (1981), and Berger (1986).

Affluence came within reach of a small segment of humanity during the twilight of the Middle Ages as economic activity expanded in Western Europe. Initially, this economic growth involved trade within cities. By the beginning of the sixteenth century, exploration of other parts of the world revealed vast commercial potential. Then, the Industrial Revolution in the eighteenth and nineteenth centuries transformed Western Europe and, soon after, North America. Industrial technology and the innovations of countless entrepreneurs created new wealth on a grand scale. At the outset, modernization theorists concede, this new wealth benefited only a few. Yet industrial technology was so productive that gradually the standard of living of even the poorest people began to rise. The specter of absolute poverty, which had cast a menacing shadow over humanity for its entire history, was finally being routed.

During the last century, the standard of living in the First World—the regions where the Industrial Revolution first began—has continued to improve. Today, industrialization confers unprecedented affluence on First-World societies and, to a lesser extent, on nations of the Second World. But without industrial technology, Third-World countries contend with the same low productivity they have endured throughout history.

The Importance of Culture

Why didn't people the world over share in the Industrial Revolution so that they, too, could enjoy material plenty? Modernization theory holds that people may or may not seek out and utilize new technology depending on whether their *cultural environment* emphasizes tradition or touts the benefits of innovation and greater productivity.

In a word, then, the greatest barrier to economic development is *traditionalism*. In societies that celebrate strong family systems and revere the past, ancient ways offer powerful guides to understanding the present and shaping the future. Predictably, this creates a form of "cultural inertia" that discourages societies from adopting technological advances that would boost their material standard of living. For example, Western innovations and technological advances have encountered fierce resistance in Iran because they threaten traditional Islamic family relationships, customs, and religious beliefs.

Max Weber (1958; orig. 1904–1905) explained that, at the end of the Middle Ages, Western Europe developed a distinctive cultural environment that favored change. As detailed in Chapter 4 ("Society"), the

Early in the nineteenth century, exhausting and dangerous work was a fact of childhood in England. An unknown artist portrayed the perilous coal mines of Britain in this 1844 painting. Initially, the Industrial Revolution did little to improve the lives of children, who had historically labored just as adults did. Gradually, however, as machinery reduced the need for labor, the role of children was transformed so that they left the mines and factories for schools.

Protestant Reformation's attack on traditional Catholicism created a progress-oriented culture. Material affluence—regarded with suspicion by the Catholic Church—became a personal virtue, and individualism steadily eroded the long-standing emphasis on kinship and community. Taken together, these changing cultural patterns nurtured the Industrial Revolution, which allowed one segment of humanity to prosper.

Rostow's Stages of Modernization

Modernization theory does not condemn poverty-stricken regions of the globe to a future as poor as their past. As technological advances diffuse around the world, all societies are gradually converging on one general form: the industrial model. According to W.W. Rostow (1960, 1978), the process of modernization follows four overarching stages.

1. **Traditional stage.** Initially, cultural traditions are strong, so poor societies resist technological innovation. Socialized to venerate the past, people in traditional societies cannot easily imagine how life could be different. They build their lives around their families and local communities, granting little individual freedom to one another, which, of course, inhibits change. Life in such communities

is often spiritually rich, but lacking in material abundance.

A century ago, much of the world was in this initial stage of economic development. And because societies like Bangladesh in central Asia and Burkina Faso in central Africa are still at the traditional stage, they remain impoverished to this day.

2. **Take-off stage.** Reaching this point, a society experiences a weakening of tradition, and the economy begins to grow. A limited market emerges as people produce goods not just for their own consumption but to profitably trade with others. Paralleling these developments, greater individualism and a stronger achievement orientation take hold, often at the expense of family ties and long-standing norms and values.

Great Britain reached the take-off stage by about 1800; the United States began take-off around 1820. Rostow determined that take-off in Canada occurred between 1890 and 1914 (Pomfret, 1981). Developing nations of the Third World, including Thailand in eastern Asia, are now at this stage.

Rostow stresses that economic "take-off" in Third-World societies depends on progressive influences—including foreign aid, the availability of advanced technology and investment capital, and schooling abroad—that only rich nations can provide.

3. **Drive to technological maturity.** By this time, a society is in full pursuit of a higher standard of living. An active, diversified economy is driven by a population eager to enjoy the benefits of industrial technology. At the same time, however, people begin to realize (and sometimes lament) that industrialization is eroding traditional life in families and local communities. Great Britain reached this point by about 1840, the United States by about 1860 and Canada between 1914 and 1950. Today, Mexico and the People's Republic of China are among the nations driving to technological maturity.

At this stage of economic development, absolute poverty has greatly declined. Cities swell with people drawn from the rural hinterlands in search of economic opportunity; occupational specialization renders relationships less personal; and heightened individualism often sparks movements for expanded political rights. Societies approaching

CRITICAL THINKING

Modernization and Women: What Are the Drawbacks?

In global perspective, gender inequality is greatest where people are poorest. Economic development, then, weakens traditional male domination and gives women opportunities to work outside the home. Birth control emancipates women from a continual routine of childbearing, and allows them to benefit from schooling and to enter the paid workforce.

Even as living standards rise, however, economic development has drawbacks for women. Investigating a poor, rural district of Bangladesh, Sultana Alam (1985) identified several problems women face as a result of modernization.

First, economic opportunity draws men from rural areas to cities in search of work, leaving women and children to fend for themselves. Men sometimes sell their land and simply abandon their wives, who are left with nothing but their children.

Second, the eroding strength of the family and neighborhood leaves women who are deserted in this way with few sources of assistance. The same holds true for women who become single through divorce or the death of a spouse. In the past, Alam reports, kin or neighbors readily took in a Bangladeshi woman who found herself alone. Today, as Bangladesh struggles to advance economically, the number of poor households headed by women is increasing. Rather than enhancing women's autonomy, Alam argues, this spirit of individualism has actually lowered the social standing of women.

Third, economic development undermines women's traditional roles as wives, sisters, and mothers, while redefining women as objects of men's sexual attention. Today, especially under the influence of the Western mass media, a modern emphasis on sexuality encourages men to desert aging spouses for women who are younger and more physically attractive.

Modernization, then, does not affect the world's women and men in the same ways. In the long run, the evidence suggests, modernization does give the sexes more equal standing. In the short run, however, the economic position of many women actually declines, and women are also forced to contend with new problems that were virtually unknown in traditional societies.

SOURCES: Based on Alam (1985) and Mink (1989).

One consequence of modernization in Third-World societies might be termed "the sexualization of women." Rather than being defined in terms of traditional kinship roles, men increasingly value women for their sexual attractiveness. It is noteworthy that many of the growing number of prostitutes in Third-World cities have discarded traditional dress for Western styles of clothing.

technological maturity also provide basic schooling for all their people, with advanced training for some. Increasingly, tradition falls into disrepute, propelling the drive for rapid social change. The social position of women steadily becomes more equal to that of men. At least initially, however, the process of development subjects women to new and unanticipated problems, as the box on page 307 explains.

4. **High mass consumption.** Economic development through industrial technology steadily raises living standards. This occurs, Rostow explains, as mass production stimulates mass consumption. Put more simply, people soon learn to "need" the expanding array of goods that is being produced. The United States reached the mass-consumption stage by the beginning of the twentieth century. Other First-World societies were not far behind. For example, Japan became a military power early in this century. After recovering from the destruction of World War II, the Japanese enjoyed high mass consumption, and Japan now rivals the United States as the world's leading economic power. The former Soviet Union claimed to be entering this stage in 1950, although the sluggish economy in the new Commonwealth of Independent States still limits the availability of many goods and services. Closing in on this level of economic development are some of the most prosperous Third-World societies in East Asia: South Korea, Taiwan, Hong Kong, and Singapore.

The Role of Rich Nations

Modernization theory claims that the First World plays a crucial role in global economic development. Far from being the *cause* of the abject poverty that afflicts much of humanity, rich societies hold the key to *solving* global inequality in the following ways:

1. **Assisting in population control.** As we have already noted, population growth is greatest in the poorest societies of the world. Rising population easily overtakes economic advances, lowering the standard of living. Curbing global population, therefore, is crucial to combating poverty. First-World nations can help control population growth by exporting birth control technology and helping to promote its use. Once economic development is under way and women's lives are no longer circumscribed by household and child-rearing chores, birth rates should decline as they have in industrialized societies.

2. **Increasing food production.** Modernization theory asserts that "high-tech" farming methods, exported from rich societies to poor nations, will raise agricultural yields. Such techniques, collectively referred to as the *green revolution*, encompass the use of new hybrid seeds, modern irrigation methods, chemical fertilizers, and pesticides for insect control.

3. **Introducing industrial technology.** Technological transfers should involve industry as well as agriculture. Rich nations can accelerate economic growth in poor societies by introducing machinery and computer technology. Such cultural diffusion helps to transform the labor force of poor countries from lower-skill agricultural work to higher-skill industrial and service work, improving the society's productivity.

4. **Instituting programs of foreign aid.** Investment capital from rich nations can boost the prospects of poor societies striving to reach the "take-off" stage. Developing countries can spend the money to purchase high technology—fertilizers and irrigation projects to raise agricultural productivity and power plants and factories to improve industrial output.

Critical evaluation. Modernization theory, which identifies how industrialization affects other dimensions of social life, has influential supporters among social scientists (Parsons, 1966; W. Moore, 1977, 1979; Bauer, 1981; Berger, 1986). Modernization theory has shaped the foreign policy of Canada, the United States, and other First-World nations for decades.

Proponents maintain that a number of poor societies have made impressive strides with the assistance of rich countries. For instance, the Asian nations of South Korea, Taiwan, the former British colony of Singapore, and the current British colony of Hong Kong each receive extensive First-World assistance, and each has an impressive record of economic development. Similarly, concerted efforts to modernize by nations like Turkey have greatly improved national living standards.

From the outset, however, modernization theory has come under fire from nations of the Second World as a thinly veiled defense of capitalism. By the 1960s, a growing number of critics in First-World societies were also citing flaws in this approach. Perhaps the most serious failing, according to critics, is that modernization theory has failed by its own standards. Instead of making the industrial model widely accessible, only limited modernization has occurred. Critics maintain that global inequality remains as striking as ever.

A second criticism lodged against modernization theory holds that this view tends to ignore historical global changes by suggesting that the same opportunities for growth that were available to First-World nations several centuries ago are still accessible to poor Third-World nations today. (Indeed, modernization theorists claim that the road to development is, in some ways, *easier* today since rich nations can offer assistance to the Third World.) However, critics claim, self-interested rich nations in today's world stand as a barrier to the development of poor nations, ensuring the perpetuation of global poverty. In essence, they argue, the First World industrialized from a position of global *strength*; the Third World cannot be expected to modernize from a position of global *weakness*.

Third, critics charge that, by treating rich and poor societies as worlds unto themselves, modernization theory offers little insight into how global development continues to affect First-World societies. As suggested in Chapter 10 ("Social Class in Canada"), the expansion of multinational corporations around the globe has brought healthy profits to wealthy industrialists in this country; at the same time, the production of industrial goods abroad has weakened many traditional Canadian industries such as steel and automobiles, eroding the economic security of rank-and-file workers.

Fourth, critics contend that modernization theory holds up the First World as the standard by which the rest of humanity should be judged, thus betraying an ethnocentric bias. As Chapter 23 ("Social Change and Modernity") explains, "progress" thus translates into reducing the cultural diversity of our world by promoting a materialistic, Western way of life around the globe.

Fifth, and finally, modernization theory draws criticism for suggesting that the causes of global poverty lie almost entirely in the poor societies themselves. This amounts to "blaming the victims" for their own plight. Instead, critics argue, an analysis of global inequality should focus as much attention on the behavior of *rich* nations as that of poor nations (Wiarda, 1987).

From all these concerns has emerged a second major approach to understanding global inequality: dependency theory.

Dependency Theory

Dependency theory is *a model of economic and social development that explains global inequality in terms of the historical exploitation of poor societies by rich societies.* Dependency theory offers a dramatically different analysis of global inequality than modernization theory, placing primary responsibility for global poverty on rich nations. Dependency theory holds that the First World has systematically impoverished the Third World so that today poor nations are dependent on richer ones. That is, while modernization theory contends that poverty is a condition that precedes development, dependency theory maintains that global poverty is caused by development (Berger, 1986). This destructive process, which continues today, extends back several centuries.

Historical Perspective

Before the Industrial Revolution, there was little of the affluence present in some of the world today. Dependency theory asserts, however, that most of the people living in what we now call the Third World were actually better off economically in the past than they are now. André Gunder Frank (1975), a noted proponent of this approach, argues that the *development* of rich societies paralleled the *underdevelopment* of poor societies:

> *Underdevelopment is not just the lack of development. Before there was development there was no underdevelopment. ... Development and underdevelopment are ... related through the common historical process that they have shared during the past several centuries. ... (1975:1)*

Dependency theory hinges on the crucial insight that the economic positions of the rich and poor nations of the world are linked and cannot be understood correctly in isolation from one another. Modernization theory, its critics argue, errs by suggesting that poor societies are lagging behind rich ones on a single "path of progress." According to dependency theory, the increasing prosperity of the First World has come largely at the expense of the Third World. In short, *some nations have grown rich only because other nations have become poor*. This complex process, which began centuries ago with the onset of global commerce, continues in much of the world today.

The Importance of Colonialism

Half a millennium has passed since Europeans set out to explore the "New World" of North America to the west, the massive continent of Africa to the south, and Asia to the east. Throughout North America, 1992 marked the quincentennial of the voyage of Christopher Columbus, who ventured from Spain believing that he could reach the Orient by sailing west. The unintended outcome of Columbus's voyage—what Europeans called "the discovery of the New World"—has long been celebrated as a stunning achievement. In recent decades, however, historians have provided a more complete understanding of this fateful collision of two worlds, as the box on page 311 explains.

What Europeans dubbed "the age of exploration" is more accurately described as an era of conquest. Colonial efforts by adventurers such as Christopher Columbus brought vast wealth to First-World nations, whose economic fortunes began to rise. By the late fifteenth century, the Third World was systematically falling under the control of European governments. Spain and Portugal colonized nearly all of Latin America. By the beginning of the twentieth century, Great Britain had colonies around the world and boasted that "The sun never sets on the British Empire." The United States, itself originally a British colony, colonized the Virgin Islands, Haiti, Puerto Rico, and part of Cuba in the Western hemisphere, and Guam and the Philippines in Asia.

Overt colonialism has largely disappeared from the world. Most Latin American nations achieved political independence during the first half of the nineteenth century, and most African and Asian colonies gained their freedom during this century. However, according to dependency theory, *political* liberation has not translated into *economic* autonomy. Far from it: poor societies of the Third World maintain economic relationships with rich nations that reproduce the colonial pattern. This neocolonialism is fueled by a capitalist world economy.

Wallerstein's Capitalist World Economy

Immanuel Wallerstein (1974, 1979, 1983, 1984) developed a model of the "capitalist world economy" to explain the origins of contemporary global

In her mixed-media work Living in the Storm Too Long, *Canadian Native artist Jane Ash Poitras shows Christopher Columbus's flagship, the* Santa Maria, *on a collision course with a buffalo, a symbol of North American Native culture. In Poitras's view, the Age of Exploration meant nothing but exploitation to the indigenous peoples, who were left powerless politically and with a bankrupt culture.*

When Worlds Collide: The Christopher Columbus Controversy

For generations, teachers across Canada told young people that the Italian explorer Christopher Columbus (1446–1505) "discovered" a "New World." Conventional accounts held that Columbus forged a link between Europe and the Americas [two continents whose names honor Amerigo Vespucci (1452–1512), who accompanied Columbus on his fateful voyage], introducing "civilization" to a land that had never known Christianity and bringing "enlightened" political and scientific ideas to replace backwardness. In short, according to conventional history, Columbus tamed a savage wilderness with the tools and thinking of a progressive culture, and set the New World on the path to economic development.

As Americans throughout the hemisphere observed the five-hundred-year anniversary of Columbus's voyage, spirited controversy surrounded this historical figure and his legacy. Against the backdrop of conventional history, the story of Columbus and his expedition is literally being rewritten by scholars informed by multicultural perspectives. These critics challenge the heroic stature of Columbus on a number of counts. First, although Columbus's discovery had enormous consequences, it was nonetheless quite accidental. Columbus sailed from Spain thinking that Asia was only three thousand miles to the west. Contrary to popular opinion, most educated people in the late fifteenth century knew that the world was round, but the planet's size was

much in doubt. The westward route from Europe to Asia is three times what Columbus imagined, with the American continents in between. Thus when Columbus and the crews of his three wooden ships stumbled onto the Bahamian Islands at the eastern edge of the Americas, they were actually quite lost.

Second, critics point out, this world was "new" only to the Europeans; the Americas had been inhabited for tens of thousands of years by a host of distinctive societies that originated in Asia. The notion that Europeans "discovered" the "New World" illustrates how, from the outset, our history has recorded contact between various cultures from the point of view of only one of them. To critics of conventional history, this amounts to a clear case of Eurocentrism—evaluating facts from a European perspective (see Chapter 3, "Culture").

Third, the consequences of contact between Europeans and the indigenous cultures of the Americas were strikingly one-sided. Columbus represented a way of life that aggressively pursued wealth; from the outset, he expected his voyage to bring him riches and power. In comparison to the Europeans, the people who received Columbus maintained a more gentle way of life. Their society, too, was hierarchical, but they lived peacefully and, typical of those with simple technology, they displayed a reverence for nature. Columbus enforced his rule with determination

and brutality. Setting a pattern for later colonizers, he looted gold and silver from the lands he controlled, subjugating Native peoples for labor. Even more tragically, Europeans unintentionally introduced to the Americas diseases against which Native peoples had no natural defenses. Taken together, violence and disease took a severe toll, decimating indigenous populations within several generations. Columbus's show of brute force to bend Native peoples to his will foreshadowed another disastrous collision of different worlds: the slave trade by which Europeans and Africans transported human beings from Africa to the United States to be sold into bondage.

The European conquest forever changed the course of life in the Americas. In at least some respects, the clash of two worlds in 1492 had long-term positive consequences. Useful instances of cultural diffusion resulted, including the introduction of horses from Europe to the Americas and the importation of corn and potatoes (and also tobacco) to Europe. Furthermore, in time, entire new societies emerged as a product of European settlement. But, from the point of view of the original inhabitants of the Americas, contact with Europeans initiated a five-hundred-year nightmare: a loss of traditional culture, centuries of oppressive colonization, and the virtual obliteration of many societies.

SOURCES: Sale (1990) and Gray (1991).

One side of the "Christopher Columbus controversy" is illustrated by artist Diego Rivera in his mural Colonial Domination. *As this painting expresses in graphic detail, the arrival of Europeans to this hemisphere initiated considerable conflict and violence, placing the Americas under the political control of European nations for more than 300 years.*

inequality.[5] Wallerstein's term *world economy* suggests that production in various nations is linked through a global economic network. He argues that this global economy results from economic expansion rooted in the First World that has steadily spilled beyond national boundaries over the last five hundred years. The dominant character of the world economy is capitalist.

Wallerstein terms the nations of the First World the *core* of the world economy. Colonialism established this core as raw materials, funneled to Western Europe from the rest of the world, fueled the Industrial Revolution. Today, multinational corporations operate profitably around the globe, drawing wealth to North America, Western Europe, and Japan. By contrast, the Third World encompasses countries at the *periphery* of the world economy. Originally drawn into the world economy by colonial exploitation, these poor countries continue to support industrial societies by providing inexpensive labor and serving as a vast market for First-World products.

---

[5] While based mostly on Wallerstein's ideas, this section also draws ideas from the work of Frank (1980, 1981), Delacroix & Ragin (1981), and Bergesen (1983).

According to Wallerstein, the world economy benefits the First World (in terms of profits) and harms the Third World (by perpetuating poverty). The world economy thus imposes a state of dependency on poor nations, which remain under the control of rich ones. This dependency arises from the following three factors:

1. **Narrow, export-oriented economies**. Unlike the economies of core nations, production in Third-World countries is not diversified. Historically, colonial powers forced farmers to stop growing a variety of traditional crops for local consumption in favor of producing just a few products for export. Thus, most colonial economies export a limited number of products—mostly raw materials. Coffee and fruits from Latin American nations, oil from Nigeria, hardwoods from the Philippines, and palm oil from Malaysia are some of the key products central to the economies of these poor societies. Multinational corporations maintain this pattern today as they purchase raw materials cheaply in poor societies and transport them to core societies where they can be processed and profitably sold. Corporations have also increased their landholdings in

Third-World nations, transforming traditional farmers into low-paid laborers in foreign-owned industries. This pattern prevents Third-World societies from developing industries of their own.

2. **Lack of industrial capacity.** Without an industrial base, poor societies face a double bind: they rely on rich nations to buy their inexpensive raw materials, and they depend on rich nations to sell them whatever expensive manufactured goods they can afford. In a classic example of this double dependency, British colonialists allowed the people of India to raise cotton, but prohibited them from manufacturing their own cloth. Instead, Indian cotton was shipped to the textile mills of Birmingham and Manchester in England, woven into cloth, and shipped back for profitable sale in India.

Dependency theorists also blast the *green revolution*, widely praised by modernization theory. To promote agricultural productivity, poor countries must purchase expensive fertilizers, pesticides, and mechanical equipment from core nations. Typically, rich countries profit more from "high-tech" farming than poor societies do.

3. **Foreign debt.** Such unequal trade patterns have plunged Third-World countries deeper and deeper in debt to industrialized nations. Collectively, the Third World owes First-World countries roughly $1 trillion, including billions of dollars owed to Canada. This staggering debt is a financial burden few poor societies can bear. Excessive debt—which drains the resources of any society—can destabilize a Third-World country's economy, making matters worse for poor nations already reeling from high unemployment and rampant inflation, and sparking widespread social unrest (Walton & Ragin, 1990). Moreover, the Third-World debt crisis requires continuous transfers of wealth from poor to rich societies—roughly $50 billion annually (United Nations Development Programme, 1991)—further impoverishing peripheral societies and increasing their dependence on rich nations. According to dependency theorists, this results in a vicious circle that makes rich nations richer and poor nations poorer.

Seeing no way out of the "debt trap," some Third-World countries have simply stopped making payments. Cuba, for example, refused to make further payments on its $7 billion foreign debt in 1986. Because failure to repay loans threatens the economic growth of rich nations, First-World countries oppose such actions, and have proposed various ways to refinance these debts.

The Role of Rich Nations

Nowhere is the difference between modernization theory and dependency theory sharper than in the role they assign to rich nations. Modernization theory holds that the *production of wealth* determines whether a nation is rich or poor. From this point of view, First-World societies create new wealth through technological innovation. Their success in this regard does not impoverish other nations. According to modernization theory, productive technology needs to be more widely adopted; as Third-World nations modernize, their level of poverty will decrease. By contrast, dependency theory casts global inequality in terms of the *distribution of wealth*. This approach asserts that rich societies have unjustly seized the wealth of the world for their own purposes. That is, the *over*development of some parts of the globe is directly tied to the *under*development of the rest of it.

Dependency theorists dismiss the idea that First-World programs of population control, agricultural and industrial technology, and foreign aid help poor societies. Instead, they contend that rich nations act simply in pursuit of profit. Selling technology makes money, and foreign aid typically goes to ruling elites (rather than the poor majority) in exchange for maintaining a favorable "business climate" for multinational corporations (Lappé, Collins, & Kinley, 1981).

Hunger activists Frances Moore Lappé and Joseph Collins (1986) claim that the capitalist culture of the First World countries encourages people to think of poverty as somehow natural. Following this line of reasoning, poverty results from having (too many) children and disasters such as droughts. But, they insist, there is nothing inevitable about global hunger. Lappé and Collins point out that the world produces enough grain so every man, woman, and child could consume 3,600 calories a day, sufficient to make everyone on the planet overweight! Even most of the poorest societies grow enough to feed all their people. The problem, however, is that many people cannot afford to buy food. Therefore, while several hundred million people in India suffer from malnutrition, that nation *exports* beef, wheat, and rice. Similarly, millions of children go hungry in Africa, a vast continent whose agricultural abundance also makes it a net food exporter.

According to Lappé and Collins, the contradiction of poverty amid plenty stems from a deliberate First-World policy of producing food for profit, not people. Rich nations cooperate with elites in the Third World to grow and export profitable crops, which eat into the production of food for local consumption. As an example, coffee, grown in much of Latin America as a crop for export, simultaneously reduces production of corn and beans, which are consumed by local people. Governments of poor societies often support the practice of growing for export rather than local consumption because food profits help to repay massive foreign debt. The problem is complex, but at its core, according to Lappé and Collins, lies the capitalist corporate structure of the First World.

Critical evaluation.   The central contribution of dependency theory—that no society develops (or fails to develop) in isolation—points up how the system of global inequality shapes the destiny of all nations. Citing Latin America and other Third-World areas, dependency theorists claim that development simply cannot proceed under the constraints presently imposed by the First World. Addressing global poverty, they conclude, demands more than internal change within poor societies. Rather, these theorists call for reform of the entire world economy so it operates in the interests of the majority of people.

Critics of the dependency approach identify some important weaknesses in the theory. First, critics charge, dependency theory wrongly contends that the wealth of the First World resulted from stealing resources from poor societies. Farmers, small-business owners, and industrialists can and do create new wealth through their imagination and drive. Wealth is not a zero-sum resource by which some gain only at the expense of others. The entire world's wealth has grown during this century, largely due to technological advances and other innovations.

Second, critics reason, if dependency theory were correct in condemning the First World for creating global poverty, then nations with the strongest ties to rich societies would be among the poorest. However, the most impoverished nations of the world (such as Ethiopia and other countries in Central Africa) have had little contact with rich societies. Similarly, critics continue, a long history of trade with rich countries has dramatically improved the economies of a number of nations including Singapore, South Korea, Japan, and Hong Kong (which became a British colony in 1841 and will remain so until 1997). On the other hand, many nations historically active as colonizers (Portugal and Spain, for example) are far from "superpowers" today.

Third, critics contend that dependency theory simplistically points the finger at a single factor—world capitalism—as the sole cause of global inequality. By directing attention to forces *outside* poor societies, dependency theory views poor societies as victims, ignoring factors *inside* these countries that may contribute to their economic plight. Sociologists have long recognized the vital role of culture in shaping human behavior. Cultural patterns vary greatly around the world; some societies embrace change readily while others staunchly resist economic development. As we noted earlier, for example, Iran's fundamentalist form of Islam deliberately discourages economic ties with other countries. Capitalist societies can hardly be blamed for Iran's resulting economic stagnation. Nor can rich societies be saddled with responsibility for the reckless and self-serving behavior of certain foreign leaders. Governments of poor societies must assume some measure of blame for widespread poverty when leaders engage in far-reaching corruption and militaristic campaigns to enhance their own power (examples include the regimes of Marcos in the Philippines, Duvalier in Haiti, Noriega in Panama, and Hussein in Iraq). Governments may even use food supplies as a weapon in internal political struggles; this occurred in Ethiopia and the Sudan in Africa. Other regimes, including many in Latin America and Africa, fail to support programs to improve the status of women or control population growth.

Fourth, critics chide dependency theorists for downplaying the economic dependency fostered by the former Soviet Union. The Soviet army seized control of most of Eastern Europe during World War II and subsequently dominated these nations politically and economically. Critics of dependency theory see the popular uprisings against Soviet-installed governments, beginning in 1989, as rebellions against Soviet domination and the resulting economic dependency. Eastern European nations were forced to buy Soviet-manufactured goods and Soviet-produced energy, and prevented from trading more profitably on the world market. The Soviets did not broadly colonize the Third World, but until recently they supported regimes in Cuba and Angola that remain highly dependent on this foreign aid.

A fifth criticism is that the policy implications of dependency theory are inherently vague. Most dependency theorists urge poor societies to sever economic ties to the First World, and to nationalize foreign-owned industries. On a broader scale, dependency theory implies that global poverty could be eliminated by a worldwide overthrow of international capitalism. What form emerging economies would take, and whether they would be capable of meeting the economic needs of a growing world population (in light of the historic shortcomings of socialist societies) remains unclear.

Canada and the Third World

Canada's approach to Third-World development reveals tension between the modernization and dependency models upon which it is based. In 1991, Canada spent $3 billion on aid to developing countries (0.45 percent of our GNP) most of which is distributed through the Canadian International Development Agency (CIDA). In the past, CIDA has concentrated on encouraging industrial development, but it has recently started to emphasize self-sufficiency and improvement of the lives of the poor through enhancement of health care, housing, education and agricultural methods. The involvement of women in development has also become a priority.

By the mid-1980s Canada had responded to changing conditions in the Third World "with increasingly sophisticated social, cultural, and economic programs for human development and self-reliance" (Tomlinson, 1991), but there remains a tension between the goal of eliminating poverty and the desire to create an environment conducive to private-sector development and debt reduction through "economic structural adjustment" (CIDA, 1987). Despite its humanitarian goals, much of Canada's aid continues to be linked to trade or the perceived potential for trade (that is, "*tied aid*"). Although in this sense Canada's role is similar to that of the U.S., some Third World countries are more comfortable accepting aid from Canada, which does not have the superpower status of the United States.

In addition to its aid and trade involvements with developing countries, Canada plays an active role in the generation and dissemination of knowledge in the Third World. Several Canadian universities are involved in overseas research and development. For example, in 1992–93, the University of Guelph had 780 foreign students—492, or 63 percent of them, from Third World countries—and about 150 faculty members with overseas experience in developing countries.

Since 1970, it has been involved in more than seventy development projects in thirty developing countries with more than $56 million in externally funded development cooperation projects.[6] Here again, the projects are aimed at both modernization and at promoting self-sufficiency or reduced dependency.

The Future of Global Inequality

North Americans, sociologists included, are discovering many ways in which global trends are linked to our lives at home. The American economy is playing a pivotal role in an unfolding global drama, as corporations based in the United States invest abroad, and business interests around the world gain control of U.S. properties. Canada, which has its own concerns about American control of vital sectors of its economy, has over $10 billion in "direct investment" in the Third World (meaning at least 10 percent equity in the enterprises involved). At the same time, large trade alliances such as the North American Free Trade Agreement (NAFTA) and the European Common Market are altering trading patterns among many First- and Second-World countries.

This process of "globalization" is reshaping inequality in Canada. Profitable investments, especially in poor nations, and lucrative sales of Canadian companies to foreign interests, have brought greater affluence to those who already have substantial wealth. At the same time, increasing industrial production abroad has cut factory jobs in this country, exerting downward pressure on wages, causing unemployment or underemployment and increased reliance on social welfare.

As this chapter has noted, however, social inequality is far more striking in global context. The concentration of wealth among First-World countries, coupled with the grinding poverty in the Third World, may well constitute the most important dilemma facing humanity in the twenty-first century. To some analysts, rich nations are the key to ending world hunger; to others, rich nations are the cause of this tragic problem. Faced with these two radically different approaches to understanding global inequality, we might wonder

---

[6] From a conversation with Dr. James Shute, Director of the Centre for International Programs. Dr. Shute also notes that the top five countries, in terms of foreign student representation at the University of Guelph, are China, Kenya, Indonesia, the U.S.A., and India—in that order.

which one is "right." As with many controversies in sociology, each view has some merit as well as inherent limitations. Table 11-2 summarizes key arguments made by advocates of each approach.

In searching for truth, we must consider empirical evidence. In some regions of the world, such as the "Pacific Rim" of Eastern Asia, the market forces endorsed by modernization theory are raising living standards rapidly and substantially. At the same time, other societies of the Third World, especially in Latin America, are experiencing economic turmoil that frustrates hopes for market-based development.

The Third-World societies that have surged ahead economically have two factors in common. First, they are relatively small.[7] Combined, the Asian nations of South Korea, Taiwan, Hong Kong, Singapore, and Japan encompass only about one-fifth of the land area and population of India. The economic problems smaller countries face are more manageable; consequently, small societies more effectively administer programs of development. Second, these "best case" societies have cultural traits in common, especially traditions emphasizing individual achievement and economic success. In other areas of the world, where powerful societal forces inhibit change and squelch individualism, even smaller nations have failed to turn development opportunities to their advantage.

---

[7] This argument was suggested by Professor Alan Frishman of Hobart College.

The picture now emerging calls into question key arguments put forward by both approaches. Theorists in both camps, for instance, are revising their views on the major "paths to development." On the one hand, few societies seeking economic growth now favor a market economy completely free of government control. This view challenges orthodox modernization theory, which endorses a free-market approach over government-directed development. Also, as recent upheavals in the former Soviet Union and in Eastern Europe demonstrate, a global reevaluation of socialism is currently under way. These events, following decades of poor economic performance and political repression, make many Third-World societies reluctant to consider this path to development. Because dependency theory has historically supported socialist economic systems, changes in world socialism will surely generate new thinking here as well.

In the immediate future, no strategy for development is likely to significantly reduce the overwhelming problems of world hunger and rapid population growth. Looking to the next century, however, there are reasons for hope. The approaches described in this chapter identify the two keys to combating global inequality. One, revealed by modernization theory, is that world hunger is partly a *problem of technology*. A higher standard of living for a surging world population depends on raising agricultural and industrial productivity. The second, derived from dependency theory, is that global inequality is also a *political issue*. Even with higher

---

TABLE 11-2 MODERNIZATION THEORY AND DEPENDENCY THEORY: A SUMMARY

	Modernization Theory	Dependency Theory
Historical pattern	The entire world was poor just two centuries ago; the Industrial Revolution brought affluence to the First World; as industrialization gradually transforms the Third World, all societies are likely to become more equal and alike.	Global parity was disrupted by colonialism, which developed the First World and simultaneously underdeveloped the Third World; barring change in the world capitalist system, rich nations will grow richer and poor nations will become poorer.
Primary causes of global poverty	Characteristics of Third-World societies cause poverty, including lack of industrial technology, traditional cultural patterns that discourage innovation, and rapid population growth.	Global economic relations—historical colonialism and the operation of multinational corporations—have enriched the First World while placing the Third World in a state of economic dependency.
Role of rich nations	First-World countries can and do assist Third-World nations through programs of population control, technology transfers that increase food production and stimulate industrial development, and by providing investment capital in the form of foreign aid.	First-World countries have concentrated global resources, advantaging themselves while producing massive foreign debt in the Third World; rich nations represent a barrier to economic development in the Third World.

Hong Kong, an economic marketplace that operates as freely as any in the world, is a monument to the power of capitalism to generate wealth. Land values in Hong Kong are among the highest anywhere, and many of the British colony's people enjoy a lavish lifestyle. At the same time, however, there is a striking contrast between the rich and the poor. In Aberdeen, shown here, thousands of Chinese people reside in a floating neighborhood with poor sanitation and few chances for improving their lives.

productivity, crucial questions concerning how resources are distributed—both within societies and around the globe—must be addressed.

As debate over global inequality continues, people are coming to recognize that the security of everyone in the world depends on reducing the destabiliz-ing extremes of contemporary global poverty. We can only hope that, as the Cold War between the superpowers winds down, energy and resources will be redirected to the needs of the vast majority of humanity, many of whom are trapped in a desperate struggle for survival.

Summary

1. Adopting a global perspective, we can discern a system of social stratification that involves all of humanity. This inequality is best perceived by dividing the globe into "three worlds," based on patterns of economic development. The First World encompasses industrialized, capitalist societies including Canada; the Second World is composed largely of industrialized societies with socialist economies in transition, including the former Soviet Union; the Third World represents the remaining poor societies that have yet to industrialize.

2. In addition to relative poverty, the Third World grapples with widespread, absolute poverty. The typical member of a Third-World society struggles to survive on an income far below that of the average person in Canada.

3. Poverty places about 20 percent of the Third-World population—at least 800 million people—at serious risk. Some 15 million people, many of them children, die of starvation every year.

4. Women are more likely than men to be poor nearly everywhere in the world. In poor, agrarian

societies, women's relative and absolute disadvantages are greater than they are in industrial societies such as Canada.

5. The poverty of Third-World societies is a complex problem whose roots lie in limited industrial technology, rapid population growth, traditional cultural patterns, internal social stratification, and barriers to development in the form of global power relationships.

6. Modernization theory maintains that acquiring advanced productive technology is crucial to economic development. Traditional cultural patterns that value kinship ties over individual achievement are viewed as a barrier to modernization.

7. Modernization theorist W.W. Rostow identifies four stages of development: traditional, take-off, drive to technological maturity, and high mass consumption.

8. Arguing that rich societies hold the keys to creating wealth, modernization theory cites four ways rich nations can assist poor nations: by bolstering population control strategies, food-producing technologies, industrial development, and investment and other foreign aid.

9. Critics of modernization theory maintain that this approach has produced limited economic development in the world, while ethnocentrically assuming that poor societies can follow the path to development taken by rich nations centuries ago.

10. Dependency theory claims global wealth and poverty are directly linked to the historical operation of the capitalist world economy.

11. The dependency of Third-World countries is rooted in colonialism. In this century, neocolonialism continues the historic exploitation of politically independent societies of the Third World through the operation of multinational corporations.

12. Immanuel Wallerstein views the First World as the advantaged "core" of the capitalist world economy; poor societies of the Third World form the global "periphery."

13. Three key factors—export-oriented economies, a lack of industrial capacity, and foreign debt—perpetuate Third-World dependency on rich nations.

14. Critics of dependency theory argue that this approach overlooks the success of some nations in creating new wealth. Contrary to the implications of dependency theory, these critics maintain, the poorest societies are not those with the strongest ties to the First World.

15. Both modernization and dependency approaches offer useful insights into the operation of global inequality. Some evidence supports each view. Less controversial is the urgent need to address the various problems brought on by worldwide poverty.

Key Concepts

colonialism the process by which some nations enrich themselves through political and economic control of other countries

dependency theory a model of economic and social development that explains global inequality in terms of the historical exploitation of poor societies by rich ones

First World industrial societies that have predominantly capitalist economies

modernization theory a model of economic and social change that explains global inequality in terms of differing levels of technological development among world societies

multinational corporation a large corporation that operates in many different countries

neocolonialism a new form of international, economic exploitation that involves not direct political control but the operation of multinational corporations

Second World industrial societies that are currently transforming their socialist economies

Third World primarily agrarian societies, in which most people are poor

Suggested Readings

This classic statement concerning global inequality sets a radical agenda.

Frantz Fanon. *The Wretched of the Earth*. New York: Grove Press, 1963.

The following publications contain recent data on the state of the global economy, and explore contrasts between the rich and poor societies of the world.

United Nations Development Programme. *Human Development Report 1991*. New York: Oxford University Press, 1991.

The World Bank. *World Development Report 1991: The Challenge of Development*. New York: Oxford University Press, 1991.

This policy statement by CIDA makes an attempt to deal with supports for capitalism (economic structural adjustment) and more humanitarian aims, including the involvement of women in development.

Canadian International Development Association (CIDA). *Sharing our Future: Canadian International Development Assistance*. Ottawa: CIDA, 1987.

This collection of essays provides an overview of Canada's perspective on Third-World issues as well as the nature of its involvement. Among the topics covered are the debt crisis, women in development, environment, and mass media.

Jamie Swift and Brian Tomlinson, eds. *Conflicts of Interest: Canada and the Third World*. Toronto: Between the Lines Press, 1991.

This useful, short paperback offers a readable introduction to the growing economic disparity between rich and poor societies.

Peter Donaldson. *Worlds Apart: The Development Gap and What It Means*. 2nd ed. New York: Penguin, 1986.

This collection of essays focuses on the frequency of revolution in the world and the global trends that underlie insurgency.

Terry Boswell, ed. *Revolution in the World-System*. New York: Greenwood Press, 1989.

These books provide a solid overview of the issue of hunger.

Arthur Simon. *Bread for the World*. Rev. ed. New York: Paulist Press, 1984; Grand Rapids: Wm. B. Erdmans Publishing Co., 1984.

Frances Moore Lappé and Joseph Collins. *World Hunger: Twelve Myths*. New York: Grove Press/Food First Books, 1986.

Bakker, J.I.H., *The World Food Crisis: Food Security in Comparative Perspective*. Toronto: Canadian Scholars' Press Inc., 1990

The first two of these books present the modernization model of development; the second pair examine and evaluate dependency theory.

W.W. Rostow. *The World Economy: History & Prospect*. Austin and London: University of Texas Press, 1978.

P.T. Bauer. *Equality, the Third World and Economic Delusion*. Cambridge, MA: Harvard University Press, 1981.

Thomas Richard Shannon. *An Introduction to the World-System Perspective*. Boulder, CO: Westview Press, 1989.

Tom Barry. *Roots of Rebellion: Land and Hunger in Central America*. Boston: South End Press, 1987.

In Chapters 6 through 8 of this book, Peter Berger presents evidence in support of modernization theory.

Peter Berger. *The Capitalist Revolution: Fifty Propositions about Prosperity, Equality, and Liberty*. New York: Basic Books, 1986.

This recent collection of essays offers a comparative analysis of capitalist economies, especially in the United States and East Asia.

Stewart R. Clegg and Gordon Redding, eds., assisted by Monica Cartner. *Capitalism in Contrasting Cultures*. Hawthorne, NY: Aldine de Gruyter, 1990.

An economic crisis of capitalism is causing decline in rich and poor societies alike, according to this collection of essays.

Richard Peet, ed. *International Capitalism and Industrial Restructuring: A Critical Analysis*. Boston: Allyn & Unwin, 1987.

The publication of this pioneering work, which points out that development might actually be lowering the status of women in Third-World countries, caused quite a stir.

Ester Boserup. *Women's Role in Economic Development*. London: George Allen & Unwin, 1970.

Among the most popular—and controversial—of recent books concerned with global inequality is this account of the Columbus expedition and its consequences.

Fitzpatrick Sale. *The Conquest of Paradise: Christopher Columbus and the Columbian Legacy*. New York: Knopf, 1990.

12

RACE AND ETHNICITY

In the kitchen, a Croatian farmer recounts a tale of horror he has heard in the village.[1] Sitting around the table, his wife and neighbors look on silently, nodding from time to time to signal agreement. The farmer explains that a band of Serbs attacked a bus full of Croats on their way to Zagreb; they blocked the road, forcing the vehicle to stop, and then pulled the Croats from the bus one by one, beating and kicking them. An old woman was clubbed to death—the farmer pauses, shuddering with anger—and no Serb moved to help her. Such brutality, he storms, shows that the Serbs are not people but animals. The man collapses into his chair. Others in the small room murmur that the fighting must continue until the Serbs are driven from the region. Or until all the Serbs are dead.

Curiously, not one person in the room has actually observed the barbarity being described. In fact, no one has ever seen a Serb commit an act of violence against a Croat, or anyone else for that matter. Some listening to the sordid tale, if isolated from the others, would even admit that most of the Serbs who live nearby are people very much like themselves, except for different religious beliefs and some distinctive customs.

---

[1] This chapter opening is adapted from an account by Celestine Bohlen (1991).

Here we see the power of ethnicity to divide humanity, to fuel anger and to provoke animosity, in much of the world today. Stories such as this one—true or not—are passed from house to house, and from generation to generation, until they become real to those who believe them. Across Eastern Europe, as the heavy hand of government control was lifted, blood feuds that have pitted categories of people against one another for centuries broke out once again. In the former republic of Yugoslavia, Croats and Serbs fell into civil war and declared their independence; throughout the former Soviet Union, Ukrainians, Moldavians, Azerbaijanis, and a host of other ethnic peoples struggled to recover their cultural identity after decades of subjugation by the Russian majority. In the Middle East, efforts continue to bring an end to decades of conflict between Arabs and Jews. In South Africa, democratic government struggles to emerge after centuries of racial separation. Throughout the Americas, the five-hundredth anniversary of the initial contact between Native people and Europeans offers an opportunity to confront and try to resolve old wounds.

All over the world, human beings are set apart—and sometimes come together viciously—based on their culture, color, and social heritage. In one of the greatest ironies of the human condition, those characteristics that most define us are often the very traits that underlie our hatred and violence toward others.

In Canada, as elsewhere, race and ethnicity trumpet personal identity and group pride while sometimes provoking conflict. This chapter examines the meaning of race and ethnicity, delves into how these social constructs have shaped our history, and explains why they continue to play such a central part—for better or worse—in the world today.

The Social Significance of Race and Ethnicity

People frequently use the terms "race" and "ethnicity" imprecisely and interchangeably. For this reason, we begin with important definitions.

Race

A **race** is *a category composed of men and women who share biologically transmitted traits deemed socially significant.* Races are commonly distinguished by physical characteristics such as skin color, hair texture, facial

features, and body shape. All humans are members of a single biological species, but the biological variations we describe as "racial characteristics" have resulted from living for thousands of generations in different geographical regions of the world (Molnar, 1983). In regions of intense heat, for example, humans developed darker skin (from the natural pigment, melanin) that offers protection from the sun; in regions with moderate climates, people have lighter skin.

Over the course of history, migration encouraged intermarriage, so that many genetic characteristics once common to a single region have spread through much of the world. In regions that historically have been "crossroads" of human migration, like the Middle East, people display striking racial variation. Among more isolated people, such as the Japanese, we find greater uniformity of racial characteristics. No society, however, lacks genetic mixture, and increasing contact among the world's people will enhance racial blending in the future.

Trying to make sense of what can be bewildering human variety, nineteenth-century biologists developed a three-part scheme of racial classifications: they labeled people with relatively light skin and fine hair as *Caucasian*; they called those with darker skin and coarser, curlier hair *Negroid*; and they described people

The range of biological variation in human beings is far greater than any system of racial classification allows. This fact is made obvious by trying to place all of the people pictured here into simple racial categories.

with yellow or brown skin and distinctive folds on the eyelids as *Mongoloid.* Such categories are misleading, however, because we now know there are no biologically pure races. In fact, the world traveler notices gradual and subtle racial variations from region to region all around the globe. The people conventionally called "Caucasians" or "whites" actually display skin color that ranges from very light to very dark, and the same variation occurs among so-called "Negroids" and "Mongoloids." Some "whites" (such as the Caucasians of southern India) actually have darker skin and hair than some "blacks" (including the blond Negroid aborigines of Australia).

Although we might think that we can readily distinguish between"black" and "white" people, research confirms that Canadians, like people throughout the world, are genetically mixed. Over many generations, the genetic traits of Negroid Africans, Caucasian Europeans, and Mongoloid Native Americans (historic descendants of people from Asia) have spread widely through the Americas. Many "black" people, therefore, have a large proportion of Caucasian genes, and many "white" people have at least some Negroid genes. Similarly, a significant proportion of the French Canadian population has some—largely unacknowledged—Native ancestry. Some of these people identify themselves as Métis while others are totally unaware of their biological roots. In short, there is a great deal of racial blending—in North America and elsewhere.

Despite the reality of biological mixing, however, people around the world place each other into racial classifications and rank these categories in systems of social inequality. In some cases, they defend this racial hierarchy by claiming that physical traits are signs of innate intelligence and other mental abilities, although there is no accepted scientific foundation for such beliefs.[2] With so much at stake, no wonder societies strive to make social rankings clear and enforceable. Earlier in this century, for example, many of the southern states in the U.S. legally defined as "colored" anyone who had at least one thirty-second African ancestry (that is, one African-American great-great grandparent or any closer ancestor). Today, with race less of a caste

distinction in the United States, the law enables parents to declare the race of a child.

Although Canada has a long-standing interest in its ethnic composition, only since the 1980s has it reinserted "black" as a separate category in the census. Generally, our attempts to determine the size of our visible minority population have been based upon self-definition and declared country of origin (or ancestry). If someone claims to be of Jamaican origin, for example, it is assumed (sometimes incorrectly) that he or she is black. Similarly, and equally incorrectly at times, someone who declares British or U.S. origins is assumed to be Caucasian. Even status or treaty Indians, whose precise numbers are known because of registration, are of mixed racial ancestry. In other words, any attempt to describe Canada in terms of racial composition is an approximation only.

Ethnicity

Ethnicity is *a shared cultural heritage.* Members of an *ethnic category* may have common ancestors, language, and religion which, together, confer a distinctive social identity. For certain purposes, as in dealing with ethnic categories that are undergoing change, it is important to distinguish between *objective* and *subjective* criteria (Isajiw, 1985): objective criteria refer to differences such as ancestry, cultural practices, dress, religion, and language, whereas subjective criteria are those involving the internalization of a distinctive social identity whereby people identify themselves as belonging to a different group or are perceived by others as doing so. Ethnic identities (the subjective component) may persist beyond cultural assimilation, sometimes over many generations, without perpetuation of traditional ethnic culture (the objective components). Whatever the degree of assimilation, ethnicity remains an important basis of social differentiation in Canada.

Over 3 million Canadians claim languages other than French and English as their mother tongues (12 percent of the population) and about half that number still speak those languages at home. Canada is now more Catholic than Protestant (see Chapter 17, "Religion"), as Catholic French-Canadians have been joined by immigrants from traditionally Catholic areas such as Italy, Poland, and Latin America. Canada's Jewish population (roughly 250,000 people) traces its ancestral ties to various countries, as do the Eastern Orthodox and Muslim people.

Race and ethnicity, then, are quite different: one is biological, the other cultural. But the two sometimes

---

[2] Philippe Rushton, a psychology professor at the University of Western Ontario, became the center of academic controversy in 1989 when he claimed that, in terms of intelligence, conformity to law, and sexual restraint, Orientals are superior to whites who, in turn, are superior to blacks. Other researchers and lay people as well were quick to point out the methodological flaws in his research: some demanded that his tenure at Western be revoked.

go hand in hand. Japanese Canadians, for example, have distinctive physical traits and—for those who maintain a traditional way of life—cultural attributes as well. But ethnic distinctiveness should not be viewed as racial. For example, Jews are sometimes described as a race although they are distinctive only in their religious beliefs as well as their history of persecution (Goldsby, 1977).

Finally, people can *change* their ethnicity by adopting a different way of life. Polish immigrants who discard their cultural background over time may cease to have a particular ethnicity. In a similar vein, people of mixed Native and non-Native heritage may have blended into the dominant francophone or anglophone populations of their respective provinces to the point where many are completely unaware of their mixed ancestry. From time to time people actually reestablish ethnic ties and identities after two or three generations, making serious efforts to return to their Polish, Jewish, or Native roots.

Minorities

A racial or ethnic **minority**[3] is *a category of people, distinguished by physical or cultural traits, who are socially disadvantaged*. While we concentrate here on ethnicity and race, it is important to realize that minorities are of many kinds, including people with physical disabilities and women (as Chapter 13, "Sex and Gender," suggests).

Minorities have two major characteristics. First, they share a *distinctive identity*. Because race is highly visible (and virtually impossible for a person to change), people of African descent in the United States or those of Chinese descent in South Africa typically have a keen awareness of their race. Visible minorities throughout Canada are equally aware of the physical characteristics that distinguish them from the majority. The significance of ethnicity (which, as noted above, can be changed) is more variable. Throughout Canada's history, some people have downplayed their historic ethnicity, while others have maintained their cultural traditions and lived in distinctive ethnic neighborhoods (Little Italy or Chinatown). Some go so far as to attempt to insulate themselves from potential assimilating influences: the Hasidic Jews of Montreal have been particularly successful in nurturing a lifestyle that effectively separates them from their neighbors. The Hutterite people of the Prairie provinces, who have the advantage of living in communal agricultural colonies, manage even more effectively to minimize contact with the "outside."

A second characteristic of minorities is *subordination*. Chapter 10 ("Social Class in Canada") explained that minorities in Canada may have lower incomes than the British and French and less occupational prestige even if, as in the case of blacks or Asians, their levels of educational attainment are as high or higher. While an ethnic category as a whole may be disadvantaged, this is not true of all members. But even the most successful individuals may be viewed negatively on the basis of their minority standing. Race or ethnicity often serves as a master status (as described in Chapter 6, "Social Interaction in Everyday Life") that overshadows personal accomplishments.

Minorities usually constitute a small proportion of a society's population, but there are exceptions. For example, blacks form a numerical majority in South Africa although they are grossly deprived of economic and political power by whites. In Canada, women represent slightly more than half the population but are still struggling to gain opportunities and privileges long enjoyed by men.

As this chapter's opening vignette suggests, social conflict between minorities and the majority is common around the world. Categories of people—African Americans in the United States, Kurds in Iraq, Christians in Egypt, Sikhs in India, Azerbaijanis in the former Soviet Union, and Native peoples in Canada—are struggling to win rights formally guaranteed by law. The Québécois and the Native peoples in Canada are looking for more than simple equality; they want *special* rights or recognition as distinct societies.[4]

Prejudice

Prejudice amounts to *a rigid and irrational generalization about an entire category of people*. Prejudice is irrational insofar as people hold inflexible attitudes that are supported by little or no direct evidence. Prejudice can be directed toward individuals of a particular social

---

[3] We use the term "minority" rather than the commonly used "minority group" because, as explained in Chapter 7 ("Groups and Organizations"), minorities are categories, not groups.

[4] Constitutional recognition of Quebec as a distinct society has twice slipped out of the bag—with the failures of the Meech and Charlottetown accords in 1990 and 1992 respectively. Native peoples, during negotiations leading to the Charlottetown Accord, suggested that they, too, should be recognized as distinct societies. The implications of such terminology are untested but undoubtedly profound.

class, sex, sexual orientation, age, political affiliation, race, or ethnicity. Prejudices are prejudgments that can be positive or negative, and most people hold some of each type. With positive prejudices, we tend to exaggerate the virtues of people like ourselves, while our negative prejudices condemn those who differ from us. Negative prejudice also runs along a continuum, ranging from mild aversion to outright hostility. Because attitudes are rooted in our culture, everyone has at least some measure of prejudice.

Stereotypes

A common form of prejudice is the **stereotype** (*stereo* is derived from Greek meaning "hard" or "solid"), *a set of prejudices concerning some category of people.* Because stereotypes often involve emotions like love (generally toward members of ingroups) or hate and fear (toward outgroups), they are hard to change even in the face of contradictory evidence. For example, some people have a stereotypical understanding of the poor as lazy and irresponsible freeloaders who would rather rely on welfare than support themselves (Waxman, 1983). As was explained in Chapter 10 ("Social Class in Canada"), this stereotype distorts reality: more than half of the poor people in Canada are children, working adults (including single mothers), and elderly people.

Stereotypes have been devised for virtually every racial and ethnic minority, and such attitudes may become deeply rooted in a society's culture. As the opening to this chapter illustrates, conflict between Serbs and Croats has long been fueled by stereotypes. In Canada, many white people stereotype Native people and other visible minorities as lacking motivation to improve their own lives, just as wealthy people stereotype the poor. Such attitudes assume that social disadvantage stems from personal deficiency. This stereotypical view ignores some key facts: that most poor people in Canada are white and that most members of visible minorities work as hard as anyone else and are *not* poor. In this case the bit of truth in the stereotype is that, proportionately, Natives and members of some other visible minorities are more likely than whites to be poor. But by building a rigid attitude out of a few selected facts, stereotypes grossly distort reality.

Racism

A powerful and destructive form of prejudice, **racism** refers to *the belief that one racial category is innately superior or inferior to another.* Racism has pervaded world history. The ancient Greeks, various peoples of India, and many Asian societies viewed anyone unlike themselves as inferior.

Racism has also been widespread in Canada: at one point, the enslavement of people of African descent or of Native people (called Panis in New France) was supported by notions of their innate inferiority—as was the placement of Indian peoples on reserves under paternalistic administration by an Ottawa-based Indian Affairs department. Today, overt racism in this country has been weakened (or rendered more subtle) by a relatively egalitarian culture and "checked by the state in order to preserve social harmony and order" (Li, 1988:49) Racism persists, though in less open and direct forms, and research continues to document the injury and humiliation that racism causes to people of color (Ramcharan, 1982; Wotherspoon and Satzewich, 1993).

Historically, the assertion that certain categories of people are *innately* inferior has provided a powerful justification for subjecting others to *social* inferiority. By the end of the last century, Great Britain, France, Spain, and the United States had forged colonial empires throughout the Third World. (Canada has never acquired external colonies—being one itself—

In an effort to improve the social standing of the lowest castes, Indian law reserves half of all government jobs for particular castes deemed to be disadvantaged. Because the government is the largest employer, higher-caste students fear they will be shut out of employment when they graduate from university. So intense are these concerns that recently eleven students killed themselves—five by fire—in public protest over this controversial policy.

but it has established a system of *internal* colonialism with respect to Indians on reservations.) Colonial exploitation often took the form of ruthless oppression, which was defended by the argument that the subjugated people were inferior beings.

Stanley Barrett (1987:5-6), an anthropologist who did field research among various white supremacist groups in Canada, notes that:

> *Racism constitutes an elaborate and systematic ideology; it acts as a conceptual tool to rationalize the division of the world's population into the privileged and the deprived. It is inherently a political phenomenon. It ... emerged with the advent of the colonization of the Third World by European nations, and thus coincided too with the development of capitalism.*

In this century, racism was central to the Nazi regime in Germany. Nazi racial doctrine proclaimed a so-called "Aryan race" of blond-haired, blue-eyed Caucasians that was allegedly superior to all others and destined to rule the world. This racist ideology was used to justify the murder of anyone deemed inferior, including some 6 million European Jews and millions of Poles, gypsies, homosexuals, and people with physical and mental disabilities.

More recently, racial conflict has intensified in Britain and Western European societies as whites confront millions of immigrants from former colonies and refugees from strife-torn Eastern Europe. Similarly, in Canada, one can observe signs of increasing racial tensions that are aggravated by tough economic times. Racism—in thought and deed—remains a serious social problem here and elsewhere.

Individual versus Institutional Racism

Stokely Carmichael and Charles Hamilton (1967) point out that we typically think of racism in terms of the acts of specific individuals who hatefully and violently strike out at people they deem inferior. This, they argue, constitutes *individual racism*, and such actions—for example, whites who prevent a black family from moving into their neighborhood—are typically denounced by the public at large.

But even greater harm can be done by *institutional racism*, which refers to racism that guides the operation of schools, hospitals, the police force, the courts and the workplace. For example, the much publicized beating of Rodney King by police officers in Los Angeles (described at the beginning of Chapter 8, "Deviance") appeared to some as an isolated case of brutality; for others, however, it epitomized a wide-ranging, systematic program of police violence directed at the city's black community. According to Carmichael and Hamilton, the public is less likely to condemn or even to recognize institutional racism because it often involves "established and respected" authority figures. Yet this kind of pervasive racism is typically more damaging.

Theories of Prejudice

If prejudice has little basis in a rational assessment of facts, what are its origins? Social scientists have offered various answers to this vexing question, citing the importance of frustration, personality, culture, and social conflict.

Scapegoat Theory of Prejudice

Scapegoat theory holds that prejudice springs from frustration. Such attitudes are common among people who are themselves disadvantaged (Dollard, 1939). A white woman earning low wages in a fish processing plant, for example, might understandably be unhappy with her situation. But she is less likely to direct her hostility at the powerful people who own and operate the plant than at powerless minority coworkers. Prejudice of this kind will not go far toward improving the woman's situation in the plant, but it serves as a relatively safe way to vent anger and it may give her the comforting feeling that at least she is superior to someone.

A **scapegoat** is thus *a person (or category of people), typically with little power, who is unfairly blamed for the troubles of others.* Because they often are "safe targets," minorities are frequently used as scapegoats. The Nazis painted the Jews as responsible for all of Germany's ills fifty years ago. A less extreme example of the same kind is the practice among British people of attributing their nation's troubles today to the presence of Pakistani and Indian immigrants. As the recession of the early 1990s grinds on, one hears increased rumblings among Canadians about lax immigration laws and about the immigrants and refugees who allegedly contribute to the shortage of jobs and the high costs of social welfare.

Authoritarian Personality Theory

T.W. Adorno (1950) and others claim that extreme prejudice forms a personality trait in certain individuals. This conclusion is supported by research showing that people who display strong prejudice against one minority are usually intolerant of all minorities. Such people exhibit *authoritarian personalities*, rigidly conforming to conventional cultural values, envisioning moral issues as clear-cut matters of right and wrong, and advocating strongly ethnocentric views. People with authoritarian personalities also look on society as naturally competitive and hierarchical, with "better" people (like themselves) inevitably dominating those who are weaker.

By contrast, Adorno found, people tolerant toward one minority are likely to be accepting of all. They tend to be more flexible in their moral judgments and believe that, ideally, society should be relatively egalitarian. They feel uncomfortable in situations in which some people exercise excessive and damaging power over others.

According to these researchers, authoritarian personalities tend to develop in people with little education and harsh and demanding parents. Raised by cold and insistent authority figures, they theorized, children may become angry and anxious, and ultimately, as adults, hostile and aggressive toward scapegoats—others they view as their social inferiors.

Cultural Theory of Prejudice

A third approach suggests that, while extreme prejudice may characterize particular people, a certain measure of prejudice is embedded in cultural values. Belief in the social superiority of some categories of people—the "charter" groups (British and French), the hard-working, reliable people of northern and western European roots—still colors Canadian culture to some extent despite concerted efforts on the part of politicians and educators to weaken or eradicate it. Canada's multicultural policies and programs have included educational initiatives to broaden the traditionally Eurocentric attitudes of Canadians by promoting appreciation of the culture and contributions of those of non-European backgrounds. Although Canadians are by no means devoid of prejudice, there is evidence that Canadians are more tolerant of racial and ethnic minorities than are their American neighbors (Lipset, 1991:112). The fact that Toronto, in a very short period of time, went from being a largely Anglo-Saxon Protestant city to one with a substantial immigrant and visible minority component without major violence or disruption suggests a fair degree of social tolerance (Artibise, 1988:244).

Emory Bogardus (1968) studied the effects of culturally rooted prejudices on interpersonal relationships for more than forty years. He devised the concept of *social distance* to assess how close or distant people feel in relation to members of various racial and ethnic

categories—seven steps, from "would admit to close kinship by marriage" to "would exclude from my country." His research in the U.S. revealed that Americans share many of the same assessments of various categories, suggesting that such attitudes are normative in their culture. They hold the most positive views toward people of white English, Canadian, and Scottish backgrounds, Bogardus explains, and welcome close relationships, including marriage, with them. Attitudes are somewhat less favorable toward the French, Germans, Swedes, and Dutch. According to Bogardus, the most negative prejudices target people of African and Asian descent. When Canadians are asked to rank various racial and ethnic categories on the Bogardus scale (Mackie, 1974) the ranking is very similar—with the British and the Americans (of the white Anglo-Saxon Protestant or WASP, variety) ranking first and second. Not only is there consistency within cultures but also between Canadian and American cultures, suggesting that such rankings are indeed normative.

A more recent survey revealed that, among Canadians, 30 percent feel that races are naturally unequal and 35 percent express concerns about letting certain minorities into "nice" neighborhoods (Fletcher, cited in *Multiculturalism and Citizenship Canada*, 1989:4). Clearly a substantial proportion of supposedly "tolerant" Canadians continue to harbor negative attitudes towards racial minorities.

With prejudice so widespread, according to the findings of Bogardus and others who have used his social distance measure, intolerance cannot be dismissed merely as a trait of a handful of abnormal people, as implied by Adorno's research. Rather, it is routinely expressed by people well adjusted to a "culture of prejudice."

Conflict Theory of Prejudice

A fourth approach views prejudice as the product of social conflict among various categories of people. According to this theory, an ideology of prejudice is used to justify the oppression of minorities. Canadians certainly did this with the Chinese laborers who were allowed to come to Canada to work—under appalling conditions—on the Canadian Pacific Railway in the 1870s and 1880s.

Conflict theories of prejudice take various forms. One argument, based on Marxist theory, holds that elites foster prejudice as a strategy to divide workers. There are numerous cases of white workers using minority coworkers as scapegoats in a process that serves the interests of capitalists insofar as such conflict decreases the chances that *all* workers will join together to advance their common interests (Geschwender, 1978; Olzak, 1989; McAll, 1990).

A different argument, recently propounded by Shelby Steele (1990), is that minorities themselves spark conflict to the extent that they encourage a climate of *race consciousness*, a political strategy to gain power and privileges for themselves. Race consciousness, Steele explains, amounts to the claim that historically disadvantaged people are now entitled to special considerations because of their race.

While this may yield short-term gains for minorities, he cautions, such policies are likely to spark a backlash from whites (or the majority) who see "special treatment" on the basis of race or ethnicity as unfair. The Québécois have made precisely that kind of claim on the basis of past injustices and the threat of assimilation in an English-speaking North America. Some non-Quebeckers feel that the wrongs of the past have now been redressed and that entrenching special status (i.e., recognition as a "distinct society") in the Constitution is going too far.

Discrimination

Closely related to prejudice is the concept of **discrimination**, *treating various categories of people unequally.* While prejudice refers to attitudes, discrimination is a matter of action. Like prejudice, discrimination can be either positive (providing special advantages) or negative (subjecting categories of people to obstacles). Discrimination also varies in intensity, ranging from subtle to blatant.

Prejudice and discrimination often occur together. A personnel manager prejudiced against members of a particular minority may refuse to hire them. Robert Merton (1976) describes such a person as an *active bigot* (see Figure 12-1). Fearing legal action, however, a prejudiced personnel manager may not discriminate, thereby becoming a *timid bigot*. What Merton calls *fairweather liberals* may discriminate without being prejudiced, perhaps in the case of a manager discriminating only because a superior demands it. Finally, Merton's *all-weather liberal* is free of both prejudice and discrimination.

Is the person prejudiced?	Does the person discriminate? Yes	No
Yes	Active Bigot (prejudiced person who discriminates)	Timid Bigot (prejudiced person who does not discriminate)
No	Fair-Weather Liberal (nonprejudiced person who discriminates)	All-Weather Liberal (nonprejudiced person who does not discriminate)

FIGURE 12-1 PATTERNS OF PREJUDICE AND DISCRIMINATION
SOURCE: Merton, 1976.

Institutional Discrimination

Like prejudice, discrimination involves both individual action and the structure of society. **Institutional discrimination** refers to *discrimination that is a normative and routine part of the economy, the educational system, or some other social institution.* As minorities in Canada have learned through painful experience, traditional ideas about a person's "place" are sometimes deeply entrenched in the operation of the workplace, the courts, and the schools.

Anderson and Frideres (1981:208) describe this kind of process as follows:

> *Bureaucracies have the job of establishing regulations and priorities as well as qualifications for particular positions in our society. Only those individuals able to meet these initial qualifications will be able to participate in the ongoing institutional structure. For example, when Native people suggested that they be hired by the Department of Indian Affairs (with a staff of about 14,000), the response by the Minister of Indian Affairs was that placement was only possible for those belonging to a particular union, and having a particular position and level of seniority in the union. Unless these requirements were met, an Indian could not be hired, and if hired without these qualifications, the union would strike.*

There was no need for the authors to point out that Natives were *not* members of the appropriate union.

Prejudice and Discrimination: The Vicious Cycle

Prejudice and discrimination persist because they tend to reinforce each other. W.I. Thomas offered a simple explanation of this fact, noted in Chapter 6 ("Social Interaction in Everyday Life"). The Thomas theorem states: *If situations are defined as real, they are real in their consequences* (1966:301; orig. 1931).

Thomas recognized that reality is a matter of how people define situations. Stereotypes become real to those who believe them, sometimes even to those who are victimized by them. Categories of people with considerable social power can enforce their prejudices to the detriment of others. Prejudice on the part of whites toward people of color, for example, does not produce *innate* inferiority but it *can* produce *social* inferiority, consigning minorities to poverty, low-prestige occupations, and poor housing in racially segregated neighborhoods. If whites interpret this disadvantage as evidence that minorities do not measure up to their standards, a new round of prejudice and discrimination is unleashed. Prejudice and discrimination thereby form a *vicious cycle*—each perpetuating the other over time, even from generation to generation, as illustrated in Figure 12-2.

FIGURE 12-2 PREJUDICE AND DISCRIMINATION— THE VICIOUS CYCLE

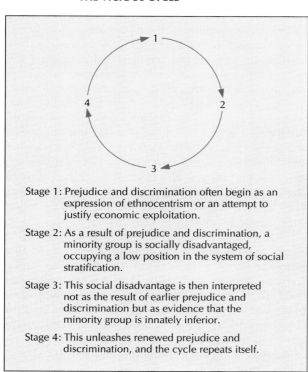

Stage 1: Prejudice and discrimination often begin as an expression of ethnocentrism or an attempt to justify economic exploitation.

Stage 2: As a result of prejudice and discrimination, a minority group is socially disadvantaged, occupying a low position in the system of social stratification.

Stage 3: This social disadvantage is then interpreted not as the result of earlier prejudice and discrimination but as evidence that the minority group is innately inferior.

Stage 4: This unleashes renewed prejudice and discrimination, and the cycle repeats itself.

Majority and Minority: Patterns of Interaction

Patterns of interaction between minorities and more privileged members of a society can be described in terms of four models: pluralism, assimilation, segregation, and genocide.

Pluralism

Pluralism is *a state in which racial and ethnic minorities are distinct but have social parity.* This means that, although categories of people are different, they are not treated in a grossly unequal manner. The relationship between Quebec—with its predominantly francophone population—and the rest of Canada provides an example of pluralism in action. Native peoples, while clearly distinct, would like to acquire social and political parity.

Social diversity has long been a source of pride in Canada. Some would argue that our multiculturalism not only acknowledges but actually celebrates our differences and encourages the perpetuation of countless "ethnic villages" or communities where people proudly maintain the cultural traditions of their immigrant ancestors. Such ethnic communities—the components of our cultural mosaic—add variety and color to the urban and rural landscapes of our country. The viability of these communities is affected by their levels of **institutional completeness,** *the complexity of community organizations that meet the needs of members.* Where communities are institutionally complete, members are

Noisy and crowded, Toronto's Kensington Market at College and Spadina reflects the changing ethnic composition of the neighborhood. Once Jewish, and then Portuguese, it is currently showing the influence of nearby Chinatown.

The ritual of Kwanza, devised in 1968, has gained popularity in recent decades as a celebration of African-American heritage. Observed soon after Chanukah and Christmas, Kwanza combines Christian and Jewish elements in a distinctly African ritual that builds the strength of families and communities.

able to live, shop, pray, and sometimes work within the boundaries of their groups: such communities might also have their own welfare and mutual aid societies, credit unions, newspapers, and radio stations. Breton (1964), who coined the term "institutional completeness," points out that the presence of these formal organizations keeps social relations within group boundaries and minimizes out-group contacts.

Canada embraces the ideal of multiculturalism, recognition of cultural heterogeneity and mutual respect among culturally diverse groups. We began to use the term "multiculturalism" in the 1960s, in recognition of the diverse backgrounds of Canadians, and adopted muticulturalism as government policy by 1971. The Canadian Multiculturalism Act of 1988 sought "to recognize all Canadians as full and equal partners in Canadian society" and in 1991 this goal was given explicit support through the creation of a new Department of Multiculturalism and Citizenship. Canada is very serious about the goal of allowing people to participate fully in all aspects of Canadian life without feeling that it is necessary to give up their ethnic identities and cultural practices: in fact, it hopes to promote unity through diversity and to enhance a Canadian identity which embraces differences. Multicultural programs provide education, consultative support, and funding for a wide range of activities including heritage language training, race relations and cross-cultural understanding programs, the ethnic press, ethnic celebrations like Toronto's Caravan and Caribana, policing and justice, and family violence programs.

Although multiculturalism is the official goal, not everyone approves of this emphasis. Critics argue that it is counterproductive in terms of immigrant adaptation and that it is divisive and detrimental to the development of a shared and coherent Canadian identity. And, while 85 percent of Canadians agree that we should make efforts to protect our racial and ethnic minorities, and 92 percent feel that working and living together should provide for increased cross-racial understanding, more than 60 percent *also* feel that immigrants should cling less to their old ways and try harder to be more like other Canadians (Fletcher, cited in *Muticulturalism and Citizenship Canada*, 1989:4).

In global perspective, Switzerland presents a rather highly evolved example of pluralism. In this European nation of more than 6 million people, strong German, French, and Italian cultural traditions run deep. The relative success of the Swiss in maintaining pluralism (albeit involving little difference in skin color) is evident in its official recognition of the languages of the three ethnicities. Just as importantly, no category is subjected to economic disadvantage (Simpson & Yinger, 1972).

Every summer, thousands of people—many of Caribbean heritage—descend upon Toronto to feast their senses on reggae, steel bands, and that colorful extravaganza, the Caribana Parade. Costumes and floats are designed and assembled over months, if not the entire year, preceding each parade.

Japanese dancers performing the Bon Odori share their heritage with "passport" holders who travel from one ethnic pavilion to another during Caravan, Toronto's week-long multicultural celebration.

Assimilation

Assimilation is *the process by which minorities gradually adopt patterns of the dominant culture*, and involves changing modes of dress, values, religion, language, or friends.

Although the United States has been seen as a "melting pot" in which various nationalities fused into an entirely new way of life, this characterization is somewhat misleading. Rather than "melting" into some completely new cultural pattern, many minorities have adopted the traits (the dress, the accent, and sometimes even the names) of the dominant English culture established by the earliest settlers. They did so to improve their social position and to escape the prejudice and discrimination directed against them (Newman, 1973).

This is not to deny the rich contributions to American culture made by various minorities; cultural contact, however, generally means more change by less powerful minorities than by members of the dominant category. Among other things, minorities in the United States (until recently) have adapted to the use of the English language. The rapid growth of the Hispanic population in recent years has created areas where Spanish is the dominant language, encouraged the study of Spanish as a second language and—as a counterforce—inspired a social movement seeking to establish English as the official language of the U.S.A.

The fact that such ethnic enclaves still exist in the U.S., where assimilation and the melting pot are the ideals, suggest that race and ethnicity endure as building blocks of American society (Glazer & Moynihan, 1970; Alba, 1985). At the other end of the continuum, in Canada, which has claimed to be a colorful mosaic in which the various pieces continue to make distinctive contributions, assimilation occurs as well. Immigrants learn to function in English and French, people from various ethnic backgrounds intermarry, ancestral cultural practices fall into disuse, and people acquire a set of shared attitudes and values that can only be called Canadian.

As a cultural process, assimilation involves changes in ethnicity but not in race. For example, many North Americans of Japanese descent have discarded their traditional way of life but still have their racial identity. However, distinguishing racial traits may diminish over generations as the result of **miscegenation**, *the biological process of interbreeding among racial categories*. Although resistance to such biological mixing remains strong, miscegenation (often outside of marriage) has occurred throughout Canadian and American history.

Segregation

Segregation refers to *the physical and social separation of categories of people.* Sometimes minorities, especially religious orders like the Hutterites, voluntarily segregate themselves. The concentration of various ethnic and racial groups in Canada's cities results, at least in part, from voluntary action. Often, however, minorities are involuntarily segregated by others who exclude them. Various degrees of segregation characterize residential neighborhoods, schools, workplaces, hospitals, and even cemeteries. While pluralism fosters distinctiveness without disadvantage, segregation enforces separation to the detriment of a minority. South Africa's system of apartheid (described in Chapter 9, "Social Stratification") exemplifies racial segregation of a rigid and pervasive nature. Alien to the cultures of Africa, apartheid was created by the European minority it favors, and it has historically been enforced through the use of brutal power (Fredrickson, 1981). Apartheid is currently being eroded in South Africa by widespread opposition among blacks and a growing number of whites. Elections, in which each individual has an equal vote (regardless of race), will be a major breakthrough in themselves. But the basic racial structure of South Africa has yet to change; it remains essentially two different societies that interact only when blacks provide services for whites.

In the United States, racial segregation has a long history. Centuries of slavery gave way to racially separated lodging, schooling, and transportation. Overt discrimination has been reduced and various efforts have been made to bring about desegregation of schools and neighborhoods, but segregation remains a fact of life in the U.S. Residential segregation has decreased little in the past decade, even for African Americans with substantial economic resources who would prefer to live in racially integrated neighborhoods (Saltman, 1991; Wilson, 1991). Furthermore, the level of social isolation is such that residents of black neighborhoods in inner cities have little social contact with the outside world (Massey and Denton, 1989).

Although Canadians might not want to think of themselves as a society that practices segregation, the evidence is clear. We have done so, historically, and we still do it today. Early black migrants—Loyalists in Nova Scotia and those brought via Underground Railroad to Ontario—found themselves living in Africville (part of Halifax) or in small rural communities like Buxton and Dawn in Ontario (see box). As a general rule, they did not receive the same kinds of land grants

This photograph from December 9, 1941 (two days after Pearl Harbor), shows a Royal Canadian Naval officer questioning a Japanese-Canadian fisherman prior to confiscating his boat. Fishermen like this were considered to be a special security risk because they were capable of communicating offshore with Japanese military vessels. Under the War Measures Act their property could be confiscated summarily, without due process of the law and with no compensation of any sort.

as other immigrants. They often attended segregated schools and were denied access to local restaurants. Residential and social segregation were a very real part of their lives.

The clearest example of segregation in Canada is apparent in our treatment of Native peoples, through the system of reserves for status Indians administered by the Department of Indian and Northern Affairs. Prior to the late 1960s, most of the education of Indian children took place in separate residential schools or on the reserves themselves. The overall effect has been one of extreme physical and social segregation, especially when the reserves are located in remote areas.

Genocide

Genocide is *the systematic annihilation of one category of people by another.* This brutal form of racism and ethnocentrism violates nearly every recognized moral standard; nonetheless, it has recurred time and again in human history.

Genocide has figured prominently in centuries of contact between Europeans and the original inhabitants of the Americas. From the sixteenth century on, the Spanish, Portuguese, English, French, and Dutch forcibly established vast colonial empires. The Native populations of North and South America were decimated after colonization began, and Europeans moved to gain control of their wealth. Some were victims of calculated killing sprees; most succumbed to diseases brought by Europeans and to which Native peoples had no natural defenses (Cottrell, 1979; Butterworth & Chance, 1981; Matthiessen, 1984; Sale, 1990; Dickason, 1992).

Genocide has also occurred in the twentieth century. Unimaginable horror befell European Jews in the 1930s and 1940s, as the Nazi regime seized control of much of Europe. During Adolf Hitler's reign of terror, known as the Holocaust, the Nazis exterminated more than 6 million Jewish men, women, and children. Between 1975 and 1980 the Communist regime of Pol Pot in Cambodia slaughtered anyone thought to represent capitalist cultural influences. Condemned to death were people able to speak any Western language and even those who wore eyeglasses, which were viewed as a symbol of capitalist culture. In the "killing fields" of Cambodia, 2 million people (one-fourth of the population) perished (Shawcross, 1979).

These four patterns of minority-majority interaction exist together in a society. For example, we proudly point to patterns of pluralism and assimilation but only reluctantly acknowledge the degree to which our society has been built on segregation and genocide. The remainder of this chapter explores the ways in which these four types of minority-majority contact have shaped the history and present social standing of major racial and ethnic categories in Canada.

Race and Ethnicity in Canada

Canada is a land of immigrants. Many thousands of years ago, the people we now call aboriginal or Native peoples came to North America over a land bridge that once connected Alaska to Siberia across the Bering Strait. The first European explorers and settlers were met by fifty-five founding nations. The French and then the British established permanent settlements in the 1600s and 1700s, conveniently ignored the aboriginal nations, and declared themselves to be the *two*

founding nations. Successive waves of immigration brought northern and then southern and eastern European people to our shores. More recently, in part as a result of changes in immigration laws, new Canadians have come from Asia, Africa, the Caribbean, and Latin America. In addition, refugees have come to Canada in unprecedented numbers over the last decade.

Table 12-1 shows the composition of Canada by ethnic origin (1991) ranked by population size. The table refers specifically to people declaring a single ethnic origin—that is, the same origin on maternal and paternal sides. Individuals of mixed origins are designated separately. It is worth keeping in mind that about 80 percent of those claiming "multiple origin" have some British or French ancestry.

Not surprisingly, considering the head start they had in settling this country, the largest ethnic categories in Canada are the French and the English. Those of Irish, Scottish, and German origin, and those proclaiming themselves simply as "Canadian"—the latter being those who are unwilling to identify any more specific origins—are also among the largest.

TABLE 12-1 THE TWENTY LARGEST ETHNIC CATEGORIES IN CANADA, 1991

Ethnic Origin*	Population	Percentage
French	6,129,680	22.7
English**	3,958,405	14.7
German	911,560	3.4
Scottish**	893,125	3.3
Canadian	765,095	2.8
Italian	750,055	2.8
Irish**	725,660	2.7
Chinese	586,645	2.2
Ukrainian	406,645	1.5
North American Indian	365,375	1.4
Dutch	358,180	1.3
East Indian	324,840	1.2
Polish	272,810	1.2
Portuguese	246,890	0.9
Jewish	245,840	0.9
Black	214,265	0.8
Filipino	157,250	0.6
Greek	151,150	0.6
Hungarian	100,725	0.4
Vietnamese	84,005	0.3
All Single Origin	19,199,790	71.1
Multiple Origins	7,794,250	28.9
Total	26,994,045	100.0

To qualify for single-origin designation, one has to claim the same ethnic origin on both paternal and maternal sides.
**When the British are combined (English, Scottish, Irish, and Welsh) the 5,611,050 people represent 20.8 percent of the Canadian population.*
SOURCE: Statistics Canada, Catalogue No. 93-315 (1991)

CRITICAL THINKING

Black Citizens of Canada: A History Ignored

Blacks were among the first settlers in Guelph, Ontario, arriving around 1830. The census recorded a black population that grew from 38 in 1861 to 107 in 1881. In 1880, this small group built the British Methodist Episcopalian Church, which still stands on Essex Street as a reminder of the vibrant community that helped to establish Guelph's multicultural roots. In terms of Canada's historical record, though, this black community—like others across the country—is essentially invisible.

Harriet Tubman, known as "Moses", had been assisted in her escape from slavery by workers on the Underground Railroad. She returned to Maryland a year later (1850) to free members of her family and then became one of the most active "conductors" on the Railroad, repeatedly risking her life to guide more than 300 slaves to freedom—many of them to Ontario. After the abolition of slavery by the Americans in 1865, many of the former slaves returned to the U.S. Others stayed in Canada.

When the average Canadian thinks about slavery, the image that comes to his or her mind is likely that of plantation slavery in the southern United States: few of us are aware of the fact that Canada has its own history of slavery. We are equally unaware of an influx of about 3,500 freed slaves who, as United Empire Loyalists, came to Nova Scotia and New Brunswick after fighting on the side of the British during the American Revolution as members of the Black Pioneers (also known as the Black Loyalists). The 30,000–40,000 escaped American slaves who made it to Canada via the Underground Railroad between 1840 and 1865, when slavery was abolished in the U.S. are unknown to most of us as well.

Slaves were on the scene in the earliest settlements of Canada (then New France). Olivier Le Jeune, who had been brought directly from Africa to Canada, was later sold in the first recorded slave sale in Canada, in 1629. By 1759, there were 3,604 slaves in New France—1,132 blacks, the rest Natives. In 1793, under the leadership of John Graves Simcoe,*

---

* When, in 1793, Governor Simcoe had dinner at the home of Mohawk leader and Loyalist, Joseph Brant (Thayendanegea), they were served by Brant's "black slaves resplendent in scarlet uniforms with white ruffles, and with silver buckles on their shoes" (Walker, 1980:21).

Note that, among the remaining largest categories, there are six visible minorities including North American Indians (or Amerindians) as well as the Vietnamese, most of whom came to Canada as refugees within the last decade. Together these six categories account for perhaps 90 percent of Canada's visible minority population.

Table 12-2 indicates the ethnic origins of the population of Canada, as well as of the provinces and territories, and suggests that ethnic and racial composition varies substantially from one part of the country to another. Anyone under the impression that Canada is dominated by those of British heritage, may be surprised to learn that only 21 percent of Canadians are single-origin English, Irish, Scottish, or Welsh—and that the British are a major category only in the Maritimes.

French-Canadians make up three quarters of the population of Quebec and a third in New Brunswick (Canada's only officially bilingual province): elsewhere, the proportions of French origin fall below 10 percent—about 3 percent in the west and north. The concentration of francophones in Quebec, coupled with their weak representation in almost all of the rest of Canada gives considerable support to the Québécois' perception of themselves as a small French island in a sea of anglophones.

People of various (non-French) European origins—whose ancestors, in some cases, were encouraged to come to Canada in order to populate the West—are predictably over-represented in Ontario and the provinces to the west, particularly in Manitoba and Saskatchewan. Those of Asian heritage, who are largely here

Upper Canada became the first British colony to legislate the (gradual) abolition of slavery. While slavery remained legal through the rest of Canada until it was abolished throughout the British Empire in 1833, it had effectively died out by about 1810. Slavery was essentially unsuited to agriculture as practiced in Canada.

Fugitives on the Underground Railroad (an informal system of people and safe houses bringing escaped slaves to freedom in the northern U.S. and eventually Canada) arrived in Ontario from the 1790s to the 1860s. These former slaves formed scattered rural settlements from Windsor to Barrie (or across the southern part of the province), where some farmed their own land while others hired themselves out as farm laborers. Some black settlements, like Buxton and Dawn,** were thriving communities

---

** Dawn was founded in 1842 by Hiram Wilson and Josiah Henson. The latter, a "conductor" on the Underground Railroad who brought about one hundred slaves to freedom, is thought to be the model for Harriet Beecher Stowe's Uncle Tom in *Uncle Tom's Cabin.*

with their own schools, blacksmith shops, and other businesses. Most of the residents of these communities and their descendants eventually abandoned their rural homes and moved, with other Canadians, to the cities. Some, however, stayed behind. Descendants of the residents of Dawn still live in Dresden, Ontario.

Though freed from slavery, blacks in Ontario and other parts of Canada experienced economic hardship as well as prejudice and discrimination—suggesting that, despite a certain smugness, Canadians are not much more tolerant than our American neighbors. Stuart McLean in *Welcome Home: Travels in Small Town Canada* (1992:75) records this conversation with Bruce and Barbara Carter of Dresden, Ontario:

"When you're brought up with discrimination," says Barbara, "you know what you can do and what you can't do. So you just abide by the rules and it's not that bad. We knew we couldn't go into the restaurants with our white girlfriends after school so we just didn't go. I never understood, however, why there were two churches. There were

two Baptist churches in town. One for the whites and one for the blacks."

"It was different for me," says Bruce. "I was a very bitter person when I was a teenager. At one time there was not one restaurant in town where I could get a cup of coffee. Toward the end of the war we had German prisoners of war around here. They were working in the sugar-beet fields under guard. The prisoners of war could go into the restaurants but a negro soldier in a Canadian army uniform couldn't. It was pretty bad. My aunt taught in a segregated school. The last one closed in the sixties."

... "We went to Disney World a while ago," says Bruce. "We went to the Canadian pavilion. They have a movie about Canada there. It's a tremendous movie—all in the round. But do you know what? There is not one black person in the whole movie. I was watching it and I thought, 'Wait a minute, where am I?' So I sat through it a second time to make sure. It's like we're a non-people. We weren't even in the crowd scenes."

SOURCES: McClain (1979); Walker (1980); DuCharme (1985); Winks (1988); McLean (1992); Nader et al. (1992)

TABLE 12-2   POPULATION BY ETHNIC ORIGIN (SINGLE ORIGIN) FOR CANADA, THE PROVINCES AND TERRITORIES, 1991*

	Can	Nfld	PEI	NS	NB	Que	Ont	Man	Sask	Alb	BC	Yuk	NWT
British	20.8	78.5	44.0	44.0	33.0	4.2	25.4	17.0	16.5	19.6	25.0	19.1	10.2
French	22.8	1.7	9.2	6.2	32.8	74.6	5.3	5.0	3.1	3.0	2.1	3.2	2.4
European	15.4	0.7	2.1	5.4	1.9	7.2	19.9	25.1	25.9	20.9	16.6	11.0	4.9
Asian	6.0	0.4	0.5	1.0	0.5	2.9	7.8	4.7	1.6	6.8	11.4	1.1	1.4
Latin American	0.3	0.0	0.1	0.0	0.0	0.4	0.4	0.3	0.1	0.3	0.2	0.1	0.0
Aboriginal	1.7	0.9	0.3	0.8	0.5	1.0	0.7	6.9	6.8	2.7	2.3	13.7	51.2
Black**	0.8	0.0	0.0	1.2	0.1	0.6	1.5	0.4	0.1	0.4	0.2	0.1	0.1
All Single Origins	71.1	82.6	56.9	59.8	70.3	94.4	67.1	62.0	57.2	57.6	60.1	51.2	72.3
Multiple Origins	28.9	17.4	43.1	40.2	29.7	5.6	32.9	38.0	42.8	42.4	39.9	48.8	27.7

* Most of the ethnic categories in this table refer to people from broad geographic regions. To qualify for single-origin designation, someone from within the British category would have to be, for example, Scottish on both sides or, within the European category, German on both sides.
** The 1986 census gave respondents the option of choosing Black as one of the ethnic categories. An additional 0.3 percent of Canadians declare Caribbean origins and another 0.1 percent declare African origins. If one assumes that most of the Caribbean- and African-origin people are Black, this raises the Black population to about 1.2 percent of the Canadian population. Most of these people live in Ontario.
SOURCE: Statistics Canada Catalogue No. 93-315 (1991).

According to some analysts, communities gather strength and people gain social confidence through emphasizing racial and ethnic identity. From another point of view, however, these processes heighten divisions within our society and fuel social conflict. Resolving the tension between appreciating our distinctive heritage and respecting our common humanity will continue to challenge us into the next century.

as part of a more recent migration flow, are a significant component of the populations in Ontario and Alberta (8 and 7 percent), whereas British Columbia is 11.4 percent Asian. Blacks, who have old and deep roots in Ontario and Nova Scotia, continue to have a presence in both provinces (with more than 1 percent representation), while Latin Americans make up less than 0.5 percent of the population in any of the provinces and territories.

Canada's *real* founding nations, the aboriginal peoples—Indian, Inuit, and Métis—together make up about 2 percent of the Canadian population. They comprise 1 percent or less of the populations of Ontario and provinces to the east, being best represented in Manitoba, Saskatchewan, the Yukon and Northwest Territories. Although *percentage* aboriginal varies from one province to another, it is important to realize that each of the provinces from Quebec through British Columbia has between 65,000 and 75,000 Native people.

Social Standing

A great deal has been written about ethnic and racial inequality in Canada and its causes (Porter, 1965; Ramcharan, 1982; Gerber, 1983; Li, 1988; Driedger, 1989; Gerber, 1990; McAll, 1990; Frideres, 1993; Wotherspoon and Satzewich, 1993). The general consensus seems to be that the workings of our capitalist economy, along with racism, prejudice, and discrimination, contribute to socio-economic inequality, with recent immigrants and visible minorities at the bottom of the scale. For a number of reasons, including a system of internal colonialism, Native peoples are the most severely disadvantaged in this regard.

Table 12-3 compares selected ethnic categories—British, French, Asian, black, and Native—on a number of socio-economic dimensions. Observations based upon this table are surprising in some respects and

TABLE 12-3   EDUCATION, EMPLOYMENT AND INCOME AMONG SELECTED ETHNIC AND RACIAL CATEGORIES, 1985–1986*

	British	French	Asian	Black	Native
Total Population	6,332,725	6,093,160	600,530	174,970	373,260
Population 15 and over	5,156,505	4,869,515	465,160	128,540	241,325
Post-secondary certification**	29.2%	29.7%	37.2%	35.8%	13.3%
Labor force participation**	62.7%	63.1%	70.8%	75.2%	50.1%
Unemployment rate	9.9%	12.7%	8.6%	12.5%	30.5%
Worked all year, full time**	32.9%	30.6%	36.5%	36.1%	15.0%
Average income (full time all year workers)	$27,602	$25,143	$23,798	$22,098	$20,988
Median income (all with income)	$13,759	$12,814	$13,132	$13,030	$7,591
Income $35,000 or more**	11.9%	8.8%	8.9%	6.2%	2.8%

* Latest data available. Note that the 1986 census asks for income and employment information for the previous year.
** Based on population 15 years of age or older.
SOURCE: Statistics Canada, Profile of Ethnic Groups—Dimensions, 1989.

consistent with expectations in others. First, Canadian Asians and blacks—some of whom were educated elsewhere before coming here as immigrants—have higher levels of post-secondary certification than the British or French. They also have higher levels of labor force participation and full-time, full-year employment. Despite this, they have lower average incomes (for full-time, year-round employment) than do the British or the French. When one looks at median income, the picture is different: the median incomes for Asians and blacks are slightly *above* that of the French. The British fare best on both average and median income measures, and have a higher percentage of adults earning $35,000 or more. On this measure, the Asians do as well as the French, while the blacks slip behind.

The Native peoples have much lower levels of post-secondary certification, labor force participation, and full-year, full-time employment than the other categories. They also have the lowest incomes on all three measures. And, despite the fact that only 50 percent of adult Natives are in the labor force, 31 percent of them are unemployed and looking for work. In that light, it is not surprising to find that only 15 percent are employed full time, all year—less than half that of any of the other categories.

On the basis of Table 12-3, one can conclude that the British are rewarded on all income measures despite the fact that they have lower levels of post-secondary certification and labor force participation. The French, who are very slightly ahead of the British on these measures, do not get the same financial rewards—in *part*, perhaps, because the economy of Quebec has been particularly sluggish. Asians and blacks, with their high levels of post-secondary education and labor force participation, should have the highest incomes—but they do not. This may be the result of racism, prejudice, and discrimination—as many analysts will be quick to point out—but date of entry into Canada also comes into the picture. Immigrants generally enter the Canadian labor market at a lower *entrance status* than they may have occupied in their countries of origin (Porter, 1965; Ujimoto, 1979; Reitz, 1980). Furthermore, recent immigrants are unlikely to have the seniority in their jobs that is associated with higher incomes.

While blacks and Asians appear to have gained access to higher education and to the labor market (including full-time employment), they appear to face barriers to equity in remuneration. Natives, on the other hand, seem to face a host of barriers—in achiev-

ing higher education, in securing employment of any kind (to say nothing of full-time employment), and in earning decent wages or salaries. Something is clearly amiss, when the First Nations (as some Native peoples prefer to be called) find themselves systematically excluded from equal participation in our educational and economic institutions.

Another glimpse into ethnic stratification is provided by Table 12-4, which shows average incomes for males and females employed full year, full time. The

TABLE 12-4 AVERAGE INCOMES FOR SINGLE ETHNIC ORIGIN* MALES AND FEMALES EMPLOYED FULL YEAR FULL TIME , BY MALE INCOME, 1985

Ethnic Origin	Male Income	Female Income
1) Jewish	$47,000	$25,171
2) Egyptian	38,568	24,332
3) Estonian	37,361	25,403
4) Latvian	36,683	25,207
5) Welsh	35,870	23,306
6) Czech	35,864	21,929
7) Slovak	35,521	24,418
8) Japanese	34,709	23,634
9) Austrian	34,130	22,147
10) Lithuanian	33,581	24,687
11) Icelandic	33,417	22,400
12) Czechoslovakian	33,309	20,944
13) Finnish	33,246	21,934
14) Scottish	33,172	20,944
15) Serbian	32,784	21,832
...		
English	30,986	19,525
...		
French	28,303	19,297
...		
48) Punjabi	26,217	16,164
49) Black	25,341	18,698
50) Filipino	25,268	19,707
51) Métis	24,701	17,331
52) Greek	24,422	16,803
53) Portuguese	24,364	15,520
54) Jamaican	24,041	15,520
55) Inuit	23,529	17,842
56) North American Indian	23,328	17,125
57) Chilean	22,610	14,879
58) Other Latin American**	22,578	15,257
59) Vietnamese	21,742	15,760
60) Haitian	20,562	14,645
61) Laotian	16,897	12,106
62) Cambodian	16,148	14,911
All Canadians	30,504	19,995

* Same ethnic origin on paternal and maternal sides.
** Other than Chilean.
SOURCE: Gerber, 1990:79 (adapted from Statistics Canada, Profile of Ethnic Groups—Dimensions, 1989) .

top and the bottom out of sixty-two ethnic and racial minorities (ranked by male income) appear in the table, along with English and French, which fall in the middle. Jewish Canadians appear at the top with an average annual income for males of $47,000. The Japanese are also in the top fifteen, as are a number of Eastern European minorities (Latvian, Estonian, Czech, and Serbian). Of the British, the Welsh and Scottish make it into the top fifteen, while the English and Irish do not: in fact, the English rank twenty-fifth.

The categories that rank the lowest are, in most cases, visible minorities. All three of Canada's Native categories (Métis, Inuit, and Indian) are in the bottom fifteen, as are blacks and a number of other minorities that are still growing as a result of recent immigration (Portuguese and Jamaican). On the lowest rungs are categories whose members are among those coming to Canada relatively recently as refugees (Chilean, Vietnamese, Haitian, Laotian, and Cambodian).

It is worth noting that, within each ethnic category, female incomes are substantially lower than those of men. In the upper ranks, female incomes tend to be about 60 to 70 percent of male incomes. In the lower ranks, the female/male income ratios are more likely to be above 70 percent—for the most part, one suspects, because male incomes are so low that female incomes cannot fall far below them.

The data we have seen so far clearly support those who argue that there *is* socio-economic stratification in Canada based upon race and ethnicity (Porter, 1965; Breton, 1979; Li, 1988; McAll, 1990). The average incomes of the lowest ranking ethnic monorities (for full-time full-year employment) are less than half of those in the upper ranks. It is also clear that, as we saw in Chapter 10 ("Social Class in Canada"), Native peoples are particularly disadvantaged (Gerber, 1990; Frideres, 1993).

Special Status Societies

On historical grounds, one might argue that the British have special status within Canada. We have a British parliamentary system, the majority of Canadians speak English, and the dominant culture is Anglo-Saxon. In the past, admission to Canada itself, to the economic elite, and to the most exclusive clubs was controlled, for the most part, by the British. You could say, as well, that the policy of multiculturalism gives special status to all of the ethnic and cultural minorities that contribute to

Canadian mosaic. Nonetheless, there are two categories that stand out because they have unique relationships with the federal government and other Canadians—the Native peoples (Indian, Inuit, and Métis) and the Québécois.

Native Peoples (First Nations)

The terms *Native* and *aboriginal* refer to fifty-five or more sovereign peoples who had established themselves on the North American continent thousands of years prior to the arrival of European explorers and settlers. Among others, these include the Inuit, Cree, Ojibwa, Micmac, Blackfoot, Iroquois, Haida, and Slavey peoples. The Métis are a socio-cultural category of biracial descent—usually French and Indian. Among the Indian peoples there are numerous categories. Registered Indians, who come under the Indian Act and are the responsibility of the Department of Indian and Northern Affairs, may be "treaty" or "non-treaty," depending on whether or not their ancestors were party to treaties. In addition, there is an undetermined number of people—who may be biologically and culturally Indian but not legally so because their ancestors, for whatever reasons, did not enter into agreements with the Crown.[5]

The 1991 census identifies more than 470,000 individuals who claim to be single-origin aboriginal (i.e., Inuit *or* Métis *or* Indian on both sides—not an Inuit-Indian mix, for example). Within the aboriginal category, there are 30,000 Inuit, 75,000 Métis, and 365,000 Indians. Frideres (1993:31) estimates that there are over 1.5 million people in Canada—registered and unregistered—with Native ancestry. In other words, almost 6 percent of the population of Canada is of Native descent.

Registered Indians who live on reserves or settlements are the special responsibility of the Department of Indian and Northern Affairs. Their relationship with Ottawa over the years could be characterized as paternalistic and bureaucratic. For example, until the 1980s, Indian children were often removed from the reserves and taken to boarding schools. There they were punished for "talking Indian" among themselves. They were forced to speak English and taught that their own

---

[5] Frideres (1993:24-46) provides a detailed explanation of the various Native and Indian categories.

languages and cultures were of no value.[6] Removed from their homes and communities for ten months of the year, the children were deprived of normal parent-child relationships. This system failed to prepare them to live effectively in either the Native or non-Native worlds. Christianity was imposed on the communities and on the children in the boarding schools. Barriers were placed in the way of economic development on the reserves, and education beyond the level of "animal husbandry" was discouraged. The effect of these measures was an erosion of the social and cultural fabric that sustained community life.

Non-status Indians, the Métis, and the Inuit were never confined to reservations and thus have escaped some of the negative effects of reservation life. Because the Inuit live in Canada's far north, they have not felt the same population pressures as the Native peoples in the rest of the country. For two reasons, however, they have experienced the same gradual erosion of traditional patterns of life. First, exploratory and drilling activities by oil, gas, and uranium companies have degraded the environment in the north and reduced the game supply. Second, many Inuit families have moved into permanent settlements, both to seek employment and to meet the legal requirement of school attendance for their children. Consequently, extended families no longer establish winter camps in traditional hunting grounds or bother to teach their children the old survival skills that used to foster a sense of self worth.

It is important to realize that there is a great deal of diversity among Native communities (Gerber, 1979) and that at a number of levels Native individuals, communities, and organizations have made real strides in dealing with the problems they face today. Where government policy once was based upon the assumption that the Indian problem would solve itself through urban migration and assimilation, there is now a recognition that Native communities on reserves and elsewhere are not only surviving but growing (Gerber, 1984). In addition, high-profile Native leaders like Ovide Mercredi, Elijah Harper, and George Erasmus have been able to articulate their demands effectively and thereby gain public support for greater self-deter-

This Winnipeg monument to Louis Riel honors the Métis leader who tried, through peace and through war, to establish the political power of his people. Despite widespread support in Manitoba and Quebec, Riel was hanged in 1885 for treason. His execution still excites controversy today, and a movement has been organized to win him a posthumous pardon.

mination. National organizations, like the Assembly of First Nations, Inuit Tapirisat, Native Council of Canada, and the Métis National Council have been instrumental in negotiating recognition of the inherent right to self-government through the Charlottetown accord (see box in Chapter 18, p. 506–7).

One dramatic result of the Native quest for self-determination will be the creation in 1999 of Nunavut, which is to be carved out of the present Northwest Territories. The new territorial government will be controlled by the Inuit majority, and an established system of cooperatives and the Inuit Broadcasting Corporation (IBC) will provide some support to the fledgling government. Political and administrative positions will being new employment prospects, potentially stimulating

---

[6] In the last five years or so, Canadians have become aware of the fact that in addition to the psychological and emotional abuse resulting from the denigration of their cultures and languages, many Indian children experienced physical and sexual abuse in some of these boarding schools.

greater educational achievement and enhancing pride. Putting control of Inuit communities back into Inuit hands will not alleviate problems overnight; the hope on the part of Native leaders, however, is that it will be one meaningful step towards dealing with a wide range of serious social problems.

The Québécois

The French presence in what is now Canada goes back to 1608, when the first permanent settlement in New France was established at Quebec City, by Samuel de Champlain, with 28 settlers—8 of whom survived over the first winter. France claimed a vast territory that extended west of the Thirteen Colonies and down to Louisiana, encompassing most of southern Ontario and the Great Lakes region. But New France grew slowly because of a lack of interest on the part of France in supporting the tiny settlement or in sending more settlers to the area. The growth in population from 8 in 1609 to just over 3,000 in 1663—spread among Quebec City, Trois-Rivières, and Montreal—was mainly the result of an "extraordinary rate of child bearing" (Beaujot and McQuillan, 1982:4). Two centuries later, at the time of Confederation, Canada's population of 3.5 million people was 31 percent French.

As a result of the size of the French population and its concentration in Quebec, the British North America Act of 1867 recognized the province's civil law tradition, Catholic schools and separate language. Confederation, which was based upon bilingualism, assumed that English- and French-speaking communities would coexist and complement each other. English and French were to be the legislative and judicial languages in federal and Quebec institutions. (Bilingualism was later strengthened and expanded by the Official Languages Act of 1969, which declared the equality of the two languages in Parliament and in the Canadian public service.)

At the time of Confederation, the province of Quebec encompassed a traditional society based upon the seigneurial system of land tenure—in which habitants worked the lands of the seigneurs. In the political vacuum left by an ineffective provincial government, the Catholic church took upon itself the task of administering many aspects of Quebec society—including education, health care, and social welfare. Once it dominated Quebec's major institutions, the church resisted change:

Uninterested in questioning the established authorities and the excesses of industrialization, and wary of new ideas, the Quebec church was more interested in maintaining its privileged position than with helping Quebeckers enter the 20th century. It extolled the virtues of rural life, cautioned against the evils of the city and the dangers of education, and preached the need to accept one's lot in life.
(Latouche, 1988)

At this time the provincial economy was dominated by a British economic and industrial elite based in Montreal. A clear linguistic class structure had developed with the unilingual English at the top, the unilingual French at the bottom, and bilingual people in the middle in supervisory positions. The unilingual French had few opportunities to better their social or financial standing and even the French-origin bilinguals could rise only so far. Individuals who rejected church domination and moved to the cities to seek employment found that a linguistic ceiling restricted upward mobility.

The 1960s brought the Quiet Revolution to Quebec which greatly diminished the political power and social influence of the Catholic Church. A newly elected premier, Jean Lesage, chose to expand the role of the state in the economic, social, and cultural life of the province. Among other things, the Lesage government established a department of education (encouraging the study of engineering, maths, sciences, and business) and nationalized Hydro-Québec (in order to attract industry with the promise of cheap electricity). It also took over the administration of Quebec's pension funds. These and other changes served to integrate Quebec into the North American economic structure (Coleman, 1984).

Quebec was now characterized by a rapidly growing working class, a declining birthrate—eliminating "the revenge of the cradle" as a tool for maintaining or improving the linguistic balance in Canada—and a decline in the influence of the church. In other words, French Canadian society was becoming more like the rest of North America—urban, secular, and industrialized. As a result, language became the primary defining characteristic of Québécois society, and francophone Quebeckers became even more aware of the relative numbers of French- and English-speaking people. They also realized that the continued existence of the small francophone minorities outside Quebec was threatened by assimilation. Reaching the conclusion that French language and culture could only be protected in the province of Quebec, they rejected their Canadian identity and began to think of themselves as Québécois only. The desire to protect their distinct language and culture led them to seek institutional dominance in Quebec, and this in turn had profound implications on federal-provincial relations.

The logical extension of a demand for institutional control was the demand for sovereignty. The late 1960s and 1970s saw an increase in Québécois nationalism and in support for the independence movement. The sentiments that gave rise to the radical terrorist Front de libération du Québec (FLQ) became more widespread and eventually paved the way for the 1976 election of the separatist Parti Québécois, led by René Lévesque.

One of the first acts of the new Parti Québécois government in Quebec was to introduce Bill 101, which made French the only official language of Quebec as well as the language of business and education. Francophones were no longer excluded from the economic elite. In addition, the children of immigrants, or of people who came to Quebec from other provinces, would be educated in French and assimilated into francophone society. The election of a separatist government and the language laws contributed to the emigration of anglophones and businesses, both large and small. In the period 1976 to 1981, Quebec's net loss through interprovincial migration doubled over the previous five-year period to include 156,000 people.

In a 1980 referendum requesting a mandate to negotiate "sovereignty-association," 60 percent of Quebeckers voted "No." The debate leading up the referendum was often divisive, especially in the city of Montreal. There, as elsewhere in the province, the referendum revealed a general pattern of increased support for sovereignty the further east one moved from the Ontario border.

Canada, under the Liberal government of Pierre Trudeau, patriated its constitution and incorporated the Charter of Rights and Freedoms in 1982. The provincial government of Quebec did not agree to the conditions of patriation and did not sign the constitution at that point. Brian Mulroney and the Progressive Conservative party won the 1984 election with massive support in Quebec, in part because they promised constitutional amendments that would alleviate Quebec's objections to the constitution.

For complex political reasons, the Meech Lake Accord (1987), which included recognition of Quebec as a "distinct society," was not ratified by all the provin-

cial legislatures before its 1990 deadline. Among the reasons for public disenchantment with "Meech" was Quebec's 1988 sign law, which banned English altogether from outdoor signs. Anglophone Canadians perceived the sign law to be a slap in the face. In turn, the failure of Meech to achieve ratification was seen by Quebeckers as a symbol of rejection by English Canada. Such symbols, as Breton (1992) points out, can have powerful political impact. Among other things, the failure of Meech spawned the separatist Bloc Québécois—a party working at the federal level to promote the cause of separation.

The Charlottetown Accord—a balanced compromise which responded to the demands of various regions and interest groups—was rejected by Canadians (including 55 percent of Quebeckers) in the referendum of Oct. 26, 1992. Subsequent levels of support for the separatist Bloc Québécois and Parti Québécois were, at least in part, the result of frustration relating to repeated failures in constitutional accommodation, as well as to the economic pain associated with a prolonged recession. The success of the two separatist parties clearly reveals that the politics surrounding the quest for special status and related powers continues to have potentially explosive consequences for Canada.

Immigration to Canada: A Hundred-Year Perspective

Canada has been—and will remain—a land of immigrants. The ten-year period from 1905 to 1914 saw the arrival of 2.5 million people, making it the peak decade for Canadian immigration. (See Figure 12-3, which details our immigration history from 1889 to 1989.) At the height of immigration to Canada, in 1913, one in every seventeen people was a newcomer—not just an immigrant but someone who had arrived within the past year. In contrast, we now admit about 200,000 immigrants per year into a population of 27 million: one in every 140 people today is a newly arrived immigrant of the current year. Knowledge of the numbers of immigrants absorbed by the tiny Canadian population of the early 1900s should give us encouragement regarding Canada's ability to absorb—even as we struggle to recover from a prolonged recession—the relatively small numbers arriving in recent years.

Race and ethnicity retain their significance in part because of the continuous flow of immigrants into our

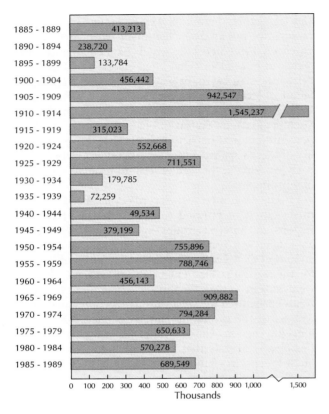

1885 - 1889	413,213
1890 - 1894	238,720
1895 - 1899	133,784
1900 - 1904	456,442
1905 - 1909	942,547
1910 - 1914	1,545,237
1915 - 1919	315,023
1920 - 1924	552,668
1925 - 1929	711,551
1930 - 1934	179,785
1935 - 1939	72,259
1940 - 1944	49,534
1945 - 1949	379,199
1950 - 1954	755,896
1955 - 1959	788,746
1960 - 1964	456,143
1965 - 1969	909,882
1970 - 1974	794,284
1975 - 1979	650,633
1980 - 1984	570,278
1985 - 1989	689,549

0 100 200 300 400 500 600 700 800 900 1,000   1,500
Thousands

FIGURE 12-3   IMMIGRATION TO CANADA, 1885–1989
SOURCE: Knowles (1992); Employment and Immigration Canada

country. The first wave of immigration after Confederation was driven by the desire to populate the West and to provide workers for the growing economy. This trend was encouraged by the controversial policies of Clifford Sifton, who was Minister of the Interior around the turn of the century (Hiller, 1991).

During the Sifton years, Canada was still trying to promote immigration from Britain—in part out of political necessity. "English Canadians took it for granted that the government would do everything possible to retain the British character of the country" (Knowles, 1992:67). By setting up an immigration office in London, England, Sifton was able to increase the flow from Britain to the point where, by 1905, about a third of our immigrants came from there. But because Sifton was primarily interested in attracting good farmers to populate the West, he also started a trickle of Ukrainian immigration that would peak in 1913, when 22,363 individuals arrived from that coun-

try (Knowles, 1992:73). These Ukrainians, along with a trickle of Doukhobors, Finns, Germans, and Scandinavians, were seen by politicians and ordinary Canadians as ignorant, unassimilable aliens who would do irreparable damage to Canada.

A series of changes to immigration policy in the early 1900s was intended to severely restrict immigration to Canada by anyone who was not white and Anglo-Saxon in origins. Unsuitable, unassimilable Southern and Eastern Europeans, as well as the Chinese, the Japanese, and American blacks were discouraged by various means from entering. Despite these efforts, migration soared—in part because politicians and businessmen believed that economic prosperity depended upon continued population growth. World War I (1914–1918), the Great Depression (1929–1939) and World War II (1939–1945) were associated with deep troughs in immigration with a short boom in the 1920s. During that short boom, immigrants from Britain and Europe were admitted along with some Jews and Russian Mennonites. By 1931, however, Canada was to close her doors to refugees—especially Jewish refugees (in part because of anti-Semitism throughout much of Canada).

After World War II there were mounting pressures (internal and international) to open the doors once again and accept large numbers of refugees. The immigrants—who, it was argued, were needed to meet labor needs, settle unpopulated areas, and expand the internal market for goods—were once again to be from "old" commonwealth countries and the U.S. By the 1950s, Germany, Italy, and the Netherlands had become important sources of immigrants and our immigration laws had been liberalized to allow more Asians, as well as Palestinian and Hungarian refugees. Further liberalization would occur under the Conservative government of John Diefenbaker, who foresaw a population of 40 million in the near future and argued that "Canada must populate or perish" (Knowles, 1992:137).

It was not until 1962, however, that Ellen Fairclough, Canada's first woman federal cabinet minister, put an end to our White Canada immigration policy. Education and occupational and language skills replaced race or national origin as the criteria of admission. After the Liberals won the 1965 election, they undertook to formalize the selection criteria and developed what we call the *points system*, which allocates specific numbers of points to education, occupation, facility in English or French, age, and the demand for

On February 24, 1942, the federal government issued an order to remove all Japanese-Canadians from coastal areas in British Columbia. About 22,000 people were moved inland to internment camps like this one, and their property was sold to discourage relocation after the war. The government was concerned with national security, but there can be little doubt that the harshness of the measures also reflected the racial hostility whites commonly directed toward people of Asian ancestry at this time in western Canada.

the applicant's skills in the Canadian labor market. The use of the points system reduces reliance upon the judgment of the individual immigration officer.

More recently, Canada has experienced waves of immigration from the West Indies and Asia (in the 1970s) and from Central and South America (in the 1980s). As Hiller (1991:173) points out, "these repeated waves of immigration reinvigorated ethnic groups already resident in Canada, and reminded residents of their own ethnicity."

The Immigration Act of 1976 recognized three classes of people as eligible for landed immigrant status: *family class* (immediate family and dependent children, parents and grandparents of Canadians or landed immigrants), *humanitarian class* (refugees or persecuted and displaced persons), and *independent class* (those who apply as individuals and are admitted on the basis of the points system). The effect of these changes, on top of the earlier ones, was to change the countries of origin of the applicants, to stimulate an unmanageable flow of refugees, and to pile up applications by family members to the point where they outnumber those under the independent category. In recent years, Canada has made a concerted effort to attract people who

are experienced in business or have significant amounts of money to invest—and has had some success in doing so (2,455 entrepreneurs with 7,446 dependents in 1991).

Table 12-5 indicates the sources of our immigrants in 1991, by geographic region of birth. Asia is by far the major source region, sending us 53 percent of our immigrants, while Europe—the source of almost all immigration in the first half of this century—has dropped down to 20 percent. Table 12-6 reveals that Britain now supplies less than 3 percent of our immigrants and ranks eleventh among source countries. China and Hong Kong, which rank first and second,

TABLE 12-5 IMMIGRANTS BY GEOGRAPHIC REGION OF BIRTH, 1991

Region	Number	%
Europe	46,651	20.2
Africa	16,530	7.2
Asia	122,228	53.0
Australasia	735	0.3
North and Central America	18,899	8.2
Caribbean-Antilles	13,046	5.7
South America	10,468	4.5
Oceania & Other Ocean Islands	2,213	1.0
Total	230,781	100.0

SOURCE: Employment and Immigration Canada, Immigration Statistics 1991.

TABLE 12-6 IMMIGRANTS BY COUNTRY OF BIRTH, 1991 (5,000 OR MORE)

Country	Number	%
China	20,621	8.9
Hong Kong	16,425	7.1
Portugal	15,737	6.8
India	14,248	6.2
Philippines	12,626	5.5
Lebanon	12,172	5.3
Vietnam	8.874	3.8
El Salvador	7,110	3.1
Sri Lanka	7.044	3.1
Iran	6,516	2.8
Great Britain	6,383	2.8
Romania	5,837	2.5
U.S.A.	5,270	2.3
Jamaica	5,103	2.2
Other	86,815	37.6
Total	230,781	100.0

SOURCE: Employment and Immigration Canada, Immigration Statistics 1991.

sent us 21,000 and 16,000 immigrants respectively in 1991 (9 and 7 percent of the total). Among the other top-ranking countries are some from which we have been receiving substantial numbers of refugees over the past few years—Romania, Vietnam, and El Salvador.

Most of the immigrants who have come to Canada in recent decades have gone to Ontario and British Columbia, with the result that immigrants make up more than 20 percent of the populations of those two provinces. As Canada Map 12-1 reveals, Alberta and Manitoba have also attracted immigrants, while the Atlantic provinces have not. Not surprisingly, the metropolitan areas of Toronto and Vancouver have the largest immigrant components (Figure 12-4, 1986 data) at 28 and 37 percent respectively: in 1986, visible minorities made up about 17 percent of the populations of the two metro areas. Within the province of Quebec, Montreal had attracted a significant immigrant component, whereas Quebec City had not. Recent immigration has clearly touched some parts of Canada more than others.

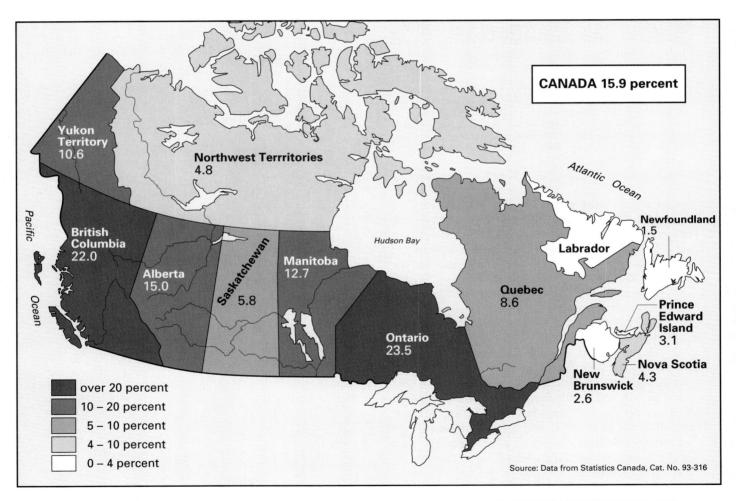

CANADA 15.9 percent

- Yukon Territory 10.6
- Northwest Terrritories 4.8
- British Columbia 22.0
- Alberta 15.0
- Saskatchewan 5.8
- Manitoba 12.7
- Ontario 23.5
- Quebec 8.6
- Labrador
- Newfoundland 1.5
- Prince Edward Island 3.1
- Nova Scotia 4.3
- New Brunswick 2.6
- Hudson Bay
- Pacific Ocean
- Atlantic Ocean

Legend:
- over 20 percent
- 10 – 20 percent
- 5 – 10 percent
- 4 – 10 percent
- 0 – 4 percent

Source: Data from Statistics Canada, Cat. No. 93-316

CANADA MAP 12-1   PERCENTAGE OF POPULATION FOREIGN-BORN FOR CANADA, THE PROVINCES AND TERRITORIES, 1991

Race and Ethnicity: Past and Future

Immigration has contributed to the development of a country which, though it started out Native, British, and French at Confederation, is now quite rightly called multicultural. The characteristics of the new-comers have stimulated the continued, and often uneasy, awareness of race and ethnicity among Canadians. Their geographic distribution has contributed to regional diversity as people with different backgrounds found themselves concentrated in various parts of the country and in different cities, giving substance to the vision of Canada as what former prime minister Joe Clark would call a "community of communities."

Canada is an experiment in multi-layered pluralism—multi-layered because the British, the French, the Native peoples, and the other ethnic and racial minorities have different kinds of relationships with each other and Canadian society as a whole. Each new wave of immigration will add to the complexity of the mosaic. Newly articulated demands and expectations on the part of the Québécois and the various Native peoples will contribute to the definition and redefinition of our unique country. If we are to survive as a nation, it will be because we have succeeded in forging an identity out of diversity. There is little to suggest that Canada could ever turn back the clock and take the other path leading to the creation of a melting pot. Diversity, it would appear, is our destiny.

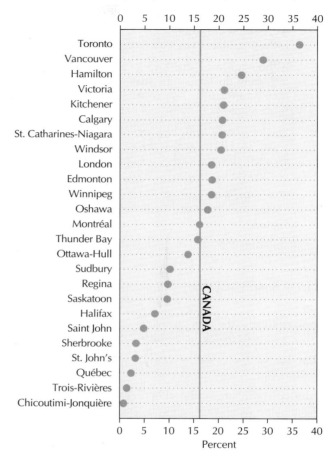

FIGURE 12-4   IMMIGRANT POPULATIONS IN CANADA'S CENSUS METROPOLITAN AREAS, 1986
SOURCE: Statistics Canada, Metropolitan Atlas Series, Cat. No. 98–106, 1989.

Summary

1. Race involves a cluster of biological traits that form three broad, overarching categories: Caucasians, Mongoloids, and Negroids. There are, however, no pure races. Ethnicity is based on shared cultural heritage. Minorities are categories of people who are socially distinctive—including those of certain races and ethnicities—and who have a subordinate social position.

2. A prejudice is an inflexible and distorted generalization about a category of people. Racism, a powerful form of prejudice, is any assertion that one race is innately superior or inferior to another.

3. Discrimination is a pattern of action by which a person treats various categories of people differently.

4. Pluralism refers to a state in which racial and ethnic categories, although distinct, have equal social

standing. Assimilation is a process by which minorities gradually adopt the patterns of the dominant culture. Segregation means the physical and social separation of categories of people. Most segregation of minorities is involuntary. Genocide is the annihilation of a category of people.

5. Although Canadians think of themselves as tolerant, they do harbor negative attitudes towards racial minorities. The consistency of these attitudes suggests a "culture of prejudice."

6. Blacks have a long history in Canada, as slaves prior to 1810, and later as Loyalists and as escaped slaves coming to Canada via the Underground Railroad.

7. The representation of racial and ethnic groups varies substantially from region to region in Canada.

8. Blacks and Asians have higher levels of education than the British and French, but their incomes tend to be lower. Natives are low on both education and income scales.

9. The Native peoples (or First Nations), who face numerous barriers to full participation in the larger society, seek self-government as a possible solution to some of their problems.

10. The Québécois feel that French language and culture can only be protected within Quebec and that they need to have maximum control of their institutions—perhaps through separation—in order to achieve this.

11. Canada, which has historically accepted large numbers of immigrants, is currently receiving most of its immigrants from Asia, especially Hong Kong.

Key Concepts

assimilation   the process by which minorities gradually adopt patterns of the dominant culture

discrimination   treating various categories of people unequally

ethnicity   a shared cultural heritage

genocide   the systematic annihilation of one category of people by another

institutional completeness   the complexity of community organizations that meet the needs of members.

institutional discrimination   discrimination that is a normative and routine part of the economy, the educational system, or some other social institution

minority   a category of people, distinguished by physical or cultural traits, who are socially disadvantaged

miscegenation   the biological process of interbreeding among racial categories

pluralism   a state in which racial and ethnic minorities are distinct but have social parity

prejudice   a rigid and irrational generalization about a category of people

race   a category composed of men and women who share biologically transmitted traits deemed socially significant

racism   the belief that one racial category is innately superior or inferior to another

scapegoat   a person (or category of people), typically with little power, who is unfairly blamed for the troubles of others

segregation   the physical and social separation of categories of people

stereotype   a set of prejudices concerning some category of people

Suggested Readings

This paperback text delves into the issues raised in this chapter.

> Harry H.L. Kitano. *Race Relations.* 4th ed. Englewood Cliffs, NJ: Prentice Hall, 1990.

These books spotlight the centrality of race and ethnicity to social stratification in Canada.

> Peter S. Li. *Ethnic Inequality in a Class Society.* Toronto: Wall and Thompson, 1988.
>
> Christopher McAll. *Class, Ethnicity, and Social Inequality.* Montreal & Kingston: McGill-Queen's University Press, 1990.

This fascinating account of white, racist, right-wing organizations in Canada is based upon extensive interviews.

> Stanley R. Barrett. *Is God Racist: the Right Wing in Canada.* Toronto: University of Toronto Press, 1987.

Novelist and essayist, Mordecai Richler, details the experience of being Jewish and anglophone in Quebec.

> Mordecai Richler. *Oh Canada! Oh Quebec! Requiem for a Divided Country.* Toronto: Penguin Books, 1992.

If cultural patterns can build community, they can also turn people against one another. Nowhere has this been truer than in the Middle East. The first book examines how ethnicity stands at the core of Middle Eastern social structure. The second book, by a noted foreign correspondent who lived in Jerusalem for five years, explores how stereotypes carry hatred into the lives of each new generation.

> Milton J. Esman and Itamar Rabinovich, eds. *Ethnicity, Pluralism, and the State in the Middle East.* Ithaca, NY and London: Cornell University Press, 1988.
>
> David K. Shipler. *Arab and Jew: Wounded Spirits in a Promised Land.* New York: Times Books, 1986.

These books investigate the social dynamics of race and ethnicity in two societies.

> John Solomos. *Race and Racism in Contemporary Britain.* London: Macmillan, 1989.
>
> Edward N. Herberg. *Ethnic Groups in Canada: Adaptations and Transitions.* Scarborough, Ontario: Nelson Canada, 1989.

Do immigrants bring innovation and economic vitality to a society or merely raise unemployment? This book paints a multidimensional portrait of newcomers to the United States and assesses the economic consequences of immigration.

> George J. Borgas. *Friends or Strangers: The Impact of Immigrants on the U.S. Economy.* New York: Basic Books, 1990.

This global analysis explores the experiences of Jews, Scots, Chinese, and other ethnic categories that have marginal standing in various societies.

> Walter P. Zenner. *Minorities in the Middle: A Cross-Cultural Analysis.* Albany, NY: SUNY Press, 1991.

This history of racial preferences examines the complex consequences of affirmative action with regard to race relations.

> Herman Belz. *Equality Transformed: A Quarter-Century of Affirmative Action.* New Brunswick, NJ: Transaction, 1991.

This book, the edited proceedings of a conference on aboriginal self-government, contains contributions from a wide range of Native leaders, as well as politicians and academics.

> Frank Cassidy, ed. *Aboriginal Self-Determination.* Montreal: The Institute for Research on Public Policy, 1991.

The following book explores Canada's immigration policy and details its consequences.

> Valerie Knowles. *Strangers at our Gates: Canadian Immigration and Immigration Policy, 1540–1990.* Toronto: Dundurn Press, 1992.

CHAPTER 13

SEX AND GENDER

Unity Dow smiled at her friends and supporters as the judge announced the court's decision; there were hugs and handshakes all around. Dow, a thirty-two-year-old lawyer and citizen of the African nation of Botswana, has won the first round in her efforts to overturn the laws by which, she maintains, her country defines women as second-class citizens.

The law that sparked Unity Dow's suit against her government regulates how citizenship is extended to children. Traditionally in Botswana, family membership is traced through men—that is, children are part of their father's family line, but not their mother's. The nation's citizenship law, which also follows the *patrilineal* model, has special significance for anyone who marries a citizen of another country as Unity Dow did. Under the law, a child of a Botswanan man and a woman of another country would be a citizen of Botswana, since legal standing passes through the father. By the same token, however, the child of a Botswanan woman and a foreign man is denied citizenship. Because she is married to a man from the United States, Unity Dow's children had no rights as citizens in the country where they were born.

The significance of the Dow case goes far beyond citizenship to the foundation of unequal legal standing of the two sexes. In rendering the decision in Dow's favor, High Court Judge Martin Horwitz declared, "The time that women were treated as chattels or were there to obey the whims and wishes of males is long past." In support of his decision, Horwitz pointed to the constitution of Botswana, which guarantees fundamental rights and freedoms to women as well as men. But not everyone agreed. Arguing the government's case against Dow, Ian Kirby, a deputy attorney general, claimed that the Botswanan constitution does allow a legal distinction between women and men. He readily conceded that the citizenship laws—and a host of other statutes—favor men, but, he added, this pattern is consistent with Botswanan culture, which has long given men power over women. To challenge such traditions in the name of Western feminism, he continued, was nothing more than cultural imperialism by which some people seek to subvert their own way of life by advancing foreign notions popular elsewhere.

Women from many African nations attended the hearing of the Dow case, some traveling great distances to bear witness to what they considered to be historic change. The case is complex and will be debated for years to come. Undoubtedly, this will be the first of many similar lawsuits—in various African societies—with the goal of establishing social equality between the sexes (Dow, 1990; Shapiro, 1991).

To many people in Canada, the Dow case may seem strange, since the notion that men and women are entitled to equal rights and privileges is widely endorsed here. But, as this chapter will explain, in our own society the two sexes are far from equal in many respects. It was not until 1981, when the new Constitution was introduced, that women and men in Canada were fully equal before the law. Section 28 guaranteed the rights and freedoms in the Charter "equally to male and female persons." Section 15, which includes racial, religious, and sexual discrimination, is the equivalent of the Equal Rights Amendment in the U.S., which American women have been trying to get into their Constitution since 1923 (Anderson, 1991).

Sex and Gender

Many people think that differences in the social standing of men and women simply reflect innate differences between the sexes. As this chapter will explain, however, the different social experiences of women and men are more a creation of society than biology. To begin, we shall explore the key concepts of sex and gender.

Sex: A Biological Distinction

Sex refers to *the division of humanity into biological categories of female and male.* Sex is determined at the moment a child is conceived through sexual intercourse. The female ovum and the male sperm, which join to form a fertilized embryo, each contain twenty-three pairs of chromosomes—biological codes that guide physical development. One of these chromosome pairs determines the child's sex. The mother always contributes an X chromosome; the father contributes either an X or a Y. A second X from the father produces a female (XX) embryo; a Y from the father yields a male (XY) embryo.

Within six weeks of conception, the sex of an embryo begins to guide its development. If the embryo is male, testicular tissues begin producing testosterone, a hormone that stimulates the development of the male genitals. Without testosterone, the embryo develops female genitals.

At birth, females and males are distinguished by **primary sex characteristics**, *the genitals used to reproduce the human species.* Further sex differentiation occurs years later when children reach puberty and their reproductive systems become fully operational. At

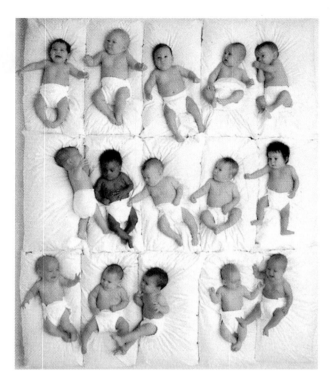

Sex is a biological distinction that develops prior to birth. Gender is the meaning that a society attaches to being female or male. That is, the range of human feelings, thoughts, and behavior is divided into what is defined as feminine or masculine. Moreover, gender differences are also a matter of power, as what is masculine typically has social priority over what is feminine. Gender differences are not evident among infants, of course, but the ways in which we think of boys and girls set in motion patterns that will continue for a lifetime.

this point, humans exhibit **secondary sex characteristics**, *physical traits other than the genitals that distinguish physiologically mature females and males.* To accommodate pregnancy, childbirth, and the nurturing of infants, adolescent females develop wider hips, breasts, and soft fatty tissue, providing a reserve supply of nutrition for pregnancy and breast-feeding (Brownmiller, 1984). Usually slightly taller and heavier than females from birth, adolescent males typically develop more muscles in the upper body, more extensive body hair, and voices deeper in tone. These are only general differences, however. Many males are smaller and lighter than many females; some males have less body hair than some females; and some males speak in a higher tone than some females.

Sex is not always a clear-cut matter. In rare cases, a hormone imbalance before birth produces a hermaphrodite (a word derived from Hermaphroditus, the offspring of the mythological Greek gods Hermes and Aphrodite, who embodied both sexes), *a human being with some combination of female and male internal and external genitalia.* Because our culture is anxious about sexual ambiguity, we generally regard hermaphrodites with confusion and even disgust. By contrast, the Pokot of Eastern Africa are indifferent to what they define as a simple biological error, and the Navajo look on hermaphrodites with awe, viewing them as the embodiment of the full potential of both the female and the male (Geertz, 1975).

Further complicating the issue, some people deliberately choose to change their sex. Hermaphrodites may have their genitals surgically altered to gain the appearance (and occasionally the function) of a sexually normal man or woman. Surgery is also commonly considered by **transsexuals**, *people who feel they are one sex though biologically they are the other.*

Sexual Orientation

Sexual orientation is *the manner in which people experience sexual arousal and achieve sexual pleasure.* For most living things, sexuality is biologically programmed. In humans, however, sexuality is bound up in the complex web of culture. The norm in all industrial societies is *heterosexuality* (*hetero* is a Greek word meaning "the other of two"), by which a person is sexually attracted to the opposite sex. However, *homosexuality* (*homo* is the Greek word for "the same"), by which a person is sexually attracted to people of the same sex, is not uncommon.

More broadly, all cultures endorse heterosexuality, although many tolerate—and some even encourage—homosexuality. Among the ancient Greeks, for instance, elite intellectual men celebrated homosexuality as the highest form of relationship, while devaluing relations with women, whom they considered to be their intellectual inferiors. In this light, heterosexuality was seen as little more than a reproductive necessity, and men who did not engage in homosexuality were defined as deviant. But because homosexual relations do not permit reproduction, no record exists of a society that has favored homosexuality to the exclusion of heterosexuality (Kluckhohn, 1948; Ford & Beach, 1951; Greenberg, 1988).

By the 1960s, homosexuals became more outspoken in opposition to heterosexual norms, and they adopted the label *gay* to describe themselves. This new terminology allowed gays to express satisfaction with their sexual orientation, amid a culture that broadly condemns homosexuality. Although stereotypes of homosexuals abound, the personalities of gay people vary as much as those of "straights."

Tolerance of gay people has increased during this century. In 1974 the American Psychiatric Association removed homosexuality from its listing of mental disorders. Gays were subject to increasing prejudice, discrimination, and violence during the 1980s, however, when the deadly disease AIDS became publicly identified with homosexual men. Today, 81 percent of the Canadian public feels that homosexuals are more accepted in society today, as compared to twenty-five years ago (Bozinzoff and MacIntosh, 1991).

Until our society becomes truly accepting of homosexuality, some gay people will understandably choose to remain "in the closet," fearfully avoiding public disclosure of their sexual orientation. Heterosexuals can begin to understand what this secrecy means by imagining never speaking about their romances to parents, roommates, or anyone else (Offir, 1982:216). For their part, many organizations of gay people are struggling to overcome the stereotypes applied to gay men and gay women (commonly called *lesbians*). In the late 1960s, a new term took hold: *homophobia* (with Greek roots meaning "fear of sameness") refers to an irrational fear of gay people (Weinberg, 1973). Instead of asking "What's wrong with gay people?" in other words, this label casts the spotlight on society itself, implying "What's wrong with people who can't accept this sexual orientation?"

The pioneering research by Alfred Kinsey (1948, 1953) suggested that about 4 percent of males and roughly 2 percent of females have an exclusively same-sex orientation. Nevertheless, roughly 10 percent of people in North America have a strong enough homosexual orientation to designate themselves as "gay" (Kirk & Madsen, 1989). In the broadest terms, at least twice this number have had at least one erotic experience with someone of the same sex. Sexual orientations, then, are not mutually exclusive; some people have a *bisexual* (combining homosexual and heterosexual) preference.

How does a person develop a particular sexual orientation? There is growing evidence that sexual orientation is rooted in biological factors present at birth and is further reinforced by the hormone balance in the body as we grow (Gladue, Green, & Hellman, 1984; Weinrich, 1987; Isay, 1989). Still other research points to the importance of the social environment in promoting particular sexual attitudes and behaviors (Troiden, 1988). According to these researchers, humans are born with the capacity and desire to be sexual, but *how* we express our sexuality is learned as our personality develops in society. Most likely, both nature and nurture play a part. To complicate matters further, sexual orientation is not established in precisely the same way for everyone. One influential study concluded that a complete explanation for sexual orientation simply does not exist at present (Bell, Weinberg, & Kiefer-Hammersmith, 1981).

Gender: A Cultural Distinction

Gender refers to *society's division of humanity, based on sex, into two distinctive categories.* Gender guides how females and males think about themselves, how they interact with others, and what positions they occupy in society as a whole.

Gender deals not only with difference—how a society constructs feminine and masculine people—but also with how society confers power on each of the sexes. Thus, gender also operates as a dimension of social inequality. This inequality, which has historically favored males, is no simple matter of biological differences between the two sexes. Females and males do, of course, differ biologically, but these disparities are complex and inconsistent. Beyond the primary and secondary sex characteristics already noted, males have more muscle in the arms and shoulders, so the average man can lift more weight than the average woman can. Furthermore, males can sustain greater strength over short periods of time. Yet, females can outperform males in some tests of long-term endurance because they can draw on the energy derived from greater body fat. Females also outperform males in life itself. Even at birth the male infant mortality rate is higher than that of females. In 1988 the male infant mortality rate was 8.2 and the female 6.4 per 1,000 (Canada Yearbook, 1993). Females born between 1985 and 1987 can expect to live almost eighty years while males born during this time can expect to live about seventy-three years (Canada Yearbook, 1993).

Adolescent males exhibit greater mathematical ability, while adolescent females outperform males in verbal skills, differences that certainly reflect different patterns of socialization and, as recent research suggests, may have some basis in biology (Maccoby & Jacklin, 1974; Baker et al., 1980; Lengermann & Wallace, 1985; Nash, 1991). In any case, however, research indicates no difference in overall intelligence between males and females.

Biologically, then, only limited differences distinguish females from males, with neither sex naturally superior. Nevertheless, the deeply rooted *cultural* notion of male superiority may seem so natural that we assume that it stems from sex itself. But society, much more than biology, is at work here, as several kinds of research reveal.

An Unusual Case Study

In 1963 a physician was performing a routine penis circumcision on seven-month-old identical twins. While using electrocautery (surgery employing a heated needle), the physician accidentally burned off the penis of one boy. Understandably, the parents were horrified. After months of medical consultation, they decided to employ further surgery to change the boy's sex and to raise him as a girl.

The child was dressed as a girl, her hair grew long, and she was treated according to cultural definitions of femininity. Meanwhile, the brother—born an exact biological copy—was raised as a boy.

Because of their different socialization, each child learned a distinctive **gender identity**, *traits that females and males, guided by their culture, incorporate into their personalities.* In this example, one child learned to think of himself in terms that our culture defines as masculine, while the other child—despite beginning life as a male—soon began to think of herself as feminine. As the twins' mother observed:

> One thing that really amazes me is that (my daughter) is so feminine. I've never seen a little girl so neat and tidy. ... She is very proud of herself, when she puts on a new dress, or I set her hair. She just loves to have her hair set; she could sit under the dryer all day long to have her hair set. She just loves it. ... (My daughter) likes for me to wipe her face. She doesn't like to be dirty, and yet my son is quite different. I can't wash his face for anything. ... She seems to be daintier. (Money & Ehrhardt, 1972:124)

However, the girl's development did not proceed smoothly, suggesting that some biological forces were coming into play. The researchers reported that, while feminine in many respects, she also displayed some masculine traits, including a desire to gain dominance among her peers. Later, researchers following the case reported that, by the time she was reaching adolescence, she was showing signs of resisting her feminine gender identity (Diamond, 1982). This complex case raises a question about whether environment can completely overcome any and all biological factors. But it also demonstrates that gender can be socially constructed to a greater degree than most people would imagine.

The Israeli Kibbutzim

Further evidence of society's power to generate gender differences is found in studies of collective settlements in Israel called *kibbutzim*. The *kibbutz* (the singular form) is important for gender research because its members historically have embraced the ideal of social equality, with men and women sharing in required work and decision making. Both sexes in the kibbutzim typically perform all kinds of work including child care, building repair, cooking, and cleaning. Boys and girls are raised in the same way and, from the first weeks of life, live in dormitories under the care of specially trained personnel. To members of kibbutzim, then, gender is barely relevant to much of everyday life.

Here, again, we find reason for caution about completely discounting biological forces. Some observers noted that women in the kibbutzim resisted spending much of the day away from their own children; as a result, many of these organizations have returned to more traditional social roles. Sociobiologists (see Chapter 3, "Culture") who have studied the kibbutzim attribute this reemergence of conventional social patterns to subtle but persistent biological dispositions. A close examination of kibbutz life suggests that nature may undermine efforts to achieve complete gender equality (Tiger & Shepher, 1975). But even if this were so—and this research has its critics—the kibbutzim certainly stand as evidence of wide cultural latitude in defining what is feminine and masculine. They also exemplify how, through conscious efforts, a society can pursue the goal of sexual equality just as it can encourage the domination of one sex by the other.

Cross-Cultural Research

Another way to determine whether gender reflects culture or some inborn imperative is to take a broad view of how the two sexes interact in many different cultures. To the extent that gender reflects the biological facts of sex, the human traits defined as feminine and masculine should be the same everywhere; if gender responds to cultural influences, these conceptions should vary.

The best-known research of this kind is a study of gender in three societies of New Guinea by anthropologist Margaret Mead (1963; orig. 1935). High in the mountains of New Guinea, Mead observed the Arapesh, whose men and women displayed remarkably similar attitudes and behavior. Both sexes, she reported, were cooperative and sensitive to others. They were, in short, what our culture would term "feminine."

Moving south, Mead then observed the Mundugumor, whose culture of head-hunting and cannibalism stood in striking contrast to the gentle ways of the Arapesh. Here, Mead reported, females and males were again alike, although they were startlingly different from the Arapesh. Both Mundugumor females and males were typically selfish and aggressive, traits defined in Canada as more "masculine."

Finally, traveling west to observe the Tchambuli, Mead discovered a culture that, like our own, defined

In every society, people assume some tasks are "naturally" feminine while others are just as obviously masculine. But, in global perspective, we see remarkable variety in such social definitions. These men of Africa's Ivory Coast are engaged in what they think of as the masculine routine of "washing day."

females and males differently. Yet the Tchambuli *reversed* many of our notions of gender: females were dominant and rational, while males were submissive, emotional, and nurturing toward children.

Based on her observations, Mead concluded that cultures can exaggerate or minimize social distinctions based on sex. Additionally, where differences are pronounced, what one culture defines as masculine may be considered feminine by another. Mead's research, therefore, strongly supports the conclusion that gender is a variable creation of society.

A broader study of more than two hundred preindustrial societies by George Murdock (1937) revealed some general agreement about which tasks tend to be viewed as feminine or masculine. Hunting and warfare, Murdock found, generally fall to males, while home-centered chores such as cooking and child care tend to be defined as female tasks. With only simple technology, preindustrial societies apparently adopt this strategy to benefit from men's greater size and short-term strength; because women bear children, their activities are likely to be more domestic.

But within these general patterns, Murdock found significant variation. Just as many societies considered agriculture—the core of preindustrial production—to be feminine as masculine. For most, in fact, farming responsibilities were shouldered by both women and men. When it came to many other tasks—from building shelters to tattooing the body—Murdock observed that societies of the world were as likely to turn to one sex as the other.

In global perspective, then, only a few specific activities are consistently defined as feminine or masculine. And as societies industrialize, with a resulting decrease in the significance of muscle power, even these distinctions are minimized (Lenski, Lenski, & Nolan, 1991). Gender, therefore, is simply too variable across cultures to be considered a simple expression of the biological categories of sex. Instead, as with many other elements of culture, what it means to be female and male is mostly a creation of society.

Patriarchy and Sexism

Although conceptions of gender do vary, one universal pattern characterizes all societies to some degree: **patriarchy** (literally, "the rule of fathers"), *a form of social organization in which males dominate females.* Despite mythical tales of societies dominated by female "Amazons," the pattern of **matriarchy**, *a form of social organi-*

zation in which females dominate males, is not at present part of the human record (Gough, 1971; Harris, 1977; Kipp, 1980; Lengermann & Wallace, 1985). While a tendency toward patriarchy may be universal, however, world societies reveal significant variation in the relative power and privilege of females and males.

Sexism, *the belief that one sex is innately superior to the other*, stands as an important ideological underpinning of patriarchy. Historically, patriarchy has been supported by a belief in the innate superiority of males who, therefore, legitimately dominate females. As Table 13-1 shows, sexism has much in common with racism, which was covered in Chapter 12 ("Race and Ethnicity"). Just as racism constitutes an ideology supporting white domination of people of color, so sexism is an ideology justifying the domination of (allegedly inferior) females by (allegedly superior) males.

Also like racism, sexism is more than a matter of individual attitudes. The notion that one sex is superior to the other is built into various institutions of our society. As we shall see presently, *institutional sexism* pervades the operation of the economy, with women highly concentrated in jobs that are less challenging and offer relatively low pay. In another example of institutional sexism, the legal system has historically minimized or overlooked entirely violence against women, especially violence perpetrated by boyfriends, husbands, and fathers (Landers, 1990). A decade ago, when an N.D.P. member of the House of Commons, Margaret Mitchell, mentioned a report on wife battering, male M.P.s burst into laughter. Such a short time ago, it was considered a non-issue. Now there are new sexual assault bills, rape crisis centers, and several hundred shelters for the estimated 1 in 8 to 1 in 10 Canadian women who are battered (Anderson, 1991; Begin, 1991; De Keseredy and Hinch, 1991).

Sexism—especially when it is institutionalized—has clear costs to women, who stand at increased risk of poverty and sexual violence. But society as a whole also pays a high price for maintaining sexism. Limiting the opportunities available to women ensures that the full talents and abilities of half the population will never be developed. And men, too, are hurt by sexism. Without denying that sexism confers on men a disproportionate share of wealth and power, this privilege comes at a high price. As Marilyn French (1985) argues, patriarchy compels men to relentlessly seek control—not only of women, but of themselves and the entire world. The consequences include far higher rates of death from suicide, violence, accidents, stress, heart attacks, and other diseases related to lifestyle. The so-called Type A

TABLE 13-1   SEXISM: ECHOES OF RACIAL STEREOTYPES

	Women	Racially Defined Visible Minorities
Link to highly visible personal traits	Secondary sex characteristics	Skin color
Assertion of innate inferiority	Women are mentally inferior. Women are irresponsible, unreliable, and emotional.	Visible minorities are mentally inferior. Visible minorities are irresponsible, unreliable, and pleasure-seeking.
Assertion that those who are disadvantaged are content with their "proper place" in society	"A woman's place is in the home." All women really enjoy being treated "like a woman."	"Visible minorities should remain in their place." Visible minorities are content living just as they do.
Assertion that victims are under the protection of their oppressors	"Men put women on a pedestal."	Whites "take care of" visible minorities.
Coping strategies on the part of victims	Behavior flattering to men; letting men think they are better even when they are not. Hiding one's real feelings. Attempting to outwit men.	Deferential behavior toward whites; letting whites think they are better even when they are not. Hiding one's real feelings. Attempting to outwit whites.
Barriers to opportunity	Women don't need an education. Confined to "women's work." Women should stay out of politics.	Visible minorities don't need an education. Confined to "visible minority occupations." Visible minorities should stay out of politics.
Criticism of those who do not "stay in their place"	Assertive women are "pushy." Ambitious women are trying to be like men. Women as traditional targets of violence by men.	Assertive visible minorities are "uppity." Ambitious visible minorities are trying to be like whites. Visible minorities as traditional targets of violence by whites.

SOURCE: Adapted from Helen Mayer Hacker, "Women as a Minority Group," Social Forces, Vol. 30 (October 1951), pp. 60–69; and "Women as a Minority Group: Twenty Years Later," in Florence Denmark, ed., Who Discriminates Against Women? (Beverly Hills, CA: Sage, 1974), pp. 124–34.

personality—characterized by chronic impatience, driving ambition, competitiveness, and free-floating hostility—is known to be linked to heart disease and is precisely the behavior that our culture defines as masculine (Ehrenreich, 1983). Furthermore, insofar as men seek control over others, they lose the ability to experience intimacy and trust (French, 1985). One recent study concluded that although competition is supposed to separate "the men from the boys," in practice it separates men from men, and from everyone else (Raphael, 1988). Overall, when human feelings, thoughts, and actions are rigidly scripted according to a culture's conceptions of gender, people cannot develop and freely express the full range of their humanity. Males are strongly pressured to be assertive, competitive, and in control, a weighty burden for many to bear. Females are constrained to be submissive, dependent, and self-effacing, regardless of their individual talents and personalities.

Is Patriarchy Inevitable?

In technologically simple societies, patriarchy stems from individuals having little control over the natural differences of sex. Pregnancy and childbirth limit the scope of women's lives, while men's greater height and strength typically allow them to overpower women. Technological advances, however, give members of industrial societies a wider range of choices in how the two sexes interact. Contraception has given women greater control over pregnancy, just as industrial machinery has diminished the primacy of muscle power in everyday life. Today, then, biological differences provide little justification for patriarchy.

Categorical social inequality—whether based on race, ethnicity, or sex—comes under attack in the more egalitarian culture of industrial societies. In many industrial nations, laws mandate equal employment opportunities for women and men and equal pay for equal efforts. Nonetheless, in all industrial societies, the two sexes continue to hold different jobs and receive unequal pay, as we will explain presently. Another indicator of patriarchy is housework; the more unequal the social standing of the two sexes, the greater the proportion of housework assigned to women. Global Map 13-1 puts housework in world perspective: although members of industrial societies share housework more than people in agrarian societies do, nowhere is housework shared equally.

Do the facts that women retain primary responsibility for the household while men control most wealth and power mean that patriarchy is inevitable? Some researchers claim that biological factors imprint different behaviors and motivations on the two sexes, mak-

WINDOW ON THE WORLD

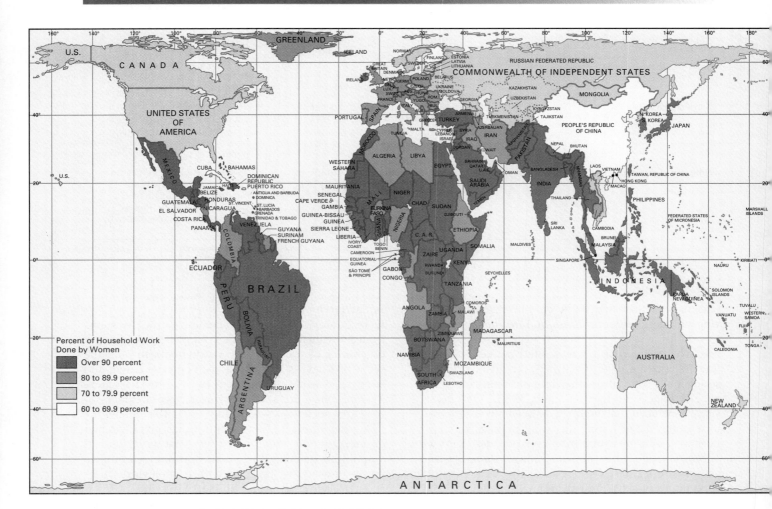

GLOBAL MAP 13-1   HOUSEWORK IN GLOBAL PERSPECTIVE

Housework—made up of necessary, although tiring and repetitive, tasks—is one good indicator of how societies construct gender. To the extent that housework is carried out by only one sex, a society differentiates its members in terms of gender. In general, the greater the proportion of housework that women perform, the greater the social dominance of men. Housework is most rigidly assigned to women in poor societies of the Third World, although in Japan and many European societies as well women do almost all these tasks. Canada is more egalitarian with regard to housework than most of the world. The People's Republic of China appears to divide housework most equally, the result of deliberate socialist policies. Even there, however, men dominate women in a host of ways.

ing the complete eradication of patriarchy difficult, if not impossible (Goldberg, 1974, 1987). Many sociologists acknowledge that biological differences between the sexes have *some* effect on human behavior (Rossi, 1985). But virtually all sociologists believe that gender is primarily a social construction. As such, it is subject to change. Simply because no society has yet eliminated patriarchy, then, does not mean that we are prisoners of the past.

To understand the persistence of patriarchy, we now examine how gender is rooted and reproduced in society, a process that spans the way we learn to think of ourselves as children to how sexual inequality affects us as adults.

Gender and Socialization

From birth until death, human feelings, thoughts, and actions reflect social definitions of the sexes. As children gain their first social experience, they quickly learn that their society defines females and males as different kinds of human beings; by about the age of three or four, they begin to apply gender standards to themselves (Kohlberg, 1966, cited in Lengermann & Wallace, 1985:37; Bem, 1981). Table 13-2 lists some of the traits that people in Canada traditionally have used to define females and males. Consider the overall pattern: not only do we tend to distinguish between the two sexes but we also define them in *opposing* terms. Polarizing humanity in terms of gender is still widespread in this country as it is elsewhere, although research suggests that most young people in Canada do not develop

TABLE 13-2 TRADITIONAL NOTIONS OF GENDER IDENTITY

Feminine Traits	Masculine Traits
Submissive	Dominant
Dependent	Independent
Unintelligent and incapable	Intelligent and competent
Emotional	Rational
Receptive	Assertive
Intuitive	Analytical
Weak	Strong
Timid	Brave
Content	Ambitious
Passive	Active
Cooperative	Competitive
Sensitive	Insensitive
Sex object	Sexually aggressive
Attractive because of physical appearance	Attractive because of achievement

consistently "feminine" or "masculine" personalities (L. Bernard, 1980).

Just as socialization incorporates gender into personal identity, so it teaches us to *act* according to cultural conceptions of what is feminine and masculine. **Gender roles** (or sex roles) are *attitudes and activities that a culture links to each sex*. Gender roles are the active expression of gender identity. In other words, insofar as our culture defines males as ambitious and competitive, we expect them to engage in team sports and seek out positions of leadership. To the extent that females are defined as deferential and emotional, we expect them to be good listeners and supportive observers.

Gender and the Family

The first question people usually ask about a newborn child—"Is it a boy or a girl?"—looms so large because the answer involves more than the infant's sex; it carries a great deal of significance for the child's entire life. Sociologist Jessie Bernard, introduced in the box on page 358, suggests that females and males live in different worlds within a single society, and that the "pink world" of girls contrasts in many respects to the "blue world" of boys (1981). In fact, gender is at work even before the birth of a child: more parents in the United States claim to want a boy (45 percent in one study) than a girl (20 percent) (cited in Lengermann & Wallace, 1985:61). While we don't have any comparable empirical data for Canada, it is reasonable to suppose that the same preferences apply here.

In global perspective, the preference for boys is even more pronounced. Societies that are strongly patriarchal place far greater value on males than on females. Many of these societies also face enormous population pressure. These two facts, taken together, set the stage for **female infanticide**, *the practice of aborting female fetuses and neglecting, or even actively killing, infant girls by parents who would prefer to raise boys.* In North Africa and most of Asia, life-threatening discrimination against females is commonplace. Researchers know that, assuming equal social treatment, a society should have about 106 females for every 100 males—a disparity that reflects the generally hardier physical condition of females. In the People's Republic of China, however, there are only 94 females for every 100 males. This means that roughly 12 percent of the females that we would expect to find are not in the records. Some of this shortfall is explained by parents not reporting the birth of a daughter. The rest may well be due to active

PROFILE

Jessie Bernard

Now in her eighties, Jessie Bernard continues to make valuable contributions

to the discipline of sociology. Her work has long focused on gender.

Bernard urges her colleagues to include women as well as men in their work. In the past, sociologists—even those critical of the status quo—have tended to disregard women. Karl Marx, for instance, paid almost no attention to women in his writings. One reason for not giving balanced attention to females and males, Bernard suggests, is that sociology, like other disciplines, has developed largely under the control of men. Many familiar sociological issues and concepts thus betray a built-in male bias.

Consider the topic of social stratification. To be a member of the upper class, a man must have considerable wealth. But this definition

neglects the other half of humanity, since a woman's social class position is traditionally derived from *men*: initially from her father and subsequently from her husband. Further, in ranking the prestige of occupations, sociologists usually ignore housework—conventionally the most common activity of women. By defining the concept of occupational prestige so that it applies primarily to men, sociologists exclude women from sociological research.

In sum, sociologists must use care to ensure that their work addresses both females and males; otherwise, the discipline investigates only half of society.

SOURCES: Based on Jessie Bernard (1981) and personal communication.

---

biases by families against daughters. Worldwide, researchers estimate, perhaps 100 million females are "missing," and many presumably have fallen victim to deadly discrimination (United Nations Development Programme, 1991).

As children grow, families continue to shape the lives of girls and boys differently. Research on parental attitudes suggests that fathers and mothers want sons who are strong, aggressive achievers while they expect daughters to be delicate, sensitive, and less assertive (Witkin-Lanoil, 1984). Parents may unconsciously convey these expectations in the way they handle their children. A researcher at an English university presented an infant dressed as either a boy or a girl to a number of women. By and large, the women handled the "female" child tenderly, with frequent hugs and caresses, while treating the "male" child more aggressively, often lifting him up high in the air or bouncing him on the knee (Bonner, 1984). Other research shows that mothers have more overall physical contact with infant boys than with infant girls (Major, 1981). The message is clear: the female world revolves around passivity and emotion, while the male world involves substantial independence and action.

Gender and the Peer Group

As children reach school age, they interact more outside the family, especially with others their own age. Peer groups further distinguish the pink and blue worlds of girls and boys. The box on page 360 explains how play groups shaped one young boy's sense of himself as masculine.

Janet Lever (1978), who spent a year observing Grade five students at play, concluded that female and male peer groups provide girls and boys with distinctive socialization. Boys, Lever reported, engage more in team sports—such as baseball and football—that involve many roles, complex rules, and clear objectives like scoring a run or making a touchdown. These games are nearly always competitive, separating winners from losers. Male peer activities reinforce masculine traits of aggression and maintaining control.

By contrast, girls in peer groups play hopscotch or jumprope, or simply talk, sing, or dance together. Spontaneous activities with few formal rules are commonplace, and this play rarely has "victory" as its ultimate goal so that girls are unlikely to oppose one another. Instead of teaching girls to be competitive,

Dorothy Smith

There are a number of Canadian sociologists who have made remarkable contributions to a feminist analysis. Mary O'Brien, Dorothy Smith, Margrit Eichler, Pat Armstrong, and Meg Luxton are just a few. Only one will be highlighted here.

Dorothy Smith is a Canadian sociologist whose contribution to feminist theory and methods goes beyond the borders of this country. Within Canada, she has influenced a generation of feminist scholarship. In 1990, Dr. Smith was the recipient of the St. John Porter Award for her book *The Everyday World as Problematic: A Feminist Sociology.* Smith's work is a radical revisioning of the way that knowledge, truth, and science have

been constructed and might be constructed in the future.

One central concept from her work is the notion of the *bifurcated consciousness.* This concept arose out of her experiences as an academic and single mother of two children. The discrepancy between the two worlds is the foundation for her critique of sociology. She advocates new methods which would begin with the experience and the conditions of women's lives based on their actual location (within and outside of the ruling powers) in society. In other words, Smith's restructuring of sociology demands a method that begins with the experiences of women and situates those experiences in the practices of people (institutions) which affect their lives.

Smith, adapting Marx's ontology and the insights derived from ethnomethodology and symbolic interaction, explains how a sociology of and for women might be accomplished. She calls the method of beginning with practical activities and showing how they are related to and constrained by external processes *institutional ethnography.* An early publication about women and psychiatry suggests how this method works. It is well known that women undergo psychotherapy more often than men. It has been believed that this is the result of women's greater psychopathology.

However, when women's experiences are actually investigated, the way that women are constrained by external forces becomes very clear. A brief quote follows:

> It is hardly surprising to find that married women go into psychotherapy a good deal more than married men. Psychiatric ideologies interpret the world for women in such a way as to create a special demand for psychiatry, particularly among women of the middle- and upper-middle classes. If a middle-class married woman is unhappy she has learned, particularly if she has been to college, to recognize that unhappiness as her cue to go to the psychiatrist. She knows already that it is a sickness and that her obligations to her marriage and to her role require her to seek expert help for what is wrong with her. She needs fixing if she is sexually unresponsive. She needs help if she can't stand her children, if she weeps or is unaccountably tired, or feels constantly irritated by her husband. She needs treatment if she is depressed.
>
> Resentment and despair are not treated as valid responses to her situation. The realities of her situation *as she feels them* are not treated as valid. For hers is not a special case. Her situation is "normal" for our society. The difficulty which psychiatry reinforces is in seeing that the routine and sanctioned features of marriage and family can ordinarily and routinely give rise to such responses. (Smith and David, 1975:6–7)

Lever explains, female peer groups promote interpersonal skills of communication and cooperation—presumably the basis for family life.

Carol Gilligan (1982) reports similar results in research concerning how children engage in moral reasoning. Boys learn to reason according to abstract principles. For them, "rightness" consists largely of "playing by the rules." In the female world, by contrast, morality is more a matter of responsibility to other people. Girls learn that "rightness" lies in maintaining close relation-

ships with others. In a host of ways, then, boys and girls draw different lessons from their peer groups.

Gender and Schooling

Even before children enter school, their reading tends to promote gender distinctions. A generation ago, the *Report of the Royal Commission on the Status of Women Canada* (1970) analyzed a selection of children's texts

Masculinity as Contest

By the time I was ten, the central fact in my life was the demand that I become a man. By then, the most important relationships by which I was taught to define myself were those I had with other boys. I already knew that I must see every encounter with another boy as a contest in which I must win or at least hold my own. ... The same lesson continued (in school), after school, even in Sunday School. My parents, relatives, teachers, the books I read, movies I saw, all taught me that my self-worth depended on my manliness, my willingness to stand up to the other boys. This usually didn't mean a physical fight, though the willingness to stand up and "fight like a man" always remained a final test. But the relationships between us usually had the character of an armed truce. Girls weren't part of this social world at all yet, just because they weren't part of this contest. They didn't have to be bluffed, no credit was gained by cowing them, so they were more or less ignored. Sometimes when there were no grownups around we would let each other know that we liked each other, but most of the time we did as we were taught.

SOURCE: Silverstein (1977).

and found that "versatile characters who have adventures are invariably males" (Mackie, 1983:185). Even math books represented males and females differently. For example, a problem focusing on the number of words typed per minute in forty-five minutes referred to the typist as female. The Commission concluded that "A woman's creative and intellectual potential is either underplayed or ignored in the education of children from their earliest years" (*Report of the Royal Commission on the Status of Women* (1970:175).

In the last decade, the growing awareness among authors, teachers, and readers that childhood learning shapes people's lives as adults has prompted changes in children's literature. Recent research suggests that today's books for children portray females and males in a more balanced way, although some sex-stereotyping persists (Purcell & Stewart, 1990).

In addition to the formal lessons of school, what Raphaela Best (1983) calls "the second curriculum"—the informal messages and experiences of school life—encourages children to embrace traditional gender patterns. By the time children reach high school, topics of study reflect the different roles females and males are expected to assume as adults. Instruction in home-centered skills such as nutrition, cooking, and sewing has long been provided to classes composed almost entirely of females. Classes in woodworking and auto mechanics, conversely, still attract a nearly all-male enrolment.

In college and university, males and females follow this same pattern, tending toward different majors.

Traditionally, the natural sciences—including physics, chemistry, biology, and mathematics—have been defined as part of the male province. Women have been encouraged to major in the humanities (such as English), the fine arts (painting, music, dance, and drama), or the social sciences (including anthropology and sociology). Today, 81 percent of all students in the natural sciences, engineering, and mathematics are male (Statistics Canada, 1993).

New areas of study quickly become linked to one sex or the other. Computer science, for example, with its grounding in engineering, logic, and abstract mathematics, predominantly appeals to men (Klein, 1984); courses in gender studies, by contrast, tend to enrol women.

Extracurricular activities also segregate the two sexes. Athletics and other activities for men benefit from more attention and greater funding than those for women. In addition, mass media coverage of men's athletics far outstrips coverage devoted to women's sports. This male dominance signals to women that they should assume supportive roles, as observers or cheerleaders, rather than excelling in their own right.

Gender and the Mass Media

Chapter 5 ("Socialization") explained that the mass media exert a powerful influence on the socialization process. Films, magazines, and television significantly affect how we think and act.

SHE'S VERY CHARLIE.

Charlie
REVLON

Some recent advertising reverses traditional gender definitions by portraying men as the submissive sex objects of successful women. Although the reversal is new, the use of gender stereotypes to sell consumer products is very old indeed.

Since it first captured the public imagination in the 1950s, television has placed the dominant segment of our population—white males—at center stage. Racial and ethnic minorities were all but absent from television until the early 1970s, and only in the last decade have a number of programs featured women in prominent roles.

Even when both sexes appear on camera, men tend to play the brilliant detectives, fearless explorers, and skilled surgeons. Men take charge, give orders, and exude competence. Women, by contrast, generally rely on men, are portrayed as less capable, and are more often the targets of comedy (Busby, 1975). Women, who have also been traditionally valued for their sexual attractiveness, are spotlighted in shows that deal with romance. Such stereotypes have persisted into the 1990s.

Change has come more slowly to advertising. Advertising, after all, sells products most successfully by conforming to widely established cultural patterns. Historically, television and magazine advertising has presented women in the home, rather than in the workplace, to sell household items such as cleaning products, food, clothing, and appliances. Men, on the other hand, predominate in ads for cars, travel, financial services, industrial companies, and alcoholic beverages. The authoritative "voiceover"—the faceless voice that describes some product in television and radio advertising—is almost always male (Holmes and Taras, 1992:261).

Despite vigorous efforts by proponents of gender equality to combat sex-based stereotyping, women are still used in advertising simply as sex objects. The controversial "Swedish bikini team" television ad campaign in 1991, in which scantily clad women descend out of nowhere to entertain beer-drinking men, would simply be impossible for viewers to imagine if the sexes were reversed.

In a systematic study of magazine and newspaper ads, Erving Goffman (1979) found other, more subtle biases. Men, he concluded, are photographed to appear taller than women, implying male superiority. Women are more frequently presented lying down (on sofas and beds) or, like children, seated on the floor. In their expressions and gestures, men exude competence and authority, whereas women are more likely to appear in childlike poses. While men tend to focus on the products being advertised, the attention of women is generally directed toward men, conveying their supportive and submissive role.

Advertising tries to persuade us that embracing traditional notions of femininity and masculinity ensures our personal and professional success. With that groundwork in place, advertising then dictates what we should consume. For example, the masculine man drives the "right" car and vacations at the "in" place. The truly feminine woman, according to the $20-billion-a-year cosmetics industry, needs a plethora of beauty aids to help her look younger and more attractive to men (Wolf, 1990).

Gender and Adult Socialization

Reinforced in so many ways by the surrounding culture, gender identity and gender roles typically come to feel "natural" well before we reach adulthood. As a result, the attitudes and behavior of adults commonly follow feminine and masculine patterns (Spender, 1980; Kramarae, 1981).

In a simple but revealing bit of research, Pamela Fishman (1977, 1978) tape-recorded two weeks of conversations by three young, white, middle-class, married couples in their homes. Even casual exchanges, she discovered, reinforced male dominance. For example, when the men began a conversation, the women usually kept it going; yet when the women initiated a conversation, the men frequently allowed it to founder. This suggests that what men have to say is considered more important. Similarly, women—but rarely men—opened conversations with remarks like "This is interesting" or "Do you know what?" This pattern, also common to the speech of children, is women's way of finding out if men really want to hear what they have to say. Starting a conversation with "This is interesting," for example, cues the listener to pay attention to what follows. Opening with "Do you know what?" amounts to stating, "I have something to say; are you willing to listen?".

The women in this research also asked many more questions than the men did, a further indication of deference to their partners. Both the men and women used a wide range of "minimal responses" (such as "yeah," "umm," and "huh"), but they used them in different ways. For the men, such responses expressed minimal interest, as if to say, "I guess I'll continue to listen if you insist on speaking". For the women, however, minimal responses more often took the form of "support work," inserted continually to show their interest in the conversation.

Years of gender-based socialization set the foundation for marriages between men and women who inhabit different social worlds. Not surprisingly, husbands and wives may have considerable difficulty simply communicating with each other. Studies of verbal interaction in marriage confirm that not talking openly—or sometimes not talking at all—is a problem common to spouses (Komarovsky, 1967; Rubin, 1976, 1983; Fitzpatrick, 1988; Tannen, 1990).

Gender and Social Stratification

Gender implies more than how people think and act. The concept of **gender stratification** refers to *a society's unequal distribution of wealth, power, and privilege*

between the two sexes. Specifically, societies allocate fewer valued resources to women than to men. This can be seen, first, in the world of work.

Working Men and Women

In 1991, 77 percent of Canadians over the age of 15 were working for income (1993 Corpus Almanac and Canadian Sourcebook, 1992). The Canadian labor force includes 84 percent of men and 71 percent of women (1993 Corpus Almanac and Canadian Sourcebook, 1992). In 1901, women comprised 13 percent of the paid work force and earned one half of men's income (Canada, 125th Anniversary Yearbook, 1992). The proportion of women who are full-year, full-time workers was about 39 percent in 1990 (Employment Income by Occupation: The Nation, 1993). The traditional view that earning an income is "man's work" thus no longer holds true.

Among the key factors altering the composition of the labor force are the growth of cities, declining family size, more flexible norms regarding appropriate roles for women, and, more recently, the increasing number of service jobs. In addition, because economic decline reduced the income of many families in Canada during the last fifteen years (see Chapter 10, "Social Class in Canada"), an increasing proportion of families require more than one income to maintain a comfortable standard of living. In 1990, dual-earner families make up 61.6 percent of all husband and wife families (Characteristics of Dual-Earner Families, Statistics Canada, 1992).

A common misconception holds that women in the labor force are single or, if married, without children. Married women with pre-school children had a 64.6 percent employment rate (1989). Married women with children between the ages of six and fifteen years had a 76.8 percent participation rate in the labor force. Married women without children under sixteen had a participation rate of 71.9 percent (*Women in the Labour Force*, 1990–1991). A very gradual increase in employer-sponsored child-care programs is giving more women and men the opportunity to combine the responsibilities of working and parenting, a trend that is especially important for divorced mothers. Over the last decade members of our three political parties have talked about a system of national day care. However, it seems unlikely that this will be developed in the near future because of the current and anticipated decrease in services and social programs.

TABLE 13-3 EMPLOYMENT BY OCCUPATION GROUP AND SEX, CANADA 1984, 1986, 1988

	Women			Men			Women as a % of Employment		
	1984	1986	1988	1984	1986	1988	1984	1986	1988
Clerical	32.1	31.0	30.8	6.2	5.9	6.1	79.1	79.9	79.8
Services	17.9	17.6	17.0	10.5	10.4	10.0	55.5	56.2	57.0
Sales	9.6	9.7	10.0	9.5	9.6	9.2	42.7	43.3	45.9
Medicine and Health	9.1	9.0	9.0	1.9	1.9	1.9	77.8	78.8	79.0
Teaching	6.0	6.2	6.1	3.1	3.0	2.9	58.8	60.9	62.2
Managerial, administrative	8.0	9.5	10.4	12.7	13.9	14.3	31.6	34.1	36.2
Product fabricating, assembling and repairing	4.7	4.5	4.2	11.5	11.4	11.4	22.9	22.9	22.5
Agriculture	2.7	2.5	2.2	5.9	5.3	4.9	25.2	25.8	25.8
Social sciences	2.2	2.2	2.3	1.3	1.3	1.3	55.2	56.8	58.4
Processing and machining	2.0	1.8	1.8	7.8	7.5	7.3	15.7	15.2	16.4
Artistic and recreational	1.5	1.7	1.8	1.8	1.7	1.8	39.0	42.5	43.8
Natural sciences	1.4	1.3	1.3	5.1	5.1	5.3	17.0	16.7	16.2
Materials handling	1.2	1.2	1.1	3.3	3.2	3.3	21.1	21.9	20.6
Other crafts and equipment operating	0.6	0.7	0.7	1.8	1.8	1.6	20.1	23.6	24.1
Transport and equipment operating	0.6	0.6	0.7	5.9	6.1	6.1	6.8	7.0	7.8
Construction trades	0.2	0.2	0.3	8.8	9.4	10.0	1.8	1.7	2.1
Religion	0.1	0.2	0.1	0.4	0.4	0.4	15.6	23.5	18.8
Forestry, logging, fishing, hunting and trapping	*	*	*	1.4	1.2	1.3	*	*	*
Mining and quarrying	*	*	*	1.0	0.9	0.9	*	*	*
Total	100.00	100.00	100.00	100.00	100.00	100.00	42.3	43.0	43.8
Total employed (000s)	4,624	4,964	5,368	6,308	6,567	6,876	...	...	...

* Numbers too small to provide reliable estimates; as a result, columns may not add up to total.
SOURCE: Statistics Canada, Labour Force Annual Averages, 1981–1988. Catalogue no. 71–529.

Gender and Occupations

While the proportions of men and women in the labor force have been converging—especially since 1970—the work done by the two sexes remains distinct. As Table 13-3 shows, clerical work employs 30 percent of all working women. In this category fall secretaries, typists, stenographers, and other workers whose efforts typically support the work of men. Not surprisingly, almost 80 percent of all such "pink-collar" jobholders are women. The second broad category is service work, performed by 17 percent of employed women. This includes waitressing and other food-service work. Both categories of jobs lie at the low end of the pay scale and offer limited opportunities for advancement.

Table 13-4 shows the ten occupations with the highest concentrations of women in 1986. Although increasing numbers of women, both married and single, are working, women remain highly segregated in the labor force because our society continues to link work to gender (Roos, 1983; Kemp & Coverman, 1989; *Women in Canada: A Statistical Report*, 1990).

TABLE 13-4 TOP TEN OCCUPATIONS* OF WOMEN, CANADA, 1986

Occupation	Occupation Group	Total Labor Force
		(000s)
Secretaries and stenographers	Clerical	425
Sales clerks and sales persons**	Sales	330
Bookkeepers and accounting clerks	Clerical	325
Cashiers and tellers	Clerical	261
Nurses***	Medicine and health	211
Food and beverage serving	Service	210
Elementary and kindergarten teachers	Teaching	152
General office clerks	Clerical	131
Receptionists and information clerks	Clerical	107
Janitors, charworkers and cleaners	Service	100

* Occupations based on the 1971 classification.
** "Sales clerks, commodities" has been combined with "Salesmen and salespersons, commodities, n.e.c.".
*** "Nurse-in-training" has been combined with "Nurses, graduate, except supervisors".
SOURCE: Statistics Canada, Labour Force Annual Averages, 1981–1988. Catalogue no. 71–529.

Men predominate in most job categories beyond the ten occupations noted in the table. The construction trades have the highest proportion of men: 97.9 percent of brickmasons, stonemasons, structural metal workers, and heavy-equipment mechanics are men. Men also hold the lion's share of positions that provide a great deal of income, prestige, and power. For example, more than 90 percent of engineers, 75 percent of judges and magistrates, 70 percent of physicians, 70 percent of corporate managers, and 65 percent of computer specialists are men (*Occupations*; Statistics Canada, 1993). Only a few women appear as the top executives of the largest corporations in Canada. Even where men and women do much the same work, titles (and consequently pay) confer greater benefits on men. A "special assistant to the president," for example, is likely to be a man, while an "executive secretary" is nearly always a woman.

There is one notable exception to this pattern, however: an increasing proportion of small businesses are now owned and operated by women. Women's share of the self-employed section rose from 18.9 percent in 1975 to 26.7 percent in 1986. In that year, women accounted for 17.7 percent of the self-employed with paid help and 34.5 percent of the self-employed without paid help (*Women in the Labour Force*, 1990–1991). Even so, the success of these talented entrepreneurs demonstrates that women have the power, incentive, and drive to create opportunities for themselves, and many find the rewards of working for themselves far greater than those offered by larger, male-dominated companies.

Overall, then, gender stratification permeates the workplace, where men tend to hold occupational positions that confer more wealth and power than those typically held by women. This gender-based hierarchy is ever present in the job setting: male physicians are assisted by female nurses, male executives have female secretaries, and male airline pilots work with female flight attendants. In any occupation, the greater a job's income and prestige, the more likely it is that the position will be held by a man.

Housework: Women's "Second Shift"

As we have already seen, housework—maintaining the home and caring for children—is the province of women throughout the world. In Canada, housework has always embodied a cultural contradiction: touted on the one hand as essential to an orderly life, and carrying little reward or social prestige on the other (Heller, 1986).

Surprisingly, women's rapid entry into the labor force has prompted little change in the pattern of responsibility for housework (Nett, 1993). On average women spend 2.5 hours per day on housework while men spend one hour per day (Canadians over fifteen in 1986). The proportion of women who indicated that they do housework on a given day is much higher than the proportion of men—85 as compared to 52 percent. (Marshall, 1990:18). Typically, couples share the disciplining of children and managing finances, but few other tasks. Men routinely perform less time-consuming tasks such as home repairs and mowing the lawn; women see to the daily shopping, cooking, and cleaning. Thus women commonly return from the workplace to face a "second shift" of unpaid work on the home front (Schooler et al., 1984; Benokraitis & Feagin, 1986; Hochschild, 1989).

Underlying changes in the workplace in recent decades is a set of contradictory attitudes. Men support the idea of women in the labor force, and many men depend on the income women earn; yet men resist modifying their own behavior to ease the pressure on women of juggling responsibilities at home and on the job (Komarovsky, 1973). Only in rare cases, such as the Israeli kibbutzim, is housework shared to any great extent. Even in Sweden—a society with a strong belief in the social equality of the sexes—only one in five couples shares housework equitably (Haas, 1981).

Gender, Income, and Wealth

Because women predominate in clerical and service jobs while men hold most business and professional positions, women earn less than men. Thus, income—a major measure of self-worth and a source of power—reinforces women's disadvantaged position in the occupational and social hierarchy.

Women's average salary is 69.6 percent of the average salary of men in Canada (*Earnings of Men and Women*, Statistics Canada, 1991). This is the lowest in all Western democracies (Anderson, 1991:142). Females who worked full-time, full-year in 1991 were estimated to earn on average $26,842 annually, whereas males were estimated to have averaged $38,567 (*Earnings of Men and Women*, Statistics Canada, 1991). Women thus cluster in low-paying positions, while men tend to rank among the more affluent. A male with eight years or less of education earned $27,116, compared to $56,522 for a university graduate. Females with eight years or less earned $18,138. Those with a university degree earned $39,723 (*Earnings of Men and Women*, Statistics Canada, 1991). The highest average male earnings were in the medicine and the health occupations, at $65,175. The highest average income for women was in the teaching occupation: $39,723 (*Earnings of Men and Women*, Statistics Canada, 1991:10).

Differences in earnings between men and women in Canada have gradually declined in recent decades. Some of this change is due to increasing opportunities for working women; mostly, however, it reflects a *decline* in the earnings of men.

This earning disparity stems primarily from the different jobs held by men and women. Taking a closer look, we discover a close link between jobs and gender: jobs with less clout are considered "women's work," and, turning the argument around, jobs have less value to the extent that they are performed by women (Parcel, Mueller, & Cuvelier, 1986). During the 1980s, this disparity was challenged by people who advocated a policy of "comparable worth," the concept that women and men should be paid not according to historical double standards but rather based on the worth of what they do. Thus women should receive equal pay for work that has equal, or comparable, worth. Several countries (including Great Britain and Australia) have national pay-equity laws, and some areas of the United States have passed legislation of this kind. In 1987, Ontario introduced pay-equity legislation, which was heralded as the most progressive piece of such legislation in North America at the time. Still, some women in this country are losing millions annually because of their sex.

A second cause of this gender-based income disparity has to do with the family. Both men and women have children, of course, but parenthood is more of a barrier to the careers of women than it is to the advancement of men. Pregnancy, childbirth, and rearing small children keep some younger women out of the labor force altogether at a time when men of the same age stand to make significant occupational gains. As a result, women workers have less job seniority than their male counterparts (Fuchs, 1986). Moreover, women who choose to have children may be reluctant or unable to maintain fast-paced jobs that demand evening and weekend work. Career women with children may seek jobs that offer a shorter commuting distance, flexible hours, and child-care services (Schwartz, 1989). The box on pages 366–67 examines a recent—and controversial—proposal to benefit corporate women. The two

factors noted so far—type of work and family responsibilities—account for roughly two-thirds of the earnings disparity between women and men. Researchers assume that a third factor—discrimination against women—accounts for the remainder (Pear, 1987). Because discrimination is illegal, it is often practiced in subtle ways, but it remains a major cause of economic disadvantage for working women (Benokraitis & Feagin, 1986). Corporate women often encounter a "glass ceiling," a barrier that, while formally denied by high company officials, effectively prevents women from rising above middle management. The traditional dominance of men at the highest corporate levels excludes women from "old boys' networks" that support many younger men on the way up. Then, too, some men are threatened by talented and ambitious women just as some are uneasy about interacting with colleagues whom they find sexually attractive.

For a variety of reasons, then, women earn less than men even within a single occupational category. As shown in Table 13-5, this disparity varies according to type of work, but in only one of these selected job classifications do women earn more than 70 percent of what men do (clerical and related occupations).

Gender and Education

Women have traditionally been discouraged, and sometimes formally excluded, from higher education because advanced schooling was thought to be unnecessary for homemakers. However, in 1990, 54 percent of all bachelor's degrees were earned by women (*Women in the Labour Force*, 1990–1991).

As noted earlier, men and women still tend to pursue different courses of study in university, although less so than in the past. However, women continue to be under-represented in two fields of study in particular, engineering and applied science (14.2 percent in engineering and 27.9 percent in mathematical and physical sciences (*Women in the Labour Force*, 1990–1991). On the other hand, women received over half of all degrees awarded in education (60.8 percent) fine and applied arts (58.9 percent) and the humanities (56.5 percent).

Women now enjoy more opportunities for postgraduate education, often a springboard to high-prestige jobs. In 1975 women earned 28.2 percent of all master's degrees, while in 1988, the figure had risen to 44.9 percent. Women earned 30.6 percent of all doctoral degrees by 1988, but education was the only

CRITICAL THINKING

Corporate Women: The "Mommy-Track" Controversy

The facts of corporate life are changing. Once the preserve of male executives and female support workers, management positions are now being occupied by women in record numbers. This is good news for corporations, because women are among the top university and business school graduates in Canada. The end of the post-World War II baby boom has reduced the supply of corporate workers, while the rapid growth in administrative positions in the new "information economy" has increased the demand for talented people. Overall, there are no longer enough men (and even fewer *good* men) to fill all the positions. Speaking purely in terms of the bottom line, corporations need women.

At the same time, the corporate world is decidedly unfriendly to women. Felice N. Schwartz—founder and president of Catalyst, an organization that promotes the careers of

women—explains the problem this way: by trying to make women equal to men in the workplace, we now ignore *maternity*, the most crucial difference between the two sexes. Many young adults want to divide their time

and energy between a career and young children. Currently, Schwartz claims, doing this is easy for men, but almost impossible for women. As evidence, she points out that, by age forty, 90 percent of executive men have children, but only 35 percent of executive women do. Men, in other words, do not face a conflict between family and career, as long as their wives take responsibility for child care.

Businesses have long been uneasy about women employees having children because, under current policies, motherhood takes women away from their jobs. Professional women usually start thinking about having children in their early thirties, after corporations have invested almost a decade in training them. Paradoxically, when a corporate woman becomes a mother, her company is likely to pressure her to decide between the company and her family. But forcing such a choice is unfair

TABLE 13-5   EARNINGS OF FULL-TIME CANADIAN WORKERS, BY SEX, 1990

Selected Occupational Categories	Income		Women's Income as a Percentage of Men's
	Men	Women	
Managerial, administrative & related occupations	$47,446	$28,299	59.6%
Occupations in social sciences and related fields	$46,485	$22,634	48.7%
Teaching and related occupations	$40,600	$26,645	65.6%
Occupations in medicine and health	$57,424	$24,331	42.4%
Clerical and related occupations	$22,549	$16,831	74.6%
Sales occupations	$27,562	$13,968	50.7%
Service occupations	$20,146	$10,266	51.0%
Farming & horticultural occupations	$15,278	$ 9,561	62.3%
Machining and related occupations	$29,152	$17,458	59.9%
Mining and quarrying (including oil and gas field) occupations	$36,565	$20,814	56.9%

SOURCE: Statistics Canada, Employment Income by Occupation: The Nation. *April 1993. Cat. No. 93-332.*

because women usually want *both* career and family. Currently, however, many mothers end up leaving their careers; when that occurs, both the corporations and the women themselves lose out.

The solution to the problem, Schwartz suggests, is for corporations to develop two tracks for women executives, a "career track" and a "career and family track." Women who wish to put their careers first (even if they have children) should be identified early and given as much opportunity and encouragement as the best and most ambitious men.

"Career and family women"—the majority of women, in Schwartz's view—value their occupations, but are willing to forgo some professional advancement so they can care for their children. These women can be a vital asset to a company, Schwartz continues, especially in the middle-management positions currently

staffed by less competent men. By creating positions of moderate responsibility, with part-time, flex-time, or job-sharing options, corporations would allow women to combine career and child rearing. Women often bring much-needed creativity and enthusiasm to jobs traditionally held by men who have stalled in their careers. Finally, a "career and family" option should never rule out women returning to the "career track" at a later time. Whatever women eventually decide to do, a twin-track program allows corporations to recover their investment from past training and gain future benefits from loyal workers whose personal needs are being met.

Schwartz's proposal has generated a heated controversy. Some critics fear that creating a "mommy track" would embolden those who claim that women have a weaker attachment to their careers, thereby undermining

women's gains in the workplace. And because such a plan is unlikely to apply to men, critics charge, it may reinforce the traditional notion that women are simply unsuited to management. Thus, critics conclude, Schwartz's proposal will compromise women's position in the corporate workplace rather than bolstering it.

Schwartz disagrees. Women, she claims, have demonstrated that they are the equal of men in any kind of work. Because roughly 40 percent of management positions are now held by women, corporations have an unprecedented responsibility to give women more choices about how they do their jobs. By expanding the range of choices open to women, corporations will defuse the conflict between careers and children. In the process, corporations will benefit from more productive and satisfied employees.

SOURCE: Schwartz (1989).

field of study where women were awarded the majority of PhDs—51.1 percent (*Women in the Labour Force,* 1990–1991).

A growing number of women are pursuing academic programs that were until recently virtually all male. Women's share of degrees in medicine, engineering, applied sciences, mathematics, and physical sciences has grown since 1975. For instance, in medicine, the percentages of degrees awarded to women rose from 24.3 percent in 1975 to 40.5 percent in 1988 (*Women in the Work Force,* 1990–1991).

However, men still outnumber women in many professional fields. In a culture that still defines high-paying professions (and the drive and competitiveness needed to succeed in them) as masculine, women may be discouraged from completing professional education after they begin their postgraduate

studies (Fiorentine, 1987). Nonetheless, the proportion of women in professional schools and the professions is rising steadily.

Gender and Politics

Before 1918, women could not vote in federal elections. Until 1919 no women were allowed to sit in the House of Commons, and until 1929, no women were allowed to sit in the Senate of Canada (*Canada 125th Anniversary Yearbook,* 1992). Women were banned from voting in national elections in the U.S.A. until 1920. It was not until 1940 that all eligible women in the country could vote in both federal and provincial elections. Table 13-6 cites milestones in women's gradual movement into Canadian political life.

Today women are involved in all levels of politics in Canada. Still, the largest proportion of women politicians is found in the municipal arena, where women can remain close to home and their caretaking responsibilities. Women are also well-represented on local schoolboards, where they can, again, act on their normative and institutionalized "responsibility" for their children.

There are, however, signs of change. Currently, 13 percent of the representatives of the House of Commons are women (Anderson, 1991:143). Just under 20 percent of the candidates in the 1988 federal election were women. Half of these female candidates ran for the N.D.P. The Canadian Advisory Council on the Status of Women has stated that, if the number of women in the House of Commons continues to increase at the rate it did between the 1984 and 1988 elections, it will take 9 elections or 45 years (approximately) before there will be equal numbers of men and women in the House.

In 1989 the N.D.P. became the first main political party to elect a woman leader—Audrey McLaughlin. In June of 1993, Kim Campbell became the first female prime minister after the resignation of the former prime minister, Brian Mulroney. At the time of writing, she had just announced an election for October 25, 1993. When you read this you will know whether or not Canada elected its first female prime minister: either Kim Campbell or Audrey McLaughlin.

Minority Women

If minorities (see Chapter 12, "Race and Ethnicity") are socially disadvantaged, are minority women doubly so? Generally speaking, yes. First, there is the disadvantage associated with race and ethnicity. Females of aboriginal background have both the lowest labor force participation rate and the second-highest unemployment rate. Their unemployment level, at 28.2 percent, is well over twice that of non-aboriginal women. The median income from all sources for aboriginal women is $6,817. Women of mixed aboriginal and non-aboriginal background fared slightly better, with a median income of $8,545 (*Women in Canada,* 1990).

Chapter 10 ("Social Class in Canada") noted that women are becoming a larger proportion of this nation's poor. The primary reason for this trend is that more families are headed by women, and this pattern puts families at risk of poverty. In 1990, 40 percent of single-parent families headed by women were poor

TABLE 13-6   MILESTONES FOR WOMEN IN CANADIAN POLITICS

Women's Rights

1916	Women in Manitoba, Alberta, and Saskatchewan gain right to vote in provincial elections.
1917	Women with property permitted to hold office in Saskatchewan. Women in British Columbia and Ontario gain right to vote in provincial elections.
1918	Women gain full federal franchise. Women in Nova Scotia gain right to vote in provincial elections.
1919	Women in New Brunswick gain right to vote in provincial elections.
1920	Uniform franchise established through the *Dominion Election Act,* making permanent the right of women to be elected to Parliament.
1922	Women in Prince Edward Island gain right to vote and to hold elected office.
1925	Women over 25 gain right to vote in Newfoundland.
1929	Women are deemed "persons" and can therefore be appointed to the Senate after the British Privy Council overturns Supreme Court of Canada's 1928 *Persons Case* decision, which had interpreted the BNA Act to mean women were not "persons" and could therefore not be appointed to the Senate.
1940	Women in Quebec gain right to vote in provincial elections, completing enfranchisement of women in Canada.
1983	*Canadian Human Rights Act* amended to prohibit sexual harassment and to ban discrimination on basis of pregnancy and family or marital status.

SOURCE: *Statistics Canada,* Canada's 125th Anniversary Yearbook, 1992. *Ottawa, October, 1991.*

(Anderson, 1991), in contrast to 4.9 percent of those headed by men.

Are Women a Minority?

In Chapter 12 ("Race and Ethnicity") a minority was defined as a category of people both socially disadvantaged and identifiable by physical or cultural traits. In a patriarchal society, women fit this definition, since they contend with a number of social barriers because of their sex, as we have explained.

Even so, most white women do *not* think of themselves as members of a minority (Hacker, 1951; Lengermann & Wallace, 1985). This is partly because, more than racial and ethnic minorities, white women belong to families at higher social levels. Yet, within every social class, women typically have less income, wealth, and power than men do. In fact, patriarchy makes women dependent for their social standing on men—first their fathers and later their husbands (J. Bernard, 1981).

Another reason that women may not consider themselves a minority is that they have been socialized to accept their situation as natural. A woman taught conventional ideas about gender believes that she should be deferential to men.

In sum, women—especially the relatively privileged—may not think of themselves as a minority. Yet as a category of people in Canada, women have both a distinctive identity and social disadvantages just as other minorities do.

Violence against Women

Perhaps the most wrenching kind of suffering that our society imposes on women is violence. As we explained in Chapter 8 ("Deviance"), official statistics reveal that criminal violence has an overwhelmingly male cast. This is not surprising since aggressiveness is a trait our culture defines as masculine. (What, for example, makes a man a "wimp" according to our norms and values? What, by contrast, makes him a "real man"?) Furthermore, a great deal of "manly" violence is directed against women, which might also be expected since much of what is culturally defined as feminine is devalued and even despised.

Because violence is commonplace in our society, and closely linked to gender, it arises most often where men and women interact most intensively. Richard Gelles (cited in Roesch, 1984) argues that, with the exception of the police and the military, the family is the most violent group in North America. Individuals are more likely to be attacked at home, Gelles continues, than they are in any other setting. Both sexes suffer from family violence although, by and large, women sustain more serious injuries than men do (Straus & Gelles, 1986; Schwartz, 1987; McLeod, 1987; Gelles & Cornell, 1990; De Keseredy and Hinch, 1991). Chapter 15 ("Family") examines family violence in more detail.

Violence against women also occurs in casual relationships. As Chapter 8 ("Deviance") explained, the notion that sexual violence involves strangers is a myth; most rapes, for instance, are perpetrated by men known (and sometimes even trusted) by women. A tendency toward sexual violence, in other words, is built into our way of life. Dianne F. Herman (1992)

argues that all forms of violence against women—from the wolf whistles that intimidate women on city streets to a pinch in a crowded subway to physical assaults that occur at home—are expressions of a "rape culture." By this, Herman means that violence is used by men as a means to dominate women. Sexual violence, then, is fundamentally about *power* rather than sex; that is why it is properly studied as a dimension of gender stratification (Griffin, 1982). Moreover, Herman argues, it is not primarily "weirdos" and misfits who engage in violence against women. Because our patriarchal way of life defines the control of women as normative, men who exercise power in this way are actually well adjusted to their surroundings. To these men, sexual violence forms a strategy to generate fear—and, ultimately, compliance—among women. No wonder surveys indicate that women are several times more likely than men to be afraid even when walking in their own neighborhoods (N.O.R.C., 1991).

Sexual Harassment

The 1991 Senate hearings in the U.S. that led to the confirmation of Supreme Court Justice Clarence Thomas drew national attention to the issue of **sexual harassment**, which can be defined as *comments, gestures, or physical contact of a sexual nature that is deliberate, repeated, and unwelcome*. Anita Hill, a law professor and former colleague, alleged that Thomas harassed her during the time they worked together for the federal government. The Senate never clearly resolved the specific allegations made by Hill and vigorously denied by Thomas; however, people across North America lined up on one side or the other as the episode touched off a debate that promises to significantly redefine the norms of workplace interaction between the sexes. Carlton Masters, formerly Ontario's Agent General to the United States, was recently forced to leave his position under charges of sexual harassment. Again, debate and controversy about the changing meanings of acceptable workplace behaviors have followed the charges.

Both men and women can be victims of sexual harassment. For two reasons, however, the victims of harassment are typically women. First, because our culture encourages men to be sexually assertive and to view women in sexual terms, sexuality can easily find its way into social interaction in the workplace, on the campus, and elsewhere. Second, most individuals in positions of power—including business executives, physicians, bureau chiefs, assembly line supervisors,

Although allegations of sexual harassment made by Anita Hill against Clarence Thomas did not prevent his appointment to the U.S. Supreme Court, the incident brought this issue to the attention of the entire continent. Just as important, mass media coverage of the case made it all too clear that national power is in the hands of men.

professors, and military officers—are men who typically oversee the work of women. Surveys carried out in widely different work settings confirm that women find the problem of sexual harassment to be widespread; generally, between one-third and one-half of respondents report receiving some form of recent unwanted sexual attention (Loy & Stewart, 1984; Paul, 1991; Canadian Advisory Council on the Status of Women, 1993). In one study of American colleges, one-third of women students reported unwanted sexual advances from their male teachers (Dziech & Weiner, 1984). Yet only four out of ten women who experience sexual harassment at work take any formal action (Canadian Advisory Council on the Status of Women, 1993). It is encouraging to note that sexual harassment has recently been ruled a compensable injury under the Ontario Workers' Compensation Act (Deverell, 1990).

Sexual harassment is sometimes blatant and direct, as when a supervisor solicits sexual favors from a subordinate coupled with threats of reprisals if the advances are refused. Behavior of this kind—which not only undermines the dignity of an individual but prevents her from earning a living—is widely condemned. Courts have declared such *quid pro quo* sexual harassment (the Latin phrase means "one thing in return for another") to be illegal and a form of discrimination that violates civil rights.

However, the problem of harassment frequently involves subtle behavior—sexual teasing, innuendos,

off-color jokes, pin-ups displayed in the workplace—none of which any individual may intend to be harassing to a specific subordinate or co-worker. In effect, however, such actions may create a *hostile environment* that is interpreted as sexual harassment (Cohen, 1991; Paul, 1991). Sexual harassment of this kind is inherently ambiguous, with each party seeing the behavior in question in a different light. For example, a man may think that showing romantic interest in a co-worker is paying the woman a compliment; she, on the other hand, may find his behavior offensive and a hindrance to her job performance.

Many women have long chafed at subtle forms of harassment. Untangling precisely what constitutes a hostile working environment, however, demands clearer standards of proper conduct than those we have now. Creating such guidelines—and educating the public to embrace them—is likely to take some time, since it means defining new forms of deviance (Cohen, 1991; Majka, 1991). In the end, courts (and, ultimately, the court of public opinion) will have to draw the line between what amounts to "reasonable friendliness" and behavior that is "unwarranted harassment."

As we have already explained, the entrance of women into the workplace has accelerated in recent decades. But merely having the two sexes working side by side does not in itself ensure that people will treat each other equally and with respect. Defining new moral and legal codes that will condemn and discourage sexual harassment will not be easy, as the controversy over the Thomas hearing revealed. But doing so is a necessary step toward protecting the rights of everyone in the workplace.

Pornography

Pornography underlies sexual violence as well. Defining pornography, however, has long been a vexing question, and the Supreme Court has been unable to formulate a single, specific standard to distinguish what is, and what is not, pornographic. Current law requires local cities and counties to decide for themselves what violates "community standards" of decency and lacks any redeeming social value. There is little doubt, however, that pornography (loosely defined) has a large following in Canada: X-rated videos, "900" telephone numbers providing sexual conversation, and a host of sexually explicit magazines together constitute a hugely profitable industry.

Traditionally, pornography was not tied to sexual violence at all. Rather, it was cast as a *moral* issue, a violation of cultural norms about how people should express their sexuality. National survey data show that pornography is still widely viewed in moral terms: 64 percent of adult women in Canada "feel that adult magazines are discriminatory towards women". In contrast, Canadian men are divided on this issue. Forty-five percent feel that adult magazines are discriminatory towards women, while 46 percent hold the opposite view (Bozinoff and Turcotte, 1993).

More recently, however, pornography has come under attack for fostering a social climate that demeans women. From this point of view, pornography is framed as a *political* issue because pornographic material graphically underscores the notion that men should control both sexuality and women. Catherine MacKinnon (1987) has denounced pornography as one foundation of male dominance because it dehumanizes women as the subservient playthings of men. Worth noting, in this context, is that the term pornography is derived from the Greek word *porne*, meaning a harlot who acts as a man's sexual slave.

A related charge asserts that pornography promotes specific acts of violence against women. Certainly anyone who has viewed recent "hard-core" videos can understand this assertion. Yet, using strict scientific standards, it is difficult to demonstrate a clear cause-and-effect relationship between what people look at and how they act. However, research does bear out the conclusion that pornography encourages men to think of women as objects rather than as people (Mallamuth & Donnerstein, 1984; Attorney General's Commission on Pornography, 1986).

Like sexual harassment, the pornography issue raises complex and sometimes conflicting concerns (*Pornography and Prostitution in Canada*, 1985; Cole, 1989). Certainly most people object to material they find offensive, but most also endorse the right of free speech and wish to safeguard artistic expression. But pressure to restrict this kind of material is building as the result of an unlikely coalition of conservatives (who oppose pornography on moral grounds) and progressives (who condemn it for political reasons).

Anti-pornography activists made human rights law a new focus for debate recently when they argued that the presence of adult magazines in corner stores is a form of discrimination against women. Because federal obscenity laws prohibit only "hard core" pornography such as sex acts involving violence, sex with children, or especially degrading or dehumanizing acts, neither explicit depictions of sex nor naked women are illegal (*Maclean's*, May 10, 1993).

Theoretical Analysis of Gender

Both the structural-functional and social-conflict paradigms point up the importance of gender to social organization.

Structural-Functional Analysis

The structural-functional paradigm views society as a complex system of many separate but integrated parts. In this view, every social structure contributes to the overall operation of society.

As explained in Chapter 3 ("Culture"), the earliest hunting and gathering societies had limited ability to challenge biological facts and forces. Lacking effective birth control, women experienced frequent pregnancies, and the responsibilities of child care kept them close to home more or less continually (Lengermann & Wallace, 1985). As a result, social norms encouraged women to center their lives around home and children. Likewise, based on their greater short-term strength, norms guided men to the pursuit of game and other tasks away from the home. This sexual division of labor created feminine and masculine worlds.

As long as technology remains simple, the biological facts of sex and the cultural facts of gender closely intertwine. This is not a matter of biological imperative so much as a cultural strategy that preindustrial societies adopt to survive. Over many generations, the sex-based division of labor becomes institutionalized, built into the structure of society and taken for granted.

Industrial technology opens up a vastly greater range of cultural possibilities. The muscles of humans and other animals no longer serve as the primary sources of energy, so the physical strength of men loses much of its earlier significance. At the same time, the ability to control reproduction gives women greater choice in shaping their lives. At this level of technological development, societies can unlock considerable amounts of talent by eroding traditional conceptions of gender. Yet change comes slowly, because gender-based assumptions about behavior are deeply embedded in social mores.

Talcott Parsons: Gender and Complementarity

In addition, as Talcott Parsons (1942, 1951, 1954) explained, gender differences form a social fabric that integrates society—at least in its traditional form. Gender lies at the heart of Parsons's theory of *complementary roles* by which men and women join together to form family units that, in turn, carry out other functions vital to the operation of society. Women are charged with maintaining the internal cohesion of the family, managing the household, and taking primary responsibility for raising children; men connect the family to the larger world, primarily by participating in the labor force. From this point of view, one would expect the increasing participation of women in the labor force to transform the traditional family.

Parsons further argued that the two sexes are exposed to distinctive patterns of socialization in order to prepare them for their respective adult roles. Boys and girls learn their appropriate gender identity and acquire skills and attitudes deemed appropriate to their sex. This explains the earlier observation that, destined for the labor force, boys are taught to be rational, self-assured, and competitive—a complex of traits that Parsons described as *instrumental*. To prepare girls for child rearing, their socialization stresses what Parsons called *expressive* qualities, such as emotional responsiveness and sensitivity to others.

Finally, according to Parsons, society promotes gender-linked behavior through various means of social control. This social guidance is partly internal: people who violate gender norms may experience guilt. It is also partly external, with the failure to display the normative gender traits provoking criticism from others. One notable method of fostering conformity, according to Parsons, is teaching each person that straying too far from accepted gender roles courts rejection by members of the opposite sex. In simple terms, women learn to view non-masculine men as sexually unattractive, while unfeminine women risk rejection by men.

Critical evaluation. Structural functionalism highlights the traditional complementarity of gender roles. From this point of view, gender integrates society both structurally (in terms of what people do) and morally (in terms of what people believe). This approach was very influential during mid-century; however, for several reasons it is rarely used today by researchers exploring the impact of gender on society.

First, critics charge that this analysis supports a vision of society that is less and less consistent with how people actually live. For example, many women have traditionally worked outside the home out of economic necessity, and the proportion doing so is rising steadily. Another problem, in the eyes of critics, is that Parsons's analysis minimizes the personal strains and social costs produced by rigid, traditional gender roles (Giele, 1988). Finally, to those whose goals include equality for the two sexes, this approach is patently unappealing. From this perspective, what Parsons describes as gender complementarity simply amounts to male domination.

Social-Conflict Analysis

From a social-conflict point of view, gender involves not just differences in action but disparities in power. Conventional gender patterns historically have benefited men while subjecting women to prejudice and discrimination comparable to that experienced by racial and ethnic minorities (Hacker, 1951, 1974; Collins, 1971; Lengermann & Wallace, 1985). Thus gender inequality promotes not cohesion but tension and conflict as men seek to protect their privileges while women challenge the status quo.

A social-conflict analysis of gender also places *sexism* at center stage. A web of notions about female inferiority that justify depriving women of opportunities and subjecting them to manipulation and violence, sexism supports lower pay for women in the workplace, the exclusion of women from positions of power in national affairs, and the subordination of women in the home.

"Hire him. He's got great legs."

SEX DISCRIMINATION ISN'T FUNNY.
SUPPORT THE NATIONAL ORGANIZATION FOR WOMEN
28 EAST 56 STREET N.Y.C. 10022

For generations, the evaluation of women in terms of physical appearance instead of job performance contributed to unequal occupational opportunities. By turning the tables, this educational poster helps people to see how grossly unfair this practice really is.

As noted in earlier chapters, the social-conflict paradigm draws heavily on the ideas of Karl Marx. Ironically, in light of his other criticisms of society, Marx paid little attention to gender, focusing his work almost exclusively on men. His friend and collaborator Friedrich Engels, however, did develop a conflict analysis of gender that brings to bear on this issue Marx's general ideas about social classes (1902; orig. 1884).

Friedrich Engels: Gender and Class

Engels suggested that, although they were different, the activities of women and men in hunting and gathering societies had comparable importance. A successful hunt may have brought men great prestige, but the vegetation gathered by women constituted most of a society's food supply (Leacock, 1978). As technological ad-

vances led to a productive surplus, however, social equality and communal sharing gave way to the notion of private property and, ultimately, to stratified social classes. At this point, men gained pronounced power over women. With surplus wealth to dispose of, men of the upper class took a keen interest in their progeny, who would inherit their estates. In Engels's view, this control of property encouraged the creation of monogamous marriage and the family. Ideally, then, men could be certain of paternity and, by identifying their offspring—especially sons—they could plan for their wealth to be passed on to the next generation of males. For their part, women built their lives around bearing and raising children. (For a feminist critique of this analysis, see the box "Patriarchy: A Feminist Perspective" in Chapter 1.)

Engels contended that capitalism intensified this male domination. First, capitalism created more wealth, which conferred greater privilege on men as the owners of property, the heirs of property, and the primary wage earners. Second, an expanding capitalist economy depended on defining people—especially women—as consumers and encouraging them to seek personal fulfilment through buying and owning products. Third, to support men working in factories, women were assigned the task of maintaining the home. The double exploitation of capitalism, then, lies in paying low wages for male labor and *no* wages for female work (Eisenstein, 1979; Barry, 1983; Jagger, 1983; Vogel, 1983).

Critical evaluation. The social-conflict paradigm stresses inequality; thus any social-conflict analysis of gender must highlight how societies place the sexes in differential positions with regard to privilege, prestige, and power. As a result, conflict approaches are decidedly critical of conventional gender roles.

Social-conflict analysis, too, has critics who cite its weaknesses. One problem, voiced by people with traditional attitudes, is that social-conflict analysis casts conventional families—historically defined by traditionalists as morally positive—as a source of social evil. Second, from a more practical point of view, social-conflict analysis minimizes the extent to which women and men live together cooperatively, and often quite happily, in families. A third problem with this approach, at least for some critics, is its contention that capitalism stands at the root of gender stratification. Societies with socialist economic systems—including the People's Republic of China and the former Soviet Union—have also been strongly patriarchal.

Feminism

Feminism is *the advocacy of social equality for the sexes, in opposition to patriarchy and sexism.* Feminism is not new to Canada. In the 1800s, a number of women worked, in isolated pockets, supporting "maternal feminism" (the spread of the purer values of home and family), temperance, and thinking of public participation as a woman's duty (Brodie and Vickers, 1985). The primary objective of the early women's movement was securing the right to vote, but after suffrage for women was achieved in 1940, other disadvantages persisted. As a response, a "second wave" of feminism (sometimes termed the "New Women's Movement") swelled in the 1960s and continues to reshape our society today.

Basic Feminist Ideas

Feminism embraces a wide range of thinking about women and men; there are many issues on which people who consider themselves feminists disagree. Generally, though, all feminists share the view that our personal experiences are significantly linked to gender. How we think of ourselves (gender identity), how we act (gender roles), and our privilege or deprivation relative to the opposite sex (gender stratification) are all derived from how our society attaches meaning and social standing to the two sexes. Here are five ideas widely considered to be central to feminism.

1. **The importance of change.** First and foremost, feminism, which is critical of the status quo, advocates equitable social standing for women and men. Thus feminism calls not only for sociological thinking but also for political action. A basic feminist contention holds that "the personal is political." A feminist perspective on human thought and interaction demands that we consider how culture defines masculinity in terms of power over others while constructing femininity as a model of altruism.

2. **Expanding human choice.** Feminists argue that cultural conceptions of gender divide the full range of human qualities into two distinct and limited spheres: the female world of emotions and cooperation, and the male world of rationality and competition. As an alternative, feminists pursue a "reintegration of humanity" (French, 1985). Feminism holds that every human being is capable of developing *all* human traits. Through a process of feminist resocialization, then, all people can pursue their human potential without limits based on gender.

3. **Eliminating gender stratification.** Feminism seeks an end to laws and cultural norms that confer privilege on men while simultaneously limiting the opportunities of women to gain education, income, and prestige from the widest range of work. Supporters of the women's movement oppose the historical pattern by which the female half of the population has been subject to decisions made by the male half—whether in the privacy of the home or in the public world of national politics.

4. **Ending sexual violence.** A major objective of the New Women's Movement is eliminating sexual violence. In a patriarchal society, sexual relationships between men and women often mirror power relationships between the sexes in the larger society (Millet, 1970; J. Bernard, 1973; Dworkin, 1987). Feminists assert that men's more powerful position in society leads to the violent subordination of women, in the form of rape, domestic abuse, sexual harassment, and the degradation of women through pornography. Thus feminism actively campaigns against all violence directed against women by working to transform the basic power relationship between the sexes.

5. **Promoting sexual autonomy.** Finally, feminism seeks to ensure that women have control of their own sexuality and decisions involving reproduction. Feminists advocate the right of women to obtain birth control information—something that was illegal in some states as recently as the 1960s. In addition, most feminists support a woman's right to choose whether to bear children or to terminate a pregnancy. Feminism as an ideology does not favor abortion, but it holds that the decision to bear children should be made by women themselves rather than by men—such as husbands, physicians, and legislators. Many feminists also support gay peoples' drive to overcome prejudice and discrimination in a culture dominated by heterosexuality. More than gay men, lesbians suffer distinct social disadvantages because they violate both the cultural norm of heterosexuality and the norm that men should control the sexuality of women (Deckard, 1979; Barry, 1983; Jagger, 1983).

Ireland is one of the few industrial societies in the world in which abortion is constitutionally banned. Irish law forbids physicians even from giving out information about how to obtain an abortion abroad. When fourteen-year-old Ann Lovett became pregnant—as the result of rape—the government initially denied her request to travel to England to terminate the pregnancy. International protest eventually drove officials to relent, and Lovett did receive the abortion she sought.

Variations within Feminism

Because the goal of sexual equality means different things to different people, and because there are various ways to promote a more equitable society, more than one kind of feminism exists today. Although the distinctions among them are far from clear-cut, three general types of feminist thinking will be described briefly (Barry, 1983; Jagger, 1983; Stacey, 1983; Vogel, 1983; Hansen & Philipson, 1990).

Liberal Feminism

Liberal feminism is rooted in classic liberal thinking that individuals should be free to develop their own abilities and pursue their own interests. Liberal feminists accept the basic organization of our society but hold that women do not yet share the same rights as men. If people are to be evaluated on their personal merits rather than according to their race or sex, in other words, the sexes must have the same opportunities to shape their lives (Jagger, 1983). To that end, much as liberals endorse the civil rights movement in support of African

Americans, liberal feminists endorse the Equal Rights Amendment and oppose prejudice and discrimination that have historically limited women's opportunities.

Those supporting this approach advocate reproductive freedom for all women. Only if women can choose whether to bear children, and only if both parents share the responsibilities of child rearing, can women and men have equal opportunities in their working lives. For the same reason, liberal feminism advocates the right of women to maternity leave and child care.

Finally, liberal feminists support the family as a social institution, but they point out that families may need to change in order to accommodate the ambitions of both women and men. With their strong belief in the rights of individuals, liberal feminists do not see all women as a single entity, thinking that all women must advance for some to advance. The key to women's liberation (and that of men) lies primarily in ending legal and cultural constraints that prevent individuals from realizing their personal goals.

Socialist Feminism

Socialist feminism evolved from Marxist conflict analysis, but largely as a criticism of this approach's inattention to gender issues. As noted earlier, Engels placed Marx's general approach in a feminist context as he claimed that the root of patriarchy is private property. Furthermore, explained Engels, although capitalism did not create patriarchy, it has intensified this form of domination by concentrating wealth and power in the hands of a small number of men.

The family, an institution basically acceptable to liberal feminists, is targeted for change by socialist feminists. The "bourgeois family," fostered by capitalism, oppresses women by keeping them in the home where they work without wages and remain economically dependent on men. In addition, this family form effectively prevents women from politically organizing with other women and men, and restricts opportunities so that women derive little personal satisfaction from any endeavors other than consuming products. In place of this family system, which Engels dismissed as "domestic slavery," socialist feminism advocates a state-centered society, which frees women by collectively performing tasks like cooking and child care. This implies that a class revolution is the prerequisite for a gender revolution.

Clearly, socialist feminists conclude that the reforms sought by liberal feminism are, by themselves, insufficient to produce equality of the sexes. Only through a socialist revolution—which simultaneously banishes private property and reorganizes life in a co-operative manner—can women and men be freed from historic oppression. Since sweeping changes are required to approach this goal, women and men must pursue their personal liberation together, rather than individually, as liberal feminists maintain. (Further discussion of socialism is found elsewhere, especially in Chapter 19, "The Economy and Work.")

Radical Feminism

Radical feminism argues that the root of sexual oppression is the concept of gender itself. The historical foundation of gender, radical feminism maintains, lies in the biological differences of sex by which women carry and bear children. The family, from this point of view, does not constitute merely an economic arrangement as Engels conceived it, but rather a system that institutionalizes heterosexual relations and inevitably confines women to the monotonous burdens of child care.

What is the alternative? Until recently, options were few because the biological process of reproduction was beyond human control. But now advancing technology has made conventional heterosexual parenting—and thus the historical family—unnecessary. So radical feminism envisions a revolution more radical than that sought by Marxists. New reproductive technology (see Chapter 15, "Family"), which already allows conception outside the body, holds the promise of separating women's bodies from the process of childbearing. With the demise of motherhood, radical feminists reason, the entire family system could be left behind, liberating the two sexes from the tyranny of gender itself.

For the radical feminist vision to be realized, four other objectives must be achieved. First, similar to the argument made by socialist feminism, technology must ensure a level of production that meets all human needs so that no one is economically dependent on anyone else. Second, responsibilities for raising children cannot fall on individuals; the tasks of parenthood must become the responsibility of society as a whole. Third, since no woman should have to bear children nor conform to conventional definitions of motherhood (or men contend with fatherhood), historical definitions of children as dependent on parents and families must be revised. Thus radical feminism advocates a program of children's rights (Jagger, 1983). Fourth, conventional thinking about sexuality itself—including norms that favor heterosexuality over homosexuality or demand that sex take place only within certain relational forms like marriage—must be abandoned (Dworkin, 1987).

If this radical feminist agenda were put in place, the resulting society would be vastly different from any known to date. From this point of view, society would evolve toward the goal of eliminating all social distinctions based on sex: that is, toward the elimination of gender.

Resistance to Feminism

Feminism has encountered resistance from both men and women who embrace dominant cultural ideas about gender. Some men oppose feminism for the same reasons that many whites have historically resisted drives for social equality for people of color: they want to preserve privileges linked to their social position. Other men, including those who are neither rich nor powerful, distrust a social movement (especially its more radical expressions) that advocates socialism or seeks to abolish traditional marriage, family, and parenthood. Further, for some men, feminism threatens an important basis of their status and self-respect: their masculinity. Men who have been socialized to value strength and dominance understandably feel uneasy about the feminist notion that they can also be gentle and warm (Doyle, 1983).

Some women, as well, shy away from feminism. For example, women who center their lives around their husbands and children may consider feminism a threat to their most cherished values. From this point of view, feminism amounts to an effort to revise the law, the workplace, and the family—in short, to remake all of society—according to the radical political agenda of a few. Feminists, then, would dispose of the traditional values that have guided life and protected individual liberties in Canada for centuries. Additionally, some women believe that, in the process of recasting the conventional "feminine" spheres of life, including the home and the family, women will lose rather than gain power and personal identity (Marshall, 1985).

Recently, federal government support for feminist organizations has decreased. Support for these organizations has been undermined by right-wing members of Parliament and a group called REAL women (Realistic Equal Active for Life). REAL women claim that their mission is to save the family as the foundation of Canadian society. They argue against abortion, day care, affirmative action, pay equity, family law reforms, and homosexuality. Yet NAC (National Action Committee on the Status of Women) which is an umbrella organization for around five hundred women's groups, representing 4 million women, pursues various feminist causes and continues to lobby the government around numerous issues on the feminist agenda such as violence against women, day care, equal pay for work of equal value, and so on.

A final area of resistance to feminism involves *how* women's social standing should be improved. Although a large majority of people in North America believe women should have equal rights, most also maintain that women should advance individually, according to their abilities. In a U.S. survey, 70 percent of respondents claimed that women should expect to get ahead on the basis of their own training and qualifications; only 10 percent thought women's rights groups represented the best approach (N.O.R.C., 1991:387). It appears that, at present, resistance to feminism is primarily directed at its socialist and radical variants; by contrast, there is widespread support for the principles that underlie liberal feminism.

Gender in the Twenty-First Century

Predictions about the future are, at best, informed speculation. Just as economists disagree about the likely inflation rate a year from now, sociologists differ in their views on the future of our society. Yet we can venture some general observations about gender, today and in the future.

To begin, change has been remarkable. The position of women in Canada a century ago was one of clear and striking subordination. Husbands controlled property in marriage, women were barred from most areas of the labor force, and no woman could vote. Although women remain socially disadvantaged, the movement toward greater equality has been dramatic. Perhaps nowhere is this change more evident than in the workplace. A century ago, women were defined as unsuitable for paid work; today's economy, by contrast, *depends* on the earnings of women (Hewlett, 1990). This economic trend will continue: two-thirds of people entering the work force during the 1990s will be women.

Many factors have contributed to this transformation. Perhaps most important, industrialization both broadened the range of human activity and shifted the nature of work from physically demanding tasks that favored male strength to jobs that require human thought and imagination, placing the talents of women and men on an even footing. Additionally, medical technology has given us control over reproduction, so women's lives are less circumscribed by unwanted pregnancies.

Many women and men have also made deliberate efforts in pursuit of social equality. Feminism seeks to end constraints imposed on people by a society that assigns activities and channels self-expression on the basis of sex. As these efforts continue, the social changes in the twenty-first century may be even greater than those we have already witnessed.

In the midst of change, strong opposition to feminism persists. Many feminists are fearful of legal changes that will undercut women's reproductive options, setting back a generation of hard-won gains. On a broader front, gender still forms an important foundation of personal identity and of family life, and it is deeply woven into the moral fabric of our society. Therefore, attempts to change cultural ideas about the two sexes will no doubt continue to provoke considerable opposition.

On balance, while dramatic and radical change in the way we understand gender may not occur in the short run, the movement toward a society in which women and men enjoy equal rights and opportunities seems certain to gain strength.

Summary

1. Sex is a biological concept; a human fetus is female or male from the moment of conception. People with the rare condition of hermaphroditism combine the biological traits of both sexes. Transsexuals are people who deliberately choose to surgically alter their sex.

2. Heterosexuality is the dominant sexual orientation in virtually every society in the world. Homosexuals make up a small but significant proportion of the population of Canada. Sexual orientation is not always clear-cut; many people are bisexual.

3. Gender refers to human traits that a culture attaches to each sex. Gender varies historically and across cultures.

4. Some degree of patriarchy exists in every society. The ideology of sexism justifies male dominance, just as racism supports racial dominance.

5. The socialization process links gender to personal identity (gender identity) and distinctive activities (gender roles). The major agents of socialization—the family, peer groups, schools, and the mass media—reinforce cultural definitions of what is masculine and feminine.

6. Gender stratification entails numerous social disadvantages for women. Although most women are now in the paid labor force, a majority of working women hold clerical or service jobs. Unpaid housework also remains predominantly a task performed by women.

7. On average, women earn about two-thirds as much as men do. This disparity is due to differences in jobs, family patterns, and discrimination.

8. Historically excluded from higher education, women now form a slight majority of all university students and receive half of all master's degrees. Men still earn a majority of doctorates and professional degrees.

9. The number of women in politics—especially on the local level—has increased sharply in recent decades. Still, the vast majority of national political officials are men.

10. Minority women have greater social disadvantages than white women. Overall, minority women earn only half as much as white men, and almost half the households headed by minority women are poor.

11. On the basis of their distinctive identity and social disadvantages, all women can be considered members of a social minority.

12. Structural-functional analysis suggests that distinctive roles for males and females constitute a survival strategy in preindustrial societies. In industrial societies, extensive gender inequality becomes dysfunctional, yet long-established cultural norms related to gender change slowly. According to Talcott Parsons, complementary gender roles serve to integrate the family and the larger society.

13. Social-conflict analysis, which views gender in terms of economic inequality and social conflict, links gender stratification to the development of private property. Friedrich Engels claimed that capitalism intensified male dominance by devaluing women as homemakers working for no pay.

14. Feminism supports the social equality of the sexes and actively opposes patriarchy and sexism. Feminism advocates a shift toward greater choice for women and men, eliminating gender stratification, ending sexual violence against women, and promoting women's control over their own sexuality.

15. There are three main variants of feminist thinking. Liberal feminism seeks equal opportunity for both sexes within the current institutional arrangements; socialist feminism advocates abolishing private property as the means to forging gender equality; radical feminism proposes ending all social distinctions based on sex to create a gender-free society.

16. Because gender distinctions stand at the core of our way of life, feminism has encountered strong resistance. Yet the Canadian Human Rights Act of 1977 forbids discrimination on the basis of sex and the constitution guarantees the rights and freedoms in the Charter equally to males and females.

Key Concepts

female infanticide the practice of aborting female fetuses and the neglecting, or even actively killing, of infant girls by parents who would prefer to raise boys

feminism the advocacy of social equality for the sexes, in opposition to patriarchy and sexism

gender society's division of humanity, based on sex, into two distinctive categories

gender identity traits that females and males, guided by their culture, incorporate into their personalities

gender roles   (sex roles) attitudes and activities that a culture links to each sex

gender stratification   a society's unequal distribution of wealth, power, and privilege between the two sexes

hermaphrodite   a human being with some combination of female and male internal and external genitalia

matriarchy   a form of social organization in which females dominate males

patriarchy   a form of social organization in which males dominate females

primary sex characteristics   the genitals, used to reproduce the human species

secondary sex characteristics   physical traits, other than the genitals, that distinguish physiologically mature females and males

sex   the division of humanity into biological categories of female and male

sexism   the belief that one sex is innately superior to the other

sexual harassment   comments, gestures, or physical contact of a sexual nature that is deliberate, repeated, and unwelcome

sexual orientation   the manner in which people experience sexual arousal and achieve sexual pleasure

transsexuals   people who feel they are one sex though biologically they are the other

Suggested Readings

These three books delve into various issues raised in this chapter.

Joyce McCarl Nielsen. *Sex and Gender in Society: Perspectives on Stratification*. 2nd ed. Prospect Heights, IL: Waveland Press, 1991.

Linda L. Lindsey. *Gender Roles: A Sociological Perspective*. Englewood Cliffs, NJ: Prentice Hall, 1990.

Sara E. Rix, ed. *The American Woman 1990–91: A Status Report*. New York: W. W. Norton, 1990.

This useful source examines the sexual lives of young people in our culture.

Jules H. Masserman and Victor M. Uribe. *Adolescent Sexuality*. New York: Charles C. Thomas, 1990.

Here are two books about homosexuality. The first takes a sociological look at sexual orientation. The second sketches the fascinating historical context for the current debate about gays and the U.S. military.

David F. Greenberg. *The Construction of Homosexuality*. Chicago: The University of Chicago Press, 1988.

Allan Berube. *Coming Out Under Fire: The History of Gay Men and Women in World War Two*. New York: The Free Press, 1990.

Here the earning disparity between women and men is analyzed in historical perspective.

Claudia Goldin. *Understanding the Gender Gap: An Economic History of American Women*. New York: Oxford University Press, 1990.

This multinational research focuses on how social changes in various global regions have affected women's work and social standing.

Setenyi Shami, Lucine Taminian, Soheir A. Morsy, Zeinab Bashir El-Bakri, and El-Wathig Kameir. *Women in Arab Society: Work Patterns and Gender Relations in Egypt, Jordan, and Sudan*. New York: Berg, 1991.

Donald Meyer. *Sex and Power: The Rise of Women in America, Russia, Sweden, and Italy*. 2nd ed. Middletown, CT: Wesleyan University Press, 1989.

One notion about gender that has changed little over the years is the importance of physical beauty for women. This book argues that our culture sets up unrealistic and destructive standards of feminine attractiveness.

Naomi Wolf. *The Beauty Myth: How Beauty Images are Used Against Women*. New York: William Morrow, 1990.

The following books are publications of the Canadian Research Institute for the Advancement of Women, Statistics Canada, or the Advisory Council on the Status of Women. The first documents the nature and extent of women's health work in the home. The second is a description of the political participation of Canadian women both today and in historical context. The third publication provides a review of the status and role of women in Canada today and in a historial context. The fourth describes women's labor force participation. The fifth and sixth document the extent of wife abuse and the various "prevention" policies and programs associated with wife abuse.

Anita Fochs Heller. *Health and Home: Women as Health Guardians*. Ottawa: Canadian Advisory Council on the Status of Women, 1986.

M. Janine Brodie and Jill M. Vickers. "Canadian Women in Politics." Ottawa: Canadian Research Institute for the Advancement of Women, 1985.

Women in Canada: A Statistical Report. Ottawa: Statistics Canada, 1990.

Morley Gunderson, Leon Muszynski, and Jennifer Keck. *Women and Labour Market Poverty*. Ottawa: Canadian Advisory Council on the Status of Women, 1990.

L. MacLeod. *Wife Battering in Canada: The Vicious Circle.* Ottawa: Advisory Council on the Status of Women, 1980. L. MacLeod. *Battered but not Beaten: Preventing Wife Battering in Canada.* Ottawa, Advisory Council on the Status of Women, 1987.

This book describes the abuse of women in the home, in the streets, and in the corporate sector.
Walter S. De Keseredy and Ronald Hinch. *Woman Abuse: Sociological Perspective.* Toronto: Thompson Educational Pub. Inc., 1991.

This is an overview of sociological data and interpretations of Canadian women in the family and in the economy.
Susanna J. Wilson. *Women, the Family and the Economy.* Toronto: Prentice Hall Canada, 1986.

This is a collection of various interpretation of women's bodies.
Dawn H. Currie and Valerie Raoul. *Anatomy of Gender: Women's Struggle for the Body.* Ottawa: University of Ottawa Press, 1992.

This book examines the thesis that gender inequity is based on the alienation of men from reproduction.
Mary O'Brien. *The Politics of Reproduction.* Boston: Routledge and Kegan Paul, 1981.

This is a description and analysis of Smith's methodology of and for women.
Dorothy Smith. *The Everyday World as Problematic: A Feminist Sociology.* Toronto: University of Toronto Press, 1987.

This is an examination of women's lives over three generations in the company town of Flin, Flon, Manitoba.
Meg Luxton. *More than a Labour of Love: Three Generations of Women's Work in the Home.* Toronto: The Women's Press, 1980.

This book provides an overview of the gendered basis of the labor force.
Hugh Armstrong and Pat Armstrong. *The Double Ghetto: Canadian Women and their Segregated Work.* Toronto: McClelland & Stewart, 1978.

This is a critique of social science from the perspective of a feminist.
Margrit Eichler. *The Double Standard: A Feminist Critique of Feminist Social Science.* New York: St. Martin's Press, 1980.

AGING AND THE ELDERLY

The book *Final Exit* shot to the top of the best seller list in 1991. This is a book about dying—not about the death of a famous person, or a philosophical treatise about death, but rather a "how-to" manual that tells people how to commit suicide. *Final Exit* gives readers specific instructions on *how to kill themselves* in a host of ways, including taking sleeping pills, self-starvation, and suffocation with a plastic bag.

The author of *Final Exit* is Derek Humphrey, a founder and executive director of The Hemlock Society. This organization, founded in 1980, offers support and practical assistance to people who wish to die. Humphrey explains that the time has come for people to have access to a straightforward manual on how to end their own lives. The immediate and remarkable popularity of *Final Exit*—especially among the elderly—suggests that millions of people agree with him.

Not surprisingly, *Final Exit* has sparked controversy. While some people applaud the book as a humane effort to assist people who are painfully and terminally ill, others claim that it has encouraged suicide by people who are experiencing only temporary depression (Angelo, 1991). Several legal battles are also under way in Canada, testing laws that prohibit physicians and others from assisting in the death of a patient.

But the appearance of *Final Exit* also raises broader questions that are no less disturbing and controversial. As we shall explain in this chapter, the ranks of the elderly are swelling rapidly as more and more men and women live longer and longer. As a result, people are uneasy about their responsibilities toward aging parents. Officials worry that the health-care system is unable to meet the needs of older people, or can do so only by shortchanging the needs of younger people. And older people themselves are, on the one hand, fearful of not being able to afford medical care they may need and, on the other hand, alarmed at the prospect of losing control of their lives to a medical establishment that often seeks to prolong life at any cost.

In the 1990s, many issues relating to aging and the elderly will command the attention of policy makers, just as they will generate intense discussion among everyone else in Canada. In some respects, growing old in Canada has never been more inviting; poverty, confronted by many elderly a generation ago, has been greatly reduced. But many stubborn problems persist: older people, for example, continue to grapple with prejudice and discrimination. And, as unprecedented numbers of women and men in our society enter old age, new and daunting problems of aging loom on the horizon.

The Stone Angel

Hagar Shipley is a ninety-year-old woman described in great depth by Margaret Laurence in her novel, *The Stone Angel*. The story, simply put, is about Hagar's last short and even bitter attempt to retain her independence, particularly from her son and daughter-in-law with whom she lives. It also involves a rebellious and defiant growth toward new self-knowledge that she experiences in the latter part of her life. A few quotes to introduce this wonderful character follow.

In the first, she discusses the things that are evidence of her life.

> My shreds and remnants of years are scattered through [the house] visibly in lamps and vases, the needlepoint fire bench, the heavy oak chair from the Shipley place, the china cabinet and walnut sideboard from my father's house. There'd not be room for these in some cramped apartment. We'd have to put them into storage, or sell them. I don't want that. I couldn't leave them. If I am not somehow contained in them and in this house, something of all change caught and fixed here, eternal enough for my purposes, then I do not know where I am to be found at all. (p. 36)

She reflects on her appearance.

> I give a sideways glance at the mirror, and see a puffed face purpled with veins as though someone had scribbled over the skin with an indelible pencil. The skin itself is the silverish white of the creatures one fancies must live under the sea where the sun never reaches. Below the eyes the shadows bloom as though two soft black petals had been stuck there. The hair which should by rights be black is yellowed white, like damask stored too long in a damp basement.
>
> Well, Hagar Shipley, you are a sight for sore eyes, all right. (p. 79)
>
> For when I look in my mirror and beyond the changing shell that houses me, I see the eyes of Hagar Currie, the same dark eyes as when I first began to remember and to notice myself ... The eyes change least of all. (p. 38)

Lastly, she reminisces about the quality of her life.

> Pride was my wilderness, and the demon that led me there was fear. I was alone, never anything else, and never free, for I carried my chains within me, and they spread out from me and shackled all I touched. (p. 292)

SOURCE: Margaret Laurence,*The Stone Angel. Toronto: McClelland & Stewart, 1964.*

The Graying of Canada

A quiet but powerful revolution is reshaping Canada: the number of elderly people—women and men aged sixty-five and over—is increasing more than twice as fast as the population as a whole. The effects of this "graying of Canada" promise to be profound.

Some statistics bring this change into sharp focus. The average annual growth of the youth population over the last one hundred and twenty years has been 1.2 percent, and that of persons over 65 has been more than double this, at 2.7 percent. Today, the population over 65 makes up 11.6 percent of the whole population (*Report on the Demographic Situation in Canada*, 1992).

In just over a century, the life expectancy of Canadians has doubled and their average number of children has declined by a half. The age/sex pyramids for the Canadian population have shown and will continue to demonstrate dramatic shape changes (see Figure 14-1). As the "baby boomers" come of age they will significantly increase the proportions of people in the age group that they are entering. Between 2001 and 2011 the biggest increase will be among those 55 to 64 (9.7 percent to 13.1 percent). Between 2011 and 2021, the largest increases will be for those between 65 and 74 (8.3 percent to 11.3). Then between 2021 and 2031 the notable jump will be among those 75 and over. By 2031, the proportion of the population aged 65 and over will have increased to almost one-quarter of the whole, 23.8 percent (*A Portrait of Seniors in Canada*, 1990). Already, the median age of Canadians has risen from 29.6 in 1981 to 31.6 in 1986 and 33.5 in 1991 (*1992 Corpus Almanac and Canadian Sourcebook*, 1992). Canada Map 14-1 shows the percentage of the population over 65, by province and territory.

What is prompting the aging of our society? Two factors stand out. The first is the baby boom that began in the late 1940s. After World War II, men and women enthusiastically settled into family life and the bearing of children. This enormous cohort of baby boomers first gained attention by forging the youth culture of the 1960s. They are setting trends as middle-aged people in the 1990s, and their numbers alone ensure that they will influence our society as they reach old age. The birth rate then took a sharp turn downward after 1965 (the so-called "baby bust"), so that our population is becoming increasingly "top-heavy" in the coming decades.

FIGURE 14-1 AGE PYRAMIDS OF CANADA FOR SELECTED YEARS SINCE EARLY 1800

SOURCE: Statistics Canada, Report on the Demographic Situation in Canada, 1992. Cat. No. 91-209, November 1992.

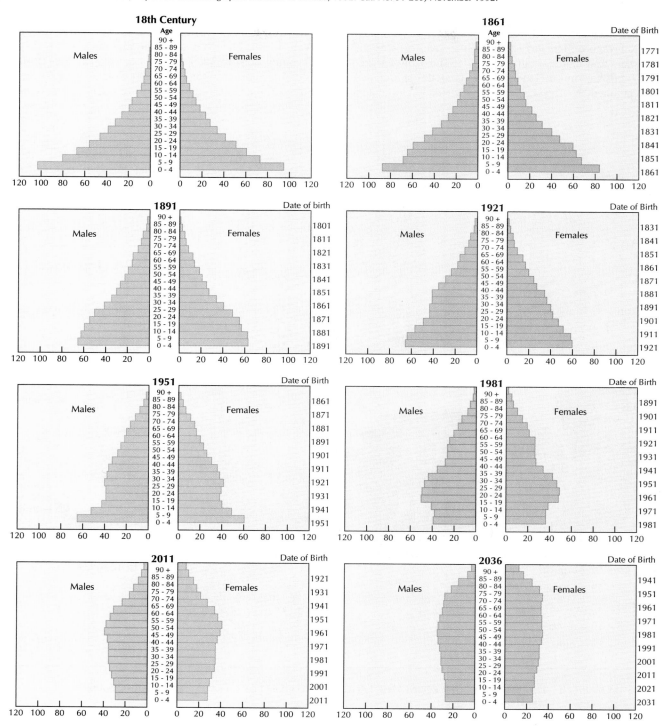

The second cause of the aging of our society is increasing life expectancy. Females born around 1800 could expect to live to be 39.8 years: males 39.3 years. By 1900 females could expect to live 50.2 years: males 47.2. Presently, females can expect to live to be about 80 years and males about 73 years (Nancarrow Clarke, 1990:60; Colombo, 1993:57). This striking increase reflects medical advances that have virtually eliminated infectious diseases such as smallpox, diphtheria, and measles, which killed many young people in the past, as well as more recent medical strides in combating cancer and heart disease, afflictions common to the elderly (Wall, 1980). The decline in mortality rates means that of women born in 1950, only 5 percent will die before becoming mothers. For every 100 women born in the 1800s, 40 died before giving birth to a child (*Report on*

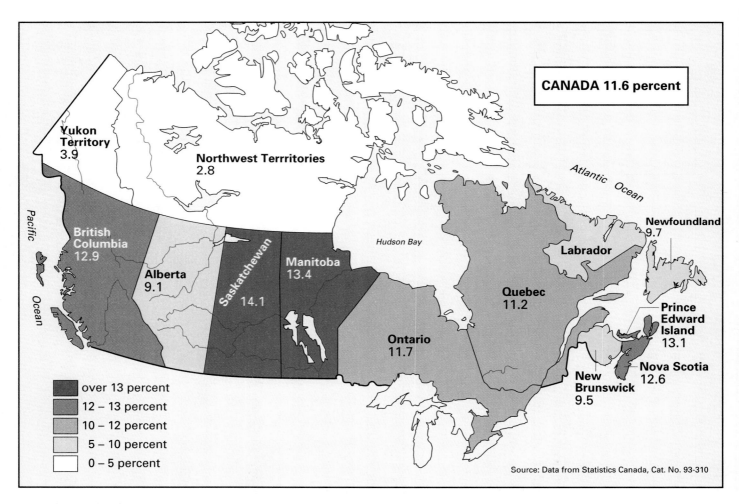

CANADA MAP 14-1   **PERCENTAGE OF THE POPULATION AGED 65 AND OVER FOR CANADA, THE PROVINCES AND TERRITORIES, 1991**

the *Demographic Situation in Canada*, 1992). In addition, a rising standard of living during this century has promoted the health of people of all ages. One clear indication of this change is that the fastest-growing segment of the entire population is people over eighty-five, who are already more than twenty times more numerous than they were at the beginning of this century. In 1991, people over 80 made up 15 percent of the population over 60. By 2001 they will comprise 19 percent and by 2011, 20 percent of the people over 65 (*Report on the Demographic Situation in Canada*, 1992).

We can only begin to imagine the consequences of this transformation. Assuming that people over sixty-five continue to retire from the labor force, the proportion of non-employed adults—already many times greater than in 1900—will soar even higher. This, in turn, will generate ever-greater demands for social resources and programs providing support for the non-working elderly. However, today's adults, especially women, are considerably different in many important ways, from previous generations. They will not be entirely like the people who are over 65 today. The elderly of the future will tend to have greater levels of education, fewer family responsibilities, better work and better conditions for saving, an improved health care system and broader access to retirement alternatives. Predicting the use of services on the basis of current use is thus very complicated (*Report on the Demographic Situation in Canada*, 1992:144). Presently, the elderly draw heavily on the health-care system. A recent study indicated that health care spending is 4.5 times greater for Canadians over 65 than for those under 65. Health care spending is 6.5 times greater for those over 75 than for those less than 65 (*Demographic Aging: The Economic Consequences*, 1991). Older people make the greatest use of physicians, hospitals, and prescription drugs. As Chapter 20 ("Health and Medicine") explains, the costs of medical care have skyrocketed in recent years, a trend that shows little evidence of slowing. Unless steps are taken to meet the medical needs of millions of additional older people—at prices that average people can *afford*—our society will face a monumental health care crisis in the next century.

Perhaps most important, in the coming decades interacting with elderly people will become commonplace. People in Canada are now accustomed to a considerable degree of age segregation. Young people rarely mingle in familiar settings with old people, so that most of the young know little about aging. In the twenty-first

During this century a remarkable change has occurred: today's youngsters have a greater chance of living beyond the age of sixty-five than infants born in 1900 had of reaching their first birthday. As a result, women and men over the age of sixty-five already outnumber teenagers and will account for one-fifth of the North American population by 2030. Will lawn bowling become more prevalent than junior hockey in the 21st century?

century, when the size of the elderly population stands at twice what it is now, those who are not elderly will have extensive daily contact with people who are.

As the proportion of older people rises, adult children will have an increased responsibility to care for aging parents. As the box on page 389 explains, many middle-aged adults already think of themselves as the "sandwich generation."

Growing Old: Biology and Culture

The graying of the population has prompted the development of a relatively new field of social science. **Gerontology** (derived from the Greek word *geron*, meaning "an old person"), is *the study of aging and the elderly*. Gerontology encompasses the biological processes of aging, a psychological focus on personality, and a more sociological look at how individual cultures define this stage of life.

Biological Changes

As we age, the body undergoes a series of gradual, yet continual, changes. How we think about these changes—whether we celebrate our maturity or bemoan our physical decline—depends largely on whether our society labels such changes as positive or negative. The culture of Canada is youth-oriented, so we tend to consider biological changes that occur early in life as positive. Growing children and adolescents approaching adulthood gain greater measures of responsibility and look forward to additional legal rights.

At the same time, our culture views biological changes that unfold later in life with a negative eye. Few people are congratulated for getting old. We commiserate with those entering old age, and make jokes about aging to avoid the harsh conclusion that the elderly are sliding down a slope of physical and mental decline. We assume, in short, that at roughly the midpoint of the life course, people cease growing *up* and begin growing *down*.

Physical problems generally complicate old age. Yet, many people in our society exaggerate the physical differences between the elderly and younger people

To many of her family, the idea seemed silly if not dangerous, but ninety-seven-year-old Beatrice Ferguson mastered the art of the hula hoop and made others rethink some of their assumptions about the elderly.

(Harris, 1976). Research in gerontology helps to separate the facts of aging from cultural stereotypes.

Gray hair, wrinkles, loss of height and weight, and an overall decline in strength and physical mobility—these all characterize the aging process that begins in middle age (Colloway & Dollevoet, 1977). After about the age of 50, bones become more brittle; falls that would be of little consequence earlier in life can result in disabling injuries. Broken bones also take longer to heal as we get older. In addition, a substantial proportion of the elderly suffer from chronic illnesses like arthritis and diabetes, which limit physical activity, and with the passing years more people contend with life-threatening conditions such as heart disease and cancer. Almost two out of three women 65 and over suffer from one sort of chronic disability or another (*Women in Canada: A Statistical Report,* 1990). Alzheimer's disease is a devastating disability that afflicts between 5 and 10 percent of the population over 65. This condition—which involves slow deterioration of the nerve fibres in the brain—is especially taxing on family members who must provide more and more care as they endure the gradual loss of a loved one.

The sensory abilities—taste, sight, touch, smell, and especially hearing—tend to diminish with age. While only about 5 percent of middle-aged people are visually impaired, 10 percent of the elderly are. The deterioration of visual abilities begins about 40 years of age but restrictive vision faces about 10 percent of people over 65. This means that there are approximately 300,000 blind or visually impaired seniors and that approximately 20 percent in 60,000 of these people are totally blind (Naeyaert, 1990). Hearing problems are more common, increasing in frequency from about 15 percent of middle-aged people to almost 50 percent of the elderly. Hearing loss increases with age (Lai, 1990). Both impairments affect men more than women (National Centre for Health Statistics, 1990). A declining ability to taste and smell can adversely affect eating habits, creating other health problems related to poor nutrition (Eckholm, 1985).

Without denying that health becomes more fragile with advancing age, the vast majority of older people are neither discouraged nor disabled by their physical condition. Only about one in ten reports trouble walking, and just one in twenty requires intensive care in a hospital or nursing home. No more than 1 percent of the elderly are bedridden. Overall, only 70 percent of men and women over the age of 65

CRITICAL THINKING

The Sandwich Generation: Who Should Care for Aging Parents?

How can anyone deny that parents who have toiled for their children in their youth, have lost many a good night's sleep when they were ill, have washed their diapers long before they could talk, and have spent about a quarter of a century bringing them up and fitting them for life, have the right to be fed by them and respected when they are old?

So asked the ancient Chinese philosopher Lin Yutang. This perennial question is taking on new meaning in Canada as the current baby boomers become the first generation in our history destined to spend as much time caring for elderly parents as for their young children. This challenge has earned them the title of the "sandwich generation," because they are facing the demands of their children, on the one hand, and those of their aging parents on the other. Why are people nearing midlife the first generation to be squeezed in this way? There are three major reasons. The first reason is *there are now more elderly people.* An explosion of the elderly population is now under way making for more older people, who will live longer and require greater support and assistance. The second factor is *adults are now having fewer children.* The number of young children in Canada actually began falling about 1960 as the baby boom came to an end. This downturn in birth rates means that the increasing number of old people will have fewer children to care for them.

Researchers estimate that a couple now have living parents for a far greater share of the life course than they have dependent children under age 20 (Preston, 1984). Further, as couples age, their caregiving responsibilities no longer come to an end; they merely shift from young children to old parents. A third factor that places more demands on today's families is that *more women are in the labor force.* The typical married couple in Canada comprises two people who work. Dual-career couples sometimes fear that they shortchange their own children; now they are also facing demands for time and attention from their aging parents. Historically, caring for the elderly has fallen to women (in their roles as daughters and daughters-in-law). Women now have less time and energy available to do this.

Who should support the elderly? An ongoing debate raises three possibilities: the elderly themselves, their adult children, and the government.

The elderly in Canada have always taken primary responsibility for their own welfare. People learn early in life that they are expected to save for their old age. But the costs of growing old threaten the security of older women and men who have tried to be self-reliant.

The extent to which adult children should be responsible for their elderly parents' care is not easily defined. Advocates of a larger role for adult children, echoing the sentiments of Lin Yutang, point out that family ties involve reciprocity and obligation; if people do not feel some obligation to care for their own parents, this argument continues, they are simply too self-centered. Furthermore, the family seems properly suited to provide the emotional support that older people require. Medical ethicist Daniel Callahan states the case simply:

> In a world of strangers or fleeting casual acquaintances, of distant government agencies and a society beyond their control, elderly parents can see in their children their only hope for someone who ought to care for them.

But not everyone is convinced that caring for aging parents is a family matter. This opposing view has roots in our culture. While our way of life stresses the duties of parents toward their young children, the obligations of children to aging parents are not clearly spelled out. Moreover, the growth of government social programs (especially Social Security and Medicare) during the last fifty years has weakened our sense of family responsibility toward the elderly. Additionally, many adult children simply do not have the resources—financial or emotional—to do as much as they would like.

A significant proportion of adults do a great deal for older parents. Research suggests that about one-fourth (mostly women) spend five hours or more every day caring for their aging parents. Further, with only one in twenty elderly people in a rest home, family members step in to perform roughly 80 percent of all home health care for elderly people who are disabled. In the future, most elderly people will be able to care for themselves—as they have in the past—without a great deal of help from anyone. But the graying of Canada means that the costs and responsibilities of supporting the elderly population will rise dramatically. With fewer adult children to meet this need, government involvement in elderly care will have to expand. Deciding precisely how to assign responsibility for meeting the needs of the elderly will command national attention for decades.

SOURCES: Based on the Institute for Philosophy and Public Policy (1988); also Gelman (1985); Callahan (1987); Stone, Cafferata, & Sangl (1987); Nett (1993); McPherson (1990); and Marshall (1987).

assess their health as "good" or "excellent," while about 30 percent characterize their overall condition as "fair" or "poor" (*Canadian Social Trends*, 1992).

Bear in mind, of course, that these patterns vary greatly within the elderly population. Generally speaking, elderly men tend to fare better than elderly women. Women live longer, on average, than men do, but they also spend more of their lives suffering from chronic disabilities like arthritis than men. In addition, as Chapter 10 ("Social Class in Canada") explained, physical health varies among the different social classes. Stated simply, this means that people who live and work in a healthful and safe environment and who can afford extensive preventive medical care have an easier time aging than those with fewer resources. In 1985 and 1990 a greater proportion of the very unhappy reported fair or poor health; whereas more of the very happy reported good or excellent health (Keith and Laudray, 1992). However, happiness level did depend somewhat on income. Fifty-six percent of men and 49 percent of women over 55 reported being very happy. Very few happy men, only 4 percent, or women, only 9 percent, had incomes of less than $10,000. The greatest proportion of very happy men, 29 percent, fell into the highest income category (Keith and Laudry, 1992).

Psychological Changes

Just as we tend to overstate the physical problems of aging, so it is easy to exaggerate the psychological changes that accompany growing old. Samuel Johnson, the famous eighteenth-century observer of British society, once reflected:

> There is a wicked inclination in most people to suppose an old man decayed in his intellect. If a young or middle-aged man, when leaving a company, does not recollect where he laid his hat, it is nothing; but if the same inattention is discovered in an old man, people will shrug their shoulders and say, "His memory is going". (cited in Berger, 1983:544)

Cultural assumptions about the various stages of life shape everyone's perceptions of human behavior; this can be true of psychologists, too. Until recently, most psychologists contended that changes in intelligence over the life course followed a simple rule: "What goes up must come down" (Baltes & Schaie, 1974). According to some research, mental decline actually begins as early as twenty-five (Wechsler, 1972). In recent years, psychologists have reassessed changes in

mental capacity brought on by aging, and few would now argue that growing old means enduring an inevitable loss in intellectual acuity. Some researchers now argue that several aspects of intelligence actually grow stronger in later years.

To clarify this matter, we need to precisely operationalize the concept of intelligence. Sensorimotor coordination, including the ability to arrange objects to match a drawing, declines steadily after midlife. Similarly, the facility to learn new material and to think quickly appear to subside among people over the age of seventy (Schaie, 1980). But the ability to use familiar ideas does not diminish with age, and verbal and mathematical skills often improve with advancing years (Baltes & Schaie, 1974). Again, education and social class affect all these capacities, and they may actually have a greater impact on intelligence than aging does (Botwinick, 1977; Riegel, 1977).

Most people wonder if they will think or feel differently when they are older. Psychologists assure us, for better or worse, that the answer is no. Personality changes little as we grow old, except that most men and women become somewhat more introverted as they age—more engaged with their own thoughts and emotions. In short, two elderly people who knew each other as children would recognize in each other many of the same personality traits that distinguished them as youngsters (Neugarten, 1971, 1972, 1977).

Aging and Culture

Sociology offers the following valuable insight: whatever changes age brings to our minds and bodies, the *significance* of growing old is very much a matter of cultural definitions.

In global perspective, one factor that shapes the meaning of aging is life expectancy, which is closely linked to a society's overall standard of living and medical technology. Throughout most of human history, people's lives were—as English philosopher Thomas Hobbes (1588–1679) put it—"nasty, brutish, and short" (although Hobbes himself managed to reach the age of ninety-one). Most people of his day married and had children in their teens, were middle-aged in their twenties, and succumbed to illnesses by their thirties or forties. It took several more centuries before a rising standard of living and technological advances began to curb infectious diseases that killed people of all ages. These factors eventually made surviving the ordeal of birth and living to, say, age forty or fifty commonplace by the beginning of this century (Mahler, 1980; Cox, 1984).

Global Map 14-1 on this page provides a comparative look at life expectancy. In the poorest nations of the Third World, including much of central Africa, the average lifespan is about fifty years. This is only slightly more than life expectancy in Europe during the Middle Ages. In the industrial societies of the world, including Canada, life expectancy is half again longer: about sev-

enty-five years. In First-World societies, people are not thought to be "old" until the mid-sixties or even later.

Reports from Abkhasia, a republic of the former Soviet Union, indicate that a surprisingly large number of people live well beyond what even we in Canada consider to be a ripe old age: to one hundred and even older. Many individuals may exaggerate their age to researchers; but, even so, Abkhasian society illustrates the important lesson that social relationships—perhaps

WINDOW ON THE WORLD

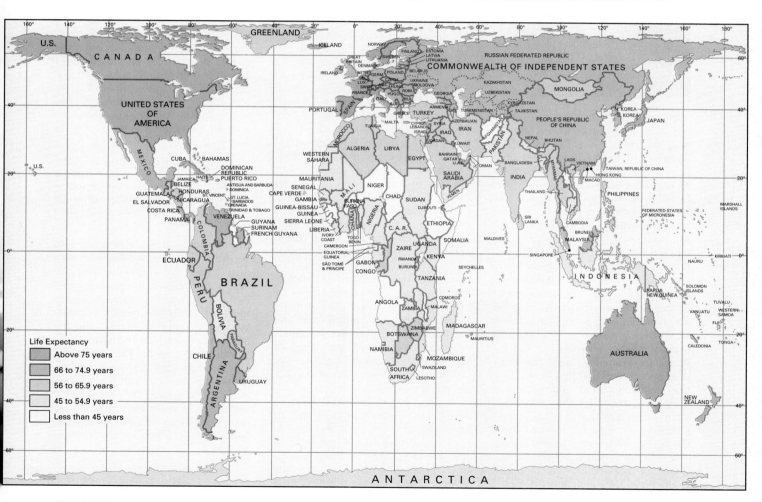

GLOBAL MAP 14-1 LIFE EXPECTANCY IN GLOBAL PERSPECTIVE
Life expectancy has shot upward over the course of this century in industrial societies including Canada, the United States, the nations of Europe, Japan, and Australia. Since poverty is the rule in much of the world, lives are correspondingly shorter elsewhere, especially in parts of Africa and Asia where life expectancy may be as low as forty years.

CROSS-CULTURAL COMPARISON

Growing (Very) Old in Abkhasia

Anthropologist Sula Benet was sharing wine and conversation with a man in Tamish, a small village in the Republic of Abkhasia in the southwest corner of the Commonwealth of Independent States. Judging the man to be about seventy, she raised her glass and offered a toast to his long life. "May you live as long as Moses," she exclaimed. The gesture of goodwill fell flat: Moses lived to 120, but Benet's companion was already 119.

An outsider—even open-minded anthropologists who study many of the world's mysteries—should be skeptical about the longevity claims made by the Abkhasians. In one village of twelve hundred visited by Benet, for example, almost two hundred people declared they were more than eighty years old, and many said they were far older than that. Research suggests that Abkhasia may well have six times more people over the age of ninety as the United States.

To her surprise, Benet discovered that some Abkhasians actually understate their age. For example,

after one man claimed to be ninety-five, his daughter (herself, eighty-one) produced a birth certificate stating his actual age as 108. Why the deception? In this instance, because the man was soon to be married. As another man (of 104) explained with a wink of his eye, "A man is a man until he is 100, you know what I mean. After that, well, he is getting old."

What accounts for the Abkhasians's remarkable longevity? The answer certainly is not the advanced medical technology in which people in Canada place so much faith; many Abkhasians have never seen a physician or a hospital. Nonetheless, their vigour and health are exceptional by our standards.

One possible explanation involves genetics: natural selection, over many centuries of gruelling warfare, has probably favored those with robust physical traits. But no clear evidence supports this hypothesis. A more likely answer has to do with lifestyle, including diet and physical activity. Abkhasians eat little saturated fat (which is linked to heart disease), use no sugar, drink no coffee or tea, and few Abkhasians smoke or chew tobacco. They do consume large amounts of healthful fruits and vegetables, and drink lots of buttermilk and low-alcohol wine. Additionally, Abkhasians maintain active lives built around regular physical work for people of all ages.

Beyond diet and lifestyle, Abkhasian culture may hold another key to long life. A clear and consistent set of traditional values and norms characterizes Abkhasian society. This gives all Abkhasians a strong sense of belonging and imbues their

lives with purpose. This is especially true of the elderly, whose active lives and accumulated experience are highly valued, in marked contrast to our own practice of pushing old people to the margins of social life. As Benet explains: "The old, when they do not simply vegetate, out of view and out of mind, keep themselves 'busy' with bingo and shuffleboard." For their part, the Abkhasians do not even have a word for old people or have a notion of retirement. Furthermore, younger people accord their elders great prestige and respect since, in their minds, advanced age confers the greatest wisdom. It is the old, rather than the young, whom people look to for decisions and guidance in everyday life. According to Benet:

> The extraordinary attitude of the Abkhasians—to feel needed at 99 or 110—is not an artificial, self-protective one; it is a natural expression, in old age, of a consistent outlook that begins in childhood. . . .

Because their society is organized to accord the greatest respect to individuals who have lived the longest, Abkhasians expect to lead long and useful lives, and have good reason to look forward to old age. Their society values its traditions highly, and the old are viewed as indispensable guardians of culture. The elders preside at important ceremonial occasions, and they transmit their knowledge to the young. They feel needed because, in their own minds and everyone else's, they are. Rather than being a burden, they are the center of society.

SOURCE: Based on Benet (1971).

even more than technological advances—are the key to a rich and long life. The box on page 392 provides details about a society in which people are reputed to live a century or even longer.

Aging and Social Stratification

Like race, ethnicity, and gender, age is one basis for socially ranking individuals. **Age stratification**, then, is defined as *the unequal distribution of wealth, power, and privileges among people of different ages*. Like other dimensions of social hierarchy, age stratification varies from one society to another.

As explained in Chapter 4 ("Society"), hunters and gatherers lack the technology to produce a surplus of food and are nomadic. Thus, they value physical strength and stamina, since these traits contribute to their survival. As people age, productivity declines along with strength and energy. Members of these societies, therefore, consider the elderly (who may actually be only thirty) as an economic burden (Sheehan, 1976).

Pastoral, horticultural, and agrarian societies have the technology to produce a material surplus; consequently, individuals may accumulate considerable wealth over a lifetime. Older people in these societies generally become richer and more powerful, so these societies tend toward **gerontocracy**, *a form of social organization in which the elderly have the most wealth, power, and privileges*. Old people, particularly the men, are honored (and sometimes feared) by their families and, as in the case of the Abkhasians, they remain active leaders of society until they die.

Additionally, the rich folk life in preindustrial societies fosters respect for the elderly, since it is they who serve as guardians of traditional wisdom and rituals—from how to plant crops to homemaking skills to marking the entry of the young into the adult community. This veneration of elders also explains the widespread practice of ancestor worship among members of agrarian societies.

Industrialization and advances in medical technology gradually increase life expectancy, but these forces also erode the power and prestige of the elderly. In part, this is because the prime source of wealth shifts from land (typically controlled by the oldest members of society) to factories and other new forms of production (often owned or managed by younger people). The growth of urban centers also divides families and forces children to depend less on their parents and more on their own earning power. Furthermore, advanced technology accelerates social change, so many of the skills, traditions, and life experiences that served the old have less relevance to the young. Over the long term, these factors transform old people from *elders* (a term with positive connotations) to the *elderly* (commanding far less prestige). Finally, the tremendous productivity of industrial societies makes the labor of everyone unnecessary; as a result, the very old and the very young often occupy nonproductive roles (Cohn, 1982).

In mature industrial societies such as Canada, economic and political leaders are generally middle-aged rather than elderly people because people at midlife usually combine experience with up-to-date skills. In rapidly changing sectors of the economy—the various high-tech fields—key executives are frequently much younger, sometimes just out of university. Older people are often consigned to marginal positions in the economy because they lack the knowledge and training demanded by a fast-changing marketplace. Certainly some elderly men and women remain at the helm of businesses they own but, more commonly, older people predominate in traditional occupations (such as barbers, tailors, and seamstresses) and jobs that involve minimal activity (night security guards, for instance) (Kaufman & Spilerman, 1982).

Industrialization also changes the relationships among the generations that make up families. Pre industrial societies favor *extended families*, with more than two generations living together, so that young and old remain in close contact. Industrial societies, as Chapter 15 ("Family") explains, promote *nuclear families* composed of just parents and their dependent children. Sixty-nine percent of people between 65 and 74 lived as members of family in 1991. 47.6 percent of those over 75 lived in a family (*Families, Number, Type, Structure*, 1992). Up to 74 years of age almost two-thirds of elderly persons live with their spouses and/or never-married children. This multigenerational pattern seems to be gaining in popularity, perhaps because of the sagging economy. Multigenerational living does not restore the historic prestige of the elderly. In such homes, adult children—rather than elderly parents—are usually defined as the heads of the household, reversing the pattern common at the beginning of this century (Dahlin, 1980).

In a few industrial societies—notably Japan—traditional cultural values and religious beliefs are still strong enough to confer high social standing on the oldest citizens. Most aged people in Japan live with an adult son or daughter and they continue to play a significant part in family life. The elderly in Japan are also more likely than their counterparts in Canada to remain in the labor force, and in many Japanese corporations the oldest employees receive the greatest respect. But even Japan is steadily becoming more like other industrial societies, in which growing old means giving up a large measure of social importance (Harlan, 1968; Cowgill & Holmes, 1972; Treas, 1979; Palmore, 1982; Yates, 1986).

Transitions and Issues of Aging

Chapter 5 ("Socialization") explained that we confront change at each stage of the life course. People must unlearn self-concepts and social patterns that no longer apply to their lives and simultaneously learn to cope with new circumstances. Of all stages of the life course, however, old age presents the greatest personal challenges.

Although physical decline in old age is less serious than most younger people think, this change can cause emotional stress among the elderly. Older people endure more pain, become resigned to limited activities, adjust to greater dependence on others, and see in the deaths of friends and relatives frequent reminders of their own mortality. Also, because our culture places such a high value on youth, physical vitality, and good looks, signs of aging may give rise to frustration, fear, and self-doubt in older people (Hamel, 1990). As one retired psychologist recently said of his old age: "Don't let the current hype about the joys of retirement fool you. They are not the best of times. It's just that the alternative is even worse" (Rubenstein, 1991:13).

Erik Erikson (1963, 1980) suggests that elderly people must resolve a tension of "integrity versus despair." No matter how much they may still be learning and achieving, older people must recognize that their lives are nearing an end. Elderly people spend much time reflecting on their past accomplishments and disappointments. To shore up their personal integrity, Erikson explains, older women and men must accept past mistakes as well as successes. Otherwise, this period may turn into a time of despair—a dead end with little positive meaning.

Research suggests that most people who find satisfaction and meaning in earlier stages of life are likely to achieve personal well-being in old age.

One of the most troublesome problems of old age is a group of illnesses called dementias. Dementias are characterized by progressive cognitive impairment including the loss of abilities such as attention span, concentration, orientation and memory. While dementias can result from several distinct diseases which affect the brain, Alzheimer's disease is the most well-known and the most common form of dementia (about 50 percent of dementia is Alzheimer's). Dementia is a serious and prevalent health problem amongst elderly Canadians. It affects between 5 and 10 percent of those over 65 and approximately 20 percent of those over 80.

Negative myths about the elderly—their health, happiness, and sexuality—abound (McPherson, 1991). Some elderly people share this dim view of their plight, but most have a more positive outlook. Table 14-1 indicates that a majority of both men and women aged 55 and over enjoy good health, and that most consider themselves to be at least "somewhat happy." Married elderly people have advantages over single cohorts in a number of different areas of their lives including morbidity, mortality, and psychological well-being. Marriage appears to be particularly advantageous for elderly males because it unites them with a network of other people more easily than singlehood (Nett, 1993). Overall, research suggests that, while personal adjustments are necessary, the experience of growing old in Canada often provides much cause for joy. However, a

TABLE 14-1 SELF-REPORTED HEALTH AND HAPPINESS STATUS OF CANADIANS AGES 55 AND OVER, 1990

	Men	Women
Health Status		
Excellent	32%	27%
Good	46	48
Fair	17	19
Poor	4	6
Not stated	1	1
Happiness Status		
Very happy	56	49
Somewhat happy	39	43
Somewhat unhappy	2	5
Very unhappy	1	1
No opinion, not stated	3	2

SOURCE: *Statistics Canada,* Canadian Social Trends, *Summer 1992, p. 26 (Catalogue No. 11-008).*

person's view does vary based on individual personality, family circumstances, social class, and financial position. People who adapt successfully to changes earlier in life can confidently look forward to deriving satisfaction and meaning from their lives later on (Neugarten, 1971; Palmore, 1979a).

Social Isolation

Elderly people are often quite isolated in our society. Retirement closes off a major source of social interaction. Then, too, negative stereotypes that depict the elderly as "over the hill" may discourage younger people from close social contact with their elders. Although a number of other events could be thought to increase the sense of loneliness among the elderly (including hearing and visual problems, disabilities of other kinds, deaths of friends, acquaintances, family members, and spouses, and geographical separation from children), studies comparing the elderly and other age groupings have shown that the elderly often suffer *less* from feelings of loneliness (Wigdor, 1991). It is as if the elderly are more able to deal with being alone than are younger people.

The greatest cause of social isolation is the inevitable death of loved ones. Few human experiences affect people as profoundly as the death of a spouse (Martin-Matthews, 1987). One study found almost three-fourths of widows and widowers cited loneliness as their most serious problem (Lund, 1989). Widows and widowers must rebuild their lives in the glaring absence of people with whom, in many instances, they spent most of their adult lives. Some survivors choose not to live at all: one study of elderly men noted a sharp increase in the incidence of mortality, sometimes by suicide, in the months following the death of their wives (Benjamin & Wallis, 1963). There are other causes for suicide among the elderly. According to the National Task Force on Suicide in Canada, 1987 these include the following: deterioration of physical health, increased incidence of mental health problems, notably depression or dementia, involuntary retirement, death of a spouse or other bereavement, social isolation, loneliness, significant financial problems, and alcohol abuse.

The problem of social isolation falls most heavily on women, who typically outlive their husbands (see Table 14-2). The more pronounced isolation among elderly women may well account for research findings that their sense of well-being is not as strong as that of elderly men in Canada and spouses in particular (Nett, 1993:307–340).

TABLE 14-2 PRIVATE HOUSEHOLD LIVING ARRANGEMENTS AMONG THE ELDERLY, 1986*

	Men	Women
	%	%
Living with spouse or unmarried children	81.1	55.1
Living with relatives	2.5	5.3
Living alone	14.7	37.7
Living with others	1.7	1.9
	100.0	100.0

* Latest data available.
SOURCE: Adapted from Statistics Canada, Population and Dwelling Characteristics, Catalogue 93-106, "Families," Part 1, Table 7, and Population and Dwelling Characteristics, Catalogue 93-104, "Dwellings and Households," Part 1, Table 2 (Ottawa: Supply and Services Canada, 1986).

Retirement

Work not only provides us with a source of income, it also figures prominently in our personal identity. Retirement from paid work, therefore, generally entails some reduction in income, diminished social prestige, and a loss of purpose in life (Chown, 1977).

Organizations may help individuals striving to ease this transition. Universities, for example, confer the title of "professor emeritus" (from Latin, meaning "fully earned") on some retired faculty members, giving them library, parking, and mail privileges. These honored retirees may, if they wish, attend faculty meetings, and some universities make office space available so they can pursue research.

For many older people, new activities and new interests minimize the personal disruption and loss of prestige brought on by retirement (Rose, 1968). Volunteer work can be personally rewarding, allowing individuals to apply their career skills to new challenges and opportunities. Seventeen percent of men and 16 percent of women report that they engage in volunteer work after retirement (Canada, 1988:19–23).

Although the notion of retirement is familiar enough to us, it is actually a recent social creation, becoming widely adopted only during the last century and only in industrial societies (Atchley, 1982). Advancing technology reduces the need for everyone to work, as well as placing a premium on up-to-date skills. Retirement permits younger workers, who presumably have the most current knowledge and training, to predominate in the labor force. In poor societies of the Third World, by contrast, most people work until they are incapacitated because everyone's labor is vital to a family's survival.

People in Canada generally consider sixty-five to be the proper age for retirement. In fact, retirement at sixty-five is closely tied to the development of pension plans. This is the age, too, when mandatory retirement (for some workers) comes into effect. In global context, however, retirement age varies significantly: some societies (including the Japanese) approve of retirement in the mid-fifties while others have no practice of retirement at all (Kii, 1979; Palmore, 1982). Not long ago, retirement was rarely an option. Before the various pension policies were put into effect, few people could afford to retire, and of course, fewer lived to retirement age. As pension programs bolstered the financial security of older people, they also promoted the idea that people *should* retire and take life easy in the later years.

In light of diverse practices in the world and over time, one might wonder if a society should formally designate any specific age for retirement. Vast differences in the interests and capacities of older people also make the notion of fixed retirement controversial. In Canada, there is an ongoing debate about whether mandatory retirement violates the individual's right to work as guaranteed under the Canadian Charter of Rights and Freedoms. But while about one half of the Canadian work force is currently subject to mandatory retirement regulations, only about 1 percent of the work force would continue to work past 65, given the choice (Tindale, 1991).

Men more than women have traditionally faced the transition to retirement. Elderly women who spend their lives as homemakers do not retire per se, although the departure of the last child from home serves as a rough parallel. But even lifelong homemakers must adjust to their husband's retirement and presence at home; this has been tagged the "husband underfoot syndrome" (Mitchell, 1972). But in adjusting to their husbands' retirement, women may also find new joys, joining their husbands in activities they previously had little time for (Keating & Cole, 1980). As the proportion of women in the labor force continues to rise, of course, both women and men will confront the changes brought on by retirement.

Aging and Income

On the whole, the image of the elderly as poverty-stricken is unfounded. As Table 14.3 shows, the rate of poverty among the elderly has declined from about 22 percent in 1980, to 9 percent in 1991 (*Poverty Profile Update for 1991*). Since 1982, in fact, poverty has been

TABLE 14-3   POVERTY RATES BY FAMILY TYPE, 1980–1991

	1980	1990	1991
Couples 65 and older	22.2%	8.5%	9.0%
Couples under 65 with children under 18	9.4%	9.6%	10.7%
Childless couples under 65	6.9%	8.3%	9.3%
Single-parent mothers under 65 with children under 18	57.7%	60.6%	61.9%

SOURCE: Poverty Profile Update for 1991. Ottawa: National Council on Welfare, Winter, 1993.

lower among the elderly than among the non-elderly (Stone, 1986). As noted in Chapter 10 ("Social Class in Canada"), children are the age category most at risk of being poor, with the incidence of poverty declining until about age fifty-five. The box "The Elderly: A Financial Windfall" examines this dramatic rise in the incomes of the elderly in more detail.

Still, for most people in Canada, retirement leads to a significant decline in income. For many, home mortgages and children's university expenses are paid off; yet the expenses for some medical and dental care, household help, and home utilities typically rise. Many elderly people do not have sufficient savings or pension benefits to be self-supporting; for this reason, various pension programs, including the Canada Pension Plan, are their greatest source of income. Because many retirees live with fixed incomes, inflation tends to affect them more severely than it does younger working people. Women and people of color are especially likely to find that growing old means growing poor.

The privation of the elderly is often hidden from view. Because of personal pride and a desire to maintain the dignity of independent living—values taught to members of our society from childhood—elderly people may conceal financial problems even from their own families. It is often difficult for people who have supported their children for years to admit that they can no longer provide for themselves, even though it may be through no fault of their own.

Abuse of the Elderly

In Canada, we seem to awaken to the problems of personal violence in stages: child abuse was first discussed in the 1960s, wife abuse came to the fore in the 1970s, and abuse of the elderly was publicly acknowledged in the 1980s. Abuse of older people takes many forms, from passive neglect to active torment, and includes verbal, emotional, financial, and physical harm. Most

A DECADE OF CHANGE

The Elderly: A Financial Windfall

A generation ago, the elderly were at high risk of poverty; today, people over sixty-five are less likely to be poor than are children. There are various reasons for this change, including better health that boosts earnings among older people, better pension programs from employers, and stock market values that tripled during the 1980s. But government policies also play a big part and, during the 1980s, federal programs favored the old over the young as never before.

The following table shows some of the progress the federal government has made in enchancing the incomes of seniors.

TABLE 14-4 SOURCES OF INCOME FOR POOR SENIORS, 1991

Source of income	Poor Couples 65 and older		Poor unattached 65 and older	
	Percent Receiving	Average Amount to Recipient	Percent Receiving	Average Amount to Recipient
Old age security pension and guaranteed income supplement	95%	$11,432	99%	$ 7,827
Canada and Quebec pension plans	69	4,278	62	2,980
Investment income			41	1,663
Welfare or provincial supplements	Samples too small		30	784
Occupational pension plans			16	2,142
Income from all sources	100	16,549	100	11,417

SOURCE: Poverty Profile Update for 1991. Ottawa: National Council on Welfare, Winter, 1993.

elderly people suffer from none of these things; but recent surveys conducted in Canada, the U.S., and Europe suggest that the incidence of elder abuse and neglect ranges from 3 to 5 percent. These findings are likely an underestimation of the problem (Wigdor, 1991). Perhaps three times as many elderly people sustain abuse at some point in time (Clark, 1986). Like violence against children or women in the home, it is difficult to determine how widespread abuse of the elderly is because victims are understandably reluctant to talk about their plight. But the trend is disturbing: as the proportion of elderly people rises, so does the incidence of abuse (Bruno, 1985).

What motivates people to abuse the elderly? Often, as suggested earlier, the cause lies in the stress of caring—financially and emotionally—for aging parents. This is especially true today because adult daughters as well as sons are now likely to be holding down jobs as well as caring for children of their own. Even in Japan—where tradition demands that adult children care for aging parents at home—more and more people find themselves unable to cope with the situation (Yates,

1986). Abuse appears to be most common where the stresses are greatest: in families with a very old person suffering from serious health problems, and where the relationship between parent and child has historically been poor. Here, family life may be grossly distorted by demands and tensions that people simply cannot endure, even if their intentions are good (Douglass, 1983; Gelman, 1985).

In sum, growing old involves serious problems and transitions. Some are brought on by physical decline. But others—including social isolation, adjustment to retirement, risk of poverty, and abuse from family members—are social problems. In the next section, we bring to bear various theoretical perspectives on how society shapes the lives of the elderly.

Theoretical Analysis of Aging

Various theories—developed from the major theoretical paradigms in sociology—help to shed light on the process of aging in Canada. We examine them each in turn.

Structural-Functional Analysis: Aging and Disengagement

Based on the ideas of Talcott Parsons—an architect of the structural-functional paradigm—Elaine Cumming and William Henry (1961) argue that aging inevitably brings on biological decline and, eventually, death. How is society to minimize the enormous disruption caused by the loss of its members? In their view, a social system ensures that tasks are performed without interruption through a gradual and orderly transfer of various statuses and roles from the old to the young. Continual turmoil would ensue if only incompetence or death brought about a changing of the guard. But a society heads off this outcome if the elderly disengage from productive roles while they are still able to perform them. Such disengagement by the elderly is also functional because, in a rapidly changing society, younger workers typically have skills and training that are more up-to-date. Formally, then, **disengagement theory** is *an analysis linking disengagement by elderly people from positions of social responsibility to the orderly operation of society.*

Disengagement may benefit elderly people as well as their society. Aging individuals with diminishing capacities presumably look forward to relinquishing some of the pressures of their jobs in favor of new pursuits of their own choosing (Palmore, 1979b). Society also grants older people greater freedom of behavior so that unusual actions on their part are construed as harmless eccentricity rather than dangerous deviance.

Critical evaluation.   In delineating one strategy societies pursue to deal with the human decline brought on by aging—by transferring responsibilities from older to younger people—disengagement theory also suggests why our society tends to define elderly people as marginal.

There are several limitations to this approach. First, workers cannot disengage from paid work unless they have sufficient financial security to fall back on. Most elderly people in Canada have had access to such resources only in recent decades, and some still do not. Second, many elderly people do not wish to disengage from their productive roles. Disengagement, after all, has high personal costs, including loss of social prestige, social isolation, and reduced income. Third, there is no clear evidence that the societal benefits of disengagement outweigh its costs, which include the loss of human resources and the need to care for people who might otherwise be able to fend better for themselves.

Then, too, any useful system of disengagement would have to take account of widely differing abilities of the elderly themselves.

Symbolic-Interaction Analysis: Aging and Activity

One critical rebuttal to disengagement theory draws heavily on the symbolic-interaction paradigm. **Activity theory** is *an analysis linking personal satisfaction in old age to a high level of activity.* Because individuals build their social identity from statuses and roles, this theory notes that disengagement in old age has the dysfunction of eroding the satisfaction and meaning many elderly people find in their lives. Therefore, what elderly people need is a source of activity beyond retirement.

Activity theory proposes that the elderly substitute new roles and responsibilities for the ones they leave behind. After all, as members of a society that values productive activity, the elderly are likely to find the prospect of disengagement as unsatisfying as a younger person would. Another problem with disengagement theory is its tendency to see old people as a monolithic category. Activity theory stresses, more accurately, that older people have distinctive needs, interests, and physical abilities that guide their activities and attitudes about aging.

Research supports the conclusion that elderly people who maintain high activity levels are the most satisfied with their lives (Friedman & Havighurst, 1954; Havighurst, Neugarten, & Tobin, 1968; Neugarten, 1977; Palmore, 1979a). But no single conclusions should be applied to the socially diverse population of elderly women and men. Many aging people find satisfaction in high levels of activity; for some older people, however, a less active schedule—or, in some cases, uninterrupted leisure—brings the greatest happiness.

Critical evaluation.   Focusing on the elderly themselves rather than on the needs of society, activity theory provides a useful counterpoint to disengagement theory. Activity theory also highlights the social diversity among elderly people, an important consideration in formulating any government policy. Further, activity theory's assertion that the elderly generally enhance their personal satisfaction by leading active lives is well supported by research.

One limitation of this approach, from a structural-functionalist point of view, is a tendency to exaggerate the well-being and competence of the elderly. Do we want active elderly people serving as physicians or airline pilots, for example? From another perspective, activity theory falls short by overlooking how many of the problems that beset older people have more to do with how well their *society* (rather than *they*) operate.

Social-Conflict Analysis: Aging and Inequality

The social-conflict approach spotlights the fact that, different age categories compete for scarce social resources. Various stages in the life course, therefore, form the basis of age stratification. In the past, middle-aged people in Canada have enjoyed the greatest social privileges, while the elderly (like children in many respects) had less power and prestige and ran a higher risk of poverty. Employers have been likely to push elderly workers aside in favor of men and women who are younger because less-senior workers typically command lower wages. The end result has been turning older people into second-class citizens (Atchley, 1982; Phillipson, 1982).

The roots of this age-based hierarchy reach into the operation of industrial-capitalist society. Following the ideas of Karl Marx, Steven Spitzer (1980) points out that, because our society has an overriding concern with profit, we devalue those categories of people who are economically unproductive. Thus, Spitzer reasons, most of the elderly have a mildly deviant status and are easily ignored. Old people are destined to be marginal members of a society consumed by material gain.

Social-conflict analysis also draws attention to social diversity in the elderly population. Differences of class, race, ethnicity, and gender divide older people as they do everyone else. Thus the fortunate seniors in higher social classes have far more economic security, greater access to top-flight medical care, and more options for personal satisfaction in old age than those with fewer privileges. Likewise, elderly WASPs (white Anglo-Saxon Protestants) typically enjoy a host of advantages denied to older people of color. And women—who represent an increasing majority of the elderly population with advancing age—suffer the social and economic disadvantages of sexism.

Critical evaluation. Social-conflict theory adds further to our understanding of the aging process by underscoring age-based inequality and focusing on ways that capitalism devalues elderly people who are less productive. The implication of this analysis is that the aged fare better in non-capitalist societies, a view validated by some research (Treas, 1979).

One shortcoming of this approach goes right to its core contention: rather than blaming *capitalism* for the lower social standing of elderly people, critics hold that *industrialization* is the true culprit, so that socialism might provide no improvement in the situation. Furthermore, the notion that capitalism dooms the elderly to economic distress is challenged by the significant rise in the income of elderly people in Canada.

Ageism

In earlier chapters, we explained how ideology—including racism and sexism—seeks to justify the social disadvantages of minorities. Sociologists use a parallel term, **ageism**, to designate *prejudice and discrimination against the elderly.*

Like racism and sexism, ageism can be blatant (as when individuals deny elderly women or men a job or access to housing simply because of their age) or subtle (as when people speak to the elderly with a condescending tone as if they were children) (Kalish, 1979). Also like racism and sexism, ageism builds physical traits into stereotypes; in the case of the elderly, graying hair, wrinkled skin, and stooped posture may be viewed as badges of personal incompetence. Negative stereotypes picture the aged as helpless, confused, resistant to change, and generally unhappy (Butler, 1975). Even supposedly positive stereotypes of older people can deny them the full range of their humanity. Sentimental depictions of sweet little old ladies and charmingly eccentric old gentlemen ignore the fact that old people are complex individuals with distinct personalities and long years of experience and accomplishment.

Ageism, like other forms of prejudice, may have some foundation in reality. Statistically speaking, old people are more likely than young people to be mentally and physically impaired. But we slip into ageism when we make unwarranted generalizations about an entire category of people, most of whom do not conform to any stereotypes. As explained earlier in this chapter, most elderly people do not suffer from significant disabilities, and most have the same needs, feelings, and diversity of views as people who are younger. Finally, despite prejudices suggesting that anyone with gray hair and wrinkles lacks sex appeal, elderly people in good health are quite capable of maintaining satisfying sexual relationships.

Media-watchers have long criticized the exclusion of the aged, and especially elderly women, from programming and advertising. Research suggests that the media do not stereotype the elderly as extensively as they do women, but television and the print media have contributed to ageism in Canada (Kubey, 1980; Buchholz & Bynum, 1982). In recent years, television and films have featured more elderly people—many in a positive light. Estimates suggest that people aged fifty and over now purchase almost half of all consumer goods, and this fact is not lost on marketing executives and media moguls (Hoyt, 1985).

On a hopeful note, some research indicates that negative stereotypes about the elderly are disappearing. Perhaps we are not as preoccupied with work as we were in the past, and are therefore less likely to devalue elderly people as nonproductive. Older men and women have also gained political clout through organizations like the Gray Panthers, National Advisory Council on Aging, and One Voice, and because of their rising affluence. But, most important, older people themselves are dispelling the negative stereotypes. Remaining active and maintaining a positive view of their lives, older people exude self-confidence, which acts as a powerful force to undermine negative social images (Tibbitts, 1979).

The Elderly: A Minority?

The evidence is clear that, as a category of people in this country, the elderly do face social disadvantages. But sociologists differ as to whether the aged form a minority in the same way as, say, people of color or women. By briefly outlining key arguments in this debate, we will point up the similarities and differences between the elderly and other categories of people that are widely known as minorities.

Three decades ago, Leonard Breen (1960) pronounced the elderly a minority. He defended this assertion by noting that, first, older people have a clear social identity based on the ascribed status of being old and, second, they are subject to prejudice and discrimination. In addition, as we have explained, the elderly are often socially isolated, and denied equal opportunity for jobs.

Other sociologists, however, were not convinced and made the counterargument that the elderly do not qualify as a minority. Gordon Streib (1968) responded

that minority status is usually both permanent and exclusive. That is, a person is a Native Canadian, of Asian descent, or a woman, *for life*, and any such standing precludes being part of the dominant category of white males. But being elderly, Streib continued, is an *open* status because people are elderly for only part of their lives. Further, he added, everyone who has the good fortune to live long enough grows old.

The elderly are marked by social diversity more than members of any sex, race, ethnicity, or social class. Not surprisingly, then, they are unlikely to define themselves collectively as old people. On the contrary, although aware of their age, the elderly commonly think of themselves in terms of other social categories.

Streib made one further point. The social disadvantages faced by the elderly are less substantial than those experienced by the minorities described in earlier chapters. For example, old people have never been deprived of the right to own property, to vote, or to hold office, as people of color and women have. In fact, older men—and, to a lesser extent, older women—exercise considerable political influence in Canada, and their risk of poverty is only slightly greater than average. Some elderly people, Streib conceded, do suffer economic disadvantages, but these do not stem primarily from old age. Instead, most of the aged poor fall into categories of people likely to be poor at any age. Streib concludes that "the poor grow old," *not* that "the old grow poor."

For all the reasons delineated here, old people do not form a minority in the same sense as other categories of people do. Nor do they even have enough characteristics in common to be called a subculture, as some have suggested (Rose, 1968). Perhaps the best way to describe the elderly is simply as a *distinctive segment* of the population of Canada.

Death and Dying

> To every thing there is a season,
> And a time to every purpose under the heaven:
> A time to be born and a time to die ...

These well-known lines from the Book of Ecclesiastes in the Bible convey two basic truths about human existence: the fact of birth and the inevitability of death. Just as life varies in striking ways across history and around the world, so does death. We conclude this chapter with a brief look at the changing character of death—the final stage in the process of growing old.

Paintings provide a dramatic record of how common death was to everyday experience in the medieval era. The Triumph of Death, by sixteenth-century Flemish artist Pieter Breughel, makes this point with chilling realism.

Historical Patterns of Death

Throughout most of human history, death was a familiar fact of life. In technologically simple hunting and gathering societies, no one dared to assume that a newborn child would live for long. This uncertainty was so great, in fact, that parents often did not name children until they reached several years of age (Herty, 1960). Surviving infancy was an achievement and a matter of good luck; but thereafter illness brought on by poor nutrition, accidents, and natural catastrophes such as drought or famine combined to make life uncertain, at best. Sometimes death was deliberate, a strategy that emerges in societies that lack the resources to feed their people. Typically, the least productive people were killed so that others could live. In some cases, societies resorted to *infanticide*, the killing of newborn infants; in others, *geronticide*, the killing of the elderly.

Agricultural technology provided far more food, which enabled societies to grow in size and establish permanent settlements. But still death remained part of the common experience. Herds of animals in close proximity to villages spread infectious disease. Larger towns devised few effective means to dispose of human waste, resulting in poor sanitation. Until about the seventeenth century, plagues brought on and spread by unsanitary conditions sometimes wiped out a town's entire population.

In sum, most of our human ancestors regarded death as an integral part of life. In medieval Europe, Christianity offered the consolation that death fit into the divine plan for human existence. To illustrate, historian Philippe Ariès describes how Sir Lancelot, one of King Arthur's fearless Knights of the Round Table, prepared for his own death when he believed himself mortally wounded:

> His gestures were fixed by old customs, ritual gestures which must be carried out when one is about to die. He removed his weapons and lay quietly upon the ground. ... He spread his arms out, his body forming a cross ... in such a way that his head faced east toward Jerusalem. (1974:7–8)

As societies gradually gained control over many causes of death, attitudes began to change. Death became less and less an everyday experience: fewer children died at birth, and accidents and disease took a smaller toll among adults. Except in times of war or other catastrophes, people came to view dying as quite *extra*ordinary, except among the very old. In 1900, about one-third of all deaths in North America occurred before the age of five, another third occurred before the age of fifty-five, and the remaining one-third of men and women died in what was then defined as old age. Now most Canadians die *after* the age of fifty-five. Thus old age and death have become fused in our culture.

The Modern Separation of Life and Death

Less a part of everyday experience, death is now looked on as something unnatural. Religious beliefs that place both life and death in a divine scheme have been eroded by the growing ability of medical technology to overcome disease and slow the physical deterioration that accompanies aging. If social conditions prepared our ancestors to accept their deaths, modern society has fostered a desire for immortality, or eternal youth. In this sense, death has become separated from life.

This denial of death, coupled with the rapid increase in the elderly population, has forced our society to confront difficult ethical questions. Should life be extended as long as technologically possible? Should we commit an increasing share of medical resources to the task of prolonging life?

Death is also *physically* removed from the rest of life. The clearest evidence of this is that many of us have never seen a person die. While our ancestors typically died at home in the presence of family and friends, death today often occurs in unfamiliar and impersonal settings such as hospitals and nursing homes (Ariès, 1974). Even hospitals commonly relegate dying patients to a special part of the building, and hospital morgues are located well out of sight of patients and visitors alike (Sudnow, 1967).

Perhaps it is no wonder that, while our ancestors accepted death as part of life, we confront the prospect of dying with fear and anxiety. No doubt, this fearful attitude has propelled the rapid increase in medical research aimed at prolonging the life of the elderly. However, we may be on the verge of forging a new norm relating to death and dying. As the opening to this chapter suggests, many aging people are less terrified of death than they are at the prospect of being kept alive at all costs. In other words, medical technology now threatens personal autonomy because doctors and hospitals rather than dying individuals are deciding a course of action. The surprising popularity of the book *Final Exit* demonstrates that people want control over their deaths no less than they seek control over their lives.

Consequently, patients and families are now taking the initiative, often times choosing not to make use of available medical technology to prolong life. Patients, families, and doctors may decide to forgo any "heroic measures" to resuscitate a person who is dying. Living Wills—statements of what medical procedures an individual wants and does not want under specific conditions—are becoming widely accepted. Certainly, there are dangers in this practice. Family members may exert subtle pressure on a failing parent to refuse medical care, for example, because others wish to be spared emotional stress or a financial burden. Patients and family members will face difficult decisions that are as much moral as they are medical; to assist them, hospitals now offer the services of biomedical ethics committees, composed of physicians, social service professionals, and members of the clergy. The trend seems clear: if decline and death remain inevitable, at least people can make their own choices about when and where and perhaps even how they will die.

Bereavement

In Chapter 5 ("Socialization"), we described the stages by which people usually confront their own death. Elizabeth Kubler-Ross (1969) claims that individuals

The infancy of photography in the 1840s was also a time of deadly epidemics in the United States, with between one-third and one-half of children dying before the age of ten. Many grieving parents rushed to capture their dead children on film. The post-mortem photograph, in most cases the only picture ever taken of someone, suggests a far greater acceptance of death during the nineteenth century. In this century, death became rare among the young so that dying is separated from life as a grim reality that people do their best to deny.

initially react with *denial*, followed by *anger*, efforts toward *negotiation* of divine intervention, gradual *resignation* and, finally, *acceptance*. But it is not only the dying person who must adjust to the approaching death but also those who will experience bereavement through the loss of a significant person.

According to some researchers, bereavement is a process that parallels the stages of dying described by Kubler-Ross. Those close to a dying person, for instance, may initially deny the reality of impending death, reaching the point of acceptance only with time. Other researchers question the use of linear stage theories, arguing that bereavement may not follow any rigid schedule (Lund, Caserta, and Diamond, 1986; Lund, 1989). But all the experts agree that how others view a death influences the attitudes of the person who is dying. That is, if family and friends accept the reality of approaching death, it helps the dying person do the same; conversely, a dying person may have difficulty accepting death if surrounded by loved ones who deny the reality of the situation. Such denial also serves to emotionally isolate the dying person, who is unable to share feelings and experiences with others.

One recent development intended to provide support to dying people is the *hospice* movement. Unlike a hospital that is designed to cure disease, a hospice helps people have a good death. These care centers for dying people work to minimize pain and suffering, and encourage family members to remain close to the patient. Hospices also help dying people avoid the social isolation that commonly accompanies terminal illness by removing obstacles for patients who wish to return home to die in familiar surroundings. In every case, the hospice staff strives to enhance the comfort and dignity of the dying person as well as family members (Stoddard, 1978).

Even under the most favorable circumstances, bereavement may persist for some time. Besides profound grief, many survivors experience social disorientation because the dead person served as a point of reference in their lives. As we suggested earlier, among the elderly—especially older women—the loss of a spouse is both common and difficult.

Research teaches us that bereavement is less intense among people who, themselves, have high self-esteem, and who understand and accept the death of a loved one (Lund et al., 1985). And survivors who feel their relationship with the dying person has reached a satisfactory resolution experience shorter and less painful grieving. By taking the opportunity to bring an appropriate closure to their relationship with a dying person, in other words, family and friends are better able to comfort and support one another after the death finally occurs (Atchley, 1983).

This chapter has described a number of consequences of the "graying of Canada." As the ranks of the elderly increase, they will become a more visible and vocal part of everyday life. Gerontology, the study of the elderly, will also gain in stature, paralleling an expansion in medical care directed toward old people. As part of this transformation, we can also expect changes in the way we view death. The growing presence of the elderly in everyday settings will almost certainly shift our perception of death from a social taboo to a natural part of the life course. Both young and old alike may benefit.

Summary

1.   Compared to about 4 percent of the population in 1900 and over 12 percent today, the elderly are expected to represent almost 25 percent of the population of Canada by the middle of the next century.

2.   Gerontology, the study of aging and the elderly, focuses on biological and psychological changes in old age, as well as how aging is defined in a culture.

3.   Growing old is accompanied by a rising incidence of disease and disability. Younger people commonly exaggerate the extent of disability among the elderly, however.

4.   Psychological research confirms that growing old does not bring about an overall loss in intelligence or great changes in individual personality.

5.   The age at which people are defined as old has varied historically: until several centuries ago, old age began as early as thirty. In poorer societies today, life expectancy is substantially lower than in North America.

6. In global perspective, industrialization fosters a decline in the social standing of elderly people.

7. As people age, they commonly experience social isolation brought on by retirement, physical disability, and the death of friends or spouse. Even so, elderly people seem to experience feelings of loneliness less often than others.

8. Retirement forces people to make various social adjustments. Although traditionally a problem faced by men, retirement will become a concern of both sexes because of the increasing participation of women in the labor force.

9. In the past decade, poverty among the elderly has dropped significantly.

10. Disengagement theory—based on structural-functional analysis—suggests that the elderly disengage from positions of social responsibility before the onset of disability or death. In this way, a society transfers statuses and roles from the old to the young in an orderly way.

11. Activity theory, based on symbolic-interaction analysis, claims that a high level of activity affords people greater personal satisfaction in old age.

12. Age stratification is a focus of social-conflict analysis. According to this paradigm, the emphasis on economic productivity in capitalist societies leads to a devaluing of those who are less productive, including the elderly. The growing affluence of the elderly—coupled to their rising numbers—underlines a trend toward older people dominating the national agenda.

13. Ageism—prejudice and discrimination against old people—serves to justify age stratification.

14. Although many old people are socially disadvantaged, the elderly encompass people of both sexes and all races, ethnicities, and social classes. Thus older people do not constitute a minority.

15. Death is no longer part of everyday life, prompting personal discomfort with the subject of death. Today most people in our society die only after reaching old age. In our attempt to isolate death from life, we have segregated dying people. Recent trends suggest that people are confronting death more directly and seeking control over the process of dying.

Key Concepts

activity theory an analysis of aging linking personal satisfaction in old age to a high level of activity

ageism prejudice and discrimination against the elderly

age stratification the unequal distribution of wealth, power, and privileges among people of different ages

disengagement theory an analysis of aging linking disengagement by elderly people from positions of social responsibility to the orderly operation of society

gerontocracy a form of social organization in which the elderly have the most wealth, power, and privileges

gerontology the study of aging and the elderly

Suggested Readings

These two texts examine a number of issues related to aging, the elderly, and the life course.

Harold Cox. *Later Life: The Realities of Aging.* 3rd ed. Englewood Cliffs, NJ: Prentice Hall, 1993.

Eric R. Kingson, Barbara A. Hirshorn, and John M. Cornman. *Ties That Bind: The Interdependence of Generations.* Washington, DC: Seven Locks Press, 1986.

The first of these books is a Pulitzer Prize-winner, first published in 1975, criticizing America's approach to aging. The second offers a more recent assessment of the issue.

Robert N. Butler. *Why Survive? Being Old in America.* New York: Harper and Row, 1985.

Richard J. Margolis. *Risking Old Age in America.* Boulder, CO: Westview, 1989.

This fascinating and richly illustrated analysis of aging highlights the treatment of the elderly in Western societies over the last one thousand years.

Herbert C. Covey. *Images of Older People in Western Art and Society.* Westport, CT: Greenwood Publishers, 1991.

A psychological approach guides this study of the adjustments to growing old.

George Thorman. *Emotional Problems of Aging.* New York: Charles C Thomas, 1989.

The following article and books examine some of the issues facing women as they grow older

E. Gee and M. Kimball. *Women and Aging.* Toronto: Butterworths, 1987.

A. Martin-Matthews. "Widowhood as an Expectable Life Event," in V. Marshall, ed., *Aging in Canada: Social Perspectives, 2nd ed.* Markham, ON: Fitzhenry and Whiteside, 1989, pp. 343–66.

The following is a government publication describing the status and role of aging Canadians.

Government of Canada. *Canada's Seniors — A Dynamic Force.* Ottawa: Seniors Secretariat, 1988.

This is an overview of the health and health services issues confronting the elderly in Canada.

N. Chappell, L. Strain and A. Blandford. *Aging and Health Care: A Social Perspective.* Toronto: Holt, Rinehart and Winston, 1986.

This book examines the social and familial relationships of elderly Canadians.

I. Connidis. *Family Ties and Aging.* Toronto: Butterworths, 1989.

This provides an overview of the living arrangements and institutionalization of elderly Canadians.

W. Forbes, J. Jackson and A. Kraus. *Institutionalization of the Elderly in Canada.* Toronto: Butterworths, 1987.

This book focuses on the demographic description of Canadian elders.

S. McDaniel. *Canada's Aging Population.* Toronto: Butterworths, 1986.

This is a comprehensive sociological text on aging in Canada.

B. McPherson. *Aging as a Social Process: An Introduction to Individual and Population Aging,* Second Edition. Toronto: Butterworths, 1990.

FAMILY

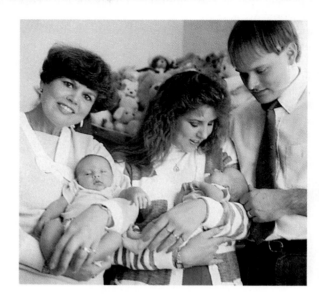

Twins were born in 1991 to Arlette Schweitzer, a forty-two-year-old librarian in the town of Aberdeen, South Dakota. While having twins is not extraordinary, the Schweitzer children made medical history as the *first case of a woman giving birth to her own grandchildren.*

Arlette Schweitzer agreed to carry and bear a child for her daughter—a woman born without a uterus and thus unable to have children on her own. Medical specialists removed eggs from the daughter's ovaries, placed them in a laboratory dish where they were fertilized with sperm from the daughter's husband, and then implanted the embryos in Arlette Schweitzer's womb (Kolata, 1991). When the twins—a girl and a boy—were born to Ms. Schweitzer, her daughter was at her side, tears of joy streaming down her face as she witnessed what would have been impossible a generation ago.

Cases of *surrogacy* like this one—in which one woman bears children using an egg from another woman—are becoming increasingly common throughout the world. In 1989 there were 118 reported cases of surrogate motherhood in Canada according to an unpublished report of the Canadian Law Reform Commission (Lipovenko, 1989). This number is likely an underestimate. In effect, new reproductive technology is

bending what were once regarded as the "rules" of family life, including the idea that only couples have children. Such techniques are blurring conventional kinship relations: what, for example, is Arlette Schweitzer's relation to the children she bore? Surrogacy is only one of many ways in which the traditional notion of family has changed in recent decades. Not long ago, the cultural ideal of the family was a working husband, a homemaker wife, and their children. This pattern still exists, of course, but now it represents slightly more than one in ten households in Canada. If a single set of characteristics ever accurately described our society's families, it simply does not today. This chapter will examine family life in Canada and elsewhere in the world, explore how families have changed over time, and explain why this important social group displays so much diversity today.

In all its forms, the family remains a major social institution in Canada, as it is in every other society. Recall from Chapter 4 ("Society") that social institutions are organizational systems a society uses to address one or more of its basic needs. Other social institutions, including schools, religion, politics, and the economy, are discussed in subsequent chapters of this book. We will see that each social institution is complex and has many consequences—negative as well as positive—for the operation of a society.

The Family: Basic Concepts

Kinship refers to *social ties based on blood, marriage, or adoption.* We develop emotional bonds toward people to whom we are "related," and kin meet many of an individual's needs. Especially in small preindustrial societies, most people cooperate with kin to secure their food and maintain their shelter. The functional significance of kinship declines somewhat in industrial societies: here people distinguish between close relatives, who interact regularly and typically live together, and distant relatives, among whom there is often little social contact.

Definitions of the family vary considerably around the world and change over time. Generally, the **family** is defined as *a relatively permanent social group of two or more people related by blood, marriage, or adoption, and who usually live together.* Family life tends to be cooperative. As the most important of our primary groups, families encourage members to share economic resources and day-to-day responsibilities. In industrial societies, people live first in a **family of orientation**, *the family into which a person is born and in which he or she receives early socialization.* Later in life, a person may live in a **family of procreation**, *a family in which people have or adopt children of their own.* In most societies of the world, families are formed by **marriage**, *a socially approved relationship, involving economic cooperation and allowing sexual activity and childbearing, that is expected to be relatively enduring.*

As we shall explain, although Canadian law only recognizes marriage as the formal union of one male and one female, marital patterns show striking variation in global perspective. The significance of marriage as the basis for procreation is evident in the traditional attachment of the label of *illegitimacy* to children born out of wedlock, and in the word *matrimony*, which is derived from Latin meaning "the condition of motherhood." This norm linking childbearing to marriage has weakened considerably, however, as the proportion of children born to unmarried women has increased.

Yet even these few generalizations cannot be applied to every family in Canada today. For example, many people object to defining as "families" only married couples and children. Thus traditional families have been increasingly complemented by various *families of affinity*: groups whose members are drawn together and who think of themselves as a family. For example, some communal groups of unrelated people who choose to live together for a period of time and share resources regard themselves as families. Similarly,

an unmarried couple and their children may live as a family, even if this pattern provokes disapproval in some quarters. Many gay and lesbian couples, some residing with children of one or both partners, also consider themselves family units.

Others, however, argue that because the family is central to our society, social approval should not be extended to any relationship simply because those involved wish to be defined as a family (Dedrick, 1990). What does or does not constitute a family, then, is now a matter of political debate. Courts play a part in this controversy: in some parts of the country, the law now recognizes the partnership of two people of one sex. Gays and lesbians are able to marry in religious ceremonies in some churches (although legal marriage remains restricted to heterosexual couples). Courts have more widely declared that unmarried partners may make claims on each other's property in the event that the relationship dissolves. Such rulings suggest that the concept of family—legally as well as socially—is taking on a broader meaning.

The Family in Cross-Cultural Perspective

Virtually all societies recognize families (Murdock, 1945), yet families are subject to significant cross-cultural variation.

As was noted in earlier chapters, industrial societies recognize the **nuclear family**, *a social unit composed of one or, more commonly, two parents and children.* Typically based on marriage, the nuclear family is also often called the *conjugal family.* In preindustrial societies, however, the **extended family**, *a social unit including parents, children, and other kin*, predominates. This is also called the *consanguine family*, meaning that it is based on blood ties. Extended families frequently include grandparents, aunts, uncles, and other kin. In Canada, extended families are not typical, but they are common among some ethnic categories, especially new immigrant groups. In addition, about one in seven elderly people lives with a relative other than a spouse, thereby forming an extended family.

Although many members of our society live in extended families, the nuclear family has been the predominant form in Canada (Nett, 1993). Industrialization intensifies the nuclear family pattern by moving productive work away from the home so that children grow up in one family (of orientation) only to leave in

In modern industrial societies, the members of extended families usually live apart from one another. However, they may assemble for rituals such as weddings, funerals, and family reunions. Here, 119 members of the Haviland clan gathered for a reunion near Brantford, Ontario.

order to pursue their careers and form a new family (of procreation). Both geographical and social mobility can tug at kinship ties, distancing members of extended families from one another.

Marriage Patterns

Cultural norms, often in the form of law, regulate whom a person may marry. These norms distinguish categories of people who *are* suitable mates from those who are *not*. One pattern that results from such norms is **endogamy**, *marriage between people of the same social group or category*. Every society has norms of endogamy that endorse marriage between people of the same age, tribe, race, religion, or social class. Some religions in Canada—especially Judaism and Catholicism—actively encourage endogamous marriage. The second pattern, also found in every society, is **exogamy**, *marriage between people of different social groups or categories*. The prohibition against gay marriage in Canada and most other societies is an obvious form of exogamy.

All societies, then, endorse some combination of endogamy and exogamy. Traditional villagers in India, for example, require a young person to marry someone from the same caste category but also from a different village. By uniting people of similar backgrounds, endogamy encourages group solidarity and helps to maintain traditional values and norms. At the same time, exogamy helps to forge useful alliances and encourages cultural diffusion.

In every industrial society, both law and cultural norms prescribe a form of marriage called **monogamy** (from Greek meaning "one union"), *marriage that joins one female and one male* . However, because divorce and remarriage occur frequently in our society, *serial monogamy*, that is, a series of monogamous marriages, more accurately describes the most prevalent pattern of matrimony in Canada. Today the average length of marriage is 12.4 years (Colombo, 1993:82). Global Map 15-1 shows that monogamy is legally prescribed throughout the Americas, in Europe, and in much of Asia.

Most marriages in the rest of the world are also monogamous. But, as Global Map 15-1 shows, many preindustrial societies—especially in Africa and southern Asia—permit **polygamy** (from Greek meaning "many unions"), *marriage that unites three or more people*. In polygamous marriage two or more nuclear families are combined to form an extended family. Polygamy takes two forms. By far the more common is **polygyny** (from the Greek, meaning "many women" or "many wives"), *marriage that joins one male with more than one female*. Islamic societies in southern Asia and Africa, for example, allow men to have up to four wives. In societies that endorse polygyny, most families are nonetheless monogamous because great wealth is required to support several wives and even more children. Polygyny was officially sanctioned by the Mormon church (formally known as the Church of Jesus Christ of Latter-Day Saints) based in Utah. In 1890, however, the Mormons banned what they termed "plural marriage" in order to win statehood for Utah from the U.S. federal government. However, some polygamous Mormon families moved north to settle in Southern Alberta in 1887, founding Cardston and numerous surrounding small towns (Parry, 1988). Even today, some Mormons live in plural marriages—one legal marriage and others performed by a local church.

Polyandry (from the Greek, meaning "many men" or "many husbands") is *marriage that joins one female with more than one male*. This pattern is extremely rare, appearing only in a few settings, such as among Tibetan Buddhists. Polyandry discourages the division of land into parcels too small to support a family and divides the burdensome costs of supporting a wife among many men. Polyandry has also been associated with female infanticide, the aborting of female fetuses or killing of female infants. This practice reduces the female population so that men must share women.

In sum, the historical record shows that in the

WINDOW ON THE WORLD

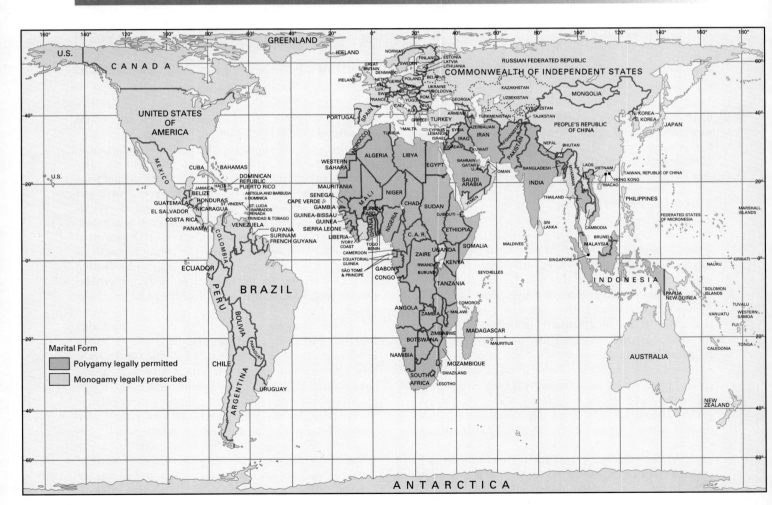

GLOBAL MAP 15-1   MARITAL FORM IN GLOBAL PERSPECTIVE
Monogamy is the legally prescribed form of marriage in all industrial societies, and throughout the Western hemisphere. In most African nations, as well as in south Asia, however, polygamy is permitted by law. In the majority of cases, this reflects the historic influence of Islam, a religion that allows a man to have no more than four wives. Even so, most marriages in these societies are also monogamous.

majority of world societies monogamy has been just one of several approved marital patterns; yet, most marriages throughout the world have been monogamous (Murdock, 1965). This cultural preference for monogamy stems from two common-sense factors: first, the financial burden of supporting multiple spouses is onerous, and second, the rough numerical parity of the sexes limits the possibility for polygamy.

Residential Patterns

Just as societies guide the process of mate selection, so they have norms that designate where a couple should reside. Most industrial societies favor **neolocality** (from the Greek, meaning "new place"), *a pattern in which a married couple establishes a new residence apart from their parents.* Although newlyweds may live with the parents of one spouse—especially if finances do not permit their setting up a new home—our cultural norm appears to be "Honor thy mother and father—but get away from them" (Blumstein & Schwartz, 1983:26).

In preindustrial societies, newlyweds often gain economic assistance and personal security by residing with one set of parents or the other. **Patrilocality** (Greek for "place of the father") is *a residential pattern in which a married couple lives with or near the husband's family.* In global perspective, this is the most prevalent pattern (Murdock, 1965). Less common in the world is **matrilocality** (meaning "place of the mother"), *a residential pattern in which a married couple lives with or near the wife's family.* Evidence suggests that patterns of locality have much to do with warfare; in bellicose societies, families favor keeping married sons at home. In addition, whether a society is matrilocal or patrilocal depends on whether daughters or sons are thought to be greater economic assets (Ember & Ember, 1971, 1991).

Patterns of Descent

Descent refers to *the system by which members of a society trace kinship over generations.* In simple terms, descent is the system of defining relatives. Industrial societies like our own recognize a pattern of **bilateral descent** ("two-sided descent"), *a system tracing kinship through both females and males.* In a bilateral society, children are linked by kinship to the families of both parents.

Most preindustrial societies, however, trace kinship only through one parent or the other. **Patrilineal descent,** *a system tracing kinship through males,* pre-dominates in these societies. This means that the father's side of the family—but not the mother's—is defined as kin; practically speaking, in patrilineal schemes only males can inherit property. Less common is **matrilineal descent,** *a system tracing kinship through females.* Here, only the mother's side of the family is considered kin, and property passes from mothers to daughters. Patrilineal descent is common among pastoral and agrarian societies, in which men produce the most valued resources. Matrilineal descent characterizes most horticultural societies, in which women are the primary breadwinners (Haviland, 1985).

Laws regarding citizenship often reflect traditional patterns of descent. As explained in the opening to Chapter 13 ("Sex and Gender"), laws in the southern African nation of Botswana until recently extended citizenship to children born to a Botswanan man and a foreign woman, but denied citizenship to the offspring of a Botswanan woman and a foreign man. This pattern was overturned in 1991 by a lawsuit brought by a woman in just such a situation; it is likely to be the first of many challenges to laws based in traditional patriarchy throughout the African continent (Shapiro, 1991).

Patterns of Authority

The predominance of polygyny, patrilocality, and patrilineal descent in the world reflects the ubiquity of some degree of patriarchy. In industrial societies such as Canada, households containing a married couple are usually headed by a man, just as men dominate most areas of social life. More egalitarian family patterns are gradually evolving, especially as increasing numbers of women enter the labor force, but the social status of wife remains lower than that of husband. Parents in Canada also still prefer boys to girls, and most children are given their father's last name.

Theoretical Analysis of the Family

As in earlier chapters, several theoretical approaches will be used to provide various insights about the family.

Functions of the Family

The structural-functional paradigm holds that the family performs several of any society's basic tasks. This explains why the family is sometimes described as "the backbone of society."

Socialization

As explained in Chapter 5 ("Socialization"), the family is the first agent in the socialization process, typically exerting more influence than peer groups, schools, churches, and the mass media. The personalities of each new generation take shape within the family, so that, ideally, adults guide children to become well-integrated and contributing members of the larger society. Early functionalists argued that the two sexes were socialized differently because the adult responsibilities of husbands (as breadwinners) and wives (as caregivers) were quite different (Parsons, 1954; Parsons & Bales, 1955). Within families of orientation, in short, boys and girls learn many of the attitudes and skills that will serve them as they establish families of procreation later on.

Regulation of Sexual Activity

Every culture restricts sexual activity because human reproduction is central to kinship organization and property rights. One universal regulation is the **incest taboo**, *a cultural norm forbidding sexual relations or marriage between certain kin.* Although the incest taboo is found throughout the world, precisely which kin are regulated in this way varies from one culture to another. The Navajo, for example, forbid their members to marry any relative of one's mother. Most people in Canada formally apply the incest taboo to both sides of the family but limit it to close relatives, including parents, grandparents, siblings, aunts, and uncles. But even here norms are not consistent. Catholics reject marriage between first cousins, for example, while Jews do not (Murphy, 1979).

Interestingly, the sexual relations that most members of our society view as immoral and unnatural have been condoned, or even encouraged, in some other cultures. Brother-sister marriages, for example, were common among the ancient Babylonian, Egyptian, Incan, and Hawaiian nobility, and reports suggest that male nobles of the Azande in eastern Africa married their daughters (Murdock, 1965; Masserman & Uribe, 1989).

The significance of the incest taboo lies primarily in social rather than biological imperatives. While sexual activity between close relatives can adversely affect the mental and physical health of offspring, this outcome, in and of itself, does not explain why the incest taboo is observed by only one form of life: human

beings. As Robert Murphy (1979) suggests, it is society more than nature that punishes incest. Why? Because the incest taboo supports family life in several ways. First, by restricting legitimate sexual activity to spouses, the incest taboo minimizes sexual competition and resulting conflict within families. Second, it forces people to marry outside their immediate family; this produces political and economic ties throughout the society. Third, in every society kinship forms an important system that determines people's rights and obligations toward one another. Allowing close relatives to reproduce would erode kinship and threaten relational chaos. It is for this reason that our society has moved cautiously to allow surrogate parenting of the kind described at the beginning of this chapter.

Social Placement

Although families are not *biologically* required for reproduction, they do provide for the *social* placement of children. Most social statuses—including race, ethnicity, religion, and social class—are ascribed at birth

The "family resemblance" of Martin and Charlie Sheen means more than sharing physical features. The range of any child's opportunities and interests depends on the social position of parents. As sociologists have discovered, the family actually serves to reproduce the class structure, a fact suggested by the way in which children typically "follow in the footsteps" of the older generation.

through the family. This fact explains the historical concern that children be born of socially sanctioned marriages. So-called "legitimate" birth—especially when parents are of similar social position—allows for the stable transmission of property and other dimensions of social standing from parents to children.

Material and Emotional Security

People turn to family members for physical protection as well as emotional and financial support. Because the family is a person's most important primary group, kin generally have intense and enduring relationships. Such personal concern seems to engender a sense of self-worth and security, two emotional elements that bolster strong physical health. Significantly, people living in families tend to be healthier than those living alone.

Critical evaluation. Structural-functional analysis identifies a number of the family's major functions. From this point of view, it is easy to see that society as we know it could not exist without families.

However, this approach has several limitations. First, in implying support for the traditional family, the structural-functional view minimizes how other institutions (like government, for example) could meet at least some of these human needs. This paradigm also overlooks the great diversity of family life in Canada. Finally, by highlighting the social cohesion that families can engender, structural-functionalism focuses little attention on the conflict and problems of family life. For example, while many families do provide emotional support to their members, violence is also common in families, with the dysfunctional effect of undermining people's self-confidence and well-being.

Social Inequality and the Family

Like the structural-functional approach, the social-conflict paradigm also links the family to the operations of society, but conflict theorists investigate how the family perpetuates patterns of social inequality. Still another "function" of the family, in other words, is to maintain the social dominance of certain categories of people at the expense of others.

The Family, Class, and Race

As noted in Chapter 13 ("Sex and Gender"), Friedrich Engels (1902; orig. 1884) traced the origin of the family to the historical development of private property. In brief, Engels argued that families emerged so individuals—at least those of the higher classes—could identify their heirs, ensuring that wealth would be passed from generation to generation. In this view, families concentrate wealth in the hands of a small proportion of the population and privilege their offspring (Mare, 1991). In industrial societies, then, the family shores up social inequality and also restrains individual social mobility. Following Engels's lead, then, the family is part and parcel of capitalism.

Moreover, racial and ethnic inequality, described in Chapter 12 ("Race and Ethnicity"), is also perpetuated through the operation of the family. Norms of endogamy guide people at each social level to marry others in the same racial and ethnic categories. As a result, social inequality persists across the generations.

The Family and Patriarchy

The family, Engels explained, also reflects and perpetuates patriarchy. The only way for men to clearly identify their progeny is by controlling the sexuality of women. Moreover, Engels continued, families turn women into both the sexual and economic property of men. A century ago in Canada the earnings of wives typically belonged to their husbands as heads of the household. Although this practice is no longer upheld by law, other examples of husbands' domination of their wives remain. Women still bear major responsibility for childrearing and housework, a pattern that has changed little even as women have entered the paid work force (Nett, 1993). Although patriarchal families offer considerable benefits to men, they too are disadvantaged by having less opportunity to share in the human satisfaction and personal growth derived from interaction with children.

Later in this chapter, we will explore how the link between the traditional family and social inequality relates to a number of conflicts and changes, such as violence against women, divorce, and the trend of women choosing to raise children outside of marriage.

Critical evaluation. Social-conflict analysis reveals another side of the family: its significant role in maintaining various kinds of social inequality. As later sections explain, inequality also shapes the family, so that various classes, races, and even the two genders experience family life in significantly different ways.

The greatest limitation of the approach taken by Engels is that even societies that have rejected the capitalist economy have families all the same. The family and social inequality are deeply intertwined, as Engels maintained, but the family appears to carry out various societal functions that are not easily accomplished by other means.

Other Theoretical Analyses

Both structural-functional and social-conflict analyses view the family in broad terms as a central structure of society. More micro-level approaches, by contrast, explore individual experiences of family life.

The Social Construction of Family Life

Chapter 6 ("Social Interaction in Everyday Life") explores the process by which people in interaction construct the reality they perceive. Applying this insight to the family, symbolic-interaction analysis argues that the reality of living in a particular household is likely to be quite different for various family members. Research supports the conclusion that women and men view their marriages very differently (Bernard, 1982). Similarly, a child and parent may share a home but understand little of each other's lives. For example, children usually think of their parents only as fathers and mothers, with little appreciation that these adults are also lovers.

Furthermore, the experiences and perceptions of parents and children alike change over time. Two people's expectations as they exchange their wedding vows usually evolve considerably when they confront the daily realities of married life. A change in the role of one spouse, such as a wife entering law school, may also alter the roles of other family members. And, of course, the arrival of a first child rewrites the rules of life for many couples. Thus the symbolic-interaction approach addresses the inadequacy of describing marriage and the family in terms of any rigid characteristics.

Social-Exchange Analysis

Social-exchange analysis is an insightful approach that casts courtship and marriage as a negotiation in which people offer each other socially valued resources and advantages (Blau, 1964). In courtship, each person assesses the likely advantages and disadvantages of taking the other as a spouse. Physical attractiveness is one critical dimension of exchange. In patriarchal societies around the world, beauty has long been a commodity offered by women on the marriage market. The social value assigned to beauty explains women's traditional concern with physical appearance and their sensitivity about revealing their age. Men, by contrast, often show-

case their financial resources so that less physically attractive men may succeed in marrying attractive women if they can offer them a high income (Melville, 1983). Dimensions of social exchange are converging for the two sexes as more women enter the labor force and become less dependent on men to support them and their children.

Critical evaluation. Micro-level analysis provides a useful counterbalance to structural-functional and social-conflict visions of the family as one of society's institutional systems. Adopting an interactional viewpoint, we gain a better sense of the individual experiences of family members, who creatively shape reality as they engage others in various ways.

The prime limitation of this approach is that the family *is*, in important respects, a system, one shaped by economic and cultural forces and traditions. Further, families in Canada do vary according to key social dimensions such as class and ethnicity and, as the next section explains, they evolve through typical stages linked to the life course.

Stages of Family Life

The family is dynamic, experiencing marked changes across the life course. Typically, family life begins with courtship, followed by settling into the realities of married life. Next, for most couples at least, is raising children, leading to the later years of marriage after children have left home to form families of their own. We will look briefly at each of these stages.

Courtship

Because family ties are vital economic assets, the members of preindustrial societies consider courtship too important to leave to prospective spouses (Stone, 1977; Haviland, 1985). An *arranged marriage* represents *an alliance between two extended families that affects the social standing of both.* Parents spend considerable time and effort investigating possibilities for marriage and, given the right opportunity, they make arrangements for marriage when their child is very young. A century ago in India, for example, children were married as early as five years of age, and half the females were married by the age of fifteen (Mayo, 1927; Mace & Mace, 1960). Today, such early marriages are less common, but still occur in traditional villages.

Arranged marriages fit into Emile Durkheim's scheme of "mechanical solidarity" (see Chapter 4, "Society"). In homogeneous traditional societies, almost any member of the opposite sex is a suitable marriage partner because all children are socialized in similar fashion to perform that society's roles of spouse and parent. While we think of marriage as joining two individuals who are *personally* compatible, in short, members of internally homogeneous societies consider that virtually any couple will be *culturally* compatible.

With industrialization, the declining importance of extended families fosters growing individuality and more personal choice in courtship. Therefore young people need to gain extensive experience in courtship because they will have a greater say in selecting their partner. The duration of courtship depends on the age at which people first marry; this, in turn, has much to do with economic security (Landale & Tolnay, 1991). Through much of this century, economic prosperity pushed down the age of first marriage. By mid-century, the typical first marriage for women occurred at age twenty (down two years from the beginning of the century) and for men at about age twenty-two (some four years earlier than at the turn of the century). Since 1970, however, real income has stalled and more women have entered the labor force to shore up their families' standard of living. In this uncertain economic climate, women and men are delaying marriage and childbearing once again as they pursue schooling or save money before beginning family life. The average age for men and women marrying for the first time was twenty-eight years for men and twenty-six years for women in 1991 (*Maclean's*, 1993).

Despite some variation, marriage concludes a long period of dating. Courtship generally begins as group dating, in which several girls and boys interact together. In time, group dating gives way to couple dating. In Canada today, courtship frequently involves a period of sexual experimentation; couples may also live together before deciding to marry.

Industrial societies such as our own elevate *romantic love* —the experience of affection and sexual passion toward another person—as the basis for marriage. The distaste for arranged marriages certainly reflects this exaltation of romantic love. For most people in Canada, marriage without love is difficult to imagine, and the mass media—from traditional fairy tales like "Cinderella" to contemporary paperback romance novels—present romantic love as the keystone of successful matrimony.

Romantic love was well established among the nobility early in the Middle Ages. Courtly love (like the term "courtship," derived from the noble courts of this earlier era) was not, however, grounds for marriage: more practical considerations of social standing held sway in the choice of a marital partner. The notion of romance was more a feudal ideal by which knights pledged themselves in service to noblewomen whom they revered from a distance but were ineligible to marry. Such love was never destined to develop into even personal intimacy. The most knights could hope to win for themselves through displays of bravery and dedication was a noblewoman's praise and respect (Beigel, 1951).

Over the centuries, romantic love grew in importance as the basis of marriage. In our more individualistic society, romantic love now functions to encourage an individual to leave the original family of orientation to form a new family of procreation. As an incentive to forming new families, romantic love is usually most intense when people first marry, sometimes helping to carry a newly married couple through the difficult adjustments to the realities of married life (Goode, 1959). Yet, the modern emphasis on romantic love also presents problems. Because it rests on feelings that may change, romantic love is a less stable foundation for marriage than social and economic considerations. Furthermore, as "Cinderella" and other folk tales suggest, romantic love can draw together people of different social backgrounds. Although social pressures discourage such pairings, they are increasing. Thus, romantic love can be a truly revolutionary force as marriages guided solely by the heart challenge racial, ethnic, religious, and social class boundaries.

Sociologists have long recognized that Cupid's arrow is aimed by society more than we like to believe. Even today, most married couples are about the same age and of the same race, religion, and social class. This pattern is called **homogamy** (literally, "like marrying like"), *marriage between people who are socially alike*.

Homogamy is common, first, because people of one social background tend to interact in the same neighborhoods, attend the same schools, and frequent the same recreational settings. Second, a common socialization encourages similar tastes and interests, so that we are likely to be attracted to people with the same social backgrounds as we have. Third, parents and peers often discourage marrying an "outsider." In some cases, this influence is subtle; in others, it is quite heavy-handed. Traditional Jews, for example, strongly oppose the marriage of their children to non-Jews. If a son or daughter should marry out of the religion, parents may "sit shiva," observing a ritual to lament the loss of a loved one. While usually done following a death, here sitting shiva signifies that by marrying an outsider the child has undergone social death and may no longer be considered a member of the family.

"Falling in love," then, may induce strong personal feelings, but the process of courtship is guided by a host of social forces. Perhaps we exaggerate the importance of romantic love to reassure ourselves that even in the midst of society we are capable of making personal choices.

Settling In: Ideal and Real Marriage

In light of the social importance of marriage, we can understand why socialization often instills highly idealized images of matrimony. Consider the following account of a thirty-one-year-old woman, married eleven years and the mother of three children:

> When I got married, I suppose I must have loved him, but at the time, I was busy planning the wedding and I wasn't thinking about anything else. I was just thinking about this big white wedding and all the trimmings, and how I was going to be a beautiful bride, and how I would finally have my own house. I never thought about problems we might have or anything like that. I don't know even if I ever thought much about him. Oh, I wanted to make a nice home for Glen, but I wasn't thinking about how anyone did that or whether I loved him enough to live with him the rest of my life. I was too busy with my dreams and thinking about how they were finally coming true. (Rubin, 1976:69)

We do not have to read between the lines to see that for this woman family life has fallen short of earlier expectations. Idealizing marriage and the family often amounts to courting disappointment. Especially for women—who, more than men, are socialized to view marriage as the key to future happiness—marital pleasures often give way to disenchantment. Courtship brings couples together for limited periods, so they may see each other only at their best. Moreover, research suggests that romantic love involves a good deal of fantasy: people fall in love with others, not necessarily as they are, but as they want them to be (Berscheid & Hatfield, 1983). Within marriage, however, spouses confront each other regularly and realistically, for better and for worse. And only after marriage do many couples face the day-to-day challenges of maintaining a household. Sobering responsibilities include paying monthly

The Wedding Portrait *(1434)*, by Flemish artist Jan Van Eyck *(1390–1441)*, is a masterpiece of its time. Here we see a young couple solemnly reciting their wedding vows—a statement of the reverence with which people of that age approached marriage. The single candle in the chandelier above their heads symbolizes Christ, and the couple's removal of their shoes indicates that they are engaged in a holy ritual.

(Jan Van Eyck, Giovanni Arnolfini and His Bride, *1434. Oil on wood. 33 x 22 1/2". The National Gallery, London.)*

bills, managing relations with in-laws, and performing mundane tasks such as shopping, cooking, and cleaning. Therefore, a great deal about marriage and one's spouse is learned only *after* the wedding.

Newly married couples may also have to make sexual adjustments. Several generations ago, cultural norms in Canada endorsed sexual activity only after marriage and, no doubt, some people married simply for this reason. Today, however, the majority of university students say they have experienced premarital intercourse (see Table 15-1). Where twenty years ago, the majority of Canadians (57 percent) felt that premarital sex was wrong, now, only 35 percent feel that it is wrong (Bozinoff & MacIntosh, 1990).

TABLE 15-1   CANADIAN SURVEYS OF PREMARITAL SEX AMONG UNIVERSITY STUDENTS

Researcher	Sample Size	University Location	Date	% Experienced Intercourse Males	Females
Mann (1967)	120	Ontario, Western	1965	35	15
Barrett (1980b)	415	Ontario, U. of Toronto	1968	40	32
Hobart (1972)	1,104	Alberta, Ontario, Que.	1968	56	44
Mann (1969)	153	Ontario, York	1969	51	31
Perlman (1973)	156	Manitoba	1970	55	37
Perlman (1978)	259	Manitoba	1975	62	45
Pool & Pool (1978)	404	Ontario, Carleton	1975	–	66
Pool & Pool (1978)	390	Ontario, U. of Ottawa	1975	–	53
Herold & Thomas (1978)	481	Ontario	1975	64	55
Hobart (1979)	2,062	Five provinces	1977	73	63
Barrett (1980b)	1,384	Ontario, U. of Toronto	1978	62	58
Herold, Way, & Kitchen	363	Ontario, Guelph	1982	60	52

SOURCE: E.S. Herold, *Sexual Behaviour of Canadian Young People* (Markham, Ont.: Fitzhenry and Whiteside, 1984), 13.

But earlier experiences do not prevent sex from proving a disappointment in marriage. In the romantic haze of falling in love, people may anticipate marriage as an extended erotic honeymoon only to find that, in time, sex becomes less than an all-consuming passion. One important U.S. study of marital sex found that 70 percent of married respondents claimed to be satisfied with the sexual dimension of their marriage, but documented a decline in sexual activity over time (Blumstein & Schwartz, 1983).

Research also suggests that couples with the most satisfying sexual relationships have the greatest overall satisfaction with their marriages. While this does not mean that sex ensures marital bliss, good sex and good relationships apparently go together (Hunt, 1974; Tavris & Sadd, 1977; Blumstein & Schwartz, 1983).

Even though there appears to be increasing tolerance for premarital sex, most Canadians are still opposed to extra-marital infidelity. Reginald Bibby (1983) found that three in four adults viewed such behavior as always wrong, and only 4 percent believed that it was not wrong at all. However, Bibby did find that there was a greater degree of tolerance for extra-marital sex among people in larger cities, the younger and more highly educated, the divorced and separated, and those with little religious faith (Nett, 1993). During the 1980s, public disapproval of extramarital sex showed a modest increase, partly because of the AIDS crisis. Thus we should bear in mind that sexual behavior involves not only moral concerns but practical fears of contracting sexually transmitted diseases.

Despite such support for fidelity, many married people do engage in extramarital sex. According to a Gallup poll, 13 percent of Canadians admitted to having an affair while married. Seventeen percent of males and 9 percent of females admitted to having an affair while married or living with someone common-law (Gallup Sexual Lifestyle Survey, 1988).

Child Rearing

The birth of a child changes marriage significantly as new demands are made on each spouse's attention, time, and energy. One thirty-year-old father described how the birth of his son had disrupted his marriage:

Those first two years were almost perfect. ... But when the baby was born everything began to change; it sort of all fell apart. It seemed [my wife] was busy with him all the time. And I felt like I didn't count anymore ... and I got resentful of Danny, then I felt terrible. What kind of father am I to feel resentful at a little kid like that? But I couldn't help how I felt. (Rubin, 1983:61)

Although some people may be ambivalent about children, Table 15-2 shows that almost all Canadians include at least one child in their conception of the ideal family. Two children is the overwhelming preference, and few people today desire four or more children—a change from two centuries ago, when *eight* children was the norm (Newman & Matzke, 1984). As Table 15-2 shows, the percent of Canadians preferring four or more children declined from 60 percent in 1945 to 13 percent in 1988, while the percent of Canadians preferring two children has increased from 17 to 58 percent during the same time period.

In preindustrial societies, production depends on

TABLE 15-2   THE IDEAL NUMBER OF CHILDREN

	Two or less	Three	Four or more
1988	58%	29%	13%
1987	58	29	13
1986	61	26	13
1985	56	33	11
1984	61	26	13
1983	56	27	17
1982	63	25	12
1980	59	27	14
1974	52	24	24
1970	34	33	33
1957	22	23	55
1945	17	23	60

SOURCE: Gallup Canada Inc., The Gallup Report, June 6, 1988, p. 2.

human labor, so adults view children as an economic asset. Then, too, having children was also regarded as a wife's duty. Birth control technology was crude and unreliable, so women frequently became pregnant whether they wanted to or not. Finally, having many babies did not necessarily mean raising a large family, as the child and infant death rate was considerably higher in the past (Nancarrow Clarke, 1990).

With industrialization, the economic equation changes drastically when it comes to children. Children today rarely become financially independent until at least age eighteen (and sometimes not until their mid-twenties), and the expense of raising them can be staggering. The total cost of raising a child to age 22 (born in 1980) in an average two-parent family is an estimated $141,673 (1982 dollars) or 21.9 percent of the net present value (1982) of family income. This includes the expenses associated with post-secondary education away from home (Olson, 1983).

The rising proportion of women in the labor force also delays marriage and reduces childbearing. Technology is also at work here, since birth control is now effective, simple to use, and easy to obtain, reducing the number of unplanned pregnancies. Abortion was declared legal in 1969 and authorized under section 18 of the Criminal Law Amendment Act. The law allowed abortion only in approved hospitals, and only if a therapeutic abortion committee, comprised of at least three physicians, certified that a continuation of the pregnancy could or would be likely to endanger the life or health of the pregnant woman. The therepeutic abortion rate, expressed as a percent of live births, grew from 13.7 in 1975 to about 18 percent in the late seventies and early eighties.

Finally, as we have seen, a significant reduction in

infant mortality has also lessened parents' need to have many children because the vast majority of infants now survive to adulthood. Taken together, these factors explain the steadily declining birth rate over the course of this century to roughly two children per family today.

This low rate of childbirth stands in sharp contrast to that in poor societies of the world. Having four or five children is typical for women in much of Latin America and Asia; in most countries of Africa, the number is closer to six. The reason for such high birth rates is that Third World women have few alternatives to bearing and raising children, and families depend on the labor of offspring to survive.

In much of the world, child rearing is a cooperative task performed by the extended family. In Canada, a nuclear family system makes the care of children the primary responsibility of parents, people who may have little preparation for this vital role. Nor does our society demand competence before men and women become parents: the privilege of driving a car requires a person to demonstrate necessary skills, but there is no comparable measure of fitness for parenthood. While we acquire many useful lessons from our parents, we often learn little about family life from their point of view (Macionis, 1978; Pollak & Wise, 1979). Thus new parents learn "on the job" from their own successes and mistakes.

As explained in Chapter 13 ("Sex and Gender"), the entry of women into the labor force in Canada has been dramatic. In 1988, 73.4 percent of women aged twenty-five to fifty-four were employed in the labor force (Statistics Canada, 1989). Moreover, most women with children were employed outside the home. But while women and men are sharing the burdens of earning an income, contemporary women still bear the traditional responsibility for raising children and doing a variety of tasks at home. Although some men in our society eagerly embrace parenting chores, most continue to resist accepting responsibility for household tasks that our culture has historically defined as feminine (Radin, 1982).

As more women join men in the labor force, public attention has focused on what are called *latchkey kids*—children whose working parents leave them to fend for themselves for a good part of the day. Defenders of traditional family values, such as REAL Women (Dubinsky, 1985), contend that many working mothers are neglecting their responsibilities to children. Husbands and fathers are rarely subject to this criticism because their income is assumed to be necessary to support their families. But the same now holds true for most mothers working outside the home (Keniston, 1985). This new reality underlies growing support for programs of childcare sponsored either by private employers or, more equitably, by the government.

Because parenting competes with other personal interests and, increasingly, the need to earn a living, more couples are choosing to delay childbirth or to remain childless. As Figure 15-1 shows, the median age of mothers giving birth to their first child in 1987 was almost 26 years, an increase of more than three years since 1971. The same is true for the increasing age of mothers who give birth to their second child (*Women in Canada:* 1980). One recent survey indicated that about two-thirds of parents in the United States would like to be able to devote far more time to child rearing (Snell, 1990). The majority of Canadian parents would likely say the same. But unless we are willing to endure a decline in our material standard of living, economic realities demand that both parents pursue careers outside the home. The child rearing patterns we have described fundamentally reflect how people are coming to terms with economic change.

The Family in Later Life

Increasing life expectancy in Canada means that, barring divorce, couples are likely to remain married for a long time. By about age fifty, most have completed the major task of raising children. The remaining years of marriage are commonly described as the "empty nest" period because, as at the beginning of marriage, cou-

ples usually have no children living in their households. This phase has been delayed (or interrupted) in recent years due to economic pressures (and sometimes divorce) that keep increasing numbers of young people living with their parents. Most single men (seven out of ten) and single women (six out of ten) between the ages of twenty and twenty-four live at home with their parents. This is up considerably from earlier in the century when it was estimated (1911) that the average age at which a young person achieved residential independence, was sixteen (Nett, 1993).

Like the birth of children, their eventual departure causes important changes in a family. Couples must make serious adjustments to losing a common focus of daily routines. Even so, spouses frequently grow closer and the marital relationship often becomes more satisfying at this point in life (Kalish, 1982). A healthy marriage at this stage of life is generally characterized by companionship. Years of living together may have diminished a couple's sexual passion for each other, but mutual understanding and commitment are likely to have grown stronger.

Personal contact with children usually continues, since most older adults live a short distance from at least one of their children (Connidis, 1989). People's incomes peak in late middle age, as the expenses of childrearing diminish. Thus at this stage in family life, parenting may involve helping children make large purchases (a car or a house) and, of course, periodically babysitting for grandchildren.

As explained in Chapter 14 ("Aging and the Elderly"), more adults in midlife face the challenge of caring for aging parents. The "empty nest" may not be filled by a parent coming to live in the home, but many adults find that parents living into their late seventies and beyond make practical, emotional, and financial demands that cannot always be met. The oldest of the "baby boomers"—now in their mid-forties—are being touted as the "sandwich generation" because they will spend as many years caring for their aging parents as they did raising their own children.

Retirement, also discussed in Chapter 14 ("Aging and the Elderly"), represents another change in family life. Traditionally, the man retired from the labor force to spend much more time at home. Although the husband's presence was often a source of pleasure to both, it sometimes undermined wives' established routines. The presence of a retired husband was little more than an intrusion to one woman, who bluntly stated: "I may have married him for better or worse, but not for lunch" (Kalish, 1982:96). Because retirement is becoming a

FIGURE 15-1   MEDIAN AGE OF MOTHERS GIVING BIRTH TO FIRST OR SECOND CHILD, 1971–1990
Source: Statistics Canada, Canadian Centre for Health Information, Health Status Section, 1991.

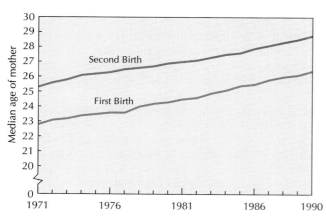

common experience for both spouses, this final stage of family life will provide the opportunity for wives and husbands to enjoy many new activities together.

The final and surely the most difficult transition in married life comes with the death of a spouse. Wives typically outlive their husbands because of their longer life expectancy and also because women usually marry men who are several years older than they are. Wives can thus expect to spend a significant period of their lives as widows. The bereavement and loneliness accompanying the death of a spouse can pose serious challenges. This experience may be even more difficult when the tables are turned: widowers usually have fewer friends than widows do, and men who have spent their lives in traditional masculine roles must adjust to the unfamiliar responsibility of housework (Berardo, 1970).

Varieties of Family Life

Social class, race and ethnicity, and gender are powerful forces that shape the lives of people in all settings and situations. Together, they generate considerable variation in marriage and family life.

Social Class

As was described in Chapter 10 ("Social Class in Canada"), social class accounts for vast differences in standards of living. A family's class position affects its financial resources and range of opportunities, as well as patterns of interaction in the home.

Affluence is no guarantee of personal happiness, nor does it ensure a successful family life. But economic advantages do permit a greater sense of security in an uncertain world. In a study of working-class families, Lillian Rubin reports the following observations of a working-class housewife:

> I guess I can't complain. He's a steady worker; he doesn't drink; he doesn't hit me. That's a lot more than my mother had, and she didn't sit around complaining and feeling sorry for herself, so I sure haven't got the right. (1976:33)

Being a steady worker, not drinking excessively, and refraining from violence, Rubin discovered, were the three attributes most frequently mentioned by working-class women as positive qualities in a husband. By con-

trast, Rubin found, these attributes were almost never mentioned by middle-class women evaluating their marriages. More privileged women were concerned with intimacy, sharing, and communication with their husbands. Of course, working-class women value these things, too, but they simply recognize that issues of relational quality are secondary to the basic need for economic and physical security.

Social scientists have also documented the negative effects of unemployment on family life (Brenner, 1976). The loss of a job is more common among people of lower social standing, who have fewer resources to begin with. For those who contend with daily economic uncertainty, unemployment sharply heightens fears and anxieties, which can erode family life. A thirty-year-old man recalls the turmoil caused by the loss of his job:

> Right after our first kid was born, I got laid off ... and I didn't have much in the way of skills to get another job with. My unemployment [payments] ran out pretty quick, and Sue Ann couldn't work because of the baby ... so we moved in with my folks. We lived there for about a year. What a mess. My mom and Sue Ann just didn't get along. (Rubin, 1976:73)

While money cannot buy happiness, as the saying goes, its absence certainly introduces strains and pressures into the lives of parents and children.

Social class also affects the relationship between spouses. Men and women of higher social class tend to be more open and expressive with each other (Komarovsky, 1967; Rubin, 1976; Fitzpatrick, 1988). This is because people of higher social standing have more schooling, and most hold jobs that emphasize verbal skills. Additionally, each social class has a distinctive pattern of socialization. As was noted in Chapter 5 ("Socialization"), working-class parents, more than their middle-class counterparts, teach their children to embrace conventional gender roles and to follow rules. By contrast, middle-class parents stress the importance of imagination and self-expression (Rubin, 1976; Kohn, 1977).

Rigid adherence to gender roles creates a rift between husbands and wives, who end up leading very different lives and sharing fewer interests. Lillian Rubin (1976) explains that men who grew up with conventional notions about masculine self-control and the need to stifle emotional expressiveness tend to be tight-lipped about their personal feelings. Women socialized to be feminine find it easier to express themselves more openly. As a result, husbands and wives may speak different languages, seeking out members of their own sex as confidants because they experience frustration in trying to simply talk to one another.

Ethnicity and Race

As Chapter 12 ("Race and Ethnicity") indicated, ethnicity and race exert powerful influences in our lives. The effects of both surface in family life.

Canada is an ethnically and racially heterogeneous country. The ethnic and racial groups vary in the extent to which they are distinguishable from the "majority". Some groups retain more aspects of their cultures (including language, religion, and even internal political and economic customs) than others. Generally, people of color are more likely to be seen and related to as if they are from a different background (experiencing discrimination, prejudice and stereotyping).

Family differences based on ethnic origin vary in the same way as other aspects of culture. Some ethnic groups strive to maintain mate selection, courtship patterns, parent-child relations, and husband-wife interaction customs from their original culture. Others may try to adapt to "Canadian" ways. Chapter 12 ("Race and Ethnicity") discusses these general issues in more depth. Here, we will simply note some of the variations that are found in some ethnic group families, particularly first and second generation immigrant families.

Families differ in the degree to which the nuclear family is separate and distinct from the extended family. Often first and second generation immigrant families, particularly those from southern Europe, Latin America, and China, maintain extended family connections by living together, visiting regularly, or being involved in each other's recreation, child care, employment, education, and religious practices.

While polygamy is characteristic of some cultural groups, including Mormons and Moslems, because it is illegal in Canada there is no accurate record of its prevalence. Now and then a case of polygamy comes to light, but it is always seen as a deviant case by the dominant majority. Among some ethnic groups, notably those of (upper-class) Middle Eastern, Japanese, and Moslem origin, arranged marriages are still practiced.

Native Canadian Families

There are more than seven hundred Native communities in Canada and more than six hundred bands or reserves. As well, there are dozens of Inuit and Métis villages and settlements. Finally, increasing numbers of Natives (at least 25 percent) live in cities and towns

Prairie families, particularly those with a strong ethnic identity, traditionally tend to maintain kinship ties. William Kurelek's painting, Manitoba Party, *evokes the earthy gaiety of a Ukrainian family reunion.*

National Gallery of Canada, Ottawa. Courtesy: Mrs. Wm. Kurelek.

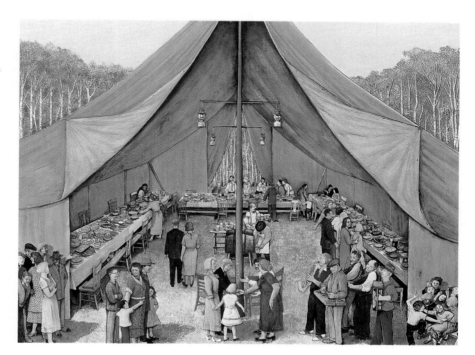

(Smith, 1993). Given this diversity, it is difficult to discuss the family patterns of Native Canadians as a homogeneous group. Indeed, as we saw in Chapter 12 ("Race and Ethnicity"), the very definition of "Native Canadian" is problematic.

Native Canadians are often among the most economically deprived members of our society, and suffer discrimination and prejudice resulting in high rates of unemployment, inadequate housing, and family instability. As one researcher says, "under these circumstances, identification with traditional cultures suffers, and their central familistic values of kin solidarity, respect for elders, and the welfare of children have been weakened" (Nett, 1993:101). Moreover, because of their political and economic subordination by Europeans, the family norms of many Native people have been threatened.

Prior to the mid-1800s (approximately) most Native peoples lived on reserves or with extended families in isolated regions. Child care was the responsibility of the extended family. Elders were highly respected and were given the task of teaching the young their language and traditions. When the Christian missionaries began to make concentrated efforts to Canadianize and Christianize Native peoples, many children were sent away from the reserves to church-run residential schools to learn another language, religion, and culture, while also learning to despise their own. In this context traditional family values began to erode. The elders lost their authority, the extended families lost their responsibilities for nurturing and caretaking. Resettlement programs often served to break up whole communities and to diminish family ties even further (Shkilnyk; 1985).

The involvement of the church and the state in Canadian Indian life has been, in many ways, troublesome. Having served to break down family traditions and solidarity, the state interfered again in the middle of this century under the auspices of social workers employed by various "Children's Aid Societies." Until the mid-1970s or so, children were taken away from parents who were no longer functioning as adequate parents because of poverty, unemployment, prejudice, alcohol abuse, and a variety of other social conditions. Many of these children were placed in non-Native foster homes, where they lost contact with their remaining Native traditions and culture. Presently, family policy is focused on maintaining children with their families whenever possible or placing them with other Native Canadian families when it is necessary to remove them (Baker, 1991).

Gender

For people of any social class, ethnicity, and race, cultural definitions of femininity and masculinity affect marriage and the family. Sociologist Jessie Bernard (1982) puts the matter simply, stating that each union is actually *two* different marriages: a female marriage and a male marriage.

> *During the last century the extent of male domination of family life has diminished to some degree, but even today few marriages are composed of socially equal partners. When Mirra Komarovsky (1973, 1976) asked college seniors to describe an ideal marriage, most—of both sexes—painted the man as dominant. The reason lies in the socialization of women to defer to men, which encourages a woman to think of her husband as superior. Similarly, few men—and even those who espouse a belief in sexual equality—wanted to marry a woman who might upstage them. Such patterns underlie our expectation that men will be older as well as taller than the women they marry. And after the wedding, even when both spouses work, most people assume that the husband's career is more important.* (McRae, 1986)

Surprisingly, in light of this male dominance, our culture promotes the idea that marriage benefits women more than men (Bernard, 1982). At bridal showers, women congratulate one of their own on her impending marriage; at bachelor parties, men sing a different song, bemoaning the loss of one of their number to his new wife. The same contrast appears in the positive stereotype of a carefree bachelor as opposed to the negative image of the lonely spinster. All this adds up to a simple conclusion: we imagine that women eagerly pursue husbands, while husbands savor their freedom until they reluctantly settle down.

The notion that marriage favors women is rooted in their historical exclusion from the labor force. A woman's financial security, that is, depended on her finding a husband. But in most respects, Jessie Bernard claims, marriage has never been beneficial for women. In comparison to single women, she notes, married women have poorer mental health, more passive attitudes toward life, and report greater unhappiness. Therefore, she concludes, *men* are the real beneficiaries of marriage. Married men generally live longer than single men, have better mental health, and report greater happiness. Bernard suggests that this also explains why, after divorce, women more than men report greater happiness, and men more than women eagerly look for a new partner. There is no better guarantor of long life, health, and happiness for a man, Bernard concludes, than a woman well socialized to perform the "duties of a wife" by devoting her life to caring for him and providing the security of a well-ordered home (see also Gove, 1972, 1979).

Bernard argues that marriage need not stifle the aspirations and happiness of women. The problem, she asserts, lies in the "anachronistic way in which marriage is structured today": husbands dominating wives and constraining them to tedious work in the home. Under these circumstances, men reap considerable advantages from marriage while women have reason to spearhead the drive to reform marital patterns.

Recent research based on a random sample of couples in the United States sorts out the connections between gender, power, and mental health in marriage (Ross, Mirowsky, & Huber, 1983; Mirowsky & Ross, 1984). Four types of marriage, the investigators found, yield different levels of depression for men and women.[1]

Type I marriages have a traditional pattern by which only the husband is employed and the wife does all housework and child rearing. Further, both partners willingly embrace conventional gender roles. Figure 15-2 shows that this arrangement appears to favor the husband, who derives income and prestige from his work. Wives in this situation, however, have higher levels of depression, presumably because their status as homemaker carries little social prestige, even though this is her preferred role.

In Type II marriages, both spouses work, although the wife performs a "second shift" by doing all the house work and child rearing. Here the wife works out of economic necessity, although she and her husband would prefer that she stay home. This arrangement, as Figure 15-2 shows, places emotional burdens on both partners: depression is high for the wife but higher still for the husband. The wife has two demanding jobs, one (or both) of which she does not want. The husband is frustrated by his own low-income job and the fact that he cannot support his family as he thinks he should. This is the only marital pattern in which husbands have poorer mental health than wives.

In Type III marriages, husband and wife are

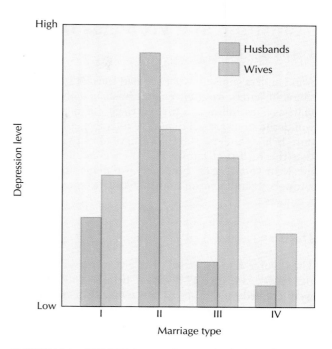

FIGURE 15-2 DEPRESSION IN FOUR TYPES OF MARRIAGE
SOURCE: Ross, Mirowsky, & Huber, 1983.

happy that the wife has a job, which provides psychological benefits for her; however, she is still responsible for all the housework. The husband benefits even more: the greater family income reduces the chance that his unemployment or any other unexpected setback will cause financial hardship for the family.

A Type IV marriage pattern has both husband and wife happily working outside the home but also sharing most family and household responsibilities. This pattern is linked to the lowest depression levels of the four types for both husbands and wives because sharing household responsibilities reduces tensions that arise when a working wife is expected to take sole responsibility for housework and children.

These findings support the conclusions by Jessie Bernard (1982) and others that more egalitarian marriages tend to be happier for husbands as well as wives. Such evidence may make us wonder why conventional and unequal marriages persist. The answer is that conventional ideas about gender are deeply rooted in our way of life; changing them involves a difficult and slow process despite evidence that both men and women benefit from doing so.

[1] As this study is based on a U.S. sample, its specific relevance to Canadian marriages needs to be determined.

Transition and Problems in Family Life

Ann Landers sums up what she had learned from thousands of letters from wives and husbands about their marriages as follows: "One marriage out of twenty is wonderful, four are good, ten are tolerable, and five are pure hell" (Landers, 1984). We have already explained that the reality of family life often falls short of the ideal. In some cases, however, problems are serious enough to undermine families and threaten family members.

Divorce

The divorce rate in Canada has grown markedly since the 1950s, as Figure 15-3 shows. Before 1968, divorces were granted only if one of the spouses was proven to have committed adultery. The Divorce Act of 1968, however, allowed for divorce in certain other circumstances: If one of the spouses had committed a matrimonial offense (such as adultery or emotional or physical cruelty), if one spouse had deserted, or if the spouses had lived apart for at least three years. In 1985, the Act was rewritten, making "marriage breakdown" the only reason for divorce. (Marriage breakdown includes separation of not less than one year, adultery, and physical and mental cruelty.) By 1990, the divorce rate was 2.94 per 1,000 and the marriage rate was 7.1 per 1,000.

One reason that divorce rates are so high in Canada is that people are highly likely to marry: about nine out of ten adults eventually do so. During the last century, however, the marriage rate has remained rela-

FIGURE 15-3   THE DIVORCE RATE, 1951–1990
SOURCE: Statistics Canada, Cat. Nos. 84-205 and 82-003S17, and Census of Canada

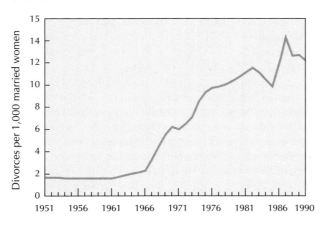

tively stable while the divorce rate has soared upward (Colombo, 1990:82). Researchers have identified seven major reasons for the rising risk of divorce (Huber & Spitze, 1980; Kitson & Raschke, 1981). First, people used to spend more of their time in family activities. Today parents and children work and play together less often; they are more active individually in schools, workplaces, and various recreational settings. We have also become more individualistic, seemingly more concerned with personal happiness than committed to the well-being of families. Second, as was noted earlier, our culture bases marriage on romantic love. Because sexual passion usually subsides with time, spouses may end a marriage in favor of a relationship that renews excitement and romance. Third, increasing participation in the labor force has reduced women's financial dependence on husbands. The growing economic strength of women also may strain conventional marriages as it gives women options to remaining in an unhappy relationship. Fourth, when both parents work outside the home, child rearing adds a considerable burden. Children do stabilize some marriages (Waite, Haggstrom, & Kanouse, 1985), but divorce is most common during the early years of marriage when many couples have young children. Fifth, divorce no longer carries the powerful negative stigma it did a century ago. Sixth, in today's transient society, marriages receive less support from extended family members and neighbors than was typical in the past The seventh reason for our high divorce rate is that, as we have seen, it is now easier to obtain a legal divorce (Thornton, 1985; Gerstel, 1987).

As Ed Kain (1990) points out, we tend to exaggerate the stability of marriage in the past—death ended as many marriages a century ago as divorce does now. But just as the dissolution of marriage was once due to forces beyond people's control, marriages are now much more likely to end simply because people want to be single—or married to somebody else.

Who Divorces?

People who marry young are the most likely to divorce. Teens who marry usually had a brief courtship and typically have less financial stability and emotional maturity. People in lower social classes, and with less education, are more likely to divorce. At all social levels, the risk of divorce rises if a couple marries in response to an unexpected pregnancy, and when the partners had only a brief acquaintance before marriage. Dissimilar social backgrounds, too, may introduce tensions that are difficult to resolve, and lead to marital breakup. In addition, people who move far away from family and friends have higher rates of divorce. Finally, men and women who divorce once are more likely to divorce again because problems tend to follow them from one marriage to another (Schlesinger, 1975; Boyd, 1983; Ambert & Baker, 1984; White, 1991; Nett, 1993). Canada Map 15-1 shows the divorce rate for the provinces and territories.

Problems of Divorce

Divorce itself is not necessarily a problem; it may merely constitute a transition that benefits each party. Even in the best case, however, ending a marriage brings as much change as beginning one.

Paul Bohannan (1970) suggests that people who divorce must make six distinct adjustments. First, there is the *emotional divorce*. A deteriorating marriage is often fraught with disappointment and frustration, if not outright hostility. Second is the formal, *legal divorce*, which involves various legal procedures and may embroil couples in complicated financial disputes. Bohannan describes a third transition as *psychic divorce*. Divorced people may experience a sense of personal failure, loneliness, and a need for personal repair. Fourth, *community divorce* refers to the need to reorganize friendships ("Were they really *my* friends or my spouse's?") and to adjust relations with parents and other family members who are accustomed to seeing someone as part of a couple.

A fifth problem, especially for women, is the *economic divorce*. Recent no-fault divorce laws have reduced the amount of alimony and child support paid by men to their former wives. Divorce courts are now likely to require that homes be sold so that marital assets can be evenly divided (Dulude, 1984). These legal changes, claim researchers, have hurt women financially. Studies suggest that, in the year following divorce, women suffer a reduction in their living standard while men experience a rise in theirs (Faludi, 1991). For the woman, especially one who does not work, this loss usually means a marked reduction in housing quality. Ex-wives often lose other forms of financial security as well, such as insurance policies, pension programs, and credit, all of which typically remain with ex-husbands. Older women who have not been in the labor force contend with economic problems that are even more severe, since they generally lack job skills (Weitzman, 1985).

A sixth and final adjustment noted by Bohannan is *parental divorce*, in which parents must resolve the difficult issues surrounding custody of children. Divorces granted under the 1986 law were less likely

Because the family is an important primary group, divorce can be a lesson in conflict and hostility for children. This four-year-old, the object of a guardianship battle between his parents, bluntly expresses his opinion as the judge awarded custody to his mother.

to involve children than those granted under the old law. In 1986, children were involved in 34 percent of divorces. Under the old Act, children were involved in approximately 52 percent of the cases (Statistics Canada, 1989). The conventional practice of awarding custody to mothers is based on the notion that women are better parents than men are. Recently, however, a growing number of fathers have sought to gain custody of their children. As a result, the trend is toward joint custody, with children having a primary home with one parent but regularly spending time with the other, or dividing their lives more or less evenly between the two parents. Although joint custody is difficult if the divorced parents live far apart or do not get along, it does have the advantage of keeping children in regular contact with both parents (Roman & Haddad, 1978; Cherlin & Furstenberg, 1983).

Because mothers usually have custody of children but fathers typically earn more income, the well-being of children often depends on fathers making court-ordered child-support payments. Yet most children of divorced parents do not receive the financial support to which they are entitled by law. What has been called "an epidemic of nonsupport" has led to legislation mandating that parents who fail to fulfill this obligation will have the payments withheld from their earnings. Still, the legislation has proven very difficult to enforce (Nett, 1993).

Conventional wisdom suggests that divorce is hardest on children. Divorce tears young people from familiar surroundings and may distance them from a parent they love. Moreover, in their own minds, children may saddle themselves with responsibility for the divorce of their parents. There is little doubt, however, that children who experience family breakup fare better than those who remain in a family racked by tension or violence (Goetting, 1981; Zill, 1984). Ideally, of course, children thrive in the absence of both family conflict and divorce.

Remarriage

Despite the rising divorce rate, marriage—and especially remarriage—remain as popular as ever. Four out of five people who divorce remarry, most within five years.

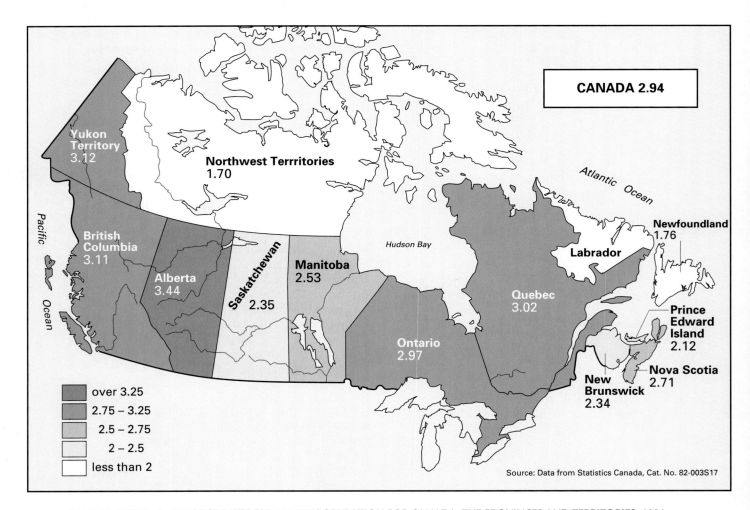

CANADA MAP 15-1   DIVORCE RATES PER 100,000 POPULATION FOR CANADA, THE PROVINCES AND TERRITORIES, 1991

Men, who derive greater benefits from marriage, are more likely to remarry than women are. This is especially true of older men who receive cultural approval for marrying younger women. For their part, because women are expected to "marry up," the older a woman is, the more education she has, and the better her job, the more difficulty she has in finding a suitable husband (Leslie & Korman, 1989).

Common sense suggests that what people learned from failed first marriages should make their subsequent marriages more successful. Yet remarriages are even more likely to end in divorce. For one thing, people who have already been through a divorce have demonstrated their willingness to end an unsatisfactory marriage. Additionally, the first divorce may have been caused by attitudes or behavior that will undermine a subsequent marriage.

The same transitions that Paul Bohannan links to divorce are present in remarriage. According to Ann Goetting (1982), *emotional remarriage* involves reestablishing a bond based on attraction, commitment, and trust. *Legal remarriage* follows, including various agreements about property and a decision about where to reside. *Psychic remarriage* suggests the need to reforge personal identity as part of a couple: often individuals must relinquish the autonomy and privacy gained after a divorce. *Community remarriage* means altering relationships with friends and family based on, once again, being married. *Economic remarriage* generally increases a couple's standard of living, since two incomes now maintain only one residence. When there are children, the more complex issue of establishing and managing child-support payments arises. Child support might flow both to and from the new household. As noted earlier, such payments are often sporadic, making economic planning difficult.

Where there are children, *parental remarriage* consists of establishing relationships with the children of the spouse, a task that often demands a huge measure of sensitivity, skill, finesse, and patience. Remarriage often gives rise to the *blended family*, composed of biological parents and stepparents. In any particular household, then, children may have two, one, or no parents in common. Since many children of blended families have one biological parent living elsewhere, the adults in their world must make special efforts to clarify who is defined as part of the child's nuclear family (Furstenberg, 1984). Children of blended families are also subject to new relationships: an only child, for example, may suddenly find she has two older broth-

ers. For these reasons, stress and conflict multiply in remarriages involving children, adding to the risk of another divorce (Kalmuss & Seltzer, 1984).

Family Violence

The ideal family serves as a safe haven from the dangers of an unfamiliar world. The disturbing reality of many homes, however, is **family violence**, *emotional, physical, or sexual abuse of one family member by another.* According to sociologist Richard J. Gelles,

> The family is the most violent group in society with the exception of the police and the military. You are more likely to get killed, injured, or physically attacked in your home by someone you are related to than in any other social context. In fact, if violence were a communicable disease, the government would consider it an epidemic. (Cited in Roesch, 1984:75)

Such facts are chilling, and in some cases, almost incredible. Public awareness is the first step toward solving this problem, which victimizes millions of adults and children.

Violence Against Women

> I guess the first time he hit me was when we had been married about eight years. I'd gone to my music lesson and had arranged for a babysitter to take the children to a school fair. When my husband got home from work the house was dark and no one was there. This enraged him, and in the driveway when I arrived, he greeted me with a punch in the kidneys. I doubled over. I didn't even know what I'd done. We never talked afterward. I swallowed my pain and tried to forget.

This incident took place in a fashionable suburban neighborhood in a family with plenty of money, beautiful children—and a lot of violence (Saline, 1984).

The common stereotype of a violent partner is a lower-class man who now and then drinks too much, loses control, and beats up his wife. In reality, although financial problems and unemployment do make the problem worse, violence against women in the home is perpetrated by men of all social classes, races, and ethnicities (Lupri, 1988:170). Furthermore, as the example above suggests, this violence often occurs at random. Family brutality frequently goes unreported to police, but researchers estimate that 20 percent of couples—or one in five—endure at least some violence each year (Lupri, 1988:171). Many of these couples experience serious incidents of violence, including kicking, biting, and punching.

Not all family turmoil involves violence by men against women. But two crucial gender-based patterns have been established by research. First, women suffer most of the serious injuries. Second, men initiate most family violence so that violence against men by women often takes the form of retaliation and self-defense (Straus & Gelles, 1986; Schwartz, 1987; Lupri, 1988).

Statistics show that almost 30 percent of women who are murdered—as opposed to 6 percent of men—are killed by spouses, ex-spouses, or unmarried partners (Lupri, 1988). In 1989, one hundred and nineteen women in Canada were murdered by former husbands or partners (Begin, 1991). Further, women are more likely to be injured by a family member than they are to be mugged or raped by a stranger or injured in an automobile accident.

Physically abused women have traditionally had few options. They may want to leave home, but many—especially those with children and without much money—have nowhere to go. Most wives are also committed to their marriages and believe (however unrealistically) that they can help abusive husbands to change. Some, unable to understand their husbands' violence, blame themselves. Others, raised in violent families, consider assault to be part of family life. Most abused women see no way out of the family violence that makes fear the centerpiece of their lives. In one study, researchers found that one-fourth of women who had entered a metropolitan hospital after attempting suicide had been victims of family violence (Stark & Flitcraft, 1979).

In the past, the law regarded domestic violence as a private concern of families. Now, a woman can obtain court protection from an abusive spouse. Legislation introduced in 1993 (known as the "stalker" legislation) was designed to improve the ability of the police and courts to protect the well-being of women and children who were being threatened and followed. Some medical personnel are also more aware today of the telltale signs of spousal violence and are more likely to report such cases to police than they were in the past.

Communities across North America are establishing shelters that provide counseling as well as temporary housing for women and children driven from their homes by violence. In 1989 in Ontario alone, seventy-eight transition houses accommodated 9,838 women,

Nations, as well as parents, can abuse children. Prior to the fall of the Ceausescu regime in 1989, the Romanian government denied women any form of birth control and banned abortion. Tens of thousands of unwanted children were the result, many of whom remain warehoused in orphanages like this one.

accompanied by 11,000 children. Eighty-seven percent of these families were in shelters because of domestic violence. Some men and women who abuse their partners are also joining self-help groups in an effort to understand and control their own behavior. In various ways, then, our society is beginning to mobilize against this serious problem.

Violence Against Children

Kelly, now an adult, will never be able to forget the sexual abuse she suffered as a child. Her stepfather regularly separated her from other members of the family and, often in a parked car, forced her to have oral sex with him. Her mother was sick at the time, and the stepfather warned Kelly that telling of their sexual relationship would cause her mother to die. "I believed him," she recalls. "I thought my mother would die and I would be left with this man" (Watson, 1984).

The vicious nature of child abuse lies in adults' use of power and trust to victimize children. Child abuse therefore inflicts both *physical* and *emotional* harm, undermining the core of family life. It is difficult to establish the extent of child abuse because, like violence against women, most instances are never reported to anyone.

Many abused children suffer in silence, believing throughout their formative years that they are to blame for their own victimization. The initial abuse, compounded by years of guilt, can leave lasting emotional scars that prevent people abused as children from forming healthy relationships as adults.

About 90 percent of child abusers are men, but they conform to no simple stereotype. As one man who entered a therapy group reported, "I kept waiting for all the guys with raincoats and greasy hair to show up. But everyone looked like regular middle-class people" (Lubenow, 1984). One trait common to abusers, however, is a history of having been abused as children, leading to the conclusion that violent behavior in personal relationships is learned (Gwartney-Gibbs, Stockard, & Bohmer, 1987). Treatment programs,

then, coupled with legal protection for victims, offer some hope of restraining offenders.

Alternative Family Forms

In recent decades, our society has displayed greater social diversity in family life. While more traditional forms are still preferred by most, marriage and the family now represent a range of legitimate lifestyles.

One-Parent Families

Figure 15-4 indicates that, in 1961, 8.4 percent of Canadian families were headed by a single parent and 91.6 percent were headed by husband-wife families. By 1991, 88.1 percent of families were headed by a husband and wife and 11.9 percent by single parents. Projections are that by 2011 two-parent families will decrease further to 83 percent (1993 *Corpus Almanac & Canadian Sourcebook*). Thus the proportion of *one-parent families* is growing rapidly, and almost 12 percent of children in Canada now live in these families. Single parenthood—about four times more common among women than among men—may result from divorce, the inability to find a suitable husband, or the desire to have a child without marriage (Kantrowitz, 1985). Now that most women are in the labor force, they have the financial resources to become single parents.

FIGURE 15-4   SINGLE-PARENT FAMILIES IN CANADA, 1961, 1976 AND 1991
SOURCE: Statistics Canada, Household and Family Projections, 1976–2001, Catalogue No. 91-522. Ottawa: Ministry of Supply and Services, Dec. 1991.

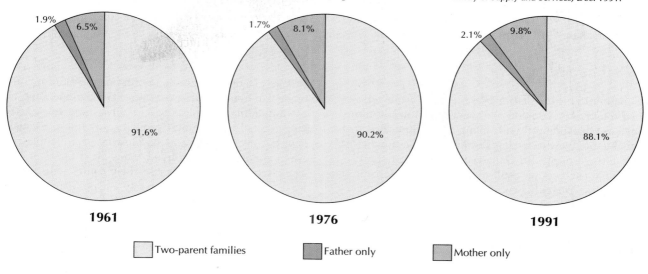

Single parenthood—when the parent is a woman—greatly increases the risks of poverty, however, because many mothers can find only low-paying jobs or are unable to work at all. This is especially true among young women. Child-care options are also limited, making full-time employment for single parents problematic as well. Estimates suggest that approximately 60 percent of women in Canada who become pregnant as teenagers give birth to live babies; 6 percent are stillborn and 36 percent are aborted (Statistics Canada, 1991). These young women with children—especially if they have the additional disadvantage of being minorities—form the core of the rising problem of child poverty.

While the negative stigma attached to being born out of wedlock has certainly declined, conventional ideas about parenthood are still echoed by a majority of adults in Canada. Public opinion holds that a woman should not become pregnant if she does not plan to raise the child with its biological father (Kelley, 1984; Tron 1993).

Most research suggests that growing up in a one-parent family can, but does not necessarily, have negative effects on children. Divorce is stressful for children, and many contend with emotional scars years later (Wallerstein & Blakeslee, 1989). Some studies link growing up in a single-parent family to low educational achievement, low income, and having children out of wedlock. But other research argues that the problems faced by families with one parent—especially if that parent is a woman—are caused by poverty rather than the absence of a second parent. Such inconsistent results show the need for continuing research about this emerging family form (Mueller & Cooper, 1984; McLanahan, 1985; Weisner & Eiduson, 1986; Astone & McLanahan, 1991; Tron, 1993).

Cohabitation

Cohabitation is *the sharing of a household by an unmarried couple.* A generation ago, widespread use of terms such as "shacking up" and "living in sin" indicated that cohabitation was viewed as deviant. Yet the number of cohabiting couples in Canada has increased sharply. Although such couples still represent only 5 percent of all couples, cohabiting is especially common on university campuses, where perhaps one-fourth of students cohabit for some period of time.

The impact of cohabiting is unclear. One American study found that the proportion of married couples who had previously cohabited had increased from about one in eight in 1970 to over one-half by 1980 (Gwartney-Gibbs, 1986). These findings suggest that cohabiting often precedes marriage, as a way of testing a serious relationship. But most cohabitation still does not lead to marriage and, in many cases, it merely serves as an intentionally temporary arrangement or one that saves money for the individuals involved. Most cases of cohabitation last several years; at that point, about 40 percent of couples marry, and the remainder split up (Blumstein & Schwartz, 1983; Macklin, 1983). As we have already explained, in Sweden cohabitation is sometimes a prelude to marriage, but for many it is a lifelong relational alternative (Popenoe, 1991).

Cohabitation, then, typically lacks the commitment (and the degree of sexual fidelity) that characterizes marriage. One twenty-four-year-old woman who married her live-in partner of five years expressed the difference between cohabitation and marriage this way: "For me, [marriage] was deciding to make a real commitment. When we were living together I felt I could walk out at any time" (Clancy & Oberst, 1985). Another clue that cohabitation is not as binding on partners as marriage is that cohabiting couples rarely have children.

However cohabiting partners define their relationship, court decisions state that individuals who live together can make claims on each other's property. In other words, as cohabitation has gained in popularity, the legal distinction between this pattern and marriage is beginning to blur.

Finally, cohabitation takes various forms. Although this relational form is most common among younger adults who are sexual partners, many elderly people with no sexual motives also choose to live together. For them, cohabitation provides some needed economic assistance or a source of companionship.

Gay and Lesbian Couples

In 1989, Denmark became the first country to formally recognize homosexual marriages, thereby extending to gay and lesbian couples the legal advantages for inheritance, taxation, and joint property ownership. Danish law, however, stops short of allowing such couples to adopt children. In the United States, recent laws in San Francisco, New York, and elsewhere confer some of the legal benefits of marriage on gay and lesbian couples. In Canada, while gays and lesbians cannot legally marry, there are churches that will sanctify such a union. The Metropolitan Community Church in Toronto is an ecumenical denomination that serves gays and lesbians with many of the rituals of the Christian Church. The marriage ceremony, for instance, is based on traditional Christian marriage vows. While gay and lesbian marriages are currently illegal, a number of institutions acknowledge homosexual partnerships in various spousal support and benefit schemes. Ontario's NDP government announced in 1993 that it would support legislation extending many rights to same-sex couples, including government controlled spousal benefits under employee insurance plans (Chisholm, 1993). Legal marriage may not be far behind.

Even though they are barred from legal marriage, many gay men and lesbians form long-term, committed partnerships and families (Bell, Weinberg, & Kiefer-Hammersmith, 1981; Gross, 1991). This is especially true of lesbian couples, who are more likely than gay couples to remain sexually exclusive (Blumstein & Schwartz, 1983).

Like heterosexual couples, gays and lesbians enter relationships with romantic ideals and then adjust to day-to-day realities; they share the strains of financial and household responsibilities. In addition, they must deal with conventional cultural values that favor masculine attributes more than feminine traits. Some homosexual couples also raise children, usually from previous heterosexual relationships, but sometimes from adoption. Artificial insemination, furthermore, now provides women with the option of having children without a male partner.

Although remaining "in the closet" is less common today than years ago, many gay men and lesbians still feel compelled to keep their relationships secret—even from other family members—to minimize prejudice and discrimination. Partners must therefore turn to each other for all the emotional, spiritual, and material support that heterosexual couples can find elsewhere. This places great strains on the gay or lesbian relationship. Yet, despite these disadvantages, many partnerships between lesbians and between gay men are strong, resilient, and long-lasting.

Singlehood

Because nine out of ten people in Canada marry, singlehood is often seen as simply a transitory stage of life that ends with marriage. In recent decades, however, more women and men have deliberately chosen the freedom and independence of living alone, remaining both single and childless (Nett, 1993).

The increase in one-person households is shown in Figure 15-5. In 1950 only about one household in

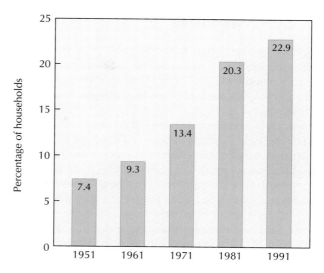

FIGURE 15-5 ONE-PERSON HOUSEHOLDS IN CANADA, 1951–1991
SOURCE: Nett, 1993:347.

twelve contained a single person. By 1990 this proportion was approaching one in four. Most will marry at some point in their lives, but an increasing number will deliberately choose to remain single.

Perhaps the greatest change in marital status is evident among young women. In 1960 about one in four women aged twenty to twenty-four were single; by 1990 the proportion was nearing two-thirds. The key to this trend is greater participation in the labor force: women who are economically secure view a husband as a matter of choice rather than a financial necessity.

By midlife, however, women who have not married confront a lack of available men. Because our culture discourages women from marrying partners much younger than they are (while encouraging men to do so), middle-aged women who do wish to marry find the odds rising against them.

New Reproductive Technology and the Family

As we saw at the beginning of this chapter, *new reproductive technology* has created new controversies for families. The benefits of this rapidly developing technology may be exciting to some, but its use raises daunting ethical questions about the creation and manipulation of life itself.

In Vitro Fertilization

Technically speaking, test-tube babies result from *in vitro fertilization*: a union of the male sperm and the female ovum "in glass" rather than in a woman's body. In this complex medical procedure, drugs stimulate the production of more than one egg in each ovary during a woman's reproductive cycle. Then doctors surgically "harvest" eggs from the ovaries and combine them with sperm in a laboratory dish. The successful fusion of eggs and sperm produces embryos, which are placed in the womb of a woman who is to bear the child. The embryos may also be frozen for use at a later time.

The benefits of *in vitro* fertilization are twofold. First, many couples cannot conceive children normally; one-fifth of these couples can be helped through this process. Second, looking to the future, many medical experts believe that new birth technologies will reduce the incidence of birth defects. In other words, by genetically screening sperm and eggs, medical specialists can increase the odds for the birth of a healthy baby (Vines, 1986).

Ethical Issues

New reproductive technology has sparked heated debate. Simply put, medical technology now provides control over life itself that would have been unthinkable only a few decades ago. (The insert describes one horrifying image of this future.) The result is a classic example of "cultural lag" (see Chapter 3, "Culture"), in which society has to catch up to the moral implications of this new technological power.

Moral quandaries abound. As with most cases of technological advance, benefits are expensive and available only to those who can afford them. Even a single attempt at *in vitro* fertilization is expensive. Usually many attempts are necessary before conception takes place. Thus, only a small fraction of infertile couples can even consider this procedure. A second problem surrounds guidelines that limit this technology to proper "families." In most cases, doctors and hospitals have been willing to apply *in vitro* fertilization only to women who are under forty years of age and are part of a heterosexual couple. Single women, older women, and lesbian couples have so far been widely excluded from this opportunity.

A third ethical problem concerns *surrogate motherhood*, in which one woman bears a child for another. Surrogate motherhood can take one of two forms. In the first type—illustrated by the case of Arlette Schweitzer—the ovum and sperm produced by a couple are joined, and the resulting embryo is implanted into the body of another woman—the surrogate—who gives birth to the child. In the second type—illustrated by the "Baby M case" several years ago—a couple contracts with a woman to bear a child for them by having the woman's own ovum artificially fertilized by the man's sperm.

Both types of surrogate motherhood raise daunting questions about who a baby's parents are. In some situations, lengthy and emotionally wrenching legal battles have been needed to resolve issues of parenthood. Until society generates moral and legal standards to clarify such cases, surrogate motherhood will remain highly controversial.

An outspoken party in controversies surrounding new reproductive technologies is the Catholic Church. As the box explains, this church has condemned all new reproductive technology as reducing human life to a manipulated object. However, many practicing Catholics do not share their Church's position.

The Family in the Twenty-First Century

Family life in Canada has changed significantly in recent decades, and new reproductive technology will surely prompt further change in the future. This possibility has led some to wonder if the family may eventually disappear entirely. Locked in debate are advocates of traditional family values, on the one hand, and proponents of new family forms and greater personal choice on the other (Berger & Berger, 1983).

We will close this chapter with five general assertions about the family with an eye toward the next century. First, divorce has become an accepted—if regrettable—element of family life. This does not mean that couples are less durable today than they were a century ago, since it was not long ago that death took a heavy toll on parents. But more couples now *choose* to end their marriages, so that the traditional view that marriage lasts "til death do us part" no longer holds true. Although the divorce rate has recently stabilized, it is unlikely that marriage will regain the durability characteristic of the 1950s. One major reason is that increasing numbers of women are able to support themselves, and traditional marriages appeal to fewer of them. Men, as well, are seeking more satisfying relationships. The higher divorce rate of the last several decades should

CRITICAL THINKING

Are New Reproductive Technologies Immoral? The Catholic Church's View

Some people in our society hail the new reproductive technologies, including *in vitro* fertilization and genetic research, as a great step forward in medical science. Others, however, are not so sure, and some are opposed to this kind of research on various ethical grounds.

The Catholic Church takes the latter view, condemning this technology as a moral danger to humanity. No child, concludes a recent report, should be "conceived as the product of an intervention of medical or biological techniques" because such techniques treat human life as an object of research and manipulation. Church officials remind us that, during the 1930s and 1940s, the Nazis conducted genetic experiments with the stated goal of improving the health of children, although these experiments were actually designed to genetically engineer a race of "superhumans."

Many scientists in Canada believe that new reproductive technology can reduce many maladies of infancy, but the Church counters that nothing can justify manipulating an embryo—a human life—in a laboratory. The Church doesn't stand alone

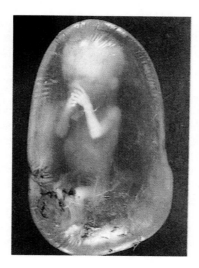

on this issue; many countries currently restrict such practices.

Less popular is the Church's opposition to using new reproductive technologies to help infertile couples have children. *In vitro* fertilization, the Church maintains, separates the act of procreation from the loving union of two parents. Catholics will recognize this argument as an extension of the Church's long-time prohibition against artificial contraception. Once separated from human sexuali-

ty, church officials fear, reproduction may quickly become as much a business as a family concern.

The popular view—even among Catholics—is that sexual intercourse between husband and wife is not the only moral way to conceive children. Since certain loving couples cannot conceive at all, they argue, artificial insemination (in which a husband's sperm is used to fertilize an ovum directly in the wife's womb) or *in vitro* fertilization has obvious value. Moreover, some Catholics complain that this prohibition strikes hardest at those people who accept the Church's view that Catholic families are incomplete without children.

Many Catholics will ignore the Church's recent pronouncements, just as many have overlooked prohibitions against artificial birth control in the past. But few people—whether Catholics or not—can easily dismiss the Church's concern that what is technologically possible may not always be morally desirable.

SOURCES: Based on Congregation for the Doctrine of the Faith (1987), Ostling (1987), and Woodward (1987).

---

probably be viewed less as a threat to families than as a sign of change in family form. After all, most divorces still lead to remarriage, casting doubt on the notion that marriage itself is becoming discredited. As women's and men's roles change, new forms of family life will emerge that may prove more stable and more fulfilling.

Second, family life in the twenty-first century will be highly variable. We have noted an increasing number of cohabiting couples, one-parent families, gay and lesbian families, and blended families created from remarriage after divorce. Each family arrangement makes for its own set of problems and satisfactions.

Some alternatives, such as singlehood and childless marriage, are unlikely to be chosen by a majority of the population. Taken together, however, they represent growing social diversity and a conception of family life as a matter of choice.

Third, in most families men play a limited role in child rearing. This process was well under way in the 1950s, a decade many people see as the "golden age" of families (Snell, 1990). Then, fathers left home each day for work, leaving the children in the care of mothers. A counter-trend has been evident for some time as many fathers—now older, on average, and more established in their careers—try to become more involved in child care. But the increasing number of women raising children outside of marriage, the rising divorce rate, and the surge in single motherhood all combine toward the same result: more and more children are growing up without social ties to their fathers. Most research suggests that the absence of fathers is not directly and significantly detrimental to children, but there is little doubt that the absence of husbands and fathers from families figures in the feminization of poverty in Canada.

Fourth, changes in the economy are affecting marriage and the family. The economic reality for most couples is that both partners must work if they are to acquire a measure of financial security. As Arlie Hochschild (1989) points out, economic changes reshape society in ways that people *feel* in family life. Marriage today is often the interaction of weary men and women; adults try their best to raise children, yet contend with suspicions that popular ideas like "quali-

ty time" are little more than ways to justify minimal parenthood (Dizard & Gadlin, 1990). Two-career couples may advance the goal of gender equality, but the long-term effects on families are likely to be mixed.

Fifth, and finally, new reproductive technology will shape families of the twenty-first century. Opposition may limit such developments, but it seems very likely that new forms of reproduction will alter traditional meanings of parenthood. At the very least, we can be sure, new technology will direct a continued focus on family life.

Despite social changes that have buffeted the family in Canada and elsewhere, most people continue to marry and seek remarriage after a divorce or widowhood. Marriage and family life have always given rise to controversy and conflicting views, and as the family evolves, this will certainly continue. But both marriage and family life will still remain the foundation of our society.

Summary

1. Societies are built on kinship; in industrial societies, the family is composed of close relatives. Family forms vary considerably across cultures, as they have across history.

2. Nuclear families have historically predominated in Canada. As in other industrial nations, marriage in our society is monogamous. Many preindustrial societies, however, allow polygamy, of which there are two types: polygyny and polyandry.

3. Cross-culturally, families differ in residential patterns. Industrial societies favor neolocality; patrilocality is more common throughout the world, and a few cultures have matrilocal households. Industrial societies recognize bilateral descent, while preindustrial societies tend to be either patrilineal or matrilineal.

4. Structural-functional analysis points to four major functions of the family: socialization of the young, regulation of sexual activity, social placement, and provision of emotional support.

5. Social-conflict theory draws attention to how the family perpetuates social inequality by strengthening social classes, ethnic and racial divisions, and gender distinctions.

6. Symbolic-interaction analysis highlights the dynamic nature of family life. This approach also explains that various family members may experience their families quite differently. The social-exchange approach highlights how people evaluate potential mates in terms of what they bring to a relationship.

7. Families originate in the process of courtship. Unlike Canada, most societies limit the role of romantic love in the choice of a mate. Even among members of our society, romantic love tends to join people with similar social backgrounds.

8. The reality of marriage usually falls short of the cultural ideal. New spouses frequently discover that they have much to learn about each other as well as about married life. Seventeen percent of males and 9 percent of females engage in sexual infidelity, although doing so still violates cultural norms.

9. Although the vast majority of married couples have children, family size has decreased over time. At the root of this trend lies industrialization, which transforms children into economic liabilities, encourages women to join the labor force, and reduces infant mortality.

10. In later life, marriage changes as children leave home to form families of their own. Couples are likely to spend more time caring for aging parents, however. Retirement may affect the relationship between spouses. The final stage of marriage begins with the death of one spouse, usually the husband.

11. Social class shapes family life by providing some families with more options and financial security than others.

12. Native Canadian families have undergone tremendous changes at the hands of the Canadian state and churches.

13. Gender affects family dynamics. Husbands continue to dominate the vast majority of families. Research suggests that marriage provides more benefits to men than to women.

14. The divorce rate today is ten times higher than it was a century ago; almost one-half of current marriages will end in divorce. Most people who divorce—especially men—remarry. Remarriage can create blended families that include children from previous marriages.

15. Violence against women and children remained major public issues in the 1980s. Both problems are widespread and underreported to authorities. Commonly, adults who abuse family members were themselves abused as children.

16. Family life in Canada has become more varied. Cohabitation and one-parent families have proliferated in recent years. Gay men and lesbians cannot legally marry but typically form long-lasting relationships. Singlehood—by chance or choice—is also increasingly common.

17. Based on current research, close to half of all marriages will end in divorce, family life will continue to take many diverse forms, the family will have to come to terms with unprecedented career demands, new reproductive technology may alter patterns of parenting, and fathers are likely to have limited importance in child rearing because of their absence from many families.

Key Concepts

bilateral descent   a system tracing kinship through both females and males

cohabitation   the sharing of a household by an unmarried couple

descent   the system by which members of a society trace kinship over generations

endogamy   marriage between people of the same social group or category

exogamy   marriage between people of different social groups or categories

extended family (consanguine family)   a social unit including parents, children, and other kin

family   a relatively permanent social group of two or more people, who are related by blood, marriage, or adoption and who usually live together

family of orientation   the family into which a person is born and receives early socialization

family of procreation   a family in which people have or adopt children of their own

family violence   emotional, physical, or sexual abuse of one family member by another

homogamy   marriage between people who are socially alike

incest taboo   a cultural norm forbidding sexual relations or marriage between certain kin

kinship   social ties based on blood, marriage, or adoption

marriage   a socially approved relationship, involving economic cooperation and allowing sexual activity and childbearing, that is expected to be relatively enduring

matrilineal descent   a system tracing kinship through females

matrilocality   a residential pattern in which a married couple lives with or near the wife's family

monogamy   a form of marriage that joins one female and one male

neolocality   a residential pattern in which a married couple lives apart from the parents of both spouses

nuclear family (conjugal family)   a social unit composed of one or, more commonly, two parents and children

patrilineal descent   a system tracing kinship through males

patrilocality   a residential pattern in which a married couple lives with or near the husband's family

polyandry   a form of marriage that joins one female with more than one male

polygamy   a form of marriage that unites three or more people

polygyny   a form of marriage that joins one male with more than one female

Suggested Readings

The first book describes and analyzes the gendered nature of the Canadian labor force.

> Pat Armstrong and Hugh Armstrong. *The Double Ghetto: Canadian Women and Their Segregated Work.* Toronto: McClelland and Stewart, 1984.

The next four books provide various overviews of the nature and condition of the family in Canadian society. The first and fourth are general texts. The second and third focus on policies that affect the family and on feminist understandings of families.

> Maureen Baker, ed. *Families: Changing Trends in Canada,* 2nd ed. Toronto: McGraw-Hill Ryerson, 1989.
> Margrit Eichler. *Families in Canada Today: Recent Changes and Their Policy Consequences.* 2nd ed. Toronto: Gage, 1988.
> Nancy Mandell and Ann Duffy. *Reconstructing the Canadian Family: Feminist Perspectives.* Toronto: Butterworths, 1988.
> Emily Nett. *Canadian Families Past and Present.* Toronto: Butterworths, 1993.

The following are government reports on child care availability and needs in Canada.

> House of Commons, Canada. *Sharing the Responsibility: Report of the Special Committee on Child Care.* Ottawa: Queen's Printer, 1987.

This article critiques some aspects of new reproductive technologies.

> National Council of Welfare. *Child Care: A Better Alternative.* Ottawa, December, 1988.
> Margrit Eichler. "Reflections on Motherhood, Apple Pie, the New Reproductive Technologies and the Role of Sociologists in Society." *Society/Société* 13(1): 1-5. 1989.

The next three books focus on "problems" within the Canadian family. The first examines Native children. The second discusses violence in the family. The third portrays the extent of poverty in Canada.

> Patrick Johnston. *Native Children and the Child Welfare System.* Toronto: Lorimer, 1983.
> Linda MacLeod. *Battered But Not Beaten ... Preventing Wife Abuse in Canada.* Ottawa: Canadian Advisory Council on the Status of Women, 1987.

> National Council of Welfare. *Poverty Profile 1988.* Ottawa, April, 1988b.

This recent best seller argues that feminism has suffered setbacks over the last decade.

> Susan Faludi. *Backlash: The Undeclared War Against American Women.* New York: Crown, 1991.

The first book, an account of several working-class families in California's Silicon Valley, highlights the effects of class, religion, and feminism to domestic patterns. The second explores changes in class and ethnicity over several generations.

> Judith Stacey. *Brave New Families: Stories of Domestic Upheaval in Late Twentieth-Century America.* New York: Basic Books, 1990.
> Corinne Azen Krause. *Grandmothers, Mothers, and Daughters: Oral Histories of Three Generations of Ethnic American Women.* Boston: Twayne Publishers/G.K. Hall & Co., 1991.

Economics exerts a strong influence inside families. The first book analyzes how making money, spending it, and giving it away affects relations among family members. The second book looks at dual-career couples and shows how clout in a marriage relates to economic power. The third book is a fascinating account of marriages in which women have more economic power than their husbands.

> Marcia Millman. *Warm Hearts and Cold Cash: The Intimate Dynamics of Families and Money.* New York: The Free Press, 1991.
> Rosanna Hertz. *More Equal Than Others: Women and Men in Dual-Career Marriages.* Berkeley: University of California Press, 1986.
> Susan McRae. *Cross-Class Families: A Study of Wives' Occupational Superiority.* New York: Oxford University Press, 1986.

This collection consists of cross-cultural essays on childbearing and family life.

> W. Penn Handwerker, ed. *Births and Power: The Politics of Reproduction.* Boulder, CO: Westview Press, 1989.

How does family life evolve among partners of different religious backgrounds? This volume takes an insightful look at the challenges of interfaith marriages.

Susan Weidman Schneider. *Intermarriage: The Challenge of Living with Differences Between Christians and Jews.* New York: The Free Press, 1989.

The first book is one of the most influential studies of the history of the African-American family in the United States. The second is a collection of essays on the current state of black families.

Herbert G. Gutman. *The Black Family in Slavery and Freedom: 1750–1925.* New York: Pantheon Books, 1976.

Harold E. Cheatham and James B. Stewart, eds. *Black Families: Interdisciplinary Perspectives.* New Brunswick, NJ: Transaction Books, 1989.

Despite our idealized vision of the family as a haven from trouble, troubled families are common in North America. These books are recent additions to the growing literature on violence in families.

Suzanne M. Retzinger. *Violent Emotions: Shame and Rage in Marital Quarrels.* Newbury Park, CA: Sage, 1991.

Richard J. Gelles and Claire Pedrick Cornell. *Intimate Violence in Families.* Newbury Park, CA: Sage, 1990.

This book takes a look at the dynamics of living in a so-called "blended family."

Anne C. Bernstein. *Yours, Mine, and Ours: How Families Change When Remarried Parents Have a Child Together.* New York: Charles Scribner's Sons, 1989.

Conventional wisdom holds that families should be self-suffi-cient units that provide for their members. These researchers claim that families are being hard pressed in an age when both parents work while they try to manage a home and raise children. The book considers both positive and negative consequences of this trend.

Jan E. Dizard and Howard Gadlin. *The Minimal Family.* Amherst: The University of Massachusetts Press, 1990.

Adults are also delaying childbirth while pursuing a career or the right relationship. This study outlines the likely effects of being a "latecomer" child.

Andrew L. Yarrow. *Latecomers: Children of Parents over 35.* New York: The Free Press, 1991.

The first of these two books examines recent changes in divorce law in the United States; the second reports on a decade-long study of divorced couples and their children.

Herbert Jacob. *Silent Revolution: The Transformation of Divorce Law in the United States.* Chicago: University of Chicago Press, 1988.

Judith S. Wallerstein and Sandra Blakeslee. *Second Chances: Men, Women, and Children a Decade After Divorce.* New York: Ticknor & Fields, 1989.

Many of the reasons that husbands and wives often communicate poorly are explored in this book.

Mary Anne Fitzpatrick. *Between Husbands and Wives: Communication in Marriage.* Newbury Park, CA: Sage, 1988.

CHAPTER 16

EDUCATION

Thirteen-year-old Naoko Masuo has just returned from school to her home in a suburb of Yokohama, Japan. She does not drop off books and head off for an afternoon of fun, as is the norm in Canada. Instead, she immediately settles into her homework. Several hours later, her mother reminds her of the time and she gathers her books once again and departs for the *juku* or "cram school" that Naoko attends for three hours three afternoons a week. Mother and daughter travel four stops on the subway to downtown Yokohama and climb to the second floor of an office building where Naoko joins dozens of other girls and boys for intensive training in Japanese, English, math, and science. Tuition at the *juku* consumes several hundred dollars of the Masuo family's monthly income. But they know well the realities of the Japanese educational system, and consider this investment in extra schooling a necessity.

The extra hours in the classroom will soon pay off when Naoko takes the national examination for children her age—a high score is the key to being admitted to a better school. Three years hence, Naoko will face another hurdle—the high-school examination—that, once again, will determine the quality of her education. Then will come the greatest challenge of all: earning admission to an exclusive national university. Only the

one-third of Japanese students who perform best on the college entrance examination enter this elite category. Once accepted to the university, a young person in Japan is virtually guaranteed a high-paying career with a prestigious company. Stumbling in the race that is Naoko's next five years will mean learning to settle for less. Like most other Japanese families, the Masuos are convinced that one cannot work too hard or begin too early in preparation for university admission (Simmons, 1989).

Education has become extremely valuable in Japan's complex and changing society, as it has in other industrial nations. **Education** refers to *the various ways in which a society transmits knowledge—including factual information and occupational skills as well as cultural norms and values—to its members.* In industrial societies, education centers on **schooling**, which is *formal instruction under the direction of specially trained teachers.* Schooling or formal education is one of the major social institutions in industrial societies.

Education: A Global Survey

Like people in Japan, we in Canada expect that children will spend much of their first eighteen years of life in school. Only a century ago, however, schooling beyond a bare minimum was a privilege restricted to a small elite. In the 1830s it is estimated that in Upper Canada about half of the children attended school—and only for an average of twelve months in total (Phillips cited in Johnson, 1968:27). In Third-World societies, even today, the vast majority of people receive little or no schooling.

Chapter 4 ("Society") explained that most people who have inhabited this planet have lived in technologically simple hunting and gathering societies. In such societies, the family was the central social institution; just as there were no governments or churches, so there was no formal system of education. Necessary knowledge and skills were simply taught to children by adults, generally within the family (Lenski, Lenski, & Nolan, 1991).

In more technologically complex agrarian societies—common in much of the world today—people routinely teach others specialized crafts and trading skills. This kind of learning is directed toward immediate needs; the opportunity to study literature, art, history, or science in schools is a privilege generally available only to wealthy people. The English word *school* is, in fact, derived from the Greek word for "leisure." In ancient Greece, renowned teachers such as Socrates, Plato, and Aristotle concentrated their efforts on a small circle of aristocratic men. Similarly, in ancient China the famous philosopher K'ung-Fu-tzu (Confucius) also taught a select few (Rohlen, 1983).

During the Middle Ages, the church expanded schooling as it established the first colleges and universities (Ballantine, 1989). But as has always been the rule in agrarian societies, schooling remained primarily a privilege of the ruling elites in both Western Europe and North America.

Johnson (1968)[1] points out that the initial developments in education in what would later become Canada took place in the early French settlements, where the three Rs (readin', writin' and religion) were taught in church-controlled schools. By 1636, the Jesuits had established a "college," which eventually became Laval University. It claims to be North America's oldest institution of higher education. By 1668 a trade or vocational school had been established at St. Joachim. In the Maritimes, an Anglican academy established in 1785 became the University of New Brunswick in 1859. The earliest primary schools in Upper Canada,

which were established in the 1780s, began to get government funding in 1792. Elitist boarding schools established in 1807 were the first step in establishing our secondary school system.

Prior to confederation (1867), we had already created separate Catholic and Protestant school systems, embraced universal education and teacher training, and put texts and curricula under control of a department of education. In 1883, Toronto became the second North American city to establish kindergarten within the school system, and by about 1920 we had compulsory education to the end of elementary school or the age of sixteen in most provinces. (In the U.S., all states had compulsory education by 1918.) In this period, secondary schools were being established and expanded across Canada. The principle of mass education had been firmly established, partly in response to the requirements of the Industrial Revolution for a literate and skilled work force.

Levels of educational attainment have increased steadily over the last fifty years, the effect being that over time larger percentages of the adult population have some post-secondary education or university degrees. Between 1961 and 1986, the proportion of Canadians twenty-five to forty-four years of age with some post-secondary education increased from 8 to about 55 percent: between 1971 and 1986—a mere fifteen years—the proportion with a university degree rose from 7 to 15 percent (Secretary of State, 1992:25–25). Clearly, Canadians are becoming aware of the educational requirements of the modern economy.[2]

Today, officially at least, only a small fraction of people are illiterate in Canada, the United States, Japan, Great Britain, Scandinavia, and parts of Europe. Finland, Australia, and the Russian-led Commonwealth of Independent States have even lower illiteracy rates. As shown in Global Map 16-1, illiteracy is considerably higher in the Americas to our south, and in Africa and Asia, *most* people neither read nor write. The reason, as Chapter 11 ("Global Inequality") explained in detail, is that agrarian societies are terribly poor, with families earning only about five percent of the income enjoyed by typical Canadian families. Faced with the need simply to survive, people in the Third World can spare little in the way of financial resources and human energy in pursuit of schooling. Except for a small number of

---

[1] The source for all of the Canadian historical material in this section is Johnson (1968).

[2] The impact of education on unemployment rates is quite apparent. "In March 1991, the rate of unemployment among those 25 years of age and older with a university degree was only 4.2 percent, compared to 18 percent for those without secondary schooling" (Secretary of State, 1992:27).

high-quality schools that cater to privileged elites, formal education is mostly of low quality, so children learn substantially less than their peers in richer societies (Hayneman & Loxley, 1983).

Yet, striking educational successes have been documented. Before the 1960 revolution that brought the Castro regime to power, schooling in Cuba was limited to a small upper class. While Castro has made little progress in reducing poverty, Cuba has widely expanded formal education and claims now to have virtually eradicated illiteracy. Such cases suggest that educational achievement is possible even in poor societies if the government defines it as a high social priority.

Before we leave the topic of illiteracy, it is important to note that official literacy and functional literacy are not the same. Although Canada claims to have minimal illiteracy by international standards, educators and others have long been voicing concerns about the extent to which Canadians have the literacy and numeracy skills required to cope with daily living and work—to

WINDOW ON THE WORLD

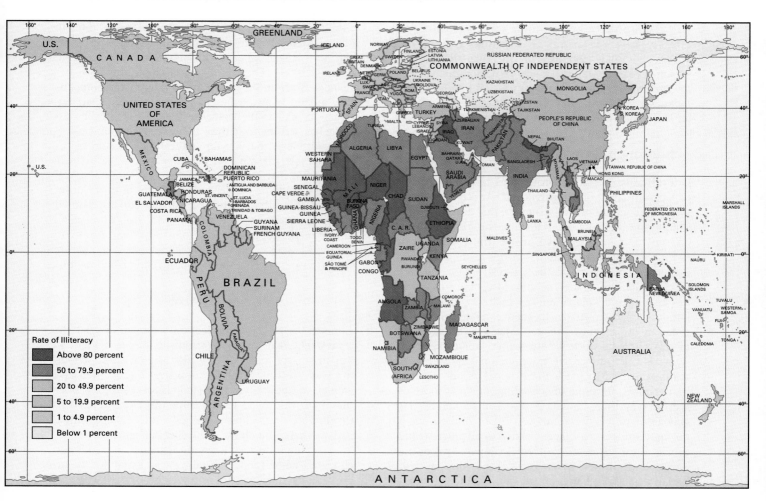

GLOBAL MAP 16-1   ILLITERACY IN GLOBAL PERSPECTIVE
Reading and writing skills are widespread in every industrial society, with illiteracy rates generally below 5 percent. Throughout Latin America, however, illiteracy is more commonplace—one consequence of limited economic development. In about a dozen nations of the world—many of them in Africa—illiteracy is the rule rather than the exception. In such societies, people rely on what sociologists call "the oral tradition" of face-to-face communication rather than communicating through the written word.

say nothing of academic pursuits. A 1989 survey carried out by the National Literacy Secretariat, concluded that 16 percent of Canada's adult population is not sufficiently literate to deal with normal everyday situations. More alarming still is the fact that the Economic Council of Canada (1992) estimates that 28 percent of Canadians aged sixteen to twenty-four cannot read a simple newspaper article and that 44 percent are not functionally numerate. The Council estimates that 1 million functionally illiterate young people will join the labor force over the next ten years unless we establish and enforce stringent standards for graduation. It has even been suggested that university graduation should require passing a literacy test (*Toronto Star,* Aug. 1, 1992:A1).

While there are grounds for questioning the effectiveness of various educational systems and approaches, it is nonetheless true that all industrial societies provide extensive schooling for their people. As the following brief descriptions of schooling in Japan, Great Britain, and the new Russian-led confederation demonstrate, each does so in a distinctive way.

Schooling in Japan

Before industrialization brought mandatory education to Japan in 1872, only a privileged few received schooling. The contemporary Japanese educational system is unique in all the world, reflecting the historical influence of China, Western Europe, the United States (which occupied Japan after World War II), and Japan's own strong traditions (Rohlen, 1983).

In the early grades, schools foster the cultural values long central to Japanese life, including obligation to family (Benedict, 1974). In their early teens, as illustrated by the account of Naoko Masuo at the beginning of this chapter, students encounter Japan's system of rigorous and competitive examinations. Written evaluations are used to place the brightest students in the best schools. In terms of schooling, Japan is more of a meritocracy than Canada or the United States. Here, college or university admission is not limited only to the best students: a bigger barrier to advanced education is the high cost involved. In Japan, by contrast, government support covers most of the financial cost of higher education; however, the performance of individuals on achievement tests literally makes or breaks rich and poor alike in terms of their academic aspirations.

More men and women in Japan (about 90 percent) graduate from high school than in Canada or the United States. At that point, competitive examinations cut down the number of college-bound Japanese youths, so that only about 30 percent of high-school graduates end up entering university—compared to about 55 percent in Canada (Secretary of State, 1992:23) and about 60 percent in the U.S. Understandably, then, Japanese students view entrance examinations with the utmost seriousness, and families send about half of all students to *juku* "cram schools" to give them an extra edge when they take their examinations.

Japanese women take such an active interest in their children's schooling that they have been dubbed *koiku mamas* (a mixture of Japanese and English that means "education mothers"). This maternal role reflects the stark reality that acceptance or rejection by a university shapes a student's career. In addition, most Japanese women, who are still not in the labor force, tend to devote themselves to the future success of their sons and, to a lesser extent, their daughters (Brinton, 1988; Simons, 1989). The payoff—or disappointment—after years of effort on the part of mother and child comes as they anxiously await the results of university examinations. So high is the suspense that observing the outcome has become something of a national pastime.

Although the Japanese educational system places considerable pressure on adolescents, the results are impressive. Especially in mathematics and science, Japanese students outperform students of every other industrial country, including Canada and the United States (Hayneman & Loxley, 1983; Rohlen, 1983). Japanese cultural traditions of hard work and loyalty to family, as well as the highly competitive examination system, appear to be a strongly motivating combination.

Schooling in Great Britain

Chapter 9 ("Social Stratification") explained that the legacy of Great Britain's feudal history is evident in British society today. During the Middle Ages, schooling was a privilege of the nobility. Young men and women of noble station studied classical subjects since they had little need for the practical skills related to earning a living. Those in schools and colleges, then, usually shared much the same elite background.

As the Industrial Revolution created a need for an educated labor force, schooling was expanded to include a greater proportion of the British people. Demands by working-class families that their children, too, be schooled accelerated this process. Today, every British child is required by law to attend school until the age of sixteen.

Traditional social distinctions, however, continue

Wealth and power in Great Britain has long been linked to "public" schools—actually privately funded boarding schools for young men and, to a lesser extent, women. The most elite of these schools transmit the way of life of the upper class not so much in the classroom as on the playing fields, in the dining halls, and in the dormitories where informal socialization goes on continuously. Elite boarding schools are especially important to new-rich families; parents with modest backgrounds and large bank accounts send their children to these schools to mix with and learn from the offspring of "old-money" families.

to shape British education. Many wealthy families send their children to what the British call *public schools*, the equivalent of private boarding schools in Canada. Elite public schools in Britain do more than teach academic subjects; they also socialize children from wealthy families into a distinctive way of life. Patterns of speech, mannerisms, and social graces are learned in the educational setting; together, these distinguish members of the upper class from everyone else. Since public schools are beyond their financial reach, most British parents send their children to state-supported day schools, just as most families do in our country.

The 1960s and 1970s saw a marked expansion in the British university system (Sampson, 1982). In order to lessen the influence of social background on schooling, British children now must compete for places in universities by taking examinations during their high-school years. The government generally pays tuition and living expenses of those who are successful. Compared with the Japanese system, the British examinations are less crucial, evident in the fact that a disproportionate number of well-to-do children still manage to attend Oxford (alma mater for eighteen British prime ministers) and Cambridge, the most prestigious British universities. Graduates of "Oxbridge" form a national elite with top positions in business and government.

Schooling in the Commonwealth of Independent States

Schooling has changed considerably in the new Russian-led commonwealth over the course of the last century. Before the socialist revolution of 1917, Russia was an agrarian society with schooling reserved primarily for nobles. By the 1930s, the Soviet Union adopted mandatory education laws and had embarked on a program to make education universal in the new socialist society. In the next two decades, political unrest and the costs and social disruption of World War II slowed educational progress, but by the end of the 1940s half the young people in the Soviet Union were attending school. In forging a national educational system, the Soviets had to contend with striking cultural diversity—still making news today—in the geographically largest country in the world. By 1975 the Soviets began to boast of having achieved virtually universal schooling (Matthews, 1983; Ballantine, 1989).

According to official Soviet policy, children of both sexes and every ethnic background had broad educational opportunities. This goal was partially realized, but Soviet women have long been overly represented in areas of study (such as education and medicine) with relatively low social prestige in that society, while men have dominated higher-prestige fields like agriculture and engineering. Similarly, although considerable strides have been made toward providing equal access to higher education for diverse ethnic groups, the Russian majority still fares better than others (Avis, 1983).

Schooling in the former Soviet Union reflects and reinforces important cultural values, just as it does in every society. Besides helping the country become an industrial power, Soviet education had important political purposes. Although changes are now under way as this society sheds its socialist past (see Chapters 18 and 19), the Soviet educational system was highly standardized under the direction of the central government so that schools taught norms and values of socialist living (Matthews, 1983; Tomiak, 1983).

As in Japan and Great Britain, competitive

examinations have long characterized the Commonwealth of Independent States. As Chapter 9 ("Social Stratification") notes, disparity of wealth was far less pronounced in the Soviet Union than in Canada, and the government paid most educational costs. This economic parity has gone a long way toward creating a level playing field for young people in the Commonwealth of Independent States—much more so than in our society. During the heyday of the Communist party, however, being the daughter or son of an important official factored in significantly when it came to either going to a selective university or simply learning a trade (Avis, 1983; Matthews, 1983; Ballantine, 1989).

This brief comparison illustrates a basic truth: education is shaped by other institutions and social forces. Societies generally adopt mandatory education laws in response to industrialization and growing political democracy. Also, schools show the influence of surrounding cultural patterns (such as the achievement orientation and intense competition of Japan), historical forces (seen in centuries of inequality in British schooling), and the political system (evident in decades of socialist education in the former Soviet Union).

Schooling in Canada

In Canada, the school reformers of the late 1800s were concerned about the fact that the "classical curriculum did not reflect the realities of the new economic order. ... Education, thus, began to be viewed as an essential precondition for national economic growth" (Gilbert, 1989:105). Wide participation and universality were important goals, and indeed education was compulsory to the age of sixteen by about 1920. Canada also has a policy of universal, publicly supported, primary and secondary schooling, including that in the separate or Catholic system. Canada has two hundred and seventy-three publicly funded post-secondary institutions, sixty-nine of which are classified as universities: tuition fees at our universities (none of which are private) cover about 15 percent of the costs, while government subsidies account for the rest.

Canada ranks second to the United States and well above the average of fourteen other developed countries in the proportion of twenty- to twenty-four-year-olds enroled in post-secondary education. It ranks above the U.S. (below only Sweden) in terms of public expenditures for education—8 percent of our gross national product or GNP (Secretary of State, 1992). These expenditures are made with the intention of giving everyone the opportunity to achieve as much as his or her individual talents and efforts allow. While this reflects our cultural ideals, it exaggerates the historical record. Women were effectively excluded from higher education until this century, and even today it is only among the higher social classes that a majority of young people attends university.

Besides trying to make schooling more widely accessible, Canadian society has long favored *practical* learning, that is, education that has a direct bearing on people's lives, and especially their occupations. The educational philosopher John Dewey (1859–1952) advanced the idea that children would readily learn information and skills they found useful. Rejecting the traditionalist emphasis on teaching a fixed body of knowledge to each generation of students, Dewey (1968; orig. 1938) endorsed *progressive education* that reflected people's changing concerns and needs. With the Quiet Revolution in Quebec in the 1960s, the classical education favored by the religious elite was replaced by a system encouraging the study of business, engineering, and science.

George Herbert Mead, the architect of the symbolic-interaction paradigm in sociology, echoed the sentiments of his friend John Dewey, claiming that "any education that is worthy of the name [provides] the solution to problems that we all carry with us" (1938:52). By contrast, Mead argued, "whatever is stored up, without immediate need, for later occasion, for display, or to pass examinations is mere information [with] no enduring place in the mind" (1906:395). Reflecting this practical emphasis, many of today's community college and university students select major areas of study with an eye toward future jobs.

The Functions of Schooling

Structural-functional analysis directs attention to ways in which formal education enhances the operation and stability of society. Central to the socialization process, schooling serves as one cultural lifeline linking the generations.

Socialization

Every society employs various strategies to transmit its way of life from one generation to the next. In technologically simple societies, most of this cultural transmission is handled by the family. As societies become more technologically complex, young people need to acquire rapidly expanding information and new skills, beyond the grasp of family members themselves, so other social institutions play a greater role in socialization. In industrial societies, schooling requires specially trained personnel to efficiently teach a wide range of knowledge.

At the primary-school level, children learn basic language and mathematical skills. Secondary school steadily builds on this foundation and, for some, college or university allow further specialization. Because industrial societies change so rapidly, schooling not only conveys specific information (which may become obsolete) but also, at its best, empowers students to teach themselves so that they will be able to adapt to future changes.

Schools also transmit cultural values and norms. Sometimes important cultural lessons are learned in subtle ways, as students experience the operation of the classroom itself. Teachers in both Canada and the U.S. give children a great deal of individual responsibility for their behavior and their tasks. However, where in the U.S., spelling bees and classroom drill are intended to foster a keen sense of competitive individualism, in Canada, there is more emphasis upon activities that encourage cooperation, sharing, and team effort. Competitiveness is actually discouraged in many Canadian classrooms because of potential damaging effects on the self-esteem of those who cannot compete successfully.

Nor is the political component of education as aggressively promoted in Canada as it is in other countries. In the United States, for example, the American political system and way of doing business are commonly championed in the classroom, and rituals such as saluting the flag and singing "The Star-Spangled

Schooling is a way of teaching the values and attitudes that a society deems important. It is also a means favored by political regimes to instill conformity and compliance into children. These children in Taiwan are receiving a lesson in "political correctness."

Banner" foster patriotism. Canada, by contrast, is almost embarrassed to express patriotism, so that very little flag waving takes place. Although our children do sing "O Canada," we place less emphasis on Canadian history or the workings of our political system than do the Americans—and a consciousness of military purpose or presence is almost completely lacking here. Instead of espousing a unified cultural identity, our classrooms try to encourage respect for all of the many cultures that make up the Canadian mosaic.

Cultural Innovation

Educational systems create as well as transmit culture. Schools attempt to stimulate intellectual inquiry and critical thinking, which lead to the development of new ideas. Today, for example, most university professors not only teach but engage in research that yields discoveries and innovations. Research in the humanities, the social sciences, and the natural sciences is changing attitudes and patterns of life throughout Canada and the larger world. Medical research, carried on mainly at major universities, has helped to increase life expectancy, just as research by sociologists and psychologists has expanded our understanding of human social life and contributed to an improved quality of life.

Social Integration

Schooling helps to forge a mass of people into a unified whole. This function is especially important in nations characterized by great social diversity, where various cultures are indifferent or even hostile to one another. The Soviet Union and Yugoslavia relied on schools to tie their disparate peoples together—without ultimately succeeding—and similar strains are now emerging in the United States. As we saw in Chapter 3 ("Culture"), Canada has had a long experience with the challenges of muticulturalism and linguistic dualism and has tried (not always successfully) to foster Canadian nationalism while accommodating a wide variety of interest groups. As a result, our educational policies have been sensitive to the problems of maintaining equality of access and unity in the face of diversity. We have been reluctant to push a national identity because of Quebec's sensitivities and our embrace of the mosaic model (Jaenen, 1981).

Societies in the Americas, Africa, and Asia, encompassing dozens of ethnic categories, all strive to foster social integration. Normally, schools try to meet this challenge, first, by establishing a common language

A   DECADE   OF   CHANGE

Trends in College Diplomas and Bachelor's Degrees

College and university attendance in Canada increased 841 percent between 1951 and 1990. College enrolments stabilized during the 1980s but universities have continued to grow. Figures 16-1 and 16-2 show that, from 1976 to 1988, the colleges graduated larger proportions of students in business and commerce, and engineering and applied sciences, while in universities the gains were largely in the social sciences.

The 1980s have also seen a steady increase in the proportion of women attending universities and graduating at the bachelor's, master's and doctoral levels (see Chapter 13, "Sex and Gender"). Figure 16-3 reveals that between 1979 and 1989, the proportion of women among those earning bachelor's and first profes-

FIGURE 16-1   COLLEGE CAREER GRADUATES BY MAJOR
FIELDS OF STUDY, 1976–1988
SOURCE: Secretary of State, Canada (1992).

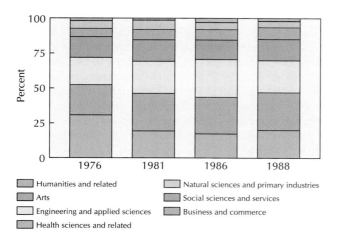

Humanities and related
Arts
Engineering and applied sciences
Health sciences and related
Natural sciences and primary industries
Social sciences and services
Business and commerce

FIGURE 16-2   BACHELOR'S AND FIRST PROFESSIONAL
DEGREE GRADUATES BY MAJOR FIELDS OF
STUDY, 1970–1989
SOURCE: Secretary of State, Canada (1992).

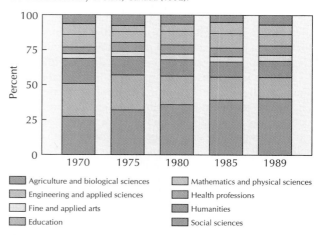

Agriculture and biological sciences
Engineering and applied sciences
Fine and applied arts
Education
Mathematics and physical sciences
Health professions
Humanities
Social sciences

to encourage broad communication and forge a national identity. Of course, some ethnic minorities resist state-sponsored schooling precisely for this reason. In the Commonwealth of Independent States, for example, Lithuanians, Ukrainians, Azerbaijanis and others long chafed at having to learn Russian, which they saw as emblematic of their domination by outsiders and a threat to their own traditions. For these reasons, the Hutterites, a culturally distinctive people in our Prairie provinces (mainly Alberta), have their children taught in schools within their own colonies (albeit using the provincial curriculum, and speaking in English for part of the day) and continue to speak a German dialect within their communities. Of course, the Quebecois perceive a threat to their distinct culture, resent the need to learn English for economic survival, and insist upon full provincial control of education—the current demand being for control of worker training. Quebec

has declared itself a unilingual province and only under special circumstances can a child be educated in English there. Native peoples in Canada have also been struggling to establish greater control of their own schools. In each of the above cases the peoples in question are resisting formal schooling in the language of the majority because of very real threats to linguistic and cultural survival.

Although there is understandable resistance to majority controlled schooling by certain segments of the population, the striking cultural diversity of our country increases the importance of formal education as a path to social integration. The expansion of educational facilities and the enactment of mandatory education laws coincided with the arrival of hundreds of thousands of immigrants from a wide variety of origins who somehow had to be transformed into Canadians. Even today, formal education plays a major role in inte-

sional degrees increased in all fields except mathematics and physical sciences. Furthermore, in 1989 women made up more than half of the degree recipients in all of the fields except mathematics/physical sciences and engineering/applied sciences.

At the PhD level, substantially larger percentages of the degrees granted are in the areas of agriculture/biological sciences, mathematics/physical sciences, and engineering and applied sciences. Women are still not as well represented at this level—espe-

cially in the three fields just listed—but as we saw in Chapter 13, they have posted gains at the PhD level in all of the major fields of study in the past decade.

SOURCE: Secretary of State (1992)

FIGURE 16-3 BACHELOR'S AND FIRST PROFESSIONAL DEGREES GRANTED TO WOMEN, BY MAJOR FIELDS OF STUDY, 1979–1989
SOURCE: Secretary of State, Canada (1992).

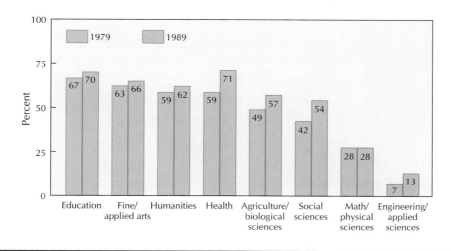

grating disparate groups, as immigrants from Asia (roughly 50 percent of recent immigrants), the Caribbean, Eastern Europe, and Latin America—and roughly 35,000 refugees a year—blend their traditions with the existing cultural mix. Although our school systems seek to provide all of them with the linguistic and other skills needed for employment and daily life, Canada has not insisted that they give up their various identities completely.

The retention of other identities is assisted, where there are concentrations of people with shared backgrounds, through our heritage language programs, which provide for formal education in traditional languages for ethnic minority children (where numbers warrant it). These programs sometimes attract other students, so that, somewhere in Canada, young people of British or Ukrainian ancestry might be studying Japanese or Italian. Furthermore, since our country is

officially bilingual and since bilingualism is needed for certain types of jobs (that of prime minister, for example), the Trudeau government established French immersion schooling throughout the country—except in Quebec where it would be redundant. About 7 percent of primary and secondary school students (outside Quebec) are enrolled in immersion programs. Canada Map 16-1 indicates that, in 1989–90, enrolment in immersion varied by province—from a low of 2.9 percent in the Northwest Territories to a high of 17.9 in New Brunswick (Canada's only officially bilingual province).

Social Placement

Formal education helps young people assume culturally approved statuses and perform roles that contribute to the ongoing life of society. To accomplish this, schooling operates as a screening process that identifies and develops people's various aptitudes and abilities. Ideally, schools evaluate student performance in terms of achievement while screening out the effects of their social background. In this ideal scheme, the "best and the brightest" are encouraged to pursue the most challenging and advanced studies, while others are guided into educational programs and occupations suited to their talents. Schooling, in short, enhances meritocracy, linking social position to personal merit.

Meritocracy has always had special significance to people who begin life with social disadvantages based on ascribed traits such as sex, race, ethnicity, and social class. For this reason, schooling has historically been the major avenue of upward social mobility in Canada.

Latent Functions of Schooling

Besides these purposeful, manifest functions of formal education, a number of latent functions are less obvious and less widely recognized. One is child care. As the numbers of one-parent families and two-career marriages rise, schools have become vital to relieving parents of some child-care duties. Among teenagers, too, schooling consumes much time and considerable energy, in many cases fostering conformity to conventional social norms at a time of life when the likelihood of unlawful behavior is high. And because many students attend school well into their twenties, education usefully engages thousands of young people for whom few jobs may be available.

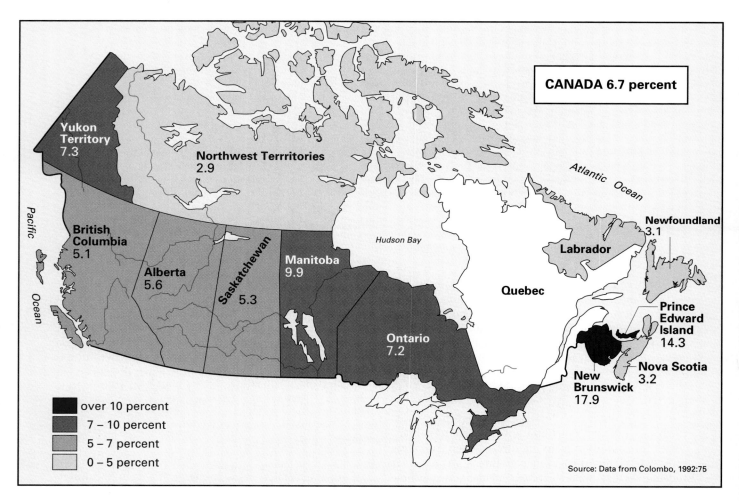

CANADA MAP 16-1   FRENCH IMMERSION ENROLMENT, (PERCENT, BY PROVINCE AND TERRITORY, 1989–90)

Another latent function of schools is to establish social relationships and networks. High schools, colleges, and universities bring together people of marriageable age, many of whom meet their future spouse as a result. Affiliation with a particular school also forms the basis of social ties that provide not only friendship, but also valuable career opportunities and resources later on in life.

Critical evaluation. Structural-functional analysis of formal education stresses the various ways in which this social institution supports the operation of an industrial society. This paradigm has usefully identified various manifest and latent functions of schooling. One key limitation of functionalism is that it overlooks how the quality of schooling is far greater for some than for others. In the next section, social-conflict analysis places the spotlight squarely on this issue.

Schooling and Social Inequality

Social-conflict analysis links formal education to patterns of social inequality. To some extent, schooling does seek to develop people's individual talents and abilities. But schools are hardly indifferent to social background, and actually perpetuate social inequality based on sex, race, ethnicity, and social class.

Throughout the world, people traditionally have thought that schooling is more important for males than for females. The education gap between women and men has been closing in recent decades, but many females and males still typically study conventionally feminine and masculine subjects. To the extent that they stress the experiences of certain types of people (say, European men) while ignoring the lives of others in the same society, schools tend to reinforce the values and importance of dominant racial, cultural, and gender categories, to the detriment of minorities. Efforts have been made across Canada to provide gender-neutral texts and library materials and to remove materials that perpetuate negative stereotypes or are offensive to various ethnic, racial, and religious minorities. Schools are also attempting to incorporate a wide range of muticultural programs and materials into their curricula to increase tolerance and understanding among youngsters of different backgrounds. The intent, in part, is to eradicate sterotypes and to raise the aspiration levels of any people who may have felt themselves to be excluded by the system. Women and francophones are among those who now are spending more time in school and proceeding to college or university (Guppy and Arai, 1993).

It is also the case that affluence affects the extent to which Canadians take advantage of educational opportunities. Along with gender, social class is a strong predictor of aspirations to attend university (Porter, Porter & Blishen, 1982): in fact, one is much more likely to attend university or college if one's parents are white-collar with post-secondary education (Guppy & Arai, 1993).

Regional variations in affluence and economic structure give rise to marked differences in educational attainment across provinces. Canada Map 16-2 reveals that, in 1989, Quebec, Ontario, and Nova Scotia had the highest levels of involvement in post-secondary education among 18–24-year-olds—above 20 percent—while levels in the Yukon and Northwest Territories were below 5 percent. Cities, too, have their own educational profiles. Figure 16-4 reveals differences in twenty-five Census Metropolitan Areas with respect to the percentages of adults (aged 20–64 years) with less than Grade 9 schooling—ranging from about 18 percent in Trois Rivières, Quebec to less than 5 percent in Victoria, B.C.

Social Control

Social-conflict analysis suggests that schooling acts as a means of social control, encouraging acceptance of the status quo with its inherent inequities. In various, often subtle ways, schools serve to reproduce the status hierarchy, although this process is not always evident to students or even to teachers.

Samuel Bowles and Herbert Gintis (1976) point out that public education grew exponentially in the late nineteenth century when capitalists were seeking a docile, disciplined, and moderately educated work force. Mandatory education laws ensured that schools would teach immigrants with diverse cultural backgrounds the English language[3] as well as cultural values supportive of capitalism. Compliance, punctuality, and discipline were—and still are—part of what is called the **hidden curriculum**, *ideas and behavior that support the status quo, taught in subtle ways to students.*

Streaming and Social Inequality

Many Canadian schools practice **streaming**, *the categorical assignment of students to different types of education-*

---

[3] Until Quebec passed Bill 101 in 1977, making French the sole official language of Quebec as well as the language of business, francophones had to be fluently bilingual in order to succeed economically. Even in Quebec, English was the language of business.

al programs. Streaming is also a common practice in many other industrial societies, including the United States, Germany, Great Britain, France, and Japan.

The educational justification for streaming is to give students the kinds of schooling appropriate to their individual aptitudes and aspirations. For a variety of reasons, including innate ability and level of motivation, some students are capable of more challenging work than others are. Also, interests differ among students, with some seeking programs preparing them for university, while others simply wish to acquire a general high-school education, and still others want to pursue job-related technical training. Streaming is intended to accommodate these divergent goals.

According to critics, however, streaming actually works to perpetuate privilege rather than to encourage or reward achievement. They point to research revealing social background has as much to do with streaming as does individual merit (Bowles & Gintis, 1976; Persell, 1977; Davis & Haller, 1981; Oakes, 1982; Porter, 1987; Hiller, 1991; Kilgore, 1991). Almost all students have the capacity to succeed in any educational program, asserts Jeannie Oakes (1985), but streaming—based on "scientific" testing—defines half of all students as below average. In practice, students from affluent families typically expect to be placed in university-bound streams while those from modest backgrounds are likely to end up learning a trade. Because students forge friendships with their classmates, streaming effectively socially segregates the advantaged from the disadvantaged (Hallinan & Williams, 1989).

In light of these criticisms, many schools are now

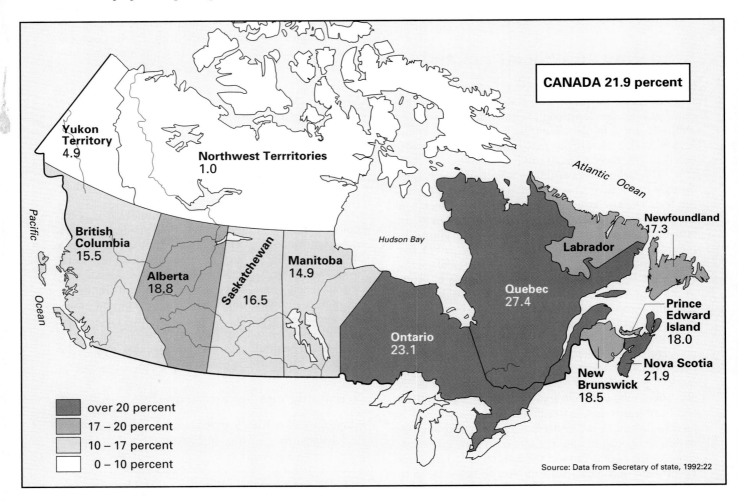

CANADA MAP 16-2   PARTICIPATION RATES OF THE 18–24 AGE GROUP IN FULL-TIME POST-SECONDARY EDUCATION, BY PROVINCE AND TERRITORY, 1989

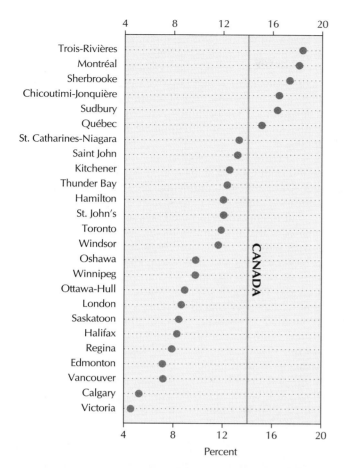

FIGURE 16-4   PERCENTAGE OF POPULATION WITH LESS THAN GRADE 9 SCHOOLING IN SELECTED CENSUS METROPOLITAN AREAS

SOURCE: Statistics Canada, Metropolitan Atlas Series, *Cat. No. 98–106, 1989.*

cautious about streaming. Recent initiatives in Ontario aimed at destreaming have been met with opposition from schools boards and teachers as well as from parents, who are concerned that their university-bound children will receive lower-quality education in destreamed classrooms. Nonetheless, the Ontario Ministry of Education and Training (1993) has come out with its destreaming schedule—one grade per year starting with Grade 9 in 1993–94.

Without streaming, less academically inclined children may be unable to compete with some of their classmates, and teachers face the difficult task of teaching students of differing abilities in one class; but these problems are not insurmountable. Streaming, on the other hand, has a clear and strong impact on students' self-concepts. Young people who spend years in higher

streams tend to see themselves as bright and able, whereas those in lower streams develop lower ambition and self-esteem (Bowles & Gintis, 1976; Persell, 1977; Rosenbaum, 1980; Oakes, 1982, 1985).

Testing and Social Inequality

Here is a question of the kind traditionally used to measure the intelligence and academic ability of school-age children.

> *Painter is to painting as _____ is to sonnet.*

> Answers: (a) *driver*
> (b) *poet*
> (c) *priest*
> (d) *carpenter*

The correct answer is (b) *poet*. A painter creates a painting as a poet creates a sonnet. This question purports to measure logical reasoning, but demonstrating this skill depends entirely on knowing what each term means. Unless students have been exposed to sonnets as a form of written verse, they are unlikely to answer the question correctly. An upper-middle-class student of European descent is likely to have more of the experiences rewarded by such tests. The same person, however, might not score as well on an intelligence test devised by the Ojibwa or the Inuit. Controversy surrounds the use of such tests, for they reflect our society's dominant culture, thereby placing the members of various minorities at a disadvantage. Children from less affluent backgrounds are also at a disadvantage because they face "tests of intelligence and cognitive skills weighted in favor of middle- and upper-class children" (Porter, Porter & Blishen, 1982:9). The motivations and attitudes transmitted to their children by middle- and upper-class parents also benefit them on these tests and in the classroom.

Ironically, intelligence tests were developed at the beginning of this century with the intention of fairly evaluating the innate ability of individuals, whatever their social background. In recent years, organizations that create these tests have carefully studied test results to eliminate the kinds of questions that seem to discriminate against certain categories of people. Any question that is found to discriminate on the basis of racial or ethnic background is deleted from future tests.

Unequal Access to Higher Education

In North America, people regard higher education as a path to occupational achievement. Not surprisingly, 79

Afrocentric schooling is currently a topic of controversy in North America. Proponents of this policy argue that teaching children African cultures—such as Egyptian hieroglyphics and Swahili vocabulary—will raise their self-esteem and strengthen their interest in learning. Critics respond that Afrocentrism promotes racial separation, precisely the problem that integrated schooling was designed to overcome. The photograph is from a summer class in African Studies at a Toronto public school.

percent of Canadians view education as "extremely important to one's future success" (Flower, 1984:27). Despite the decline in the proportion of the population that is eighteen to twenty-four years of age, enrolment in post-secondary education has risen dramatically in the post-war period.[4] While, in 1988, about 55 percent of high school graduates went directly on to post-secondary education, of the eighteen to twenty-four age cohort only 22 percent were enrolled in full-time post-secondary education (Secretary of State, 1992:22–23).

There are many reasons why most people in Canada do not graduate from community college or university. Some high-school students want to enter the labor force right away; others cannot afford to continue their education because of the costs of tuition and deferred income. The intellectual demands of the curriculum may also dissuade some students with limited talents. Yet most of our young people would like to attend college or university, and doing so is certainly within the academic ability of the vast majority.

In one respect at least, we have moved closer to the goal of equal access to higher education in Canada: as noted above, women and men now attend university in roughly equal numbers. Low or moderate family income, however, remains a formidable barrier to enrolment: young people with lower family incomes or

fathers in blue-collar occupations are much less likely to go to university (Wotherspoon, 1991). Most universities provide financial assistance to students in the form of bursaries and scholarships, and governments make loans available to those of limited means. Nevertheless, many people cannot afford the remaining costs. The problem has been accentuated in recent years as cutbacks in government funding have forced tuition increases.

Figure 16-5 shows that the Asian and black communities in Canada actually have *higher* levels of educational attainment (completing secondary or university education) than either the British or the French. However, it is important to note that the arrival of relatively well educated immigrants in the Asian and black categories may mean that the high levels of educational achievement are not necessarily characteristic of members of those minorities who are born or schooled in Canada. The figures for the Native population suggest that we have not effectively removed barriers to minority educational achievement. Furthermore, the educational attainments of Asians and blacks in Canada do not place them among the top income-earners: in terms of median income, they rank between the British (top) and French, while on other measures of income they rank below the two "charter" groups. See Chapter 10 ("Social Class in Canada") for a more detailed discussion.

Whatever kind of community college or universi-

FIGURE 16-5 EDUCATIONAL ATTAINMENT FOR SELECTED CATEGORIES OF PEOPLE,* 1986.**
* Percentages are based upon populations aged 15 and older, who claimed to be "single origin": i.e., with the same background on both paternal and maternal sides.
** Latest data available.
SOURCE: Statistics Canada, Catalogue No. 93-315.

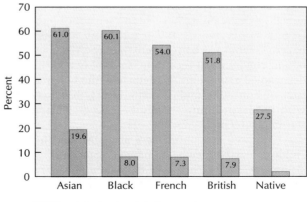

---

[4] While university enrolments have risen substantially, those in community colleges have leveled off since 1986.

ty one attends, higher education expands career opportunities and increases earnings. Figure 16-6 shows average annual incomes for full-time workers of various ages according to level of educational attainment. At each level, income increases with age (reflecting seniority or experience) and for each age category, income increases with level of schooling. Having a university degree makes a substantial difference to incomes in the two older categories. Furthermore, having a university degree, as opposed to a community college diploma, decreases the likelihood that one will be unemployed two years after graduation: as one progresses from bachelor's through master's and doctoral degrees, the likelihood of being unemployed is further reduced (Secretary of State, 1992:40).

Certainly many people find schooling to be its own reward, but the income figures shown here indicate that schooling is also a sound investment in financial terms, increasing income by hundreds of thousands of dollars over a person's working life. Bear in mind, of course, that the higher earnings of more educated people may stem from more than schooling. As we have seen, university graduates are likely to come from relatively well-to-do families and to enjoy social and economic advantages—including "old boy" networks, knowledge of how the system works, and a strong desire to achieve.

Credentialism

As modern societies have become more technologically advanced, culturally diverse, and socially mobile, credentials, such as diplomas and degrees, have assumed some of the significance once attached to family background. That is, instead of sizing people up by asking who their parents are, we now check their resumes and count their degrees.

Credentialism, then, is *the requirement that a person hold some particular diploma or degree as a condition of employment.* Structural-functional analysis suggests that credentialism is simply the way our technologically complex society goes about ensuring that important jobs are filled by well-trained people. By contrast, social-conflict analysis holds that credentials often bear little relation to the skills and responsibilities of a specific job. Employers in an insurance agency, for example, may expect applicants for managerial positions to have a university degree, but they really do not expect them to know much about the insurance business, since management trainees will go through the company's own training program in any case.

Then why are degrees so important? Collins (1979) argues that they have a latent function of allowing in only the kind of people who will fit into the corporate world, with the manners and attitudes desirable for high-prestige occupations. Credentials, in short, work as a gate-keeping strategy that restricts powerful and lucrative occupations to a small segment of the population.

Finally, this emphasis on credentials in Canada and the United States has encouraged **overeducation,** *a situation in which workers have more formal education than the performance of their occupations requires.* Many new and specialized jobs obviously demand advanced schooling. Research indicates, however, that educational achievement has actually outpaced the demands of the labor market (Berg, 1970; Rumberger, 1981). In fact, close to half of all university graduates (at bachelor's, master's and doctoral levels) are *underemployed,*

**FIGURE 16-6
AVERAGE ANNUAL EMPLOYMENT INCOME FOR FULL-TIME WORKERS, BY LEVEL OF SCHOOLING AND AGE GROUP, 1985**
SOURCE: Secretary of State, Canada, 1992.

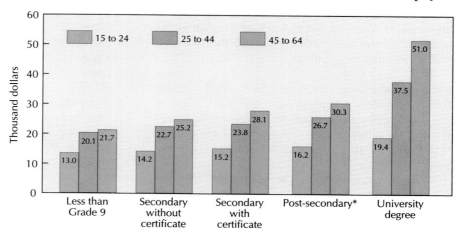

* Does not include university degrees

working at jobs that do not require their educational qualifications (Secretary of State, 1992:41). This does not negate the intellectual value of schooling; it simply points out the inconsistency between more and more schooling for our population and the expansion of low-skill service jobs over the last few decades, a trend described in Chapter 10 ("Social Class in Canada"). Why are we intent on gaining more education if available jobs do not require it? Val Burris (1983) suggests that if we define credentials as the key to getting a job, people will invest in schooling whether or not jobs demand it. This emphasis on schooling may make some dissatisfied with their jobs, but it does improve their chances of getting better work and gaining access to a host of other opportunities for social advancement (Shockey, 1989).

Privilege and Personal Merit

One of the themes of social-conflict analysis deserves to be highlighted: *schooling turns social privilege into personal merit.* Attending university, in other words, is more or less a rite of passage for men and women from well-to-do families, and a real challenge for young people from families with fewer financial resources whose parents have little experience with the world of higher education.

But the North American cultural emphasis on individual achievement pushes us to see credentials as "badges of ability" as Richard Sennett and Jonathan Cobb (1973) put it, rather than as symbols of family affluence. While some people certainly rise from modest beginnings by studying long and hard, we need to recognize that when we congratulate the typical new graduate, we often overlook the social resources that made this achievement possible. In the same way, we are quick to condemn the high-school dropout as personally deficient with little thought to the social circumstances that surround that person's life.

Critical evaluation.   Social-conflict analysis explores formal education in terms of social inequality. Thus we see that schooling is unequal for different categories of people; schooling can also serve to transform privilege into personal ability and social disadvantage into personal deficiency.

Social-conflict analysis can be criticized for ignoring how different kinds of schooling may actually meet the needs of socially and individually diverse students. This approach also minimizes the extent to which schooling develops everyone's talents and abilities.

Finally, without denying that personal ability and privilege are closely linked, there has always been considerable meritocracy in our educational system, and the historical record shows that schooling has led to upward social mobility for many talented women and men.

Problems in the Schools

Although Canadians have long debated the value and quality of education, the debate has intensified over the past decade or two. Table 16-1 reveals that the percentage of people who are dissatisfied with the education their children are receiving has been increasing—from 41 percent in 1973 to 56 percent in 1992—and that the levels of dissatisfaction are greatest in Ontario and British Columbia. Somewhat surprisingly, in light of current concerns with government deficits and taxes, a majority of Canadians (68 percent) favor increased government funding to all educational sectors (*Toronto Star*, Sept. 7, 1992:A11). Many parents feel that formal education standards at all levels have declined in recent decades. Discipline appears to be lax and children go through school without learning "the basics."

School Discipline

Canadians and Americans alike believe that schools should inculcate personal discipline and that the job is not being done properly. The U.S. government estimates that several hundred thousand students and at least one thousand teachers are physically assaulted on school grounds every year. This violence at school is blamed on poverty-stricken urban environments that breed drug use as well as violence on the street and at home. All too often, violence in the community and at school involves the use of guns. The National Education Association estimates that 100,000 American students carry a gun to school (Hull, *Time*, Aug. 2, 1993:30). Canada's school discipline problems are not of the same type or magnitude, but there have been many instances of assault upon students and teachers; students have been found at school with knives—most often in specific violence-prone schools—but very rarely with guns. At the post-secondary level, the 1989 killing of 14 female engineering students—by Marc Lepine at Montreal's l'Ecole Polytechnique—shocked Canadians across the country, driving home the realization that, even within our schools, we are not immune to deadly violence.

TABLE 16-1 PARENTS' DISSATISFACTION WITH CHILDREN'S EDUCATION, 1973, 1978, 1992

Are you satisfied or dissatisfied with the education children are getting today?

Canada	Satisfied	Dissatisfied	Don't know
1992	35%	56%	9%
1978	34	53	13
1973	51	41	8
Regional breakdown (1992)			
Atlantic	41	54	6
Quebec	37	55	8
Ontario	30	61	10
Prairies	49	45	6
B.C.	25	63	12

Note: percentages may not add exactly to 100, due to rounding.
SOURCE: Toronto Star, September 7, 1992, p. A11.

In some cities in the United States, the level of violence has escalated to the point that parents fear for their children not only while traveling to and from school but also while in school. These two brothers, aged 4 and 5, set off for school in New York City wearing bulletproof jackets.

More commonly, however, the discipline problems in our schools involve students who display disdain for learning, are rude to their teachers or challenge their authority, skip classes, disrupt the classroom, or otherwise interfere with the formal education of themselves and others. "When *I* was young," parents will say, "we did what the teacher told us." Selective memory notwithstanding, there undoubtedly has been a gradual decline in classroom discipline over the past few decades related to larger societal trends. In teachers' college, discussion of educational theory and the finer points of pedagogy do nothing to prepare would-be teachers for their first field placements, where the most pressing question is one of how to "maintain *control* in the classroom."[5] Teachers, who are trained to teach but find that their energies are diverted into policing students, experience frustration and disillusionment on the job.

Bureaucracy and Student Passivity

Another problem experienced within the school system is pervasive *student passivity* or the failure of students to take an active role in their own learning. This problem is not confined to any particular type of school: it can

[5] From a lecture by Ian Gomme of Memorial University.

be found in private as well as public schools and at all grade levels (Coleman, Hoffer, & Kilgore, 1981).

Schooling is a wonderful opportunity, and one that is rare in human history. In medieval Europe, children assumed many adult responsibilities before they were teenagers; a century ago, Canadian children worked long hours for little pay in factories, on farms, and in coal mines. Today, by contrast, the major task facing young people is to study their human heritage—to learn the effective use of language, master the manipulation of numbers, and acquire knowledge and skills that should enhance their comprehension, enjoyment, and participation in the surrounding world.

Dropping Out

If many students are disruptive in class, others are not there at all. The problem of dropping out—quitting school before completing a high school diploma—leaves young people (many of whom are disadvantaged to begin with) ill-equipped for the world of work, and at high risk for poverty.

Numerous Canadian officials, business representatives, and educators have been very concerned about Canada's drop-out rate, which seemed to be exceptionally high when compared to those of other countries. In 1970 and 1990, the U.S. rates were 12.2 and 10.7 percent respectively, indicating a slight decline. Measured differently,[6] the Canadian rates were 48 and 32 percent in 1970–71 and 1990–91 respectively. A recently refined measure suggests that the more realistic drop-out rate for Canada in 1991 was 18 percent, with considerable regional variation (see Table 16-2); many who appear to be drop-outs are really only stop-outs, who leave and return at a later date to complete their secondary school programs (Fennel, *Maclean's*, June 14, 1993:49). Detailed follow-up of such individuals by several school boards suggests that even the levels in Table 16-2 (column 3) are too high; the new numbers—based upon Statistics Canada's *School Leavers Survey* (Gilbert et al., 1993)—are more reassuring than the earlier figures, but even at 18 percent there is cause for concern.

In the report *Leaving School*, which compares school leavers and high school graduates, Gilbert et al. note that leavers are more likely:

1. to be from single-parent or no-parent families
2. to have parents with lower educational attainment
3. to be married and to have dependent children (especially the women)
4. to have lower grade averages
5. to have failed a grade in elementary school
6. to have worked more than 20 hours per week during the final school year
7. to use alcohol (regularly) and drugs.

Aboriginal people have a very high dropout rate (40 percent), while immigrants have a low level (11 per-

TABLE 16-2   DROPOUT RATES IN CANADA

	1970–1971	1990–1991	Latest Study 1991
Canada	48%	32%	18%
British Columbia	46	34	16
Alberta	40	35	14
Saskatchewan	32	24	16
Manitoba	45	27	19
Ontario	38	34	17
Quebec	54	28	22
New Brunswick	38	15	20
Nova Scotia	N/A	25	22
Prince Edward Island	43	24	25
Newfoundland	62	25	24

SOURCE: Macleans, June 14, 1993.

[6] The American rates are based upon the proportion of the population between fourteen and twenty-four that had left school without a high school diploma (U.S. Bureau of the Census, 1991). The Statistics Canada figures reflect the number of students who did not enter and graduate from the same high school within four years (*Maclean's*, June 14, 1993:49). Those who changed schools or left and came back were counted as dropouts.

cent). In addition, it is noted that school leavers are currently more likely to be unemployed (34 percent) than are the graduates (23 percent).

For young people who drop out of school in a credential-based society, the risks of unemployment or becoming stuck in a low-paying job are easy to imagine. Faced with this reality, many of those who leave school return to the classroom at a later time.

Education and the World of Work

Recently, the province of New Brunswick took a novel approach to education in its utilitarian role of preparing workers who are capable of participating in a changing and, hopefully, expanding labor market. While Premier Frank McKenna was actively recruiting businesses to establish in or relocate to New Brunswick, some of his schools were making a special, complementary offer. Their graduates would enter the work force with "guaranteed" skills: if the employer were to find them wanting, they could be returned for upgrading at the schools' expense. Strategic spending in education has helped to decrease the overall dropout rate in New Brunswick as well. An appropriately educated, bilingual work force is one of the factors allowing Moncton, New Brunswick, to entice a wide range of companies to relocate there. Moncton (population 106,503) is attracting international attention, and has been chosen as one of the top five "Best Cities for Business" by *The Globe and Mail: Report on Business* (August, 1993:55). Advanced telecommunications technology is one of the factors allowing many companies to move to an area without a large population base.

A large study, *Making the Match,* involving twenty companies and five universities (Evers, Rush, Krmpotic & Duncan-Robinson, 1993) was designed to assess the skill development experiences of Canadian university students and graduates as well as the fit between these skills and the needs of corporations. The skills most in demand (and shortest in supply) were not the technical skills (like using the computer) but a skill composite which was labeled "Mobilizing Innovation and Change"—(the abilities to integrate and use information, adapt to change, take reasonable risks, and conceptualize the future). Leadership and conflict management are also scarce skills. The educational system needs to develop technical skills, but, in addition, it should consider innovative approaches of its own to foster the skills needed by industry. Interestingly, there is a link between these skills and the educational "aims and objectives" espoused by many of our universities.

Functional Illiteracy: Must We Rethink Education?

Imagine being unable to read labels on cans of food, instructions for assembling a child's toy, the dosage on a medicine bottle, or even the information on your own paycheque. These are some of the debilitating experiences of **functional illiteracy**, *reading and writing skills inadequate for carrying out everyday responsibilities.*

As schooling became universal, the Canadian government confidently concluded that illiteracy had been all but eliminated. The truth of the matter, according to the National Literacy Secretariat, is that only 62 percent of Canadians have sufficient literacy and numeracy skills to deal with everyday tasks: about 15 percent have difficulty recognizing familiar words or doing simple addition and subtraction. Canadians are not alone in this respect, though, for it is estimated that about one in four adults in the United States is functionally illiterate, and that the proportions are higher among the elderly and minorities.

Functional illiteracy is a complex social problem. It is caused partly by an educational system that passes children from one grade to the next whether they learn or not. Another cause is community indifference to local schools that prevents parents and teachers from working together to improve children's learning. Still another cause is that millions of children grow up with illiterate parents who offer little encouragement to learn language skills.

Functional illiteracy costs the North American economy more than $100 billion a year. This cost includes decreased productivity (by workers who perform their jobs improperly) and increased accidents (by people unable to understand written instructions). It also reflects the costs of supporting those unable to read and write well enough to find work and end up receiving public assistance or in prison.

Correcting this national problem requires one approach for young people and another for adults. To stop functional illiteracy before it happens, the public must demand that children not be graduated from school until they have learned basic language skills. For adults, the answer begins with diagnosis—a difficult task since many feel shame at their plight and avoid disclosing their need for help. Once such people are identified, however, adult education programs must be provided and utilized. Canada has an elaborate set of literacy programs, but they are not reaching their target groups.

It should be noted that in some cases, illiteracy is not an inability to read at all, but an inability to read in English or French—and that Canada does have an active program teaching English as a second language (ESL) to the constantly replenished body of immigrant schoolchildren and adults.

Our society is one of the most affluent on earth, yet several other countries have more literate populations than we do. For those living in a world of incomprehensible symbols, functional illiteracy is a personal disaster; for all of us, it is an urgent national problem.

SOURCE: Based on Kozol (1980, 1985); Columbo, (1992:76).

Make bedtime *story* time.

After you have dressed, fed, played, scolded, consoled and cared for your child, remember to do just one more thing. Read together, to help ensure your child's future in a world dictated by words.

When you tuck your child under the covers, take the time to open a cover. It just might be the most important part of the day.

ABC CANADA

THE FOUNDATION TO PROMOTE LITERACY IN CANADA

Distribution of this message was made possible by the Canadian Advertising Foundation

Education for Tomorrow

As a society, Canada is undergoing a series of changes with implications for our educational system.

Firstly, we are dealing with increasing diversity as a result of steady immigration, cultural pluralism (partly in response to our policy of multiculturalism), ethnic nationalism (most visibly amongst the Québecois and Native peoples) as well as continuing regional and class divisions. In this context, the educational system is required: 1) to promote equality of access, participation, and outcome; and 2) to play an integrative role, in part by fostering a Canadian identity that overrides our differences.

Secondly, Canada is experiencing technological change involving the expanded use of computers and robots—which in turn has an impact on organizational patterns (for example, the possibilty of working at home while "hooked up" to the office). The school must prepare young people—and adults involved in upgrading their skills—for a world of electronic communication and continuous, rapid technological development. Although they cannot teach everything, computers must become an integral part of the learning milieu, for they increasingly shape the world in which we live, work, and play.

And thirdly, we are facing a shrinking world of shifting political alliances, economic restructuring, multinational corporations, and global competition—in the context of which we strive to maintain our quality of life. Insofar as education is responsible for the development of skills that are relevant to the labor market, our schools must develop in students both technical skills and an ability to be innovative, flexible, and analytical.

Education is intricately involved with change as 1) a catalyst, 2) an adaptive mechanism, and 3) a force for maintaining tradition and continuity. It is simultaneously an explosive irritant and one of the ingredients in the glue that binds us together.

Summary

1. Education is a major social institution for transmitting knowledge and skills, as well as teaching cultural norms and values, to young people. In preindustrial societies, education occurs informally within the family; industrial societies are characterized by formal schooling.

2. Structural-functional analysis, which highlights the role of schooling in socialization, delves into how formal education promotes social integration, places people in the social hierarchy, and encourages cultural innovation. Latent functions of schooling include child care and forging lasting personal relationships.

3. Social-conflict analysis points out that the opportunity for formal education is unequally distributed across the population. This approach also explains that schooling acts as a means of social control, instilling the value of discipline that produces compliant adult workers.

4. Critics have charged that standardized intelligence tests are culturally biased in favor of some categories of people while placing others at a disadvantage.

5. Allegedly based on individual talents, streaming is also strongly related to students' social background. Streaming confers greater educational resources on more privileged students, thereby perpetuating social inequality and transforming social privilege into personal merit.

6. The majority of Canadian young people attend publicly funded schools at the primary and secondary levels. Most privately funded schools are affiliated with religious organizations. A very small proportion of young people—generally of privileged social background—attend private preparatory schools.

7. Canada is a "credential society." By requiring degrees for higher-paying occupations, employers ensure that workers have learned norms and attitudes appropriate to the business setting.

8. Many people are critical of public schools. Lack of discipline, questionable standards, and student passivity are seen as problems. In addition, perhaps 20 percent of young women and men drop out of high school, thereby placing themselves at high risk of unemployment and poverty.

9. Declining academic standards are reflected in lower average scores on academic achievement tests and functional illiteracy among a significant proportion of high-school graduates.

10. Canada has parallel Catholic and non-Catholic school systems throughout the provinces. Its schooling also reflects cultural diversity and the policies of bilingualism and multiculturalism.

Key Concepts

credentialism   the requirement that a person hold an advanced degree as a condition of employment

education   the various ways in which knowledge—including factual information and occupational skills as well as cultural norms and values—is transmitted to members of a society

functional illiteracy   the lack of basic reading and writing skills needed for everyday life

hidden curriculum   ideas and behavior that support the status quo, taught in subtle ways to students

overeducation   a situation in which workers have more formal education than the performance of their occupations requires

schooling   formal instruction under the direction of specially trained teachers

streaming   categorically assigning students to different types of educational programs

Suggested Readings

This textbook is a good resource for the sociological analysis of education.

> Jeanne H. Ballantine. *The Sociology of Education.* 2nd ed. Englewood Cliffs, NJ: Prentice Hall, 1989.

The first of the following books on schooling and gender examines how academia is being transformed by feminist thinking. The second book, based on the lives of sixty-two women, asserts that women continue to have a marginal existence in the academic world.

> Carol S. Pearson, Donna L. Shavik, and Judith G. Touchton. *Educating the Majority: Women Challenge Tradition in Higher Education.* New York: Macmillan, 1989.
>
> Nadya Aisenberg and Mona Harrington. *Women of Academe: Outsiders in the Sacred Grove.* Amherst: The University of Massachusetts Press, 1988.

The first of these books is a best-seller that helped launch the current debate over "political correctness" on the university campus. The second echoes these conservative sentiments, indicting "PC" for undermining higher education.

> Allan Bloom. *The Closing of the American Mind: How Higher Education Has Failed Democracy and Impoverished the Souls of Today's Students.* New York: Simon & Schuster, 1987.
>
> Dinesh D'Souza. *Illiberal Education: The Politics of Race and Sex on Campus.* New York: The Free Press, 1991.

These researchers investigate how a "culture of romance" erodes the career aspirations of women on university campuses.

> Dorothy C. Holland and Margaret A. Eisenhart. *Educated in Romance: Women, Achievement, and College Culture.* Chicago: University of Chicago Press, 1990.

This collection of essays asks why so few African Americans have entered scientific fields and makes suggestions for increasing the numbers.

> Willie Pearson, Jr. and H. Kenneth Bechtel, eds. *Blacks, Science, and American Education.* New Brunswick, NJ: Rutgers University Press, 1989.

Schooling boys and girls separately was common in Europe until recently; how and why did the United States develop the policy of coeducation?

> David Tyack and Elisabeth Hansot. *Learning Together: A History of Coeducation in America.* New Haven: Yale University Press, 1990.

This is an excellent reader for detailed and concise explorations of current educational issues.

> Ratna Ghosh and Douglas Ray, eds. *Social Change and Education in Canada.* Toronto: Harcourt Brace Jovanovich, 1991.

This report of a large scale cross-sectional study argues that Canada's meritocratic educational system does not benefit the majority of working-class children.

> John Porter, Marion Porter, and Bernard R. Blishen. *Stations and Callings.* Toronto: Methuen, 1982.

This collection of articles approaches the sociology of education from a critical perspective, showing how schools perpetuate inequalities.

> Terry Wotherspoon, ed. *The Political Economy of Canadian Schooling.* Toronto: Methuen, 1987.

A national survey comparing school leavers and high school graduates on a wide range of variables is the basis of this provocative publication.

> Sid Gilbert, Lynn Barr, Warren Clark, Mathew Blue, and Deborah Sunter. *Leaving School.* Ottawa: Government of Canada, 1993.

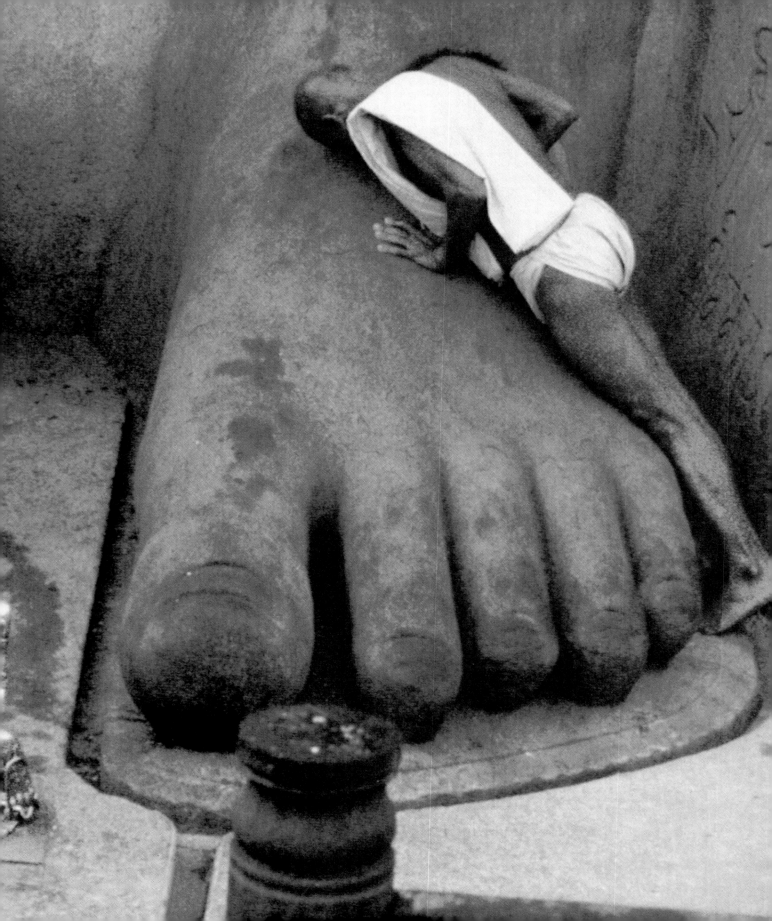

CHAPTER 17

RELIGION

Davⁱd Van Horn found himself facing a jail term in 1990 for simply doing his job—at least, that's the way he saw it. Van Horn works as a contract archaeologist for developers, who are legally required to investigate a site for scientifically valuable artifacts before building on it. Digging on a desolate stretch of prairie near the southern California town of Indian Wells, Van Horn came upon a handful of bone chips. Following routine scientific procedures, he sent the fragments to a laboratory for analysis. His hunch—later confirmed by tests—was that they were human remains charred by cremation, which dated back centuries before Europeans inhabited the region.

But David Van Horn got some other news as well: officials notified him that he had run afoul of the law. A California statute requires anyone who unearths human remains to report the discovery—and to turn over what is found—to the local coroner. The law was enacted in response to leaders of the Native community, who claim that perhaps a million of their ancestors have been unearthed by scientists like Van Horn or, worse still, by simple "grave robbers" looking for anything of value to sell to local souvenir shops (Mydans, 1991).

For their part, scientists like David Van Horn have no desire to offend anyone. On the contrary, they see

their work as helping us to understand and appreciate the ways of life of people who inhabited our lands long ago. From this point of view, the remains unearthed by Van Horn provide important evidence about the diets, diseases, and standard of living of people who lived centuries ago. To Native people, however, this work constitutes sacrilege. From this perspective, excavating another people's burial place amounts to defiling sacred ground and transforming revered ancestors into laboratory specimens or mere trinkets.

This confrontation between scientists and Native people illustrates a dynamic dimension of social life that guides this chapter: what one person defines as an everyday article, another may view as a sacred object commanding reverence and respect. As we shall explain, this distinction between the otherworldly and the ordinary lies at the heart of *religion*, a major social institution.

Religion: Basic Concepts

The scientific point of view takes a matter-of-fact approach to investigating human society as well as the natural world. Although many members of our society consider scientific inquiry to be an expression of human

The Other-Worldly and the Ordinary: W.O. Mitchell's Who Has Seen the Wind

Who and where God is, and whether or not God exists, are fundamental human questions which all peoples have grappled with, in many different ways. In *Who Has Seen the Wind*, W.O. Mitchell describes the initiation of Brian (one of the boys in the following excerpt) into the meanings of birth, death, life, freedom, and justice. The wind in the novel, the beautiful, powerful, and perpetual Prairie wind, symbolizes God. In this excerpt Brian and his friend Forbsie are trying to figure out who and where God is.

"It's where God stays," said Brian, "heaven."

"No it ain't," said Forbsie. He lifted his arm and pointed. "God lives right in town. Over there. I seen Him lots of times."

"Where?"

"At His house."

"You have not!"

"Oh, yes! He's all grapes and bloody. He carries around a lamb."

Brian got up. "Let's us go over to His place."

Forbsie got up. "I guess I'll go home. I don't feel so much like going."

"I've got something to say to Him. I'm going to get Him after my gramma. You show me where He lives."

"All right," said Forbsie.

[...]

Brian sang, "Step on a crack, break my gramma's back!" He did not miss stepping upon a single crack in the three blocks that took him to the great, gray, sandstone church: Knox Presbyterian—1902.

"Is this it?" asked Brian.

Forbsie said that it was.

"Let's go see Him, then."

"I'm going home, I think. It's suppertime, and I better get home."

"Not yet." Brian started up the stone steps; when he turned at the top, he saw that Forbsie was halfway down the block, his head turned back over his shoulder. Brian knocked on the church door. As he did, he felt the wind ruffling his hair. Forbsie was down by the corner now.

A woman came out of the little brown house next to the church. She shook a mop, then turned to re-enter the house. She stopped as she saw Brian; stood watching him. A fervent whirlwind passed the brown house with the woman standing on the porch; at the trees before the church, it rose suddenly, setting every leaf in violent motion, as though an invisible hand had gripped the trunks and shaken them.

Brian wondered why Forbsie had not wanted to come. He knocked again. It was simply that God was in the bathroom and couldn't come right away.

As he turned away from the door, he saw the woman staring at him. She ought to know if God was in. He went down the steps and to the opening in the hedge.

"I guess God isn't anywhere around."

"Why—what do you mean?"

"That's His house, isn't it?"

"Yes."

"I'm going to see Him."

The woman stared at him silently a moment; under the slightly gray hair pulled severely back, her face wore an intense look. "God isn't—He isn't the same as other people, you know. He's a spirit."

"What's that?

"It's someone—something you can't hear—or see, or touch."

---

curiosity, for most of our history on earth, human beings living in small societies attributed birth, death, and whatever happened in between to the operation of supernatural forces. At the time of the Industrial Revolution, for example, most Europeans framed their life experiences as expressions of divine will. Gradually, however, science emerged as an alternative world view, one that seeks to explain our surroundings through systematic observation.

Sometimes, science and traditional beliefs collide. More broadly, however, science and our human fascination with the supernatural often go hand in hand since, as our scientific knowledge advances, the universe seems all the more awesome and mysterious.

French sociologist Emile Durkheim, whose ideas we explored in detail in Chapter 4 ("Society"), claimed that religions the world over share a focus on "all sorts of things that surpass the limits of our knowledge" (1965:62; orig. 1915). Human beings, Durkheim explained, define any idea, object, event, or experience in one of two ways. Most things we consider **profane** (from the Latin for "outside the temple"), meaning *ordinary elements of everyday life.* But some things, Durkheim continued, are set apart as **sacred**, *that which is defined as extraordinary, inspiring a sense of awe, reverence, and even fear.* Throughout human history, distinguishing between the profane and the sacred has been the key to all religious belief. In brief, then, **religion** is *a system of beliefs and practices based on recognizing the sacred.*

Because religion deals with ideas that transcend everyday experience, neither common sense nor sci-

[...]
"Does He smell?"

"No, he doesn't. I think you better talk with my husband. He's the minister and he could tell you much more about this than I could," she said, with relief loosening the words.

"Does he know God pretty well?"

"Pretty well. He—he tells people about Him."

"Better than you do? Does he know better than you do?"

"It's—it's his job to know God."

"My dad is a druggist. He works for God, I guess."

"He works for God," the woman agreed.

"My Uncle Sean isn't a sheep-herder—neither is Ab. Ab's got a thing on his foot, and one foot is shorter, so he goes up and down when he walks."
[...]
"Has your husband got calfs?" Brian asked her.

"No—he hasn't any calfs—calves." She looked quickly back over her shoulder.

"He looks after the sheep and the sheep pups."

"Looks after the ... !"

"I'm going to get God after my gramma," Brian confided. "She has a thing on her leg too. It is not the same as Ab's. You only see it on the heel. She's got room-a-ticks in a leg."

The woman cast another anxious look over her shoulder.

"She belshes," said Brian, "a lot."

"Perhaps your grandmother has stomach trouble."

"If your husband works for God, then he could take me in His house for a while, couldn't he?"

"Perhaps he could. Tomorrow."

"Not now?"

"Tomorrow—in the morning—after breakfast." She turned to the doorway.

"Does God like to be all grapes and bloody?"

"All what?"

"That's what I want to see."

"But what do you mean ... ?"

"Something's burning," said Brian. I'll come back."

She hurried in to her burning dinner.

Brian walked back towards his home. He did not turn down Bison Avenue where it crossed the street upon which the church was, but con-tinued on, a dark wishbone of a child wrapped in reflection.

The wind was persistent now, a steady urgency upon his straight back, smoking up the dust from the road along the walk, lifting it and carrying it out to the prairie beyond. Several times Brian stopped: once to look up into the sun's unbearable radiance and then away with the lingering glow stubborn in his eyes; another time when he came upon a fox-red caterpillar making a procession of itself over a crack that snaked along the walk. He squashed it with his foot. Further on he paused at a spider that carried its bead of a body between hurrying thread-legs. Death came for the spider too.

He looked up to find that the street had stopped. Ahead lay the sudden emptiness of the prairie. For the first time in his four years of life he was alone on the prairie.

SOURCE: W.O. Mitchell, *Who Has Seen the Wind. Toronto: Macmillan, 1976.*

ence can establish religious truth. Religion is a matter of **faith**, *belief anchored in conviction rather than scientific evidence.* In the New Testament of the Bible, Christians are said to "walk by faith, not by sight" (II Corinthians 5:7), and faith is described as "the conviction of things not seen" (Hebrews 11:1).

In global perspective, matters of faith vary greatly. Nothing is placed in the category of sacred or profane by everyone on earth; anything may become one or the other depending on how a community of people defines it. In Canada, for example, we view most books as profane or secular, but the Torah (the first five books of the Hebrew Bible, or Old Testament) is defined as sacred by Jews, as is the entire Bible by Christians and the Qur'an (Koran) by Muslims. Similarly, most cities fall within the profane world, but Jerusalem is considered sacred by members of all three of these religions.

Durkheim (1965:62) explained that we understand profane things in terms of their everyday usefulness; we sit down at a computer or turn the key of a car to accomplish various jobs. What is defined as sacred, however, we separate from everyday life and denote as "set apart and forbidden" so that it evokes a reverent and submissive response. For instance, followers of Islam demand that people remove their shoes before entering a mosque—a sacred place of worship that is not to be symbolically defiled by shoes that have touched the profane ground outside.

As this example suggests, the sacred is addressed through **ritual**, *formal, ceremonial behavior.* Holy communion is the central ritual for most Christians; the wafer and wine consumed during communion are never defined as food—they are sacred symbols of the body and blood of Jesus Christ.

Religion and Sociology

Some people with strong religious beliefs are disturbed by the thought of sociologists, archaeologists, or other scientists studying what they hold to be sacred. In truth, however, the sociological study of religion carries no threat to anyone's faith. Because sociologists recognize that religion is central to virtually every culture on earth, they seek to understand how religious beliefs and practices guide human societies.

In doing this, sociology does not pass judgment on religion, nor does it make any claim about whether any specific matter of faith is right or wrong. As a science, sociological analysis is concerned with the social consequences of religious activity. Therefore, while sociologists can explain how religion is tied to other dimensions of social life, science offers no insights at all about the properly religious matters of the *meaning and purpose* of human existence. While some sociologists have interpreted the *consequences* of religion as positive, others as negative, and still others in a neutral manner, sociological analysis can never assess the *validity* of religious doctrine, which is a matter of faith rather than empirical evidence. Sociologists, like other

Every religion distinguishes the sacred from the secular. Followers of Islam reverently remove their shoes—which touch the profane ground—before entering this sacred mosque in the Persian Gulf nation of Brunei.

people, may have one or another religious orientation: some are not believers, while others participate fully in their religions.

Theoretical Analysis of Religion

Whatever their personal religious beliefs, sociologists agree that religion is a major social institution that must be understood in the context of society. Each of the major theoretical paradigms explores how religion affects social life.

The Functions of Religion

Emile Durkheim believed that each one of us confronts the power of society every day. Society, he claimed, has an existence of its own that goes beyond the life of any individual. Thus society itself is "godlike"; unlike individuals, society does not die, it has the power to shape the lives of all of us, and it evokes a sense of reverence and awe. Then, too, society demands that individuals submit to its values and norms. According to Durkheim (1965; orig. 1915), then, the sacred lies at the heart of society: as people develop religious beliefs, they celebrate the awesome power of their society.

This explains why, in every society, people transform certain everyday objects into sacred symbols. The sacred represents the collective immortality of individual mortal beings. The members of technologically simple societies, Durkheim explained, exemplify the power of their society by a **totem**, *an object in the natural world that is imbued with sacred qualities.* The totem—perhaps an animal or an elaborate work of art—becomes the centerpiece of ritual, symbolizing the power of society to transform individuals into a well-integrated collectivity.

In the modern world, the apparent weakening of traditional religion led Durkheim to fear the erosion of society itself. His concept of *anomie* or normlessness captures the idea that modern society, steeped in science and rational skepticism, cannot duplicate religion's historical power to imbue our lives with meaning and unite us into a human community. Thus, reasoned Durkheim, we moderns are left to celebrate a profane world, becoming caught up in the individualistic pursuit of money and possessions, often at the expense of our concern for spiritual values, our neighbors, or even our families.

Note that Durkheim's analysis of the parallel

One way that religions support social inequality is by restricting leaders to certain categories of people. Historically, this has meant the dominance of white men, but this pattern has eroded in recent years. In 1989, for example, Barbara Harris became the first woman of color to be ordained as a bishop in the Episcopal Church.

between the sacred and society ignores the question of whether a divine power exists or not. Either way, he concluded, religious beliefs and practices arise to reflect the power of society in all our lives. From this general beginning, Durkheim went on to identify several specific functions of religion for the operation of society.

Social Cohesion

Religion promotes social cohesion by uniting members of a society through shared symbolism, values, and norms. In simple societies, the visible expression of this unity is the totem. Complex societies, too, foster cohesion with such symbolism. The beaver, the maple leaf, the trillium, and the *fleur de lis* are quasi-religious totems in Canada. The recitation of the Lord's Prayer all across the country, until very recently, implied a kind of common religious belief. Local communities across Canada also gain a sense of unity through totem-like symbolism attached to sports teams: from the Montreal Canadiens, to the Toronto Blue Jays, the Calgary Stampeders, and the Vancouver Canucks.

Social Control

Every society tries to promote some degree of social conformity. To do this, cultural norms, especially those that deal with reproduction, birth, marriage, and death,

are imbued with religious meaning. More broadly, religion also confers legitimacy on the political system. In medieval Europe, this process was quite explicit, as monarchs claimed to rule by divine right. Few of today's political leaders would claim to be picked by God, but many publicly ask for divine blessing and guidance, implying to the rest of us that their efforts are right and just.

Providing Meaning and Purpose

In the face of human failings, disease, and death, life can seem hopelessly chaotic. Religious beliefs offer the comforting sense that the vulnerable human condition serves some greater purpose. Strengthened by such convictions, people are less likely to collapse with despair when confronted by life's uncertainties and calamities. Major life transitions—including birth, marriage, and death—are usually marked by religious observances that place these events in a context of meaning. To many people, religion also figures in the vital human dimension of *love*, the emotional and spiritual connection to others (Wright & D'Antonio, 1980). Religion, then, addresses ultimate issues of life, death, and attachment that transcend both common sense and science.

Critical evaluation. Durkheim's work provides the foundation of the structural-functional analysis of religion. This approach emphasizes that the sharing of religious beliefs—whatever they may be—produces social cohesion and stability, and enhances a sense of meaning and purpose.

The major weakness of this approach is in downplaying the dysfunctions of religion—especially the capacity of strong beliefs to generate destructive social conflict. During the early Middle Ages, for example, religious faith was used to justify the Crusades, in which European Christians waged a military campaign against Muslims in the Middle East. Muslims, in turn, were driven by moral duty to fight the invading Christians. Conflict among Muslims, Jews, and Christians has been a source of political instability in various parts of the world ever since. Social divisions in Northern Ireland, too, turn partly on conflict between Protestant and Catholic religious beliefs, while Dutch Calvinism historically supported apartheid in South Africa (Renick, 1991). Religious conflict also continues to divide India, Sri Lanka, Malaysia, and other nations. Ironically, in light of our assumption that religion is a force for good in the world, differences in faith have provoked more violence in the world than differences of social class.

The Social Construction of the Sacred

The symbolic-interaction paradigm views all of society as a human construction. "Society," asserts Peter Berger (1967:3) "is a human product and nothing but a human product, that yet continuously acts back upon its producer." Once formed through social interaction, then, society shapes the existence of its creators.

Religion, in Berger's view, is also a social construction (although perhaps inspired by divine forces). Various religious practices, from everyday rituals like saying grace before meals to periodic religious services, teach individuals what their society defines as sacred.

Why should societies construct the sacred? Echoing Durkheim's insights, Berger explains that the sacred legitimizes and stabilizes social life. As a human creation, society is inherently precarious and subject to disruption. Placing everyday events within a "cosmic frame of reference" confers on the fallible, transitory creations of human beings "the semblance of ultimate security and permanence" (1967:35–36).

Marriage is a good example. If it is seen only as a contract between two people, marriage can be ended as easily as it is begun. But if two people negotiate a relationship defined as *holy matrimony*, this bond has far greater claims on both of them. In the same way, cultural norms that regulate sexual activity are made stronger if violations are viewed as *sin*. When humans confront uncertainty and life-threatening situations—such as illness, war, and natural disaster—sacred symbols come to the fore. Even people who are otherwise not very religious may pray as loved ones are dying, just as soldiers have traditionally gone to war "with God on their side." In short, the social construction of the sacred lifts humanity above the ultimate reality of death, so that society—if not its individual members—becomes immortal.

Critical evaluation.   The symbolic-interaction approach suggests that, as we negotiate the life course, we place many natural experiences and events under a "sacred canopy" of meaning (Berger, 1967). But, as Berger points out, the sacred can only legitimize and stabilize society if the socially constructed character of the sacred goes unrecognized or people attribute the process to divine inspiration. The conception of holy matrimony is less compelling if we think of it merely as a social strategy to shore up relationships. Faced with life-threatening disaster, human beings could also derive little strength from sacred beliefs they viewed simply as

devices for coping with tragedy. This reminds us again of the reason many people are uncomfortable with the sociological study of religion: it may be disconcerting to think that we have constructed the sacred in the same manner as we have created the rest of society.

Religion and Social Inequality

The social-conflict paradigm offers additional insights about religion by focusing on how religion supports social inequality. Religion, according to Karl Marx, amounts to an ideology that serves ruling elites by legitimizing the status quo and diverting people's attention from social inequities.

In Great Britain, the monarch has traditionally been crowned by the head of the Church of England, illustrating the close alliance between religious and political elites. In practical terms, working for political change may well mean opposing the church—and, by implication, God. Moreover, when religious leaders declare that existing social arrangements are morally just, it weakens people's drive to change a system marred by a grossly unequal distribution of social resources, with privileges allocated for the few at the expense of the many. Religion, Marx continued, encourages people to look hopefully to a "better world to come," patiently enduring social problems of *this* world. In one of his best-known statements, Marx offered a stinging criticism of religion as "the sigh of the oppressed creature, the sentiment of a heartless world, and the soul of soulless conditions. It is the opium of the people" (1964:27; orig. 1848).

An additional link between religion and social inequality involves gender. Virtually all the world's major religions have reflected and encouraged male dominance of social life, as the box explains.

During Marx's lifetime, powerful Christian nations of Western Europe used the "conversion of heathens" as one justification for colonial exploitation of societies in Africa, Asia, and throughout the Americas. In the United States, major churches in the South declared the enslavement of African Americans to be consistent with God's will. Until well into this century, many churches actively supported segregation and other forms of racial inequality. Some religious organizations still do so today.

But religion has another side—one that promotes change, sometimes on a grand scale. Consider the analysis of nineteenth-century European society by Max

Weber (1958; orig. 1904–1905). As Chapter 4 ("Society") explains in detail, Weber viewed industrial- capitalist societies as the product not of social conflict, but of the rational world view embodied by early Calvinism. In Weber's terms, the "Protestant ethic"— an approach to life based on discipline, thrift, and a desire to carry out God's will on earth—worked as an engine of change. From this religious ethic evolved the "spirit" of capitalism, a way of thinking and acting that eventually transformed much of Western Europe. Weber's analysis of the social consequences of Calvinism helps us to see that religion does not always support established hierarchies and the status quo.

Critical evaluation.   Social-conflict analysis shows that the power of religion can legitimize social inequality. This has been true in Canada as elsewhere.

Yet critics of religion's conservative face, Marx included, minimize ways in which religion has promoted not only change but social equality. In Canada, the social gospel movement, headed by Tommy Douglas, was instrumental in the development of much of the social safety net presently available in Canada. Many clergy now support revolutionary change in Latin America and elsewhere, and churches in Canada have offered asylum to refugees from El Salvador, Nicaragua, Guatemala, and other politically unstable countries to our south. In global context, much the same pattern emerges: in South Africa, for example, some of the strongest voices for dismantling the system of racial apartheid come from inside churches. Marx apparently underestimated the extent to which religion would promote social change in the twentieth century.

Liberation Theology

Significantly, religion has mixed with the sociological thinking of Karl Marx to form a recipe for change called *liberation theology*. Christianity shares with many world religions a longstanding concern for the suffering of poor and oppressed people. Traditionally, the Christian response has been to strengthen the faith of the believer in a better life to come. In recent decades, however, some church leaders and theologians have embraced Karl Marx's pursuit of social equality in *this* world.

Formally, **liberation theology** is *a fusion of Christian principles with political activism, often Marxist in character*. This social movement developed in the late 1960s within Latin America's Roman Catholic Church. Liberation theology begins with the church's estab-

lished teaching that Christianity offers liberation from human sin. What is new—and controversial—is the assertion that the church cannot be content with addressing people's spiritual needs; it must also help people liberate themselves from the abysmal poverty of the Third World, as described in Chapter 11 ("Global Inequality").

Although they disagree among themselves on many issues, advocates of liberation theology embrace three general principles. First, human suffering in the world is tragic and beyond the imagination of most secure, comfortable people in Canada. Second, this massive anguish runs counter to Christian morality, by threatening the survival of a large share of humanity. Third, global poverty is preventable and, as an expression of faith and conscience, Christians must act to reduce this suffering. Many—but not all—clergy who support this kind of change see in Marxism a path toward a better future for those who have endured a lifetime of suffering.

A growing number of Catholic men and women have allied themselves with the poor in a political struggle against the ruling powers in some Latin American societies. The costs of opposition have been high. Church members have been killed in the violence that engulfs much of that region. In 1980, Oscar Arnulfo Romero, the archbishop of San Salvador (the capital of El Salvador) and an outspoken advocate of the poor, was gunned down inside his church while celebrating mass. In 1989, during the continuing civil unrest in El Salvador, six Jesuit priests were murdered in their home by government troops.

The radicalization of the Latin American Church has attracted some additional support from the people of the region (Neuhouser, 1989). But it has also polarized the Catholic community. With strong advocates on one side, liberation theology also has powerful adversaries, among them Pope John Paul II, who condemns this movement for tainting traditional church doctrine with politics. The Vatican claims that liberation theology endangers the Catholic faith by diverting attention from the other worldly concerns of Christianity, and embroiling the church in political controversy. Thus, the pope has forbidden church officials to participate in political conflicts. Nonetheless, the liberation theology movement is gaining strength in Latin America—especially El Salvador and Brazil—fueled by the belief that Christian faith and a sense of basic human justice demand efforts to mitigate the plight of the world's poor (Boff, 1984).

Religion and Patriarchy: Does God Favor Males?

Most people in North America envision God as male (Cawley, 1992). Because we link attributes like wisdom and power to men, it is not surprising that we think of God in masculine terms. By and large, organized religions also favor males, as seen in passages from many of the sacred writings of major world religions.

The Qur'an (Koran)—the sacred text of Islam—asserts that men are to have social dominance over women:

> Men are in charge of women. ... Hence good women are obedient. ... As for those whose rebelliousness you fear, admonish them, banish them from your bed, and scourge them. (cited in Kaufman, 1976:163)

Christianity—the dominant religion of the Western world—has also supported patriarchy. While Christians do revere Mary, the mother of Jesus, the New Testament also includes the following passages:

> A man ... is the image and glory of God; but woman is the glory of man. For man was not made from woman, but woman from man. Neither was man created for woman, but woman for man. (I Corinthians 11:7–9)
> As in all the churches of the saints, the women should keep silence in the churches. For they are not permitted to speak, but should be subordinate, as even the law says. If there is anything

they desire to know, let them ask their husbands at home. For it is shameful for a woman to speak in church. (I Corinthians 14:33–35)

> Wives, be subject to your husbands, as to the Lord. For the husband is the head of the wife as Christ is the head of the church. ... As the church is subject to Christ, so let wives also be subject in everything to their husbands. (Ephesians 5:22–24)

Male Orthodox Jews include the following words in daily prayer:

> Blessed art thou, O Lord our God, King of the Universe, that I was not born a gentile. Blessed art thou, O Lord our God, King of the Universe, that I was not born a slave. Blessed art thou, O Lord our God, King of the Universe, that I was not born a woman.

In another dimension of religious patriarchy, the major religions have long excluded women from the clergy, although this is now being widely challenged. Islam continues to exclude women from such positions, as does the Roman Catholic Church. A growing number of Protestant denominations, however, have overturned historical practices and now ordain women. While Orthodox Judaism still upholds the traditional prohibition against women serving as rabbis, Reform Judaism has long elevated women to this role (and is the

largest denomination of the major religions to ordain gay and lesbian people). In 1985, the first woman became a rabbi in the Conservative branch of Judaism. The proportion of women among students in seminary schools across Canada has never been higher, so that further change is only a matter of time.

Challenges to the patriarchal structure of organized religion—from women entering the clergy to revisions in the language in hymnals and prayers—spark heated controversy, delighting progressives while outraging traditionalists. Propelling these developments is a lively strain of feminism within most religious communities today. According to feminist Christians, for example, patriarchy in the church stands in stark contrast to the largely feminine image of Jesus Christ in the Scriptures as "nonaggressive, noncompetitive, meek and humble of heart, a nurturer of the weak and a friend of the outcast" (Sandra Schneiders, cited in Woodward, 1989:61). Moreover, they argue, unless traditional notions of gender are removed from our understanding of God, women will never share equally with men in the church. Theologian Mary Daly puts the matter bluntly: "If God is male, then male is God" (cited in Woodward, 1989:58).

Types of Religious Organizations

Because there are hundreds of different religious organizations in North America, sociologists have developed schemes to categorize them. The most widely used model takes the form of a continuum with "churches" on one pole and "sects" on the other. We can describe any actual religious organization, then, in relation to these two ideal types by locating it on the church-sect continuum.

Church and Sect

Max Weber deserves the credit for drawing the general distinction between church and sect—and his student Ernst Troeltsch (1931) elaborated on this polar model. A **church**, described in ideal terms, is *a type of religious organization that readily seeks accommodation with the larger society.* Church-like organizations are well established, typically persisting for centuries and usually including all members of a particular family over many generations. Churches favor formality in their organization, with extensive bureaucratic regulations and an approved program of training leading to the ordination of officials.

As they address the realm of the sacred, Troeltsch explained, churches strive to broaden their appeal. Thus they conceive of God in highly intellectualized terms (for example, as a force for good in the world), and generally favor abstract moral standards (such as "do unto others as you would have them do unto you") over specific codes that guide actual day-to-day behavior.

Troeltsch pointed out that in their drive for universality, churches not only develop an intellectualized vision of God but also seek accommodation and compromise with their secular surroundings. By teaching morality in safely abstract terms, churches can wink at specific social arrangements that run counter to their principles. For example, a church may pronounce all human beings brothers and sisters, but raise no objection to laws that deny equal rights to people of one race or sexual orientation. Similarly, churches urge their members to pursue moral righteousness, but usually shy away from specifics when it comes to which behaviors (regarding sex, for instance) should be praised or condemned. Such generality simultaneously gives these religious organizations wide appeal and minimizes conflict between the church and the political state (Troeltsch, 1931; O'Dea & Aviad, 1983).

In global perspective, the range of human religious activity is truly astonishing. Members of one Christian cult in the Latin American nation of Guatemala observe Good Friday by vaulting over fire, an expression of their faith that God will protect them.

Some church-like organizations are tied to the government. An **ecclesia** is *a church that is formally allied with the state.* Ecclesias have been common in human history: the Catholic Church was for centuries allied with the Roman Empire; the Anglican Church is now the official Church of England; Confucianism was the state religion in China until early in this century; and Islam is today the official religion of Pakistan and Iran. Empowered by the state, ecclesias claim all people in a society as members. Membership in the official church, then, is usually required by law, virtually eliminating religious freedom of choice. Because church and state are fused, an ecclesia most clearly exemplifies religious acceptance of political arrangements in the larger society.

A second type of church is a **denomination**, *a church, not linked to the state, in a society that recognizes religious pluralism.* Canadian society "officially" favors the denominational model in which many church-like organizations coexist with one another. The historical split between Roman Catholic Lower Canada and Church of England Upper Canada has given way to a remarkable religious diversity in Canada. Our society comprises dozens of church-like Christian denominations—including Catholics, Baptists, Methodists, and Lutherans—as well as denominations within Judaism, Hinduism, Buddhism and other religious traditions.

A second general religious form is the **sect**, *a type of religious organization that resists accommodation with the larger society.* Simply stated, sect members place their religious convictions ahead of what others around them may hold to be true. In extreme cases, members of a sect may withdraw completely in order to practice their religion without interference from outsiders. The Mennonites, described in Chapter 3 ("Culture"), are one North American sect that has long sought isolation from outsiders (Fretz, 1989). More commonly, however, members of sects participate in the world more or less as other people do; the difference is that sect members are more likely than most people to view their beliefs as the only true religion, which puts them at odds with the doctrine of religious pluralism. For this reason, members of church-like organizations sometimes perceive sectarians as dogmatic in their insistence that their religious community represents "authentic" faith in contrast to those who have made too many compromises with the world (Stark & Bainbridge, 1979).

In organizational terms, many sects shun the rigid formality of established churches. They do so in order to rejoice in the personal experience of God's presence, again in contrast to churches, which practice more subdued and formal ritual. Thus members of sects often exude a spontaneity and emotional fervor as they worship, while members of churches tend to be passive and attentive to the formal leader. Put otherwise, sects reject the intellectualized approach of churches, stressing instead the fundamental experience of a divine power. We can pinpoint this distinction in patterns of prayer, as Rodney Stark (1985:314) points out: the sense of a distant God, found in "church" prayer—"Our Father, who art in Heaven"—contrasts sharply with the image of a more immediate God typical of sects—"Lord, bless this poor sinner kneeling before you now."

A further distinction between church and sect turns on patterns of leadership. The more church-like a religious organization is, the more likely that its leaders are formal officials with approved training, such as priests, rabbis, and ministers. Because more sect-like organizations celebrate the personal presence of God, members expect their leaders to embody divine inspiration in the form of **charisma**, which, in religious context, means *evidence of God's favor in the behavior of an individual*. This term has Greek roots meaning "divine favor." A charismatic leader, then, is presumably endowed with divine inspiration that awakens feelings of spiritual joy in an audience, infusing followers with the emotional experience that sects value so highly.

Traditionally, many sects relied heavily on outsiders joining their ranks. This underlies the practice of actively recruiting, or *proselytizing*, outsiders. Sects tout the experience of **conversion**, *a personal transformation resulting from adopting new religious beliefs*. Members of Jehovah's Witnesses, for example, have long encouraged the faithful to share their beliefs with others. But proselytizing often does more to increase the commitment of those who already believe than to actually attract new members.

Troeltsch and later researchers have noted that churches and sects differ in their social composition. Generally speaking, people of high social standing favor well-established churches. This is not surprising, since privileged people accommodate the larger society most comfortably. By contrast, sects attract people of lower social position. A sect's openness to new members and promise of salvation and personal fulfilment holds special appeal to people who perceive themselves as social outsiders. However, as we shall explain presently, many of the more established churches in Canada have lost

membership to sects in recent decades (*1993 Corpus Almanac and Canadian Sourcebook*, 1992). As a consequence, sects now find themselves with more affluent members.

Sects usually form as breakaway groups from established churches or other religious organizations; sects, in short, emerge from religious schism (Bibby, 1987). In some cases, as a religious organization becomes more established by accommodating the secular world, some members (especially those of lower social position) may defect to create a new organization that better meets their spiritual needs. The psychic intensity and lack of formal structure characteristic of sects make them less stable than churches; some sects, therefore, blossom only to disappear soon after. By and large, sects that endure become more and more like churches, losing religious fervor as they become more bureaucratic, established, and respectable. Both the Puritan and the Quaker colonists who came to the United States from England were members of breakaway sects. Each of these sects has subsequently evolved into an established church, although further schism leading to the creation of new sects has also occurred. In sum, the concepts of church and sect are opposite ends of a dynamic continuum on which religious organizations may move over time.

Cult

A **cult** is *a religious organization with roots outside the dominant religious traditions of a society*. Whereas a sect emerges from division and reform within a conventional religious organization, a cult represents something almost entirely new. Because some cult principles or practices seem unconventional to members of a particular society, the popular view of cults pictures them as deviant or even evil. In recent decades, negative media publicity given to a few cults has raised suspicion about any unfamiliar religious organization. Thus, some scholars note, to call a religious community a cult amounts to declaring it to be unworthy (Richardson, 1990).

This is unfortunate because there is nothing intrinsically wrong with this kind of religious organization; many long-standing religions—Christianity, Islam, and Judaism included—began as cults. The product of religious *innovation* or cultural *diffusion*, a cult may become popular, but most do not. Cults formed through innovation typically center around a highly charismatic leader who offers a new and unprecedented message. This was the case when Jesus of Nazareth began attracting followers in a remote part of the Roman Empire two millennia ago. More recently, Joseph Smith founded the Church of Jesus Christ of Latter-Day Saints (the Mormons) in New York State in 1830. Smith accepted many established Christian principles—cults are rarely entirely novel—but he distinguished early Mormonism with several unconventional religious ideas, including the practice of polygamy or plural marriage. In the following 150 years, Mormons became steadily more church-like, abandoning unorthodox practices. Spurred by a doctrine of proselytizing, Mormonism is now one of the fastest-growing religious organizations in North America (*1993 Corpus Almanac and Canadian Sourcebooks*, 1992; Stark, 1984).

Cultural diffusion produces a cult as religious ideas from one society (where they are conventional) are carried to another society (where they are not). Transcendental Meditation (TM) developed here when Maharishi Mahesh Yogi introduced Hindu principles and practices to North American society in the late 1950s. During the 1970s, TM became widely popular. Since then, however, its fortunes have faded and TM has relatively few followers in North America today (Bainbridge & Jackson, 1981).

To the extent that they are novel, cults may be even more at odds with conventional society than sects are. Some cults demand that members not only adopt distinctive religious beliefs but also embrace an entire *lifestyle* involving a radical change in self-identity. It is cases of this kind that have sparked popular press reports of cult leaders brainwashing new members into renouncing their past lives. While this has happened, it is not very common.

In a complex and changing world, cults arise regularly. They gain importance when people are anxious about their lives, disenchanted with established religions, and thus are ready to embrace new answers. But, in most cases, cults arise only to quickly fade. Many cults actively proselytize, but usually with little success. Most people show only a passing interest in cults and do not join; those who do may or may not remain members for long, and only rarely is anyone psychologically harmed from such an experience. Of course some cults have considerable success in attracting and retaining members. By and large, however, cults that flourish tend to become more church-like over time (Barker, 1981; Kilbourne, 1983).

Religion in History

Religion shapes every society of the world. And, like other social institutions, religion shows considerable variation historically and cross-culturally.

Religion in Preindustrial Societies

Religion extends further back in the human record than written history. How do we know? Because archaeologists have collected evidence that our human ancestors routinely engaged in religious rituals at least forty thousand years ago.

Among early hunters and gatherers, religion took the form of **animism** (from Latin meaning "the breath of life"), *the belief that elements of the natural world are conscious forms of life that affect humanity.* Animistic people may view forests, oceans, mountains, or the wind as spiritual forces responsible for shaping human experience. Many Native societies that flourished throughout the Americas have been animistic, which accounts for their deeply respectful view of the natural environment. For such people, religion is not a distinctive sphere of life; hunting and gathering societies carry out religious activity entirely within the family. They may look to a *shaman* or religious leader, but shamanism is not a full-time, specialized activity.

Belief in a single divine power responsible for creating the world evolved more recently, roughly coinciding with the development of horticulture and agriculture. As single-deity religions take root, religious life starts to reach beyond the family; at this stage, religion is often fused with politics. To illustrate, ancient leaders such as the Egyptian pharaoh and the early Chinese emperor ruled as both kings and priests.

In agrarian societies, religion stands alone as a powerful social institution; the centrality of the church in medieval Europe exemplifies this supremacy. The physical design of the medieval city even casts this dominance in stone, with the cathedral rising above all other structures.

Religion in Industrial Societies

The Industrial Revolution ushered in a growing emphasis on science, diminishing the scope of religious thinking. Increasingly, people in distress looked to physicians and other practitioners of science for the comfort they had earlier sought from religious leaders.

Yet religion continues to thrive in a scientific world, largely because science is powerless to address issues of ultimate meaning in human life. In other words, learning *how* the world works falls to scientific investigators; but *why* we and the surrounding universe exist at all constitutes both a more important question and one about which scientists have nothing to say. Therefore, many traditional religions have endured during the twentieth century, and new religions have also emerged. Whatever the benefits of science to our material lives, then, religion has a unique capacity to address the spiritual dimension of human existence.

Because religion and science represent powerful but distinct ways of viewing the universe, the two sometimes fall into an uneasy relationship. Earlier in this century, controversy over the origin of humanity focused on whether schools in the States should teach the scientific theory of evolution, or the biblical creation story to students. This debate puts scientific "facts" about human evolution in opposition to religious "beliefs" commonly called *creationism*. The issue still rages in parts of the United States, and emerges from time to time in Canada as well.

World Religions

Religion is found virtually everywhere on our planet and, remarkably, the diversity of religious expression is almost as wide-ranging as culture itself. Many of the thousands of different religions are highly localized with few followers. A few may be termed *world religions* because they have millions of adherents and are known throughout the world. We shall briefly describe six world religions, which together claim the support of 3.8 billion people—almost three-fourths of humanity. Clearly, the societies of our world remain significantly tied to religion.

Christianity

Christianity is the most widespread religion, with 1.7 billion adherents, which amounts to roughly one-third of humanity. Most Christians live in Europe or throughout the Americas; more than 85 percent of North Americans identify with Christianity. As shown in Global Map 17-1, however, Christians represent a significant share of the population in many other world regions, with the notable exceptions of Northern Africa and Asia. This pattern reflects the diffusion of Christianity by European colonizers during the last five hundred years. The dominant influence of Christianity in the Western Hemisphere is evident in the Western practice of numbering years on the calendar beginning with the birth of Christ.

The roots of Christianity lie in Middle-Eastern Judaism. Christianity originated as a cult, although it retained many of the teachings and practices of Judaism, which dates back much further. Like many cults, Christianity was propelled by the personal charisma of a leader, Jesus of Nazareth, who preached a message of personal, spiritual salvation. From a sociological point of view, one reason for the success of this new religion was that Jesus did not seek to antagonize the political powers-that-be; rather he accepted edicts from the Roman Empire, calling on his followers to "Render therefore to Caesar things that are Caesar's" (Matthew 22:21). Yet, from a moral standpoint, Jesus's message was quite revolutionary, offering the promise of human triumph over sin and death through faith. Jesus preached a universal message that all people should join in spiritual love.

Christianity is one example of **monotheism**, *belief in a single divine power*. This new religion challenged the Roman Empire's traditional **polytheism**, *belief in many gods*. Yet Christianity has a unique vision of the Supreme Being as a sacred Trinity: God the Creator; Jesus Christ, Son of God and Redeemer; and the Holy Spirit, a Christian's personal experience of God's presence.

The claim that Jesus was imbued with divinity rests on accounts of his final days on earth. Tried and sentenced to death in Jerusalem, by officials who sensed that his ideas were a threat to established political leaders, Jesus endured a cruel execution by crucifixion, which transformed the cross into a sacred Christian symbol. According to Christian belief, Jesus was resurrected—that is, he rose from the dead—showing that he was the Son of God.

At the time, the Roman Empire imposed a broad peace in the Mediterranean region. This so-called *Pax Romana* allowed the Apostle Paul and others to travel safely, spreading Christianity widely. Although the Romans initially persecuted Christians, by the fourth century Christianity became an ecclesia—the official religion of the Roman Empire. What had begun as a cult four centuries before had been transformed into an established church.

Soon afterward, Rome declined, but the eastern part of the empire, based in the city of Constantinople (now Istanbul, Turkey), flourished until the fifteenth century. A religious division in the eleventh century resulted in twin centers of Christianity: the Roman Catholic Church based in Rome and the Orthodox Church centered in Constantinople.

Further divisions splintered Christianity toward the end of the Middle Ages, when religious leaders such as Martin Luther (1483–1546) protested established church doctrine. The Reformation in Europe spawned numerous Protestant organizations and ushered in a period of religious pluralism.

While not the oldest of the world religions, Christianity has most influenced Western civilization. Through division, diffusion, and innovation, we now see Christian organizations that resemble churches, sects, and cults. What they all share is the belief that a historical figure named Jesus of Nazareth was sent by God to provide salvation from sin, and that he still offers everlasting life to those who accept him as their personal savior (Smart, 1969; Kaufman, 1976; Stavrianos, 1983).

Islam

Islam has almost 1 billion followers (18 percent of humanity) who are called Muslims (or Moslems). A majority of people in the Middle East are Muslims, which explains the tendency of people in the West to link Islam to Arabs in that region of the world. But most Muslims are not Arabs; Global Map 17-2 shows that a majority of people throughout Northern Africa and Western Asia are Muslims. Moreover, significant concentrations of Muslims are found in Pakistan, India, Bangladesh, Indonesia, and the southern republics of the Commonwealth of Independent States. Although representing only a tiny share of the population, estimates place the Muslim population of North America at roughly 5 million, and the number is rapidly growing (Roudi, 1988; Weeks, 1988).

Islam is the word of God as revealed to the prophet Muhammad, who was born in the city of Mecca (in western Saudi Arabia) about the year 570. To Muslims, Muhammad was a prophet, not a divine being as Christians define Jesus. The Qur'an (Koran), sacred to Muslims, is the word of God—in Arabic, Allah—as transmitted through Muhammad, God's messenger. In Arabic, the word Islam means both "submission" and "peace," and the Qur'an urges submission to Allah as the path to inner peace. Muslims express this spiritual devotion in a daily ritual of five prayers.

Islam spread rapidly after the death of Muhammad, although divisions arose as they did within Christianity. All Muslims, however, accept the Five Pillars of Islam: (1) recognizing Allah as the one, true God, and Muhammad as God's messenger; (2) ritual prayer; (3) giving alms to the poor; (4) fasting during the month of Ramadan; and (5) making a pilgrimage once to the Sacred House of Allah in Mecca (Weeks, 1988; El-Attar, 1991). Like many religions, Islam holds people accountable to God for their deeds on earth. Those who live obediently will be rewarded in heaven, while nonbelievers will suffer unending punishment.

Muslims are also obligated to defend their faith. Sometimes this tenet has justified holy wars against nonbelievers (in roughly the same way that medieval Christians joined the Crusades to recapture the Holy Land from the Muslims). In recent decades, especially

This page from a Persian manuscript, dated about 1540, depicts The Ascent of the Prophet Mohammed to Heaven. Rising from earth through a host of angels, the prophet Mohammed is about to enter Paradise in the presence of Allah. Note that the prophet's face is blank—apparently because the artist deemed it sacred and unsuitable for reproduction.

(Ascent of the Prophet Mohammed to Heaven. British Library, London.)

in Iran, Muslims have sought to rid their societies of Western social influences they regard as morally compromising (Martin, 1982; Arjomand, 1988).

Like most religions, Islam is linked to the domination of women by men. Westerners often view Muslim women as among the most socially oppressed people on earth. Muslim women do lack many of the personal freedoms enjoyed by Muslim men, yet patriarchy was already well established in the Middle East at the time of Muhammad's birth. Some defenders argue that Islam actually improved the social position of women by demanding that husbands deal justly with their wives. Further, although Islam permits a man to

have up to four wives, it warns men to have only one wife if more than one will encourage him to treat these women unjustly (Qur'an, "The Women," Verse 3).

Hinduism

Hinduism is the oldest of all the world religions, originating in the Indus River Valley some 4,500 years ago. Hindus number some 700 million (13 percent of humanity). Global Map 17-3 shows that Hinduism remains the predominant religion of Pakistan and India today; in addition, a significant Hindu popula-

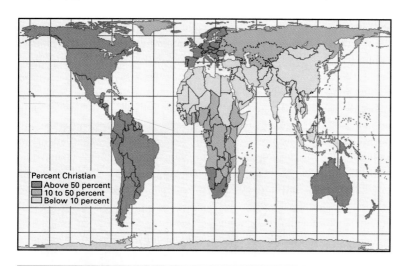

GLOBAL MAP 17-1   CHRISTIANITY IN GLOBAL PERSPECTIVE

Percent Christian
Above 50 percent
10 to 50 percent
Below 10 percent

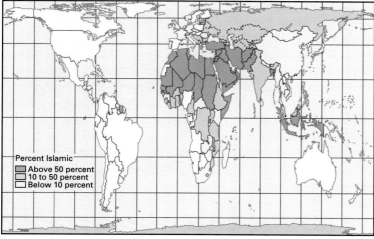

GLOBAL MAP 17-2   ISLAM IN GLOBAL PERSPECTIVE

Percent Islamic
Above 50 percent
10 to 50 percent
Below 10 percent

tion is found in a few societies of southern Africa and in Indonesia. Over the centuries, Hinduism and Indian culture have become intertwined, so that now one is not easily described apart from the other. Because of this intermingling of culture and religion, Hinduism, unlike Christianity and Islam, has experienced relatively little diffusion (Schmidt, 1980). However, an estimated 1 million adherents in the United States makes Hinduism a significant part of the religious diversity of our country.

Hinduism also differs from Christianity and Islam in several other key ways. First, it is not linked to the life of any single person. Second, it has no sacred writings comparable to the Bible or the Qur'an. Third, Hinduism does not even envision God as a specific entity. For this reason, Hinduism—like other Asian religions, as we shall see—is sometimes thought of as an "ethical religion." Hindu beliefs and practices vary widely, but all Hindus recognize that the moral force of our universe confronts everyone with responsibilities known as *dharma*. One traditional example of dharma is the duty to act in concert with the traditional caste system, described in Chapter 9 ("Social Stratification").

A second Hindu principle, called *karma*, refers to the belief in the spiritual progress of the human soul. To a Hindu, every action we take has a spiritual consequence; proper living enhances moral development, while improper living results in moral decline. Karma works through *reincarnation*, a cycle of new birth following death, so that the individual is reborn into a spiritual state corresponding to the moral quality of a previous life. Unlike Christianity and Islam, Hinduism proclaims no ultimate justice at the hands of a supreme god, although in the cycle of rebirth, each person reaps exactly what is sown. The sublime state of *nirvana* represents spiritual perfection; when a soul reaches this rarefied existence, it is spared further rebirth.

Looking at Hinduism, we realize that not all religions can be neatly labeled monotheistic or polytheistic. Hinduism may be described as monotheistic because it envisions the universe as a single moral system; yet Hindus see evidence of this moral order in every element of nature. While central to a Hindu's life, rituals are also quite variable. Such variety stems from weaving religion into daily lives in countless Indian villages over thousands of years. Most Hindus, however, practice private devotions, including, for example, ritual cleansing following contact with a person of lower caste position. Many also participate in massive public events, such as the Kumbh Mela, which occurs every twelve years. At this time, millions of Hindus make a pilgrimage to the sacred Ganges River to bathe in its ritually purifying waters.

Hinduism is still unfamiliar to most Westerners. But, like religions more well known to us, Hinduism is a powerful force offering both explanation and guidance in life (Pitt, 1955; Sen, 1961; Embree, 1972; Kaufman, 1976; Schmidt, 1980).

Buddhism

India also gave rise to Buddhism, a religion that emerged about 2,500 years ago. Today more than 300 million people (6 percent of humanity) embrace Buddhism, and almost all are Asians. As shown in Global Map 17-4, adherents to Buddhism represent over half the populations of Myanmar, Thailand, Cambodia, and Japan; Buddhism is also widespread in India and the People's Republic of China. Of the world religions considered so far, Buddhism most resembles Hinduism in doctrine, but, like Christianity, its inspiration springs from the life of one individual.

Siddhartha Gautama was born to a high-caste Indian family about 563 B.C.E. As a young man, he was preoccupied with spiritual matters. At the age of twenty-nine, he underwent a radical personal transformation. Setting off for years of travel and meditation, he finally achieved what Buddhists describe as *bodhi*, or

A general trait of most Eastern religions is that they recognize no god of judgment; rather, they provide a model for spiritually healthful everyday living.

enlightenment. Understanding the essence of life, Gautama became a Buddha.

Energized by Buddha's personal charisma, followers spread his teachings—the *dhamma*—across India. During the third century B.C.E., the ruler of India joined the ranks of Buddhism, and subsequently sent missionaries throughout Asia, elevating Buddhism to the status of a world religion.

Central to Buddhist belief is the notion that human existence involves suffering. Buddhism does not forbid pleasure, but rather holds that such experience is transitory. This belief stems from Buddha's own travels throughout a society rife with poverty. But Buddhism rejects wealth as a solution to suffering; on the contrary, in this world view materialism inhibits spiritual development. Buddhism's response to world problems is for individuals to pursue personal, spiritual transformation.

Buddhism closely parallels Hinduism in its belief in reincarnation; here again, only full enlightenment ends the cycle of death and rebirth, thereby liberating a person from the suffering of the world. Also like Hinduism, Buddhism recognizes no god of judgment, but, rather, sees spiritual consequences in each daily action.

Like Christianity, Buddhism originated in the life of a charismatic teacher. However, its conception of a moral universe in which spiritual development occurs

WINDOW ON THE WORLD

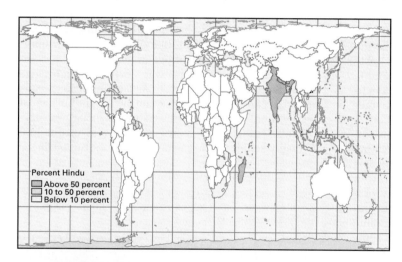

GLOBAL MAP 17-3 HINDUISM IN GLOBAL PERSPECTIVE

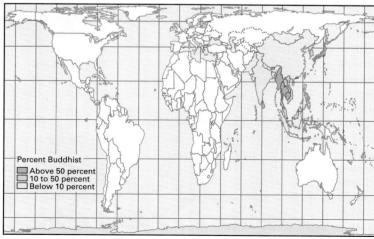

GLOBAL MAP 17-4 BUDDHISM IN GLOBAL PERSPECTIVE

over many lifetimes places Buddhism closer to Hinduism overall (Schumann, 1974; Thomas, 1975).

Confucianism

From about 200 B.C.E. until the beginning of this century, Confucianism was an ecclesia—the official religion of China. Following the 1949 revolution, religion was suppressed by the Communist government of the People's Republic of China. Hundreds of millions of Chinese are influenced by Confucianism, although the government provides little in the way of official data to establish more precise numbers. Almost all adherents of Confucianism live in the People's Republic of China, but cultural diffusion and Chinese immigration have introduced this religion to other societies in Southeast Asia. Estimates hold that 100,000 followers of Confucianism live throughout North America.

This religion was founded by K'ung-Fu-tzu, known to Westerners as Confucius, who lived between 551 and 479 B.C.E. Confucius shared with Buddha a deep concern for the problems and suffering of the world. Buddha encouraged a more sect-like spiritual withdrawal from the world; Confucius, however, instructed his followers to engage the world but to do so with correct moral conduct. Thus, Confucianism became fused with the traditional culture of China. Here we see a second example of what might be called a "national religion": as Hinduism has remained largely synonymous with Indian culture, Confucianism is enshrined in the Chinese way of life.

A central concept of Confucianism is *jen*, meaning humaneness. In practice, this means that self-interest must always be subordinated to moral concerns. In the family, the individual must display loyalty and consideration for others. Likewise, families must remain mindful of their duties toward the larger community. In this way, an overarching morality integrates society as a whole: personal loyalty builds strong families; strong families form wholesome communities, and so on. Unlike Jesus and Buddha, then, Confucius directed attention *to* the world, not *away from* it; he also sought guidance in the past for actions in the present, while Christianity and Buddhism look more to the future for salvation and spiritual fulfilment.

Most of all, Confucianism stands out because it lacks a clear sense of the sacred. We could view Confucianism as the celebration of society itself as sacred, in the sense that Durkheim described that process. Alternatively, we might argue that Confucianism is less a religion than a model for leading a disciplined life based on Chinese traditions. Certainly the historical dominance of Confucianism helps to explain why Chinese culture has long taken a skeptical attitude toward the supernatural. If we conclude that Confucianism is best thought of as a disciplined and scholarly way of life, we must also recognize that it shares with religion a body of beliefs and practices that have as their goals goodness and the promotion of social unity (Kaufman, 1976; Schmidt, 1980; McGuire, 1987).

Judaism

Speaking purely in numerical terms, Judaism is less a world religion than any of the others we have considered, with about 17 million adherents (0.3 percent of humanity). Only in Israel is Judaism a majority religion. But Judaism has special significance to our society because the largest concentration of Jews (some 7 million people) live in North America. Followers of Judaism are also found in every other region of the world, with most of the remainder living in Europe and the Middle East.

Like Confucianism, Judaism has deep roots: Jews look to the past as a source of guidance in the present and for the future. Jewish history extends back some 4,000 years before the birth of Christ to the ancient

Chanukah is an important Jewish ritual of commemoration that serves to teach young people their long and rich history.

cultures of Mesopotamia. At that time, Jews were animistic, but this belief was to change after Jacob—grandson of Abraham, the earliest great ancestor—led his people to Egypt.

Under Egyptian rule, Jews endured centuries of slavery. In the thirteenth century B.C.E., a turning point came as Moses, the adopted son of an Egyptian princess, was called by God to lead the Jews from bondage. This exodus (the word's Latin and Greek roots mean "a marching out") from Egypt is commemorated by Jews today in the celebration of Passover. As a result of the Jews' liberation from bondage, Judaism became monotheistic, recognizing a single, all-powerful God.

A distinctive concept of Judaism is the *covenant*, a special relationship with God by which Jews became a "chosen people." The covenant also implies a duty to observe God's law, especially the Ten Commandments as revealed to Moses on Mt. Sinai. Jews regard the Bible (or, in Christian terms, the Old Testament) as both a record of their history and a statement of the general obligations of Jewish life. Of special importance are the first five books of the Bible (Genesis, Exodus, Leviticus, Numbers, and Deuteronomy), designated as the *Torah* (a word roughly meaning "teaching" and "law"). In contrast to Christianity's central concern with personal salvation, Judaism (not unlike Confucianism) emphasizes moral behavior in this world.

Judaism is composed of various denominations distinguished by interpretations of doctrine. Orthodox Jews strictly observe traditional beliefs and practices, including historical forms of dress, segregation of men and women at religious services, and consumption of only kosher foods. Such distinctive practices set off Orthodox Jews as the most sect-like. In the mid-nineteenth century, many Jews sought greater accommodation to the larger society, leading to the formation of the more church-like Reform Judaism. More recently, a third segment—Conservative Judaism—has established a middle ground between the other two denominations.

All Jews, however, share a keen awareness of their cultural history, which has included considerable prejudice and discrimination. A collective memory of centuries of slavery in Egypt, conquest by Rome, and persecution in Europe has shaped Jewish awareness and identity. Interestingly, the urban ghetto (derived from the Italian word *borghetto*, meaning settlement outside the city walls) was first home to Jews in medieval Italy; this form of residential segregation soon spread to other parts of Europe.

Jewish emigration to North America began in the mid-1600s. Many early immigrants prospered and many were also assimilated into largely Christian communities. But as more and more Jews joined the Great Immigration during the final decades of the nineteenth century, prejudice and discrimination against them—commonly termed *anti-Semitism*—increased. During this century, anti-Semitism reached a vicious peak when Jews experienced the most horrific persecution in modern times. During the Holocaust, the Nazi regime in Germany systematically annihilated some 6 million Jewish people during the 1930s and 1940s. The killing was so extensive and methodical that many in North America and Europe initially did not comprehend the scope of this genocide (Abzug, 1985).

Despite its historical themes, Judaism has changed considerably over thousands of years. Like Christianity and Islam, Judaism recognizes a single God; like Hinduism and Confucianism, it emphasizes moral directives in this world rather than hope for salvation in a world to come. The history of Judaism also points up a tragic dimension of the human record—the extent to which religious minorities have been the target of hatred and even slaughter (Bedell, Sandon, & Wellborn, 1975; Holm, 1977; Schmidt, 1980; Seltzer, 1980; B. Wilson, 1982; Eisen, 1983).

Religion in Canada

Canada has experienced remarkable changes over the course of its brief history, with transformation in all social institutions including religion. Some wonder if the Industrial Revolution, the establishment of universal schooling, and the advancing role of science and technology together have undermined traditional religion. Yet the evidence shows that religion continues to play a central role in our way of life (Bibby, 1987).

Religious Affiliation

National surveys reveal that almost 90 percent of adults in Canada identify with a particular religion (Baril and Mori, 1991). Traditionally, Canada has been fairly evenly divided between Catholics and Protestants. For more than a century, until about 1971, Protestants outnumbered Catholics. Now the reverse is true. Table 17-1 records survey results showing that Catholicism is embraced by approximately 45 percent of respondents, while Protestants make up almost one-third of the population, and about 10 percent claim to have no religious affiliation. One percent identify with Judaism.

TABLE 17-1 DISTRIBUTION OF RELIGIONS IN CANADA,* 1985–1990

		1985	1986	1988	1989	1990
Roman	000s	8,845	9,014	9,203	9,161	9,270
Catholic	%	45.0	45.3	45.6	45.2	45.2
Mainline Protestant						
United	000s	2,850	2,674	2,757	2,271	2,521
	%	14.5	13.4	13.7	11.2	12.3
Anglican	000s	2,017	1,773	1,929	1,781	1,892
	%	10.3	8.9	9.6	8.8	9.2
Other	000s	1,626	1,691	1,634	1,566	1,746
	%	8.3	8.5	8.1	7.7	8.5
No religion	000s	2,054	2,023	2,183	2,651	2,492
	%	10.4	10.2	10.8	13.1	12.1
Other**	000s	2,095	2,416	2,080	2,409	1,851
	%	10.7	12.1	10.3	11.9	9.0
Not stated	000s	181	308	407	408	358
	%	0.9	1.5	2.0	2.0	1.7
Total	**000s**	**19,668**	**19,898**	**20,194**	**20,248**	**20,526**
	%	**100.0**	**100.0**	**100.0**	**100.0**	**100.0**

*Population aged 15 and over.
**Including Judaism which accounted for about 1.2% of the population in 1981 (Census of Canada).
SOURCE: Canadian Social Trends, Autumn 1991, p. 22.

About 24 percent of adults in Canada report that they attend religious instruction classes weekly. In the vast majority of counties, about 8 percent of Canadians go to church at least once a month (Gallup Report, 1991). Almost a third of the adult population claims to pray daily and more than half say that they read the Bible or other religious literature at least occasionally (Nemeth, 1993).

Canadian society has no official religion, and the separation of church and state is enshrined in the Constitution. The population of Canada is also more religiously diverse than that of most other countries on earth—one result of our historically high level of immigration.

Religiosity

Religiosity is a general concept that refers to *the importance of religion in a person's life.* Quantitative measures of religiosity in Canada vary depending on exactly how this concept is operationalized. Years ago, Charles Glock (1959, 1962) identified five distinct dimensions of religiosity. *Experiential* religiosity refers to the strength of a person's emotional tie to a religion. *Ritualistic* religiosity deals with frequency of ritual activity such as prayer and church attendance. *Ideological* religiosity concerns an individual's degree of belief in religious doctrine. *Consequential* religiosity has to do with how much religious beliefs influence a person's daily behavior. Finally, *intellectual* religiosity refers to a person's knowledge of the history and doctrines of a particular religion. Anyone is likely to be more religious on some dimensions than on others; this inconsistency

Heaven and hell were never portrayed more vividly than by Jan Van Eyck (1390–1441) in his painting The Last Judgment *(c. 1420). While the modern understanding of heaven and hell may by different from that expressed by Van Eyck, belief in the afterlife is still strong among Canadians.*

compounds the difficulty of measuring the concept of religiosity.

How religious, then, are members of our society? Canada Map 17-1 shows the percentage of respondents in each province that stated they had "no religion" on the 1990 census. The figures range from a low of 1.6 percent in Newfoundland to a high of 33.7 percent in the Yukon. The figure for Canada as a whole is 12.3 percent

Nevertheless, a large majority of Canadians (86 percent) claim to believe in God. Seventy-one percent believe in some type of heaven, 34 percent believe in hell and 30 percent believe there is a devil. Surprisingly, only 88 percent of declared Protestants believe in God (Bozinoff and MacIntosh, 1990). In terms of expe-

riential religiosity, then, people in Canada seem to be notably religious, although they tend to believe in the more positive doctrinal aspects, such as God and heaven, rather than the more negative aspects such as hell and the devil.

However, there have been significant changes in the religious characteristics of the Canadian population. One of the largest changes overall is the growth in the proportion of Canadians who state that they have no religion. In 1990 those with no religion accounted for 12 percent of adult Canadians, compared to 7 percent in 1981. This trend parallels a considerable drop in church attendance, as shown in Figure 17.1. If those who rarely or never attend church are included, the proportion with no religion grows to 37 percent.

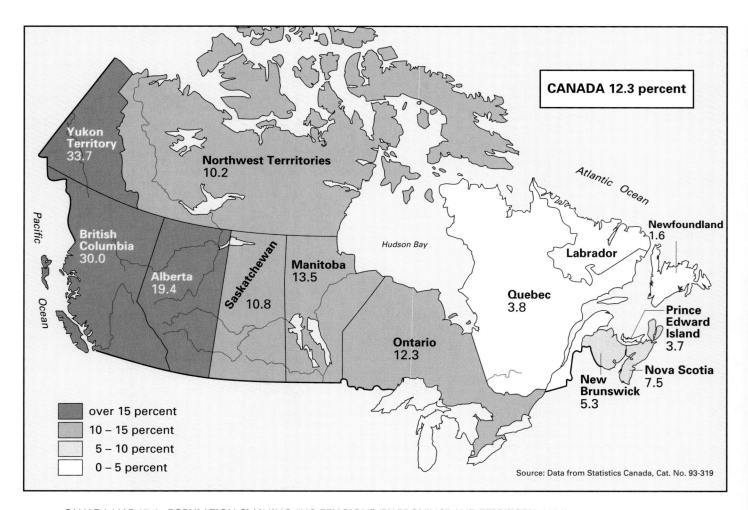

CANADA MAP 17-1   POPULATION CLAIMING "NO RELIGION" (BY PROVINCE AND TERRITORY, 1991)

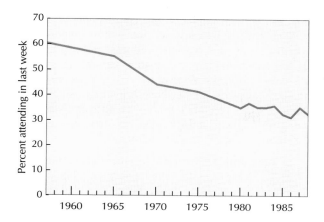

FIGURE 17-1 CHURCH OR SYNAGOGUE ATTENDANCE,*
1957–1988
* Adults aged 18 and over
SOURCE: *Canadian Social Trends*, Autumn 1991, p. 24.

The question "How religious are we?" thus yields no easy answers. Keep in mind, too, that belief in God is normative in our culture so that people may make such a claim simply to conform. Similarly, we should not assume that everyone who attends services does so for religious reasons; a synagogue, mosque, or church can provide a sense of identity and belonging, a means of satisfying family members, a way to serve the community, or a source of social prestige. Our general conclusion, then, is that most people in Canada are at least somewhat religious, and a large minority deeply so.

Religiosity also varies among different religious organizations. In a classic study of religious diversity, Rodney Stark and Charles Glock (1968) found Catholics to be generally more religious than Protestants. And members of sects, they concluded, are typically more religious than members of Catholic or Protestant churches.

Correlates of Religious Affiliation

Sociologists study religion not only to comprehend how people address the sacred but because religious affiliation is related to a host of familiar social patterns.

Social Class
Religious organizations are socially stratified. As noted earlier in this chapter, members of sect-like organizations typically have a lower social position than that of more church-like religious communities.

Protestant denominations with the highest social

position are those whose membership is mainly of Northern European background, including many families whose ancestors came to Canada more than a century ago. They encountered little prejudice and discrimination and have had the most time to establish themselves socially. Roman Catholics, frequently Quebec based, have contended with greater social barriers based on being a minority religion.

Jews have unexpectedly high social standing considering that many are fairly recent immigrants who confronted anti-Semitism from some members of the Christian majority. Jewish traditions place great value on achievement and education. Although a large proportion of Jews immigrated to Canada in poverty, an intense desire for learning led parents to ensure that their children were extensively schooled. As a result, the social position of many Jews—although certainly not all—rose in subsequent generations.

Ethnicity and Race
Around the world, religion is strongly linked to ethnicity. Many religions predominate in a geographical region, sometimes in a single society. The vast majority of Muslims, for example, live in the Eastern Hemisphere; Hinduism is virtually synonymous with the culture of India, as is Confucianism with the culture of China.

Religion is also fused with national identity in Canada. The social diversity of our society, for example, includes *Anglo-Saxon* Protestants, *French* Catholics, *Russian* Jews, and *Greek* Orthodox. This linking of nation and creed results from the influx of immigrants to Canada from societies with a single major religion. Beyond these broad patterns, however, nearly every ethnic group in this country displays at least some religious diversity. People of English ancestry, for instance, include members of many Protestant denominations, Roman Catholics, Jews, and adherents of other religions.

Political Attitudes
The Roman Catholic Church continues to hold to fairly traditional doctrines, especially about sexuality. Most practicing Catholics ignore their leaders, however: 91 percent approve of artificial birth control, 82 percent condone premarital sex, and only 20 percent support the outright opposition of the church to abortion.

On most issues, members of the United Church of Canada are more liberal than those of other religious heritages. As a church they are more likely to speak out on social issues. And, in spite of a split within the denomination, they were vocal about accepting homosexual clergy. Even so, some 20 percent of all those who belong to the United Church feel that the church is presently too liberal. Religiously "conservative" Protestant denominations, who comprise approximately 8 percent of the population (including Baptists, Pentecostals, Mennonites etc.) are more active church supporters .

Perhaps surprisingly, Canadians tend not to vote along religious lines. In fact, in the 1988 federal election, approximately equal numbers from each denomination supported each of the three major political parties (Nemeth, 1993).

Religion in a Changing Society

Every society changes over time, which implies a transformation of social institutions. Just as family life and schooling have changed over the course of this century, so has our society's religious life.

Secularization

One of the most important and controversial patterns of social change is **secularization**, *a historical trend away from the supernatural and the sacred.* For society as a whole, secularization points to a declining influence of religion in everyday life. For religious organizations, becoming more secular means that they direct attention less to other worldly issues (like life after death) and more to worldly affairs (like whether women or gay people should be ordained as clergy).

Secularization, a concept derived from a Latin word meaning "the present age," is generally associated with modern, technologically advanced societies (Cox, 1971; O'Dea & Aviad, 1983). Conventional wisdom holds that secularization is one result of the increasing importance of science to human understanding. Imagine the early scientist Sir Isaac Newton (1642–1727) sitting under a tree observing an apple falling to the ground. Had he thought the way most Europeans did during the Middle Ages, Newton might have taken an other-worldly view of the event, concluding that apples grow and fall according to the will of God. But living in an age when human beings were adopting the logic of science to understand the natural world, his observation led him to formulate the far more worldly law of gravity.

Evidence of contemporary secularization can be

seen in the fact that, since mid-century, public schools have taught children less and less about religion. More broadly, adults perceive birth, illness, and death less as the work of a divine power than as natural stages in the life course that are now more likely to occur in the presence of physicians (whose knowledge is based on science) than religious leaders (whose knowledge is based on faith). Theologian Harvey Cox comments on the diminishing sphere of religion:

> The world looks less and less to religious rules and rituals for its morality or its meanings. For some, religion provides a hobby, for others a mark of national or ethnic identification, for still others an aesthetic delight. For fewer and fewer does it provide an inclusive and commanding system of personal and cosmic values and explanations. (1971:3)

If Cox is correct, one might wonder if religion will some day completely disappear. But this is not the consensus among sociologists (Hammond, 1985; McGuire, 1987). Recall that the vast majority of people in Canada continue to profess a belief in God, and most are affiliated with a religious organization. While Canadians in the

William Kurelek's self portrait, Lord That I Might See, *captures something of the painful perplexity of the Christian penitent seeking God's guidance and help.*

mainline denominations may not be attending religious services as frequently as they were in the past, the majority still identify with the historically dominant groups. It is not appropriate to equate attendance decreases with religious disaffiliation. Religion, especially among the major, mainline denominations, is fused with the family, identity, biography, and culture of the individual (Bibby, 1987:51).

However, the fact that Canadians tend to identify with particular denominations, to see themselves as spiritual, and to believe in God is not a reflection of the overall health of the mainline denominations. Reginald Bibby (1993) argues that the Canadian churches are in full-scale crisis. Even though Canadians yearn for meaning and fulfillment, their needs are not being met by the mainline denominations. Canadian churches, Bibby argues, are failing in four ways to attract and maintain adherents. First, they have a distribution problem: As he put it in an interview in *The Globe and Mail*, "they can-

not get the faith out of the warehouse" (Sept. 9, 1993: 1–2). The mainline churches tend to be homogeneous, inward looking social clubs that fail to appeal to outsiders. Second, because they depend so heavily on volunteers, the organizations lack structures to handle the balance needed between national, regional, and local interests. Third, some have emphasized social action to such an extent as to virtually extinguish their reason for being together—a belief in God. Fourth, their marketing skills are inadequate and they, as organizations, have been unable to target their audiences with any accuracy. Bibby predicts large drops in affiliation with mainline denominations in the next quarter of a century.

But even though the mainline denominations are expected to decline even further in the future, growth is expected to occur in the smaller conservative and evangelical churches (Bibby, 1993). Secularization, therefore, does not signal the impending death of religion. More accurately, secularization is an uneven

CROSS-CULTURAL COMPARISON

Civil Religion In the United States

The inconsistent character of secularization is illustrated in what Robert Bellah (1975) has called **civil religion**, *a quasi-religious loyalty binding individuals in a basically secular society*. The term *civil* refers to the ordinary life of citizens of a political state; patriotism and various national rituals, in other words, have the power to evoke religious feelings. The ascendancy of civil rites offset, at least to some degree, the declining prominence of religion.

The United States is a case in point. Just as religion presents a blueprint for leading a good life, a vast majority of people in the United States believe that their political and economic systems exemplify what is good, and that American involvement in world affairs benefits other countries. By contrast, most Americans think of communism as an evil system (N.O.R.C.,1991). Thus the collapse of communist governments in much of the world in recent years has

been widely perceived by Americans as a moral triumph for their country (Williams & Demerath, 1991).

Civil religion also encompasses a wide range of rituals. Before the opening of sporting events, spectators rise respectfully for the playing of the "Star Spangled Banner." Public parades and celebrations held regularly during the year (and especially on the Fourth of July) foster patriotism and build social unity. Roughly like the cross to Christians and the Star of David to Jews, the flag serves Americans as a sacred symbol of their national identity. Patriotism also evokes a similar sense of wonder and awe in many Americans as more traditional religious experiences. The explanation lies in Emile Durkheim's insight that all ritual allows us to experience our collective identity— the power of society.

Civil religion is not a specific religious doctrine, of course. But civil religion does incorporate many ele-

ments of traditional religion into the political system of a secular society. The belief shared by most people in the U.S.A. that their society stands as a force for good in the world (based more on faith than on clear and convincing evidence) amounts to one vital religious expression in a modern, secular society.

In many respects religion undergirds society in Canada as well, although not as extensively or overtly as in the States. Notice that in courtrooms we are asked to "swear" to tell the truth on the Bible. Until recently, school policy in all parts of Canada included saying the Lord's Prayer as part of morning exercises for all school children. Canadians, too, have infused patriotism with religion. Brian Mulroney immortalized the notion that Canada's social programs are a "sacred trust." We, too, in Canada, cherish parts of our way of life—for example, medicare—as if they had religious significance.

process of change in which a decline in some dimensions of religiosity parallels an increase in others. Similarly, while some religious organizations have lost significant membership in recent decades, others are rapidly gaining in popularity. Finally, in global perspective we see that while religion is declining in importance in some world regions (the Scandinavian countries, for example), religious fervor is rising in others (like Algeria) (Cox, 1990).

Given the complexity of secularization, public attitudes concerning its merits vary significantly. Some people lament secularization as the loss of traditional values. More secular religious organizations, these critics fear, are no longer addressing other-worldly needs and are preaching instead a doctrine of greater permissiveness in behavior, even sanctioning actions previously viewed as deviant. But others celebrate secularization, touting this drive as a liberation from the all-encompassing beliefs of the past and a way for people to assume greater responsibility for what they choose to believe. Further, secularization has brought the practices of many religious organizations in line with widespread social attitudes. As an example, more women are becoming religious leaders.

Religious Revival

A great deal of change is going on inside the world of organized religion. As we have seen, membership in established, "mainstream" churches like the Anglican and Presbyterian denominations has decreased, while that in more sect-like churches has grown. Between 1981 and 1991 the decrease in the Presbyterian was 22 percent, in the United, 18 percent, in the Anglican and Lutheran, 10 percent, and in the Baptist, 5 percent. Most of the smaller denominations, including the Spiritualist, Evangelical, Christian and Missionary Alliance, New Apostolic, and Missionary churches grew significantly in the same time period. The Jewish and Eastern Orthodox churches grew by 7 percent. This suggests that secularization is a self-limiting process. In other words, as the most church-like organizations become more worldly in their orientation, people abandon them in favor of other, more sect-like religious communities that better address their spiritual concerns (Bibby, 1987).

Religious Fundamentalism

A significant element in modern religions is the growth of **religious fundamentalism**, *a conservative religious*

doctrine that opposes intellectualism and worldly accommodation in favor of restoring a traditional other-worldly focus. In Canada, fundamentalism has made the biggest inroads among Protestants. But fundamentalism has proliferated beyond Protestant denominations; it is also gaining popularity among Roman Catholics and Jews.

While fundamentalism is hardly new, its influence has steadily increased during this century (Bromley & Shupe, 1984). In the nineteenth century, fundamentalism fueled opposition to the teaching of evolution in schools and promoted later efforts to keep religious instruction in the classroom. To many people in Canada however, fundamentalism emerged as a key political and social force when conservative Christian organizations publicly supported the conservative social agenda of the Conservative Party. More recently, the Reform and Christian Heritage parties have received the backing of fundamentalist groups.

Throughout its history, religious fundamentalism has defended traditional beliefs against the tide of change. During the nineteenth century, North American society was in the throes of rapid change as schooling was becoming universal and science was gaining ground on traditional religious thinking. Compounding this transformation, immigrants were streaming into the country in increasing numbers, and industrial cities soon eclipsed in size and productive power the farms and villages familiar to earlier generations.

In times of tumultuous social change, such as the nineteenth century when greater social diversity was eroding traditions and fostering secularization, religious conservatives respond by trying to restore what followers hold to be *fundamental* religious practices and beliefs (Hunter, 1983, 1985, 1987, 1989; Wilcox, 1989). Four fundamentalist tenets stand out. First, fundamentalists *interpret Scripture literally.* They charge that worldly accommodation and increasing intellectualism lead more liberal religious organizations to lose sight of God's message. For example, fundamentalists accept the idea that God created the world precisely as described in Genesis. Second, fundamentalists *reject religious diversity* on the grounds that tolerance and relativism water down personal faith. Third, members of fundamentalist organizations *pursue the personal experience of God's presence.* In contrast to the worldliness and intellectualism of other religious organizations, fundamentalism seeks to propagate "good old-time religion" and spiritual revival. To fundamentalist Christians, the experience of being "born again," meaning they establish a personal relationship with Jesus, is expected to translate clearly into their everyday life. Fourth, fundamentalism *opposes worldly accommodation* because the broader society is viewed as a dangerous source of "secular humanism" that undermines religious conviction. Taken together, these traits suggest why some people consider fundamentalism to be somewhat rigid and self-righteous. At the same time, this brief sketch helps us understand why others find in fundamentalism—with its greater religious certainty and its emphasis on personally experiencing God's presence—an appealing alternative to the more intellectual, tolerant, and worldly "mainstream" denominations.

The label "fundamentalist" applies better to some religious organizations than to others. Generally, the term is used by conservative Christian organizations in the evangelical tradition, including Pentecostals, Associated Gospel, Baptists, and the Seventh-Day Adventists.

Although Christian fundamentalism has typically shunned worldly concerns, in 1980 it took on a decidedly political character; it emerged as the *New Christian Right* (Viguerie, 1981; Hunter, 1983; Speer, 1984; Ostling, 1985). Jerry Falwell, a fundamentalist preacher, led what he labeled the "Moral Majority" through most of the 1980s in the United States. His target was what he termed the "liberal agenda," including the Equal Rights Amendment, abortion as a matter of choice, the civil rights of gay people, and the widespread availability of pornography. Moral Majority members also sought to bring back prayer in public schools, which they view as bastions of permissiveness and secular humanism. The REAL Women's Movement in Canada, claiming to be pro-family, has a similar conservative social agenda and vociferously opposes women's organizations such as the National Action Committee, along with day care, the paid employment of mothers outside of the home, and abortion. To a certain extent, their efforts have been successful. The movement helped launch a decade of conservative and anti-feminist policies.

The Electronic Church

Finally, conservative religious organizations have received a boost through skilful use of the mass media to generate religious excitement and gain converts. In contrast to small village congregations of years past, "gatherings" now take the form of radio and television audiences who support what is commonly called the *electronic church* dominated by "prime-time preachers" (Bibby, 1987). Although many members of more liberal churches contend that "prime-time preaching" undermines religion with emotional simplicity, many people have become regular participants in this new form of religious activity. Others argue that the decline is related to being able to "attend" church in the comfort of their own homes and that religious TV is a substitute for formal attendance. People are not "turning off," rather "tuning in" (Bibby, 1987:32).

At the beginning of the 1980s, electronic religion was unique to the United States and included approximately 1,400 radio stations and sixty television stations (including many cable television channels). Aided by their electronic churches, religious leaders such as Oral Roberts, Robert Schuller, and Jim and Tammy Bakker and Canadian TV evangelists such as David Mainse and Terry Winter have become better known than all but a few clergy were in the past. Estimates hold that about 4 percent of the national television audience regularly tune in to religious television. Moreover, the majority of people who watch religious programs on TV are also regular church-goers. Almost 80 percent attend weekly (68 percent) or monthly (11 percent).

Sending religious messages via the mass media prompted two notable developments during the 1980s. On the one hand, regular solicitation of contributions brought a financial windfall to some religious organizations. Broadcasting with 3,200 stations in half the countries in the world, for example, Jimmy Swaggart received $180 million in contributions in 1986 alone. On the other hand, some media-based ministries were corrupted by the power of money. In 1989, Jim Bakker (who, with his ex-wife Tammy, began his television career in 1965 hosting a children's puppet show) was jailed following a conviction for defrauding contributors. Such cases, although few in number, attracted enormous national attention and eroded public support as people began to wonder whether television preachers were more interested in raising cash or moral standards. In the middle of 1986, there was a proposed pay TV channel called the Canadian Interfaith Network (C.I.N). It was to be inter-denominational and geared toward a multi-denominational audience. It fell through, however, because several major denominations were not supportive (e.g., Anglican and Roman Catholic). C.I.N. evolved into Vision TV and the church groups that were originally opposed to C.I.N. have been more receptive. While Canadians, having watched the debates in religious broadcast leadership of the United States as mentioned above, were skeptical, Canadian TV evangelists such as David Mainse and Terry Winter, true to the "Canadian personality," are relatively low-key and have exhibited fewer public "sins" (Bibby, 1987:34–36).

The Future of Religion

The popularity of media ministries, the rapid growth of religious fundamentalism, religious innovation and cult formation, and the continued adherence of millions more people to the "mainstream" churches all clearly demonstrate that secularization is not squeezing the religion from our society (Bibby, 1987). The world is becoming more complex, with rapid changes almost outstripping our capacity to keep pace. But rather than undermining religion, these processes end up firing the religious imagination of people everywhere who, more than ever, long for a sense of religious community, meaning, and purpose. Science is simply unable to address these central human needs and questions. Against this backdrop of uncertainty, it is little wonder that many people turn to their faith for assurance and hope (Cox, 1977; Barker, 1981).

Summary

1. Religion is a major social institution based on distinguishing the sacred from the profane. Religion is a matter of faith, not scientific evidence, which people express through various rituals.

2. Sociology analyzes the social consequences and correlates of religion, but makes no claims as to the ultimate truth or falsity of any religious belief.

3. Emile Durkheim argued that religion expresses the power of society over individuals. His structural-functional analysis suggests that religion promotes social cohesion, enhances social control, and confers meaning and purpose on life.

4. Using the symbolic-interaction paradigm, Peter Berger explains that religious beliefs are socially constructed. These beliefs provide a vital source of individual meaning and security, just as religious rituals overlay relationships like marriage, and major life events from birth to death with sacred significance.

5. Using the social-conflict paradigm, Karl Marx linked religion to social inequality. While religion does perpetuate inequality in some respects, religious ideals also motivate people to seek greater social equality.

6. A church is one kind of religious organization that seeks accommodation with the larger society. A further distinction among churches is made between an ecclesia, or state-sponsored church, and a denomination, which recognizes religious pluralism.

7. A sect, another type of religious organization, resists accommodation with the larger society.

Sects emerge as a result of religious division and often have charismatic leadership.

8. Cults are religious organizations that embrace beliefs and practices that are unconventional from the point of view of the surrounding society. By making distinctions among churches, sects, and cults, sociologists do not judge one type of religious organization as more valid or worthy than another.

9. Technologically simple human societies were generally animistic; in more complex societies, religion emerges as a distinct social institution.

10. Followers of six world religions—Christianity, Islam, Hinduism, Buddhism, Confucianism, and Judaism—represent three-fourths of all humanity.

11. Almost all adults in Canada identify with a religion; about 60 percent have a formal religious affiliation, with the largest number belonging to the Roman Catholic church.

12. How religious our nation is depends on how religiosity is operationalized. The vast majority of people claim to believe in God, although attendance at church services has declined greatly, and the number of people indicating "no religion" on the census has grown.

13. Canada has considerable religious diversity, with affiliation linked to social class, ethnicity, and race.

14. Secularization, an important dimension of social change, involves declining attention to the supernatural and the sacred. Religious organizations become more secular (church-like) as they

become more intellectual and conceive of God in more distant terms. Some people view secularization as a breakdown of traditional morality; others perceive it as a form of liberation and a source of greater tolerance.

15. Membership in more liberal "mainstream" churches has declined sharply in recent decades; however, more conservative religious organizations (notably Christian sects) have been surging in popularity. These parallel trends suggest that secularization will not result in the demise of religion.

16. Civil religion is a quasi-religious belief by which people profess loyalty to their society, often in the form of patriotism. The United States is a notable example of a society where civil religion thrives.

17. Fundamentalism opposes religious accommodation to the world and stresses a more other-worldly focus. Fundamentalist Christianity also stresses literal interpretation of the Bible, rejects religious diversity, and pursues the personal experience of God's presence. During the 1980s, some fundamentalist Christian organizations actively supported conservative political goals in Canada.

18. Despite the historical process of secularization, the shifting of support toward fundamentalist organizations and the continued expression of religious beliefs by people in Canada casts doubt on the notion that religion is eroding. Rather, evidence abounds that religion still addresses many timeless questions about human experiences and needs.

Key Concepts

animism   the belief that natural objects are conscious forms of life that can affect humanity

charisma   in religious terms, evidence of God's favour in the behaviour of an individual

church   a type of religious organization that readily seeks accommodation with the larger society

civil religion   quasi-religious loyalty binding individuals in a basically secular society

conversion   a personal transformation resulting from adopting new religious beliefs

cult   a religious organization with roots outside the dominant religious traditions of a society

denomination   a church, not linked to the state, in a society that recognizes religious pluralism

ecclesia   a church that is formally allied with the state

faith   belief that is anchored in conviction rather than scientific evidence

liberation theology   a fusion of Christian principles with political activism, often Marxist in character

monotheism   belief in a single divine power

polytheism   belief in many gods

profane   that which is defined as an ordinary element of everyday life

religion   system of beliefs and practices based on recognizing the sacred

religiosity   the importance of religion in a person's life

religious fundamentalism   a conservative religious doctrine that opposes intellectualism and worldly accommodation in favor of restoring a traditional other-worldly focus

ritual   formal, ceremonial behavior

sacred   that which is defined as extraordinary, inspiring a sense of awe, reverence, and even fear

sect   a type of religious organization that resists accommodation with the larger society

secularization   a historical trend away from the supernatural and the sacred

totem   an object in the natural world that is imbued with sacred qualities

Suggested Readings

This is a comprehensive analysis of religion in Canada based on three national surveys conducted in 1975, 1980, and 1985.

Reginald W. Bibby. *Fragmented Gods, The Poverty and Potential of Religion in Canada.* Toronto: Irwin, 1987.

This is a special issue of this journal, dedicated to comparing religion in Canada and the United States.

Canadian Journal of Sociology 3(2) (Spring 1978).

This is the first sociological study of religion in Canada. It focuses on the growth of various religious groups in Alberta between the 1920s and 1940s.

W.E. Mann. *Sect, Cult and Church in Alberta.* Toronto: University of Toronto Press, 1955.

This is a government publication that provides a demographic review of religion in Canada.

George A. Mori. *Religious Affiliation in Canada: Canadian Social Trends.* Ottawa: Statistics Canada, 1990.

The following book is an interesting study of Jehovah's Witnesses in Canada.

James M. Penton. *Jehovah's Witnesses in Canada: Champions of Freedom of Speech and Worship.* Toronto: Macmillan, 1976.

This book examines views on social justice of a variety of religious groups in Canada.

John R. Williams, ed. *Canadian Churches and Social Justice.* Toronto: Lorimer, 1984.

This book explains why Canadian churches are in a state of decline and makes some future predictions.

Reginald W. Bibby. *Unknown Gods.* Toronto: Stoddart, 1993.

Focusing on the life of St. Paul, the first of these books argues that charisma is not merely a personal trait but a collective phenomenon generated in response to a social need. The second, an intellectual history of the concept of charisma, draws on the work of Weber, Durkheim, and Freud.

Anthony J. Blasi. *Making Charisma: The Social Construction of Paul's Public Image.* New Brunswick, NJ: Transaction, 1991.

Charles Lindholm. *Charisma.* Cambridge, MA: Basil Blackwell, 1990.

This book comprises nine essays that survey religion in global perspective.

James A. Beckford and Thomas Luckmann, eds. *The Changing Face of Religion.* Newbury Park, CA: Sage, 1989.

These two books focus on the Catholic Church. The first, a personal exploration of "charismatic Catholics," reveals that Catholicism is not always highly formal and ritualized. The second, challenging the view that the Catholic Church is a conservative force in the world, shows the progressive agenda of the church in Brazil.

Mary Jo Neitz. *Charisma and Community: A Study of Religious Commitment Within the Charismatic Renewal.* New Brunswick, NJ: Transaction, 1987.

Scott Mainwaring. *The Catholic Church and Politics in Brazil, 1916–1985.* Palo Alto, CA: Stanford University Press, 1986.

This book, written by a sociologist who survived the Holocaust, attempts to explain why some Christians risked their lives to save Jews.

Nechama Tec. *When Light Pierced the Darkness: Christian Rescue of Jews in Nazi-Occupied Poland.* New York: Oxford University Press, 1986.

This book examines life in five Islamic communities in the United States, shedding light on a religion about which many North Americans know little.

Yvonne Yazbeck Haddad and Adair T. Lummis. *Islamic Values in the United States: A Comparative Study.* New York: Oxford University Press, 1987.

Religion has long played a major role in the social relations between the sexes. This collection of ten essays examines both the ideal and the real social position of women in Islamic societies.

Freda Hussain, ed. *Muslim Women.* New York: St. Martin's Press, 1984.

This collection of essays delves into the process of secularization.

Philip E. Hammond, ed. *The Sacred in a Secular Age: Toward Revision in the Scientific Study of Religion.* Berkeley, CA: University of California Press, 1985.

POLITICS AND GOVERNMENT

One thousand years ago, halfway around the world, a man stood by the side of the road, surveying his homeland in the wake of war. As the cold wind swirled around him, he could see that the soldiers had left, but the graves of those who were not so lucky seemed to be everywhere. He noticed oxen-drawn carts weighted down with crops grinding slowly toward the distant city; he knew that they would soon return with other goods, just as they had before the fighting began. He watched families nervously looking about as they hunched over in the fields, scavenging for food. He heard people trying to assure themselves that life was returning to normal. But, as the man walked to his house, he knew that all was not the same. He sat and wrote the following lines (Chang Pin, "Lament for Ten Thousand Men's Graves"):

> The war ended on the Huan border,
> And the trading roads are open again;
> Stray crows come and go,
> Cawing in the wintry sky.
> Alas for the white bones,
> Heaped together in desolate graves;
> All had sought military honors for their leader.

Chang Pin's poem raises a number of timeless points: how power is distributed within a society; why people often feel that they have little control over their lives; and why the many sometimes die in service to the few. His thoughts also draw us to the broader question of why nations fall into conflict. The sobering fact is that warfare has been present—at least somewhere in the world—continually, virtually without end, from long before Chang Pin's lifetime right down to our own.

At several levels, this chapter investigates the dynamics of power in and between societies. A central concept of this inquiry is **politics**, *the institutionalized system by which a society distributes power and makes decisions.* We shall begin by examining the role of power in social organization, survey political systems around the world and examine the operation of government in Canada, and conclude the chapter with a look at the military, asking why nations go to war and how they might, instead, pursue peace.

Power and Authority

Political life fuels disagreement and often ignites conflict. Early in this century, Max Weber (1978; orig. 1921) recognized these facts when he defined **power** as *the ability to achieve desired ends despite possible resistance from others.* History shows that *force*—physical might or psychological coercion—constitutes the most basic form of power. But no society exists for long if its power derives solely from force, because people will break rules they do not respect at the first opportunity. Coercing people's compliance through terror is both difficult and limited in effectiveness. By contrast, durable social organization depends on significant agreement about proper goals (cultural values) and the suitable means of attaining them (cultural norms). But in what circumstances do members of a society define the use of power as just? Weber viewed power with justice as the essence of the concept of **authority**, which he defined as *power people perceive as legitimate rather than coercive.*

Whether people perceive power as legitimate or coercive depends on the social context. To illustrate, consider the power of teachers to assign term papers to their classes. Although students may greet such assignments with groans, they usually do the work according to their teacher's directions. Students complete the task for the same reason that the teacher assigns it in the first place: the ritual of assigning a paper is built on the roles we expect people to follow in the classroom. In short, power used in a normative fashion is transformed into authority.

On the other side of the coin, a teacher who threatens a student with a poor grade in order to obtain sexual favors violates cultural norms as well as university regulations. Such behavior constitutes coercive power rather than legitimate authority. So while power and authority both produce compliance, they differ in the meanings people attach to the actions involved.

Notice, too, that when authority is at work those who command are bound by cultural norms just as much as those who obey.

What, then, are the roots of authority? Max Weber identified three, which come together in many everyday experiences of power.

Traditional Authority

Traditional authority, claimed Weber, is *power legitimized by respect for long-established cultural patterns.* Traditional authority pervades preindustrial societies in which change happens slowly. People come to think of traditional social patterns—their society's collective memory—as nearly sacred. In ancient China, the power of the emperor rested on tradition, as did the rule of monarchs in medieval Europe. Traditional authority is commonly exercised by families whose members may reign for centuries. The near-sacred character of traditional authority gives many traditional leaders a god-like standing; some even claim to rule by divine right.

As a society industrializes, tradition no longer holds sway as a means of legitimizing power. Hannah Arendt (1963) explains that traditional authority is compelling only so long as everyone in a society shares one historical world view; this form of authority, then, is undermined by the cultural diversity that accompanies immigration. Because ours is a nation of immigrants, national leaders in Canada rely little on traditional authority—no prime minister, for example, would claim

Leaders want to have legitimacy in the eyes of the people they rule because such acceptance affords stability to a government. Becoming established in this way, however, is no easy task; a look at many nations of the world reveals that a thin line separates political authority from military power.

to rule by grace of God. However, we still have a monarch, Queen Elizabeth II, as our head of state, although the more democratic culture of today's world has shifted real power to commoners popularly elected to office. On the recommendation of our prime minister, the Queen appoints the Governor General, who performs largely ceremonial functions such as opening parliament. Despite this minimal role, there are many Canadians who are uncomfortable with any attachment to the monarchy.

If traditional authority plays a smaller part in politics, it continues to be present in many dimensions of everyday life. Patriarchy, the traditional domination of women by men, is still widespread, although increasingly challenged, in Canada. Less controversial is the traditional authority parents exert over their young children. Family life also shows us that traditional authority enables some people to direct the actions of others based on their status rather than the wisdom of their commands. To children who ask *why* they should obey, parents have long retorted, "Because I said so!" To debate the merits of a command would, after all, place parent and child on the same level.

Rational-Legal Authority

As explained in Chapter 7 ("Groups and Organizations"), Weber viewed bureaucracy as the organizational backbone of industrial societies. Bureaucracy is one expression of our modern, rational view of the world, an outlook that erodes traditional customs and practices. Rather than venerating the past, members of industrial societies typically build their lives around formal rules, often in the form of law. But rational law, like tradition, serves to legitimize power. Thus Weber defined **rational-legal authority** (sometimes called *bureaucratic authority*) as *power legitimized by legally enacted rules and regulations*. Rational-legal authority is closely linked to **government**, *formal organizations that direct the political life of a society*.

Rationally enacted rules not only guide government in Canada, they also underlie much of our everyday life. The authority of classroom teachers, for example, rests primarily on their official status in bureaucratic colleges and universities. Likewise, officers of the law strive to maintain the public peace. In such cases, authority flows, not from family background, but from offices in formal organizations. In other words, what is important today is less the person and more the office so that, while a queen is always a queen, a prime

minister accepts and relinquishes power as given by law to the office itself. To put the matter in different terms, traditional authority is transmitted by ascription, while bureaucratic authority follows achievement. A modern officeholder exercises rational-legal authority not on the basis of birth but rather based on talent, special training, and, in the case of the prime minister, on electoral success.

Charismatic Authority

Max Weber was intrigued by charisma—exceptional personal qualities, as discussed in Chapter 17 ("Religion"). Broadening this religious concept to take account of all kinds of leadership, Weber defined **charismatic authority** as *power legitimized through extraordinary personal abilities that inspire devotion and obedience*. Charisma, therefore, provides a third way in which power can be transformed into authority. But unlike tradition and rational law, charisma is less a quality of social organization than a dimension of individual personality.

Members of every society regard some of their number as especially forceful, creative, and magnetic. In modern societies, these may include famous artists, entertainers, and political leaders. In traditional societies, Weber noted, charisma can enhance the stature of a traditional leader, but it can also empower an individual to challenge tradition, leading others away from established beliefs and practices. Likewise, the prospects of would-be politicians in Canada rise or fall according to their degree of personal charisma. Among our more charismatic prime ministers, John Diefenbaker (1957–63) and Pierre Elliott Trudeau (1968–79, 1980–84) were able were able to inspire Canadians with oratory and a vision of Canada. The "Trudeaumania" that accompanied Trudeau into his first term of office is a phenomenon that has not been matched since. René Lévesque, premier of Québec from 1976–85, also had charismatic appeal. The clash between these two "champions" and their respective visions during Quebec's referendum on sovereignty-association in 1980 heightened the political drama of that moment in history.

For Weber, charismatic authority was most clearly expressed in founding new ways of life. By motivating an audience to follow their lead, charismatics often are able to make their own rules, as if drawing on some higher power. Driven by individual visions for radical change, some charismatics have left their mark on global politics. Vladimir Lenin guided the former Soviet

Union's overthrow of feudal monarchy, Mahatma Gandhi inspired the struggle to free India from British colonialism, and Martin Luther King, Jr., galvanized the civil rights movement in the United States.

Charisma may arise from personality, but it also reflects a society's expectations about what kind of people emerge as leaders. Patriarchy encourages us to tap men as our national leaders, while steering charismatic women more toward the arts, the family, and other social contexts traditionally defined as feminine. Yet, in recent years, charismatic women—including Indira Gandhi of India, Benazir Bhutto of Pakistan, and Margaret Thatcher of the United Kingdom—gained national political prominence. A few years down the road, history will pass judgment on the charismatic appeal—or lack thereof—of our own Kim Campbell.

Because charismatic authority emanates from a single individual, any charismatic movement, whether religious or political, faces a crisis of survival upon the death of its leader. The persistence of a charismatic movement, Max Weber reasoned, requires **routinization of charisma**, *the transformation of charismatic authority into some combination of traditional and bureaucratic authority.* Christianity, for example, began as a cult driven by the personal charisma of Jesus of Nazareth. After the death of Jesus, the Roman Catholic Church gradually emerged on the twin foundations of tradition and bureaucracy, and it continues to flourish today, two thousand years later. Oftentimes, however, there is no routinization of charisma; most charismatic movements simply disintegrate upon the departure of the inspirational leader.

Politics in Global Perspective

Like most other dimensions of social life, politics varies significantly from one society to another. To survey this diversity, we begin with a look back in time; then we turn to political systems in today's world.

Politics in History

Glancing back over human history, we see that politics has not always been a major social institution. With few specialized roles and minimal material wealth, technologically simple hunting and gathering societies operated like a large family. In general, members recognized as their leader a man with unusual strength, hunting skill, or personal charisma. But such leaders exercised little power over others, since they had few resources to reward supporters or to punish challengers. In simple societies, then, leaders were barely discernible from everyone else, and politics as a sphere of life remained on the fringe (Lenski, Lenski, & Nolan, 1991).

Agrarian societies, which are larger and more complex, benefit from more specialized activity and a plentiful material surplus. In these societies, hierarchy becomes increasingly pronounced, as wealth and power are concentrated among a small elite. Such inequality thrusts politics outside the family so that it becomes a social institution in its own right. Elites whose families have maintained their privileged position for generations may acquire traditional authority, sometimes claiming divine right to rule. These leaders may benefit

Neoclassical artist Jacques Louis David *(1748–1825) painted* The Death of Socrates *(1787) to memorialize that Greek philosopher as he was about to drink the cup of hemlock that would end his life. Like Christ, the artist suggests, Socrates is being put to death by a society that fails to understand his message—note that he is surrounded by twelve disciples as he defends virtue even at the cost of his own life. To many thinkers of this age, the eighteenth century promised a triumph of reason over numbing tradition.*

(Jacques Louis David, The Death of Socrates. *1787. Oil on canvas. 59 x 78". The Metropolitan Museum of Art. New York. Wolfe Fund, 1931. Catharine Lorillard Wolfe Collection.)*

further from Weber's rational-legal authority to the extent that they are served by a bureaucratic political administration and a system of law.

As politics expands in scope, societal power eventually takes the form of a **political state**, *a formal government claiming the legitimate use of coercion to support its rule.* Governments claim authority, in other words, based on some combination of tradition, law, and charismatic leadership. But governments rarely stand as the sole source of power in a society. Political revolutions, after all, have occurred throughout human history.

Historically, the political state has developed slowly because the power of government depends on technology; only a few centuries ago, communication over even short distances was uncertain and the transportation of armies and supplies was slow and cumbersome. Thus governments could confidently control only limited areas. Even early political empires (such as Mesopotamia in the Middle East about 5,000 years ago) constituted a collection of small *city-states* rather than a single nation (Stavrianos, 1983). The greatest political power in the ancient world was Rome, the center of a far-reaching empire for some 500 years beginning in the first century B.C.E. By today's standards, the government of the Roman Empire seems as inefficient and unwieldy as the weapons used by the Roman armies. Unable to effectively control its vast empire, Rome eventually collapsed.

In the modern world, political organization has evolved toward *nation-states*. Currently, the world has roughly one hundred and eighty-five independent nation-states, which differ in countless ways including culture, technology, and political system. In industrial societies, the political state is most broadly involved in the everyday lives of the population, providing a host of services ranging from income assistance and schooling to enforcing safety standards in the workplace.

Contemporary Political Systems

Several types of political systems manage the affairs of contemporary nation-states. Despite significant differences, all types of government strive to legitimize their power by winning the hearts and minds of the population.

Monarchy

Monarchy (a word with Latin and Greek roots meaning "ruling alone") is *a type of political system in which*

power is passed from generation to generation in a single family. Monarchy dates back very far as a form of government; great kings and queens even take center stage in the Bible. In Weber's terms, monarchy is legitimized primarily by tradition. In Great Britain, the royal family (as well as many members of the traditional aristocracy) trace their ancestry back through centuries of nobility. Typically, a monarch enjoyed the support of a governmental organization; sometimes the power of a monarch was enhanced by personal charisma. But the core of royal authority lies in deeply rooted tradition.

During the medieval era, *absolute monarchy*, in which hereditary rulers claimed a virtual monopoly of power based on divine right, flourished from England to China and in some parts of the Americas. Monarchy remained widespread even early in this century. On a spring morning in 1910, seventy national leaders assembled in London for the funeral of King Edward VII; of these rulers, more than fifty were hereditary monarchs (Baltzell, 1964).

Not all monarchs wield unlimited power. Over the course of this century, monarchs have gradually given way to elected officials. In European nations that have retained their royalty—including Great Britain, Spain, Norway, Sweden, Belgium, Denmark, and the Netherlands—these families now preside over *constitutional monarchies* in which monarchs are little more than symbolic heads of state. Actual governing is now the responsibility of elected officials, led by a prime minister, and guided by a constitution. In these countries, then, the nobility may reign, but elected officials actually rule (Roskin, 1982).

Democracy

The historical trend in the modern world has favored **democracy**, *a political system in which power is exercised by the people as a whole.* The members of democratic societies rarely participate directly in routine decision making; numbers alone make this an impossibility. In a system more precisely termed *representative democracy*, citizens place authority in the hands of elected leaders, who must answer to the people for their performance in office. Legitimacy, then, is based on popular support, measured by lawful elections. In most societies that think of themselves as democratic, many eligible voters never go to the polls. In the 1992 presidential election in the United States, for example, only 50 percent of eligible voters cast a ballot.

Democratic political systems are common in First-World industrial societies that are relatively rich by world standards (Hannan & Carroll, 1981). Economic development and democratic government go together because both depend on a motivated and literate populace. A monarchy derives legitimacy from a strong sense of tradition and little desire for change—a condition common to agrarian societies but one that dissipates in the winds of industrialization. A democratic political system is based on rational-legal authority that functions by means of a rational election process. Elections place leaders in offices that confer authority limited by law. Thus democracy and rational-legal authority are linked just as monarchy and traditional authority are.

But modern political systems consist not just of leaders and followers; they are built on extensive bureaucracy. Formal organization is necessary to carry out the increasing range of government activities found in democratic societies; yet, democracy and bureaucracy exist in uneasy alliance. The actual task of public administration in Canada involves close to 1 million people as federal, provincial, and municipal employees—making government Canada's largest employer. These bureaucrats, though part of the governing apparatus of this country, were never elected and are unknown to the public they purport to serve. To elect them would be impractical given their numbers and the need for highly specialized training. So, ironically, while the public focuses attention on elected leaders, most everyday decision-making is carried out by career bureaucrats who are not directly accountable to the people (Scaff, 1981; Edwards, 1985; Etzioni-Halevy, 1985).

Democracy and Freedom: Contrasting Approaches

Virtually all industrialized nations have claimed to be democratic and politically free, even though they have forged very different political systems. This curious fact prompts us to take a closer look at what it means to be "free" in various societies.

Canada, the United States, and the nations of Western Europe—together known as "the West"—are societies shaped by the free-market principles of capitalism. The operation of a market system requires that individuals enjoy a high measure of personal freedom to pursue whatever goals advance their self-interest. Thus, the Western tradition of political freedom means the personal *freedom to* vote for one's preferred leader or otherwise act with minimal interference from government.

As Chapter 19 ("The Economy and Work") explains, however, capitalism fosters considerable inequality of wealth, which has fueled criticism of Western societies as neither free nor democratic because wealth gives some people the power to impose their will on others. From this standpoint, popular elections are unlikely to change the capitalist system, so political rituals have little practical importance or impact. Whoever is elected presides over a society that permits some to enjoy lavish housing, extensive education, and abundant health care while necessities are denied to others.

For most of this century, the Soviet Union and the nations of Eastern Europe had centralized, government-controlled economies. Socialist governments in these societies demanded that individuals act in ways that officials deemed socially responsible, and leaders monitored social life in order to provide every citizen with a job, housing, schooling, and medical care. The socialist governments of the Eastern Bloc defended these policies on the basis that they created a more or less equal standard of living for everyone. Thus the Soviet socialist tradition defined "freedom" quite differently from countries in the West: as *freedom from* basic want. By Western standards, at least, these societies lacked the basic elements of democracy, in that their people had no right to elect political leaders, to form opposition parties, or to freely act in their own interests. But officials called theirs a democratic system because government was responsive to the needs of people.

In light of the changes in the socialist world, however, it may be reasonable to ask if economic equality and political liberty are compatible. To foster economic equality, socialism—and the heavy hand of government—infringed on individual initiative. But, by the same token, as these nations have moved toward Western-style political liberty, they are encountering far greater economic inequality.

The political transformation of much of the socialist world has led many analysts in our own society to trumpet the expansion of democracy. The box, which reviews global political shifts during the last decade, explains that an unprecedented share of the world's people now have sufficient political rights and civil liberties to be called "free." A graphic illustration of this transformation appears in Global Map 18-1.

Authoritarianism and Totalitarianism

Despite evidence of a trend toward democracy in some parts of the world, not all nations try to involve their people in politics. **Authoritarianism** refers to *any political system that denies popular participation in government*. As we have already explained, no society involves all its citizens in the daily activities of government, so every political system is authoritarian to some

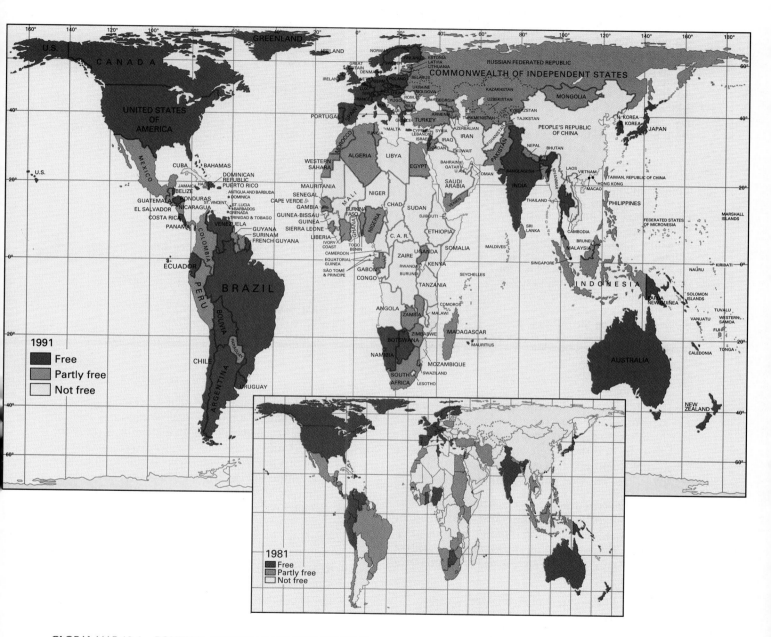

GLOBAL MAP 18-1   POLITICAL FREEDOM IN GLOBAL PERSPECTIVE

In 1991, sixty-seven of the world's nations that contained almost 40 percent of all people were politically "free." Another fifty nations that included almost 30 percent of the world's people were "partly free." Another thirty nations with about one-third of humanity remained "not free." Comparing the two maps shows that, during the 1980s, democratic gains were made in Eastern Europe, the former Soviet Union, and South America. Political rights are most extensive in the rich nations of the world and least extensive in poorer countries of Africa and Asia.

A DECADE OF CHANGE

The 1980s: A Decade of Democracy

Beginning with the rise of the Polish trade union Solidarity in the late 1970s, popular opposition to socialist governments swelled throughout Eastern Europe. The "opening" of these tightly controlled societies intensified after 1985 when Mikhail Gorbachev came to power in the Soviet Union and initiated his program of *perestroika* or "restructuring." In the final months of 1989, the people of Eastern Europe toppled unpopular socialist governments like so many dominoes first in Poland, then in Hungary, East Germany, Bulgaria, Czechoslovakia, and Romania. Long-time dissatisfaction erupted into action when it became clear that the former Soviet Union lacked the power or the will to sustain their existing socialist governments.

The future of political life in these countries is far from clear, as

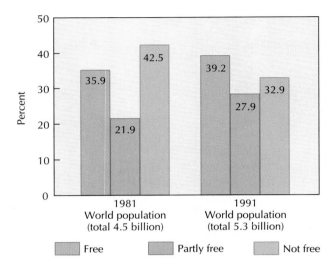

FIGURE 18-1   GLOBAL DEMOCRACY, 1981 AND 1991
SOURCES: Based on Mathews (1991) and McColm et al. (1991).

degree. Therefore, we should reserve this term for political systems that are broadly indifferent to people's lives, in which leaders cannot be legally removed from office, and that provide the people with little or no way to voice their opinions. Polish sociologist Wlodzimierz Wesolowski (1990:435) puts the matter this way:

> [In a democracy,] the self-organizing principle of society takes precedence over the organizing activity of the state, so that society is the ultimate source of power. The authoritarian philosophy argues for the supremacy of the state [over other] organized social activity.

Although absolute monarchies are now rare, they illustrate highly authoritarian political systems. A more common example of an authoritarian political system in the modern world is the military dictatorship. Examples include the regime of Juan and Eva Peron in Argentina during the 1940s and 1950s, and the military juntas that have ruled Chile, the Philippines, Haiti, and Panama. Here, again, we can point to nations that have become more democratic in recent years.

The greatest measure of political control of a society by government is termed **totalitarianism,** *a political system that denies popular participation in government and also extensively regulates people's lives.* Totalitarian governments are relatively new to the world; they emerged within the last century along with the technological means to rigidly regulate the lives of citizens. The Soviet government as well as the Nazi regime in Germany both had the military power and the electronic technology to broadly monitor the lives of their people. Still more sophisticated equipment for electronic surveillance and computers that store vast amounts of information have increased the potential for government manipulation of a large population.

Totalitarian leaders sometimes claim to embody the will of the people, but more accurately they try to bend people to the will of the government. Such governments form *total* concentrations of power, permitting no organized opposition. Denying the populace the right to assemble for political purposes, totalitarian regimes thrive in an environment of fear and social atomization. Such governments also limit the access of

they struggle to gain a greater measure of economic security. What seems all but certain, however, is that political *pluralism*, meaning many political parties competing for popular support, is replacing the monopoly of power held by Communist parties since World War II.

In 1991, the Communist party's historic monopoly on power also came to an end in the Soviet Union. The former Baltic republics, Latvia, Estonia, and Lithuania, won back the independence they had lost during World War II when the Soviet armies moved westward, and, in 1992, most of the remaining republics formed a new Commonwealth of Independent States.

While Eastern Europe and the former Soviet Union have made dramatic strides toward political freedom, democratic forces are making gains elsewhere as well. Multiple parties are more in evidence now across the continent of Africa; Latin America continues a struggle to recover democratic institutions; and South Asian nations grapple to sustain a drive toward democracy. There are also new threats to democratic institutions— especially the reemergence of nationalism and ethnicity, which has turned people against one another from Ireland to the former Soviet Union to the dividing nation of Yugoslavia and politically tense India. But, on balance, the 1990s opened with greater prospects for political democracy in the world than have existed in recent memory.

According to Freedom House, a New York-based organization that tracks global political trends, almost 40 percent of the world's people—more than 2 billion out of a total of 5.3 billion—are now living in "free" societies with extensive political rights and civil liberties. As shown in Figure 18-1, another 28 percent (1.5 billion) people are "partially free," with more limited rights and liberties. The final one-third of the world's people remain in countries where government sharply restricts individual initiative. Comparing these figures with the percentages a decade ago, the trend toward democracy is unmistakable. Additionally, in 1991—for the first time on record— more of the world's people lived in "free" societies than in nations deemed "not free."

SOURCES: Based on Mathews (1991) and McColm et al. (1991).

---

citizens to information: in the former Soviet Union, for example, the mass media have only recently begun to act independently of the government. Further, that totalitarian state weakened the public capacity for collective action by restricting access to items such as telephone directories, accurate city maps, and copying machines. Another typical tactic of totalitarian governments is to encourage citizens to disclose the allegedly unpatriotic activities of other people—a sure recipe for widespread terror. After the 1989 crackdown on the Beijing democracy movement in the People's Republic of China, for example, officials demanded that citizens report anyone—even their own family members—who had challenged the government.

Because totalitarian governments demand not only outward conformity but inward commitment to their rule, socialization in such societies is intensely political. Schools and the mass media are government controlled, presenting only official versions of events. In North Korea, among the most totalitarian states in the modern world, political banners and pictures of leaders are found everywhere, and pedestrians rarely gain respite from partisan slogans that blare over loudspeakers. These messages serve as constant reminders that the government expects and commands the total support of each citizen. Government indoctrination is especially intense whenever political opposition surfaces. In the aftermath of the prodemocracy movement, for example, Chinese officials subjected students at the sixty-seven Beijing universities to mandatory political "refresher" courses (Arendt, 1958; Kornhauser, 1959; Friedrich & Brzezinski, 1965; Nisbet, 1966; Goldfarb, 1989).

Although they always coerce a population toward conformity with the party line, totalitarian governments span the political spectrum from the far right (Nazi Germany) to the far left (North Korea and Albania). Unlike Canadians, who are more accustomed to government regulation of the economy, many people in the United States view socialist societies as totalitarian by definition. Yet socialism (an economic system) is not synonymous with totalitarianism (a political system). Socialism generally means pervasive government involvement in everyday life. But limited socialism—as it exists in Canada and, to a greater extent, in Sweden,

The concept of political liberty burned in the minds of many European thinkers during the eighteenth and nineteenth centuries; authoritarian regimes were often just as intent on stamping out dissent. In The Third of May, 1808, the Spanish painter Francisco Goya (1746–1828) commemorates the death of Madrid citizens at the hands of faceless soldiers. The martyrs shown here are dying not for religious salvation, as in so much medieval art, but for the modern principle of political freedom.

—meshes quite easily with political democracy. Then, too, some societies with capitalist economies, including Chile and South Africa, exercise totalitarian control over the lives of most of their citizens.

Politics in Canada

Canada's national existence arises on the other side of the political upheaval that gave birth to the United States. As Seymour Martin Lipset points out, "The United States is the country of the revolution, Canada of the counterrevolution." The Americans sought "a form of rule derived from the people and stressing individualism," while Canadians desired "free institutions within a strong monarchical state" (1991:1). Life, liberty and the pursuit of happiness would be the goals of our neighbors to the south: we chose peace, order and good government.

Part of the impetus for Confederation was economic, but the leaders in various parts of what was to become Canada were all watching a little nervously over their shoulders, fearing economic and political absorption, if not military conquest, by the increasingly populous and aggressive United States. The various parts of Canada came together somewhat reluctantly: Newfoundlanders initially rejected confederation in a 1869 election and the people of Nova Scotia would have done the same had they been asked to vote on the issue. Nowhere did political union occur without vig-

orous debate and passionate opposition. Table 18-1 reveals that Canada, as we know it today, was formed in bits and pieces from 1867 to 1949, when Newfoundland had been enticed, at last, to vote yes to confederation in a referendum.[1]

It is important to realize that, because the provinces joined Canada at different times and through various kinds of agreements, they have never had uniform relationships with the federal government. Furthermore, Quebec was seen as unique from the beginning because of its French-speaking Catholic majority. Canada is a rather loose confederation in that important powers were left in provincial hands. Questions of federal-provincial jurisdiction (i.e., the centralization or decentralization of power) have been with us since 1867: they are old and persistent questions that we cannot expect to resolve for all time. Canada's provincial structure, its geographic size and diversity, and its immigration and settlement history have added an important regional dimension to our collective identity and to Canadian politics. The presence of Quebec as the only entity with a French-speaking majority in North America adds a special dimension to our "Canadian" experience in terms of identity, federal-provincial relations, and unity. Our existence as a "fragile federation" (Marsden & Harvey, 1979), ever mindful of the factors that divide and unite us, is expressed in our

---

[1] The most influential proponent of Newfoundland's union with Canada was the soon-to-be premier, Joseph Smallwood.

The members of the House of Commons represent the 295 electoral districts distributed across the country according to population. The daily "Question Period" gives members of the opposition parties a chance to grill the prime minister and cabinet ministers in front of the television cameras.

The government of the Northwest Territories is conducted in eight languages, including Inuktitut, Slavey, and Dogrib. Translation occurs simultaneously from the language of the speaker into English and from English into the other seven languages of the listeners. Here we see the Dogrib interpreters in action.

TABLE 18-1 DATES OF ENTRY INTO CONFEDERATION	
New Brunswick	July 1, 1867
Nova Scotia	July 1, 1867
Ontario	July 1, 1867
Quebec	July 1, 1867
Manitoba	July 15, 1870
North-West Territory*	July 15, 1870
British Columbia	July 20, 1871
Prince Edward Island	July 1, 1873
Newfoundland	March 31, 1949

*Rupert's Land (including central to northern Ontario and Quebec) and the area west to B.C. and north to the Arctic purchased from the Hudson's Bay Company.
SOURCE: Waite, 1988.

periodic (or seemingly continuous) constitutional navel-gazing.

Canadians are represented in Parliament by the Senate (an appointed body with 104 seats apportioned on a regional basis to the Maritimes, Ontario, Quebec, and the West[2]) and the House of Commons (with 295 seats distributed roughly on the basis of population). The fact that Quebec and Ontario together elect 59 percent, or 174, of the 295 members of Parliament means that they have a decisive impact on which party wins the most seats, and therefore on who becomes prime minister. In addition, the predominance of MPs from

Ontario and Quebec reduces the likelihood that legislation unfavorable to the interests of central Canada will be passed by Parliament. The unhappiness of the peripheral provinces with the political clout of central Canada at both House of Commons and Senate levels is behind the quest for a *Triple-E senate* that is equal, effective, and elected. Equal representation for all provinces at the Senate level would counter the Quebec-Ontario dominance in the House.

Culture, Economics, and Politics

Unlike Americans, who embrace individualism wholeheartedly, Canadians endorse it with ambivalence: our individualism is tempered by a sense of communal responsibility, a recognition of legitimate *group* interests, and a recognition that we are, in the words of former prime minister Joe Clark, a "community of communities." When the Trudeau government gave us our Charter of Rights and Freedoms in 1982, analysts pointed out that, in a sense, we had moved closer to embracing the individualism of the United States:

> *The most striking change in the north was the 1982 incorporation in the constitution of a due-process bill of rights. The Canadian Charter of Rights and Freedoms is not the American Bill of Rights. It preserves the principle of parliamentary supremacy and places less emphasis upon individual, as distinct from group, rights than does the American document. But the Charter brings Canada much closer to the*

---

[2] There are twenty-four seats for each of the regions named plus six for Newfoundland and one each for the Yukon and Northwest Territories.

American stress on protection of the individual and acceptance of judicial supremacy with its accompanying encouragement to litigiousness than is true of other parliamentary countries. (Lipset, 1990:3)

In accordance with our (still strong) emphasis on the collectivity, Canadians expect and endorse a broadly interventionist government. Although in recent years, Canadians have been increasingly worried about the costs of government activity, they nonetheless expect one or another level of government to deal with national defense, law and order, international relations, radio and television broadcasting, stabilization of the economy, regional development, pensions, unemployment insurance, welfare, roads, railways, buses and subways, education (right up through university), and medical care. In fact, to the extent that we can articulate a "Canadian" identity, it is based upon some of the government services that make us a tolerant and caring society. The widespread anxiety about free trade with the United States arose, certainly, from the fear of job loss, but also from the fear that resulting pressures to harmonize with our powerful neighbor to the south would threaten our social welfare programs and particularly our medicare system.

Government in Canada is more involved in the daily lives of its citizens than is the American government, but this does not mean that there is complete agreement among Canadians regarding the appropriateness of that involvement. Some people feel that governments should take an even *more* activist role in areas like child care, job creation, minority rights, employment or pay equity, and environmental protection. Others feel that government already does far too much, at too great expense, and that it should be withdrawing many of its programs, and encouraging privatization of services where feasible. These differences in perspective are in part a function of socio-economic status and regional subculture, and are reflected in the policies and platforms of Canada's political parties.

Political Parties

Since about the time of Confederation, Canadians have joined together to form **political parties**, *organizations operating within the political system that seek control of the government.* Although we take political parties for granted today as part of a democratic system, the party system had tentative beginnings here (and was hotly debated in the United States, where George Washington and Benjamin Franklin, among others, feared that

parties would tear their fledgling nation apart).

The political parties that we know today trace their roots to the period after 1940, when the United Provinces of Upper and Lower Canada came into being. In fact, it was a "Liberal-Conservative" coalition of factions under Sir George Etienne Cartier and Sir John A. Macdonald that provided sufficient political stability to allow for the negotiation of Confederation. The first House of Commons had, among others, "Tory" (Conservative) and "Grit" (Liberal) factions that, by 1867, were beginning to align themselves with specific sets of policies and supporters. The Tories were "firmly protectionist, expansionist, and pro-business," while the Grits were "anti-railroad, anti-protectionist, and pro-agrarian" (Van Loon & Whittington, 1981:326–7). After the First World War, a number of minor parties appeared on the scene, the most long-lived of which was the anti-capitalist CCF-NDP, or the Cooperative Commonwealth Federation, which became the New Democratic party after 1961.

In recent years, Canada has had close to twenty registered political parties at the federal level alone. Although each of these has fielded candidates in ridings across the country, only the Progressive Conservative, Liberal, New Democratic, and Social Credit parties have elected MPs in significant numbers over extended periods of time. In fact, by the elections of 1980, 1984, and 1988, Social Credit was no longer winning any seats, leaving three major contenders.

Of the remaining parties, many of which are regional (such as the Bloc Québécois) or appeal to a specific interest group (for example the Green Party), almost all are very serious about particular issues and winning seats. The notable exception is the Rhinoceros party which was founded in 1963 with the express purpose of making fun of politicians and the political process. With their outrageous clothes and even *more* outrageously humorous election platforms, Rhinoceros Party candidates provide an outlet for those who want to protest the whole political process without simply spoiling their ballots: at the same time, they add to the entertainment value of Canadian politics for the rest of us. In the 1984 election, eighty-nine Rhino candidates across the country won 99,207 votes or an astounding 0.8 percent of the national vote (Bernard, 1988). The largest chunk of this support came from a small number of ridings in the center of Montreal.

Functions of Political Parties

Political parties in Canada and elsewhere have the following key societal functions:

In the Bathrooms of the Nation?

When Pierre Trudeau was Minister of Justice in the Pearson government, he brought forward a divorce reform bill and amendments to the Criminal Code which liberalized laws on homosexuality and abortion. Trudeau caught the attention of Canadians by announcing in front of television cameras that "The state has no place in the bedrooms of the nation" (Clarkson and McCall, 1990:107)

In this excerpt from their book, Van Loon and Whittington play on Trudeau's quip.

If it is true as one prominent Canadian public figure once stated that "the government has no place in the bedrooms of the nation," it is clear that government has surely found a place in every other room of the house. Picture for a moment a middle-aged political scientist standing in front of his bathroom mirror about to

scrape the excess hair from his haggard features. "In here," he might be over-heard to say with satisfaction, "the government certainly has no place."

But then he might pause and ponder his immediate surroundings. He notices that there is a little note etched on the corner of the mirror which indicates that this particular piece of glass meets a certain government standard. The label on the aerosol can containing his shaving cream warns him, "Do not puncture or incinerate." A government agency somewhere has decided that such warnings are neccessary. The same label tells him that the can contains "350 mL" (however much that is!), because still another government agency has abolished fluid ounces; moreover, the government requires that the information on the label be repeated in the two official languages. As he brushes his teeth, our hero, by now on the verge of paranoia, remembers that

the electricity and the water in the small room are supplied by public utilities, and that the municipality puts various chemicals in the water to protect him from typhoid, dysentery, tooth decay, and sundry other public health horrors. Trembling with the embarrassment of how public his bathroom has become, he glances out the window and notices an elderly gentleman walking his dog along the municipally owned and operated sidewalk. The dog is on a leash because a municipal by-law decrees it; and, as if to add insult to injury, the man is carrying a small shovel and a little plastic "doggie bag" because the municipality is very concerned about keeping its streets clean.

SOURCE: *Richard J. Van Loon & Michael S. Whittington. The Canadian Political System: Environment, Structure, and Process. 3rd ed. Toronto: McGraw-Hill Ryerson, 1981:1.*

1. **Promoting political pluralism.** Political parties create centers of power independent of the government. This is why totalitarian governments routinely quash all political parties, save their own.

2. **Increasing political involvement.** Parties draw people into the political process by articulating various points of view about controversial issues. They function as reference groups that help people shape their individual opinions. Political campaigns encourage public debate, helping to make government more responsive to the people.

3. **Selection of political candidates.** Political parties nominate candidates to run for office. Through nomination meetings in each constituency, local party members choose the candidates who will run for office in the next election.[3] Whenever the

national or provincial parties are selecting new leaders, the riding associations elect the delegates who go to the leadership conventions.[4]

4. **Forging political coalitions.** While parties can divide a society, they often forge broad coalitions among people interested in various specific issues. Party platforms usually incorporate a wide range of proposals so that the party will appeal to many people, making victory at the polls more likely. Many nations have dozens of narrowly based political parties. Canada might be characterized as having a two-and-a-half party system in that, although the NDP has won twenty to forty seats almost consistently since 1965, it has never managed to form the government at the federal level.

5. **Maintaining political stability.** By maintaining relatively consistent positions on a number of issues,

---

[3] In the 1993 pre-election period, the Liberal party ruffled more than a few feathers by promoting and even appointing certain hand-picked candidates. In some cases, "stars" from outside the ridings were "parachuted" in despite bitter local protest. One of the goals of the Liberal party at that time was to have 25 percent female candidates.

[4] Another approach is to have the members-at-large, throughout a province for example, vote for a new leader directly rather than indirectly by electing delegates to a convention. The Alberta Conservatives used this approach in 1993 to elect Ralph Klein as their leader.

the major parties promote political stability. For that reason, of course, those who seek radical change in Canada may lambast political parties in general.

Political Ideology

People commonly label their political views in terms of the political spectrum, a continuum ranging from communism on the left and extreme conservatism on the right. Many Canadians, upon surveying the political scene, conclude that there are no ideological differences among our major political parties (at least not between the Liberals and Conservatives). William Christian (1983) disagrees, noting that there are some very clear and consistent ideological strains that have characterized our parties over time. Our parties and their ideological orientations are the result of our unique political history and European roots, as evidenced by the fact that they are very different from those in the United States. It is certainly true, however, that the ideological *mix* in our parties makes it difficult to accurately place them on a left-right continuum. For example, we have "Red" and "Pink" Tories in our "Progressive" Conservative party.

The political left in Canada can be described as anti-capitalist (or anti-big business), egalitarian, collectivist, and interventionist. It is supportive of universal child care, education, and medicare, as well as a broad safety net of social welfare programs. Government or public ownership and regulation of major industries, unionization, inheritance taxes, and rates of taxation that increase with income (progressive taxation) are also part of its policy wish list. Free trade with the United States (the FTA) or with the United States and Mexico (NAFTA) are not supported by the left because of its apparent and potential negative effects upon employment (especially in manufacturing) and social programs.

As one might expect, those on the political right espouse a different set of values and goals. They are in favor of private enterprise, big business, and free markets. Although they might be elitist and individualistic in some respects, they also have collectivist sentiments. Competitiveness, globalization, restructuring, deficit reduction, and privatization (of Crown corporations) are laudable goals in the eyes of the right, as are private property rights, tax exemptions for capital gains, the FTA and NAFTA. Those on the right generally feel that, while government expenditures on social programs are necessary, they should be restricted by our ability to pay for them.

Parties on the Political Spectrum

As noted above, one places Canadian parties on a left-right continuum with some hesitation, knowing that each party, in itself, is a mixed bag and that there is always some movement in party positions. All three of our major parties have moved a little to the right in the past few years, in response to developments in the U.S. and widespread anxieties about government deficits and debt. Nevertheless, Figure 18-2 suggests the approximate location of some of our national parties on this scale.

It would be difficult to place some of our other parties on the left-right axis in Figure 18-2. The Bloc Québécois has as its central aims disruption of the House of Commons and the political independence of Quebec, environmental or ecological issues are the *raison d'être* of the Green party, and the Rhinoceros party is engaged in generalized protest and fun.

Party Support

Although many Canadians live their lives as supporters of *one* particular political party, and may even come from families which for generations have supported the same one, most of us are considerably more fickle. As a result of changes in party platforms, leaders, dominant issues, or the general economic and political climate, as well as social or geographic mobility at the individual level, there are people who can say they have voted for all three of the major parties (and maybe even a minor or protest party) at some point in their lives. It is also

FIGURE 18-2   SELECTED CANADIAN POLITICAL PARTIES ON A LEFT-RIGHT CONTINUUM

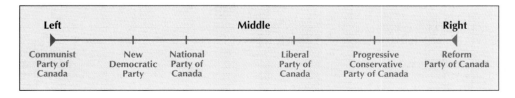

very common for Canadians to vote for different parties at federal and provincial levels, even when the elections are only weeks or months apart. Many observers of the Quebec political scene argue that the Québécois hedge their bets by voting for a separatist party (Parti Québécois) at the provincial level and the Liberals or Conservatives federally, or the Bloc Québécois federally and the Liberals provincially. As strange as it might seem to an outside observer, this kind of split voting can be the result of cool calculation rather than confusion on the part of the voter.

Fickleness notwithstanding, there *are* observable patterns in party support (Meisel. 1975; Gerber 1986; Bashevkin, 1993). People are more likely to support the NDP if they are blue-collar workers, unionized, and male. When they live in a homogeneous working-class neighborhood or riding, or in a province where the NDP has a reasonable chance of assuming power, the tendency to vote NDP is reinforced. Ridings in which a large proportion of the population is employed in mining or manufacturing tend to be supportive of the NDP. The Progressive Conservatives are supported in affluent areas where residents are well-educated, British, and Protestant, but *also* in farming communities and non-unionized working-class neighborhoods. In other words, the PCs are supported at both ends of the affluence scale (Gerber, 1986). The Liberals are more likely to be supported by the affluent and highly educated as well as by recent immigrants. In addition, historically, the Liberals have been able to count on widespread support in Quebec and among French-Canadians in other provinces: the major exceptions in Quebec occurred in the "Diefomania" election of 1958 and the Mulroney landslides of 1984 and 1988 when the Conservatives took fifty, fifty-eight, and sixty-three seats (out of seventy-five) respectively.

Figure 18-3 reveals the variation in support, by province and territory for various political parties in the 1988 election. Conservative support ranged from over 50 percent in Quebec and Alberta to 26 percent in the Northwest Territories: the party won the election with 43 percent of the popular vote and 57 percent of the seats.[5] Overall, the PCs had their strongest support

---

[5] Note that the lack of fit between percentage of the popular vote and percentage of seats is due to the fact that the winner is the person who has the *most* votes. One can win at the riding level with 40 percent of the vote or even less if there are five or more parties fielding candidates.

FIGURE 18-3 SUPPORT FOR THE THREE MAJOR POLITICAL PARTIES IN THE 1988 FEDERAL ELECTION
SOURCE: Report of the Chief Electoral Officer, 1988; Colombo, 1992:150.

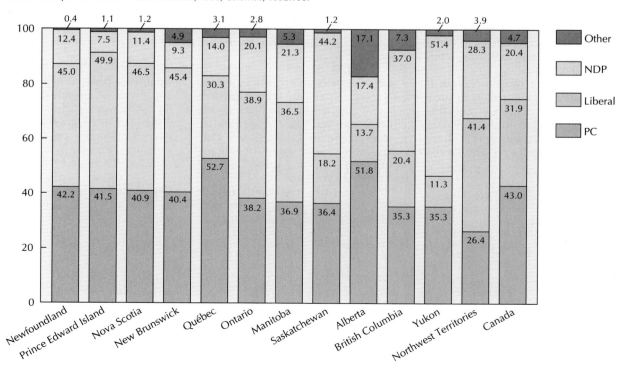

Native Self-Government

Canada's Native peoples have never been treated just like other Canadians—and there have been good historical reasons for distinctive treatment. When the first European explorers and settlers arrived in Canada, they encountered fifty-five *founding nations* or *First Nations* (Dickson, 1992), distinct linguistic and cultural groups spread across the continent and north to the Arctic. The groups were self-governing within traditional territories and had formal relationships between tribes. In the case of the Iroquois or Six Nations Confederacy*, they had an elaborate constitution and federal structure. Fifty hereditary peace chiefs met yearly to deal with common problems and make new laws. "The laws and decisions of the Confederacy, though unwritten, were passed on by word of mouth and recorded in wampum, arguably the world's oldest constitution, predating the American Constitution by 200 years" (Nader et al., 1992). Some aspects of this constitution, which takes seven days to recite, were incorporated into the federal structures of both the United States and Canada.

The First Nations taught the explorers and early settlers to survive on this harsh continent, and introduced the settlers to the agricultural production of corn, squash, beans, potatoes, and tobacco. The fur trade

*Known as the League of Five Nations (Mohawk, Cayuga, Onondaga, Oneida, and Seneca) until they were joined by the Tuscorora in 1722.

Constitutional affairs minister, Joe Clark, and Ovide Mercredi, leader of the Assembly of First Nations, participated in the negotiations that led to the Charlottetown Accord. Had it been supported in the constitutional referendum of October 26, 1992, the inherent right to self-government by aboriginal peoples would have been given constitutional recognition.

would have been impossible without Native expertise, labor, and the *canoe*, the design of which has not been improved (Nader at al. 1992). If most of the Six Nations, with their widespread reputation for military prowess, had not sided with the British against the French in the 1750s and with the British and the Loyalists (1777) during the American Revolution, Canada might now be either French or part of the U.S.A. As the Americans launched their attack on Canada in 1812, the British had concluded that "Amerindian support was vital to the preservation of Britain's remaining North American colonies" (Dickson, 1992:217).

As settlers began to flow into Canada, the old fur trade partners and military allies found themselves in conflict as pressures built up over land. In order to avoid the kind of Native resistance to settlement that had occurred in the United States, a number of treaties were negotiated with some groups, dating from the pre-Confederation period in the Maritimes through to 1921 in the Northwest Territories. The descendants of the Natives who signed treaties are now called *treaty or status Indians*.

The terms of the treaties varied over time and across the country (Frideres, 1993) but most commonly they involved the surrender of lands in exchange for reserves and other guarantees. The interpretation of the treaties has been the subject of considerable debate for, in some cases, the actual wording of the treaties did not coincide with the understandings Native people had about their contents. More importantly, in light of the current quest for self-government, there is debate about whether or not the existence of treaties implied recognition of Native sovereignty. Whatever the technicalities (and there *are* indications that sovereignty was recognized) many Native peoples believe that they *were* sovereign prior to the treaties and that the treaties did not extinguish that sovereignty. Of course, Native groups who were never party to treaties could not have extinguished sovereignty by that means.

When Canada's Constitution was finally patriated in 1982, section 35 recognized and affirmed the existing aboriginal and treaty rights of aboriginal peoples, including Indian, Inuit, and Métis. Five years later,

when the Meech Lake accord was negotiated in an effort to get Quebec to sign on to the Constitution, Native people's request that it recognize their right to self-government was ignored altogether. A technicality in Manitoba allowed a Native member of the Legislative Assembly, Elijah Harper, the historic opportunity to scuttle "Meech" just before its ratification deadline in 1990.

During the next round of constitutional negotiation, representatives of four Native organizations sat at the negotiation table with provincial representatives and later the premiers, with the result that the Charlottetown accord of August 1992 recognized the *inherent*** right to self-government of Native people. The "Canada Clause" notes that "the Aboriginal peoples of Canada, being the first peoples to govern this land, have the right to promote their languages, cultures and traditions and to ensure the integrity of their societies, and their governments constitute one of three orders of government in Canada." The defeat of this accord in the referendum of October 26, 1992 (see Canada Map 18-1) was a bitter disappointment to the Native negotiators. The likelihood is small that a combination of historic conditions, political personalities, and public mood will

***This terminology is very important because it implies that the right to self-government is neither granted to them by the Canadian government nor subject to repeal. Instead, the right is based on aboriginal status and granted by their Creator.

generate a similar compromise in the foreseeable future.

In the meantime, a number of Native communities have proceeded to manage their affairs as if the constitutional accord had been ratified, and the Royal Commission on Aboriginal Peoples (Platiel, *Globe and Mail*, Aug. 19, 1993:A4) has declared that the right of Aboriginal peoples to govern themselves pre-dates Confederation, has a basis in Canadian law, and is already protected in our Constitution. A number of formal self-government agreements have already been negotiated between various Native groups, the federal government, and their respective provinces, and new ones are under consideration.

The most dramatic development in the area of self-government is taking place in the Northwest Territories, which decided in a 1992 plebescite to carve a new territory out of its eastern region. Nunavut, with one-fifth of Canada's land mass and a clear Inuit majority, will become a distinct entity with its own territorial government in 1999. Although the development of Nunavut will be enhanced by the existence of the Inuit Broadcasting Corporation (IBC), numerous successful cooperatives, and experienced Inuit business people, the Inuit people will still face formidable challenges. Low levels of educational attainment (Gerber, 1990), devastating social problems, and weak pan-Inuit traditions will complicate the situation as the people of Nunavut assume the tasks of territorial self-government.

in the Maritimes, Quebec, and Alberta, the Liberals in the Maritime provinces, and the NDP in Saskatchewan, BC, and the Territories. In other words, support for the various parties is *not* evenly distributed across the country. To the extent that such patterns persist over time, they suggest the existence of distinct regional political cultures.

Politics and the Individual

The Canadian political system, being democratic, responds in principle to the needs and judgments of the electorate. But how do people acquire political attitudes in the first place? And to what extent do we use our right to participate in the political system?

Political Socialization

Pierre Trudeau and Brian Mulroney are among the prime ministers of Canada who raised young children at 24 Sussex Drive and Harrington Lake, the prime minister's official summer residence. Although both of these parents probably shielded them from many aspects of political life, their children undoubtedly learned the basic tenets of liberalism and conservatism from their fathers. These families are unusual in that they are intensely involved in politics: as a result of more intimate exposure one would expect their children to be very much aware of politics and, at a tender age, to have clear party affiliations.

Political attitudes, like other elements of culture, are aquired through the socialization process. The major agents of socialization, which also shape our political views, are the family, the schools, and the mass media (see Chapter 5, "Socialization"). Of these, the family is in a position to exert the earliest influence.

The family is a powerful agent of socialization; not surprisingly, then, children typically come to share many opinions held by their parents. Because neighborhoods and schools tend to be relatively homogeneous in socio-economic terms, a child's initial peer groups are likely to reinforce ideas about the world learned at home. In Canada, a large minority of children express a partisan preference by Grade 4 and by Grade 8 a majority do so (Van Loon & Whittington, 1981:122).

Children are more likely to learn about politics if their families are actively involved, if there is a great deal of political "talk" in the household, and if their families are are of higher socio-economic status. Also male children absorb political information and identify

political symbols at an earlier age than their female counterparts.

As described in Chapter 16 ("Education"), schools teach the culture's dominant political values, one of them being respect for authority. Our school children also learn to recognize political symbols, such as the flag, the prime minister, and the Queen, and like children elsewhere, start off with warm, fuzzy feelings about these political icons. Interestingly, in grades 4 and 5, over 70 percent of children choose the Queen as their favorite (over the prime minister or governor general) and not until Grade 8 does a majority (53 percent) realize that the prime minister is more powerful that the Queen, whose role is entirely ceremonial (Van Loon & Whittington, 1981:121).

Canada did not have its own flag until 1965, and our children sang *God Save the Queen* until we adopted *O Canada* as our national anthem in 1980. Furthermore, very few schools offer anything like the formal "civics" classes found in American schools. Our political socialization appears to be both more subtle and more informal that that in the U.S.

The mass media, too, convey values and opinions pertaining to politics. Conservatives sometimes charge the media with having a "left-wing agenda," while critics on the left complain that what is packaged as "news" really amounts to support for the status quo. Specific newspapers are frequently identified as having "Liberal" or "Conservative" sympathies, and some of the francophone media in Quebec have been labeled as separatist.

Although the media may have their specific ideological slants, it is not entirely clear that they are successful in converting their readers or viewers at a basic philosophical level. On the other hand, there is little doubt that the media are active players in the day to day conduct of politics and that their involvement has changed the way that politics is "done." Good "soundbites" and catchy phrases are gold to the politician, especially when uttered in time for the evening news. Advertising consumes a major part of election campaign budgets, and image takes precedence over substance.

The image projected on nightly television can help to make or break a political career as our former, short-term prime ministers Joe Clark and John Turner have learned. Televised debates between the leaders of political parties are *almost* mandatory in today's political climate, and can have a significant impact on the voters' impressions of the party leaders (Widdis Barr, 1991).

As we saw in Chapter 2 ("Sociological Investigation"), opinion polls are particularly worrisome to some observers of the political scene. Do polls reflect or shape public opinion? If Conservative fortunes seem to be rising, does the appearance of increasing support, in turn, pull more people onto the PC party wagon? Since the polls measure change as it is happening, it is very difficult to determine cause and effect.

Other agents of political socialization are the many organizations to which people belong. Some of these are professional, ethnic, or voluntary associations, unions, or special interest organizations like women's groups. From time to time, some churches attempt to mobilize their members behind a particular cause such as fighting abortion or arranging for the sponsorship of refugees. Seniors clubs might form initially to encourage social interaction among elders but find themselves marching on Ottawa to protest the deindexing of pensions. Political parties themselves would normally recruit people already inclined to be political activists, but, having done so, they may increase participation levels, political knowledge and sophistication, and partisanship. Some of these organizations are founded for political purposes: others with a wide range of nonpolitical goals become political only as a result of specific circumstances.

Political Participation

Needless to say, socialization does not increase *everyone's* political involvement or enthusiasm for our system of government; on the contrary, significant segments of our population learn that the political system responds little, if at all, to their needs. Indifference or even hostility toward the political system is evident among those who are disadvantaged and feel powerless to remedy the situation. In other cases, those who become committed and actively involved in political action may turn away disillusioned when they see how the political system actually works. In fact, as the Spicer Commission reported in 1991, Canadians have become increasingly cynical about politicians and the political process in general.

Years ago, Lester Milbrath (1965) proposed a typology reflecting a *hierarchy of participation* in electoral politics. He classified individual participation as falling into *gladiatorial, transitional and spectator* roles. At the gladiatorial level, participants are actually involved in the political fray (as in attending strategy meetings or running for political office); at the transitional level, one might contact a politician, contribute time in a campaign, or give money to a political party; and, as a spectator one might express interest in poli-

tics, expose oneself to political information, and vote (and then sit back to watch the returns on television).

According to a 1974 survey, at most 5 percent of Canadians are involved at the gladiatorial level. Another 40 percent participate at the transitional level, most commonly attending a rally or "all candidates" meeting and trying to influence the votes of friends or coworkers. At the opposite extreme, only 5 percent said that they had *never* voted in a federal election: 80 to 90 percent engage in informal discussion about elections with friends and follow the campaign to some extent through the media. Although people are a little less inclined to vote in provincial than federal elections, other types of participation seem to be similar at both levels of government (Van Loon & Whittington. 1981).

In any specific federal election about 75 percent or more of the eligible voters come out to the polls (compared to roughly 50 to 55 percent in the U.S.). Turnout for provincial elections is generally a little lower and in municipal elections lower still. To the extent that elections constitute spectator sport, turnout improves if it is a good race.

Canadian participation levels were high at every stage of the constitutional negotiations leading to the defeat of the Charlottetown accord in 1992. After the

Here a Canadian of Sikh origin acts as a scrutineer during an election, checking voter eligibility and, later, counting ballots. Fifty years ago, he (like other Asians) would not have had the right to vote in Canada.

defeat of the Meech Lake accord, public demands for wider participation in future constitutional discussions led to the creation in November, 1990, of the Spicer Commission, which involved town-hall and home meetings. In the end more than 400,000 Canadians had participated in the sometimes painful, intensely introspective debate about our constitution.

On the basis of the Spicer report and other input, the government presented twenty-eight constitutional proposals (September, 1991) through widely distributed pamphlets, and the *Globe and Mail* published a "Constitutional Primer" to facilitate discussion across the country. The Beaudoin-Dobbie Commission (Jan. 1992) organized five regional conferences on the major themes. Again, a cross-section of Canadians responded to the invitation to participate. Canada Map 18-1 reveals tremendous variation from east to west in support for the Charlottetown accord—from 74 percent in PEI to 32 percent in B.C. While opinions varied considerably across the country, a remarkable 72 percent of eligible voters turned out to say "yes" or "no" to this very complex document. Canadians, although divided, were certainly not apathetic about their constitutional future.

The Participation of Women

The women's suffrage movement began in Canada in the 1880s, but since it had to function simultaneously at the provincial and federal levels, it was subject to all "the regional conflicts and divisions that characterized

other Canadian social movements" (Bashevkin, 1993: 4). Despite divisions that were especially damaging to this movement, women in Canada finally acquired the right to vote at the federal level in 1918. Manitoba was the first province to extend the franchise to women (1916), while Quebec was the last (1940).

The extension of the franchise to women set the scene for a series of political firsts. Agnes Macphail quickly ran for and won federal political office (1921), but she had to deal with numerous obstacles—including people who said "We can't have a woman." It was not until 1957 that Canada had its first female cabinet minister at the federal level, Ellen Fairclough, and 1984 before women were given portfolios other than those deemed most "suited" to women, like health, education, or the status of women. Brian Mulroney broke this pattern at the federal level by appointing Pat Carney to international trade, Barbara McDougall to junior finance, and Kim Campbell to the justice portfolio (Bashevkin, 1993:88). Audrey McLaughlin became the first federal party leader in 1989, and Kim Campbell's leadership win in 1993 automatically made her Canada's first female prime minister. Although in ideological and practical terms the NDP has been most persistent, over the long term, in the promotion of women, these firsts involve all three of the major parties.

Despite these highly visible firsts, it is important to realize that, overall, women are underrepresented in politics. The tendency has been for women to be on the support staff of the political party rather than the candi-

When Kim Campbell won the leadership of the Progressive Conservative Party in June of 1993, she automatically became Canada's first female prime minister. Polls conducted immediately after Campbell became prime minister showed that PC support had increased substantially among women.

date: the higher one goes within the party hierarchy, the smaller the representation of women. Where women have been candidates, it has been for minor parties or in ridings where a win would be unlikely. One also finds that the proportion female among those running for office and winning is greatest at the municipal level, somewhat lower at the provincial level and lower still at the federal level.

There has been a steady increase in the number of women elected at the federal level in recent years, with the representation of females among the successful candidates increasing from 5 percent in 1980 to 9.6 percent in 1984 and 13.2 percent in 1988. This figure is high compared with the United States, Britain, and France, which have legislatures that are about 6 percent female,

but low when compared with Finland, Sweden, Norway, and Denmark where 32 to 38 percent of MPs are female (Bashevkin, 1993:87, 153–4).[7] Among the barriers to women's participation are socialization, lack of financing or contacts, and the electoral system itself. To the extent that gender stereotypes contribute to resistance on the part of voters and reluctance on the part of potential female candidates, the arrival of Kim Campbell in the prime minister's office may expand horizons—but then Agnes Macphail thought that many women would immediately follow in her footsteps.

---

[7] The NDP government elected in Ontario in 1990 was 27 percent female.

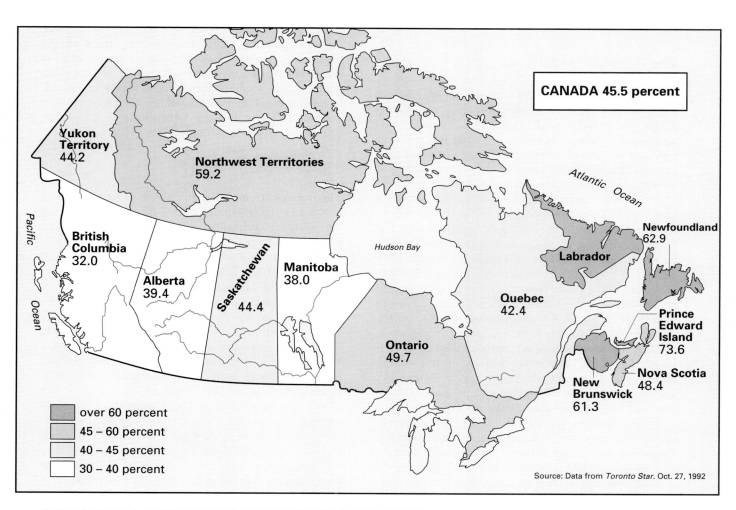

CANADA 45.5 percent

Yukon Territory 44.2

Northwest Territories 59.2

British Columbia 32.0

Alberta 39.4

Saskatchewan 44.4

Manitoba 38.0

Ontario 49.7

Quebec 42.4

Hudson Bay

Atlantic Ocean

Labrador

Newfoundland 62.9

Prince Edward Island 73.6

Nova Scotia 48.4

New Brunswick 61.3

Pacific Ocean

over 60 percent
45 – 60 percent
40 – 45 percent
30 – 40 percent

Source: Data from *Toronto Star*. Oct. 27, 1992

CANADA MAP 18-1   SUPPORT FOR THE CHARLOTTETOWN ACCORD:REFERENDUM 1992 (PERCENT VOTING "YES," BY PROVINCE AND TERRITORY)

Theoretical Analysis of Power in Society

For most of this century, sociologists and political scientists have debated the answers to some basic questions about power in our society: How is power distributed? Who makes the decisions? Whose interests does government serve?

Power is among the most difficult topics of scientific research because decision making is complex and often occurs behind closed doors. Moreover, as Plato recognized more than 2,000 years ago, theories about power are difficult to separate from the beliefs and interests of social thinkers themselves. From this mix of facts and values, two competing models of power have emerged.

The Pluralist Model

Formally, the **pluralist model** is *an analysis of politics in which power is dispersed among many competing interest groups*. The pluralist model is linked to the structural-functional paradigm in sociology; from this point of view, the political system responds to the needs of various constituencies that make up the society, trying to fashion agreements and to strike compromises.

Pluralists claim, first, that politics is an arena of negotiation. There are thousands of interest groups in Canada, most of which seek rather narrow goals. The Canadian Association of University Teachers (CAUT), for example, responds to issues that affect university faculty, leaving to others debates over health policy, the death penalty, or gun control. But even with limited objectives, no organization holds sufficient power to realize all its goals. As a result, organizations often operate as *veto groups*, realizing some success while keeping competitors from achieving all their goals. The political process, then, relies heavily on negotiating alliances and compromises that bridge differences among various interest groups and produce policies that have wide support (Dahl, 1961, 1982).

Government officials play a key role in transforming special interests into popular public policy. They do so by taking account of lobbying efforts on the part of organizations, as well as monitoring public opinion polls and election results. Officials of the federal government also must coordinate their efforts with those of provincial and municipal governments, which,

in turn, are influenced by still more interest groups. In sum, pluralists see power as widely dispersed throughout our society.

A second pluralist assertion holds that power has many sources—including wealth, political office, social prestige, and personal charisma. Only in exceptional cases do all these sources of power fall into the same hands. Here, again, we conclude that power is diffused across a wide spectrum.

In *The Vertical Mosaic: An Analysis of Social Class and Power in Canada* (1965), John Porter addresses the question of who makes the major decisions (or exercises power) in Canada and, on the basis of extensive research, decides that there are competing elites at the top of five major organizational clusters: economic, political, bureaucratic, labor, and ideological (i.e., church, education, and the media). Of the five, the economic or corporate elite and the bureaucratic elite are the most powerful. While there is competition among these elites because of the opposing interests of their respective institutions, Porter also points out that these powerful and wealthy elites are also highly integrated. In order to keep the system working, they are willing to accommodate each other. As a result, we have what one might call cooperative pluralism.

The Power-Elite Model

The **power-elite model** is *an analysis of politics holding that power is concentrated among the rich*. This second approach is closely allied with the social-conflict paradigm in sociology.

The term *power elite* is a lasting contribution of C. Wright Mills (1956), who argued that the upper class holds the bulk of society's wealth, enjoys most of its prestige, and exercises the lion's share of power. The power elite are the "super-rich," families who forge alliances primarily with one another—in corporate boardrooms and at the altar. In this way, Mills noted, a handful of families perpetuate their privileges and ensure that their priorities become the national agenda. This coalition of families dominates the major sectors of society. According to Mills, individual men and women circulate from one sector to another, consolidating their power as they go. Before becoming prime minister, Brian Mulroney was a labor lawyer and then vice-president of Iron Ore Company of Canada. Since stepping down as prime minister, he has returned to Montreal to practice law within the corporate context. It is not unusual for national political leaders to enter public life from powerful and highly paid positions in business—and return to the corporate world later on.

From the perspective of the power-elite model, the concentration of wealth and power in a political democracy like Canada is simply too great for the average person's voice to be heard. Rejecting pluralist assertions that various centers of power serve as checks and balances on one another, the power-elite model maintains that those at the top have no real opposition.

In another important study of Canada's elite, *The Canadian Corporate Elite: Economic Power in Canada* (1975), Wallace Clement argues that Canada is ruled by an economic or corporate elite that is becoming increasingly powerful. As a result of the dense networks that bind the various elites, the economic, political, and bureaucratic elites are blending into one group under corporate elite domination. The members of this group are very likely to have upper class origins and to have a vested interest in maintaining the capitalist system. Clement rejects the pluralist model, noting that the state and private capital are complimantary and mutually dependent. In effect, the state and the capitalists act as one.

Critical evaluation. Table 18-2 summarizes the pluralist and elite models of power, presenting very different analyses and reaching opposing conclusions about the nature of contemporary politics.

Overall, there is probably greater empirical support for the power-elite model. Marked concentration

of wealth and barriers to equal opportunity faced by minorities get in the way of a truly pluralist democracy in Canada. Although this does not mean that the pluralist model is completely wrong, it does suggest that our political system is not as democratic as most people think it is. Although each adult has the right to vote, the choices we make in elections usually are limited to positions acceptable to the most powerful segments of our society. Conservative and Liberal party leaders may offer different approaches to helping the poor, for example, but neither has suggested radically redistributing wealth or abolishing the capitalist system. Even the NDP talks of controlling or regulating the capitalist system rather than overthrowing or replacing it.

On the other hand, even the most powerful members of our society do not always get their way. As long as ordinary people continue to form political associations or express themselves in the context of various interest groups, our society will retain a substantial degree of pluralism. There are numerous examples of situations where the Québécois, Natives, environmentalists, labor unions, or feminists have won concessions and inspired policy changes that are anathema to big business.

Both the pluralist and the power-elite models of social power offer insights into our country's political system. Our political system does afford each person basic rights and offers every segment of the population a political voice—at times a powerful voice. On the other hand, the persistence of social inequality and

TABLE 18-2 THE PLURALIST AND POWER-ELITE MODELS: A COMPARISON

	Pluralist Model	Power-Elite Model
How is power distributed in Canada?	Highly dispersed.	Highly concentrated.
How many centers of power are there?	Many, each with a limited scope.	Few, with power that extends to many areas.
How do centers of power relate to one another?	They represent different political interests and thus provide checks on one another.	They represent the same political interests and face little opposition.
What is the relation between power and the system of social stratification?	Some people have more power than others, but even minority groups can organize to gain power. Wealth, social prestige, and political office rarely overlap.	Most people have little power, and the upper class dominates society. Wealth, social prestige, and political office commonly overlap.
What is the importance of voting?	Voting provides the public as a whole with a political voice.	Voting cannot promote significant political change.
What, then, is the most accurate description of the Canadian political system?	A pluralist democracy.	An oligarchy—rule by the wealthy few.

unequal access to politically relevant resources ensures that some people will continue to have more power than others.

Power Beyond the Rules

Politics is always a matter of disagreement about goals and the means to achieve them. Yet a political system tries to resolve controversy within a system of rules. The Canadian Constitution and Charter of Rights and Freedoms enunciate the values and determine the shape of our political system. Countless other laws and regulations guide the hand of every political official from the prime minister to the enumerator who is hired for a week or two to establish the list of eligible voters before each election. But political activity sometimes exceeds—or tries to do away with—established practices.

Revolution

As we have already explained, political stability depends on transforming power into legitimate authority. Sometimes political systems that lose legitimacy make way for radical alternatives. **Political revolution** is *the overthrow of one political system in favor of another.*

Political revolution is more profound than mere reform. Reform involves change *within* the system's rules; revolution implies change *of the system itself.* Moreover, reform may spark conflict, but it rarely escalates into violence. The extreme case of reform is the overthrow of one leader by another—a *coup d'état* (in French, literally "stroke concerning the state"), which typically involves violence on a limited scale. By contrast, revolution often produces widespread violence. The 1989 pro-democracy movement in the People's Republic of China was revolutionary because participants envisioned a new and more open political system. The government recognized the threat and responded brutally, causing thousands of deaths before the uprising was ended. In the successful week-long revolution against Romanian dictator Nicolae Ceaucescu in 1989, thousands of citizens perished, victims of attacks by state soldiers on unarmed crowds. But revolution can sometimes occur nonviolently. In other Eastern European countries, the sweeping transformations of the late 1980s took place with little or no bloodshed.

Closer to home, one sees revolutionary potential in Quebec's quest for greater autonomy. If the Québé-cois were to vote *for* sovereignty in a future referendum, they would set in motion a process that would dismantle Canada as presently constituted and force the creation of two new and very different political entities, assuming that the rest of Canada survives in one piece. Such a revolution, should it come about, could be a peaceful one, consistent with Canada's tradition of evolutionary change, but there are no iron-clad guarantees. A number of issues such as the definition of the *boundaries* of a newly independent Quebec might well be the source of painful conflict (Gerber, 1992).

No type of political system is immune to revolution; nor does revolution invariably produce any one kind of government. The American Revolution ended the colonial control of the British monarchy and produced a democratic government. French revolutionaries in 1789 also overthrew a monarch, summarily executing members of the feudal aristocracy only to observe, within a decade, the return of monarchy in the person of Napoleon. In 1917, the Russian Revolution replaced the czarist monarchy with a socialist government built on the ideas of Karl Marx. In 1992, the Soviet Union formally came to an end, launching revolutionary change toward political democracy and a market system.

Despite their striking variety, analysts of revolution have pointed out several common patterns (Tocqueville, 1955, orig. 1856; Davies, 1962; Brinton, 1965; Skocpol, 1979; Lewis, 1984).

1. **Rising expectations.** Common sense suggests that revolution would be more likely in bad times than good, but history shows that political upheaval usually takes place when people's lives are improving. Extreme deprivation can be paralyzing, while a rising standard of living stimulates the desire for an even better life so that expectations may outpace reality. Crane Brinton explains that revolutions are typically "not started by down-and-outers, by starving, miserable people," but are "born of hope and their philosophies are formally optimistic" (1965:250).

2. **Deprivation and social conflict.** Revolutionary aspiration is propelled by a sense of injustice. The appeal of insurgency rises to the extent that people think they deserve more than they have while seeing little chance for improving their lot within the confines of the prevailing political system (Griffin & Griffin, 1989).

3. **Nonresponsiveness of the old government.** Revolutions gain momentum if a political regime is

unable or unwilling to reform, especially when demands for change are made by large numbers of people or powerful segments of society (Tilly, 1986). The Ceaucescu regime in Romania, for example, defied popular calls for economic and political reforms, making revolution increasingly likely.

4. **Radical leadership by intellectuals.** The English philosopher Thomas Hobbes (1588–1679) observed that political rebellion in seventeenth-century England often was centered at the universities. This pattern has been repeated at other times and places. Recently, students were instrumental in initiating the pro-democracy movement in the People's Republic of China. Students stand at the forefront of so many of these insurrections because intellectuals formulate the principles that justify radical change. Marx also pointed out the central role of the intelligentsia in any revolutionary change.

5. **Establishing a new legitimacy.** The overthrow of a political system is rarely easy, but more difficult still is ensuring a revolution's long-term success. Revolutionary movements are sometimes unified by hatred of the past government. After the first taste of success, divisions within a revolutionary movement may intensify. A political regime also faces the task of legitimizing its newly won power, and it must guard against counterrevolution as past leaders maneuver to regain control. This explains the speed and ruthlessness with which victorious revolutionaries typically dispose of past leaders.

Terrorism

The 1980s was a decade characterized by heightened concern over **terrorism**, *violence or threat of violence employed by an individual or a group as a political strategy.* Like revolution, terrorism is a political act entirely beyond the rules of the established political system. Paul Johnson (1981) links terrorism to concepts introduced earlier in this chapter.

First, explains Johnson, terrorists try to paint violence as a legitimate political tactic. Terrorists generally have difficulty winning the support of their audience since violent intimidation is condemned as immoral by virtually every culture. Terrorists also set themselves up for criticism as they reject established channels of political negotiation. But from the terrorist's point of view,

the political system under attack is both inherently unjust and unresponsive. More practically speaking, terrorism can greatly enhance the power of a small number of individuals. The Front de libération du Québec (FLQ), which may have comprised fewer than thirty people, used terrorism to promote its goal of an independent, socialist Quebec. From 1963 to 1971, it was involved in two hundred or more bombings of increasing seriousness and in 1970 it kidnapped Pierre Laporte (a Quebec cabinet minister) and James Cross (the British trade commissioner) and murdered Laporte. The FLQ clearly caught the attention of the country.

Second, Johnson continues, terrorism is not only a tactic employed by groups, it is also a strategy used by governments against their own people. **State terrorism** refers to *the use of violence, generally without support of law, against individuals or groups by a government or its agents.* While inconsistent with democratic political systems, state terrorism may be formal and lawful within authoritarian and totalitarian governments, which survive by inciting fear and intimidation. The left-wing Stalinist regime in the Soviet Union and the right-wing Nazi regime in Germany each employed widespread terror. More recently, government-backed "death squads" have sought to eliminate opposition to military governments in Latin America, and terror campaigns are periodically used by the government of the People's Republic of China to quell dissent.

Third, although democratic systems reject state terrorism, democratic societies are especially vulnerable to terrorism by individuals. This is the case, Johnson explains, because they afford extensive civil liberties to their people and have minimal police networks. This susceptibility helps to explain the tendency of democratic governments to suspend civil liberties if officials think themselves under attack. After the Japanese attack on Pearl Harbor at the outset of World War II, the Canadian government responded to widespread fears that Japanese Canadians might engage in terrorism or espionage by rounding them up from their B.C. communities, confiscating their properties, and moving them to internment camps in the interior for the duration of the war. More recently, civil liberties were suspended in 1970 when, in response to the murder of Pierre Laporte by the FLQ, Pierre Trudeau invoked the War Measures Act and arrested more than 450 people, many of whom were suspected of being FLQ members and sympathizers.

During the 1980s, global terrorism increased in frequency and severity. Terrorists seized embassies and consulates of more than fifty nations; they also kidnapped (and sometimes murdered) hundreds of political officials, business leaders, teachers, and Olympic athletes, as well as several world leaders (Jenkins, 1982). Even the Pope was a victim of a terrorist attack in 1981. Canadian citizens have rarely been the targets of terrorist attacks abroad, in part because we are not a major power, and perhaps because of our country's role as peacekeeper or mediator in international disputes. (In fact, Ken Taylor, Canada's ambassador to Iran, became a hero to Americans when, in 1980, he engineered the escape of six American Embassy staff members whose colleagues had been taken hostage.) In 1985, an Air India 747 went down near Ireland with 280 Canadians, most of Indian origin, on board. The assumed cause was a terrorist bomb aimed not at Canada but at India.

Assuming that those responsible have been identified, how should governments respond to terrorist acts? Because terrorist groups are nearly always shadowy organizations with no formal connection to any established state, targeting reprisals may be impossible. Furthermore, threats that are not carried out may tend to encourage other terrorist groups to target that country (Jenkins, cited in Whitaker, 1985:29). The dilemma posed by terrorism, then, is the urge on the one hand to respond—in some way—to violent attack, and the fear on the other hand of broadening the conflict and confronting other governments.

A final dimension of terrorism involves political definitions. In any society, the state claims to rule justly and asserts its right to employ violence to maintain "law and order." Further, the state generally has the power to convince much of the population of the rightness of its actions, even when they are violent. Thus governments use force to "uphold the law," while their opponents who use violence are branded as "terrorists." Similarly, given political differences in a society and around the world, one person's "terrorist" may be another's "freedom fighter."

War and Peace

We conclude our discussion with a look at what is perhaps the most critical political issue of all, war. Formally defined, **war** is *armed conflict among the people of various societies, directed by their governments.* As we suggested at the beginning of this chapter, war is as old as humanity. But if the presence of violent conflict remains the same, understanding it now takes on a new

Because governments can direct military force at their people, the most destructive form of terrorism is directed by the state. During 1992, the government of Thailand called out troops to crush a popular opposition to an undemocratic prime minister, which resulted in a week of violence and scores of deaths as soldiers fired into crowds of demonstrators on the streets of Bangkok.

urgency. Because we have the technological capacity to destroy ourselves, war poses unprecedented danger to the entire planet. Most scholarly investigation of war has as its ultimate aim promoting **peace**, which is *the absence of war*, although not necessarily the lack of all conflict.

Although many people think of war as extraordinary, rather than a common element of life, global peace is actually what is rare, existing only for brief periods throughout this century. At most points in time, there is armed conflict occurring in various locations worldwide. Most wars are localized, while others, like the two World Wars, are widespread. Canada's involvement in several of these wars cost Canadian lives: 60,661 were killed in WWI: 42,042 in WWII; and 312 in the Korean War. In the Vietnam War, some Canadian individuals signed up to fight in the American forces but Canada's official role involved serving on truce commissions and supplying medical or technical assistance. Since Vietnam, Canada has generally been involved in the world's trouble-spots as a peacekeeper.

The Causes of War

The frequency of war in human affairs might imply that there is something "natural" about armed confrontation. Certainly members of every culture come to embrace certain symbols and principles—such as patriotism and freedom—to the point that they are willing to fight to defend (or extend) them. But while evidence supports the conclusion that some animals are naturally aggressive (Lorenz, 1966), research provides no basis for concluding that human beings inevitably go to war under any particular circumstances. As Ashley Montagu (1976) reminds us, governments around the world must resort to considerable coercion in order to enlist the support of their people for wars. Moreover, armies are deliberately constructed of small social groups in which soldiers are motivated to fight in order to protect close companions as well as themselves. Loyalty to small groups, rather than allegiance to abstract principles, stands at the heart of war as it is experienced on the battlefield (Hruschka, 1990).

Like all forms of social behavior, warfare is one product of *society* that varies in frequency and purpose from culture to culture. The Tasaday in the Philippines, among the most peace-loving of the world's people, rarely resort to violence. In contrast, the Yanomamö, described in Chapter 3 ("Culture"), are quick to wage war with others. These patterns follow from social arrangements: Napoleon Chagnon (1988) explains that the ferocity of Yanomamö men stems from a system of rewards that confers prestige and the society's most desirable women on successful warriors.

If society holds the key to war or peace, under what circumstances *do* humans engage in warfare? Based on the work of Quincy Wright (1987), we can identify five factors that promote war.

1. **Perceived threats.** Societies mobilize their members when leaders perceive a threat to people, territory, or culture. On the other hand, the likelihood of peace increases in the absence of such threats.

2. **Social problems.** Internal problems that generate widespread frustration encourage a society's leaders to become aggressive toward their neighbors. Sometimes, in effect, enemies are "socially constructed" as a form of scapegoating. Political leaders are well aware that warfare tends to raise their popularity, just as it turns attention away from troublesome domestic problems. The lack of economic development in the People's Republic of China, for example, has sparked that nation's hostility toward Vietnam, Tibet, and the former Soviet Union.

3. **Political objectives.** Leaders sometimes settle on war as a desirable political strategy. Poor societies, such as Vietnam, have fought wars to end foreign domination. For powerful societies like the United States, a periodic "show of force" (such as the invasions of Grenada and Panama, and the Gulf War) may enhance global political objectives. A deliberate decision to escalate conflict may also win concessions from an opponent unwilling or unable to do the same (Patchen, 1987).

4. **Moral objectives.** Rarely do populations support going to war simply for tangible rewards, such as territory or wealth. Recognizing this, leaders infuse military campaigns with moral urgency, inspiring people to fight for causes like "religion", "freedom," "making the world safe for democracy," or the "fatherland." Leaders often paint an enemy as wicked, as Iranian officials did when they tagged the United States as the "great Satan," or as U.S. President George Bush did when he rallied his country to war against Iraq by casting that country's leader, Saddam Hussein, as a modern-day Adolf Hitler.

5. **The absence of alternatives.** A fifth factor that encourages armed conflict is the absence of other means to resolve international disputes. Societies establish political systems partly to reduce conflict through the rule of law. Article 1 of the United Nations' Charter defines that organization's task as "maintaining international peace," but its ability to resolve tensions among strongly nationalistic societies, while at times significant, has been limited.

Militarism and the Arms Race

Many people accept the idea that there are "just wars," armed conflicts that are necessary to oppose evil. But there is no doubt that the costs of wars and the militarism that sustains them is high indeed. These costs extend considerably beyond those of actual fighting. Together, the world's community of nations spends more than $5 billion annually on militarism. In addition to these direct expenditures, additional indirect costs include the diverting of resources that might otherwise be used in the struggle for survival by millions of desperately poor people throughout the world (see

Chapter 11, "Global Inequality"). Assuming the will and the political wisdom of doing so, there is little doubt that resources currently spent on militarism could be used to eradicate global poverty. A large proportion of the world's top scientists also direct their talents toward military research; this is another vital resource that is siphoned away from other activity that might benefit humanity.

Although the armies of some countries stand out as far larger than others, every nation on earth has some military power. The former Soviet Union had the world's largest armed forces in terms of men and women in uniform, with some 5 million soldiers. The United States, which has the world's mightiest military capacity based on nuclear bombs and other high technology weapons, historically has allocated more money to defense than to any other single purpose—currently about 25 percent of all government spending. Canada, which in effect depends on the U.S. for its defense, allocates about 8 percent of government spending to defense and maintains its armed forces strength at about 85,000 volunteer men and women.

The extraordinary expense of militarism is largely due to the **arms race**, *a mutually reinforcing escalation of military might*, which for decades involved the two military "superpowers," the United States and the Soviet Union. The United States became a superpower as it emerged victorious from World War II with newly developed nuclear weapons. The atomic bomb was first used in war by U.S. forces to crush Japan in 1945. But the Soviet Union exploded a bomb of its own in 1949 unleashing the "cold war," so that each superpower leader became convinced that the other was committed to military superiority. For the next four decades, both nations aggressively developed more and more powerful nuclear weaponry, and more efficient means to deliver a rain of death on the enemy.

The irony—and the tragedy—of the arms race is that the United States and the Soviet Union pursued a policy that neither nation wanted nor could afford. The dissolution of the Soviet Union in 1992 has produced, at first glance at least, the possibility that each of these two military superpowers may no longer view the other as an adversary. This warming of relations, coupled with serious economic problems that have turned the attention of both nations homeward, offers what is probably the best chance yet for an end to the arms race.

But turning this tide will not be easy. The world remains a dangerous place in part because of destabilization throughout the area that was once the Soviet Union and the continued existence of nuclear arms in the hands of the newly independent nations. Furthermore, the conventional American wisdom holds that military strength ensures peace, and the arms race has had positive economic consequences for the U.S. Sam Marullo (1987) points out that the arms race has provided wages to tens of thousands of American workers, swelled the profits of hundreds of corporations, and resulted in research discoveries that led to new civilian products. Even so, he concludes, the enormous resources allocated for the arms race would probably be better spent for the U.S. people if invested in conventional industries.

C. Wright Mills (1956, 1958) took a more narrow view of militarism, linking the arms race to the interests of the power elite. Drawing on the ideas of Karl Marx, Mills viewed the expanding of the military-industrial complex as highly profitable for the small number of capitalists who control the economy. From Mills's point of view, military expenditures are antithetical to the interests of the population as a whole, but enrich the capitalist class.

Ironically, another argument against growing militarism was advanced by a decorated army general who went on to become president of the United States. In his last official speech as president in 1961, Dwight Eisenhower warned of the increasing power of the **military-industrial complex**, *the close association between the United States federal government and defense industries*. In rough agreement with the contention of C. Wright Mills, Eisenhower claimed that a power elite dominating both the economy and defense establishment had acquired unparalleled control over the U.S. government. The military-industrial complex, he observed, had the potential to undermine democracy as it became less and less responsive to the American people.

Nuclear Weapons and War

Technological advance has made warfare more deadly than ever. The typical warhead on one of today's MX missiles is far more destructive than the relatively "puny" atomic device that obliterated the Japanese city of Hiroshima nearly fifty years ago.

Not only are nuclear weapons more powerful, but there are many more of them. As the 1990s began, the world contained some 50,000 nuclear weapons, representing a destructive power roughly equivalent to five tons of TNT for every human being on the planet. This level of "overkill" means that, should even a fraction of this arsenal be consumed in war, life as we know it would cease to exist on much of the earth.

Albert Einstein, whose genius contributed to the development of nuclear weapons, reflected on this achievement with these sobering words: "The unleashed power of the atom has changed everything *save our modes of thinking*, and we thus drift toward unparalleled catastrophe." In short, nuclear weapons have rendered unrestrained war unthinkable in a world not yet capable of peace.

At present, the vast majority of nuclear weapons are held by the United States and Russia. Three other nations—Great Britain, France, and the People's Republic of China—have a substantial nuclear arsenal. Even as superpower tensions are diminished, the danger of catastrophic war increases with **nuclear proliferation**, *the acquisition of nuclear weapons by more and more societies.* Most analysts agree that several additional nations (including Israel, India, Pakistan, and South Africa) already possess nuclear weapons. Evidence exists that still more countries (including Algeria, Argentina, Brazil, Iraq, Libya, North Korea, Syria, and Taiwan) have been or currently are developing nuclear technology that could lead to weapons. By the end of this decade, estimates suggest, between twenty-five and fifty nations will have the ability to engage in nuclear war. Because many of these countries have long-standing conflicts with their neighbors, nuclear proliferation places the entire world at risk (Spector, 1988).

The Pursuit of Peace

The final question to consider in completing this survey of war and the military is how the world might reduce the dangers of war. We shall sketch out several approaches to promoting peace.

1. **Maintaining the status quo.** The logic of the present arms race suggests that security is derived from a balance of terror between the superpowers. A policy that has been tagged *mutually assured destruction* (MAD) states that either superpower launching a first-strike nuclear attack against the other would itself suffer massive retaliation. The strength of this notion of deterrence is that it appears to have kept the peace for forty years. But it does have three flaws. First, by encouraging the arms race, deterrence burdens the economies of the United States and the Commonwealth of Independent States. Second, as military technology becomes more complex—as missiles deliver their warheads more quickly and computers have less time to react to an apparent attack—the risks of unintended war

increase. Third, deterrence cannot control nuclear proliferation which, as we have already explained, will only increase in the future. For the long term, an alternative strategy is obviously needed.

2. **High-technology defense.** One alternative to deterrence that emerged during the 1980s is the American *strategic defense initiative* (SDI). Under this proposal, a complex system of satellites and ground installations would provide a protective shield against enemy attack. In principle, the system detects enemy missiles soon after launch and destroys them with lasers and particle beams before they can reenter the atmosphere. If perfected, advocates argue, the "star wars" defense will render nuclear weapons obsolete.

The SDI proposal has prompted heated controversy. Some claim that such a program, even after years and trillions of dollars have been spent on research and development, would produce at best a leaky umbrella in the event of war. Just as seriously, leaders of the former Soviet Union viewed SDI as an offensive system, able to assist the United States in making a first strike on them. For this reason, its development and deployment would likely provoke countermeasures, with both sides taking one more costly step in the arms race (Kurtz, 1988).

3. **Diplomacy and disarmament.** Still another approach views peace as a diplomatic challenge rather than a technological problem (Dedrick & Yinger, 1990). If diplomacy can ease nations toward disarmament, both military costs and stockpiles of weapons will decrease. The idea behind disarmament is simple: a build-up of weapons in the past can lead to a mutual process of build-*down* in the future.

Disarmament also has limitations. No country wants to increase its vulnerability by reducing its defenses. Successful diplomacy, then, depends not on allowing "soft" concessions or making "hard" demands, but on everyone involved sharing responsibility for a common problem (Fisher & Ury, 1988). Disarmament proceeds best in a climate of mutual trust, but self-interest alone should motivate nations to seriously consider this approach to peace.

The leaders of the United States and the former Soviet Union recorded modest success in negotiating arms-control agreements. Given the rising costs of the arms race, the pressing domestic social problems of the two superpowers, and the easing of the cold war in the 1990s, the world may look toward significant disarmament with guarded optimism.

4. **Resolving underlying conflict.** In the end, success in reducing the dangers of nuclear war will depend on resolving deep-rooted conflicts that have fueled the arms race. Even with rapid transformation in the former Soviet Union, political differences between the superpowers will surely keep the two sides wary.

But other sources of conflict are found all around the globe. Despite the improving relations between Washington and Moscow, regional conflicts continue unabated in Latin America, Africa, Eastern Europe, the Middle East, and Asia. According to one estimate, the world currently spends 3,000 times as much money on militarism as it does on peacekeeping efforts (Sivard, 1988). In some cases, superpowers can assist efforts to reach fair and reasonable settlements of regional problems. In other situations, powerful nations need to recognize their part in creating these problems. The United States, for example, has helped fuel conflict in several Latin American countries by supporting repressive regimes and even by covertly destabilizing governments unfriendly to U.S. interests.

Ever since Canadian prime minister Lester B. Pearson proposed the creation of a United Nations peacekeeping force in 1956 (for which he was awarded the 1957 Nobel Peace Prize) Canada has seen its international role mainly in terms of mediation and peacekeeping. Although we did participate in the Allied attack on Iraq during the Gulf War, after the war Canadians helped patrol the demilitarized zone. Our role in Yugoslavia has been largely limited to peacekeeping and medical assistance.

The danger of war remains great: around the globe we see vast stockpiles of weapons, the proliferation of nuclear technology, and a powerful military-industrial establishment with a real interest in maintaining international tensions. Forces working for peace also marshall great resources and the power of imagination: organizations such as the United Nations are promoting stability in the world, we see international cooperation in expanding trade worldwide, and improving superpower relations are lessening the threat of global annihilation. Perhaps most crucial is the growing realization that the aspirations of billions of people for a better life depend on a nonviolent solution to the age-old problem of war.

Summary

1. Politics is a major social institution by which a society distributes power and organizes decision making. Any political system seeks legitimacy. Max Weber explained that three social contexts transform power into authority: tradition, rationally enacted rules and regulations, and the personal charisma of a leader.

2. Traditional authority predominates in preindustrial societies; industrial societies legitimize power through bureaucratic organizations and law. Charismatic authority arises in every society and if organizations founded by charismatic leaders are to endure they must become routinized into traditional or rational-legal authority.

3. All members of technologically simple societies have roughly the same amount of power, and they engage in no distinct political life. Political systems separate from family life arise only as societies generate a material surplus.

4. Monarchy is based on traditional authority and is common in preindustrial societies. As industrialization introduces egalitarian forces, including widespread individual rights and schooling, politics becomes more democratic and is based on rational-legal authority and extensive bureaucracy.

5. Democracy is a type of political system in which the population as a whole has considerable power. At the beginning of the 1990s, most of the world's nations were democratic for the first time in human history.

6. Authoritarian political systems prevent popular participation in government, and display indiffer-

ence to the aspirations and initiatives of the population. Totalitarian political regimes also involve little popular participation, but exert extensive control over the everyday lives of the people.

7. The government of Canada is based upon an elected House of Commons and an appointed Senate. Because representation in the House of Commons is based (roughly) on population, Quebec and Ontario together have 59 percent of the seats. This weighting in favor of central Canada is a source of concern for the peripheral provinces.

8. Canada has three major political parties at the federal level. The Progressive Conservative party leans to the right on social and economic issues, the Liberal party is closer to the center, and the New Democratic party is farther to the left. Since *each* of the parties is a bit of a mixed bag, accurate placement on a left-right continuum is difficult.

9. One of the major political struggles going on in Canada involves the centralization versus the decentralization of power, or provincial versus federal power.

10. Canadian government takes an active role in the daily lives of its citizens. Canadian political culture supports widespread intervention in social and economic spheres.

11. Quebec separation, should it occur, would be a revolutionary act that would dismantle Canada as

we know it today. The tradition of peaceful resolution of problems in Canada might make this a non-violent transition but there are no guarantees.

12. Native self-government is a current issue that has deep historic roots. Many Native groups are currently practising some level of self-government under a wide range of agreements, but constitutional recognition of an *inherent* right to self-government is still an important goal.

13. The pluralist model holds that political power is widely dispersed; the power-elite model takes an opposing view, arguing that power is concentrated in a small, wealthy segment of the population.

14. Revolution brings radical transformation to a political system. Revolutions aim at different political objectives and meet with varied degrees of success.

15. Terrorism is the use of violence in pursuit of political goals. Although attention has long focused on group terrorism, state terrorism is potentially far more powerful.

16. War is armed conflict between governments. The development of nuclear weapons, and their proliferation, has increased the possibility of global catastrophe. Enhancing world peace ultimately depends on resolving social problems and the conflicts that underlie militarism.

Key Concepts

arms race a mutually reinforcing escalation of military might

authoritarianism any political system that denies popular participation in government

authority power that people perceive as legitimate rather than coercive

charismatic authority power legitimized through extraordinary personal abilities that inspire devotion and obedience

democracy a type of political system in which power is exercised by the people as a whole

government formal organizations that direct the political life of a society

military-industrial complex the close association between government and defense industries

monarchy a type of political system in which power is passed from generation to generation in a single family

nuclear proliferation the acquisition of nuclear-weapons technology by more and more societies

peace the absence of war

pluralist model an analysis of politics in which power is dispersed among many competing interest groups

political parties organizations operating within the political system that seek control of government

political revolution   the overthrow of one political system in order to establish another

political state   a formal government claiming the legitimate use of coercion to support its rule

politics   the institutionalized system by which a society distributes power and makes decisions

power   the ability to achieve desired ends despite possible resistance from others

power-elite model   an analysis of politics holding that power is concentrated among the rich

rational-legal authority   (also bureaucratic authority) power legitimized by legally enacted rules and regulations

routinization of charisma   the transformation of charismatic authority into some combination of traditional and bureaucratic authority

state terrorism   the use of violence, generally without support of law, against individuals or groups by a government or its agents

terrorism   violence or the threat of violence employed by an individual or group as a political strategy

totalitarianism   a political system that denies popular participation in government and extensively regulates people's lives

traditional authority   power that is legitimized through respect for long-established cultural patterns

war   armed conflict among the people of various societies, directed by their governments

Suggested Readings

Here are two general texts dealing with politics and society.
> Anthony M. Orum. *Introduction to Political Sociology: The Social Anatomy of the Body Politic.* 3rd ed. Englewood Cliffs, NJ: Prentice Hall, 1988.
> Mildred A. Schwartz. *A Sociological Perspective on Politics.* Englewood Cliffs, NJ: Prentice Hall, 1990.

The exercise of power goes beyond government to the way we interact in countless everyday situations. This analysis explores social life in terms of three types of power: exploitation, negotiation, and cooperation.
> Kenneth E. Boulding. *Three Faces of Power.* Newbury Park, CA: Sage, 1989.

Law is deeply shaped by gender. In sixteen essays, this feminist legal scholar explains why many issues we often think of as moral and criminal—including rape, pornography, and sex discrimination—are also thoroughly political.
> Catherine A. MacKinnon. *Feminism Unmodified: Discourses on Life and Law.* Cambridge: Harvard University Press, 1987.

This analysis of the contemporary political scene investigates recent trends and probes the consequences of proliferating individual "rights."
> Mary Ann Glendon. *Rights Talk: The Impoverishment of Political Discourse.* New York: The Free Press, 1991.

Another current debate surrounds the effects of the media on our political system.
> Frederick J. Fletcher (ed.). *Media and Voters in Canadian Election Campaigns.* Toronto: Dundurn Press, 1991

This classic analysis of politics and society is based on a journey through the United States made by a brilliant French aristocrat in the early 1830s. Many of Tocqueville's insights remain as fresh and valuable today as when he wrote them.
> Alexis de Tocqueville. *Democracy in America.* Garden City, NY: Doubleday-Anchor Books, 1969 (orig. 1834–1840).

Here are the two classics that frame much of political sociology and present the contrasting elite and pluralist models.
> C. Wright Mills. *The Power Elite.* New York: Oxford University Press, 1956.
> Robert A. Dahl. *Who Governs?* New Haven, CT: Yale University Press, 1961.

The exercise of power by multiple or single elites is the topic of these two Canadian classics.
> John Porter. *The Vertical Mosaic: An Analysis of Social Class and Power in Canada.* Toronto: University of Toronto Press, 1965
> Wallace Clement. *The Canadian Corporate Elite: Economic Power in Canada.* Toronto: McClelland and Stewart, 1975

This anthology of almost thirty articles brings together some of the most timely and convincing arguments on the topic of international terrorism.
> Charles W. Kegley, Jr., ed. *International Terrorism: Characteristics, Causes, Controls.* New York: St. Martin's Press, 1990.

This thoughtfully analytical and easy to read book is a must for political sociologists.

Raymond Breton. *Why Meech Failed: Lessons for Canadian Constitutionmaking*. Toronto: C.D. Howe Institute, 1992.

The following book provides a comprehensive analysis of women's political participation in Canada.

Sylvia B. Bashevkin. *Toeing the Lines: Women and Party Politics in English Canada* (2nd ed.). Toronto: Oxford University Press, 1993.

This collection of articles deals with many aspects of Native policy, rights, land claims and self-government.

J. Anthony Long and Menno Boldt (eds.). *Governments in Conflict? Provinces and Indian Nations in Canada*. Toronto: University of Toronto Press, 1988

CHAPTER 19

THE ECONOMY AND WORK

"When you compare what my dad looked forward to against what I'm looking forward to, he expected that things would be better for us and that my children would have it better than I have. But there isn't that feeling anymore." Ian Crump, a 45-year-old father of three, put three generations of experience in a nutshell as he pondered the situation of the descendants of Kitty and Henry Neville Compton Crump who had gathered at the old prairie homestead south of Regina. The family had felt the effects of the restructured economy, high taxes, and deficits that were contributing to a sense of economic malaise across the country.

Ian's cousin, Tom Crump, went through an experience that very clearly illustrates the changing job environment. As a hospital administrator in Vancouver he had been preparing to lay off fifty people when his boss came in and said it would be fifty-one. A senior position and seventeen years with the same employer proved to be no protection from ongoing economic upheaval and no base for launching his children into middle-class security. Downsizing and restructuring were leading to lay-offs at all levels, including middle management, and breaking the link that once bound company and employee for a much longer period—possibly through the entire working life of the employee. "By the stan-

dards of his parents, the job was a brief interlude; by the expectations of his children, an eternity" (Greenspon, *The Globe and Mail*, July 31, 1993:D1, 5).

This chapter examines the economy as a social institution, explores the character of work in today's world, and explains some of the consequences of the emerging global marketplace for people in Canada. We will see that a good deal of the conventional wisdom about economic life no longer applies in the face of sweeping changes in North America and around the world.

The Economy: Historical Overview

The **economy** is *the institutionalized system for production, distribution, and consumption of goods and services.* The range of economic activity is immense, involving any material object or human activity that has value. *Goods* range from necessities (such as food, clothing, and shelter) to luxury items (such as automobiles, yachts, and swimming pools). *Services* include all the things people do that benefit others (such as the work of religious leaders, physicians, police officers, and telephone operators).

We value goods and services because they ensure survival or because they make life easier, more interesting, or more aesthetically pleasing. What we produce and the things we consume are also important for our self-concepts and social identities. The distribution of goods and services, then, shapes the lives of everyone in basic ways.

The complex economies that mark modern industrial societies are themselves the product of centuries of technological innovation and social change. As Chapter 4 ("Society") explained, technologically simple societies of the past produced only what they immediately consumed. These small nomadic groups lived off the land—hunting game, gathering vegetation, and fashioning rudimentary clothing, tools, and shelters. Production, distribution, and consumption were all part of family life.

The Agricultural Revolution

Agriculture emerged as human inventiveness harnessed plows to animal power. Agrarian societies are ten to twenty times more productive than hunting and gathering societies, so they produce a significant surplus and establish permanent settlements. Because producing food no longer consumes the time and energy of all, individuals assume specialized economic roles, producing crafts, designing tools, and constructing dwellings. Trading networks link more and more towns, facilitating the exchange of food, animals, and other goods (Jacobs, 1970). These four factors—agricultural technology, productive specialization, permanent settlements, and trade—were the keys to a revolutionary expansion of the economy.

As noted in previous chapters, this economic expansion also increases social inequality. In contrast to relatively egalitarian hunters and gatherers, agrarian elites control most of the land—the primary productive resource. Greater productivity, therefore, does not necessarily enhance the standard of living of everyone.

In agrarian societies, the economy becomes a social institution distinct from family life, although people's work is typically done close to home. In medieval Europe, for instance, most people farmed nearby fields. City dwellers often worked in their homes—a pattern called *cottage industry*. What they produced they sold in regularly scheduled outdoor markets (the historical origin of contemporary "flea markets," suggesting that not everything was of the highest quality).

In London three centuries ago, for example, a home may have included several rooms used for baking, under the direction of the husband, who held the status of master baker. His wife could expect to be no more than his lifelong assistant, due to the pronounced patriarchy of the times. In addition, the household usually included several younger male apprentices working for wages as they developed their skills, and perhaps a young man or woman working as a servant (Laslett, 1984).

The Industrial Revolution

Beginning in mid-eighteenth-century England, industrialization introduced five revolutionary changes to the economies of Western societies.

1. **New forms of energy.** Since the earliest hunting and gathering societies, energy had been produced by the muscles of human beings and animals. At the dawn of industrialization in 1765, James Watt pioneered the application of steam power to machinery. Surpassing muscle power a hundred-fold, steam engines soon made production far more efficient than ever before.

2. **The spread of factories.** Steam-driven machinery soon rendered cottage industries uncompetitive and thus obsolete. Factories—centralized workplaces apart from the home—spread rapidly. Although more productive, factory work lacked the personal feeling and close ties that had characterized family-based cottage industries.

3. **Manufacturing and mass production.** Before the Industrial Revolution, most work involved propagating raw materials, such as crops, wool, and wood. The industrial economy shifted that focus to manufacturing raw materials into a wide range of salable products. For example, factories mass-produced clothing from wool and transformed lumber into furniture.

4. **Specialization.** A worker in a cottage industry fashioned a product from beginning to end based on skill acquired from years of apprenticeship. Factory work, by contrast, is highly specialized; laborers repeat a single task, making only a small contribution to the finished product. Thus factories raised productivity, but they also lowered the skill level required of the average worker (Warner & Low, 1947).

5. **Wage labor.** Instead of working for themselves or joining with other members of a household in a productive enterprise, industrial workers became wage laborers. In essence, they sold their labor to strangers who often cared less about them than about the machines they operated. Supervision of workers became routine and intense. The impact of the Industrial Revolution gradually rippled outward from the factories to transform all of society. Greater productivity steadily raised the standard of living as countless new products and services filled an expanding economy. Especially at the outset, these benefits were shared very unequally. Some factory owners made vast fortunes, while the majority of industrial workers remained perilously close to poverty. Children were soon working as

[handwritten in left margin: Poverty for workers, employed rich]

SOCIAL DIVERSITY

The French-Canadians of Manchester, New Hampshire

The Amoskeag Manufacturing Company, once the largest textile factory in the world, was the pillar of economic life in Manchester, New Hampshire. From its founding in 1837 to its closing in 1935, the Amoskeag plant provided the major source of employment and controlled the development of the city of Manchester. The company initially founded a community of young women, from rural New England, who worked together and *lived* together in boardinghouses with ten p.m. curfews and compulsory church attendance. Irish immigrant families, willing to work for lower wages, eventually replaced the mill girls.

In the 1870s, French-Canadian immigrants who had been forced out of impoverished farming areas by a scarcity of land, found their way in substantial numbers from rural Quebec to the Amoskeag mills. The mill owners soon concluded that French-Canadians were the ideal labor force, and Amoskeag proceeded to recruit them actively. Mill agents scanned the Quebec countryside for possible recruits and advertisements in Quebec newspapers extolled the virtues of Amoskeag and Manchester.

French-Canadian workers were ideal in part because they had large families. Entire family groups were brought into the mills (including the children) and could be counted on to draw kinfolk as well as their own large families. So numerous were the Canadians, in the end, that the mill bosses

French-Canadians were probably well represented on the Amoskeag Textile Club Baseball Team (ca. 1920). The Textile Club, to which any Amoskeag employee over 18 could belong, hosted a wide range of activities including golf, dances, card games, and Christmas parties for children.

were forced to learn a little French. This large group was appreciated by management because it proved to be a "docile," "industrious," and "stable" labor force with a family-based structure that discouraged union involvement. Despite their numbers, however, not one French-Canadian was promoted into the supervisory ranks. Native-born Americans or immigrants of British and Northern European stock filled the latter.

Migration from Quebec to Manchester, a convenient stop on the railway linking Montreal and Boston, was

so substantial that, by 1910, French-Canadians made up 35 percent of the Amoskeag labor force and 38 percent of the population of Manchester. Some of the families that migrated to Manchester stayed only long enough to save some money before returning to their farms in Quebec. Others put down permanent roots and contributed to life with a French flavor in the section of Manchester that is still called Little Canada.

SOURCE: Based on Hareven and Langenbach (1978).

wage laborers in factories and deep in coal mines for pennies a day. Women factory workers were among the lowest paid of all.

The Postindustrial Society

Industrialization is an ongoing process. In Europe and North America, workers gradually organized into labor unions in opposition to factory owners. During this century, governments outlawed child labor, forced wages upward, improved workplace safety, and extended schooling and political rights to a larger segment of the population.

By the mid-twentieth century, Canada was becoming a **postindustrial economy**, *a productive system based on service work and high technology*. Computerized machinery has reduced the role of human labor in production. Simultaneously, bureaucracy has expanded the ranks of clerical workers and managers. Robert Heilbroner (1985) points out that, over the past century, the proportion of employees in managerial positions has risen dramatically. Service industries—such as public relations, advertising, banking, and sales—now employ most of Canada's labor force (75 percent in 1991). Distinguishing the postindustrial era, then, is a shift by workers from industrial production to service jobs.

The crucial technology of a postindustrial age concerns information. The computer stands at the center of an *Information Revolution* in North America and elsewhere in the industrial world, generating a host of new, specialized occupations. Just as gaining technical skills was the key to success in the past, now women and men must enhance their literacy skills. People unable to speak, write, or otherwise communicate effectively face less and less economic opportunity.

The postindustrial society also brings further change in the location of work. Industrialization initially centralized the workforce in factories where enormous machinery and energy sources were situated. Today, however, computers, fax machines, and other new information technologies allow workers to perform many jobs at home or even while driving in their cars. More educated and skilled workers also no longer require—and often do not tolerate—the close supervision that marked yesterday's factories.

Sectors of the Modern Economy

In line with the broad historical changes just described, we can see a shifting balance among three sectors of a society's economy. The **primary sector** is *the part of the economy that generates raw materials directly from the natural environment*. The primary sector, which includes agriculture, animal husbandry, fishing, forestry, and mining, dominates economies of preindustrial, agrarian societies. Early in our nation's history, for example, most work involved agriculture and other primary-sector activities. Table 19-1 indicates that the primary sector in Canada has declined from 41 percent of the economy in 1870 to less than 5 percent in 1991.

Globally, the economies of developing nations of the world such as India and the People's Republic of China are still dominated by the primary sector. Global Map 19-1 illustrates the importance of the primary sector in the world's economies.

The **secondary sector** is *the part of the economy that transforms raw materials into manufactured goods* and, as such, gains prominence as societies industrialize. Secondary-sector production includes refining petroleum, and manufacturing tools, building materials, and automobiles. In societies that are still industrializing—such as Yugoslavia and Greece—the secondary sector of the economy has grown to roughly the same size as the primary sector.

Global Map 19-2 illustrates the share of the economy claimed by industrial production around the world. The map is essentially a reverse image of Global Map 19-1: First-World economies with the smallest primary sectors have the largest industrial sectors.

As industrial societies mature, the secondary sector peaks and eventually declines. In Canada the manufacturing sector peaked at around one quarter of the labor force, dropping to below 17 percent by 1991. In place of manufacturing, growth has occurred in the **tertiary sector**, *the part of the economy that generates services rather than goods*. The wide range of service occupations includes secretarial and clerical work, positions in food service, sales, law, advertising, and teaching. Accounting for only a tiny share of work in preindustrial economies, the tertiary sector grows with industrialization and becomes the dominant economic

TABLE 19-1   THE CANADIAN ECONOMIC STRUCTURE 1870–1991

Sector	1870	1961	1991
Primary	41.2%	12.8%	4.6%
Secondary	22.4	24.7	16.5
Tertiary	36.0	58.2	75.0

SOURCE: Statistics Canada, Catalogue. Nos. 93-151 (1986), 93–327 (1991); Watson (1988).

sector in postindustrial societies. Seventy-five percent of Canada's labor force today is engaged in the tertiary sector, an increase of 17 percent in just over thirty years (Figure 19-1).

Comparative Economic Systems

Two overarching models—capitalism and socialism—have dominated analysis of economic systems during this century. No society has an economy that is purely capitalist or purely socialist; these models represent two ends of a continuum on which an actual economy can be placed. Further, societies toward each end of the continuum have undergone extensive change.

Capitalism

Capitalism is *an economic system in which productive resources are privately owned.* Ideally, a capitalist economy has three distinctive features.

1. **Private ownership of property.** A capitalist economy supports the right of individuals to own almost

---

W I N D O W   O N   T H E   W O R L D

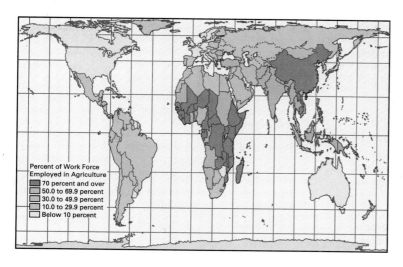

GLOBAL MAP 19-1   AGRICULTURAL EMPLOYMENT IN GLOBAL PERSPECTIVE

The primary sector of the economy predominates in societies with the least economic development. Thus, in the poor countries of Africa and Asia, half, or even three-fourths, of all workers are farmers. The picture is altogether different among First-World nations—including the United States, Canada, Great Britain, and Australia—which have less than 10 percent of their workforce in agriculture.

Percent of Work Force Employed in Agriculture
- 70 percent and over
- 50.0 to 69.9 percent
- 30.0 to 49.9 percent
- 10.0 to 29.9 percent
- Below 10 percent

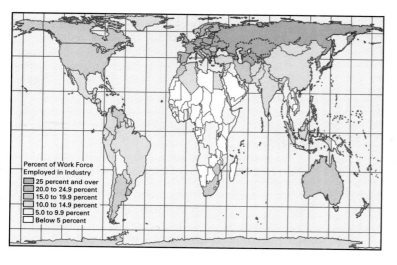

GLOBAL MAP 19-2   INDUSTRIAL EMPLOYMENT IN GLOBAL PERSPECTIVE

The Third World, by and large, has yet to industrialize. For this reason, in the countries of Latin America, Africa, and Asia, a small proportion of the labor force engages in industrial work. The industrial nations of the Second World—including the Commonwealth of Independent States—have the largest share of their workers in industry. In the First World, we see a reverse of this trend, with more and more workers moving from industrial jobs to service work. Thus, the postindustrial economy of Canada now has about the same share of workers in industrial jobs as the much poorer nation of Argentina.

Percent of Work Force Employed in Industry
- 25 percent and over
- 20.0 to 24.9 percent
- 15.0 to 19.9 percent
- 10.0 to 14.9 percent
- 5.0 to 9.9 percent
- Below 5 percent

anything, from forests and other natural resources to factories and retail businesses. While all societies permit individuals to have personal possessions, the more capitalist an economy is, the more private ownership extends to wealth-producing property.

2. **Pursuit of personal profit.** A capitalist society encourages the accumulation of private property and defines a self-centered, profit-minded orientation as natural and simply a matter of "doing business." In practical terms, according to Scottish economist Adam Smith (1723–1790), when individuals pursue their own self-interest, the entire society benefits from greater "wealth and prosperity" (1937:508; orig. 1776).

3. **Free competition and consumer sovereignty.** A purely capitalist economy would operate without interference from the government. The state thereby assumes a *laissez-faire* (a French expression meaning "to leave alone") approach to the marketplace. Adam Smith claimed that a freely competitive economy regulates itself by the "invisible hand" of the laws of supply and demand.

According to Smith, whose *An Inquiry into the Nature and Causes of the Wealth of Nations* (1776) became the bible of the free-trade movement, the market system is dominated by consumers who compare quality and price, buying those goods and services that provide the greatest value. Producers compete with one another to offer the highest-quality goods and services at the lowest possible price. And prodded by competition to be as efficient as possible, producers readily embrace technological innovations that end up benefiting consumers even more. Although both producers and consumers are motivated by personal gain, the overall economy grows as production becomes more efficient, technology advances, and consumers enjoy ever-increasing value. Smith's time-honored maxim holds that from narrow self-interest comes the greatest good for the greatest number of people.

If we were to think of an economy as a vast and complex ship, Smith's argument suggests that the self-interested actions of individual crew members with no single captain would ensure that the ship remains on course (Albrecht, 1983:47). From another perspective, Smith argued that government control of an economy would inevitably upset the complex market system, sapping producer motivation, diminishing the quality of goods produced, and thereby shortchanging consumers.

Socialism

Socialism is *an economic system in which productive resources are collectively owned*. In its ideal form, a socialist economy opposes each of the three characteristics of capitalism just described.

1. **Collective ownership of property.** An economy is socialist to the extent that it limits the rights to private property, especially property used in producing goods and services. Socialist economies direct the production of food, clothing, and other goods and services toward meeting the needs of the population as a whole, not just those of some privileged segment of society. A socialist society, for example, defines housing as a right of all instead of a private commodity to be traded in the marketplace for profit.

Karl Marx asserted that private ownership of productive property spawns social classes and invariably generates a powerful economic elite. Because socialism regards such classes as opposing the interests of the broader population, socialist law prevents class formation by forbidding the private ownership of property.

2. **Pursuit of collective goals.** The individualistic pursuit of profit also stands at odds with the collective orientation of socialism. Cultural values and norms in socialist societies define as illegal what capitalists call the entrepreneurial spirit. For this reason, private trading is branded as illegal "black market" activity.

3. **Government control of the economy.** Socialism rejects the idea that a free-market economy regulates itself. Instead of a laissez-faire approach, socialist societies place the economy under government control. Thus, socialism creates a *centrally controlled economy*. From a socialist point of view, individuals acting on the basis of narrow self-interest—Adam Smith's ship without a captain—should flounder or, worse still, destroy themselves on the rocks. In the absence of the guiding hand of government, the economy will endure spasms of growth and recession, inflation and unemployment, that adversely affect everyone.

Socialism rejects the contention that consumers guide capitalist production through their purchases. Marx maintained that consumers often lack the information necessary to evaluate the performance and potential dangers of various products. Nor is advertising much help; from this point of view, ads manipulate people to buy what is profitable rather than what they genuinely need. Commercial advertising thus plays a small role in a socialist economy.

Socialism and Communism

As the realization of the ideal spirit of socialism, **communism** is *a hypothetical economic and political system in which all members of society have economic and social equality.* Karl Marx viewed socialism as a transitory stage on the path toward the ideal of a communist society devoid of all class divisions and conflict. In many socialist societies today, the dominant political party describes itself as communist, but nowhere has the communist goal been achieved.

Why? For one thing, social stratification involves differences of power as well as wealth. Socialist societies have generally succeeded in reducing disparities in income and wealth only through expanding government bureaucracies, giving officials extensive power over the people. In the process, government has not "withered away" as Karl Marx imagined. On the contrary, during this century political elites have gained enormous power and privilege in socialist societies.

Marx would have been the first to agree that a communist society is a *utopia* (from Greek words meaning "not a place"). His writings provide only a vague description of true communism. Yet Marx considered communism a worthy goal, and would probably have disparaged existing "Marxist" societies like the People's Republic of China and Cuba for falling far short of his communist ideal.

Democratic Socialism

Many nations of Western Europe espouse **democratic socialism,** *an economic and political system that combines significant government intervention in the economy with free elections.* Democratic-socialist societies recognize advantages in both the market economy and government regulation. They also embrace open political contests and, in fact, typically have a far greater share of their citizens casting votes than is the case in the United States, the leading capitalist society (see Chapter 18, "Politics and Government").

In most countries of this kind, the government owns at least many of the largest industries and services, such as mining, transportation, utilities, the mass media, education, and health care. Private industry also exists, but it is subject to extensive regulation. High taxation (aimed especially at the rich) transfers wealth, through various social welfare programs, to less advantaged members of society. In Great Britain, about 15 percent of the economy is nationalized. In Sweden, Italy, and France, roughly 12 percent of production is state-controlled. In all these Western European countries, public support for social welfare programs is strong (Roskin, 1982; Gregory & Stuart, 1985; Pedersen, 1990).

Canada falls in between the democratic socialism of Western Europe and the individualistic capitalism of the U.S in its policies. The role of government here is substantially greater than in the U.S., but not as great as in Western Europe.

Relative Advantages of Capitalism and Socialism

The recent economic changes that are reshaping many societies of the world sparked debate over the relative advantages of capitalism and socialism. Assessing these economic models is difficult because nowhere do they exist in their pure states. Societies mix capitalism and socialism to varying degrees, and each also has distinctive cultural attitudes toward work, unequal natural resources, different levels of technological development, and disparate patterns of trade. Finally, the destructive effects of war burden some societies more than others (Gregory & Stuart, 1985). Despite these complicating factors, some crude comparisons seem possible.

Productivity

Table 19-2 compares economic performance in a number of societies, divided into those with predominantly capitalist economies and those that, until recently, were predominantly socialist. "Gross Domestic Product" (GDP) is the total value of all goods and services produced annually within the country's borders; "per capita" (or per person) GDP allows us to compare societies of different size. Because each country uses its own currency system, the table presents per capita GDP in 1990 U.S. dollars.

Among the societies with predominantly capitalist economies (collectively termed the First World), the United States had the highest per capita GDP ($17,615), closely followed by Canada ($16,375) and the former Federal German Republic (West Germany) ($14,730). Greece had the lowest per capita GDP

The productivity of capitalist Hong Kong is evident in the fact that streets are choked with advertising and shoppers. Socialist Beijing, by contrast, is dominated by government buildings rather than a central business district. Here bicyclists glide past the Great Hall of the People.

($5,500). There is considerable variation in GDP among these countries, due to complicating factors already noted. But, by world standards, per capita GDP in these eleven predominantly capitalist societies is high, with an unweighted average (ignoring the unequal population size) of $13,345. This average figure is a rough measure of the value of goods and services produced annually per person in predominantly capitalist societies.

Looking at the former Soviet Union and the nations of Eastern Europe just before their upheavals at the end of the last decade, the German Democratic Republic (East Germany prior to German reunification) had the highest economic output per person ($8,000), while Albania had the lowest ($2,000). Overall, these socialist economies produced considerably less than their capitalist counterparts. The unweighted average is $5,000 or 37 percent of the figure for capitalist societies. The comparison between what were West and East Germany is especially interesting, because this is a case of a single society divided at the end of World War II into two parts—one capitalist and one socialist. In the late 1980s, per capita GDP in the socialist German Democratic Republic was about 54 percent that of the capitalist Federal Republic of Germany.

Distribution of Income

How income is distributed is also important in comparing capitalist and socialist economies. Table 19-3 gives an idea of the extent of income inequality in several societies with predominantly capitalist and predomi-

nantly socialist economies during the 1960s and 1970s. The income ratios indicate how many times more income was received by highly paid people than was earned by poorly paid people.[1]

Of the five primarily capitalist societies listed in Table 19-3, the United States had the greatest income inequality, with a rich person earning almost thirteen times more than a poor person. The income ratios of Canada (12.0) and Italy (11.2) were only slightly lower. Both Sweden (5.5) and Great Britain (5.0) had much less income inequality because they incorporate socialist principles into traditionally capitalist economies. The unweighted average shows that a rich person earned more than nine times as much as a poor person in predominantly capitalist societies.

With an unweighted average of 4.5, the socialist societies had about half as much income inequality. This comparison of economic performance supports the conclusion that *capitalist economies are relatively more productive but they also generate greater social inequality; socialist economies produce greater social equality, but with a lower standard of living.*

Chapter 18 ("Politics and Government") explained that a society's economic and political systems are closely linked. Capitalism depends on the freedom of producers and consumers to interact in a market setting without extensive interference from the state. Thus

---

[1] Specifically, income ratio is derived by dividing the ninety-fifth percentile income by the fifth percentile income. The authors are unaware of more recent data on global inequality.

TABLE 19-2   ECONOMIC PERFORMANCE OF CAPITALIST
AND SOCIALIST ECONOMIES, 1988

	Per Capita GDP (U.S. dollars)
Predominantly Capitalist Economies	
Austria	12,386
Belgium	13,140
Canada	16,375
Federal Republic of Germany (the former West Germany)	14,730
France	13,961
Great Britain	12,270
Greece	5,500
Hong Kong	13,900
Japan	13,135
Sweden	13,780
United States	17,615
Unweighted average	13,345
Predominantly Socialist Economies	
Albania	2,000
Bulgaria	4,750
Czechoslovakia	7,750
German Democratic Republic (the former East Germany)	8,000
Hungary	4,500
Poland	4,000
Romania	3,000
Soviet Union	6,000
Yugoslavia	5,000
Unweighted average	5,000

SOURCE: United Nations Development Programme. Human Development Report 1990. New York: Oxford University Press, 1990:129.

TABLE 19-3   DISTRIBUTION OF INCOME IN CAPITALIST
AND SOCIALIST ECONOMIES

	Income Ratio
Predominantly Capitalist Economies	
United States (1968)	12.7
Canada (1971)	12.0
Italy (1969)	11.2
Sweden (1971)	5.5
Great Britain (1969)	5.0
Unweighted average	9.3
Predominantly Socialist Economies	
Soviet Union (1966)	5.7
Czechoslovakia (1965)	4.3
Hungary (1964)	4.0
Bulgaria (1963-1965)	3.8
Unweighted average	4.5

SOURCE: Adapted from P.J.D. Wiles, Economic Institutions Compared (New York: Halsted Press, 1977), as cited in Paul R. Gregory and Robert C. Stuart, Comparative Economic Systems, 2nd ed. (Boston: Houghton Mifflin, 1985):503.

economic capitalism is linked to extensive civil liberties and political freedom. Socialist societies strive to maximize economic and social equality. This requires considerable state intervention in the economy, limiting the personal freedom of citizens.

Changes in Socialist Countries

During the last decade, a profound transformation has taken place in many socialist countries of the world. Beginning in the shipyards of Poland's port city of Gdansk in 1980, workers began organizing in opposition to their socialist government. Despite struggle and setback, the Solidarity movement eventually succeeded in dislodging the Soviet-backed party officials, electing their own leader, Lech Walesa, as national president. The Poles are now in the process of introducing market principles to their economy.

Other countries of Eastern Europe, all of which fell under the political control of the former Soviet Union at the end of World War II, also shook off socialist regimes during 1989 and 1990. These nations— including the German Democratic Republic[2] Czechoslovakia, Hungary, Romania, and Bulgaria— have likewise introduced capitalist elements into what had for decades been centrally controlled economies. In 1992, the Soviet Union itself formally dissolved, a process that, along the way, liberated the Baltic states of Estonia, Latvia, and Lithuania and forged a loose federation out of most of the remaining republics, now called the Commonwealth of Independent States.

The reasons for the sweeping changes in what Chapter 11 ("Global Inequality") described as Second-World socialism are many and complex. In light of earlier discussions, however, two factors stand out. First, these predominantly socialist economies have not been as productive as their capitalist counterparts. As we have explained, they were successful in achieving economic equality; living standards for everyone, however, were low compared to those in Western European countries. Second, the brand of socialism that was imprinted on Eastern Europe by the former Soviet Union encouraged heavy-handed and unresponsive government that rigidly controlled the media as well as

---

[2] The reunification of East and West Germany (Oct. 3, 1990) means that the mode and speed of introduction of capitalism into the East are quite different from other Eastern-bloc countries. Currently, West Germany is reeling under the burden of incorporating the East into its economic and political systems.

the ability of individuals to move about, even in their own countries. Put in other words, the socialist revolutions in these nations *did* do away with economic elites (as Karl Marx predicted); but, as Max Weber might have foreseen, they *expanded* the clout of political elites as party bureaucracies grew massive.

Now that the expansive party apparatus has been all but dismantled and these countries are moving toward market systems, what can we expect in the future? In light of the unexpected twists and turns in this region of the world, few people are confident about what lies ahead. What we can say, at this early stage, is that the consequences of market reforms are uneven, with some nations faring better than others. Further, for the short term at least, the introduction of market forces has sparked rapid price increases, which have further eroded living standards. In the long term, officials in these nations contend, this change will raise everyone's standard of living through greater productivity. At the same time, to the extent that these countries gradually come to resemble their neighbors farther to the West, a rising standard of living will be accompanied by increasing economic disparity.

Work in the Postindustrial Economy

Change is not restricted to the socialist world; the economy of Canada has also changed dramatically during the last century. The Industrial Revolution transformed the Canadian work force a century ago; further changes are taking place today.

In 1991, 14 million Canadians were in the labor force, representing two-thirds of those over the age of fifteen. As has been the case historically, a larger proportion of men (74.8 percent) than women (58.2 percent) are in the labor force. As noted in Chapter 13 ("Sex and Gender"), however, the gender gap in labor force participation has diminished in recent decades among Canadians. The figure for males has not increased since 1980, but the female rate is up from 46.7 percent.

Table 19-4 provides labor force participation figures for males and females by age for selected racial and ethnic categories, and reveals some very interesting patterns. For instance, labor force participation is virtually identical for the British and the French, except that, for

TABLE 19-4   LABOR FORCE PARTICIPATION* BY AGE AND SEX FOR SELECTED CATEGORIES**, 1986

	British	French	Asian	Black	Native
Males					
15–24 years	71.3	67.7	61.3	59.5	47.9
25 and over	75.2	77.6	83.2	88.4	67.4
Total	74.4	75.5	78.0	80.4	60.7
Females					
15–24 years	63.9	61.2	60.8	56.9	35.9
25 and over	48.8	49.1	64.8	75.2	42.3
Total	51.5	51.5	64.0	70.6	40.2

*Based upon population 15 years of age and older.
**Refers to single origin only — i.e., those who are of the same origin on both paternal and maternal sides.
SOURCE: Statistics Canada, Profile of Ethnic Groups—Dimensions, Catalogue No. 93-154, 1989.

both males and females, the British have slightly higher rates in the fifteen to twenty-four year age category. Asians and blacks have slightly lower participation rates in the younger age category, but their rates for those twenty-five and over and their total rates (for those fifteen and over) are substantially *higher* than those of the British or French, especially among females. *Seventy-five percent* of black females twenty-five years old and over are in the labor force, compared with only 49 percent of their British and French counterparts. In Canada, 70.6 percent of black females fifteen and over were in the labor force in 1991: among black women in the U.S. (sixteen and over in 1991) the figure was 57 percent. The comparable figures for black males are 80.4 and 69.5 in Canada and the U.S. respectively.

However, the Native population exhibits markedly lower labor force participation rates for both males and females in each of the age categories. The rates among Asian and black males and females suggest that race may not be the effective barrier to participation for Natives: it may instead be the result of a history of internal colonialism, *de facto* segregation, rural isolation, and cultural dislocation (Gerber, 1990; Frideres, 1993).

It should be noted that age affects labor force participation in ways that are not apparent in Table 19-4. For both women and men, participation is relatively low in the teens and picks up in the early twenties. During the childbearing years, women's participation levels off. After about the age of forty-five, the working profiles of the two sexes again become similar, with a marked withdrawal from the labor force as people approach age sixty-five. After that point in life, only a small proportion of each sex continues to work.

The Decline of Agricultural Work

At the beginning of this century, Canada was still largely rural, with about 35 percent of the labor force engaged in farming. By 1961, this proportion had fallen to almost 13 percent, and by 1991 to less than 5 percent (Table 19-1). Still, because today's agriculture involves more machinery and fewer people, it is more productive than ever. A century ago, a typical farmer could feed five people; today, a farmer grows food for seventy-five. This dramatic rise in productivity also reflects new types of crops, pesticides that promote higher yields, greater energy consumption, and other advances in farming techniques. The average Canadian farm has more than doubled in size from about 250 acres 1950 to about 600 today. This process signals the eclipse of "family farms," which are declining in number and produce only a small part of our agricultural yield; more and more production is carried out by *corporate agribusinesses* (Bakker & Winson, 1993). But, more productive or not, this transformation has wrought painful adustments for farming communities across the country, as a way of life is lost. The rest of us are affected indirectly by this change: prices have generally been kept low by the rising productivity of agribusiness, although a growing proportion of people are concerned about the effect of widespread use of pesticides and chemicals on crops.

From Factory Work to Service Work

Industrialization swelled the ranks of blue-collar workers early in this century. As shown in Table 19-1, by 1961 the manufacturing sector had peaked at about one quarter of the work force or about double the share employed in agriculture. By that time, another transformation had begun, as the white-collar revolution carried a majority of workers into service occupations. By 1991, three-quarters of employed men and women held service jobs, and manufacturing employed only about 17 percent of the labor force.

Looking back, the growth of white-collar occupations is one reason for the widespread—if misleading—description of Canada as a middle-class society. As explained in Chapter 10 ("Social Class in Canada"), much so-called "white-collar" work is more accurately termed "service work," including sales positions, secretarial jobs, and employment in fast-food restaurants.

Such work yields little of the income, prestige, and other benefits of traditional white-collar occupations. In other words, more and more of the jobs being created in this postindustrial era provide only a modest standard of living.

The Dual Labor Market

We can also describe the change from factory work to service jobs in terms of a shifting balance between two different *labor markets* (Edwards, 1979). The **primary labor market** includes *occupations that provide extensive benefits to workers.* This segment of the labor market encompasses the traditional white-collar professions and high management positions. These are jobs that people think of as *careers*: work in the primary labor market provides high income and job security and is also personally challenging and intrinsically satisfying. Such occupations require a broad education rather than specialized training, and they offer solid opportunity for advancement.

But few of these advantages apply to work in the **secondary labor market**, *jobs providing minimal benefits to workers.* This segment of the labor force consists of low-skill, blue-collar work like routine assembly-line operations, and low-level white-collar jobs including clerical positions. The secondary labor market offers workers much lower income, and affords little job security. Even if workers attain more schooling, they face little opportunity for advancement. In truth, many of these jobs are dead ends, often lacking even the benefits of a seniority system. Not surprisingly, then, workers in the secondary labor market are most likely to experience alienation and dissatisfaction (Mottaz, 1981; Kohn & Schooler, 1982).

Another term used to describe some of these workers is the **reserve army of labor**, *that part of the labor force that is last hired during expansion and first fired when the economy contracts.* These problems are especially serious for women, other minorities, and especially Natives, who tend to be overly represented in this segment of the labor force (Kemp & Coverman, 1989; Gerber, 1990; Frideres, 1993). A growing proportion of the jobs being created in the emerging postindustrial economy fall within the secondary labor market. Like manufacturing jobs in factories a century ago, these positions require workers to perform unchallenging tasks, for low wages, under poor working conditions (Edwards, 1979; Gruenberg, 1980).

My Financial Career

Stephen Leacock (1869–1944), the English-speaking world's best known humorist in the early 1900s, grew up on a farm at Orillia, Ontario, near Lake Simcoe. He was a prolific writer of humor and of social, political, and economic commentary. Leacock was the long-term department head of McGill's department of Economics and Political Science until his retirement in 1936. He was active in the Conservative party and, in 1911, helped defeat Sir Wilfrid Laurier's Liberal government, which was proposing free trade with the United States (Lynch, 1988). Here, Leacock exposes the intimidation experienced by many in their initial dealings with what was once a more formal banking establishment. Although most of us take banking for granted, there are still some members of our society (the poor and illiterate among them) who shy away from contact with this central economic institution.

When I go into a bank I get rattled. The clerks rattle me; the wickets rattle me, the sight of the money rattles me; everything rattles me.

The moment I cross the threshold of a bank and attempt to transact business there, I become an irresponsible idiot.

I knew this beforehand, but my salary had been raised to fifty dollars a month and I felt that the bank was the only place for it.

So I shambled in and looked timidly round at the clerks. I had an idea that a person about to open an account must consult the manager.

I went up to wicket marked 'Accountant'. The accountant was a tall, cool devil. The very sight of him rattled me. My voice was sepulchral.

'Can I see the manager?' I said, and added solemnly, 'alone.' I don't know why I said 'alone.'

'Certainly,' said the accountant, and fetched him.

The manager was a grave, calm man. I held my fifty-six dollars clutched in a crumpled ball in my pocket.

'Are you the manager?' I said. God knows I didn't doubt it.

'Yes,' he said.

'Can I see you,' I asked 'alone?' I didn't want to say 'alone' again, but without it the thing seemed self-evident.

The manager looked at me in some alarm. He felt that I had an awful secret to reveal.

'Come in here,' he said, and led the way to a private room. He turned the key in the lock.

'We are safe from interruption here,' he said: 'sit down.'

We both sat down and looked at each other. I found no voice to speak.

'You are one of Pinkerton's men, I presume,' he said.

He had gathered from my mysterious manner that I was a detective. I knew what he was thinking, and it made me worse.

'No, not from Pinkerton's,' I said, seeming to imply that I came from a rival agency.

'To tell the truth,' I went on, as if I had been prompted to lie about it, 'I am not a detective at all. I have come to open an account. I intend to keep all my money in this bank.'

The manager looked relieved but still serious: he concluded now that I was a son of Baron Rothschild or a young Gould.

Labor Unions

Labor unions are *organizations of workers that attempt to improve wages and working conditions through strategies including negotiations and strike.* In Canada, union membership has been remarkably stable over the last twenty years at just over one third of the labor force, peaking at 35.1 percent in 1983. The involvement of women increased slightly while that of men decreased to the point where, in 1990, women constituted 40 percent of union membership in Canada (Statistics Canada, Cat. No. 71-202, 1990). As well, the involvement of Canadian workers in international unions has dropped off dramatically while national unions and government unions have grown. As Figure 19-1 shows, the highest level of union membership is found in government or public administration at over 70 percent, the manufacturing and service sectors are both around the one third mark, while mining and the trades lag behind.

It is also worth noting that there is substantial interprovincial variation in levels of unionization. In Newfoundland, 55.1 percent of the labor force is unionized: at the other end of the spectrum is Alberta at 26.6 percent (Statistics Canada, Cat. No. 71-202, 1990). The other relatively highly unionized provinces are Quebec, B.C., and Ontario. The differences are not entirely due to the economic structures of the various provinces, for even within the same industry there can be substantial variation: the level of unionization within the construction industry, for example, varies from 81 percent in Quebec to 25 percent in Prince Edward Island.

In global perspective, union membership in industrialized countries varies substantially—from a low of 16 percent of the work force in the U.S. to about

'A large account, I suppose,' he said.

'Fairly large,' I whispered. 'I propose to deposit fifty-six dollars now and fifty dollars a month regularly.'

The manager got up and opened the door. He called to the accountant.

'Mr Montgomery,' he said unkindly loud, 'this gentleman is opening an account, he will deposit fifty-six dollars. Good morning.'

I rose.

A big iron door stood open at the side of the room.

'Good morning,' I said, and stepped into the safe.

'Come out,' said the manager coldly, and showed me the other way.

I went to the accountant's wicket and poked the ball of money at him with a quick convulsive movement as if I were doing a conjuring trick.

My face was ghastly pale.

'Here,' I said, 'deposit it.' The tone of the words seemed to mean, 'Let us do this painful thing while the fit is on us.'

He took the money and gave it to another clerk.

He made me write the sum on a slip and sign my name in a book. I no longer knew what I was doing. The bank swam before my eyes.

'Is it deposited?' I asked in a hollow, vibrating voice.

'It is,' said the accountant.

'Then I want to draw a cheque.'

My idea was to draw out six dollars of it for present use. Someone gave me a cheque-book through a wicket and someone else began telling me how to write it out. The people in the bank had the impression that I was an invalid millionaire. I wrote something on the cheque and thrust it in at the clerk. He looked at it.

'What! are you drawing it all out again?' he asked in surprise. Then I realized that I had written fifty-six instead of six. I was too far gone to reason now. I had a feeling it was impossible to explain the thing. All the clerks had stopped writing to look at me.

Reckless with misery, I made a plunge.

'Yes, the whole thing.'

'You withdraw your money from the bank?'

'Every cent of it.'

'Are you not going to deposit any more?' said the clerk, astonished.

'Never.'

An idiot hope struck me that they might think something had insulted me while I was writing the cheque and that I had changed my mind. I made a wretched attempt to look like a man with a fearfully quick temper.

The clerk prepared to pay the money.

'How will you have it?' he said.

'What?'

'How will you have it?'

'Oh.'—I caught his meaning and answered without even trying to think—'in fifties.'

He gave me a fifty-dollar bill.

'And the six?' he asked dryly.

'In sixes,' I said.

He gave it to me and I rushed out.

As the big door swung behind me I caught the echo of a roar of laughter that went up the ceiling of the bank. Since then I bank no more. I keep my money in cash in my trousers pocket and my savings in silver dollars in a sock.

SOURCE: Leacock (1965):23ff.

one third in Canada, Switzerland and Japan, one half in Great Britain, and a high of more than 90 percent in Denmark and Sweden. Clearly, some cultures are more receptive to unions than others: those with social-democratic values tend to have the higher levels of unionization. The U.S. with its pro-capitalist values has never been particularly supportive of the union movement. Unions there have been declining steadily since the 1970s, from a high of about a third of the labor force to the present level of about 16 percent. The political climate of the 1980s, under the Reagan and Bush administrations, was generally hostile to union interests (Goldfield, 1987), and the decline of U.S. manufacturing industries (relative to services) has made a big dent in union membership there. Canada, where the manufacturing sector has always been relatively small, has been less affected by this decline.

FIGURE 19-1 TOTAL UNION MEMBERSHIP AS A PERCENTAGE OF ALL PAID WORKERS, BY SELECTED INDUSTRY, 1985
SOURCE: Statistics Canada, Catalogue No. 71-202.

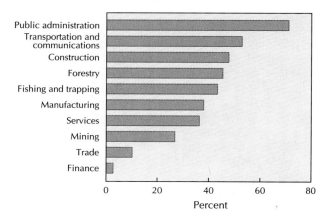

Professions

The *professions* constitute a privileged category of work in Canada's postindustrial economy. Many kinds of work are commonly called professional: we speak of professional tennis players, professional exterminators, even professional con artists. Used this way, a professional pursues some activity for a living in contrast to the *amateur* (from Latin meaning "lover"), who acts simply out of love for the activity itself.

In its more traditional usage, a **profession** is *a prestigious, white-collar occupation that requires extensive formal education*. The term suggested that certain work involved a profession—or public declaration—of faith or willingness to abide by certain principles. Traditional professions include the ministry, medicine, law, and academia (W. Goode, 1960). Today, we recognize more occupations as professions, to the extent that they have the following four characteristics (Ritzer, 1972).

1. **Theoretical knowledge.** Mere jobs involve technical skills, but professionals claim a theoretical understanding of some field based on extensive schooling and regular interaction with peers. Anyone can master first-aid skills, for example, but physicians are set apart because of their theoretical understanding of human health and illness.

2. **Self-regulated training and practice.** While most workers are directly accountable to superiors and are subject to routine, on-the-job supervision, professionals are more likely to be self-employed (Zald, 1971). Professionals participate in associa-

tions that set standards for performing or "practicing." Associations also expect their members to conform to a formal code of ethics.

3. **Authority over clients.** Many jobs—sales work, for example—require people to respond directly to the desires of customers. By contrast, professionals expect their "clients" to follow their direction and advice. Professionals claim this authority based on possessing knowledge that "lay people" lack.

4. **Community orientation rather than self-interest.** The traditional "professing" of faith or obligation was a way for professionals to declare their intentions to serve the needs of clients or the broader community rather than their own self-interest. Most business executives readily admit to working in pursuit of personal financial gain, and this is one reason that engaging in commerce was not one of the traditional professions. Professionals such as priests or university professors, however, rarely admit to such motives. They prefer to think of their work as contributing to the well-being of others. Some professionals, including physicians, are even barred by professional codes from advertising. This aura of altruism also makes many professionals reluctant to discuss the fees that contribute to their high incomes.

Besides the traditional professions, a number of other occupations can be described as *new professions*. These occupations, which include architecture, social work, and accounting, share most of the characteristics just presented.

Many new service occupations in the postindustrial economy have also sought professional standing, a process known as *professionalization*. Members of an occupation often initiate a claim to professional standing by labeling their work in a new way. The new name suggests that they employ special, theoretical knowledge and has the added benefit of distancing them from their field's previously less distinguished reputation. Government bureaucrats, for example, become "public policy analysts," and dogcatchers are reborn as "animal control specialists." Interested parties may form a professional association that will formally attest to their specialized skills. This organization then begins to lobby for the legal right to license those who perform the work in question. It also develops a code of ethics, modeled on those of traditional professions, which emphasizes the occupation's contribution to the community. A professional association may also establish schools or other training facilities, and perhaps start a

Unionized workers who feel they have been dealt a bad hand in labor negotiations may avail themselves of their right to strike. Here striking nurses in Alberta point out the potential danger to patients in government-mandated job cuts.

professional journal. All of this is done in an attempt to win public acceptance of the occupation's professional standing (Abbott, 1988).

Not every category of workers tries to claim full professional status. Some *paraprofessionals*, including paralegals and medical technicians, possess specialized skills but lack the extensive theoretical education required of professionals.

Self-Employment

Self-employment—in effect, earning a living without working for a large organization—was once common-place in North America. Rural farms were owned and operated by families, and self-employed workers in the cities owned shops and other small businesses or sold their skills on the open market. C. Wright Mills (1951) estimated that in the early nineteenth century about 80 percent of the U.S. labor force was self-employed, but, with the onset of the Industrial Revolution, that picture changed dramatically. Self-employment plummeted to one third, one fifth and even lower in both Canada and the United States.

In recent years, Canada has experienced increases in self-employment. By about 1990, self-employment accounted for roughly 14 percent of the labor force. The increasing importance of self-employment is illustrated by the fact that, between 1975 and 1987 in Canada, the number of self-employed workers grew by 60 percent while the rest of the work force grew by only 26 percent (Neill, 1990). Figure 19-2 reveals that the highest levels of self-employment are to be found in fishing, trapping, and agriculture. Not surprisingly, very little mining, maufacturing, or educating is done by the lone entrepreneur.

Professionals—like lawyers—have always been well represented among the self-employed because their schooling and skills have high market value. But most self-employed workers in Canada are not professionals. They are small business owners, plumbers, carpenters, free-lance writers, editors, artists, and long-distance truck drivers. Overall, the self-employed are more likely to have blue-collar than white collar occupations.

Our society has always painted an appealing picture of working independently: no time clocks to punch, no rigid routines, and no one looking over your shoulder. For those excluded from organizations by prejudice or discrimination, self-employment has served as a strategy to increase economic opportunity (Evans, 1989). Further, self-employment holds the potential—although rarely realized—of earning a great

D'Arcy Moses is a Gitksan Native who grew up in Alberta. Incorporating aboriginal themes and issues in his creations, Moses has become a popular and highly successful fashion designer working out of Montreal.

FIGURE 19-2   SELF-EMPLOYED AS A PERCENTAGE OF ALL WORKERS, 1987
SOURCE: Statistics Canada, Cat. No. 93-326.

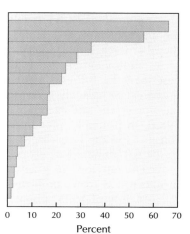

deal of money. But for all its advantages, self-employment presents workers with special problems. Many are vulnerable to fluctuations in the economy: during the recession of the early 1990s, small businesses filed for bankruptcy in alarming numbers. Another common problem is that the self-employed lack pension and health-care benefits generally provided to employees of large organizations.

Unemployment

Work serves as a source not only of income but of personal satisfaction, social prestige, and individual identity. For this reason, unemployment causes both financial hardship and psychological stress (Riegle, 1982).

Some unemployment is found in every society. Few young people entering the labor force find a job immediately; some older workers temporarily leave the labor force while seeking a new job or because of a strike; others suffer from long-term illnesses; and others who are illiterate or without skills find themselves locked out of the job market.

Although people may be quick to blame themselves if they find themselves out of work, unemployment is not just a personal problem; it is also a product of the economy itself. Capable and willing workers lose their jobs when economic recession occurs, if occupations become obsolete, or as factories close in the face of rising foreign competition. As illustrated by the story of Tom Crump at the beginning of this chapter, mergers and downsizing can also lead to the dismissal of employees from all levels of an organization. The emerging postindustrial economy has shattered the job security of workers in many traditional blue-collar occupations as well (Kasarda, 1983).

In predominantly capitalist societies like Canada, the unemployment rate rarely dips below 5 percent of the labor force. Public officials generally view this level of unemployment as natural, and sometimes even describe it as "full employment." An "unemployment problem" is publicly acknowledged only when the unemployment rate exceeds 7 or 8 percent (Albrecht, 1983). In principle, predominantly socialist societies consider work to be each person's right and obligation, so the government may create jobs to keep the unemployment rate low. In practice, however, unemployment is just as great a problem in these societies.

In July of 1993, Canada's unemployment rate climbed to 11.6 percent, the highest rate since the previous November. Forty-three thousand jobs, almost all

of which were full-time, disappeared that July, wiping out close to half of the 99,000 jobs created in June (Vardy, *The Financial Post*, Aug 7, 1993:1). Equally disturbing is the fact that part-time work now makes up 18 percent of all employment, and 40 percent of that work is done by "involuntary part-timers" or people who would rather have full-time jobs.

The national unemployment rate only tells part of the story, for in some provinces, like Newfoundland and P.E.I., unemployment may approach twice the national rate. Canada Map 19-1 reveals the regional pattern in unemployment rates, while Figure 19-3 shows that even cities or metropolitan areas have widely divergent rates. In 1986, for example, unemployment rates ranged from about 5.5 percent in Toronto to 17 percent in Chicoutimi-Jonquière.

Table 19-5 shows the unemployment rates for various segments of the Canadian population in 1986. Looking at the rates for males first, you will note that

The Great Depression of the 1930s was a time of catastrophic unemployment in Canada. The photograph shows members of the Single Men's Unemployed Association parading down Bathurst Street in Toronto during a march for jobs. The sign held by the man in the foreground makes an interesting, if unintentional, reference to labelling theory.

those of French origin have higher unemployment rates than those of British origin. Rates for Asian Canadians, in either age category or overall, are lower than for the British, while those for black Canadians are higher than those for any of the categories to the left in the table. The unemployment rates for the Native category are about two or three times the rates of the others. Note that the pattern for females is roughly the same and that, in each case, fifteen- to twenty-four-year-olds have higher unemployment rates than do older people.

Figure 19-4 looks at employment from a different perspective, indicating the proportion of people fifteen years of age and over who are employed full-time all year. From this perspective, Canadians of Asian and

TABLE 19-5 UNEMPLOYMENT RATES* BY AGE AND SEX FOR SELECTED CATEGORIES,** 1986

	British	French	Asian	Black	Native
Males					
15–24 years	17.2	20.7	16.2	21.6	43.2
25 and over	7.3	9.8	7.0	11.0	27.8
Total	9.2	11.9	8.7	13.2	32.0
Females					
15–24 years	16.4	21.0	12.5	21.3	41.3
25 and over	9.3	11.7	7.6	9.5	22.7
Total	10.8	13.8	8.5	11.9	28.2

*Based on population in labor force.
**Refers to single origin only (i.e., those who are of the same origin on both paternal and maternal sides).
SOURCE: Statistics Canada, Cat. No. 93-154. Profile of Ethnic Groups—Dimensions, 1989.

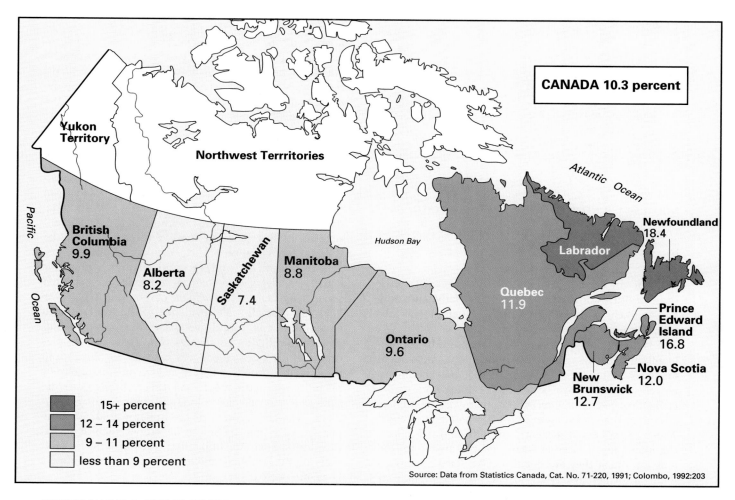

CANADA MAP 19-1   UNEMPLOYMENT RATES (PERCENT OF LABOR FORCE BY PROVINCE, 1991)

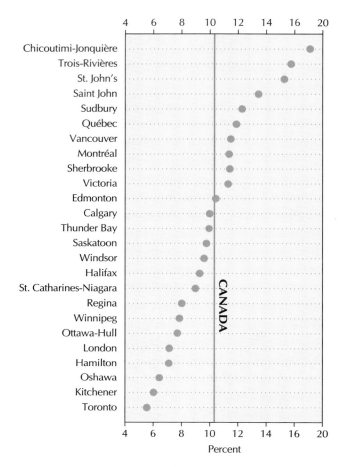

FIGURE 19-3   UNEMPLOYMENT RATES FOR SELECTED METROPOLITAN AREAS, 1986*

* Latest data available. Although actual unemployment rates may vary over time, the disparity between cities is always fairly large.
SOURCE: Statistics Canada, Metropolitan Atlas Series, *1986.*

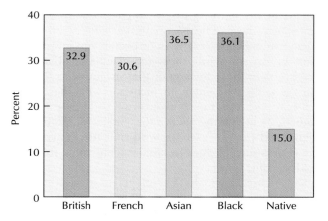

FIGURE 19-4   FULL-TIME ALL-YEAR EMPLOYMENT FOR PEOPLE AGED 15 AND OVER FOR SELECTED CATEGORIES, 1985*

* Latest data available.
SOURCE: Statistics Canada, Profile of Ethnic Groups—Dimensions, *1989.*

might better be described as *underemployed*. Official statistics also may overlook the fact that some people who are out of work receive income from odd jobs or illegal activity. Overall, however, the actual level of unemployment is probably several percentage points above the official figure.

The Underground Economy

Unlike socialist economies that have traditionally condemned market forces, the capitalist North American economy embraces "free enterprise." Yet, even in Canada, economic transactions are subject to government regulations that require extensive records and regular reports. Any violation of these regulations places transactions within the **underground economy**, *economic activity involving income or the exchange of goods and services that is not reported to the government.*

On a small scale, evidence of the underground economy can be found everywhere: sales representatives from different companies swap customer samples on a weekly basis; teenagers baby-sit for parents in their neighborhoods; a family makes some extra money by holding a garage sale. All these things generate income that people are unlikely to report to the government. A larger segment of the underground economy consists of crime. Income from crimes such as illegal drug sales, cigarette smuggling, prostitution, bribery, theft, illegal gambling, and loan-sharking almost always goes unreported.

But the single largest segment of the underground economy involves "honest" people who fail to

black origin have better employment experience than those of British or French origin, while Natives are only half as likely as the other groups to be employed full-time all year.

Official unemployment statistics, based on monthly national surveys, generally understate unemployment for two reasons. First, to be counted among the unemployed, a person must be actively seeking work. Especially during economic recessions, many people become discouraged after failing to find a job and stop looking. These "discouraged workers" are not counted among the unemployed. Second, many people unable to find jobs for which they are qualified take "lesser" employment: a former university teacher, for example, may drive a taxi while seeking a new teaching position. Such people are included among the employed, although they

accurately report their legally obtained income on income tax forms. Self-employed people like various tradespeople or owners of small businesses may understate their incomes; waiters, waitresses, and other service workers may not report their full income from tips. Even relatively small omissions and misrepresentations on individual income tax returns add up to billions of dollars in the underground economy (Simon & Witte, 1982; Dalglish, *Maclean's*, Aug. 9, 1993).

Exactly how large is the underground economy? Roger Smith of the University of Alberta estimates that, in Canada, the underground economy accounted for some 15 to 20 percent of economic activity in 1990, up from about 10 percent a decade earlier (cited in Dalglish, *Maclean's*, Aug. 9, 1993:20). A survey by the Canadian Home Builder's Association estimated that 55 percent of all renovations in 1992 were done on the black market. At the same time, Statistics Canada suggests that underground activity accounts for only 3.5 percent of GDP. Although estimates of the magnitude of the problem are all over the map, the existence and growth of the underground economy is not disputed.

A recent increase in underground economic activity is attributed to high tax levels in general and, in particular, to the imposition of the Goods and Services Tax in 1991. The effect of taxing services for the first time was to provide an incentive for under-the-table cash payment. One indication of this trend is a 57 percent increase, between 1991 and 1992, in the use of hard *cash* rather than credit cards or cheques (Dalglish, 1993).

Technology and Work

The central feature of the emerging postindustrial economy is the computer and other new information technologies. Throughout history, technology has defined the kinds of skills that a society seeks and rewards; to some extent, then, technology also determines what kinds of *people* join in the productive system. The industrial era, with its emphasis on physically demanding factory work, was skewed toward men. The rise of information technology has encouraged the entry of women into the labor force.

The computer-based Information Revolution is changing the conditions of work and the workplace. Shoshana Zuboff (1982) points to five ways in which computers have already altered the character of work. First, she suggests, *computers are deskilling labor.* Just as industrial machinery deskilled the master craftwork-

er of an earlier era, so computers now threaten the skills of managers. Why? Simply because more and more business decisions are based on computer modeling, in which a machine signals a company to "buy" or "sell," or leads a passive manager to approve or reject a loan. Second, *work is becoming more abstract.* Industrial workers typically have a "hands-on" relationship with their product; postindustrial workers manipulate symbols in pursuit of some abstract business goal. Third, Zuboff explains, *computers limit workplace interaction.* The Information Revolution often leads to social isolation as workers perform most of their work at computer terminals. Fourth, *computers demand new standards for productivity.* Because information can be processed so quickly, organizations must redefine their expectations for employees who utilize new technology. Fifth, *computers enhance the supervision and control of workers.* Using computers, supervisors can monitor worker output precisely and continuously. Workers now have to contend with ever-present management, which is far from typical in the industrial workplace.

Zuboff's broader point is that technology is not socially neutral; rather it shapes the way we work. Understandably, then, while workers may find some dimensions of the Information Revolution pleasing, they are likely to oppose others.

Corporations

Corporations lie at the core of today's capitalist economies. A **corporation** is *an organization with a legal existence including rights and liabilities apart from those of its members.* An organization that is legally incorporated, in other words, becomes an entity unto itself able to enter into contracts and own property.

The idea of legal incorporation arose about a century ago to provide two benefits to owners of large businesses. First, incorporation shields owners from the legal liabilities of their businesses. This legal strategy protects personal wealth from lawsuits arising from business debts or harm to consumers.

Most large corporations operating in Canada (many of which are mutlinational) are owned by thousands of stockholders (as well as by other corporations) rather than by single families. This dispersion of corporate ownership has to some extent spread wealth by making more people small-scale capitalists. Ralf Dahrendorf (1959) adds that the day-to-day operation of a corporation is the task of white-collar executives who are responsible to the stockholders. In practice,

CRITICAL   THINKING

Regional Economic Disparities

Although there is debate about the definition of "region" (Brodie, 1989), there is some justification for defining regions as units with institutional or political boundaries (Breton, 1981; Matthews, 1983). Furthermore, trying to measure regional disparities is easier if data (for example census data) are collected regularly for the units in question. For these reasons, throughout this text, regions are defined in terms of provinces and territories.

Figure 19-5 in this box shows the variation in the percentage of the labor force employed in manufacturing industries—considered by some to be the real wealth-creating engine of the economy—for Canada's regions or provinces. Despite consistent official efforts to promote regional development and to spread the manufacturing base more evenly across the country, Ontario and Quebec continue to contain the manufacturing core of the Canadian economy, with 18 to 19 percent of their workers involved. The

Atlantic provinces have between 8 and 12 percent of workers in manufacturing, the prairie provinces between 6 and 11 per cent, and B.C. 12 percent. Saskatchewan has the weakest manufacturing base of all the provinces, and B.C. for all its affluence, is still a peripheral province in this respect, undiversified economically and overwhelmingly dependent upon forestry alone (Marchak, 1986). Another way of looking at the manufacturing clout of Ontario and Quebec is to note that, with 62 percent of the population, they have 76 percent of the manufacturing jobs.

Brym points out that two types of explanations have been offered for these kinds of disparities: the "mainstream" approach and the "radical" or political economy approach. The mainstream approach focuses upon the geographic causes of diversity: distance from markets, physical barriers (like mountains), natural resources (in more or less high demand), the federal

system of government, and population characteristics. From the radical perspective, inequities derive from human actions rather than nature. Confederation allowed "powerful central Canadian economic interests to drain wealth from the weak peripheral or hinterland regions, such as the prairies and the maritimes" (Brym, 1986:8). The policies of capitalists (or industrialists) and politicians serve to accentuate the disparities.

Once policies are enacted that concentrate capital, productive capacity, and jobs in a particular region, population flows to that region. Increased population translates into political power (i.e., increased representation in Parliament), and eventually into new policies strengthening the economic center. With one half of Canada's population in the Windsor-Quebec City corridor, it is difficult to reverse these tendencies.

SOURCE: Based on Brym (1986).

FIGURE 19-5   PERCENTAGE OF LABOR FORCE EMPLOYED IN MANUFACTURING INDUSTRIES FOR CANADA AND THE PROVINCES, 1991
SOURCE: Adapted from Statistics Canada; Colombo, 1992.

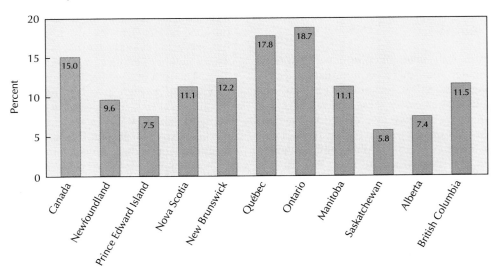

however, a great deal of corporate stock is owned by a small number of the corporation's top executives and directors who, in Canada, may be members of a very small number of families (Clement, 1975; Francis, 1986). These major stockholders comprise a small economic elite, which owns and operates the richest and most powerful Canadian businesses. Thus the proliferation of corporations has not substantially changed how large businesses operate or affected the distribution of wealth in Canada.

Economic Concentration

Profit-making corporations range in size from one-person businesses to veritable giants, such as Bell Canada Enterprises (124,000 employees), and Canadian Pacific (63,000). Many of Canada's corporations are small, with less than $100,000 in assets, but the largest of these corporations dominate the Canadian economy and periodically expand their empires through mergers and buy-outs of smaller firms. In a pattern that differs from the U.S., Canada's banks and other financial institutions (though not always the largest employers) are well represented among the top corporations in terms of revenues and profits.

Canada's problems of corporate concentration stem from: 1) the inordinate wealth and power of specific individuals, families, and corporations; 2) interlocking directorships that bind otherwise diverse corporations; 3) geographic centralization of investment in Ontario and Quebec; and 4) the tendency of corporations to expand or diversify by merging or buy-

ing existing firms instead of developing new productive capacity. The latter tendency was exacerbated by the Free Trade Agreement with the United States, as evidenced by a $20 billion boom in acquisitions and mergers in the first few months of 1989 (Bronson, 1993: 204). This has been referred to as "paper entrepreneurship," an activity which does nothing to contribute to Canada's wealth: "the pie remains the same size, but the pieces are cut differently" (Francis, 1986:229).

Diane Francis, currently editor of *The Financial Post,* has expressed concern about what she sees as increased corporate concentration in her 1986 book *Controlling Interest: Who Owns Canada?* In it, she profiles thirty-two of Canada's most powerful families who, "along with five conglomerates, already control about one-third of the country's non-financial assets, nearly double what they controlled just four years before" (1986:1).

Table 19-6 ranks, by profit, the top 15 companies that are traded on the Canadian stock exchanges. BCE or Bell Canada Enterprises topped the list with nearly $1.5 billion in profits. BCE revenues were in excess of $21 billion and the corporation employs 124,000 people. Bell Canada, the separate telecommunications company, also had hefty profits and is a major employer as well. Note that three of Canada's banks also appear among the top performers.

Foreign Ownership

The Trudeau government was sufficiently concerned about foreign investment in Canada to create the For-

TABLE 19-6 CORPORATE PERFORMANCE* IN CANADA RANKED BY PROFITS, 1991

Company	Profit ($thousands)	Revenue ($ thousands)	Assets ($thousands)	Number of Employees
BCE Inc.	1,390,000	21,270,000	48,312,000	124,000
Bell Canada	1,006,100	7,904,500	18,414,400	52,897
Bank of Nova Scotia	676,224	8,420,179	97,660,809	29,888
Northern Telecom	548,300	8,521,100	9,379,300	57,955
Bank of Montreal	640,000	8,847,000	109,035,000	32,126
Seagram Co. Ltd.	474,000	5,206,000	10,104,000	14,000
Toronto-Dominion Bank	408,000	6,138,000	74,133,000	25,353
Imasco Ltd.	380,400	7,989,800	48,519,000	86,863
TransCanada PipeLines	328,700	4,007,600	8,236,600	1,791
TransAlta Utilities	233,100	1,305,200	3,939,000	2,500
Thomson Corp.	182,000	6,033,000	7,907,000	45,700
American Barrick Resources	174,940	553,767	1,504,293	1,845
British Columbia Telephone	205,700	2,063,400	3,934,900	14,524
Imperial Oil	195,000	9,026,000	13,192,000	10,152
CT Financial Services	193,227	4,094,468	44,264,510	17,019

* *Publicly owned corporations listed on Canadian stock exchanges.*
SOURCE: The Globe and Mail: Report on Business, *July 1993.*

eign Investment Review Agency (FIRA) in 1973.[3] This was, in part, a response to a task force report, produced under Herb Gray, which revealed that, overall, foreign control of Canadian manufacturing had reached 60 percent, while the rubber and petroleum industries were 90 percent under foreign control. Most of the foreign control, then and now, was American, and that amount of control by one foreign country raised questions in many minds about our economic and political sovereignty.

There are a large number of companies, with names that are familiar to most Canadians, that are not traded on Canadian stock exchanges because they are 100 percent American owned (*Globe and Mail: Report on Business,* July, 1993). Among them are General Motors, Chrysler, IBM, Safeway, Amoco, Proctor & Gamble, Mobil Oil, General Electric, McDonald's, Goodyear, Hewlett-Packard, Motorola, and John Deere. Honda Canada is held by Japanese (50.4 percent) and (not Canadian but) U.S. investors (49.6 percent). The concerns about these companies, as well as those owned by Japanese, British, Swiss, or other interests, revolve around profits leaving Canada, avoidance of taxation within Canada, the lack of research and development or high-level management functions on Canadian soil, and even political interference.

Concern about the extent of American investment in Canada, and the related processes of "integration, rationalization, and harmonization with the United States economically, socially, and politically..." (Hurtig, 1992), has even spawned a brand new political party. As part of its platform, the National Party of Canada promises to "end the growth of foreign ownership and control" as well as to reverse the "growth of excessive corporate concentration."

Conglomerates and Corporate Linkages

Economic concentration has spawned **conglomerates**, *giant corporations composed of many smaller corporations.* Conglomerates, which begin as corporations, seek greater profits by entering new markets. In the past, corporations grew as they spun off new companies; during the 1980s, "takeovers" of existing companies became more common. Forging a conglomerate is also a way to diversify a company, so that new products can provide a hedge against declining profits in the original market.

Sometimes these mergers are extremely diverse, as illustrated by the Irving empire, discussed in the box on page 547, which combines timber, buses, drugs, hardware, and pre-fab housing, to name a few. Similarly, when the American firm, R.J. Reynolds, was faced with declining sales of tobacco products it merged with Nabisco foods, forming a conglomerate called RJR-Nabisco. Beatrice Foods, which was a Canadian company (until it was purchased by American interests through Merrill Lynch Capital in 1991) is another corporate "umbrella," containing more than fifty smaller corporations that manufacture well-known products including Hunt's foods, Tropicana fruit juices, La Choy foods, Orville Redenbacher popcorn, Max Factor cosmetics, Playtex clothing, and Samsonite luggage.

Besides conglomerates, corporations are also linked by extremely wealthy families who own their stock (Clement, 1975). Among the Canadian families who have large and varied corporate holdings in Canada (in addition to the Irvings) are the McCains, the Molsons, the Steinbergs, the Eatons, the Desmarais, the Campeaus, the Blacks, the Richardsons, the Mannixes, the Belzbergs, and the Bentleys (Francis, 1986). Most of these families, though spread across Canada, know each other, interact socially, and have business interests in common.

Today, linkage often takes the form of corporations owning each other's stock. Because they are able to own property just as individuals do, corporations invest heavily in one another. Joint ventures, which promise to benefit all parties, frequently accompany stock linkages (Herman, 1981).

One more type of linkage among corporations is the **interlocking directorate**, *a social network of people who serve simultaneously on the boards of directors of many corporations.* These connections, which give corporations access to insider information that can be extremely valuable, remain an important trait of corporate life (Clement, 1975; Marlios, 1975; Herman, 1981; Scott & Griff, 1985). Peter Bentley of Vancouver personally sits on more than a dozen "blue ribbon boards," has "titled Europeans on his boards and has served on theirs," and has "entered into countless partnerships with English and German firms" (Francis, 1986).

Finally, not all corporate linkages are formal. Gwen Moore (1979) has described how social networks (discussed in Chapter 7, "Groups and Organizations") informally link members of the corporate elite. In other words, corporate executives travel in many of the same social circles, allowing them to exchange valuable information. Such networks enhance not only

---

[3] A more pro-U.S. government under Brian Mulroney later changed the role and the name of the agency. As of 1985, it has been called Investment Canada. Although FIRA was supposed to block foreign takeovers, in fact, it turned back only a handful of applications.

C R I T I C A L   T H I N K I N G

The Irving Empire

Among the family dynasties examined by Diane Francis in *Controlling Interest: Who Owns Canada?* is that of K.C. Irving, based in New Brunswick. "New Brunswick is a company town," claims Francis, "and its proprietor is K.C. Irving." She goes on to describe his empire:

> The Irving group of companies is big by anybody's standards. It includes the country's largest shipyard and drydock facilities. Irving Oil is one of Canada's ten largest oil companies, with 3,000 service stations in Atlantic Canada and the Ottawa Valley, the country's largest refinery, as well as untold hold-

ings in oil and gas discoveries in western Canada. K.C.'s forestry business is world-scale, including half a dozen pulp and paper mills and sawmills and title to 1.5 million acres of timberlands in New Brunswick and Maine, an area equivalent to the size of Prince Edward Island. These landholdings, which he owns outright, make him the largest private landowner in the Maritimes. He also owns fleets of ships, trucks, buses, and railway cars, most of the media in the province, stores selling cars, food, hardware, drugs, and construction materials, and factories spewing out everything from pre-fab housing to concrete, steel, and hundreds more products. It is hard to get

an exact picture of the scope of the Irving empire. None of the companies are publicly owned, and the Irvings fiercely protect their privacy through a complicated and impenetrable corporate structure ...

Francis argues that this kind of corporate concentration is damaging to the Canadian economy. The prosperity of the Irvings has been based, in part, on the ability to lobby politicians, on erecting barriers against competitors, and on a virtual media monopoly.

SOURCE: Francis (1986:16).

---

the economic clout of big businesses, they also expand the influence of corporate leaders in political, social, and charitable organizations (Clement, 1975; Useem, 1979; Francis, 1986).

Corporate linkages do not necessarily oppose the public interest, but they do concentrate power and they sometimes encourage illegal activity. Price-fixing, for example, is legal in much of the world (the Organization of Petroleum Exporting Countries—OPEC—meets regularly to try to set oil prices), but not in Canada and the United States. By their nature, however, linkages encourage price-fixing, especially when a few corporations control an entire market.

Corporations and Competition

The capitalist economic model assumes businesses operate independently and competitively. In Canada, however, the entire economy is not competitive. On the contrary, the competitive sector includes mostly smaller businesses and self-employed people. Large corporations at the core of the North American economy fall within the *noncompetitive sector*. Large corporations are not truly competitive, first, because of their extensive linkages, and second, because many markets are dominated by a small number of corporations. Diane Francis puts this quite bluntly, arguing that com-

petition among Canadian capitalists "rarely breaks out in the absence of any meaningful combines laws within or foreign rivalry from without. This means that instead of a lively, competitive marketplace yielding jobs, innovations or opportunities for new entrepreneurs, Canada has far too many cash cows controlled by far too few proprietors" (1986:3).

From a business point of view, a company would maximize profits by achieving a **monopoly**, *domination of a market by a single producer*. With no competitors, a company can simply dictate prices. A century ago, the American government saw the public danger in this and limited monopolies by law through the Sherman Anti-Trust Act of 1890. Canada does not have comparable legislation, but when it does allow monopolies, the companies have to submit to government regulation: Bell Canada had a monopoly for years, but had to apply to the government for permission to increase rates.

Although total monopolies may be eliminated or at least controlled in North America, another limitation on competition persists in the form of **oligopoly**, or *domination of a market by a few producers*. Oligopoly seems to be inherent in industrial-capitalism. Entering the automobile manufacturing market today, for example, would take a staggering investment of billions of dollars, and even then there is no certainty of competing effectively against existing automobile manufacturers that have merged to form ever-larger corporations.

Certainly the successful entry of foreign-owned corporations into the North American automobile market shows that oligopolies can be challenged. But from the point of view of big business, competition means *risk*, and amounts to a threat to corporate profits.

Growing corporate power has implications for government. The capitalist model minimizes government intervention in the economy in favor of allowing market forces free reign. But corporate power is now so great and competition among corporations so limited that government regulation is often the only means to protect the public interest. Government oversight of at least much of the economy is now a fact of life in Canada. Yet, in the view of some critics, the government can hardly be called an adversary of large corporations. The government is, they point out, the single biggest customer of large corporations, and it frequently intervenes to support struggling companies. In effect, corporations and government typically work in concert in an attempt to make the entire economy more stable and to make businesses more profitable (Madsen, 1980).

Corporations and the Global Economy

Corporations have grown in size and power so fast that they will soon account for most of the world's economic activity. The largest corporations, centered in the United States, Canada, Japan, and Western Europe, have spilled across national borders and now view the entire world as one vast marketplace.

As discussed in Chapter 11 ("Global Inequality"), multinationals are large corporations that produce and market products in many different nations. Beatrice Foods operates factories in thirty countries and sells products in more than one hundred. Canada's Northern Telecom is among the huge corporations that earn much (and in some cases most) of their profits outside their own countries.

Corporations become multinational in pursuit of their primary goal: making money. About three-fourths of the world's people live in Third-World societies where most of the planet's resources are found. Worldwide operations, then, offer access to vast markets, cheap labor, and plentiful raw materials. Developing an international profile has the added bonuses of permitting corporations to lower their tax bills and to move money from country to country, profiting from fluctuating currency values.

The effects of capitalist expansion to the poor societies of the Third World are hotly debated, as Chapter 11 ("Global Inequality") explains in detail. On one side of the controversy, modernization theorists argue that multinationals are the key to world economic development (Rostow, 1978; Madsen, 1980; Berger, 1986). Multinationals unleash the great productivity of

The expansion of Western multinational corporations has altered patterns of consumption throughout the world, creating a homogeneous "corporate culture" that is—for better or worse—undermining countless traditional ways of life.

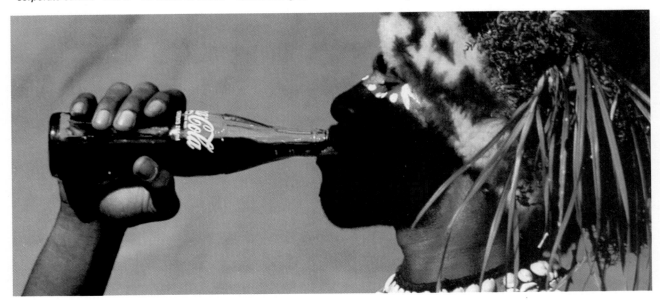

the capitalist economic system, draw Third World countries into their economic spheres, stimulate technology transfer and provide jobs in the developing countries themselves.

Corporate expansion, modernization theorists argue, provides poor societies with needed employment in the secondary (manufacturing) and tertiary (service) sectors. Multinationals also import capital to the Third World and introduce new technology, especially manufacturing techniques, that together accelerate economic growth. Multinationals thus offer countries in which they operate short-term advantages by paying wages and taxes, and stimulate long-term development by expanding the local economy with new products and services.

On the other side, dependency theorists claim that multinationals have intensified global inequality (Vaughan, 1978; Wallerstein, 1979; Delacroix & Ragin, 1981; Bergesen, 1983). Multinational investment, they argue, actually creates few jobs. Instead, tremendously powerful multinationals frequently inhibit the development of labor-intensive local industries, the real source of employment. Critics of multinationals also charge that they generally produce expensive consumer goods for export to rich societies, rather than generating food and other necessities needed by the local people.

Far from assisting in the economic development of Third-World societies, dependency theorists conclude, multinationals make poor societies poorer and increasingly reliant on rich societies of the capitalist First World. From this perspective, the growth of multinational corporations amounts to little more than an extension of historical colonialism: a neocolonialism now concerned with profit rather than direct political control. As one defender of multinationals asserted, "We are not without cunning. We shall not make Britain's mistake. Too wise to govern the world, we shall simply own it" (cited in Vaughan, 1978:20).

The Economy of the Twenty-first Century

In recent years the rate of economic change has accelerated, just as it did in 1890, as if to anticipate the arrival of a new century. The biggest changes have reverberated through socialist societies of Eastern Europe and the former Soviet Union. Socialism, which at its peak organized the productive lives of about one-fourth of humanity, seems to be in decline, although the People's

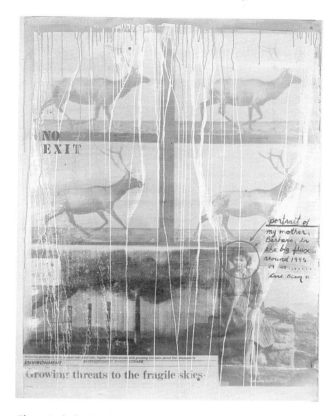

The arrival of Columbus, and the European migration that followed, brought to North America a whole new perspective on man's relation to nature. The polluting effect of industrial civilization is graphically conveyed in Ojibway artist Carl Beam's etching entitled No Exit. It comes from his 1992 collection, The Columbus Boat.

Republic of China, Cuba, and other nations still hold steadfastly to government-based economies.

Capitalism, too, has seen marked changes and now operates with a significant degree of government regulation. The most significant change in the capitalist system is the emergence of global corporations. The global reach of today's giant businesses means that North American corporations have expanded into more parts of the world. On the other side of the coin, corporations based outside North America are increasing their investments here. Canadians have worried mainly about U.S. control of our economy, but corporations based in Germany, Japan, the Netherlands, and Switzerland (in that order) have also invested heavily in Canada.[4]

---

[4] In 1985, Canada had $54 billion in direct investment abroad, while foreign direct investment in Canada was $87 billion. The figures for 1990 were $87 billion and $125 billion respectively. Direct investment means at least 10 percent of the equity in an enterprise (Statistics Canada; Colombo, 1992:183).

Canadians and Americans alike have become conscious of Japanese direct investment on this continent as well as its influence on corporate philosophy and structure (see Chapter 7, "Groups and Organizations"). The 1989 purchase of New York's Rockefeller Center—a prominent symbol of U.S. capitalism—by Japan's Mitsubishi corporation undoubtedly caught the attention of many Americans. Canadians have seen Japanese interests buy the Banff Springs Hotel and become very active in the development of ski resorts and golf courses throughout the western provinces in particular.

Growing industrial production overseas, benefiting from new factories, a highly motivated workforce, and the latest technology, has reduced Canadian and American competitiveness in numerous areas. The world's largest steel corporations and automobile manufacturers are now Japanese, as is virtually the entire North American market in home electronics.

What will be the long-term effects of all these changes? One conclusion seems clear: our economic future will depend less on the performance of individual *national* economies. Instead, the world's societies are becoming increasingly interconnected in a global economic system, as illustrated by Canada's free trade agreements and the European Economic Community. The emergence of the postindustrial economy in Canada is certainly linked to increasing industrial production abroad, especially in Asia's Pacific Rim. Finally, the ever-pressing issue of global inequality looms large. Whether the world economy ultimately reduces or deepens the disparity between rich and poor societies will likely steer our planet toward peace or belligerence.

Summary

1. The economy is a major social institution by which goods and services are produced, distributed, and consumed.

2. In technologically simple societies, economic activity is subsumed within the family. In agrarian societies, the economy becomes distinct from the family. Industrialization sparks significant economic expansion due to new sources of energy, factories, mass production, and specialization. In postindustrial economies, the majority of workers provide services rather than contributing to the manufacture of goods.

3. The primary sector of the economy generates raw materials; the secondary sector manufactures various goods; the tertiary sector produces services. In preindustrial societies, the primary sector predominates; the secondary sector is of greatest importance in industrial societies; the tertiary sector prevails in postindustrial societies.

4. The economies of today's industrial societies may be described in terms of two models. Capitalism is based on private ownership of productive property and the pursuit of personal profit in a competitive marketplace. Socialism is based on collective ownership of productive property and the pursuit of collective well-being through government control of the economy.

5. Although the Canadian economy is predominantly capitalist, our government is widely involved in economic life. Government plays an even greater economic role in the democratic socialist societies of Western Europe. The former Soviet Union has slowly introduced some market elements into its historically centralized economy; many nations of Eastern Europe are making similar changes, with some limited success.

6. Capitalism is highly productive, providing a high overall standard of living. Socialist economies are less productive but generate more economic equality.

7. Agricultural work has declined in Canada during this century. The number of blue-collar jobs has also diminished; such work now involves only one-fourth of the labor force. Today, close to two-thirds of Canadian workers have white-collar service jobs.

8. A profession is a special category of white-collar work based on theoretical knowledge, occupational autonomy, authority over clients, and an emphasis on community service.

9. Work in the primary labor market provides far more rewards than work in the secondary labor market. Most new jobs are in the secondary labor market's service sector.

10. Today, 14 percent of Canada's workers are self-employed. Although many professionals fall into this category, most self-employed workers have blue-collar occupations.

11. Capitalist societies tend to maintain an unemployment rate of at least 5 percent. Socialist societies, too, struggle with high unemployment.

12. The underground economy represents perhaps 15 to 20 percent of the economic activity in Canada, including most criminal business as well as legal income unreported on income tax forms.

13. Corporations form the core of the Canadian economy. The largest corporations, which are conglomerates, account for most corporate assets and profits.

14. The competitive sector of the Canadian economy encompasses smaller businesses. Large corporations dominate the noncompetitive sector.

15. Multinational corporations have grown in number and size during this century. The consequences for global economic development are a matter of continuing controversy.

Key Concepts

capitalism an economic system in which productive resources are privately owned

communism a hypothetical economic and political system in which all members of society have economic and social equality

conglomerates giant corporations composed of many smaller corporations

corporation an organization with a legal existence including rights and liabilities apart from those of its members

democratic socialism an economic and political system that combines significant government intervention in the economy with free elections

economy the institutionalized system for production, distribution, and consumption of goods and services

interlocking directorate a social network of people who serve simultaneously on the boards of directors of many corporations

labor unions organizations of workers that attempt to improve wages and working conditions through various strategies, including negotiations and strikes

monopoly domination of a market by a single producer

oligopoly domination of a market by a few producers

postindustrial economy a productive system based on service work and high technology

primary labor market occupations that provide extensive benefits to workers

primary sector the part of the economy that generates raw materials directly from the natural environment

profession a prestigious, white-collar occupation that requires extensive formal education

secondary labor market jobs that provide minimal benefits to workers

secondary sector the part of the economy that transforms raw materials into manufactured goods

reserve army of labor the part of the labor force that is last hired during expansion and first fired when the economy contracts

socialism an economic system in which productive resources are collectively owned

tertiary sector the part of the economy that generates services rather than goods

underground economy economic activity involving income or the exchange of goods and services that is not reported to the government

Suggested Readings

One of sociology's best contemporary thinkers examines the social consequences of capitalism.

> Peter L. Berger. *The Capitalist Revolution: Fifty Propositions about Prosperity, Equality, and Liberty.* New York: Basic Books, 1986.

This textbook focuses on patterns of conflict within the workplace.

> George Ritzer and David Walczak. *Working: Conflict and Change.* 4th ed. Englewood Cliffs, NJ: Prentice Hall, 1990.

The first of these books, a sociological classic, explores the emergence of a postindustrial society. The second, published a decade later, argues that manufacturing remains crucial to the economy and to our ability to develop high-wage service occupations.

> Daniel Bell. *The Coming of Post-Industrial Society: A Venture in Social Forecasting.* New York: Harper Colophon, 1976.
>
> Stephen S. Cohen and John Zysman. *Manufacturing Matters: The Myth of the Post-Industrial Economy.* New York: Basic Books, 1987.

In light of the economic struggles currently going on in Eastern Europe, this collection of essays, exploring this region's social and economic history, takes on new importance.

> Daniel Chirot, ed. *The Origins of Backwardness in Eastern Europe: Economics and Politics from the Middle Ages Until the Early Twentieth Century.* Berkeley: University of California Press, 1989.

This is among the first sociological accounts of the economic and political changes in Eastern Europe.

> William Echikson. *Lighting the Night: Revolution in Eastern Europe.* New York: Morrow, 1990.

Technology and corporate expansion have also worked to transform both the First and Second Worlds.

> Richard McKenzie and Dwight Lee. *Quicksilver Capital: How the Rapid Movement of Wealth Has Changed the World.* New York: The Free Press, 1991.

This study suggests that traditional notions about gender continue to shape the workplace today.

> Rita Mae Kelly. *The Gendered Economy: Work, Careers, and Success.* Newbury Park, CA: Sage, 1991.

How have specific occupational groups, such as physicians and lawyers, historically claimed the right to control particular services as professional jurisdictions?

> Andrew Abbott. *The System of Professions: An Essay on the Division of Expert Labor.* Chicago: University of Chicago Press, 1988.

This analysis highlights the economic reasons for tax evasion and other dimensions of the underground economy.

> Frank A. Cowell. *Cheating the Government: The Economics of Evasion.* Cambridge, MA: The MIT Press, 1990.

Although farming has received growing attention in recent decades, the role of women in farming is rarely studied. This book describes farmwork, household work, and community life among farm women today.

> Rachel Ann Rosenfeld. *Farm Women: Work, Farm, and Family in the United States.* Chapel Hill, NC: University of North Carolina Press, 1985.

This comparative study probes one important dimension of the economy—attitudes toward work.

> Tomotsu Sengoku. *Willing Workers: The Work Ethics in Japan, England, and the United States.* Westport, CT: Quorum Books, 1985.

The very Canadian problem of regional dependency is given sophisticated treatment here.

> Ralph Matthews. *The Creation of Regional Dependency.* Toronto: University of Toronto Press, 1983.

The first title is a Canadian classic dealing with the small group of people that controls our economy. The relationships among them are also explored. The second is a highly readable, though disturbing, account of the the wealthiest Canadian families and the corporations they control.

> Wallace Clement. *The Canadian Corporate Elite.* Toronto: McClelland and Stewart, 1975.
>
> Diane Francis. *Controlling Interest: Who Owns Canada?* Toronto: Macmillan, 1986.

20

HEALTH AND MEDICINE

Corey Smith is a university student, away from home for the first time and living in residence at a university on the Prairies. She is the youngest of four girls. All of the others had left home by the time Corey entered high school. Her sisters seem to her to be very successful. They are all married and settled in their careers: two as nurses and one as a teacher. Corey doesn't think that she can live up to their models. She has never dated. While her marks are very good, she is preoccupied with her appearance, with getting a date, falling in love, and getting married. The first step on that glorious path remains elusive. Corey feels she is too fat, but she is starving. At 5 feet 6 inches, she weighs only 89 pounds. Her friends in residence are really worried. They know that she is not eating, but they don't know how to convince her that she has a problem.

Corey Smith's problem, familiar to many university students, is *anorexia nervosa* (Currie, 1988; Orbach, 1986), a disorder characterized by what specialists term "severe caloric restriction," or intense, often compulsive dieting. Another eating disorder, *bulimia*, involves binge eating coupled with induced vomiting to inhibit weight gain. The two diseases have similar victim profiles (cf. Striegel-Moore, Silberstein, & Rodin, 1986). Like many diseases, anorexia nervosa has social as well as biological sources: not only are 90 to 95 percent of its victims *females*, but most of them are *white* and from *affluent* families. Many women who contend with eating disorders are strongly pressured by their parents to be high achievers. Although Corey Smith's case is unusually severe, research suggests that one-third to one-half of university-aged women actively try to lose weight, although most of them would not be considered overweight. In North America in 1990, one to two percent of women between the ages of fourteen and twenty-five suffered from anorexia nervosa (National Eating Disorder Information Centre, 1993).

To better appreciate the social foundation of eating disorders for women, consider a comment once made by the Duchess of Windsor: "A woman," she observed, "cannot be too rich or too thin." Women fall victim to eating disorders because our culture places such importance on their physical appearance, with slenderness the ideal of femininity (Parrott, 1987). Some researchers suggest that this society socializes young women to believe that they are never "too thin to feel fat." Such an attitude pushes women toward a form of "mass starvation" that some critics claim "compares with foot-binding, lip-stretching, and other forms of woman mutilation" found in other cultures (Wooley, Wooley, & Dyrenforth, 1979; Levine, 1987).

Health is the concern of physicians and other

medical professionals. Sociologists, too, study health because, as this chapter explains, social forces greatly shape the well-being of the population and people throughout the world.

What Is Health?

Common sense suggests that health is simply the absence of disease. The World Health Organization, however, defines the ideal of **health** as *a state of complete physical, mental, and social well-being* (1946:3). This more sociological definition underscores the major theme of this chapter, that *health is as much a social as a biological issue.*

Health and Society

The health of any population is shaped by important characteristics of the surrounding society as a whole.

1. **Health relates to a society's cultural patterns.** People evaluate health based on standards that vary from culture to culture. Rene Dubos (1980; orig. 1965) points out that early in this century, yaws, a contagious skin disease, was so common in tropical Africa that societies there considered it normal. There is some truth, then, in the observation that health is having the same diseases as one's neighbors (Quentin Crisp, cited in Kirk & Madsen, 1989).

    What the members of a society view as healthy is also closely linked to what they deem to be *morally* good; by the same token, they often define as illness what they judge to be ethically wrong. Because many people in Canada object to homosexuality on moral grounds, they sometimes call this sexual orientation "sick," although it is quite natural from a medical point of view. Many members of our society, especially men, view as normal and desirable a competitive, stressful way of life, even though stress is related to some two-thirds of physician visits. Stress also underlies heart disease, which is the leading cause of death in Canada (Wallis, 1983). Ideas about what constitutes good health, therefore, mesh into a type of social control that promotes conformity to cultural norms.

    Because they are embedded in culture, standards of health change over time. Early in this century,

some prominent physicians condemned women who pursued a university education, warning that doing so placed an unhealthy strain on the female brain; others denounced people who masturbated as ruining their own health (Smith-Rosenberg & Rosenberg, 1984; Money, 1985). During the same era, few physicians recognized that the growing popularity of cigarette smoking posed a threat to health. Today, of course, we view each of these issues quite differently.

2. **Health relates to a society's technology and social resources.** The level of health people come to define as normal also depends on their society's technology. Looking back to a time when we had little control over the environment and living standards were low, people routinely contended with malnutrition, poor or nonexistent sanitation, all sorts of occupational hazards, and a host of infectious diseases. Only as industrialization raised the standard of living did conceptions of health correspondingly rise.

    In global perspective, contrasts of this kind persist today. What many people throughout the Third World learn to accept as the norm for health, most people in Canada would consider intolerable. In the most disadvantaged societies of the world, half the babies born each year die in infancy as a direct result of poverty (George, 1977; Harrison, 1984).

3. **Health relates to social inequality.** Every society on earth unequally distributes the resources that promote personal well-being. The physical, mental, and emotional health of wealthier women and men in Canada is far better than that of poor people, as we shall explain presently. This pattern starts at birth, with infant mortality highest among the poor; it persists through old age. Affluent people, on average, live years longer than poor people do.

Historical Patterns of Health

Because health has an important social dimension, we find pronounced changes in human well-being over the long course of history. What we commonly think of as revolutionary events of the past—the development of agriculture, the Industrial Revolution, and the emergence of scientific medicine—have all had a major impact on patterns of health.

Health in Preindustrial Societies

Members of the earliest hunting and gathering societies, described in Chapter 4 ("Society"), labored continually to secure an adequate supply of food. Simple technology greatly limited their ability to sustain a healthful environment. As Gerhard and Jean Lenski (1991) suggest, because each mother had to breast-feed an infant for a year or more, a food shortage or the birth of another child often meant abandoning at least one child. But children fortunate enough to survive infancy were still vulnerable to a host of injuries and illnesses. Nearly half the members of hunting and gathering societies died before age twenty, and few lived to see forty.

The agricultural revolution that marked the onset of "civilization" greatly expanded the supply of food and other resources. While this development enhanced the health of elites, peasants and slaves fared no better than before, typically living in crowded, unsanitary shelters. Facing a daily struggle with hunger, hard work, and fre-

Medieval medical practice was heavily influenced by astrology, so that physicians and lay people alike attributed disease to astral influence; this is the root of our word "influenza." In this woodcut by Swiss artist Jost Amman (1580), midwives attend a childbirth as astrologers cast a horoscope for the newborn.

quently abusive treatment, this peasant majority suffered from widespread poor health.

Through much of history, the growth of cities threatened health even more. Concentrations of people living in conditions of little or no sanitation meant disease was ever-present and easily spread. In medieval Europe, for example, even rich urbanites lived amid human waste and other refuse, and the situation only became worse as the cities grew (Mumford, 1961). From time to time, the spread of infectious disease, including plague, wiped out a sizable portion of a city's population. A great plague struck London in 1665, for example, and killed thousands of people during the better part of a year. Reddish spots on the skin accompanied by sneezing marked the onset of the plague, and people could only fill their pockets with herbs and flowers hoping these would ward off the disease. So frightening was the experience of this plague centuries ago that it remains with us still in the form of an innocent children's rhyme (Gray 1970, cited in Spates & Macionis, 1987:57):

> *Ring-a-ring-a-roses,*
> *A pocket full of posies*
> *'Tishoo, 'tishoo,*
> *We all fall down.*

Health in Industrial Societies

The Industrial Revolution in Europe and North America had a dramatic effect on health, but not immediately. At the outset, as factories in the mid-eighteenth century drew millions of people from the countryside to the cities, health problems actually became worse. Even the few workers who were well paid lived in crowded, contaminated tenements, and rich and poor alike traversed city streets that were rife with crime. Factory smoke fouled the air, and the hazard this presented to people went unrecognized until well into the twentieth century. Factories were dangerous, and workplace accidents happened routinely. No laws protected the safety of early industrial workers and few employers thought these hired hands worthy of much concern.

During the nineteenth century, health in Western Europe and North America gradually began to improve. At first glance, this change may seem to be a result of medical advances, which occurred after mid-century, but the death rate in Western Europe and North America actually began to decline even before that (Illich, 1976; McKeown, 1979; Mahler, 1980). Industrialization itself—apart from any medical breakthroughs—brought improving health by slowly raising the standard of living, giving more people access to better nutrition and safer housing.

But scientific medicine did play a part in people's improving health, especially in cities plagued with infectious diseases. To illustrate, in 1854 John Snow examined residential patterns of cholera victims in London and traced the source of this disease to contaminated drinking water (Mechanic, 1978). Before long, scientists identified the cause of cholera as bacteria, and eventually they developed protective vaccines. Armed with this knowledge, early environmentalists also campaigned against the age-old practice of discharging raw sewage into rivers used for drinking water. By the early twentieth century, death rates from infectious diseases declined sharply.

Over the long term, industrialization has had a dramatic, beneficial effect on people's health. Leading killers in 1900 were influenza and pneumonia, which together accounted for one-fourth of all deaths. Today these diseases cause fewer deaths in Canada. As Figure 20.1 indicates, the rate of infant deaths which were frequently due to infectious diseases has declined dramatically for both boy and girl infants since 1931, while the life expectancy at birth, for both, has climbed steadily.

With infectious diseases now brought under control, chronic conditions like heart disease, cancer, and cerebrovascular diseases such as stroke eventually claim the majority of the population of Canada, as Figure 20-2 shows. Changing social patterns play a part here, too: the increasing use of work-saving devices reduces healthful exercise in the course of daily life, and people are smoking cigarettes, a practice rare a century ago. Also, our diet draws heavily on meat and eggs, pro-

viding considerable cholesterol. Consequently, we are now more likely to die from heart disease than are the Japanese, whose diet is based on fish (Wallis, 1984). Because people today succumb from chronic conditions rather than acute infections, death is now associated with advancing age. A century and a half ago, both men and women lived to be approximately thirty-nine years of age on average in Canada (Nancarrow Clarke, 1990). For people born in 1990, by contrast, government estimates place life expectancy at more than seventy-two years for men and more than seventy-nine years for women. In essence, we are now fortunate to live long enough to die from the chronic illnesses of old age, heart disease, cancer, and stroke.

Global Patterns of Health

In contrast to our remarkable progress in combating infectious disease, in the Third World striking poverty (see Chapter 11, "Global Inequality") makes health much worse than in industrial societies. People in poor countries expect to live roughly sixty years, ten years less than the First-World average (Mahler, 1980). In Africa, life expectancy is barely fifty, and in the poorest societies in the world, such as Cambodia and Ethiopia, the figure drops to forty.

According to the World Health Organization, one billion of the world's people—one in five—suffer from poor health due to poverty. Ill health stems directly from the cruel reality of malnutrition—not having enough to eat or consuming only one kind of food, as the box explains.

In impoverished countries, sanitary drinking

FIGURE 20-1   TRENDS IN LIFE EXPECTANCY AND INFANT MORTALITY
SOURCE: Canada's 125th Anniversary Yearbook, 1992. Ottawa: Statistics Canada, October 1991:96.

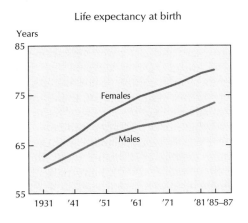

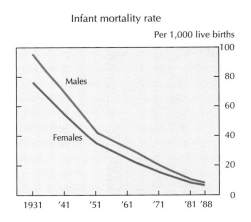

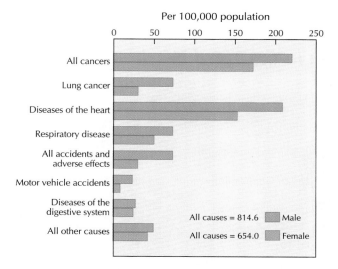

Per 100,000 population

All cancers

Lung cancer

Diseases of the heart

Respiratory disease

All accidents and adverse effects

Motor vehicle accidents

Diseases of the digestive system

All other causes

All causes = 814.6 Male
All causes = 654.0 Female

FIGURE 20-2   STANDARDIZED DEATH RATES, BY SELECTED CAUSE AND SEX, 1988
SOURCE: Canada's 125th Anniversary Yearbook, 1992. Ottawa: Statistics Canada, October 1991:97.

water may be as scarce as the chance for a balanced diet. Unsafe water is a major cause of the infectious diseases that imperil Third-World adults and children. The leading causes of death in Canada a century ago, including influenza, pneumonia, and tuberculosis, are still widespread killers in poor societies. Only 10 percent of all children receive protection from measles, tuberculosis, whooping cough, polio, tetanus, and diphtheria in the developing world. Five million children still die from these diseases and an additional 5 million are disabled annually (Nancarrow Clarke, 1990). Additionally, substandard sanitation promotes the growth of parasites such as hookworms, tapeworms, and roundworms, giving rise to additional illnesses (Harrison, 1984; Newman & Matzke, 1984).

To make matters worse, medical personnel are few and far between in the Third World. In some of the poorest societies—in central Africa, for example—many people never consult a physician. Global Map 20-1 illustrates the state of medical care throughout the world.

Against this backdrop of overarching poverty and minimal medical care, it is no wonder that Third-World societies have high death rates at all stages of life, especially in childhood. Paul Harrison (1984) estimates that 10 percent of Third-World children die in their first year of life; in the poorest societies, half the children never reach adulthood. Children of the Third World today, that is, die at the same rate as European children did in 1750 (George, 1977).

Improving Third-World health poses a monumental challenge. First, poverty and poor health form a vicious cycle: poverty (through malnutrition and inadequate medical care) breeds disease, which, in turn, limits people's ability to work to improve their economic situation (Harrison, 1984). As was explained in Chapter 11 ("Global Inequality"), the combined effects of simple technology in the Third World and concentrations of wealth in the First World make it unlikely that we will soon see a dramatic reduction in global poverty. The prognosis for improving the physical, mental, and social well-being of the world's poorest people, then, remains bleak.

One issue further complicates the problem of world health: as new medical technology brings infectious diseases under control, the populations of poor nations increase. But poor countries lack the resources to ensure the well-being of the populations they have now, so population growth only makes matters worse. Thus, reducing death rates through medical advances carries with it the moral obligation to help reduce birth rates as well.

Health in Canada

In comparison with the Third World, Canada has very favorable patterns of health. To survey health in our society, we begin with an overview of how health is distributed throughout the population, and then move on to examine several contemporary issues that affect the health of everyone.

Social Epidemiology: The Distribution of Health

Social epidemiology is *the study of how health and disease are distributed throughout a society's population.* Early social epidemiologists examined the origin and spread of epidemic diseases; John Snow's research on cholera, noted earlier, is but one example. Modern social epidemiologists try to link patterns of health to physical and social environments (Cockerham, 1986). For example, they might investigate rates of heart disease for people of various age categories, the two sexes, or according to class and race.

Age and Sex

During this century, a rising standard of living and improved medical care in Canada have enhanced the

CROSS-CULTURAL COMPARISON

Poverty: The Leading Cause of Death in the Third World

Widespread famine in Africa during the 1980s brought home to people in affluent Canada the image of starving children. Some of the children portrayed by the mass media appeared bloated, while others seemed to have shriveled to little more than skin drawn tightly over bones. Both of these deadly conditions are direct consequences of poverty.

Children with bloated bodies are suffering from protein deficiency. In West Africa this condition is known as *kwashiorkor*, which means literally "one-two." The term derives from the mothers' common practice of abruptly weaning a first child upon the birth of a second. Deprived of mother's milk, an infant may receive virtually no protein. Children with shrivelled bodies are being deprived of both protein and calories, the result of eating little food of any kind.

In either case, children usually do not die of starvation, strictly speaking. More precisely, their weakened condition makes them vulnerable to stomach ailments such as gastroenteritis or diseases like measles. The death rate from measles is a thousand times greater in parts of Africa than in North America.

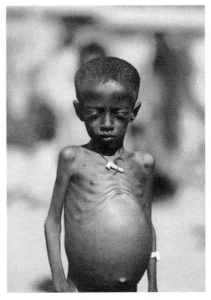

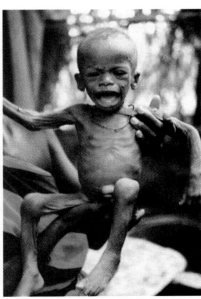

Depending on a single food also undermines nutrition, causing a deficiency of protein, vitamins, and minerals. Millions of people in the Third World suffer from goiter, a debilitating, diet-related disease of the thyroid gland. Pellagra, a disease common to people who consume only corn, is equally serious, frequently leading to insanity. Those who con-

sume mostly processed rice are prone to beriberi.

A host of diseases virtually unknown to members of rich societies are a common experience of life—and death—in the Third World.

SOURCE: Based, in part, on George (1977).

---

health of people of almost every age. One exception is young adults, who suffer more accidental deaths than in the past, mostly due to automobile mishaps. Generally, however, members of our society are blessed with good health and substantial longevity.

Women live somewhat longer lives than men, although they do suffer more sickness during their lives. Females have a biological advantage that renders them less likely than males to die before or immediately after birth. Then, as socialization takes over, males learn to be more aggressive and individualistic, resulting in higher rates of accidents, violence, and suicide. Our cultural definition of masculinity encourages males to be competitive at work, to repress their emotions, and to

engage in hazardous behaviors like smoking and excessive drinking. While providing men with greater social and economic privileges, then, conventional gender distinctions also entail greater health risks.

Social Class and Race

Social epidemiologists have established a strong link between health and social class from the beginning of life. Infant mortality—the death rate among newborns—is twice as high among the poor as it is for privileged people. While the richest children in our society have health that rivals that found anywhere in the world, our poorest children are as vulnerable as those in many Third-World countries, including Sudan and Lebanon.

Table 20-1 shows that both life expectancy and life expectancy free of disability vary significantly from income level to income level, and by neighborhood quality. Those in the highest income levels live longer, and have more years free of disability, than those in the poorest income levels. There is some debate about the causal direction in such findings (that is, whether people get sick because they are poor, or people are poor because they are sick). It appears that for the most part

class is the independent variable and health is the dependent. At times, however, sickness may lead to a decline in income over a long period of time.

Native Canadians continue to live shorter lives than non-Native Canadians. In 1990, the life expectancy for a Native male was 66.9 years (compared to about 73 years for non-Native males), and 74 years for Native females (as compared to about 80 years for non-Native females) (*Canada's 125th Anniversary Yearbook*, 1992). The causes of death also tend to be different for Native Canadians. Between 1982 and 1992, injury (violence

WINDOW ON THE WORLD

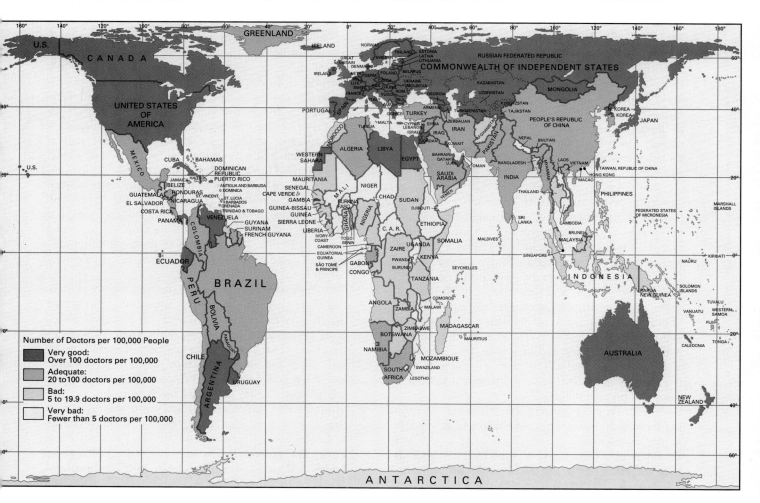

GLOBAL MAP 20-1 MEDICAL CARE IN GLOBAL PERSPECTIVE
Medical doctors, widely available to people in the First World, are perilously scarce in poor societies. While traditional forms of healing do improve health, antibiotics and vaccines—vital for controlling the infectious diseases that plague the Third World—are often in short supply. In poor societies, therefore, death rates are high, especially among infants.

TABLE 20-1 DISTRIBUTION OF HEALTH EXPECTANCY IN CANADA, BY SEX, LATE 1970S

	Life Expectancy			Disability-free Life		
	Male	Female	Total	Male	Female	Total
Income Level						
Lowest	67.1	76.6	71.9	50.0	59.9	54.9
Second	70.1	77.6	73.8	57.9	61.8	59.9
Third	70.9	78.5	74.7	61.1	64.3	62.7
Fourth	72.0	79.0	75.5	62.6	63.5	63.1
Highest	73.4	79.4	76.4	64.3	67.5	65.9
Local Area						
Poor neighbor-hood	61.4	70.9	66.1	49.2	54.0	51.6
Middle-class district	72.2	78.2	75.2	62.9	66.9	64.9

SOURCE: *R. Wilkins and O.B. Adams, Healthfulness of Life: A Unified View of Mortality, Institutionalization, and Non-Institutionalized Disability in Canada, 1978. Montreal: The Institute for Research on Public Policy, 1983:126.*

and accidents) and poisoning have been the major causes of death for Natives, although there are dramatic declines in these causes (43 percent since 1987). The second and third major causes of death parallel those for the non-Native population: circulatory diseases and neoplasms (*Basic Departmental Data*, 1992).

In Canada, as elsewhere in the world, poverty condemns people to crowded, unsanitary environments that breed infectious diseases. Although tuberculosis is no longer a widespread threat to health in Canada, the rate of TB is once again on the rise (Hurst, 1992). Their higher risk of poverty makes Native Canadians more likely than non-Natives to die from this disease.

Native people, and poor people of all races, also suffer from nutritional deficiencies. A large percentage of our population try to get by with a substandard diet and minimal medical care. The results are predictable: while wealthy women and men typically die in old age of chronic illnesses such as heart disease and cancer, poor people generally die younger from infectious diseases that prey on the poor.

There is some concern that AIDS may be spreading more quickly among Native men and women, particulary women who live on reserves. According to the World Health Organization, nine hundred and sixty Native Canadians presently have AIDS and as many as 1,500 carry the HIV infection (*Windspeaker*, 1991). Some argue that Natives are hit first when it comes to an epidemic because their immune systems, having faced fewer diseases, are not as strong as non-Native Canadians (*Windspeaker*, 1991).

But, in some respects, privilege also carries risks to health. In fact, when affluence results from stress-producing competition, or encourages a sedentary lifestyle and the consumption of rich food, the wealthy pay the price in terms of high death rates from heart disease (Fuchs, 1974; Wallis, 1984). Nevertheless, wealth also confers decided health advantages: a safer environment, living with less fear, and access to better medical care when illness strikes (Lin & Ensel, 1989). The facts are conclusive: affluent people live longer and suffer less from illness than do other members of our society. Here again we see how the distribution of health depends on how society operates.

Environmental Pollution

In global perspective, the idea that human beings must live in harmony with the natural world has formed a central theme of many cultures, especially in Asia. Only recently, however, have we in the West come to embrace this position, and only after causing considerable damage to the environment. Table 20-2 presents an overview of the top twenty environmental disasters over the last twenty years. The first eight are general phenomena, while those that follow are specific events that occurred in various parts of the world.

By their very nature, industrial societies disrupt the ecological balance. Few members of our society can imagine living without automobiles and factories, but they both pollute the air, producing a well-documented threat to health. Thus modern technology, while raising our standard of living, has also introduced new health hazards.

Industrial wastes arouse public concern as well. For more than half a century, some industries across the country have been haphazardly disposing of poisonous chemicals. They have poured toxic substances into local sewage systems or discharged them directly into rivers and streams. Dumps that dot our national landscape now contain steel drums filled with dangerous chemicals that gradually leach into the soil and groundwater. International attention was drawn to the issue of toxic wastes in 1980, when the residents of Love Canal, a neighborhood in Niagara Falls, New York, discovered deadly dioxin seeping into their homes and yards, which had been built on the site of an old petrochemical dump.

A final environmental issue that affects human health is nuclear power. An inexpensive source of energy, nuclear power also spares finite supplies of coal and oil. But nuclear power has the major drawback that a serious malfunction could release radiation—as deadly as fallout from an atomic bomb—into the atmosphere, threatening life for hundreds of miles. This danger is more than hypothetical: accidents at nuclear reactor plants have been reported since they first began operating in the early 1950s. Serious malfunctions occurred at reactors near Ottawa (1952), near Liverpool, England (1957), and at Three Mile Island near Harrisburg,

---

TABLE 20-2 TOP TWENTY ENVIRONMENTAL DISASTERS

1. Atmospheric deterioration   Global warming, ozone depletion. Continual heavy pollution over Mexico City.

2. Soil degradation   An area about the size of China and India combined has suffered moderate to extreme soil degradation, caused mainly by agricultural activities, deforestation and overgrazing in the past 45 years, according to a new United Nations Environment Program study. This area—1.2 billion hectares—represents almost 11 percent of the Earth's vegetated surface.

3. Deforestation   Europe has no old-age growth forests left. There are a few in North America. We are busily chewing our way through the remnants of the tropical forests at the rate of nearly 17 million hectares per year.

4. Coral reefs   Coral reefs are the underwater analogue of tropical forests. The most species-rich of ecosystems—up to 3,000 species may live on just one reef in Southeast Asia—they are also probably the oldest. Many are now endangered.

5. Toxification   Poisoning by mercury, cadmium, heavy metals, chlorine, DDT, PCBs, and a wide range of other substances. Acid rain. The accumulation of oil and plastic in the oceans. Daily leakage from tankers dwarfs the amount of oil spilled by the Exxon Valdez and during the Gulf War.

6. Depletion of fisheries   The United Nations' Food and Agricultural Organization reported in 1990 that the most traditional marine fish stocks have reached full exploitation.

7. Loss of biodiversity   All of the above contribute to the loss of biodiversity—defined as the variety among living organisms and the ecological communities they inhabit. Best estimates put the total number of species between 5 million and 30 million. Most are minute; only 1.4 million have been named by taxonomists.

8. The nuclear mess   The military mess dwarfs the civil catastrophes. The bill for dismantling the U.S. network of nuclear weapons facilities is currently estimated to be $130 billion.

9. Michigan (1973–74)   All 9 million people living in the state of Michigan during this period had measurable levels of a highly toxic chemical—PBB—in their tissues. A consignment of PBB was mistakenly delivered to agricultural feed company and mixed into cattle food. For nine months, contaminated milk, meat, and eggs were sold across the state.

10. Seveso (July 10, 1976)   A reactor used in the manufacture of trichlorophenol exploded at a chemical plant near Milan owned by Givaudan, a subsidiary of the Swiss pharmaceutical giant Hoffman-La Roche. It was 10 days before the company publicly admitted that the resultant toxic cloud contained dioxin, one of the most persistent and poisonous synthetic chemicals. In the year following the accident, the rate of birth defects in the area increased by the more than 40 percent.

11. Love Canal (summer–fall 1978)   Industrial sludge from a leaking dump turned a town near Niagara Falls, N.Y., into America's "first toxic ghost town." Though people are moving back, scientists are still assessing the damage.

12. Amoco Cadiz (March 16, 1978)   This supertanker, flying the Liberian flag and manned by an Italian crew, went aground on the Brittany coast, disgorging her cargo of 200,000 tonnes of crude oil. More than 200 km of coastline were smothered.

13. Three Mile Island (March 28, 1979)   America's worst commercial nuclear-reactor accident. Decontamination work continues; the human cost is harder to assess. The amount of radiation vented from the crippled plant and the amount of fallout that descended on the surrounding counties are still matters of dispute.

14. Antarctic ozone hole (1981)   The depletion of the ozone layer over Antarctica each spring was first noticed by scientist Joe Farman at the British Antarctic Survey. The subsequent ozone crisis offered the first evidence that human activity could actually threaten global systems. Ozone depletion in the northern hemisphere was discovered subsequently.

15. Bhopal (Dec. 3–4, 1984)   More than 30 tonnes of methyl-isocyanate, a gaseous toxin, escaped from a Union Carbide pesticide factory in Bhopal, India. According to current estimates, more than 3,500 people died, and tens of thousands of others are believed to have been injured by the gas.

16. Chernobyl (April 26, 1986)   A vast concrete dome now encases the site of the first accident at Chernobyl, which claimed 30 lives immediately and contaminated vast areas of the former Soviet Union and northern Europe.

17. Exxon Valdez (March 24, 1989)   Ran aground in Prince William Sound, Alaska, releasing 232,000 barrels (11 million gallons) of oil.

18. Gulf War (Jan. 19, 1991)   The Kuwaiti oil fires; the Gulf spill (the largest in history); the release into the environment of radioactive materials and toxic chemicals when Iraqi chemical warfare factories and refineries were bombed.

19. Aral Sea (April 1991)   Once the fourth-biggest lake in the world, the Aral Sea—located in Uzbekistan and Kazakhastan—is now sixth largest, having lost a volume of water equivalent to $1\frac{1}{2}$ times that of Lake Erie between 1973 and 1989. The cause: the diversion of the two great rivers that fed the Aral to irrigate millions of acres of cotton.

20. Chelyabinsk (revealed summer 1991)   A secret report for Mikhail Gorbachev described the true extent of the problems at this nuclear military complex, which was the Soviet Union's primary facility for manufacturing nuclear weapons for 43 years. Its 80 square miles are the most polluted spot on Earth. If you multiply Chernobyl a hundred times, you have the picture.

SOURCE: *Montreal Gazette, Sunday June 7, 1992:A1.*

Pennsylvania (1979). The most serious accident to date—a meltdown of the reactor core at the Chernobyl plant near Kiev in the former Soviet Union in 1986—spread radiation throughout much of the world. The immediate death toll was only thirty but, over the long term, casualties from radiation exposure will probably reach the thousands.

In addition to the danger of reactor accidents, nuclear power plants produce waste materials that remain highly radioactive for hundreds of thousands of years. Currently, we have no way to dispose of such wastes without risking future contamination of the environment.

Cigarette Smoking

Many threats to health are matters of individual behavior, and cigarette smoking tops the list of preventable hazards. Cigarette smoking became common in Canada only about the time of World War I. Despite evidence of its dangers—especially rising rates of lung cancer a generation later—most people remained unaware of the harm posed by cigarettes and viewed smoking as socially acceptable and even fashionable. Now smoking is recognized as the leading preventable cause of illness and death among people in Canada, and this practice is coming to be defined as a mild social deviance.

Despite continued advertising by cigarette manufacturers (banned from television and radio in 1971), per capita consumption of cigarettes has decreased from 43 to 33 percent from 1969 to 1989. This decrease is accounted for mostly by males whose rate of smoking declined from 52 to 35 percent. The rate among females changed only slightly, from 34 to 31 percent. Even so, in 1991, Canadian tobacco companies manufactured 46.81 billion cigarettes, down from 48.66 billion in 1990 ("Tobacco Production Edges Up," *Montreal Gazette*, Jan. 25, 1992:PE1). The popularity of smoking has definitely peaked, and more and more businesses and governments across the country are responding to the health hazards of smoking tobacco by banning the practice in public buildings.

As most smokers realize, the nicotine in cigarette smoke is physically addictive. Thus people may become physically dependent on tobacco, as well as relying on the drug as a means of coping with stress. This psychological dependency explains why the divorced and separated are more likely to smoke, as are the unemployed and people in the military services. Blue-collar workers tend to smoke more than white-collar workers, and people with less schooling smoke more than their more

educated counterparts. Men (35 percent) still smoke more than women (31 percent).

During the 1930s, medical researchers noted a sharp rise in smoking-related diseases such as lung cancer. Studies showed that roughly twenty years of smoking was generally required for lung cancer to develop. But not until the 1960s did the government take the dangers of tobacco use seriously. The official turnaround was partly provoked by a rising incidence of lung cancer among women, who had begun smoking in large numbers during the 1940s. By the mid-1960s, reports revealed a direct link between smoking cigarettes—as well as cigars and pipes—and heart disease; cancer of the mouth, throat, and lungs; and lung diseases such as bronchitis and emphysema. Lung cancer is the leading cause of cancer death for men and in competition with breast cancer as the leading cause of death among women. As recently as 1961, lung cancer death rates for men were over six times higher than they were for women. But as women's rate of smoking has increased so too have their rates of lung cancer. Over the last twenty years, the annual rate of increase for lung cancer mortality for women aged twenty-five to forty-

Fifty years ago, film celebrities were hired by tobacco companies to help sell cigarettes, despite growing evidence of the harm caused by smoking.

four has been 3.6 percent (Probert, et. al., 1992). These increases in smoking and mortality among females have been attributed in part to advertisements that have increasingly targeted women and adolescents. The average age at which individuals begin to smoke is 12.5 years (Probert et al., 1992). Canada Map 20-1 indicates the deaths due to cancers of the respiratory system (mainly lung cancer) per 10,000 population in various provinces and territories, as well as for Canada as a whole.

Beyond raising their risk of fatal illnesses, smokers also experience more frequent minor illnesses such as flu, and pregnant women who smoke increase the likelihood of spontaneous abortion and prenatal death. Research indicates that even nonsmokers exposed to cigarette smoke have a higher risk of smoking-related diseases (Shephard, 1982).

Tobacco is still a huge industry in Canada. The tobacco industry still maintains that because the precise link between cigarettes and disease has not been specified, the health effects of smoking remain "an open question" (Rudolph, 1985). But the tobacco industry is not breathing as easily today as it once did. Laws mandating a smoke-free environment are rapidly proliferating. In the winter of 1993, the health minister for the Federal Conservative government, Benoit Bouchard, introduced a bill designed to make it difficult for a young person to buy cigarettes. The *Sale of Tobacco to Young Person's Act* raised the legal age for buying cigarettes from sixteen to eighteen, restricted the locations

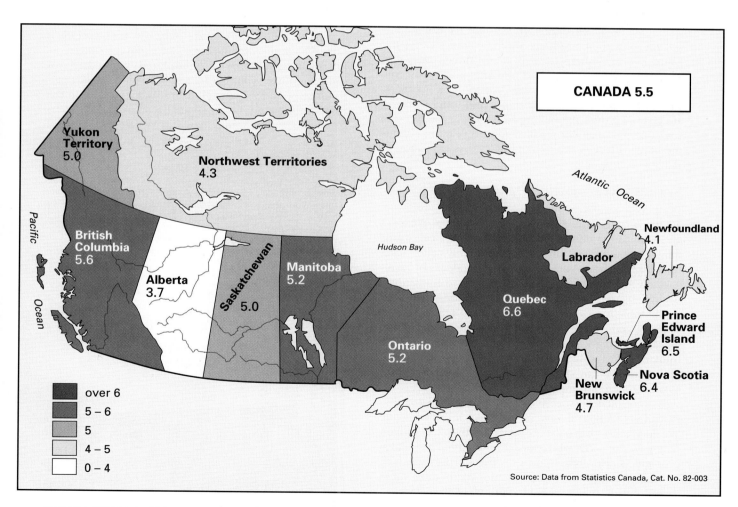

CANADA MAP 20-1   DEATHS FROM CANCERS OF THE RESPIRATORY SYSTEM (PER 10,000 POPULATION, BY PROVINCE AND TERRITORY, 1991)

of cigarette vending machines, and imposed fines of up to $50,000 for selling tobacco to minors (Doyle, *Toronto Star*, Feb. 5, 1993:A14).

A number of municipalities across the country have introduced more or less extensive anti-smoking bylaws. The city of Toronto, for instance, has declared workplaces and public indoor areas in Toronto smoke-free unless there is a fully enclosed and separately ventilated area. Smoking has been barred at the Skydome, Maple Leaf Gardens, shopping malls, recreation centers, bowling alleys, theaters, and cinemas. Restaurants too, have been required to increase their no-smoking areas from 30 to 50 percent (MacLeod, *Globe and Mail*, Dec. 3, 1992). Furthermore, courts have increased the liability of cigarette manufacturers in lawsuits brought by victims of smoking-related illnesses, or their survivors.

One response of the tobacco industry has been to sell more of their products abroad—especially in the Third World—where regulation of tobacco sales and advertising is less strict, and anti-smoking sentiments have not dampened enthusiasm for tobacco products. In North America, however, more and more smokers are giving up the habit, taking advantage of the fact that someone who has not smoked for ten years has about the same pattern of health as a lifelong nonsmoker.

Sexually Transmitted Diseases

Sexual activity, while a source of individual pleasure and vital to the continuation of the species, can transmit a large number of illnesses. Commonly called *venereal diseases* (from Venus, the Roman goddess of love), sexually transmitted illnesses date back to humanity's beginnings; references to these maladies are even found in the Bible. Canadian culture has traditionally viewed sex with ambivalence; while we celebrate it in advertising and throughout the mass media, we also tend to think of sex as sinful. Not surprisingly, then, some people regard venereal diseases not simply as illnesses, but as punishment for immorality.

In global perspective, sexually transmitted diseases (STDs) pose a very serious health problem; the World Health Organization estimates that 250 million new cases of STD are reported annually. This health problem is also great—and growing—in Canada. The incidence of STDs—there are fifty of them in all—soared during the "sexual revolution" of the 1960s. In essence, this revolution redefined sex as a natural and pleasant way to express affection that could be enjoyed

whether or not people were married. Before this time, estimates held that two out of three men but only about one in ten women had premarital sexual intercourse; by 1990, the figures had risen to three out of four men and two out of three women.

In this climate of sexual permissiveness, sexually transmitted diseases became an exception to the general pattern by which infectious diseases have declined during this century. With the rise in STDs—and especially acquired immune deficiency syndrome (AIDS)—the second half of the 1980s witnessed a sexual counterrevolution that prompted individuals to reexamine their values and behavior (Kain, 1987; Kain & Hart, 1987). The following sections provide a brief overview of several common STDs.

Gonorrhea and Syphilis

Gonorrhea and syphilis are very old diseases, each caused by a microscopic organism almost always transmitted by sexual contact. Untreated, gonorrhea can cause sterility; syphilis can damage major organs and result in blindness, mental disorders, and death. In the past, our society severely stigmatized victims of gonorrhea and syphilis, seeing these diseases as the "wages of sin" among social outcasts such as prostitutes.

Experts—and the public—disagree as to the best strategy for combating the spread of HIV. Liberals support the distribution of condoms to young people because condom use significantly reduces the chances for sexual transmission of the virus. Conservatives object to this policy, claiming it encourages casual sex, which, for them, is the heart of the problem. From this point of view, rethinking the notion that young people should be sexually active is a better approach.

Roughly 1,441 cases of gonorrhea and syphilis were reported in Canada in 1990, although the actual number may well be several times greater. Generally speaking, poorer people and particularly visible minorities have higher rates of various STDs than those from the higher social classes. Most cases of gonorrhea and syphilis are easily cured with penicillin, an antibiotic drug developed in the 1940s. Although some strains of these diseases resist efforts at treatment, neither disease currently represents a serious health threat in Canada.

Genital Herpes

Genital herpes received widespread public attention during the 1980s. Physicians are not required by law to report cases of genital herpes, unlike gonorrhea and syphilis. However, an estimated 20 to 30 million adults in the United States (one in seven) are infected with the genital herpes virus (Moran et al., 1989), and the rate is likely similar in Canada.

Although far less serious than gonorrhea and syphilis, herpes is currently incurable. Patients may exhibit no symptoms or they may experience periodic, painful blisters on the genitals accompanied by fever and headache. Although it is not fatal to adults, women with active genital herpes can transmit the disease to a child during a vaginal delivery, and it can be deadly to a newborn. In such cases, therefore, women usually give birth by cesarean section.

AIDS

The most serious of all sexually transmitted diseases is acquired immune deficiency syndrome, or AIDS. Although AIDS may have appeared as early as the 1960s, researchers identified it only in 1981. Although much has been learned since then, AIDS is incurable and fatal.

The first AIDS case in Canada was reported by the Laboratory Centre for Disease Control (LCDC) in February 1982. From this first case to July 1992, there have been 6,560 cases reported in Canada. If we consider delayed and under-reporting, the real number may be closer to 8,400 cases. The highest incidence was recorded in 1989 at 1,200 cases (over three Canadians per day). This rate declined somewhat in 1990. We may be beginning to see some of the results of the widespread education campaign, and subsequent behavior changes in sex practices, and drug and intravenous use. Approximately one adult Canadian in 10,000 is living with AIDS today, and approximately 30,000 are infected with HIV.

Women have accounted for less than 7 percent of all of the AIDS cases reported in Canada. From 1982 to 1984, twenty women were diagnosed with AIDS. Between 1988 and 1989, one hundred and fifty-seven women contracted the disease. As of February 1989, there were forty-one children diagnosed with AIDS and close to half of these were under one year of age. In 1989, AIDS became one of the top four overall contributors to potential years of life lost (PYLL) for men in Canada, and presently contribute more PYLL in men than diseases such as diabetes, and chronic lung and kidney disease (Remis, 1993).

AIDS is caused by a human immunodeficiency virus (HIV). This virus attacks white blood cells, the core of the immune system that the body mobilizes to fight infections. As these cells are destroyed, a person with AIDS becomes vulnerable to a wide range of infectious diseases that eventually bring on death. Technically, then, AIDS kills people indirectly by rendering them unable to fight off common infections.

Estimates place the number of people worldwide who are infected with HIV as high as 10 million, a figure that could increase three- or fourfold by the end of this decade. Global Map 20-2 shows that the African continent (more specifically, countries below the Sahara Desert) has the highest HIV infection rate and currently accounts for almost two-thirds of all cases worldwide. In the cities of central African nations such as Burundi, Rwanda, Uganda, and Kenya, roughly one-fifth of all young adults are infected with HIV (Tofani, 1991). North America represents about 10 percent of global HIV.

People carrying HIV do not immediately contract AIDS, however. On the contrary, the majority of people with the virus show no symptoms whatever, and most are unaware of their own infection. Symptoms of AIDS usually do not appear for at least a year. Within about five years, some 25 percent of infected persons will develop AIDS; most infected people will eventually develop the disease. As the death toll mounts, AIDS has turned out to be nothing less than catastrophic—potentially the most serious epidemic of modern times.

Today all donated blood is checked for HIV before being transfused However, the Canadian Hemophiliac Society has accused the Canadian Red Cross of "bureaucratic foot-dragging" that led to the infection of at least 750 hemophiliacs with the HIV virus, and potentially many other transfusion recipients in the mid-1980s. Several high-profile lawsuits have been launched against the Red Cross.

While fear of AIDS is rampant, there is some

grounds for comfort. Transmission of HIV almost always occurs through blood, semen, or breast milk. This means that AIDS is not spread through casual contact with an infected person; one cannot become infected by shaking hands or hugging an infected person. There is no recorded case of the virus being transmitted through coughing and sneezing, through the sharing of towels, dishes, or telephones, or through water in a bath, pool, or hot tub. The risk of transmitting AIDS through saliva (as in kissing) is extremely low. Infected women can pass HIV to their newborn children, although present evidence indicates that there is less than a 50 percent chance of this occurring. The bottom line is that AIDS is a deadly disease—but it is also hard to get through casual contact.

Oral and especially genital sex are dangerous,

WINDOW ON THE WORLD

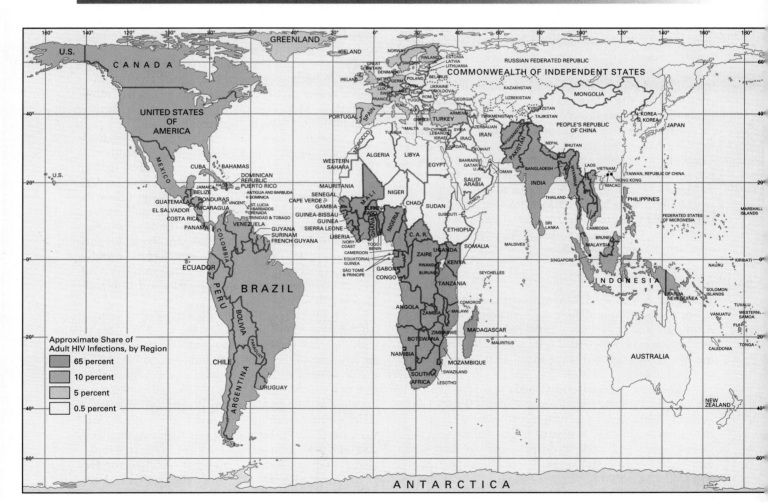

GLOBAL MAP 20-2   HIV INFECTION OF ADULTS IN GLOBAL PERSPECTIVE
Infection of adults with HIV is not spread evenly around the world. Approximately two-thirds of all cases in the world are recorded in sub-Saharan Africa where, in many countries, HIV has become a runaway epidemic. Such a high infection rate reflects the prevalence of other venereal diseases and infrequent use of condoms, both of which enhance heterosexual transmission of HIV. Regions of the world with moderate rates of infection include South and Southeast Asia, which together account for 10 percent of global infections, and South and North America, which each represent another 10 percent of all cases of HIV. The incidence of infection is lower still in Europe. Least affected by HIV are the societies of North Africa and the Middle East and also the nations of Australia and New Zealand.

however. The risk of transmitting the infection can be greatly reduced, but not eliminated, by use of latex condoms. In the age of AIDS, abstinence or an exclusive relationship with an uninfected person is the only sure way to avoid sexual transmission of AIDS. Self-interest demands that no one enter a sexual relationship lightly or casually.

These facts suggest that people can protect themselves by avoiding the behaviors that place them at high risk for becoming infected with HIV. The first is *anal sex*, which can cause rectal bleeding that allows easy transmission of HIV from one person to another. Anal sex is therefore extremely dangerous and, the greater the number of sexual partners, the greater the risk. Anal sex is commonly practiced by gay men, in some cases with multiple partners. This is the reason that homosexual and bisexual men comprise about 60 percent of those with AIDS. In response to the devastating effect of AIDS on gay communities across North America, gays (as well as nongays) have shunned sexual promiscuity in recent years (McKusick et al., 1985; Remis, 1993).

Sharing needles used to inject drugs is the second most prevalent high-risk behavior. Casual sex sometimes accompanies drug use; therefore, having sex with an intravenous drug user also constitutes a high-risk behavior. The association of this kind of drug use with people of lower socio-economic levels is another reason that there are class correlates in the incidence of AIDS.

Using any drug, including alcohol, also increases the risk of being infected with HIV to the extent that it impairs judgment. In other words, even people who understand what places them at risk of infection may act less responsibly once they are under the influence of alcohol, marijuana, or some other drug.

HIV prevalence among actively homosexual men is probably in the range of 10 to 15 percent. Approximately 22,500 men among the estimated 200,000 to 300,000 gay and bisexual men may be infected with HIV in Canada. The prevalence of AIDS amongst heterosexuals is much lower. Some estimate that perhaps 6 percent of infected adults contracted the disease through heterosexual contact (Remis, 1993). The likelihood of a runaway "breakout" of AIDS into the heterosexual population now seems less likely than it did several years ago (Fumento, 1989). Heterosexual activity can and does transmit AIDS, however, and the risk rises with the number of sexual partners a person has, especially if any partner falls into a high-risk category. Worldwide, heterosexual relations are the primary means of HIV transmission, accounting for two-thirds of all infections (Eckholm & Tierney, 1990).

In the U.S.A., the "third wave" of AIDS—after gay men and intravenous drug users—is now ravaging the urban poor. HIV is already getting out of control in cities such as Miami and New York, where the use of crack cocaine fuels casual sex and prostitution, which spread the deadly virus. Although the incidence of crack cocaine in Canada is much much smaller than in the U.S.A., its use, associated as it is with casual sex and prostitution, cannot help but ensure a higher rate of AIDS among users.

AIDS goes far beyond a medical problem and individual tragedies; it has also thrown our health-care system into financial crisis. The cost of treating a single person with AIDS already runs to hundreds of thousands of dollars and this figure may rise as new

Paul Marcus's sculpture The Junkie *graphically depicts the loss of humanity that often accompanies serious drug abuse. The age of AIDS has added another deadly consequence of intravenous drug use: the transmission of HIV through the sharing of needles. Some cities now have programs providing clean needles to addicts despite opposition on the grounds that doing so encourages illegal drug use.*

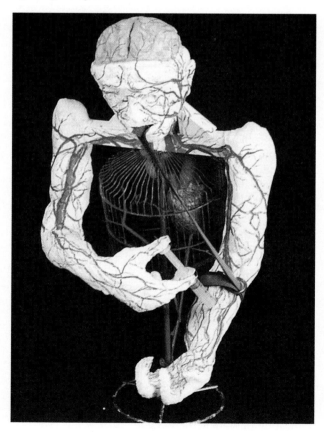

therapies are developed. Added to the direct costs of treatment and research are tens of billions of dollars in lost earnings and productivity. Medicare, private insurance, and personal savings will meet only a small fraction of this total. Taking all these factors into account, then, we see that AIDS represents both a medical and a social problem of monumental proportions.

It has been suggested that governments have responded slowly to the AIDS crisis largely because gays and intravenous drug users are widely viewed as deviant. More recently, money allocated for AIDS research has increased rapidly, and progress is being made. This is partly the result of the activism of the gay community, through groups such as ACT-UP, who have been successful in increasing public knowledge about the need for AIDS funding. For example, researchers have found that some drugs, such as AZT, suppress the symptoms of the disease but do not as yet lengthen the lives of people infected with HIV. Nevertheless, educational programs remain the most effective weapon against AIDS, since prevention is the only way to stop a disease that currently has no cure.

Ethical Issues: Confronting Death

Health involves not only medical concerns but also ethical issues. For example, Chapter 14 ("Aging and the Elderly") explained that our society is now facing a dilemma as to whether we should continue to allocate more and more resources to provide medical care for elderly people at the expense of the growing needs of the young (Callahan, 1987). Other vexing ethical issues surround death. These questions arise mainly because technological changes now give human beings greater control over life itself.

When is a person dead?   In defining death, common sense suggests that we reach this point when breathing ceases and the heart stops beating. But advancing medical technology has made this definition obsolete. Respiration can be sustained by machines, just as a heart that has stopped beating can be revived or even replaced. Furthermore, both breathing and heartbeat may continue in the absence of any brain activity.

Today, in short, experts confront the difficult question of specifying the line that separates life and death. Currently, medical and legal experts view death as an irreversible state involving no response to stimulation, no movement or breathing, no reflexes, and no indication of brain activity (Ladd, 1979; Wall, 1980).

Do people have a right to die?   Today, medical personnel, family members, and patients themselves face the agonizing burden of deciding when a terminally ill person should die. In 1992, Parliament abolished attempted suicide as a crime but retained the prohibition against assisting in suicide (Section 241(b) of the Criminal Code). Individuals periodically challenge this law. One such challenge was that mounted by Sue Rodriguez, a terminally ill British Columbia woman with Lou Gehrig's disease. At the time of printing, Rodriguez had approximately two to fourteen months of life left to live. The disease process meant that she would eventually be unable to swallow, to speak, to walk, or even to turn over without assistance. She would need a respirator to breathe. As her condition worsened, and she expected to be less likely to want to continue to live, her ability to end her life would be reduced. She wanted permission for a doctor, at a given time in the future, to set up an intravenous tube filled with a lethal dose of medication. Her case spawned both widespread support and fervent opposition from such groups as churches, anti-abortion activists, and both the provincial and federal governments (Wood, 1993). On September 30, 1993, the Supreme Court decided with a vote of 5–4, that Rodriguez's rights were not violated by the federal law against assisting in suicides. The court ruled that the state interest in protecting the sanctity of life took precedence over the individual right to a dignified death. (Wilson and Fine, *Globe and Mail*, Oct. 1, 1993:1.)

Despite this decision, we can be sure that the issue will not go away, as thousands of men and women, faced with a terminal illness that may cause suffering, consider ending their own life. Courts and government commissions will continue to wrestle with the ethical dilemma pitting *patients' rights* against the medical principle that we should provide all appropriate care to those in need.

What about mercy killing?   *Mercy killing* is the common term for **euthanasia**, *assisting in the death of a person suffering from an incurable disease.* Euthanasia (from the Greek, meaning "a good death") poses an ethical dilemma, since such an act is, on the one hand, an expression of kindness that, on the other hand, causes the death of another person.

Although legal support for a patient's right to die has increased, assisting in the death of another person is still quite controversial. In 1992, for example, Jack Kevorkian, a physician who helped two women end their lives with his "suicide machine," was arrested in

Michigan and charged with murder. No one thinks that the women involved—who ended their lives rather than continuing to suffer from terminal illnesses— thought of Kevorkian as their murderer. But our society is uneasy about legally empowering physicians to actively end a life in response to a patient's request.

The debate breaks down roughly as follows. Those who view life—even with suffering—as preferable to death categorically reject euthanasia. People who recognize circumstances under which death is preferable to life support euthanasia, but they face the practical problem of determining just when a person's life is no longer worth living. Such a decision is always difficult, and family members confront this matter at a time already marked by stress and sorrow. People may express their love of a dying person in various ways, as these examples suggest. After requesting physicians to revive the heart of her dying father, one daughter recently said:

> I'm glad they brought him back. He was old, but that doesn't mean he should stop living. He was still alive, and as long as he's alive, he should be saved.

Another daughter, however, insisted that physicians not prolong the life of her ninety-eight-year-old mother:

> If my mother's heart stopped beating, I don't want them pounding on her chest and destroying her body any more than it was. For what? Revive her for another day or another two weeks? (cited in Kleiman, 1985:11)

Adding to the burden of family members who must decide the fate of a dying patient is the ever-present concern with medical expenses. A single attempt to revive a patient whose heart has stopped may cost $1,500. Two weeks of heroic lifesaving efforts may cost the already overburdened medical system tens of thousands of dollars. While in Canada patients do not have to pay these amounts directly, opponents of euthanasia fear that such costs might lead physicians, or society in general, to place undue pressure on families to discontinue heroic treatment.

Ethical standards for dealing with dying patients are gradually emerging, a product of the interplay of physicians, lawyers, clergy, philosophers, patient rights groups, and others (Flynn, 1991). Such standards— and hospital bioethics committees to interpret them— are needed more than ever before, since many deaths now occur while people are attached to life-prolonging equipment (Humphrey, 1991). Presently, wide support

The vexing problem of whether or when a society should allow suffering people to die is nowhere better illustrated than in the life of Dax Cowart. After being critically burned in a propane-gas explosion, Cowart begged for a gun to shoot himself, and protested every effort by medical specialists to save him. Now almost twenty years later, Cowart has forged a life worth living—he graduated from law school and is married. But he still maintains that doctors should have complied with his wishes and let him die.

exists for the concept of *passive* euthanasia (or, in common language, "pulling the plug"), in which heroic treatment is withheld. Support is weaker for *active* euthanasia, illustrated by the Kevorkian case, in which a family member or physician directly assists in ending a life.

Medicine

Medicine is *an institutionalized system for combating disease and improving health.* Medicine forms a vital part of a broader concept of **health care**, which is *any activity intended to improve health.* Medicine has undergone many changes over the course of its long history.

Throughout most of human history, individuals and their families did what they could to enhance their own health. Medicine emerges as a multifaceted social institution when societies become more complex and their members assume various formal, specialized roles. Traditional preindustrial societies recognize medical specialists, who have knowledge of the healing properties of certain plants, and who often combine such skills with astute insights into the emotional and spiritual needs of the ill (Ayensu, 1981). Traditional healers—from acupuncturists to herbalists—are sometimes dismissed by the ethnocentric members of industrial societies as "witch doctors," but they do improve human health, and they continue to combat some of the world's greatest health problems.

As societies industrialize, a system of formal training and licensing empowers people to assist patients in improving their health. Although families still treat their own minor illnesses, they increasingly rely on a host of specialists—from anesthesiologists to x-ray technicians—to provide health care in offices and hospitals established for these purposes.

The Rise of Scientific Medicine

Health care in Canada is now dominated by *scientific medicine*, which applies the logic of science to research and the treatment of illness. Originally, various approaches to medicine distinguished herbalists, druggists, midwives, and even ministers. In the seventeenth century, about one in 600 adults engaged in some form of healing arts—about the same proportion as today—but there was little consensus about how this work should be done (Stevens, 1971; Nancarrow Clarke, 1990). Even the medical elite of the time—men who had received formal medical training in Europe—still knew little by today's standards, and their skills were often surpassed by those of herbalists and midwives. Unsanitary instruments, lack of anesthesia, and a large measure of ignorance made surgery a terrible ordeal in which surgeons killed as many patients as they saved.

Gradually, however, specialists learned more about human anatomy, physiology, and biochemistry. Early in the nineteenth century, medical societies appeared in Canada as doctors established themselves as self-regulating professionals (Blishen, 1991). Formal colleges of medicine offered training in the field. The increase in the number of medical schools paralleled the growth in the number of hospitals (Stevens, 1971). Medical societies required those who wished to practice or teach medical skills to obtain licenses, and these organizations enforced conformity to specific medical standards.

Advances in scientific medicine during the 19th century sparked stunning achievements in the field of disease control. At the same time, the number of women healers was also drastically reduced, particularly midwives. This is a picture of Emily Howard Stowe, Canada's first female doctor. After being refused admittance to medical schools in Canada, she received a degree from the New York Medical College for Women. She practiced medicine in Toronto for 13 years before finally being granted a license, in 1880.

The standards that lay at the heart of this new profession were established largely through the efforts of the allopathic doctors (Blishen, 1991). The establishment in 1865 of the General Council of Medical Education and Registration in Upper Canada signified acceptance of the scientific model of medicine, and the organization widely publicized the medical successes of its members to further improve their own public image. Scientific researchers were touted for tracing the cause of life-threatening illnesses to bacteria and viruses, and also for developing vaccines to prevent disease.

Still, alternative approaches to health care, such as regulating nutrition, also had many defenders. The allopathic doctors responded boldly—some thought arrogantly—to these challenges by asserting the superiority of their own approach. They established the Canadian Medical Association (CMA) in 1867. Once they had won control of the certification process, they were able to define what constituted medical acts and practice. Thus they, through the provincial colleges, could determine what the various "para-medical" occupations could and could not do. Before long, the practice of medicine was limited mainly to those with an M.D. degree. In the process, as the CMA intended, both the prestige and income of physicians rose dramatically. Men and women with M.D. degrees have become among the highest-paid workers in Canada.

Other practitioners—such as naturopaths, herbal healers, and midwives—held to their traditional roles, but at a high cost: all have been relegated to fringe areas of the medical profession. With far less social prestige and income than physicians, such professionals now have a small, if devoted, following in Canada (Nancarrow Clarke, 1990; Blishen, 1991).

The rise of scientific medicine, taught in expensive, urban medical schools, also changed the social profile of doctors. There is and has long been an over-representation of medical school students from higher-level social backgrounds. Their fathers have tended to have higher education than average, and to be employed in managerial and professional levels of the labor force (Blishen, 1991). Medicine is also a traditionally male-dominated profession. Women were long considered unfit to practice (Starr, 1982; Huet-Cox, 1984; Nancarrow Clarke, 1990). In 1992, more than 80 percent of physicians were men, while approximately 97 percent of nurses were women.

In sum, as the allopaths and their association (CMA) established physicians as scientific professionals, it simultaneously restricted the practice of medicine to a small, affluent elite—those admitted to expensive and often discriminatory medical schools. Medicine, in effect, became dominated by white men, most of them from urban, privileged families (Stevens, 1971; Starr, 1982; Blishen, 1991). The result has been a shortage of physicians in rural areas as well as a lack of physicians drawn from the ranks of women and other minorities.

Holistic Medicine

The achievements of the scientific medical model are impressive. Yet, especially in recent decades, this model has been tempered by the more traditional notion of **holistic medicine**, *an approach to health care that emphasizes prevention of illness and takes account of the whole person within a physical and social environment.*

A holistic approach is not necessarily in opposition to the model of scientific medicine. But advocates of holistic medicine point out that rigidly adhering to

the scientific orientation focuses on diseases and injuries rather than on prevention of illness and overall well-being. Holistically oriented practitioners charge that some physicians have become preoccupied with drugs, surgery, artificial organs, and high technology; in the process, these healers have narrowed their focus, concentrating on symptoms rather than people, and disease rather than health. Drugs and surgery can be vital forms of treatment, and holistic healers do not discount them. But they contend that these techniques should fit within a broader view of health that takes account of a person's entire life and environment. Thus holistic medicine reaches beyond medical doctors to include a wide variety of other trained personnel—physical therapists, nutritionists, counselors, clergy, and even acupuncturists and teachers of meditation—who can work with physicians as a team to improve the physical, mental, and social well-being of patients. In the holistic approach to health care, then, the following are major concerns (Gordon, 1980)

1. **Patients are people.** Holistic practitioners are concerned not only with symptoms, but with how each person's environment and lifestyle encourage or inhibit health. For example, the likelihood of illness increases under stress caused by the death of a family member, engaging in intense competition at work, or the daily burden of poverty (Duhl, 1980). This broad approach also leads holistic practitioners to expand the bounds of conventional medicine to actively combat environmental pollution and other dangers to public health.

2. **Responsibility, not dependency.** Holistic medicine tries to shift responsibility for health from physicians to people themselves. At the extreme, scientific medicine defines health as a complex issue only doctors can understand, thereby fostering dependency on the part of patients. While recognizing the need for experts, especially in a crisis, the holistic approach holds that professional healers should work to empower people by helping them to engage in health-promoting behavior (Ferguson, 1980). Holistic medicine favors an *active* approach to *health*, whereas scientific medicine more often takes a *reactive* approach to *disease*.

3. **Personal treatment environment.** Conventional medicine has shifted health care from the home to impersonal offices and hospitals, which are disease-centered rather than health-oriented, and which reinforce uninformed reliance on medical experts. While holistic medicine understands the

need for hospitalization in cases of severe illness, it favors situating health care in personal, relaxed settings.

4. **Optimum health for all.** In principle, the holistic view extends health care beyond treating disease to promoting the highest possible level of well-being for everyone. Even women and men who think they are "well" can work to realize "a state of extraordinary vigor, joy, and creativity" (Gordon, 1980:17).

On the broadest level, holistic medicine seeks to reestablish the personal social ties that commonly united healers and patients before the era of impersonal specialists. The CMA currently recognizes more than fifty specific areas of medical practice, and a growing proportion of M.D.s are entering these high-paying specialties rather than more holistic family practice. Thus, while technological advances surely improve medicine in some respects, they may actually diminish the profession in others.

Medicine and Economics in Global Perspective

As medicine has come to rely on high technology, the costs of health care in industrial societies have skyrocketed. Various countries use different strategies to help people meet these expenses.

Medicine in Socialist Societies

In societies with predominantly socialist economies, the government provides medical care directly to the people. It is an axiom of socialism that all citizens have the right to medical care on the same terms. To translate this ideal of equity into reality, people do not rely on their private financial resources to pay physicians and hospitals; rather, the government funnels public funds to pay medical costs. The state owns and operates medical facilities and pays salaries to practitioners, who are government employees.

People's Republic of China.　The People's Republic of China, a poor, agrarian society that is only beginning to industrialize, faces the daunting task of attending to the health of more than a billion people. Traditional healing arts, including acupuncture and the prescription of medicinal herbs, are still widely practiced in China. In addition, a holistic concern for the interplay of mind and body—a tradition whose roots extend back

thousands of years—figures prominently in the Chinese approach to health care (Sidel & Sidel, 1982b; Kaptchuk, 1985).

As part of experimental market reforms, China introduced some private forms of medical care during the 1980s, but by the end of the decade the government had reestablished tight control over every area of life, including health care. Consequently, all medical facilities are now government operated. China's so-called barefoot doctors, roughly comparable to paramedics in Canada, have brought some modern methods of medical care to millions of peasants in remote rural villages. Glancing back at Global Map 20-1, we can see that medical care in China—measured in terms of the number of doctors—is adequate by world standards.

The Commonwealth of Independent States.　The former Soviet Union is in the process of sweeping transformation as its state-dominated economy moves toward a market system. In line with these momentous shifts, the scheme for providing medical care is also likely to change. Until 1992, at least, the government provided medical care funded from taxes (Fuchs, 1974; Knaus, 1981). As is the case in the People's Republic of China, people did not choose their own physician, but reported to a government health facility near their home.

While providing basic care for the people, the medical system of the former Soviet Union has been highly impersonal and bureaucratic. In this Moscow hospital—one of the nation's best—a team of surgeons performs eye operations on eight patients in assembly-line fashion.

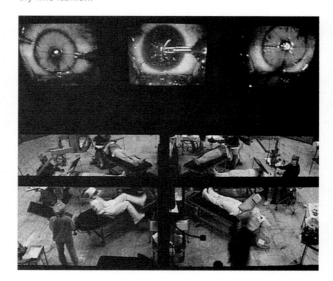

Physicians in the former Soviet Union have had lower prestige and income than their counterparts in Canada. They have received about the same salary as skilled industrial workers, a reflection of socialist attempts at economic equality. During the recent market-driven price increases, many physicians complained that their salaries had dropped in value to the point that they could scarcely afford to buy food. Worth noting, too, is that about 70 percent of Commonwealth physicians are women, compared with about 20 percent in Canada, and, as in Canada, occupations dominated by women offer fewer financial rewards.

Under the Soviet system, the number of physicians was high by world standards, and these women and men succeeded in meeting most of the basic needs of a large population. However, rigid bureaucracy resulted in highly standardized and impersonal medical care. As the nation adopts market reforms, uniformity will likely diminish and consumer choices will increase. But disparities in quality of care among various segments of the population may well intensify.

Medicine in Capitalist Societies

Societies with predominantly capitalist economies limit government welfare programs, including health care. Citizens provide for themselves in accordance with their own resources and personal preferences. As Chapter 19 ("The Economy and Work") explains, capitalist societies have substantial economic inequality. Paying for good health is simply beyond the means of a significant part of the population. Therefore every capitalist society provides some government assistance. Most of these nations—with the noteworthy exception of the United States—offer a comprehensive health program to the entire population.

Canada. The Canadian government pays doctors and hospitals—who operate privately—for the services they provide according to a schedule of fees set annually by the federal government and provincial governments in consultation with professional medical associations. Thus Canada has government-funded and -regulated medical care but, because practitioners operate privately, not true socialized medicine.

The system of universal medical care that presently exists in Canada is the result of a long history. In 1919, Mackenzie King introduced the idea of universal medical care as a part of the Liberal party platform. Subsequently, numerous other interest groups, especially organized labor, advocated medical coverage for all Canadians. In 1961, a Royal Commission on Health

Service was appointed by the federal government under Supreme Court Justice Emmett Hall. The recommendations of the Commission became law across Canada in 1972. The four basic characteristics of the scheme were as follows:

1. Universality. The plan was to be eligible to all residents of Canada on equal terms regardless of such differences as previous health records, age, lack of income, non-membership in a group, or other considerations. The federal government stipulated that at least 95 percent of the population was to be covered within two years of the provincial adoption of the plan.

2. Portability. The benefits were to be portable from province to province.

3. Comprehensive coverage. The benefits were to include all necessary medical services, and certain surgical services performed by a dental surgeon in hospital.

4. Administration. The plan was to be run on a non-profit basis.
(Nancarrow Clarke, 1993:186).

See Table 20-3 for a summation of the development of state medical insurance.

Canada's system has the advantage of providing care for everyone at a total cost that is proportionally significantly less than that needed to operate the (non-universal) medical system in the United States (see Table 20-4).

However, there have been some criticisms of the Canadian system. One is that it does not make effective use of state-of-the-art technology, as is done south of the border. However, in the United States such technology is available primarily for the wealthy and the well-insured. The vast majority of Americans do not reap the benefits of these technological advances, and do not have the access to medical care that Canadians do. For example, death from cervical cancer is still a major threat in the U.S., especially for poor women. In contrast, Canada has, because of the ready availability of pap smears, all but eliminiated death from cervical cancer. Another current criticism of the Canadian system is that it is slower to respond and that people may have to wait long periods of time prior to treatment. Again, the answer is that at least people are not denied the possibility of treatment because they are unable to pay for it.

The United States. The United States is unique among the industrialized societies of the world in

TABLE 20-3   TIME LINE: THE DEVELOPMENT OF STATE MEDICAL INSURANCE

Germany and Western Europe introduced social welfare insurance, including health insurance, in the 1880s. New Zealand introduced social welfare insurance, including health insurance, in the early part of the twentieth century. Great Britain introduced national health insurance in 1948.

CANADA

1919	Platform of the Liberal Party under Mackenzie King includes Medicare.
1919	End of World War I: organized labor began what was to become an annual statement by the CCL concerning the importance of national health insurance.
1919–1920	Talk of Medicare in the U.S.A.: several states passed medicare legislation that was later withdrawn.
1934	Canadian Medical Association appointed a Committee on Medical Economics, which produced a report outlining the CMA position in support of national health insurance, with several provisos.
1934	Legislation passed for provincial medical insurance in Alberta. Government lost power before it could be implemented.
1935	British Columbia introduced provincial medical insurance legislation. Despite public support via a referendum, this legislation was never implemented because of a change in governments.
1935	Employment and Social Insurance Act including a proposal for research into the viability of a national medical insurance scheme was introduced.
1942	Beveridge report on Britain's need for a National Health Service published in Great Britain—the subject of much discussion in Canada.
1945	Dominion-Provincial Conference on Reconstruction included proposals for federally supported medical insurance. Conference broke down in the wake of federal-provincial dispute.
1947	Saskatchewan implemented hospital insurance.
1951	A Canadian Sickness Survey completed. It demonstrated income differences in illness.
1958	Hospital Insurance and Diagnostic Services Act passed.
1962	Saskatchewan introduced provincial medical insurance.
1962	Royal Commission appointed to investigate medical services. Saskatchewan Doctors' Strike.
1966	Federal legislation for state medical insurance passed.
1968	Federal legislation implemented.
1972	Federal legislation included the Yukon and Northwest Territories.
1977	Federal government changed the funding formula with the provinces.
1984	Canada Health Act. Reinforced the policy that medical care to be financed out of the public purse.
1987	Ontario Doctor's Strike
1993	The high cost of health care becomes an issue in the federal election campaign.

SOURCE: J.N. Clarke, 1990:187.

TABLE 20-4   HEALTH EXPENDITURES AS PERCENTAGES OF THE GROSS NATIONAL PRODUCT, CANADA AND THE UNITED STATES, 1960–1991

Year	Canada	United States
1960	5.5	5.3
1965	6.0	5.9
1970	7.1	7.4
1975	7.2	8.4
1980	7.3	9.2
1985	8.5	10.5
1986	8.8	10.7
1987r	8.8	10.9
1988r*	8.7	11.1
1989r*	8.9	11.5
1990r*	9.4	12.2
1991*	9.9	13.2

rRevised figures
*Provisional estimates
SOURCE: Policy, Planning and Information Branch March, 1993. Health Expenditures in Canada Summary Report 1987–1991, Health Canada, 1993. Reproduced with permission of the Minister of Supply and Services Canada, 1993.

having no government-sponsored medical program for every citizen. The government does pay most medical expenses, but only for some categories of people. For example, the Medicare program covers some of the medical expenses of men and women over age sixty-five. In 1990, about 13 percent of the U.S. population was covered under this program. Another 61 percent were at least partially covered through a family-member's employer or labor union, while 14 percent purchased medical insurance privately. Overall, three-quarters of the U.S. population have some private medical insurance (Health Insurance Association of America, 1991; U.S. Bureau of the Census, 1991).

For the most part, then, medicine in the United States is a private, profit-making industry in which more money buys better care. Called a **direct-fee system**, theirs is *a medical-care system in which patients pay directly for the services of physicians and hospitals.* Affluent people in the United States can purchase top-flight medical care, yet the poor fare far worse than their counterparts in Europe and Canada. This translates into relatively high death rates among both infants and adults in the United States (Fuchs, 1974; United Nations, 1991).

Health insurance became a central issue in the 1992 presidential campaign. Both major political parties endorsed a greater government role in funding medical care, and the idea won new support from both the AMA and insurance companies. It appears that the U.S. will soon join other industrial nations in guaranteeing at least some medical coverage for everyone.

Japan. Physicians in Japan operate privately, and a combination of private insurance and government programs pays medical costs. As Chapter 7 ("Groups and Organizations") notes, Japanese corporations take a wide-ranging interest in the welfare of their employees, and many provide medical care as an employee benefit. For those outside such privately funded programs, government medical insurance covers 70 percent of all costs, and the elderly receive free care (Vogel, 1979).

Great Britain. In 1948 Great Britain instituted socialized medicine as an outgrowth of a medical insurance program begun in 1911. However, the British did not do away with private care; instead, they devised a "dual system" of medical services. Thus all British citizens are entitled to medical care provided by the National Health Service, but those who can afford to may purchase more extensive—and expensive—care from doctors and hospitals that operate privately.

Sweden. In 1891 Sweden instituted a compulsory, comprehensive system of government medical care. Citizens pay for this program with their taxes, which are among the highest in the world. Typically physicians receive salaries from the government rather than fees from patients, and most hospitals are government managed. Because this medical system resembles that of socialist societies, it is often described as **socialized medicine**, *a medical-care system in which most medical facilities are owned and operated by the government, and most physicians are salaried government employees.*

Theoretical Analysis of Health and Medicine

Each of the major theoretical paradigms in sociology provides a means of organizing and interpreting the facts and issues presented in this chapter.

Structural-Functional Analysis

Structural-functional analysis rests on the image of society as a complex system that is stable and internally well-integrated. Talcott Parsons (1951) included the good health of its members as a societal imperative. From a social-systems point of view, Parsons viewed illness as dysfunctional, undermining individuals' ability to contribute to the operation of society. Parsons also recognized that every society must have an established means for dealing with those who are ill. How this is done, of course, depends on a society's available technology and cultural system. Our society is among the most technologically complex in the world, and our medical care reflects this.

The Sick Role

One of the most important ideas contributed by the structural-functional analysis of health is the **sick role**, *patterns of behavior defined as appropriate for people who are ill.* As developed by Parsons, the sick role has four characteristics.

1. **Illness provides exemption from routine responsibilities.** In everyday life, individuals perform their roles as students, parents, and employees. Serious illness, Parsons claims, relaxes or suspends normal social responsibilities. To prevent abuse of this license, people cannot simply declare themselves ill; they must enlist the support of others—especially a recognized medical expert—before assuming the sick role.

2. **A person's illness is not deliberate.** We assume that sick people are not responsible for their ailments; illness is something that has happened to them. Therefore, the failure of ill people to fulfill routine responsibilities should carry no threat of punishment.

3. **A sick person must want to be well.** We also assume that the people who are ill want to be well. Thus people suspected of feigning illness to escape responsibility or to receive special attention have no legitimate claim to the sick role.

4. **An ailing person must seek competent help.** An additional obligation assumed by people who are ill is seeking competent assistance and cooperating with health-care practitioners. Anyone who fails to seek medical help or to follow doctor's orders gives

up any claim on the sick role's exemption from routine responsibilities.

The Physician's Role

Parsons perceived the sick person and the healer as functionally linked. He described the physician's role as providing medical care as needed by the patient. Just as a person in the sick role is expected to pursue health by seeking competent help, so the physician is expected to do whatever will cure illness. Sometimes doing so is impossible, but physician and patient initially work from the premise that the patient will recover.

Parsons claimed that the physician's role confers power over the patient. This hierarchy is rooted in the cultural norm that ailing individuals must cooperate with physicians, and it is strengthened by the physician's special knowledge. Physicians expect patients to comply with their requests and to supply personal information, even that shared with no one else. Parsons noted that the power of physicians also carries responsibility to use this information only for legitimate medical purposes.

The physician's role varies from society to society, and reflects a country's attitude toward hierarchy. In Japan, for example, strong tradition gives physicians considerable authority, so that they share less information with patients than their counterparts in the West.

Critical evaluation. Parsons's functionalist analysis explains how notions about illness and strategies for providing medical care fit into broader patterns of social organization. The concept of the sick role, in other words, represents the accommodation of society to illness. Others have noted that the sick role also applies to some non-illness situations, such as pregnancy (Myers & Grasmick, 1989). One limitation of this concept is that it is more easily applied to acute conditions (like the flu) than chronic disease (like heart disease), which may not be reversible. Moreover, affluent people have more opportunity to assume the sick role than poor people, who cannot afford not to work even when they are ill.

Critics charge that Parsons's view of the physician's role supports the idea that doctors—rather than people themselves—bear the primary responsibility for health. Treatment-oriented physicians respond to acute illness, of course, but a more prevention-oriented approach to health would cast physicians as equal partners along with patients in the pursuit of health.

Symbolic-Interaction Analysis

Viewed according to the symbolic-interaction paradigm, society appears less as a grand system than a complex and changing reality. This means that health and medical care are human creations based on social definitions.

The Social Construction of Illness

Any state of health or illness is a matter of socially constructed reality, as described in Chapter 6 ("Social Interaction in Everyday Life"). In a society where most people suffer from malnutrition, therefore, they may consider an underfed child to be quite normal. Similarly, for decades the members of our own society defined smoking cigarettes as a matter of personal taste, and today many people give little thought to the deleterious effects on health of a rich diet.

How we *respond* to serious illness is also based on social definitions which may or may not square with medical facts. For instance, people with AIDS contend with fear and sometimes outright bigotry that has no basis in medical fact.

Even the "expert opinions" of medical professionals are influenced by nonmedical factors. In one piece of research, David Mechanic (1978) noted that during periods when productivity lagged behind demand in the former Soviet Union, physicians were less likely to excuse workers from their jobs. Similarly, military doctors may define flu symptoms as illness during peacetime but overlook this evidence in desperate times of war. Closer to home, university students have been known to dismiss signs of illness on the eve of a vacation, yet dutifully march into the infirmary before a difficult examination. In each case, people and medical experts do not simply assess health in some objective way; rather, they negotiate the definition of a situation based on a host of considerations.

How a medical situation is defined can also affect how somebody actually feels. Medical experts have long noted the existence of *psychosomatic* disorders (a fusion of Greek words for "mind" and "body"), in which a person's state of mind influences physical well-being (Hamrick, Anspaugh, & Ezell, 1986). Sociologist W.I. Thomas (1931) pointed out that as a situation is defined as real, it becomes real in its consequences.

The Social Construction of Treatment

In Chapter 6 ("Social Interaction in Everyday Life"), we used the dramaturgical approach of Erving Goffman to explain how physicians craft their physical surroundings ("the office") and present themselves to others to foster specific impressions of competence and power.

Sociologist Joan Emerson (1970) further illustrates this process of reality construction by analyzing a situation familiar to women, a gynecological examination carried out by a male doctor. After observing seventy-five such examinations, she explains that this situation is especially precarious because it is vulnerable to misinterpretation. Why? Simply because the man's touching of a woman's genitals—conventionally viewed as a sexual act and possibly even an assault—must, in this case, be defined as impersonal and professional. To ensure that this reality dominates the setting, the medical staff carefully structure their personal performances to remove sexual connotations as completely as possible.

Emerson notes several ways in which the medical staff seeks to do this. The examination is restricted to a specific setting used for no other purpose—a room whose decor and equipment are decidedly medical in character. All personnel wear medical uniforms, never clothing that could be worn in other, nonmedical situations. The staff tries to make the patient feel that such examinations are simply routine although, from the patient's point of view, they may be quite unusual.

Furthermore, although rapport between physician and patient is important, this is established before the examination begins. Once under way, the male physician's performance is matter of fact, suggesting to the patient that inspecting the genitals is no different from surveying any other part of the body. A woman is usually present during the examination in the role of nurse. Not only does she assist the physician, but her presence dispels any impression that a man and woman are "alone in a room" (Emerson, 1970:81).

The need to manage situational definitions has long been overlooked by medical schools. This omission is unfortunate because, as Emerson's analysis shows, understanding how reality is socially constructed in the examination room is just as crucial as mastering the medical skills involved. Fortunately, medical professionals are gradually coming to recognize the importance of sociological insights. For example, Professor David Hemsell of Southwestern Medical School in Texas urges all his medical students to gain a better understanding of this process from the patient's point of view by actually climbing onto an examination table and placing their feet in the metal stirrups with their legs apart. Hemsell claims, "The only way to understand women's feelings is to be there." He adds, "You can see the impact of being in that position hit them in the face like a two-by-four." Imagine the even greater impact on the men if they were required to do this without wearing their trousers.

Critical evaluation. One strength of the symbolic-interaction paradigm lies in revealing the relative meaning of sickness and health. What is normal or deviant, healthful or harmful, depends on a host of factors, many of which are not, strictly speaking, medical. Another contribution lies in showing how all medical procedures involve a subtle interaction between patient and physician.

A problem with this approach is that it seems to deny that there are any objective standards of well-being. Certain physical conditions do indeed cause specific, negative changes in human capacities, however we define them. And people who lack sufficient nutrition and safe water, for example, suffer the ill effects of their unhealthy environment however they define their surroundings.

Social-Conflict Analysis

Social-conflict analysis takes a different approach by linking health and medical care to social inequality. Sociologists using this paradigm have developed three major criticisms of capitalist societies with regard to health.

Unequal Access to Medical Care

Personal health is the foundation of social life. Yet by defining medical care as a commodity for purchase, capitalist societies skew health in favor of the wealthy. As we have already noted, this problem is especially serious in the United States, which stands out as having no comprehensive national medical-care program.

Medical Care and the Profit Motive

For others, however, even a program of socialized medicine does not go far enough. More radical critics claim that patterns of health in capitalist countries inevitably reflect the class system itself. Thus, they maintain, the strikingly unequal distribution of wealth in Canada makes equal medical care impossible, despite government efforts. Only a significant redistribution of economic resources would make medical care uniformly available (Bodenheimer, 1977; Navarro, 1977; Nancarrow Clarke, 1990).

From this point of view, capitalist medical care amounts to another big business that provides a poor product. The thalidomide disaster of the 1950s and 1960s is a case in point. The ingestion of thalidomide by pregnant mothers (prescribed as the safest possible sleeping pill) resulted in the births of at least 115 babies with phocomelia in Canada (the absence of limbs and the presence of seal-like flippers instead). All of this was in spite of the fact that serious questions had been asked about the safety of thalidomide for several years in several different countries, and that it had already been banned from use in the U.S.A.

From the 1940s to the 1960s DES (diethylstilbestrol) was prescribed to pregnant women who had a history of miscarriages, diabetes, or toxemia during pregnancy. Approximately four million women took DES over this time; 400,000 in Canada. The children later developed a variety of problems ranging from a rare vaginal cancer, to a variety of apparently benign structural changes in the uterus, vagina, and cervix amongst women. About thirty percent of the male children have genital trait and semen abnormalities, including cysts, and extremely small or undescended testicles (Nancarrow Clarke, 1990).

Physicians, hospitals, and producers of drugs and medical supplies comprise multibillion-dollar corporate conglomerates (Ehrenreich, 1978). The quest for ever-increasing profits, these critics suggest, encourages questionable medical practices, including performing unnecessary tests and surgery and an overreliance on drugs (Kaplan et al., 1985). Then there are periodic scandals about unsafe medical products and procedures. For example, thousands of women had silicone breast implants under the assumption that the commonly used plastic packets of silicone were safe. Recently, however, it became clear that these implants—which have a tendency to rupture, causing significant harm—are not safe enough, a fact apparently known to Dow Corning, their major manufacturer, for decades.

Many surgical procedures performed in Canada each year are "elective", meaning that they were not prompted by a medical emergency. Critics charge that the extent of such surgery reflects not just the medical needs of patients but the financial interests of surgeons and hospitals (Illich, 1976). Some suggest that at least 10 percent of elective surgery could safely be refused or deferred, saving the health care system a great deal of money. More important, since about one in two hundred patients dies from elective surgery (because surgery itself is dangerous), lives are needlessly lost (Sidel & Sidel, 1982a). Finally, critics point out, Canada has been all too tolerant of physicians having a direct financial interest in the tests, procedures, and drugs they order for their patients. For some critics, this crystallizes the core problem with medicine: health care should be motivated by a concern for people, not profits.

Medicine as Social Control

A final issue raised by social-conflict analysts is that medical care operates as a means of social control. Because we think of science as a path to objective truth, our scientifically based medical establishment has enjoyed broad support. But is scientific medicine as politically neutral as it claims to be?

For one thing, the medical establishment has long been ambivalent about government-administered medical insurance. C.M.A. officials often decry state involvement as eroding quality care, interfering in the near-sacred doctor-patient relationship and constraining the way doctors can practice medicine. Moreover, the medical establishment has a history of racial and sexual discrimination, invoking through the years "scientific" facts to protect the interests of the wealthy white men who dominate the medical profession (Leavitt, 1984). The box provides several illustrations of how the banner of science has been used to support sexism. Such practices may decrease as more women and people of color join the ranks of physicians, although critics contend that such biases—albeit more subtle—still pervade the medical establishment (Zola, 1978; Brown, 1979; Blishen, 1991).

Even today critics view scientific medicine as a means of maintaining class inequality. A scientific approach to illness tends to focus on bacteria, viruses, and biological processes, while giving short shrift to social patterns that affect health such as wealth and poverty. From the scientific perspective, in other words, indigent people become ill because of poor sanitation and a diet lacking in vital nutrients, even though poverty may lie at the root of these ills. In this way, critics charge, scientific medicine effectively depoliticizes the issue of health by reducing social and political issues to simple biology.

Critical evaluation. Social-conflict analysis provides still another view of the relationships among health, medicine, and our society. There is little doubt that many people think of medicine in terms of artificial hearts, CAT scans, and other sophisticated technology while overlooking the fact that many people lack the most basic medical care.

Medicine and Victorian Women: Science or Sexism?

A century ago medical science reacted strongly to the changing roles of women. With men firmly in control, the medical establishment staunchly opposed greater sexual equality.

Medical opinion labeled conventional gender distinctions as both natural and inevitable (Mitchinson, 1991). Beyond differences in size and strength, physicians pronounced men inherently rational while claiming that women were dominated by emotions, and had hypersensitive nervous and reproductive systems. Thus women's highest calling was childbearing. Writing in 1890, one physician remarked that "the Almighty, in creating the female sex, had taken the uterus and built up a woman around it" (cited in Smith-Rosenberg & Rosenberg, 1984:13). In short, as far as women were concerned, medical opinion equated health with motherhood, arguing that childless women risked a life wreaked by physical and mental illness.

The Victorian medical establishment also obstructed women's demands for schooling. Physicians warned that too much thinking rendered a woman weak and sickly and decreased her capacity to bear healthy children. Confronting the notion of an educated woman in 1901, one gynecologist complacently predicted, "She may become highly cultured and accomplished and shine in society, but her future husband will discover too late that he has married a large outfit of headaches, backaches, and spine aches, instead of a woman fitted to take up the duties of life" (cited in Smith-Rosenberg & Rosenberg, 1984:16). Another member of the Harvard medical faculty warned that "If she puts as much force into her brain education as a boy, the brain or the special apparatus [the reproductive system] will suffer" (cited in Bollough & Voght, 1984:30).

Victorian physicians also drew on so-called scientific reasoning to oppose women's control over their sexuality. Women, they argued, had no interest in sexual activity beyond having children, and had neither the desire nor the ability to achieve orgasm. By contrast, if a man failed to reach sexual climax, he risked a dangerous buildup of nervous energy. Male orgasms, unimpeded by contraceptive devices such as condoms, were also said to enhance a woman's health by "bathing the female reproductive organs" (cited in Smith-Rosenberg & Rosenberg, 1984:19). Well into this century, in fact, the American Medical Association opposed contraception and abortion, citing allegedly medical grounds.

Some Victorians saw this pseudo-science for what it was. Martha Carey Thomas, president of Bryn Mawr College, won much support for her contention that men holding such ungenerous attitudes toward women were themselves "pathological, blinded by neurotic mists of sex, unable to see that women form one-half of the kindly race of normal, healthy human creatures in the world" (cited in Bollough & Voght, 1984:34).

One objection to the conflict approach is that it minimizes the advances in health wrought by scientific medicine. While there is plenty of room for improvement, the overall health of the population has become better in recent decades.

To sum up, sociology's three major theoretical paradigms convincingly argue that health and medicine are social issues. The famous French scientist Louis Pasteur (1822–1895) spent much of his life studying how bacteria cause disease. Before his death, the record indicates, he remarked that health depends much less on bacteria than on the social environment in which bacteria operate (Gordon, 1980:7). Explaining Pasteur's insight is sociology's essential contribution to understanding human health.

Summary

1. Health is a social and biological issue and depends on the extent and distribution of a society's resources. Culture shapes definitions of health as well as patterns of health care.

2. Through most of human history, health has been poor by today's standards. Health improved dramatically in Western Europe and North America in the nineteenth century, first because

industrialization raised living standards, and later as medical advances brought infectious diseases under control.

3. Infectious diseases were the major killers at the beginning of this century. Today most people in Canada die in old age of heart disease, cancer, or stroke.

4. Health in the Third World is generally poor, because of inadequate sanitation and malnutrition. Life expectancy is about twenty years less than in Canada; in the poorest nations, half the children do not survive to adulthood.

5. In Canada, three-fourths of children born today can expect to live to at least age sixty-five. Throughout the life course, women have relatively better health than men, and people of high social position enjoy better health than others.

6. Industrialization has raised our society's standard of living and thus improved health. However, environmental pollution, especially from industrial wastes, threatens the future health of our population.

7. Cigarette smoking increased during this century to become the greatest preventable cause of death in Canada. Now that the health hazards of smoking are known and social tolerance for tobacco use has declined, cigarette consumption has waned.

8. Sexually transmitted diseases are a health issue of growing concern. In the 1980s the spread of genital herpes transformed patterns of sexuality away from casual sex toward greater selectivity and commitment. The spread of AIDS, a fatal and incurable disease, has reinforced this shift.

9. Because of advancing medical technology, an increasing number of ethical issues surround death and the rights of the dying. Because of the capability to sustain life artificially, death now commonly results from a human decision.

10. Historically a family concern, health care is now the responsibility of trained specialists. The model of scientific medicine underlies the Canadian medical establishment.

11. The holistic approach to medicine balances science and technology with other procedures that promote health as well as treat disease. Highlighting the need for professional healers to gain personal knowledge of patients and their environment, holistic healers encourage people to assume greater responsibility for their own health.

12. Socialist societies define medical care as a right that governments offer equally to everyone. Capitalist societies view medical care as a commodity to be purchased, although most capitalist governments support medical care through socialized medicine or national health insurance. The United States is the only industrialized society with no comprehensive medical-care program. Instead, it uses a direct-fee system, in which users must pay for their own medical coverage.

13. Canada's medical system involves a schedule of fees set up by governments in consultation with physicians, which regulates how much physicians may bill for various procedures. Most medical care is paid for by the medicare system.

14. Structural-functional analysis links health and medicine to other social structures. Central to structural-functional analysis is the concept of the sick role, in which illness allows release from routine social responsibilities as long as patients seek to regain their health.

15. The symbolic-interaction paradigm investigates how health and treatments for illness are largely matters of subjective perception and social definition.

16. Social-conflict analysis focuses on the unequal distribution of health and medical care. It criticizes North American medical care for its over-reliance on drugs and surgery and for over-emphasizing the biological rather than the social causes of illness.

Key Concepts

direct-fee system a medical-care system in which patients pay directly for the services of physicians and hospitals

euthanasia (mercy killing) assisting in the death of a person suffering from an incurable illness

health a state of complete physical, mental, and social well-being

health care any activity intended to improve health

holistic medicine an approach to health care that emphasizes prevention of illness and takes account of the whole person within a physical and social environment

medicine an institutionalized system for combating disease and improving health

sick role patterns of behavior that are defined as appropriate for those who are ill

social epidemiology the study of how health and disease are distributed in a society's population

socialized medicine a health-care system in which most medical facilities are owned and operated by the government, and most physicians are salaried government employees

Suggested Readings

This book probes many of the issues raised in this chapter.
Peter E.S. Freund and Meredith B. McGuire. *Health, Illness, and the Social Body.* Englewood Cliffs, NJ: Prentice Hall, 1991.

Describing rituals of exorcism in Sri Lanka, the first of the following books explores forms of healing that defy understanding in Western terms. The second, a collection of essays, examines the wide variety of approaches to health care in African societies.
Bruce Kapferer. *A Celebration of Demons.* New York: Berg, 1990.
Brian M. de Toit and Ismail H. Abdalla, eds. *African Healing Strategies.* New York: Trado-Medic, 1985.

These books delve into the history of medicine from the perspective of gender conflict. The first reports on women's exclusion from the emerging medical establishment. The second explains how female midwives were gradually replaced by male obstetricians.
Regina Markell Morantz-Sanchez. *Sympathy and Science: Women Physicians in American Medicine.* New York: Oxford University Press, 1985.
Jane B. Donegan. *Women & Men Midwives: Medicine,*

Morality, and Misogyny in Early America. Westport, CT: Greenwood Press, 1985.

Few issues reveal the interplay of medicine and ethics as clearly as abortion. This reference work provides a comprehensive overview of publications on all sides of this topic.
Richard Fitzsimmons and Joan P. Diana. *Pro-Choice/Pro-Life: An Annotated, Selected Bibliography.* Westport, CT: Greenwood Press, 1991.

The effects of illness often ripple through an entire family, straining and distorting relationships. Alcoholism is a case in point.
Ramona M. Asher. *Women With Alcoholic Husbands: Ambivalence and the Trap of Codependency.* Chapel Hill: University of North Carolina Press, 1992.

Here are three recent books concerned with the AIDS epidemic. The first highlights the social dimensions of this catastrophic disease; the second is of special concern to faculty and students; and the third criticizes the medical establishment and the press for exaggerating the scope of the AIDS epidemic.
Dorothy Nelkin, David P. Willis, and Scott V. Parris, eds. *A Disease of Society: Cultural and Institutional Responses*

to AIDS. Cambridge, UK: Cambridge University Press, 1991.

Jackie R. McClain and Tom E. Matteoli. *Confronting AIDS on the Campus and in the Classroom: A Guide for Higher Education.* Washington, DC: College and University Personnel Association, 1989.

Michael Fumento. *The Myth of Heterosexual AIDS.* New York: Basic Books, 1989.

This is an overview of the structure and culture of the work of medical doctors in Canada today.

Bernard R. Blishen. *Doctors in Canada.* Toronto: University of Toronto Press, 1991.

This is a reader with extensive coverage of a wide variety of issues related to the Canadian medical care system. For the most part the writers are from a variety of social science disciplines.

Singh Bolaria and Harley D. Dickenson, eds. *Sociology of Health Care in Canada.* Toronto: Harcourt Brace Jovanovich, 1988.

This is a comprehensive overview of issues in the sociology of Canadian illness and medicine.

Barry Edginton. *Health, Disease and Medicine in Canada.* Toronto: Butterworths, 1989.

This is a description of the work, life, and culture of chiropractors.

Merrijoy Kelner, Oswald Hall, and Jan Coultner. *Chiropractors: Do They Help.* Toronto: Fitzhenry and Whiteside, 1980.

This is a critical study of the pharmaceutical industry in Canada.

Joel Lexchin. *The Real Pushers: A Critical Analysis of the Canadian Drug Industry.* Vancouver: New Star Books, 1984.

This is an historical examination of how doctors viewed women's bodies in Victorian Canada.

Wendy Mitchinson. *The Nature of Their Bodies: Women and Their Doctors in Victorian Canada.* Toronto: University of Toronto Press, 1991.

This is based on qualitative interviews with women about the impact of cancer on their lives.

Juanne Nancarrow Clarke. *It's Cancer: The Personal Experiences of Women Who Have Received a Cancer Diagnosis.* Toronto: IPI Publishing, 1985.

This is an overview of medical sociology and the sociology of health and illness from a paradigmatic perspective.

Juanne Nancarrow Clarke. *Health, Illness and Medicine in Canada.* Toronto: McClelland & Stewart, 1990.

These last two books, written by a medical reporter, provide a critical examination of a variety of issues in the Canadian medical and pharmaceutical industries.

Nicholas Regush. *Canada's Health Care System: Condition Critical.* Toronto: Macmillan, 1987.

Nicholas Regush. *Safety Last: The Failure of the Consumer Health Protection System in Canada.* Toronto: Key Porter Books, 1993.

POPULATION AND URBANIZATION

In 1519 a band of Spanish conquistadors led by Hernando Cortés reached Tenochtitlán, the capital of the Aztec empire. What they saw stunned them—a lake-encircled city, teeming with over 300,000 people, more than the population of any European city at that time. Gazing down broad streets, exploring stone temples, and entering the magnificent royal palace filled with golden treasures, Cortés and his soldiers wondered if they were dreaming.

Cortés soon woke up and set his mind to looting the city. At first, he was unable to overcome the superior forces of the Aztecs and their leader Montezuma, but the determined leader spent two years raising a vast army and finally managed to destroy Tenochtitlán. In its place, Cortés constructed a new city in the European fashion—*Ciudad Imperial de Mexico*—Mexico City.

Today Mexico City is once more fighting for its life. Its population has soared in recent decades and experts predict that, by the end of the 1990s, the city will be home to 30 million people—one hundred times the number that astonished Cortés. This huge population is grappling with a host of problems common to Third-World societies, including poverty, foreign debt, poor health, and a rapidly deteriorating environment.

Rising populations, vast urban sprawl, and desperate poverty—this combination burdens much of the world today. This chapter examines both population growth and urbanization—two powerful forces that have shaped and reshaped our planet for thousands of years. Increasing population may turn out to be the most serious problem facing the world in the coming century; it is all but certain that this vital drama will be played out in cities of unprecedented size.

Demography: The Study of Population

From the point at which the human species emerged some 200,000 years ago until recently, the population of the entire earth remained quite low at some 20 million—about seven million less people than live in Canada today. Life for our ancestors was anything but certain, as they were vulnerable to a wide range of diseases and frequent natural disasters. Across hundreds of centuries, however, our species has managed to flourish. Ironically, perhaps, global population is now so large (about 5.4 billion in 1992) and growing so rapidly (by almost 100 million each year) that the future of humanity is again uncertain.

The causes and consequences of this growth form

the core of **demography**, *the study of human population.* Demography (from the Greek, meaning "description of people") is closely related to sociology, but focuses on the size, age, and sex composition of a population as well as people's movements from one region to another. Although much demographic research is quantitative, demography is more than a numbers game. The discipline poses crucial questions about the effects of population growth and how it may be controlled.

Demographic analysis proceeds from several basic concepts.

Fertility

Any study of human population must concern itself with how many people are born. **Fertility** is *the incidence of childbearing in a society's population.* Women are capable of childbearing from the onset of menstruation (typically in the early teens) to menopause (usually in the late forties). During this time, a woman could conceivably bear more than twenty children, but this *fecundity,* or potential childbearing, is sharply reduced by health, financial concerns, cultural norms, and personal choice.

Demographers often measure fertility using the **crude birth rate,** *the number of live births in a given year for every thousand people in a population.* A crude birth rate is calculated by dividing the number of live births in a given year by a society's total population, and multiplying the result by 1,000. In Canada in 1991 there were 411,910 live births in a population of 27 million. According to this formula, then, there were 15.2 live births for every thousand people, or a crude birth rate of 15.2.

This birth rate is "crude" because it is based on the entire population, not just women and men in their childbearing years. For this reason, making comparisons using crude birth rates can be misleading because one society may have a higher proportion of women of childbearing age than another. A crude birth rate also tells us nothing about how birth rates differ among people of various races, ethnicities, and religions. But this measure does have the strength of being easy to calculate, and it is widely regarded as a good measure of a society's overall fertility. Table 21-1 shows that the crude birth rates of Canada and other industrial societies are low in world context. Canada Map 21-1 reveals that crude fertility rates within Canada vary dramatically—from a 1991 low of 13.6 in Newfoundland, to a high of 28.2 (like the Mexican rate) in the Northwest Territories where the Native population is in the majority.

TABLE 21-1 FERTILITY AND MORTALITY RATES IN GLOBAL PERSPECTIVE, 1990

	Crude Birth Rate	Crude Death Rate	Infant Mortality Rate
North America			
Canada	14	7	7
United States	17	9	10
Europe			
Belgium	12	11	6
Commonwealth of Independent States	18	10	24
Denmark	12	11	6
France	14	9	6
Spain	11	8	6
United Kingdom	14	11	7
Latin America			
Chile	21	6	18
Cuba	18	7	12
Haiti	45	16	107
Mexico	29	5	33
Nicaragua	39	8	65
Puerto Rico	19	8	17
Africa			
Algeria	37	9	87
Cameroon	42	15	120
Egypt	34	10	90
Ethiopia	45	15	116
Nigeria	46	17	119
South Africa	35	8	52
Asia			
Afghanistan	44	18	154
Bangladesh	42	14	136
India	30	11	89
Israel	22	7	9
Japan	11	7	5
Vietnam	30	8	50

SOURCE: U.S. Bureau of the Census, Statistical Abstract of the United States 1991. Washington, DC: U.S. Government Printing Office, 1991.

Mortality

Population size is also affected by **mortality**, *the incidence of death in a society's population.* Corresponding to the crude birth rate, demographers use a **crude death rate**, defined as *the number of deaths in a given year for every thousand people in a population.* The crude death rate is calculated as the number of deaths in a given year divided by the total population, and multiplied by 1,000. In 1991, there were 191,700 deaths in the Canadian population of 27 million yielding a crude death rate of 7.1. As Table 21-1 shows, this rate is low by world standards, even lower than that of the U.S.

A third widely-used demographic measure is the **infant mortality rate**, *the number of deaths in the first year of life for each thousand live births in a given year.*

This rate is derived from dividing the number of deaths of children under one year of age by the number of live births during the same year and multiplying the result by 1,000. In 1991 Canada's infant mortality rate was 7 per 1,000 births. This is lower than the rate in the U.S., but above that of most European and Scandinavian countries or Japan.

Like other demographic variables, this rate conceals considerable variation among segments of the Canadian population. For example, infant mortality rates are higher among the poor, in isolated communities, and among the Native peoples. Nonetheless, infant mortality offers a good general measure of overall quality of life and is therefore used as one indicator of socio-economic development. Table 21-1 shows that infant mortality in Canada is low by world standards.

Note that the United States has a relatively high rate when compared to other industrialized nations, especially those with government-sponsored medical care.

Societies with a low infant mortality rate have a high **life expectancy**, *the length of time a person, on the average, can expect to live.* Canadian males born in 1991 can expect to live seventy-four years, while females can expect to live eighty-one years—two years longer than males and females in the United States. Life expectancy in rich, First-World countries is about twenty years greater than it is in poor, Third-World societies.

Migration

Population size also changes as people move from one place to another. Demographers define **migration** as *the*

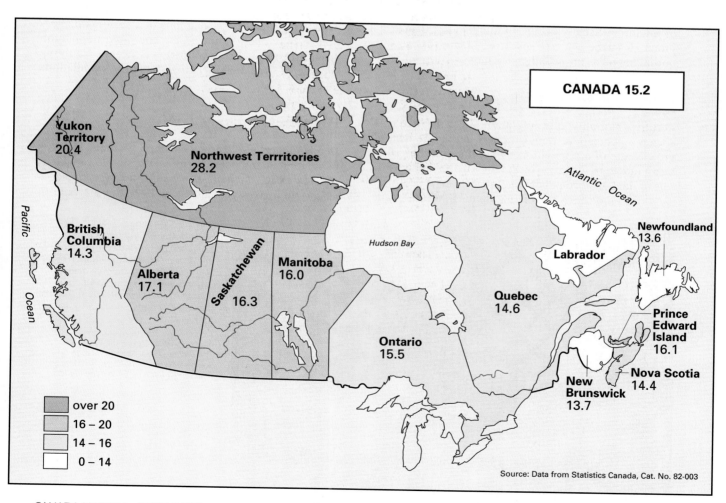

CANADA MAP 21-1   BIRTH RATES (BY PROVINCE AND TERRITORY, 1991)

movement of people into and out of a specified territory. Migration is sometimes involuntary, as illustrated by the forcible transport of 10 million Africans to the Western Hemisphere as slaves (Sowell, 1981). Other migration is voluntary; in this case, people typically are motivated to move by complex "push-pull" factors. Dissatisfaction with life in a poor rural village may "push" people to begin the process of migration. A common "pull" factor is the attraction of a big city, where people assume opportunity is greater. As we shall explain later in this chapter, migration underlies much of rapid urban growth in the Third World. The movement of people into a territory—commonly termed *immigration*—is measured as an *in-migration rate* calculated as the number entering an area for every thousand people in the population. Movement out of a territory—or *emigration*—is measured as an *out-migration rate*, that is, the number leaving for every thousand people. Both types of migration usually occur simultaneously; demographers describe the net result of in-migration and out-migration as the *net-migration rate*.

Population Growth

Fertility, mortality, and migration affect the size of a society's population. Demographers derive the *natural growth rate* of a population by subtracting the crude death rate from the crude birth rate. The natural growth rate of the Canadian population in 1991 was 8 per thousand (the crude birth rate of 15.2 minus the crude death rate of 7.2), or 0.8 percent annually. During the 1990s, demographers predict, the growth rate of the Canadian population will remain low, but this is not the case for many regions of the world, as is shown in Global Map 21-1.

The global map shows that the population growth in the industrialized regions of the world is well below average. In Europe, the current rate of growth is just 0.2 percent, and it is falling rapidly in Japan and elsewhere in the First World. By contrast, annual growth rates equal or exceed the world average throughout the Third World—including Asia (currently about 1.7 percent) and Latin America (overall, about 1.8 percent). The greatest population surge is in Africa, where annual growth averages 3.1 percent. To understand the significance of these figures, consider that an annual growth of 2 percent (as in Latin America) doubles a population in thirty-five years, and a 3 percent growth rate (as in Africa) reduces the *doubling time* of a society's population to only twenty-four years. The rapid population growth of the poorest countries is deeply troubling because of their inability to support the populations they have now.

Population Composition

Demographers also study the composition of a society's population at any point in time. One simple variable is the **sex ratio**, *the number of males for every hundred females in a given population.* In 1991 the sex ratio in

African-American artist Jacob Lawrence completed a series of paintings that he titled The Migration of the Negro (1940-1941) to document a major population movement among people of color from the rural South to the urban centers of the Northeast and Midwest.

Jacob Lawrence, The Migration of the Negro. Panel 1: During the World War There Was a Great Migration North by Southern Negroes. 1940-41. Tempera on masonite. 11 1/2 x 17 1/2". The Phillips Collection.

Canada was 97.2 or 97 men for every 100 females. Sex ratios typically fall below 100 because, as was noted in Chapter 20 ("Health and Medicine"), women tend to outlive men.

A more complex and subtle way to describe the composition of a population is the **age-sex pyramid**, *a graphic representation that divides a population into various categories based on age and sex.* Figure 21-1 presents the age-sex pyramids for Canada in 1971, 1981, and 1991. The left side indicates the distribution of males of different ages, while the right side shows the corresponding distribution of females. The rough pyramid shape results from higher mortality as people age. Also note that, after about age thirty, women increasingly outnumber men in Canada. The greater population share between the ages of twenty and forty-four represents the high birth rate from the mid-1940s to the late 1960s, commonly called the *baby boom*. The contraction

WINDOW ON THE WORLD

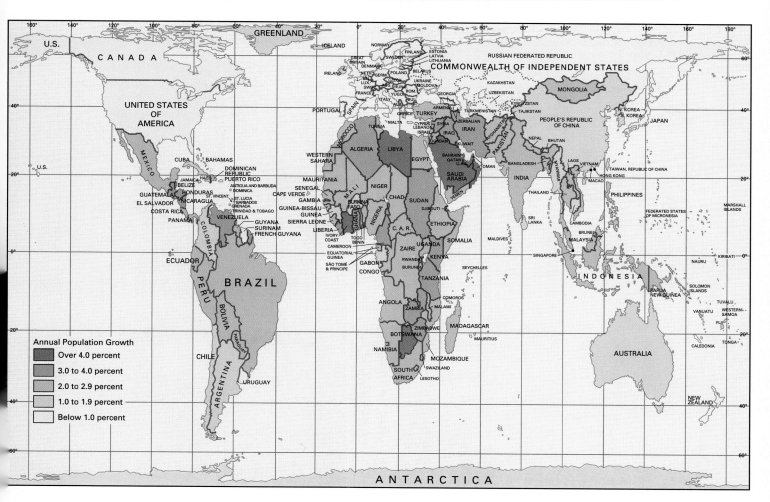

GLOBAL MAP 21-1   POPULATION GROWTH IN GLOBAL PERSPECTIVE

The richest societies of the world—including Canada, the United States, and the nations of Europe—have growth rates below 1 percent. The nations of Latin America and Asia typically have growth rates of about 2 percent, which double a population in thirty-five years. The continent of Africa has an overall growth rate of 3.1 percent, which cuts the doubling time to less than twenty-four years. In global perspective, we see that a society's standard of living is closely related to its rate of population growth, meaning that population is rising fastest in the world regions that can least afford to support more people.

just below age twenty shows that the baby boom was followed by a *baby bust*: a sharp decline in the birth rate. From a peak of 28.2 in 1955, the crude birth rate dropped to 14.4 in 1987 (and rose again to 15.2 by 1991). The bulges in the three pyramids in Figure 21-1 reveal the upward motion of the baby boom generation over a 20-year period. Figure 14-1 in Chapter 14 ("Aging and the Elderly") on page 385 projects the baby boom movement to the year 2036.

The bulges and contractions in a society's age-sex pyramid provide important clues to its demographic history. Figure 21-2 compares the age-sex pyramids of a rich country, Switzerland, and a poor nation, Bangla-

desh. The relatively boxlike pyramid for Switzerland reveals a birth rate that has long been very low, and which recently has dropped even further. With fewer women entering their childbearing years, population growth is likely to remain low. The Swiss pattern is more or less replicated by other industrial societies.

Bangladesh, a typical Third-World society, offers a dramatic contrast. The sharp point near the top of the pyramid is produced by high death rates after what we think of as middle age. The extremely wide base reveals the birth rate to be very high. Fertility is likely to rise even more, since the majority of females have yet to enter their childbearing years. Worldwide, the median

FIGURE 21-1   AGE-SEX POPULATION PYRAMID FOR CANADA, 1971–1991*
* Note that, in 1971, the baby boom shows up in the 5–9 year age category; by 1991, the baby boom is in the 25–39 year age categories.
SOURCE: Adapted from Statistics Canada, Catalogue No. 93-310, 1971, 1981, 1991.

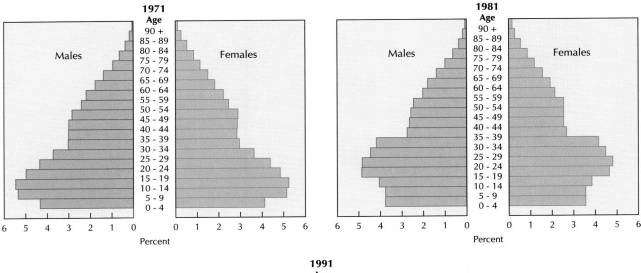
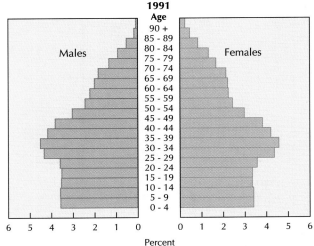

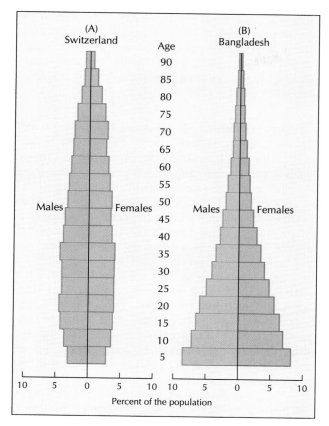

(A)
Switzerland

(B)
Bangladesh

Age

90
85
80
75
70
65
60
55
50
45
40
35
30
25
20
15
10
5

Males   Females   Males   Females

10   5   0   5   10   10   5   0   5   10

Percent of the population

FIGURE 21-2   THE DEMOGRAPHIC COMPOSITION OF SWITZERLAND AND BANGLADESH
SOURCE: Newman & Matzke, 1984.

age is only twenty-four—compared to thirty-four in Canada and thirty-five in Europe—making future population increases in poor countries all but inevitable. Unless effective birth control is available and utilized, exploding population will further strain limited social resources throughout the Third World.

History and Theory of Population Growth

Through most of human history, people considered large families desirable since human labor was the key to productivity. Additionally, until the development of rubber condoms 150 years ago, birth control was uncertain at best. Paralleling high birth rates were high death rates—the result of the diseases for which there was no cure. Occurring together, high fertility and high mortality more or less canceled each other out, so population grew slowly. The world's population at the

dawn of civilization in about 6000 B.C.E. (no more than 50 million) increased steadily if slowly across the millennia that followed, as is shown in Figure 21-3. When societies did manage population gains, they were often abruptly erased by periodic outbreaks of deadly plague, such as the Black Death, which swept across Western Europe in the mid-fourteenth century.

A demographic shift occurred about 1750 as the earth's population turned sharply upward, reaching 1 billion a century later. As we shall see, this increase was more the result of a drop in mortality than a jump in fertility. But the result was dramatic. Reaching a global population of 1 billion had taken forty thousand years to accomplish, but the 2 billion mark was attained in 1930—in just another eighty years. In other words, not only was population increasing, but the *rate* of growth was also rising quickly. A third billion was added by 1962—after just thirty-two years—and a fourth billion by 1974, a scant twelve years later. Although the rate of growth has recently stabilized, this pace continues, with our planet passing the 5 billion level in 1987. In no previous century did the world's population even double. In the twentieth century, however, it has increased *fourfold*.

Demographic projections are really informed guesswork. Currently, experts predict that world population will exceed 6 billion early in the coming century, and will probably reach 8 billion by 2025. Little wonder, then, that global population has become a matter of urgent concern.

Malthusian Theory

It was the sudden population growth some two centuries ago that sparked the development of demogra-

FIGURE 21-3   THE GROWTH OF WORLD POPULATION

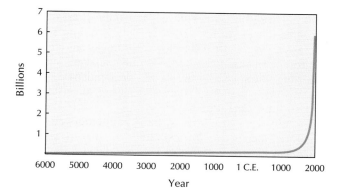

7
6
5
4
3
2
1

Billions

6000   5000   4000   3000   2000   1000   1 C.E.   1000   2000

Year

Among the poorest countries on earth, Bangladesh is struggling to meet the needs of approximately 120 million people in a land area less than one-sixth the size of Ontario. With a high birth rate, that nation's population problem is likely to become more serious in the future.

phy as a discipline in the first place. One of the first efforts to explain population growth was made by Thomas Robert Malthus (1766–1834), an English clergyman and economist. His conclusion was as much a warning as an explanation, since he saw population growth driving the world toward social chaos.

Malthus (1926; orig. 1798) began by arguing that population growth was the simple result of the timeless passion between the sexes. As people reproduce, he continued, population should increase faster and faster according to what mathematicians call a geometric progression, as illustrated by the series of numbers 2, 4, 8, 16, 32, and so on. Malthus was left with the sobering realization that world population could soon soar out of control.

Malthus was confident that food production would also increase, but not as fast as people would multiply. Resources would expand only in arithmetic progression (as in the series 2, 3, 4, 5, 6, and so on) because, even with technological innovations in agriculture, farmland is limited. Malthus's analysis led to a startling vision of a future in which population would outstrip our planet's resources, leading ultimately to catastrophic starvation.

But what of efforts to limit population growth? Malthus imagined two possibilities. First were *positive checks* to growth, such as famine, disease, and war. Second were *preventive checks*, including artificial birth control, sexual abstinence, and delayed marriages. The

clergyman's religious principles precluded birth control, and his common sense told him people would not abstain from sex or marry later, unless they were facing imminent famine. His forecast ended on a decidedly pessimistic note, earning him the title of the "dismal parson."

Critical evaluation.   Fortunately, Malthus's predictions were flawed in several ways. First, by the middle of the nineteenth century, the birth rate in Europe began to drop—partly because children were becoming less of an economic asset, and partly because people did embrace artificial birth control. Second, Malthus underestimated human ingenuity: advances in irrigation, fertilizers, and pesticides greatly increased the output of farmers, and industrial technology resulted in unforeseen increases in the production of other goods.

But Malthus was also criticized, not for his answers, but for asking the wrong questions. Karl Marx denounced Malthus for ignoring the role of social inequality as a cause of abundance or a source of famine. According to Marx (1967; orig. 1867), Malthus seemed to think that human suffering was a "law of nature," rather than a result of human mischief in the form of the capitalist economy.

Still, we should not entirely dismiss Malthus's dire prediction. First, daunting problems of population growth and limited resources remain. As Malthus suggested, habitable land, clean water, and unpolluted air are certainly finite. Moreover, technology is no miracle solution to our problems. As technology has boosted economic productivity, it has also created new and threatening problems, such as environmental pollution, described in Chapter 20 ("Health and Medicine"). Similarly, medical advances have lowered the death rate but, in so doing, have increased world population.

Second, the press of population growth and the gnawing effects of hunger are less evident to North Americans than to people in the Third World. In the poorest societies of Africa, Asia, and Latin America, rapid population growth is approaching the catastrophe Malthus envisioned. The 3 percent growth rate currently found in much of Africa, for example, will double that region's population before the year 2020. And, throughout the Third World, almost one-fifth of the world's people are already in jeopardy due to poverty.

Third, although there is no doubt that short-run population growth has been far less than that feared by Malthus, in the long run, as Paul Ehrlich (1978) points out, *no rate of increase can be sustained indefinitely.* For this reason, the entire world has a direct interest in planning and programs that will control our planet's population.

Demographic Transition Theory

Malthus's rather crude analysis of population growth has been superseded by **demographic transition theory**, *the thesis that population patterns are linked to a society's level of technological development.*

This relationship is evident by comparing the three stages of technological development shown in Figure 21-4. Stage 1—preindustrial agrarian societies—have high birth rates because adults value children as a source of labor and because effective birth control does not exist. Death rates, too, are high, since a low standard of living and primitive medical technology promote deadly infectious diseases. Overall, high mortality neutralizes high fertility, yielding slow population growth, a trend that lasted for thousands of years before the Industrial Revolution began in eighteenth-century Europe.

Stage 2—the onset of industrialization—brings a demographic transition as population surges upward. This increase results from expanding food supplies and more effective controls on disease so that, while birth rates remain high, death rates fall sharply. Malthus developed his ideas in this context, which explains his pessimism about the future. Most Third-World societies today are in this high-growth stage.

In Stage 3—a fully industrialized economy—the birth rate drops, curbing population growth once again. This happens, first, because sophisticated technology makes effective birth control widely available. People embrace this technology because a higher standard of living makes children expensive to raise, effectively transforming them from economic assets to liabilities. Having fewer children also permits women more time

to work outside the home. As birth rates begin to fall into line with low death rates, fertility and mortality are balanced and once again population growth is slow.

Western industrial societies have been in this third stage for much of this century. Recall, for example, that annual growth rates for populations in Europe and North America are now below 1 percent. A few poor societies, such as the People's Republic of China, have managed to hold population growth at about 2 percent through sweeping government programs. But, without industrial development, most Third-World societies appear to be locked in a spiral of dangerously high population growth.

Critical evaluation. Demographic transition theory suggests that technology holds the key to population growth. Instead of the runaway population increase Malthus feared, in other words, this analysis foresees limited population growth and material plenty as a result of technological development.

Demographic transition theory dovetails with modernization theory, one approach to global development detailed in Chapter 11 ("Global Inequality"). Modernization theorists take the optimistic view that the Third World will solve its population problem as poor societies gradually adopt industrial technology and raise their living standards. But critics—notably those who endorse dependency theory—argue that current global economic arrangements will only ensure the continued poverty of Third-World societies. Unless there is a significant redistribution of global resources, they claim, our planet will become increasingly divided into industrialized "haves" enjoying low population growth and nonindustrialized "have-nots" struggling in vain to feed soaring populations.

World Population Today

Drawing on demographic transition theory, we can briefly highlight important differences in the demographic standing of industrial and developing societies.

Industrial Societies

Soon after the Industrial Revolution began, annual population growth in Western Europe and North America peaked at about 3 percent: then, as industrialization proceeded, it declined, and since 1970, annual growth has remained below 1 percent. Well within Stage 3 of demographic transition theory, rich nations appear close to the population replacement level of 2.1 births

FIGURE 21-4 DEMOGRAPHIC TRANSITION THEORY

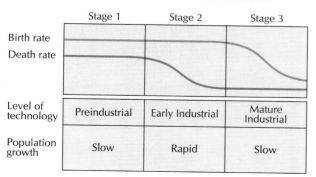

Il paraît que je suis un phénomène socio-culturel.

LA FRANCE A BESOIN D'ENFANTS.

The birthrate in Europe has dropped so low that some analysts foresee an absolute decline in population in this world region. In France, the government has turned to advertising to encourage people to have children. The ad implies children are becoming so rare that this baby can remark: "It appears that I am a socio-cultural phenomenon." At the bottom right is added, "France needs children."

per woman, a point termed **zero population growth**, *the level of reproduction that maintains population at a steady state.* Several European societies have already shown a decrease in population, prompting some analysts to suggest that postindustrial societies may experience a fourth demographic stage, as populations actually decline (van de Kaa, 1987). Because the Canadian population is still relatively young—with a median age of thirty-four—population growth is expected to continue for at least several decades. But the "graying of Canada," discussed in Chapter 14 ("Aging and the Elderly"), partly reflects the smaller proportion of children to older people as well as the trend of people living longer.

Factors pushing fertility downward include the higher costs of raising children, the increasing proportion of women in the labor force, and the growing number of people choosing to marry at a later age or to remain childless. Contraceptive use and voluntary sterilization have increased dramatically. Even Catholics, whose religious doctrine prohibits artificial birth control, no longer differ significantly from other Canadians in their contraceptive practices. (In fact, Quebec, which is more than 85 percent Catholic, has one of the lower fertility rates in Canada.) Abortion has been legal since 1969, and each year Canadian women terminate more

than 70,000 pregnancies in hospitals and another 20,000 in clinics.[1]

Overall, however, population growth in Canada and other industrial societies is not perceived as a problem. If anything, Canada worries about a low population growth rate and seeks to augment it through immigration. Quebec seeks immigrants but also has policies designed to encourage child-bearing.

Less-Developed Societies

Today only disappearing hunting and gathering societies (see Chapter 4, "Society") are still within demographic transition theory's Stage 1. These isolated societies, until recently untouched by industrial technology, have high birth and death rates and, consequently, low population growth. Most world societies—in Latin America, Africa, and Asia—have predominantly agrarian economies with limited industrialization, placing them in Stage 2. Advanced medical technology supplied to these areas by industrial societies has sharply reduced death rates, but birth rates remain high. Figure 21-5 shows the predictable result. These countries have experienced 80 percent of the world's population increase during this century, and they currently account for about two-thirds of the earth's people. Demographers predict that this percentage will increase to more than three-fourths when the global population exceeds 6 billion (U.S. Bureau of the Census, 1991).

Birth rates are high in the Third World today for the same reasons they were high everywhere for most of human history. In agrarian societies, children are vital economic assets, frequently working eight- or ten-hour days to contribute to their families' income. Parents also look to their offspring for economic support in old age. The economic value of children, coupled with high infant mortality, understandably encourages parents to have large families. Throughout the Third World, families average four or five children; in rural areas, the number may reach six or even eight (The World Bank, 1991).

The social position of women also figures as a crucial factor in today's population picture. Agrarian societies are strongly patriarchal, defining women's primary responsibilities as bearing and raising children. In Latin America, a combination of economic need, traditional patriarchy, and Roman Catholic doctrine discourages

---

[1] In Canada, there is one abortion for every five live births. In the U.S. the ratio is 1 to 3.

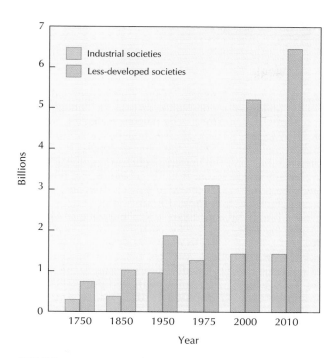

FIGURE 21-5 POPULATION DISTRIBUTION, INDUSTRIAL AND LESS-DEVELOPED SOCIETIES, 1750–2010
SOURCE: Piotrow, 1980; U.S. Bureau of the Census, 1991.

many women from using birth control devices, with predictable demographic consequences. In much of Africa, many women in poor villages have never had the opportunity to use effective birth control (Salas, 1985). In some Asian countries, women have little access to effective contraception, although in others—notably India and China—governments have launched bold, even intrusive, programs to control fertility. The current situation in the People's Republic of China, the world's most populous society, is examined in the box.

There is a further connection between the social position of women and population growth. In short, if restricted to the traditional roles of child rearing and homemaking, women are likely to have many children. Similarly, men without economic and educational opportunities are more likely to define their masculinity in terms of virility. Thus formal education and rewarding work—for women as well as men—hold the keys not only to a society's economic development, but to population control as well. Research suggests, to cite just two examples, that in Sudan (Africa) and Colombia (South America) women with seven years of schooling had half as many children as those with no schooling at all (Ross, 1985; Salas, 1985).

Efforts to control fertility have met with some

success: in many Third-World countries, average family size fell by over 20 percent between 1975 and 1985 (Salas, 1985). This decline appears to be continuing, although perhaps at a slower rate. But the capacity to control population growth depends on reducing fertility sharply, since death rates are falling in most parts of the world.

In point of fact, population growth in the Third World is due *primarily* to declining death rates. After about 1920, when Europe and North America began to export advances in scientific medicine, nutrition, and sanitation to Third-World countries, mortality in these societies fell dramatically. Since that time, inoculations against infectious diseases and the use of antibiotics and insecticides have continued to curb death rates with stunning effectiveness. For example, in Sri Lanka, malaria caused half of all deaths in the mid-1930s; a decade later, the use of insecticide to kill malaria-carrying mosquitoes cut the death toll from this disease by 50 percent (Ehrlich, 1978). Although we hail such an achievement, over the long term this technological advance sent Sri Lanka's population soaring. Similarly, India's infant mortality rate fell from 130 in 1975 to 90 in 1990, but this decline helped boost that nation's population to more than 850 million.

In sum, although infant mortality and life expectancy in Third-World countries are still unfavorable when compared to richer nations, both have improved. More children throughout the world now survive to adulthood; however, they then proceed to have children of their own. This is why birth control programs are now vital in parts of the world where "death control" policies worked well several generations ago (Piotrow, 1980).

The Importance of Demography

Demographic analysis sheds light on how and why the world is experiencing unprecedented population growth. Only through such study can humankind address this pressing problem.

But even if we grasp the causes and scope of the problem, controlling global population is a monumental task. As we have seen, the rate of population growth is currently greatest in the poorest societies of the world, those that lack the productive capacity to support their present populations, much less their future ones. Although, as privileged inhabitants of the First World, we are spared the trauma of poverty, we can recognize the consequences of adding almost 100 million people to our planet each year. Beyond the drain

CROSS-CULTURAL COMPARISON

Birth Control in China

Third-World governments have responded to rapid population growth with a variety of programs aimed at reducing fertility. The People's Republic of China has one-fifth of the world's people, with a population of 1.2 billion in 1990. Furthermore, more than half the Chinese people are under thirty, raising the specter of a baby boom without parallel in human history. As a result, since 1979, the Chinese government has pursued a tough policy limiting couples to a single child.

Local officials strongly encourage couples to delay childbirth and, once a child is born, to submit to sterilization or abort subsequent pregnancies. One-baby couples receive income bonuses, and single children are promised priority in school enrollment, health care, and, later, in employment and housing. In various ways, the government transmits a clear message: family planning is each couple's social responsibility. The results of this program have been significant, as the annual growth rate dropped from 2.0 percent in the 1960s to about 1.8 percent in the 1980s.

But like many government policies, this program spawned a number of unexpected problems. First, widespread sterilization during the early 1980s provoked international protest that China was forcing its people to undergo surgery. Second, the one-child policy has encouraged parents to abort female fetuses or even to kill female infants. Chinese cultural traditions confer on sons the duty of caring for elderly parents; daughters, by contrast, serve their husband's parents. Thus most Chinese couples shudder at the prospect of growing old without a son. A third problem is that privileges accorded to only children are now disproportionately enjoyed by sons, increasing sexual inequality in China.

By 1990, the government reacted to these strains with some leniency. Yet the price of unregulated growth appears higher: at the present rate of growth, the population will double by 2025, undermining the struggle of a vast society to raise its standard of living.

SOURCES: *The World Bank (1984), Brophy (1989a, 1989b), and Tien (1989).*

---

on food supplies, however, these millions need housing, education, and employment—all in tragically short supply. The well-being of the entire world may ultimately depend on resolving many of the economic and social problems of poor, overly populated countries and bridging the widening gulf between the "have" and "have-not" societies. Describing recent population growth as "a great wave," one official concluded:

> *I see the world population movement as the effort to construct a breakwater—a structure that will stop the wave and prevent it from engulfing and sweeping away centuries of human development and civilization.* (cited in Gupte, 1984:323)

Urbanization: The Growth of Cities

For most of human history, the small populations found around the world lived in nomadic groups, moving as they depleted vegetation or following migratory game. As civilization emerged in the Middle East some 8,000 years ago, widely scattered settlements were built for the first time, but these held only a small fraction of the earth's people. Today the largest single cities contain as many people as the entire planet did then, and these cities will likely become even larger.

Urbanization, then, is *the concentration of humanity into cities.* Urbanization both redistributes population in a society and transforms many patterns of social life. We will follow these changes in terms of three urban revolutions—the emergence of cities, the growth of industrial cities, and the explosive growth in Third-World cities—that are the focus of much of the rest of this chapter.

The Evolution of Cities

In the long course of human history, cities are a recent development. After hundreds of thousands of years of evolutionary development, our ancestors grasped the idea of the city only about 10,000 years ago. Two factors set the stage for the *first urban revolution*, the emergence of permanent settlements.

One factor was the changing ecology: as glaciers began to melt at the end of the last ice age, people migrated toward warm regions with fertile soil. The second was changing technology: at about the same time, humans discovered how to raise animals and crops. Whereas hunting and gathering had required small bands of people to continually migrate, pastoralism and horticulture forced people to remain in one place and build permanent settlements (Lenski, Lenski, & Nolan, 1991). Domesticating animals and plants also generated a material surplus, which freed some people from the need to produce food in favor of activities like building shelters, making tools, weaving clothing, and leading religious rituals. In this context, the founding of cities stands as a truly revolutionary move; cities raised living standards significantly and enhanced productive specialization to a degree never seen before.

The First Cities

Historians believe the first city was Jericho, a settlement to the north of the Dead Sea in disputed land currently occupied by Israel. About 8000 B.C.E., Jericho contained some 600 people (Kenyon, 1957; Hamblin, 1973; Spates & Macionis, 1987). By 4000 B.C.E., cities had become far more numerous, flourishing across the Fertile Crescent between the Tigris and Euphrates rivers in present-day Iraq and, soon afterward, along the Nile River in Egypt. Some settlements, with populations as high as 50,000, became centers of urban empires dominating large regions. Priest-kings wielded absolute power over lesser nobility, administrators, artisans, soldiers, and farmers. Slaves, captured in frequent military campaigns, provided labor to build monumental structures like the pyramids of Egypt (Wenke, 1980; Stavrianos, 1983; Lenski, Lenski, & Nolan, 1991).

Early urban settlement in Latin America often took the form of ceremonial centers. Here is the massive Pyramid of the Sun at Teotihuacan, near Mexico City.

Cities originated independently in at least three other areas of the world. Several large, complex cities dotted the Indus River region of present-day Pakistan by about 2500 B.C.E. Scholars date Chinese cities from around 2000 B.C.E. In Central and South America, urban centers began somewhat later, about 1500 B.C.E. In North America, however, Native American societies rarely formed settlements; significant urbanization, therefore, did not begin until the arrival of European settlers in the sixteenth century (Lamberg-Karlovsky, 1973; Change, 1977; Coe & Diehl, 1980).

Preindustrial Cities in Europe

Urbanization in Europe began about 1800 B.C.E. on the Mediterranean island of Crete. Spreading throughout Greece, the drive for urbanization gave rise to more than one hundred city-states, of which Athens is the most famous. During its Golden Age, lasting barely a century after 500 B.C.E., Athens exemplified the positive potential of urban life. The Athenians, numbering about 300,000 and living in an area of roughly one square mile, developed and advanced cultural elements still central to the Western way of life, including philosophy, the arts, the principles of democracy, and a mixture of physical and mental fitness symbolized by the Olympic games (Mumford, 1961; Carlton, 1977; Stavrianos, 1983). Yet for all its achievements, Athenian society depended on the labor of slaves, who made up nearly one-third of the population. And democratic principles notwithstanding, Athenian men denied the rights of citizenship to women and foreigners (Mumford, 1961; Gouldner, 1965).

As Greek civilization faded, the city of Rome grew to almost 1 million inhabitants and became the center of a vast empire. By the first century C.E., the militaristic Roman Empire encompassed much of northern Africa, Europe, and the Middle East. In the process, Rome widely diffused its language, arts, and technological innovations. After centuries of regional domination, the Roman Empire gradually fell into disarray by the fifth century C.E., a victim of its own gargantuan size, internal corruption, and militaristic appetite. In many respects, Athens and Rome were polar opposites, one moderate and learned, the other drawn to excess and militarism. Yet, between them, the Greeks and Romans founded cities all across Europe, including London, Paris, and Vienna.

The fall of the Roman Empire initiated an era of urban decline and stagnation that lasted some 600 years. Cities drew back within defensive walls, typically with no more than about 25,000 people. Competing warlords battled for territory, inhibiting trade and cultural exchange. About the eleventh century, the "dark ages" came to an end as a semblance of peace allowed economic activity to bring cities to life once again.

As trade increased, medieval cities slowly removed their walls, but they retained their narrow, winding, and usually filthy streets. As their economies expanded, London, Brussels, and Florence teemed with people from all walks of life: artisans, merchants, priests, peddlers, jugglers, nobles, and servants. Typically, different occupational groups such as bakers, keymakers, and carpenters lived in distinct sections or "quarters"; evidence of this practice remains today in the names of streets in many old cities. In the medieval cities of Europe, cathedrals towered above all other buildings, signifying the preeminence of Christianity.

By today's standards, medieval cities were surprisingly personal (Sjoberg, 1965). Family ties were strong, and the people inside each city "quarter" shared a trade and sometimes a religious and ethnic tradition. In some cases, this clustering was involuntary; religious and ethnic minorities were restricted by law to certain districts. For example, Jews were targets of extensive prejudice and discrimination in an era dominated by the Roman Catholic Church. Laws in Venice and later in most of Europe confined Jews to areas known as *ghettos*.

Industrial-Capitalist Cities in Europe

Throughout the Middle Ages, commerce steadily increased, creating an affluent urban middle class or *bourgeoisie* (a French word meaning "of the town"). By the fifteenth century, the wealth-based power of the bourgeoisie rivaled the traditional dominance of the hereditary nobility. The expanding European colonization of much of the world further bolstered the might of the new trading class.

By about 1750 the trade-based economy of most cities was given an enormous boost as the Industrial Revolution got under way. In a short span of time, this tremendous economic expansion triggered a *second urban revolution* beginning in Europe and soon spreading to North America. Factories unleashed vast new productive power, drawing people to cities in unprecedented numbers. As Table 21-2 shows, during the nineteenth century the population of Paris soared from 500,000 to over 3 million, and London exploded from 800,000 to 6.5 million (A. Weber, 1963, orig. 1899; Chandler & Fox, 1974). Most of this increase was due to migration from rural areas by people seeking a better standard of living.

As industrialization proceeded, cities changed in more ways than just the size of their populations. Because business stood at its heart, the industrial-capitalist city evolved a typical urban form. The old, irregular alleys that marked the medieval city gave way to broad, straight streets that could accommodate the flow of ever-increasing commercial traffic, including motor vehicles. Steam and electric trolleys also criss-crossed the new cities, sometimes on the ground, sometimes above (the "elevated lines") and sometimes below (the "subways"). Cities also took on a patchwork character, as Lewis Mumford (1961) explains, because commercial interests dictated that land be divided into regular-sized lots that facilitated the real-estate industry. Finally, the cathedrals—icons of the medieval cities—were soon dwarfed by the epitome of industrial-capitalist living: the brightly lit, towering, and frantic central business district. In this center of the New City, corporate-owned skyscrapers proclaimed the power of the capitalist economy.

Industrialization also transformed urban social life. With increasing size and a focus on business rather than family ties, cities became impersonal; people could "walk lonely in the crowd." Crime rates rose. Inequality remained striking, with a handful of industrialists living in palatial splendor while most men, women, and children performed exhausting work in factories for bare subsistence.

Table 21-2 shows that European cities continued to grow into the twentieth century, although at a declining rate. As the frenetic pace of growth subsided, organized efforts by workers to improve their plight led to legal regulation of the workplace, better housing, and the right to vote. Early in this century, residents of

TABLE 21-2   POPULATION GROWTH IN SELECTED INDUSTRIAL CITIES OF EUROPE (IN THOUSANDS)

City	Year			
	1700	1800	1900	1990*
Amsterdam	172	201	510	725
Berlin	100	172	2,424	3,022
Lisbon	188	237	363	2,396
London	550	861	6,480	9,170
Madrid	110	169	539	4,451
Paris	530	547	3,330	8,709
Rome	149	153	487	3,021
Vienna	105	231	1,662	2,313

* for urban area
SOURCE: Based on data from Tertius Chandler and Gerald Fox, 3000 Years of Urban History. *New York: Academic Press, 1974:17-19; and U.S. Bureau of the Census,* World Population Profile, *Washington, DC: U.S. Government Printing Office, 1991.*

virtually every city boasted of access to public services including water, sewerage, and electricity. While many city-dwellers, even today, remain in poverty, the city has partly fulfilled its historic promise—to provide a rising standard of living for most people.

The Growth of North American Cities

Inhabiting this continent over tens of thousands of years, Native North Americans were mainly migratory peoples, establishing few permanent settlements. Cities first took root only after European colonization began. The Spanish made an initial settlement at St. Augustine, Florida, in 1565, and the English founded Jamestown, Virginia, in 1607. Around the same time, Samuel de Champlain founded a trading post at Québec (1608). New Amsterdam, later called New York, was established by the Dutch in 1624, Montreal was founded by Maisonneuve in 1642, Halifax was founded in 1749 by the British (to counter the French influence in North America) and York (now Toronto) was founded in 1793 by John Graves Simcoe in a location where it could be protected from American invasion.

These tentative intrusions onto Indian lands were accompanied by an expanded fur trade, an invasion of rural settlers, colonial expansion, and a struggle for control over lands involving Natives, the British, and the French—all of which led to massive immigration and gradual urbanization. By 1990, the United States con-

tained 195 cities with a population of more than 100,000, while, according to the 1991 census, Canada had 35 cities of that size—and both countries have more than three quarters of their populations living in areas that are designated as urban. An examination of the transformation of North America over a three-hundred-and-fifty-year period must begin in the colonial era.

Colonial Settlement in North America: 1624–1800

What we think of today as the metropolises of New York and Boston were, at the time of founding, tiny settlements in a vast wilderness. Dutch New Amsterdam at the tip of Manhattan Island (1624) and English Boston (1630) each resembled medieval towns of Europe, with narrow, winding streets that still delight pedestrians (and frustrate motorists) in lower Manhattan and downtown Boston. New Amsterdam was walled on its north side, the site of today's Wall Street. Boston, the largest colonial settlement, had a population of only 7,000 in 1700.

The rational and expansive culture of capitalism soon transformed these quiet villages into thriving towns with grid-like streets bustling with activity. Figure 21-6 contrasts the traditional shape of colonial New Amsterdam with the regular design of Philadelphia founded in 1680 after an additional half-century of economic development.

Toronto (York) was founded on July 30, 1793 by John Graves Simcoe, commander of the Queen's

FIGURE 21-6 THE STREET PLANS OF COLONIAL NEW AMSTERDAM (NEW YORK), AND PHILADELPHIA
The plan of colonial New Amsterdam (1624) reflects the preindustrial urban pattern of walls enclosing a city of narrow, irregular streets. Colonial Philadelphia (1681) reflects the industrial urban pattern of accessible cities containing wide, regularly spaced, parallel and perpendicular streets to facilitate economic activity.

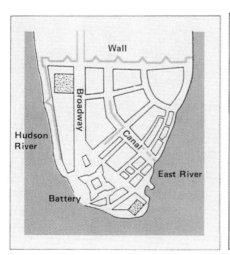
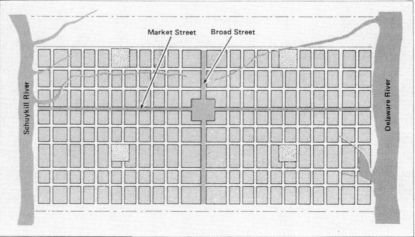

Rangers and later the first lieutenant-governor of Upper Canada. Montreal, by that time, was already a bustling city of over 5,500, but in Upper Canada there were only about fifteen settler families between Burlington Bay and the Bay of Quinte—a distance of two hundred kilometers (Benn, 1993).

Simcoe's intent was to move the capital from its vulnerable location near Niagara Falls to one where it could be protected from American invasion. He also wanted to establish a civilian community and a naval base. The map of York Harbour in Figure 21-7 shows the location of "the Garrison" (now called Fort York) and the settlement of York. The grid-like settlement plan (similar to that of Philadelphia in Figure 21-6) is near the area where Toronto's St. Lawrence Market stands today (Benn, 1993). The north-south lines above Queen Street mark the parcels of land that were granted by Simcoe to some of his regimental comrades and others in an effort to entice them to settle in York as a local aristocracy. The members of that "Family Compact" dominated Upper Canada until the 1830s: the lines separating their land allotments still show up as major north-south arteries on Toronto road maps.

Even as the first settlements grew, North America remained overwhelmingly rural. In 1790 the United States government's first census counted a national population of only 4 million, a scant 5 percent of whom lived in cities. Around the time of Confederation in Canada (1867), the U.S. population of about 40 million was 20 percent urban, while Canada's population of about 3 million was almost as urban at 18 percent. In both countries, the vast majority of people lived on farms and in small villages. The small Canada-U.S. gap in levels of urbanization had essentially disappeared by 1940 and today Canada has inched ahead of the U.S (77 and 75 percent urban respectively). Table 21-3 shows Canada's population growth and levels of urbanization from its first post-confederation census to the present: the U.S. population has consistently been roughly ten times that of Canada, but its urbanization levels have been almost identical.

Urban Expansion

Throughout the nineteenth century, towns sprang up across the North American continent—somewhat later

FIGURE 21-7 MAP OF YORK (TORONTO)

York (1793) was designed on a grid pattern as a temporary capital for Upper Canada. It was located on a protected bay where it could be shielded from potential attack by the Americans.

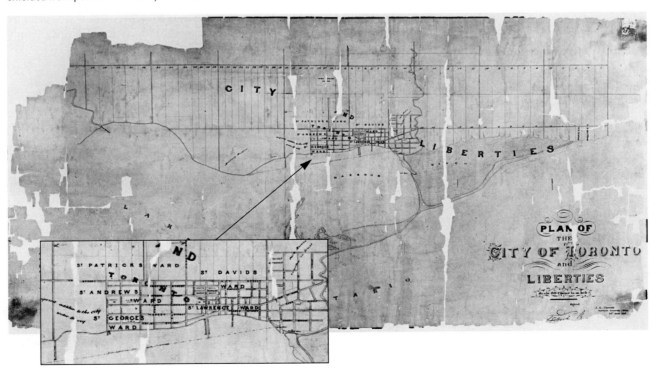

TABLE 21-3 THE URBAN POPULATION OF CANADA, 1871–1991

Year	Population (000s)	Percent Urban
1871	3,689	18.3
1881	4,325	23.3
1891	4,833	29.8
1901	5,371	34.9
1911	7,207	41.8
1921	8,788	47.4
1931	10,377	52.5
1941	11,507	55.7
1951	14,009	62.4
1961	18,238	69.7
1971	21,568	76.1
1981	24,343	75.8
1991	27,297	76.6

SOURCE: Colombo, 1992:40; Artibise & Stelter, 1988.

in Canada than in the United States. Waterways as well as new roads and railway lines encouraged the growth of these towns and cities. British Columbia agreed to enter into Confederation in 1871 on the condition that a transcontinental railway would be completed within ten years. The last spike was not driven until 1885, but the Canadian Pacific Railway (CPR) gave a powerful boost to settlement and economic development, especially in towns and cities located on the railway line itself. Calgary was incorporated as a town in 1884 (one year after the arrival of the CPR) and by 1891 had a population of 3,876: it became a city two years later.

By 1920 and 1931, American and Canadian censuses repectively revealed that more than 50 percent of their populations were living in cities. To some, increased urbanization constituted progress toward better living, but others mourned the gradual passing of traditional agrarian life. Over time, rural-urban tensions grew more pronounced, with adversaries trading negative stereotypes that pitted "ignorant country cousins" against "shady city slickers" (Callow, 1969).

Interestingly, urbanization took hold at different rates in various sectors of the continent. The Industrial Revolution proceeded far more rapidly in the northern states than in the American South, which experienced limited urbanization. By the time of the Civil War, New York City's population was ten times that of Charleston. Historians cite the tension between the industrial-urban North and the agrarian-rural South as one of the major causes of the Civil War (Schlesinger, 1969). In Canada, Ontario, and to a lesser extent Quebec, urbanized more rapidly than the Atlantic or Prairie provinces. Complaints about the political and economic power of industrialized central Canada (i.e., Ontario and Quebec)

have been common in the rest of the country and sometimes lead to talk of the separation of Eastern or Western provinces. Quebec has not had a monopoly on such sentiments.

The Metropolitan Era

The American Civil War gave an enormous boost to industrialization in the U.S., as factories strained to produce the instruments of combat. Much later the First and Second World Wars stimulated war-related production in both Canada and the United States. These only added to structural economic changes that were encouraging rural-urban migration and paving the way for huge waves of immigrants, mostly from Europe. Throughout North America, tens of millions of newcomers were blending their various ways of life into the dynamic new urban mix.

As the Industrial Revolution picked up momentum, cities teemed with unprecedented numbers of people. In 1900, New York boasted 4 million residents, Montreal had a population of about 400,000, and Toronto was approaching 200,000. Table 21-4 shows the population growth (1966–1991) of the thirty-five Canadian cities that had reached 100,000 by 1991. Table 21-5 ranks the ten largest Canadian cities in 1966 and 1991, indicating considerable change over time: only Montreal and Edmonton retain their ranks—first and fifth—over the twenty-five-year period involved.

The dizzying growth and concentration of population marked the coming of the **metropolis,** *a large city that socially and economically dominates the surrounding area.* This development began before 1900 in the U.S. and perhaps forty years later in Canada. The current Canadian definition of a Census Metropolitan Area (CMA) involves a population of at least 100,000 spread out among one or more municipalities with economic and commuting ties. These metropolises, and their counterparts in the U.S., became the manufacturing, commercial, and residential centers of North America.

As their populations grew, the physical shape of the metropolis continued to change as well. In 1850, few buildings could be found that exceeded three or four stories. By the 1880s, industrial technology was producing steel girders and mechanical elevators so that builders were raising structures ten stories above the ground. And this, of course, was only the beginning. In 1975, Toronto's CN Tower was completed. At 553.3 meters, it is still the world's tallest free-standing structure. City centers contain these kinds of monuments as well as clusters of soaring buildings of

TABLE 21-4 POPULATION GROWTH IN CANADA'S LARGEST CITIES 1966–1991 (POPULATION IN THOUSANDS)

	1966	1976	1981	1986	1991
Brampton, Ont.	36.3	103.5	149.0	188.5	234.4
Burlington, Ont.	65.9	104.3	114.9	116.7	129.6
Calgary, Alta.	330.6	469.9	592.7	636.1	710.7
East York, Ont.*	74.2	107.0	102.0	101.1	102.7
Edmonton, Alta.	376.9	461.4	532.2	574.0	616.7
Etobicoke, Ont.	219.5	297.1	298.7	303.0	310.0
Gloucester, Ont.	23.2	56.5	72.9	89.8	101.7
Halifax, N.S.	86.8	117.9	114.6	113.6	114.5
Hamilton, Ont.	298.1	312.0	306.4	306.7	318.5
Kitchener, Ont.	93.3	131.9	139.7	150.6	168.3
Laval, Que.	196.1	246.2	268.3	284.1	314.4
London, Ont.	194.4	240.4	254.3	269.1	303.2
Longueuil, Que.	25.6	122.4	124.3	125.4	129.9
Markham, Ont.	7.8	56.2	77.0	114.6	153.8
Mississauga, Ont.	93.5	250.0	315.1	374.0	463.4
Montréal, Que.	1222.3	1080.5	980.4	1015.4	1017.7
Nepean, Ont.	43.9	76.9	84.4	95.5	107.6
North York, Ont.	399.5	558.4	559.5	556.3	562.6
Oakville, Ont.	52.8	69.0	75.8	87.1	114.7
Oshawa, Ont.	78.1	107.0	117.5	123.7	129.3
Ottawa, Ont.	290.7	304.5	295.2	300.8	314.0
Québec, Que.	167.0	177.1	166.5	164.6	167.5
Regina, Sask.	131.1	149.6	162.6	175.0	179.2
Richmond, B.C.**	50.5	80.0	96.1	108.5	126.6
St. Catharines, Ont.	97.1	123.4	124.0	123.5	129.3
Saskatoon, Sask.	115.9	133.8	154.2	177.6	186.1
Scarborough, Ont.	278.4	387.1	443.4	484.7	524.6
Surrey, B.C.**	81.8	116.5	147.1	181.4	189.3
Thunder Bay, Ont.	104.5	111.5	112.5	112.3	114.0
Toronto, Ont.	664.6	633.3	599.2	612.3	635.4
Vancouver, B.C.	410.4	410.2	414.3	431.1	471.8
Vaughan, Ont.	n.a.	17.8	29.7	65.1	111.4
Windsor, Ont.	192.5	196.5	192.1	193.1	191.4
Winnipeg, Man.	257.0	560.9	564.5	594.6	616.8
York, Ont.	134.7	141.4	134.6	135.4	140.5

* Incorporated as a Borough.
** Incorporated as a District Municipality.
SOURCE: Statistics Canada, Cat. No. 93-305; Colombo, 1992:52–53.

TABLE 21-5 THE TEN LARGEST CITIES IN CANADA, 1966 AND 1991 (POPULATION IN THOUSANDS)

	1966		1991	
Rank	City	Population	City	Population
1	Montreal	1,222.3	Montreal	1,017.7
2	Toronto	664.6	Calgary	710.7
3	Vancouver	410.4	Toronto	635.4
4	North York	399.5	Winnipeg	616.8
5	Edmonton	376.9	Edmonton	616.7
6	Calgary	330.6	North York	526.6
7	Hamilton	298.1	Scarborough	524.6
8	Ottawa	290.7	Vancouver	471.8
9	Scarborough	278.4	Mississauga	463.4
10	Winnipeg	257.0	Ottawa	314.0

SOURCE: Statistics Canada, Cat. No. 93-305; Colombo, 1992:52–53.

glass, concrete, and steel, while public transit and road-ways allow for lower-density city sprawl that stretches for miles.

Canada has twenty-five CMAs, ranging in size from Toronto at almost 4 million population to Thunder Bay, Ont., at 124,000 (see Table 21-6).

Urban Decentralization

The industrial metropolis reached its peak about 1950 in the U.S. and 1975 in Canada. Since then, something of a turnaround has occurred as people have deserted the downtowns in a process known as *urban decentralization* (Edmonston & Guterbock, 1984). Another look at Table 21-4 shows that some of the largest cities

TABLE 21-6   POPULATION OF METRO* AREAS IN CANADA 1951–1991 (POPULATION IN THOUSANDS)

	1951	1961	1971	1981	1991	Land Area (sq. km) 1986
Calgary, Alta.	142.3	279.1	403.3	592.6	754	5,056.0
Chicoutimi-Jonquière, Que.	91.2	127.6	133.7	135.2	161	1,723.3
Edmonton, Alta.	193.6	359.8	495.7	656.9	840	11,396.7
Halifax, N.S.	138.4	193.4	222.6	277.7	321	2,508.1
Hamilton, Ont.	281.9	401.1	498.5	542.1	600	1,358.5
Kitchener, Ont.	107.5	154.9	226.8	287.8	356	823.6
London, Ont.	167.7	226.7	286.0	283.7	382	2,105.1
Montreal, Que.	1,539.3	2,215.6	2,743.2	2,828.3	3,127	3,508.6
Oshawa, Ont.	n.a.	n.a.	120.3	154.2	240	894.2
Ottawa-Hull, Ont.-Que.	311.6	457.0	602.5	718.0	921	5,138.3
Quebec, Que.	289.3	379.1	480.5	576.0	646	3,150.3
Regina, Sask.	72.7	113.7	140.7	164.3	192	3,421.6
St. Catharines-Niagara, Ont.	189.0	257.8	303.4	304.4	365	1,399.8
St. John's, Nfld.	80.9	106.7	131.8	154.8	172	1,130.0
Saint John, N.B.	80.7	98.1	106.7	114.0	125	2,904.8
Saskatoon, Sask.	55.7	95.6	126.4	154.2	210	4,749.4
Sherbrooke, Que.	n.a.	n.a.	n.a.	125.2	139	915.8
Sudbury, Ont.	80.5	127.4	155.4	149.9	158	2,612.1
Thunder Bay, Ont.	73.7	102.1	112.1	121.4	124	2,202.6
Toronto, Ont.	1,261.9	1,919.4	2,628.0	2,998.7	3,893	5,613.7
Trois-Rivières, Que.	46.1	53.5	55.9	111.4	136	871.9
Vancouver, B.C.	586.2	826.8	1,082.4	1,268.1	1,603	2,786.3
Victoria, B.C.	114.9	155.8	195.8	233.5	288	1,951.1
Windsor, Ont.	182.6	217.2	258.6	246.1	262	861.7
Winnipeg, Man.	357.2	476.5	540.3	584.8	652	3,294.8

* For census metropolitan areas which include neighboring municipalities from which the major urban center draws its work force. Population is based on CMA boundaries at the time of each census.

n.a.—not available as these areas had not reached the critical 100,000 population level.

SOURCE: Census of Canada; Colombo (1992):53.

stopped growing or actually lost population between 1976 and 1981, while a few showed further decline by 1986. But decentralization has not brought an end to urbanization: on the contrary, cities are evolving into a different form. In addition to our densely populated central cities, we now have vast urban regions encompassing expanded suburbs. Together these city cores and their outlying suburban areas form metropolitan areas. Many of the expanding cities, like Etobicoke, Scarborough, and North York, for example, are the suburban parts of Metropolitan Toronto.

Suburbs and Central Cities

Just as central cities flourished a century ago, we have recently witnessed the expansion of **suburbs**, *urban areas beyond the political boundaries of a city*. Suburbanization really took off throughout North America by about 1940, as public transit and improved roadways

enabled people to live beyond the commotion of the city while still being able to commute to work "downtown" (Warner, 1962). The first suburbanites were the well-to-do people imitating the pattern of the European nobility who alternated between their country estates and town houses (Baltzell, 1979). But the growth of suburbs has been fueled by racial and ethnic intolerance as well: rising immigration was adding to the social diversity of central cities, prompting many people to flee to homogeneous, high-prestige enclaves beyond the reach of the masses. In time, of course, less wealthy people also came to view a single-family house on its own piece of leafy suburban ground as essential to happiness and the proper raising of children.

The economic boom of the late 1940s, and the mobility provided by increasingly affordable automobiles, made this dream come true for more and more people. After World War II, men and women eagerly returned to family life, igniting the baby boom described earlier in this chapter. Since central cities offered little space for new housing construction, suburbs blossomed almost overnight.

Today, well over half of Canada's urbanites live in municipalities outside the central cities, or in newer central cities, like those on the Prairies, which are largely suburban in style. As a result of the overall flight to the suburbs by young families and the fact that more people are living alone in their downtown homes, even vigorous construction in the central cities has not been sufficient to stem the decline in some central city populations (Michelson, 1988:86).[2] As population decentralized, businesses also began to migrate to the suburbs. Older people today can recall trips "downtown" to shop but, by the 1970s, the suburban mall had replaced "main street" as the center of retail trade (Rosenthal, 1974; Tobin, 1976; Geist, 1985). Manufacturing interests, too, began to eye the suburbs where there was relief from high taxes, escalating property costs, and traffic congestion.

Decentralization was not good news for everyone, however. Rapid suburban growth meant financial difficulties for the older central cities. Population decline meant reduced tax revenues: cities lost their more affluent residents to the suburbs and were left to provide expensive social programs for the poor who remained.

In 1953, in response to this disparity between the core of the city and outlying areas, the Province of Ontario created "Metropolitan Toronto" by combining the central city of Toronto with twelve of its suburbs. The province had to impose the solution initially, as none of the municipalities was exactly enamoured of the prospect. But, as a result of the success of Metropolitan Toronto, other urban regions across Canada have followed suit, while Metro Toronto itself has continued to add to the number of funtions carried out at the upper tier.

The benefits of this model of urban development are clear when we look at the situation in the United States. Since American cities rarely adopt a metropolitan-type government, they tend to suffer much more from decaying inner-cities. "Canadian metropolitan areas suffer fewer of the glaring contrasts in welfare, infrastructure, and supportive services differentiating American central cities and suburbs" (Michelson, 1988:97).

When several adjacent metropolitan regions get so large that they bump up against each other and form a continuous urban band, they form what is called a

megalopolis, *a vast urban region containing a number of cities and their surrounding suburbs.* Gottman (1961) first coined the term, megalopolis, in reference to the area between and including Boston and Washington. In Canada, our closest equivalent is the area known as the "Golden Horseshoe," which stretches from Oshawa through Toronto to St. Catharines, although the Windsor–Quebec City corridor forms another looser version. The dominance of this region in the political and economic scheme of things is quite apparent in the fact that the Golden Horseshoe alone contains about one third of Canada's population while the larger Windsor–Quebec City corridor contains about one half (Hiller, 1991:16).

Inter-Regional Population Movement

Any country, but particularly any large country, is likely to experience population shifts from one of its regions to another. In the United States, the major shift is taking population from the cities of the Northeast and the Midwest and redistributing it in the south: from the Snowbelt to the Sunbelt. Southern cities like San Diego, San Antonio, and Phoenix are growing rapidly, while ones in the North like Detroit, Chicago, and Baltimore are losing population.

Canada—alas—does not have a sunbelt, but that does not stop us from moving from one part of the country to another in search of opportunities. Table 21-7 shows the net gains and losses (through interprovincial migration) for each province in each five-year period between 1956 and 1991. In some parts of the country, the losses are consistent and large: the Atlantic provinces, overall, lost population in every five- year period except 1971–76; Quebec lost in every period, but most dramatically in 1966–71 and 1976–81[3]; Manitoba and Saskatchewan suffered consistent losses; Ontario and Alberta lost in some periods and gained in others[4]; while B.C. shows up as the only province to have consistent gains in every five-year interval. In this sense, B.C. is the equivalent of our sunbelt in that there is lifestyle and retirement migration

---

[2] Note that the population of Toronto (Table 21-4) declined between 1976 and 1981, but regained its losses by 1991.

[3] This is the period immediately following the election in 1976 of the separatist Parti Québécois which, in 1977, passed Bill 101 making French the language of business and restricting English-language schooling. Several head offices moved out of Montreal at that time, an outflow of anglophone people took place, and real estate prices plummeted.

[4] Alberta gained substantially during the sixties and seventies when world oil prices zoomed skyward and all eyes turned to Alberta oil. When oil prices fell, Alberta began to lose population once again.

TABLE 21-7   NET INTERPROVINCIAL MIGRATION IN CANADA, 1956–1991

When Canadians move from one province to another, it tends to be directly related to economic conditions. This was most apparent from 1976–1981 when the resource boom in Alberta caused a large influx there from other provinces. But falling international oil prices in the early 1980s led to a reversal of this trend as Canadians moved east, especially to Ontario. In recent years, those moving to another province have tended to head to British Columbia.
The following table shows net interprovincial migration—the number of persons moving into a province minus the number of persons moving out of that province.

	Nfld	PEI	NS	NB	Que	Ont	Man	Sask	Alta	BC
1956–1961	−4,671	−1,099	−15,295	−5,270	−7,756	34,345	−15,957	−33,557	16,787	33,230
1961–1966	−15,213	−2,969	−27,124	−25,680	−19,859	85,369	−23,471	−42,094	−1,983	77,747
1966–1971	−19,344	−2,763	−16,396	−19,599	−122,736	150,712	−40,690	−81,399	32,005	114,964
1971–1976	−1,857	3,754	11,307	16,801	−77,610	−38,560	−26,827	−40,752	58,571	92,285
1976–1981	−18,983	−829	−7,140	−10,351	−156,496	−57,826	−42,218	−9,716	186,364	122,625
1981–1986	−15,051	751	6,895	−65	−81,254	121,767	−2,634	−2,974	−31,676	7,382
1986–1991	−15,282	−885	−5,302	−3,798	−39,934	68,730	−35,417	−63,155	−43,282	141,077

SOURCE: Statistics Canada; Colombo, 1992:69.

taking place, with British Columbia as the destination. Trade with the Pacific Rim also opens up opportunities for British Columbians.

Understanding Cities: Theory and Method

Having sketched out the historical development of cities, we turn to various theoretical insights and research observations about city life. In short, what difference does urbanization make to social life?

European Theory: Urban Life versus Rural Life

Various European sociologists were among the first to contrast urban and rural life. We will briefly introduce the contributions of two German sociologists, Ferdinand Toennies and Georg Simmel.

Ferdinand Toennies: *Gemeinschaft* and *Gesellschaft*

In the late nineteenth century, when his society was awash in rapid change, the German sociologist Ferdinand Toennies (1855–1936) set out to chronicle the social traits emerging in the industrial metropolis (1963; orig. 1887). He contrasted rural and urban life using two concepts that have become an established part of sociology's terminology.

Toennies used the term *Gemeinschaft* (a German word roughly meaning "community") to refer to *a type of social organization in which people are bound closely together by kinship and tradition*. Rural villagers, Toennies explained, sustain enduring ties of kinship, neigh-

borhood, and friendship. *Gemeinschaft*, then, describes any social setting in which people form what amounts to a single primary group. *Gemeinschaft* is essentially synonymous with Emile Durkheim's *mechanical solidarity*, discussed in Chapter 4 ("Society").

By and large, argued Toennies, *Gemeinschaft* is rarely found in the industrial city. On the contrary, urbanization enhances *Gesellschaft* (this German word roughly means "association"), which is *a type of social organization in which people typically have weak social ties and a great deal of self-interest*. As part of *Gesellschaft*, women and men are motivated by their own needs and desires rather than a desire to advance the well-being of everyone. City dwellers, Toennies suggested, have little sense of community and therefore look at others merely as the means of achieving their individual goals. *Gesellschaft* finds its parallel in Durkheim's concept of *organic solidarity*.

In short, then, to Toennies urbanization is the steady march from *Gemeinschaft* to *Gesellschaft*: the erosion of kinship and tightly integrated neighborhoods as society shifts to allow for greater cultural diversity, tolerance, and self-interest (cf. Wilson, 1991). Further, Toennies explained, *Gesellschaft* provides the social climate—the temporary and impersonal ties—characteristic of a society centered on economic pursuits. Thus Toennies took a basically negative view of modern, urban society—more so than Durkheim who, you will recall, saw in the urban world the benefits of expanding freedom and personal privacy.

Georg Simmel: The Blasé Urbanite

We have already encountered the ideas of Georg Simmel in our discussion of how size affects the social dynamics of small groups (see Chapter 7, "Groups and

Marc Chagall's painting I and the Village *(1911) conveys the essential unity of rural life forged by tradition and common work on the land. By contrast, in his painting* The City *(1919), Ferdinand Léger communicates the disparate images and discontinuity of experience that are commonplace in urban areas. Taken together, these two paintings capture Toennies's distinction between* Gemeinschaft *and* Gesellschaft.

(Marc Chagall, I and the Village. *1911. Oil on canvas, 63⁵/₈ x 59⁵/₈". Collection, The Museum of Modern Art, New York. Mrs. Simon Guggenheim Fund; Fernand Léger,* The City. *1919. 91 x 117 ¹/₂. The Philadelphia Museum of Art [The A.E. Gallatin Collection.])*

Organizations"). Simmel also turned his characteristically micro-level focus to the question of how urban life shaped people's behavior and attitudes (1964; orig. 1905).

From the point of view of the individual, Simmel explained, the city is a crush of people, objects, and events. Understandably, he continued, the urbanite is easily overwhelmed with stimulation. Consequently, city people typically develop what Simmel termed a *blasé attitude*, as they learn to respond selectively to their surroundings. That is, they tune out much of what goes on around them in order to focus attention on what seems to be important. City dwellers are not without sensitivity and compassion for others, although they sometimes may seem "cold and heartless." But urban detachment, as Simmel saw it, is better understood as a strategy for social survival by which people have to hold themselves aloof from much of their surroundings if they are to have the time and energy to engage those who really matter.

Observing the City

Sociologists in the United States (there were no sociology departments in Canada yet) soon joined their European colleagues in exploring the rapidly growing cities. The first major sociology program in the United States took root at the University of Chicago. In the late nineteenth century, Chicago was a major metropolis bursting with population and cultural diversity. Chicago's social life was the focus for generations of sociologists, and these researchers produced a rich understanding of many dimensions of urban life. The work of the Chicago School had a major impact on Canadian urban sociologists.

While these early sociologists were inspired by the ideas of theorists like Toennies and Simmel, their unique contribution was in making the city a laboratory for actual research. Perhaps the greatest urban sociologist of all was Robert Park, who for decades provided the leadership that established sociology as a respected academic discipline in North America. Park is introduced in the box.

Louis Wirth: Urbanism as a Way of Life

A second major figure in the Chicago School of urban sociology was Louis Wirth (1897–1952). Wirth's (1938) best-known contribution is a brief essay in which he systematically organized the ideas of Toen-

Robert Ezra Park (1864–1944)

I suspect that I have actually covered more ground, tramping about in cities in different parts of the world, than any other living man. (1950:viii)

Robert Ezra Park was a man with a single consuming passion—the city. On the streets of the great cities of the world, he found the full range of human triumph and troubles. Through his thirty-year career at the University of Chicago, he led a group of dedicat-ed sociologists in the direct, systematic observation of urban life.

Park acknowledged his debt to European sociologists such as Ferdinand Toennies and Georg Simmel (with whom Park studied in Germany). But Park created a new dimension in urban sociology by advocating the *direct observation* of the city rather than what he considered the armchair theorizing of the Europeans. At Park's urging, generations of sociologists at the University of Chicago rummaged through practically every corner of their city.

From this research, Park came to understand the city as a highly ordered mosaic of distinctive regions, including ethnic communities, vice areas, and industrial districts. These so-called "natural areas" all evolved in relation to one another over time. To Park, the city was a living social organism: truly the human kaleidoscope. This stunning variety of human experience, Park maintained, is the key to people's timeless attraction to cities:

The attraction of the metropolis is due in part to the fact that in the long run every individual finds somewhere among the varied manifestations of city life the sort of environment in which he expands and feels at ease; he finds, in short, the moral climate in which his particular nature obtains the stimulations that bring his innate dispositions to full and free expression. It is, I suspect, motives of this kind ... which drove many, if not most, of the young men and young women from the security of their homes in the country into the big, booming confusion and excitement of city life. (1967:41; orig. 1925)

Park was well aware that many people saw the city as disorganized and even dangerous. Park recognized the element of truth in these concerns but, still, he found cities fascinating. So enamored was he that he devoted much of his life to exploring cities throughout the world. He firmly believed that urban places offered a better way of life—the promise of greater human freedom and opportunity—than could be found anywhere else.

SOURCES: Based on Park (1967; orig. 1925) and Park (1950).

nies, Simmel, Park, and others into a comprehensive theory of urban life.

Wirth began by identifying three factors that define urbanism: large population, dense settlement, and social diversity. These essential traits, he argued, make urban life impersonal, superficial, and transitory. Living among millions of others, urbanites have contact with many more people than rural residents do. Thus if city residents notice others at all, they know them in terms of *what they do*: as the school bus driver, the florist, or the clerk in the grocery store. Just as urban social relationships are highly specialized, Wirth continued, they are also an expression of self-interest. For example, shoppers see grocers as a source of food while grocers view shoppers as a source of income. These men and women may pleasantly exchange greetings, but they are both aware that friendship is not the reason for their interaction.

Limited interpersonal involvement, coupled with great social diversity, also make city dwellers more tolerant than rural villagers. Rural communities often jealously maintain their narrow traditions, but the heterogeneous population of a city rarely imposes a code of moral values on local residents (Wilson, 1985). Thus, concluded Wirth, cities operate like social "melting-pots."

Wirth's vision of the city belies a mixed view of urban living. While he acknowledged the freedom and privacy of urban living (echoing Durkheim and Park), he also saw in the anonymous rush of city life the loss of personal ties and the erosion of traditional morality (here, recalling Toennies). In sum, people find new excitement and opportunities in the city, but many important interpersonal connections are lost.

Critical evaluation. Both in Europe and the United

States, early sociologists concentrated their research efforts on the city. After decades of additional research, however, we are in a better position to assess their conclusions.

Are cities distinctive? Yes, but probably not to the extent that some of the urban pioneers claimed. By and large, urban settings do have a weaker sense of community than do rural areas, but we can easily underestimate the strength of urban social ties just as we can exaggerate the social cohesion of rural life. While urbanites do treat most people impersonally, they also have a smaller number of close personal relationships. Further, the public anonymity of cities may mean that some people are lonely and aloof, but the majority remain well integrated with others and welcome the public privacy that cities afford (Keller, 1968; Cox, 1971; Macionis, 1978; Wellman, 1979; Lee et al., 1984). In addition, we need to remind ourselves that conflict has long characterized life in the countryside as well as the city.

On another level, we can now see that pioneering sociologists fell victim to another distortion: implying that urbanism neutralizes the effects of class, race, and ethnicity. Herbert Gans (1968) responded to Wirth's notion that urbanism is a single, general way of life by pointing out that there are many brands of urbanites: rich and poor, white and black, Anglo and Hispanic, women and men—all such categories are distinctive in the lives their members lead in cities. In fact, cities often intensify social differences. That is, we see the extent of social inequality and striking cultural diversity more clearly in cities—where categories of people have the greatest "critical mass" (Spates & Macionis, 1987).

Urban Ecology

Research into the social correlates of urbanism also extends to **urban ecology,** *the study of the link between the physical and social dimensions of cities.* Chapter 3 ("Culture") spotlighted cultural ecology, the investigation of how cultural patterns are related to the physical environment. Urban ecology is one application of this approach; it points up that cities are both physical and social realities and that these two facets of urbanism dovetail in many ways.

Consider, for example, why cities are located where they are. The first cities that accompanied the emergence of agriculture were established in fertile regions. Preindustrial societies concerned with defense built their cities on mountains or in other ways took advantage of the natural environment for self-protec-

tion. Athens is situated on an outcropping of rock; Paris and Mexico City are centered on islands. After the Industrial Revolution, the unparalleled importance of economics situated cities near rivers and natural harbors that facilitated trade.

Urban ecologists also study the physical design of cities. They have developed several models explaining urban form.

The concentric zone model. In 1925 Ernest W. Burgess, a student and colleague of Robert Park, visualized land use in Chicago and several other U.S. cities as a series of concentric zones rather like a bulls-eye. At the center of the city, Burgess observed, is a central business district, surrounded by a ring of factories. Beyond this commercial zone lie a succession of residential rings with housing that is more and more expensive the farther it stands from the noise and pollution of the city's center.

The sector model. Investigating a greater number of cities, Homer Hoyt (1939) expanded the scope of Burgess's research. Hoyt concluded that distinctive districts often form wedge-shaped sectors. For example, a particularly fashionable area may be built along a finger of high ground. Similarly, industrial development in many cities extends outward along railroad lines or following the twists and turns of a river. In this way, Hoyt observed, specialized districts of a city grow in wedge-shaped sectors.

The multiple-nuclei model. Chauncy Harris and Edward Ullman (1945) made an additional contribution to the urban ecology literature as they documented the onset of urban decentralization. As population spreads outward, they concluded, cities lose their single-center form in favor of a multiple-nuclei model, with many centers of business and manufacturing.

Looking closely at this process, Harris and Ullman identified two major reasons that specific endeavors spread out across a city. First, some activities may be antagonistic to others. Few people wish to live in the shadow of industrial areas, for example, and owners of fashionable retail shops want to distance themselves from pornography and vice areas. Thus the complexity and diversity of urban life yields a mosaic of distinctive districts. Second, economics also comes into play here. Industry usually prefers outlying industrial parks, where land is readily available and cheap, to the older, congested inner cities. People, too, are drawn to lower-cost land in the suburbs and, eventually, retail businesses follow them, giving rise to shopping malls miles from downtown. As a result, cities now have many distinctive centers of activity.

Social area analysis. Social area analysis adds a new twist to urban ecology by investigating what people in specific neighborhoods have in common. Research in industrial cities has focused on three factors that explain a great deal about where people end up living: *family type*, reflecting marital status and family size; *social standing*, based on income and prestige; and *race and ethnicity* (Shevky & Bell, 1955; Johnston, 1976).

Researchers have concluded that families with children gravitate to areas offering large apartments or single-family homes and good schools. The rich generally seek high-prestige neighborhoods away from low-income people—sometimes in the suburbs, and often in exclusive central-city areas. People with a common cultural heritage tend to cluster together. The poor and some minorities, whose choices are limited, also live in distinct areas.

An integrated analysis. Each of the models we have described provides a partial understanding of urban land use. Attempting to integrate them all, Brian Berry and Philip Rees (1969) argue that each factor plays a part in shaping the city. In accordance with Burgess's theory, distinctive types of families disperse population in concentric zones, at least assuming there are no other influences. Families with few children tend toward the city's center, while those with more children live farther away. Differences of social standing generate the sector-shaped districts described by Hoyt; that is, the rich often occupy one "side of the tracks," while the poor inhabit the other. Racial and ethnic groups cluster together at various points throughout the city, in support of Harris and Ullman's multiple-nuclei model and the findings of social area analysis.

Critical evaluation. After almost a century of research, urban ecologists have succeeded in linking the physical and social dimensions of urban life. But as ecologists themselves concede, their conclusions paint a very idealized picture of city life. Critics chime in that urban ecology errs by implying that cities take shape simply due to the choices people make; more accurately, from their point of view, urban development is guided by power elites rather than by "average" people (Molotch, 1976; Feagin, 1983). Another pro-

blem is that urban ecologists studied cities during a single historical period. What they have learned about industrializing cities has limited value for understanding preindustrial towns; similarly, even among industrial cities, socialist settlements are quite unlike their capitalist counterparts. Taken together, such concerns offer good reason to doubt that any single ecological model will account for the full range of urban diversity.

Third-World Urbanization

Twice in human history the world has experienced a revolutionary expansion of cities. The first urban revolution began about 8000 B.C.E. when the first cities emerged, and this change spanned thousands of years as urban settlements sprang up on the various continents. The second urban revolution began about 1750 and lasted for two centuries as the Industrial Revolution sparked the rapid growth of cities in Europe and North America.

A third urban revolution was under way by 1950, but this time the change is not occurring in the industrial societies of the world where, as shown in Global Map 21-2, 75 percent of people already are city dwellers. Extraordinary urban growth is now taking place in the Third World, where, in 1950, only 25 percent of people lived in cities. Since then, about 40 percent of the Third-World population has clustered in cities; by 2000, half are expected to be urbanites. Put in other words, in 1950, only seven cities in the world had populations of over 5 million, and only two of these were in the Third World. By 1985, twenty-six cities had more than 5 million residents, and eighteen were in the Third World (Fornos, 1986). By the end of this century, some Third-World cities will literally dwarf all but a few of the cities in industrialized societies.

Table 21-8 compares the size of the world's ten largest urban areas in 1980 with population estimates for 2000. In 1980, six of the top ten were in industrial societies. By the beginning of the next century, however, only four of the top ten will be situated in industrial nations: two in Japan, one in South Korea, and one in the United States. Most will be in less economically developed societies of the Third World. These urban areas not only will be the world's largest, they will contain unprecedented populations. Relatively rich societies like Japan may have the resources to provide for urban settlements approaching 30 million people, but for poor societies, such as Mexico and Brazil, huge populations concentrated in limited areas will strain already overburdened services.

Causes of Third-World Urban Growth

To understand the third urban revolution, recall that many nonindustrial societies are now entering the high-growth stage of demographic transition. Declining death rates caused by improved technology have fueled a population explosion in Latin America, Africa, and Asia. For urban areas, the rate of growth is *twice* as

high because, in addition to high birth rates, millions of migrants leave the countryside each year in search of a better standard of living in the city. The urban areas offer more jobs, superior health care, better schools, and even basic conveniences such as running water and electricity. Political events have also intensified urban migration; in many societies, the seizure of land by elites has forced peasants to migrate to cities (London, 1987).

Cities do offer more opportunities than rural areas, but they provide no panacea for the massive

WINDOW ON THE WORLD

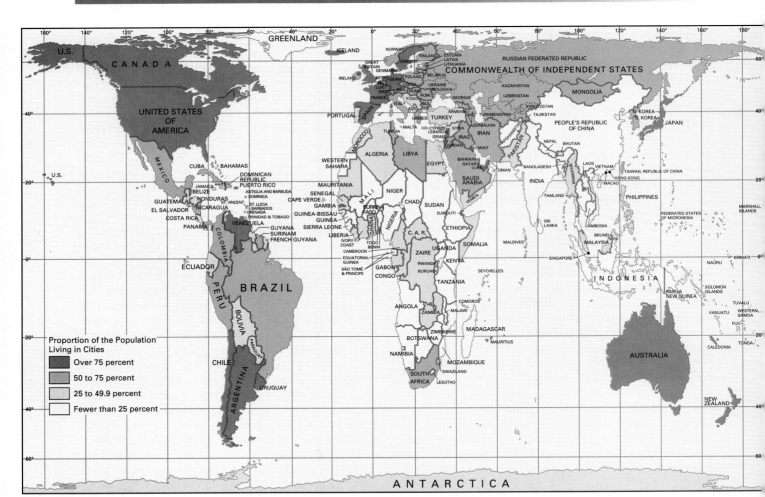

GLOBAL MAP 21-2 URBANIZATION IN GLOBAL PERSPECTIVE
Urbanization is closely linked to economic development. Thus First-World nations—including Canada and the United States—have more than three-fourths of their populations in cities, while in the poorest countries of the Third World—found in Africa and Asia—fewer than one-fourth of the people live in urban centers. Urbanization is now extremely rapid in the Third World, however, with emerging "supercities" of unprecedented size.

TABLE 21-8 THE WORLD'S TEN LARGEST URBAN AREAS, 1980 AND 2000

1980

Urban Area	Population (in millions)
New York, U.S.A.	16.5
Tokyo-Yokohama, Japan	14.4
Mexico City, Mexico	14.0
Los Angeles-Long Beach, U.S.A.	10.6
Shanghai, China	10.0
Buenos Aires, Argentina	9.7
Paris, France	8.5
Moscow, U.S.S.R.	8.0
Beijing, China	8.0
Chicago, U.S.A.	7.7

2000 (projected)

Urban Area	Population (in millions)
Tokyo-Yokohama, Japan	30.0
Mexico City, Mexico	27.9
São Paulo, Brazil	25.4
Seoul, South Korea	22.0
Bombay, India	15.4
New York, U.S.A.	14.7
Osaka-Kobe-Kyoto, Japan	14.3
Tehran, Iran	14.3
Rio de Janeiro, Brazil	14.2
Calcutta, India	14.1

SOURCES: United Nations and U.S. Bureau of the Census.

Hong Kong, the British colony on the Chinese mainland, is scarcely 1,000 square kilometres but contains some 6 million people. This yields a population density of about 6,000 people per square kilometre, among the highest densities in the world.

problems generated by an escalating population and poverty. Many Third-World cities, such as Mexico City, described at the beginning of this chapter, are simply unable to meet the needs of much of their population. Thousands of rural people stream into Mexico City every day, although more than 10 percent of *current* residents have no running water in their homes, 15 percent lack sewage facilities, and half the trash and garbage produced each day cannot be processed. To make matters worse, exhaust from factories and cars chokes everyone, rich and poor alike (Friedrich, 1984). Like other major cities throughout Latin America, Africa, and Asia, Mexico City is surrounded by wretched shantytowns—settlements of makeshift homes built from discarded materials. As explained in Chapter 11 ("Global Inequality"), even city dumps are home to thousands of poor people, who pick through the waste hoping to find enough food and fuel to ensure their survival for another day.

The Future of Third-World Cities

The problems now facing Third-World cities seem to defy solution, and the end of this remarkable urban growth is nowhere in sight. What hope is there of relieving the plight of people in these emerging megacities?

Earlier chapters have suggested two different answers to this question. One view, linked with modernization theory, holds that as the Third World undergoes industrialization (as Western Europe and North America did two centuries ago), greater productivity will push living standards upward and ease population growth. A second view, associated with dependency theory, dismisses such progress as illusory as long as Third-World societies remain economically dependent on rich societies.

Urbanist Jane Jacobs (1984), combining elements of each approach, asserts that expanding trade may solve some of these problems, but only if Third-World nations break trading ties with rich societies and build trading networks among themselves. Then their economies can move beyond providing only raw materials and inexpensive labor to wealthy corporate interests in rich societies.

Jacobs's argument, which embraces a middle ground, has drawn controversy from both camps. Analysts on the side of modernization theory warn that contact with rich societies is necessary for developing nations to obtain much-needed technology. Critics on the side of dependency theory assert that even breaking those ties would not resolve the growing crisis of Third-World cities: what is needed is a revolutionary redistribution of the wealth that is now controlled by a small segment of the population (Gilbert & Gugler, 1983). But almost everyone agrees on one important point: whatever the course of events, the drama of overpopulation in the Third World will be played out in the cities.

The Historical Importance of Cities

Having finished our survey of urbanization, we end by stepping back and reflecting on the place of cities in the drama of human history. There can be no doubt that the city has figured strongly in our past. In fact the root of the word civilization is the Latin word *civis*—meaning a "city dweller." Like the ancient Romans, the early Greeks recognized this link; their word *polis*—meaning "city"—is the root of politics, which was the core of Greek life.

At the same time, cities have often been disparaged. The English author and Nobel Prize winner Rudyard Kipling, after visiting Chicago, exclaimed, "Having seen it, I urgently desire never to see it again. It is inhabited by savages" (cited in Rokove, 1975:22). Why do cities provoke such spirited and divergent reactions?

The answer lies in their ability to encapsulate and intensify human culture. Cities have spawned some of the greatest human virtues (the cultural developments of classical Athens) as well generated some of the greatest human failings (the militarism and violence of classical Rome or Nazi Berlin). Industrial societies have undergone concerted urbanization as people have sought a better way of life, but ironically, many social problems—such as poverty, crime, racial tensions, and environmental pollution—are most pronounced in cities. In short, the city is an intricate weave of noble accomplishments and wretched shortcomings.

As we approach the twenty-first century, the greatest test of urban living will occur in societies of the Third World. Mexico City, São Paulo, and Bombay will contain almost unimaginable numbers of people. Throughout history, the city improved people's standard of living more than any other settlement pattern. The question facing humanity now is whether cities in poor societies will be able to meet the needs of vastly larger populations in the next century. The answer—which carries implications for international relations, global economic relations, and simple human justice—will affect all of us.

Summary

1. Fertility and mortality, measured as crude birth rates and crude death rates, are major components of population growth. In global terms, fertility, mortality, and population growth in North America are relatively low.

2. Migration, another key demographic concept, has special importance to the historical growth of cities.

3. Age-sex pyramids allow demographers to describe the composition of a population and to project future population patterns.

4. Historically, world population grew slowly because high birth rates were largely offset by high death rates. In about 1750, however, a demographic transition began as world population rose sharply, mostly as a result of declining death rates.

5. Malthus claimed that population would grow faster than food supplies, eventually resulting in social calamity. Contradicting Malthus's omin-

ous predictions, demographic transition theory holds that technological advance brings gradually declining birth rates. This leveling off has occurred in industrial societies, where population growth is now low. In the Third World, however, declining death rates coupled with continued high birth rates are swelling population to unprecedented levels.

6. Research has shown that lower birth rates and improved economic productivity in the Third World both result from bolstering the social position of women.

7. World population is expected to reach 8 billion by the year 2025. If this occurs, social problems related to poverty may overwhelm Third-World societies, where population growth is now greatest.

8. Closely related to population growth is urbanization. The first urban revolution began with the appearance of cities after 8000 B.C.E.; by the start of the common era, cities had emerged in every region of the world.

9. While members of nonurban societies must continually search for food, city dwellers engage in a wide range of productive specialization.

10. Preindustrial cities are characterized by small buildings and narrow, winding streets, personal social ties, and rigid patterns of social inequality.

11. A second urban revolution began about 1750 as the Industrial Revolution prompted rapid urban growth in Europe. The structure of cities changed, as planners created wide, regular streets, and social anonymity increased.

12. Urbanism came to North America with European settlers. A string of colonial towns dotting the Atlantic coastline gave way by the late 1800s to hundreds of new cities from coast to coast.

13. By 1931, a majority of the Canadian population lived in urban areas: twenty-five metropolises encompassing 100,000 to 4 million residents now dominate the urban scene.

14. Since 1950 Canadian cities have decentralized, moving out of central cities into suburban settings.

15. This decentralization has generated vast urban areas, metropolises, that Statistics Canada calls Census Metropolitan Areas. As urban areas expand and bump up against each other they form what is called a megalopolis.

16. Rapid urbanization in Europe during the nineteenth century led early sociologists to contrast rural and urban life. Ferdinand Toennies explained the process of urbanization in terms of the concepts of *Gemeinshaft* and *Gesellschaft*; Georg Simmel claimed that the overstimulation of city life produced a blasé attitude in urbanites.

17. At the University of Chicago, Robert Park hailed cities for permitting greater social freedom. Louis Wirth suggested that the size, density, and social heterogeneity of cities generated a way of life characterized by impersonality, self-interest, and tolerance of people's differences.

18. Urban ecology studies the interplay of the physical and social environment of the city. The concentric zone, sector, multiple-nuclei, and social area models each provide insights into urban land use.

19. A third urban revolution is now occurring in the Third World, where most of the world's largest urban areas will soon be found.

Key Concepts

age-sex pyramid   a graphic representation that divides a population into various categories based on age and sex

crude birth rate   the number of live births in a given year for every thousand people in a population

crude death rate   the number of deaths in a given year for every thousand people in a population

demographic transition theory   the thesis that population patterns are linked to a society's level of technological development

demography   the study of human population

fertility   the incidence of childbearing in a society's population

Gemeinschaft   a type of social organization in which people are bound closely together by kinship and tradition

Gesellschaft   a type of social organization in which people have weak social ties and a great deal of self-interest

infant mortality rate   the number of deaths in the first year of life for each thousand live births in a given year

life expectancy   the length of time a person, on the average, can expect to live

megalopolis   a vast urban region containing a number of cities and their surrounding suburbs

metropolis   a large city that socially and economically dominates an urban area

migration   the movement of people into and out of a specified territory

mortality   the incidence of death in a society's population

sex ratio   the number of males for every hundred females in a given population

suburbs   urban areas beyond the political boundaries of a city

urban ecology   the study of the link between the physical and social dimensions of cities

urbanization   the concentration of humanity into cities

zero population growth   the level of reproduction that maintains population at a steady state

Suggested Readings

This text probes various demographic topics.
> John R. Weeks. *Population: An Introduction to Concepts and Issues*. 4th ed. Belmont, CA: Wadsworth, 1989.

This comparative analysis of twenty nations focuses on the availability of contraception and the effect of contraception policies on fertility.
> Elise F. Jones, Jacqueline Darroch Forrest, Stanley K. Henshaw, Jane Silverman, and Aida Torres. *Pregnancy, Contraception, and Family Planning in Industrialized Countries*. New Haven, CT: Yale, 1989.

These two books by noted population experts describe the current state of world population and offer straightforward suggestions about how to limit population growth.
> Rafael M. Salas. *Reflections on Population*. New York: Pergammon Press, 1984.
> Werner Fornos. *Gaining People, Losing Ground: A Blueprint for Stabilizing World Population*. Washington, DC: The Population Institute, 1986.

This is a textbook that provides a historical and contemporary analysis of cities in North America and throughout the world.
> James L. Spates and John J. Macionis. *The Sociology of Cities*. 2nd ed. Belmont, CA: Wadsworth, 1987.

This paperback examines the nature of community in today's world and considers how sociologists study community life.
> Larry Lyon. *The Community in Urban Society*. Chicago: Dorsey, 1987.

This book deals with the choices we make between the private and the public good—often to the disadvantage of the less powerful and affluent.
> David Popenoe. *Private Pleasure-Public Plight*. New Brunswick, New Jersey: Trans-Action Books. 1985

The following provides a wide-ranging comparison of urban development in Canada and the United States.
> Michael Goldberg and John Mercer. *The Myth of the North American City*. Vancouver: University of British Columbia Press. 1986.

This overview of research on urban communities in Canada covers a broad range of topics.
> Peter McGahan. *Urban Sociology in Canada*. Toronto: Butterworths. 1982.

An examination of rural social structures and change is undertaken here.
> S. Dasgupta. *Rural Canada*. Toronto: Mellon. 1987.

CHAPTER 22

COLLECTIVE BEHAVIOR AND SOCIAL MOVEMENTS

On February 1, 1990, four men walked into Woolworth's in Greensboro, North Carolina, to share a meal. They sat down to what seemed to be an ordinary breakfast of eggs, grits, bacon, and coffee served by a smiling waitress. But the men were treated as celebrities and the event was news around the world.

Why? Thirty years earlier to the day, the same four—then college students—had seated themselves at the same lunch counter and requested a meal from the same waitress. She refused to serve them because, as African Americans, they were unwelcome in the segregated Greensboro Woolworth. The four young men sat there nervously, ignored by her but closely observed by a white police officer who periodically slapped his billy club into his bare hand. After an hour, the men got up and peacefully left. Their courageous action called attention to the racial exclusion then commonplace throughout the U.S. and helped ignite a major social movement for civil rights that sought to end such legal segregation.

People typically engage in organized and controversial action in order to transform the world in one way or another. A major focus of this chapter is **social movements**, *organized activity that encourages or discourages social change*. Social movements are perhaps the most important type of **collective behavior**, *activity involving a large number of people, often spontaneous, and typically in violation of established norms*. Other forms of collective behavior—each giving rise to controversy and some provoking change—are fashions and fads, riots, crowds, mass hysteria, and public opinion. This chapter surveys various topics that form the broad and internally diverse field of collective behavior. It then focuses on social movements, such as the women's movement in Canada and the democratic movements that recently swept through Eastern Europe and the former Soviet Union.

Collective Behavior

Sociological inquiry into collective behavior in North America dwindled about 1950, when sociologists shifted their focus to more established social patterns like the family and social stratification. Because collective behavior focused on actions generally deemed as unusual or deviant, many analysts apparently thought this area of inquiry to be less worthy. The numerous social movements that burst on the scene in the tumultuous 1960s, however, renewed sociological interest in various types of collective behavior (Breton, 1972;

Weller & Quarantelli, 1973; G. Marx & Wood, 1975; Marsden & Harvey, 1979; Reitz, 1980; Aguirre & Quarantelli, 1983; Turner & Killian, 1987; McAdam, McCarthy, & Zald, 1988; Ponting, 1989).

Studying Collective Behavior

Collective behavior presents sociologists with several significant challenges. First, the concept of collective behavior is *broad*, embracing a sometimes bewildering array of phenomena. It is far from obvious, for example, what traits fads, rumors, and mob behavior have in common. Furthermore, each of these activities has very different consequences for social change. Rumors may disrupt the life of a small town, clothing fads often challenge conventional standards of appearance, and mob behavior can result in loss of life and property as people confront authorities or one another.

A second difficulty is that collective behavior is *complex*. A rumor seems to come out of nowhere and circulates in countless different settings. For no apparent reason, one new form of dress "catches on" while another does not. Why would millions of people in Eastern Europe, after patiently enduring undemocratic rule for decades, suddenly and decisively sweep away their leaders?

Third, some collective behavior is *transitory*. Sociologists have extensively studied the family because it is an enduring element of social life. Fashions, rumors, and riots, by contrast, tend to arise and dissipate so quickly that they are difficult to track and study systematically.

Some researchers into collective behavior acknowledge these problems but add that they apply to most of the issues sociologists study. Benigno Aguirre and E.L. Quarantelli (1983) ask what social behavior is *not* complex and dynamic? Moreover, collective behavior is not always so elusive; no one is surprised by the crowds that form at sports events and musical festivals, and sociologists can study these gatherings firsthand or by examining videotapes or audio records. Researchers can even anticipate some natural disasters in order to study the human response they provoke. We know, for example, that forty to eighty major tornadoes occur in particular regions of the United States each year; therefore, sociologists can be prepared to initiate research on short notice (Miller, 1985). Researchers may also use historical documents to reconstruct details of an unanticipated natural disaster or riot.

But sociologists have not resolved all the problems inherent in this area of study. The most serious problem, Aguirre and Quarantelli maintain, is that theory still does not link all the diverse actions that fall under the term collective behavior. At present, here is how the situation stands. All collective behavior involves the action of a **collectivity**, by which sociologists mean *a large number of people whose minimal interaction occurs in the absence of well-defined and conventional norms*. Collectivities are of two kinds. *Localized collectivities* involve people in physical proximity to one another; this type is illustrated by crowds and riots. *Dispersed collectivities* comprise people who influence one another despite being spread over great distances; examples here include rumors, public opinion, and fashion (Turner & Killian, 1987).

Sociologists distinguish collectivities from social groups (see Chapter 7, "Groups and Organizations"), on the basis of three characteristics.

Sociologists distinguish between a group and a collectivity on the basis of the extent of interaction, clarity of social boundaries, and character of norms. These people enjoying an antilogging protest concert by Australian rock group Midnight Oil at Clayoquot Sound, British Columbia, are a loose collectivity rather than a well-defined group.

1. **Limited social interaction.** Group members interact directly and frequently. Interaction in localized collectivities such as mobs is limited and temporary. People participating in dispersed collectivities like a fad typically do not interact at all.

2. **Unclear social boundaries.** Limited interaction makes for weak social boundaries. Group members have a sense of common identity, which people engaged in collective behavior typically lack. Localized crowds may have a common object of attention (such as a despondent person on a ledge high above the street), but these people exhibit little sense of unity. Individuals involved in dispersed collectivities, such as "the public" that intends to vote for some political candidate, have even less of a sense of shared membership. The exception to this rule is a social movement that gives rise to well-defined factions; even here, however, it is often difficult to discern who falls within the ranks of, say, the pro-life or pro-choice movement.

3. **Weak and unconventional norms.** Conventional cultural norms usually regulate the behavior of group members. Some collectivities, such as people traveling on an airplane, operate according to social norms, but they usually amount to little more than respecting the privacy of the person sitting in the next seat. Other collectivities—such as emotional soccer fans who destroy property as they leave a stadium—rather spontaneously develop decidedly unconventional norms (Weller & Quarantelli, 1973; Turner & Killian, 1987).

Crowds

An important concept in the study of collective behavior is the **crowd**, *a temporary gathering of people who share a common focus of attention and whose members influence one another.* Historian Peter Laslett (1984) points out that crowds are a modern development; in medieval Europe, 25,000 people assembled in one place only when major armies faced off on the field of combat. Crowds of this size routinely form in industrial societies; they are found at sporting events, rock concerts, and even the registration halls of large universities.

But all crowds are not alike. Herbert Blumer (1969) organized crowds into four types. A *casual crowd* is a loose collection of people who interact little, if at all. People who gather on the beach or collect at the scene of an automobile accident have only a passing

awareness of one another. Few social patterns are typical of casual crowds beyond the momentary sharing of an interest.

A *conventional crowd* results from deliberate planning, as illustrated by a country auction, a university lecture, or a somber funeral. In each case, interaction typically conforms to norms deemed appropriate for the situation.

An *expressive crowd* forms around an event with emotional appeal, such as a religious revival, a wrestling match, or the Stanley Cup parade. Excitement is the main reason people join expressive crowds in the first place, and this fact makes expressive crowds relatively spontaneous and exhilarating to those involved.

An *acting crowd* is a collectivity fueled by an intense, single-minded purpose, as in the case of people rushing the doors of a concert hall or fleeing from a building that is on fire. Acting crowds are ignited by emotions more powerful than those typical of expressive crowds, often reaching feverish intensity that sometimes erupts into mob violence.

Any gathering of people can change from one type of crowd to another. In 1985, for example, 60,000 fans assembled in a soccer stadium near Brussels, Belgium, to watch the European Cup Finals between Italy and Great Britain. Initially, they formed a conventional crowd. But by the time the game started, many of the British fans had become intoxicated and were taunting the Italians sitting in an adjacent part of the stands. At this point, an expressive crowd had formed. When the two sides began to throw bottles at each other, the scene exploded as the British surged like a human wave toward the Italians. An estimated 400 million television viewers watched in horror as this acting crowd became a rampaging mob trampling hundreds of helpless spectators. In minutes, thirty-eight people were dead and another 400 injured (Lacayo, 1985).

Deliberate action by a crowd is not the product simply of rising emotions. Participants in *protest crowds*—a fifth category that can be added to Blumer's list—engage in a variety of actions, including strikes, boycotts, sit-ins, and marches, that have political goals (McPhail & Wohlstein, 1983). For example, university campuses and government legislatures frequently witness protest crowds that express views about a wide range of issues. These crowds vary in emotional intensity, ranging from conventional to acting crowds. Sometimes a protest gathering begins peacefully, but its members become aggressive when confronted with counter-demonstrators. In July, 1990, during the Oka crisis, an unexpectedly violent clash occurred between the police and 4,000 residents of Quebec's South Shore when the latter came out to protest the Mohawk takeover of the Mercier Bridge into Montreal.

Mobs and Riots

As an acting crowd turns violent we may witness the birth of a **mob**, *a highly emotional crowd that pursues some violent or destructive goal.* Despite, or perhaps because of, their intense emotion, mobs tend to dissipate rather quickly. The duration of a mob incident also depends on whether its leadership tries to inflame or stabilize the crowd, and on the mob's precise objectives.

Lynching is the most notorious example of mob behavior. This term is derived from Charles Lynch, a Virginia colonist who sought to maintain law and order in his own way before formal courts were established. The word soon became synonymous with terrorism and murder outside the legal system. Lynching has always been colored by race. After the Civil War in the U.S., as slaves gained political rights and economic opportunities, these free people of color presented a threat to many whites who no longer had legally sanctioned superiority. Especially in the South, whites' efforts to maintain their domination fueled lynch mobs as a highly effective form of social control. African Americans who questioned white superiority, or were

even suspected of doing so, risked hanging or being burned alive at the hands of vengeful whites. Blacks and occasionally their white defenders became all-purpose scapegoats.

Lynch mobs—typically composed of low-status whites most threatened by the emancipation of slaves—reached a peak between 1880 and 1930. About 5,000 lynchings were recorded by police in that period; no doubt, many more occurred. Most of these crimes were committed in the Deep South, where an agrarian economy still depended on a cheap and docile labor force, but lynchings took place in virtually every state and victimized every minority. For example, on the western frontier, lynch mobs frequently targeted people of Mexican and Asian descent (White, 1969, orig. 1929; Grant, 1975)

A violent crowd without any particular purpose is a **riot**, *a social eruption that is highly emotional, violent, and undirected.* Unlike the action of a mob, a riot usually has no clear goal. Long-standing anger generally fuels riots, which are sparked by some minor incident (Smelser, 1962). Rioters then indulge in seemingly random violence against property or persons. Whereas a mob action usually ends when a specific violent goal has been achieved (or decisively prevented), a riot tends to disperse only as participants run out of steam or as community leaders or the police gradually bring them under control.

Riots often serve as collective expressions of social injustice. Industrial workers, for example, have rioted to vent rage at their working conditions, and race riots have occurred with striking regularity. In Canada, in response to steady migration from China (of what was seen to be unfairly competitive cheap labour) and a sudden influx of over 8,000 Japanese in 1907, a riot broke out, during which the people of Vancouver lashed out violently against Japanese individuals and looted their businesses. In Los Angeles in 1992, an especially destructive riot was triggered by the acquittal of police officers involved in the beating of Rodney King. The turmoil left more than fifty dead, caused thousands of injuries, and millions of dollars' worth of property damage. These riots were followed almost immediately by race riots on the streets of Toronto.

Riots are not always fired by hate: they can also stem from positive feelings. In Montreal, the celebration of the 1993 Stanley Cup victory turned into a night of looting and violence: days later, in anticipation of further violence, the Montreal Canadiens were protected during their victory parade by hundreds of policemen and the riot squad.

This picture taken by a Montreal press photographer is a good illustration of a riot that developed from high spirits rather than a sense of grievance or hatred. On June 10, 1993, thousands of hockey fans went on a rampage through the streets of Montreal to celebrate their team's victory over the Los Angeles Kings in the Stanley Cup final.

Contagion Theory

What makes the behavior of crowds unconventional? Social scientists have developed several different explanations over the last century. One of the first, formulated by French sociologist Gustave Le Bon (1841–1931), is *contagion theory*. The essence of Le Bon's (1960; orig. 1895) argument is that crowds exert a hypnotic influence on their members. In the anonymity of a crowd, he claimed, people evade personal responsibility and surrender to a collective mind. As a crowd assumes a life of its own, individual members slip their social restraints and become irrational automatons driven by contagious emotion. As fear or hate resonates through the crowd, emotional intensity builds, hypnotizing individuals toward an unrestrained outburst. The predictable result, Le Bon concluded, is destructive violence.

Critical evaluation. Some of Le Bon's assertions —that crowds generate anonymity and sometimes emotion—are widely accepted as true. Yet, as Clark McPhail (1991) points out, Le Bon (and others who followed his lead) embraced the idea of "the maddening crowd" without systematic study. More recently, investigators who have completed empirical research have concluded that a crowd does not take on a life of its own, apart from the thoughts and intentions of members. In other words, the individuals in Vancouver, who rioted against the Japanese in 1907, harboured personal racist sentiments that found an outlet in group action.

Convergence Theory

Convergence theory holds that motivations for collective action originate not in a crowd itself but rather in the setting where the action takes place. From this point of view, crowds form as like-minded individuals converge on the basis of a common attitude or interest. In 1985 a number of whites in southwest Philadelphia banded together to pressure an African-American couple to move from their neighborhood. Fearing violence, the couple fled; at this point, the crowd burned down the couple's home. In such instances, convergence theorists contend, the crowd itself did not generate violence; rather, racial hostility had been simmering for some time among many local people. This crowd, then, grew out of a convergence of people sharing an attachment to their traditionally white neighborhood, who opposed the presence of black residents, and who already had a propensity for violent action.

Critical evaluation. By linking crowds to broader social forces that operate in a particular setting, convergence theory places collective action in a clear context. From this perspective, crowd behavior is not irrational, as Le Bon maintained, but a result of individual decision-making (Berk, 1974).

It is probably true, however, that people do some things in a crowd that they would not have the courage to do alone. In addition, crowds can intensify sentiments simply by creating a critical mass of like-minded people.

Emergent-Norm Theory

Ralph Turner and Lewis Killian (1987) have developed an *emergent-norm theory* of crowd dynamics. While these researchers concede that crowds are not entirely predictable, they dismiss the notion that crowds are irrational, as Le Bon claimed. Similar interests may draw people together, but distinctive patterns of behavior emerge within the crowd itself.

Turner and Killian maintain that crowds begin as collectivities in which people have mixed interests and motives. Entering conventional or casual crowds, members understand what norms will guide their behavior. But the norms that steer less stable types of crowds— expressive, acting, and protest crowds—frequently surface only in particular settings. Usually leaders start the process of norm construction. For example, one

Whether a crowd of people intent on changing society is lionized for courage or condemned for disruptive behavior is a matter of political positions and value judgments. These Algerian marchers, who recently opposed Islamic fundamentalism as a threat to democracy, won their share of both praise and blame.

member of the crowd at a rock concert holds up a lit cigarette lighter to signal praise for the performers, and others follow suit; or a few people in an angry street crowd throw bricks through store windows, and a riot ensues.

In the infamous New Bedford, Massachusetts tavern rape in 1983, one man assaulted a twenty-one-year-old woman who had entered the bar to buy cigarettes, and raped her on the floor. Five other men then joined in, repeatedly raping the woman for an hour and a half. Still others in the bar cheered the rapists: apparently as some people sized up the situation, they concluded that this brutal action was somehow acceptable, while the rest were too intimidated to voice opposition. In any case, no one in the bar responded in the conventional way by calling the police (*Time*, March 5, 1984).

Critical evaluation. Emergent-norm theory represents a symbolic-interaction approach to crowd dynamics. Turner and Killian maintain that crowd behavior is neither as irrational as contagion theory suggests, nor as purposeful as convergence theory implies. So while crowd behavior responds to participants' motives, it is guided by norms that emerge in a setting as the situation unfolds. This means that decision making plays a significant role in crowd behavior, even though it may not be evident to casual observers. For example, frightened people clogging the exits of a burning theater may appear to be victims of irrational panic but, from their point of view, fleeing a life-threatening situation is certainly a rational alternative to death (1972:10). Experience and com-mon sense play a part in precisely how people respond to any such event, of course; leaders on the scene also have a hand in guiding crowd response.

Further, although people in a crowd may experience some pressure to conform, emergent-norm theory points out that not every participant embraces the emerging norms. Some assume leadership roles, others become lieutenants, rank-and-file followers, inactive bystanders, or opponents (Weller & Quarantelli, 1973; Zurcher & Snow, 1981).

Crowds, Politics, and Social Change

In May of 1919, labor negotiations, in which building and metal workers sought collective bargaining rights and improved working conditions, broke down in Winnipeg. In response, close to 30,000 public- and private-sector workers walked off the job in what became known as the Winnipeg General Strike. This massive strike effectively paralyzed the city and shortened official tempers. A charge into a crowd of strikers by the Royal North-West Mounted Police resulted in 30 injuries and one death. Government intervention forced the Winnipeg workers back to their jobs, but not without sparking a series of sympathy strikes across the country. Although decades passed before collective bargaining became a reality, the crowds of strikers in Winnipeg helped to fuel a social movement and bring about social change (Reilly, 1988).

Because crowds are linked to social change, they often provoke controversy. Defenders of the established social order have long feared and hated them. Gustave Le Bon's negative view of crowds as "only powerful for destruction" echoed the sentiments of members of the aristocracy (1960:18; orig. 1895). But collective action that is condemned by privileged people as destructive may be cheered by the disadvantaged as rightful protest against social wrongs.

But crowds do not share a single political cast: some call for change, some resist it. Throngs of Romans rallying to the Sermon on the Mount by Jesus of Nazareth, bands of traditional weavers destroying new industrial machinery that was making their skills obsolete, masses of marchers carrying banners and shouting slogans for or against abortion—these and countless other instances across the centuries show crowds to be an important means by which people challenge or support their society (Rude, 1964; Canetti, 1978).

Rumor and Gossip

Collective behavior is not limited to people in physical proximity. Sociologists use the term **mass behavior** to refer to *collective behavior among people dispersed over a wide geographical area.*

One example of mass behavior is **rumor**, *unsubstantiated information spread informally, often by word of mouth.* Rumors are a familiar part of social life. In the past, people spread rumors through face-to-face communication. Although this is still frequently the case, our modern technology—including telephones, computers, and especially the mass media—allows rumors to be transmitted more rapidly to a greater number of people.

Rumor has three essential characteristics.

1. **Rumor thrives in a climate of ambiguity.** Rumor grows when people lack definitive information about a topic they care about. For example, workers fearing a massive layoff may hear little from

management, and may be suspicious of what they are told. Rumor, then, is an attempt to define reality in the absence of substantiated facts (Shibutani, 1966; Rosnow & Fine, 1976).

2. **Rumor is unstable.** As people spread a rumor, they alter its content so that, before long, many variations of truth emerge. People tend to change rumors by accentuating the parts that serve their interests. For example, workers play up the shortcomings of management as they transmit rumors; for their part, management tries to "spin" information in its own way.

3. **Rumor is difficult to stop.** The number of people aware of a rumor increases in geometric progression as one person spreads information to several others. Of course, some rumors dissipate with time but, in general, only clear, substantiated information that is widely dispersed will stop a rumor.

Rumor can trigger the formation of crowds or other collective behavior. For this reason, authorities often establish rumor-control hotlines in times of crisis as a form of information management and social control.

Closely related to rumor is **gossip**, *rumor about the personal affairs of others.* As Charles Horton Cooley (1962; orig. 1909) pointed out, while rumor involves issues or events of interest to a large segment of the public, gossip concerns a small circle of people who know a particular person. While rumors spread widely, then, gossip is typically localized. Gossip can be an effective strategy for social control as its targets become aware that they are the subject of praise or scorn. People may also gossip about others to elevate their own standing as "insiders" in a social group. Those who gossip *too* often, however, may find themselves dismissed as disreputable. The need to control gossip suggests the power of this form of communication.

Public Opinion

One form of highly dispersed collective behavior is *public opinion*, which was defined in Chapter 5 ("Socialization") as widespread attitudes toward controversial issues. Although we frequently speak about "the public" in singular terms, no single issue is of concern to everyone. More accurately, societies contain many publics. In industrial nations, publics wax and wane around issues such as water fluoridation, air pollution, handguns, foreign relations, child care, and thousands of other debates and activities. Although the members

of a public may share an interest in a particular issue, typically they have a range of opinions about it. Public issues are thus important matters about which people disagree (Lang & Lang, 1961; Turner & Killian, 1987).

Because most individuals possess a wide range of interests and group affiliations, they belong simultaneously to many publics. Yet, on any given issue, 5 or 10 percent of people will offer no opinion because of ignorance or apathy. As interest in an issue rises or falls, the public involved grows larger or smaller. For example, interest in the social position of women in Canada was strong during the decades of the women's suffrage movement but declined after women won the right to vote—federally in 1918 and provincially when Quebec became the last province to extend the franchise to women in 1940. Since the 1960s, a second wave of feminism has again inspired in the public strong opinions about a host of gender-related issues.

On any issue, not everyone's opinion carries the same clout. Some categories of people have more social influence than others because they are wealthier, more powerful, or better educated. Many special-interest groups shape public policy even though they represent only a small fraction of the population. In general, privileged people make use of their affluence, prestige, and social contacts to promote their opinions more effectively than others do.

Political leaders, special-interest groups, and businesses all seek to influence public tastes and attitudes by using **propaganda**, *information presented with the intention of shaping public opinion.* Although the term has negative connotations, propaganda is not necessarily false. What determines whether or not we should view information as propaganda is the intention behind it. People generate propaganda to win over some audience to a particular viewpoint, not to encourage others to think carefully for themselves. Political speeches, commercial advertising, and even some university lectures disseminate propaganda with the goal of making people think or act in some specific way. Input from Canada's business community during the 1987 debate over free trade with the U.S. was denounced by opponents as propaganda, as were all of the pronouncements of the three major federal political parties during the 1992 referendum on the Charlottetown "accord."

Panic and Mass Hysteria

Panic and mass hysteria are closely related forms of collective behavior. A **panic** is a form of localized collective behavior by which people react to a threat or other stimulus with emotional, irrational, and often self-destructive behavior. The classic illustration of a panic is people responding to a fire in a crowded theater. As they flee in fear, they trample one another and block exits so that few actually escape. In other cases, the stimulus sparking a panic may be something desirable, like a sudden half-price sale in a popular discount store.

Mass hysteria is *a form of dispersed collective behavior by which people respond to a real or imagined event with irrational, frantic behavior.* Mass hysteria differs from a panic in that the people involved have little direct contact with one another. Mass hysteria is commonly a response to a perceived threat, although a positive event such as a film celebrity's appearance on campus might provoke such a reaction.

Whatever triggers the mass hysteria may or may not be real. The key is that a large number of people *think* it is and take it seriously. Parents' fears that their children may become infected with HIV from a schoolmate who has AIDS may stir as much hysteria in a community as the very real danger of an approaching hurricane. Moreover, actions of people in the grip of mass hysteria generally make the situation worse. At the extreme, mass hysteria leads to chaotic flight and crowds in panic. People who see others overcome by fear may become more afraid themselves, as hysteria feeds on itself.

On the night before Halloween in 1938, CBS radio broadcast a dramatization of H.G. Wells's novel *War of the Worlds* (Cantril, Gaudet, & Herzog, 1947; Koch, 1970). From a New York studio, a small group of actors began by presenting a program of "live dance music" heard by an estimated 10 million people across the United States. The program was suddenly interrupted by a "news report" of explosions on the surface of the planet Mars, and the subsequent crash landing of a mysterious cylinder near a farmhouse in New Jersey. The program then switched to an "on-the-scene reporter" who presented a chilling account of giant monsters equipped with death-ray weapons emerging from the spaceship. An "eminent astronomer," played by Orson Welles, somberly informed the audience that Martians had begun a full-scale invasion of Earth. At a time when most people relied on their radios for factual news and many were prepared to believe that intelligent life existed on Mars, this episode was chilling.

At the beginning, middle, and end of the program, an announcer identified the broadcast as a fictitious dramatization. Yet more than 1 million people apparently believed that the events were actually taking place as described. By the time the show was over, thousands were hysterical, gathering in the streets spreading news of the "invasion" while others flooded telephone switchboards with warnings to friends and relatives. Among those who jumped into their cars and fled were a college senior and his roommate.

> *My roommate was crying and praying. He was even more excited than I was—or more noisy about it anyway; I guess I took it out in pushing the accelerator to the floor. ... After it was all over, I started to think about that ride, I was more jittery than when it was happening. The speed was never under 70. I thought I was racing against time. ... I didn't have any idea exactly what I was fleeing from, and that made me all the more afraid.* (Cantril, Gaudet, & Herzog, 1947:52).

Mass hysteria, then, can build in a vicious cycle. The box on page 627 describes another classic example of mass hysteria in U.S. history, generated by totally fictitious accounts of witches in colonial Massachusetts.

Fashions and Fads

Two additional types of collective behavior—fashions and fads—affect people dispersed over a large area. A **fashion** is *a social pattern favored for a time by a large number of people.* In contrast to more established norms, fashion is transitory, sometimes lasting only for months. Fashion characterizes the arts (including painting, music, drama, and literature), automobiles, language, architecture, and public opinion. The most widely recognized examples of fashion are clothing and other aspects of personal appearance.

Lyn Lofland (1973) suggests that, in preindustrial societies, clothing and personal adornment reflect traditional *style* that changes little over the years. Categories of people—women and men, and members of various social classes and occupations—are easily recognized by distinctive clothes and characteristic hairstyles that visibly mark their social standing.

In industrial societies, however, style gives way to fashion for two reasons. First, modern people are less tied to tradition and often eagerly embrace new ways of living. Second, the high social mobility of industrial societies heightens the significance of what people consume. German sociologist Georg Simmel (1971; orig. 1904) explained that people use fashion to craft their presentation of self, and seek approval and prestige as they do so. According to Simmel, affluent people are

CRITICAL THINKING

The Witches of Salem: Can Whole Towns Go Crazy?

The best-known example of mass hysteria in early U.S. history took place in 1692 in the village of Salem, Massachusetts, fifteen miles north of Boston. It is an example of mass hysteria that swept up an entire town, with deadly results.

The story began in the home of a local minister, Samuel Parris. He owned a slave woman named Tituba, who hailed from Barbados and was well-versed in the art of black magic. Tituba regularly enthralled a group of young girls by spinning tales that were undoubtedly beyond the bounds of conventional conversation in this devoutly pious Puritan community. Before long, two of the youngest girls began to display the most extraordinary behavior, writhing on the ground in apparent convulsions. Other young girls throughout the village soon mimicked this bizarre behavior, and horrified parents reached what seemed to be the only sensible conclusion: their children were bewitched.

The clergy stepped forward to demand that the girls identify those responsible for this "Satanic" outbreak. The girls pointed not only to Tituba but to two other older women. Brought to trial for witchcraft, Tituba provided an eerie and detailed account of beliefs about the "underworld" that she had learned in her youth, and she hinted that many people in Salem were witches.

When the girls were pressed to identify other culprits, they spewed forth so many names that the jail soon overflowed with suspected sorceresses. As townspeople watched these events unfold, everyone became as terrified of being named a witch as they were of confronting one. Understandably, few were willing to defend any of the accused, lest they too be labeled as members of the evil coven. By the end of the summer of 1692, twenty people convicted of witchcraft had been put to death. After reaching a fever pitch, the witchcraft hysteria began to subside. In the wake of the executions, some of Salem's citizens finally began to question the girls' accusations. No doubt, the young girls had been carried away by the immense power they were exercising over their patriarchal Puritan colony. They even accused strangers of sorcery. But as the accusations shifted from "outsiders" like Tituba to some of the founding fathers of the community, people with power began to fight back. It was then that, as quickly as they had invaded Salem, the "witches" departed.

SOURCE: Based on Erikson (1966).

---

typically the trend setters, since they have the money to spend on luxuries that bespeak privilege. In the lasting phrase of U.S. sociologist Thorstein Veblen (1953; orig. 1899), fashion involves *conspicuous consumption*, meaning that people spend money simply to show off their wealth to one another.

Less affluent people understandably long to own the trappings of wealth, so they snap up less expensive copies of items that have become fashionable. In this way, a fashion moves downward in society. But as this happens the fashion eventually loses its prestige, with the wealthy moving on to something new. Fashions, in short, are born at the top of the social hierarchy, then they rise to mass popularity in bargain stores across the country, and soon are all but forgotten by everyone.

A curious reversal of this pattern sometimes occurs among more egalitarian-minded people. In this case, a fashion that originates among people of lower social position is mimicked by the rich who wish to identify with the masses. A classic example is the "upward mobility" of blue jeans, or dungarees (from a Hindi word for a coarse and inferior fabric). First worn by manual laborers, jeans gained popularity among the affluent, especially those who supported the struggles of the socially disadvantaged. Jeans became the uniform of political activists in the civil rights and antiwar movements in the 1960s and, gradually, of university students across North America. Author Tom Wolfe (1970) coined the phrase "radical chic" to satirize the desire of some rich people to look fashionably poor. By the 1980s, expensive designer jeans had become the rage among people of every political persuasion.

A **fad** is *an unconventional social pattern that people embrace briefly but enthusiastically.* Fads, sometimes called *crazes*, are commonplace in industrial societies and often define a decade. During the 1950s, two young entrepreneurs in California produced a brightly colored plastic version of a popular Australian toy, a three-foot-diameter hoop that one swung around the body by gyrating the hips. Dubbed the "hula hoop," this odd device soon became a North American craze. Hula hoops disappeared almost as quickly as they emerged, but—decades later—they have surfaced once again, this time in China. Streaking—running naked in public—had an even briefer moment in the sun, lasting only a few months in early 1974. Their fleeting existence suggests that fads happen almost at random. But research reveals that the popularity of any fad depends on its acceptance by high-prestige people. In addition, as we see in the case of streaking, fads fade from the scene if subjected to official repression by police or other authority figures (Aguirre, Quarantelli, & Mendoza, 1988).

Fads and fashions share similar characteristics: both involve dispersed collectivities and last only a short time. But they also differ in several respects (Blumer, 1968; Turner & Killian, 1987). Fads are truly passing fancies—enthusiasms that capture the mass imagination but quickly burn out and disappear. Fashions, by contrast, reflect fundamental cultural values like individuality and sexual attractiveness and tend to evolve over time. In this way, a fashion but rarely a fad becomes incorporated into a society's culture. Streaking, for instance, came out of nowhere and soon vanished, while blue jeans originated in the rough mining camps of Gold Rush California a century ago and still influence clothing designs today. Such persistence explains the positive connotation of being called *fashionable* in contrast to the mildly insulting label *faddish*.

Social Movements

Crowds, rumors, fashions, and the other forms of collective behavior we have examined usually have little enduring significance for society as a whole. Social movements, however, are deliberate and consequential forms of collective behavior. As noted at the beginning of the chapter, a social movement involves organized activity that promotes or resists some dimension of change. Social movements stand apart from other types of collective behavior in three respects: they have a high degree of internal organization, they last longer, and their purpose is to reorganize or defend society in some respect.

Social movements are far more common today than in the past. Preindustrial societies are tightly integrated by tradition, making the emergence of social movements for change extremely rare. Industrial societies, however, foster diversity in the form of subcultures and countercultures so that social movements develop around a wide range of public issues. In recent decades, for example, homosexual men and women—supported by heterosexuals sympathetic to their political aims—have organized to win economic and legal parity with everyone else. Like any social movement that challenges conventional practices, this one has sparked a countermovement as traditionalists try to block greater social acceptance of homosexuality. Right-wing organizations in Canada, including the Ku Klux Klan and the Western Guard, are opposed to any extension of privileges to blacks, immigrants, Jews—or homosexuals (Barrett, 1987). In today's society, almost every significant public issue gives rise to both a social movement favoring change and an opposing countermovement (Lo, 1982).

There are three major dynamic sources of social change in Canada: class relations, regional identity, and the bilingual and multicultural nature of Canadian society (Marsden and Harvey, 1979:4). In fact, many of Canada's social movements arise from one of four sources.

1. **Quebec**, as its francophone majority seeks to reshape its relationship with the rest of the country or possibly to establish its sovereignty.

2. **The regions**, as they respond to economic and political inequities and numerous cultural differences.

3. **Native peoples**, as they struggle to gain recognition of an *inherent* right to self-government.

4. **Ethnic and racial minorities** that want to participate as equals within the larger society without completely losing their identities.

Types of Social Movements

Sociologists classify social movements in various ways (Aberle, 1966; Cameron, 1966; Blumer, 1969). One variable is *breadth*, since some movements target selected people while others try to change everyone. A second variable is *depth*, with some movements attempting to render only superficial changes in how we live, as others pursue radical transformation. Combining these variables, we can identify four types of social movements, shown in Figure 22-1.

Alternative social movements are the least threatening to the established social order, seeking limited change only in some segment of the population. Planned Parenthood, one example of an alternative social movement, encourages individuals of childbearing age to take the consequences of their sexual activity more seriously by practicing birth control.

Redemptive social movements also have a selective focus, but they attempt radical change in those they engage. Examples include fundamentalist Christian organizations that seek new members through conversion. The resulting transformation is sometimes so momentous that converts describe their experience as being "born again."

Reformative social movements, which generally work within the existing political system, seek only limited social change but encompass the entire society. They can be progressive (promoting a new social pattern) or reactionary (countermovements trying to preserve the status quo or to return to past social patterns). In the ongoing debate about abortion in Canada, both the pro-life and pro-choice organizations are reformative social movements. Right-wing movements such as the Western Guard, the National Citizen's Coalition, and the Ku Klux Klan are examples of reactionary countermovements. *Revolutionary social movements* have the most severe consequences of all. They seek basic transformation of a society. Sometimes pursuing specific goals, sometimes spinning utopian dreams, followers of these social movements reject existing social institutions as flawed while favoring some radically new alternatives. The nationalist or sovereigntist (i.e., separatist) movement in Quebec is in the revolutionary category because it seeks, at the very least, a radical restructuring of federal institutions to give Quebec more political and economic autonomy; failing that, Quebec nationalists would argue, the need to protect their distinct society requires the establishment of an independent state, and the complete overthrow of existing institutions.

Until recently, some people might have assumed a link between revolutionary social movements and left-wing politics, but events in Eastern Europe and the Commonwealth of Independent States have shown that socialism, too, is subject to popular overthrow.

The goals of the First Nations and other native groups are more varied. Some Native peoples, like the Six Nations and Kahnawake, are reluctant to rock the boat because they consider themselves to be sovereign nations under treaties with Canada: others seek a new kind of relationship involving settlement of land claims, constitutional recognition of their inherent right to self-government and a new basis for resource allocation that would allow them to actually practice self-government. The latter groups are more clearly revolutionary in intent, but if they are successful, even the Six Nations and Kahnawake will be functioning within a dramatically altered context.

Deprivation Theory

Because social movements are typically organized and enduring, sociologists find this form of collective behavior somewhat easier to explain than fleeting incidents of mob behavior or mass hysteria. One approach, *deprivation theory*, holds that social movements arise as

FIGURE 22-1   FOUR TYPES OF SOCIAL MOVEMENTS
SOURCE: Aberle, 1966.

		BREADTH OF CHANGE	
		Specific individuals	Entire society
DEPTH OF CHANGE	Limited	1 Alternative social movement	3 Reformative social movement
	Radical	2 Redemptive social movement	4 Revolutionary social movement

a response to a perception of being deprived of what is deemed fair. People who think they lack sufficient income, satisfactory working conditions, important political rights, or basic social dignity may engage in organized collective behavior to bring about a more just state of affairs (Morrison, 1978; Rose, 1982).

The emancipation of Americans of African descent after the Civil War seemed to signal an end to white domination. However, the economic prosperity of many white farmers depended on low-cost black labor, so that many whites felt threatened by the apparent rise in the social position of African Americans. The whites' sense of loss was especially keen during economic downturns. As a result, various social movements emerged from the desire to keep African Americans "in their place" (Dollard et al., 1939). Some whites organized in support of segregationist Jim Crow laws, while others forged terrorist organizations like the Ku Klux Klan. The success of these movements enabled threatened whites to hold on to some relative advantages.

The deprivation approach is also evident in Karl Marx's prediction that industrial workers would organize in opposition to capitalism. Marx asserted that capitalism deprived workers by giving them low wages and little social power, thereby alienating them from their own creative potential. Labor unions and various political organizations of workers have arisen to redress grievances stemming from the deprivation experienced by working-class men and women.

As we noted in Chapter 7 ("Groups and Organizations"), deprivation is a relative concept (Stouffer et al., 1949; Merton, 1968). Regardless of their absolute amount of money and power, people tend to evaluate themselves in relation to some category of others or some standard of justice. **Relative deprivation**, then, is *a perceived disadvantage arising from some specific comparison.*

More than a century ago Alexis de Tocqueville (1955; orig. 1856) studied the social uprising that sparked the French Revolution. Why, he asked, did rebellion occur in progressive France rather than in more traditional Germany where, by any objective measure, peasants were worse off? Tocqueville's answer was that, as bad as their condition was, German peasants had known nothing but feudal servitude and thus had no basis for feeling deprived. French peasants, by contrast, had experienced various improvements in their lives, which whetted their appetites for even greater progress. Thus the French—not the Germans—felt a keen sense of relative deprivation. In analyzing this apparent paradox, Tocqueville pinpointed one of the notable ironies of human history, that increasing prosperity, far from satisfying the population, is likely to promote a spirit of unrest (1955:175; orig. 1856).

Echoing Tocqueville's insight, James C. Davies (1962) suggests that as life gets better, people often take their rising fortunes for granted and come to expect even more. Relative deprivation can set in if the standard of living suddenly stops improving or, worse, begins to drop. As Figure 22-2 illustrates, social movements aimed at changing society are most likely to arise when an extended period of improvement in the standard of living is followed by a shorter period of decline.

Critical evaluation. Deprivation theory reveals the limits of common sense as a predictor of discontent. People do not organize in opposition to their situation simply because they are suffering in an absolute sense; social movements aimed at change are propelled by a perception of relative deprivation. We can discern the broad appeal of this insight by noting that it is found in the work of thinkers as diverse as Marx and Tocqueville.

But since most people experience some sense of discontent all the time, we are left wondering why social movements emerge among certain categories of people and not others. A second problem is that deprivation theory has a tendency toward circular reasoning: deprivation is assumed to cause social movements, but the only evidence of deprivation is the social movement itself (Jenkins & Perrow, 1977). A third limitation of this approach is that it focuses more on the setting in

Under the domination of the Israeli government, Palestinians in the disputed territories claim that they have been reduced to second-class citizens. This keen sense of deprivation has led to years of protest, drawing both sides into violent conflict.

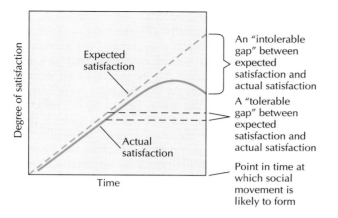

FIGURE 22-2 RELATIVE DEPRIVATION AND SOCIAL MOVEMENTS
In this diagram, the solid line represents a rising standard of living over time. The dotted line represents the expected standard of living, which is typically somewhat higher. Davies describes the difference between the two as "a tolerable gap between what people want and what they get." If the standard of living suddenly drops in the midst of rising expectations, however, this gap grows to an intolerable level. At this point, social movements can be expected to form.
SOURCE: Davies, 1962.

which a social movement develops than on the movement itself (McAdam, McCarthy, & Zald, 1988). Fourth, some research suggests that relative deprivation turns out not to be a very good predictor of social movements (Muller, 1979).

Mass-Society Theory

William Kornhauser's *mass-society theory* (1959) suggests that social movements attract socially isolated people who feel personally insignificant as part of the masses of large, complex societies. In this view, social movements are more *personal* than *political* in that they confer a sense of purpose and belonging on people otherwise adrift in society (Melucci, 1989). In this view, categories of people with weak social ties are most readily mobilized into a social movement. In societies characterized by strong social integration, on the other hand, social movements rarely come to the fore. Like Gustave Le Bon, whose ideas were explored earlier, Kornhauser offers a conservative and critical view of social movements. He regards activists as psychologically motivated individuals prone to deviance who join groups in which leaders can easily manipulate them. Thus extremist social movements on both ends of the political spectrum typically gain their most ardent support from people who belong to few social groups.

Critical evaluation. The strength of Kornhauser's theory lies in its analysis of social movements in terms of both the people who join them and the characteristics of the larger society. One practical criticism is that, beginning with the contention that mass societies foster social movements, researchers run up against the problem of having no simple standard against which to measure the extent to which people form a "mass society." A more political criticism holds that placing the roots of social movements in human psychology tends to dismiss the importance of social justice. Put otherwise, this theory suggests that flawed people, rather than a flawed society, underlie the emergence of social movements.

Some research supports this approach; other evidence disputes its contentions. Research by Frances Piven and Richard Cloward (1977) shows that a breakdown of routine social patterns seems to contribute to social movements among poor people. Also, in a study of the New Mexico State Penitentiary, Bert Useem (1985) found that suspending prison programs that promoted social ties among inmates led to an increase in chaotic and violent protest activity. On the other hand, a number of studies conclude that most people recruited by the Nazi movement in Germany were *not* socially isolated (Lipset, 1963; Oberschall, 1973) nor are the people involved in Canada's radical right (Barrett, 1987). Similarly, urban rioters in the 1960s typically had strong ties to their communities (Sears & McConahay, 1973). Evidence also suggests that young people who join religious cults do not have particularly weak family ties (Wright & Piper, 1986). Finally, researchers who have examined the biographies of 1960s political activists find evidence of deep and abiding commitment to political goals rather than isolation from society or personal aberration (McAdam, 1988, 1989; Whalen & Flacks, 1989).

Structural-Strain Theory

One of the most influential approaches to understanding social movements is *structural-strain theory*, developed by Neil Smelser (1962). This analysis identifies six factors that foster social movements. The more prevalent these conditions are, the greater the likelihood that a social movement will develop. Smelser's theory also offers clues as to what situations spark unorganized mobs or riots and which give rise to highly organized social movements. The pro-democracy movement that transformed Eastern Europe during the late 1980s illustrates Smelser's six factors.

1. **Structural conduciveness.** The roots of social movements lie in significant problems that beset a society. The generally low standard of living in Eastern Europe in recent decades, coupled with the lack of political participation by the majority of people, created widespread dissatisfaction.

2. **Structural strain.** Relative deprivation and other kinds of strain flow from the inability of a society to meet the expectations of its people. The prodemocracy movement in Eastern Europe gained strength because people there could readily see that their quality of life was far lower than that of their counterparts in Western Europe or than years of propaganda about prosperous socialism had led them to expect.

3. **Growth and spread of an explanation.** Any coherent social movement depends on a clear statement of a problem, its causes, and likely solutions. To the extent that solutions are well articulated, people are likely to express their dissatisfaction in an organized way. If not, frustration may eventually explode in the form of unorganized rioting. Intellectuals propounded the notion that the plight of Eastern Europe was caused by deep economic and political flaws; energies were directed into political action because movement leaders proposed solutions involving strategies to increase democracy.

4. **Precipitating factors.** Discontent frequently festers for a long time, only to be transformed into collective action by a specific event. When Mikhail Gorbachev came to power in the Soviet Union in 1985 and implemented his program of *perestroika*, people in Eastern Europe seized a historic opportunity to reorganize their political and economic life, as Moscow relaxed its rigid control.

5. **Mobilization for action.** Widespread concern about a public issue sets the stage for collective action in the form of rallies, leafleting, building of alliances with sympathetic organizations, and similar activities. The initial success of the Solidarity movement in Poland—covertly aided by the Reagan Administration in the United States and the Vatican—mobilized people throughout Eastern Europe to press for change. The rate of change accelerated as reform movements gained strength: progress that had taken a decade in Poland required only months in Hungary, and only weeks in other countries.

6. **Lack of social control.** The responses of established authorities, such as political officials, the police, and the military, largely determines the outcome of any social movement. Firm repression by the state can weaken or even destroy a social movement, as was seen by the crushing of prodemocracy forces in the People's Republic of China. By contrast, Gorbachev adopted a policy of nonintervention in Eastern Europe, which propelled the drive for change there. Ironically, the forces his program unleashed in these neighboring nations soon spread to the Soviet Union itself, ending the historic domination of the Communist party and leading to a new political confederation in 1992. It also laid the groundwork for the three Baltic states—Estonia, Latvia, and Lithuania—to break away from the former Soviet Union and establish themselves as fully independent nations.

Critical evaluation. Smelser's approach recognizes the complexity of social movements and suggests how various factors encourage or inhibit their development. Structural-strain theory also explains how social problems may give rise to either organized social movements or more spontaneous mob action or rioting. It also is distinctly *social*, rather than psychological, in focus.

Yet Smelser's theory contains some of the same circularity of argument found in Kornhauser's analysis. Social movements are caused by strain, he maintains, but the only evidence of this underlying strain appears to be the emerging social movement itself. Finally, this theory overlooks several key factors, including the important role of resources such as the mass media or international alliances in the success or failure of a social movement (Oberschall, 1973; Jenkins & Perrow, 1977; McCarthy & Zald, 1977; Olzak & West, 1991). Canada's native peoples have been particularly adept at gaining media coverage and winning support for their cause in the U.S., Europe, the United Nations, and among the Canadian public.

Resource-Mobilization Theory

Resource-mobilization theory adds an important dimension to our understanding of social movements. Drives for change are unlikely to succeed—or even get off the ground—without substantial resources, including money, human labor, office and communications facilities, contacts with the mass media, and a positive public image. In short, any social movement rises or falls on its ability to attract resources and mobilize people. The collapse of socialism in Eastern Europe was largely the work of dissatisfied people in those countries. But assistance from outside, in the form of fax machines, copiers, telecommunications equipment, money, and moral support, was critical in allowing first the Poles and then people in other countries to successfully oppose their leaders.

As this example demonstrates, outsiders are as important as insiders to the victory of a social movement, often playing a crucial role in supplying resources (McCarthy & Zald, 1977; Killian, 1984; Baron, Mittman, & Newman, 1991; Burstein, 1991). Socially disadvantaged people, by definition, lack the money, contacts, leadership skills, and organizational know-how that a successful movement requires, and it is here that sympathetic outsiders fill the resource gap. In Canada, people with all manner of skills, resources, and contacts have been involved in CASNP (the Canadian Alliance in Solidarity with Native Peoples). Well-to-do whites, including university students, performed a vital service to the black civil rights movement in the 1960s. Even a small core of powerful resource people can sometimes be enough to link a fledgling social movement to a larger sympathetic audience and the practical resources it needs to get off the ground (Snow, Zurcher, & Ekland-Olson, 1980; Snow, Rochford, Jr., Worden, & Benford, 1986).

On the other side of the coin, a lack of resources frustrates efforts toward intentional change. The history of the AIDS epidemic offers a case in point. Initially, the American government made a minimal response as the incidence of AIDS rose in the early 1980s. To a large extent, gay communities in cities like San Francisco and New York were left to shoulder the responsibility for treatment and educational programs on their own. Gradually, as the general public in both Canada and the U.S. began to grasp the dimensions of the problem, various levels of government in both countries started to allocate more resources. Galvanizing the public, members of the entertainment industry lent not only money and visibility but their prestige and credibility to the movement to combat the disease—and helped to transform a fledgling social movement into a well organized global coalition of political leaders, educators, and medical specialists.

Critical evaluation.   The strength of resource-mobilization theory lies in its recognition that resources as well as discontent are necessary to the success of a social movement. This theory also emphasizes the interplay between social movements and other groups and organizations that are capable of providing or withholding valuable resources. Continuing research in this area suggests that a movement's position in the power structure also affects the strategies it can employ; violence, for example, is a resource that can be used by people initially seeking entry into a political system, but it can only be used defensively once an organization becomes established (Grant & Wallace, 1991).

Critics of this approach maintain that even relatively powerless segments of a population can promote successful social movements if they manage to organize effectively and have strongly committed members. Research by Aldon Morris (1981) shows that people of color drew largely on their own skills and resources to fuel the American civil rights movement of the 1950s and 1960s. A second problem with this theory is that it overstates the extent to which powerful people are willing to challenge the status quo. Some powerful whites did provide valuable resources to the black civil rights movement but, generally speaking, white elites remained unsympathetic (McAdam, 1982, 1983).

Overall, the success or failure of a social movement turns on the outcome of a political struggle between challengers and supporters of intentional change. A strong and united establishment, perhaps aided by a countermovement, decreases the chances that any social movement will effect meaningful change. If, however, the established powers are divided, a movement's chances for success multiply. This is very clearly apparent in the native struggle for constitutional recognition in Canada. For close to two decades, native peoples faced a united front of provincial leaders who were unwilling to give in to demands for native participation in constitutional negotiations: by 1991, the election of several new premiers who were more open to native involvement set the stage for their active participation in the negotiations leading up to the Charlottetown accord.

"New Social Movements" Theory

During the 1980s one more theoretical approach to social movements emerged. What is now called *new social movements theory* investigates the distinctive features of recent social movements in mature industrial societies of North America and Western Europe (Melucci, 1980; McAdam, McCarthy, & Zald, 1988; Kriesi, 1989).

Environmentalists are a prominent example of what are called "new social movements." Such efforts for change typically involve people in many countries and are concerned with "quality of life" issues that participants believe are vital to the future of humanity.

The most familiar contemporary social movements deal with global ecology, women's and gay rights, peace, Native or aboriginal rights, and animal rights, among others. One distinctive feature of these movements is their national scope. As Chapter 18 ("Politics and Government") explained, the state has expanded to become the dominant center of power in all industrial societies, and government now sets countless policies that affect entire populations. Not surprisingly, then, social movements have also assumed national (and sometimes international) proportions. While traditional social movements such as labor organizations are concerned primarily with economic issues, new social movements tend to focus on cultural change and enhancing the quality of our social and physical surroundings. The international ecology movement, for example, opposes practices that aggravate global warming and other environmental dangers. Third, whereas traditional social movements that strive for economic equality tend to elicit strong support from working-class people, the new social movements with their non-economic agendas usually draw disproportionate support from middle-class people.

Critical evaluation. Because the new social movements theory is a recent development, sociologists are still assessing its utility. One clear strength of this analysis is its understanding of the vast power of the state to shape society, making government the target of large-scale social movements. This approach also spotlights the power of the mass media to unite people around the world in pursuit of political goals.

This approach garners criticism, however, for exaggerating the differences between "traditional" and "new" social movements. The women's movement, for example, focuses on many of the same issues—workplace conditions and pay—that have consumed the energies of labor organizations for decades. Similarly, Canadian Native peoples are involved in an international movement affecting indigenous peoples on several continents, but a large part of their struggle is economic.

Each of the five theories we have presented explains part of the complex process by which social movements arise. Table 22-1 summarizes the theories.

Stages in Social Movements

Despite the many differences that set one social movement apart from others, all efforts at intentional change unfold in similar stages. Researchers have identified four phases in the life of the typical social movement (Blumer, 1969; Mauss, 1975; Tilly, 1978).

Stage 1: Emergence. Social movements are driven by the perception that all is not well. Some, such as the civil rights and women's movements, are born of widespread dissatisfaction. Others emerge only as a small vanguard group increases public awareness of some issue, as gay activists have done with respect to the threat posed by AIDS.

Stage 2: Coalescence. After emerging, a social movement must define itself clearly and develop a strategy for "going public." Leaders must determine policies, select tactics, build morale, and recruit new members. At this stage, the movement may engage in collective action like rallies or demonstrations to attract media attention in hopes of capturing the notice of the public. Additionally, the movement may form alliances with other organizations to gain necessary resources.

Stage 3: Bureaucratization. To become an established political force, a social movement must assume bureaucratic traits, as described in Chapter 7 ("Groups and Organizations"). As it becomes routinized, a social

TABLE 22-1 THEORIES OF SOCIAL MOVEMENTS: A SUMMARY

Deprivation Theory	People join as a result of experiencing relative deprivation. Social movement is a means of seeking change that brings participants greater benefits. Social movements are especially likely when rising expectations are frustrated.
Mass-Society Theory	People who lack established social ties are mobilized into social movements. Periods of social breakdown are likely to spawn social movements. Social movement is a means of gaining a sense of belonging and social participation.
Structural-Strain Theory	People join because of their shared concern about the inability of society to operate as they believe it should. The growth of a social movement reflects many factors, including a belief in its legitimacy and some precipitating event that provokes action.
Resource-Mobilization Theory	People may join for all of the reasons noted above and also because of social ties to existing members. The success or failure of a social movement depends largely on the resources available to it. Also important is the extent of opposition to its goals within the larger society.
New Social Movement Theory	People join motivated by a concern for "quality of life," not necessarily economic issues. Mobilization is national or international in scope. New social movements are a response to the expansion of the mass media, and also the power of the state in modern industrial societies to affect people's lives for good or ill.

movement depends less on the charisma and talents of a few leaders and relies more on a capable staff. Some social movements do not become established in this way, however. Many activist organizations on university campuses during the late 1960s were energized by a single charismatic leader and, consequently, did not endure for long. On the other hand, the well established National Action Committee on the Status of Women (NAC), despite changing leadership, offers considerable continuity in its activist role at the helm of the women's movement in Canada.

At the same time, bureaucratization can sometimes hinder a social movement. Frances Piven and Richard Cloward (1977), reviewing social movements in U.S. history, noted that leaders sometimes become so engrossed in building an organization that they neglect the need to sustain sentiments of insurgency among their followers. In such cases, the radical edge of protest is lost.

Stage 4: Decline. Social movements are inherently dynamic, so a decline is not necessarily a demise (Wright, 1987). Eventually, however, most social movements lose their influence. Frederick Miller (1983) suggests four reasons why this may occur.

First, decline may simply signal success, as members see nothing more to accomplish. For example, the women's suffrage movement declined after it won the right to vote for women in the United States and Canada. Such clear-cut successes are rare, however, since few social movements have one specific goal.

More commonly, gaining one victory adds impetus to new campaigns. Because issues related to gender extend far beyond voting, the women's movement has been reborn.

Second, a social movement may flag due to organizational factors, such as poor leadership, loss of interest among members, exhaustion of resources, repression by authorities, or excessive bureaucratization. Some people attracted by the dynamism of a new social movement lose interest when formal routines replace the excitement of early efforts at change. Fragmentation due to internal conflicts over goals and tactics is another common problem. Political parties with radical goals like those of Quebec's Parti Québécois (formed in 1968 with sovereignty as its central aim) can lose some of their more committed and activist members when they have to modify their platforms, however temporarily, in order to govern or to ensure reelection (as the PQ did in 1984).

Third, a social movement may degenerate if the established power structure, through offers of money, prestige, and other rewards, succeeds in diverting leaders from their goals. "Selling out" is one facet of the iron law of oligarchy, noted in Chapter 7 ("Groups and Organizations"), by which organizational leaders may use their positions to enrich themselves. Jerry Rubin, a political activist of the late 1960s, parlayed his celebrity status as a rebel into a career in the New York financial world. But it actually works both ways: there are people who have left lucrative, high-prestige occupations to become activists too. Cat Stevens, a famous rock star of the 1970s, became a Muslim, changed his name to Yusuf Islam, and now promotes the spread of his religion.

Fourth and finally, the demise of a social movement may stem from repression. Those in power may crush a movement for social change by frightening away participants, discouraging new recruits, or even imprisoning leaders. The intensity of the state's reaction depends on how much of a threat the movement is deemed to be by officials with the power to crack down on it. In the 1960s, the Front de libération du Québec (FLQ)—a revolutionary movement whose aim was an independent socialist Quebec—was using bombs, kidnapping, and murder to promote its cause. In 1970, Prime Minister Pierre Trudeau invoked the War Measures Act in peacetime to suspend civil liberties and facilitate the arrest of FLQ members and sympathizers. By 1971, the FLQ had folded.

Beyond the reasons noted by Miller, a fifth cause of decline is that a social movement may "go mainstream." Some movements become an accepted part of the system—typically after realizing at least some of their goals—to the point that they no longer challenge the status quo. Canada's socialist movement as embodied in the New Democratic Party (NDP) has traditionally supported, firstly, an expanded government role in providing social services and, secondly, the rights of workers rather than of employers. In 1993, one finds three NDP provincial governments facing huge deficits, debt loads and publics who are fearful of any increases in spending. Bob Rae, the NDP premier of Ontario, finds himself in the extremely uncomfortable position of being the one to spearhead a 5 percent roll-back in public service salaries and make other cuts in services. Not surprisingly, he has been criticized by unions and members of his own party for acting in the interests of big business and capitalism—just like any other "mainstream" political party.

Although separated for centuries by social barriers, there is now hope that blacks and whites in South Africa will be able to forge a racially unified society. In a 1992 referendum, whites voiced their support for continued negotiations with the black majority towards a democratic government.

Figure 22-3 provides a graphic summary of the various stages of social movements.

Social Movements and Social Change

Social movements exist to encourage—or to resist—social change. Whatever the intention, their success varies from case to case. Gender equality, still only a partially realized goal, has been advanced by the actions of numerous women's groups in Canada and elsewhere. Environmentalists, as well, have experienced some major successes and changed public awareness dramatically. The younger generation is growing up taking for granted some of the things that other people struggled so hard to win: a woman's right to vote, collective bar-

FIGURE 22-3   STAGES IN THE LIVES OF SOCIAL MOVEMENTS

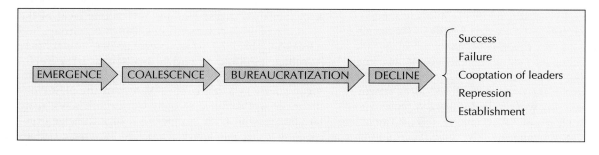

EMERGENCE → COALESCENCE → BUREAUCRATIZATION → DECLINE →
Success
Failure
Cooptation of leaders
Repression
Establishment

gaining, limited working hours, and recycling are but a few examples.

This all leads to one overarching conclusion: we can draw a direct link between social movements and change. Social transformations such as the Industrial Revolution and the rise of capitalism sparked alliances among people intent on changing some dimension of their lives. By the same token, the efforts of workers, women, racial and ethnic minorities, and gay people have sent ripples of change throughout our society. Thus, social change is both the cause and the consequence of social movements.

Summary

1. A collectivity differs from a social group in its limited social interaction, its vague social boundaries, and its weak and often unconventional norms.

2. Crowds, an important type of collective behavior, take various forms: casual crowds, conventional crowds, expressive crowds, acting crowds, and protest crowds.

3. Crowds that become emotionally intense and even violent spawn mobs and riots. Mobs pursue a specific goal; rioting is undirected destructiveness.

4. Contagion theory views crowds as anonymous, suggestible, and subject to escalating emotions. Convergence theory links crowd behavior to the traits of participants. Emergent-norm theory holds that crowds may develop their own behavioral norms.

5. Crowds have figured heavily in social change throughout history. Depending on political orientation, the observer perceives crowds as either detrimental or constructive.

6. Rumor, which thrives in a climate of ambiguity, is concerned with public issues; gossip, a closely related concept, deals with personal issues of local interest.

7. Public opinion consists of people's positions on issues of widespread importance. Such attitudes reflect people's social background. On any public issue a small proportion of the population claims to hold no opinion.

8. Mass hysteria is a type of collective behavior by which people anxiously respond to a significant event, real or imagined. In a spiral of panic, hysteria may lead to ineffective action, which provokes further frenzy.

9. In industrial societies, people employ fashion to gain social prestige. A fad, which is more unconventional than a fashion, is also of shorter duration but is embraced with greater enthusiasm.

10. A social movement entails deliberate activity intended to promote or discourage change. Social movements vary in the breadth and depth of their goals.

11. According to deprivation theory, social movements arise out of relative deprivation rather than anyone's absolute circumstances.

12. Mass-society theory suggests that people join social movements to gain a sense of belonging and social significance.

13. Structural-strain theory explains the development of social movements as a cumulative consequence of six factors. Well-formulated grievances and goals encourage the organization of social movements; undirected anger and frustration promote rioting.

14. Resource-mobilization theory ties the success or failure of a social movement to the availability of resources like money, human labor, and alliances with other organizations.

15. A typical social movement proceeds through specific stages. First, emergence occurs as leaders define a public issue requiring action; second, coalescence represents a movement's entry into public life; third, bureaucratization refers to a movement's increasingly formal organization, and fourth, a movement declines as a result of failure or, sometimes, success.

16. The accomplishment of social movements is evident in characteristics of society that people now take for granted. Just as movements produce change, so change itself sparks social movements.

Key Concepts

collective behavior   activity involving a large number of people, often spontaneous, and typically in violation of established norms

collectivity   a large number of people whose minimal interaction occurs in the absence of well-defined and conventional norms

crowd   a temporary gathering of people who share a common focus of attention and whose members influence one another

fad   an unconventional social pattern that people embrace briefly but enthusiastically

fashion   a social pattern favored for a time by a large number of people

gossip   rumor about the personal affairs of others

mass behavior   collective behavior among people dispersed over a wide geographical area

mass hysteria   a form of dispersed collective behavior by which people respond to a real or imagined event with irrational, frantic behavior

mob   a highly emotional crowd that pursues some violent or destructive goal

panic   a form of localized collective behavior by which people react to a threat or other stimulus with emotional, irrational, and often self-destructive behavior

propaganda   information presented with the intention of shaping public opinion

relative deprivation   a perceived disadvantage arising from some specific comparison

riot   a social eruption that is highly emotional, violent, and undirected

rumor   unsubstantiated information spread informally, often by word of mouth

social movement   organized activity that encourages or discourages social change

Suggested Readings

These books probe in greater detail some topics covered in this chapter.

> Ralph H. Turner and Lewis M. Killian. *Collective Behavior.* 3rd ed. Englewood Cliffs, NJ: Prentice Hall, 1987.
> William Gamson. *The Strategy of Social Protest.* 2nd ed. Belmont, CA: Wadsworth, 1990.

Here is an historical account of how and why sociologists have understood (or, more accurately, misunderstood) crowd behavior.

> Clark McPhail. *The Myth of the Maddening Crowd.* New York: Aldine De Gruyter, 1991.

This recent analysis further builds on the mass-society approach to social movements.

> Alberto Melucci. *Nomads of the Present: Social Movements and Individual Needs in Contemporary America.* Philadelphia: Temple University Press, 1989.

This collection of articles deals with the development of Social Gospel movements, Social Credit, the Cooperative Commonwealth Federation (CCF), unions, and Quebec nationalism.

> S.D. Clark, J. Paul Grayson, & Linda M. Grayson. *Prophecy and Protest: Social Movements in Twentieth-Century Canada.* Toronto: Gage, 1975.

This book analyzes three important social movements of a turbulent decade: the antiwar movement, the women's movement, and the civil rights movement.

> Stewart Burns. *Social Movements of the 1960s: Searching for Democracy.* Boston: G.K. Hall/Twayne, 1990.

The first of these books offers an historical overview of the gay and lesbian movements in the United States. The second concludes that when compared with the black civil rights movement, the gay movement has failed because of poor strategies.

> Barry D. Adam. *The Rise of a Gay and Lesbian Movement.* Boston: Twayne, 1987.
> Marshall Kirk and Hunter Madsen. *After the Ball.* Garden City, NY: Doubleday, 1989.

This account of one of the most stunning examples of collective behavior in recent years tries to explain the mass suicide of some 900 members of a sect called the People's Temple in Jonestown, Guyana.

> John R. Hall. *Gone from the Promised Land: Jonestown in American Cultural History.* New Brunswick, NJ: Transaction, 1987.

The following takes a close look at the people involved in several right-wing organizations in Canada. Based on interviews, it gives a real sense of the beliefs and commitments behind organizations such as the Western Guard and the Ku Klux Klan.

Stanley R. Barrett. *Is God a Racist?: The Right Wing in Canada.* Toronto: University of Toronto Press, 1987.

Here is a personal account of a teenager's experiences during the Cultural Revolution in China from 1966 to 1969, which has been dubbed a mass movement out of control.

Gao Yuan. *Born Red: A Chronicle of the Cultural Revolution.* Stanford, CA: Stanford University Press, 1987.

These two books look at social movements in world perspective. The first explores how organizations of workers brought about change in Spain after the death of dictator Francisco Franco; the second highlights the tension between support for change and the status quo in poor societies of the Third World.

Robert M. Fishman. *Working-Class Organization and the Return to Democracy in Spain.* Ithaca, NY: Cornell University Press, 1990.

John Walton. *Reluctant Rebels: Comparative Studies of Revolution and Underdevelopment.* New York: Columbia University Press, 1984.

This is an excellent book on social movements.

Gary Rush and Serge Denisov. *Social and Political Movements.* New York: Appleton-Century-Crofts, 1971.

CHAPTER 23

SOCIAL CHANGE AND MODERNITY

The firelight flickers in the gathering darkness. Chief Kanhonk sits, as he has done every evening for many years, ready to begin an evening of animated talk and storytelling.[1] These are the hours of every day when the Kaiapo, a small society of Brazil's Amazon region, celebrate their culture. Since the Kaiapo are a traditional people with no written language, the elders rely on evenings before the fire to instruct their grandchildren in their people's history and way of life. In the past, evenings like this have been filled with tales of brave Kaiapo warriors fighting off Portuguese traders who came in pursuit of slaves and gold.

But as the minutes slip by, only a few older villagers assemble for the evening ritual. None of the children is to be found. "It is the Big Ghost," one old man grumbles, explaining the poor turnout. The "Big Ghost" has indeed descended upon them: its presence is evident in the soft glow spilling from windows of homes throughout the village. The Kaiapo children—and many adults as well—are watching television. The consequences of installing a satellite dish in the village three years ago have turned out to be greater than any-

one imagined. In the end, what their enemies failed to do to the Kaiapo with guns they may do to themselves with prime-time programming. Those around the fire sit in gloomy silence, knowing that their culture is once again under attack and may soon be gone (Simons, 1989).

The Kaiapo are distinctive members of the 230,000 Native people who inhabit the country we call Brazil. They are easily identified by their striking body paint and ornate ceremonial dress. Recently, they have become rich as profits from gold mining and harvesting mahogany trees have flowed into the settlement. A favorite topic of conversation in the village is whether their new-found fortune is a blessing or a curse. To some, affluence means the opportunity to learn about the outside world through travel and television. Others, like Chief Kanhonk, express a different view. Sitting by the fire, he thinks aloud about how their wealth can help the Kaiapo to live better: "I have been saying that people must buy useful things like knives and fishing hooks. Television does not fill the stomach. It only shows our children and grandchildren white people's things." Bebtopup, the oldest priest, nods in agreement and adds, "The night is the time the old people teach the young people. Television has stolen the night" (Simons 1989:37).

---

[1] This opening is a selective adaptation of the account provided by Simons (1989).

The transformation of the Kaiapo raises profound questions about what causes social change; their current plight forces us to wonder whether change—even toward a higher material standard of living—is always for the better. Moreover, the drama of the Kaiapo is being played out around the globe as more and more traditional cultures are drawn away from their past by a materialistic way of life modeled on the rich societies of the First World.

Canadians can look within their own boundaries to find peoples who are grappling with the same kinds of concerns about the influence of television in particular. In a part of the Northwest Territories, which in 1999 years will become the separate territory of Nunavut, the Inuit people have long been concerned about the damaging effects of television programming originating in the U.S and southern Canada. With financial assistance from the federal government, they have created the Inuit Broadcasting Corporation (IBC) which produces news, documentaries, children's programs (including cartoons and puppet shows), and talk shows that deal with issues of relevance to the region—in its own language, Inuktitut. With the IBC, the Inuit people have been able to mitigate some of the intrusive and damaging impacts of television upon their culture.

This chapter, then, examines social change as a process with both positive and negative consequences. Of particular interest is what sociologists call *modernity*, the product of social changes beginning with the Industrial Revolution. But we shall also consider how rich and powerful nations, like Canada and the United States, are involved in changes affecting the rest of the world.

What Is Social Change?

Earlier chapters have examined human societies in terms of both stability and change. The relatively *static* social patterns include status and roles, social stratification, and the various social institutions. The dynamic forces that sometimes recast human consciousness, behavior, and needs include social conflict, innovations in technology, the development of formal organizations, the growth of cities, and social movements. It is factors of this kind that fuel **social change**, *the transformation of culture and social institutions over time*. The process of social change has four general characteristics.

1. **Social change is universal although the rate of change varies.** "Nothing is constant except death and taxes," as the saying goes. However, social patterns related to death and dying have changed in recent centuries, as Chapter 5 ("Socialization") explained. Additionally, people today die at a much later age than in the past. And taxes, which emerged along with complex social organization, were unknown to most of our ancestors. In short, one would be hard pressed to identify anything that is not subject to the twists and turns of social change.

   Still, some societies change faster than others. Chapter 4 ("Society") explained that hunting and gathering societies were remarkably stable over thousands of years. As technology becomes more complex, a society's rate of social change increases (Lenski, Lenski, & Nolan, 1991), because technological advance multiplies the effect of discovery as any single invention is combined with cultural elements already in place.

   Moreover, even in a given society, some cultural elements change more quickly than others. William Ogburn's (1964) theory of *cultural lag* recognizes that material culture (that is, things) usually changes faster than nonmaterial culture—ideas and attitudes (see Chapter 3, "Culture"). For example, medical devices that prolong the life of a seriously ill person have developed more rapidly than have ethical standards for deciding when and how to employ this technology.

2. **Social change is sometimes intentional but often unplanned.** Industrial societies actively encourage many kinds of change. For example, scientists seek more efficient forms of energy, advertisers try to convince consumers that a new gadget is a "necessity," and government officials seek ways to increase equality of opportunity among various categories of people. Yet even the experts rarely envision all the consequences of the changes they propose. Early automobile manufacturers understood that cars would allow people to travel in a single day distances that had required weeks or months a century before. But no one foresaw how profoundly the mobility provided by automobiles would affect families and reshape cities and suburbs, not to mention resulting in some three to four thousand accidental deaths in Canada each year.

Increasing technological sophistication and the expansion of multinational corporations have made the world seem smaller, as products familiar to us are now eagerly consumed on the other side of the globe. Does this mean that thousands of historically distinctive ways of life will become a single global McCulture? What are the advantages and drawbacks of this expansion of First-World influence?

3. **Social change often generates controversy.** The historical record provides ample evidence that social change yields both good and bad consequences. Politically speaking, in other words, every social transformation wins support from some people and provokes opposition from others. Capitalists welcomed the Industrial Revolution because advancing technology increased productivity and profits. Many workers, however, fearing that machines would make their skills obsolete, strongly resisted "progress." Similarly, South African blacks have spoken almost with a single voice in support of the gradual weakening of apartheid. Although a majority of whites supported the 1992 referendum to end this system of racial separation, many harbor doubts about the long-term effects of this change.

In Canada, changing patterns of social interaction between the majority of Canadians and the Québecois, aboriginal peoples, and other racial or ethnic minorities or between women and men, and gays and heterosexuals give rise to tensions, misunderstandings, and an overall sense of unease. These kinds of changes play a role in the continuing quest for a national identity, which is revealed in our interminable constitutional struggles.

4. **Social change has variable consequences.** Some social changes have only passing significance, whereas other transformations have far-reaching ramifications. At one extreme, fads, such as the "Teenage Mutant Ninja Turtles," arise and dissipate quickly. At the other, members of our society are still adjusting to powerful technological advances such as television half a century after its introduction. Today we can scarcely imagine how the computer-based Information Revolution will transform the entire world during the next century. Like the automobile and television, computers will have both positive and negative impacts, opening up new kinds of jobs while eliminating old ones, and facilitating the processing of information while compromising personal privacy.

Causes of Social Change

Many factors underlie social change. Some change emerges within a particular society. But in a world linked by sophisticated communication and transportation technology, change in one place often prompts change elsewhere.

Culture and Change

Culture is a dynamic system of symbols that continually gains new elements and loses others. Chapter 3 ("Culture") identified three important sources of cultural change. First, *invention* produces mechanical objects, ideas, and social patterns that reshape society to varying degrees. Rocket-propulsion research, beginning in the 1940s, has produced increasingly sophisticated vehicles for space flight. Today we take such technology for granted, and during the next century probably a significant number of people will travel in space.

A second process, *discovery*, occurs when people recognize existing elements of the world they hadn't noticed before or learn to see them in a new way. For example, medical advances offer a growing understanding of how the human body operates. Beyond the direct effects for human health, medical discoveries have also stretched life expectancy, setting in motion here what Chapter 14 ("Aging and the Elderly") calls the "graying of Canada."

Third, *diffusion* creates change as cultural elements spread from one society to another through trade, migration, and mass communication. Ralph Linton (1937) recognized that many familiar elements of our culture have come to us from other lands—for example, cloth (developed in Asia), clocks (invented in Europe), and coins (devised in Turkey). Generally, material things diffuse more readily than nonmaterial cultural traits. The Kaiapo, introduced at the beginning of this chapter, were quick to adopt television but have been reluctant to embrace the materialism and individualism that gradually seizes those who spend hours watching Western, commercial programming.

During its entire history, Canada has been transformed by cultural diffusion accompanying immigration. In recent decades, people from Southern and Central Europe, Asia, Latin America, and the Carribean have been introducing new cultural patterns, clearly evident in the tastes, sights, smells, and sounds of cities across the country. Little Italies, Chinatowns, Caribana parades, ethnic festivals like Toronto's Caravan, outdoor cafés, reggae music, pizza, perogies, fajitas, and sushi have become part of the fabric of life for many Canadians.

Social Structure and Change

Tension and conflict within a society also produce social change. The link between social structure and social change stands at the core of Karl Marx's ideas (see especially Chapter 4, "Society," and Chapter 9, "Social Stratification"). Marx pointed to conflict between social classes as the engine of social change. In industrial-capitalist societies, he explained, the struggle between capitalists and workers drives society toward a system of socialist production. In the century since Marx's death, this model has proven simplistic; yet, he correctly foresaw that social conflict arising from inequality (involving race and gender as well as social class) would propel every society, including Canada, toward change. The last chapter ("Collective Behavior and Social Movements") described how movements supported by Native peoples, the Québecois, labor, people of color, women, and gay men and lesbians are continuing to reshape our society.

Ideas and Change

Max Weber, too, contributed to our understanding of social change. While Weber acknowledged the importance of conflict based on material production, he traced the roots of social change to the world of ideas. He illustrated his argument by showing how people who display charisma (described in Chapters 17, "Religion," and 18, "Politics and Government") can convey a message that sometimes changes the world. Weber also spotlighted the importance of ideas by revealing how the world view of early Protestants drove them to embrace industrial capitalism (see Chapter 4, "Society"). Because industrial capitalism developed primarily in areas of Western Europe where the Protestant work ethic was strong, Weber (1958; orig. 1904–1905) concluded that the disciplined rationality of Calvinist Protestants was instrumental in this change.

Ideas also fuel social movements. Chapter 22 ("Collective Behavior and Social Movements") explained that a social movement may emerge from the decision to modify society in some manner (say, to clean up the environment) or from a sense that existing social arrangements must be reformed (Smelser, 1962). The international gay rights movement draws strength from the contention that homosexuals have been the targets of prejudice and discrimination, and that lesbians and gay men should enjoy rights equal to those of the heterosexual majority. The persisting opposition to the gay rights movement indicates the power of ideas—as ideology—to inhibit as well as to advance social change.

The Natural Environment and Change

Because human societies interact with their natural environment, change in one tends to produce change in the other. Many Native cultures viewed the natural world with reverence, living according to natural rhythms. European settlers who came to North America saw nature in a strikingly different way: as an adversary to be tamed and then molded to human purposes. Confronting a wilderness, these newcomers systematically cut down forests to provide space and materials for building, established towns, extended roads in every direction, and dammed rivers as sources of water and energy. Today, the conversion of farmers' fields, virgin forests or traditional Native hunting grounds into urban landscapes, massive hydroelectric power plants or simply wastelands continues unabated. Such construction reveals both our cultural determination to master the natural environment and the centrality of ideas like "growth" in our capitalist culture.

Despite its advantages, technological development increasingly threatens the natural environment. With our high standard of living, Canadians generate tens of billions of pounds of refuse each year—along with considerable debate and conflict over where it

should be dumped. The operation of millions of motor vehicles, thousands of factories, and the routine use of dozens of household products all release hazardous chemicals into the air. Only in the last few decades have we begun to understand and take seriously the devastating effects of our way of life on our natural surroundings; devising and agreeing upon real solutions to this problem will require greater public awareness, political pressure and time.

Our way of life is also based on very high consumption of energy. As Global Map 23-1 shows, residents of rich countries, including Canada, are by far the

WINDOW ON THE WORLD

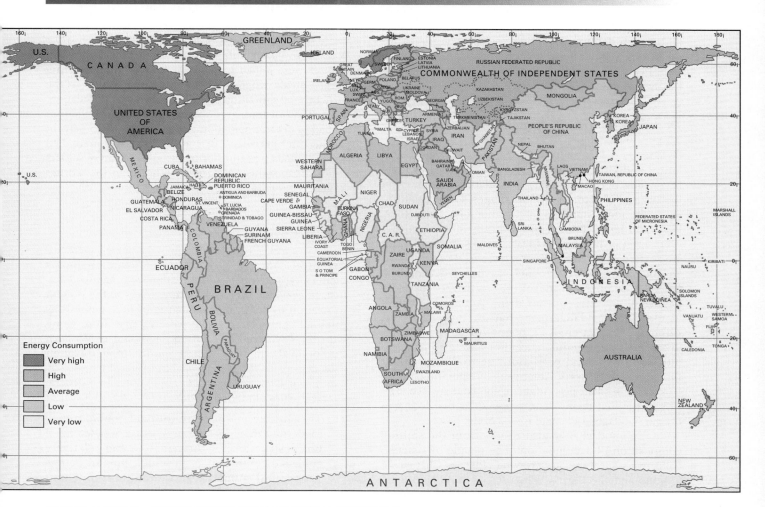

GLOBAL MAP 23-1   ENERGY CONSUMPTION IN GLOBAL PERSPECTIVE
The members of industrial societies consume far more energy than others on the planet. The typical U.S. resident uses the same amount of energy in a year as one hundred people in the Central African Republic. This means that the most economically productive societies are also those that place the greatest burden on the natural environment.

highest energy users in the world, consuming one hundred times as much energy as people who live in the poorest societies of the Third World. Not only does this pattern raise concerns about conservation of finite resources, it also highlights once again the material disparity that divides people of the world.

Just as people act on the natural environment, so does nature affect human societies, sometimes with devastating effect. Throughout history, entire civilizations have succumbed to natural disasters in the form of floods, volcanic eruptions, and earthquakes. A thriving civilization in ancient India was destroyed in about 1500 B.C.E. as the waters of the Indus River gradually rose. Four centuries later, devastating earthquakes ended an early civilization on the island of Crete (Hamblin, 1973; Stavrianos, 1983). Today, life is still disrupted by such natural calamities. In recent years, earthquakes have killed tens of thousands in Armenia and Iran, just as droughts in central Africa have devastated the lives of millions.

Demography and Change

Demographic factors (described in Chapter 21, "Population and Urbanization") also cause social change. Increasing population places escalating demands on the natural environment and shapes social relationships. In some small countries, notably the Netherlands and Japan, limited space already affects virtually every facet of life. For example, homes in Amsterdam are small and narrow in comparison to those in Canada, and staircases are extremely steep in order to make efficient use of space. In Tokyo, bus drivers routinely negotiate city streets that many American drivers would consider dangerously narrow for even a car. Although Canada enjoys a bounty of physical space, urbanization and industrialization have also changed our way of life and will continue to do so. About three-fourths of North Americans live in cities, which cover only a small percentage of the land surface. The way of life that results barely resembles that found in the rural villages and small towns of the past.

Profound change also results from the shifting composition of a population. The people of Canada, collectively speaking, are growing older, as Chapter 14 ("Aging and the Elderly") explained. In 1991, almost 12 percent of Canadians were over sixty-five, more than double the proportion in 1901, and Statistics Canada estimates that by the year 2036, seniors will account for *one quarter* of the population. Medical research and health-care services will increasingly focus on the elderly, and common stereotypes about old people will be challenged as more men and women enter this stage of life (Barberis, 1981). Life may change in countless additional ways as homes are redesigned (perhaps extending to "granny flats" in suburban backyards) and household products altered to meet the needs of older consumers. Societal concerns about the retirement age, familial responsibility for eldercare, pensions, and medical coverage undoubtedly will be subject to vigorous public debate.

Migration within and among societies is another demographic factor that often promotes dramatic social change. Since the early 1800s tens of millions of immigrants have come to Canada, initially to participate in the fur trade or to establish farming homesteads but more recently to seek a better life in the growing urban areas. The immigrants who arrived in Canada's urban centers were joined by a steady flow of migrants from rural Canada where high fertility and changes in the structure of agriculture resulted in surplus population. As a result of immigration and rural–urban migration Canada's urban population grew from 18 to 76 percent of the total between 1871 and 1991. In a mere 120 years, Canada was transformed from a nation of settlers to an urban-industrial society with one of the world's largest economies.

Modernity

A central concept in the study of social change is **modernity**, *patterns of social life linked to industrialization*. In everyday usage, modernity refers to the present in relation to the past. Sociologists include within this catch-all concept the social patterns that arose along with the Industrial Revolution beginning in Western Europe in the mid-eighteenth century. **Modernization** thus designates *the process of social change initiated by industrialization*. Peter Berger (1977) notes four general characteristics of modernization.

1. **The decline of small, traditional communities.** Modernity involves "the progressive weakening, if not destruction, of the concrete and relatively cohesive communities in which human beings have found solidarity and meaning throughout most of history" (Berger, 1977:72). For thousands of years, in the camps of hunters and gatherers and in the rural villages of early North American settlers, people lived in small-scale settlements

with family and neighbors. Each person had a well-defined place in a traditional world, based on sentiments and beliefs that were passed from generation to generation. Living in small primary groups certainly limited the range of personal experience, but it conferred a strong sense of identity, belonging, and purpose.

Since Canada has a land mass of close to 10 million square kilometers (the second largest in the world) and a population density of only 2.8 per square kilometer, and since about 80 percent of its population lives within 160 kilometers of the U.S. border, it goes without saying that there is a great deal of space through which to scatter isolated communities. Small, isolated communities—many of them with far fewer than 100 members—still exist in Canada, but they are now home to only a small percentage of our population. Many of these people are Indian, Métis, or Inuit. Through most of rural Canada, efficient communication—increasingly through satellites—and rapid transportation have changed the meaning of physical space so that few communities are now isolated from events in the society as a whole and in the larger world. For almost everyone, the family has ceased to be the unrivaled center of everyday life. As Talcott Parsons (1966) noted, modern living is played out in distinct institutional settings including schools, workplaces, hospitals, prisons, and places of worship.

2. **The expansion of personal choice.** People in traditional, preindustrial societies view their lives as being shaped by forces beyond human control—gods, spirits, or simply fate. Jealously protecting their traditions, these societies grant members a narrow range of personal choices.

As the power of tradition diminishes, a society's members come to see their lives as an unending series of options. Berger calls this process *individualization*. Many people in Canada, for instance, adopt one "lifestyle" or another, since a way of life that one person finds suitable may hold little appeal for another. Recognizing alternatives in everyday life, of course, parallels a willingness to embrace change. Modern people, then, readily imagine the world being different from what it is.

3. **Increasing diversity in beliefs.** In preindustrial societies, strong family ties and powerful religious beliefs enforce conformity, discouraging diversity and change. Modernization promotes a more rational, scientific world view, in which traditional beliefs lose their force and morality becomes a matter of individual attitude. The growth of cities, the expansion of impersonal, formal organizations, and the social mix of immigrants from around the

In response to the accelerated pace of change in the late nineteenth century, Paul Gauguin (1848–1903) left his native France for the South Seas where he was captivated by a simpler and seemingly timeless way of life. He romanticized this environment in his 1894 painting Mahana no Atua (Day of the Gods).

Paul Gauguin, Day of the Gods [Mahana no Atua]. 1894. Oil on canvas. 68.3 x 91.5 cm. The Art Institute of Chicago, Helen Birch Bartlett Memorial Collection.

world combine to foster a diversity of beliefs and behavior as well as a tolerant openness to those who differ from ourselves.

Chapter 17 ("Religion") spotlighted *secularization*, the historical decline in the importance of religion. The weakening of religious doctrine, and especially the separation of church and state (which has been relatively recent in Canada), frees people to embrace a wider range of personal beliefs. Secularization meant that religious organizations in Canada gradually lost control of colleges and universities, primary and secondary institutions, and health care: in Quebec, the process also meant loss of control of several daily newspapers, and of the political process itself (Nock, 1986).

When compared with Americans, Canadians are less likely to believe in God, attend church regularly, or adhere to evangelical or moralistic beliefs (Lipset, 1990). While fundamentalist religious activity flourishes in the U.S. (Stark & Bainbridge, 1981; Johnstone, 1983), Canadians distinguish themselves by declaring "no religion"—7.4 percent nationally in 1981, with a high of 20.9 percent in British Columbia (Nock, 1986). Despite its slow start, one might argue that secularization is further advanced north of the border.

4. **Future orientation and growing awareness of time.** People in modern societies share a distinctive appreciation of time. First, we tend to think more about the future, while preindustrial people are past-oriented and guided by traditions. Modern people, moreover, look toward the future, typically imagining that life will be enhanced by inventions and discoveries. Second, modern societies organize daily routines according to precise units of time. With the introduction of clocks in the late Middle Ages, Europeans began to think in terms of hours and minutes. Why? Because of the growing importance of economic activity. Industrial technology depends on the precise measurement of time; in addition, the Industrial Revolution prompted capitalists, preoccupied with profits, to proclaim, "Time is money!" Berger suggests that one shorthand way of gauging a society's degree of modernization is to note what proportion of people wear wristwatches.

According to Berger, then, modernization emancipates people from the tyranny of tradition, but leaves them without the comforting security of heritage and roots. No longer do people live in tightly knit communities where traditional religious beliefs provide each person with a strong sense of belonging but little individual freedom. Modern societies offer far more autonomy but less sense of purpose and fewer enduring social ties.

Finally, recall that modernization is one of the causes of sociology itself. As Chapter 1 ("The Sociological Perspective") explained, the discipline originated in the wake of the Industrial Revolution in Western Europe, at a time and place where social change was proceeding most intensely. Early European and American sociologists attempted to describe and explain the rise of modern society and its consequences—both good and bad—for human beings.

Ferdinand Toennies: The Loss of Community

The German sociologist Ferdinand Toennies, who is introduced in the box, produced a highly influential account of modernization, detailed in Chapter 21 ("Population and Urbanization"). Like Peter Berger, whose work he influenced, Toennies viewed modernization as the progressive loss of human community, or *Gemeinschaft*, which provided personal ties, a sense of group membership, and loyalty within small communities. The Industrial Revolution undermined this strong social fabric by introducing a businesslike emphasis on facts and efficiency. European and North American societies gradually became rootless and impersonal and people came to associate mostly on the basis of self-interest—a state Toennies called *Gesellschaft* (1963; orig. 1887).

Much of North America early in this century approximated Toennies's concept of *Gemeinschaft*. Families that had lived in small villages and towns for many generations were tightly integrated into a hard-working, slow-moving way of life. This social world was circumscribed in space as well as in its way of life. Telephones (invented in 1876) were rare even after 1915, when the first coast-to-coast call made history. Living without television (introduced in 1939 and rare until the 1950s), families entertained themselves, often gathering with friends in the evening—much like Brazil's Kaiapo—to share stories, sorrows, or song. Without rapid transportation (although Henry Ford's assembly line began in 1908, cars became common only after World War II), many people thought of their own town as their entire world.

PROFILE

Ferdinand Toennies (1855–1936)

Can traditional human virtues such as selflessness and honor survive in the modern world? This question guided the work of Ferdinand Toennies, who, along with Max Weber and Georg Simmel, helped to establish sociology as an academic discipline in Germany.

Born to a wealthy family in the German countryside, Toennies received an extensive education. He also learned a great deal from observing the world about him—especially how the Industrial Revolution was transforming Germany and other European countries. Toennies's work reveals a deep concern with the common-sense notion of "progress"; he had serious qualms about whether "progress" was actually improving the quality of life in modern societies. His influential book *Gemeinschaft and*

Gesellschaft (1963; orig. 1887) is therefore both a chronicle of modernization and an indictment of an increasingly impersonal world.

Toennies's thesis is that traditional societies, built on kinship and

neighborhood, nourish collective sentiments, morality, and honor. Modernization washes across traditional society like an acid, eroding human community and unleashing rampant individualism. Toennies stopped short of asserting that modern society was in a basic sense "worse" than societies of the past, and he made a point of praising the spread of rational, scientific thinking. Nevertheless, the growing individualism and selfishness of modern society troubled him considerably. Knowing there could be no return to the past, he looked to the future, hoping that perhaps some new form of social organization would combine traditional collective responsibility and modern rationality.

SOURCE: Based on Cahnman & Heberle (1971).

Inevitable tensions and conflicts—sometimes based on race, ethnicity, and religion—characterized small communities of the past. According to Toennies, however, the traditional ties of *Gemeinschaft* bound people of a community together, "essentially united in spite of all separating factors" (1963:65).

Modern societies are closer to Toennies's concept of *Gesellschaft*, in which people are "essentially separated in spite of uniting factors" (1963:65). In large cities, for example, most people live among strangers, and ignore people they pass on the street.

An important contributor to a sense of rootlessness in neighborhoods is our high level of geographic mobility. Table 23-1 on page 650 shows that one in six households in either Canada or the United States reported moving during the previous year, with over 85 percent of the moves taking place within provincial or state boundaries. Table 23-2 reveals that, when residential mobility is measured over either a one- or a five-year period, people between the ages of 20 and 34 are most likely to have moved—over a five-year interval between 60 and 70 percent have done so. The high level of mobility in the youngest age categories is prob-

ably due to the search for larger accommodation by the 20- to 34-year-old parents of these small children. The General Social Survey (1985) reveals that the most frequently stated reasons for the moves to the respondents' current homes were: 1) to puchase or build a home; 2) to live in a larger home; 3) to live in a better neighborhood; 4) to live near work; and 5) to establish an independent household. Each of these top-ranked reasons is consistent with movement among 20- to 34-year-olds, who are leaving the homes of their parents, getting married, and having children.

Modern life is not completely devoid of *Gemeinschaft*. Even in a world of strangers, friendships are often strong and lasting. Traditions are especially pronounced in many ethnic neighborhoods where residents maintain their local community ties. But in cosmopolitan districts of large cities, an indifference to those outside of an immediate circle—the attitude that disturbed Toennies in the 1880s—continues to pose an ethical dilemma today.

Critical evaluation. Toennies's theory of *Gemeinschaft* and *Gesellschaft* is the most widely cited model

William Kurelek's painting All Things Betrayest Thee Who Betrayest Me *is an unforgettable evocation of the anxiety-ridden solitude afflicting the modern person divorced from traditional support systems of human community, what Ferdinand Toennies called* Gemeinschaft. *The title of the painting comes from a line in Francis Thompson's poem "The Hound of Heaven."*

TABLE 23-1   MOVING ON IN CANADA AND THE UNITED STATES

	Canada	United States
Place of Residence One Year Ago		
	1990–91	1989–90
Same House	83.6	82.1
Different House/ Same Province or State	14.3	13.9
Different House/ Different Province or State	1.2	3.3
Different House/ Different Country	0.9	0.7

SOURCES: U.S. Census Bureau, Geographical Mobility; Statistics Canada, Cat. No. 93-322.

TABLE 23-2   CANADIAN MOBILITY STATUS BY AGE GROUP (DIFFERENT PLACE OF RESIDENCE ONE AND FIVE YEARS AGO)

Percentage Movers in Each Age Category		
	1990–91	1986–91
Total Population*	16.4	46.7
1–4 years	21.4	n.a.
5–9 years	15.4	56.5
10–14 years	12.1	46.5
15–19 years	15.8	40.0
20–24 years	34.7	60.2
25–34 years	27.2	71.9
35–44 years	14.0	48.2
45–54 years	9.1	32.9
55–64 years	6.9	26.2
65 and over	5.8	22.2

* Mobility status is measured by recording a change of address from June 4, 1990, to June 4, 1991 (left column), or from June 4, 1986, to June 4, 1991 (right column). The left column is based upon individuals one year of age and over, since those who are under one year of age did not have an address on June 4, 1990. Similarly, the right column is baded upon the population 5 years of age and older: younger individuals were not yet born on June 4, 1986.
SOURCE: Statistics Canada, Cat. No. 93-322.

for describing modernization. The theory's strength lies in its synthesis of various dimensions of change—growing population, the rise of cities, greater impersonality. However, Toennies's approach falls short by failing to specify which factors are cause and which are effect. Critics have also asserted that Toennies favored—perhaps even romanticized—traditional societies.

Emile Durkheim: The Division of Labor

The French sociologist Emile Durkheim, whose work is discussed in Chapter 4 ("Society"), shared Toennies's interest in the profound social changes wrought by the Industrial Revolution. For Durkheim, modernization is marked by the increasing *division of labor*, or specialized economic activity, that accompanies industrialization (1964b; orig. 1893). Whereas everyone in traditional societies performs similar daily activities, modern societies function by having people carry out highly distinctive roles.

Durkheim claimed that members of preindustrial societies are held together by *mechanical solidarity*—

social bonds that result from shared moral sentiments and a sense that everyone is basically alike and belongs together. Mechanical solidarity depends on a minimal division of labor so that, guided by tradition, everyone's life is basically the same. Durkheim's mechanical solidarity mirrors Toennies's *Gemeinschaft.*

As the division of labor becomes more pronounced, a society develops *organic solidarity*—bonds of mutual dependency based on specialization. In simple terms, modern societies lose their bonds of likeness but, in the process, discover a new source of solidarity in their differences. Now specialized in their pursuits, people find that they are dependent on others to meet most of their needs. Organic solidarity corresponds to Toennies's concept of *Gesellschaft*.

Despite obvious similarities, Durkheim and Toennies interpreted modernity somewhat differently. To Toennies, modern *Gesellschaft* lacks social solidarity—the inevitable result of the gradual change from "natural" and "organic" traditions of the rural past to the "artificial" and "mechanical" life of contemporary, industrial cities. Durkheim disagreed, maintaining that the modern city is no less natural than the village. He made this point by reversing Toennies's language: labeling modern society as "organic" and traditional societies as "mechanical" because they were so regimented. Thus Durkheim viewed modernization not so much as a loss of community as a *change* in the basis of community—from bonds of likeness (kinship and neighborhood) to economic interdependence (the division of labor). Durkheim's view of modernity is both more complex and more positive than that of Toennies.

Critical evaluation. Durkheim's work stands alongside that of Toennies, which it closely resembles, as a highly influential analysis of modernity. Of the two, Durkheim is clearly the more optimistic; still, he feared that modern societies would become so internally diverse that they would collapse into *anomie*, a condition in which norms and values are so weak and inconsistent that society provides little moral guidance to individuals. As noted in Chapter 4 ("Society"), modern individuals prone to anomie will tend toward egocentrism, placing their own needs above those of others.

Evidence supports Durkheim's contention that anomie plagues modern societies. Suicide rates, which Durkheim considered a prime index of anomie, have risen during this century in both Canada and the U.S.: in Canada, the rates have doubled. In 1986 there were 22.8 suicides per 100,000 Canadian males, whereas females commit suicide at a much lower rate (6.4). Older men (aged 70 and over) committed suicide at a rate of 34.9 per 100,000. Among Native people, especially males, rates are more than double those of the general population. There were 56.3 suicides for every 100,000 Native men (1986) and more than 100 per 100,000 among Native males aged 15–29 (Beneteau, 1990). These figures are consistent with increases in *anomie* resulting from rapid social change, a breakdown in normative structures, and reduced social solidarity.

Even though modernization is associated with numerous indicators of stress or distress, shared norms and values are still strong enough to give the majority of people a sense of meaning and purpose. Despite the hazards of anomie and atomization, most people seem to value the privacy and personal autonomy that modern society affords.

Max Weber: Rationalization

Max Weber held that ideas and beliefs stand out as causes of social change; his thesis is detailed in Chapter 4 ("Society"). For Weber, then, modernity amounts to the progressive replacement of a traditional world view by a rational way of thinking.

In preindustrial societies, tradition acts as a constant brake to change. To traditional people, "truth" is roughly synonymous with *what has always been* (1978:36; orig. 1921). In modern societies, however, people see truth as the product of deliberate calculation. Because they value efficiency more than reverence for the past, individuals embrace whatever new social patterns allow them to achieve their goals. A rational view of the world, then, leads people to seek out and assess various options according to their specific consequences rather than according to any absolute standard of rightness.

Echoing the claim of Toennies and Durkheim that industrialization weakens tradition, Weber declared that modern society had become "disenchanted." What were once unquestioned truths have become subject to matter-of-fact calculations in a more rational world. Embracing rational, scientific thought, in short, modern society turns away from the gods.

Weber's work thus explores various modern "types"—notably the capitalist, the scientist, and the bureaucrat—all of whom share the rational and detached world view he believed was coming to dominate human interaction.

Critical evaluation. Compared with Toennies, and especially Durkheim, Weber was a profound critic of modern society. He recognized that science could produce technological wonders, yet he worried that it was carrying us away from more basic questions about the meaning and purpose of human existence. Weber feared that rationalization, especially in bureaucracies, would erode the human spirit with endless rules and regulations.

Some critics of Weber maintained that the alienation he attributed to bureaucracy actually stems from social inequality. This contention leads us to the ideas of Karl Marx.

Karl Marx: Capitalism

While other analysts of modernity examined shifting patterns of social order, Marx focused on social conflict. For Marx, modern society was synonymous with capitalism; in his view, the Industrial Revolution was primarily a *capitalist revolution*. As Chapter 4 ("Society") explained, Marx asserted that the bourgeoisie emerged in medieval Europe as a social class intent on wresting control of society from the feudal nobility. The bourgeoisie were finally successful when the Industrial Revolution placed a powerful new productive system under their control.

Marx agreed that modernity weakened small-scale communities (as described by Toennies), increased the division of labor (as noted by Durkheim), and fostered a rational world view (as asserted by Weber). But he saw these factors simply as conditions necessary for capitalism to flourish. Capitalism draws people from farms and small towns into an ever-expanding market system centered in the cities; specialization underlies efficient factories; and rationality is exemplified by the capitalist's relentless quest for profits.

Earlier chapters painted Marx as a spirited critic of capitalist society, but his vision of modernity also contains significant optimism. Unlike Weber, who viewed modern society as an "iron cage" of bureaucracy, Marx believed that social conflict in capitalist social systems would produce revolutionary social change and, ultimately, lead to an egalitarian form of socialism. Such a society, he claimed, would allow the wonders of

industrial technology to enrich the lives of the many rather than the few—and thereby rid the world of the prime source of social conflict and dehumanization. While Marx's evaluation of modern capitalist society was highly negative, then, he envisioned a future with greater human freedom, blossoming human creativity, and a renewed sense of human community.

Critical evaluation.   Marx's theory of modernization draws together many threads of change in a fabric dominated by capitalism. Yet Marx may have underestimated the significance of bureaucracy in shaping modern societies. The stifling effects on humanity of centralized bureaucracy in socialist societies may, in fact, be worse than the dehumanizing impacts of capitalism. The recent upheavals in Eastern Europe and the former Soviet Union reveal the depth of popular opposition to entrenched bureaucracies.

Understanding Modernity: The Theory of Mass Society

The rise of modernity is a complex process involving many transformations, described in previous chapters and summarized in Table 23-3. How is one to make sense of so many changes going on all at once? One broad approach—drawing on the ideas of Toennies, Durkheim, and Weber—understands modernization as the formation of *mass societies* (Dahrendorf, 1959; Kornhauser, 1959; Nisbet, 1966, 1969; Baltzell, 1968; Stein, 1972; Berger, Berger, & Kellner, 1974).

Formally defined, a **mass society** is *a society in which industrialization proceeds and bureaucracy expands while traditional social ties grow weaker.* A mass society emerges with the erosion of traditional kinship and neighborhood. Socially atomized, the members of modern societies typically experience feelings of uncertainty and personal powerlessness.

Why? Because, first, the scale of modern life increases to the point that impersonality and cultural diversity overwhelm the individual and drain meaning from people's lives. Second, the government expands to the extent that it manages many aspects of daily life, taking over tasks that used to be carried out by strong families and cohesive neighborhoods (like social welfare programs for the indigent and care of the elderly). In place of kith and kin, in short, we now contend with the directives of strangers—often nameless officials in distant and unresponsive bureaucracies. We now take a closer look at each of these two arguments.

A sure sign of modernization is that people shun traditional activities such as farming in favor of specialized productive roles. Hoping to secure a day's work in Mexico City, these men offer their services as electricians, contractors, painters, and plumbers.

TABLE 23-3   TRADITIONAL AND MODERN SOCIETIES: DIMENSIONS OF DIFFERENCE

	Characteristics of Traditional Societies	Characteristics of Modern Societies
Scale of Life		
	Small scale; population typically small and widely dispersed in rural villages and small towns	Large scale; population typically large and concentrated in cities
Cultural Patterns		
Values	Homogeneous; sacred character; few subcultures and countercultures	Heterogeneous; secular character; many subcultures and countercultures
Norms	High moral significance; little tolerance of diversity	Variable moral significance; high tolerance of diversity
Orientation	Present linked to past	Present linked to future
Technology	Preindustrial; human and animal energy	Industrial; advanced energy sources
Social Structure		
Status and role	Few statuses, most ascribed; few specialized roles	Many statuses, some ascribed and some achieved; many specialized roles
Relationships	Typically primary; little anonymity and privacy	Typically secondary; considerable anonymity and privacy
Communication	Face-to-face	Face-to-face communication supplemented by mass media
Social control	Informal gossip	Formal police and legal system
Social stratification	Rigid patterns of social inequality; little mobility	Fluid patterns of social inequality; considerable mobility
Gender patterns	Pronounced patriarchy; women's lives centered on the home	Declining patriarchy; increasing number of women in the paid labor force
Family	Extended family as the primary means of socialization and economic production	Nuclear family retains some socialization function but is more a unit of consumption than of production
Religion	Religion guides world view; little religious pluralism	Religion weakens with the rise of science; extensive religious pluralism
Education	Formal schooling limited to elites	Basic schooling becomes universal, with growing proportion receiving advanced education
State	Small-scale government; little state intervention into society	Large-scale government; considerable state intervention into society
Economy	Based on agriculture; some manufacturing within the home; little white-collar work	Based on industrial mass production; factories become centers of production; increasing white-collar work
Health	High birth and death rates; brief life expectancy because of low standard of living and simple medical technology	Low birth and death rates; longer life expectancy because of higher standard of living and complex medical technology
Social Change		
	Slow; change evident over many generations	Rapid; change evident within a single generation

Expanding Scale of Social Life

Mass-society theory argues, first, that the scale of modern life has increased exponentially. Before the Industrial Revolution, Europe and North America formed an intricate mosaic of countless rural villages and small towns. In these small communities, which inspired Toennies's concept of *Gemeinschaft*, people lived out their lives surrounded by kin and guided by a shared heritage. In these communities, gossip was an informal, yet highly effective, means of ensuring rigid conformity to community standards. Limited community size, social isolation, and a strong, traditional religion combined to generate cultural homogeneity—the mechanical solidarity described by Durkheim. For example, in England before 1690, law and local custom demanded that everyone regularly participate in the Christian ritual of Holy Communion (Laslett, 1984). Because social differences were repressed, subcultures and countercultures rarely flourished and the pace of social change was slow. Also, social position was more or less set at birth, with little social mobility.

A surge in population, the growth of cities, and the specialization of economic activity during the Industrial Revolution gradually changed all this. People came to be known by their function (for example, as the "doctor" or the "bank clerk") rather than by their kinship group or hometown. The majority of people regarded others simply as a mass of strangers. The face-to-face communication of the village was eventually replaced by the mass media—newspapers, radio, and television—that only furthered the process of social atomization. Large organizations steadily assumed more and more responsibility for daily needs that had once been fulfilled by family, friends, and neighbors; universal public education enlarged the scope of learning; police, lawyers, and courts supervised a formal criminal justice system. Even charity became the work of faceless bureaucrats working for the Red Cross, large voluntary associations, and various public welfare agencies.

Geographical mobility, mass communications, and exposure to diverse ways of life undermined traditional values. Less certain about what was worth believing, people became more tolerant of social diversity, more and more trumpeting the merits of individual rights and freedom of choice. Subcultures and countercultures multiplied. Making categorical distinctions among people fell out of favor; to treat someone a particular way based on race, sex, or religion came to be defined as backwards and unjust. In the process, minorities who had long lived at the margins of society gained greater power and broader participation. Yet, mass-society theorists fear, transforming people of various backgrounds into a generic mass may end up dehumanizing everyone.

The Rise of the State

In the small-scale, preindustrial societies of Europe, government amounted to little more than a local noble, who had limited control over the population. A royal family formally reigned over an entire nation but, without efficient transportation or communication, the power of even absolute monarchs fell far short of that wielded by today's political leaders.

Technological innovation allowed government to expand, and the centralized state grew in size and importance. At the time of confederation, government, either federal or provincial, had limited functions. Since then, government has entered more and more areas of social life—establishing publicly-owned enterprises in the areas of transportation, communication and natural resources, regulating wages and working conditions, establishing standards for products of all kinds, educating the population, delivering medical care, protecting the environment, and providing financial assistance to the ill, the aged, and the unemployed. Taxes have correspondingly soared, so that today's average worker labors for six months a year merely to pay for various government services.

In a mass society, power resides in large bureaucracies, leaving people in local communities little control over their lives. For example, government officials mandate that local schools must have a standardized educational program, local products must be government-inspected and carry government-approved labels, and every citizen must maintain extensive records for purposes of taxation. While such regulations may protect people and enhance uniformity of treatment, they depersonalize human decision making and limit the autonomy of neighborhoods, families, and individuals.

Critical evaluation.   The theory of mass society acknowledges that the transformation of small-scale societies has positive aspects, but tends to see in historical change the loss of an irreplaceable heritage. Modern societies increase individual rights, magnify tolerance for social differences, and raise standards of living. But they seem prone to what Max Weber feared most—excessive bureaucracy—as well as to Toennies's self-centeredness and to Emile Durkheim's anomie. Their size, complexity, and tolerance of diversity all but doom traditional values and family patterns, leaving individuals isolated, powerless, and materialistic.

Critics of mass-society theory contend that it

romanticizes the past. They remind us that many people in the small towns of Canada's past were actually quite eager to set out for a better life in the cities. And who would actually wish to give up the improved standard of living that industrial technology has made possible? Another limitation of the mass-society approach is that it offers little praise for deliberate efforts to lessen social inequality. Mass-society analysis, critics claim, attracts support from social and economic conservatives who defend conventional morality and capitalist values, while showing indifference to the historical plight of women and other minorities.

Understanding Modernity: The Theory of Class Society

A second interpretation of modernity derives largely from the ideas of Karl Marx. From this point of view, modernity takes the form of a **class society**, *a capitalist society with pronounced social stratification*. According to this theory, the widespread feelings of powerlessness in modern society stem from pervasive social inequality. While this approach concurs that modern societies have grown to a mass scale, class-society theorists claim that the heart of modernization is an expanding capitalist economy. Inherent in capitalist societies are pronounced inequality and social conflict, even if the extent of inequality has diminished to some degree compared to what it was a century ago (Miliband, 1969; Habermas, 1970; Clement, 1975: Polenberg, 1980; Blumberg, 1981; Harrington, 1984; Brym, 1985)

Capitalism

Class-society theory holds that the increasing scale of social life in modern times has resulted from the insatiable appetite of capitalism. Because a capitalist economy pursues ever-increasing profits, both production and consumption expand as long as there is money to be made. Marx considered the Industrial Revolution to be a significant stage in the enlarging capitalist economic system.

According to Marx, capitalism emphasizes "naked self-interest" and individual greed (1972:337; orig. 1848). This self-centeredness undermines the social ties that once cemented small-scale communities. Capitalism also fosters impersonality and anonymity by transforming people into commodities, both as a source of labor and a market for capitalist production. The net

result is that capitalism reduces human beings to cogs in the machinery of material production.

Science, the key to greater productivity, also serves as a modern ideology to justify capitalism. In preindustrial Europe, the nobility defended their right to rule with traditional notions of moral obligation and responsibility. In modern societies, capitalists legitimize their way of life by encouraging people to view their own well-being as a *technical* puzzle to be solved by engineers and other experts rather than through the pursuit of social justice (Habermas, 1970). A capitalist culture, for example, encourages us to find the solution to illness in scientific medicine rather than in eliminating poverty, which for many people undermines health in the first place.

Businesses also raise the banner of scientific logic when they claim that efficiency is achieved only through continual growth. As Chapter 19 ("The Economy and Work") explained, capitalist corporations have reached enormous size and control almost unimaginable wealth. Nevertheless, to increase profits even more, they have gained "global reach" by becoming multinationals that operate throughout the world. From the class-society point of view, then, the expanding scale of life is not so much a function of *Gesellschaft* as it is the inevitable and destructive consequence of capitalism.

The Persistence of Social Inequality

Modernity has gradually eroded some of the rigid categorical distinctions that divided preindustrial societies. Class-society theory maintains, however, that elites persist albeit in a different form: capitalist millionaires, rather than family-based nobility, now occupy society's highest echelons. Canada, as economist Diane Francis (1986) points out, has more billionaire families per capita than does the United States: Canada has six, while the U.S. (with an economy twelve times larger) has only double that number (i.e., twelve billionaire families). Furthermore, the distribution of family income is clearly skewed in Canada: from 1951 to 1985, with minor fluctuations, families in the top 20 percent earned about 40 percent of all income while the bottom fifth earned just over 6 percent (Fréchette, 1988).

Clearly, a small minority continues to enjoy great wealth while many people live in a state of desperate poverty. What of the state, which mass-society theory suggests has an expanding role in combating social problems? Marx was skeptical that government could accomplish more than minor reforms. The capitalist state, he reasoned, could not bring about meaningful change because it was designed to protect the wealth and privileges of capitalists. Other class-society theorists add that, while it may be true that working people and minorities enjoy greater political rights and economic benefits today than in years past, these changes are the fruits of political struggle, not expressions of government benevolence. And, they continue, despite our pretensions of democracy, power still rests primarily in the hands of those with money.

Critical evaluation. Table 23-4 spells out key differences in the interpretations of modernity offered by class-society theory and mass-society theory. In place of mass-society theory's focus on the increasing scale of social life and the rise of large organizations, class-society theory stresses the expansion of capitalism and persistent social inequality. Class-society theory also dismisses Durkheim's argument that people in modern societies suffer from moral collapse and anomie. Instead, in this view, the malaise of modern life has as its roots alienation and powerlessness.

Critics of the class-society approach point out that this theory implies that a centralized economy would cure the ills of modern living. But few people would argue that socialism, at least in its various expressions around the world, has proved itself capable of generating a high standard of living. Furthermore, many social problems found in Canada —including unemployment, homelessness, industrial pollution, and unresponsive government—were commonplace in the formerly socialist nations of Eastern Europe and in the former Soviet Union.

Modernity and the Individual

Both mass- and class-society theories focus on broad patterns of social change since the Industrial Revolution. Each "macro-level" approach also offers "micro-level" insights into how modernity shapes individual lives.

Mass Society: Problems of Identity

Modernity liberated individuals from small, tightly knit communities of the past. In historical context, most people in today's modern societies possess unprecedented privacy and freedom to express their individuality. Mass-society theory suggests, however, that extensive social diversity, atomization, and rapid social

TABLE 23-4 TWO INTERPRETATIONS OF MODERNITY: A SUMMARY

	Key Process of Modernization	Key Effects of Modernization
Mass-society theory	Industrialization; growth of bureaucracy	Increasing scale of life; rise of the state and other formal organizations
Class-society theory	Rise of capitalism	Expansion of capitalist economy; persistence of social inequality

change make it difficult for many people to establish any internally coherent identity at all (Wheelis, 1958; Riesman, 1970; Berger, Berger, & Kellner, 1974). Canadians have had considerable difficulty articulating a national identity—and, indirectly, personal identities—to the point where Lipset (1991:42) states that national identity "is the quintessential Canadian issue." Proximity to the United States, regional tensions, ethnic and cultural diversity, bilingualism, and rapid social change make clear self-definition more difficult for Canadians (Hiller, 1991; Taras, Rasporich & Mandel, 1993).

Chapter 5 ("Socialization") explained that people forge distinctive personalities based on their social experience. The small, homogeneous, and slowly changing societies of the past gave each member a firm foundation for building a meaningful personal identity. For example, the Hutterite communities that still flourish in Canada's prairie provinces (in Alberta in particular) provide their members with strong historical, religious, and cultural roots. Their young people know the meaning of being Hutterite—that is, they understand how they should think and behave—and most learn to embrace this life as "natural" and right. Everything is shared in common—property, work, meals—in these tiny communal societies that have perpetuated the Hutterite way of life, largely unchanged, for over 400 years. Under these circumstances, which contrast sharply with those of modern mass society, it is relatively easy to establish a coherent and secure sense of personal identity.

Mass societies, with their characteristic diversity and rapid change, provide only shifting sands on which to build a personal identity. Left to make their own life decisions, people confront a bewildering range of options. Autonomy has little value without standards for making choices; in a tolerant mass society, no one path seems more compelling than the next. Not surprisingly, many people shuttle from one identity to another, changing their lifestyle in search of an elusive "true self." They may join one or another social movement in search of purpose and belonging, and even experiment with various religions hoping to find a system of beliefs that "fits" them. This difficulty in developing an identity is not psychological, although it is often treated as an individual problem. Rather, many people grappling with modern life suffer from the widespread "relativism" of their society, unsure which way the moral compass points because they have lost the security and direction once made clear by tradition.

For David Riesman (1970; orig. 1950), modernization brings on changes in **social character**, that is, *personality patterns common to members of a society.* Preindustrial societies promote what Riesman terms **tradition-directedness**, *rigid personalities based on conformity to time-honored ways of living.* Members of traditional societies model their lives on what has gone before so that what is "good" is equivalent to "what has always been." Tradition-directedness, then, brings to the level of individual experience Toennies's *Gemeinschaft* and Durkheim's mechanical solidarity. Tradition-directed character makes people culturally conservative so that they think and act alike. Unlike the conformity found in modern societies, this uniformity is not an attempt to mimic one another. Instead, because everyone draws on the same cultural foundation, defined as the one proper way to live, homogeneity is the result. Hutterite women and men exemplify people with tradition-directed character; in the Hutterite culture, conformity ties ancestors and their descendents in an unbroken chain of communal living as ordained by God.

A tradition-directed personality is likely to be defined as deviant by members of a diverse and rapidly changing society. Modern people, by and large, prize personal flexibility, the capacity to adapt, and sensitivity. Riesman calls this type of social character **other-directedness**, *highly variable personality patterns among people open to change and likely to imitate the behavior of others.* Because their socialization occurs within societies that are continuously in flux, other-directed people typically display greater superficiality, inconsistency, and change. They try on different roles and identities, sometimes like so many pieces of new clothing, and engage in various "performances" as they move from setting to setting (Goffman, 1959). In a traditional society, such "shiftiness" marks a person as untrustworthy, but in a modern society, the ability to

fit in virtually anywhere is a valued personal trait (Wheelis, 1958).

In societies that value the up-to-date rather than the traditional, people look to members of their own generation as significant role models rather than looking up to their elders. Following the same reasoning, "peer pressure" can sometimes seem irresistible to people with no enduring standards to guide them. Our society urges individuals to be true to themselves. But when social surroundings change so rapidly, how can people determine to which self they should be true? This problem is at the root of the identity crisis so widespread in industrial societies today. "Who am I?" is a question that many of us struggle to answer. Many Canadians will answer this question in the negative, saying only that they are "*not* American". In sociological terms, this personal problem doesn't reflect a personal crisis but rather the inherent complexity and instability of modern mass society.

Class Society: Problems of Powerlessness

Class-society theory paints a different picture of modernity's effects on individuals. This approach maintains that persistent social inequality undermines modern society's promise of individual freedom. For some, modernity delivers great privilege, but for others, modern life means coping every day with powerlessness. For visible minorities and the Native population in particular, the challenges of modern life are typically even greater. Similarly, women enjoy increasing participation in modern societies, but they continue to run up against the traditional barrier of sexism. Elderly people as well encounter the impediment of ageism. In short, this approach rejects mass-society theory's claim that people suffer from too much freedom. Instead, class-society theory holds that a majority of people in societies like Canada are still denied full participation in social life.

Class-society theorists hail the struggle to empower individuals, which has been gaining strength. For example, employees seek greater control of the workplace, consumers press for more say in the marketplace, and citizens try to make government more responsive to their needs (Toffler, 1981). On a global scale, as Chapter 11 ("Global Inequality") explained, the expanding scope of world capitalism has placed more of the earth's population under the influence of multinational corporations. As a result, about two-thirds of the world's income is concentrated in the richest societies, which contain only about 15 percent of its people. Class-society theorists therefore ask: Is it any wonder that throughout the Third World people are also seeking greater power to shape their own lives?

Such problems led Herbert Marcuse (1964) to challenge Max Weber's contention that modern society is rational. Marcuse labels modern society irrational because it fails to meet the basic needs of so many people. While modern capitalist societies produce unparalleled wealth, poverty remains the daily plight of millions and, in global terms, billions of people. Moreover, Marcuse argues, technological advances rarely empower people; instead, technology tends to reduce their control over their own lives. High technology generally means that a corps of specialists—not the vast majority of people themselves—control events and dominate discussion, whether the issue is energy production for communities or health care for individuals. Specialists define ordinary people as ill-equipped for decision making, so that the public learns to defer to elites of one kind or another. And elites, from this point of view, have little concern for the common interest. Despite the popular view that technology *solves* the world's problems, Marcuse concludes, it may be more accurate to say it *causes* them. In sum, class-society theory asserts that people suffer because modern societies have concentrated both wealth and power in the hands of a privileged few.

Mass-society theory explains the collapse of the social fabric as the result of rapid social change and the erosion of tradition. Class-society theory, by contrast, suggests that social inequality diminishes the likelihood of meaningful human community.

Modernity and Progress

In modern societies, most people expect—and applaud—social change. People link modernity to the idea of *progress* (from Latin, meaning "a moving forward"), a state of continual improvement. By contrast, we denigrate stability as a form of stagnation.

This chapter began by describing the Kaiapo of Brazil, for whom affluence has broadened opportunities but weakened traditional heritage. In examining the Kaiapo, we notice that social change is too complex to be simply equated with progress. More precisely, whether or not we see a given change as progress depends on our underlying values. A rising standard of living among the Kaiapo—or, historically, among Canadians—has helped make lives longer and more comfortable. But affluence has also fueled materialism at the expense of spiritual life, creating ambivalence toward change in the minds of many people.

Modern society's recognition of basic human rights is valued by most people. The assertion that individuals have rights simply by virtue of their humanity is a distinctly modern idea that can be found in the *Canadian Charter of Rights and Freedoms,* the American *Declaration of Independence* and the United Nations' *Declaration of Human Rights.* But, as Chapter 3 ("Culture") explained, we now have something of a "culture of rights" that often overlooks the duties and obligations we have to one another. The contrast between the modern idea of individual dignity and the traditional notion of personal duty and honor is highlighted in the box on page 659.

In principle, the idea that individuals should have considerable autonomy in shaping their own lives has wide support in Canada. Thus many people will applaud the demise of traditional conceptions of honor as progress. Yet, as people exercise their freedom of choice, they inevitably challenge social patterns cherished by those who maintain a more traditional lifestyle. For example, people may choose not to marry. Some may remain single, others may live with someone without marrying, have children outside of marriage, or form partnerships with members of their own sex. To those who support individual choice, such changes symbolize progress; to those who value traditional family patterns, however, these developments signal societal decay (Wallis, 1985).

Even technological advance has controversial aspects. Rapid transportation and efficient communication have improved our lives in many respects. However, complex technology has also weakened traditional attachments to hometowns and even to family. Industrial technology has also unleashed an unprecedented threat to the natural environment and, in the form of nuclear weapons, imperiled the future of humanity. In short, then, social change gives rise to uncertainty, unforeseen complexity, and controversy, making sweeping assumptions about the modern world—whether ringing endorsements of "progress" or stinging indictments of unfamiliar new social forms—risky at best.

Modernization in Global Perspective

Sometimes social change proceeds haphazardly, sometimes deliberately. Some change that is desperately needed has not occurred at all, as in much of the Third World, where almost 1 billion people struggle daily against life-threatening poverty.

Two competing views of the causes of global poverty were presented in Chapter 11 ("Global Inequality"). *Modernization theory* claims that in the past the entire world was poor and that technological change, especially the Industrial Revolution, has enhanced human productivity and raised living standards. From this point of view, the solution to global poverty lies in encouraging technological development in less developed regions.

For reasons suggested earlier, however, global modernization may be difficult. Recall that David Riesman portrayed preindustrial people as *tradition-directed*. By embracing a way of life rooted in the past, they may resist change. According to modernization theory, the world's rich societies should deliberately intervene in poor societies to encourage productive innovation.

Traditional Honor and Modern Dignity

Honor occupies about the same place in contemporary usage as chastity. An individual asserting it hardly invites admiration, and one who claims to have lost it is an object of amusement rather than sympathy (1974:83). Honor is a human virtue that seems distinctly out of place in modern society. Honor means acting according to traditional cultural norms. Since traditional norms varied for different categories of humanity, honor also means behaving like the kind of person you are. Men and women gain honor by acting differently, for example. *He* is expected to act protectively toward *her*, while *she* is expected to be mindful of traditional norms including the need to defer graciously to *him*. Honor, in short, cannot be separated from strong morality and rigid social distinctions—between men and women, nobles and serfs, one's own family and outsiders. Through conformity, however, honor is available to people of every social station. During the Middle Ages, European nobles claimed honor when they per-

formed their feudal obligations toward their social inferiors and displayed proper respect for their peers. Similarly, commoners acted honorably when they fulfilled their duties to their superiors and everyone else.

With modernization, cultural norms have become weaker and more variable, and categorical distinctions among people have been challenged by drives for social equality. Modern culture holds that all people should be treated as social equals. Therefore, although the concept of honor survives among some ethnic categories and traditional occupations, such as the military, it has less appeal to most members of modern societies.

Modernization enhances concern for people as *individuals*, which is expressed in the concept of *dignity*. Whereas various categories of people have distinctive codes of honor, dignity is a universal human trait, originating in the inherent value of everyone. We recognize the dignity of others when we acknowledge our

common humanity by overlooking social differences.

In the spirit of modern dignity, women may object to men treating them as women rather than as individuals. The male practices of holding open a door for a woman and paying for a shared meal may be honorable in the traditional sense, but are more likely to be viewed as affronts to the dignity of women by underscoring social differences based on sex.

As a result, the significance of honor is fading in modern societies. The cultural diversity and rapid social change sweeping across modern societies makes traditional scripts for living suspect, at best. In contrast to codes of honor that guided human interaction in the past, human beings now value individual self-worth and aspirations to self-determination. This forms the essence of dignity.

SOURCE: Based on Berger, Berger, & Kellner (1974).

First-World nations must export technology to the Third World, welcome students from abroad, and provide foreign aid to stimulate economic development.

The review of modernization theory in Chapter 11 suggests that the success of these policies has been limited. Even where the greatest efforts have been made, resistance to change has compromised the results. Traditional people such as Brazil's Kaiapo have gained wealth by selling their resources on world markets, but only at the cost of being drawn into the "global village," where concern for money replaces traditional values. In some societies, notably some Islamic societies like Iran, rapid modernization has sparked a powerful backlash from segments seeking to restore traditional culture.

A daunting problem facing advocates of modernization theory, then, is that modernity may bring high-

The future of our world lies not in isolation, by which societies jealously protect their culture, nor in confederation, by which everyone enthusiastically embraces a single way of life. The challenge of the next century will be managing diversity, a skill made more necessary as communications technology, economic expansion, and the need to confront global problems draw the disparate peoples of the world closer together. In the emerging conversation of nations, we should not assume that the richest and most powerful societies of the world should do all the talking. On the contrary, the keys to long-term peace and ecological survival may well lie in rediscovering the many human truths that form the common sense of our more traditional neighbors.

er living standards but in the process sweep a society into a global mass culture of Western pop music, trendy clothes, and fast food. One Brazilian anthropologist expressed uncertainty about the future of the Kaiapo: "At least they quickly understood the consequences of watching television. . . . Now [they] can make a choice" (Simons, 1989:37).

But not everyone views modernization as a viable option. According to a second approach to global inequality, *dependency theory*, contemporary poor societies are at a distinct disadvantage even if they want to pursue modernization. From this point of view, the major barrier to economic development is not traditionalism but the global domination of rich, capitalist societies of the First World. Initially, as Chapter 11 ("Global Inequality") explained, this system took the form of colonialism, whereby European societies seized control of much of Latin America, Africa, and Asia. Trading relationships soon enriched England, Spain, and other colonial powers, as their colonies at the same time grew poorer. Almost all societies subjected to this form of domination are now politically independent, but colonial-style ties continue in the form of multinational corporations based in rich societies operating throughout the world.

In effect, dependency theory asserts, rich societies achieved their modernization at least partly at the expense of poor nations, which provided valuable resources and human labor. Even today, Third-World countries remain locked in a disadvantageous economic relationship with those of the First World, dependent on rich societies to buy their raw materials and in return provide them with whatever high-priced manufactured products they can afford. Continuing ties with rich societies appear likely to perpetuate current patterns of global inequality.

Dependency theory implies that social change occurs outside the control of individual societies. In this view, the fate and fortune of individual nations worldwide is tied to their position in the global economy. Thus, change to improve the plight of people in the Third World will require corresponding changes in First-World societies.

Whichever approach is found to be more convincing, we can no longer isolate the study of Canada from that of the rest of the world. At the beginning of the twentieth century, a majority of people in even the richest societies lived in relatively small settlements with limited awareness of others. Now, at the threshold of the twenty-first century, people everywhere participate in a far larger human drama. The world seems smaller because the lives of all its people are increasingly linked. We now discuss the relationships among societies in the same way that people a century ago talked about the expanding ties among towns and cities. Surely one of the essential tasks of the twenty-first century will be managing global diversity as the people of the world find their lives linked in more and more ways.

The century now coming to an end has witnessed unparalleled human achievement. Yet solutions to many of the timeless problems of human existence— including finding meaning in life, eradicating poverty, and resolving internal conflicts—remain elusive. To this list of pressing matters, new concerns have been added, such as managing the global environment and maintaining world peace. One source of optimism as we approach the twenty-first century is that we look ahead with an unprecedented understanding of human society.

Summary

1. Every society changes continuously, although with varying speed and consequences. Whether social change is intentional or unplanned, it is usually controversial.

2. Social change occurs in several ways, including the cultural processes of invention and discovery within a society, and cultural diffusion from one society to another. Another source of social change is found in social structure—tensions and conflicts within society itself. Patterns of culture and ways of thinking can either encourage or inhibit social change. Finally, the natural environment and population dynamics also influence the pace and direction of social change.

3. Modernity refers to the social consequences of industrialization. According to Peter Berger, the general characteristics of modernity are the weakening of small traditional communities, the expansion of personal choice, the increasing diversity in patterns of belief, and a keener awareness of time, especially the future.

4. Ferdinand Toennies described modernization as the transition from *Gemeinschaft* to *Gesellschaft*. This process signifies the progressive loss of community amid growing individualism.

5. Emile Durkheim linked modernization to an expanding division of labor. Mechanical solidarity, based on common activities and shared beliefs, gradually gives way to organic solidarity, in which specialization makes people interdependent.

6. Max Weber described the rise of modernity as the replacement of traditional patterns of thought by rationality. He feared that rational organization would dehumanize modern society.

7. According to Karl Marx, modernity amounts to the triumph of capitalism over feudalism. Viewing capitalist societies as fraught with social conflict, he anticipated revolutionary change leading to a more egalitarian socialist society.

8. In the view of mass-society theorists, modernity increases the scale of life and transfers to government and other formal organizations the responsibility for many tasks previously performed informally by the family and neighbors. Mass-society theory holds that cultural diversity and rapid social change lead individuals in modern societies to develop variable personal identities and to have difficulty finding certainty and meaning in their lives.

9. Class-society theory holds that capitalism underlies Western modernization. According to this approach, widespread powerlessness in modern societies stems from capitalism's propensity to concentrate wealth and power in the hands of a few.

10. People in industrialized countries commonly associate modernity with social progress. This simplistic view overlooks the often deleterious effects of social change. Social change is an exceedingly complex process; from any point of view, the consequences of modernity can be perceived as good and bad.

11. In a global context, modernization theory advocates intentional intervention to stimulate the development of poor societies. Advocates of this approach argue that global poverty primarily stems from traditionalism.

12. Dependency theory argues that a society's potential for development depends on its position in the world economic system. Poor Third-World societies are unlikely to duplicate the path to modernization of rich First-World societies because they have become dependent on these rich societies.

Key Concepts

class society a capitalist society with pronounced social stratification

mass society a society in which industrialization proceeds and bureaucracy expands while traditional social ties grow weaker

modernity patterns of social life linked to industrialization

modernization the process of social change initiated by industrialization

other-directedness highly variable personality patterns among people open to change and likely to imitate the behavior of others

social change the transformation of culture and social institutions over time

social character personality patterns common to members of a society

tradition-directedness rigid personalities based on conformity to time-honored ways of living

Suggested Readings

This paperback text surveys social change in a world perspective.
> Daniel Chirot. *Social Change in the Modern Era*. New York: Harcourt Brace Jovanovich, 1986.

This collection of articles by an unusually wide range of authors takes a fascinating look at the question of Canadian identity from national and regional perspectives.
> David Taras, Beverly Rasporich and Eli Mandel (eds.). *A Passion for Identity: An Introduction to Canadian Studies*. Scarborough, Ontario: Nelson, 1993.

Many people think of growth as inherently good. The notion of growth is hardly simple, however, as this book explains.
> Henry Teune. *Growth*. Newbury Park, CA: Sage, 1988.

The following highly readable books are filled with fascinating insights about the modern world.
> Peter Berger, Brigitte Berger, and Hansfried Kellner. *The Homeless Mind: Modernization and Consciousness*. New York: Vintage Books, 1974.
> Peter L. Berger. *Facing Up to Modernity: Excursions in Society, Politics, and Religion*. New York: Basic Books, 1977.

Here we grasp the implications of modernity through detailed comparisons with preindustrial England.
> Peter Laslett. *The World We Have Lost: England Before the Industrial Age*. 3rd ed. New York: Charles Scribner's Sons, 1984.

This article looks at class formation in Canada in comparison with the U.S., Sweden, Norway, and Finland, taking gender into account.
> Wallace Clement. "Comparative Class Analysis: Locating Canada in a North American and Nordic Context." *Canadian Review of Sociology and Anthropology* 27(4), 1990.

Many of the consequences of major events in history are unpredictable. This book examines changes in U.S. society—attitudes toward sex, gender, and homosexuality —that were part of the legacy of World War II.
> John Costello. *Virtue Under Fire: How World War II Changed Our Social and Sexual Attitudes*. Boston: Little, Brown, 1986.

These two books—the first a collection of articles by many well-known thinkers—delve into the implications of technological changes during this century and suggest likely future developments.
> Albert H. Teich, ed. *Technology and the Future*. 5th ed. New York: St. Martin's Press, 1990.
> O.B. Hardison, Jr. *Disappearing Through the Skylight: Culture and Technology in the Twentieth Century*. New York: Viking, 1989.

This very readable study deals with the experience of people, long caught in impoverished rural areas, who are finally forced to migrate to urban areas to seek a livelihood.
> S.D. Clark. *The New Urban Poor*. Toronto: McGraw-Hill Ryerson, 1978.

This book is about those "other Canadians who refuse to accept the urban dream and goal" and are left behind in the retreat from rural areas.

Ralph Matthews. *"There's No Better Place than Here": Social Change in Three Newfoundland Communities.* Toronto: Peter Martin Associates, 1978.

This book examines social change in traditional societies with a focus on music: how Western music is influencing traditional musical patterns in a number of countries.

Bruno Nettl. *The Western Impact on World Music: Change, Adaptation, and Survival.* New York: Schirmer Books, 1985.

This analysis of the U.S. economy and workforce offers projections about change over the 1990s.

William B. Johnston and Arnold E. Packer. *Workforce 2000: Work and Workers for the Twenty-First Century.* Indianapolis: Hudson Institute, 1987.

Probing economic development and the changes that accompany it, this analysis contrasts rural and urban development as well as its different consequences for men and women.

Tony Barnett. *Social and Economic Development: An Introduction.* New York: Guilford Press, 1989.

A well-known social critic explores the state of politics, religion, and progress in today's world in this wide-ranging discussion.

Christopher Lasch. *The True and Only Heaven: Progress and Its Critics.* New York: W.W. Norton, 1991.

This critical analysis of the 1980s stresses the need for grassroots activism to reshape the world of the next century.

David C. Korten. *Getting to the 21st Century: Voluntary Action and the Global Agenda.* West Hartford, CT: Kumarian Press, 1990.

This collection of essays offers crucial insights into how change in the United States affects transformations in other societies of the world.

Mike Featherstone, ed. *Global Culture: Globalization, Nationalism, and Modernity.* Newbury Park, CA: Sage, 1990.

absolute poverty a deprivation of resources that is life threatening

achieved status a social position that is assumed voluntarily and that reflects a significant measure of personal ability and effort

activity theory an analysis of aging linking personal satisfaction in old age to a high level of activity

Afrocentrism highlighting the viewpoint of people of African descent

ageism prejudice and discrimination against the elderly

age-sex pyramid a graphic representation that divides a population into various categories based on age and sex

age stratification the unequal distribution of wealth, power, and privileges among people of different ages

agriculture the technology of large-scale farming using plows powered by animals or advanced energy

alienation the experience of separation resulting from powerlessness

animism the belief that natural objects are conscious forms of life that can affect humanity

anomie Durkheim's designation of a condition in which society provides individuals with little moral guidance

anticipatory socialization the process of social learning directed toward gaining a desired position

arms race a mutually reinforcing escalation of military might

ascribed status a social position that is received at birth or involuntarily assumed later in the life course

assimilation the process by which minorities gradually adopt patterns of the dominant culture

authoritarianism any political system that denies popular participation in government

authority power that people perceive as legitimate rather than coercive

bilateral descent a system tracing kinship through both females and males

blue-collar occupations work involving mostly manual labor

bureaucracy an organizational model rationally designed to perform complex tasks efficiently

bureaucratic inertia the tendency of bureaucratic organizations to persist over time

bureaucratic ritualism a preoccupation with organizational rules and regulations as ends in themselves rather than as the means to organizational goals

capitalism an economic system in which productive resources are privately owned

capitalists people who own factories and other productive enterprises

caste system a system of social stratification based on ascription

cause and effect a relationship between two variables in which change in one (the independent variable) causes change in another (the dependent variable)

charisma in religious terms, evidence of God's favor in the behavior of an individual

charismatic authority power legitimized through extraordinary personal abilities that inspire devotion and obedience

church a type of religious organization that readily seeks accommodation with the larger society

civil religion a quasi-religious loyalty binding individuals in a basically secular society

class conflict Marx's term for the struggle between social classes over the distribution of wealth and power in society

class consciousness Marx's term for workers' recognition of their unity as a social class in opposition to capitalists and to capitalism itself

class society a capitalist society with pronounced social stratification

class system a system of social stratification based on individual achievement

cohabitation the sharing of a household by an unmarried couple

cohort a category of people with a common characteristic, usually their age

collective behavior activity involving a large number of people, often spontaneous, and typically in violation of established norms

collectivity a large number of people whose minimal interaction occurs in the absence of well-defined and conventional norms

colonialism the process by which some nations enrich themselves through political and economic control of other countries

communism a hypothetical economic and political system in which all members of society have economic and social equality

concept a mental construct that represents some part of the world, inevitably in a somewhat simplified form

concrete operational stage Piaget's term for the level of human development at which people first use logic to understand their surroundings

conglomerates giant corporations composed of many smaller ones

content analysis a methodology that involves the counting or coding of the content of written, aural, or visual materials

control the ability to neutralize the effect of one variable in order to assess the relationships among other variables

conversion a personal transformation resulting from adopting new religious beliefs

corporation an organization with a legal existence including rights and liabilities apart from those of its members

correlation a relationship between two (or more) variables

counterculture social patterns that strongly oppose popular culture

credentialism the requirement that a person hold an advanced degree as a condition of employment

crime the violation of norms formally enacted into criminal law

crimes against property (property crimes) crimes that involve theft of property belonging to others

crimes against the person (violent crimes) crimes against people that involve violence or the threat of violence

criminal justice system a formal system that responds to alleged violations of the law using police, courts, and punishment

criminal recidivism subsequent offenses by people previously convicted of crimes

crowd a temporary gathering of people who share a common focus of attention and whose members influence one another

crude birth rate the number of live births in a given year for every thousand people in a population

crude death rate the number of deaths in a given year for every thousand people in a population

cult a religious organization with roots outside the dominant religious traditions of a society

cultural integration the close relationship among various parts of a cultural system

cultural lag disruption in a cultural system resulting from the unequal rates at which different cultural elements change

cultural materialism a theoretical paradigm that explores the relationship of human culture and the physical environment

cultural relativism the practice of judging a culture by its own standards

cultural transmission the process by which one generation passes culture to the next

cultural universals traits found in every culture

culture the beliefs, values, behavior, and material objects shared by a particular people

culture shock personal disorientation that accompanies exposure to an unfamiliar way of life

deductive logical thought reasoning that transforms general ideas into specific hypotheses suitable for scientific testing

democracy a type of political system in which power is exercised by the people as a whole

democratic socialism an economic and political system that combines significant government intervention in the economy with free elections

demographic transition theory the thesis that population patterns are linked to a society's level of technological development

demography the study of human population

denomination a church, not linked to the state, in a society that recognizes religious pluralism

dependency theory a model of economic and social development that explains global inequality in terms of the historical exploitation of poor societies by rich ones

dependent variable a variable that is changed by another (independent) variable

descent the system by which members of a society trace kinship over generations

deterrence the attempt to discourage criminality through punishment

deviance the recognized violation of cultural norms

direct-fee system a medical-care system in which patients pay directly for the services of physicians and hospitals

discrimination treating various categories of people unequally

disengagement theory an analysis of aging linking disengagement by elderly people from positions of social responsibility to the orderly operation of society

division of labor specialized economic activity

dramaturgical analysis the investigation of social interaction in terms of theatrical performance

dyad a social group with two members

ecclesia a church that is formally allied with the state

economy the institutionalized system for production, distribution, and consumption of goods and services

education the various ways in which knowledge—including factual information and occupational skills as well as cultural norms and values—is transmitted to members of a society

ego Freud's designation of a person's conscious attempt to balance innate pleasure-seeking drives with the demands of society

empirical evidence information we are able to verify with our senses

endogamy marriage between people of the same social group or category

ethnicity a shared cultural heritage

ethnocentrism the practice of judging another culture by the standards of one's own culture

ethnomethodology the study of the everyday, common-sense understandings that people have of the world

Eurocentrism the dominance of European (esp. English) culture

euthanasia (mercy killing) assisting in the death of a person suffering from an incurable illness

exogamy marriage between people of different social groups or categories

experiment a research method for investigating cause and effect under highly controlled conditions

expressive leadership group leadership that emphasizes collective well-being

extended family (consanguine family) a social unit including parents, children, and other kin

fad an unconventional social pattern that people embrace briefly but enthusiastically

faith belief anchored in conviction rather than scientific evidence

false consciousness Marx's description of any belief suggesting that the shortcomings of individuals, rather than society, are responsible for widespread social problems

family a relatively permanent social group of two or more people, who are related by blood, marriage, or adoption and who usually live together

family of orientation the family into which a person is born and receives early socialization

family of procreation a family in which people have or adopt children of their own

family violence emotional, physical, or sexual abuse of one family member by another

fashion a social pattern favored for a time by a large number of people

female infanticide the practice of aborting female fetuses and neglecting, or even actively killing, infant girls by parents who would prefer to raise boys

feminism the advocacy of social equality for the sexes, in opposition to patriarchy and sexism

feminization of poverty a trend by which women represent an increasing proportion of the poor

fertility the incidence of childbearing in a society's population

First World industrial societies that have predominantly capitalist economies

folkways norms that have little moral significance

formal operational stage Piaget's term for the level of human development at which people use highly abstract thought and are able to imagine alternatives to reality

formal organization a large secondary group that is formally organized to facilitate achieving its goals efficiently

functional illiteracy the lack of basic reading and writing skills needed for everyday life

Gemeinschaft a type of social organization in which people are bound closely together by kinship and tradition

gender society's division of humanity, based on sex, into two distinctive categories

gender identity traits that females and males, guided by their culture, incorporate into their personalities

gender roles (sex roles) attitudes and activities that a culture links to each sex

gender stratification a society's unequal distribution of wealth, power, and privilege between the two sexes

generalized other George Herbert Mead's term for widespread cultural norms and values we use as a reference in evaluating ourselves

genocide the systematic annihilation of one category of people by another

gerontocracy a form of social organization in which the elderly have the most wealth, power, and privileges

gerontology the study of aging and the elderly

Gesellschaft a type of social organization in which people have weak social ties and a great deal of self-interest

gossip rumor about the personal affairs of others

government formal organizations that direct the political life of a society

groupthink a limited understanding of some issue due to group conformity

Hawthorne effect a change in a subject's behavior caused by the awareness of being studied

health a state of complete physical, mental, and social well-being

health care any activity intended to improve health

hermaphrodite a human being with some combination of female and male internal and external genitalia

hidden curriculum ideas and behavior that support the status quo, taught in subtle ways to students

holistic medicine an approach to health care that emphasizes prevention of illness and takes account of the whole person within a physical and social environment

homogamy marriage between people who are socially alike

horticulture technology based on using hand tools to cultivate plants

humanizing bureaucracy fostering an organizational environment that develops human resources

hunting and gathering simple technology to hunt animals and gather vegetation

hypothesis an unverified statement of a relationship between variables

id Freud's designation of the human being's basic drives

ideal culture social patterns consistent with cultural values and norms

ideal type an abstract statement of the essential characteristics of any social phenomenon

incest taboo a cultural norm forbidding sexual relations or marriage between certain kin

income occupational wages or salaries and earnings from investments

independent variable a variable that causes change in another (dependent) variable

inductive logical thought reasoning that builds specific observations into general theory

industrialism technology that powers sophisticated machinery with advanced fuels

infant mortality rate the number of deaths in the first year of life for each thousand live births in a given year

ingroup a social group commanding a member's esteem and loyalty

institutional completeness the complexity of community organizations that meet the needs of members

institutional discrimination discrimination that is a normative and routine part of the economy, the educational system, or some other social institution

instrumental leadership group leadership that emphasizes the completion of tasks

intergenerational social mobility upward or downward social mobility of children in relation to their parents

interlocking directorate a social network of people who serve simultaneously on the boards of directors of many corporations

interpretive research an interpretive method whose goal is to understand meanings and the way people construct meanings as they create their social worlds

interview a series of questions administered personally by a researcher to respondents

intragenerational social mobility a change in social position occurring during a person's lifetime

juvenile delinquency the violation of legal standards by the young

kinship social ties based on blood, marriage, or adoption

labeling theory the assertion that deviance and conformity result from the response of others

labor unions organizations of workers that attempt to improve wages and working conditions through various strategies, including negotiations and strikes

language a system of symbols that allows members of a society to communicate with one another

latent functions the unrecognized and unintended consequences of any social pattern

liberation theology a fusion of Christian principles with political activism, often Marxist in character

life expectancy how long a person, on average, can expect to live

looking-glass self Cooley's assertion that the self is based on how others respond to us

macro-level orientation a focus on broad social structures that characterize society as a system

manifest functions the recognized and intended consequences of any social pattern

marriage a socially approved relationship, involving economic cooperation and allowing sexual activity and childbearing, that is expected to be relatively enduring

mass behavior collective behavior among people dispersed over a wide geographical area

mass hysteria a form of dispersed collective behavior by which people respond to a real or imagined event with irrational, frantic behavior

mass media impersonal communications directed toward a vast audience

mass society a society in which industrialization proceeds and bureaucracy expands while traditional social ties grow weaker

master status a status that has exceptional importance for social identity, often shaping a person's entire life

material culture tangible elements of culture such as clothing and cities

matriarchy a form of social organization in which females dominate males

matrilineal descent a system tracing kinship through females

matrilocality a residential pattern in which a married couple lives with or near the wife's family

mean the arithmetic average of a series of numbers

measurement the process of determining the value of a variable in a specific case

mechanical solidarity Durkheim's term for social bonds, common to preindustrial societies, based on shared moral sentiments

median the value that occurs midway in a series of numbers arranged in order of magnitude or, simply, the middle case

medicalization of deviance the transformation of moral and legal issues into medical matters

medicine an institutionalized system for combating disease and improving health

megalopolis a vast urban region containing a number of cities and their surrounding suburbs

meritocracy a system of social stratification based on personal merit

metropolis a large city that socially and economically dominates an urban area

micro-level orientation a focus on situational patterns of social interaction

migration the movement of people into and out of a specific territory

military-industrial complex the close association between the federal government and defense industries

minority a category of people, distinguished by physical or cultural traits, who are socially disadvantaged

miscegenation the biological process of interbreeding among racial categories

mob a highly emotional crowd that pursues some violent or destructive goal

mode the value that occurs most often in a series of numbers

modernity patterns of social life linked to industrialization

modernization the process of social change begun by industrialization

modernization theory a model of economic and social development that explains global inequality in terms of differing levels of technological development among world societies

monarchy a type of political system in which power is passed from generation to generation in a single family

monogamy a form of marriage that joins one female and one male

monopoly domination of a market by a single producer

monotheism belief in a single divine power

mores norms that have great moral significance

mortality the incidence of death in a society's population

multiculturalism a policy of encouraging ethnic or cultural heterogeneity

multinational corporation a large corporation that operates in many different countries

neocolonialism a new form of international, economic exploitation that involves not direct political control but the operation of multinational corporations

neolocality a residential pattern in which a married couple lives apart from the parents of both spouses

network a web of social ties that links people who may have little common identity and interaction

nonmaterial culture intangible elements of culture such as values and norms

nonverbal communication communication using body movements, gestures, and facial expressions rather than speech

norms rules and expectations by which a society guides the behavior of its members

nuclear family (conjugal family) a social unit composed of one or, more commonly, two parents and children

nuclear proliferation the acquisition of nuclear-weapons technology by more and more societies

objectivity the state of personal neutrality in conducting research

oligarchy the rule of the many by the few

oligopoly domination of a market by a few producers

operationalizing a variable specifying exactly what is to be measured in assigning a value to a variable

organic solidarity Durkheim's designation of social bonds, common to industrial societies, based on specialization

organizational environment a range of factors outside an organization that affect its operation

other-directedness highly variable personality patterns among people open to change and likely to imitate the behavior of others

outgroup a social group toward which one feels competition or opposition

overeducation a situation in which workers have more formal education than the performance of their occupations requires

panic a form of localized collective behavior by which people react to a threat or other stimulus with emotional, irrational, and often self-destructive behavior

participant observation a method in which researchers systematically observe people while joining in their routine activities

pastoralism technology that supports the domestication of animals

patriarchy a form of social organization in which males dominate females

patrilineal descent a system tracing kinship through males

patrilocality a residential pattern in which a married couple lives with or near the husband's family

peace the absence of war

peer group people who interact regularly, usually with common interests, social position, and age

personality a person's fairly consistent pattern of thinking, feeling, and acting

personal space the surrounding area over which a person makes some claim to privacy

plea bargaining a legal negotiation in which the prosecution reduces a defendant's charge in exchange for a guilty plea

pluralism a state in which racial and ethnic minorities are distinct but have social parity

pluralist model an analysis of politics in which power is dispersed among many competing interest groups

political parties organizations operating within the political system that seek control of government

political revolution the overthrow of one political system in order to establish another

political state a formal government claiming the legitimate use of coercion to support its rule

politics the institutionalized system by which a society distributes power and makes decisions

polyandry a form of marriage that joins one female with more than one male

polygamy a form of marriage that unites three or more people

polygyny a form of marriage that joins one male with more than one female

polytheism belief in many gods

population the people who are the focus of research

positivism a means to understand the world based on science

positivist social science an approach that seeks to model itself on the physical sciences through criteria such as objectivity, replicability, causality, experimentation, quantification, and generalization

postindustrial economy a productive system based on service work and high technology

power the ability to achieve desired ends despite possible resistance from others

power-elite model an analysis of politics holding that power is concentrated among the rich

prejudice a rigid and irrational generalization about a category of people

preoperational stage Piaget's term for the level of human development in which the individual first uses language and other symbols

primary group a small social group in which relationships are both personal and enduring

primary labor market occupations that provide extensive benefits to workers

primary sector the part of the economy that generates raw materials directly from the natural environment

primary sex characteristics the genitals, used to reproduce the human species

profane that which is defined as an ordinary element of everyday life

profession a prestigious white-collar occupation that requires extensive formal education

proletariat people who provide labor necessary for the operation of factories and other productive enterprises

propaganda information presented with the intention of shaping public opinion

public opinion the attitudes of people throughout a society about one or more controversial issues

qualitative research inquiry based on subjective impressions

quantitative research inquiry based on the analysis of numerical data

questionnaire a series of questions presented to subjects

race a category composed of men and women who share biologically transmitted traits deemed socially significant

racism the belief that one racial category is innately superior or inferior to another

rationality deliberate, matter-of-fact calculation of the most efficient means to accomplish any particular goal

rationalization of society Weber's characterization of the historical change from tradition to rationality as the dominant mode of thought

rational-legal authority (bureaucratic authority) power legitimized by legally enacted rules and regulations

real culture actual social patterns that typically only approximate cultural values and norms

reference group a social group that serves as a point of reference for people making evaluations or decisions

rehabilitation reforming the offender to preclude subsequent offenses

relative deprivation a perceived disadvantage arising from some specific comparison

relative poverty the deprivation of some people in relation to those who have more

reliability the quality of consistent measurement

religion a system of beliefs and practices based on recognizing the sacred

religiosity the importance of religion in a person's life

religious fundamentalism a conservative religious doctrine that opposes intellectualism and worldly accommodation in favor of restoring a traditional otherworldly focus

replication repetition of research by others in order to assess its accuracy

research method a strategy for systematically conducting research

reserve army of labor the part of the labor force that is last hired during expansion and first fired when the economy contracts

resocialization deliberate control of an environment intended to radically alter an inmate's personality

retribution an act of moral vengeance by which a society subjects an offender to suffering comparable to that caused by the offense

retrospective labeling the interpretation of someone's past consistent with present deviance

riot a social eruption that is highly emotional, violent, and undirected

ritual formal, ceremonial behavior

role patterns of expected behavior attached to a particular status

role conflict incompatibility among the roles corresponding to two or more different statuses

role set a number of roles attached to a single status

role strain incompatibility among roles corresponding to a single status

routinization of charisma the transformation of charismatic authority into some combination of traditional and bureaucratic authority

rumor unsubstantiated information spread informally, often by word of mouth

sacred that which is defined as extraordinary, inspiring a sense of awe, reverence, and even fear

sample a part of a population selected to represent the whole

Sapir-Whorf hypothesis the assertion that people perceive the world only in terms of the symbols provided by their language

scapegoat a person (or category of people), typically with little power, who is unfairly blamed for the troubles of others

schooling formal instruction under the direction of specially trained teachers

science a logical system that bases knowledge on direct, systematic observation

secondary analysis a research method in which a researcher utilizes data collected by others

secondary group a large and impersonal social group based on some special interest or activity

secondary labor market jobs that provide minimal benefits to workers

secondary sector the part of the economy that transforms raw materials into manufactured goods

secondary sex characteristics physical traits, other than the genitals, that distinguish physiologically mature females and males

Second World industrial societies that are currently transforming their socialist economies

sect a type of religious organization that resists accommodation with the larger society

secularization a historical trend away from the supernatural and the sacred

segregation the physical and social separation of categories of people

self George Herbert Mead's term for a dimension of personality encompassing an individual's self-conception

sensorimotor stage Piaget's term for the level of human development in which people experience the world only through sensory contact

sex the division of humanity into biological categories of female and male

sexism the belief that one sex is innately superior to the other

sex ratio the number of males for every hundred females in a given population

sexual harassment comments, gestures, or physical contact of a sexual nature that is deliberate, repeated, and unwelcome

sexual orientation the manner in which people experience sexual arousal and achieve sexual pleasure

sick role patterns of behavior appropriate for those who are ill

social change the transformation of culture and social institutions over time

social character personality patterns common to members of a society

social conflict struggle between segments of society over valued resources

social-conflict paradigm a framework for building theory based on the assumption that society is a complex system characterized by inequality and conflict that generate social change

social construction of reality the process by which individuals creatively shape reality through social interaction

social control the process by which members of a society encourage conformity to cultural norms

social dysfunction the undesirable consequence of any social pattern for the operation of society

social epidemiology the study of how health and disease are distributed in a society's population

social fact Durkheim's term for any social pattern that people confront as an objective reality beyond themselves

social function the consequence of any social pattern for the operation of society

social group two or more people who identify with one another and have a distinctive pattern of interaction

social institution a major sphere of social life organized to meet a basic human need

social interaction the process by which people act and react in relation to others

socialism an economic system in which productive resources are collectively owned

socialization lifelong social experience by which individuals develop human potential and learn patterns of their culture

socialized medicine a health-care system in which most medical facilities are owned and operated by the government, and most physicians are salaried government employees

social marginality the state of being excluded from social activity as an "outsider"

social mobility changes in people's positions in a system of social stratification

social movement organized activity that encourages or discourages social change

social protection rendering an offender incapable of further offenses either temporarily during a period of incarceration or permanently by execution

social stratification a system by which society ranks categories of people in a hierarchy

social structure a relatively stable pattern of social behavior

society people who interact in a limited territory and share a culture

sociobiology a theoretical paradigm that studies ways in which biological forces affect human culture

sociocultural evolution the Lenskis' term for the process of social change that results from gaining new cultural information, particularly technology

socioeconomic status a composite social ranking based on various dimensions of social inequality

sociology the scientific study of human society

spurious correlation an apparent, although false, relationship between two (or more) variables caused by some other variable

state terrorism the use of violence, generally without support of law, against individuals or groups by a government or its agents

status a recognized social position that an individual occupies

status consistency consistent standing across various dimensions of social inequality

status set all the statuses a person holds at a given time

stereotype a set of prejudices concerning some category of people

stigma a powerfully negative social label that radically changes a person's self-concept and social identity

streaming categorically assigning students to different types of educational programs

structural-functional paradigm a framework for building theory based on the assumption that society is a complex system whose parts work together to promote stability

structural social mobility a shift in the social position of large numbers of people due more to changes in society than to individual efforts

subculture cultural patterns that distinguish some segment of a society's population

suburbs urban areas beyond the political boundaries of a city

superego Freud's designation of the presence of culture within the individual in the form of internalized values and norms

survey a research method in which subjects respond to a series of questions in a questionnaire or interview

symbol anything that carries a particular meaning recognized by members of a culture

symbolic-interaction paradigm a theoretical framework based on the assumption that society is continuously recreated as human beings construct reality through interaction

technology the application of cultural knowledge to the task of living in a physical environment

terrorism violence or the threat of violence employed by an individual or group as a political strategy

tertiary sector the part of the economy that generates services rather than goods

theoretical paradigm a set of fundamental assumptions that guides thinking and research

theory the process of linking facts together to explain something

Third World primarily agrarian societies, in which most people are poor

Thomas theorem the assertion that situations that are defined as real are real in their consequences

total institution a setting in which people are isolated from the rest of society and manipulated by an administrative staff

totalitarianism a political system that denies popular participation in government and extensively regulates people's lives

totem an object in the natural world imbued with sacred qualities

tradition sentiments and beliefs passed from generation to generation

traditional authority power that is legitimized through respect for long-established cultural patterns

tradition-directedness rigid personalities based on conformity to time-honored ways of living

transsexuals people who feel they are one sex though biologically they are the other

triad a social group with three members

underground economy economic activity involving income or the exchange of goods and services that is not reported to the government

urban ecology the study of the link between the physical and social dimensions of cities

urbanization the concentration of humanity into cities

validity the quality of measuring precisely what one intends to measure

values culturally defined standards of desirability, goodness, and beauty that serve as broad guidelines for social life

variable a concept whose value changes from case to case

victimless crimes violations of law in which there are no readily apparent victims

war armed conflict among the people of various societies, directed by their governments

wealth the total amount of money and valuable goods that any person or family controls

white-collar crime crimes committed by people of high social position in the course of their occupations

white-collar occupations higher-prestige work involving mostly mental activity

zero population growth the level of reproduction that maintains population at a steady state

REFERENCES

ABBOTT, ANDREW. *The System of Professions: An Essay on the Division of Expert Labor*. Chicago: University of Chicago Press, 1988.

ABERLE, DAVID F. *The Peyote Religion Among the Navaho*. Chicago: Aldine, 1966.

ABZUG, ROBERT H. *Inside the Vicious Heart: Americans and the Liberation of Nazi Concentration Camps*. New York: Oxford University Press, 1985.

ADAMS, P. F., and V. BENSON. "Current Estimates from the National Health Interview Survey, 1989." U. S. National Center for Health Statistics. *Vital Health Statistics*, Vol. 10, No. 176. Washington, DC: U. S. Government Printing Office, 1990.

ADORNO, T. W., et al. *The Authoritarian Personality*. New York: Harper and Brothers, 1950.

AGUIRRE, B. E., E. L. QUARANTELLI, and JORGE L. MENDOZA. "The Collective Behavior of Fads: Characteristics, Effects, and Career of Streaking." *American Sociological Review*. Vol. 53, No. 4 (August 1988):569–84.

AGUIRRE, BENIGNO E., and E. L. QUARANTELLI. "Methodological, Ideological, and Conceptual-Theoretical Criticisms of Collective Behavior: A Critical Evaluation and Implications for Future Study." *Sociological Focus*. Vol. 16, No. 3 (August 1983):195–216.

AKERS, RONALD L., MARVIN D. KROHN, LONN LANZA-KADUCE, and MARCIA RADOSE-VICH. "Social Learning and Deviant Behavior." *American Sociological Review*. Vol. 44, No. 4 (August 1979):636–55.

ALAM, SULTANA. "Women and Poverty in Bangladesh." *Women's Studies International Forum*. Vol. 8, No. 4 (1985):361–71.

ALBA, RICHARD D. *Italian Americans: Into the Twilight of Ethnicity*. Englewood Cliffs, NJ: Prentice Hall, 1985.

ALBON, JOAN. "Retention of Cultural Values and Differential Urban Adaptation: Samoans and American Indians in a West Coast City." *Social Forces*. Vol. 49, No. 3 (March 1971):385–93.

ALBRECHT, WILLIAM P., JR. *Economics*. 3rd ed. Englewood Cliffs, NJ: Prentice Hall, 1983.

ALLAN, EMILIE ANDERSEN, and DARRELL J. STEFFENSMEIER. "Youth, Underemployment, and Property Crime: Differential Effects of Job Availability and Job Quality on Juvenile and Young Adult Arrest Rates." *American Sociological Review*. Vol. 54, No. 1 (February 1989):107–23.

ALLEN, MICHAEL PATRICK, and PHILIP BROYLES. "Campaign Finance Reforms and the Presidential Campaign Contributions of Wealthy Capitalist Families." *Social Science Quarterly*. Vol. 72, No. 4 (December 1991):738–50.

ALLSOP, KENNETH. *The Bootleggers*. London: Hutchinson and Company, 1961.

ALTMAN, DREW, et al. "Health Care for the Homeless." *Society*. Vol. 26, No. 4 (May/June 1989):4–5.

AMBERT, A.M. and M. BAKER. "Marriage Dissolution: Structural and Ideological Changes." In M. Baker, ed., *The Family*. Toronto: McGraw Hill Ryerson, 1984.

AMERICAN COUNCIL ON EDUCATION, as reported in "Number of Black Students Still Falling, Study Finds." *The Chronicle of Higher Education*. Vol. XXXIV, No. 11 (November 11, 1987):2.

AMERICAN COUNCIL ON EDUCATION. "Senior Women Administrators in Higher Education: A Decade of Change, 1975–1983." Washington, DC: 1984.

AMERICAN SOCIOLOGICAL ASSOCIATION. "Code of Ethics." Washington, DC: 1984.

ANDERSON, ALAN B. and JAMES S. FRIDERES. *Ethnicity in Canada: Theoretical Perspectives*. Toronto: Butterworths, 1981.

ANDERSON, DANIEL R., and ELIZABETH PUGZLES LORCH. "Look at Television: Action or Reaction?" In Jennings Bryant and Daniel R. Anderson, eds., *Children's Understanding of Television: Research on Attention and Comprehension*. New York: Academic Press, 1983:1–33.

ANDERSON, DORIS. *The Unfinished Revolution*. Toronto: Doubleday Books, 1991.

ANDERSON, JOHN and M. GUNDERSON. *Union Management Relations in Canada*. Don Mills, Ontario: Addison-Wesley, 1982.

ANDO, FAITH H. "Women in Business." In Sara E. Rix, ed., *The American Woman: A Status Report 1990–91*. New York: W. W. Norton, 1990:222–30.

ANG, IEN. *Watching Dallas: Soap Opera and the Melodramatic Imagination*. London: Methuen, 1985.

ANGELO, BONNIE. "Assigning the Blame for a Young Man's Suicide." *Time*. Vol. 138, No. 2 (November 18, 1991):12–14.

———. "The Pain of Being Black" (an interview with Toni Morrison). *Time*. Vol. 133, No. 21 (May 22, 1989):120–22.

APOSTLE, RICHARD. "Subjective Dimensions of Social Class in Canada." Paper presented at Atlantic Association of Sociology & Anthropology, St. John's, Newfoundland.

ARCHER, DANE, and ROSEMARY GARTNER. *Violence and Crime in Cross-National Perspective*. New Haven: Yale University Press, 1987.

ARENDT, HANNAH. *Between Past and Future: Six Exercises in Political Thought*. Cleveland, OH: Meridian Books, 1963.

———. *The Origins of Totalitarianism*. Cleveland, OH: Meridian Books, 1958.

ARIÈS, PHILIPPE. *Centuries of Childhood: A Social History of Family Life*. New York: Vintage Books, 1965.

———. *Western Attitudes Toward Death: From the Middle Ages to the Present*. Baltimore, MD: The Johns Hopkins University Press, 1974.

ARJOMAND, SAID AMIR. *The Turban for the Crown: The Islamic Revolution in Iran*. New York: Oxford University Press, 1988.

ARMSTRONG, PAT and H. ARMSTRONG. *The Double Ghetto: Canadian Women and Their Segregated Work*, rev. ed. Toronto: McClelland & Stewart, 1984.

ARTIBISE, ALAN F.J. "Canada as an Urban Nation." *Daedalus* 117, Fall, 1988.

———, and GIL STELTER. "Urbanization." *The Canadian Encyclopedia*. 2nd ed. Edmonton: Hurtig Publishers, 1988: 2235–36.

ASANTE, MOLEFI KETE. *Afrocentricity*. Trenton, NJ: Africa World Press, 1988.

———. *The Afrocentric Idea*. Philadelphia: Temple University Press, 1987.

ASCH, SOLOMON. *Social Psychology*. Englewood Cliffs, NJ: Prentice Hall, 1952.

ASTONE, NAN MARIE, and SARA S. MCLANAHAN. "Family Structure, Parental Practices and High School Completion." *American Sociological Review*. Vol. 56, No. 3 (June 1991):309–20.

ATCHLEY, ROBERT C. "Retirement as a Social Institution." *Annual Review of Sociology*. Vol. 8. Palo Alto, CA: Annual Reviews, Inc., 1982:263–87.

———. *Aging: Continuity and Change*. Belmont, CA: Wadsworth, 1983; 2nd ed., 1987.

AVIS, GEORGE. "Access to Higher Education in the Soviet Union." In J. J. Tomiak, ed., *Soviet Education in the 1980s*. London: Croom Helm, 1983:199–239.

AYENSU, EDWARD S. "A Worldwide Role for the Healing Powers of Plants." *Smithsonian.* Vol. 12, No. 8 (November 1981):87–97.

BABBIE, EARL. *The Practice of Social Research.* 6th ed. Belmont, CA: Wadsworth, 1992.

BACHRACH, PETER, and MORTON S. BARATZ. *Power and Poverty.* New York: Oxford University Press, 1970.

BAHL, VINAY. "Caste and Class in India." Paper presented to the Southern Sociological Society, Atlanta, April, 1991.

BAILEY, WILLIAM C. "Murder, Capital Punishment, and Television: Execution Publicity and Homicide Rates." *American Sociological Review.* Vol. 55, No. 5 (October 1990):628–33.

BAILEY, WILLIAM C., and RUTH D. PETERSON. "Murder and Capital Punishment: A Monthly Time-Series Analysis of Execution Publicity." *American Sociological Review.* Vol. 54, No. 5 (October 1989):722–43.

BAINBRIDGE, WILLIAM SIMS, and DANIEL H. JACKSON. "The Rise and Decline of Transcendental Meditation." In Bryan Wilson, ed., *The Social Impact of New Religious Movements.* New York: The Rose of Sharon Press, 1981: 135–58.

BAKER, MARY ANNE, CATHERINE WHITE BERHEIDE, FAY ROSS GRECKEL, LINDA CARSTARPHEN GUGIN, MARCIA J. LIPETZ, and MARCIA TEXLER SEGAL. *Women Today: A Multidisciplinary Approach to Women's Studies.* Monterey, CA: Brooks/Cole, 1980.

BAKER, MAUREEN, in Lorne Tepperman and R. Jack Richardson, eds., Toronto: McGraw Hill Ryerson, 353–381, 1991.

BAKKER, J.I. (HANS), ed. *The World Food Crisis: Food Security in Comparative Perspective.* Toronto: Canadian Scholar's Press, 1990.

———, and ANTHONY WINSON. "Rural Sociology." In Peter S. Li and B. Singh Bolaria, eds. *Contemporary Sociology: Critical Perspectives.* Toronto: Copp Clark Pitman, 1993: 500–517.

BALDUS, BERND and VERNA TRIBE. "The Development of Perceptions and Evaluations of Social Inequality Among Public School Children." *Canadian Review of Sociology and Anthropology,* 15(1), 1978: 50–60.

BALES, ROBERT F. "The Equilibrium Problem in Small Groups." In Talcott Parsons et al., eds., *Working Papers in the Theory of Action.* New York: Free Press, 1953:111–15.

———, and PHILIP E. SLATER. "Role Differentiation in Small Decision-Making Groups." In Talcott Parsons and Robert F. Bales, eds., *Family, Socialization and Interaction Process.* New York: Free Press, 1955:259–306.

BALLANTINE, JEANNE. *The Sociology of Education.* 2nd ed. Englewood Cliffs, NJ: Prentice Hall, 1989.

BALTES, PAUL B., and K. WARNER SCHAIE. "The Myth of the Twilight Years." *Psychology Today.* Vol. 7, No. 10 (March 1974):35–39.

BALTZELL, E. DIGBY. *The Protestant Establishment: Aristocracy and Caste in America.* New York: Vintage, 1964.

———. "Introduction to the 1967 Edition." In W. E. B. DuBois, *The Philadelphia Negro: A Social Study.* New York: Schocken, 1967; orig. 1899.

———, ed. *The Search for Community in Modern America.* New York: Harper & Row, 1968.

———. "The Protestant Establishment Revisited." *The American Scholar.* Vol. 45, No. 4 (Autumn 1976):499–518.

———. *Philadelphia Gentlemen: The Making of A National Upper Class.* Philadelphia, PA: University of Pennsylvania Press, 1979; orig. 1958.

———. *Puritan Boston and Quaker Philadelphia.* New York: Free Press, 1979.

———. "The WASP's Last Gasp." *Philadelphia Magazine.* Vol. 79 (September 1988):104–7, 184, 186, 188.

BANFIELD, EDWARD C. *The Unheavenly City Revisited.* Boston, MA: Little, Brown, 1974.

BARASH, DAVID. *The Whispering Within.* New York: Penguin Books, 1981.

BARBERIS, MARY. "America's Elderly: Policy Implications." *Population Bulletin.* Vol. 35, No. 4 (January 1981). Population Reference Bureau.

BARIL, ALAIN and GEORGE A. MORI. "Canadian Social Trends." Cat. no. T1-008E, no. 22: Ottawa: Statistics Canada 1991:22–24

BARKER, EILEEN. "Who'd Be a Moonie? A Comparative Study of Those Who Join the Unification Church in Britain." In Bryan Wilson, ed., *The Social Impact of New Religious Movements.* New York: The Rose of Sharon Press, 1981: 59–96.

BARON, JAMES N., BRIAN S. MITTMAN, and ANDREW E. NEWMAN. "Targets of Opportunity: Organizational and Environmental Determinants of Gender Integration within the California Civil Service, 1979–1985." *American Journal of Sociology.* Vol. 96, No. 6 (May 1991):1362–1401.

BARONE, MICHAEL, and GRANT UJIFUSA. *The Almanac of American Politics.* Washington, DC: Barone and Co., 1981.

BARR, CATHY WIDDIS. "The Importance and Potential of Leaders Debates." In Frederick J. Fletcher, ed., *Media and Voters in Canadian Election Campaigns.* Toronto: Dundurn Press, 1991: 107–156.

BARRETT, STANLEY R. *Is God a Racist? The Right Wing in Canada.* Toronto: University of Toronto Press, 1987.

BARROW, GEORGE M., and PATRICIA A. SMITH. *Aging, the Individual, and Society.* 2nd ed. St. Paul, MN: West, 1983.

BARRY, KATHLEEN. "Feminist Theory: The Meaning of Women's Liberation." In Barbara Haber, ed., *The Women's Annual 1982–1983.* Boston: G. K. Hall, 1983:35–78.

BASHEVKIN, SYLVIA B. *Toeing the Lines: Women and Party Politics in Canada.* 2nd ed. Toronto: Oxford University Press, 1993

Basic Departmental Data. Department of Indian Affairs & Northern Development. Ottawa: Statistics Canada, 1992.

BASSETT, ISABEL. *The Bassett Report: Career Success and Canadian Women.* Toronto: Collins, 1985.

BASSUK, ELLEN J. "The Homelessness Problem." *Scientific American.* Vol. 251, No. 1 (July 1984):40–45.

BATESON, C. DANIEL, and W. LARRY VENTIS. *The Religious Experience: A Social-Psychological Perspective.* New York: Oxford, 1982.

BAUER, P. T. *Equality, the Third World, and Economic Delusion.* Cambridge, MA: Harvard University Press, 1981.

BEATRICE COMPANY, INC. *Annual Report 1985.* Chicago: Beatrice, 1985.

BEAUJOT, RODERIC and KEVIN MCQUILLAN. *Growth and Dualism: The Demographic Development of Canadian Society.* Toronto: Gage, 1982.

BECKER, HOWARD S. *Outside: Studies in the Sociology of Deviance.* New York: Free Press, 1966.

BEDELL, GEORGE C., Leo Sandon, Jr., and Charles T. Wellborn. *Religion in America.* New York: Macmillan, 1975.

BEEGHLEY, LEONARD. *The Structure of Social Stratification in the United States.* Needham Heights, MA: Allyn & Bacon, 1989.

BEGIN, PATRICIA. *Violence Against Women: Current Response.* Cat. no. 1391B67. Ottawa: Ministry of Supply and Services, Sept. 1991.

BEIGEL, HUGO G. "Romantic Love." *American Sociological Review.* Vol. 16, No. 3 (June 1951):326–34.

BELL, ALAN P., MARTIN S. WEINBERG, and SUE KIEFER-HAMMERSMITH. *Sexual Preference: Its Development in Men and Women.* Bloomington, IN: Indiana University Press, 1981.

BELLAH, ROBERT N. *The Broken Covenant.* New York: Seabury, 1975.

———, RICHARD MADSEN, WILLIAM M. SULLIVAN, ANN SWIDLER, and STEVEN M. TIPTON. *Habits of the Heart: Individualism and Commitment in American Life.* New York: Harper & Row, 1985.

BELSKY, JAY, RICHARD M. LERNER, and GRAHAM B. SPANIER. *The Child in the Family.* Reading, MA: Addison-Wesley, 1984.

BEM, SANDRA LIPSITZ. "Gender Schema Theory: A Cognitive Account of Sex-Typing." *Psychological Review.* Vol. 88, No. 4 (July 1981):354–64.

BENEDICT, RUTH. "Continuities and Discontinuities in Cultural Conditioning." *Psychiatry.* Vol. 1 (May 1938):161–67.

———. *The Chrysanthemum and the Sword: Patterns of Japanese Culture.* New York: New American Library, 1974; orig. 1946.

BENET, SULA. "Why They Live to Be 100, or Even Older, in Abkhasia." *The New York Times Magazine* (December 26, 1971):3, 28–29, 31–34.

BENETEAU, RENÉE. "Trends in Suicide." in Craig McKie and Keith Thompson, eds., *Canadian Social Trends*. Toronto: Thompson Educational Publishing, 1990.

BENJAMIN, BERNARD, and CHRIS WALLIS. "The Mortality of Widowers." *The Lancet*. Vol. 2 (August 1963):454–56.

BENJAMIN, LOIS. *The Black Elite: Facing the Color Line in the Twilight of the Twentieth Century*. Chicago: Nelson-Hall, 1991.

BENN, CARL. *Historic Fort York, 1793–1993*. Toronto: Natural Heritage, 1993.

BENNETT, NEIL G., DAVID E. BLOOM, and PATRICIA H. CRAIG. "The Divergence of Black and White Marriage Patterns." *American Journal of Sociology*. Vol. 95, No. 3 (November 1989):692–722.

BENNETT, STEPHEN EARL. "Left Behind: Exploring Declining Turnout among Noncollege Young Whites, 1964–1988." *Social Science Quarterly*. Vol. 72, No. 2 (June 1991):314–33.

BENOKRAITIS, NIJOLE, and JOE FEAGIN. *Modern Sexism: Blatant, Subtle, and Overt Discrimination*. Englewood Cliffs, NJ: Prentice Hall, 1986.

BERARDO, F. M. "Survivorship and Social Isolation: The Case of the Aged Widower." *The Family Coordinator*. Vol. 19 (January 1970):11–25.

BERESFORD-HOWE, CONSTANCE. *A Serious Widow*. Toronto: McClelland & Stewart, 1991.

BERG, IVAR. *Education and Jobs: The Great Training Robbery*. New York: Praeger, 1970.

BERGER, BRIGITTE, AND PETER L. BERGER. *The War Over the Family: Capturing the Middle Ground*. Garden City, NY: Anchor/Doubleday, 1983.

BERGER, PETER L. *Invitation to Sociology*. New York: Anchor Books, 1963.

———. *Facing Up to Modernity: Excursions in Society, Politics, and Religion*. New York: Basic Books, 1977.

———. *The Capitalist Revolution: Fifty Propositions About Prosperity, Equality, and Liberty*. New York: Basic Books, 1986.

———. *The Sacred Canopy: Elements of a Sociological Theory of Religion*. Garden City, NY: Doubleday & Company, Inc., 1967.

———, BRIGITTE BERGER, and HANSFRIED KELLNER. *The Homeless Mind: Modernization and Consciousness*. New York: Vintage Books, 1974.

BERGER, PETER L. and HANSFRIED KELLNER. *Sociology Reinterpreted: An Essay on Method and Vocation*. Garden City, NY: Anchor Books, 1981.

BERGER, PETER L., and THOMAS LUCKMANN. *The Social Construction of Reality: A Treatise in the Sociology of Knowledge*. Garden City, NY: Anchor, 1967.

BERGESEN, ALBERT, ed. *Crises in the World-System*. Beverly Hills, CA: Sage Publications, 1983.

BERK, RICHARD A. *Collective Behavior*. Dubuque, IA: Wm. C. Brown, 1974.

BERNARD, JESSIE. *The Female World*. New York: Free Press, 1981.

———. *The Future of Marriage*. New Haven, CT: Yale University Press, 1982; orig. 1973.

BERNARD, LARRY CRAIG. "Multivariate Analysis of New Sex Role Formulations and Personality." *Journal of Personality and Social Psychology*. Vol. 38, No. 2 (February 1980):323–36.

BERRY, BRIAN L., and PHILIP H. REES. "The Factorial Ecology of Calcutta." *American Journal of Sociology*. Vol. 74, No. 5 (March 1969):445–91.

BERSCHEID, ELLEN, and ELAINE HATFIELD. *Interpersonal Attraction*. 2nd ed. Reading, MA: Addison-Wesley, 1983.

BERTON, PIERRE. *The Dionne Years: A Thirties Melodrama*. Toronto: McClelland & Stewart, 1977.

BERUBE, ALLAN. *Coming Out Under Fire: The History of Gay Men and Women in World War Two*. New York: The Free Press, 1990.

BEST, RAPHAELA. *We've All Got Scars: What Boys and Girls Learn in Elementary School*. Bloomington, IN: Indiana University Press, 1983.

BIBBY, REGINALD W. *Fragmented Gods: The Poverty and Potential of Religion in Canada*. Toronto: Irwin, 1987.

———. "The Moral Mosaic: Sexuality in Canada 80's." *Social Indicators Research*, 13, 1983: 171–84.

———. *Unknown Gods*. Toronto: Stoddart, 1993.

———, and D.C. POSTERSKI. *The Emerging Generation*. Toronto: Irwin Publishing, 1985.

BINGHAM, AMY. "Division I Dilemma: Making the Classroom a Priority for Athletes." *The Kenyon Journal*. Vol. II, No. 3 (November 1987):2.

Black Issues in Higher Education. "Black Graduate Students Decline." Vol. 4, No. 8 (July 1, 1987):1–2.

BLACK, NAOMI. "Agnes MacPhail." *The Canadian Encyclopedia* (2nd ed.), Edmonton: Hurtig Publishers, 2, 1988: 1281.

BLAU, JUDITH R., and PETER M. BLAU. "The Cost of Inequality: Metropolitan Structure and Violent Crime." *American Sociological Review*. Vol. 47, No. 1 (February 1982):114–29.

BLAU, PETER M. *Exchange and Power in Social Life*. New York: Wiley, 1964.

———. *Inequality and Heterogeneity: A Primitive Theory of Social Structure*. New York: The Free Press, 1977.

———, TERRY C. BLUM, and JOSEPH E. SCHWARTZ. "Heterogeneity and Intermarriage." *American Sociological Review*. Vol. 47, No. 1 (February 1982): 45–62.

BLAU, PETER M., and OTIS DUDLEY DUNCAN. *The American Occupational Structure*. New York: John Wiley, 1967.

BLAUSTEIN, ALBERT P., and ROBERT L. ZANGRANDO. *Civil Rights and the Black American*. New York: Washington Square Press, 1968.

BLISHEN, BERNARD R. "The Construction and Use of an Occupational Class Scale." *Canadian Journal of Economics and Political Science*. XXIV, 1958: 519–525.

———. *Doctors in Canada*. Toronto: University of Toronto Press, 1991.

———, W. CARROLL and C. MOORE. "The 1981 socio-economic index for occupations in Canada." *Canadian Review of Sociology and Anthropology* 24, 1987: 465–488.

BLISS, MICHAEL. *The Discovery of Insulin*. Toronto: McClelland & Stewart, 1982.

BLOOM, LEONARD. "Familial Adjustments of Japanese-Americans to Relocation: First Phase." In Thomas F. Pettigrew, ed., *The Sociology of Race Relations*. New York: Free Press, 1980:163–67.

BLUM, ALAN, and GARY FISHER. "Women Who Kill." In Delos H. Kelly, ed., *Criminal Behavior: Readings in Criminology*. New York: St. Martin's Press, 1980:291–301.

BLUMBERG, ABRAHAM S. *Criminal Justice*. Chicago: Quadrangle Books, 1970.

BLUMBERG, PAUL. *Inequality in an Age of Decline*. New York: Oxford University Press, 1981.

BLUMER, HERBERT G. "Fashion." In David L. Sills, ed., *International Encyclopedia of the Social Sciences*. Vol. 5. New York: Macmillan and Free Press, 1968:341–45.

———. "Collective Behavior." In Alfred McClung Lee, ed., *Principles of Sociology*. 3rd ed. New York: Barnes & Noble Books, 1969:65–121.

BLUMSTEIN, PHILIP, and PEPPER SCHWARTZ. *American Couples*. New York: William Morrow, 1983.

BNA COMMUNICATIONS INC. "The Challenge of Diversity: Equal Employment and Managing Difference in the 1990s." Summary report. Washington, DC: The Bureau of National Affairs, 1990.

BODENHEIMER, THOMAS S. "Health Care in the United States: Who Pays?" In Vicente Navarro, ed., *Health and Medical Care in the U. S.: A Critical Analysis*. Farmingdale, NY: Baywood Publishing Co., 1977:61–68.

BOFF, LEONARD and CLODOVIS. *Salvation and Liberation: In Search of a Balance Between Faith and Politics*. Maryknoll, NY: Orbis Books, 1984.

BOGARDUS, EMORY S. "Comparing Racial Distance in Ethiopia, South Africa, and the United States." *Sociology and Social Research*. Vol. 52, No. 2 (January 1968):149–56.

BOHANNAN, PAUL. *Divorce and After*. Garden City, NY: Doubleday & Company, 1970.

BOHLEN, CELESTINE. "Where the Fires of Hatred are Easily Stoked." *The New York Times* (August 4, 1991):E3.

BOHM, ROBERT M. "American Death Penalty Opinion, 1936–1986: A Critical Examination of the Gallup Polls." In Bohm, Robert M., ed.,*The Death Penalty in America: Current Research*. Cincinnati: Anderson Publishing Co., 1991:113–45.

BOLDT, MENNO. *Surviving as Indians: The Challenge of Self Government*. Toronto: University of Toronto Press, 1983.

BOLLOUGH, VERN, and MARTHA VOGHT. "Women, Menstruation, and Nineteenth-Century Medicine." In Judith Walzer Leavitt, ed.,*Women and Health in America*. Madison, WI: The University of Wisconsin Press, 1984:28–37.

BONILLA-SANTIAGO, GLORIA. "A Portrait of Hispanic Women in the United States." In Sara E. Rix, ed.,*The American Woman 1990–91: A Status Report*. New York: W. W. Norton, 1990:249–57.

BONNER, JANE. Research presented in "The Two Brains." Public Broadcasting System telecast, 1984.

BOOTH, ALAN, and LYNN WHITE. "Thinking About Divorce." *Journal of Marriage and the Family*. Vol. 42, No. 3 (August 1980):605–16.

BOSERUP, ESTER. *Women's Role in Economic Development*. London: George Allen & Unwin, 1970.

BOSWELL, TERRY E. "A Split Labor Market Analysis of Discrimination Against Chinese Immigrants, 1850–1882." *American Sociological Review*. Vol. 51, No. 3 (June 1986):352–71.

BOTT, ELIZABETH. *Family and Social Network*. New York: Free Press, 1971; orig. 1957.

BOTWINICK, JACK. "Intellectual Abilities." In James E. Birren and K. Warner Schaie, eds., *Handbook of the Psychology of Aging*. New York: Van Nostrand Reinhold, 1977:580–605.

BOULDING, ELISE. *The Underside of History*. Boulder, CO: Westview Press, 1976.

BOWLES, JACQUELINE, and WILLIAM A. ROBINSON. "PHS Grants for Minority Group HIV Infection Education and Prevention Efforts." *Public Health Reports*. Vol. 104, No. 6 (November–December 1989):552–59.

BOWLES, SAMUEL, and HERBERT GINTIS. *Schooling in Capitalist America: Educational Reform and the Contradictions of Economic Life*. New York: Basic Books, 1976.

BOYD, MONICA. "The Social Demography of Divorce in Canada." In K. Ishwaran, ed., *Marriage and Divorce in Canada*. Toronto: Methuen, 1983.

———, JOHN GOYDER, FRANK E. JONES, HUGH A. MCROBERTS, PETER PINEO and JOHN PORTER. "status attainment in canada: findings of the canadian mobility study." *Canadian Review of Sociology and Anthropology* 18, 1981: 657–673.

BOYER, ERNEST L. *College: The Undergraduate Experience in America*. Prepared by The Carnegie Foundation for the Advancement of Teaching. New York: Harper & Row, 1987.

BOZINOFF, LORNE and ANDRÉ TURCOTTE. "Majority of Women Feel Adult Magazines are Discriminatory." Toronto: Gallup Poll, Sunday, April 25, 1993.

BOZINOFF, LORNE and PETER MACINTOSH. "Only 24% Believe Premarital Sex is Wrong." Toronto: Gallup Report, Monday, February 12, 1990.

———. "Vast Majority of Canadians Believe in God and Heaven." Toronto: Gallup Report, Thur., Aug. 30, 1990.

———. "Society Regarded as More Accepting of Homosexuals." Toronto: Gallup Report, September 25, 1991.

BRAITHWAITE, JOHN. "The Myth of Social Class and Criminality Reconsidered." *American Sociological Review*. Vol. 46, No. 1 (February 1981):36–57.

BRAND, DAVID. "The New Whiz Kids." *Time*. Vol. 130, No. 9 (August 31, 1987):42–46, 49, 51.

BREEN, LEONARD Z. "The Aging Individual." In Clark Tibbitts, ed., *Handbook of Social Gerontology*. Chicago: University of Chicago Press, 1960:145–62.

BRENNER, HARVEY. *Estimating the Social Costs of National Economic Policy: Implications for Mental and Physical Health and Criminal Aggression*. Joint Economic Committee, 94th Congress, October 26, 1976.

BRETON, RAYMOND. "Institutional completeness of ethnic communities and the personal relations of immigrants." *American Journal of Sociology* 70, 1964: 193–205.

———. "The Socio-Political Dynamics of the October Events." *Canadian Review of Sociology and Anthropology* IX, 1972:33–56.

———. "Ethnic Stratification Viewed from Three Theoretical Perspectives." In James E. Curtis and William G. Scott, eds., *Social Stratification: Canada*. 2nd ed. Scarborough, Ontario: Prentice Hall, 1979: 270–294.

———. "Regionalism in Canada." In David Cameron, ed. *Regionalism and Supranationalism*. Montreal: Institute for Research on Public Policy, 1981.

———. "French-English Relations." In James Curtis and Lorne Tepperman, eds., *Understanding Canadian Society*. Toronto: McGraw-Hill Ryerson, 1988: 557–585.

———. *Why Meech Failed: Lessons for Canadian Constitutionmaking*. Toronto: C.D. Howe Institute, 1992.

BRINTON, CRANE. *The Anatomy of Revolution*. New York: Vintage Books, 1965.

BRINTON, MARY C. "The Social-Institutional Bases of Gender Stratification: Japan as an Illustrative Case." *American Journal of Sociology*. Vol. 94, No. 2 (September 1988):300–34.

BRODIE, JANINE. "The Political Economy of Regionalism." In Wallace Clement and Glen Williams, eds., *The New Canadian Political Economy*. Montreal: McGill-Queen's University Press, 1989: 138–159.

———, and JILL M. VICKERS. "Canadian Women in Politics." Ottawa: Canadian Research Institute for the Advancement of Women, 1982.

BROMLEY, DAVID G., and ANSON D. SHUPE, Jr. *New Christian Politics*. Macon, GA: Mercer University Press, 1984.

BRONSON, HAROLD. "Economic Concentration and Corporate Power." In Peter S. Li and B. Singh Bolaria, eds., *Contemporary Sociology: Critical Perspectives*. Toronto: Copp Clark Pitman, 1993: 203–222.

BROPHY, GWENDA. "China, Part I." *Population Today*. Vol. 17, No. 3 (March 1989a):12.

———. "China: Part II." *Population Today*. Vol. 17. No. 4 (April 1989b):12.

BROWN, E. RICHARD. *Rockefeller Medicine Men: Medicine and Capitalism in America*. Berkeley, CA: University of California Press, 1979.

BROWNMILLER, SUSAN. *Femininity*. New York: Linden Press, Simon and Schuster, 1984.

BROWNSTEIN, RONALD, and NINA EASTON. *Reagan's Ruling Class: Portraits of the President's Top One Hundred Officials*. New York: Pantheon, 1983.

BROYLES, J. ALLEN. "The John Birch Society: A Movement of Social Protest of the Radical Right." In Louis E. Genevie, ed., *Collective Behavior and Social Movements*. Itasca, IL: F. E. Peacock, 1978:338–45.

BRUCE, ERIKA and ALAN F. FOX. "The Social Sciences in Canada." *International Social Science Journal*, 39, 1 (Feb.) 1990: 127–34.

BRUNO, MARY. "Abusing the Elderly." *Newsweek* (September 23, 1985):75–76.

BRYM, ROBERT J. "The Canadian Capitalist Class, 1965–1985." In Robert, J. Brym, ed., *The Structures of the Canadian Capitalist Class*. Toronto: Garamond, 1985: 1–20.

———, ed. *Regionalism in Canada*. Toronto: Irwin, 1986.

BUCHHOLZ, MICHAEL, and JACK E. BYNUM. "Newspaper Presentation of America's Ages: A Content Analysis of Image and Role." *The Gerontologist*. Vol. 22, No. 1 (February 1982):83–88.

BUMPASS, L. "Children and Marital Disruption: A Replication and Update." *Demography*. Vol. 21, No. 1 (February 1984):71–82.

BURCH, ROBERT. Testimony to House of Representatives Hearing in "Review: The World Hunger Problem." October 25, 1983, Serial 98–38.

BURNHAM, WALTER DEAN. *Democracy in the Making: American Government and Politics*. Englewood Cliffs, NJ: Prentice Hall, 1983.

BURNS, JAMES A. "Discipline: Why Does It Continue To Be a Problem? Solution Is in Changing School Culture." *National Association of Secondary School Principals Bulletin*. Vol. 69, No. 479 (March 1985):1–47.

BURRIS, VAL. "The Social and Political Consequences of Overeducation." *American Sociological Review*. Vol. 48, No. 4 (August 1983):454–67.

BURSTEIN, PAUL. "Legal Mobilization as a Social Movement Tactic: The Struggle for Equal Employment Opportunity." *American Journal of Sociology*. Vol. 96, No. 5 (March 1991):1201–25.

BUSBY, LINDA J. "Sex Role Research on the Mass Media." *Journal of Communications.* Vol. 25 (Autumn 1975):107–13.

BUTLER, ROBERT N. *Why Survive? Being Old in America.* New York: Harper & Row, 1975.

BUTTERWORTH, DOUGLAS, and JOHN K. CHANCE. *Latin American Urbanization.* Cambridge, UK: Cambridge University Press, 1981.

"Buy America while Stocks Last." *The Economist.* Vol. 313, No. 7633 (December 16, 1989):63–66.

CAHNMAN, WERNER J., and RUDOLF HEBERLE. "Introduction." In *Ferdinand Toennies on Sociology: Pure, Applied, and Empirical.* Chicago: University of Chicago Press, 1971:vii–xxii.

CALLAHAN, DANIEL. *Setting Limits: Medical Goals in an Aging Society.* New York: Simon & Schuster, 1987.

CALLOW, A. B., JR., ed. *American Urban History.* New York: Oxford University Press, 1969.

CALMORE, JOHN O. "National Housing Policies and Black America: Trends, Issues, and Implications." In *The State of Black America 1986.* New York: National Urban League, 1986:115–49.

CAMERON, WILLIAM BRUCE. *Modern Social Movements: A Sociological Outline.* New York: Random House, 1966.

CAMPBELL, ANNE. *The Girls in the Gang.* 2nd ed. Cambridge, MA: Basil Blackwell, 1991.

Canada's 125th Anniversary Yearbook, 1992. Ottawa: Statistics Canada, October 1991.

"Canada: The Community Health Centre in Canada, 1972." In *Canada's 125th Anniversary Yearbook, 1992.* Ottawa: Statistics Canada, 1991.

CANADIAN ADVISORY COUNCIL ON THE STATUS OF WOMEN

Canadian Guidelines for the Prevention, Diagnosis, Management and Treatment of Sexually Transmitted Diseases in Neonates, Children, Adolescents, and Adults. Ottawa: Laboratory Centre for Disease Control, Health Protection Branch, Department of National Health and Welfare, 1992.

CANADIAN INTERNATIONAL DEVELOPMENT AGENCY (CIDA). *Sharing our Future: Canadian International Development Assistance.* Ottawa: Ministry of Supply and Services Canada, 1987.

CANETTI, ELIAS. *Crowds and Power.* New York: The Seabury Press, 1978.

CANTOR, MURIAL G., and SUZANNE PINGREE. *The Soap Opera.* Beverly Hills, CA: Sage Publications, 1983.

CANTRIL, HADLEY, HAZEL GAUDET, and HERTA HERZOG. *Invasion from Mars: A Study in the Psychology of Panic.* Princeton, NJ: Princeton University Press, 1947.

CAPLOW, THEODORE, et al. *Middletown Families.* Minneapolis, MN: University of Minnesota Press, 1982.

CARLEY, KATHLEEN. "A Theory of Group Stability." *American Sociological Review.* Vol. 56, No. 3 (June 1991):331–54.

CARLSON, NORMAN A. "Corrections in the United States Today: A Balance Has Been Struck." *The American Criminal Law Review.* Vol. 13, No. 4 (Spring 1976):615–47.

CARLTON, ERIC. *Ideology and Social Order.* London: Routledge & Kegan Paul, 1977.

CARMICHAEL, STOKELY, and CHARLES V. HAMILTON. *Black Power: The Politics of Liberation in America.* New York: Vintage, 1967.

CARRIGAN, D. OWEN. *Crime and Punishment in Canada: A History.* Toronto: McClelland & Stewart, 1991.

CARROLL, GINNY. "Who Foots the Bill?" *Newsweek.* Special Issue (Fall/Winter, 1990):81–85.

CARROLL, WILLIAM K. *Corporate Power and Canadian Capitalism.* Vancouver: University of British Columbia Press, 1986.

CARTER, STEPHEN L. *Reflections of an Affirmative-Action Baby.* New York: Basic Books, 1991.

CASSIDY, FRANK, ed., *Aboriginal Self-Determination.* Montreal: The Institute for Research on Public Policy, 1991.

CAWLEY, JANET. "On the Way to Female Imagery of God." In Dawn H. Curie and Valerie Raoul, eds., *The Anatomy of Gender.* 1992: 53–65.

CEBOTAREV, E.A. "Women, Human Rights and the Family in Development Theory and Practice (with reference to Latin America and the Caribbean)." *Canadian Journal of Development Studies* IX (2), 1988: 187–200.

CENTER FOR THE STUDY OF SPORT IN SOCIETY. *1991 Racial Report Card: A Study in the NBA, NFL, and Major League Baseball.* Boston: Northeastern University, 1991.

CENTERS FOR DISEASE CONTROL. Report included in "Blacks' Syphilis Rate Up Sharply." *The New York Times* (May 17, 1991):A19.

HIV/AIDS Surveillance. Vol. 40, Nos. 51 & 52 (January 3, 1992). Atlanta: The Centers, 1992.

CHAGNON, NAPOLEON A. *Yanomamö.* 3rd ed. New York: Holt, Rinehart and Winston, 1983.

———. "Life Histories, Blood Revenge, and Warfare in a Tribal Population." *Science.* Vol. 239, No. 4843 (February 26, 1988):985–92.

CHANDLER, TERTIUS, and GERALD FOX. *3000 Years of Urban History.* New York: Academic Press, 1974.

CHANGE, KWANG-CHIH. *The Archaeology of Ancient China.* New Haven, CT: Yale University Press, 1977.

CHAPPELL, NEENA L., and BETTY HAVENS. "Old and Female: Testing the Double Jeopardy Hypothesis." *The Sociological Quarterly.* Vol. 21, No. 2 (Spring 1980):157–71.

CHAPPLE, STEVE, and REEBEE GAROFALO. *Rock 'n' Roll Is Here to Pay: The History and Politics of the Music Industry.* Chicago: Nelson-Hall, 1977.

Characteristics of Dual Earner Families. Ottawa: Statistics Canada, 1992.

CHERLIN, ANDREW, and FRANK F. FURSTENBERG, JR. "The American Family in the Year 2000." *The Futurist.* Vol. 17, No. 3 (June 1983):7–14.

CHERLIN, ANDREW. *Marriage, Divorce, Remarriage.* Cambridge, MA: Harvard University Press, 1981.

CHILDREN'S DEFENSE FUND. *Child Poverty in America.* Washington, DC, 1991.

CHIP1 Social Survey Software. Datasets by J. Bruner and J. J. Macionis. Hanover, NH: Zeta Data/Englewood Cliffs, NJ: Prentice Hall, 1991.

CHISHOLM, PATRICIA. "To Celebrate Our Love Publicly." *Maclean's,* June 28, 1993: 29.

CHOMSKY, NOAM and EDWARD S. HERMAN. *Manufacturing Consent: The Political Economy of the Mass Media.* New York: Pantheon Books, 1988.

CHOWN, SHEILA M. "Morale, Careers and Personal Potentials." In James E. Birren and K. Warner Schaie, eds., *Handbook of the Psychology of Aging.* New York: Van Nostrand Reinhold, 1977:672–91.

CHRISTIAN, WILLIAM. "Ideology and Politics in Canada." In John H. Redekop, ed., *Approaches to Canadian Politics.* 2nd ed. Scarborough, Ontario: Prentice Hall, 1983.

CLANCY, PAUL, and GAIL OBERST. "First Comes Love, Then Comes Live-In." *USA Today* (March 28, 1985):1A, 2A.

CLARK, CURTIS B. "Geriatric Abuse: Out of the Closet." In *The Tragedy of Elder Abuse: The Problem and the Response.* Hearings before the Select Committee on Aging, House of Representatives, July 1, 1986:49–50.

CLARK, JUAN M., JOSE I. LASAGA, and ROSE S. REGUE. *The 1980 Mariel Exodus: An Assessment and Prospect: Special Report.* Washington, DC: Council for Inter-American Security, 1981.

CLARK, MARGARET S., ed., *Prosocial Behavior.* Newbury Park, CA: Sage, 1991.

CLARK, S.D. *The Suburban Society.* Toronto: University of Toronto Press, 1966.

———. *The New Urban Poor.* Toronto: McGraw-Hill Ryerson, 1978.

———, J. PAUL GRAYSON, and LINDA GRAYSON. *Prophecy and Protest: Social Movements in Twentieth Century Canada.* Toronto: Gage, 1975.

CLARK, THOMAS A. *Blacks in Suburbs.* New Brunswick, NJ: Rutgers University Center for Urban Policy Research, 1979.

CLARKE, JUANNE NANCARROW. *Health, Illness & Medicine in Canada.* Toronto: McClelland & Stewart, 1990.

———. "Media Portrayal of Disease from the Medical, Political Economy and Life Style Perspectives." *Qualitative Health Research*, vol. 1, no. 3, 1991: 287–308.

———. "Cancer, Heart Disease and AIDS: What Do the Media Tell Us About These Diseases?" *Health Communication*, 4(2), 1992: 105–120, .

CLEMENT, WALLACE. *The Canadian Corporate Elite: Economic Power in Canada.* Toronto: McClelland & Stewart, 1975.

———. "Approaches Toward a Canadian Sociology." In L. Tepperman and J. Curtis, eds., *Readings in Sociology: An Introduction* Toronto: McGraw-Hill Ryerson, 1988: 31–42.

———. "Comparative Class Analysis: Locating Canada in a North American and Nordic Context." *Canadian Review of Sociology and Anthropology.* 27 (4), 1990.

CLINARD, MARSHALL B. *Cities with Little Crime*: The Case of Switzerland. Cambridge, UK: Cambridge University Press, 1978.

———, and DANIEL ABBOTT. *Crime in Developing Countries.* New York: Wiley, 1973.

CLOWARD, RICHARD A., and LLOYD E. OHLIN. *Delinquency and Opportunity: A Theory of Delinquent Gangs.* New York: Free Press, 1966.

COAKLEY, JAY J. *Sport in Society: Issues and Controversies.* 3rd ed. St. Louis, MO: C. V. Mosby, 1986; 4th ed., 1990.

COCKERHAM, WILLIAM C. *Medical Sociology.* 2nd ed. Englewood Cliffs, NJ: Prentice Hall, 1982; 3rd ed., 1986.

COE, MICHAEL D., and RICHARD A. DIEHL. *In the Land of the Olmec.* Austin, TX: University of Texas Press, 1980.

COHEN, ALBERT K. *Delinquent Boys: The Culture of the Gang.* New York: Free Press, 1971; orig. 1955.

COHEN, LLOYD R. "Sexual Harassment and the Law." *Society.* Vol. 28, No. 4 (May–June, 1991):8–13.

COHEN, MICHAEL. "Restructuring the System." *Transaction.* Vol. 26, No. 4 (May/June 1989):40–48.

COHN, BOB. "The Lawsuit Cha-Cha." *Newsweek* (August 26, 1991):58–59.

COHN, RICHARD M. "Economic Development and Status Change of the Aged." *American Journal of Sociology.* Vol. 87, No. 2 (March 1982):1150–61.

COLE, SUSAN. *Pornography and the Sex Crisis.* Toronto: Amanita Enterprises, 1989.

COLEMAN, JAMES S., and THOMAS HOFFER. *Public and Private High Schools: The Impact of Communities.* New York: Basic Books, 1987.

COLEMAN, JAMES, THOMAS HOFFER, and SALLY KILGORE. *Public and Private Schools: An Analysis of Public Schools and Beyond.* Washington, DC: National Center for Education Statistics, 1981.

COLEMAN, JOHN R. "Homeless on the Streets of New York." In John J. Macionis and Nijole V. Benokraitis, eds., *Seeing Ourselves: Classic, Contemporary, and Cross-Cultural Readings in Sociology.* 2nd ed. Englewood Cliffs, NJ: Prentice Hall, 1992.

COLEMAN, RICHARD P., and BERNICE L. NEUGARTEN. *Social Status in the City.* San Francisco, CA: Jossey-Bass, 1971.

COLEMAN, RICHARD P., and LEE RAINWATER. *Social Standing in America.* New York: Basic Books, 1978.

COLEMAN, WILLIAM D. *The Independence Movement in Quebec 1945–1980.* Toronto: University of Toronto Press, 1984.

COLLINS, RANDALL. "A Conflict Theory of Sexual Stratification." *Social Problems.* Vol. 19, No. 1 (Summer 1971):3–21.

———. *The Credential Society: An Historical Sociology of Education and Stratification.* New York: Academic Press, 1979.

———. *Sociological Insight: An Introduction to Nonobvious Sociology.* New York: Oxford University Press, 1982.

———. *Weberian Sociological Theory.* Cambridge, UK: Cambridge University Press, 1986.

COLLOWAY, N. O., and PAULA L. DOLLEVOET. "Selected Tabular Material on Aging." In Caleb Finch and Leonard Hayflick, eds., *Handbook of the Biology of Aging.* New York: Van Nostrand Reinhold, 1977:666–708.

COLOMBO, JOHN ROBERT. *The Canadian Global Almanac 1993: A Book of Facts.* Toronto: Macmillan, 1992.

Community Colleges and Related Institutions: Postsecondary Enrolment and Graduates, 1990–1991. Cat. no. 81–222. Ottawa: Statistics Canada, 1993.

COMTE, AUGUSTE. *Auguste Comte and Positivism: The Essential Writings.* Gertrud Lenzer, ed. New York: Harper Torchbooks, 1975.

CONGREGATION FOR THE DOCTRINE OF THE FAITH. *Instruction on Respect for Human Life in Its Origin and on the Dignity of Procreation: Replies to Certain Questions of the Day.* Vatican City, 1987.

CONNIDIS, INGRID A. *Family Ties and Aging.* Toronto: Butterworths, 1989.

CONRAD, PETER, and JOSEPH W. SCHNEIDER. *Deviance and Medicalization: From Badness to Sickness.* Columbus, OH: Merrill, 1980.

CONTRERAS, JOSEPH. "A New Day Dawns." *Newsweek* (March 30, 1992):40–41.

COOLEY, CHARLES HORTON. *Human Nature and the Social Order.* New York: Schocken Books, 1964; orig. 1902.

———. *Social Organization.* New York: Schocken Books, 1962; orig. 1909.

COPPOCK, MARJORIE L. "Women's Leadership Involvement in Community Volunteer Organizations." Paper presented to Southwestern Sociological Association, Dallas, Texas, 1987.

CORNELL, STEPHEN. *The Return of the Native: American Indian Political Resurgence.* New York: Oxford University Press, 1988.

Corpus Almanac and Canadian Sourcebook. Barbara Law, ed. Don Mills: Southam Information and Technology Group, 1992.

CORSARO, WILLIAM A., and THOMAS A. RIZZO. "Discussione and Friendship: Socialization Processes in the Peer Culture of Italian Nursery School Children." *American Sociological Review.* Vol. 53, No. 6 (December 1988): 879–94.

COSER, LEWIS A. *Masters of Sociological Thought: Ideas in Historical and Social Context,* 2nd ed. New York: Harcourt Brace Jovanovich, 1977.

COTTLE, THOMAS J. "What Tracking Did to Ollie Taylor." *Social Policy.* Vol. 5, No. 2 (July–August 1974):22–24.

COTTRELL, JOHN, and THE EDITORS OF TIME-LIFE. *The Great Cities: Mexico City.* Amsterdam: 1979.

COUNCIL ON INTERNATIONAL EDUCATIONAL EXCHANGE. *Educating for Global Competence: The Report of the Advisory Committee for International Educational Exchange.* New York: The Council, 1988.

COUNTS, G. S. "The Social Status of Occupations: A Problem in Vocational Guidance." *School Review.* Vol. 33 (January 1925):16–27.

COURTNEY, ALICE E., and THOMAS W. WHIPPLE. *Sex Stereotyping in Advertising.* Lexington, MA: D. C. Heath, 1983.

COWGILL, DONALD, and LOWELL HOLMES. *Aging and Modernization.* New York: Appleton-Century-Crofts, 1972.

COX, HAROLD. *Later Life: The Realities of Aging.* Englewood Cliffs, NJ: Prentice Hall, 1984.

COX, HARVEY. *The Secular City.* Rev. ed. New York: Macmillan, 1971; orig. 1965.

———. *Turning East: The Promise and Peril of the New Orientalism.* New York: Simon and Schuster, 1977.

———. "Church and Believers: Always Strangers?" In Robbins, Thomas, and Dick Anthony. *In Gods We Trust: New Patterns of Religious Pluralism in America.* 2nd ed. New Brunswick, NJ: Transaction, 1990:449–62.

CREESE, GILLIAN, NEIL GUPPY and MARTIN MEISSNER. *Ups and Downs on the Ladder of Success.* Ottawa: Statistics Canada, 1991.

CRISPELL, DIANE. "Working in 2000." *American Demographics.* Vol. 12, No. 3 (March 1990):36–40.

CROUSE, JAMES, and DALE TRUSHEIM. *The Case Against the SAT.* Chicago: University of Chicago Press, 1988.

CRYSTAL, GRAEF S. "How Much CEOs Really Make." *Fortune* (June 17, 1991):72–80.

CUFF, E. C., and G. C. F. PAYNE, eds. *Perspectives in Sociology.* London: Allen and Unwin, 1979.

CULLETON, BEATRICE. *In Search of April Raintree.* Winnipeg: Pemmican Publications Inc., 1983.

CUMMING, ELAINE, and WILLIAM E. HENRY. *Growing Old: The Process of Disengagement.* New York: Basic Books, 1961.

CURRIE, DAWN H. "Starvation Amidst Abundance: Female Adolescents and Anorexia." In B.S. Bolaria and H.D. Dickenson, eds., *The Sociology of Health Care in Canada.* Toronto: Harcourt Brace Jovanovich, 1988: 198–215.

CURRIE, ELLIOTT. *Confronting Crime: An American Challenge.* New York: Pantheon, 1985.

CURTIS, JAMES E. and WILLIAM G. SCOTT, eds. *Social Stratification: Canada.* 2nd ed. Scarborough, Ontario: Prentice Hall, 1979.

CURTIS, JAMES, EDWARD GRABB, NEIL GUPPY and SID GILBERT, eds. *Social Inequality in Canada: Patterns, Problems and Policies.* Toronto: Prentice Hall, 1988.

CURTISS, SUSAN. *Genie: A Psycholinguistic Study of a Modern-Day "Wild Child."* New York: Academic Press, 1977.

CUTRIGHT, PHILLIP. "Occupational Inheritance: A Cross-National Analysis." *American Journal of Sociology.* Vol. 73, No. 4 (January 1968):400–16.

DAHL, ROBERT A. *Who Governs?* New Haven, CT: Yale University Press, 1961.

———. *Dilemmas of Pluralist Democracy: Autonomy vs. Control.* New Haven, CT: Yale University Press, 1982.

DAHLIN, MICHAEL. "Perspectives on Family Life of the Elderly in 1900." *The Gerontologist.* Vol. 20, No. 1 (February 1980):99–107.

DAHRENDORF, RALF. *Class and Class Conflict in Industrial Society.* Stanford, CA: Stanford University Press, 1959.

DALGLISH, BRENDA. "Cheaters." *Maclean's,* Aug. 9, 1993: 18–21.

DALY, MARTIN, and MARGO WILSON. *Homicide.* New York: Aldine De Gruyter, 1988.

DAMON, WILLIAM. *Social and Personality Development.* New York: W. W. Norton, 1983.

DANIELS, ROGER. "The Issei Generation." In Amy Tachiki et al., eds., *Roots: An Asian American Reader.* Los Angeles: UCLA Asian American Studies Center, 1971:138–49.

DANNEFER, DALE. "Adult Development and Social Theory: A Reappraisal." *American Sociological Review.* Vol. 49, No. 1 (February 1984):100–116.

DARNTON, NINA, and YURIKO HOSHIA. "Whose Life Is It, Anyway?" *Newsweek.* Vol. 113, No. 4 (January 13, 1989):61.

DAVIES, CHRISTIE. *Ethnic Humor Around the World: A Comparative Analysis.* Bloomington: Indiana University Press, 1990.

DAVIES, JAMES C. "Toward a Theory of Revolution." *American Sociological Review.* Vol. 27, No. 1 (February 1962):5–19.

DAVIES, MARK, and DENISE B. KANDEL. "Parental and Peer Influences on Adolescents' Educational Plans: Some Further Evidence." *American Journal of Sociology.* Vol. 87, No. 2 (September 1981):363–87.

DAVIS, JAMES A. *Social Differences in Contemporary America.* New York: Harcourt Brace Jovanovich, 1987.

DAVIS, KINGSLEY. "Extreme Social Isolation of a Child." *American Journal of Sociology.* Vol. 45, No. 4 (January 1940):554–65.

———. "Final Note on a Case of Extreme Isolation." *American Journal of Sociology.* Vol. 52, No. 5 (March 1947):432–37.

———, and WILBERT MOORE. "Some Principles of Stratification." *American Sociological Review.* Vol. 10, No. 2 (April 1945):242–49.

DAVIS, SHARON A., and EMIL J. HALLER. "Tracking, Ability, and SES: Further Evidence on the 'Revisionist-Meritocratic Debate.'"*American Journal of Education.* Vol. 89 (May 1981):283–304.

DECKARD, BARBARA SINCLAIR. *The Women's Movement: Political, Socioeconomic, and Psychological Issues.* 2nd ed. New York: Harper & Row, 1979.

DEDRICK, DENNIS K. Personal communication, 1990.

———, and RICHARD E. YINGER. "MAD, SDI, and the Nuclear Arms Race." Manuscript in development. Georgetown, KY: Georgetown College, 1990.

DEGLER, CARL. *At Odds: Women and the Family in America From the Revolution to the Present.* New York: Oxford University Press, 1980.

DeKESEREDY, WALTER S. and RONALD HINCH. *Woman Abuse: Sociological Perspectives.* Toronto: Thompson Educational Publishing, 1991.

DELACROIX, JACQUES, and CHARLES C. RAGIN. "Structural Blockage: A Crossnational Study of Economic Dependency, State Efficacy, and Underdevelopment." *American Journal of Sociology.* Vol. 86, No. 6 (May 1981):1311–47.

Demographic Aging: The Economic Consequences. Ottawa: Ministry of Supply and Services, 1991.

DEMOTT, JOHN S. "Wreaking Havoc on Spring Break." *Time.* Vol. 127, No. 14 (April 7, 1986):29.

DePARLE, JASON. "Painted by Numbers, 1980s are Rosy to G. O. P., While Democrats See Red." *The New York Times* (September 26, 1991a):B10.

———. "Poverty Rate Rose Sharply Last Year as Incomes Slipped." *The New York Times* (September 27, 1991b):A1, A11.

DEPEW, ROBERT. "Policing Native Communities: Some Principles and Issues in Organizational Theory." *Canadian Journal of Criminology,* 34, 1992.

DER SPIEGEL. "Third World Metropolises Are Becoming Monsters; Rural Poverty Drives Millions to the Slums." In *World Press Review* (October 1989).

DEVINE, JOEL A. "State and State Expenditure: Determinants of Social Investment and Social Consumption Spending in the Postwar United States." *American Sociological Review.* Vol. 50, No. 2 (April 1985):150–65.

DEWEY, JOHN. *Experience and Education.* New York: Collier Books, 1968; orig. 1938.

DIAMOND, MILTON. "Sexual Identity, Monozygotic Twins Reared in Discordant Sex Roles and a BBC Follow-Up." *Archives of Sexual Behavior.* Vol. 11, No. 2 (April 1982):181–86.

DICKASON, OLIVE PATRICIA. *Canada's First Nations: A History of Founding Peoples from the Earliest Times.* Toronto: McClelland & Stewart, 1992.

DICKENS, CHARLES. *The Adventures of Oliver Twist.* Boston: Estes and Lauriat, 1886; orig. 1837–1839.

DIPRETE, THOMAS A. "Unemployment over the Life Cycle: Racial Differences and the Effect of Changing Economic Conditions." *American Journal of Sociology.* Vol. 87, No. 2 (September 1981):286–307.

DIZARD, JAN E., and HOWARD GADLIN. *The Minimal Family.* Amherst: The University of Massachusetts Press, 1990.

DOBSON, RICHARD B. "Mobility and Stratification in the Soviet Union." *Annual Review of Sociology.* Vol. 3. Palo Alto, CA: Annual Reviews, Inc., 1977: 297–329.

DOBYNS, HENRY F. "An Appraisal of Techniques with a New Hemispheric Estimate." *Current Anthropology.* Vol. 7, No. 4 (October 1966):395–446.

DOLLARD, JOHN, et al. *Frustration and Aggression.* New Haven, CT: Yale University Press, 1939.

DOMHOFF, G. WILLIAM. *Who Rules America?* Englewood Cliffs, NJ: Prentice Hall, 1967.

———. *The Higher Circles: The Governing Class in America.* New York: Vintage, 1971.

———. *The Powers That Be: Processes of Ruling Class Domination in America.* New York: Vintage, 1979.

———. *Who Rules America Now? A View of the '80s.* Englewood Cliffs, NJ: Prentice Hall, 1983.

———. "The Growth Machine and the Power Elite: A Theoretical Challenge to Pluralists and Marxists Alike." Paper presented to the American Political Science Association. Washington, DC: 1984.

DONOVAN, VIRGINIA K., and RONNIE LITTENBERG. "Psychology of Women: Feminist Therapy." In Barbara Haber, ed., *The Women's Annual 1981: The Year in Review.* Boston: G. K. Hall, 1982:211–35.

DOUGLAS, JACK. *The Social Meanings of Suicide.* Princeton, N.J.: Princeton University Press, 1967.

DOUGLASS, RICHARD L. "Domestic Neglect and Abuse of the Elderly: Implications for Research and Service." *Family Relations.* Vol. 32 (July 1983): 395–402.

DOW, UNITY. Personal communication, 1990.

DOYAL, LESLEY, with Imogen Pennell. *The Political Economy of Health*. London: Pluto Press, 1981.

DOYLE, JAMES A. *The Male Experience*. Dubuque, IA: Wm. C. Brown, 1983.

DOYLE, PATRICK. "Ottawa to Raise Legal Smoking Age." *The Toronto Star*, Fri., Feb. 5, 1993: A14.

DRIEDGER, LEO, ed. *Ethnic Canada: Identities and Inequalities*. Toronto: Copp Clark Pitman, 1987.

———, ed. *The Ethnic Factor: Identity in Diversity*. Toronto: McGraw-Hill Ryerson, 1989.

DUBINSKY, KAREN. *Lament for a Patriarchy Lost? Anti-feminism, Anti-abortion and R.E.A.L. Women in Canada*. Ottawa: Canadian Research Institute for the Advancement of Women, 1985.

DUBOIS, W. E. B. "The Social Effects of Emancipation (1913)." In John J. Macionis and Nijole V. Benokraitis, eds., *Seeing Ourselves: Classic, Contemporary, and Cross-Cultural Readings in Sociology*. 2nd ed. Englewood Cliffs, NJ: Prentice Hall, 1992.

DUBOIS, W. E. B. *The Philadelphia Negro: A Social Study*. New York: Schocken, 1967; orig. 1899.

DUBOS, RENE. *Man Adapting*. New Haven, CT: Yale University Press, 1980; orig. 1965.

DUCHARME, MICHELE. "The History of Guelph's Black Community." *The Ontarion*, March 26, 1985: 7. (Archival Collections: University of Guelph Library)

DUHL, LEONARD J. "The Social Context of Health." In Arthur C. Hastings et al., eds., *Health for the Whole Person: The Complete Guide to Holistic Medicine*. Boulder, CO: Westview Press, 1980:39–48.

DULUDE, LOUISE. *Love, Marriage and Money*. Ottawa: Canadian Advisory Council on the Status of Women, 1984.

DURDEN, GAREY C., JASON F. SHOGREN, and JONATHAN I. SILBERMAN. "The Effects of Interest Group Pressure on Coal-Strip Mining Legislation." *Social Science Quarterly*. Vol. 72, No. 2 (June 1991):239–50.

DURKHEIM, EMILE. *The Division of Labor in Society*. New York: Free Press, 1964a; orig. 1895.

———. *The Rules of Sociological Method*. New York: Free Press, 1964b; orig. 1893.

———. *The Elementary Forms of Religious Life*. New York: Free Press, 1965; orig. 1915.

———. *Suicide*. New York: Free Press, 1966; orig. 1897.

———. *Selected Writings*. Anthony Giddens, ed. Cambridge, UK: Cambridge University Press, 1972.

———. *Sociology and Philosophy*. New York: Free Press, 1974; orig. 1924.

DUROCHER, RENÉ. "Quiet Revolution." *The Canadian Encyclopedia*. 2nd ed. Edmonton: Hurtig Publishers, 3, 1988: 1813–4.

DWORKIN, ANDREA. *Intercourse*. New York: Free Press, 1987.

DZIECH, BILLIE WRIGHT, and LINDA WEINER. *The Lecherous Professor: Sexual Harassment on Campus*. Boston, MA: Beacon Press, 1984.

Earnings of Men and Women. Ottawa: Statistics Canada, 1991.

EBAUGH, HELEN ROSE FUCHS. *Becoming an EX: The Process of Role Exit*. Chicago: University of Chicago Press, 1988.

ECKHOLM, ERIK. "Malnutrition in Elderly: Widespread Health Threat." *The New York Times* (August 13, 1985):19–20.

———, and JOHN TIERNEY. "AIDS in Africa: A Killer Rages On." *The New York Times* (September 16, 1990):A1, 14.

EDGERTON, ROBERT B. *Deviance: A Cross-Cultural Perspective*. Menlo Park, California: Cummings, 1976.

EDMONSTON, BARRY, and THOMAS M. GUTERBOCK. "Is Suburbanization Slowing Down? Recent Trends in Population Deconcentration in U. S. Metropolitan Areas." *Social Forces*. Vol. 62, No. 4 (June 1984):905–25.

EDWARDS, DAVID V. *The American Political Experience*. 3rd ed. Englewood Cliffs, NJ: Prentice Hall, 1985.

EDWARDS, RICHARD. *Contested Terrain: The Transformation of the Workplace in the Twentieth Century*. New York: Basic Books, 1979.

EHRENREICH, BARBARA. *The Hearts of Men: American Dreams and the Flight from Commitment*. Garden City, NY: Anchor, 1983.

———. *Fear of Falling: The Inner Life of the Middle Class*. New York: Harper Collins, 1990.

EHRENREICH, JOHN. "Introduction." In John Ehrenreich, ed., *The Cultural Crisis of Modern Medicine*. New York: Monthly Review Press, 1978:1–35.

EHRLICH, PAUL R. *The Population Bomb*. New York: Ballantine Books, 1978.

EICHLER, MARGRIT. "Women as Personal Dependents." In Marylee Stephenson, ed., *Women in Canada*, rev. ed. Don Mills, Ont.: General Publishing, 1977: 51–69.

———. "Women's Unpaid Labour." *Atlantis*, 3, part 2, 1978: 52–62.

———. *Families in Canada Today: Recent changes and their policy consequences*. 2nd ed., Toronto: Gage, 1988.

EISEN, ARNOLD M. *The Chosen People in America: A Study of Jewish Religious Ideology*. Bloomington, IN: Indiana University Press, 1983.

EISENSTEIN, ZILLAH R., ed. *Capitalist Patriarchy and the Case for Socialist Feminism*. New York: Monthly Review Press, 1979.

EISLER, BENITA. *The Lowell Offering: Writings by New England Mill Women 1840–1845*. Philadelphia and New York: J. B. Lippincott Company, 1977.

EITZEN, D. STANELY. *Social Problems*. Boston: Allyn and Bacon, 1980.

EKMAN, PAUL. "Biological and Cultural Contributions to Body and Facial Movements in the Expression of Emotions." In A. Rorty, ed., *Explaining Emotions*. Berkeley: University of California Press, 1980a:73–101.

———. *Face of Man: Universal Expression in a New Guinea Village*. New York: Garland Press, 1980b.

———. *Telling Lies: Clues to Deceit in the Marketplace, Politics, and Marriage*. New York: W. W. Norton, 1985.

———, WALLACE V. FRIESEN, and JOHN BEAR. "The International Language of Gestures." *Psychology Today* (May 1984):64–69.

EL-ATTAR, MOHAMED. Personal communication, 1991.

ELIAS, ROBERT. *The Politics of Victimization: Victims, Victimology and Human Rights*. New York: Oxford University Press, 1986.

ELAM, STANLEY M., LOWELL C. ROSE, and ALEC M. GALLUP. "The 23rd Annual Gallup Poll of the Public's Attitudes Toward Public Schools." *Phi Delta Kappan*, Vol. 73 (September 1991):41–56.

ELKIN, FREDERICK, and GERALD HANDEL. *The Child and Society: The Process of Socialization*. 4th ed. New York: Random House, 1984.

ELKIND, DAVID. *The Hurried Child: Growing Up Too Fast Too Soon*. Reading, MA: Addison-Wesley, 1981.

ELLIOT, DELBERT S., and SUZANNE S. AGETON. "Reconciling Race and Class Differences in Self-Reported and Official Estimates of Delinquency." *American Sociological Review*. Vol. 45, No. 1 (February 1980):95–110.

ELLIS, D. and L. SAWYER. *When I Grow Up: Career Expectations and Aspirations of Canadian School Children*. Ottawa: Women's Bureau, 1986.

ELMER-DEWITT, PHILIP. "The Revolution that Fizzled." *Time*. Vol. 137, No. 20 (May 20, 1991):48–49.

EMBER, MELVIN, and CAROL R. EMBER. "The Conditions Favoring Matrilocal versus Patrilocal Residence." *American Anthropologist*. Vol. 73, No. 3 (June 1971):571–94.

———. *Anthropology*. 6th ed. Englewood Cliffs, NJ: Prentice Hall, 1991.

EMBREE, AINSLIE T. *The Hindu Tradition*. New York: Vintage Books, 1972.

EMERSON, JOAN P. "Behavior in Private Places: Sustaining Definitions of Reality in Gynecological Examinations." In H. P. Dreitzel, ed., *Recent Sociology*. Vol. 2. New York: Collier, 1970:74–97.

Employment by Income and Occupation: The Nation. Ottawa: Statistics Canada, April 1993.

ENGELS, FRIEDRICH. *The Origin of the Family*. Chicago: Charles H. Kerr and Company, 1902; orig. 1884.

ERIKSON, ERIK H. *Childhood and Society*. New York: W. W. Norton, 1963; orig. 1950.

———. *Identity and the Life Cycle*. New York: W. W. Norton, 1980.

ERIKSON, KAI T. *Wayward Puritans: A Study in the Sociology of Deviance*. New York: John Wiley, 1966.

———. *Everything in Its Path: Destruction of Community in the Buffalo Creek Flood*. New York: Simon and Schuster, 1976.

ERIKSON, ROBERT S., NORMAN R. LUTTBEG, and KENT L. TEDIN. *American Public Opinion: Its Origins, Content, and Impact*. 2nd ed. New York: Wiley, 1980.

ETZIONI, AMITAI. "Too Many Rights, Too Few Responsibilities." *Society*. Vol. 28, No. 2 (January/February 1991):41–48.

ETZIONI, AMITAI. *A Comparative Analysis of Complex Organization: On Power, Involvement, and Their Correlates*. Revised and enlarged ed. New York: Free Press, 1975.

ETZIONI-HALEVY, EVA. *Bureaucracy and Democracy: A Political Dilemma*. Rev. ed. Boston: Routledge & Kegan Paul, 1985.

EVANGELAUF, JEAN. "Student Financial Aid Reaches $20. 5 Billion, but Fails to Keep Pace with Rising College Costs, Study Finds." *The Chronicle of Higher Education*. Vol. XXXIV, No. 14 (December 2, 1987):A33, A36.

EVANS, M. D. R. "Immigrant Entrepreneurship: Effects of Ethnic Market Size and Isolated Labor Pool." *American Sociological Review*. Vol. 54, No. 6 (December 1989):950–62.

EVE, SUSAN BROWN. "Age Strata Differences in Utilization of Health Care Services among Adults in the United States." *Sociological Focus*. Vol. 17, No. 2 (April 1984):105–20.

EVERS, FREDERICK T., JAMES C. RUSH, JASNA A. KRMPOTIC, JOANNE DUNCAN-ROBINSON. *Making the Match: Phase II (Final Technical Report)*, Universities of Guelph and Western Ontario, 1993.

FALK, GERHARD. Personal communication, 1987.

FALLOWS, JAMES. "Immigration: How It's Affecting Us." *The Atlantic Monthly*. Vol. 252 (November 1983):45–52, 55–62, 66–68, 85–90, 94, 96, 99–106.

FALUDI, SUSAN. *Backlash: The Undeclared War Against American Women*. New York: Crown, 1991.

Family Economics Review. "Updated Estimates of the Cost of Raising a Child." Vol. 2, No. 4 (1989):30–31.

FANTINI, MARIO D. *Regaining Excellence in Education*. Columbus, OH: Merrill, 1986.

FARRELL, MICHAEL P., and STANLEY D. ROSENBERG. *Men at Midlife*. Boston, MA: Auburn House, 1981.

FEAGIN, JOE. *The Urban Real Estate Game*. Englewood Cliffs, NJ: Prentice Hall, 1983.

———. "The Continuing Significance of Race: Antiblack Discrimination in Public Places." *American Sociological Review*. Vol. 56, No. 1 (February 1991):101–16.

FEATHERMAN, DAVID L., and ROBERT M. HAUSER. *Opportunity and Change*. New York: Academic Press, 1978.

FENNELL, MARY C. "The Effects of Environmental Characteristics on the Structure of Hospital Clusters." *Administrative Science Quarterly*. Vol. 29, No. 3 (September 1980):489–510.

FENNELL, TOM. "A Measure of Hope." *Maclean's*. June 14, 1993: 48–49.

FERGUSON, TOM. "Medical Self-Care: Self Responsibility for Health." In Arthur C. Hastings et al., eds., *Health for the Whole Person: The Complete Guide to Holistic Medicine*. Boulder, CO: Westview Press, 1980:87–109.

FERGUSSON, D. M., L. J. HORWOOD, and F. T. SHANNON. "A Proportional Hazards Model of Family Breakdown." *Journal of Marriage and the Family*. Vol. 46, No. 3 (August 1984): 539–49.

FIFE, SANDY. "The Total Quality Muddle." *The Globe and Mail: Report on Business,* Nov. 1992: 64–74.

FINKELHOR, DAVID. *Child Sexual Abuse: New Theory and Research*. New York: The Free Press, 1984.

FINKELSTEIN, NEAL W., and RON HASKINS. "Kindergarten Children Prefer Same-Color Peers." *Child Development*. Vol. 54, No. 2 (April 1983):502–8.

FIORENTINE, ROBERT. "Men, Women, and the Premed Persistence Gap: A Normative Alternatives Approach." *American Journal of Sociology*. Vol. 92, No. 5 (March 1987):1118–39.

FIREBAUGH, GLENN, and KENNETH E. DAVIS. "Trends in Antiblack Prejudice, 1972–1984: Region and Cohort Effects." *American Journal of Sociology*. Vol. 94, No. 2 (September 1988):251–72.

FISCHER, CLAUDE S., et al. *Networks and Places: Social Relations in the Urban Setting*. New York: Free Press, 1977.

FISCHER, CLAUDE W. *The Urban Experience*. 2nd ed. New York: Harcourt Brace Jovanovich, 1984.

FISHER, ELIZABETH. *Woman's Creation: Sexual Evolution and the Shaping of Society*. Garden City, NY: Anchor/Doubleday, 1979.

FISHER, ROGER, and WILLIAM URY. "Getting to YES." In William M. Evan and Stephen Hilgartner, eds.,*The Arms Race and Nuclear War*. Englewood Cliffs, NJ: Prentice Hall, 1988:261–68.

FISHMAN, PAMELA M. "Interactional Shitwork." *Heresies: A Feminist Publication on Art and Politics*. Vol. 2 (May 1977):99–101.

FISHMAN, PAMELA M. "The Work Women Do." *Social Problems*. Vol. 25, No. 4 (April 1978):397–406.

FISKE, ALAN PAIGE. "The Cultural Relativity of Selfish Individualism: Anthropological Evidence that Humans Are Inherently Sociable." In Margaret S. Clark, ed., *Prosocial Behavior*. Newbury Park, CA: Sage, 1991:176–214.

FITZPATRICK, JOSEPH P. *Puerto Rican Americans: The Meaning of Migration to the Mainland*. Englewood Cliffs, NJ: Prentice Hall, 1971.

———. "Puerto Ricans." In *Harvard Encyclopedia of American Ethnic Groups*. Cambridge, MA: Harvard University Press, 1980:858–67.

FITZPATRICK, MARY ANNE. *Between Husbands and Wives: Communication in Marriage*. Newbury Park, CA: Sage, 1988.

FLAHERTY, MICHAEL G. "A Formal Approach to the Study of Amusement in Social Interaction." *Studies in Symbolic Interaction*. Vol. 5. New York: JAI Press, 1984:71–82.

———. "Two Conceptions of the Social Situation: Some Implications of Humor." *The Sociological Quarterly*. Vol. 31, No. 1 (Spring 1990).

FLETCHER, FREDERICK J., ed. *Media and Voters in Canadian Election Campaigns*. Toronto: Dundurn Press, 1991.

FLORIDA, RICHARD, and MARTIN KENNEY. "Transplanted Organizations: The Transfer of Japanese Industrial Organization to the U. S." *American Sociological Review*. Vol. 56, No. 3 (June 1991):381–98.

FLOWER, G.E. *Speaking Out: The 1984 CEA poll of Canadian opinion on education*. Toronto: Canadian Education Association, 1984.

FLYNN, PATRICIA. "The Disciplinary Emergence of Bioethics and Bioethics Committees: Moral Ordering and its Legitimation." *Sociological Focus*. Vol. 24, No. 2 (May 1991):145–56.

Forbes. Special Issue. "The Forbes 500 Annual Directory." Vol. 147, No. 9 (April 29, 1991).

FORD, CLELLAN S., and FRANK A. BEACH. *Patterns of Sexual Behavior*. New York: Harper & Row, 1951.

FORM, WILLIAM. "Self-Employed Manual Workers: Petty Bourgeois or Working Class?" *Social Forces*. Vol. 60, No. 4 (June 1982):1050–69.

FORNOS, WERNER. "Growth of Cities Is Major Crisis." *Popline*. Vol. 8, No 3 (March 1986):4.

FORREST, HUGH. "They Are Completely Inactive ..." *The Gambier Journal*. Vol. 3, No. 4 (February 1984):10–11.

FOWLER, FLOYD J., JR., and THOMAS W. MANGIONE. *Standardized Survey Interviewing: Minimizing Interviewer-Related Error*. Newbury Park, CA: Sage, 1989.

FRANCIS, DIANE. *Controlling Interest: Who Owns Canada?* Toronto: Macmillan, 1986.

FRANK, ANDRE GUNDER. *On Capitalist Underdevelopment*. Bombay: Oxford University Press, 1975.

———. *Crisis: In the World Economy*. New York: Holmes & Meier, 1980.

————. *Reflections on the World Economic Crisis.* New York: Monthly Review Press, 1981.

FRANKLIN, JOHN HOPE. *From Slavery to Freedom: A History of Negro Americans.* 3rd ed. New York: Vintage Books, 1967.

FRASER, SYLVIA. *In My Father's House.* Toronto: Collins Paperback, 1987.

FRAZIER, E. FRANKLIN. *Black Bourgeoisie: The Rise of a New Middle Class.* New York: Free Press, 1965.

FRÉCHETTE, PIERRE. "Income Distribution." *The Canadian Encyclopedia.* 2nd ed. Edmonton: Hurtig Publishers, 2, 1988:1051–1052.

FREDRICKSON, GEORGE M. *White Supremacy: A Comparative Study in American and South African History.* New York: Oxford University Press, 1981.

FREEMAN, DEREK. *Margaret Mead and Samoa: The Making and Unmaking of an Anthropological Myth.* Cambridge, MA: Harvard University Press, 1983.

FRENCH, MARILYN. *Beyond Power: On Women, Men, and Morals.* New York: Summit Books, 1985.

FRETZ, WINFIELD. *The Waterloo Mennonites: A Community in Paradox.* Waterloo: Wilfrid Laurier Press, 1989.

FRIDERES, JAMES S. *Native Peoples in Canada: Contemporary Conflicts.* 4th ed. Scarborough, Ontario: Prentice Hall, 1993.

FRIEDMAN, EUGENE A., and ROBERT J. HAVIGHURST. *The Meaning of Work and Retirement.* Chicago: University of Chicago Press, 1954.

FRIEDRICH, CARL J., and ZBIGNIEW BRZEZINSKI. *Totalitarian Dictatorship and Autocracy.* 2nd ed. Cambridge, MA: Harvard University Press, 1965.

FRIEDRICH, OTTO. "A Proud Capital's Distress." *Time.* Vol. 124, No. 6 (August 6, 1984):26–30, 33–35.

————. "United No More." *Time.* Vol. 129, No. 18 (May 4, 1987):28–37.

FUCHS, VICTOR R. *Who Shall Live.* New York: Basic Books, 1974.

————. "Sex Differences in Economic Well-Being." *Science.* Vol. 232 (April 25, 1986):459–64.

FUGITA, STEPHEN S., and DAVID J. O'BRIEN. "Structural Assimilation, Ethnic Group Membership, and Political Participation among Japanese Americans: A Research Note." *Social Forces.* Vol. 63, No. 4 (June 1985):986–95.

FUJIMOTO, ISAO. "The Failure of Democracy in a Time of Crisis." In Amy Tachiki et al., eds., *Roots: An Asian American Reader.* Los Angeles: UCLA Asian American Studies Center, 1971:207–14.

FUMENTO, MICHAEL. *The Myth of Heterosexual AIDS.* New York: Basic Books, 1989.

FURSTENBERG, FRANK F., JR. "The New Extended Family: The Experience of Parents and Children after Remarriage." Paper presented to the Changing Family Conference XIII: The Blended Family. University of Iowa, 1984.

————, J. BROOKS-GUNN, and S. PHILIP MORGAN. *Adolescent Mothers in Later Life.* New York: Cambridge University Press, 1987.

FUSFELD, DANIEL R. *Economics: Principles of Political Economy.* Glenview, IL: Scott, Foresman, 1982.

GAGLIANI, GIORGIO. "How Many Working Classes?" *American Journal of Sociology.* Vol. 87, No. 2 (September 1981):259–85.

Gallup Sexual Life Style Survey. Toronto: Gallup Report, Saturday, September 3, 1988.

GALLUP, GEORGE, JR. *Religion in America.* Princeton, NJ: Princeton Religion Research Center, 1982.

GALSTER, GEORGE. "Black Suburbanization: Has It Changed the Relative Location of Races?" *Urban Affairs Quarterly.* Vol. 26, No. 4 (June 1991):621–28.

GANS, HERBERT J. *The Urban Villagers: Group and Class in the Life of Italian-Americans.* New York: Free Press, 1982; orig. 1962.

————. *People and Plans: Essays on Urban Problems and Solutions.* New York: Basic Books, 1968.

————. *Deciding What's News: A Study of CBS Evening News, NBC Nightly News, Newsweek and Time.* New York: Vintage, 1980.

GARDNER, R. ALLEN, and BEATRICE T. GARDNER. "Teaching Sign Language to a Chimpanzee." *Science.* Vol. 165 (1969):664–72.

GARFINKEL, HAROLD. "Conditions of Successful Degradation Ceremonies." *American Journal of Sociology.* Vol. 61, No. 2 (March 1956):420–24.

————. *Studies in Ethnomethodology.* Cambridge, UK: Polity Press, 1967.

GASKELL, JANE, ARLENE MCLAREN and MYRA NOVOGRODSKY. *Claiming An Education: Feminism and Canadian Schools.* Toronto: Our Schools/Our Selves Education Foundation and Garamond Press, 1989.

GEE, ELLEN M. and MEREDITH M. KIMBALL. *Women and Aging.* Toronto: Butterworths, 1987.

GEERTZ, CLIFFORD. "Common Sense as a Cultural System." *The Antioch Review.* Vol. 33, No. 1 (Spring 1975):5–26.

GEIST, WILLIAM. *Toward a Safe and Sane Halloween and Other Tales of Suburbia.* New York: Times Books, 1985.

GELLES, RICHARD J., and CLAIRE PEDRICK CORNELL. *Intimate Violence in Families.* 2nd ed. Newbury Park, CA: Sage, 1990.

GELMAN, DAVID. "Who's Taking Care of Our Parents?" *Newsweek* (May 6, 1985):61–64, 67–68.

GEORGE, SUSAN. *How the Other Half Dies: The Real Reasons for World Hunger.* Totowa, NJ: Rowman & Allanheld, 1977.

GERBER, LINDA M. "The Development of Canadian Indian Communities: A Two-Dimensional Typology Reflecting Strategies of Adaptation to the Outside World." *Canadian Review of Sociology and Anthropology* 16(4), 1979: 123–50.

————. "Ethnicity Still Matters: Socio-Demographic Profiles of the Ethnic Elderly in Ontario." *Canadian Ethnic Studies* XV (3), 1983: 60–80.

————. "Community characteristics and out-migration from Canadian Indian communities: path analyses." *Canadian Review of Sociology and Anthropology* 21, 1984: 145–165.

————. "Multiple Jeopardy: A Socio-economic Comparison of Men and Women among the Indian, Métis and Inuit Peoples of Canada." *Canadian Ethnic Studies* XXII(3), 1990: 69–84.

————. "Referendum Results: Defining New Boundaries for an Independent Quebec." *Canadian Ethnic Studies* XXIV(2), 1992: 22–34.

GERSTEL, NAOMI. "Divorce and Stigma." *Social Problems.* Vol. 43, No. 2 (April 1987):172–86.

GERTH, H. H., and C. WRIGHT MILLS, eds. *From Max Weber: Essays in Sociology.* New York: Oxford University Press, 1946.

GESCHWENDER, JAMES A. *Racial Stratification in America.* Dubuque, IA: Wm. C. Brown, 1978.

GHOSH, RATNA and DOUGLAS RAY, eds. *Social Change and Education in Canada.* Toronto: Harcourt Brace Jovanovich, 1991.

GIBBONS, DON C. *Delinquent Behavior.* 3rd ed. Englewood Cliffs, NJ: Prentice Hall, 1981.

GIBBONS, DON C., and MARVIN D. KROHN. *Delinquent Behavior.* 4th ed. Englewood Cliffs, NJ: Prentice Hall, 1986.

GIBBS, NANCY. "The Clamor on Campus." *Time.* Vol. 137, No. 22 (June 3, 1991b):54–55.

GIBBS, NANCY. "When Is It Rape?" *Time.* Vol. 137, No. 22 (June 3, 1991a): 48–54.

GIDDENS, ANTHONY. *Sociology: A Brief but Critical Introduction.* New York: Harcourt Brace Jovanovich, 1982.

GIELE, JANET ZOLLINGER. "Women's Work and Family Roles." In Janet Zollinger Giele, ed., *Women in the Middle Years: Current Knowledge and Directions for Research and Policy.* New York: John Wiley and Sons, 1982:115–50.

GIFFEN, P.J. "Official rates of crime and delinquency." In W.T. McGrath, ed., *Crime and Its Treatment in Canada.* Toronto: Macmillan, 1976.

GILBERT, ALAN, and JOSEF GUGLER. *Cities, Poverty, and Development.* New York: Oxford University Press, 1983.

GILBERT, DENNIS, and JOSEPH A. KAHL. *The American Class Structure: A New Synthesis.* 3rd ed. Homewood, IL: The Dorsey Press, 1987.

GILBERT, S.N. "The Forgotten Purpose and Future Promise of University Education." *Canadian Journal of Community Mental Health* 8(2), 1989:103–122.

GILBERT, SID, LYNN BARR, WARREN CLARK, MATTHEW BLUE and DEBORAH SUNTER. *Leaving School: Results from a national survey comparing school leavers and high school graduates 18 to 20 years of age.* Ottawa: Government of Canada (LM-294-07-93E), 1993.

GILLETT, CHARLIE. *The Sound of the City: The Rise of Rock and Roll.* New York: Pantheon, 1983.

GILLIGAN, CAROL. *In a Different Voice: Psychological Theory and Women's Development.* Cambridge, MA: Harvard University Press, 1982.

GIMENEZ, MARTHA E. "Silence in the Classroom: Some Thoughts about Teaching in the 1980s." *Teaching Sociology.* Vol. 17, No. 2 (April 1989):184–91.

GINSBURG, PAUL B. "Market-Oriented Options in Medicare and Medicaid." In Jack B. Meyer, ed., *Market Reforms in Health Care: Current Issues, New Directions, Strategic Decisions.* Washington, DC: American Enterprise Institute for Public Policy Research, 1983:103–18.

GIOVANNINI, MAUREEN. "Female Anthropologist and Male Informant: Gender Conflict in a Sicilian Town." In John J. Macionis and Nijole V. Benokraitis, eds., *Seeing Ourselves: Classic, Contemporary, and Cross-Cultural Readings in Sociology.* 2nd ed. Englewood Cliffs, NJ: Prentice Hall, 1992:27–32.

GLAAB, CHARLES N. *The American City: A Documentary History.* Homewood, IL: Dorsey Press, 1963.

GLADUE, BRIAN A., RICHARD GREEN, and RONALD E. HELLMAN. "Neuroendocrine Response to Estrogen and Sexual Orientation." *Science.* Vol. 225, No. 4669 (September 28, 1984):1496–99.

GLASS, DAVID V., ed. *Social Mobility in Britain.* London: Routledge & Kegan Paul, 1954.

GLAZER, NATHAN, and DANIEL P. MOYNIHAN. *Beyond the Melting Pot.* 2nd ed. Cambridge, MA: M.I.T. Press, 1970.

GLENN, CHARLES L., and FRANMARIE KENNEDY-KEEL. "Commentary." *Education Week.* Vol. V, No. 21 (February 5, 1986):21.

GLENN, NORVAL D., and BETH ANN SHELTON. "Regional Differences in Divorce in the United States." *Journal of Marriage and the Family.* Vol. 47, No. 3 (August 1985):641–52.

The Globe & Mail. "Women Neglected Majority, UN Says." Tues., May 25, 1993.

GLOCK, CHARLES Y. "The Religious Revival in America." In Jane Zahn, ed., *Religion and the Face of America.* Berkeley, CA: University of California Press, 1959:25–42.

———. "On the Study of Religous Commitment." *Religious Education.* Vol. 62, No. 4 (1962):98–110.

GLUCK, PETER R., and RICHARD J. MEISTER. *Cities in Transition.* New York: New Viewpoints, 1979.

GLUECK, SHELDON, and ELEANOR GLUECK. *Unraveling Juvenile Delinquency.* New York: Commonwealth Fund, 1950.

GOETTING, ANN. Personal communication, 1989.

———. "Divorce Outcome Research." *Journal of Family Issues.* Vol. 2, No. 3 (September 1981):350–78.

———. "The Six Stations of Remarriage: Developmental Tasks of Remarriage after Divorce." *Family Relations.* Vol. 31, No. 2 (April 1982):213–22.

GOFFMAN, ERVING. *The Presentation of Self in Everyday Life.* Garden City, NY: Anchor, 1959.

———. *Asylums: Essays on the Social Situation of Mental Patients and Other Inmates.* Garden City, NY: Anchor, 1961.

———. *Stigma: Notes on the Management of Spoiled Identity.* Englewood Cliffs, NJ: Prentice Hall, 1963.

———. *Interactional Ritual: Essays on Face to Face Behavior.* Garden City, NY: Anchor, 1967.

———. *Gender Advertisements.* New York: Harper Colophon, 1979.

GOLD, ALLAN R. "Increasingly, Prison Term is the Price for Polluters." *The New York Times* (February 15, 1991):B6.

GOLDBERG, STEVEN. *The Inevitability of Patriarchy.* New York: William Morrow and Co., 1974.

———. Personal communication, 1987.

GOLDEN, FREDERIC. "Here Come the Microkids." *Time.* Vol. 119, No. 18 (May 3, 1982):50–56.

GOLDFARB, JEFFREY C. *Beyond Glasnost: The Post-Totalitarian Mind.* Chicago: University of Chicago Press, 1989.

GOLDFIELD, MICHAEL. *The Decline of Organized Labor in the United States.* Chicago and London: University of Chicago Press, 1987.

GOLDSBY, RICHARD A. *Race and Races.* 2nd ed. New York: Macmillan, 1977.

GOLDSMITH, H. H. "Genetic Influences on Personality from Infancy." *Child Development.* Vol. 54, No. 2 (April 1983):331–35.

GOODE, WILLIAM J. "The Theoretical Importance of Love." *American Sociological Review.* Vol. 24, No. 1 (February 1959):38–47.

———. "Encroachment, Charlatanism, and the Emerging Profession: Psychology, Sociology and Medicine." *American Sociological Review.* Vol. 25, No. 6 (December 1960):902–14.

GORDON, JAMES S. "The Paradigm of Holistic Medicine." In Arthur C. Hastings et al., eds., *Health for the Whole Person: The Complete Guide to Holistic Medicine.* Boulder, CO: Westview Press, 1980:3–27.

GORDON, MILTON M. *Assimilation in American Life.* New York: Oxford University Press, 1964.

GORING, CHARLES BUCKMAN. *The English Convict: A Statistical Study.* Montclair, NJ: Patterson Smith, 1972; orig. 1913.

GORTMAKER, STEVEN L. "Poverty and Infant Mortality in the United States." *American Journal of Sociology.* Vol. 44, No. 2 (April 1979):280–97.

GOTTMANN, JEAN. *Megalopolis.* New York: Twentieth Century Fund, 1961.

GOUGH, KATHLEEN. "The Origin of the Family." *Journal of Marriage and the Family.* Vol. 33, No. 4 (November 1971):760–71.

GOULD, STEPHEN J. "Evolution as Fact and Theory." *Discover* (May 1981):35–37.

GOULDNER, ALVIN. *Enter Plato.* New York: Free Press, 1965.

———. "The Sociologist as Partisan: Sociology and the Welfare State." In Larry T. Reynolds and Janice M. Reynolds, eds., *The Sociology of Sociology.* New York: McKay, 1970a:218–55.

———. *The Coming Crisis of Western Sociology.* New York: Avon Books, 1970b.

———. "Sex, Marital Status, and Psychiatric Treatment." *Social Forces,* Vol. 58, No. 3 (September 1979):89–94.

GOVE, WALTER R. "The Relationship Between Sex Roles, Marital Status, and Mental Illness." *Social Forces,* Vol. 51, No. 3 (September 1972):34–44.

GOYDER, JOHN C. and JAMES E. CURTIS. "Occupational mobility in Canada over four generations." In James E. Curtis and William G. Scott, eds., *Social Stratification: Canada.* 2nd ed. Scarborough, Ontario: Prentice Hall, 1979.

GRANOVETTER, MARK. "The Strength of Weak Ties." *American Journal of Sociology.* Vol. 78, No. 6 (May 1973):1360–80.

GRANT, DON SHERMAN II, and MICHAEL WALLACE. "Why Do Strikes Turn Violent?" *American Journal of Sociology.* Vol. 96, No. 5 (March 1991):1117–50.

GRANT, DONALD L. *The Anti-Lynching Movement.* San Francisco, CA: R and E Research Associates, 1975.

GRANT, KAREN R. "The Inverse Care Law in the Context of Universal Free Health Insurance in Canada: Toward Meeting Health Needs Through Public Policy." *Sociological Focus.* Vol. 17, No. 2 (April 1984):137–55.

GRAY, J.H. *Booze: The Impact of Whiskey on the Prairie West.* Scarborough, Ontario: New American Library, 1972.

GRAY, PAUL. "Whose America?" *Time.* Vol. 137, No. 27 (July 8, 1991):12–17.

GREELEY, ANDREW M. *Why Can't They Be Like Us? America's White Ethnic Groups.* New York: E. P. Dutton, 1971.

———. *Ethnicity in the United States: A Preliminary Reconnaissance.* New York: John Wiley, 1974.

———. *Religious Change in America.* Cambridge: Harvard University Press, 1989.

GREENBERG, DAVID F. *The Construction of Homosexuality.* Chicago: University of Chicago Press, 1988.

GREENSPON, EDWARD. "The Incredible Shrinking Middle Class." *The Globe and Mail*. July 31, 1993:D1,5.

GREER, SCOTT. *Urban Renewal and American Cities*. Indianapolis: Bobbs-Merrill, 1965.

GREGORY, PAUL R., and ROBERT C. STUART. *Comparative Economic Systems*. 2nd ed. Boston, MA: Houghton Mifflin, 1985.

GRIFFIN, RICHARD WAYNE, and SANDRA KERANEN GRIFFIN. "Theoretical Aspects of Insurgency Among the Powerless." Paper presented to the Southwestern Sociological Association, Little Rock, Arkansas, 1989.

GRISWOLD, WENDY. "The Fabrication of Meaning: Literary Interpretation in the United States, Great Britain, and the West Indies." *American Journal of Sociology*. Vol. 92, No. 5 (March 1987):1077–1117.

GROSS, JANE. "New Challenge of Youth: Growing Up in a Gay Home." *The New York Times* (February 11, 1991):A1, B7.

GRUENBERG, BARRY. "The Happy Worker: An Analysis of Educational and Occupational Differences in Determinants of Job Satisfaction." *American Journal of Sociology*. Vol. 86, No. 2 (September 1980):247–71.

GUNDERSON, MORLEY, LEON MUSZYNSKI and JENNIFER KECK. *Women and Labour Market Poverty*. Ottawa: Canadian Advisory Council on the Status of Women, 1990.

GUPPY, NEIL and A. BRUCE ARAI. "Who Benefits from Higher Education? Differences by Sex, Social Class, and Ethnic Background." In James Curtis, Edward Grabb, and Neil Guppy, (1993) *Social Inequality in Canada: Patterns, Problems, Policies*. 2nd ed. Scarborough: Prentice Hall, 1993: 214–232.

GUPTE, PRANAY. *The Crowded Earth: People and the Politics of Population*. New York: W. W. Norton, 1984.

GURAK, DOUGLAS T., and JOSEPH P. FITZPATRICK. "Intermarriage among Hispanic Ethnic Groups in New York City." *American Journal of Sociology*. Vol. 87, No. 4 (January 1982):921–34.

GUTMAN, HERBERT G. *The Black Family in Slavery and Freedom, 1750–1925*. New York: Pantheon Books, 1976.

GWARTNEY-GIBBS, PATRICIA A. "The Institutionalization of Premarital Cohabitation: Estimates from Marriage License Applications, 1970 and 1980." *Journal of Marriage and the Family*. Vol. 48, No. 2 (May 1986):423–34.

——, JEAN STOCKARD, and SUSANNE BOHMER. "Learning Courtship Aggression: The Influence of Parents, Peers, and Personal Experiences." *Family Relations*. Vol. 36, No. 3 (July 1987):276–82.

GYORGY, JANE. "Learning the Language of the Snows." *The Globe and Mail*, Tuesday, May 25, 1993: A22.

HAAS, LINDA. "Domestic Role Sharing in Sweden." *Journal of Marriage and the Family*. Vol. 43, No. 4 (November 1981):957–67.

HABERMAS, JURGEN. *Toward a Rational Society: Student Protest, Science, and Politics*. Jeremy J. Shapiro, trans. Boston, MA: Beacon Press, 1970.

HACKER, HELEN MAYER. "Women as a Minority Group." *Social Forces*. Vol. 30 (October 1951):60–69.

HACKER, HELEN MAYER. "Women as a Minority Group: 20 Years Later." In Florence Denmark, ed., *Who Discriminates Against Women*. Beverly Hills, CA: Sage, 1974:124–34.

HADDEN, JEFFREY K., and CHARLES E. SWAIN. *Prime Time Preachers: The Rising Power of Televangelism*. Reading, MA: Addison-Wesley, 1981.

HAGAN, JOHN. *Disreputable Pleasures: Crime and Deviance in Canada*. 2nd ed. Toronto: McGraw-Hill Ryerson, 1984.

——, A. R. GILLIS, and JOHN SIMPSON. "The Class Structure of Gender and Delinquency: Toward a Power-control Theory of Common Delinquent Behavior." *American Journal of Sociology*. Vol. 90, No. 6 (May 1985): 1151–78.

HAGAN, JOHN, and PATRICIA PARKER. "White-Collar Crime and Punishment: The Class Structure and Legal Sanctioning of Securities Violations." *American Sociological Review*. Vol. 50, No. 3 (June 1985):302–16.

HAGAN, JOHN, JOHN SIMPSON, and A. R. GILLIS. "Class in the Household: A Power-Control Theory of Gender and Delinquency." *American Journal of Sociology*. Vol. 92, No. 4 (January 1987):788–816.

HAIG, ROBIN ANDREW. *The Anatomy of Humor: Biopsychosocial and Therapeutic Perspectives*. Springfield, IL: Charles C. Thomas, 1988.

HALBERSTAM, DAVID. *The Reckoning*. New York: Avon, 1986.

HALE, SYLVIA. "The Documentary Construction of Female Mismanagement" *Canadian Review of Sociology and Anthropology*, 24(4), Nov. 1987: 489–513.

The Halifax Chronicle Herald, Sat., Feb. 29, 1992.

HALLETT, M.E. "Nellie McClung." *The Canadian Encyclopedia*. 2nd ed. Edmonton: Hurtig Publishers, vol. 2, 1988: 1257.

HALLINAN, MAUREEN T., and RICHARD A. WILLIAMS. "Interracial Friendship Choices in Secondary Schools." *American Sociological Review*. Vol. 54, No. 1 (February 1989):67–78.

HAMBLIN, DORA JANE. *The First Cities*. New York: Time-Life, 1973.

HAMEL, RUTH. "Raging Against Aging." *American Demographics*. Vol. 12, No. 3 (March 1990):42–45.

HAMMOND, PHILIP E. "Introduction." In Philip E. Hammond, ed., *The Sacred in a Secular Age: Toward Revision in the Scientific Study of Religion*. Berkeley, CA: University of California Press, 1985:1–6.

HAMRICK, MICHAEL H., DAVID J. ANSPAUGH, and GENE EZELL. *Health*. Columbus OH: Merrill, 1986.

HANDELMAN, DON and ELLIOTT LEYTON. "Bureaucracy and World View: Studies in the Logic of Official Interpretation." St. John's: Institute of Social and Economic Research, 1978.

HANDLER, JOEL F., and YEHESKEL HASENFELD. *The Moral Construction of Poverty: Welfare Reform in America*. Newbury Park, CA: Sage, 1991.

HANDLIN, OSCAR. *Boston's Immigrants 1790–1865: A Study in Acculturation*. Cambridge, MA: Harvard University Press, 1941.

HANEY, CRAIG, CURTIS BANKS, and PHILIP ZIMBARDO. "Interpersonal Dynamics in a Simulated Prison." *International Journal of Criminology and Penology*. Vol. 1 (1973):69–97.

HANNAN, MICHAEL T., and GLENN R. CARROLL. "Dynamics of Formal Political Structure: An Event-History Analysis." *American Sociological Review*. Vol. 46, No. 1 (February 1981):19–35.

HANSEN, KAREN V., and ILENE J. PHILIPSON, eds. *Women, Class, and the Feminist Imagination: A Socialist-Feminist Reader*. Philadelphia: Temple University Press, 1990.

HARBERT, ANITA S., and LEON H. GINSBERG. *Human Services for Older Adults*. Columbia, SC: University of South Carolina Press, 1991.

HARDEN, MIKE. "Rest Assured that Eventually You'll Get Your Money's Worth." *The Columbus Dispatch* (November 19, 1989):C1.

HARDER, SANDRA. *Women in Canada: Socio-Economic Status and Other Contemporary Issues* Cat no. 1291R05. Ottawa: Minister of Supply and Services, 1991–92.

HARDOY, JORGE E. "Two Thousand Years of Latin American Urbanization." In Jorge E. Hardoy, ed., *Urbanization in Latin America: Approaches and Issues*. Garden City, NY: Anchor Books, 1975.

HAREVEN, TAMARA K. "The Life Course and Aging in Historical Perspective." In Tamara K. Hareven and Kathleen J. Adams, eds., *Aging and Life Course Transitions: An Interdisciplinary Perspective*. New York: Guilford Press, 1982:1–26.

——, and RANDOLPH LANGENBACH. *Amoskeag: Life and Work in an American Factory City*. New York: Pantheon Books, 1978.

HARLAN, WILLIAM H. "Social Status of the Aged in Three Indian Villages." In Bernice L. Neugarten, ed., *Middle Age and Aging: A Reader in Social Psychology*. Chicago: University of Chicago Press, 1968:469–75.

HARLOW, CAROLINE WOLF. *Female Victims of Violent Crime*. Bureau of Justice Statistics report. Washington, DC: U. S. Government Printing Office, 1991.

HARLOW, HARRY F., and MARGARET KUENNE HARLOW. "Social Deprivation in Monkeys." *Scientific American*. Vol. 207 (November 1962):137–46.

HARRIES, KEITH D. *Serious Violence: Patterns of Homicide and Assault in America*. Springfield, IL: Charles C. Thomas, 1990.

HARRINGTON, MICHAEL. *The New American Poverty*. New York: Penguin Books, 1984.

HARRIS, CHAUNCEY D., and EDWARD L. ULLMAN. "The Nature of Cities." *The Annals.* Vol. 242 (November 1945):7–17.

HARRIS, LOUIS, AND ASSOCIATES. *The Myth and Reality of Aging in America.* Washington, DC: National Council on Aging, 1976.

HARRIS, MARVIN. *Cows, Pigs, Wars and Witches: The Riddles of Culture.* New York: Vintage Books, 1975.

———. "Why Men Dominate Women." *New York Times Magazine* (November 13, 1977):46, 115–23.

———. *Good to Eat: Riddle of Food and Culture.* New York: Simon and Schuster, 1985.

———. *Cultural Anthropology.* 2nd ed. New York: Harper & Row, 1987.

HARRISON, PAUL. *Inside the Third World: The Anatomy of Poverty.* 2nd ed. New York: Penguin Books, 1984.

HARRON, DON. *Debunk's Illustrated Guide to the Canadian Establishment.* Toronto: Macmillan, 1984.

HARTMANN, BETSY, and JAMES BOYCE. *Needless Hunger: Voices from a Bangladesh Village.* San Francisco: Institute for Food and Development Policy, 1982.

HAVIGHURST, ROBERT J., BERNICE L. NEUGARTEN, and SHELDON S. TOBIN. "Disengagement and Patterns of Aging." In Bernice L. Neugarten, ed., *Middle Age and Aging: A Reader in Social Psychology.* Chicago: University of Chicago Press, 1968:161–72.

HAVILAND, WILLIAM A. *Anthropology.* 4th ed. New York: Holt, Rinehart and Winston, 1985.

HAYNEMAN, STEPHEN P., and WILLIAM A. LOXLEY. "The Effect of Primary-School Quality on Academic Achievement Across Twenty-nine High- and Low-Income Countries." *American Journal of Sociology.* Vol. 88, No. 6 (May 1983):1162–94.

HEALTH INSURANCE ASSOCIATION OF AMERICA. *Source Book of Health Insurance Data.* Washington, DC: The Association, 1991.

HEILBRONER, ROBERT L. *The Making of Economic Society.* 7th ed. Englewood Cliffs, NJ: Prentice Hall, 1985.

HELGESEN, SALLY. *The Female Advantage: Women's Ways of Leadership.* New York: Doubleday, 1990.

HELLER, ANITA FOCHS. *Health and Home: Women as Health Guardians.* Ottawa: Canadian Advisory Council on the Status of Women, March, 1986.

HELMES-HAYES, R. *A Quarter-Century of Sociology and the University of Toronto. 1963–1988.* Toronto: Canadian Scholars' Press, 1988.

HELMUTH, JOHN W. "World Hunger Amidst Plenty." *USA Today.* Vol. 117, No. 2526 (March 1989):48–50.

HENLEY, NANCY, MYKOL HAMILTON, and BARRIE THORNE. "Womanspeak and Manspeak: Sex Differences in Communication, Verbal and Nonverbal." In John J. Macionis and Nijole V. Benokraitis, eds., *Seeing Ourselves: Classic, Contemporary, and Cross-Cultural Readings in Sociology,* 2nd ed. Englewood Cliffs, NJ: Prentice Hall, 1992:10–15.

HERITAGE, JOHN. *Garfinkel and Ethnomethodology.* Cambridge, UK: Polity Press, 1984.

HERMAN, DIANNE F. "The Rape Culture." In John J. Macionis and Nijole V. Benokraitis, eds., *Seeing Ourselves: Classic, Contemporary, and Cross-Cultural Readings in Sociology.* 2nd ed. Englewood Cliffs, NJ: Prentice Hall, 1992.

HERMAN, EDWARD S. *Corporate Control, Corporate Power: A Twentieth Century Fund Study.* New York: Cambridge University Press, 1981.

HERRIAM, NATHAN, M.D. "Confusion and Dementia." *Mental Health and Aging.* N.A.C.A. Ottawa: Statistics Canada, March, 1991.

HERRNSTEIN, RICHARD J. *IQ and the Meritocracy.* Boston: Little, Brown, 1973.

HERRSTROM, STAFFAN. "Sweden: Pro-Choice on Child Care." *New Perspectives Quarterly.* Vol. 7, No. 1 (Winter 1990): 27–28.

HERTY, ROBERT. "The Collective Representation of Death." In *Death and the Right Hand.* Aberdeen: Cohen and West, 1960:84–86.

HESS, STEPHEN. "Reporters Who Cover Congress." *Society.* Vol. 28, No. 2 (January–February 1991):60–65.

HEWLETT, SYLVIA ANN. "The Feminization of the Work Force." *New Perspectives Quarterly.* Vol. 7, No. 1 (Winter 1990):13–15.

HEWLETT, SYLVIA ANN. *A Lesser Life: The Myth of Women's Liberation in America.* New York: William Morrow, 1986.

HILLARD, DAN C. "Media Images of Male and Female Professional Athletes: An Interpretive Analysis of Magazine Articles." *Sociology of Sport Journal,* 1, 1, 1984: 251–62.

HILLER, HARRY H. *Canadian Society, A Macro Analysis.* 2nd ed. Scarborough: Ontario, 1991.

HILSMAN, ROGER. *The Politics of Governing America.* Englewood Cliffs, NJ: Prentice Hall, 1985.

HILTS, PHILIP J. "Demands to Fix U. S. Health Care Reach a Crescendo." *The New York Times* (June 9, 1991):1, 5.

HIMMELFARB, ALEXANDER and C. JAMES RICHARDSON. *Sociology for Canadians: Images of Society.* Toronto: McGraw-Hill, August 1982.

HINCH, RONALD. "Inconsistencies and contradictions in Canada's sexual assault law." *Canadian Public Policy. XIV(3)* 1988: 282–294.

HIROSHI, MANNARI. *The Japanese Business Leaders.* Tokyo: University of Tokyo Press, 1974.

HIRSCHI, TRAVIS. *Causes of Delinquency.* Berkeley, CA: University of California Press, 1969.

———, and MICHAEL GOTTFREDSON. "Age and the Explanation of Crime." *American Journal of Sociology.* Vol. 89, No. 3 (November 1983):552–84.

HIRSCHMAN, CHARLES, and MORRISON G. WONG. "Socioeconomic Gains of Asian Americans, Blacks, and Hispanics: 1960–1976." *American Journal of Sociology.* Vol. 90, No. 3 (November 1984):584–607.

HOCHSCHILD, ARLIE, with ANNE MACHUNG. *The Second Shift: Working Parents and the Revolution at Home.* New York: Viking, 1989.

HODGE, ROBERT W., DONALD J. TREIMAN, and PETER H. ROSSI. "A Comparative Study of Occupational Prestige." In Reinhard Bendix and Seymour Martin Lipset, eds., *Class, Status, and Power: Social Stratification in Comparative Perspective.* 2nd ed. New York: Free Press, 1966:309–21.

HOERR, JOHN. "The Payoff from Teamwork." In *Business Week,* No. 3114 (July 10, 1989):56–62.

HOGAN, DENNIS P., and EVELYN M. KITAGAWA. "The Impact of Social Status and Neighborhood on the Fertility of Black Adolescents." *American Journal of Sociology.* Vol. 90, No. 4 (January 1985):825–55.

HOLLAND, DOROTHY C., and MARGARET A. EISENHART. *Educated in Romance: Women, Achievement, and College Culture.* Chicago: The University of Chicago Press, 1990.

HOLM, JEAN. *The Study of Religions.* New York: Seabury Press, 1977.

HOLMES, HELEN and DAVID TARAS. *Selling Ourselves: Media, Power and Policy in Canada.* Toronto: Harcourt Brace Jovanovich, 1992.

HOLMES, LOWELL. "A Tale of Two Studies." *American Anthropologist.* Vol. 85, No. 4 (December 1983):929–35.

HOLT, THOMAS C. "Afro-Americans." In *Harvard Encyclopedia of American Ethnic Groups.* Cambridge, MA: Harvard University Press, 1980:5–23.

HONEYWELL, ROY J. *The Educational Work of Thomas Jefferson.* Cambridge, MA: Harvard University Press, 1931.

HOOK, ERNEST B. "Behavioral Implications of the XYY Genotype." *Science.* Vol. 179 (January 12, 1973):139–50.

HOSTETLER, JOHN A. *Amish Society.* 3rd ed. Baltimore: Johns Hopkins University Press, 1980.

HOUSE OF REPRESENTATIVES. *A. I. D. and Third World Women, the Unmet Potential.* Hearing held May 11, 1988. Washington, DC: U. S. Government Printing Office, 1988.

HOUT, MICHAEL, and ANDREW M. GREELEY. "The Center Doesn't Hold: Church Attendance in the United States, 1940–1984." *American Sociological Review.* Vol. 52, No. 3 (June 1987):325–45.

HOWE, NEIL, and WILLIAM STRAUSS. "America's 13th Generation." *The New York Times* (April 16, 1991).

HOWLETT, DEBBIE. "Cruzan's Struggle Left Imprint: 10,000 Others in Similar State." *USA Today* (December 27, 1990):3A.

HOYT, HOMER. *The Structure and Growth of Residential Neighborhoods in American Cities.* Washington, DC: Federal Housing Administration, 1939.

HOYT, MARY FINCH. "The New Prime Time." *USA Weekend* (December 13–15, 1985):4.

HRUSCHKA, PETER D. Personal communication, 1990.

HSU, FRANCIS L. K. *The Challenge of the American Dream: The Chinese in the United States.* Belmont, CA: Wadsworth, 1971.

HUBER, JOAN, and GLENNA SPITZE. "Considering Divorce: An Expansion of Becker's Theory of Marital Instability." *American Journal of Sociology.* Vol. 86, No. 1 (July 1980):75–89.

HUET-COX, ROCIO. "Medical Education: New Wine in Old Wine Skins." In Victor W. Sidel and Ruth Sidel, eds., *Reforming Medicine: Lessons of the Last Quarter Century.* New York: Pantheon Books, 1984:129–49.

HULL, JON D. "A Boy and His Gun." *Time,* Aug. 2, 1993: 29–35.

HULS, GLENNA. Personal communication, 1987.

HUMPHREY, DEREK. *Final Exit: The Practicalities of Self-Deliverance and Assisted Suicide for the Dying.* Eugene, OR: The Hemlock Society, 1991.

HUMPHRIES, HARRY LEROY. *The Structure and Politics of Intermediary Class Positions: An Empirical Examination of Recent Theories of Class.* Unpublished Ph. D. dissertation. Eugene, OR: University of Oregon, 1984.

HUNNICUT, BENJAMIN K. *Work Without End.* Philadelphia: Temple University Press, 1988.

———. "Are We All Working Too Hard? No Time for God or Family." *The Wall Street Journal* (January 4, 1990).

HUNT, MORTON. *Sexual Behavior in the 1970s.* Chicago: Playboy Press, 1974.

HUNTER, ALFRED A. *Class Tells: On Social Inequality in Canada.* 2nd ed. Toronto: Butterworths, 1986.

HUNTER, FLOYD. *Community Power Structure.* Garden City, NY: Doubleday, 1963; orig. 1953.

HUNTER, JAMES DAVISON. *American Evangelicalism: Conservative Religion and the Quandary of Modernity.* New Brunswick, NJ: Rutgers University Press, 1983.

———. "Conservative Protestantism." In Philip E. Hammond, ed., *The Sacred in a Secular Age.* Berkeley, CA: University of California Press, 1985:50–66.

———. *Evangelicalism: The Coming Generation.* Chicago: The University of Chicago Press, 1987.

HURN, CHRISTOPHER. *The Limits and Possibilities of Schooling.* Boston: Allyn and Bacon, 1978.

HURST, L. "Tuberculosis Makes a Quiet Return." *The Toronto Star,* Nov. 8, 1992: A1, A10.

HURTIG, MEL. *A New and Better Canada: Principles and Polices of a New Canadian Political Party.* Toronto: Stoddart, 1992.

HWANG, SEAN-SHONG, STEVEN H. MURDOCK, BANOO PARPIA, and RITA R. HAMM. "The Effects of Race and Socioeconomic Status on Residential Segregation in Texas, 1970–1980." *Social Forces.* Vol. 63, No. 3 (March 1985):732–47.

HYMAN, HERBERT H., and CHARLES R. WRIGHT. "Trends in Voluntary Association Memberships of American Adults: Replication Based on Secondary Analysis of National Sample Survey." *American Sociological Review.* Vol. 36, No. 2 (April 1971):191–206.

ILLICH, IVAN. *Medical Nemesis: The Expropriation of Health.* New York: Pantheon Books, 1976.

Immigration Statistics. Ottawa: Minister of Supply and Services, Canada, 1992.

INNIS, HAROLD. *Essays in Canadian Economic History* (rev. ed.). Toronto: University of Toronto Press, 1956.

INSTITUTE FOR PHILOSOPHY AND PUBLIC POLICY. "The Graying of America." Vol. 8, No. 2 (Spring 1988):1–5.

IRISH, MARIAN D., JAMES W. PROTHRO, and RICHARD J. RICHARDSON. *The Politics of American Democracy.* 7th ed. Englewood Cliffs, NJ: Prentice Hall, 1981.

IRWIN, JOHN. *Prison in Turmoil.* Boston, MA: Little, Brown, 1980.

ISAJIW, WSEVELOD W. "Definitions of Ethnicity." In Rita M. Bienvenue and Jay E. Goldstein. *Ethnicity and Ethnic Relations in Canada.* 2nd ed. Toronto: Butterworths, 1985: 5–18.

ISAY, RICHARD A. *Being Homosexual: Gay Men and Their Development.* New York: Farrar, Straus, Giroux, 1989.

JACOB, JOHN E. "An Overview of Black America in 1985." In James D. Williams, ed., *The State of Black America 1986.* New York: National Urban League, 1986:i–xi.

JACOBS, DAVID. "Inequality and Police Strength." *American Sociological Review.* Vol. 44, No. 6 (December 1979):913–25.

JACOBS, JANE. *The Death and Life of Great American Cities.* New York: Random House, 1961.

———. *The Economy of Cities.* New York: Vintage, 1970.

———. *Cities and the Wealth of Nations.* New York: Random House, 1984.

JACQUET, CONSTANT H., and ALICE M. JONES. *Yearbook of American and Canadian Churches 1991.* Nashville, TN: Abingdon Press, 1991.

JAEGER, ART, and ROBERT GREENSTEIN. "Poverty Rate and Household Income Stagnate as Rich-Poor Gap Hits Post-War High." Washington, DC: Center on Budget and Policy Priorities, 1989.

JAENEN, CORNELIUS. "Mutilated Multiculturalism." In J. Donald Wilson, ed., *Canadian Education in the 1980s.* Calgary: Detselig Enterprises, 1981.

JAGAROWSKY, PAUL A., and MARY JO BANE. *Neighborhood Poverty: Basic Questions.* Discussion paper series H-90-3. John F. Kennedy School of Government. Cambridge: Harvard University, 1990.

JAGGER, ALISON. "Political Philosophies of Women's Liberation." In Laurel Richardson and Verta Taylor, eds., *Feminist Frontiers: Rethinking Sex, Gender, and Society.* Reading, MA: Addison-Wesley, 1983.

JAMES, DAVID R. "City Limits on Racial Equality: The Effects of City-Suburb Boundaries on Public-School Desegregation, 1968–1976." *American Sociological Review.* Vol. 54, No. 6 (December 1989):963–85.

JANIS, IRVING. *Crucial Decisions: Leadership in Policymaking and Crisis Management.* New York: Free Press, 1989.

JANIS, IRVING. *Victims of Groupthink.* Boston, MA: Houghton Mifflin, 1972.

JAYNES, GERALD DAVID, and ROBIN M. WILLIAMS, eds. *A Common Destiny: Blacks and American Society.* Washington, DC: National Academy Press, 1989.

JEFFERSON, THOMAS. Letter to James Madison, October 28, 1785. In Julian P. Boyd, ed., *The Papers of Thomas Jefferson.* Princeton: Princeton University Press, 1953:681–83.

JENCKS, CHRISTOPHER, et al. *Inequality: A Reassessment of the Effect of Family and Schooling in America.* New York: Basic Books, 1972.

JENCKS, CHRISTOPHER. "Genes and Crime." *The New York Review* (February 12, 1987):33–41.

JENKINS, BRIAN M. "Statements About Terrorism." In *International Terrorism, The Annals of the American Academy of Political and Social Science.* Vol. 463 (September 1982). Beverly Hills, CA: Sage Publications:11–23.

JENKINS, BRIAN M. "Terrorism Remains a Threat." Syndicated column, *The Columbus Dispatch* (January 14, 1990):D-1.

JENKINS, J. CRAIG, and CHARLES PERROW. "Insurgency of the Powerless: Farm Worker Movements (1946–1972)." *American Sociological Review.* Vol. 42, No. 2 (April 1977): 249–68.

JOHNSON, DIRK. "Census Finds Many Claiming New Identity: Indian." *The New York Times* (March 5, 1991):A1, A116.

JOHNSON, F. HENRY. *A Brief History of Canadian Education.* Toronto: McGraw-Hill, 1968.

JOHNSON, HOLLY. "Violent Crime." In Craig McKie and Keith Thompson, eds., *Canadian Social Trends.* Toronto: Thompson Educational Publishing, 1990.

JOHNSON, JULIE. "Do We Have Too Many Lawyers?" *Time.* Vol. 138, No. 8 (August 26, 1991):54–55.

JOHNSON, NORRIS R. "Panic at 'The Who Concert Stampede': An Empirical Assessment." *Social Problems.* Vol. 34, No. 4 (October 1987):362–73.

JOHNSON, PAUL. "The Seven Deadly Sins of Terrorism." In Benjamin Netanyahu, ed., *International Terrorism.* New Brunswick, NJ: Transaction Books, 1981:12–22.

JOHNSTON, R. J. "Residential Area Characteristics." In D. T. Herbert and R. J. Johnston, eds., *Social Areas in Cities. Vol. 1: Spatial Processes and Form.* New York: Wiley, 1976:193–235.

JOHNSTONE, RONALD L. *Religion in Society: A Sociology of Religion.* 2nd ed. Englewood Cliffs, NJ: Prentice Hall, 1983.

JOINT ECONOMIC COMMITTEE. *The Concentration of Wealth in the United States: Trends in the Distribution of Wealth Among American Families.* Washington, DC: United States Congress, 1986.

JONES, DAVID A. *History of Criminology: A Philosophical Perspective.* Westport, CT: Greenwood Press, 1986.

JONES, RANDY. "What Goes Up Must Come Down." *The Halifax Chronicle Herald,* Tues., Jan. 19, 1993: A5.

JONES, RUTH, and WARREN E. MILLER. "Financing Campaigns: Macro Level Innovation and Micro Level Response." *The Western Political Quarterly.* Vol. 38, No. 2 (June 1985):187–210.

JONES, TERRY. "Foul Ball in the Front Office: Racial Practices in Baseball Management." *The Black Scholar.* Vol. 18, No. 3 (May/June 1987):16–24.

JOSEPHY, ALVIN M., JR. *Now That the Buffalo's Gone: A Study of Today's American Indians.* New York: Alfred A. Knopf, 1982.

KAELBLE, HARTMUT. *Social Mobility in the 19th and 20th Centuries: Europe and America in Comparative Perspective.* New York: St. Martin's Press, 1986.

KAIN, EDWARD L. "A Note on the Integration of AIDS Into the Sociology of Human Sexuality." *Teaching Sociology.* Vol. 15, No. 4 (July 1987):320–23.

———. *The Myth of Family Decline: Understanding Families in a World of Rapid Social Change.* Lexington, MA: Lexington Books, 1990.

———, and SHANNON HART. "AIDS and the Family: A Content Analysis of Media Coverage." Presented to National Council on Family Relations, Atlanta, 1987.

KALISH, CAROL B. "International Crime Rates." Bureau of Justice Statistics *Special Report,* May 1988. Washington, DC: U. S. Government Printing Office, 1988.

KALISH, RICHARD A. "The New Ageism and the Failure Models: A Polemic." *The Gerontologist.* Vol. 19, No. 4 (August 1979):398–402.

———. *Late Adulthood: Perspectives on Human Development.* 2nd ed. Monterey, CA: Brooks/Cole, 1982.

KALMUSS, DEBRA, and JUDITH A. SELTZER. "Continuity of Marital Behavior in Remarriage: The Case of Spouse Abuse." Unpublished paper. November 1984.

KAMINER, WENDY. "Volunteers: Who Knows What's in It for Them." *Ms.* (December 1984):93–94, 96, 126–28.

KANE, MARY JO. "The Post Title IX Female Athlete in the Media." *Journal of Physical Education, Recreation, and Dance,* March 1989: 58–62.

KANTER, ROSABETH MOSS. *Men and Women of the Corporation.* New York: Basic Books, 1977.

———. *The Change Masters: Innovation and Entrepreneurship in the American Corporation.* New York: Simon and Schuster, 1983.

———. "All That Is Entrepreneurial Is Not Gold." *The Wall Street Journal* (July 22, 1985):18.

———. *When Giants Learn to Dance: Mastering the Challenges of Strategy, Management, and Careers in the 1990s.* New York: Simon and Schuster, 1989.

KANTER, ROSABETH MOSS, and BARRY A. STEIN. "The Gender Pioneers: Women in an Industrial Sales Force." In R. M. Kanter and B. A. Stein, eds., *Life in Organizations.* New York: Basic Books, 1979:134–60.

———. *A Tale of "O": On Being Different in an Organization.* New York: Harper & Row, 1980.

KANTROWITZ, BARBARA. "Mothers on Their Own." *Newsweek* (December 23, 1985):66–67.

KAPICA, JACK. "Churches told to try the old hard sell." *The Globe and Mail,* Sept. 9, 1993: 1–20.

KAPLAN, ERIC B., et al. "The Usefulness of Preoperative Laboratory Screening." *Journal of the American Medical Association.* Vol. 253, No. 24 (June 28, 1985):3576–81.

KAPTCHUK, TED. "The Holistic Logic of Chinese Medicine." In Shepard Bliss et al., eds., *The New Holistic Health Handbook.* Lexington, MA: The Steven Greene Press/Penguin Books, 1985:41.

KARP, DAVID A., and WILLIAM C. YOELS. "The College Classroom: Some Observations on the Meaning of Student Participation." *Sociology and Social Research.* Vol. 60, No. 4 (July 1976):421–39.

KASARDA, JOHN D. "Entry-Level Jobs, Mobility and Urban Minority Employment." *Urban Affairs Quarterly.* Vol. 19, No. 1 (September 1983):21–40.

KAUFMAN, MARC. "Becoming 'Old Old'." *The Philadelphia Inquirer* (October 28, 1990):1-A, 10-A.

KAUFMAN, POLLY WELTS. "Women and Education." In Barbara Haber, ed., *The Women's Annual, 1981: The Year in Review.* Boston, MA: G. K. Hall and Company, 1982:24–55.

KAUFMAN, ROBERT L., and SEYMOUR SPILERMAN. "The Age Structures of Occupations and Jobs." *American Journal of Sociology.* Vol. 87, No. 4 (January 1982): 827–51.

KAUFMAN, WALTER. *Religions in Four Dimensions: Existential, Aesthetic, Historical and Comparative.* New York: Reader's Digest Press, 1976.

KEATING, NORAH C., and PRISCILLA COLE. "What Do I Do with Him 24 Hours a Day? Changes in the Housewife Role After Retirement." *The Gerontologist.* Vol. 20, No. 1 (February 1980):84–89.

KEITH, JULIE and LAURA LAUDREY. "Well-being of Older Canadians." In Craig McKie and Keith Thompson, eds., *Canadian Social Trends.* Toronto: Thompson Educational Publishing, 1990.

KELLER, HELEN. *The Story of My Life.* New York: Doubleday, Page and Company, 1903.

KELLER, SUZANNE. *The Urban Neighborhood.* New York: Random House, 1968.

KELLEY, JACK. "Births Out of Wedlock Opposed." *USA Today* (August 16, 1985):6A.

KELLEY, ROBERT. *The Shaping of the American Past. Vol. 2: 1865 to the Present.* 3rd ed. Englewood Cliffs, NJ: Prentice Hall, 1982.

KEMP, ALICE ABEL, and SHELLEY COVERMAN. "Marginal Jobs or Marginal Workers: Identifying Sex Differences in Low-Skill Occupations." *Sociological Focus.* Vol. 22, No. 1 (February 1989):19–37.

KENISTON, KENNETH. "Working Mothers." In James M. Henslin, ed., *Marriage and Family in a Changing Society.* 2nd ed. New York: Free Press, 1985: 319–21.

KENNICKELL, ARTHUR, and JANICE SHACK-MARQUEZ. "Changes in Family Finances from 1983 to 1989: Evidence from the Survey of Consumer Finances." *Federal Reserve Bulletin* (January 1992):1–18.

KENYON, KATHLEEN. *Digging Up Jericho.* London: Ernest Benn, 1957.

KERCKHOFF, ALAN C., RICHARD T. CAMPBELL, and IDEE WINFIELD-LAIRD. "Social Mobility in Great Britain and the United States." *American Journal of Sociology.* Vol. 91, No. 2 (September 1985):281–308.

KESSLER, RONALD D., and PAUL D. CLEARY. "Social Class and Psychological Distress." *American Sociological Review.* Vol. 45, No 3 (June 1980):463–78.

KII, TOSHI. "Recent Extension of Retirement Age in Japan." *The Gerontologist.* Vol. 19, No. 5 (October 1979):481–86.

KILBOURNE, BROCK K. "The Conway and Siegelman Claims Against Religious Cults: An Assessment of Their Data." *Journal for the Scientific Study of Religion.* Vol. 22, No. 4 (December 1983):380–85.

KILGORE, SALLY B. "The Organizational Context of Tracking in Schools." *American Sociological Review.* Vol. 56, No. 2 (April 1991):189–203.

KILLIAN, LEWIS M. "Organization, Rationality and Spontaneity in the Civil Rights Movement." *American Sociological Review.* Vol. 49, No. 6 (December 1984):770–83.

KING, KATHLEEN PIKER, and DENNIS E. CLAYSON. "The Differential Perceptions of Male and Female Deviants." *Sociological Focus.* Vol. 21, No. 2 (April 1988):153–64.

KING, MARTIN LUTHER, JR. "The Montgomery Bus Boycott." In Walt Anderson, ed., *The Age of Protest.* Pacific Palisades, CA: Goodyear, 1969:81–91.

KING, PATRICIA. "When Desegregation Backfires." *Newsweek.* Vol. 144, No. 5 (July 31, 1989):56.

KINSEY, ALFRED, et al. *Sexual Behavior in the Human Male.* Philadelphia: W. B. Saunders, 1948.

————. *Sexual Behavior in the Human Female.* Philadelphia: W. B. Saunders, 1953.

KIPP, RITA SMITH. "Have Women Always Been Unequal?" In Beth Reed, ed., *Towards a Feminist Transformation of the Academy: Proceedings of the Fifth Annual Women's Studies Conference.* Ann Arbor, MI: Great Lakes Colleges Association, 1980:12–18.

KIRK, MARSHALL, and PETER MADSEN. *After the Ball: How America Will Conquer its Fear and Hatred of Gays in the '90s.* New York: Doubleday, 1989.

KITANO, HARRY H. L. "Japanese." In *Harvard Encyclopedia of American Ethnic Groups.* Cambridge, MA: Harvard University Press, 1980:561–71.

KITANO, HARRY H. L. *Race Relations.* 3rd ed. Englewood Cliffs, NJ: Prentice Hall, 1985.

KITSON, GAY C., and HELEN J. RASCHKE. "Divorce Research: What We Know, What We Need to Know." *Journal of Divorce.* Vol. 4, No. 3 (Spring 1981):1–37.

KITTRIE, NICHOLAS N. *The Right To Be Different: Deviance and Enforced Therapy.* Baltimore, MD: The Johns Hopkins University Press, 1971.

KLEIMAN, DENA. "Changing Way of Death: Some Agonizing Choices." *The New York Times* (January 14, 1985):1, 11.

KLEIN, SUSAN SHURBERG. "Education." In Sarah M. Pritchard, ed., *The Women's Annual, Number 4, 1983–1984.* Boston, MA: G. K. Hall and Company, 1984:9–30.

KLEUGEL, JAMES R., and ELIOT R. SMITH. *Beliefs About Inequality: Americans' Views of What Is and What Ought to Be.* New York: Aldine de Gruyter, 1986.

KLUCKHOHN, CLYDE. "As An Anthropologist Views It." In Albert Deuth, ed., *Sex Habits of American Men.* New York: Prentice Hall, 1948.

KNAUS, WILLIAM A. *Inside Russian Medicine: An American Doctor's First-Hand Report.* New York: Everest House, 1981.

KNOKE, DAVID, and RICHARD B. FELSON. "Ethnic Stratification and Political Cleavage in the United States, 1952–1968." *American Journal of Sociology.* Vol. 80, No. 3 (November 1974):630–42.

KNOWLES, VALERIE. *Strangers at Our Gates: Canadian Immigration and Immigration Policy, 1540–1990.* Toronto: Dundurn, 1992.

KOCH, HOWARD. *The Panic Broadcast: Portrait of an Event.* Boston: Little, Brown, 1970.

KOHLBERG, LAWRENCE, and CAROL GILLIGAN. "The Adolescent as Philosopher: The Discovery of Self in a Postconventional World." *Daedalus.* Vol. 100 (Fall 1971):1051–86.

KOHN, MELVIN L. *Class and Conformity: A Study in Values.* 2nd ed. Homewood, IL: The Dorsey Press, 1977.

————, and CARMI SCHOOLER. "Job Conditions and Personality: A Longitudinal Assessment of Their Reciprocal Effects." *American Journal of Sociology.* Vol. 87, No. 6 (May 1982):1257–83.

KOLATA, GINA. "When Grandmother Is the Mother, Until Birth." *The New York Times* (August 5, 1991):1, 11.

KOMAROVSKY, MIRRA. *Blue Collar Marriage.* New York: Vintage Books, 1967.

————. "Cultural Contradictions and Sex Roles: The Masculine Case." *American Journal of Sociology.* Vol. 78, No. 4 (January 1973):873–84.

————. *Dilemmas of Masculinity: A Study of College Youth.* New York: W. W. Norton, 1976.

KORNHAUSER, WILLIAM. *The Politics of Mass Society.* New York: Free Press, 1959.

KOZOL, JONATHAN. *Prisoners of Silence: Breaking the Bonds of Adult Illiteracy in the United States.* New York: Continuum, 1980.

————. "A Nation's Wealth." *Publisher's Weekly* (May 24, 1985):28–30.

————. *Illiterate America.* Garden City, NY: Doubleday, 1985.

————. *Rachel and Her Children: Homeless Families in America.* New York: Crown Publishers, 1988.

KRAMARAE, CHERIS. *Women and Men Speaking.* Rowley, MA: Newbury House, 1981.

————, BARRIE THORNE, and NANCY HENLEY. "Sex Similarities and Differences in Language, Speech, and Nonverbal Communication: An Annotated Bibliography." In Barrie Thorne, Cheris Kramarae, and Nancy Henley, eds., *Language, Gender and Society.* Cambridge: Newbury House, 1983:150–331.

KRIESI, HANSPETER. "New Social Movements and the New Class in the Netherlands." *American Journal of Sociology.* Vol. 94, No. 5 (March 1989): 1078–16.

KRISBERG, BARRY, and IRA SCHWARTZ. "Rethinking Juvenile Justice." *Crime and Delinquency.* Vol. 29, No. 3 (July 1983):333–64.

KUBEY, ROBERT W. "Television and Aging: Past, Present, and Future." *The Gerontologist.* Vol. 20, No. 1 (February 1980):16–35.

KUBLER-ROSS, ELISABETH. *On Death and Dying.* New York: Macmillan, 1969.

KUHN, THOMAS. *The Structure of Scientific Revolutions.* 2nd ed. Chicago: University of Chicago Press, 1970.

KURTZ, LESTER R. *The Nuclear Cage: A Sociology of the Arms Race.* Englewood Cliffs, NJ: Prentice Hall, 1988.

KUZNETS, SIMON. *Modern Economic Growth: Rate, Structure, and Spread.* New Haven, CT: Yale University Press, 1966.

————. "Economic Growth and Income Inequality." *The American Economic Review.* Vol. XLV, No. 1 (March 1955):1–28.

Labour Force Activity: The Nation. Ottawa: Statistics Canada, 1993.

LACAYO, RICHARD. "Blood in the Stands." *Time.* Vol. 125, No. 23 (June 10, 1985):38–39, 41.

————. "Law and Disorder." *Time.* Vol. 137, No. 13 (April 1, 1991):18–21.

LADD, JOHN. "The Definition of Death and the Right to Die." In John Ladd, ed., *Ethical Issues Relating to Life and Death.* New York: Oxford University Press, 1979:118–45.

LADNER, JOYCE A. "Teenage Pregnancy: The Implications for Black Americans." In James D. Williams, ed., *The State of Black America 1986.* New York: National Urban League, 1986:65–84.

LAI, H. M. "Chinese." In *Harvard Encyclopedia of American Ethnic Groups.* Cambridge MA: Harvard University Press, 1980:217–33.

LAI, SIMON. *Living with Sensory Loss: Hearing.* National Advisory Council on Aging. Cat. no. 711–08. Ottawa: Statistics Canada, March 1990.

LAMAR, JACOB V., JR. "Redefining the American Dilemma." *Time.* Vol. 126, No. 19 (November 11, 1985):33, 36.

LAMBERG-KARLOVSKY, C. C., and MARTHA LAMBERG-KARLOVSKY. "An Early City in Iran." In *Cities: Their Origin, Growth, and Human Impact.* San Francisco: Freeman, 1973:28–37.

LANDALE, NANCY S., and STEWART E. TOLNAY. "Group Differences in Economic Opportunity and the Timing of Marriage: Blacks and Whites in the Rural South, 1910." *American Sociologial Review.* Vol. 56, No. 1 (February 1991):33–45.

LANDERS, ANN. Syndicated column: *The Dallas Morning News* (July 8, 1984):4F.

LANDERS, RENE M. "Gender, Race, and the State Courts." *The Radcliffe Quarterly.* Vol. 76, No. 4 (December 1990):6–9.

LANE, CHARLES. "Defying the Stereotypes." *Newsweek* (July 15, 1991):18–19.

LANE, DAVID. "Social Stratification and Class." In Erik P. Hoffman and Robbin F. Laird, eds., *The Soviet Polity in the Modern Era.* New York: Aldine, 1984: 563–605.

LANG, KURT, and GLADYS ENGEL LANG. *Collective Dynamics.* New York: Thomas Y. Crowell, 1961.

LAPPE, FRANCES MOORE, and JOSEPH COLLINS. *World Hunger: Twelve Myths.* New York: Grove Press/Food First Books, 1986.

LAPPE, FRANCES MOORE, JOSEPH COLLINS, and DAVID KINLEY. *Aid as Obstacle: Twenty Questions about Our Foreign Policy and the Hungry.* San Francisco: Institute for Food and Development Policy, 1981.

LAPRAIRIE, CAROL P. " Community Types, Crime and Police Services on Canadian Indian Reserves." *Journal of Research in Crime and Delinquency* 25(4) 1988: 375–91.

LASLETT, BARBARA. "Family Membership, Past and Present." *Social Problems.* Vol. 25, No. 5 (June 1978):476–90.

LASLETT, PETER. *The World We Have Lost: England Before the Industrial Age.* 3rd ed. New York: Charles Scribner's Sons, 1984.

LATOUCHE, DANIEL. "Québec." *The Canadian Encyclopedia*. 2nd ed. Edmonton: Hurtig Publishers, 3, 1988: 1793–1802.

LAXER, GORDON. *Open for Business: The Roots of Foreign Ownership in Canada*. Toronto: Oxford University Press, 1989.

LE BON, GUSTAVE. *The Crowd: A Study of the Popular Mind*. New York: The Viking Press, 1960; orig. 1895.

LEACOCK, ELEANOR. "Women's Status in Egalitarian Societies: Implications for Social Evolution." *Current Anthropology*. Vol. 19, No. 2 (June 1978): 247–75.

LEACOCK, STEPHEN. "My Financial Career." In Stephen Leacock, *The Best of Leacock*. Toronto: McClelland & Stewart, 1965.

LEAVITT, JUDITH WALZER. "Women and Health in America: An Overview." In Judith Walzer Leavitt, ed., *Women and Health in America*. Madison, WI: University of Wisconsin Press, 1984:3–7.

LEE, BARRETT A., R. S. OROPESA, BARBARA J. METCH, and AVERY M. GUEST. "Testing the Decline of Community Thesis: Neighborhood Organization in Seattle, 1929 and 1979." *American Journal of Sociology*. Vol. 89, No. 5 (March 1984):1161–88.

LEERHSEN, CHARLES. "Unite and Conquer." *Newsweek* (February 5, 1990):50–55.

LEIFER, ERIC M. "Inequality Among Equals: Embedding Market and Authority in League Sports." *American Journal of Sociology*. Vol. 96, No. 3 (November 1990):655–83.

LEMERT, EDWIN M. *Social Pathology*. New York: McGraw-Hill, 1951.

————. *Human Deviance, Social Problems, and Social Control*. 2nd ed. Englewood Cliffs, NJ: Prentice Hall, 1972.

LENGERMANN, PATRICIA MADOO, and RUTH A. WALLACE. *Gender in America: Social Control and Social Change*. Englewood Cliffs, NJ: Prentice Hall, 1985.

LENSKI, GERHARD. *Power and Privilege: A Theory of Social Stratification*. New York: McGraw-Hill, 1966.

————, and JEAN LENSKI. *Human Societies: An Introduction to Macrosociology*. 3rd ed. New York: McGraw-Hill, 1978; 4th ed., 1982; 5th ed., 1987.

LENSKI, GERHARD, JEAN LENSKI, and PATRICK NOLAN. Human Societies: *An Introduction to Macrosociology*. 6th ed. New York: McGraw-Hill, 1991.

LENSKYJ, HELENE. *Out of Bounds: Women, Sport and Sexuality*. Toronto: Women's Press, 1986.

LENTON, RHONDA L. "Homicide in Canada and the U.S.A.: A Critique of the Hagan Thesis." In Alexander Himelfarb and C. James Richardson, eds., *Sociology for Canadians*. 2nd ed. Toronto: McGraw-Hill Ryerson, 1989.

LEONARD, EILEEN B. *Women, Crime, and Society: A Critique of Theoretical Criminology*. New York: Longman, 1982.

LESLIE, GERALD R., and Sheila K. Korman. *The Family in Social Context*. 7th ed. New York: Oxford University Press, 1989.

LESTER, DAVID. *The Death Penalty: Issues and Answers*. Springfield, IL: Charles C. Thomas, 1987.

LEVER, JANET. "Sex Differences in the Complexity of Children's Play and Games." *American Sociological Review*. Vol. 43, No. 4 (August 1978): 471–83.

LEVIN, B. "Tuition Fees and University Accessibility." *Canadian Public Policy*, vol. 16, no. 1, March, 1993.

LEVIN, JACK, and WILLIAM C. LEVIN. *Ageism: Prejudice and Discrimination Against the Elderly*. Belmont, CA: Wadsworth, 1980.

LEVINE, MICHAEL P. *Student Eating Disorders: Anorexia Nervosa and Bulimia*. Washington, DC: National Educational Association, 1987.

LEVINSON, DANIEL J., with CHARLOTTE N. DARROW, EDWARD B. KLEIN, MARIA H. LEVINSON, and BRAXTON MCKEE. *The Seasons of a Man's Life*. New York: Alfred A. Knopf, 1978.

LEVITAN, SAR A., and ISAAC SHAPIRO. *Working but Poor: America's Contradiction*. Baltimore, MD: Johns Hopkins University Press, 1987.

LEVY, FRANK. *Dollars and Dreams: The Changing American Income Distribution*. New York: Russell Sage Foundation, 1987.

LEWIS, FLORA. "The Roots of Revolution." *The New York Times Magazine* (November 11, 1984):70–71, 74, 77–78, 82, 84, 86.

LEWIS, OSCAR. *The Children of Sanchez*. New York: Random House, 1961.

LEWONTIN, R. C., STEVEN ROSE, and LEON J. KAMIN. *Not In Our Genes: Biology, Ideology, and Human Nature*. New York: Pantheon, 1984.

LI, PETER S. *Ethnic Inequality in a Class Society*. Toronto: Wall and Thompson, 1988.

LIAZOS, ALEXANDER. "The Poverty of the Sociology of Deviance: Nuts, Sluts and Preverts." *Social Problems*. Vol. 20, No. 1 (Summer 1972):103–20.

LICHTER, DANIEL R. "Race, Employment Hardship, and Inequality in the American Nonmetropolitan South." *American Sociological Review*. Vol. 54, No. 3 (June 1989):436–46.

LIEBERSON, STANLEY. *A Piece of the Pie: Black and White Immigrants Since 1880*. Berkeley, CA: University of California Press, 1980.

LIEBOW, ELLIOT. *Tally's Corner*. Boston, MA: Little, Brown, 1967.

LIN, NAN, and WALTER M. ENSEL. "Life Stress and Health: Stressors and Resources." *American Sociological Review*. Vol. 54, No. 3 (June 1989): 382–99.

LIN, NAN, WALTER M. ENSEL, and JOHN C. VAUGHN. "Social Resources and Strength of Ties: Structural Factors in Occupational Status Attainment." *American Sociological Review*. Vol. 46, No. 4 (August 1981):393–405.

LINCOLN, JAMES R., and ARNE L. KALLEBERG. "Work Organization and Workforce Commitment: A Study of Plants and Employees in the U. S. and Japan." *American Sociological Review*. Vol. 50, No. 6 (December 1985):738–60.

LING, PYAU. "Causes of Chinese Emigration." In Amy Tachiki et al., eds., *Roots: An Asian American Reader*. Los Angeles, CA: UCLA Asian American Studies Center, 1971:134–38.

LINK, BRUCE G., BRUCE P. DOHRENWEND, and ANDREW E. SKODOL. "Socio-Economic Status and Schizophrenia: Noisome Occupational Characteristics As a Risk Factor." *American Sociological Review*. Vol. 51, No. 2 (April 1986): 242–58.

LINK, BRUCE G., Francis T. Cullin, James Frank, and John F. Wozniak. "The Social Rejection of Former Mental Patients: Understanding Why Labels Matter." *American Journal of Sociology*. Vol. 92, No. 6 (May 1987): 1461–1500.

LINTON, RALPH. "One Hundred Percent American." *The American Mercury*. Vol. 40, No. 160 (April 1937):427–29.

LINTON, RALPH. *The Study of Man*. New York: D. Appleton-Century, 1937.

LIPOVENKO, DOROTHY. "Study undertaken for law reform body turns up 118 surrogate-mother cases." *The Globe and Mail*, February 10, 1989: A1–2.

LIPSET, SEYMOUR MARTIN. *Political Man: The Social Bases of Politics*. Garden City, NY: Doubleday Anchor Books, 1963.

————. *Continental Divide: The Values and Institutions of the United States and Canada*. New York: Routledge, 1991.

————. *Canada and the United States*. Charles F. Donan and John H. Sigler, eds., Englewood Cliffs, N.J.: Prentice Hall Stable for Hajidorn La.

————, and REINHARD BENDIX. *Social Mobility in Industrial Society*. Berkeley, CA: University of California Press, 1967.

LISKA, ALLEN E. *Perspectives on Deviance*. 3rd ed. Englewood Cliffs, NJ: Prentice Hall, 1991.

————, and BARBARA D. WARNER. "Functions of Crime: A Paradoxical Process." *American Journal of Sociology*. Vol. 96, No. 6 (May 1991):1441–63.

LISKA, ALLEN E., and MARK TAUSIG. "Theoretical Interpretations of Social Class and Racial Differentials in Legal Decision Making for Juveniles." *Sociological Quarterly*. Vol. 20, No. 2 (Spring 1979):197–207.

LITTMAN, MARK S. "Poverty in the 1980s: Are the Poor Getting Poorer?" *Monthly Labor Review*. Vol. 112, No. 6 (June 1989):13–18.

LO, CLARENCE Y. H. "Countermovements and Conservative Movements in the Contemporary U. S." *Annual Review of Sociology*. Vol. 8. Palo Alto, CA: Annual Reviews, Inc., 1982:107–34.

LOFLAND, LYN. *A World of Strangers*. New York: Basic Books, 1973.

LOGAN, JOHN R., and MARK SCHNEIDER. "Racial Segregation and Racial Change in American Suburbs, 1970–1980." *American Journal of Sociology*. Vol. 89, No. 4 (January 1984):874–88.

LOHR, STEVE. "British Health Service Faces A Crisis in Funds and Delays." *The New York Times* (August 7, 1988):1, 12.

LONDON, BRUCE. "Structural Determinants of Third World Urban Change: An Ecological and Political Economic Analysis." *American Sociological Review.* Vol. 52, No. 1 (February 1987):28–43.

LONG, EDWARD V. *The Intruders: The Invasion of Privacy by Government and Industry.* New York: Frederick A. Praeger, 1967.

LONG, J. ANTHONY and MENNO BOLDT, eds., *Governments in Conflict? Provinces and Indian Nations in Canada.* Toronto: University of Toronto Press, 1988.

LORD, WALTER. *A Night to Remember.* Rev. ed. New York: Holt, Rinehart and Winston, 1976.

LORENZ, KONRAD. *On Aggression.* New York: Harcourt, Brace and World, 1966.

LOWREY, PETER. "Spiritual Escape." *Calgary Herald*, Sat., Oct. 26, 1985:4.

LOY, PAMELA HEWITT, and LEA P. STEWART. "The Extent and Effects of Sexual Harassment of Working Women." *Sociological Focus.* Vol. 17, No. 1 (January 1984):31–43.

LUBENOW, GERALD C. "A Troubling Family Affair." *Newsweek* (May 14, 1984):34.

LUCAS, REX A. *Men in Crisis: A Study of a Mine Disaster.* New York: Basic Books, 1969.

LUKAS, J. ANTHONY. "Wilding—As American as Tom Sawyer." *The New York Times* (May 28, 1989):sec. 4, p. 15.

LUND, DALE A. "Conclusions about Bereavement in Later Life and Implications for Interventions and Future Research." In Dale A. Lund, ed., *Older Bereaved Spouses: Research With Practical Applications.* Taylor-Francis-Hemisphere, 1989:217–31.

LUND, DALE A., MARGARET F. DIMOND, MICHAEL S. CASERTA, ROBERT J. JOHNSON, JAMES L. POULTON, and J. RICHARD CONNELLY. "Identifying Elderly With Coping Difficulties After Two Years of Bereavement." *Omega.* Vol. 16, No. 3 (1985):213–24.

LUPRI, EUGENE. "Male Violence in the Home." In Craig McKie and K. Thompson, eds., *Social Trends in Canada.* Toronto: Thompson Educational Publishers, 1988: 170–172.

LUTZ, CATHERINE A. *Unnatural Emotions: Everyday Sentiments on a Micronesia Atoll and Their Challenge to Western Theory.* Chicago: University of Chicago Press, 1988.

LUTZ, CATHERINE, and GEOFFREY M. WHITE. "The Anthropology of Emotions." In Bernard J. Siegel, Alan R. Beals, and Stephen A. Tyler, eds., *Annual Review of Anthropology.* Palo Alto, CA: Annual Reviews, Inc. Vol. 15 (1986):405–36.

LUXTON, MEG. *More Than a Labour of Love.* Toronto: Women's Press, 1980.

LYNCH, GERALD. "Stephen Leacock." *The Canadian Encyclopedia.* 2nd ed. Edmonton: Hurtig Publishers, 2, 1988: 1192.

LYND, ROBERT S. *Knowledge For What? The Place of Social Science in American Culture.* Princeton, NJ: Princeton University Press, 1967.

———, and HELEN MERRELL LYND. *Middletown in Transition.* New York: Harcourt, Brace & World, 1937.

MA, LI-CHEN. Personal communication, 1987.

MACCOBY, ELEANOR EMMONS, and CAROL NAGY JACKLIN. *The Psychology of Sex Differences.* Palo Alto, CA: Stanford University Press, 1974.

MACE, DAVID, and VERA MACE. *Marriage East and West.* Garden City, NY: Doubleday (Dolphin), 1960.

MACIONIS, JOHN J. "Intimacy: Structure and Process in Interpersonal Relationships." *Alternative Lifestyles.* Vol. 1, No. 1 (February 1978):113–30.

———. "The Search for Community in Modern Society: An Interpretation." *Qualitative Sociology.* Vol. 1, No. 2 (September 1978):130–43.

———. "A Sociological Analysis of Humor." Presentation to the Texas Junior College Teachers Association, Houston, 1987.

———. "Sociology in the 1990s: Reaching for the World." *VUES: Newsletter of the Section on Undergraduate Education* (Summer 1991):4. Washington, DC: American Sociological Association.

MACKAY, DONALD G. "Prescriptive Grammar and the Pronoun Problem." In Barrie Thorne, Cheris Kramarae, and Nancy Henley, eds., *Language, Gender and Society.* Cambridge: Newbury House, 1983:38–53.

MACKIE, MARLENE. "Ethnic Stereotypes and Prejudice: Alberta Indians, Hutterites and Ukrainians." *Canadian Ethnic Studies X*, 1974: 118–129.

———. *Exploring Gender Relations: A Canadian Perspective.* Toronto: Butterworths, 1983.

MACKLIN, ELEANOR D. "Nonmarital Heterosexual Cohabitation: An Overview." In Eleanor D. Macklin and Roger H. Rubin, eds., *Contemporary Families and Alternative Lifestyles: Handbook on Research and Theory.* Beverly Hills, CA: Sage, 1983:49–74.

Maclean's, "Beauty and the Breast." March 9, 1992: 38–45.

Maclean's. "The Age of Caution." CTV Poll. Jan. 4, 1993.

Maclean's. "The Centrefold War. Do Skin Magazines Violate Human Rights?" May 10, 1993: 14–16.

Maclean's. "The Home Stretch." CTV Poll. June 14, 1993: 10–14.

MACLEOD, L. "The John Porter Award." *Society*, vol. 14, no. 3, October 1990.

MACLEOD, LINDA. *Wifebattering in Canada: The Vicious Circle.* Ottawa: Advisory Council on the Status of Women, 1980.

———. *Battered But Not Beaten: Preventing Wifebattering in Canada.* Ottawa: Advisory Council on the Status of Women, 1987.

MACLEOD, ROBERT. "New Bylaw Weeds Out Smokers." *The Globe and Mail*, Thurs., Dec. 3, 1992.

MADSEN, AXEL. *Private Power: Multinational Corporations for the Survival of Our Planet.* New York: William Morrow, 1980.

MAHLER, HALFDAN. "People." *Scientific American.* Vol. 243, No. 3 (September 1980): 67–77.

MAJKA, LINDA C. "Sexual Harassment in the Church." *Society.* Vol. 28. No. 4 (May–June, 1991):14–21.

MAJOR, BRENDA. "Gender Patterns in Touching Behavior." In Clara Mayo and Nancy M. Henley, eds., *Gender and Nonverbal Behavior.* New York: Springer Verlag, 1981:15–37.

MALTHUS, THOMAS ROBERT. *First Essay on Population 1798.* London: Macmillan, 1926; orig. 1798.

MANGAN, J. A., and ROBERTA J. PARK. *From Fair Sex to Feminism: Sport and the Socialization of Women.* London: Frank Cass, 1987.

MAO, YOUNG, LAURIER GIBBONS and TINA WONG. "The Impact of the Decreased Prevalence of Smoking in Canada." *Canadian Journal of Public Health*, vol. 83, no. 6, 1992: 413–16.

MARCHAK, PATRICIA. *Ideological Perspectives on Canadian Society.* Toronto: McGraw Hill, 1975.

———. "The Rise and Fall of the Peripheral State: The Case of British Columbia." In Robert J. Brym, ed., *Regionalism in Canada.* Toronto: Irwin, 1986: 123–160.

MARCUSE, HERBERT. *One-Dimensional Man.* Boston, MA: Beacon Press, 1964.

MARE, ROBERT D. "Change and Stability in Educational Stratification." *American Sociological Review.* Vol. 46, No. 1 (February 1981):72–87.

———. "Five Decades of Educational Assortative Mating." *American Sociological Review.* Vol. 56, No. 1 (February 1991):15–32.

MARGOLICK, DAVID. "Rape in Marriage Is No Longer Within the Law." *The New York Times* (December 13, 1984):6E.

MARKOFF, JOHN. "Remember Big Brother? Now He's a Company Man." *The New York Times* (March 31, 1991):7.

MARLIOS, PETER. "Interlocking Directorates and the Control of Corporations: The Theory of Bank Control." *Social Science Quarterly.* Vol. 56, No. 3 (December 1975):425–39.

MARRY, MARCUS. "New Hope for Old Unions?" *Newsweek* (February 24, 1992):39.

MARSDEN, LORNA R. and EDWARD B. HARVEY *Fragile Federation: Social Change in Canada.* Toronto: McGraw-Hill Ryerson, 1979.

MARSDEN, PETER. "Core Discussion Networks of Americans." *American Sociological Review.* Vol. 52, No. 1 (February 1987):122–31.

MARSHALL, SUSAN E. "Ladies Against Women: Mobilization Dilemmas of AntiFeminist Movements." *Social Problems*. Vol. 32, No. 4 (April 1985): 348–62.

MARSHALL, VICTOR W. *Aging in Canada*. 2nd ed., Toronto: Fitzhenry and Whiteside, 1986.

MARTIN, RICHARD C. *Islam: A Cultural Perspective*. Englewood Cliffs, NJ: Prentice Hall, 1982.

MARTIN, WILLIAM. "The Birth of a Media Myth." *The Atlantic*. Vol. 247, No. 6 (June 1981):7, 10, 11, 16.

MARULLO, SAM. "The Functions and Dysfunctions of Preparations for Fighting Nuclear War." *Sociological Focus*. Vol. 20, No. 2 (April 1987):135–53.

MARX, GARY T., and JAMES L. WOOD. "Strands of Theory and Research in Collective Behavior." In Alex Inkeles et al., eds., *Annual Review of Sociology*. Vol. 1. Palo Alto, CA: Annual Reviews, Inc., 1975:363–428.

MARX, KARL. "Theses on Feuer." In Robert C. Tucker, ed., *The Marx-Engels Reader*. New York: W. W. Norton, 1972:107–9; orig. 1845.

———. *Capital*. Friedrich Engels, ed. New York: International Publishers, 1967; orig. 1867.

———. Excerpt from "A Contribution to the Critique of Political Economy." In Karl Marx and Friedrich Engels, *Marx and Engels: Basic Writings on Politics and Philosophy*. Lewis S. Feurer, ed. Garden City, NY: Anchor Books, 1959:42–46.

———. *Karl Marx: Early Writings*. T. B. Bottomore, ed. New York: McGraw-Hill, 1964a.

———. *Karl Marx: Selected Writings in Sociology and Social Philosophy*. T. B. Bottomore, trans. New York: McGraw-Hill, 1964.

———. *The Marx-Engels Reader*. Robert C. Tucker, ed. New York: W. W. Norton, 1977.

MARX, KARL, and FRIEDRICH ENGELS. "Manifesto of the Communist Party." In Robert C. Tucker, ed., *The Marx-Engels Reader*. New York: W. W. Norton, 1972:331–62; orig. 1848.

MASHEK, JOHN W., and PATRICIA AVERY. "Women Politicians Take Off the White Gloves." *U. S. News and World Report* (August 15, 1983):41–42.

"Massacre in Montreal." *Maclean's*, 102, #51, Dec. 18, 1989: 14–18.

MASSERMAN, JULES H., and VICTOR M. URIBE. *Adolescent Sexuality*. New York: Charles C. Thomas, 1990.

MASSEY, DOUGLAS S., and NANCY A. DENTON. "Hypersegregation in U. S. Metropolitan Areas: Black and Hispanic Segregation Along Five Dimensions." *Demography*. Vol. 26, No. 3 (August 1989):373–91.

MASTERS, WILLIAM H., VIRGINIA E. JOHNSON, and ROBERT C. KOLODNY. *Human Sexuality*. 3rd ed. Glenview, IL: Scott, Foresman/Little, Brown, 1988.

MATHEWS, ANNE MARTIN. "The Newfoundland Migrant Wife." *Atlantis: A Woman's Studies Journal*, 2.2, Spring, 1977.

MATTHEWS, MERVYN. "Long Term Trends in Soviet Education." In J. J. Tomiak, ed., *Soviet Education in the 1980s*. London: Croom Helm, 1983:1–23.

MATTHEWS, RALPH. *"There's No Better Place Than Here: Social Change in Three Newfoundland Communities."* Toronto: Peter Martin, 1978.

———. *The Creation of Regional Dependency*. Toronto: University of Toronto Press, 1983.

MATTHIESSEN, PETER. *In the Spirit of Crazy Horse*. New York: Viking Press, 1983.

———. *Indian Country*. New York: Viking Press, 1984.

MATZA, DAVID. *Delinquency and Drift*. New York: John Wiley, 1964.

MAURO, TONY. "Cruzan's Struggle Left Imprint: Private Case Triggered Public Debate." *USA Today* (December 27, 1990):3A.

MAUSS, ARMAND L. *Social Problems of Social Movements*. Philadelphia, PA: Lippincott, 1975.

MAY, ELAINE TYLER. "Women in the Wild Blue Yonder." *The New York Times* (August 7, 1991):21.

MAYO, KATHERINE. *Mother India*. New York: Harcourt, Brace and Co., 1927.

McADAM, DOUG. *Political Process and the Development of Black Insurgency, 1930–1970*. Chicago: University of Chicago Press, 1982.

———. "Tactical Innovation and the Pace of Insurgency." *American Sociological Review*. Vol. 48, No. 6 (December 1983):735–54.

———. *Freedom Summer*. New York: Oxford University Press, 1988.

———. "The Biographical Consequences of Activism." *American Sociological Review*. Vol. 54, No. 5 (October 1989):744–60.

———, JOHN D. McCARTHY, and MAYER N. ZALD. "Social Movements." In Neil J. Smelser, ed., *Handbook of Sociology*. Newbury Park, CA: Sage, 1988:695–737.

McAll, CHRISTOPHER. *Class, Ethnicity and Social Inequality*. Montreal and Kingston: McGill-Queen's University Press, 1990.

McBROOM, WILLIAM H., and FRED W. REED. "Recent Trends in Conservatism: Evidence of Non-Unitary Patterns." *Sociological Focus*. Vol. 23, No. 4 (October 1990):355–65.

McCARTHY, JOHN D., and MAYER N. ZALD. "Resource Mobilization and Social Movements: A Partial Theory." *American Journal of Sociology*. Vol. 82, No. 6 (May 1977):1212–41.

McCLAIN, PAULA DENISE. *Alienation and Resistance: The Political Behavior of Afro-Canadians*. Palo Alto, California: R&E Research Associates, 1979.

McDANIEL, SUSAN A. *Canada's Aging Population*. Toronto: Butterworths, 1986.

McGRATH, ELLIE. "Preparing to Wield the Rod." *Time*. Vol. 121, No. 4 (January 23, 1984):57.

McGUIRE, MEREDITH B. *Religion: The Social Context*. 2nd ed. Belmont, CA: Wadsworth, 1987.

McHENRY, SUSAN. "Rosabeth Moss Kanter." In *Ms*. Vol. 13 (January 1985): 62–63, 107–8.

McKEOWN, THOMAS. *The Role of Medicine: Dream, Mirage, or Nemesis?* Princeton, NJ: Princeton University Press, 1979.

McKIE, CRAIG and KEITH THOMPSON, eds. *Canadian Social Trends*. Toronto: Thompson Educational Publishing, 1990.

McKUSICK, LEON, et al. "Reported Changes in the Sexual Behavior of Men at Risk for AIDS, San Francisco, 1982–84—The AIDS Behavioral Research Project." *Public Health Reports*. Vol. 100, No. 6 (November–December 1985):622–29.

McLANAHAN, SARA. "Family Structure and the Reproduction of Poverty." *American Journal of Sociology*. Vol. 90, No. 4 (January 1985):873–901.

McLEAN, STUART. *Welcome Home: Travels in Smalltown Canada*. Toronto: Viking, 1992.

McNEIL, DONALD G., JR. "Should Women Be Sent Into Combat?" *The New York Times* (July 21, 1991):E3.

McPHAIL, CLARK. *The Myth of the Maddening Crowd*. New York: Aldine De Gruyter, 1991.

———, and RONALD T. WOHLSTEIN. "Individual and Collective Behaviors Within Gatherings, Demonstrations, and Riots." *Annual Review of Sociology*. Vol. 9. Palo Alto, CA: Annual Reviews, Inc., 1983:579–600.

McPHERSON, BARRY D. *Aging as a Social Process: An Introduction to Individual and Population Aging*. 2nd ed. Toronto: Butterworths, 1990.

McRAE, SUSAN. *Cross-Class Families: A Study of Wives' Occupational Superiority*. New York: Oxford University Press, 1986.

McROBERTS, HUGH A., and KEVIN SELBEE. "Trends in Occupational Mobility in Canada and the United States: A Comparison." *American Sociological Review*. Vol. 46, No. 4 (August 1981):406–21.

MEAD, GEORGE HERBERT. "Teaching of Science in College." *Science*. Vol. 24 (1906):390–97.

———. *Mind, Self, and Society*. Charles W. Morris, ed. Chicago: University of Chicago Press, 1962; orig. 1934.

MEAD, MARGARET. *Coming of Age in Samoa*. New York: Dell, 1961; orig. 1928.

———. *Sex and Temperament in Three Primitive Societies*. New York: William Morrow, 1963; orig. 1935.

MECHANIC, DAVID. *Medical Sociology*. 2nd ed. New York: Free Press, 1978.

MEISEL, J. *Working Papers on Canadian Politics*. Montreal: McGill-Queen's University Press, 1975.

MELTZER, BERNARD N. "Mead's Social Psychology." In Jerome G. Manis and Bernard N. Meltzer, eds., *Symbolic Interaction: A Reader in Social Psychology*. 2nd ed. Boston, MA: Allyn & Bacon, 1977:15–27; 3rd ed., 1978.

MELUCCI, ALBERTO. "The New Social Movements: A Theoretical Approach." *Social Science Information*. Vol. 19, No. 2 (May 1980):199–226.

———. *Nomads of the Present: Social Movements and Individual Needs in Contemporary Society*. Philadelphia: Temple University Press, 1989.

MELVILLE, KEITH. *Marriage and Family Today*. 3rd ed. New York: Random House, 1983.

MERTON, ROBERT K. "Social Structure and Anomie." *American Sociological Review*. Vol. 3, No. 6 (October 1938):672–82.

———. "Discrimination and the American Creed." In *Sociological Ambivalence and Other Essays*. New York: The Free Press, 1976:189–216.

———. *Social Theory and Social Structure*. New York: Free Press, 1968.

MESSNER, STEVEN R. "Economic Discrimination and Societal Homicide Rates: Further Evidence of the Cost of Inequality." *American Sociological Review*. Vol. 54, No. 4 (August 1989):597–611.

MICHELS, ROBERT. *Political Parties*. Glencoe, IL: Free Press, 1949; orig. 1911.

MICHELSON, WILLIAM. "Urbanization and Urbanism." In James Curtis and Lorne Tepperman, eds., *Understanding Canadian Society*. Toronto: McGraw-Hill Ryerson, 1988: 73–104.

MILGRAM, STANLEY. "Behavioral Study of Obedience." *Journal of Abnormal and Social Psychology*. Vol. 67, No. 4 (1963):371–78.

———. "Group Pressure and Action Against a Person." *Journal of Abnormal and Social Psychology*. Vol. 69, No. 2 (August 1964):137–43.

———. "Some Conditions of Obedience and Disobedience to Authority." *Human Relations*. Vol. 18 (February 1965):57–76.

MILIBAND, RALPH. *The State in Capitalist Society*. London: Weidenfield and Nicolson, 1969.

MILLER, ARTHUR G. *The Obedience Experiments: A Case of Controversy in Social Science*. New York: Praeger, 1986.

MILLER, DAVID L. *Introduction to Collective Behavior*. Belmont, CA: Wadsworth, 1985.

MILLER, FREDERICK D. "The End of SDS and the Emergence of Weatherman: Demise Through Success." In Jo Freeman, ed., *Social Movements of the Sixties and Seventies*. New York: Longman, 1983:279–97.

MILLER, MARK. "Under Cover, In the Closet." *Newsweek* (January 14, 1991):25.

MILLER, MICHAEL. "Lawmakers Begin to Heed Calls to Protect Privacy." *The Wall Street Journal* (April 11, 1991):A16.

MILLER, WALTER B. "Lower Class Culture as a Generating Milieu of Gang Delinquency." In Marvin E. Wolfgang, Leonard Savitz, and Norman Johnston, eds., *The Sociology of Crime and Delinquency*. 2nd ed. New York: John Wiley, 1970:351–63; orig. 1958.

MILLET, KATE. *Sexual Politics*. Garden City, NY: Doubleday, 1970.

MILLS, C. WRIGHT. *White Collar: The American Middle Classes*. New York: Oxford University Press, 1951.

———. *The Power Elite*. New York: Oxford University Press, 1956.

———. *The Social Causes of World War Three*. New York: Simon and Schuster, 1958.

———. *The Sociological Imagination*. New York: Oxford University Press, 1959.

MINK, BARBARA. "How Modernization Affects Women." *Cornell Alumni News*. Vol. III, No. 3 (April 1989):10–11.

MINTZ, BETH, and MICHAEL SCHWARTZ. "Interlocking Directorates and Interest Group Formation." *American Sociological Review*. Vol. 46, No. 6 (December 1981):851–69.

MIROWSKY, JOHN. "The Psycho-Economics of Feeling Underpaid: Distributive Justice and the Earnings of Husbands and Wives." *American Journal of Sociology*. Vol. 92, No. 6 (May 1987):1404–34.

MIROWSKY, JOHN, and CATHERINE ROSS. "Working Wives and Mental Health." Presentation to the American Association for the Advancement of Science. New York, 1984.

———. *The Social Causes of Psychological Distress*. Hawthorne, NY: Aldine de Gruyter, 1989.

MITCHELL, WILLIAM L. "Lay Observations on Retirement." In Frances M. Carp, ed., *Retirement*. New York: Behavioral Publications, 1972:199–217.

MITCHINSON, WENDY. *The Nature of Their Bodies: Women and Their Doctors in Victorian Canada*. Toronto: University of Toronto Press, 1991.

MOLNAR, STEPHEN. *Human Variation: Races, Types, and Ethnic Groups*. 2nd ed. Englewood Cliffs, NJ: Prentice Hall, 1983.

MOLOTCH, HARVEY. "The City as a Growth Machine." *American Journal of Sociology*. Vol. 82, No. 2 (September 1976):309–33.

———, and DEIRDRE BODEN. "Talking Social Structure: Discourse, Domination, and the Watergate Hearings." *American Sociological Review*. Vol. 50, No. 3 (June 1985):273–88.

MONEY, JOHN. *The Destroying Angel: Sex, Fitness & Food in the Legacy of Degeneracy Theory, Graham Crackers, Kellogg's Corn Flakes & American Health History*. Buffalo, NY: Prometheus Books, 1985.

———, and ANKE A. EHRHARDT. *Man and Woman, Boy and Girl*. New York: New American Library, 1972.

MONK-TURNER, ELIZABETH. "Sex, Educational Differentiation, and Occupational Status: Analyzing Occupational Differences for Community and Four-Year Entrants." *The Sociological Quarterly*. Vol. 24, No. 3 (July 1983):393–404.

———. "The Occupational Achievement of Community and Four-Year College Graduates." *American Sociological Review*. Vol. 55, No. 5 (October 1990):719–25.

MONTAGUE, ASHLEY. *The Nature of Human Aggression*. New York: Oxford University Press, 1976.

Montreal Gazette. "Tobacco Production Edges Up." Sat., Jan. 25, 1992:PE1.

MOORE, GWEN. "The Structure of a National Elite Network." *American Sociological Review*. Vol. 44, No. 5 (October 1979):673–92.

———. "Structural Determinants of Men's and Women's Personal Networks." *American Sociological Review*. Vol. 55, No. 5 (October 1991):726–35.

MOORE, JOAN, and HARRY PACHON. *Hispanics in the United States*. Englewood Cliffs, NJ: Prentice Hall, 1985.

MOORE, WILBERT E. "Modernization as Rationalization: Processes and Restraints." In Manning Nash, ed., *Essays on Economic Development and Cultural Change in Honor of Bert F. Hoselitz*. Chicago: University of Chicago Press, 1977:29–42.

———. *World Modernization: The Limits of Convergence*. New York: Elsevier, 1979.

MORAN, JOHN S., S. O. ARAL, W. C. JENKINS, T. A. PETERMAN, and E. R. ALEXANDER. "The Impact of Sexually Transmitted Diseases on Minority Populations." *Public Health Reports*. Vol. 104, No. 6 (November–December 1989): 560–65.

MORRIS, ALDON. "Black Southern Sit-in Movement: An Analysis of Internal Organization." *American Sociological Review*. Vol. 46, No. 6 (December 1981):744–67.

MORRISON, DENTON E. "Some Notes Toward Theory on Relative Deprivation, Social Movements, and Social Change." In Louis E. Genevie, ed., *Collective Behavior and Social Movements*. Itasca, IL: F. E. Peacock, 1978:202–9.

MORROW, LANCE. "Rough Justice." *Time*. Vol. 137, No. 13 (April 1, 1991): 16–17.

MOSKOS, CHARLES C. "Female GIs in the Field." *Society*. Vol. 22, No. 6 (September/October 1985):28–33.

MOTTAZ, CLIFFORD J. "Some Determinants of Work Alienation." *The Sociological Quarterly*. Vol. 22, No. 4 (Autumn 1981):515–29.

MUELLER, DANIEL P., and PHILIP W. COOPER. "Children of Single Parent Families: How Do They Fare as Young Adults?" Presentation to the American Sociological Association, San Antonio, Texas, 1984.

MULLER, EDWARD N. *Aggressive Political Participation*. Princeton, NJ: Princeton University Press, 1979.

MULLER, THOMAS, and THOMAS J. ESPENSHADE. *The Fourth Wave: California's Newest Immigrants*. Washington, DC: The Urban Institute Press, 1985.

MUMFORD, LEWIS. *The City in History: Its Origins, Its Transformations, and Its Prospects.* New York: Harcourt, Brace & World, 1961.

MURDOCK, GEORGE P. "Comparative Data on the Division of Labor by Sex." *Social Forces.* Vol. 15, No. 4 (May 1937):551–53.

————. "The Common Denominator of Cultures." In Ralph Linton, ed., *The Science of Man in World Crisis.* New York: Columbia University Press, 1945:123–42.

————. *Social Structure.* New York: Free Press, 1965; orig. 1949.

MURPHY, ROBERT F. *An Overture to Social Anthropology.* Englewood Cliffs, NJ: Prentice Hall, 1979.

MURRAY, MEGAN BALDRIDGE. "Innovation Without Geniuses." In *Yale Alumni Magazine and Journal.* Vol. XLVII, No. 6 (April 1984):40–43.

MURRAY, PAULI. *Proud Shoes: The History of an American Family.* New York: Harper & Row, 1978.

MYDANS, SETH. "Study of Indians' Remains: Science or Sacrilege?" *The New York Times* (October 19, 1990).

MYERS, DAVID G. *Psychology.* New York: Worth, 1986.

MYERS, SHEILA, and HAROLD G. GRASMICK. "The Social Rights and Responsibilities of Pregnant Women: An Application of Parsons' Sick Role Model." Paper presented to Southwestern Sociological Association, Little Rock, Arkansas, March 1989.

N. O. R. C. *General Social Surveys, 1972–1991: Cumulative Codebook.* Chicago: National Opinion Research Center, 1991.

NADER, RALPH, NADIA MILLERON and DUFF CONACHER. *Canada Firsts.* Toronto: McClelland & Stewart, 1992.

NAEYAERT, KATHLEEN. *Living with Sensory Loss: Vision.* (National Advisory Council on Aging.) Ottawa: 1990.

NATIONAL CENTER FOR EDUCATION STATISTICS. *Digest of Education Statistics 1983–84.* Washington, DC: U. S. Government Printing Office, 1983.

NATIONAL CENTER FOR EDUCATION STATISTICS. *Digest of Education Statistics: 1990.* Washington, DC: U. S. Government Printing Office, 1991:244.

NATIONAL COMMISSION ON EXCELLENCE IN EDUCATION. *A Nation at Risk.* Washington, DC: U. S. Government Printing Office, 1983.

NATIONAL EATING DISORDER INFORMATION CENTRE, 1993.

NATIONAL INSTITUTE OF DRUG ABUSE. U. S. Department of Health and Human Services. *National Household Survey on Drug Abuse: Main Findings 1990.* Rockville, MD: U. S. Government Printing Office, 1991.

NAVARRO, VICENTE. "The Industrialization of Fetishism or the Fetishism of Industrialization: A Critique of Ivan Illich." In Vicente Navarro, ed., *Health and Medical Care in the U.S.: A Critical Analysis.* Farmingdale, NY: Baywood Publishing Co., 1977:38–58.

NAWAZ, MOHAMED. *Potsmoking and Illegal Conduct: Understanding the Social World of University Students.* Canada: Diliton Publications, 1978.

NEIDERT, LISA J., and REYNOLDS FARLEY. "Assimilation in the United States: An Analysis of Ethnic and Generation Differences in Status and Achievement." *American Sociological Review.* Vol. 50, No. 6 (December 1985):840–50.

NEILL, SHIRLEY. "Unionization in Canada." In Craig McKie and Keith Thompson, eds., *Canadian Social Trends.* Toronto: Thompson Educational Publishing, 1990.

NELSON, HARRY, and ROBERT JERMAIN. *Introduction to Physical Anthropology.* 3rd ed. St. Paul, MN: West, 1985:22–24.

NEMETH, MARY. "God is Alive." *Maclean's.* Toronto: April 12, 1993.

NETT, EMILY, M. *Canadian Families: Past and Present.* 2nd ed. Toronto: Butterworths, 1993.

NEUGARTEN, BERNICE L. "Grow Old with Me. The Best Is Yet to Be." *Psychology Today.* Vol. 5 (December 1971):45–48, 79, 81.

————. "Personality and the Aging Process." *The Gerontologist.* Vol. 12, No. 1 (Spring 1972):9–15.

————. "Personality and Aging." In James E. Birren and K. Warner Schaie, eds., *Handbook of the Psychology of Aging.* New York: Van Nostrand Reinhold, 1977:626–49.

NEUHOUSER, KEVIN. "The Radicalization of the Brazilian Catholic Church in Comparative Perspective." *American Sociological Review.* Vol. 54, No. 2 (April 1989):233–44.

New Haven Journal Courier. "English Social Structure Changing." November 27, 1986.

NEWMAN, JAMES L., and GORDON E. MATZKE. *Population: Patterns, Dynamics, and Prospects.* Englewood Cliffs, NJ: Prentice Hall, 1984.

NEWMAN, WILLIAM M. *American Pluralism: A Study of Minority Groups and Social Theory.* New York: Harper & Row, 1973.

1991 Green Book. U. S. House of Representatives. Washington, DC: U. S. Government Printing Office, 1991.

NISBET, ROBERT A. *The Sociological Tradition.* New York: Basic Books, 1966.

————. "Sociology as an Art Form." In *Tradition and Revolt: Historical and Sociological Essays.* New York: Vintage Books, 1970.

NOCH, D. A. "Religion." In K. Ishwaran, ed., *Sociology: An Introduction.* Don Mills, Ontario: Addison-Wesley, 1986.

NORBECK, EDWARD. "Class Structure." In *Kodansha Encyclopedia of Japan.* Tokyo: Kodansha, 1983:322–25.

NUMBERS, RONALD L. "Creationism in 20th-Century America." *Science.* Vol. 218, No. 5 (November 1982):538–44.

NUNN, CLYDE Z., HARRY J. CROCKETT, JR., and J. ALLEN WILLIAMS, JR. *Tolerance for Nonconformity.* San Francisco, CA: Jossey-Bass Publishers, 1978.

O'BRIEN, MARY. *The Politics of Reproduction.* London: Routledge and Kegan Paul, 1981.

O'DEA, THOMAS F., and JANET O'DEA AVIAD. *The Sociology of Religion.* 2nd ed. Englewood Cliffs, NJ: Prentice Hall, 1983.

O'HARE, WILLIAM. "In the Black." *American Demographics.* Vol. 11, No. 11 (November 1989):25–29.

————. "The Rise of Hispanic Affluence." *American Demographics.* Vol. 12, No. 8 (August 1990):40–43.

————, and JAN LARSON. "Women in Business: Where, What, and Why." *American Demographics.* Vol. 13, No. 7 (July 1991):34–38.

O'REILLY, JANE. "Wife Beating: The Silent Crime." *Time.* Vol. 122, No. 10 (September 5, 1983):23–24, 26.

OAKES, JEANNIE. "Classroom Social Relationships: Exploring the Bowles and Gintis Hypothesis." *Sociology of Education.* Vol. 55, No. 4 (October 1982):197–212.

OAKES, JEANNIE. *Keeping Track: How High Schools Structure Inequality.* New Haven, CT: Yale University Press, 1985.

OBERSCHALL, ANTHONY. *Social Conflict and Social Movements.* Englewood Cliffs, NJ: Prentice Hall, 1973.

OFFIR, CAROLE WADE. *Human Sexuality.* New York: Harcourt Brace Jovanovich, 1982.

OGBURN, WILLIAM F. *On Culture and Social Change.* Chicago: University of Chicago Press, 1964.

OKIMOTO, DANIEL. "The Intolerance of Success." In Amy Tachiki et al., eds., *Roots: Asian American Reader.* Los Angeles, CA: UCLA Asian American Studies Center, 1971:14–19.

OLSEN, LAWRENCE. *Costs of Children.* Toronto: D.C. Heath and Company, 1983.

OLZAK, SUSAN. "Labor Unrest, Immigration, and Ethnic Conflict in Urban America, 1880–1914." *American Journal of Sociology.* Vol. 94, No. 6 (May 1989):1303–33.

————, and ELIZABETH WEST. "Ethnic Conflict and the Rise and Fall of Ethnic Newspapers." *American Sociological Review.* Vol. 56, No. 4 (August 1991): 458–74.

ORBACH S. *Hunger Strike: The Anorectic's Struggle as a Metaphor for our Age.* New York: Norton, 1986.

ORLANSKY, MICHAEL D., and WILLIAM L. HEWARD. *Voices: Interviews with Handicapped People.* Columbus, OH: Charles E. Merrill, 1981:85, 92, 133–34, 172. Copyright 1981. Reprinted by permission of the publisher.

ORSHANSKY, MOLLIE. "How Poverty is Measured." *Monthly Labor Review.* Vol. 92, No. 2 (February 1969):37–41.

OSSENBERG, RICHARD J. "Social Class and Bar Behavior during an Urban Festival." In James E. Curtis and William G. Scott, eds. *Social Stratification: Canada.* 2nd ed. Scarborough, Ontario: Prentice Hall, 1979.

OSTLING, RICHARD N. "Jerry Falwell's Crusade." *Time.* Vol. 126, No. 9 (September 2, 1985):48–52, 55, 57.

———. "Technology and the Womb." *Time.* Vol. 129, No. 12 (March 23, 1987):58–59.

OSTRANDER, SUSAN A. "Upper Class Women: The Feminine Side of Privilege." *Qualitative Sociology.* Vol. 3, No. 1 (Spring 1980):23–44.

———. *Women of the Upper Class.* Philadelphia, PA: Temple University Press, 1984.

OUCHI, WILLIAM. *Theory Z: How American Business Can Meet the Japanese Challenge.* Reading, MA: Addison-Wesley, 1981.

OWEN, DAVID. *None of the Above: Behind the Myth of Scholastic Aptitude.* Boston, MA: Houghton Mifflin, 1985.

PALMORE, ERDMAN. "Advantages of Aging." *The Gerontologist.* Vol. 19, No 2 (April 1979b):220–23.

———. "Predictors of Successful Aging." *The Gerontologist.* Vol. 19, No. 5 (October 1979a):427–31.

———. "What Can the USA Learn from Japan About Aging?" In Steven H. Zarit, ed., *Readings in Aging and Death: Contemporary Perspectives.* New York: Harper & Row, 1982:166–69.

PAMPEL, FRED C., KENNETH C. LAND, and MARCUS FELSON. "A Social Indicator Model of Changes in the Occupational Structure of the United States: 1947–1974." *American Sociological Review.* Vol. 42, No. 6 (December 1977):951–64.

PARCEL, TOBY L., CHARLES W. MUELLER, and STEVEN CUVELIER. "Comparable Worth and Occupational Labor Market: Explanations of Occupational Earnings Differentials." Paper presented to the American Sociological Association, New York, 1986.

PARENTI, MICHAEL. *Inventing Reality: The Politics of the Mass Media.* New York: St. Martin's Press, 1986.

PARK, ROBERT E. "The City: Suggestions for the Investigation of Human Behavior in the Human Environment." In Robert E. Park and Ernest W. Burgess, *The City.* Chicago: University of Chicago Press, 1967; orig. 1925:1–46.

———. *Race and Culture.* Glencoe, IL: The Free Press, 1950.

PARKINSON, C. NORTHCOTE. *Parkinson's Law and Other Studies in Administration.* New York: Ballantine Books, 1957.

PARROTT, JULIE. "The Effects of Culture on Eating Disorders." Paper presented to Southwestern Social Science Association, Dallas, Texas, March 1987.

PARRY, KEITH. "Mormons." *The Canadian Encyclopedia.* 2nd ed. Edmonton: Hurtig Publishers, 1988: 1390.

PARSONS, TALCOTT. "Age and Sex in the Social Structure of the United States." *American Sociological Review.* Vol. 7, No. 4 (August, 1942):604–16.

———. *Essays in Sociological Theory.* New York: Free Press, 1954.

———. *The Social System.* New York: Free Press, 1964; orig. 1951.

———. *Societies: Evolutionary and Comparative Perspectives.* Englewood Cliffs, NJ: Prentice Hall, 1966.

———, and ROBERT F. BALES, eds. *Family, Socialization and Interaction Process.* New York: Free Press, 1955.

PATCHEN, MARTIN. "The Escalation of Inter-Nation Conflicts." *Sociological Focus.* Vol. 20, No. 2 (April 1987):95–110.

PATTERSON, GREGORY A. "Black Middle Class Debates Merits of Cities and Suburbs." *The Wall Street Journal* (August 6, 1991):B1.

PAUL, ELLEN FRANKEL. "Bared Buttocks and Federal Cases." *Society.* Vol. 28. No. 4 (May–June, 1991):4–7.

PEAR, ROBERT. "Women Reduce Lag in Earnings, But Disparities With Men Remain." *The New York Times* (September 4, 1987):1, 7.

———, with ERIK ECKHOLM. "When Healers are Entrepreneurs: A Debate Over Costs and Ethics." *The New York Times* (June 2, 1991):1, 17.

PEDERSEN, DANIEL. "The Swedish Model: Lessons for the Left." *Newsweek* (March 5, 1990):30–31.

PENNINGS, JOHANNES M. "Organizational Birth Frequencies: An Empirical Investigation." *Administrative Science Quarterly.* Vol. 27, No. 1 (March 1982): 120–44.

PEREZ, LISANDRO. "Cubans." In *Harvard Encyclopedia of American Ethnic Groups.* Cambridge, MA: Harvard University Press, 1980: 256–60.

PERSELL, CAROLINE HODGES. *Education and Inequality: A Theoretical and Empirical Synthesis.* New York: Free Press, 1977.

PESCOSOLIDO, BERNICE A., and SHARON GEORGIANNA. "Durkheim, Suicide, and Religion: Toward a Network Theory of Suicide." *American Sociological Review.* Vol. 54, No. 1 (February 1989):33–48.

PESSEN, EDWARD. *Riches, Class, and Power: America Before the Civil War.* New Brunswick, NJ: Transaction, 1990.

PETER, LAURENCE J., and RAYMOND HULL. *The Peter Principle: Why Things Always Go Wrong.* New York: William Morrow, 1969.

PETERS, THOMAS J., and ROBERT H. WATERMAN, JR. *In Search of Excellence: Lessons From America's Best-Run Companies.* New York: Warner Books, 1982.

PETRIE, A. ROY. *Alexander Graham Bell.* Don Mills, Ont.: Fitzhenry and Whiteside Ltd., 1975.

PHILLIPSON, CHRIS. *Capitalism and the Construction of Old Age.* London: The Macmillan Press, 1982.

PHYSICIANS' TASK FORCE ON HUNGER IN AMERICA. "Hunger Reaches Blue-Collar America." Report issues 1987.

PILLEMER, KARL. "Maltreatment of the Elderly at Home and in Institutions: Extent, Risk Factors, and Policy Recommendations." In U. S. Congress. House, Select Committee on Aging and Senate, Special Committee on Aging. *Legislative Agenda for an Aging Society: 1988 and Beyond.* Washington, DC: U. S. Government Printing Office, 1988.

PINDERHUGHES, DIANNE M. "Political Choices: A Realignment in Partisanship Among Black Voters?" In James D. Williams, ed., *The State of Black America 1986.* New York: National Urban League, 1986:85–113.

PINES, MAYA. "The Civilization of Genie." *Psychology Today.* Vol. 15 (September 1981):28–34.

PIOTROW, PHYLLIS T. *World Population: The Present and Future Crisis.* Headline Series 251 (October 1980). New York: Foreign Policy Association.

PIRANDELLO, LUIGI. "The Pleasure of Honesty." In *To Clothe the Naked and Two Other Plays.* New York: Dutton, 1962:143–98.

PITT, MALCOLM. *Introducing Hinduism.* New York: Friendship Press, 1955.

PIVEN, FRANCES FOX. and RICHARD A. CLOWARD. *Poor People's Movements: Why They Succeed, How They Fail.* New York: Pantheon, 1977.

PIVEN, FRANCES FOX. *Why Americans Don't Vote.* New York: Pantheon, 1988.

PLATIEL, RUDY. "Natives have legal right to self-rule, inquiry finds." *The Globe and Mail,* Aug. 19, 1993: A4.

PLEWES, BETTY and RIEKY STUART. "Women and Development Revisited: The Case for a Gender and Development Approach." In Jamie Swift and Brian Tomlinson, eds., *Conflicts of Interest: Canada and the Third World.* Toronto: Between the Lines, 1991:107–132.

PLOMIN, ROBERT, and TERRYL T. FOCH. "A Twin Study of Objectively Assessed Personality in Childhood." *Journal of Personality and Sociology Psychology.* Vol. 39, No. 4 (October 1980):680–88.

POLENBERG, RICHARD. *One Nation Divisible: Class, Race, and Ethnicity in the United States Since 1938.* New York: Pelican Books, 1980.

POLLACK, OTTO, and ELLEN S. WISE. *Invitation to a Dialogue: Union and Separation in Family Life.* New York: SP Medical and Scientific Books, 1979.

POLSBY, NELSON W. "Three Problems in the Analysis of Community Power." *American Sociological Review.* Vol. 24, No. 6 (December 1959):796–803.

POMER, MARSHALL I. "Labor Market Structure, Intragenerational Mobility, and Discrimination: Black Male Advancement Out of Low-Paying Occupations, 1962–1973." *American Sociological Review.* Vol. 51, No. 5 (October 1986): 650–59.

POMFRET, RICHARD. *The Economic Development of Canada.* Toronto: Methuen, 1981.

PONTING, J. RICK, ed. *Arduous Journey: Canadian Indians and Decolonization.* Toronto: McClelland & Stewart, 1989.

POPENOE, DAVID. "Family Decline in the Swedish Welfare State." *The Public Interest.* No. 102 (Winter 1991):65–77.

POPKIN, SUSAN J. "Welfare: Views from the Bottom." *Social Problems*. Vol. 17, No. 1 (February 1990):64–79.

PORTER, JOHN. *The Vertical Mosaic: An Analysis of Social Class and Power in Canada*. Toronto: University of Toronto Press, 1965.

———. "Education Equality and the Just Society." In John Porter, ed., *The Measure of Canadian Society: Education Equality and Opportunity*. Ottawa: Carleton University, 1987: 242–280.

———, MARION PORTER, and BERNARD R. BLISHEN. *Stations and Callings*. Toronto: Methuen, 1982.

PORTES, ALEJANDRO. "The Rise of Ethnicity: Determinants of Ethnic Perceptions Among Cuban Exiles in Miami." *American Sociological Review*. Vol. 49, No. 3 (June 1984):383–97.

———, and LEIF JENSEN. "The Enclave and the Entrants: Patterns of Ethnic Enterprise in Miami Before and After Mariel." *American Sociological Review*. Vol. 54, No. 6 (December 1989):929–49.

A Portrait of Seniors in Canada. Cat. no. 89–59. Ottawa: Statistics Canada, September 1990.

Poverty Profile: Update for 1991. Ottawa: National Council on Welfare, 1993.

POWELL, CHRIS, and GEORGE E. C. PATON, eds. *Humour in Society: Resistance and Control*. New York: St. Martin's Press, 1988.

PREMACK, DAVID. *Intelligence in Ape and Man*. Hillsdale, NJ: Lawrence Erlbaum Associates, 1976.

PROBERT, ADAM, HOWARD MORRISON, ROBERT SEMINCIW, and YOUNG MAO. "Recent Trends in Lung Cancer among Canadians Ages 25–44." *Canadian Journal of Public Health*, vol. 83, no. 6, 1992: 426–28.

PURCELL, PIPER, and LARA STEWART. "Dick and Jane in 1989." *Sex Roles*. Vol. 22, Nos. 3–4 (1990):177–85.

PUTKA, GARY. "SAT To Become A Better Gauge." *The Wall Street Journal* (November 1, 1990):B1.

———. "Whittle Develops Plan to Operate Schools for Profit." *The Wall Street Journal* (May 15, 1991):B1.

QUEENAN, JOE. "The Many Paths to Riches." *Forbes*. Vol. 144, No. 9 (October 23, 1989):149.

QUINNEY, RICHARD. *Class, State and Crime: On the Theory and Practice of Criminal Justice*. New York: David McKay, 1977.

RADIN, NORMA. "Primary Caregiving and Role-Sharing Fathers." In Michael E. Lamb, ed., *Nontraditional Families: Parenting and Child Development*. Hillsdale, NJ: Lawrence Erlbaum Aassociates, 1982:173–204.

RAMCHARAN, SUBHAS. *Racism: Nonwhites in Canada*. Toronto: Butterworths, 1982.

RANDALL, VICKI. *Women and Politics*. London: Macmillan Press, 1982.

RAPHAEL, RAY. *The Men from the Boys: Rites of Passage in Male America*. Lincoln and London: University of Nebraska Press, 1988.

RECKLESS, WALTER C. "Containment Theory." In Marvin E. Wolfgang, Leonard Savitz, and Norman Johnstone, eds., *The Sociology of Crime and Delinquency*. 2nd ed. New York: John Wiley, 1970:401–5.

———, and SIMON DINITZ. "Pioneering with Self-Concept as a Vulnerability Factor in Delinquency." *Journal of Criminal Law, Criminology, and Police Science*. Vol. 58, No. 4 (December 1967):515–23.

REED, RODNEY J. "Administrator's Advice: Causes and Remedies of School Conflict and Violence." *National Association of Secondary School Principals Bulletin*. Vol. 67, No. 462 (April 1983):75–79.

REICH, ROBERT B. "As the World Turns." *The New Republic* (May 1, 1989):23, 26–28.

———. *The Work of Nations: Preparing Ourselves for 21st-Century Capitalism*. New York: Alfred A. Knopf, 1991.

REID, SUE TITUS. *Crime and Criminology*. 3rd ed. New York: Holt, Rinehart and Winston, 1982; 6th ed. Fort Worth, TX: Holt, 1991.

REIMAN, JEFFREY H. *The Rich Get Richer and the Poor Get Prison: Ideology, Class, and Criminal Justice*. 2nd ed. New York: John Wiley & Sons, 1984; 3rd ed., 1990.

REIMERS, CORDELIA W. "Sources of the Family Income Differentials Among Hispanics, Blacks, and White Non-Hispanics." *American Journal of Sociology*. Vol. 89, No. 4 (January 1984):889–903.

REITZ, JEFFREY G. *The Survival of Ethnic Groups*. Toronto: McGraw-Hill Ryerson, 1980.

Religions in Canada. Cat. no. 93-319.Ottawa: Statistics Canada, June 1993.

REMIS, ROBERT S. "The Epidemiology of HIV and AIDS in Canada: Current Perspectives and Future Needs." *Canadian Journal of Public Health*, vol. 84, no. 1, Jan./Feb., 1993: 534, 536.

REMOFF, HEATHER TREXLER. *Sexual Choice: A Woman's Decision*. New York: Dutton/Lewis, 1984.

RENICK, TIMOTHY M. "From Apartheid to Liberation: Calvinism and the Shaping of Ethical Belief in South Africa." *Sociological Focus*. Vol. 24, No. 2 (May 1991):129–43.

Report on the Demographic Situation in Canada. Ottawa: Statistics Canada, 1992.

RICHARDSON, JAMES T. "Definitions of Cult: From Sociological-Technical to Popular Negative." Paper presented to the American Psychological Association, Boston, August, 1990.

RICHLER, MORDECAI. *Oh Canada! Oh Quebec! Requiem for a Divided Country*. Toronto: Penguin Books, 1992.

RIDGEWAY, CECILIA L. *The Dynamics of Small Groups*. New York: St. Martin's Press, 1983.

RIDGEWAY, CECILIA, and DAVID DIEKEMA. "Dominance and Collective Hierarchy Formation in Male and Female Task Groups." *American Sociological Review*. Vol. 54, No. 1 (February 1989):79–93.

RIEFF, PHILIP. "Introduction." In Charles Horton Cooley, *Social Organization*. New York: Schocken Books, 1962.

RIEGEL, KLAUS F. "History of Psychological Gerontology." In James E. Birren and K. Warner Schaie, eds., *Handbook of the Psychology of Aging*. New York: Van Nostrand Reinhold, 1977:70–102.

RIEGLE, DONALD W., JR. "The Psychological and Social Effects of Unemployment." *American Psychologist*. Vol. 37, No. 10 (October 1982):1113–15.

RIESMAN, DAVID. *The Lonely Crowd: A Study of the Changing American Character*. New Haven, CT: Yale University Press, 1970; orig. 1950.

RILEY, MATILDA WHITE, ANNE FONER, and JOAN WARING. "Sociology of Age." In Neil J. Smelser, ed., *Handbook of Sociology*. Newbury Park, CA: Sage Publications, 1988:243–90.

RITZER, GEORGE. *Man and His Work: Conflict and Change*. New York: Appleton-Century-Crofts, 1972.

RITZER, GEORGE. *Sociological Theory*. New York: Alfred A. Knopf, 1983:63–66.

ROBERTS, J. DEOTIS. *Roots of a Black Future: Family and Church*. Philadelphia, PA: The Westminster Press, 1980.

ROBINSON, DAWN. "Toward a Synthesis of Sociological and Psychological Theories of Eating Disorders." Paper presented to Southwestern Social Science Association, Dallas, Texas, March 1987.

ROBINSON, VERA M. "Humor and Health." In Paul E. McGhee and Jeffrey H. Goldstein, eds., *Handbook of Humor Research, Vol II, Applied Studies*. New York: Springer-Verlag, 1983:109–28.

ROESCH, ROBERTA. "Violent Families." *Parents*. Vol. 59, No. 9 (September 1984): 74–76, 150–52.

ROETHLISBERGER, F. J., and WILLIAM J. DICKSON. *Management and the Worker*. Cambridge, MA: Harvard University Press, 1939.

ROHLEN, THOMAS P. *Japan's High Schools*. Berkeley, CA: University of California Press, 1983.

ROKOVE, MILTON L. *Don't Make No Waves, Don't Back No Losers*. Bloomington, IN: Indiana University Press, 1975.

ROMAN, MEL, and WILLIAM HADDAD. *The Disposable Parent: The Case for Joint Custody*. New York: Holt, Rinehart and Winston, 1978.

ROOF, WADE CLARK. "Socioeconomic Differentials Among White Socioreligious Groups in the United States." *Social Forces*. Vol. 58, No. 1 (September 1979):280–89.

————. "Unresolved Issues in the Study of Religion and the National Elite: Response to Greeley." *Social Forces.* Vol. 59, No. 3 (March 1981):831–36.

————, and WILLIAM MCKINNEY. *American Mainline Religion: Its Changing Shape and Future.* New Brunswick, NJ: Rutgers University Press, 1987.

ROOS, PATRICIA. "Marriage and Women's Occupational Attainment in Cross-Cultural Perspective." *American Sociological Review.* Vol. 48, No. 6 (December 1983):852–64.

ROSE, ARNOLD M. "The Subculture of the Aging: A Topic for Sociological Research." In Bernice L. Neugarten, ed., *Middle Age and Aging: A Reader in Social Psychology.* Chicago: University of Chicago Press, 1968:29–34.

ROSE, JERRY D. *Outbreaks.* New York: Free Press, 1982.

ROSEN, ELLEN ISRAEL. *Bitter Choices: Blue-Collar Women in and out of Work.* Chicago: University of Chicago Press, 1987.

ROSENBAUM, RON. "A Tangled Web for the Supreme Court." *The New York Times* Magazine (March 12, 1989):60.

ROSENFELD, RACHEL A., and ARNE L. KALLEBERG. "A Cross-National Comparison of the Gender Gap in Income." *American Journal of Sociology.* Vol. 96, No. 1 (July 1990):69–106.

ROSENTHAL, ELISABETH. "Canada's National Health Plan Gives Care to All, With Limits." *The New York Times* (April 30, 1991):A1, A16.

ROSENTHAL, JACK. "The Rapid Growth of Suburban Employment." In Lois H. Masotti and Jeffrey K. Hadden, eds., *Suburbia in Transition.* New York: New York Times Books, 1974:95–100.

ROSKIN, MICHAEL G. *Countries and Concepts: An Introduction to Comparative Politics.* Englewood Cliffs, NJ: Prentice Hall, 1982.

ROSNOW, RALPH L., and GARY ALAN FINE. *Rumor and Gossip: The Social Psychology of Hearsay.* New York: Elsevier, 1976.

ROSS, CATHERINE E., JOHN MIROWSKY, and JOAN HUBER. "Dividing Work, Sharing Work, and In-Between: Marriage Patterns and Depression." *American Sociological Review.* Vol. 48, No. 6 (December 1983):809–23.

ROSS, SUSAN. "Education: A Step Ladder to Mobility." *Popline.* Vol. 7, No. 7 (July 1985):1–2.

ROSSI, ALICE S. "Gender and Parenthood." In Alice S. Rossi, ed., *Gender and the Life Course.* New York: Aldine, 1985:161–91.

ROSSIDES, DANIEL W. *Social Stratification: The American Class System in Comparative Perspective.* Englewood Cliffs, NJ: Prentice Hall, 1990.

ROSTOW, W. W. *The Stages of Economic Growth: A Non-Communist Manifesto.* Cambridge, UK: Cambridge University Press, 1960.

————. *The World Economy: History and Prospect.* Austin, TX: University of Texas Press, 1978.

ROUDI, NAZY. "The Demography of Islam." *Population Today.* Vol. 16, No. 3 (March 1988):6–9.

ROWE, DAVID C. "Biometrical Genetic Models of Self-Reported Delinquent Behavior: A Twin Study." *Behavior Genetics.* Vol 13, No. 5 (1983):473–89.

————, and D. WAYNE OSGOOD. "Heredity and Sociological Theories of Delinquency: A Reconsideration." *American Sociological Review.* Vol. 49, No. 4 (August 1984):526–40.

RUBENSTEIN, ELI A. "The Not So Golden Years." *Newsweek* (October 7, 1991):13.

RUBIN, BETH A. "Class Struggle American Style: Unions, Strikes and Wages." *American Sociological Review.* Vol. 51, No. 5 (October 1986):618–31.

RUBIN, KEN. "Privacy." *The Canadian Encyclopedia.* 2nd ed. Edmonton: Hurtig Publishers, (3): 1761, 1988.

RUBIN, LILLIAN B. *Intimate Strangers: Men and Women Together.* New York: Harper & Row, 1983.

RUBIN, LILLIAN BRESLOW. *Worlds of Pain: Life in the Working-Class Family.* New York: Basic Books, 1976.

RUBINSON, RICHARD. "Class Formation, Politics, and Institutions: Schooling in the United States." *American Journal of Sociology.* Vol. 92, No. 3 (November 1986):519–48.

RUDE, GEORGE. *The Crowd in History: A Study of Popular Disturbances in France and England, 1730–1848.* New York: John Wiley & Sons, 1964.

RUDOLPH, BARBARA. "Tobacco Takes a New Road." *Time.* Vol. 126, No. 20 (November 18, 1985):70–71.

RUMBERGER, RUSSELL. *Overeducation in the U. S. Labor Market.* New York: Praeger, 1981.

RUSSELL, DIANA E. H. *Rape in Marriage.* New York: Macmillan, 1982.

RYAN, WILLIAM. *Blaming the Victim.* Rev. ed. New York: Vintage, 1976.

RYTINA, JOAN HUBER, WILLIAM H. FORM, and JOHN PEASE. "Income and Stratification Ideology: Beliefs About the American Opportunity Structure." *American Journal of Sociology.* Vol. 75, No. 4 (January 1970):703–16.

SABATO, LARRY J. *PAC Power: Inside the World of Political Action Committees.* New York: Norton, 1984.

SACKS, HOWARD L. Letter to the author, 1986.

SAGAN, CARL. *The Dragons of Eden.* New York: Ballantine, 1977.

SALAS, RAFAEL M. "The State of World Population 1985: Population and Women." *Popline.* Vol. 7, No. 7 (July 1985):4–5.

SALE, KIRKPATRICK. *The Conquest of Paradise: Christopher Columbus and the Columbian Legacy.* New York: Knopf, 1990.

SALHOLZ, ELOISE. "The Future of Gay America." *Newsweek* (March 12, 1990):20–25.

SALINE, CAROL. "Bleeding in the Suburbs." *Philadelphia.* Vol. 75, No. 3 (March 1984):81–85, 144–51.

SALTMAN, JULIET. "Maintaining Racially Diverse Neighborhoods." *Urban Affairs Quarterly.* Vol. 26, No. 3 (March 1991):416–41.

SAMPSON, ANTHONY. *The Changing Anatomy of Britain.* New York: Random House, 1982.

SAMPSON, ROBERT J. "Urban Black Violence: The Effects of Male Joblessness and Family Disruption." *American Journal of Sociology.* Vol. 93, No. 2 (September 1987):348–82.

————, and JOHN H. LAUB. "Crime and Deviance Over the Life Course: The Salience of Adult Social Bonds." *American Sociological Review.* Vol. 55, No. 5 (October 1990):609–27.

SAPIR, EDWARD. "The Status of Linguistics as a Science." *Language.* Vol. 5 (1929):207–14.

————. *Selected Writings of Edward Sapir in Language, Culture, and Personality.* David G. Mandelbaum, ed. Berkeley, CA: University of California Press, 1949.

SAUNDERS, JANICE MILLER, and JOHN N. EDWARDS. "Extramarital Sexuality: A Predictive Model of Permissive Attitudes." *Journal of Marriage and the Family.* Vol. 46, No. 4 (November 1984):825–35.

SAUNDERS, JOHN. "What Executives Earn." *The Globe and Mail,* April 3, 1993: B1, 4.

SCAFF, LAWRENCE A. "Max Weber and Robert Michels." *American Journal of Sociology.* Vol. 86, No. 6 (May 1981):1269–86.

SCHAEFER, RICHARD T. *Racial and Ethnic Groups.* Boston: Little, Brown, 1979.

SCHAIE, K. WARNER. "Intelligence and Problem Solving." In James E. Birren and R. Bruce Sloane, eds., *Handbook of Mental Health and Aging.* Englewood Cliffs, NJ: Prentice Hall, 1980:262–84.

SCHEFF, THOMAS J. *Being Mentally Ill: A Sociological Theory.* 2nd ed. New York: Aldine, 1984.

SCHELLENBERG, JAMES A. *Masters of Social Psychology.* New York: Oxford University Press, 1978:38–62.

SCHELLENBERG, KATHRYN. *The Pendulum Swings: A Case Study of High-Tech Turbulence and Turnover.* University of Utah: unpublished Ph.D. dissertation, 1991.

SCHLAFLY, PHYLLIS. "Mothers, Stay Home; Your Kids Need You." *USA Today* (May 30, 1984):10A.

SCHLESINGER, ARTHUR, JR. "The Cult of Ethnicity: Good and Bad." *Time.* Vol. 137, No. 27 (July 8, 1991):21.

SCHLESINGER, ARTHUR. "The City in American Civilization." In A. B. Callow, Jr., ed., *American Urban History.* New York: Oxford University Press, 1969: 25–41.

SCHLESINGER, B. "Women and Men in Second Marriages." In S.P. Wakil, ed., *Marriage, Family and Society*. Scarborough, Ont.: Butterworths, 1975.

SCHMIDT, ROGER. *Exploring Religion*. Belmont, CA: Wadsworth, 1980.

SCHOOLER, CARMI, JOANNE MILLER, KAREN A. MILLER, and CAROL N. RICHTAND. "Work for the Household: Its Nature and Consequences for Husbands and Wives." *American Journal of Sociology*. Vol. 90, No. 1 (July 1984):97–124.

SCHREINER, TIM. "Your Cost to Bring Up Baby: $142,700." *USA Today* (October 19, 1984):1D.

SCHUMANN, HANS WOLFGANG. *Buddhism: An Outline of Its Teachings and Schools*. Wheaton, IL: The Theosophical Publishing House, Quest Books, 1974.

SCHUR, EDWIN M. *Labeling Women Deviant: Gender, Stigma, and Social Control*. New York: Random House, 1984.

SCHUTT, RUSSELL K. "Objectivity versus Outrage." *Society*. Vol. 26, No. 4 (May/June 1989):14–16.

SCHWARTZ, FELICE N. "Management, Women, and the New Facts of Life." *Harvard Business Review*. Vol. 89, No. 1 (January–February 1989):65–76.

SCHWARTZ, JOE. "Rising Status." *American Demographics*. Vol. 11, No. 1 (January 1989):10.

SCHWARTZ, MARTIN D. "Gender and Injury in Spousal Assault." *Sociological Focus*. Vol. 20, No. 1 (January 1987):61–75.

SCHWARTZ-NOBEL, LORETTA. *Starving in the Shadow of Plenty*. New York: McGraw-Hill, 1981.

SCOTT, D.B. "Lean Machine." *The Globe and Mail: Report on Business*, Nov. 1992: 90–99.

SCOTT, JOHN, and CATHERINE GRIFF. *Directors of Industry: The British Corporate Network, 1904–1976*. New York: Blackwell, 1985.

SCOTT, W. RICHARD. *Organizations: Rational, Natural, and Open Systems*. Englewood Cliffs, NJ: Prentice Hall, 1981.

SEARS, DAVID O., and JOHN B. MCCONAHAY. *The Politics of Violence: The New Urban Blacks and the Watts Riot*. Boston: Houghton Mifflin, 1973.

SECRETARY OF STATE CANADA. *Profile of Higher Education in Canada* (S2-196/1991). Ottawa: Ministry of Supply and Services, 1991.

SEELEY, JOHN R. et al. *Crestwood Heights: A Study of the Culture of Suburban Life*. New York: Wiley, 1963.

SELIMUDDIN, ABU K. "The Selling of America." *USA Today*. Vol. 117, No. 2525 (March 1989):12–14.

SELLIN, THORSTEN. *The Penalty of Death*. Beverly Hills, CA: Sage Publications, 1980.

SELTZER, ROBERT M. *Jewish People, Jewish Thought: The Jewish Experience in History*. New York: Macmillan, 1980.

SEN, K. M. *Hinduism*. Baltimore, MD: Penguin, 1961.

SENGOKU, TAMOTSU. *Willing Workers: The Work Ethics in Japan, England, and the United States*. Westport, CT: Quorum Books, 1985.

SENNETT, RICHARD, and JONATHAN COBB. *The Hidden Injuries of Class*. New York: Vintage, 1973.

SEWELL, WILLIAM H., ARCHIBALD O. HALLER, and GEORGE W. OHLENDORF. "The Educational and Early Occupational Status Attainment Process: Replication and Revision." *American Sociological Review*. Vol. 35, No. 6 (December 1970):1014–27.

SHAFFIR, W. *Life in a Religious Community: The Lubavitcher Chassidim in Montreal*. Toronto: Holt, Rinehart and Winston of Canada, 1974.

SHANAS, ETHEL. "Social Myth as Hypothesis: The Case of the Family Relations of Old People." *The Gerontologist*. Vol. 19, No. 1 (February 1979):3–9.

SHAPIRO, MARTIN. *Getting Doctored: Critical Reflections on Becoming a Physician*. Toronto: Between the Lines, 1978.

SHAPIRO, NINA. "Botswana Test Case." *Chicago Tribune* (September 15, 1991):1.

SHAW, CLIFFORD R., and HENRY D. MCKAY. *Juvenile Delinquency in Urban Areas*. Chicago: University of Chicago Press, 1972; orig. 1942.

SHAWCROSS, WILLIAM. *Sideshow: Kissinger, Nixon and the Destruction of Cambodia*. New York: Pocket Books, 1979.

SHEEHAN, TOM. "Senior Esteem as a Factor in Socioeconomic Complexity." *The Gerontologist*. Vol. 16, No. 5 (October 1976):433–40.

SHEEHY, GAIL. *Passages: Predictable Crises of Adult Life*. New York: E. P. Dutton, 1976.

SHELDON, WILLILAM H., EMIL M. HARTL, and EUGENE MCDERMOTT. *Varieties of Delinquent Youth*. New York: Harper, 1949.

SHELER, JEFFERY L. "Lobbyists Go for It." *U. S. News & World Report*. Vol. 98, No. 23 (June 17, 1985):30–34.

SHEPHARD, ROY J. *The Risks of Passive Smoking*. London: Croom Helm, 1982.

SHERRID, PAMELA. "Hot Times in the City of London." *U. S. News & World Report* (October 27, 1986):45–46.

SHEVKY, ESHREF, and WENDELL BELL. *Social Area Analysis*. Stanford, CA: Stanford University Press, 1955.

SHIBUTANI, TAMOTSU. *Improvised News: A Sociological Study of Rumor*. Indianapolis, IN: Bobbs-Merrill, 1966.

SHIPLER, DAVID K. *Russia: Broken Idols, Solemn Dreams*. New York: Penguin Books, 1984.

SHIPLEY, JOSEPH T. *Dictionary of Word Origins*. Totowa, NJ: Roman & Allanheld, 1985.

SHKILNYK, ANASTASIA M. *A Poison Stronger than Love: The Destruction of an Ojibwa Community*. New Haven: Yale University Press, 1985.

SHOCKEY, JAMES W. "Overeducation and Earnings: A Structural Approach to Differential Attainment in the U. S. Labor Force (1970–1982)." *American Sociological Review*. Vol. 54, No. 5 (October 1989):856–64.

SIDEL, RUTH, and VICTOR W. SIDEL. *A Healthy State: An International Perspective on the Crisis in United States Medical Care*. Rev. ed. New York: Pantheon, 1982a.

————. *The Health Care of China*. Boston, MA: Beacon Press, 1982b.

SILLS, DAVID L. "The Succession of Goals." In Amitai Etzioni, ed., *A Sociological Reader on Complex Organizations*. 2nd ed. New York: Holt, Rinehart and Winston, 1969:175–87.

SILVERSTEIN, MICHAEL. In Jon Snodgrass, ed., *A Book of Readings for Men Against Sexism*. Albion, CA: Times Change Press, 1977:178–79.

SIMMEL, GEORG. *The Sociology of Georg Simmel*. Kurt Wolff, ed. New York: Free Press, 1950:118–69.

————. "The Mental Life of the Metropolis." In Kurt Wolff, ed., *The Sociology of Georg Simmel*. New York: Free Press, 1964:409–24; orig. 1905.

————. "Fashion." In Donald N. Levine, ed., *Georg Simmel: On Individuality and Social Forms*. Chicago: University of Chicago Press, 1971; orig. 1904.

SIMON, CARL P., and ANN D. WITTE. *Beating the System: The Underground Economy*. Boston: Auburn House, 1982.

SIMON, DAVID R., and D. STANLEY EITZEN. *Elite Deviance*. 3rd ed. Boston: Allyn & Bacon, 1990.

SIMON, RITA J. and N. SHARMA. "Women and Crime: Does the American Experience Generalize?" In F. Adler and R.J. Simon, eds., *Criminology of Deviant Women*. Boston: Houghton Mifflin, 1979.

SIMONS, CAROL. "Japan's *Kyoiku* Mamas." In John J. Macionis and Nijole V. Benokraitis, eds., *Seeing Ourselves: Classic, Contemporary, and Cross-Cultural Readings in Sociology*. Englewood Cliffs, NJ: Prentice Hall, 1989:281–86.

SIMONS, MARLISE. "The Amazon's Savvy Indians." *The New York Times Magazine* (February 26, 1990):36–37, 48–52. Copyright a 1989 by The New York Times Company.

SIMPSON, GEORGE EATON, and J. MILTON YINGER. *Racial and Cultural Minorities: An Analysis of Prejudice and Discrimination*. 4th ed. New York: Harper & Row, 1972.

SINGER, DOROTHY. "A Time to Reexamine the Role of Television in Our Lives." *American Psychologist*. Vol. 38, No. 7 (July 1983):815–16.

SINGER, JEROME L., and DOROTHY G. SINGER. "Psychologists Look at Television: Cognitive, Developmental, Personality, and Social Policy Implications." *American Psychologist*. Vol. 38, No. 7 (July 1983):826–34.

SIVARD, RUTH LEGER. *World Military and Social Expenditures, 1987–88*. 12th ed. Washington, DC: World Priorities, 1988.

SIZER, THEODORE R. *Horace's Compromise: The Dilemma of the American High School*. Boston, MA: Houghton Mifflin, 1984.

SJOBERG, GIDEON. *The Preindustrial City*. New York: Free Press, 1965.

SKOCPOL, THEDA. *States and Social Revolutions: A Comparative Analysis of France, Russia, and China*. Cambridge, UK: Cambridge University Press, 1979.

SKOLNICK, ARLENE. *The Psychology of Human Development*. New York: Harcourt Brace Jovanovich, 1986.

———. *The Intimate Environment: Exploring Marriage and the Family*. 5th ed. New York: HarperCollins, 1992.

SLATER, PHILIP E. "Contrasting Correlates of Group Size." *Sociometry*. Vol. 21, No. 2 (June 1958):129–39.

SLATER, PHILIP. *The Pursuit of Loneliness*. Boston, MA: Beacon Press, 1976.

SMART, NINIAN. *The Religious Experience of Mankind*. New York: Charles Scribner's Sons, 1969.

SMELSER, NEIL J. *Theory of Collective Behavior*. New York: Free Press, 1962.

SMILGAS, MARTHA. "The Big Chill: Fear of AIDS." *Time*. Vol. 129, No. 7 (February 16, 1987):50–53.

SMITH, ADAM. *An Inquiry into the Nature and Causes of the Wealth of Nations*. New York: The Modern Library, 1937; orig. 1776.

SMITH, DAN. *The Seventh Fire: The Struggle for Aboriginal Self-Government*. Toronto: Key Porter, 1993.

SMITH, DOROTHY E. "Women, the Family and Corporate Capitalism." In M. Stephenson, ed., *Women in Canada*, Don Mills, Ont.: General Publishing, 1977: 32–48.

———. "Women's Inequality and the Family." Department of Sociology, Ontario Institute for Studies in Education, Mimeograph, 1979.

———. "Women, Class and the Family." In R. Miliband and J. Saville, eds. *The Socialist Register*. London: Merlin Press, 1983.

———. *The Everyday World as Problematic: A Feminist Sociology*. Toronto: University of Toronto Press, 1987.

———, and SARA J. DAVID, eds., *Women Look at Psychiatry*. Vancouver, B.C.: Press Gang Publishers, 1975.

SMITH, DOUGLAS A. "Police Response to Interpersonal Violence: Defining the Parameters of Legal Control." *Social Forces*. Vol. 65, No. 3 (March 1987): 767–82.

———, and CHRISTY A. VISHER. "Street-Level Justice: Situational Determinants of Police Arrest Decisions." *Social Problems*. Vol. 29, No. 2 (December 1981):167–77.

SMITH, DOUGLAS A., and PATRICK R. GARTIN. "Specifying Specific Deterrence: The Influence of Arrest on Future Criminal Activity." *American Sociological Review*. Vol. 54, No. 1 (February 1989):94–105.

SMITH, ROBERT ELLIS. *Privacy: How to Protect What's Left of It*. Garden City, NY: Anchor Press/Doubleday, 1979.

SMITH-LOVIN, LYNN, and CHARLES BRODY. "Interruptions in Group Discussions: The Effects of Gender and Group Composition." *American Journal of Sociology*. Vol. 54, No. 3 (June 1989):424–35.

SMITH-ROSENBERG, CAROL, and CHARLES ROSENBERG. "The Female Animal: Medical and Biological Views of Woman and Her Role in Nineteenth Century America." In Judith Walzer Leavitt, ed.,*Women and Health in America*. Madison, WI: University of Wisconsin Press, 1984:12–27.

SNELL, MARILYN BERLIN. "The Purge of Nurture." *New Perspectives Quarterly*. Vol. 7, No. 1 (Winter 1990):1–2.

SNIDERMAN, PAUL M., DAVID A. NORTHRUP, JOSEPH F. FLETCHER, PETER H. RUSSELL and PHILIP E. TETLOCK. "Psychological and Cultural Foundations of Prejudice: The Case of Anti-Semitism in Quebec." *Canadian Review of Sociology and Anthropology*, 30(2), May 1993: 242–270.

SNOW, DAVID A., E. BURKE ROCHFORD, JR., STEVEN K. WORDEN, and ROBERT D. BENFORD. "Frame Alignment Processes, Micromobilization, and Movement Participation." *American Sociological Review*. Vol. 51, No. 4 (August 1986):464–81.

SNOW, DAVID A., LOUIS A. ZURCHER, JR., and SHELDON EKLAND-OLSON. "Social Networks and Social Movements: A Macrostructural Approach to Differen-

tial Recruitment." *American Sociological Review*. Vol. 45, No. 5 (October 1980):787–801.

SNOWMAN, DANIEL. *Britain and America: An Interpretation of Their Culture 1945–1975*. New York: Harper Torchbooks, 1977.

SOUTH, SCOTT J., and STEVEN F. MESSNER. "Structural Determinants of Intergroup Association: Interracial Marriage and Crime." *American Journal of Sociology*. Vol. 91, No. 6 (May 1986):1409–30.

SOWELL, THOMAS. *Ethnic America*. New York: Basic Books, 1981.

SOYINKA, WOLE. "Africa's Culture Producers." *Society*. Vol. 28, No. 2 (January/February 1991):32–40.

SPATES, JAMES L. "Sociological Overview." In Alan Milberg, ed., *Street Games*. New York: McGraw-Hill, 1976a:286–90.

———. "Counterculture and Dominant Culture Values: A Cross-National Analysis of the Underground Press and Dominant Culture Magazines." *American Sociological Review*. Vol. 41, No. 5 (October 1976b):868–83.

———. "The Sociology of Values." In Ralph Turner, ed., *Annual Review of Sociology*. Vol. 9. Palo Alto, CA: Annual Reviews, 1983:27–49.

———, and JOHN J. MACIONIS. *The Sociology of Cities*. 2nd ed. Belmont, CA: Wadsworth, 1987.

SPATES, JAMES L., and H. WESLEY PERKINS. "American and English Student Values." *Comparative Social Research*. Vol. 5. Greenwich, CT: Jai Press, 1982:245–68.

SPECTOR, LEONARD S. "Nuclear Proliferation Today." In William M. Evan and Stephen Hilgartner, eds., *The Arms Race and Nuclear War*. Englewood Cliffs, NJ: Prentice Hall, 1988:25–29.

SPEER, JAMES A. "The New Christian Right and Its Parent Company: A Study in Political Contrasts." In David G. Bromley and Anson Shupe, eds., *New Christian Politics*. Macon, GA: Mercer University Press, 1984:19–40.

SPEIZER, JEANNE J. "Education." In Barbara Haber, ed., *The Women's Annual 1982–1983*. Boston: G. K. Hall, 1983:29–54.

SPENCER, GARY. *Projections of the Population of the United States, by Age, Sex, and Race: 1988 to 2080*. Washington, DC: U. S. Government Printing Office, 1989.

SPENCER, META. *Foundations of Modern Sociology*. Canadian 2nd ed. Toronto: Prentice Hall, 1981.

SPENDER, DALE. *Man Made Language*. London: Routledge & Kegan Paul, 1980.

SPITZER, STEVEN. "Toward a Marxian Theory of Deviance." In Delos H. Kelly, ed., *Criminal Behavior: Readings in Criminology*. New York: St. Martin's Press, 1980:175–91.

SRINIVAS, M. N. *Social Change in Modern India*. Berkeley, CA: University of California Press, 1971.

STACEY, JUDITH. *Patriarchy and Socialist Revolution in China*. Berkeley: University of California Press, 1983.

STACK, CAROL B. *All Our Kin: Strategies for Survival in a Black Community*. New York: Harper & Row, 1975.

STAHURA, JOHN M. "Suburban Development, Black Suburbanization and the Black Civil Rights Movement Since World War II." *American Sociological Review*. Vol. 51, No. 1 (February 1986):131–44.

STAPLES, BRENT. "Where Are the Black Fans?" *New York Times Magazine* (May 17, 1987):26–34, 36.

STAPLES, ROBERT, and ALFREDO MIRANDE. "Racial and Cultural Variations Among American Families: A Decennial Review of the Literature on Minority Families." *Journal of Marriage and the Family*. Vol. 42, No. 4 (August 1980):157–72.

STARK, EVAN, and ANN FLITCRAFT. "Domestic Violence and Female Suicide Attempts." Presentation to American Public Health Association, New York, 1979.

STARK, RODNEY. "The Rise of a New World Faith." *Review of Religious Research*. Vol. 26, No. 1 (September 1984):18–27.

———. *Sociology*. Belmont, CA: Wadsworth, 1985.

———, and WILLIAM SIMS BAINBRIDGE. "Of Churches, Sects, and Cults: Preliminary Concepts for a Theory of Religious Movements." *Journal for the Scientific Study of Religion*. Vol. 18, No. 2 (June 1979):117–31.

———. "Secularization and Cult Formation in the Jazz Age." *Journal for the Scientific Study of Religion*. Vol. 20, No. 4 (December 1981):360–73.

STARK, RODNEY, and CHARLES Y. GLOCK. *American Piety: The Nature of Religious Commitment*. Berkeley, CA: University of California Press, 1968.

STARR, PAUL. *The Social Transformation of American Medicine*. New York: Basic Books, 1982.

Statistics Canada Health Reports, 1989, vol. 3 (no. 1), 7, Ottawa: Statistics Canada, 1991.

Statistics of Income Bulletin. Vol. 11, No. 3 (Winter 1991–92).

STAVRIANOS, L. S. *A Global History: The Human Heritage*. 3rd ed. Englewood Cliffs, NJ: Prentice Hall, 1983.

STEELE, SHELBY. *The Content of Our Character: A New Vision of Race in America*. New York: St. Martin's Press, 1990.

STEIN, MAURICE R. *The Eclipse of Community: An Interpretation of American Studies*. Princeton, NJ: Princeton University Press, 1972.

STEINMETZ, GEORGE, and ERIK OLIN WRIGHT. "The Fall and Rise of the Petty Bourgeoisie: Changing Patterns of Self-Employment in the Postwar United States." *American Journal of Sociology*. Vol. 94, No. 5 (March 1989): 973–1018.

STEPHENS, JOHN D. *The Transition from Capitalism to Socialism*. Urbana, IL: University of Illinois Press, 1986.

STERNLIEB, GEORGE, and JAMES W. HUGHES. "The Uncertain Future of the Central City." *Urban Affairs Quarterly*. Vol. 18, No. 4 (June 1983):455–72.

STEVENS, GILLIAN, and GRAY SWICEGOOD. "The Linguistic Context of Ethnic Endogamy." *American Sociological Review*. Vol. 52, No. 1 (February 1987): 73–82.

STEVENS, ROSEMARY. *American Medicine and the Public Interest*. New Haven, CT: Yale University Press, 1971.

STIEHM, JUDITH HICKS. *Arms and the Enlisted Woman*. Philadelphia: Temple University Press, 1989.

STOCKWELL, EDWARD G., DAVID A. SWANSON, and JERRY W. WICKS. "Trends in the Relationship Between Infant Mortality and Socioeconomic Status." *Sociological Focus*. Vol. 20, No. 4 (October 1987):319–27.

STODDARD, SANDOL. *The Hospice Movement: A Better Way to Care for the Dying*. Briarcliff Manor, NY: Stein and Day, 1978.

STONE, LAWRENCE. *The Family, Sex and Marriage in England 1500–1800*. New York: Harper & Row, 1977.

STONE, ROBYN. *The Feminization of Poverty and Older Women*. Washington, DC: U. S. Department of Health and Human Services, 1986.

———, GAIL LEE CAFFERATA, and JUDITH SANGL. *Caregivers of the Frail Elderly: A National Profile*. Washington, DC: U. S. Department of Health and Human Services, 1987.

STOUFFER, SAMUEL A., et al. *The American Soldier: Adjustment During Army Life*. Princeton, NJ: Princeton University Press, 1949.

STRANG, DAVID. "From Dependency to Sovereignty: An Event History Analysis of Decolonization 1870–1987." *American Sociological Review*. Vol. 55, No. 6 (December 1990):846–60.

STRAUS, MURRAY A., and RICHARD J. GELLES. "Societal Change and Change in Family Violence from 1975 to 1985 as Revealed by Two National Surveys." *Journal of Marriage and the Family*. Vol. 48, No. 4 (August 1986):465–79.

STREIB, GORDON F. "Are the Aged a Minority Group?" In Bernice L. Neugarten, ed., *Middle Age and Aging: A Reader in Social Psychology*. Chicago: University of Chicago Press, 1968:35–46.

STRIEGEL-MOORE, RUTH, LISA R. SILBERSTEIN, and JUDITH RODIN. "Toward an Understanding of Risk Factors for Bulimia." *American Psychologist*. Vol. 41, No. 3 (March 1986):246–63.

SUDNOW, DAVID N. *Passing On: The Social Organization of Dying*. Englewood Cliffs, NJ: Prentice Hall, 1967.

SUMNER, WILLIAM GRAHAM. *Folkways*. New York: Dover, 1959; orig. 1906.

SUNG, BETTY LEE. *Mountains of Gold: The Story of the Chinese in America*. New York: Macmillan, 1967.

SURO, ROBERTO. "Hispanics in Despair." *The New York Times: Education Life* (November 4, 1990):section 4a, page 25.

SURTEES, LAWRENCE. "Northern Telecom: The morning after." *The Globe and Mail,* July 5, 1993: B1, 4.

SUTHERLAND, EDWIN H. "White Collar Criminality." *American Sociological Review*. Vol. 5, No. 1 (February 1940):1–12.

———, and DONALD R. CRESSEY. *Criminology*. 3rd ed. Philadelphia: J. B. Lippincott, 1930; 8th ed., 1970; 10th ed., 1978.

SUZUKI, DAVID, and PETER KNUDTSON. *Genethics: The Clash Between the New Genetics and Human Values*. Cambridge, MA: Harvard University Press, 1989.

SWARTZ, STEVE. "Why Michael Milken Stands to Qualify for Guinness Book." *The Wall Street Journal*. Vol. LXX, No. 117 (March 31, 1989):1, 4.

SWIFT, JAMIE and BRIAN TOMLINSON, eds., *Conflicts of Interest: Canada and the Third World*. Toronto: Between the Lines, 1991.

SYZMANSKI, ALBERT. *Class Structure: A Critical Perspective*. New York: Praeger, 1983.

SZASZ, THOMAS S. *The Manufacturer of Madness: A Comparative Study of the Inquisition and the Mental Health Movement*. New York: Dell, 1961.

———. *The Myth of Mental Illness: Foundations of a Theory of Personal Conduct*. New York: Harper & Row, 1970; orig. 1961.

TAEUBER, KARL, and ALMA TAEUBER. *Negroes in Cities*. Chicago: Aldine, 1965.

TAJFEL, HENRI. "Social Psychology of Intergroup Relations." *Annual Review of Psychology*. Palo Alto, CA: Annual Reviews, 1982:1–39.

TANNEN, DEBORAH. *You Just Don't Understand Me: Women and Men in Conversation*. New York: William Morrow, 1990.

TANNENBAUM, FRANK. *Slave and Citizen: The Negro in the Americas*. New York: Vintage Books, 1946.

TARAS, DAVID, BEVERLY RASPORICH, and ELI MANDEL. *A Passion for Identity: An introduction to Canadian Studies*. Scarborough, Ontario: Nelson, 1993.

TAVRIS, CAROL, and CAROLE WADE. *The Longest War: Sex Differences in Perspective*. 2nd ed. New York: Harcourt Brace Jovanovich, 1984.

TAVRIS, CAROL, and SUSAN SADD. *The Redbook Report on Female Sexuality*. New York: Delacorte Press, 1977.

TAYLOR, JOHN. "Don't Blame Me: The New Culture of Victimization." *New York Magazine* (June 3, 1991):26–34.

TEEPLE, GARY. "The Capitalist Economy and the State." In Peter S. Li and B. Singh Bolaria, eds., *Contemporary Sociology: Critical Perspective*. Mississauga, ON: Copp Clark Pitman, 1993:180–202.

TEPPERMAN, LORNE. "A Simulation of Social Mobility in Industrial Societies." *Canadian Review of Sociology and Anthropology* 13 1976: 26–42.

TERKEL, STUDS. *Working*. New York: Pantheon Books, 1974:1–2, 57–59, 65, 66, 69, 221–22. Copyright a 1974 by Pantheon Books, a Division of Random House, Inc.

THE WORLD BANK. *World Development Report 1984*. New York: Oxford University Press, 1984.

———. *World Development Report 1991: The Challenge of Development*. New York: Oxord University Press, 1991.

THEEN, ROLF H. W. "Party and Bureaucracy." In Erik P. Hoffmann and Robbin F. Laird, eds., *The Soviet Polity in the Modern Era*. New York: Aldine, 1984:131–65.

THEODORSON, GEORGE A., and ACHILLES G. THEODORSON. *A Modern Dictionary of Sociology*. New York: Barnes and Noble Books, 1969.

THOITS, PEGGY A. "Self-labeling Processes in Mental Illness: The Role of Emotional Deviance." *American Journal of Sociology*. Vol. 91, No. 2 (September 1985):221–49.

THOMAS, EDWARD J. *The Life of Buddha as Legend and History*. London: Routledge & Kegan Paul, 1975.

THOMAS, PIRI. *Down These Mean Streets*. New York: Signet, 1967.

THOMAS, W. I. "The Relation of Research to the Social Process." In Morris Janowitz, ed., *W. I. Thomas on Social Organization and Social Personality*. Chicago: University of Chicago Press, 1966:289–305; orig. 1931.

————, and F. ZNANIECKI. *The Polish Peasant in Europe and America.* New York: Octagon Books, (1919) 1971.

THOMPSON, ANTHONY PETER. "Emotional and Sexual Components of Extramarital Relations." *Journal of Marriage and the Family.* Vol. 46, No. 1 (February 1984):35–42.

THORNBERRY, TERRANCE, and MARGARET FARNSWORTH. "Social Correlates of Criminal Involvement: Further Evidence on the Relationship Between Social Status and Criminal Behavior." *American Sociological Review.* Vol 47, No. 4 (August 1982):505–18.

THORNE, BARRIE, CHERIS KRAMARAE, and NANCY HENLEY, eds. *Language, Gender and Society.* Cambridge: Newbury House, 1983.

THORNTON, ARLAND. "Changing Attitudes Toward Separation and Divorce: Causes and Consequences." *American Journal of Sociology.* Vol. 90, No. 4 (January 1985):856–72.

THUROW, LESTER C. "A Surge in Inequality." *Scientific American.* Vol. 256, No. 5 (May 1987):30–37.

TIBBITTS, CLARK. "Can We Invalidate Negative Stereotypes of Aging?" *The Gerontologist.* Vol. 19, No. 1 (February 1979):10–20.

TIEN, H. YUAN. "Second Thoughts on the Second Child." *Population Today.* Vol. 17, No. 4 (April 1989):6–9.

TIENDA, MARTA, and DING-TZANN LII. "Minority Concentration and Earnings Inequality: Blacks, Hispanics, and Asians Compared." *American Journal of Sociology.* Vol. 93, No. 1 (July 1987):141–65.

TIGER, LIONEL, and JOSEPH SHEPHER. *Women in the Kibbutz.* New York: Harcourt Brace Jovanovich, 1975.

TILLY, CHARLES. *From Mobilization to Revolution.* Reading, MA: Addison-Wesley, 1978.

————. "Does Modernization Breed Revolution?" In Jack A. Goldstone, ed., *Revolutions: Theoretical, Comparative, and Historical Studies.* New York: Harcourt Brace Jovanovich, 1986:47–57.

Time. "The Crime That Tarnished a Town." Vol. 123, No. 10 (March 5, 1984):19.

TINDALE, JOSEPH A. N.A.C.A. "Older Workers in an Aging Workforce." Ottawa: Statistics Canada, 1991.

TITTLE, CHARLES R., and WAYNE J. VILLEMEZ. "Social Class and Criminality." *Social Forces.* Vol. 56, No. 22 (December 1977):474–502.

————, and DOUGLAS A. SMITH. "The Myth of Social Class and Criminality: An Empirical Assessment of the Empirical Evidence." *American Sociological Review.* Vol. 43, No. 5 (October 1978):643–56.

TOBIN, GARY. "Suburbanization and the Development of Motor Transportation: Transportation Technology and the Suburbanization Process." In Barry Schwartz, ed., *The Changing Face of the Suburbs.* Chicago: University of Chicago Press, 1976.

TOCH, THOMAS. "The Exodus." *U. S. News and World Report.* Vol. 111, No. 24 (December 9, 1991):68–77.

TOCQUEVILLE, ALEXIS DE. *Democracy in America.* Garden City, NY: Doubleday Anchor Books, 1969; orig. 1834–1840.

————. *The Old Regime and the French Revolution.* Stuart Gilbert, trans. Garden City, NY: Doubleday Anchor Books, 1955; orig. 1856.

TOENNIES, FERDINAND. *Community and Society (Gemeinschaft und Gesellschaft).* New York: Harper & Row, 1963; orig. 1887.

TOFANI, LORETTA. "AIDS Ravages a Continent, and Sweeps a Family." *The Philadelphia Inquirer* (March 24, 1991):1, 15-A.

TOFFLER, ALVIN. *The Third Wave.* New York: Bantam Books, 1981.

TOMIAK, JANUSZ. "Introduction." In J. J. Tomiak, ed., *Soviet Education in the 1980s.* London: Croom Helm, 1983:vii–x.

TOMLINSON, BRIAN. "Development in the 1990s: Critical Reflections on Canada's Economic Relations with the Third World." In Jamie Swift and Brian Tomlinson, eds., *Conflicts of Interest: Canada and the Third World.* Toronto: Between the Lines, 1991.

TOOLE, DAVID. "We've Got Their Number: Our fourth annual ranking of Canada's 50 richest." *The Financial Post: Moneywise.* May 1989: 25–37.

TOOMEY, BEVERLY, RICHARD FIRST, and JOHN RIFE. Research described in "Number of Rural Homeless Greater than Expected." Ohio State *Quest* (Autumn 1990):2.

TREAS, JUDITH. "Socialist Organization and Economic Development in China: Latent Consequences for the Aged." *The Gerontologist.* Vol. 19, No. 1 (February 1979):34–43.

TREIMAN, DONALD J. "Industrialization and Social Stratification." In Edward O. Laumann, ed., *Social Stratification: Research and Theory for the 1970s.* Indianapolis, IN: Bobbs-Merrill, 1970.

TROELTSCH, ERNST. *The Social Teaching of the Christian Churches.* New York: Macmillan, 1931.

TROIDEN, RICHARD R. *Gay and Lesbian Identity: A Sociological Analysis.* Dix Hills, NY: General Hall, 1988.

TRON, JACQUELINE. "Young Women Speak: The Experience of Teenage Pregnancy and Motherhood." Honours Sociology Thesis, Wilfrid Laurier University, May 1993.

TUMIN, MELVIN M. "Some Principles of Stratification: A Critical Analysis." *American Sociological Review.* Vol. 18, No. 4 (August 1953):387–94.

————. *Social Stratification: The Forms and Functions of Inequality.* 2nd ed. Englewood Cliffs, NJ: Prentice Hall, 1985.

TURNER, R., ed. *Ethnomethodology: Selected Readings.* Harmondsworth: Penguin, 1974.

TURNER, RALPH H., and LEWIS M. KILLIAN. *Collective Behavior.* 2nd ed. Englewood Cliffs, NJ: Prentice Hall, 1972; 3rd ed., 1987.

TYGIEL, JULES. *Baseball's Great Experiment: Jackie Robinson and His Legacy.* New York: Oxford University Press, 1983.

TYLER, S. LYMAN. *A History of Indian Policy.* Washington, DC: United States Department of the Interior, Bureau of Indian Affairs, 1973.

TYREE, ANDREA, MOSHE SEMYONOV, and ROBERT W. HODGE. "Gaps and Glissandos: Inequality, Economic Development, and Social Mobility in 24 Countries." *American Sociological Review.* Vol. 44, No. 3 (June 1979):410–24.

U. S. BUREAU OF JUSTICE STATISTICS. *Recidivism of Prisoners Released in 1983.* Washington, DC: U. S. Government Printing Office, 1989.

U. S. BUREAU OF THE CENSUS. "Get the Scoop on 1990 Metro Area Population." *Census and You.* Vol. 29, No. 9 (September 1991). Washington, DC: U. S. Government Printing Office, 1991.

U. S. BUREAU OF THE CENSUS. "Where Does Your City Rank?" *Census and You.* Vol. 26, No. 7 (July 1991). Washington, DC: U. S. Government Printing Office, 1991.

U. S. BUREAU OF THE CENSUS. Current Population Survey. Unpublished data for March 1991. Supplied by the bureau, 1992.

U. S. BUREAU OF THE CENSUS. *Fertility of American Women: June 1990.* Current Population Reports, Series P-20, No. 454. Washington, DC: U. S. Government Printing Office, 1991.

U. S. BUREAU OF THE CENSUS. *Household and Family Characteristics: March 1990 and 1989.* Current Population Reports, Series P-20, No. 447. Washington, DC: U. S. Government Printing Office, 1990.

U. S. BUREAU OF THE CENSUS. *Marital Status and Living Arrangements: March 1990.* Current Population Reports, Series P-20, No. 450. Washington, DC: U. S. Government Printing Office, 1991.

U. S. BUREAU OF THE CENSUS. *Money Income of Households, Families, and Persons in the United States: 1990.* Current Population Reports, Series P-60, No. 174. Washington, DC: U. S. Government Printing Office, 1991.

U. S. BUREAU OF THE CENSUS. Press release on homeless count (CB91-117). Washington, DC: U. S. Government Printing Office, 1991.

U. S. CONGRESS. HOUSE. Select Subcommittee On Children, Youth, And Families. *U. S. Children and Their Families: Current Conditions and Recent Trends, 1989.* Washington, DC: U. S. Government Printing Office, 1989.

U. S. DEPARTMENT OF COMMERCE. *United States Department of Commerce News.* CB91-221. Washington, DC: U. S. Government Printing Office, 1991.

U. S. DEPARTMENT OF EDUCATION. National Center for Education Statistics. *The Condition of Education, 1991, Vol. 2, Postsecondary Education.* Washington, DC: U. S. Government Printing Office, 1991.

U. S. Department of Energy. *Annual Energy Review 1990*. Washington, DC: U.S. Government Printing Office, 1991.

U. S. Department of Health and Human Services. *Alcohol, Drug Abuse, and Mental Health News*. Vol. 15, No. 8 (October 1989). U. S. Department of Health and Human Services. *Vital and Health Statistics: Current Estimates from the National Health Interview Survey, 1990*. Series 10, No. 181. Hyattsville, MD: U. S. Government Printing Office, 1991.

U. S. Department of Justice. *Criminal Victimization in the United States, 1987*. Washington, DC: U. S. Government Printing Office, 1987.

U. S. Department of Labor. Bureau of Labor Statistics. *Employment and Earnings*. Vol. 38, No. 9 (September). Washington, DC: U. S. Government Printing Office, 1991.

U. S. Department of Labor. Bureau of Labor Statistics. *Employment and Earnings*. Vol. 39, No. 1 (January). Washington, DC: U. S. Government Printing Office, 1992.

U. S. Federal Bureau of Investigation. *Crime in the United States 1990*. Washington, DC: U. S. Government Printing Office, 1991.

U. S. Federal Election Commission. *FEC Final Report on 1988 Congressional Campaigns Shows $459 Million Spent*. Washington, DC: The Commission, 1989a.

U. S. Federal Election Commission. *Federal Election Commission Record*. Vol. 15, No. 8 (August 1989b).

U. S. House of Representatives, Select Committee on Children, Youth, and Families. *Abused Children in America: Victims of Neglect*. Washington, DC: U. S. Government Printing Office, 1987.

U. S. National Center for Health Statistics. *Current Estimates from the National Health Survey, 1989*. Washington, DC: U. S. Government Printing Office, 1990.

U. S. National Center for Health Statistics. *Vital Statistics of the United States, 1988, Vol. 1, Natality*. Washington DC: U. S. Government Printing Office, 1990.

U. S. Women's Bureau. *Employers and Child Care: Benefiting Work and Family*. Washington, DC: U. S. Government Printing Office, 1989.

Ubelacker, Sheryl. "Brave New Womb." *Chatelaine*, August 1993: 30–36.

Uchitelle, Louis. "But Just Who is That Fairy Godmother?" *The New York Times* (September 29, 1991):section 4, page 1.

Ujimoto, K. Victor. "Postwar Japanese Immigrants in British Columbia: Japanese Culture and Job Transferability." In Jean Leonard Elliott, ed., *Two Nations, Many Cultures: Ethnic Groups in Canada*. Scarborough, Ontario: Prentice Hall, 1979.

United Nations Development Programme. *Human Development Report 1991*. New York: Oxford University Press, 1991.

United Nations. *World Economic Survey 1988: Current Trends and Policies in the World Economy*. New York: United Nations Publications, 1988.

Unruh, John D., Jr. *The Plains Across*. Urbana: University of Illinois Press, 1979.

Useem, Bert. "Disorganization and the New Mexico Prison Riot of 1980." *American Sociological Review*. Vol. 50, No. 5 (October 1985):677–88.

Useem, Michael. "The Social Organization of the Corporate Business Elite and Participation of Corporate Directors in the Governance of American Institutions." *American Sociological Review*. Vol. 44, No. 4 (August 1979): 553–72.

———. "Corporations and the Corporate Elite." In Alex Inkeles et al., eds., *Annual Review of Sociology*. Vol. 6. Palo Alto, CA: Annual Reviews, 1980:41–77.

———, and Jermoe Karabel. "Pathways to Corporate Management." *American Sociological Review*. Vol. 51, No. 2 (April 1986):184–200.

Vallee, Frank. "John Porter." *The Canadian Encyclopedia*. 2nd ed. Edmonton: Hurtig Publishers, vol. 3, 1988: 1726.

Van De Kaa, Dirk J. "Europe's Second Demographic Transition." *Population Bulletin*. Vol. 42, No. 1 (March 1987). Washington, DC: Population Reference Bureau.

Van Den Haag, Ernest, and John P. Conrad. *The Death Penalty: A Debate*. New York: Plenum Press, 1983.

Van Loon, Richard J. and Michael S. Whittington. *The Canadian Political System: Environment, Structure and Process*. 3rd ed. Toronto: McGraw-Hill Ryerson, 1981.

Van Valey, T. L., W. C. Roof, and J. E. Wilcox. "Trends in Residential Segregation." *American Journal of Sociology*. Vol. 82, No. 4 (January 1977): 826–44.

Vardy, Jill. "Job hopes take sharp nosedive." *The Financial Post*, Aug. 7, 1993:1.

Vatz, Richard E., and Lee S. Weinberg. *Thomas Szasz: Primary Values and Major Contentions*. Buffalo, NY: Prometheus Books, 1983.

Vaughan, Mary Kay. "Multinational Corporations: The World as a Company Town." In Ahamed Idris-Soven et al., eds., *The World as a Company Town: Multinational Corporations and Social Change*. The Hague: Mouton Publishers, 1978:15–35.

Vayda, Eugene, and Raisa B. Deber. "The Canadian Health Care System: An Overview." *Social Science and Medicine*. Vol. 18, No. 3 (1984):191–97.

Veblen, Thorstein. *The Theory of the Leisure Class*. New York: The New American Library, 1953; orig. 1899.

Viguerie, Richard A. *The New Right: We're Ready to Lead*. Falls Church, VA: The Viguerie Company, 1981.

Vines, Gail. "Whose Baby Is It Anyway?" *New Scientist*. No. 1515 (July 3, 1986):26–27.

Vinovskis, Maris A. "Have Social Historians Lost the Civil War? Some Preliminary Demographic Speculations." *Journal of American History*. Vol. 76, No. 1 (June 1989):34–58.

Vogel, Ezra F. *Japan as Number One: Lessons for America*. Cambridge, MA: Harvard University Press, 1979.

Vogel, Lise. *Marxism and the Oppression of Women: Toward a Unitary Theory*. New Brunswick, NJ: Rutgers University Press, 1983.

Vold, George B., and Thomas J. Bernard. *Theoretical Criminology*. 3rd ed. New York: Oxford University Press, 1986.

Von Hirsh, Andrew. *Past or Future Crimes: Deservedness and Dangerousness in the Sentencing of Criminals*. New Brunswick, NJ: Rutgers University Press, 1986.

Vonnegut, Kurt, Jr. "Harrison Bergeron." In *Welcome to the Monkey House*. New York: Delacorte Press/Seymour Lawrence, 1968:7–13; orig. 1961.

Waite, Linda J., Gus W. Haggstrom, and David E. Kanouse. "The Consequences of Parenthood for the Marital Stability of Young Adults." *American Sociological Review*. Vol. 50, No. 6 (December 1985):850–57.

Waite, P.B. "Confederation." *The Canadian Encyclopedia*. 2nd ed. Edmonton: Hurtig Publishers, 1988: 488–9.

Waitzkin, Howard. "A Critical Theory of Medical Discourse: Ideology, Social Control and the Processing of Social Context in Medical Encounters." *Journal of Health and Social Behavior*, vol. 30, June 1989: 220–239.

Walker, Jack L. "The Origins and Maintenance of Interest Groups in America." *The American Political Science Review*. Vol. 77, No. 2 (June 1983):390–406.

Walker, James W. St. G. *A History of Blacks in Canada*. Ottawa: Ministry of Supply and Services Canada, 1980.

Walker, Susan. "Literacy tests urged at U of T." *The Toronto Star*, Aug. 1, 1992: A1.

Wall, Thomas F. *Medical Ethics: Basic Moral Issues*. Washington, DC: University Press of America, 1980.

Wallerstein, Immanuel. "Crises: The World Economy, the Movements, and the Ideologies." In Albert Bergesen, ed., *Crises in the World-System*. Beverly Hills, CA: Sage Publications, 1983:21–36.

Wallerstein, Immanuel. *The Capitalist World-Economy*. New York: Cambridge University Press, 1979.

Wallerstein, Immanuel. *The Modern World-System: Capitalist Agriculture and the Origins of the European World-Economy in the Sixteenth Century*. New York: Academic Press, 1974.

Wallerstein, Immanuel. *The Politics of the World Economy: The States, the Movements, and the Civilizations*. Cambridge (UK): Cambridge University Press, 1984.

WALLERSTEIN, JUDITH S. "Children Having Children." *Time*. Vol. 126, No. 23 (December 9, 1985):78–82, 84, 87, 89–90.

WALLERSTEIN, JUDITH S. "Hold the Eggs and Butter." *Time*. Vol. 123, No. 13 (March 26, 1984):56–63.

WALLERSTEIN, JUDITH S. and SANDRA BLAKESLEE. *Second Chances: Men, Women, and Children a Decade after Divorce*. New York: Ticknor & Fields.

WALLIS, CLAUDIA. "Stress: Can We Cope?" *Time*. Vol. 121, No. 23 (June 6, 1983):48–54.

WALTON, JOHN, and CHARLES RAGIN. "Global and National Sources of Political Protest: Third World Responses to the Debt Crisis." *American Sociological Review*. Vol. 55, No. 6 (December 1990):876–90.

WARNER, SAM BASS, JR. *Streetcar Suburbs*. Cambridge, MA: Harvard University and M. I. T. Presses, 1962.

WARNER, W. LLOYD, and J. O. LOW. *The Social System of the Modern Factory*. Yankee City Series, Vol. 4.

WARNER, W. LLOYD, and PAUL S. LUNT. *The Social Life of a Modern Community*. New Haven, CT: Yale University Press, 1941.

WATSON, JOHN B. *Behaviorism*. Rev. ed. New York: W. W. Norton, 1930.

WATSON, RUSSELL. "A Hidden Epidemic." *Newsweek* (May 14, 1984):30–36.

WATSON, WILLIAM. "Economy." *The Candian Encyclopedia*. 2nd ed. Edmonton: Hurtig Publishers, 1988: 652–56.

WATTEL, H. "Levittown: A Suburban Community." In William Dobriner, ed., *The Suburban Community*. New York: G. P. Putnam's Sons, 1958:287–313.

WAXMAN, CHAIM I. *The Stigma of Poverty: A Critique of Poverty Theories and Policies*. 2nd ed. New York: Pergamon Press, 1983.

WEBER, ADNA FERRIN. *The Growth of Cities*. New York: Columbia University Press, 1963; orig. 1899.

WEBER, MAX. *The Protestant Ethic and the Spirit of Capitalism*. New York: Charles Scribner's Sons, 1958; orig. 1904–1905.

———. *General Economic History*. Frank H. Knight, trans. New York: Collier Books, 1961; orig. 1919–1920.

———. *Economy and Society*. G. Roth and C. Wittich, eds. Berkeley, CA: University of California Press, 1978.

WECHSLER, D. *The Measurement and Appraisal of Adult Intelligence*. 5th ed. Baltimore, MD: Williams and Wilkins, 1972.

WEEKS, JOHN R. "The Demography of Islamic Nations." *Population Bulletin*. Vol. 43, No. 4 (December 1988).

WEINBERG, GEORGE. *Society and the Healthy Homosexual*. Garden City, NY: Anchor Books, 1973.

WEINER, ANNETTE B. "Ethnographic Determinism: Samoa and the Margaret Mead Controversy." *American Anthropologist*. Vol. 85, No. 4 (December 1983):909–19.

WEINRICH, JAMES D. *Sexual Landscapes: Why We Are What We Are, Why We Love Whom We Love*. New York: Charles Scribner's Sons, 1987.

WEISNER, THOMAS S., and BERNICE T. EIDUSON. "The Children of the 60s as Parents." *Psychology Today* (January 1986):60–66.

WEITZMAN, LENORE J. *The Divorce Revolution: The Unexpected Social and Economic Consequences for Women and Children in America*. New York: Free Press, 1985.

———, DEBORAH EIFLER, ELIZABETH HODAKA, and CATHERINE ROSS. "Sex-Role Socialization in Picture Books for Preschool Children." *American Journal of Sociology*. Vol. 77, No. 6 (May 1972):1125–50.

WELLER, JACK M., and E. L. QUARANTELLI. "Neglected Characteristics of Collective Behavior." *American Journal of Sociology*. Vol. 79, No. 3 (November 1973):665–85.

WELLFORD, CHARLES. "Labeling Theory and Criminology: An Assessment." In Delos H. Kelly, ed., *Criminal Behavior: Readings in Criminology*. New York: St. Martin's Press, 1980:234–47.

WELLMAN, BARRY and S.D. BERKOWITZ, eds., *Social Structures: A Network Approach*. Cambridge: Cambridge University Press, 1988.

WELLMAN, BARRY. "The Community Question: Intimate Networks of East Yorkers." *American Journal of Sociology*. Vol. 84, No. 5 (March 1979):1201–31.

WELLMAN, BARRY. "The Community Question: The Intimate Networks of East Yorkers." *American Journal of Sociology* 84(5), 1979: 1201–1231.

WENKE, ROBERT J. *Patterns of Prehistory*. New York: Oxford University Press, 1980.

WERMAN, JILL. "Who Makes What?" *Working Woman* (January 1989):72–76, 80.

WESOLOWSKI, WLODZIMIERZ. "Transition from Authoritarianism to Democracy." *Social Research*. Vol. 57, No. 2 (Summer 1990):435–61.

WESTERMAN, MARTY. "Death of the Frito Bandito." *American Demographics*. Vol. 11, No. 3 (March 1989):28–32.

WESTHUES, KENNETH. "The Established Church as an Agent of Change." *Sociological Analysis*, 334(2) 1973:106–23.

WESTOFF, CHARLES F., and ELISE F. JONES. "The Secularization of U. S. Catholic Birth Control Practices." *Family Planning Perspective*. Vol. X, No. 5 (September/October 1977):203–7.

WHALEN, JACK, and RICHARD FLACKS. *Beyond the Barricades: The Sixties Generation Grows Up*. Philadelphia, PA: Temple University Press, 1989.

What We Heard: Issues and Questions Raised During Public Hearings. Ottawa: Royal Commission on New Reproductive Technology, 1991.

WHEELIS, ALLEN. *The Quest for Identity*. New York: W. W. Norton, 1958.

WHITAKER, MARK. "Ten Ways to Fight Terrorism." *Newsweek* (July 1, 1985): 26–29.

WHITE, L.K. "Determinants of Divorce: A Review of Research in the Eighties." In A. Booth, ed., *Contemporary Families: Looking Forward, Looking Back*. Minneapolis, Minn.: National Council on Family Relations, 1991.

WHITE, RALPH, and RONALD LIPPITT. "Leader Behavior and Member Reaction in Three 'Social Climates.'" In Dorwin Cartwright and Alvin Zander, eds., *Group Dynamics*. Evanston, IL: Row, Peterson, 1953:586–611.

WHITE, WALTER. *Rope and Faggot*. New York: Arno Press and *The New York Times*, 1969; orig. 1929.

WHITMAN, DAVID. "Shattering Myths about the Homeless." *U. S. News & World Report* (March 20, 1989):26, 28.

WHITNEY, CRAIG R. "British Health Service, Much Beloved but Inadequate, is Facing Changes." *The New York Times* (June 9, 1991):11.

WHORF, BENJAMIN LEE. "The Relation of Habitual Thought and Behavior to Language." In *Language, Thought, and Reality*. Cambridge, MA: The Technology Press of M.I.T. /New York: Wiley, 1956:134–59; orig. 1941.

WHYTE, DONALD R. and FRANK G. VALLEE. "Sociology." *The Canadian Encyclopedia*. 2nd ed. Edmonton: Hurtig Publishers, 3, 1988: 2035–36.

WHYTE, WILLIAM FOOTE. *Street Corner Society*. 3rd ed. Chicago: University of Chicago Press, 1981; orig. 1943.

WHYTE, WILLIAM H., JR. *The Organization Man*. Garden City, NY: Anchor, 1957.

WIARDA, HOWARD J. "Ethnocentrism and Third World Development." *Society*. Vol. 24, No. 6 (September–October 1987):55–64.

WIATROWSKI, MICHAEL A., DAVID B. GRISWOLD, and MARY K. ROBERTS. "Social Control Theory and Delinquency." *American Sociological Review*. Vol. 46, No. 5 (October 1981):525–41.

WIGDOR, BLOSSOM. *Elder Abuse: Major Issues from a National Perspective*. Ottawa: National Advisory Council on Aging, 1991.

———. "Mental Health and Aging." *Mental Health and Aging*. Ottawa: Statistics Canada, 1991.

WILCOX, CLYDE. "Support for the Christian Right Old and New: A Comparison of Supporters of the Anti-Communism Crusade and the Moral Majority." *Sociological Focus*. Vol. 22, No. 2 (May 1989):87–97.

WILKERSON, ISABEL. "Interracial Marriage Rises, Acceptance Lags." *The New York Times* (December 2, 1991):1, 10.

WILKINS, R. and O.B. ADAMS. *Healthfulness of Life: A Unified View of Mortality, Institutionalization, and Non-institutionalized Disability in Canada*. Montreal: The Institute for Research on Public Policy, 1983: 126.

WILL, GEORGE F. "No Psycho-Socio Babble Lessens the Fact That Evil Was the Crux of Central Park Rape." *The Philadelphia Inquirer* (May 1, 1989).

WILLIAMS, RHYS H., and N. J. DEMERATH III. "Religion and Political Process in an American City." *American Sociological Review.* Vol. 56, No. 4 (August 1991):417–31.

WILLIAMS, ROBIN M., JR. *American Society: A Sociological Interpretation.* 3rd ed. New York: Alfred A. Knopf, 1970.

WILLIAMSON, JEFFREY G., and PETER H. LINDERT. *American Inequality: A Macroeconomic History.* New York: Academic Press, 1980.

WILSON, ALAN B. "Residential Segregation of Social Classes and Aspirations of High School Boys. "*American Sociological Review.* Vol. 24, No. 6 (December 1959):836–45.

WILSON, BRYAN. *Religion in Sociological Perspective.* New York: Oxford University Press, 1982.

WILSON, CLINTY C., II, and FELIX GUTIERREZ. *Minorities and Media: Diversity and the End of Mass Communication.* Beverly Hills, CA: Sage Publications, 1985.

WILSON, EDWARD O. *Sociobiology: The New Synthesis.* Cambridge, MA: Belknap Press of the Harvard University Press, 1975.

———. *On Human Nature.* New York: Bantam Books, 1978.

WILSON, J. DONALD. "Religion and Education: The Other Side of Pluralism." In J. Donald Wilson, ed., *Canadian Education in the 1980s.* Calgary: Detselig Enterprises, 1981: 97–113.

WILSON, JAMES Q. *Bureaucracy: What Government Agencies Do and Why They Do It.* New York: Basic Books, 1991.

———, and RICHARD J. HERRNSTEIN. *Crime and Human Nature.* New York: Simon and Schuster, 1985.

WILSON, JOHN. *Religion in American Society: The Effective Presence.* Englewood Cliffs, NJ: Prentice Hall, 1978.

WILSON, LOGAN. *American Academics Then and Now.* New York: Oxford University Press, 1979.

WILSON, THOMAS C. "Urbanism and Tolerance: A Test of Some Hypotheses Drawn from Wirth and Stouffer." *American Sociological Review.* Vol. 50, No. 1 (February 1985):117–23.

———. "Urbanism, Migration, and Tolerance: A Reassessment." *American Sociological Review.* Vol. 56, No. 1 (February 1991):117–23.

WILSON, WILLIAM JULIUS. "The Black Underclass." *The Wilson Quarterly.* Vol. 8 (Spring 1984):88–99.

———. "Studying Inner-City Social Dislocations: The Challenge of Public Agenda Research." *American Sociological Review.* Vol. 56, No. 1 (February 1991):1–14.

Windspeaker. "Preventative Measures Needed to Halt AIDS Spread." Ann Arbor, Michigan: Apr. 12, 1991: 19.

———. "AIDS Figures Chilling." Ann Arbor, Michigan: April 12, 1991:4.

WINKS, ROBIN W. "Slavery." *The Canadian Encyclopedia.* 2nd ed. Edmonton Hurtig Publishers, 3, 1988: 2010–11.

WINN, MARIE. *Children Without Childhood.* New York: Pantheon Books, 1983.

WINNICK, LOUIS. "America's 'Model Minority.'" *Commentary.* Vol. 90, No. 2 (August 1990):22–29.

WIRTH, LOUIS. "Urbanism As a Way of Life." *American Journal of Sociology.* Vol. 44, No. 1 (July 1938):1–24.

WITKIN-LANOIL, GEORGIA. *The Female Stress Syndrome: How to Recognize and Live with It.* New York: Newmarket Press, 1984.

WOLF, NAOMI. *The Beauty Myth.* Toronto: Random House, 1990.

WOLFE, DAVID B. "Killing the Messenger." *American Demographics.* Vol. 13, No. 7 (July 1991):40–43.

WOLFE, TOM. *Radical Chic.* New York: Bantam, 1970.

WOLFGANG, MARVIN E., ROBERT M. FIGLIO, and THORSTEN SELLIN. *Delinquency in a Birth Cohort.* Chicago: University of Chicago Press, 1972.

WOLFGANG, MARVIN E., TERRENCE P. THORNBERRY, and ROBERT M. FIGLIO. *From Boy to Man, From Delinquency to Crime.* Chicago: University of Chicago Press, 1987.

WOLFINGER, RAYMOND E., and STEVEN J. ROSENSTONE. *Who Votes?* New Haven, CT: Yale University Press, 1980.

WOLFINGER, RAYMOND E., MARTIN SHAPIRO, and FRED J. GREENSTEIN. *Dynamics of American Politics.* 2nd ed. Englewood Cliffs, NJ: Prentice Hall, 1980.

Women in Canada: A Statistical Report (Second Edition). Ottawa: Statistics Canada, 1990.

Women in the Labour Force. 1990–91 Edition. Women's Bureau, Labour Canada. Ottawa: Statistics Canada, 1990.

Women in the Labour Force. Ottawa: Statistics Canada, 1990–91:990.

WONG, BUCK. "Need for Awareness: An Essay on Chinatown, San Francisco." In Amy Tachiki et al., eds., *Roots: An Asian American Reader.* Los Angeles, CA: UCLA Asian American Studies Center, 1971:265–73.

WOOD, DANIELL. "Death Wish: Would You Choose an Assisted Suicide." *Chatelaine,* July 1993, 25–29, 94.

WOODWARD, C. VANN. *The Strange Career of Jim Crow.* 3rd rev. ed. New York: Oxford University Press, 1974.

WOODWARD, KENNETH L. "Rules for Making Love and Babies." *Newsweek.* Vol. 109, No. 12 (March 23, 1987):42–43.

———. "Feminism and the Churches." *Newsweek.* Vol. 13, No. 7 (February 13, 1989):58–61.

———. "Talking to God." *Newsweek.* Vol. 119, No. 1 (January 6, 1992):38–44.

WOOLEY, ORLAND W., SUSAN C. WOOLEY, and SUE R. DYRENFORTH. "Obesity and Women—II: A Neglected Feminist Topic." *Women's Studies International Quarterly.* Vol. 2 (1979):81–92.

WORLD HEALTH ORGANIZATION. *Constitution of the World Health Organization.* New York: World Health Organization Interim Commission, 1946.

WOTHERSPOON, TERRY, ed. *The Political Economy of Canadian Schooling.* Toronto: Methuen, 1987.

———. "Transforming Canada's Education System: The Impact on Educational Inequalities, Opportunities and Benefits." In B. Singh Bolaria, ed., *Social Issues and Contradictions in Canadian Society.* Toronto: Harcourt Brace Jovanovich, 1991: 448–463.

———, and VIC SATZEWICH. *First Nations: Race, Class, and Gender Relations.* Scarborough, Ontario: Nelson, 1993.

WREN, CHRISTOPHER S. "In Soweto-by-the-Sea, Misery Lives On as Apartheid Fades." *The New York Times* (June 9, 1991):1, 7.

WRIGHT, ERIK OLIN, and BILL MARTIN. "The Transformation of the American Class Structure, 1960–1980." *American Journal of Sociology.* Vol. 93, No. 1 (July 1987):1–29.

WRIGHT, JAMES D. "Address Unknown: Homelessness in Contemporary America." *Society.* Vol. 26, No. 6 (September/October 1989):45–53.

WRIGHT, QUINCY. "Causes of War in the Atomic Age." In William M. Evan and Steven Hilgartner, eds., *The Arms Race and Nuclear War.* Englewood Cliffs, NJ: Prentice Hall, 1987:7–10.

WRIGHT, STUART A. "Social Movement Decline and Transformation: Cults in the 1980s." Paper presented to the Southwestern Social Science Association, Dallas, Texas, March 1987.

WRIGHT, STUART A., and ELIZABETH S. PIPER. "Families and Cults: Familial Factors Related to Youth Leaving or Remaining in Deviant Religious Groups." *Journal of Marriage and the Family.* Vol. 48, No. 1 (February 1986):15–25.

———, and WILLIAM V. D'ANTONIO. "The Substructure of Religion: A Further Study." *Journal for the Scientific Study of Religion.* Vol. 19, No. 3 (September 1980):292–98.

WRONG, DENNIS H. "The Oversocialized Conception of Man in Modern Sociology." *American Sociological Review.* Vol. 26, No. 2 (April 1961):183–93.

YATES, RONALD E. "Growing Old in Japan; They Ask Gods for a Way Out." *Philadelphia Inquirer* (August 14, 1986):3A.

YBARRA, LEA. *Conjugal Role Relationships in the Chicano Family.* Unpublished doctoral dissertation, University of California, 1977 (cited in Nielsen, 1990).

YODER, EDWIN M., JR. "Offering Sociology as Theology." *The Philadelphia Inquirer* (May 5, 1989).

YODER, JAN D., and ROBERT C. NICHOLS. "A Life Perspective: Comparison of Married and Divorced Persons." *Journal of Marriage and the Family.* Vol. 42, No. 2 (May 1980):413–19.

YORK, GEOFFREY. "UN body chastises Canada on poverty." *The Globe and Mail,* June 25, 1993: A1–2.

ZALD, MAYER N. *Occupations and Organizations in American Society.* Chicago: Markham, 1971.

ZANGWILL, ISRAEL. *The Melting Pot.* Macmillan, 1921; orig. 1909.

ZASLAVSKY, VICTOR. *The Neo-Stalinist State: Class, Ethnicity, and Consensus in Soviet Society.* Armonk, NY: M. E. Sharpe, 1982.

ZEITLIN, IRVING M. *The Social Condition of Humanity.* New York: Oxford University Press, 1981.

ZHOU, MIN, and JOHN R. LOGAN. "Returns of Human Capital in Ethnic Enclaves: New York City's Chinatown." *American Sociological Review.* Vol. 54, No. 5 (October 1989):809–20.

ZILL, NICHOLAS. National Survey conducted by Child Trends, Inc., Washington, DC, 1984. Reported by Marilyn Adams. "Kids Aren't Broken by the Breakup." *USA Today* (December 20, 1984):5D.

ZIMBARDO, PHILIP G. "Pathology of Imprisonment." *Society.* Vol. 9 (April 1972):4–8.

ZIPP, JOHN F. "Perceived Representativeness and Voting: An Assessment of the Impact of 'Choices' vs. 'Echoes.'" *The American Political Science Review.* Vol. 79, No. 1 (March 1985):50–61.

———, and JOEL SMITH. "A Structural Analysis of Class Voting." *Social Forces.* Vol. 60, No. 3 (March 1982):738–59.

ZOLA, IRVING KENNETH. "Medicine as an Institution of Social Control." In John Ehrenreich, ed., *The Cultural Crisis of Modern Medicine.* New York: Monthly Review Press, 1978:80–100.

ZUBOFF, SHOSHANA. "New Worlds of Computer-Mediated Work." *Harvard Business Review.* Vol. 60, No. 5 (September–October 1982):142–52.

ZURCHER, LOUIS A., and DAVID A. SNOW. "Collective Behavior and Social Movements." In Morris Rosenberg and Ralph Turner, eds., *Social Psychology: Sociological Perspectives.* New York: Basic Books, 1981:447–82.

ingway, 329; Chester Higgins Jr./Photo Researchers, 330; Canapress/Victor Fisher, 331 (t.); Japanese Cultural Centre. Photographer Phil Doi, 331 (b.); National Archives of Canada/PA-37468, 332; Linda Gerber, 334 (l.); Culver Pictures Inc., 334 (r.); Terrence McCarthy/*The New York Times*, 336; Henry Kalen, 339; National Archives of Canada/C-24452, 343.

CHAPTER 13 Larry Fried/The Image Bank, 348; Jacky Gucia/The Image Bank, 349; Michel Tcherevkoff/The Image Bank, 350; Co Rentmeester/The Image Bank, 353; Courtesy of Pennsylvania State University, 358; Liza McCoy/Photographer, 359; Courtesy of Revlon, 361; Charles Gupton/Stock, Boston, 366; Rob Crandall/Picture Group, 370; Courtesy of the National Organization of Women, 373; Robert Fox/Impact Visuals, 375.

CHAPTER 14 Paul Liebhardt, 382; Rob Crandall/Picture Group, 383; Dick Hemingway, 387; Sharon Farmer, from "Songs of My People." © New African Visions, Inc., 388; Eve Arnold/Magnum Photos, 392; Scala/Art Resource, 401; Stanley B. Burns, M.D./The Burns Archives, 402.

CHAPTER 15 Collection of Marilyn Lanfear, Texas. Photo courtesy Bernice Steinbaum Gallery, New York City, 406; Michael O'Neill, 407; *The Toronto Star*/G. Stephen, 409; Steve Sands/Outline Press, 412; The National Gallery, London, 416; National Gallery of Canada, Ottawa, 421; David Schreiber/The Torrance (CA) Daily Breeze, 425; James Skovmand, *The San Diego Union-Tribune*, 428; Stu Rossner/Stock, Boston, 433.

CHAPTER 16 Robert Caputo, 438; Richard Kalvar/Magnum Photos, 439; Hans Neleman/The Image Bank, 443; Paul Liebhardt, 445; Photographer: Marko Shark, 452; AP/Wide World Photos, 455; ABC Canada, Harrod & Mirlin Advertising, 457.

CHAPTER 17 Raghu Rai/Magnum Photos, 460; Eric Haase/CONTACT/Woodfin Camp & Associates, 461; Hans Hoefer/Woodfin Camp & Associates, 464; Ira Wyman/Sygma, 465; Gilles Peress/Magnum Photos, 469; British Library, London. Bridgeman/Art Resource, 473; Paul Liebhardt, 475; Jan Lukas/Photo Researchers, 477; The Metropolitan Museum of Art, New York. Fletcher Fund, 479; Reprinted by permission of the estate of William Kurclek, courtesy The Isaacs/Inuit Gallery, Toronto, 482.

CHAPTER 18 Andy Hernandez/SIPA, 490; Eve Arnold/Magnum Photos, 491; JB Pictures, 492; The Metropolitan Museum of Art, New York. Wolfe Fund, 494; The Prado, Madrid. Giraudon/Art Resource, 500; Photographer: W.J. Gibbons, NCC/CNN, 501 (l.); Tess McIntosh, Department of Culture and Communications, Government of the Northwest Territories, 501 (r.); Canapress/Blaise Edwards, 506; Elections Canada, 509; Canapress/Chuck Stoody, 510; Reuters/Bettmann, 516.

CHAPTER 19 Louis Psihoyos/Matrix, 524; Canadawide Features Service/Moira Welsh, 525; Courtesy of the Manchester (New Hampshire) Historic Association, 527; Harald Sund/The Image Bank, 532 (l.); Sygma, 532 (r.); Roy Antal/*Regina Leader Post*, 538; Photographer: Christopher Morris, 539; Public Archives of Canada/C29397, 540; Mayer/Gamma Liaison, 548; Arnold Gottlieb Gallery, 549.

CHAPTER 20 Frank Fournier/Contact/Woodfin Camp & Associates, 554; Susan Rosenberg/Photo Researchers, 555; The Granger Collection, 557; W. Campbell/Sygma, 560 (l.); Peter Magubane/Black Star, 560 (r.); Cecil Fox/Science Source/Photo Researchers, 564; Marty Katz, 566; P.P.O.W. Gallery, New York, 569; Ruven Afanadore, 571; National Archives of Canada/C9480, 572; Sam Garcia, 574.

CHAPTER 21 Hunter Museum of Art, Chattanooga, Tennessee. Gift of the Benwood Foundation, 586; Stephanie Maze/Woodfin Camp & Associates, 587; The Phillips Collection, 590; Terry Madison/The Image Bank, 594; N. Maceschal/The Image Bank, 596; Erich Hartmann/Magnum Photos, 599; Collection, The Museum of Modern Art, New York. Mrs. Simon Guggenheim Fund, 608 (l.); The Philadelphia Museum of Art. The A. E. Gallatin Collection, 608 (r.); City of Toronto Archives, 602; The University of Chicago Library, 609; Fred Mayer/Magnum Photos, 613.

CHAPTER 22 Ron Haviv/SABA, 618; AP/Wide World Photos, 619; Photographer: Jeff Vinnick, 620; Canapress/Jacques Boissinot, 622; Jalil Bonhar/Wide World Photos, 623; The Granger Collection, 627; Shlomo Arad/JB Pictures, 630; Donna Binder/Impact Visuals, 634; Jon Jones/Sygma, 636.

CHAPTER 23 James Willis/Tony Stone Worldwide, 640; Mauri Rautkari/WWF Photolibrary, 641; G. V. Faint/The Image Bank, 643; The Art Institute of Chicago. Helen Birch Bartlett Memorial Collection, 647; Bildarchiv Preussischer Kulturbesitz, 649; Reprinted by permission of the estate of Wiliam Kurelek, courtesy of The Isaacs/Inuit Gallery, Toronto, 650; Stephanie Maze/Woodfin Camp & Associates, 652; Andrew Holbrooke/Black Star, 658; Kevin Bubriski/The Film Study Center, Harvard University, 660.

Readers wishing further information on data provided through the cooperation of Statistics Canada may obtain copies of related publications by mail from: Publications Sales, Statistics Canada, Ottawa, Ontario, Canada K1A 0T6, or by calling 1-613-951-7277 or toll-free 1-800-267-6677. Readers may also facsimile their order by dialing 1-613-951-1584.

Name Index

Abbott, Daniel, 231, 233, 539
Aberle, David F., 629
Abzug, Robert H., 478
Adams, O.B., 562
Adorno, T. W., 326
Ageton, Suzanne S., 222, 231
Aguirre, Benigno, 620, 628
Akers, Ronald L., 222
Akihito, Emperor (of Japan) 250
Alam, Sultana, 307
Alba, Richard D., 331
Albrecht, William P., Jr., 530
Allan, Emilie Andersen, 219
Allsop, Kenneth, 218
Ambert, A.M., 425
Amman, Jost, 557
Anderson, Daniel R., 143
Anderson, Doris, 350, 354, 368
Anderson, Elijah, 56
Anderson, Maria, 328
Ang, Ien, 144
Angelo, Bonnie, 383
Anspaugh, David J., 578
Aquinas, St. Thomas, 12
Arai, A. Bruce, 449
Arendt, Hannah, 492, 499
Ariès, Phillippe, 146, 401, 402
Aristotle, 12, 83, 252, 440
Arjomand, Said Amir, 474
Armstrong, Pat, 359
Artibise, Alan F.J., 327
Asch, Solomon, 185, 186
Astone, Nan Marie, 430
Astor, John Jacob, 257
Atchley, Robert C., 395, 403
Aurelius, Marcus, 12
Aviad, Janet O'Dea, 469, 482
Avis, George, 443, 444
Ayensu, Edward S., 572

Bahl, Vinay, 246
Bailey, William C., 239
Bainbridge, William Sims, 469, 471, 648
Baker, Mary Anne, 352, 422
Baker, Maureen, 425
Bakker, J.I., 535
Bakker, Jim, 485
Bakker, Tammy, 485
Baldus Bernd, 141
Bales, Robert F., 184, 185, 412
Ballantine, Jeanne, 141, 440, 443, 444
Baltes, Paul B., 390

Baltzell, E. Digby, 21, 257, 495, 605, 653
Banfield, Edward, 284
Banks, Curtis, 46
Banting, Frederick, 83
Barash, David, 69, 92
Barberis, Mary, 645
Baril, Alain, 478
Barker, Eileen, 471, 486
Baron, James N., 633
Barr, Cathy Widdis, 508
Barrett, Stanley R., 326, 628, 631
Barry, Kathleen, 92, 373–374
Bashevkin, Sylvia B., 505, 510, 511
Bassett, Isabel, 199
Bassuk, Ellen J., 287
Bauer, P. T., 305, 308
Beach, Frank A., 351
Bear, John, 168
Becker, Howard S., 210, 219
Becker, Rosa, 56
Bedell, George C., 478
Begin, Patricia, 3, 354, 428
Beigel, Hugo G., 415
Bell, Alan P., 352, 431
Bell, Alexander Graham, 83
Bell, Wendell, 611
Bellah, Robert N., 75, 93, 483
Belsky, Jay, 141
Bem, Sandra Lipsitz, 357
Bendix, Reinhard, 247
Benedict, Ruth, 147, 148, 442
Benet, Sula, 392
Benford, Robert D., 633
Benjamin, Bernard, 395
Benn, Carl 602
Benokraitis, Nijole V., 177, 364, 365
Bentley, Peter, 546
Berardo, F.M., 420
Beresford-Howe, Constance, 149
Berg, Ivar, 453
Berger, Brigitte, 432, 653, 657, 660
Berger, Peter L., 3, 4, 42, 153, 162, 261, 305, 308, 309, 390, 432, 466, 548, 646, 653, 657, 660
Bergesen, Albert, 312, 549
Berk, Richard A., 623
Bernard, Jessie, 274, 358, 369, 374, 414, 422, 423
Bernard, Larry Craig, 357
Bernard, Thomas J., 212, 222, 225
Berscheid, Ellen, 416
Berton, Pierre, 130
Best, Charles, 83

Best, Raphaela, 142, 360
Bhutto, Benazir, 494
Bibby, Reginald, 417, 470, 478, 483–386
Black, Naomi, 23
Blau, Judith, 235
Blau, Peter, 22, 44, 190, 231, 235, 247, 414
Blishen, Bernard R., 449, 451, 572, 573, 580
Blumberg, Abraham, 235
Blumberg, Paul, 656
Blumer, Herbert, 621, 628, 629, 634
Blumstein, Philip, 411, 417, 430, 431
Bodenheimer, Thomas S., 579
Boff, Leonard, 467
Bogardus, Emory, 327
Bohannan, Paul, 425
Bohlen, Celestine, 321
Bohm, Robert, 239
Bohmer, Susanne, 429
Bollough, Vern, 581
Bonner, Jane, 358
Botwinick, Jack, 390
Boulding, Kenneth E., 104, 105
Bowles, Samuel, 20, 449–451
Boyd, Monica, 249, 425
Bozinoff, Lorne, 371, 416, 480
Braithwaite, John, 231
Brant, Joseph, 335
Brenner, Harvey, 420
Breton, Raymond, 330, 338, 341, 544, 619
Breughel, Pieter, 401
Brinton, Crane, 514
Brinton, Mary C., 250
Brodie, M. Janine, 374, 544
Brody, Charles, 168
Bromley, David G., 484
Brophy, Gwenda, 598
Brough, James, 130
Brown, E. Richard, 580
Brown, John George, 257
Brownmiller, Susan, 168, 229
Bruce, Erika, 15
Bruno, Mary, 397
Brym, Robert J., 544, 656
Brzezinski, Zbigniew, 499
Buchholz, Michael, 400
Burch, Robert, 302
Burgess, Ernest W., 610
Burris, Val, 454
Burstein, Paul, 633
Busby, Linda J., 361

Bush, George, 251, 517
Butler, Robert N., 399
Butterworth, Douglas, 333
Bynum, Jack E., 400

Cafferata, Gail Lee, 389
Cahnman, Werner J., 649
Callahan, Daniel, 389, 570
Callow, A.B., Jr., 603
Calvin, John, 116
Cameron, William Bruce, 629
Campanis, Al, 27
Campbell, Anne, 225
Campbell, Kim, 368, 494, 510, 511
Campbell, Richard T., 249
Canetti, Elias, 624
Cantor, Murial G., 144
Cantril, Hadley, 626
Capernicus, 12
Capone, Al, 218
Carley, Kathleen, 189, 190
Carlson, Norman A., 239
Carlton, Eric, 599
Carmichael, Stokely, 326
Carnegie, Andrew, 257
Carney, Pat, 510
Carpov, Stephan, 109
Carrigan, D. Owen, 206, 218, 224, 225
Carroll, Glenn R., 495
Carter, Barbara, 335
Carter, Bruce, 335
Cartier, George Etienne, 502
Castro, Fidel, 441
Cawley, Janet, 468
Ceaucescu, N., 515
Cebotarev, E.A., 302
Chagall, Marc, 608
Chagnon, Napoleon, 65, 66, 79, 83, 102, 517
Chamberlain, Neville, 170
Chance, John K., 333
Chandler, John K., 16
Chandler, Tertius, 600
Change, Kwang-Chih, 599
Chapple, Steve, 215
Cherlin, Andrew, 425
Chisholm, Patricia, 431
Chomsky, Noam, 74
Chown, Sheila, 395
Christian, William, 504
Clancy, Paul, 430
Clark, Curtis B., 397
Clark, Dick, 215

Clark, Joe, 181, 345, 501, 506
Clark, Margaret S., 258
Clark, S.D., 14
Clark, Warren, 191
Clarke, Juanne Nancarrow, 54, 88, 91, 162, 386, 418, 558, 559, 572, 573, 575, 576, 579, 580
Clarkson, Stephen, 503
Clayson, Dennis E., 226
Clegg, Johnny, 247
Clement, Wallace, 258, 269, 276, 513, 545–547, 656
Clinard, Marshall, 231, 233
Cloward, Richard, 216, 631, 635
Coakley, Jay J., 25, 27
Cobb, Jonathan, 288, 454
Cockerham, William C., 559
Coe, Michael D., 599
Cohen, Albert, 217
Cohen, Lloyd R., 370
Cohn, Bob, 181
Cohn, Richard M., 393
Cole, Priscilla, 396
Coleman, James, 455
Coleman, William D., 340
Collins, Joseph, 313
Collins, Randall, 117, 372, 453
Colloway, N.O., 388
Colombo, John Robert, 4, 8, 81, 282, 286, 386, 457, 549, 603, 607
Columbus, Christopher, 310–312
Colville, Alex, 58, 93
Como, Perry, 215
Comte, Auguste, 12, 13, 17, 18
Confucius, 12, 194, 440, 477
Connidis, Ingrid A., 419
Conrad, John P., 239
Conrad, Peter, 221
Contreras, Joseph, 247, 253
Cooley, Charles Horton, 138, 182, 183, 625
Cooper, Philip W., 430
Coppock, Marjorie L., 191
Cornell, Clarie Pedrick, 369
Corsaro, William A., 137
Cortés, Hernando, 82, 587
Coser, Lewis A., 138, 183
Cottrell, John, 333
Counts, G.S., 44, 269
Courtney, Alice E., 144
Coverman, Shelley, 363, 535
Cowart, Dax, 571
Cowgill, Donald, 394
Cox, Harold, 391
Cox, Harvey, 482, 483, 484, 486, 610
Creese, Gillian, 271, 274, 280, 281
Cressey, Donald R., 225
Crisp, Quentin, 556
Cross, James, 515
Crump, Ian, 525
Cuff, E. C., 115
Culleton, Beatrice, 152
Cumming, Elaine, 398
Currie, Elliot, 232, 555
Curtis, James, 281
Curtiss, Susan, 134
Cutright, Phillip, 247
Cuvelier, Steven, 365

D'Antonio, William V., 465
Dahlin, Michael, 393

Dahrendorf, Ralf, 258, 543, 653
Dalglish, Brenda, 543
Daly, Martin, 212
Damon, William, 136, 137
Dannefer, Dale, 148
Darwin, Charles, 19, 90, 131
David, Jacques Louis, 359, 494
Davies, Christie, 177
Davies, James C., 514, 630, 631
Davies, Mark, 143
Davis, Kingsley, 129, 133, 134, 253, 263
Davis, Linda, 33, 34
Davis, Sharon A., 450
Day, Doris, 215
De Berry, Duc, 253
Deckard, Barbara Sinclair, 374
Dedrick, Dennis K., 408, 519
DeKeseredy, Walter S., 3, 226, 228, 229, 354, 369
Delacroix, Jacques, 312, 549
Demerath, N.J., III, 483
Denton, Nancy, 332
Depew, Robert, 235
Desmarais, Jacqui, 267
Desmarais, Paul, 267
DeVilliers, Priscilla, 238
Dewey, John, 444
Dhillon, Baltej Singh, 80
Diamond, Milton, 353, 403
Dickason, Olive Patricia, 333
Dickens, Charles, 145
Dickson, William J., 46, 195, 506
Diefenbaker, John, 493
Diehl, Richard A., 599
Diekema, David, 184
Dinitz, Simon, 212
Dobson, Richard B., 252
Dollard, John, 326, 630
Dollevoet, Paula L., 388
Domhoff, G. William, 258
Donovan, Virginia K., 135
Douglas, Jack, 41
Douglass, Richard L., 397
Dow, Unity, 349
Doyle, James A., 376
Driedger, Leo, 336
Dubinsky, Karen, 418
Dubois, W.E.B., 21
Dubos, Rene, 556
DuCharme, Michelle, 335
Duhl, Leonard J., 573
Dulude, Louise, 425
Duncan, Otis Dudley, 44, 247
Duncan-Robinson, Joanne, 456
Durkheim, Emile, 5, 12, 18, 53, 100, 109, 120–124, 164, 214, 462–464, 483, 607, 650–653, 657
Dworkin, Andrea, 374
Dyrenforth, Sue R., 555
Dziech, Bille Wright, 370

Ebaugh, Helen Rose Fuchs, 162
Eckholm, Erik, 73, 388, 569
Edmonston, Barry, 604
Edwards, David V., 496, 535
Edwards, Richard, 258
Ehrenreich, Barbara, 355
Ehrenreich, John, 580
Ehrhardt, Anke A., 352

Ehrlich, Paul, 594, 597
Eichler, Margrit, 43, 44, 359
Eiduson, Bernice T., 430
Einstein, Albert, 42, 191, 373
Eisen, Arnold M., 478
Eisenhart, Margaret A., 33, 34, 45, 142
Eisenhower, Dwight, 518
Ekland-Olson, Sheldon, 633
Ekman, Paul, 69, 166, 168, 170, 171
Elias, Robert, 231
Elkin, Frederick, 131
Elkind, David, 147
Elliot, Delbert S., 222, 231
Ember, Carol R., 411
Ember, Melvin M., 411
Embree, Ainslie T., 475
Emerson, Joan, 579
Engels, Friedrich, 24, 112, 373, 413
Ensels, Walter M., 562
Erasmus, George, 339
Erikson, Erik, 394
Erikson, Kai, 46, 214, 627
Etzioni, Amitai, 191
Etzioni-Halevy, Eva, 496
Evans, M.D.R., 539
Evers, Frederick T., 456
Ezell, Gene, 578

Fairbanks, Douglas, 267
Fairclough, Ellen, 510
Falk, Gerhard, 74
Faludi, Susan, 425
Falwell, Jerry, 485
Farnsworth, Margaret, 231
Farrell, Michael P., 149
Feagin, Joe R., 177, 364, 365, 611
Ferguson, Beatrice, 388
Ferguson, John, 573
Figlio, Robert M., 231
Fine, Gary Alan, 625
Fine, Sean, 570
Finkelstein, Neal W., 141
Fiorentine, Robert, 367
Fischer, Claude S., 191
Fisher, Elizabeth, 102, 104, 105
Fisher, Roger, 519
Fishman, Pamela, 362
Fiske, Alan Paige, 258
Fitzpatrick, Joseph P., 190
Fitzpatrick, Mary Anne, 362, 420
Flacks, Richard, 631
Flaherty, Michael, 177
Fletcher, Frederick J., 327
Flitcraft, Ann, 428
Flynn, Patricia, 571
Foch, Terryl T., 132
Foner, Anne, 140, 151
Ford, Clellan S., 351
Ford, Henry, 648
Fornos, Werner, 611
Fowler, Floyd J., Jr., 48
Fox, Alan F., 15
Fox, Gerald, 16, 600
Francis, Diane, 267, 545–547, 656
Frank, André Gunder, 309, 312
Franklin, Benjamin, 502
Frazier, 231
Fréchette, Pierre, 268, 269
Fredrickson, George M., 247, 332
Freeman, Derek, 43
French, Marilyn, 354, 355, 374

Fretz, Winfield, 86, 469
Freud, Sigmund, 134, 135
Frideres, James S., 328, 336, 338, 534, 535
Friedman, Eugene A., 398
Friedrich, Carl J., 499
Friedrich, Otto, 253, 613
Friesen, Wallace, 168
Frishman, Alan, 316
Fu-tzu, K'ung, 12, 194, 440, 477
Fuchs, Victor R., 365, 562, 574, 576
Fumento, Michael, 569
Furstenberg, Frank F., Jr., 425, 427

Galileo, 12
Gandhi, Indira, 494
Gandhi, Mahatma, 494
Gans, Herbert, 143, 144, 610
Gardner, Allen, 73
Gardner, Beatrice, 73
Garfinkel, Harold, 164, 165, 220
Garofalo, Reebee, 215
Gartin, Patrick R., 222
Gaudet, Hazel, 626
Gautama, Siddhartha, 475
Geertz, Clifford, 351
Geist, William, 606
Gelles, Richard J., 369, 427, 428
Gelman, David, 389, 397
Genovese, Kitty, 651
George, Susan, 556, 559, 560
Georgianna, Sharon, 5
Gerber, Linda M., 231, 273, 283, 336, 338, 339, 505, 514, 534, 535
Gerstel, Naomi, 424
Gerth, H. H., 116
Geschwender, James A., 328
Gibbons, Don C., 212
Gibbs, Nancy, 228, 229
Giddens, Anthony, 258
Giele, Janet Zollinger, 148, 372
Gilbert, Dennis, 275
Gilbert, Sid, 444
Gillett, Charlie, 215
Gilligan, Carol, 136, 137, 359
Gillis, A.R., 230
Gintis, Herbert, 20, 449–451
Giovannini, Maureen, 44
Glass, David V., 247
Glaude, Brian A., 351
Glazer, Nathan, 331
Glock, Charles, 479, 481
Glueck, Eleanor, 212
Goetting, Ann, 426, 427
Goffman, Erving, 22, 27, 151, 165, 192, 220, 361, 658
Goldberg, Steven, 357
Goldfarb, Jeffrey C., 499
Goldfield, Michael, 537
Goldsby, Richard A., 324
Goldsmith, H. H., 132
Goode, William J., 415, 538
Gorbachev, Mikhail, 195, 251, 498
Gordon, James S., 573, 574, 581
Goring, Charles Buckman, 211
Gottfredson, Michael, 230
Gottman, Jean, 606
Gough, Kathleen, 354
Gouldner, Alvin, 42, 43, 599
Gove, Walter R., 423
Goya, Francisco, 500

Goyder, John, 281
Granovetter, Mark, 190
Grant, Don Sherman, II, 633
Grant, Donald L., 622
Grasmick, Harold G., 578
Gray, Herb, 546
Gray, Paul, 311, 557
Green, Richard, 351
Greenberg, David F., 351
Greenspon, Edward, 525
Gregory, Paul R., 531
Gretzky, Wayne, 255
Griff, Catherine, 546
Griffin, Richard Wayne, 514
Griffin, Sandra Keranen, 514
Griswold, David B., 217
Griswold, Wendy, 164
Gross, Jane, 431
Gruenberg, Barry, 535
Guppy, Neil, 271, 280, 449
Gupte, Pranay, 598
Gurak, Douglas T., 190
Guterbock, Thomas, 604
Gutierrez, Felix, 145
Gwartney-Gibbs, Patricia A., 429, 430
Gyorgy, Jane, 73

Haas, Linda, 364
Habermas, Jürgen, 656
Hacker, Helen Mayer, 355, 368, 372
Haddad, William, 425
Hagan, John, 225, 230
Haggstrom, Gus W., 424
Halberstam, David, 195
Hale, Sylvia, 44
Hall, Emmett, 575
Haller, Archibald O., 44
Haller, Emil J., 450
Hallett, M.E., 23
Hallinan, Maureen T., 450
Hamblin, Dora Jane, 68, 599, 645
Hamel, Ruth, 394
Hamilton, Charles, 326
Hamilton, Mykol, 168, 169, 172
Hamrick, Michael H., 578
Handel, Gerald, 131
Handleman, Don, 120
Haney, Craig, 46
Hannan, Michael T., 495
Hansen, Karen V., 375
Harden, Mike, 243
Hareven, Tamara K., 149, 527
Harlan, William H., 394
Harlow, Harry, 132
Harlow, Margaret, 132
Harron, Don, 274, 275
Harper, Elijah, 339
Harries, Keith D., 231
Harrington, Michael, 656
Harris, Barbara, 465
Harris, Chauncy, 610, 611
Harris, Marvin, 67, 73, 84, 89, 354, 388
Harrison, Paul, 556, 559
Hart, Shannon, 566
Harvey, Edward B., 500, 628
Haskins, Ron, 141
Hatfield, Elaine, 416
Haviland, William A., 411, 414
Havinghurst, Robert J., 398
Hayneman, Stephen P., 441, 442

Heberle, Rudolf, 649
Heilbroner, Robert, 528
Helgesen, Sally, 201
Heller, Anita Fochs, 364
Hellman, Ronald E., 351
Helmes-Hayes, R., 15
Helmuth, John W., 301
Hemsell, David, 579
Henley, Nancy, 168, 169, 172, 173
Henry, William, 398
Henson, Josiah, 335
Herman, Dianne F., 369
Herman, Edward S., 74, 546
Herold, E.S., 417
Herrnstein, Richard J., 132, 212
Herzog, Herta, 626
Hill, Anita, 369, 370
Hillard, Dan C., 26
Hiller, Harry H., 71, 342, 343, 450, 606, 657
Hinch, Ronald, 3, 226, 228, 229, 354, 369
Hiroshi, Mannari, 250
Hirschi, Travis, 217, 219, 230
Hitler, Adolf, 170, 517
Hobbes, Thomas, 12, 17, 390, 515
Hochschild, Arlie, 148, 364, 434
Hodge, Robert W., 44, 247, 269
Hoffer, Thomas, 455
Holland, Dorothy C., 33, 34, 45, 142
Holm, Jean, 478
Holmes, Helen, 43, 144, 145, 361
Holmes, Lowell, 394
Homans, George, 22
Hook, Ernest B., 212
Horwitz, Martin, 349
Hoyt, Homer, 610
Hoyt, Mary Finch, 400
Huber, Joan, 423, 424
Huet-Cox, Rocio, 573
Hull, Jon D., 454
Hull, Raymond, 196
Huls, Glenna, 210
Humphrey, Derek, 383, 571
Hunt, Morton, 417
Hunter, James Davison, 485
Hurst, Charles E., 562
Hurtig, Mel, 546

Illich, Ivan, 557, 580
Innis, Harold, 14
Irving, K.C., 547
Irwin, John, 152
Isajiw, Wsevelod, W., 323

Jacklin, Carol Nagy, 352
Jackson, Daniel H., 471
Jacobs, David, 235
Jacobs, Jane, 526, 613
Jaenen, Cornelius, 445
Jagger, Alison, 373–376
Janis, Irving L., 186
Jencks, Christopher, 212
Jenkins, Brian M., 516
Jenkins, J. Craig, 630, 632
Jesus, 471–473, 624
John Paul II, Pope, 467
Johnson, F. Henry, 181, 440
Johnson, Julie, 173
Johnson, Paul, 515

Johnston, R.J., 611
Johnstone, Ronald L., 648
Jones, David A., 211
Jones, Terry, 27

Kahl, Joseph A., 275
Kain, Edward L., 424, 566
Kalish, Carol B., 232
Kalish, Richard A., 419
Kalleberg, Arne L., 203
Kalmuss, Debra, 427
Kandel, Denise, 143
Kane, Mary Jo, 26
Kanhonk, Chief, 641
Kanter, Rosabeth Moss, 199–201
Kantrowitz, Barbara, 429
Kaplan, Eric B., 169, 580
Kaptchuk, Ted, 574
Kasarda, John D., 540
Kaufman, Robert L., 393
Kaufman, Walter, 473, 475, 477
Keating, Norah C., 396
Keith, Julie, 390
Keller, Suzanne, 610
Kelley, Jack, 430
Kellner, Hansfried, 42, 653, 657, 660
Kelly, Orville, 159
Kemp, Alice Abel, 363, 535
Kenyon, Kathleen, 599
Kerckhoff, Alan C., 249
Kevorkian, Jack, 570
Kiefer-Hammersmith, Sue, 352, 431
Kii, Toshi, 396
Kilbourne, Brock K., 471
Kilgore, Sally B., 450, 455
Killian, Lewis M., 620, 621, 623–625, 628, 633
King, Kathleen Piker, 226
King, Mackenzie, 575
King, Martin Luther, Jr., 494
King, Rodney Glen, 209, 326
Kinley, David, 313
Kinsey, Alfred, 92, 351
Kipling, Rudyard, 614
Kipp, Rita Smith, 354
Kirby, Ian, 349
Kirk, Marshall, 351, 556
Kitson, Gay C., 424
Kittrie, Nicholas N., 235, 239
Kleiman, Dena, 571
Klein, Ralph, 503
Kluckhohn, Clyde, 351
Knaus, William A., 574
Knowles, Valerie, 342
Knudtson, Peter, 212
Koch, Howard, 626
Kohlberg, Lawrence, 136, 357
Kohn, Melvin L., 141, 420, 535
Kolata, Gina, 407
Komarovsky, Mirra, 362, 364, 420
Korman, Sheila K., 427
Kornhauser, William, 499, 631, 653
Kozol, Jonathan, 48, 287, 457
Kramarae, Cheris, 173, 362
Krisberg, Barry, 230
Krmpotic, Jasna A., 456
Krohn, Marvin D., 212
Kubey, Robert W., 400
Kübler-Ross, Elisabeth, 150, 402
Kuhn, Thomas, 18
Kurelek, William, 482

Kurtz, Lester R., 519
Kuznets, Simon, 261, 262

Lacayo, Richard, 210, 621
Ladd, John, 570
Lai, H. M., 388
Lamberg-Karlovsky, C.C., 599
Lamberg-Karlovsky, Martha, 599
Landale, Nancy S., 415
Landers, Ann, 6, 424
Lane, David, 251
Lang, Gladys Engel, 625
Lang, Kurt, 625
Laporte, Pierre, 515
Lappé, Frances Moore, 313
LaPrairie, Carol P., 235
Laslett, Peter, 248, 621, 653
Latouche, Daniel, 340
Laub, John H., 217
Lauder, Estée, 267
Laudrey, Laura, 390
Laurence, Margaret, 383
Lawrence, Jacob, 590
Laxer, Gordon, 54
Le Bon, Gustave, 623, 624, 631
Le Jeune, Olivier, 334
Leacock, Eleanor, 102, 373
Leacock, Stephen, 536, 537
Leavitt, Judith Walzer, 580
Lee, Barrett A., 610
Leifer, Eric M., 27
Lengermann, Patricia Madoo, 274, 352, 354, 357, 368, 372
Lenin, Vladimir, 114, 493
Lenski, Gerhard, 99–102, 104, 261, 354, 440, 494, 557, 599, 642
Lenski, Jean, 99–102, 104, 261, 354, 440, 494, 557, 599, 642
Lenskyj, Helene, 26
Lenton, Rhonda L., 239
Leonard, Eileen B., 226
Lepine, Marc, 1, 3, 211, 454
Lerner, Richard M., 141
Leslie, Gerald R., 427
Lester, David, 239
Lever, Janet, 141, 358
Lévesque, René, 493
Levin, B., 5
Levine, Michael, 555
Levinson, Daniel J., 148
Levy, Frank, 269
Lewis, Flora, 514
Lewis, Oscar, 284
Leyton, Elliot, 120
Li, Peter S., 325, 336, 338
Liazos, Alexander, 222
Lin, Nan, 191, 562
Lincoln, James R., 203
Link, Bruce G., 222
Linton, Ralph, 160, 644
Lippitt, Ronald, 185
Lipset, Seymour Martin, 76, 247, 327, 500, 631, 648, 657
Liska, Allen E., 212, 218, 231
Littenberg, Ronnie, 135
Littlechild, George, 163, 223
Lo, Clarence Y.H., 628
Locke, John, 17
Lofland, Lyn, 626
Logan, Jim, 26

Lombroso, Caesare, 211
London, Bruce, 612
Long, Edward V., 196
Lorch, Elizabeth Pugzles, 143
Lord, Walter, 243
Lorenz, Konrad, 517
Low, J.O., 526
Loxley, William A., 441, 442
Loy, Pamela Hewitt, 370
Lubenow, Gerald C., 429
Luckmann, Thomas, 162
Lund, Dale A., 403
Lunt, Paul S., 275
Lupri, Eugene, 427, 428
Luther, Martin, 473
Lutz, Catherine A., 166
Luxton, Meg, 55, 56, 359
Lynd, Robert, 75

Ma, Li-Chen, 270
Maccoby, Eleanor Emmons, 352
Macdonald, John A., 502
Mace, David, 414
Mace, Vera, 414
MacIntosh, Peter, 416, 480
Macionis, John J., 7, 185, 293, 294, 304, 418, 557, 599, 610
MacKay, Donald G., 173
MacKenzie, Helen, 73
Mackie, Marlene, 54
MacKinnon, Catherine, 371
Macleod, Linda, 3
Madonna, 215
Madsen, Peter, 351, 548, 556
Magellan, Ferdinand, 100
Mahesh Yogi, Maharishi, 471
Mahler, Halfdan, 391, 557, 558
Mainse, David, 485
Majka, Linda C., 370
Major, Brenda, 358
Malthus, Thomas Robert, 594
Mandel, Eli, 657
Mangan, J. A., 26
Mangione, Thomas W., 48
Manning, Preston, 195
Marchak, Patricia, 15
Marcus, Paul, 569
Marcuse, Herbert, 659
Markoff, John, 202
Marlios, Peter, 546
Marsden, Peter, 191, 500, 620, 628
Marshall, Susan E., 364, 389
Martin, Alicia, 181
Martin, Richard C., 474
Martineau, Harriet, 23
Marullo, Sam, 518
Marx, Gary, 620
Marx, Karl, 17, 18, 21, 24, 43, 87, 100, 108–114, 123, 124, 213, 223, 251, 252, 255, 259, 260, 263, 275, 276, 327, 373, 466, 467, 514, 518, 531, 534, 594, 644, 652, 655, 656
Masserman, Jules H., 412
Massey, Douglas, 332
Masters, Carlton, 369
Masuo, Naoko, 439
Mathews, Anne Martin, 56
Matthews, Mervyn, 443, 444, 544
Matthiessen, Peter, 333
Matza, David, 222

Matzke, Gordon E., 417, 559
Mauss, Armand L., 634
Mayo, Katherine, 414
McAdam, Doug, 620, 631, 633
McAll, Christopher, 258, 328, 336, 338
McCarthy, John D., 620, 631–633
McClain, Jackie R., 335
McClung, Nellie, 23
McConahay, John B., 631
McDougall, Barbara, 510
McGuire, Meredith B., 477
McHenry, Susan, 200
McKay, Henry D., 222
McKenna, Frank, 456
McKeown, Thomas, 557
McKusick, Leon, 77, 569
McLanahan, Sara S., 430
McLaughlin, Audrey, 368, 510
McLean, Stuart, 335
McLeod, L., 369
McPhail, Agnes, 23, 510, 511
McPhail, Clark, 621, 623
McPherson, Barry D., 389, 394
McRae, Susan, 422
Mead, George Herbert, 22, 137–140, 153, 444
Mead, Margaret, 42, 147, 353
Mechanic, David, 558, 578
Meisel, J., 505
Meissner, Martin, 271
Melucci, Alberto, 631, 633
Mercredi, Ovide, 339, 506
Merton, Robert K., 19, 161, 187, 198, 215, 216, 225, 328
Messner, Steven, 190, 231
Michels, Robert, 199
Michelson, William, 606
Milbrath, Lester, 509
Milgram, Stanley, 185, 186
Miliband, Ralph, 656
Miller, Arthur G., 185
Miller, David L., 620
Miller, Frederick, 635
Miller, Michael, 197
Miller, Walter, 217
Millet, Kate, 374
Mills, C. Wright, 9, 11, 116, 512, 518, 539
Mink, Barbara, 307
Mirowsky, John, 187, 423
Mirvish, Ed, 248
Mitchell, Margaret, 354
Mitchell, W.O., 462
Mitchell, William L., 396
Mitchinson, Wendy, 581
Mittman, Brian S., 633
Molotch, Harvey L., 611
Money, John, 352, 556
Monik, Bonnie Shnier, 269
Montagu, Ashley, 517
Moore, Gwen, 191, 546
Moore, Wilbert, 253, 263, 308
Moran, John S., 567
Morgan, J. P., 257
Mori, George A., 478
Morita, Akio, 204
Morris, Aldon, 633
Morrison, Denton E., 630
Morrow, Lance, 210
Moses, 478
Moses, D'Arcy, 539

Mottaz, Clifford J., 535
Moynihan, Daniel Patrick, 331
Mueller, Charles W., 365, 430
Muhammad, 473, 474
Muller, Edward N., 631
Mulroney, Brian, 267, 368, 508, 510, 512, 546
Mumford, Lewis, 557, 599, 600
Murdock, George, 86, 354, 408, 411, 412
Murphy, Robert, 412
Murray, Megan Baldridge, 200
Mydans, Seth, 461
Myers, Sheila, 578

Nader, Ralph, 335, 506
Naeyaert, Kathleen, 388
Napoleon, 514
Navarro, Vincente, 579
Neill, Shirley, 539
Nemeth, Mary, 479, 482
Nett, Emily M., 364, 389, 395, 408, 413, 417, 419, 422, 425, 431
Neugarten, Bernice L., 390, 395, 398
Neuhouser, Kevin, 467
Newman, Andrew E., 633
Newman, James L., 417, 559
Newman, William M., 331
Newton, Isaac, 12, 482
Nisbet, Robert A., 42, 499, 653
Noch, 648
Nolan, Patrick, 100, 102, 104, 261, 354, 440, 494, 599, 642
Norbeck, Edward, 250

O'Brien, Mary, 24, 359
O'Dea, Thomas F., 469, 482
Oakes, Jeannie, 20, 450, 451
Oberschall, Anthony, 631, 632
Oberst, Gail, 430
Offir, Carole Wade, 351
Ogburn, William, 83, 642
Ohlendorf, George W., 44
Ohlin, Lloyd, 216
Olson, Clifford, 238, 418
Olzak, Susan, 328, 632
Orbach, S., 555
Osgood, D. Wayne, 212
Ossenberg, Richard J., 278
Ostling, Richard N., 433, 485
Ouchi, William, 202

Palmore, Erdman, 394–396, 398
Parcel, Toby L., 365
Parenti, Michael, 143
Park, Robert Ezra, 608–610
Park, Roberta J., 26
Parker, Patricia, 225
Parkinson, C. Northcote, 196
Parris, Samuel, 627
Parrott, Julie, 555
Parry, Keith, 410
Parsons, Talcott, 18, 86, 185, 308, 372, 398, 412, 577, 578, 647
Pasteur, Louis, 581
Patchen, Martin, 517
Paton, George E. C., 177
Paul, Ellen Frankel, 370
Payne, G. C. F., 115

Pear, Robert, 365
Pearson, Lester B., 520
Pedersen, Daniel, 531
Pennings, Johannes M., 202
Peron, Eva, 498
Peron, Juan, 498
Perri, Rocco, 216, 218
Perrow, Charles, 630, 632
Persell, Caroline Hodges, 450, 451
Pescosolido, Bernice A., 5
Pessen, Edward, 257
Peter, Laurence J., 196
Peters, Thomas J., 200
Peterson, Ruth D., 239
Phillips, Kevin, 440
Phillipson, Chris, 375
Piaget, Jean, 135–137
Pin, Chang, 491
Pines, Maya, 134
Pingree, Suzanne, 144
Piotrow, Phyllis T., 597
Piper, Elizabeth S., 631
Pirandello, Luigi, 162
Pitt, Malcolm, 475
Piven, Frances, 631, 635
Plato, 12, 252, 440, 512
Plewes, Betty, 302
Plomin, Robert, 132
Poitras, Jane Ash, 310
Pol Pot, 333
Polenberg, Richard, 656
Pollack, Otto, 418
Ponting, J. Rick, 620
Popenoe, David, 430
Porter, John, 14, 276, 336–338, 449–451, 512
Porter, Marion, 449, 451
Powell, Chris, 177
Premack, David, 73
Presley, Elvis, 215
Probert, Adam, 565
Purcell, Piper, 360

Quarantelli, E.L., 620, 621, 624, 628
Quayle, Dan, 181
Queen Elizabeth II, 493
Quinney, Richard, 223

Radin, Norma, 418
Ragin, Charles C., 312, 549
Raleigh, Sir Walter, 78
Ramcharan, Subhas, 325, 336
Raphael, Ray, 355
Raschke, Helen J., 424
Rasporich, Beverly, 657
Reckless, Walter, 212, 213
Rees, Philip, 611
Reich, Robert B., 269
Reid, Sue Titus, 235
Reilly, 624
Reitz, Jeffrey G., 337, 620
Remis, Robert S., 567, 569
Remoff, Heather Trexler, 92
Renick, Timothy M., 465
Richardson, James T., 470
Richler, Mordecai, 49
Ridgeway, Cecilia L., 184, 185, 190
Riegel, Klaus F., 390
Riel, Louis, 339
Rife, John, 183

Riley, Matilda White, 140
Ritzer, George, 109, 538
Rivera, Diego, 312
Rizzo, Thomas A., 137
Roberts, Mary K., 217
Roberts, Oral, 485
Robinson, Jackie, 27
Rochford, E. Burke, Jr., 633
Rockefeller, John D., 254
Rodin, Judith, 555
Rodriguez, Sue, 570
Roesch, Roberta, 369, 427
Roethlisberger, F. J., 46, 195
Rohlen, Thomas P., 440, 442
Rokove, Milton L., 614
Roman, Mel, 425
Romero, Oscar Arnulfo, 467
Roos, Patricia, 363
Rose, Arnold M., 395
Rose, Jerry D., 630
Rosenbaum, Ron, 236, 451
Rosenberg, Charles, 556, 581
Rosenberg, Stanley D., 149
Rosenthal, Jack, 606
Roskin, Michael G., 495, 531
Rosnow, Ralph L., 625
Ross, Catherine E., 423
Ross, Susan, 597
Rossi, Alice S., 357
Rossi, Peter H., 44, 269
Rostow, Walt W., 306, 548
Rowe, David C., 212
Rubenstein, Eli A., 394
Rubin, Jerry, 635
Rubin, Ken, 197
Rubin, Lillian Breslow, 362, 416, 417, 420
Rudé, George, 624
Rudolph, Barbara, 565
Rumberger, Russell, 453
Rush, James C., 456
Rushton, Philip, 132, 323
Ryan, William, 284

Sadd, Susan, 417
Sagan, Carl, 68
Salas, Rafael M., 597
Sale, Kirkpatrick, 311, 333
Saline, Carol, 427
Saltman, Juliet, 332
Sampson, Anthony, 443
Sampson, Robert J., 217, 231
Sandon, Leo, Jr., 478
Sangl, Judith, 389
Sansom, William, 166
Sapir, Edward, 74
Satzewich, Vic, 258, 325, 336
Scaff, Lawrence A., 496
Schaie, K. Warner, 390
Schawrtz, Martin D., 430
Scheff, Thomas J., 220
Schellenberg, James A., 138
Schellenberg, Kathryn, 202
Schlesinger, Arthur, Jr., 425, 603
Schmidt, Roger, 475, 477, 478
Schneider, Joseph W., 221
Schneiders, Sandra, 468
Schooler, Carmi, 364, 535
Schuller, Robert, 485
Schur, Edwin, 226
Schwartz, Felice N., 365–367
Schwartz, Ira, 230

Schwartz, Martin D., 369, 428
Schwartz, Pepper, 411, 417, 431
Schweitzer, Arlette, 407
Scott, John, 546
Sears, David O., 631
Sellin, Thorsten, 231, 239
Seltzer, Judith A., 427
Seltzer, Robert M., 478
Semyonov, Moshe, 247
Sen, K.M., 475
Sengoku, Tamotsu, 203
Sennett, Richard, 288, 454
Sewell, William H., 44
Shakespeare, William, 12
Shames, Stephen, 217
Shapiro, Martin, 113
Shapiro, Nina, 349, 411
Shaw, Clifford R., 222
Shawcross, William, 333
Sheehan, Tom, 149, 393
Sheen, Charlie, 412
Sheen, Martin, 412
Sheldon, William, 211, 212
Shephard, Roy J., 565
Shepher, Joseph, 353
Sherrid, Pamela, 249
Shevky, Eshref, 611
Shibutani, Tamotsu, 625
Shipler, David K., 251
Shipley, Joseph T., 198
Shkilnyk, Anastasia M., 422
Shockey, James W., 454
Shore, Dinah, 267
Shupe, Anson D., Jr., 484
Shute, James, 315
Sidel, Ruth, 574, 580
Sidel, Victor W., 574, 580
Sifton, Clifford, 342
Sills, David L., 198
Silverstein, Michael, 360, 555
Simcoe, John Graves, 600
Simmel, Georg, 188, 607, 626, 649
Simmons, Carol, 439
Simon, Carl P., 543
Simons, Marlise, 641, 661
Simpson, George Eaton, 330
Simpson, John, 230
Singer, Dorothy G., 143
Singer, Jerome L., 143
Sivard, Ruth Leger, 300, 520
Sjoberg, Gideon, 600
Skocpol, Theda, 514
Skolnick, Arlene S., 136, 137
Slater, Philip E., 93, 184, 190
Smart, Ninian, 473
Smelser, Neil J., 622, 631, 632
Smilgas, Martha, 77
Smith, Adam, 17, 530
Smith, Corey, 555
Smith, Dan, 422
Smith, Dorothy, 55, 56, 359
Smith, Douglas A., 222, 231, 235
Smith, Joseph, 471
Smith, Robert Ellis, 196, 197
Smith, Roger, 543
Smith-Lovin, Lynn, 168
Smith-Rosenberg, Carol, 556, 581
Snell, Marilyn Berlin, 419, 433
Snow, David A., 624, 633
Snowman, Daniel, 249
Solheim, Olaf, 53
South, Scott J., 190
Soyinka, Wole, 66

Spanier, Graham B., 141
Spates, James L., 25, 76, 82, 293, 557, 599
Spector, Leonard S., 519
Speer, James A., 485
Speizer, Jeanne J., 191
Spencer, Herbert, 18, 19, 121
Spencer, Meta, 15
Spender, Dale, 362
Spilerman, Seymour, 393
Spitze, Glenna, 424
Spitzer, Steven, 223
Srinivas, M. N., 245
St. Augustine, 294
Stacey, Judith, 375
Staples, Brent, 27
Stark, Evan, 428
Stark, Rodney, 469–471, 481, 648
Starr, Paul, 573
Stavrianos, L.S., 104, 473, 495, 599, 645
Steele, Shelby, 328
Steffensmeier, Darrell J., 219
Stein, Barry A., 199, 200
Stein, Maurice R., 653
Stephens, George, 258
Stevens, Cat, 635
Stevens, Rosemary, 572, 573
Stewart, Lara, 360
Stewart, Lea P., 370
Stinchcombe, Arthur L., 260
Stockard, Jean, 429
Stoddard, Sandol, 403
Stone, Lawrence, 414
Stone, Robyn, 389, 396
Stouffer, Samuel A., 187, 630
Stowe, Emily Howard, 572
Stowe, Harriet Beecher, 335
Strang, David, 303
Straus, Murray A., 369, 428
Streib, Gordon, 400
Striegel-Moore, Ruth, 555
Stuart, Robert C., 302, 531
Sudnow, David N., 402
Summer, William Graham, 77
Suzuki, David, 212
Swain, Sally, 75
Szasz, Thomas, 220

Tajfel, Henri, 188
Tannen, Deborah, 362
Taras, David, 144, 145, 361, 657
Tausig, Mark, 231
Tavris, Carol, 140, 417
Taylor, Ken, 516
Teeple, Gary, 258
Tepperman, Lorne, 252, 275
Thatcher, Margaret, 494
Theen, Rolf H. W., 251
Theodorson, Achilles G., 115
Theodorson, George A., 115
Thoits, Peggy A., 220
Thomas, Clarence, 369, 370
Thomas, W.I., 54, 163, 328, 578
Thornberry, Terrance, 231
Thorne, Barrie, 168, 169, 172, 173
Thornton, Arland, 424
Tibbits, Clark, 400
Tien, H. Yuan, 598
Tierney, John, 569
Tiger, Lionel, 353
Tilly, Charles, 515

Tindale, Joseph A., 396
Tittle, Charles R., 231
Tobin, Gary, 606
Tobin, Sheldon S., 398
Tocqueville, Alexis de, 17, 514, 630
Toennies, Ferdinand, 607, 609, 648–652, 657
Tofani, Loretta, 567
Toffler, Alvin, 658
Tolnay, Stewart E., 415
Tomiak, Janusz, 443
Tomlinson, Brian, 315
Treas, Judith, 394, 399
Treiman, Donald J., 44, 247, 269
Tribe, Verna, 141
Troeltsch, Ernst, 468, 469
Troiden, Richard R., 352
Tron, Jacqueline, 430
Trudeau, Pierre Elliott, 251, 267, 493, 503, 508, 515
Truman, Harry, 203
Tubman, Harriet, 334
Tumin, Melvin M., 245, 255
Turcotte, André, 371
Turner, Ralph, 620
Tygiel, Jules, 27
Tyree, Andrea, 247

Uchitelle, Louis, 259
Ujimoto, K. Victor, 337
Ullman, Edward, 610, 611
Uribe, Victor M., 412
Ury, William, 519
Useem, Bert, 631
Useem, Michael, 547

Vallee, Frank G., 15
Van Buren, Abigail, 6
van de Kaa, Dirk J., 596
van den Haag, Ernest, 239
Van Eyck, Jan, 416, 479
Van Gogh, Vincent, 237, 285
Van Horn, David, 461
Van Loon, Richard J., 503, 508, 509
Vardy, Jill, 540
Vatz, Richard E., 220
Vaughan, Mary Kay, 549
Veblen, Thorstein, 627
Vercheres, Madeleine de, 78
Vespucci, Amerigo, 311
Vickers, Jill M., 374
Viguerie, Richard A., 485
Villemez, Wayne J., 231
Vines, Gail, 432
Visher, Christy A., 231, 235
Vogel, Lise, 373, 375
Voght, Martha, 581
Vold, George B., 212, 222, 225
von Hirsh, Andrew, 221
Vonnegut, Kurt, Jr., 263

Wade, Carole, 140
Waite, Linda J., 424
Waitzkin, Howard, 166
Walker, Jack L., 335
Wall, Thomas F., 386, 570
Wallace, Michael, 633
Wallace, Ruth A., 274, 352, 354, 357, 368, 372
Wallerstein, Immanuel, 311, 312, 549

Wallis, Chris, 395
Wallis, Claudia, 556, 562, 659
Ward, Lester, 13
Waring, Joan, 140, 151
Warner, Barbara D., 218, 605
Warner, W. Lloyd, 275, 526
Washington, George, 502
Waterman, Robert H., Jr., 200
Watson, John B., 132
Watson, Russell, 429
Watson, William, 528
Waxman, Chaim I., 325
Weber, Adna Ferrin, 600
Weber, Max, 22, 40, 42, 100, 109,
    114–120, 123, 192, 196, 198,
    255, 259, 260, 275, 305, 467,
    491–495, 644, 649, 652, 655,
    659
Wechsler, D., 390
Weinberg, Lee S., 220
Weinberg, Martin S., 351, 352, 431
Weiner, Annette B., 43
Weiner, Linda, 370
Weinrich, James D., 351
Weisner, Thomas S., 430
Weitzman, Lenore J., 149, 425
Welford, Charles, 222
Wellborn, Charles T., 478

Weller, Jack M., 620
Wellman, Barry, 191, 610
Wells, Herbert G., 626
Wenke, Robert J., 68, 599
Werman, Jill, 256
Wesolowski, Wlodzimierz, 498
West, Elizabeth, 632
Westerman, Marty, 84
Whalen, Jack, 631
Wheelis, Allen, 657, 658
Whipple, Thomas W., 144
Whitaker, Mark, 516
White, Geoffrey M., 166
White, Lynn, 425
White, Ralph, 185
White, Walter, 622
Whitman, David, 287
Whittington, Michael S., 503, 508,
    509
Whorf, Benjamin, 74
Whyte, Donald R., 15
Whyte, William Foote, 51, 52
Whyte, William H., Jr., 198
Wiarda, Howard J., 309
Wiatrowski, Michael A., 217
Wigdor, Blossom, 395
Wilkins, R., 562
Williams, 75, 86, 258

Williams, Rhys H., 483
Williams, Richard A., 450
Wilson, Bryan, 478
Wilson, Clinty C., II, 141, 145
Wilson, Deborah, 570
Wilson, Edward O., 93
Wilson, Hiram, 335
Wilson, James Q., 607
Wilson, Margo, 212
Wilson, Thomas C., 609
Wilson, William Julius, 332
Winfield-Laird, Idee, 249
Winks, Robin W., 335
Winn, Marie, 147
Winson, Anthony, 535
Winter, Terry, 485
Wirth, Louis, 184, 608
Wise, Ellen S., 418
Witkin-Lanoil, Georgia, 131, 140, 358
Witte, Ann D., 543
Wohlstein, Ronald T., 621
Wolf, Naomi, 361
Wolfe, Tom, 628
Wolfgang, Marvin E., 231
Wood, Daniell, 570
Wood, James L., 620
Woodward, Kenneth L., 433, 468
Wooley, Orland W., 555

Wooley, Susan C., 555
Worden, Steven K., 633
Worthington, Peter, 238
Wotherspoon, Terry, 258, 325, 336
Wren, Christopher S., 247
Wright, Quincy, 517, 635
Wright, Stuart A., 465, 631
Wrong, Dennis, 153

Yates, Ronald E., 394, 397
Yeltzin, Boris, 251
Yinger, J. Milton, 330
Yinger, Richard E., 519
York, Geoffrey, 282
Yutang, Lin, 389

Zald, James, 620, 631–633
Zald, Mayer N., 538
Zaslavsky, Victor, 251
Zeitlin, Irving, 111
Zill, Nicholas, 426
Zimbardo, Philip, 46, 57
Znaniecki, F., 54
Zola, Irving Kenneth, 580
Zuboff, Shoshana, 543
Zurcher, Louis A., 624, 633

Subject Index

Abkhasia, 392
Absolute poverty, 282, 290
Achieved status, 159, 178
Activity theory, 398, 404
Adolescence, 147
Adulthood, 147–149
Afrocentrism, 81, 95
Age stratification, 393, 404
Age-sex pyramid, 591, 615
Ageism, 399, 400, 404
Aging, 149–151, 383–405
    abuse of elderly, 396, 397
    biological changes, 387–390
    culture, and, 390–393
    death and dying, 400–403
    family life, as stage of, 419, 420
    income, and, 396
    psychological changes, 390
    retirement, 395, 396
    social isolation, 395
    social stratification, 393, 394
    theoretical analysis, 397
Agricultural revolution, 526
Agriculture, 104, 125
AIDS, 567–571
Alienation
    capitalism and, 113, 114
    defined, 113, 125
    industrial capitalism, and, 113
    rationality and, 119, 120
Ancestry, 272
Animism, 471, 487
Anomie, 122, 125
Anticipatory socialization, 143, 154

Apartheid, 245, 246
Arms race, 518, 521
Ascribed status, 158, 178
Ascription, 272
Assimilation, 331, 346
Authoritarianism, 496–498, 521
Authority, 492, 521

Bangladesh, 592–594
Bereavement, 402, 403
Bias-free words, 174
Bilateral descent, 411, 435
Blue-collar occupations, 258, 264
Buddhism, 475–477
Bureaucracy
    bureaucratic inertia, 198, 206
    bureaucratic ritualism, 198, 206
    bureaucratic waste/incompetence,
        196–198
    characteristics of, 192–194
    defined, 192, 206
    humanizing, 200, 201
    informal side of, 195
    information revolution, and, 197
    limitations of, 195, 196
    origins of, 192
    small groups, vs., 194, 195

Canada
    abortion rate, 596
    age-sex population pyramid, 592
    ancestry, 272

black citizens, 334
corporations. See Corporations
criminal statistics, 227
gender, 273, 274
graying of, 384–387
health, 559–562
history of sociology, 14, 15
homelessness, 285–288
immigration, 341–344
income, 268, 269, 290
languages spoken in, 81
lower class, 278, 279
medicine, 575
Meech Lake Accord, 341
middle class, 277, 278
Native Peoples. See Native Peoples
    (First Nations)
occupational status for
    males/females, 269–271
political parties, 502–508
politics, 500–511
poverty, 282–288
power, 269
punishment, 236
Quebec, anti-semitism in, 49, 50
Quebecois, 340, 341
race and ethnicity, 272, 273,
    333–345
regional economic disparities, 544
religion, 478–482
schooling, 271, 272, 444
social classes, 274–279
social mobility, 280, 281
social standing, 336–338

    Third World, and, 315
    unemployment, 540, 541
    upper class, 276, 277
    urban population, 603–605
    values, 76
    working class, 277, 278
Capitalism, 652, 656
    alienation, and, 113, 114
    class conflict, and, 112, 113
    defined, 529, 551
    deviance and, 223, 224
Capitalists, 110, 125
Caste and class systems, 245–253
    caste system, defined, 245, 264
    class system, defined, 247, 264
    Great Britain, in, 248, 249
    India, in, 245, 246
    Japan, in, 249, 250
    South Africa, in, 245–247
    Soviet Union, in, 250–252
Cause and effect, 38, 60
Change. See Social change
Charisma, 470, 487
Charismatic authority, 493, 521
Charlottetown Accord, 506, 510
Child rearing, 417–419
Childhood, 145–147
China
    birth control in, 598
    medicine in, 574
Christianity, 472, 473
Church, 468, 487
Cigarette smoking, 564–566
Cities. See Urbanization

Civil religion, 483, 487
Class conflict, 112, 125
Class consciousness, 113, 125
Class society
    defined, 655, 663
    problems of powerlessness, 658, 659
Class systems. *See* Caste and class systems
Cohabitation, 430, 435
Cohort, 151, 154
Collective behavior, 619–628, 638
Collectivity, 620, 638
Colonialism, 303, 318
Commonwealth of Independent States. *See* Soviet Union
Communism, 531, 551
Concept, 36, 60
Concrete operational stage, 136, 154
Conglomerates, 546, 551
Contagion theory, 623
Content analysis, 54, 60
Control, 39, 60
Convergence theory, 623
Conversion, 470, 487
Corporations
    competition, and, 547, 5478
    defined, 543, 551
    economic concentration, 545
    foreign ownership, 545, 546
    global economy, and, 548, 549
    mergers/amalgamations, 546, 547
Correlation, 38, 60
Counterculture, 82, 95
Courtship, 414–416
Credentialism, 453, 459
Crime. *See also* Deviance
    defined, 210, 240
    global perspective, 232, 233
    statistics, 227–229
    "street" criminal, 229–232
    types, 227
Criminal justice system, 211, 234–240
Criminal recidivism, 239, 240
Crowd, 621, 638
Crude birth rate, 588, 615
Crude death rate, 588, 615
Cult, 470, 487
Cultural integration, 95
Cultural lag, 95
Cultural materialism, 89, 95
Cultural relativism, 84, 95
Cultural transmission, 95
Cultural universals, 86, 95
Culture, 65–96
    aging and, 390–393
    components, 69–80
    constraint, as, 93
    defined, 66, 95
    freedom, as, 93, 94
    human freedom, and, 93, 94
    human intelligence, and, 68, 69
    theoretical analysis, 86–93
    nature of, 66, 67
Culture shock, 95

Data collection, 45–55
Data, methods of interpreting sociological, 55
Date rape, 228
Davis-Moore thesis, 253–255, 263

Death, 149, 150, 400–403, 570, 571
Deductive logical thought, 57, 60
Democracy, 495, 496, 498, 499, 521
Democratic socialism, 531, 551
Demographic transition theory, 595, 615
Demography, 587–593
    change, and, 645
    defined, 588, 615
    importance of, 597, 598
Denomination, 469, 487
Dependency theory, 309–315
    defined, 318
    summary, 316
Dependent variable, 38, 60
Deprivation theory, 629–631
Descent, 411, 435
Deterrence, 237, 240
Deviance, 209–241
    biological context, 211, 212
    capitalism, and, 223, 224
    defined, 240
    gender, and, 225, 226
    personality factors, 212, 213
    social foundations of, 213, 214
    structural-functional analysis, 214–219
    symbolic-interaction analysis, 219–222
    nature of, 210–214
    white-collar crime, 224, 225, 240
Deviant subcultures, 216, 217
Dignity, 660
Dionne Quintuplets, 130
Direct-fee system, 576, 583
Discrimination, 328, 329, 346
Diseases, media perception of, 91
Disengagement theory, 398, 404
Division of labor, 122, 123, 125, 650–652
Divorce, 424–426
Dramaturgical analysis, 165–172, 178
Dyad, 189, 206
Dying, 149, 150, 400–403, 570, 571

Ecclesia, 469, 487
Economy, 525–553
    comparative economic systems, 529–534
    corporations. *See* Corporations
    defined, 525, 551
    future, in the, 549, 550
    historical overview, 525–529
    sectors of modern, 528
Education, 439, 459. *See also* Schooling
Ego, 135, 154
Elderly. *See* Aging
Embarrassment, 170–172
Emergent-norm theory, 623, 624
Empirical evidence, 60
Endogamy, 409, 435
Environmental disasters, 563
Environmental pollution, 562–564
Ethnicity, 323, 346. *See also* Race
Ethnocentrism, 83–85, 95
Ethnomethodology, 24, 164, 178
Eurocentrism, 80, 95
Euthanasia, 570, 583
Evangelists, 485
Exogamy, 409, 435

Experiments, 45–47, 55, 60
Expressive leadership, 184, 206
Extended family, 408, 435

Fad, 628, 638
Faith, 463, 487
False consciousness, 111, 125
Family, 140, 141, 408–437
    alternative forms
        cohabitation, 430
        gay/lesbian couples, 430, 431
        one-parent families, 429, 430
        singlehood, 431
    basic concepts, 408
    cross-cultural perspective, in, 408–411
    ethnicity/race, effect of, 421, 422
    functions of, 411–413
    future, in the, 432–434
    gender and, 357, 358
    gender, effect of, 422, 423
    later life, in, 419, 420
    new reproductive technology and, 431, 432
    social class, effect of, 420, 421
    social inequality and, 413, 414
    theoretical analysis, 411–414
    violence, 427–429
Family life
    problems in
        divorce, 424–426
        remarriage, 426, 427
    stages of
        child rearing, 417–419
        courtship, 414–416
        old age, 419, 420
        reality of marriage, 416, 417
    varieties of, 420–423
Family of orientation, 408, 435
Family of procreation, 408, 435
Family violence, 427–429, 435
Fashion, 626, 638
Female infanticide, 357, 378
Feminism, 23, 24, 374–378
Feminist research, 55–57
Feminization of poverty, 283, 290
Fertility, 588, 615
First World, 294, 295, 318
Folkways, 77, 95
Formal operational stage, 137, 154
Formal organizations, 191–206
Functional illiteracy, 457, 459

Gays and lesbians, 351, 430, 431
Gemeinschaft, 607, 615, 648, 649
Gender
    adult socialization, 361, 362
    Canada, in, 273, 274
    cultural distinction, 352–354
    defined, 352, 378
    deviance and, 225, 226
    education, and, 365–367
    family, and, 357, 358
    family, effect on, 422, 423
    income and wealth, and, 364, 365
    language and, 172–174
    mass media, and, 360, 361
    organizations, in, 199, 200
    peer group, and, 358, 359
    politics, and, 367, 368

research, and, 43–45
    schooling, and, 359, 360
    sex and, 350–357
    social stratification, and, 362–371
    socialization, and, 357–362
    theoretical analysis, 371–374
    twenty-first century, in, 377
Gender identity, 352, 378
Gender roles, 357, 379
Gender stratification, 362, 379
Generalized other, 139, 154
Genital herpes, 567
Genocide, 332, 346
Gerontocracy, 393, 404
Gerontology, 387, 404
Gesellschaft, 607, 615, 648–651
Global inequality, 213–319
Gonorrhea, 566
Gossip, 625, 638
Government, 493, 521. *See also* Politics
Great Britain
    class and caste system, 248, 249
    medical system, 577
    schooling in, 442, 443
Groups and organizations, 181–207
Groupthink, 187, 206

Hawthorne effect, 60
Health, 555–584. *See also* Medicine
    Canada, in, 559–562
    cigarette smoking, 564–566
    death, confronting, 570, 571
    defined, 556, 583
    environmental pollution, 562–564
    global patterns of, 558, 559
    historical patterns of, 556–558
    medical care in global perspective, 561
    medicine. *See* Medicine
    sexually transmitted diseases, 566–571
    society, and, 556
    theoretical analysis, 577–581
Health care, 571, 583
Hermaphrodite, 351, 379
Hidden curriculum, 449, 459
Hinduism, 474, 475
Holistic medicine, 573, 583
Homelessness, 285–288
Homogamy, 415, 435
Homosexuals, 351, 430, 431
Honor, 660
Horticulture, 102, 125
Housework, 356, 364
Humanizing bureaucracy, 200, 206
Humor, 173–177
Hunting and gathering societies, 101, 125
Hypothesis, 45, 60

Id, 135, 154
Ideal culture, 78, 95
Ideal type, 115, 125
Idealization, 169, 170
Ideology, 252–254, 264
Illiteracy, 441, 457, 459
In vitro fertilization, 432, 433
Incest taboo, 412, 435
Income, 268, 290

Income disparity, 262
Independent variable, 38, 60
India
    caste and class system, 245, 246
    poverty, 304
Inductive logical thought, 57, 60
Industrial revolution, 526–528
Industrialism, 105, 125
Infant mortality rate, 588, 615
Information revolution, 197
Ingroup, 188, 206
Institutional completeness, 346–328, 346
Institutional discrimination, 328, 346
Instrumental leadership, 184, 206
Intergenerational social mobility, 280, 290
Interlocking directorate, 546, 551
Interpretive research, 56, 60
Interview, 48, 60
Intragenerational social mobility, 280, 290
Islam, 473, 474
Israel, 353

Japan
    class and caste system, 249, 250
    formal organizations, 202–204
    medical system, 577
    schooling, 439, 442
    social stratification, 249, 250
Judaism, 477, 478
Juvenile delinquency, 210, 240

Kinship, 408, 435
Kuznets Curve, 261, 262

Labor unions, 536, 537, 551
Language, 70–75
    defined, 95
    gender issue, 172–174
    global perspective, 72
Latent functions, 19, 29
Liberation theology, 467, 487
Life expectancy, 589, 615
Looking-glass self, 139, 154

Macro-level orientation, 22, 29
Manifest functions, 19, 30
Marriage
    defined, 408, 435
    depression, 423
    patterns, 409–411
    realities of, 416, 417
    remarriage, 426, 427
Mass behavior, 624, 638
Mass hysteria, 626, 638
Mass media, 143, 154, 360, 361
Mass society
    defined, 653, 663
    problems of identity, 657, 658
Mass-society theory, 631
Master status, 159, 178
Material culture, 78, 95
Matriarchy, 354, 379
Matrilineal descent, 411, 435
Matrilocality, 411, 435
Mean, 37, 60

Measurement, 37, 61
Mechanical solidarity, 122, 125
Median, 37, 61
Medicalization of deviance, 221, 240
Medicine, 571–584. *See also* Health
    Canada, in, 575
    Commonwealth of Independent States, in, 574, 575
    defined, 571, 583
    Great Britain, in, 577
    holistic, 573, 574
    Japan, in, 577
    scientific, rise of, 572, 573
    Sweden, in, 577
    theoretical analysis, 577–581
    United States, in, 575–577
Meech Lake Accord, 341
Megalopolis, 606, 615
Meritocracy, 255, 264
Metropolis, 603, 615
Micro-level orientation, 22, 30
Migration, 589, 615
Military-industrial complex, 518, 521
Minority, 324, 346
Miscegenation, 331, 346
Mob, 622, 638
Mode, 37, 61
Modernity, 645–662
    defined, 646, 663
    global perspective, in, 660–662
    individual, and the, 657–659
    modernization, characteristics, 646–648
    progress, and, 659, 660
Modernization, 646, 663. *See also* Modernity
Modernization theory, 305–309
    defined, 318
    summary, 316
Monarchy, 495, 521
Monogamy, 409, 436
Monopoly, 547, 551
Monotheism, 472, 487
Montreal Massacre, 1–3, 7
Mores, 77, 95
Mortality, 588, 615
Multiculturalism, 80–82, 95, 346
Multinational corporations, 304, 318

Name changes, 6
Native Peoples (First Nations), 338–340
    families, 421, 422
    native self-government, 506, 507
Neocolonialism, 304, 318
Neolocality, 411, 435
Network, 190, 206
"New social movements" theory, 633, 634
Norms, 77, 95
Nuclear family, 408, 436
Nuclear proliferation, 519, 521
Nutrition, 301

Objectivity, 40, 61
Oligarchy, 199, 206
Oligopoly, 547, 551
Operationalizing a variable, 37, 61
Organic solidarity, 123, 125
Organizational environment, 201, 206

Organizations, 191–205
Other-directedness, 658, 663
Outgroup, 188, 206
Overeducation, 453, 459

Panic, 625, 638
Parkinson's Law, 196
Participant observation, 50–55, 61
Pastoralism, 103, 125
Patriarchy
    defined, 354, 379
    feminist perspective, 24
    religion and, 468
    sexism, and, 354–356
Patrilineal descent, 411, 436
Patrilocality, 411, 436
Peace
    defined, 516, 521
    pursuit of, 519, 520
Peer group, 142, 154
Personal space, 169, 178
Personality, 131, 154
Peter Principle, 196
Plea bargaining, 235, 240
Pluralism, 329, 330, 346
Pluralist model, 512, 513, 521
Police, 234, 235
Political parties, 502–508, 521
Political revolution, 514, 522
Political state, 495, 522
Politics, 491–523
    Canada, in, 500–511
    contemporary political system, 495–500
    defined, 491, 522
    global perspective, in, 494–500
    history, in, 494, 495
Polyandry, 410, 436
Polygamy, 409, 436
Polygyny, 409, 436
Polytheism, 472, 487
Population, 590, 591
    composition, 590–593
    defined, 61
    history/theory of population growth, 593–595
    sample, and, 47, 48
    world population today, 595–598
Pornography, 371
Positivism, 13, 30
Positivist social science
    concepts, variables, measurement, 36–40
    defined, 61
    elements, 36–45
    limitations, 40, 41
    objectivity, 40
    subjective interpretation, 42
Positivist sociological investigation, 34–36
Postindustrial economy, 528, 551
Poverty
    absolute, 300
    Canada, in, 282–288
    India, in, 304
    relative, 300
    Third World, in, 298–305
Power
    beyond the rules, 514–516
    defined, 491, 522
    theoretical analysis, 512–514

Power-elite model, 512, 513, 522
Prejudice, 324–328, 346
Preoperational stage, 136, 154
Presentation of self, 165, 178
Primary group, 182, 206
Primary labor market, 535, 551
Primary sector, 528, 551
Primary sex characteristics, 350, 379
Privacy, 197
Profane, 462, 487
Profession, 538, 551
Proletariat, 110, 125
Propaganda, 625, 638
Property crimes, 227, 240
Prostitution, 234
Public opinion, 145, 154, 625
Punishment, 235–239

Qualitative research, 51, 61
Quantitative research, 51, 61
Quebecois, 340, 341
Questionnaire, 48, 61

Race, 321–347
    Canada, in, 272, 273
    defined, 322, 346
    family, effect on, 421, 422
    organizations, in, 199, 200
    religion, effect on, 481
Racism, 325, 326, 346
Rational-legal authority, 493, 522
Rationality, 116–120, 125
Rationalization, 652
Rationalization of society, 116, 125
Real culture, 78, 95
Reference group, 187, 206
Rehabilitation, 237, 240
Relative deprivation, 630, 638
Relative poverty, 282, 290
Reliability, 37, 61
Religion, 461–489
    basic concepts, 461–464
    Canada, in, 478–482
    defined, 462, 487
    evangelists, 485
    functions of, 464, 465
    future of, 486
    patriarchy, and, 468
    religious revival, 484, 485
    secularization, 482–484
    social inequality, and, 466, 467
    theoretical analysis, 464–468
    types of religious organization, 468–472
    world religions, 472–478
Religious fundamentalism, 484, 487
Remarriage, 426, 427
Replication, 40, 61
Research
    ethics, 45
    feminist, 55–57
    gender and, 43–45
    interpretive, 56, 57
    politics and, 42, 43
    survey, 47–50
Research method, 45, 61
Reserve army of labor, 535, 551
Resocialization, 151, 154
Resource-mobilization theory, 632, 633
Retirement, 395, 396

Retribution, 237, 240
Retrospective labeling, 220, 240
Revolution, 114, 514, 515
Riot, 622, 638
Ritual, 463, 487
Rock and roll, 215
Role, 160, 178
Role conflict, 161, 178
Role set, 161, 178
Role strain, 161, 178
Routinization of charisma, 494, 522
Rumor, 624, 638

Sacred, 462, 487
Salaries, 256
Salem, 627
Samoa, 42, 43
Sample, 47, 61
"Sandwich generation", 389
Sapir-Whorf hypothesis, 74, 95
Scapegoat, 326, 346
Schooling, 141, 142, 439–459
    Canada, in, 271, 272
    defined, 439, 459
    discipline, school, 454, 455
    dropping out, 455, 456
    functions, 444–449
    future, in the, 458
    gender and, 359, 360
    global survey, 439–444
    illiteracy, 441, 457, 459
    problems, 454–457
    social inequality, and, 449–454
    student passivity, 455
    testing, 451
    unequal access to higher
        education, 451–453
    work, and, 456, 457
Second World, 296, 297, 318
Secondary analysis, 53, 55, 61
Secondary group, 183, 206
Secondary labor market, 535, 551
Secondary sector, 528, 551
Secondary sex characteristics, 350, 379
Sect, 469, 487
Secularization, 482–484, 487
Segregation, 332, 346
Self, 137, 154
Self-employment, 539, 540
Sensorimotor stage, 135, 154
Sex, 350, 379
Sex and gender, 349–380
Sex ratio, 590, 615
Sexism, 354, 379
Sexual harassment, 369–371, 379
Sexual orientation, 351, 379
Sick role, 577, 583
Singlehood, 431
Small groups, vs. bureaucracy, 194,
    195
Social change, 641–645
    causes, 643
    defined, 642, 663
    social movements and, 636, 637
    nature of, 642, 643
Social character, 657, 663
Social class in Canada. See under
    Canada
Social conflict, 110, 125

Social construction of reality, 162–165
Social control, 77, 95
Social Darwinism, 19, 132
Social dysfunctions, 20, 30
Social epidemiology, 559, 583
Social fact, 120, 125
Social functions, 18, 30
Social groups, 182–191, 206
Social inequality
    family, and, 413, 414
    persistence of, 656
    religion and, 466, 467
    schooling and, 449–454
Social institution, 126
Social interaction, 157–179
Social isolation, 132–134
Social marginality, 9, 30
Social mobility, 244, 264, 280, 281
Social movements, 628–637
    social change, and, 636
    stages, 634–636
    theories, 635
    types, 629
Social protection, 238, 240
Social stratification, 243–265
    aging and, 393, 394
    ascription and, 272–274
    caste and class systems. See Caste
        and class systems
    conflict, and, 255
    defined, 244, 264
    facts and values, 263
    functions of, 253–255
    gender, and, 362–371
    social-conflict paradigm, 260
    structural-functional paradigm,
        260
    technology, and, 261
    Third-World poverty, 303
    nature of, 244, 245
Social-conflict paradigm, 20, 30
Socialism
    changes in socialist countries, 533
    communism, and, 531
    compared to capitalism, 531–534
    defined, 530, 551
    democratic, 531
Socialization, 129–155
    agents of, 140–145
    defined, 130, 154
    human freedom, and, 152, 153
    life course, and, 145–151
    resocialization (total institutions),
        151, 152
    social experience, importance of,
        129–134
    social isolation, 132–134
    understanding, process, 134–140
Socialized medicine, 577, 583
Societies
    agrarian, 104, 105
    horticultural and pastoral,
        102–104
    hunting and gathering, 101, 102
    industrial, 105–107
    traditional and modern, 654
Society, 99–126
    conflict, and, 108–114
    defined, 99, 126
    four visions of, 123, 124

function, and, 120–123
    health and, 556
    production, and, 110, 111
    rationalization of, 114–120
    technology, and, 100–108
Sociobiology, 90–93, 95
Sociocultural evolution, 100, 106, 107,
    126
Socioeconomic status, 260, 264
Sociological investigation, 33–62
    ten steps in, 57–59
Sociological perspective, 1–12
Sociological theory, 17–29
Sociology
    defined, 2, 30
    origins, 12–17
    science and, 12–14
    social changes, and, 14–17
    social crisis, and, 9, 10
    social diversity, and, 9
    social marginality, and, 9
South Africa
    apartheid, 245, 246
    caste and class system, 245–247
Soviet Union
    class and caste system, 250–252
    medicine, 574, 575
    schooling, 443, 444
Sports, 25–28
Spurious correlation, 39, 61
State terrorism, 515, 522
Status, 158, 178
Status consistency, 248, 264
Status set, 158, 178
Stereotype, 325, 346
Streaming, 449–451, 459
"Street" criminal, 229–232
Structural social mobility, 252, 264
Structural-functional paradigm, 18, 30
Structural-strain theory, 631, 632
Subculture, 80, 95
Suburbs, 605, 606, 616
Suicide, 5
Superego, 135, 154
Survey, 47, 61
Sweden
    medical system, 577
Symbol, 69, 95
Symbolic-interaction paradigm, 22, 30
Syphilis, 566

Tact, 170–172
Taipei, 88, 89
Technology
    changing status of women, and,
        104
    defined, 95
    limits of, 107, 108
    material culture and, 78–80
    society and, 100–108
    stratification and, 261
    work, and, 543
Television, 143–145
Terrorism, 515, 516, 522
Tertiary sector, 528, 551
Theoretical paradigm, 18, 30
Theory, 17, 30
Theory of class society, 655–657
Theory of mass society, 653–655

Third World, 297, 298
    Canada and, 315
    defined, 318
    poverty, 298–305
    urbanization, 611–614
Thomas theorem, 163, 178
Titanic, 243
Total institution, 151, 154
Totalitarianism, 498–500, 522
Totem, 464, 487
Tradition, 116, 125
Tradition-directedness, 657, 663
Traditional authority, 492, 522
Transsexual, 351, 379
Triad, 189, 206

Underground economy, 542, 543, 551
Unemployment, 540–542
United States
    civil religion in, 483
    medicine in, 575–577
    values, 76
Urban ecology, 610, 616
Urbanization
    cities, evolution, 598–601
    cities, growth of North American,
        601–605
    cities, historical importance, 614
    defined, 598, 616
    inter-regional population
        movement, 606, 607
    Metropolitan Era, 603, 604
    suburbs and central cities, 605, 606
    theory and method, 607–610
    Third-World urbanization,
        611–614
    urban decentralization, 604, 605
    urban ecology, 610, 611
    urban expansion, 602, 603

Validity, 38, 61
Values, 75–77, 95
Variable, 36, 61
Victimless crimes, 227, 240
Violent crimes, 227, 240

War, 516, 522
Wealth, 269, 290
White-collar crime, 224, 225, 240
White-collar occupations, 264
Women
    medicine and Victorian, 581
    minority, 368
    modernization and, 307
    politics, participation in, 510, 511
    poverty, and, 286
    technology, effects of 104
    Third World, 302
    violence against, 369–371, 427,
        428
Work, 534–543

Yugoslavia, 321

Zero population growth, 596, 615

JOHN J. MACIONIS

John J. Macionis (pronounced ma-SHOW-nis) was born and raised in Philadelphia, Pennsylvania. He received his bachelor's degree from Cornell University and his doctorate in sociology from the University of Pennsylvania. His publications are wide-ranging, focusing on community life in the United States, interpersonal intimacy in families, effective teaching, the importance of global analysis to sociology, and the anatomy of humor. He is coauthor of the popular urban text *The Sociology of Cities*, and he has coedited *Seeing Ourselves: Classic, Contemporary, and Cross-Cultural Readings in Sociology*. He has also written a brief version of this book, *Society: The Basics*.

John Macionis is currently professor of sociology at Kenyon College in Gambier, Ohio. He has served as chair of the Anthropology-Sociology Department, director of Kenyon's multidisciplinary program in humane studies, and chair of the college's faculty.

Professor Macionis teaches a wide range of upper-level courses, but his favorite course is Introduction to Sociology, which he teaches every semester.

LINDA M. GERBER

Linda M. Gerber has spent most of her life in or near Toronto. Her first degree was in nursing, and then she turned her attention to graduate studies in sociology. While still a graduate student, she became involved as a consultant in highway planning doing socio-economic impact assessment. After completing her master's and doctoral degrees at the University of Toronto, she spent three years as a research associate at Harvard's Center for Population Studies before joining the faculty in the Department of Sociology and Anthropology at the University of Guelph.

Professor Gerber's research has focused upon Canada's Native peoples, Canadian politics and ethnicity, but she has a broader interest in Canadian society (its demographic processes, its identity, and its fragility). Her publications are in the areas of Native studies, voting behavior, gerontology, ethnic relations and Quebec separatism. While she has taught a wide range of undergraduate and graduate courses over the years, she continues to teach one introductory sociology course each year.

JUANNE NANCARROW CLARKE

Juanne Nancarrow Clarke was born and raised in that part of Southwestern Ontario just outside of Toronto that is now called Mississauga. She received her bachelor's degree from the University of Windsor, her master's degree from York University in Toronto, and her doctoral degree from the University of Waterloo. Professor Clarke has been teaching at Wilfrid Laurier University in Waterloo since 1971. During that time she has taught a number of different courses and has always taught methods of social research and the sociology of health, illness and medicine. She has served as department chair and has coordinated the Woman's Studies program. Her publications range from studies of methodology, to gender, to various aspects of health, illness and medicine. She is currently researching gender differences in the experience of chronic fatigue syndrome and the mother-daughter relationship when the mother has breast cancer during the teenage years of her daughter. Professor Clarke has always enjoyed teaching Introductory Sociology.